The History of Science and Religion in the Western Tradition: An Encyclopedia

Garland Reference Library of the Humanities (Vol. 1833)

ADVISORY BOARD

THE HISTORY OF SCIENCE AND RELIGION IN THE WESTERN TRADITION: AN ENCYCLOPEDIA

GARY B. FERNGREN
General Editor

Professor of History
Oregon State University
Corvallis, Oregon

Edward J. Larson
Co-editor

Richard B. Russell Professor
of History and Law
University of Georgia
Athens, Georgia

Darrel W. Amundsen
Co-editor

Professor of Classics
Western Washington University
Bellingham, Washington

Anne-Marie E. Nakhla
Assistant Editor

Independent Scholar
Seattle, Washington

GARLAND PUBLISHING, INC.
A MEMBER OF THE TAYLOR & FRANCIS GROUP
NEW YORK & LONDON
2000

Published in 2000 by Garland Publishing, Inc.
A member of the Taylor & Francis Group
29 West 35th Street
New York, NY 10001

10   9   8   7   6   5   4   3   2   1

Library of Congress Cataloging-in-Publication Data
The history of science and religion in the western tradition : an encyclopedia / Gary B. Ferngren, general editor ; Edward J. Larson, Darrel W. Amundsen, co-editors ; Anne-Marie E. Nakhla, assistant editor.
     p.   cm.— (Garland reference library of the humanities ; o. 1833)
    Includes bibliographical references and index.
    ISBN 0-8153-1656-9 (alk. paper)
    1. Religion and science—History.   I. Ferngren, Gary B.   II. Larson, Edward J. (Edward John)   III. Amundsen, Darrel W.   IV. Series.
    BL245.H57   2000
    291.1'75—dc21

00-025153

Printed on acid-free, 250-year-life paper
Manufactured in the United States of America

CONTENTS

PREFACE

Andrew Dickson White's *A History of the Warfare of Science with Theology in Christendom* (1896) was published just over a century ago. In it White argued that Christianity had a long history of opposing scientific progress in the interest of dogmatic theology. White's thesis, supported by John William Draper in his *History of the Conflict between Religion and Science* (1874), struck a responsive chord in American thought, which was, at the turn of the twentieth century, increasingly committed to a secular outlook and to recognizing the central role that science played in modern society. The Draper-White thesis, as it has come to be known, was enormously influential among academics. During much of the twentieth century, it has dominated the historical interpretation of the relationship of science and religion. It wedded a triumphalist view of science with a dismissive view of religion. Science was seen to be progressing continually, overcoming the inveterate hostility of Christianity, which invariably retreated before its awesome advance. Popular misconceptions doubtless underlay the widespread presumption that religion was, by its very nature, opposed to science. Based on faith, religion seemed bound to suffer when confronted by science, which was, of course, based on fact.

While some historians had always regarded the Draper-White thesis as oversimplifying and distorting a complex relationship, in the late twentieth century it has undergone a more systematic reevaluation. The result has been the growing acknowledgment among professional historians that the relationship of religion and science has been a much more positive one than is usually thought. While popular images of controversy continue to exemplify the supposed hostility of Christianity to new scientific theories, a number of studies have shown that Christianity has sometimes nurtured and encour-

aged scientific endeavor, while at other times the two have coexisted without either tension or attempts at harmonization. If Galileo and the Scopes Trial come to mind as examples of conflict, they were exceptions rather than the rule. In the words of David C. Lindberg, writing on medieval science and religion for this volume:

> There was no warfare between science and the church. The story of science and Christianity in the Middle Ages is not a story of suppression, nor one of its polar opposite, support and encouragement. What we find is an interaction exhibiting all of the variety and complexity that we are familiar with in other realms of human endeavor: conflict, compromise, understanding, misunderstanding, accommodation, dialogue, alienation, the making of common cause, and the going of separate ways (p. 266).

What Lindberg writes of medieval Europe can be said to describe much of Western history. The recognition that the relationship of science and religion has exhibited a multiplicity of attitudes, which have reflected local conditions and particular historical circumstances, has led John Hedley Brooke to speak of a "complexity thesis" as a more accurate model than the familiar "conflict thesis." But old myths die hard. While Brooke's view has gained acceptance among professional historians of science, the traditional view remains strong elsewhere, not least in the popular mind.

The purpose of this volume is to provide a comprehensive survey of the historical relationship of the Western religious traditions to science from the time of the Greeks of the fifth century before Christ to the late twentieth century. The editors' decision to limit the volume's coverage to the West reflects both our own professional backgrounds and our belief that, underlying the diversity of the several streams that have fed Western civilization, there exists a basic substratum, formed by the West's dual heritage of the classical world of Greece and Rome and the monotheistic traditions of Judaism, Christianity, and Islam. The more than one hundred articles that we have commissioned demonstrate that, within that heritage, science and religion have enjoyed a varied and multifaceted association. From the beginning, the editors intended to produce a volume that would provide a convenient summary of recent historical scholarship. In assigning the articles, we have been fortunate in enlisting the cooperation of many of the leading scholars in the field.

Our contributors have been drawn from a variety of backgrounds. No single point of view—in respect to either religion or historical interpretation—can be said to monopolize these pages. While many of our contributors share the view of the editors that the historical relationship of science and religion has been a complex one—sometimes harmonious, sometimes conflictive, often merely coexisting—others retain a less benign view of Western religions as they have interacted with science. Moreover, readers will find some overlap in the subjects treated. Rather than strive vigorously to avoid duplication, we have commissioned several essays that deal with different aspects of the same subject. Our desire throughout has been that each article should provide a comprehensive treatment of its subject.

It hardly needs to be said that this volume adopts a historical approach to the subjects it treats. We have attempted to avoid imposing presentist and essentialist approaches, which have too often distorted the modern understanding of both religion and science of the past; hence our inclusion of the occult sciences, for example, which would not fall under the rubric of science today. Science has long enjoyed a kind of privileged reputation as empirically based and, therefore, rigorously objective. By contrast, it has been widely recognized that religious

traditions are neither monolithic nor static. They have developed over time and reflect the diverse circumstances of their geography and culture. Less well known is the fact that definitions and conceptions of science, too, have changed over the centuries. Indeed, they continue to arouse vigorous debate in our own day. "Science," wrote Alfred North Whitehead, "is even more changeable than theology" (*Science and the Modern World*. 1925. Reprint. New York: New American Library 1960, 163). If the historical landscape is littered with discarded theological ideas, it is equally littered with discarded scientific ones. Failure to understand this historical reality has led those who see the march of science as one of inexorable progress to view controversies between science and religion as disputes in which (to quote Whitehead again) "religion was always wrong, and . . . science was always right. The true facts of the case are very much more complex, and refuse to be summarised in these simple terms" (ibid., loc. cit.).

Recognition that both science and religion are historically conditioned does not necessarily imply a relativist point of view. It does, however, at least require an awareness of the cultural factors that are imposed on all societies, ideas, and disciplines, including, of course, our own. It demands a view of the past that is neither patronizing nor disparaging but capable of appreciating the power of ideas that we do not share or that have fallen out of fashion in our own day. If the study of the intersection of religion and science demonstrates anything, it is the enduring vitality and influence of some of the most basic concepts of the Western world—religious, philosophical, and scientific—which retain their ability to shape ideas and inform our culture in the twenty-first century.

Gary B. Ferngren

ACKNOWLEDGMENTS

The general editor owes an enormous debt of gratitude to the members of our Advisory Board: John Hedley Brooke, Owen Gingerich, John Henry, David C. Lindberg, and Ronald L. Numbers. Without their constant advice and encouragement, this volume would not have been completed. Ronald Numbers gave much helpful advice in the early stages of the project, and John Henry in its final stages. Jitse M. van der Meer and Donald McNally of the Pascal Centre for Advanced Studies in Faith and Science, Redeemer College, Ancaster, Ontario, made a number of useful suggestions at the beginning.

The following have given generously of their time in reading essays: John Burnham, Ronald E. Doel, Paul Farber, Carl-Henry Geschwind, Jonathan Katz, Mary Jo Nye, Robert Nye, and Lisa Sarasohn. Many of the essays have been improved in style and logic by the lucid pen of Heather Ferngren. Bill Martin lent ready assistance in problems of software conversion. The support of my wife, Agnes Ferngren, in many ways and on many occasions, is beyond my ability adequately to acknowledge.

This project received the support of a joint grant from the Office of Research and the College of Liberal Arts, Oregon State University. Paul Farber facilitated its timely completion by rescheduling my teaching load at a crucial stage.

"Creationism Since 1859" by Ronald L. Numbers is abridged from "The Creationists," in *God and Nature: Historical Essays on the Encounter between Christianity and Science*, ed. by David C. Lindberg and Ronald L. Numbers (Berkeley and Los Angeles: University of California Press, 1986), pp. 391–423, and is used with the permission of the University of California Press. Complete documentation, including citations to sources quoted, can be found in the original essay.

"Cosmogonies from 1700 to 1900" by Ronald L. Numbers is extracted from *Creation by Natural Law: Laplace's Nebular Hypothesis in American Thought* (Seattle: University of Washington Press, 1977). Complete documentation, including citations to sources quoted, can be found in the original volume.

The first three-fourths of "Theories of Religious Insanity in America" by Ronald L. Numbers, Janet S. Swain, and Samuel B. Thielman is extracted from Ronald L. Numbers and Janet S. Numbers, "Millerism and Madness: A Study of 'Religious Insanity' in Nineteenth-Century America," *Bulletin of the Menninger Clinic* 49 (1985): 289–320, and is reprinted with permission. Complete documentation, including citations to sources quoted, can be found in the original article.

CONTRIBUTORS

Richard J. Blackwell
Professor of Philosophy and Danforth Chair in the
Humanities
Saint Louis University
St. Louis, Missouri
Galileo Galilei

Peter J. Bowler
Professor of History and Philosophy of Science
The Queen's University of Belfast
Belfast, Northern Ireland
Evolution

Thomas Broman
Associate Professor of the History of Science
University of Wisconsin-Madison
Madison, Wisconsin
The Enlightenment

Robert M. Burns
Lecturer, Department of Historical and
Cultural Studies
Goldsmiths' College
University of London
London, England
Miracles

William F. Bynum
Professor of the History of Medicine
University College, University of London, and the
Wellcome Institute for the History of Medicine
London, England
The Great Chain of Being

Charles D. Cashdollar
University Professor of History
Indiana University of Pennsylvania
Indiana, Pennsylvania
Positivism

Robin Collins
Assistant Professor of Philosophy
Messiah College
Grantham, Pennsylvania
Scientific Naturalism

Walter H. Conser Jr.
Professor of Philosophy and Religion
University of North Carolina-Wilmington
Wilmington, North Carolina
Baconianism

Deborah J. Coon
Assistant Professor of Psychology and Adjunct Assistant
Professor of History
University of New Hampshire
Durham, New Hampshire
Pragmatism; Spiritualism

William Lane Craig
Research Professor of Philosophy
Talbot School of Theology
La Mirada, California
The Anthropic Principle

Michael J. Crowe
Professor of Liberal Studies
University of Notre Dame
Notre Dame, Indiana
The Plurality of Worlds and Extraterrestrial Life

Lisle W. Dalton
Instructor of Religious Studies
University of Wisconsin-Oshkosh
Oshkosh, Wisconsin
Phrenology

Edward B. Davis
Associate Professor of the History of Science
Messiah College
Grantham, Pennsylvania
Early-Modern Protestantism; Scientific Naturalism

William A. Dembski
Senior Fellow
Center for the Renewal of Science and Culture,
Discovery Institute
Seattle, Washington
The Design Argument

Alnoor Dhanani
Independent scholar
Lexington, Massachusetts
Islam

Charles E. Dinsmore
Associate Professor of Anatomy
Rush Medical College
Chicago, Illinois
Premodern Theories of Generation

LeRoy E. Doggett†
Formerly Chief of the Nautical Almanac Office
United States Naval Observatory
Washington, D.C.
The Calendar

William Eamon
Professor of History
New Mexico State University
Las Cruces, New Mexico
Magic and the Occult

H. Tristram Engelhardt Jr.
Professor of Medicine
Center for Ethics, Medicine, and Public Issues
Baylor College of Medicine
Houston, Texas
Orthodoxy

Paul Farber
Distinguished Professor of History
Oregon State University
Corvallis, Oregon
Evolutionary Ethics

Edward Grant
Distinguished Professor Emeritus of History and
Philosophy of Science and Professor Emeritus of
History
Indiana University
Bloomington, Indiana
Aristotle and Aristotelianism; The Eternity of the World

Frederick Gregory
Professor of History
University of Florida
Gainesville, Florida
Materialism

David Ray Griffin
Professor of Philosophy of Religion
Claremont School of Theology and the Claremont
Graduate University, and Codirector,
Center for Process Studies
Claremont, California
Process Philosophy and Theology

Douglas Groothuis
Associate Professor of Philosophy of Religion and
Ethics
Denver Seminary
Denver, Colorado
Blaise Pascal

Steven J. Harris
Fellow, the Jesuit Institute
Boston College
Boston, Massachusetts
Roman Catholicism Since Trent

D. G. Hart
Librarian and Associate Professor of Church History
and Theological Bibliography
Westminster Theological Seminary
Philadelphia, Pennsylvania
Nineteenth-Century Biblical Criticism

Peter M. Hess
Associate Program Director
Science and Religion Course Program
Center for Theology and the Natural Sciences
Berkeley, California
Earthquakes; Natural History

Kenneth J. Howell
John Henry Newman Scholar in Residence
The Newman Foundation at the University of Illinois
Champaign, Illinois
Augustine of Hippo; Theodicy

Edward W. Hughes
Director, St. George Institute
Methuen, Massachusetts
Orthodoxy

Sarah Hutton
Reader in Renaissance and Seventeenth-Century Studies
Middlesex University
London, England
The Cambridge Platonists

Stanley L. Jaki
Distinguished University Professor
Seton Hall University
South Orange, New Jersey
God, Nature, and Science

David M. Knight
Professor of History and Philosophy of Science
University of Durham
Durham, England
Taxonomy

James Lattis
Director, Space Place
University of Wisconsin-Madison
Madison, Wisconsin
Pre-Copernican Astronomy

Thomas M. Lennon
Professor of Philosophy
University of Western Ontario
London, Ontario, Canada
Cartesianism

David N. Livingstone
Professor of Geography and Intellectual History
The Queen's University of Belfast
Belfast, Northern Ireland
Ecology and the Environment; Geography; The Origin and Unity of the Human Race

Peter Losin
Division of Education Programs
National Endowment for the Humanities
Washington, D.C.
Plato and Platonism

Craig Sean McConnell
Department of the History of Science
University of Wisconsin-Madison
Madison, Wisconsin
Twentieth-Century Cosmologies

Emerson Thomas McMullen
Associate Professor of History
Georgia Southern University
Statesboro, Georgia
Anatomy and Physiology to 1700

Stephen C. Meyer
Associate Professor of Philosophy
Whitworth College
Spokane, Washington
Senior Fellow, Discovery Institute
Seattle, Washington
The Demarcation of Science and Religion

Sara Miles
Dean of Undergraduate Programs and Associate
Professor of History and Biology
Eastern College
St. Davids, Pennsylvania
Gender

James R. Moore
Reader in History of Science and Technology
The Open University
Milton Keynes, England
Charles Darwin

Mark A. Noll
McManis Professor of Christian Thought
Wheaton College
Wheaton, Illinois
Evangelicalism and Fundamentalism

David R. Oldroyd
Professor, School of Science and Technology Studies
University of New South Wales
Sydney, New South Wales, Australia
Theories of the Earth and Its Age Before Darwin

Richard Olson
Professor of History and Willard W. Keith Jr. Fellow
in Humanities
Harvey Mudd College
Claremont, California
Physics

Margaret J. Osler
Professor of History
University of Calgary
Calgary, Alberta, Canada
Mechanical Philosophy; Skepticism; Varieties of Providentialism

Wade E. Pickren
Director, Archives and Library Services
American Psychological Association
Washington, D.C.
European Psychology

John Polkinghorne
Past President and Fellow, Queen's College
Cambridge University
Cambridge, England
Chaos Theory

Lawrence M. Principe
Senior Lecturer in Chemistry
Johns Hopkins University
Baltimore, Maryland
Alchemy

Jon H. Roberts
Professor of History
University of Wisconsin-Stevens Point
Stevens Point, Wisconsin
Psychology in America

Ira Robinson
Professor of Judaic Studies
Concordia University
Montreal, Quebec, Canada
Judaism Since 1700

David B. Ruderman
Joseph Meyerhoff Professor of Modern Jewish History
Director, Center for Judaic Studies
University of Pennsylvania
Philadelphia, Pennsylvania
Judaism to 1700

Nicolaas A. Rupke
Professor, Institut für Wissenschaftgeschichte
Georg-August-Universität Göttingen
Göttingen, Germany
Geology and Paleontology from 1700 to 1900; German Nature Philosophy

Colin A. Russell
Emeritus Professor in History of Science
and Technology
The Open University
Bedford, England
The Conflict of Science and Religion; Views of Nature

Lisa Sarasohn
Professor of History
Oregon State University
Corvallis, Oregon
Epicureanism

Robert J. Schadewald
Writer
Burnsville, Minnesota
Flat-Earthism; Geocentricity

Sara Schechner Genuth
Scholar in Residence
Center for History of Physics
American Institute of Physics
College Park, Maryland
Comets and Meteors

Rennie B. Schoepflin
Associate Professor of History
La Sierra University
Riverside, California
America's Innovative Nineteenth-Century Religions

Jole Shackelford
Assistant Professor, Program in the History of Science
and Technology
University of Minnesota
St. Paul, Minnesota
Hermeticism

Allyne L. Smith Jr.
Assistant Professor, Department of Health Care
Administration
University of Osteopathic Medicine and Health Science
Des Moines, Iowa
Orthodoxy

Laura A. Smoller
Assistant Professor of History
University of Arkansas-Little Rock
Little Rock, Arkansas
Astrology

Peter G. Sobol
Honorary Fellow, Department of the History of Science
University of Wisconsin-Madison
Madison, Wisconsin
The Cabala; Numbers; Theories of the Soul

John Stenhouse
Senior Lecturer, Department of History
University of Otago
Dunedin, New Zealand
Genesis and Science

Rodney L. Stiling
Lecturer, Integrated Liberal Studies Program
University of Wisconsin-Madison
Madison, Wisconsin
The Genesis Flood

Dennis Stillings
Director, Archaeus Project
Kamuela, Hawaii
Electricity

Frederick Suppe
Professor of Philosophy and Chair of the History and
Philosophy of Science Program
University of Maryland
College Park, Maryland
Epistemology

Janet S. Swain
Chief Psychologist
Department of Psychiatry
Dean Medical Center
Madison, Wisconsin
Theories of Religious Insanity in America

Ferenc M. Szaz
Professor of History
University of New Mexico
Albuquerque, New Mexico
Modern American Mainline Protestantism

Samuel B. Thielman
Adjunct Assistant Professor of Psychiatry
Duke University School of Medicine
Durham, North Carolina
Theories of Religious Insanity in America

Robert B. Todd
Professor, Department of Classical, Near-Eastern, and
Religious Studies
University of British Columbia
Vancouver, British Columbia, Canada
Stoicism

William A. Wallace
Professor Emeritus of Philosophy and History
The Catholic University of America
Washington, D.C.
Professor of Philosophy
University of Maryland
College Park, Maryland
Thomas Aquinas and Thomism

Richard Weikart
Assistant Professor of History
California State University at Stanislaus
Turlock, California
Genetics

Stephen P. Weldon
Visiting Scholar
Cornell University
Ithaca, New York
*Deism; Postmodernism; Secular Humanism; The Social
Construction of Science*

Richard S. Westfall†
Formerly Distinguished Professor of
History and Philosophy of Science
Indiana University
Bloomington, Indiana
Isaac Newton

David B. Wilson
Professor of History, Mechanical Engineering,
and Philosophy
Iowa State University
Ames, Iowa
The Historiography of Science and Religion

Leonard G. Wilson
Professor Emeritus of the History of Medicine
University of Minnesota
Minneapolis, Minnesota
Uniformitarianism and Actualism

Michael P. Winship
Assistant Professor of History
University of Georgia
Athens, Georgia
Early-Modern Protestantism

† indicates that the author is deceased

PART I

The Relationship of Science and Religion

1. The Historiography of Science and Religion

David B. Wilson

The history of science and religion has been a contentious subject. In addition to the usual scholarly disputes present in any academic area, this historical subject has been enmeshed in more general historiographical debates and influenced by the religious or antireligious beliefs of some historians. After considering some basic issues, this essay discusses several works written during the previous century and a half, while focusing on the last fifty years. Recent decades have seen a radical shift in point of view among historians of science.

Although historians have espoused various approaches to the past, it will make our subject more manageable if we concentrate on the polar opposites around which views have tended to cluster. One approach has been to examine past ideas as much as possible in their own context, without either judging their long-term validity or making the discussion directly relevant to present issues. Another approach has been to study past ideas from the perspective of the present, taking full advantage of the hindsight provided by later knowledge to judge which ideas have proven to be valid. The second approach has apparent advantages. It does not exclude current knowledge that can assist us in the historical task. It also keeps present issues to the fore by insisting that historians draw lessons from the past that are relevant to current issues. However, historians have tended to regard the second approach as precariously likely to lead to distortion of the past in the service of present concerns. Dismissing this as "presentism," therefore, historians of science have come to favor the first, or contextualist, approach.

Whichever method historians use, they might reach one of several possible conclusions about the historical relationship between science and religion. Conflict, mutual support, and total separation are three obvious candidates. One of these models might long have predominated, or the relationship might have changed from time to time and place to place. The discovery of conflict might raise the further questions of which side emerged victorious and which side ought to have done so. The discovery of mutual support might lead to the question of whether either science or religion contributed to the other's continued validity or even to its origin.

The Conflict Thesis

The most prominent view among both historians and scientists in the twentieth century has been a presentist conflict thesis that argues as follows. To engage in the history of science, one must first know what science is. It is certainly not religion, and, indeed, it is quite separate from religion, as can clearly be seen in science as practiced in the modern world. The historian of science, then, should properly examine the internal development of the scientific ideas that made modern science possible (that is, to the exclusion of such external factors as religion). The proponents of some ideas in the past were closer to the right track in this process than others. Those who expanded the realm of religion too far were on the wrong track, so that religion improperly intruded on the realm of science. In such instances, conflict ensued between science and religion, with scientific advances eventually making the truth clear to all and invariably (and rightly) emerging victorious. The historical process need not have occurred in this way, but it so often did that conflict has been the primary relationship between science and religion. Science's best-known victories were those of Copernicanism and Darwinism. Presentism, internalism, and the conflict thesis coalesced into a de facto alliance, with the result that the conflict model is still widely accepted by academics (historians and scientists alike), though generally no longer by historians of science. A gulf in point of view thus marks the immediate setting of any scholarly treatment of the subject for a popular audience.

That this alliance was not a necessary one can be seen in the work of William Whewell (1794–1866), the most prominent historian of science during the first half of the nineteenth century. Known today primarily as a historian and philosopher of science, Whewell was, first of all, a mathematical physicist, but also an Anglican clergyman and a moral theorist. His philosophy of science featured a series of what he called "fundamental ideas" (like the idea of space) that, as part of man's mind created in the image of God, figured crucially in scientific knowledge of God's other creation, nature. Moral knowledge was structured similarly. Both moral and scientific knowledge were progressive. Scientists, for example, gradually became aware of the existence and implications of fundamental ideas. The study of history, that is, disclosed (a sometimes lurching) progress toward the present or, at any rate, Whewell's particular version of the present. Great scientists, such as Isaac Newton (1642–1727), were both intellectually strong and morally good.

Whewell did not think that conflict between science and religion had been especially significant historically, nor, indeed, was it in Whewell's own day. From his vantage point, he could give medieval science the uncomplimentary epithet "stationary" for several reasons that did not particularly include religious repression. The Roman Catholic Church had acted against Galileo (1564–1642), to be sure, but, for Whewell, that episode was an aberration. A tightly knit, biblical-historical-philosophical-moral-scientific-theological unity was manifested in Whewell's major, mutually reinforcing, books: *History of the Inductive Sciences* (1837), *Foundation of Morals* (1837), *Philosophy of the Inductive Sciences* (1840), and *Elements of Morality* (1845).

John William Draper (1811–82), author of *History of the Conflict Between Religion and Science* (1874), and Andrew Dickson White (1832–1918), author of *The Warfare of Science* (1876) and *A History of the Warfare of Science with Theology in Christendom* (1896), lived in an age that was different from Whewell's. While the Darwinian debates of the 1860s preceded Draper's book, what really alarmed him during that decade was the formulation of the doctrine of papal infallibility and the Roman Catholic Church's pronouncement that public institutions teaching science were not exempt from its

authority. In his *History*, Draper depicted these developments as merely the latest phase in a long history of "the expansive force of the human intellect," in conflict not with religion generally, but with that "compression" inflicted by Catholicism. White developed and first published his views at about the same time as Draper. White's insights stemmed from his presidency of the new Cornell University, which was founded as a secular institution that stood in sharp contrast to the traditional religious sponsorship of colleges and universities. The withering criticism and innuendo directed at him personally by some religious figures led eventually to the writing of his books. Like those of Draper, White's books did not condemn all religion. They attacked what White called "that same old mistaken conception of rigid Scriptural interpretation" (White 1876, 75). White proclaimed that whenever such religion sought to constrain science, science eventually won but with harm to both religion and science in the process. Science and "true religion," however, were not at odds.

Had Whewell still been alive, White and Draper might have told him how their circumstances had helped them improve on his writing of history. Unlike Whewell, they believed that they had stood in the shoes, as it were, of those who had been persecuted. White seemed especially to identify with Galileo. Their improved awareness had, they thought, enabled them to observe factors that he had overlooked. In any case, their books were highly influential. Moreover, it was not their whispered qualifications but their screaming titles that were to thunder through the decades, remaining audible more than a century later.

Differences of opinion did not seem to alter what was to become the widely current views of Draper and White. In *Metaphysical Foundations of Modern Physical Science* (1924), E. A. Burtt argued that the foundations of science were often theological. Galileo's God, for example, labored as a geometrician in creating the world, with the result that man, who knew some mathematics as well as God did, was capable of grasping nature's essential mathematical logic. In *Science and the Modern World* (1926), Alfred North Whitehead maintained that the origin of modern science depended upon medieval theology, which had long insisted on God's rationality and hence also the rationality of his creation. Yet, in the 1930s, when his research suggested that seventeenth-century English Puritanism had fostered science, Robert K. Merton found that prevailing scholarly opinion, which had been shaped by the books of Draper and White, held that science and religion were inherently opposed and necessarily in conflict. Of course, the 1920s were the decade not only of Burtt and Whitehead, but also of the Scopes trial, which was generally interpreted as yet another in a long series of confrontations between science and religion. Also, during the 1920s and 1930s (and for some time afterward), the still undeveloped discipline of the history of science was pursued mainly by men trained in the sciences, who found presentist internalism a natural point of view.

Reaction to the Conflict Thesis

The Whig Interpretation of History (1931), written by the young general historian Herbert Butterfield, was eventually to influence the history of science deeply. Butterfield argued that historians had tended to be Protestant in religion and Whig in politics. They liked to divide the world into friends and enemies of progress—progress, that is, toward their own point of view. History was thus peopled by progressives and reactionaries, Whigs and Tories, Protestants and Catholics. Whig historians made the mistake of seeing Martin Luther, for example, as similar to modern Protestants rather than, as was actually the case, closer to sixteenth-century Catholics. By reading the present into the past in this way, Whig historians ratified the present, but only by misshaping the past. A better way was to assume that the sixteenth century was quite different from the twentieth and to explore the sixteenth century on its own terms, letting any similarities emerge from historical research rather than from prior assumption.

Butterfield's *Origins of Modern Science* (1949) applied this methodology to the history of science, including the relationship between science and religion, during the scientific revolution. By not viewing scientists of the past as necessarily similar to modern scientists, it was possible to reach historical insights quite different from those of, say, Whewell or White. Overall, the scientific revolution resulted not from accumulating new observations or experimental results, but from looking at the same evidence in a new way: It was a "transposition" in the minds of the scientists. The alleged revolutionary Copernicus (1473–1543) could now be understood as a "conservative," much akin to the Greek astronomers with whom he disagreed. Religion was not necessarily either opposed to or separate from science in the modern sense but could, in principle, be viewed in any relationship,

depending on the historical evidence. Reading the evidence in a non-Whiggish way, Butterfield saw variety. There was, to be sure, theological opposition to the Copernican system, but it would not have been very important if there had not also been considerable scientific opposition. Even Galileo did not actually prove the earth's motion, and his favorite argument in favor of it, that of the tides, was a "great mistake." Christianity favored the new mechanical worldview because it allowed a precise definition of miracles as events contrary to the usual mechanical regularity. Newton's gravitational theory required God's continued intervention in the universe he created, and one of Newton's possible explanations of gravity "made the existence of God logically necessary" (Butterfield 1949, 157). Butterfield's *Christianity and History* (1949) made his own Christian faith explicit, but his religious views did not make *Origins of Modern Science* into a Christian tract, though they guaranteed that Christian factors received a fair hearing.

Whatever the exact influence of Butterfield on them, three books published during the 1950s revealed the progress of non-Whiggish studies of science and religion during the scientific revolution. Alexandre Koyré, influenced by Burtt, had already published studies like "Galileo and Plato" (1943) a few years before Butterfield's *Origins of Modern Science.* In *From the Closed World to the Infinite Universe* (1957), Koyré argued that the revolution involved philosophy and theology as well as science and that all three dimensions of thought usually existed in "the very same men," such as Johannes Kepler (1571–1630), René Descartes (1596–1650), Isaac Newton, and Gottfried Wilhelm Leibniz (1646–1716). Koyré thus portrayed the conflict between Newton and Leibniz, one that involved Leibniz's stiff opposition to Newton's gravitational theory, as primarily a theological conflict. He contrasted Newton's "work-day God" (who caringly involved himself in the operation of his universe) with Leibniz's "God of the sabbath" (who created the world skillfully enough for it to run by itself). In his *The Copernican Revolution* (1957), Thomas Kuhn adopted the "unusual" approach of treating astronomers' philosophical and religious views as "equally fundamental" to their scientific ones. For the early Copernicans, at the center of the universe resided the sun, "the Neoplatonic symbol of the Deity" (Kuhn 1957, 231). Unlike Koyré's and Kuhn's books, Richard Westfall's *Science and Religion in Seventeenth-Century England* (1958) examined a variety of better- and lesser-known men of science (virtuosi) in a particular national context. In general, the virtuosi regarded their scientific discoveries as confirmation of their religious views, thus answering charges that studying nature both led man to value reason over revelation and made it difficult to know the nonmaterial side of existence. While there existed in the seventeenth century a multiplicity of ways to dovetail science and religion, there was a general movement from revealed religion to a natural theology that prepared the way for the deism of the next century.

The 1950s witnessed non-Whiggish studies of science and religion, not only in the century of Galileo and Newton, but in Darwin's century, too. In his "second look" in *Isis* at Charles Gillispie's *Genesis and Geology* (1951), Nicolaas Rupke credited Gillispie with transforming the historiography of geology by going beyond the great ideas of great men as defined by modern geology to the actual religious-political-scientific context of British geology in the decades before Darwin's *Origin of Species* (1859). Explicitly rejecting the conflict thesis of Draper and White, Gillispie saw "the difficulty between science and Protestant Christianity . . . to be one of religion (in a crude sense) *in* science rather than one of religion *versus* science" (Gillispie 1951, ix). Writing about a period in which geologists were often themselves clergymen, Gillispie thought "that the issues discussed arose from a quasi-theological frame of mind within science" (Gillispie 1951, x). At the end of the decade, John Greene published *The Death of Adam* (1959), an examination of the shift from the "static creationism" of Newton's day to the evolutionary views of Darwin's. Without making any particular point of rejecting the Draper-White conflict thesis, Greene nevertheless did so implicitly, calling attention "to the religious aspect of scientific thought" (Greene 1959, vi) and infusing his book with examples of a variety of connections between religion and science. Thus, Georges Louis Leclerc, Comte de Buffon (1707–88), was forced to fit his science to the religious views of the day but found evolution contrary to Scripture, reason, and experience. William Whiston (1667–1752) employed science to explain scriptural events, rejecting alternative biblical views that were either too literal or too allegorical. Charles Darwin (1809–82) jousted with fellow scientists Charles Lyell (1797–1875) and Asa Gray (1810–88) about the sufficiency of natural selection as opposed to God's guidance and design in evolutionary processes.

Christian Foundations of Modern Science

If these notable books of the 1950s rejected the conflict thesis in various ways, two books from the early 1970s went even further, turning the thesis on its head to declare (echoing Whitehead) that Christianity had made science possible. The first was Reijer Hooykaas's *Religion and the Rise of Modern Science* (1972). The Protestant historian Hooykaas (1906–94) had explored the relations between science and religion for several years. His *Natural Law and Divine Miracle* (1959), for example, showed the compatibility of what he called "a Biblical concept of nature" with nineteenth-century biology and geology. In 1972, he went further by arguing for a Christian, especially Calvinistic, origin of science itself. After discussing Greek concepts of nature, Hooykaas concluded that, in the Bible, "in total contradiction to pagan religion, nature is not a deity to be feared and worshipped, but a work of God to be admired, studied and managed" (Hooykaas 1972, 9). Not only did the Bible "de-deify" nature, Calvinism encouraged science through such principles as voluntaristic theology, a "positive appreciation" of manual work, and an "accommodation" theory of the Bible. Voluntarism emphasized that God could choose to create nature in any way he wanted and that man, therefore, had to experience nature to discover God's choice. This stimulus to experimental science was reinforced by the high value that Christianity placed on manual labor. The view that, in biblical revelation, God had accommodated himself to ordinary human understanding in matters of science meant that Calvinists generally did not employ biblical literalism to reject scientific findings, particularly Copernican astronomy.

Stanley L. Jaki's *Science and Creation* (1974) also expanded themes that were present in his earlier chapter "Physics and Theology" in his *The Relevance of Physics* (1966). Jaki was a Benedictine priest with doctorates in both theology and physics. His *Science and Creation,* a book of breathtaking scope, examined several non-Western cultures before focusing on the origin of science within the Judeo-Christian framework. Jaki argued that two barriers to science pervaded other cultures: a cyclic view of history and an organic view of nature. Endless cycles of human history made men too apathetic to study nature. Even when they did, their concept of a living, willful nature precluded discovery of those unvarying patterns that science labels natural laws. The Judeo-Christian view, in contrast, historically regarded nature as the nonliving creation of a rational God, not cyclic but with a definite beginning and end. In this conceptual context (and only in this context), modern science emerged, from the thirteenth through the seventeenth centuries. Earlier adumbrations of science were pale, short-lived imitations, doomed by hostile environments. Unfortunately, Jaki thought, amidst attacks on Christianity in the twentieth century, there had arisen the theory of an oscillating universe, which was another unwarranted, unscientific, cyclic view of nature. Hence, consideration of both past and present disclosed the same truth: "the indispensability of a firm faith in the only lasting source of rationality and confidence, the Maker of heaven and earth, of all things visible and invisible" (Jaki 1974, 357).

The Continuing Influence of the Conflict Thesis

Despite the growing number of scholarly modifications and rejections of the conflict model from the 1950s on, the Draper-White thesis proved to be tenacious, though it is probably true that it had been more successfully dispelled for the seventeenth century than for the nineteenth. At any rate, in the 1970s leading historians of the nineteenth century still felt required to attack it. In the second volume of his *The Victorian Church* (1970), Owen Chadwick viewed the conflict thesis as a misconception that many Victorians had about themselves. His *The Secularization of the European Mind* (1975) presented Draper's antithesis as the view to attack by way of explaining one aspect of nineteenth-century secularization. Writing about Charles Lyell in 1975, Martin Rudwick also deplored distortions produced by Draper and White, arguing that abandoning their outdated historiography would solve puzzles surrounding Lyell's time at King's College, London. Examining nineteenth-century European thought in *History, Man, and Reason* (1971), the philosopher-historian Maurice Mandelbaum rejected what he called "the conventional view of the place of religion in the thought of the nineteenth century," which "holds that science and religion were ranged in open hostility, and that unremitting warfare was conducted between them" (Mandelbaum 1971, 28).

Why did these historians believe that the conflict thesis was sufficiently alive and well to require refuta-

tion? For one thing, even those historians who were most significant in undermining the conflict thesis did not reject it entirely. Moreover, they made statements that could be construed as more supportive of the thesis than perhaps they intended. "Conflict with science" was the only subheading under "Religion" in the index to Gillispie's *The Edge of Objectivity* (1960), and it directed the reader to statements that seemed to support the conflict model. What geology in the 1830s "needed to become a science was to retrieve its soul from the grasp of theology" (Gillispie 1960, 299). "There was never a more unnecessary battle than that between science and theology in the nineteenth century" (Gillispie 1960, 347). Even Gillispie's *Genesis and Geology* was criticized by Rudwick in 1975 as only a more sophisticated variety of the "positivist" historiography of Draper and White. Westfall, in a preface to the 1973 paperback edition of his book, wrote: "In 1600, Western civilization found its focus in the Christian religion; by 1700, modern natural science had displaced religion from its central position" (Westfall 1973, ix). Greene introduced the subjects of the four chapters in his *Darwin and the Modern World View* (1961) as four stages in "the modern conflict between science and religion" (Greene 1961, 12). Surely, the most widely known book written by a historian of science, Kuhn's *Structure of Scientific Revolutions* (1962), excluded those philosophical and religious views that Kuhn had earlier (in his *Copernican Revolution* [1957]) labeled "equally fundamental" aspects of astronomy. This exclusion undoubtedly aided the view that a conflict existed, a view that was the ally of internalism. The 1970s were a period in which past scientists' religious statements could still be dismissed as "ornamental or ceremonial flourishes" or as "political gestures." The "orthodoxy" of internalism among historians of science in the 1960s and early 1970s was the target of the fascinating autobiographical account of life as a student and teacher at Cambridge University by Robert Young in his contribution to *Changing Perspectives in the History of Science* (1973). And even Young, whose own pathbreaking nonconflictive articles from around 1970 were later reprinted in *Darwin's Metaphor* (1985), wrote in his 1973 piece that "the famous controversy in the nineteenth century between science and theology was very heated indeed" (Young 1973, 376).

A second factor was the prevailing view among scientists themselves, which influenced historians of science, who either had their own early training in science or maintained regular contact with scientists, or both. In this regard, we might consider the work of the scientist-historian Stephen Jay Gould, one of the most successful popularizers of both science and the history of science. A collection of his popular essays appeared in 1977 as *Ever Since Darwin*. Gould stoutly rejected the "simplistic but common view of the relationship between science and religion—they are natural antagonists" (Gould 1977, 141). However, the book's specific instances came preponderantly from the conflict theorist's familiar bag of examples: the Church's disagreeing with Galileo; T. H. Huxley's "creaming" Bishop "Soapy Sam" Wilberforce; natural selection's displacing of divine creation; and, as Freud said, man's losing his status as a divinely created rational being at the center of the universe because of the science of Copernicus, Darwin, and Freud himself. Gould's most sympathetic chapter was his discussion of Thomas Burnet's late-seventeenth-century geological explanations of biblical events like Noah's flood. Even here, however, Gould regarded the views of Burnet's opponents as dogmatic and antirationalist, reflecting the same unhappy spirit that, wrote Gould, later possessed Samuel Wilberforce, William Jennings Bryan, and modern creationists. "The Yahoos never rest" (Gould 1977, 146).

Whatever the reasons for the continued survival of the conflict thesis, two other books on the nineteenth century that were published in the 1970s hastened its final demise among historians of science. In 1974, Frank Turner carved out new conceptual territory in *Between Science and Religion*. He studied six late Victorians (including Alfred Russel Wallace, the co-inventor of the theory of evolution by natural selection) who rejected both Christianity and the agnostic "scientific naturalism" of the time. In their various ways, they used different methods, including the empiricism of science (but not the Bible), to support two traditionally religious ideas: the existence of a God and the reality of human immortality. Even more decisive was the penetrating critique "Historians and Historiography" that James Moore placed at the beginning of his *Post-Darwinian Controversies* (1979). In what would have been a small book in itself, Moore's analysis adroitly explored the historical origins of Draper and White's "military metaphor" and went on to show how the metaphor promulgated false dichotomies: between science and religion, between scientists and theologians, between scientific and religious institutions. The metaphor simply could not handle, for

example, a case of two scientist-clergymen who disagreed about a scientific conclusion partly because of their religious differences. Finally, Moore called for historians to write "non-violent" history, of which the remainder of his book was a prodigious example. Examining Protestant responses to Darwin's ideas, he concluded that it was an "orthodox" version of Protestantism that "came to terms" with Darwin more easily than did either a more liberal or a more conservative version and, in addition, that much anguish would have been spared had this orthodoxy prevailed.

The Complexity Thesis

By the 1980s and 1990s, there had been nearly a complete revolution in historical methodology and interpretation. Setting aside his own views of science and religion, the historian was expected to write non-Whiggish history to avoid what Maurice Mandelbaum called the "retrospective fallacy." This fallacy consisted of holding an asymmetrical view of the past and the future, in which the past was seen as like a solid, with all of its parts irrevocably fixed in place, while the future was viewed as fluid, unformed, and unforeseen. The problem for the historian was to transpose his mind to such an extent that a historical figure's future (which was part of the historian's own past) lost the fixity and inevitability that the historian perceived in it and, instead, took on the uncertainty that it had for the historical figure. The concern for what led to the present, and the extent to which it was right or wrong by present standards, thus dissipated. A good test for the historian was whether he could write a wholly sympathetic account of a historical figure with whom he totally disagreed or whose ideas he found repugnant. Would the historical figure, if by some magic given the chance to read the historian's reconstruction, say that, indeed, it explained what he thought and his reasons for doing so? To be valid, any broader historical generalization had to be based on specific, non-Whiggish studies that accurately represented past thought.

This radically different methodology yielded a very different overall conclusion about the historical relationship of science and religion. If "conflict" expressed the gist of an earlier view, "complexity" embodied that of the new. The new approach exposed internalism as incomplete and conflict as distortion. Past thought turned out to be terribly complex, manifesting numerous combinations of scientific and religious ideas, which, to be fully understood, often required delineation of their social and political settings.

From this mainstream perspective, moreover, historians could deem other approaches unacceptable. Zeal for the triumph of either science or religion in the present could lure historians into Whiggish history. The works not only of Draper and White, but also of Hooykaas and Jaki fell into that category. Kenneth Thibodeau's review in *Isis* of Jaki's *Science and Creation,* for example, declared it "a lopsided picture of the history of science" that "minimizes" the accomplishments of non-Christian cultures and "exaggerates" those of Christian ones (Thibodeau 1976, 112). In a review in *Archives Internationale d'Histoire des Sciences,* William Wallace found Hooykaas's *Religion and the Rise of Modern Science* to be "a case of special pleading." In their historiographical introduction to the book they edited, *God and Nature* (1986), David Lindberg and Ronald Numbers judged that Hooykaas and Jaki had "sacrificed careful history for scarcely concealed apologetics" (Lindberg and Numbers 1986, 5). Likewise, some historians found Moore's nonviolent history unacceptable: He "sometimes seems to be writing like an apologist for some view of Christianity" (La Vergata 1985, 950), criticized Antonella La Vergata in his contribution to *The Darwinian Heritage* (1985).

Among the multitude of articles and books that argued for a relatively new, non-Whiggish complexity thesis, two exemplars were Lindberg and Numbers's *God and Nature* and John Brooke's *Science and Religion* (1991). Though similar in outlook, they differed in format. The first was a collection of eighteen studies by leading scholars in their own areas of specialty, while the second was a single scholar's synthesis of a staggering amount of scholarship, an appreciable portion of which was his own specialized research.

Turning in their introduction to the contents of their own volume, Lindberg and Numbers rightly observed that "almost every chapter portrays a complex and diverse interaction that defies reduction to simple 'conflict' or 'harmony'" (Lindberg and Numbers 1986, 10). Medieval science, for example, was a "handmaiden" to theology (but not suppressed), while the close interlocking of science and religion that developed by the seventeenth century began to unravel in the eighteenth. To examine briefly the complexity of only one chapter, consider James Moore's (nonapologetic) discussion of "Geologists and Interpreters of Genesis in the Nine-

teenth Century." Moore focused on British intellectual debates occurring in a variegated context of geographical, social, generational, institutional, and professional differences. Around 1830, professional geologists (that is, those with specialist expertise) tended to "harmonize" Genesis and geology by using geology to explain the sense in which the natural history of Genesis was true. They were opposed by nonprofessional "Scriptural geologists," who used Genesis to determine geological truths. By the 1860s, a new generation of professional geologists did their geology independently of Genesis. They were in agreement with a new generation of professional biblical scholars in Britain, who believed that Genesis and geology should be understood separately. Meanwhile, the earlier conflicting traditions of harmonization and scriptural geology were kept going by amateurs. Hence, while debate over how to meld Genesis and geology was a social reality in late-Victorian Britain, it did not perturb the elite level of the professionals. Numbers expanded his own chapter in *God and Nature* into *The Creationists* (1992), an outstanding treatment of such issues at the nonelite level in the twentieth century.

Brooke's volume targeted general readers in a way that Lindberg and Numbers's did not. In his historiographical remarks, Brooke considered the very meanings of the words "science" and "religion," resisting specific definitions for them. The problem, Brooke explained, was that the words had so many meanings. It could even be misleading to refer to Isaac Newton's "science," when Newton called what he was doing "natural philosophy," a phrase connoting quite different issues in the seventeenth century than did "science" in the twentieth. As did Lindberg and Numbers, Brooke found complexity: "The principal aim of this book," he wrote, "has been to reveal something of the complexity of the relationship between science and religion as they have interacted in the past" (Brooke 1991, 321). As for Lindberg and Numbers, so also for Brooke, complexity did not preclude general theses. He concluded, for example, that science went from being "subordinate" to religion in the Middle Ages to a position of relative equality in the seventeenth century, not separate from religion but "differentiated" from it.

Conclusion

This essay, in rejecting presentist histories of science and religion, may itself seem somewhat presentist. Though it tries fairly to present the opposite point of view, it favors the recent historiographical revolution in advocating a contextualist approach, with all its attendant complexities. Though the new point of view has decided advantages over the old, it has the potential of leading historians astray. Pursuit of complexity could produce ever narrower studies that are void of generalization. Moreover, awareness of the great variation of views in different times and places could lead to the mistaken conclusion that those ideas were nothing but reflections of their own "cultures." Instead, in thinking about science and religion, as in most human endeavors, there have always been the relatively few who have done their work better than the rest. Existence of differences among them does not mean that they have not thought through and justified their own positions. In fact, that they have done so is an example of a contextualist generalization—one that is not only in harmony with the evidence of the past, but also relevant to present discussions.

Indeed, the whole non-Whiggish enterprise might inform the present in other ways, too, though scholars are understandably wary of drawing very specific lessons from history for the present. Consider, however, a few general points. Study of past ideas on their own terms might provide a kind of practice for working out one's own ideas or for nourishing tolerance for the ideas of others. There have been and, no doubt, always will be disagreements among our strongest thinkers, as well as questions of the relationship between their ideas and those of the population at large. Moreover, things always change, though not predictably or necessarily completely. Indeed, the most influential thinkers seem fated to have followers who disagree with them, even while invoking their names. Even the most well-founded, well-argued, and well-intentioned ideas about science and religion are liable to later change or eventual rejection. The same is true for historiographical positions, including, of course, the complexity thesis itself.

See also Conflict of Science and Religion

BIBLIOGRAPHY

Brooke, John Hedley. *Science and Religion: Some Historical Perspectives.* Cambridge: Cambridge University Press, 1991.

Butterfield, Herbert. *The Whig Interpretation of History.* 1931. Reprint. New York: Norton, 1965.

Daston, Lorraine. "A Second Look. History of Science in an Elegiac Mode: E. A. Burtt's *Metaphysical Foundations of Modern Physical Science* Revisited." *Isis* 82 (1991): 522–31.

Draper, John William. *History of the Conflict Between Religion and Science.* 1874. Reprint. New York: Appleton, 1928.

Fisch, Menachem, and Simon Schaffer, eds. *William Whewell: A Composite Portrait.* Oxford: Clarendon, 1991.

Gillispie, Charles Coulton. *Genesis and Geology: A Study in the Relations of Scientific Thought, Natural Theology, and Social Opinion in Great Britain, 1790–1850.* 1951. Reprint. New York: Harper Torchbooks, 1959.

———. *The Edge of Objectivity: An Essay in the History of Scientific Ideas.* Princeton, N.J.: Princeton University Press, 1960.

Gould, Stephen Jay. *Ever Since Darwin: Reflections in Natural History.* New York: Norton, 1977.

Greene, John C. *The Death of Adam: Evolution and Its Impact on Western Thought.* Ames: Iowa State University Press, 1959.

———. *Darwin and the Modern World View.* 1961. Reprint. New York: New American Library, 1963.

Hooykaas, R. *Natural Law and Divine Miracle: The Principle of Uniformity in Geology, Biology, and Theology.* 2d imp. Leiden: E.J. Brill, 1963.

———. *Religion and the Rise of Modern Science.* 1972. Reprint. Edinburgh: Scottish Academic Press, 1973.

Jaki, Stanley L. *The Relevance of Physics.* Chicago: University of Chicago Press, 1966.

———. *Science and Creation: From Eternal Cycles to an Oscillating Universe.* Edinburgh: Scottish Academic Press, 1974.

Koyré, Alexandre. "Galileo and Plato." *Journal of the History of Ideas* 4 (1943): 400–28.

———. *From the Closed World to the Infinite Universe.* Baltimore: Johns Hopkins University Press, 1957.

Kuhn, Thomas S. *The Copernican Revolution: Planetary Astronomy in the Development of Western Thought.* New York: Vintage Books, 1957.

———. *The Structure of Scientific Revolutions.* 1962. 2d ed. Chicago: University of Chicago Press, 1970.

La Vergata, Antonello. "Images of Darwin: A Historiographic Overview." In *The Darwinian Heritage,* ed. by David Kohn, with bibliographical assistance from Malcolm J. Kottler. Princeton, N.J.: Princeton University Press, 1985, 901–72.

Lindberg, David C., and Ronald L. Numbers, eds. *God and Nature: Historical Essays on the Encounter Between Christianity and Science.* Berkeley: University of California Press, 1986.

Mandelbaum, Maurice. *History, Man, and Reason: A Study in Nineteenth-Century Thought.* Baltimore: Johns Hopkins University Press, 1971.

Merton, Robert K. *Science, Technology and Society in Seventeenth Century England.* 1938. Reprint. New York: Harper and Row, 1970.

Moore, James R. *The Post-Darwinian Controversies: A Study of the Protestant Struggle to Come to Terms with Darwin in Great Britain and America, 1870–1900.* Cambridge: Cambridge University Press, 1979.

Rudwick, Martin. "The Principle of Uniformity." Review of R. Hooykaas, *Natural Law and Divine Miracle. History of Science* 1 (1962): 82–6.

————. "Charles Lyell, F.R.S. (1797–1875) and His London Lectures on Geology, 1832–1833." *Notes and Records of the Royal Society of London* 29 (1975): 231–63.

Rupke, Nicolaas A. "A Second Look. C. C. Gillispie's *Genesis and Geology*." *Isis* 85 (1994): 261–70.

Thibodeau, Kenneth F. Review of *Science and Creation,* by Stanley L. Jaki. *Isis* 67 (1976): 112.

Turner, Frank Miller. *Between Science and Religion: The Reaction to Scientific Naturalism in Late Victorian England.* New Haven, Conn.: Yale University Press, 1974.

Wallace, William A. Review of R. Hooykaas, *Religion and the Rise of Modern Science,* and J. Waardenburg, *Classical Approaches to the Study of Religion. Archives Internationale d' Histoire des Sciences* 25 (1975): 154–6.

Westfall, Richard S. *Science and Religion in Seventeenth-Century England.* 1958. Reprint. Ann Arbor: University of Michigan Press, 1973.

Westman, Robert S. "A Second Look. Two Cultures or One? A Second Look at Kuhn's *The Copernican Revolution*." *Isis* 85 (1994): 79–115.

White, Andrew Dickson. *The Warfare of Science.* New York: Appleton, 1876.

————. *A History of the Warfare of Science with Theology in Christendom.* 2 vols. New York: Appleton, 1897.

Wilson, David B. "On the Importance of Eliminating *Science* and *Religion* from the History of Science and Religion: The Cases of Oliver Lodge, J. H. Jeans, and A. S. Eddington." In *Facets of Faith and Science,* ed. by Jitse M. van der Meer. Vol. 1: *Historiography and Modes of Interaction.* Lanham, Md.: The Pascal Centre for Advanced Studies in Faith and Science/University Press of America, 1996, 27–47.

Young, Robert M. "The Historiographic and Ideological Contexts of the Nineteenth-Century Debate on Man's Place in Nature." In *Changing Perspectives in the History of Science: Essays in Honour of Joseph Needham,* ed. by Mikulas Teich and Robert M. Young. London: Heinemann, 1973, 344–438. Reprinted in Robert M. Young, *Darwin's Metaphor: Nature's Place in Victorian Culture.* Cambridge: Cambridge University Press, 1985, 164–247.

————. *Darwin's Metaphor: Nature's Place in Victorian Culture.* Cambridge: Cambridge University Press, 1985.

2. THE CONFLICT OF SCIENCE AND RELIGION

Colin A. Russell

The Conflict Thesis

The history of science has often been regarded as a series of conflicts between science and religion (usually Christianity), of which the cases of Galileo Galilei (1564–1642) and Charles Darwin (1809–82) are merely the most celebrated examples. Some would go further and argue that such conflict is endemic in the historical process, seeing these and other confrontations as occasional eruptions of a deep-seated inclination that is always present, if not always quite so spectacularly visible. There is usually the additional assumption, implicit or explicit, that the outcome of such conflict will always and inevitably be the victory of science, even if only in the long term. Such a view of the relations between science and religion has been variously described as a "conflict thesis," a "military metaphor," or simply a "warfare model."

The considerable literature on this subject began with two famous works of the nineteenth century: John William Draper's *History of the Conflict Between Religion and Science* (1874) and Andrew Dickson White's *A History of the Warfare of Science with Theology in Christendom* (1896). A more mature work of the twentieth century, J. Y. Simpson's *Landmarks in the Struggle Between Science and Religion* (1925), adds to the vocabulary of metaphors by positing a struggle between science and religion. The first two books achieved a wide circulation and have been repeatedly reprinted. They were written at a time when science seemed triumphant at home and abroad, and each author had his particular reasons for settling old scores with organized religion. Draper, a professor of chemistry and physics in a medical school in New York, feared the power wielded by the Roman Catholic Church and was worried by the promulgation of the dogma of papal infallibility of 1870. White, professor of history at the University of Michigan and later president of Cornell (the first private nonsectarian university in the United States), was not surprisingly opposed by the advocates of sectarian theology. White's book thus became a manifesto directed (in the last version) not so much against religion as against dogmatic theology.

For nearly a century, the notion of mutual hostility (the Draper-White thesis) has been routinely employed in popular-science writing, by the media, and in a few older histories of science. Deeply embedded in the culture of the West, it has proven extremely hard to dislodge. Only in the last thirty years of the twentieth century have historians of science mounted a sustained attack on the thesis and only gradually has a wider public begun to recognize its deficiencies.

Issues of Contention

First, it may be helpful to spell out briefly the chief issues of contention around which the real or imagined conflict revolves. Initially these issues were in the area of epistemology: Could what we know about the world through science be integrated with what we learn about it from religion? If not, a situation of permanent conflict seemed probable. Such epistemological issues were first raised on a large scale by the Copernican displacement of the earth from the center of the solar system, which was clearly incompatible with what seemed to be the biblical world picture of a geocentric universe. The question, though posed by Copernicus (1473–1543) himself, caused little public stir until the apparent conflict became inextricably intertwined with other clerico-political disagreements at the time of Galileo. With hindsight, it is truly remarkable that, as early as the sixteenth century, Copernicus and his disciple Georg Joachim Rheticus (1514–74) resolved the issue to their satisfaction by invoking the patristic distinction between the Bible's teaching on spiritual and eternal realities and its descriptions of the natural world in the language of ordinary people. Rheticus specifically appealed to Augustine's doctrine of "accommodation," asserting that the Holy Spirit accommodated himself on the pages of Scripture to the everyday language and terminology of appearances. What began to emerge was what later became the distinction between world picture and worldview, the former being mechanistic, tentative, and expendable, while the latter concerned values and principles that were likely to endure. This same principle imbued the work both of Galileo and his followers and of Johannes Kepler (1571–1630) and effectively defused the issue for a majority of Christian believers. If they were right, there was an absence of conflict not only over the specific case of cosmology but, in principle, over anything else in which scientific and biblical statements appeared to be in contradiction. A "conflict thesis" would have seemed untenable because there was nothing to fight about. However, the historical realities were such that these lessons were not quickly learned.

Despite the advent in the late eighteenth century of evidence for a much older Earth than had been imagined on the basis of the Mosaic account in Genesis, little opposition arose until the emergence in early-Victorian England of a disparate but vocal group of "scriptural geologists." They were not, as is often claimed, a group of naive scientific incompetents, but, indeed, were often rather able men who saw a distinction between biblical descriptions of the present natural world and of events in the past, respectively corresponding to their understandings of physical science and history. While for the most part happy to accept "accommodation" over biblical references to the sun and Earth, they were not prepared to extend it to what appeared to be descriptions of history, including chronology. The potential for conflict was greatest where science had a historical content (as in geology or biology). The war cries of the "scriptural geologists" were echoed by those who, in due course, assailed Darwinian evolution on the same grounds.

A second, and related, area of contention has been in the realm of methodology. Here we find the age-old polarization between a science based on "facts" and a theology derived from "faith," or between a naturalistic and a religious worldview. Naturalism has had a long his-

tory, going back to the early Middle Ages and beyond, with a spectacular revival in nineteenth-century England that was dignified by the title of "scientific naturalism." It was a view that denied the right of the church to "interfere" in the progress of science by introducing theological considerations into scientific debates. By the same token, any appeal to divine purpose as an explanation of otherwise inexplicable phenomena has been a famous hostage to fortune. This philosophy of "God of the gaps" has generated special heat when one of the "gaps" has later been filled naturalistically. In these cases, conflict has certainly appeared, though whether it is really about methodological issues may be doubted. It has also been argued in a veritable torrent of informed and scholarly works that the methodologies of science and of religion are complementary rather than contradictory, and local instances of dispute have been assigned to other causes. Yet, this confusion still penetrates popular thinking, and the conflict thesis has been thereby sustained.

The third potential for conflict has been in the field of ethics. Most recently this has been realized in such questions as genetic engineering, nuclear power, and proliferation of insecticides. Past debates on the propriety of such medical procedures as vaccination and anesthesia have been replaced by impassioned conflict over abortion and the value of fetal life. In Victorian times, one of the more serious reasons for opposing Darwin was the fear that his theories would lead to the law of the jungle, the abandonment of ethical constraints in society. Yet, in nearly all of these cases, it is not so much science as its application (often by nonscientists) that has been under judgment.

Fourth, some opposition between science and religion has arisen from issues of social power. In Catholic cultures in continental Europe, the polarity between sacred and secular was often much sharper than in Britain and the United States, with the result that progressive science-based ideologies were more frequently in explicit contention with conservative political and ecclesiastical forces. In early-nineteenth-century Britain, certain high-church Anglicans turned on science for threatening their dominant role in society. While this debate was formally about the authority of Scripture, in reality it was about the growing spirit of liberalism within the universities. Not surprisingly, the community of science resented such attacks and, in due course, turned the table on the enemy.

Their response came in the form of a concerted effort by certain scientific naturalists in Victorian

England, most notably those associated with Thomas Henry Huxley (1825–95), to overthrow the hegemony of the English church. The movement, which was accompanied by bitter conflict, generated a flood of articles, lay "sermons," and verbal attacks on the clergy and included conspiratorial attempts to get the "right men" in to key positions in the scientific establishment. It involved lectures, secular Sunday schools, and even a successful lobby to have Charles Darwin's body interred in Westminster Abbey. Yet, it was not a battle between science and religion except in the narrowest sense. Unlike White, who averred that he opposed not religion but dogmatic theology, Huxley sought to undermine organized religion, though his rhetoric frequently sought to convey the impression of a disinterested defence of truth. One recent writer identifies the driving force behind at least the Victorian struggles as "the effort by scientists to improve the position of science. They wanted nothing less than to move science from the periphery to the centre of English life" (Heyck 1982, 87). It was at this time that science became professionalized, with the world's first professional institute for science, the Institute of Chemistry, established in 1877. In Europe, it was also the period when scientific leadership began to slip from Britain to Germany, generating a fierce rearguard reaction by some British scientists against anything that could diminish their public standing. If the Church was seen to be in their way, it must be opposed by all means, including the fostering of a conflict myth, in which religion routinely suffered defeat at the hands of triumphalist science.

The Weaknesses of the Conflict Thesis

The conflict thesis, at least in its simple form, is now widely perceived as a wholly inadequate intellectual framework within which to construct a sensitive and realistic historiography of Western science. Nor was it merely a case of British controversy. Ronald L. Numbers has suggested that "the war between science and theology in colonial America has existed primarily in the cliché-bound minds of historians." He regards the polemically attractive warfare thesis as "historically bankrupt" (Numbers 1985, 64, 80). In the composite volume *God and Nature: Historical Essays on the Encounter between Christianity and Science* (1986), edited by Numbers and his colleague at the University of Wisconsin, David C. Lindberg, an effort is made to correct the stereotypical view of conflict between Christianity and science.

The shortcomings of the conflict thesis arise from a multiplicity of reasons, some of which may be briefly summarized as follows.

First, the conflict thesis hinders the recognition of other relationships between science and religion. At different phases of their history, they were not so much at war as largely independent, mutually encouraging, or even symbiotic. Certainly there are well-documented cases, such as those of Galileo and Darwin, in which science and religion seemed to wage open war with each other. But recent scholarship has demonstrated the complexity of the issues at stake in even these cases, with ecclesiastical politics, social change, and personal circumstances as relevant as questions of science and religion. Quite apart from those considerations, such cases have been too often taken as typical, and, consequently, a generalized conflict thesis has been erected on insubstantial foundations. As a historical tool, the conflict thesis is so blunt that it is more damaging than serviceable. One has only to consider the "two books" of Francis Bacon (1561–1626)—nature and Scripture—each of which had a role complementary to that of the other. They were held not to be at odds with each other, because they dealt with different subjects. Again, for many major scientific figures in the seventeenth and eighteenth centuries, Christianity played a central role in fostering and even shaping their scientific endeavors: The instances of Kepler, Robert Boyle (1627–91), Isaac Newton (1642–1727), and René Descartes (1596–1650) are the most conspicuous. The historical relations between religion and science are certainly more rich and complex than a simple conflict thesis suggests.

Second, and more specific, the conflict thesis ignores the many documented examples of science and religion operating in close alliance. This was most obviously true of the seventeenth and eighteenth centuries, as evidenced by the names of Boyle, Newton, Blaise Pascal (1623–62), Marin Mersenne (1588–1648), Pierre Gassendi (1592–1655), and Isaac Beeckman (1588–1637). Since then, a continuous history of noted individuals making strenuous efforts to integrate their science and religion has testified to the poverty of a conflict model. This was particularly true in Britain, where representatives in the nineteenth century included most famously Michael Faraday (1791–1867), James Joule (1818–89), James Clerk Maxwell (1831–79), William Thomson (Lord Kelvin

[1824–1907]), and George Gabriel Stokes (1819–1903). In the next century, a number of distinguished scientists of religious persuasion were ready to join societies like the Victoria Institute in London or its successors in Britain and the United States, which were dedicated to bringing together religious and scientific ideas. The English-speaking world was not unique in this quest for integration but has certainly been the most subject to historical scrutiny.

Third, the conflict thesis enshrines a flawed view of history in which "progress" or (in this case) "victory" has been portrayed as inevitable. There appears to be no inherent reason why this should be so, though it is readily understandable why some should wish it to be the case. This approach represents and embraces a long demolished tradition of positivist, Whiggish historiography.

Fourth, the conflict thesis obscures the rich diversity of ideas in both science and religion. Neither of these has ever been monolithic, and there was seldom a unified reaction from either. Thus, in the case of Galileo, it was the Roman Catholic, not the Protestant, wing of Christianity that appeared to be at odds with science. In the Darwinian controversy, a uniform response was lacking even within one branch of Protestantism, for Anglicans of low-, high-, or broad-church persuasion tended to respond to Darwin's theories in different ways. Moreover, the scientific community was deeply divided over religion in Victorian England, the mathematical physicists being far more sympathetic than the scientific naturalists. The conflict thesis fails to recognize such variety.

Fifth, the conflict thesis engenders a distorted view of disputes resulting from other causes than those of religion versus science. Given this expectation, conflict is not difficult to find in every circumstance, whether or not justified by the available historical evidence. A classic case is that of the alleged opposition to James Young Simpson (1811–70) for his introduction of chloroform anesthesia in midwifery. Despite repeated claims of clerical harassment, the evidence is almost nonexistent. Insofar as there was any conflict, it was between the London and Edinburgh medical establishments or between obstetricians and surgeons. The origins of that myth may be located in an inadequately documented footnote in White (1896, 2.63).

Finally, the conflict thesis exalts minor squabbles, or even differences of opinion, to the status of major conflicts. The confrontation between Samuel Wilberforce (1805–73) and Huxley in 1860 has been so frequently paraded as a one-sided battle on a vast scale that one is liable to forget that, in fact, it was nothing of the kind. Such exaggeration is an almost inevitable accompaniment to the exposition of a conflict theory. It is excellent drama but impoverished history, made credible only by a prior belief that such conflict is inevitable. Of such material are legends made, and it has been well observed that "the dependence of the conflict thesis on legends that, on closer examination, prove misleading is a more general defect than isolated examples might suggest" (Brooke 1991, 40).

Reasons for Its Endurance

Given, then, that the warfare model is so inaccurate, one may wonder why it has lasted so long. This is, indeed, a major question for historians. The explanation may lie at least partly in the celebrated controversy of Huxley and his friends with the Anglican and Roman Catholic churches. In addition to the strategies mentioned above, they had another tactic, more subtle and yet more bold than anything else they accomplished. By establishing the conflict thesis, they could perpetuate a myth as part of their strategy to enhance the public appreciation of science. Thus, Huxley could write, with a fine disregard for what history records:

> Extinguished theologians lie about the cradle of every science as the strangled snakes beside that of Hercules; and history records that wherever science and orthodoxy have been fairly opposed, the latter have been forced to retire from the lists, bleeding and crushed if not annihilated; scotched if not slain.

The Huxleyite warriors were outstandingly successful in this respect, and their ideals were enshrined in the works of Draper and White, best understood as polemical tracts that advanced the same cause. Yet, Draper takes such liberty with history, perpetuating legends as fact, that he is rightly avoided today in serious historical study. The same is nearly as true of White, though his prominent apparatus of prolific footnotes may create a misleading impression of meticulous scholarship. With an astonishing breadth of canvas, his writing exudes confidence in his thesis and conveys a sense of truly comprehensive analysis. Yet, with his personal polemic agenda, selectivity was inevitable. As such, it exposed him to the criticism that he was trapped by his own presuppositions of an inherent antagonism between the theological and the scientific views of the universe. His book, which he commenced writing in the 1870s, is no longer regarded as even a reliable secondary source for historical study. It is, however, an accurate reflection of how certain liberal-minded men of his day perceived the relationship between religion and science and of how "history" (or a version of it) was pressed into service for their cause. The remarkable thing about the whole conflict thesis is how readily the Victorian propaganda in all of its varied forms has become unconsciously assimilated as part of the received wisdom of our own day. However, it is salutary to note that serious historical scholarship has revealed the conflict thesis as, at best, an oversimplification and, at worst, a deception. As a rare example of the interface between contemporary public opinion and historical scholarship, it is high time for a robust exposure of its true character.

See also Charles Darwin; Early Christian Attitudes
    Toward Nature; Galileo Galilei; Historiography of
    Science and Religion; Medieval Science and Religion

BIBLIOGRAPHY

Brooke, John Hedley. *Science and Religion: Some Historical Perspectives.* Cambridge: Cambridge University Press, 1991.

Corsi, P. *Science and Religion: Baden Powell and the Anglican Debate, 1800–1860.* Cambridge: Cambridge University Press, 1988.

Draper, John William. *History of the Conflict Between Religion and Science.* London, 1874.

Farr, A. D. "Religious Opposition to the Obstetric Anaesthesia: A Myth?" *Annals of Science* 40 (1983): 159–77.

Gilley, S., and A. Loades. "Thomas Henry Huxley: The War Between Science and Religion." *Journal of Religion* 61 (1981): 285–308.

Heyck, T. W. *The Transformation of Intellectual Life in Victorian England.* London: Croom Helm, 1982.

Hooykaas, R. *Religion and the Rise of Modern Science.* Edinburgh: Scottish Academic Press, 1972.

———. *G. J. Rheticus' Treatise on Holy Scripture and the Motion of the Earth.* Amsterdam: North Holland, 1984.

Jensen, J. V. "Return to the Wilberforce-Huxley Debate." *British Journal for the History of Science* 21 (1988): 161–79.

Lindberg, David C., and Ronald L. Numbers, eds. *God and Nature: Historical Essays on the Encounter between Christianity and Science.* Berkeley: University of California Press, 1986.

———. "Beyond War and Peace: A Reappraisal of the Encounter between Christianity and Science." *Perspectives on Science and Christian Faith* 39 (1987): 140–5.

Livingstone, David N. *Darwin's Forgotten Defenders: The Encounter Between Evangelical Theology and Evolutionary Thought.* Edinburgh: Scottish Academic Press, 1987.

Lucas, J. R. "Wilberforce and Huxley: A Legendary Encounter." *Historical Journal* 22 (1979): 313–30.

Moore, James R. *The Post-Darwinian Controversies: A Study of the Protestant Struggle to Come to Terms with Darwin in Great Britain and America, 1870–1900.* Cambridge: Cambridge University Press, 1979, 20–49.

Numbers, Ronald L. "Science and Religion." *Osiris* 2d ser. (1985): 58–80.

Russell, C. A. "Some Approaches to the History of Science." Unit 1 of undergraduate course *AMST 283, Science and Belief: From Copernicus to Darwin.* Milton Keynes, U.K.: The Open University Press, 1974, 30–49.

———. *Cross-Currents: Interactions Between Science and Faith.* 1985. Reprint. London: Christian Impact, 1995.

———. "The Conflict Metaphor and Its Social Origins." *Science and Christian Belief* 1 (1989): 3–26.

Russell, C. A., N. G. Coley, and G. K. Roberts. *Chemists by Profession.* Milton Keynes, U.K.: Royal Institute of Chemistry/Open University Press, 1977.

Simpson, James Y. *Landmarks in the Struggle Between Science and Religion.* London: Hodder and Stoughton, 1925.

White, A. D. *A History of the Warfare of Science with Theology in Christendom.* 2 vols. New York: Appleton, 1897.

3. THE DEMARCATION OF SCIENCE AND RELIGION

Stephen C. Meyer

Introduction

What is science? What is religion? How do the two intersect? Historians of science address these questions by analyzing how the scientific and religious beliefs of particular scientists or cultures have interacted at specific times. Philosophers of science and religion, however, have sought to characterize the relationship between them in more general terms. Their endeavor has required defining science and religion in order to distinguish or "demarcate" them from each other by clear and objective criteria. During modern times, theologians and philosophers of science have attempted to make categorical demarcations between science and religion on various definitional grounds.

Defining Differences: Some Philosophical Context

The neo-orthodox theologian Karl Barth (1886–1968), for example, asserted that science and religion have different objects of interest. Religion and theology focus on God's self-revelation through Christ; science studies the natural world. Barth maintained that science and religion use different methods of obtaining knowledge. Scientists can know the external world through rational and empirical investigation. Yet, because of human sin, man cannot know God from the visible testimony of the creation, that is, "from the things that are made" (Romans 1:20), as Saint Paul put it. Instead, human knowledge of God comes only if God reveals himself directly to man in a mystical or an a-rational way.

Existentialist philosophers such as Søren Kierkegaard (1813–55) and Martin Buber (1878–1965) also accepted a fundamental epistemological distinction between science and religion. According to both, scientific knowledge is impersonal and objective, whereas religious knowledge is personal and subjective. Since science concerns itself with material things and their functions, objective knowledge is possible, at least as an ideal. Religion, however, involves a personal relationship with the object known (God) and a personal or moral response to him. Therefore, radical subjectivity characterizes religious endeavor. Or, to use Buber's well-known terminology, science fosters an "I-it" relationship between the knower and the known; religion, an "I-Thou" relationship.

A group of early-twentieth-century philosophers known as logical positivists also insisted that science and religion occupy separate and nonoverlapping domains, but for different reasons. According to the positivists, only empirically verifiable (or logically undeniable) statements are meaningful. Since science makes statements about observable material entities, its statements have meaning. Religious or metaphysical beliefs, however, refer to unobservable entities such as God, morality, salvation, free will, and love. Hence, by positivistic definition, they lack meaning. As Frederick Coppleston has explained, the principal tenet of positivism was that, since experience alone provides the basis for knowledge, "the scientific method was the only means of acquiring anything that could be called knowledge" (Coppleston 1985, 117–18). Hence, positivism not only distinguishes between science and religion, but it does so on grounds that deny objective warrant to religious belief.

Models of Interaction: Defining the Issues

Contemporary philosophers of science and religion generally recognize that science and religion do represent two distinct types of human activity or endeavor. Most acknowledge that they require different activities of their practitioners, have different goals, and ultimately have different objects of interest, study, or worship. For these reasons, some have suggested that science and religion occupy either completely separate "compartments" or "complementary" but nonoverlapping domains of discourse and concern. These perspectives have been formalized as two models of science-religion interaction known, respectively, as compartmentalism and complementarity. Compartmentalism (associated with Barth, Kierkegaard, and positivists) asserts that science and religion inevitably offer different types of descriptions of different types of realities. Complementarity (as articulated principally by neuroscientist Donald M. Mackay in the 1970s) allows that science and religion may sometimes speak about the same realities but insists that the two always describe reality in categorically different but complementary ways (that is, with so-called "incommensurable" languages). Both of these models deny the possibility of either conflict or specific agreement between science and religion. Science, properly understood, can neither support nor undermine religion since the two represent distinct and nonintersecting planes of experience and knowledge. Both complementarity and compartmentalism thus presuppose the metaphysical or religious neutrality of all scientific theories.

Contemporary philosophers such as Alvin Plantinga, Roy Clouser, and J. P. Moreland have questioned the strict separation of science and religion. They point out that it does not follow from the real differences between them that science and religion must differ qualitatively in every respect. Thus, philosophers have noted that religions as well as sciences make truth claims. Moreover, science and religion often seem, at least, to make claims about the same subject in clear propositional language. For example, both make claims about the origin and nature of the cosmos, the origin of life, and the origin of man; both make claims about the nature of human beings, the history of certain human cultures, and the nature of religious experience. Religions, like sciences, may be right or wrong about these subjects, but few contemporary philosophers of science (though not necessarily theologians or scientists) now agree that science and religion never make intersecting truth claims. Historical religions in particular (such as Judaism, Christianity, and Islam) make specific claims

about events in time and space that may either contradict or agree with particular scientific theories.

Indeed, as Plantinga has argued, many (though not all) scientific theories have metaphysical and religious implications. Plantinga cites several examples of scientific theories, which, if taken as claims about truth rather than merely as instrumental devices for ordering experience or generating hypotheses, have clear metaphysical import. He notes that various cosmological explanations for the fine-tuning of the physical constants (the so-called "anthropic" coincidences) either support or deny a theistic conclusion; that sociobiology and theism give radically different accounts of human altruism; and that neo-Darwinian evolutionary theory, *contra* theism, denies any detectable design or purpose in creation.

On this latter score, many evolutionary biologists agree with Plantinga's assessment. Francisco Ayala, Stephen Jay Gould, William Provine, Douglas Futuyma, Richard Dawkins, Richard Lewontin, and the late G. G. Simpson, for example, all agree that neo-Darwinism (taken as a realistic portrayal of the history of life) postulates an exclusively naturalistic mechanism of creation, one that allows no role for a directing intelligence. As Simpson put it: "man is the result of a purposeless and natural process that did not have him in mind" (Simpson 1967, 344–5). In any case, these theories deny, *contra* classical theism, any discernable evidence of divine purpose, direction, or design in the biological realm. From a Darwinian point of view, any appearance of design in biology is illusory, not real. Thus, even if God exists, his existence is not manifest in the products of nature. As Francisco Ayala has explained: "The functional design of organisms and their features would . . . seem to argue for the existence of a designer. It was Darwin's greatest accomplishment to show [however] that the directive organization of living beings can be explained as the result of a natural process, natural selection, without any need to resort to a Creator or other external agent" (Ayala 1994, 4–5). As Richard Lewontin and many other leading neo-Darwinists have noted, organisms only "appear" to have been designed.

Statements such as these clearly illustrate why attempts to impose a strict separation between science and metaphysics or science and religion have been increasingly questioned. Where scientific theories and religious doctrines are taken as truth claims (as both scientists and religious believers usually require), some scientific theories may be taken as either supporting or contradicting religious doctrines. Indeed, many would argue that there is no reason to exclude the possibility that some truth claims of religion may be evaluated rationally on the basis of public evidences. Several of the examples cited above suggest that scientific discoveries or theories may well contradict religious doctrines. Other examples suggest the possibility that science may also provide support for the truth claims of religion. Archaeological evidence may support biblical assertions about the history of Israel or early Christianity; cosmological or biological evidence may support various theological conceptions of creation; and neurophysiological or psychological evidence may support religiously derived understandings of consciousness and human nature. While many religious practitioners would acknowledge with Barth and Buber that religious commitment requires more than intellectual assent to doctrinal propositions, it does not follow that the propositional truth claims of religion may not have an evidential or rational basis.

Hence, recent work on the relationship between science and religion has suggested limits to the complementarity and compartmentalism models. While most philosophers of science and religion would agree that compartmentalism and complementarity model some aspects of the relationship between science and religion accurately, many now assert that these models do not capture the whole of the complex relationship between science and religion. Real conflict and real agreement between scientific and religious truth claims has occurred and is possible. Theories of science may not always be religiously or metaphysically neutral.

Yet, contemporary defenders of the complementary model contend that the alleged metaphysical implications of scientific theories represent illicit or unsupported extensions of scientific theory, not the science itself. They assert that statements such as those cited above about the meaning of Darwinism, for example, do not represent science per se, but "para-scientific" reflection about science or a pseudoscientific "apologetic" for philosophical naturalism. Such reflection may reveal the metaphysical predilections of scientists (for example, Gould or Simpson), but it does not demonstrate any real metaphysical implications of science.

Those critical of complementarity agree that Ayala's and Simpson's statements do reflect metaphysical biases and that these statements may lack empirical support.

Yet, for them it does not follow that either Gould's or Simpson's articulation of Darwinism is inaccurate. Nor does it follow that Darwinism does not constitute a scientific theory. Many scientific theories reflect the biases of scientific theorists. Some are inadequately supported or fallible. Does that mean that they are necessarily unscientific? This discussion begs a more fundamental question. Can scientific theories have metaphysical implications? If not, why not? Could Darwin, for example, formulate a scientific theory specifying that life arose as a result of *exclusively* naturalistic forces such as natural selection and random variation? Could he, as a scientist, deny that divine guidance played a causal role in the process by which new species are created? Many historians of science now agree that Darwin meant to exclude a causal role for God in his theory of evolution. They also agree that competing theories implied just the opposite. Is Darwinism, then, unscientific? Indeed, was all nineteenth-century biology prior to Darwin unscientific? If so, on what grounds? What exactly is science?

History of the Demarcation Issue

Such questions lead inevitably to the center of one of the most vexing issues in the philosophy of science, namely, the demarcation issue. Identifying scientific theories or truth claims and distinguishing them from religious or metaphysical truth claims (as opposed to religious practices or rituals) seems to require a set of criteria for defining science. But what exactly makes a theory scientific? And how can scientific theories be distinguished or demarcated from pseudoscientific theories, metaphysical theories, or religious beliefs? Indeed, should they be?

In a seminal essay, "The Demise of the Demarcation Problem" (Laudan 1988a, 337–50), Larry Laudan explains that contemporary philosophers of science have generally lost patience with attempts to distinguish scientific theories from nonscientific theories. Demarcation criteria (criteria that purport to distinguish true science from pseudoscience, metaphysics, and religion) have inevitably fallen prey to death by a thousand counterexamples. Many theories that have been repudiated on evidentiary grounds express the very epistemic and methodological virtues (for example, testability, falsifiability, repeatability, and observability) that have been alleged to characterize true science. By contrast, some highly esteemed theories lack one or more of the allegedly necessary features of science.

Laudan notes that, following Aristotle, science was first distinguished from nonscience by the degree of certainty associated with scientific knowledge. Science, it was thought, could be distinguished from nonscience because science produced certain knowledge (*episteme*), whereas other types of inquiry, such as philosophy or theology, produced opinion (*doxa*). Yet, this approach to demarcation ran into difficulties. Unlike mathematicians, scientists rarely provided strict logical demonstrations (deductive proofs) to justify their theories. Instead, scientific arguments often utilized inductive inference and predictive testing, neither of which produced certainty. Moreover, these limitations were clearly understood by philosophers and scientists by the late Middle Ages. For example, William of Ockham (c. 1280–c. 1349) and Duns Scotus (c. 1265–c. 1308) specifically refined Aristotelian inductive logic in order to diminish (but not eliminate) the fallibility known to be associated with induction. Further, as Owen Gingerich has argued, some of the reason for Galileo's conflict with the Roman Catholic Church stemmed from his inability to meet scholastic standards of deductive certainty, standards that he regarded as neither relevant to, nor attainable by, scientific reasoning. By the late Middle Ages, and certainly during the scientific revolution, scientists and philosophers understood that scientific knowledge, like other knowledge, is subject to uncertainty. Hence, attempts to distinguish science from nonscience began to change. No longer did demarcationists attempt to characterize science on the basis of the superior epistemic status of scientific theories; rather they attempted to do so on the basis of the superior methods science employed to produce theories. Science came to be defined by reference to its method, not its certainty or its content.

This approach also encountered difficulties, not the least of which was the consistent presence of disagreement about what the method of science actually entails. During the seventeenth century, the so-called mechanical philosophers insisted, contrary to Aristotelians, that scientific theories must provide mechanistic explanations. Yet, Isaac Newton (1642–1727) formulated a theory that provided no such mechanistic explanation. Instead, his theory of universal gravitation described mathematically, but did not explain, the gravitational motion of the planetary bodies. Despite provocation from Gottfried Wilhelm Leibniz (1646–1716), who defended the mechanistic ideal, Newton expressly refused to give any explanation for the mysterious "action at a distance" associated with his theory of gravitational attraction.

Similar debates about scientific method occurred during the nineteenth century. Some scientists and philosophers regarded the inductive procedures of John Stuart Mill (1806–73) and William Herschel (1738–1822) as representative of the true scientific method. Others articulated the so-called *vera causa* ideal, which limited science to previously known or observable causes. Still others, such as C. S. Peirce (1839–1914) and William Whewell (1794–1866), insisted that predictive success constituted the most important hallmark of true science, whether or not theoretical entities could be observed directly. Yet, Peirce and Whewell also acknowledged that explanatory power, as opposed to predictive success, characterized scientific theorizing in some contexts. Such lack of agreement brought havoc upon the demarcationist enterprise. If scientists and philosophers cannot agree about what the scientific method is, how can they distinguish science from disciplines that fail to use it? In any case, there may well be more than one scientific method. Historical sciences, for example, use distinctive types of explanations, inferences, and modes of testing. If more than one scientific method exists, then attempts to mark off science from nonscience by using a single set of methodological criteria will almost inevitably fail.

As problems with using methodological considerations grew, the demarcationist enterprise again shifted ground. Beginning in the 1920s, philosophy of science took a linguistic, or semantic, turn. The logical-positivist tradition held that scientific theories could be distinguished from nonscientific theories not because scientific theories had been produced via unique or superior methods, but because such theories were more meaningful. Logical positivists asserted that all meaningful statements are either empirically verifiable or logically undeniable. According to this "verificationist criterion of meaning," scientific theories were more meaningful than philosophical or religious ideas because scientific theories referred to observable entities, whereas philosophy and religion referred to unobservable entities. This approach also subtly implied the inferior status of metaphysical beliefs.

Yet, positivism eventually self-destructed. Philosophers came to realize that positivism could not meet its own verificationist criterion of meaning: The verificationist criterion turned out to be neither empirically verifiable nor logically undeniable. Furthermore, positivism misrepresented much actual scientific practice. Scientific theories refer to unverifiable and unobservable entities such as forces, fields, atoms, quarks, and universal laws. Meanwhile, many disreputable theories (for example, the flat-Earth theory) appeal only to "common sense" observations. Clearly, positivism's verifiability criterion would not achieve the demarcation for which philosophers of science had hoped.

With the demise of positivism, demarcationists took a different tack. Karl Popper (1902–94) proposed falsifiability as a demarcation criterion. According to Popper, scientific theories can be distinguished from metaphysical theories because scientific theories can be falsified (as opposed to verified) by prediction and observation, whereas metaphysical theories cannot. Yet, this, too, proved to be a problematic criterion. First, falsification turns out to be difficult to achieve. Rarely are the core commitments of scientific theories directly tested via prediction. Instead, predictions occur when core theoretical commitments are conjoined with auxiliary hypotheses (hence, always leaving open the possibility that auxiliary hypotheses, not core commitments, are responsible for failed predictions). Newtonian mechanics, for example, assumed as its core three laws of motion and the theory of universal gravitation. On the basis of these assumptions, Newton made a number of predictions about the positions of planets in the solar system. When observations failed to corroborate Newton's predictions, he did not reject his core assumptions. Rather, he altered some of his auxiliary hypotheses to explain the discrepancies between theory and observation. For example, he amended his working assumption that planets were perfectly spherical and influenced only by gravitational force. As Imre Lakatosh has shown, Newton's refusal to repudiate the core of his theory even in the face of anomalies enabled him to refine his theory and eventually led to its tremendous success (Lakatosh 1970, 189–95). The explanatory flexibility of Newton's theory did not function to confirm its "nonscientific status," as the Popperian demarcation criterion would imply.

Studies in the history of science have shown the falsificationist ideal to be simplistic. The role of auxiliary hypotheses makes many scientific theories, including those in the so-called hard sciences, difficult, if not impossible, to falsify conclusively on the basis of one failed prediction or anomaly. Yet, some theories (for example, of flat Earth, phlogiston, and heliocentrism) have been

eventually falsified in practice by the judgment of the scientific community regarding the preponderance of data. This fact raises a difficult question for demarcationists. Since the theories of phlogiston and a flat Earth have been overwhelmingly falsified, they must be falsifiable and, therefore, scientific. Are such falsified theories more scientific than currently successful theories that have the flexibility to avoid falsification by a single anomaly? Is a demonstrably false theory more scientific than one that has wide explanatory power and may well be true? Further, Laudan shows that it is absurdly easy to specify some prediction, any prediction, that, if false, would count as a conclusive test against a theory (Laudan 1988b, 354). Astrologers and phrenologists can do it as easily as, indeed, astronomers and physiologists.

Such contradictions have plagued the demarcationist enterprise from its inception. As a result, most contemporary philosophers of science regard the question, "What methods distinguish science from nonscience?" as both intractable and uninteresting. What, after all, is in a name? Certainly not automatic epistemic warrant or authority. Increasingly, then, philosophers of science have realized that the real issue is not whether a theory is scientific, but whether a theory is true or warranted by the evidence. Hence, as philosopher Martin Eger has summarized it: "[d]emarcation arguments have collapsed. Philosophers of science don't hold them anymore. They may still enjoy acceptance in the popular world, but that's a different world." Or, as Laudan expresses it: "If we could stand up on the side of reason, we ought to drop terms like 'pseudo-science'. . . . they do only emotive work for us" (Laudan 1988a, 349).

Demarcation Arguments in the Creation-Evolution Debate

Despite the rejection of demarcation criteria by philosophers of science, these criteria continue to be employed in various ideologically charged scientific debates. Perhaps the most dramatic example has occurred in the so-called creation-evolution debate. Both sides have asserted that theories espoused by the other depart from established canons of the scientific method. Creationists such as Duane Gish and no less a personage than Karl Popper himself have referred to Darwinian evolutionary theory as an unscientific "metaphysical research program" (Popper 1988, 145). For their part, defenders of evolution have employed these same tactics to discredit any possibility of a scientific theory of creation and to exclude the teaching of creationist interpretations of biological evidence in U.S. public high schools.

In 1981–82, during the Arkansas trial over the legitimacy of teaching "creation science," the Darwinist philosopher of science Michael Ruse cited five demarcation criteria as the basis for excluding any creationist theory from public education. According to Ruse, for a theory to be scientific it must be (1) guided by natural law, (2) explanatory by natural law, (3) testable against the empirical world, (4) tentative, and (5) falsifiable. Ruse testified that creationism, with its willingness to invoke divine action as a cause of certain events in the history of life, could never meet these criteria. He concluded that creationism might be true but that it could never qualify as science. Presiding Judge William Overton agreed, ruling in favor of the American Civil Liberties Union (ACLU), at whose behest Ruse had testified, and citing Ruse's five demarcation criteria in his ruling.

After the trial, some philosophers of science, including Larry Laudan and Philip Quinn (neither of whom supported creationism's empirical claims), repudiated Ruse's testimony as either ill-informed about the status of the demarcation problem or disingenuous. Both argued that Ruse's criteria could not distinguish the a priori scientific status of creationist and evolutionary theory. They insisted that only specific empirical, as opposed to methodological, arguments could accomplish this.

Indeed, upon further examination, Ruse's demarcation criteria have proven problematic, especially as applied to the debate about biological origins. For example, insofar as both creationist and evolutionary theories constitute historical theories about past causal events, neither explains exclusively by reference to natural law. The theory of common descent, arguably the central thesis of Darwin's *Origin of Species* (1859), does not explain by natural law. Common descent does so by postulating a hypothetical pattern of historical events that, if actual, would account for a variety of currently observed data. In the fifth chapter of the *Origin,* Darwin (1809–82) himself refers to common descent as the *vera causa* (the actual cause or explanation) of a diverse set of biological observations. In Darwin's theory of common descent, as in historical theories generally, postulated causal events (or patterns thereof) do the explanatory work. Laws do not. Hence, Ruse's second demarcation criterion, if applied consistently, would require classify-

ing *both* creationist theory and the Darwinian theory of common descent as unscientific.

Similar problems have afflicted Ruse's remaining demarcation criteria. Theories about the past rarely employ the exclusively predictive methods of testing required by Popper's falsifiability criterion. Theories of origins generally make assertions about what happened in the past to cause present features of the universe to arise. Such theories necessarily attempt to reconstruct unobservable past causal events from present clues or evidences. Methods of testing that depend upon the prediction of novel or future events have minimal relevance to historical theories of whatever type. Those who insist that testing must involve prediction, rather than compare the explanatory power of competing theories, will find little that is scientific in any origins theory, evolutionary or otherwise.

Analyses of the other demarcation criteria articulated by Ruse have shown them similarly incapable of discriminating the a priori scientific status of creationist and evolutionary theories. Accordingly, during a talk before the American Association for the Advancement of Science (AAAS) in 1993, Ruse repudiated his previous support for the demarcation principle by admitting that Darwinism (like creationism) "depends upon certain unprovable metaphysical assumptions."

The Future of the Demarcation Issue

The demarcationist arguments employed in the origins controversy almost inevitably presuppose a positivistic or neopositivistic (that is, Popperian) conception of science. Some have wondered, therefore, whether new developments in the philosophy of science might make demarcation tenable on other grounds. Yet, recent nonpositivistic accounts of scientific rationality seem to offer little hope for a renewed program of demarcation.

Philosophers of science Paul Thagard and Peter Lipton have shown, for example, that a type of reasoning known as "inference to the best explanation" is widely employed not only in science, but also in historical, philosophical, and religious discourse. Such work seems to imply that knowledge is not as easily classified on methodological or epistemological grounds as compartmentalists and demarcationists once assumed. Empirical data may have metaphysical implications, while unobservable (even metaphysical) entities may serve to explain observable data or their origins.

More recent work on the methods of the historical sciences has suggested that the methodological and logical similarity between various origins theories (in particular) runs quite deep. Philosopher of biology Elliot Sober has argued that both classical creationistic design arguments and the Darwinian argument for descent with modification constitute attempts to make retrodictive inferences to the best explanation. Other work in the philosophy of science has shown that both creationist and evolutionary programs of research attempt to answer characteristically historical questions; both may have metaphysical implications or overtones; both employ characteristically historical forms of inference, explanation, and testing; and, finally, both are subject to similar epistemological limitations. Hence, theories of creation or "intelligent design" and naturalistic evolutionary theories appear to be what one author has termed "methodologically equivalent." Both prove equally scientific or equally unscientific provided the same criteria are used to adjudicate their scientific status (provided that metaphysically neutral criteria are used to make such assessments). These two theories may not, of course, be equivalent in their ability to explain particular empirical data, but that is an issue that must be explored elsewhere.

See also Design Argument; Epistemology; God, Nature, and Science

BIBLIOGRAPHY

Ayala, Francisco. *Creative Evolution.* Ed. by John H. Campbell and J. W. Schoff. New York: Jones and Bartlett, 1994.

Behe, Michael. *Darwin's Black Box.* New York: Free Press, 1996.

Clouser, Roy. *The Myth of Religious Neutrality.* Notre Dame, Ind.: Notre Dame University Press, 1993.

Coppleston, Frederick. *A History of Philosophy.* Book 3, Vol. 8. New York: Doubleday, 1985.

Dembski, William. *The Design Inference: Eliminating Chance Through Small Probabilities.* Cambridge: Cambridge University Press, 1998.

Eger, Martin. "A Tale of Two Controversies: Dissonance in the Theory and Practice of Rationality." *Zygon* 23 (1988): 291–326.

Gillespie, Neal. *Charles Darwin and the Problem of Creation.* Chicago: University of Chicago Press, 1979.

Gingerich, Owen. "The Galileo Affair." *Scientific American* 247 (August 1982): 133–43.

Lakatos, Imre. "Falsification and the Methodology of Scientific Research Programmes." In *Criticism and the Growth of Knowledge,* ed. by Imre Lakatos and Alan Musgrave. Cambridge: Cambridge University Press, 1970, 91–195.

Laudan, Larry. "The Demise of the Demarcation Problem." In *But Is It Science?* ed. by Michael Ruse. Buffalo, N.Y.: Prometheus Books, 1988a, 337–50.

———. "Science at the Bar: Causes for Concern." In *But Is It Science?* ed. by Michael Ruse. Buffalo, N.Y.: Prometheus Books, 1988b, 351–5.

Lipton, Peter. *Inference to the Best Explanation.* London: Routledge, 1991.

Mackay, Donald M. "'Complementarity' in Scientific and Theological Thinking." *Zygon* 9 (1974): 225–44.

Meyer, Stephen C. "Of Clues and Causes: A Methodological Interpretation of Origin of Life Studies." Ph.D. thesis, Cambridge University, 1990.

———. "The Methodological Equivalence of Design and Descent: Can There be a Scientific Theory of Creation?" In *The Creation Hypothesis,* ed. by J. P. Moreland. Downers Grove, Ill.: InterVarsity, 1994, 67–112, 300–12.

———. "The Nature of Historical Science and the Demarcation of Design and Descent." In *Facets of Faith and Science,* ed. by Jitse van der Meer. Vol. 4: *Interpreting God's Action in The World.* Lanham, Md.: University Press of America, 1996, 91–130.

Moreland, J. P. *Christianity and the Nature of Science.* Grand Rapids, Mich.: Baker Books, 1989.

Plantinga, Alvin. "Methodological Naturalism." *Origins and Design* 18(1) (1996): 18–27.

———. "When Faith and Reason Clash: Evolution and the Bible." *Christian Scholars Review* 21(1) (1991): 8–32.

Popper, Karl. "Darwinism as a Metaphysical Research Program." In *But Is It Science?* ed. by Michael Ruse. Buffalo, N.Y.: Prometheus Books, 1988, 144–55.

Ruse, Michael, ed. *But Is It Science?* Buffalo, N.Y.: Prometheus Books, 1988.

Simpson, George Gaylord. *The Meaning of Evolution.* Cambridge, Mass.: Harvard University Press, 1967.

Sober, Elliot. *Philosophy of Biology.* Oxford: Oxford University Press, 1993.

Thaxton, C., W. Bradley, and R. Olsen. *The Mystery of Life's Origin.* Dallas: Lewis and Stanley, 1992.

Van Till, Howard, Davis Young, and Clarence Menninga. *Science Held Hostage.* Downers Grove, Ill.: InterVarsity Press, 1988.

4. Epistemology

Frederick Suppe

Epistemology is that branch of philosophy concerned with investigating the natures of knowledge and belief and their relations to each other and to such concepts as evidence, faith, rationality, and sensory experience. Both religion and science attempt to bring order, understanding, and even control to the cosmos that human beings inhabit. In recent generations, the understanding that religion provides has been increasingly stigmatized as inferior to that of science. Where the two clash, religious understanding has usually suffered, for religious beliefs are frequently taken to be merely matters of *faith,* whereas science is said to yield *knowledge.*

This Standard Perspective drives much of the contemporary "science and religion" literature, such as "God of the gaps" defenses that increasingly marginalize religious understanding to the ever-narrowing "gaps" in scientific understanding. It even drives religious attempts to discredit evolution on the ground that evolution theory does not meet the evidential standards of real science, from which it is concluded either that evolution is every bit as much a matter of faith as competing religious beliefs or, with disingenuous inversion, that competing creationist views are as legitimate a scientific theory as evolution.

Modern epistemology is dominated to a surprising degree by seventeenth- and eighteenth-century rationalist and empiricist philosophical developments that do not support the Standard Perspective. Only with Immanuel Kant (1724–1804) was the basis for the Standard Perspective laid: While science concerns objects of experience, God is not such an object, and religion is grounded in the moral imperatives by which humans must live. Today, epistemology is strongly conditioned by modern reworkings of rationalist, empiricist, and Kant-

ian concerns. Although the focus in this essay is on recent developments, the impact of these historical influences is emphasized.

Epistemological findings have little informed contemporary science-versus-religion debates, which tend to turn appreciably on uncritically accepted and poorly articulated epistemological assumptions that are often at odds with opponents' equally deficient assumptions. Later developments in epistemology have not supported contentions that science is epistemically privileged over religion or vice versa.

Internalist Epistemologies

The classic twentieth-century articulation of the Standard Perspective has come from logical positivists, who attempted to demarcate *cognitively significant* claims (exemplified by science, mathematics, and logic) from *metaphysical nonsense* (exemplified by the metaphysical postulates of philosophical idealism and other a priori views about reality). Logical positivists variously analyzed cognitively significant beliefs as those that are either reducible to truths of mathematics and formal logic or else verifiable, testable, or confirmable on the basis of sensory evidence or publicly experienced events such as the outcomes of scientific experiments. Anything else—even the cognitive-significance criteria—was metaphysical nonsense.

Although positivistic doctrines have been exploited to discredit religious beliefs as cognitively *in*significant faith, positivists such as Rudolf Carnap (1891–1970) were much more circumspect in their assessment of religious beliefs, especially Western ones. Attempts to prove the existence of God via ontological and other arguments that invoked a priori metaphysical "first principles" such as *ex nihilo nihil* (nothing comes from nothing) were relegated to the status of metaphysical nonsense and, hence, not a source of real knowledge. But Carnap and others were explicit in arguing that religious beliefs, to the extent that they could be tested against experience, *were* cognitively significant and that those passing evidential muster were as genuine as scientific knowledge.

Such emphases are consonant with central Judeo-Christian doctrines of the progressive revelation of a personal God to persons through religious experiences judged veridical on the basis of intersubjective experience (for example, the appearance of Jesus on the road to Emmaus or Moses's parting of the Red Sea) or by meeting canons of evidence such as Ignatius of Loyola's (1491–1556) "Rules for the Discernment of Spirits" or Pope Benedict XIV's (b. 1675, p. 1740–58) *Heroic Virtue,* which are still used in beatification proceedings. Many other religions have various ordeals or tests for public demonstrations of the veracity of their claims.

Contemporary discussions of a priori knowledge center upon mathematics and so are relatively tangential to science-religion debates. Our focus is the epistemology of the a posteriori and its relevance to scientific-versus-religious knowledge. On most contemporary epistemologies, scientific and a posteriori religious claims fare comparably.

The positivistic analysis exemplifies a foundationalist approach prominent since the Enlightenment. According to this view, a class of epistemologically secure *base knowledge*—typically, a class of experience-based beliefs—is distinguished from the remaining problematic knowledge claims. *Amplification principles* are then sought whereby the base knowledge can provide adequate evidence for some nonbase claims to qualify as knowledge. For example, on the basis of observations of vapor trails in cloud chambers, physicists may conclude both the existence of unseen subatomic charged particles and certain general principles about their behavior. The vapor-trail observations would be the base knowledge, and inductive or other ampliative epistemological principles would extend the evidence to more problematic claims about unseen particles and general laws.

The earliest foundationalisms posited that base knowledge must be *incorrigibly certain* ("beyond doubt") and thereby immediately confronted grave difficulties. Considerations of optical illusions and hallucinations indicate that ordinary perceptual experiences can be mistaken and, hence, do not qualify as incorrigible base knowledge. False prophets and the like indicate that compelling religious experiences are also corrigible and, hence, do not qualify. Inductive generalizations from instances to generalized laws are uncertain since unexperienced counterinstances may lurk ahead. Some sort of ampliative *inductive principle* stating that the experienced instances are representative of unexperienced cases must be added to secure certainty; however, that principle itself must be beyond doubt. David Hume (1711–76) showed that, if such principles were a posteriori, empirical attempts to establish them with certainty would lead to a vicious infinite regress. Kant construed them as *synthetic* a priori principles necessary and sufficient for perception, which he unsuccessfully attempted to prove via transcendental arguments.

Some foundationalists argued that one could not be mistaken about one's sensory experiences and identified incorrigible base knowledge with such private *sense data.* Knowledge about even ordinary macro objects such as tables and chairs was thereby rendered as problematic as atomic particles leaving vapor trails in cloud chambers. Attempts to distinguish certain aspects of sense data (for example, John Locke's [1632–1704] primary qualities) as veridical representations of external objects were unsuccessful. *Causal analyses* attempted to use scientific laws mediating the experience of physical objects to extrapolate the physical events causing one's sensory experiences. Such attempts succumb to a variation of Hume's regress, since those laws are empirical generalizations that must be validated on the basis of evidence about the relationships holding between sense data and external events, and the latter can be obtained only via recourse to already established laws.

Modern foundationalisms such as positivism's abandoned the requirement that knowledge must be certain, allowing either corrigible sense data or intersubjective publicly observable events to serve as corrigible base knowledge. Some, taking a cue from Thomas Reid (1710–96), allowed that religious experiences could qualify as corrigible base knowledge. Ampliative principles warranting nonbase knowledge were advanced, often construed probabilistically. Depending upon the approach to inductive logic taken, such attempts required inductive principles that either could not be justified on a priori grounds or else encountered probabilistic analogues to Hume's regress. Many concluded that such inductive principles could only be unsubstantiated *presuppositions of induction.*

Coherentist analyses begin with the supposition that knowledge need not be certain, but they reject foundationalism's basic/nonbasic bifurcation. Instead, it is supposed that, at any given time, a person has a coherent set of beliefs and is free to add new beliefs that do not render one's belief set incoherent. Development of this basic idea in a manner consistent with scientific evidential practices—such as new experiences impeaching prior beliefs—requires imposing further conditions that restrict the addition of new beliefs and the restructuring of a person's belief set. Such analyses also allow the possibility that different groups of people will come up with coherent but incompatible belief sets, resulting in relativistic epistemological pluralism.

Coherentist and foundationalist analyses share the assumption that knowledge consists of true beliefs for which one has adequate evidence. If corrigible knowledge is allowed, then it is possible to have adequate evidence for false beliefs. Intuitively, adequate evidence for a belief B should be adequate evidence for any belief B' that is entailed by B. Edmond Gettier (b. 1927) showed that the supposition of adequate evidence for false beliefs combined with the entailment condition for adequate evidence led to paradox: Inappropriately held true beliefs B' qualify as knowledge under these twin suppositions. A series of attempts to restrict the circumstances in which evidence for B accrued to entailed B' resulted in variant paradoxes. Thus, most foundationalisms and coherentist analyses have ultimately proved unsatisfactory in their attempts to account for even ordinary knowledge of physical objects, let alone nonbasic scientific or religious knowledge. Such foundationalisms and coherentisms lend little support to the idea that religious belief is epistemologically disadvantaged relative to science.

Foundationalists construe truth as a correspondence between belief and the world, whereas coherentists construe it as a compatibility of reasonably held beliefs—essentially reducing truth to adequacy of evidence. Paul Feyerabend (1924–94) argued that a correspondence truth condition was liable to the same sort of regresses as were causal analyses, and so he urged that knowledge should be reduced to evidentially supported complexes of belief that include unsubstantiated presuppositions. Thomas Kuhn (1922–96) and others followed suit. Such moves do not by themselves serve to differentiate scientific from religious belief. Indeed, Kuhn likens change of scientific presuppositions to religious conversion and

sees science normally operating within presuppositions (a *paradigm*) held as a matter of faith or conviction.

Skepticism and the KK Thesis

Foundationalist and coherentist developments ultimately reinforce epistemological skepticisms wherein even routine knowledge of macro physical objects is difficult or problematic unless knowledge is reduced to congeries of group opinion. That skepticism is driven by a tacitly held principle known as the *KK Thesis*:

S knows that P entails *S knows that S knows that P*

which implies that to know that P you must know that P is true and must know that your evidence is adequate.

Inductive knowledge depends on applying an ampliative inductive principle to a set of observations representative of the general case G. Hume's argument against induction further requires that you must *know* that the inductive principle applies to the general case and concludes that the latter knowledge is impossible on pain of regress. Hume's argument tacitly invokes the KK Thesis and concludes that one does not know that G *is true* even when the observational instances do, in fact, represent the general case (hence, generalizations true of the observational instances *are* true of all cases). Deny the KK Thesis as a requirement for knowledge, and Hume's argument against induction collapses. So, too, do the variant regress arguments against causal analyses and correspondence truth. Even skeptical arguments against taking ordinary perception-based beliefs as base knowledge presuppose the KK Thesis. Inability to be certain that one's perceptions are not hallucinations, dreams, optical illusions, or the effects of a malevolent demon may show that you cannot be certain that your experiences are veridical evidence—even in circumstances in which perception *is* operating in a normal reliable fashion. But only via invocation of something like the KK Thesis does it follow that your evidence for belief is inadequate when perception *does* operate in a normal reliable fashion.

Externalist Epistemologies

Internalist epistemologies reduce the evidential base for knowledge to the subjective or perceptual experiences of individuals whose base is augmented by ampliative principles. *Externalisms* allow much of the evidential burden for knowledge to be borne by things external to the knower *S*'s sensory experiences, such as empirical regularities governing perceptual interaction with the external world and the cognitive operations involved in processing sensory stimuli. Doing so without succumbing to the regresses that befell foundationalist causal analyses requires rejecting the KK Thesis and other principles demanding prior knowledge of such processes as a condition for basing knowledge upon them. For externalisms, such processes constitute the core of one's evidential basis for knowledge.

Allowing the functioning of empirical and cognitive processes to be evidential for knowledge undercuts foundationalist basic/nonbasic bifurcations of beliefs on the basis of, for instance, direct perceptual experience of an event. Consider the knowledge that one has a full gas tank, which is gained by looking at the gauge. Mediating perception of the gauge is a set of empirical regularities of light transmission, retinal stimulation, and cognitive processing. The gauge reading is, in turn, mediated by a set of electromechanical regularities holding between float valves connected to potentiometers, the transference of small currents, and their conversion to a meter readout. My perception of the gas level is mediated by both the instrumental and the perceptual sets of regularities. Both my "direct" perception of the gauge reading R and my "indirect" perception of the gas tank level G are causally remote from my sensory experiences and mediated via complex empirical regularities. I know the gauge reading R only if the regularities at work in this context suitably tie my sensory experiences to the specific reading R—making my experience E be a *detector* for R. (For example, if I would not have this specific sensory experience E now *unless* the gauge were reading R, then E is a detector for R.) So, too, I know the gas level G by looking at the gauge only if the regularities at work make my sensory experience E a detector for the specific gas level G. Both "direct" and "indirect" perceptual knowledge thus are either problematic or veridical in precisely the same manners. There is no epistemologically significant difference between "direct" and "indirect" perceptual knowledge.

Reliabilisms are externalisms that locate evidential adequacy in the cognitive and sensory processes of belief formation. Knowledge thus consists in those (true) beliefs that are formed in reliable manners in response to sensory experiences. *Causal reliabilisms* identify knowledge of P with beliefs suitably *caused* by P. But most reliabilisms focus upon the proper functioning of cognitive and perceptual mechanisms, intellectual hygiene, or strategies for belief formation. *Nonreliabilist externalisms* separate belief-formation processes from evidential adequacy, the latter construed in terms of sensory or cognitive states as decisive *indicators* of the truth of the associated beliefs. Thus, in the case of the gas gauge, when, in response to seeing the gauge read three-quarters full, I form the belief that there are fifteen gallons of fuel left, I would know that there are fifteen gallons if the gauge reading were indicative of that fact under the circumstances.

Externalisms generally do an excellent job of accommodating common-garden perceptual knowledge, although they often result in difficulties blocking counterexamples that center on unrealistic exotic cases. Some nonreliabilist externalisms have been especially impressive in their ability to accommodate scientific knowledge based on sophisticated experiments, statistical analyses, and even computer modeling. No internalist analysis successfully accommodates such scientific knowledge.

Do such externalist successes with science disadvantage religious knowledge claims? There is no reason in principle why godly events cannot cause religious beliefs to be formed or why sensory or cognitive experiences cannot be indicative of religious truths. Many religions postulate both natural and supernatural regularities that impinge cognitively upon humans. If one supposes, as some "God of the gaps" views do, that God is restricted to exploiting *just* natural regularities (as does science), then the march of science increasingly minimizes the scope for supernatural knowledge. But any such attempt to preclude externalist epistemic exploitation of both supernatural and natural regularities smacks of question-begging scientism. The spirit of externalisms is to allow the epistemic exploitation of *whatever* regularities happen to obtain.

The KK Thesis effectively collapses the evidential basis for *knowledge* to the considerations one can adduce in defense of *knowledge claims* that inevitably fall short of proving the claim. Externalist and other epistemologies denying the KK Thesis effectively drive a wedge between the evidential basis for knowledge that P and considerations adduced in defense of claims to know that P. Thus, while acknowledging that the latter considerations generally *underdetermine* the truth of the *claim* to know that P, one can impose the evidential requirement that, for knowledge itself, the indicator states must be decisive in the sense that they contextually *guarantee* the truth of the belief that P. Doing so automatically blocks the whole family of Gettier-inspired paradoxes (since no false belief can have adequate evidence) and simultaneously provides the epistemic power to accommodate sophisticated scientific knowledge.

One characteristic of scientific knowledge is that it imposes regimens of peer evaluation on knowledge claims before admitting them into the realm of scientific doctrine. So, too, many religions have standards for evaluating the genuineness of revelation, the authenticity of miracles, the truth of oracles, the quality of theological deliberation on such experiences, and the like. In realms such as the law, there exist similar gatekeeping institutions. From an externalist perspective, one is free to insist that authenticated scientific, religious, or legal knowledge (for example) must *both* satisfy the epistemology's evidential requirements for knowledge *and* meet the *credentialing standards* that the associated social institution imposes for admission into its *public knowledge* corpus. In science, we have peer review; in the law, judicial review; and in religion, ecclesiastical review (as well as rules for the discernment of spirits, standards for Heroic Virtue, and the like) as requirements that credentialed knowledge claims must meet. Again, unless question begging, such externalisms prove quite catholic in their accommodation of both scientific and religious knowledge—whether construed as private or public.

Social Dimensions of Knowledge

Philosophers have traditionally viewed knowledge as private cognitive achievements, and they have underemphasized social dimensions of knowledge, including the credentialing of public knowledge. In the late twentieth century, philosophical awareness of social dimensions of knowledge has expanded, beginning with the awareness that propositional knowledge claims are couched in shared public language, and extending to the concerns of Thomas Kuhn, feminists, and others who emphasize the social construction of public knowledge.

The problem that most social epistemologies address is rooted in the skepticism endemic to private epistemologies that assume the KK Thesis. Social epistemologists attempt to invert private skepticism by seeking socially constituted objectivity. Eschewing both evidential certainty and correspondence truth, they typically view knowledge as an inherently biased social construct. Knowledge reduces to knowledge claims that pass muster under some socially constituted standards, which inevitably are biased and question begging. The focal epistemological enterprise becomes preserving some sense of "objectivity" for knowledge that rescues it from the debasement of an "anything goes" relativism, which deconstructs continuity with Enlightenment notions of correspondence truth and rational comprehension of reality.

Feminist and other *standpoint epistemologies* argue that the perspectives of discriminated minorities who survive in a majority-controlled world are more objective than the uncritical biases of the discriminating majority—a view that could be extended to the relative epistemic legitimation of the experiences of early Christians over their repressors and to liberation theologians today over the establishment church. So, too, other social epistemologies stress the fact that some social groups are epistemically advantaged by virtue of the questions they ask and the ways they seek to form their beliefs. Still others stress the relationship between knowledge and power, especially as it involves the power to manipulate nature to produce decisive indicators or to compel social acceptance of particular beliefs.

These are dimensions that potentially might redress alleged epistemological advantages of science over religion. None of these social epistemologies claims to establish absolute objectivity for knowledge or knowledge claims, but rather only relative epistemic advantage of one group's claims over another. To an appreciable degree, they attempt to legitimate minority claims to knowledge in the face of majority dismissal. And in today's scientist society, religious claims are minority claims. If such relativistic epistemologies disadvantage *all* religious knowledge claims over scientific knowledge, they are examples of question-begging scientism.

However, religious knowledge holding its own in such a relativistic manner seems a hollow victory, amounting to a crude version of the modernist-versus-postmodernist debates wherein science is demoted to the discredited state to which modernism earlier had relegated religion. But just as there is growing realization that the modernist-versus-postmodernist debates are inadequately drawn, so, too, are the oppositions between those epistemologies that locate knowledge solely in the personal realm and the upstart social epistemologies. Once one abandons the KK Thesis and comes to appreciate the power of driving a sharp wedge between knowledge and claims to know—between the externalist evidential basis for knowledge and the more internalist base one typically adduces in defense of claims to know—externalist versions of more traditional objectivity constraints by evidence can be combined with the credentialing insights of those who stress the social dimensions of knowledge.

Both science and religion have strong, constructive aspects to the public knowledge they proclaim. Both science and religion purport to exploit the experiences of individuals as a basis for knowledge, yet subject the resulting knowledge claims to evaluation and possible credentialing into a public body of accepted doctrine and putative knowledge. In both cases, such publicly credentialed knowledge is genuine scientific or religious knowledge *if* it also is the personal knowledge of persons supplying it. Individuals may possess far more knowledge about the subjects that either science or religion addresses, but, lacking such credentialing, their knowledge will fail to be accepted as scientific or religious doctrine. There are false prophets in both realms. Only by dogmatic invocation of question-begging scientistic or religious assumptions do recent developments in epistemology afford distinctive advantage to either science or religion.

Reconciling Science and Religion: The Role of Epistemology

Contemporary debates over the compatibility of science and religion have been poorly informed by the epistemology literature—a literature that gives little consolation to those who seek to find radical disparities in the qualities of knowledge that religion and science are capable of providing. The reason for this may be that epistemology literature is poorly attuned to the sophistication and nuances of either real experimental scientific knowledge or actual religious experience, of either theoretical scientific results or sophisticated theological investigation. Yet, the epistemological literature itself addresses nuances and subtleties of knowledge to which the science and religion literatures seem oblivious. Epistemology, philosophy of science, and the science and religion fields tend to focus on their own concerns and literatures to the exclusion of the typical experienced realities of sci-

entific practice, religious experience, or the lived experience of knowers. Nevertheless, there is reason to hope that more inclusive treatments sufficiently informed by all these fields of meta-analysis *and* the realities of both scientific practice and religious experience will enhance, and perhaps transform, our understanding of all five intertwined dimensions.

See also Demarcation of Science and Religion; Postmodernism; Social Construction of Science

BIBLIOGRAPHY

Alston, William. *Perceiving God: The Epistemology of Religious Experience.* Ithaca, N.Y.: Cornell University Press, 1991.

Benedict XIV [Prosper Lambertini]. *Treatise of Benedict XIV on the Beatification and Canonization of the Servants of God.* c. 1740–1758. Portions translated as *Heroic Virtue.* 3 vols. Durbin and Derby: Thomas Richardson and Son, 1850.

Bloor, David. *Knowledge and Social Imagery.* 2d ed. Chicago: University of Chicago Press, 1991.

BonJour, Lawrence. *The Structure of Empirical Knowledge.* Cambridge, Mass.: Harvard University Press, 1985.

Carnap, Rudolf. "The Elimination of Metaphysics Through Logical Analysis of Language." 1932. Reprint. In *Logical Positivism,* ed. by A. J. Ayer. New York: Free Press, 1959.

Chisholm, Roderick. *Foundations of Knowing.* Minneapolis: University of Minnesota Press, 1982.

Dretske, Fred. *Seeing and Knowing.* Chicago: University of Chicago Press, 1969.

Feyerabend, P. "An Attempt at a Realistic Interpretation of Experience." *Proceedings of the Aristotelian Society* n.s. 58 (1958): 143–70.

Hilpinnen, Risto. "Knowing That One Knows and the Classic Definition of Knowledge." *Synthese* 21 (1970): 109–32.

Hume, David. *Enquiries Concerning the Human Understanding,* ed. by L. a. Selby-Bigge. 1748. Reprint. 2d ed. Oxford: Clarendon, 1902.

Ignatius of Loyola. *The Spiritual Exercises of St. Ignatius.* Ed. by Louis J. Puhl. 1548. Reprint. Chicago: Loyola University Press, 1951.

Kant, Immanuel. *Critique of Pure Reason.* Trans. by N. K. Smith. 2d ed. 1787. Reprint. New York: St. Martin's, 1961.

Kuhn, Thomas. *The Structure of Scientific Revolutions.* Rev. ed. Chicago: University of Chicago Press, 1970.

Lehrer, Keith. *Theory of Knowledge.* Boulder, Colo.: Westview, 1990.

Locke, John. *Essay Concerning Human Understanding.* Ed. by A. C. Fraser. 1659. Reprint. 2 vols. New York: Dover, 1959.

Longino, Helen E. *Science as Social Knowledge.* Princeton, N.J.: Princeton University Press, 1990.

Nielson, Joyce McCarl. *Feminist Research Methods: Exemplary Readings in the Social Sciences.* Boulder, Colo.: Westview, 1990.

Plantinga, Alvin. *Warrant: The Current Debate.* New York: Oxford University Press, 1993.

Plantinga, Alvin, and Nicholas Wolterstorff, eds. *Faith and Rationality: Reason and Belief in God.* Notre Dame, Ind.: University of Notre Dame Press, 1983.

Reid, Thomas. *Essays on the Intellectual Powers of Man.* 1785. Reprint. Cambridge, Mass.: MIT Press, 1969.

Rouse, Joseph. *Knowledge and Power: Toward a Political Philosophy of Science.* Ithaca, N.Y.: Cornell University Press, 1987.

Suppe, Frederick. "Credentialing Scientific Claims." *Perspectives on Science* 1 (1973): 153–203.

———. *The Structure of Scientific Theories.* 2d ed. Urbana: University of Illinois Press, 1977.

———. *The Semantic Conception of Theories and Scientific Realism.* Urbana: University of Illinois Press, 1989.

5. CAUSATION

John Henry

The nature of causation, how one event or process might be said to produce and so explain another, has been recognized as a site of major philosophical interest in which a number of interconnected difficulties have been discerned. Are all events caused? Can all causes be expressed in the form of general laws? Is there a necessary connection between cause and effect or is the supposed connection merely the result of inductive inference? Does the concept of cause depend upon a notion of power? Must causes always precede their effects? Fascinating as these and other associated questions are, we do not pursue them here. The aim of this essay is simply to consider theological theories about the role of God in causation and the way these ideas impinged upon and interacted with naturalistic theories of causation. As the theories of causation themselves are not pursued here, we do not even consider the fortunes of teleological accounts of the natural world and the notion of what are called final causes (the purposive reasons why particular outcomes are brought about), even though there is a case for saying, as did Sir Thomas Browne (1605–82), author of *Religio Medici* (1642), that God's providence hangs upon the existence of final causes.

Essentially, the theological account is easily told. God was regarded as the first or primary cause, the sine qua non, of the universe and everything in it. On this much everyone in the Judeo-Christian tradition was agreed. There were, however, two principal sources of disagreement. First, opinions were divided about the extent of God's direct involvement in the workings of the universe, some (although this was always a minority view) regarding God as the sole active agent at work in the universe, others recognizing a hierarchy of secondary (or natural) causes descending below God. Second, those who acknowledged that God chose to operate not directly, but by delegating various causal powers to the world's creatures, disagreed about the fine detail that this picture involved. The resulting disputes seem to be about the level of God's supervision of, and involvement in, the secondary causes, some thinkers insisting that God's omnipotence is best illustrated by assuming that he delegates all things to secondary causes, others preferring to suppose that he leaves some room for his own direct intervention. These questions were frequently bound up with considerations of the nature of providence—that is, with differing opinions about what it meant to say that God was omnipotent. All were essentially agreed that God could do anything that did not involve a contradiction, but just what was contradictory and what was not was fiercely disputed. For some, God could not create a substance without accidents (roughly speaking, an object without any properties) or create matter that could think. For others, however, such things easily came within God's ability, but it made no sense to say that he could break the law of the excluded middle (according to which, a particular state of affairs either is or is not; there is no third alternative) or create a weight so heavy that his omnipotence could not lift it. In what follows, we try to confine ourselves strictly to the subject of causation, without straying into discussions of providentialism, but it should be borne in mind that this is a somewhat artificial distinction.

Determinism versus Occasionalism

Although the religion of the ancient Greeks was polytheistic, it has been recognized that, among the naturalist philosophers, there was a marked tendency toward monotheism. Believing in a supreme intelligence capable of ordering and creating the world, they argued that a true god need not struggle with other gods to exert his will (as in the various polytheistic myths), and they developed a notion of god that was far removed from human limitations. Deriving principally from their wish to explain all natural phenomena in terms of physical causes, the one god of the philosophers essentially represented the principle of universal and immutable order and was not only physically transcendent but also morally so. The unified divinity of Greek philosophers was unconcerned by the plight of mortals even though, as for example in some interpretations of the "Unmoved Mover" of Aristotle's cosmology, it might have been indirectly responsible, through the chain of cause and effect, for their plight. In Greek natural philosophy, therefore, it followed that accounts of natural processes did not refer back to the divinity (except in the case of creation myths like that presented in Plato's *Timaeus*), it being assumed that nature was entirely and unalterably regular in its operations.

The earliest suggestions that such ideas made an impression upon Christian theology can be seen in discussions among the early Fathers of God's omnipotence, in which it is affirmed that, although God can enact anything through his power, he chooses to enact things in a fitting way, according to what is "just" or correct. This can be seen as a response to criticisms of pagan thinkers like Galen (A.D. 129–c. 210), the great medical authority, who ridiculed the Christians for believing that God could make a horse or a bull out of ashes in contrast to the pagan view that God would not attempt such a natural impossibility but would choose "the best out of the possibilities of becoming" (*On the Usefulness of the Parts of the Body* 11.14). The implication seems to have been that there was some natural necessity that, for a horse really to be a horse, it had to be made of flesh and bone. Something like this idea even seems to have surfaced in Christian popular culture. In a work attributed to the Venerable Bede (c. 673–735), we learn of "a country saying" that "God has the power to make a calf out of a block of wood. Did he ever do it?" Comments like this seem to suggest a recognition among early Christians that nature is best understood in terms of its regular operations and appearances.

In the Muslim tradition, however, the response to Greek philosophy took a somewhat different turn, giving rise to a major examination of theories of causation. As a result of the impact of Greek ideas, beginning in the eighth century and proceeding through the ninth, Muslim theologians were led to emphasize the supreme omnipotence of God. Among the followers of the theologian al-Ash'ari (d. 935), belief in this omnipotence culminated in the rejection of the natural efficacy of "secondary" agents. Based at first on an interpretation of the Koran, in which it says, for example, that God "created you and your deeds" (37: 94), it was later given philosophical underpinning in a critical analysis of causality written by al-Ghazali (1058–1111). Rejecting the determinism of Aristotelian philosophy, which did not allow for any supernatural intervention, al-Ghazali insisted that there is no necessary correlation between what is taken as the cause and what is taken as the effect. The supposed necessary connection between contingencies in the natural world is based on nothing more than psychological habit. Logical necessity is a coherent notion, al-Ghazali declared, but causal necessity is inadmissible, being based on the fallacious assumption that, because an effect occurs with a cause, it must occur through the cause.

Al-Ghazali's rejection of causation went hand in hand with the so-called occasionalist metaphysics of the Muslim Mutakallims, which had been established since the middle of the ninth century. Seeking to prove that God was the sole power, the sole active agent at work in the universe, the Mutakallims had embraced a form of atomism. Believing, not unreasonably, that the existence of indivisible magnitudes in space entailed the existence of indivisibles of time (since, if time were continuous, two indivisible particles might pass each other and be frozen in time at a point when they were halfway past each other, which, of course, is impossible if they are indivisibles), the Mutakallims argued that God must re-create the world from one moment to the next. Just as God created the atomic particles, so he creates the indivisible moments of time one after another. In re-creating the world in this way, God re-creates everything as he did before, though with numerous changes. What seems like a continuous pageant of changes in accordance with natural laws of cause and effect is, therefore, merely the result of God's way of re-creating the world in self-imposed accordance with strict patterns and rules. When a natural entity is seen to act, it does not act by its own operation; it is, rather, God who acts through it. There is no other meaning to the notion of cause and effect.

This occasionalism (so-called because it was held that an event did not cause an effect but merely signaled the occasion at which God acts) was vigorously opposed by the Muslim Aristotelian philosopher Averroës (1126–98) and by the Jewish Aristotelian philosopher Moses Maimonides (1135–1204). Both critics insisted that the reality of causal operations could be inferred from sensory experience and argued that knowledge itself depended upon causality, since the distinction between what is knowable and what is not depends upon whether or not causes can be assigned to the thing in question. This last point depends upon acceptance of the important Aristotelian concept of form. A body, according to Aristotle (384–322 B.C.), is made up of matter and form, and it is the form that gives the body its identity, which includes not only its principle of existence, but also its principle of activity. Additionally, Averroës objected to the suggestion that activity is legitimately attributable only to an agent having will and consciousness. The distinction between natural and voluntary activity must be maintained, Averroës insisted, because natural agents always act in a uniform way (fire cannot fail to heat), while voluntary agents act in different ways at different times. Besides, by emphasizing God's voluntary action, the Mutakallims were anthropomorphizing God, seeing him as a capricious and despotic ruler of the creation. According to Averroës, voluntary action cannot be attributed to God because it implies that he has appetites and desires that move his will.

The Averroistic position led, however, to an extreme determinism that seemed to circumscribe the power of God. This, among other Averroistic doctrines, enjoyed a certain success with early scholastic natural philosophers in the revival of learning in the Latin West and was included in the condemnation of 219 philosophical propositions issued by the bishop of Paris, Etienne Tempier, in 1277. But what was to become one of the main alternatives in the orthodox Christian view had by then already been worked out by Thomas Aquinas (c. 1225–74). Aquinas wished to maintain the notion of divine providence, effectively rejected in Averroism, while combining it with a recognition of the usefulness of the Aristotelian notion of natural efficacy. The difficulty here, however, is that there seems to be a duplication of effort. If the divine power suffices to produce any given effect, there is no need of a secondary natural cause. Similarly, if an event can be explained in terms of natural causes, there is no need for a divinity. Drawing upon Neoplatonic traditions, Aquinas suggested an emanationist hier-

archy of secondary causes in which inferior causes depend ultimately upon the primary cause because they are held to emanate from it in the way that radiance emanates from a light source. This was supposedly in keeping with God's goodness, since it was a case of God's communicating his "likeness" to things, not merely by giving them existence, but by giving them the ability to cause other things.

This was to become the dominant view of causation in Christian orthodoxy. Before pursuing that subject, however, it is worth noting that occasionalism reappeared during the seventeenth century in the Christian West. It emerged from the mechanical philosophy of René Descartes (1596–1650). Seeking to eliminate all unexplained or occult conceptions from his natural philosophy, Descartes tried to explain all physical phenomena in terms of the interactions of invisibly small particles of matter in motion. Apart from the force of impact, resulting from a body's motion, he rejected all explanations in terms of forces or powers, regarding them as occultist notions. To characterize the different ways in which moving bodies behaved, Descartes introduced his three laws of nature and, following on from his third law (in which he gives a broad characterization of force of impact), seven rules of impact. By applying Descartes's rules, it is possible in principle to understand or predict how colliding bodies will interact with one another (although, in fact, Descartes's rules incorporate a number of false assumptions).

In keeping with his wish to eliminate occult concepts from his philosophy, however, Descartes was anxious to clarify what he meant by the force of a body's motion: "It must be carefully observed what it is that constitutes the force of a body to act on another body," he wrote in his *Principia Philosophiae* (1644). "It is simply the tendency of everything to persist in its present state so far as it can (according to the first law)." But Descartes had already made clear in his discussion of his first law that the tendency of everything to persist in its present state is not the property of a body itself but the result of the immutability of God. Because of his immutability, God preserves motion "in the precise form in which it occurs at the moment that he preserves it, without regard to what it was a little while before." This accounts for the continued motion of projectiles after leaving contact with the projector and for the tangential motion of a body released from a sling. If the precise motions of bodies depend upon an attribute of God (his immutability), it follows that the motions must be directly caused by God. As Descartes wrote in *Le Monde:* "It must be said, then, that God alone is the author of all the movements in the universe."

Although Descartes presented a picture in which God is directly responsible for the motions of every particle in the universe and seems to operate in a discontinuist way, re-creating motions from moment to moment, as did the God of the Mutakallims, he was rather coy about drawing attention to the theological implications. A number of his followers took up these ideas, however, with varying degrees of explicitness. The fullest system of occasionalism was developed by Nicolas de Malebranche (1638–1715), who was driven by his own religious commitments to push Cartesianism in a theocentric direction. But there were also several philosophical difficulties with the nature of causation that were avoided by taking an occasionalist line. It was by no means clear to Descartes's contemporaries, for example, that motion could be transferred in a collision from one particle of matter to another, particularly if, as Descartes insisted, the matter was completely passive and inert. As Henry More (1614–87), the Cambridge theologian, wrote in response to the Cartesian account of collision in 1655: "For Descartes himself scarcely dares to assert that the motion in one body passes into the other. . . . [I]t is manifest that one arouses the other from sleep as it were, and in this way aroused bodies transfer themselves from place to place by their own force." Clearly, More's account is too occultist to be acceptable to a Cartesian, but it nicely raises the philosophical issue of causality that confronted Descartes's philosophy. It also illustrates for the modern reader the Humean point that our assumptions about cause and effect are habits of thinking. No modern reader would have any hesitation in accepting the suggestion that motion is transferred from one body to another in a collision, but for thinkers in an earlier age, with different habits of mind, such a view was as absurd as expecting color to be transferred from one object to another in a collision.

Although occasionalism could extricate Descartes from his philosophical difficulties with causation, it brought along with it a number of theological difficulties. For Isaac Barrow (1630–77), the Cartesian system reduced God to a "carpenter or mechanic repeating and displaying *ad nauseam* his one marionettish feat." But worse, as Henry More pointed out, was that God seemed to be directly responsible for all of the evil of the world, and, hence, human free will was made nonsense.

The Absolute and the Ordained Powers of God

In spite of powerful support in both of its historical manifestations, occasionalism never succeeded in becoming part of the philosophical or theological mainstream. The alternative view, that God invests his creatures with causative principles of their own, was certainly the dominant view in the Christian tradition. When Aquinas struck his middle way between the antiprovidential determinism of Averroism and the theistic excesses of occasionalism, he was drawing upon an already established approach, in which the Greek notion of natural efficacy was accommodated to the Christian view of an omnipotent deity. The chief means of making this accommodation was through the distinction between the absolute power of God and his so-called ordained power (*potentia dei absoluta et ordinata*). Although this distinction is not made fully explicit until 1235, when it was used by Alexander of Hales (c. 1170–1245), he was clearly not the first to have thought of it. In about 1260, when it appears in the *Summa Theologiae* of Albertus Magnus (1193–1280), we are told that the distinction is customary. It has been suggested, with some plausibility, that it derives from the earlier distinction, made by Origen (c. A.D. 185–c. 251) and others, between what God can do and what he deems fitting or "just," which was brought to the fore by Peter Damian's (1007–72) *De divina omnipotentia,* an attack on the excessive reliance on logical argument in theology.

By his absolute power, it was held, God could do anything. But, having decided upon the complete plan of Creation, God holds his absolute power in abeyance and uses his ordained power to maintain the preordained order that he chose to effect. Although God is entirely able to use his absolute power to change things, it is safe to assume that all will proceed in accordance with his ordained power. Furthermore, it was generally assumed that, by his ordained power, God had invested his creatures with their own natural powers. Accepting the Aristotelian idea that the natural powers of a particular body were part of its identity, it was believed that, if a body was devoid of any activity of its own, its existence would be pointless. God's ordained power was not, therefore, used to carry out all changes from moment to moment, as in occasionalism. It was a creative power that established the system of the world, delegating causal powers to things, and, subsequently, its role was to uphold the system. To thwart atheistic suggestions that the system was capable of operating without God, it was usually held that the *potentia ordinata* was required to keep the whole system in being. But, given that its existence was maintained, the system functioned by itself in accordance with the laws of nature that God had imposed upon it. Indeed the so-called laws of nature were recognized to be a shorthand way of referring to the sum total of causal powers possessed by bodies. Inanimate objects were incapable of obeying laws, but natural powers always operated in specific and uniform ways so that bodies might appear to be operating according to law.

Within this broad tradition of causation, however, there were nuances. William of Ockham (c. 1280–c. 1349), accepting the condemnation of 219 Aristotelian propositions of 1277, developed a radical empiricism based on an emphasis on God's absolute power. All that exists are contingencies created by the arbitrary will of God. There are no necessary connections between things: Whatever might be performed by secondary causes might be performed directly by God. So, in a particular case of combustion, an assumption that it was caused by fire might be ill founded if God had directly intervened. Causal relations could be established, therefore, only by experience, not by reason, and even our experiences might be mistaken. Ockham's empiricism proved influential, especially among theological voluntarists, who wished to emphasize the role of God's arbitrary will in Creation, even though it was usually tempered by a perceived need to accept the real and reliable action of secondary causes. The emphasis on experimentalism in the scientific method of Robert Boyle (1627–91) and other leading members of the Royal Society in the late seventeenth century, for example, can be seen to be based on the same kind of theological concern with the unconstrained freedom of God's will, although in other respects Boyle and his colleagues were entirely at ease with the notion of secondary causes and their uniform mode of action.

The famous dispute between Samuel Clarke (1675–1729), speaking for Isaac Newton (1642–1727), and Gottfried Wilhelm Leibniz (1646–1716) included a number of differences over the nature of causation. Ultimately, these differences can be traced back to their opposed positions on the nature of providence, Newton being a voluntarist (who emphasized God's arbitrary will and held him free to make any kind of world he chose) and Leibniz a necessitarian or intellectualist (who held God's reason to be his primary attribute and who believed, therefore, that God was constrained by coeternal rational and moral principles to create only this world—which must be the best of all possible worlds). Even so, both thinkers subscribed to the general belief that God, the primary cause, had delegated causal efficacy to secondary causes. Leibniz famously suggested that Newton's God was a poor workman, continually obliged to set his work right "by an extraordinary concourse." But this was to take too literally Newton's efforts to forestall suggestions that the mechanical philosophy could explain all phenomena without recourse to God. Being aware that atheists could appropriate to their cause a mechanical system of the world in which motions were always preserved, Newton insisted that the motions of the heavenly bodies were in gradual decay and that God's periodic intervention was required to correct this decay. Although it was not unreasonable for Leibniz to assume that Newton must have had a miraculous intervention in mind—that is to say, intervention by God's absolute power—it is clear from unpublished comments by Newton that he believed that comets were the secondary causes through which the ordained power of God operated to replenish the motions of the planets.

The Rise of Secondary Causation

Natural theology, which achieved its heyday at the end of the seventeenth and the beginning of the eighteenth centuries, was entirely based upon the traditional distinction between God and secondary causes. And, as is well known, this distinction led to the flourishing of deism, which accepted the existence of an omnipotent Creator and was willing to discuss the Creator's attributes as revealed by the intricate contrivance of his creation, but denied the validity of theological and religious doctrines supposedly gleaned from revelation. When defenders of religious orthodoxy introduced reports of miracles into their attempts to defend the importance of revelation, a number of the more radical deists even went so far as to deny the possibility of miracles. Peter Annet (1693–1769), for example, used the immutability of God to argue that he could not, or would not, interrupt the normal course of nature. Deism can be seen, therefore, as an extreme version of the tradition of attributing natural efficacy to secondary causes, at the opposite end of the *potentia absoluta et ordinata* spectrum from occasionalism. It can also be seen, of course, as a major source for atheistic appropriations of explanations by secondary causes, in which the need for a primary cause is denied.

By the nineteenth century, natural philosophers were so used to developing their theories in terms of secondary causes alone—without introducing the deity—that the origin of new species of plants and animals caused some embarrassment. The fossil record seemed to suggest that new species of animals and plants had appeared on the earth at different times; creatures that were not found in earlier rock strata suddenly appear in abundance. The comparatively new science of geology was called upon to account for the changing face of both the earth and the habitat, which made it possible, perhaps for the first time, for such new creatures to thrive. But geology and paleontology could say nothing about the origins of the new creatures themselves. Secondary causation did not seem capable of extending that far. Here, then, were the limits of natural science. The origin of species became the "mystery of mysteries," to be left to the man of religion. As William Whewell (1794–1866) said, it was a problem to which "men of real science do not venture to return an answer."

Needless to say, this abdication of the rights of science did not persist for long. A group of biological scientists seeking to find the answer to this mystery developed theories of biological evolution. Once again, these theories could be presented as the workings of secondary causes established by God. As Charles Darwin (1809–82) wrote in 1842, before he became an agnostic:

> It accords with what we know of the law impressed on matter by the Creator: that the creation & extinction of forms, like the birth and death of individuals, should be the effect of secondary laws. It is derogatory that the Creator of countless systems of worlds should have created each of the myriads of creeping parasites and slimy worms which have swarmed each day of life on land and water on this globe.

For many believers, Darwin's theory of evolution pointed the way to a "grander view of the Creator," in which God was able to demonstrate his wisdom and omnipotence by ensuring the self-development of different life forms through the workings of secondary causes.

It is perhaps an indication of the strong links between theories of secondary causation and belief in the existence of God that anti-Darwinist Christians tried to dismiss Darwinism on the ground that it relied upon chance, rather than cause and effect. This charge was vigorously rejected by "Darwin's bulldog," T. H. Huxley (1825–95), who argued that evolution involved chance no more than the scene of chaos presented at a seashore in a heavy gale: "The man of science knows that here, as everywhere, perfect order is manifested; that there is not a curve of the waves, not a note in the howling chorus, not a rainbow glint on a bubble, which is other than a necessary consequence of the ascertained laws of nature." In our postquantum age, in which Werner Heisenberg's (1901–76) uncertainty principle holds sway, it would be harder for a scientist to talk so confidently of the necessary consequences of cause and effect, but this does not mean that the uncertainty principle thwarted religious interpretations of the physical world. On the contrary, believers immediately saw Heisenberg's principle as a way of rejecting the determinism that had been all too often appropriated to the cause of atheism. It would seem that theists are ever resourceful in their use of contemporary scientific theory to support belief in God.

In later-twentieth-century physics, there has been a tendency to rely on mathematical formalism, rather than cause-and-effect accounts, to lead from one claim about the physical world to another. It has even been remarked that the word "cause" hardly appears in the discourse of modern physics. It seems unlikely, however, that Albert Einstein (1879–1955) remains unique among modern physicists in believing that there must be a real world controlled by causal mechanisms underwriting the mathematical formalisms discerned in quantum physics. Moreover, causal accounts continue to be the raison d'être of most other sciences. Given the richness of the distinction between God's absolute and ordained powers and the tradition of secondary causation, it seems hardly surprising that many scientists continue to combine their science with a devout belief in God.

See also Cartesianism; Medieval Science and Religion; Miracles; Physics; Varieties of Providentialism

BIBLIOGRAPHY

Alexander, H. G., ed. *The Leibniz-Clarke Correspondence: With Extracts from Newton's* Principia *and* Opticks. Manchester, U.K.: Manchester University Press/New York: Barnes and Noble, 1956.

Beauchamp, T. L., and A. Rosenberg. *Hume and the Problem of Causation.* New York: Oxford University Press, 1981.

Brooke, John Hedley. *Science and Religion: Some Historical Perspectives.* Cambridge: Cambridge University Press, 1991.

Brown, Stuart, ed. *Nicolas Malebranche: His Philosophical Critics and Successors.* Assen and Maastricht: Van Gorcum, 1991.

Burns, R. M. *The Great Debate on Miracles: From Joseph Glanvill to David Hume.* London and Toronto: Associated University Presses, 1981.

Courtenay, William J. "The Critique on Natural Causality in the Mutakallimun and Nominalism." *Harvard Theological Review* 66 (1973): 77–94.

Fakhry, Majid. *Islamic Occasionalism and Its Critique by Averroës and Aquinas.* London: Allen and Unwin, 1958.

Funkenstein, Amos. *Theology and the Scientific Imagination: From the Middle Ages to the Seventeenth Century.* Princeton, N.J.: Princeton University Press, 1986.

Gillispie, Charles C. *Genesis and Geology: The Impact of Scientific Discoveries upon Religious Beliefs in the Decades Before Darwin.* Cambridge, Mass.: Harvard University Press, 1951.

Hatfield, Gary C. "Force (God) in Descartes's Physics." *Studies in the History and Philosophy of Science* 10 (1979): 113–40.

Huxley, T. H. "On the Reception of the *Origin of Species.*" In *The Life and Letters of Charles Darwin,* ed. by F. Darwin. 3 vols. London: John Murray, 1887, Vol. 2, 179–204.

Jolley, Nicholas. "The Reception of Descartes' Philosophy." In *The Cambridge Companion to Descartes,* ed. by John Cottingham. Cambridge: Cambridge University Press, 1992, 393–423.

Kubrin, David. "Newton and the Cyclical Cosmos: Providence and the Mechanical Philosophy." *Journal of the History of Ideas* 28 (1967): 325–46.

Mackie, J. L. *The Cement of the Universe: A Study of Causation.* Oxford: Clarendon, 1974.

Oakley, Francis. *Omnipotence, Covenant, and Order: An Excursion in the History of Ideas from Abelard to Leibniz.* Ithaca, N.Y., and London: Cornell University Press, 1984.

Ospovat, Dov. *The Development of Darwin's Theory: Natural History, Natural Theology, and Natural Selection, 1838–1859.* Cambridge: Cambridge University Press, 1981.

Shanahan, Timothy. "God and Nature in the Thought of Robert Boyle." *Journal of the History of Philosophy* 26 (1988): 547–69.

6. Views of Nature

Colin A. Russell

The nature of nature has not only intrigued human beings since the beginning of recorded history. It has also in many important ways helped determine their attitudes to the world and, indeed, to themselves and God. Amidst all of the bewildering and kaleidoscopic changes of attitude over history, we can discern three major paradigms, or models, each with its own distinctive characteristics, each exclusive of the others, and each varying in prominence over time and space. In a word, nature has, to various persons and groups, seemed to possess the attributes of a divinity, an organism, or a mechanism. These different conceptions have overlapped in the past, but only at the end of the twentieth century have all three appeared together as popular competitors in the Western world. Today, the dilemma facing postmodernism is which of them to choose. In previous ages, there appeared to be little choice. We shall consider each model in turn.

Divinity

Belief in a godlike character of nature goes back to the ancient pre-Christian world. In a seminal study of speculative thought in the ancient Near East, two writers made the following comment:

> When we read in Psalm xix that "the heavens declare the glory of God; and the firmament showeth his handiwork" we hear a voice which mocks at the beliefs of the Egyptians and Babylonians. The heavens, which were to the psalmist but a witness of God's greatness, were to the Mesopotamians the very majesty of godhead, the highest ruler, Anu. To the Egyptians the heavens signified the mystery of the divine mother through whom

man was reborn. In Egypt and Mesopotamia the divine was comprehended as immanent; the gods were in nature (Frankfort and Frankfort 1951, 257).

At Heliopolis, the Egyptians worshiped their all-powerful sun god Ra, for, in the Near East, that heavenly body was clearly of blazing importance. Throughout the region, the deification of nature was most obviously evident in the case of the earth. She was a divine power, Nintu, "the lady who gives birth," and also "the fashioner of everything wherein is the breath of life" (Frankfort and Frankfort 1951, 257–8). This deification of the earth is still to be encountered in many cultures that have been relatively untouched by the ideologies of the West. It was widespread in the ancient world, though, of course, its nature and extent varied greatly. The Greek atomists, for example, would have none of it, and in Aristotle (384–322 B.C.) it was relatively unobtrusive, though it remains a feature of his four elements (earth, air, fire, and water), which were named after Olympian gods. Aristotle was an organicist because he took principles derived from the study of living things and applied them to all of nature (for example, metals mature in the earth, and all things have natures that control their development). Plato (c. 427–347 B.C.), on the other hand, represents a strong version of the organic view of nature, actually endowing the cosmos and all of its parts with life. Like many of his predecessors, Plato spoke of a *psyche,* a world soul that moves and animates the universe, in which stars, planets, sun, and moon were described as that "heavenly tribe of the gods." The influence of Greek ideas persisted long into the Middle Ages and affected European attitudes to nature. But from about the thirteenth century, Aristotelian natural philosophy prevailed over Plato's ideas, though a strong undercurrent of Platonic thought, to say nothing of popular mythology, kept alive a tenuous belief in a divine universe until the resurgence of Neoplatonism during the Renaissance, when it blossomed once again as a major component of Western thought.

Yet, one exception, as the Frankforts observed, turned out to be of immense importance: the Hebrew scriptures. In them, not merely the psalmists but also the prophets denounced the worship of "the queen of heaven" and of the gods of the forest grove. Yahweh alone must be worshiped, the God who is above all nature and the Creator of it. From the very first page of Genesis, nature is portrayed as the product of God's creative activity, never as part of himself. The worship of all other gods was incompatible with the Hebrew devotion to Yahweh, and those gods included both the deities of neighboring tribes and natural objects like trees and animals. The Israelite was not even permitted to adore a replica of these objects that he had made with his own hands.

These components of a rigorously enforced monotheism became part of the Judeo-Christian tradition. In the early years of the Christian church, they posed particular problems to the patristic writers, who were acutely aware of the parallel stream of Greek ideas that survived alongside Christian theology, not least because they must have seemed much more "natural" to many people. Hence, the divinity of nature was to become a matter of some controversy among the early Fathers, though all were agreed on the otherness of God from his universe and fearful of a lapse into nature worship. At the time of the Renaissance, the revival of Neoplatonism gave rise to a philosophy that was in essence pantheistic. It acknowledged the sun as the supreme god of the heavens and justified the (supposed) circularity of the planets' motion as a proper expression of their divinity. Moreover, in popular consciousness, a divine cosmos had lingered for many centuries. The Jacobean doctor Robert Fludd (1574–1637) wondered if "this splendid Nature . . . is herself god, or whether god himself is she" (Godwin 1979). Fludd may seem to have been working in the last twilight of a divinized nature. Shortly afterward, with the mechanization of the universe, such theological imaginings finally disappeared from science. Nature was effectively de-deified.

Organism

Even when men were reluctant to speak of nature as divine, for fifteen hundred years another tradition lingered on in which the cosmos, if not deified, was at least regarded as having an inner life of its own. It would be a mistake to suggest an absolute distinction between the divine and the animate conceptions of nature, but for much of the time the difference is clear enough. This organismic view of nature persisted at almost every level of European society. Sometimes it is hard to tell whether phrases are carelessly used as mere colloquialisms and figures of speech or whether they are conscious expressions of views about the world. Nevertheless, there is abundant evidence that, for many people, the world was alive with influences, occult forces, and mysterious powers.

The church, however, had its reservations. Thus, Origen (c. A.D.185–c. 251) believed that the heavenly bodies had their own special "intelligences," for which daring speculation he was condemned in A.D. 553. Augustine of Hippo (354–430) could not decide whether "this world of ours is animate, as Plato and many other philosophers think," admitting that "I do not affirm that it is false that the world is animate, but I do not understand it to be true" (Dales 1980, 533). Despite the doubts of Origen and Augustine, the strategies of the early church Fathers included a deanimation of nature. In so doing, they were drawing heavily upon the Hebrew tradition they had inherited in the Old Testament. This tendency to deanimate nature persisted through the Middle Ages. But it was not the end of the story.

One phrase that often appears particularly significant is "Mother Earth." It takes us back to primitive times and seems to have predated even the idea of "Mother Nature." Mircea Eliade writes: "The image of the Earth-Mother, pregnant with every kind of embryo, preceded the image of Nature." It arose from a projection of life on to the cosmos, thus sexualizing it, "the culmination and expression of an experience of mystical sympathy with the world." He adds:

It is not a matter of making objective or scientific observation but of arriving at an appraisal of the world around us in terms of life, of anthropocosmic destiny, embracing sexuality, fecundity, death and rebirth (Eliade 1962, 52, 34).

"Mother Earth" seems to have first appeared in Mesopotamia at about 2000 B.C. or earlier and has been well described by the Assyriologist Thorkild Jacobsen, according to whom the universe was seen not only as a living, sexualized organism, but also as a cosmic state, ruled over by a hierarchy of powerful gods.

With the rise of Greek civilization, some of these Mesopotamian notions of "Mother Earth" began to appear in altered forms. "Mother Earth" came to be called Gaia, a reincarnation of the Mesopotamian Ninhursaga. In the subsequent development of Greek protoscientific ideas, however, she plays little part, though in Roman literature she makes an occasional appearance (for example, in Virgil and Horace).

In the early centuries of the Christian church, the Fathers occasionally touched upon related subjects. Eusebius (c. 260–c. 340), for example, writes of nature (not the Earth) as a universal mother, who is nonetheless subject to God's laws and commands; he denies the possibility of spontaneous causation. The patristic writers emphasized the biblical traditions in contrast to those of the Greek atomists with their totally impersonal, even materialistic, conception of nature. By the tenth century, the Muslim philosophers al-Farabi (873–950) and Avicenna (Ibn Sina [980–1037]) were proposing a life-giving force with origins beyond the material world itself, manifesting itself as animal, vegetative, and mineral souls, each being a different aspect of one World Soul. This is perhaps the nearest that Islamic philosophy got to the concept of an Earth Mother.

Throughout the Middle Ages, the ideas of the Christian church were almost inextricably bound up with those of Aristotle and Plato. Common in the Aristotelian tradition was the notion of inherent tendencies: An arrow eventually fell to Earth, for example, because it had some kind of "homing instinct." Within the Christian tradition, Francis of Assisi (1181/2–1226) composed his famous *Song of the Creatures,* which referred to "our sister water," "our brother fire," and "our mother the earth, which . . . bringeth forth divers fruits and flowers of many colors and grass." In this celebration of nature, while Saint Francis managed to avoid endowing it with divine qualities, his references to its own life were far from poetic conceits.

Abundant evidence indicates that, for many people living at the close of the Middle Ages, the world was alive with influences, occult forces, and mysterious powers. This was even true of science and medicine. With the Renaissance came a revival of Platonic thought. This Neoplatonism seems to have influenced Copernicus (1473–1543), for it was well represented in the great library at Cracow and rife in Bologna, at both of whose universities he was an impressionable student. This may explain the residual organicism in his view of nature,

leading him to endow the sun with mysterious virtue and to suggest that the earth was in some way "fertilized by the sun." Such was the power of these strange "influences" acting over great distances that Robert Fludd, wishing to heal a battle wound, applied his salve, not to the injury, but to the arrow that caused it. Again, William Gilbert (1544–1603), physician to Queen Elizabeth I and father of the science of magnetism, had a thoroughly animistic view of the earth. Although recognizing it as a giant magnet, he asserted that the whole universe was animate and that "this glorious earth" had a soul and "the impulse of self-preservation" (Gilbert 1600, 104). It was a natural view to take, for magnetism and life do have much in common, as Thales (fl. 585 B.C.) had recognized two millennia before. An organismic or animated cosmos, or at least a living earth, appears frequently in poetry from Spenser to Wordsworth and other Romantics of the nineteenth century. And while it disappeared from the technical literature of science, it sometimes surfaced in the rhetoric of scientists such as Humphry Davy (1778–1829) and T. H. Huxley (1825–95).

Mechanism

With the scientific revolution a process came to fruition that one author has called "the mechanization of the world-picture" (Dijksterhuis 1961). It involved a recognition of the lawlike behavior of nature, of its openness to new kinds of rational inquiry (including the experimental method), and of the moral rectitude of investigating it (for the glory of God and the relief of man's estate). It has been variously called a "deanimation," a "demythologization," or a "mechanization" of nature. It marked a fundamental shift in human perception of the world, comparable with its de-deification and sometimes associated with it. After this, the appropriate metaphor for nature was certainly not a divinity and not even an organism, but rather a *mechanism.*

Although the widespread adoption of this worldview can be located in seventeenth-century Europe, the machine metaphor was hinted at centuries before. Thus, the notion of natural law was embedded in the nominalism of William of Ockham (c. 1280–c. 1349) and later theologians. Although the existence of laws does not necessarily imply mechanism, a mechanism must be lawlike in behavior. The laws of nature, impressed on inanimate matter, were an expression of the providence of God, gloriously manifesting his power and goodness. So it was that, for all of his animistic leanings, Copernicus as early as 1543 could speak of "the machinery of the world, which has been built for us by the best and most orderly Workman of all" (Copernicus 1543, 508).

It is pertinent to observe that this mechanical model of the universe was, of necessity, interpreted mathematically, and some have suggested that a mathematical vision of the cosmos constitutes a fourth model of nature. It looks back to Pythagoras (sixth century B.C.) and Plato in the ancient world and forward to Albert Einstein (1879–1955) and Arthur Eddington (1882–1944) in the twentieth century. Nevertheless, it is not so much an ontological view of the world as a methodological tool. It can apply to divine, animistic, or mechanical conceptions of the universe and has done so in the past to all three. It was, however, most obviously indispensable in its application to a vision of the world as a machine.

A fully blown mechanical philosophy emerged in different forms at different places. One of the first to make the pilgrimage from organicism to mechanism was Johannes Kepler (1571–1630). In 1597 he was thinking in animistic terms, but by 1605 he had announced his intention "to show that the celestial machine is to be likened not to a divine organism but rather to clockwork" (Westman and McGuire 1977, 41). Later he had doubts, but these were resolved by 1621. An early mechanical philosopher of the scientific revolution was Isaac Beeckman (1588–1637) of the Netherlands. He had inherited a Calvinist tradition, which was to prove generally favorable to the mechanistic approach to nature, with its strong emphasis on the otherness and providence of God as expressed in nature through scientific laws. The Roman Catholic Church also had its own prominent representative in René Descartes (1596–1650). Inspired by a dream in 1619, Descartes regarded the pursuit of mathematical and mechanical science a divine vocation. He moved to Holland, where he published his great *Discourse on Method* in 1637. Other Roman Catholic mechanists included Marin Mersenne (1588–1648) and Pierre Gassendi (1592–1655).

In seventeenth-century England, Puritanism seems to have played an important part both in the early progress of the new Royal Society, which was founded in 1660, and in the promotion of the mechanical view of nature. After 1700, other theological groups have been credited with promoting Newtonian mechanism, including Anglicans not of the high-church persuasion and promoters of the dissenting academies. Meanwhile,

Robert Boyle (1627–91) had condemned the Aristotelians for denying that the universe was created by God, although they "were obliged to acknowledge a provident and powerful being that maintained and governed the universe which they called nature" (Boyle 1688, 36). His assertion that the universe was "like a rare clock, such as may be that at Strasbourg" was as clear an indication as any of the appropriateness of the mechanical metaphor. Descartes, Boyle, and others sought to explain such diverse earthly phenomena as heat, falling bodies, the spherical nature of drops, magnetism, the behavior of gases, and the colors of chemistry in terms of matter and motion only. Early discussions in the fledgling Royal Society were shot through with the conviction that the earth was a machine and part of an even greater mechanism, the whole visible universe.

Of course, the full implications of a wholly mechanistic view of nature took time to be explored. In England, the fear that expulsion of nonmechanical forces from nature would lead inexorably to atheism strengthened the hands of the Neoplatonist school at Cambridge led by Henry More (1614–87) and Ralph Cudworth (1617–88) in their opposition to Descartes. Isaac Newton (1642–1727), despite his monumental achievement in discovering universal gravitation, continued to study alchemy and to believe in occult forces in nature. Insisting that occasional divine intervention was necessitated by the facts of astronomy, he failed to take the ultimate step of reducing all physical phenomena to mechanistic categories. That step was taken by his successors, however, especially by Pierre Laplace (1749–1827), whose *Système du monde* (1796) and *Mécanique céleste* (1799–1825) rendered Newton's "God of the gaps" superfluous.

By around 1850, a mechanical world was nearly universal in physics, exemplified by Michael Faraday's (1791–1867) work in electricity and James Clerk Maxwell's (1831–79) on the kinetic theory of matter. William Thomson (Lord Kelvin [1824–1907]) said that he could not understand a thing unless he could make a mechanical model of it. In organic chemistry, the old idea of a vital force was slowly eroded after Friedrich Wöhler's (1800–82) synthesis of urea from allegedly nonorganic materials in 1828. Biologists worked in expectation that their subject might one day be reduced to chemistry and physics. Even in geology, a mechanical explanation of fossils began to replace an explanation in terms of "plastic forces" at work in the earth, an organismic idea revived briefly in the nineteenth century by religious people whom Hugh Miller (1802–56) called "the anti-geologists" (Miller 1881, 348–82). However, as early as 1833, it had been banished as a "favorite dogma" from Charles Lyell's (1797–1875) *Principles of Geology*. Since then, geology has been mechanized almost beyond recognition by developments in, successively, glacier theories, volcanology, and plate tectonics.

It is clear that, paradoxically, the mechanistic view of nature has been seen as both an enemy and an ally of religion. This is because it was a complex set of ideas whose effects were widely varied. The element of design implied in the clock mechanism spoke of the consummate skill of the clockmaker. Hence, from Newton to Darwin a mechanistic nature became a routine tool of Christian apologetics in the form of natural theology. In this case, mechanism and religion were in close accord.

But there were also negative points. Mechanism seemed to lead directly to materialism. A reductionist view that the cosmos is nothing but an assemblage of atoms and forces might be conducive to atheism. The argument was occasionally employed in antireligious polemics from the Enlightenment onward. Further anxieties arose over another feature of mechanism: the element of self-sufficiency. The clockwork image could restrict the clockmaker to an initial act of creation. Further unease was aroused by the possibility that a purely mechanical universe might seem to be entirely deterministic. If so, there were legitimate questions to pose about both human free will and divine providence. Finally, there was the question of abuse. A mechanical universe can be abused with impunity, whereas one that is alive or even divine deserves more respect. There is, of course, no logical justification for abusing a machine (particularly if it belongs to someone else) merely because it is a machine, but the argument has a certain emotional appeal to those disposed on other grounds to demechanize the earth and reinstate an organism in its place.

These apparent threats to Christianity from mechanistic nature proved to be less menacing than might have been expected. In their rebuttal, attention was drawn to the fallacy of reductionism, to the alternative to deism of a comprehensive biblical theism, and to the potential complementarity between determinism and freedom. Indeed, with modern physics, the possibility of an iron determinism in nature seemed to be undercut by advances in thermodynamics, in quantum theory and (some would say) in chaos theory. On balance, it seems clear that both science

and Christianity had good reasons for retaining a mechanical world view.

The Dilemma of Postmodernism

The late twentieth century has seen the growth of a movement to revert to the idea of an organic or even a divine nature. It has been triggered by a reaction against the rationality of the Enlightenment and a new awareness of our environmental crisis. A critical question may be put in the following form: Given the current ecological crisis, how should we readjust our ideas of nature? Two common responses have been given. The first is to retain the status quo (that is, to maintain a mechanistic view of nature but hope that environmental problems associated with it will somehow be solved). A second answer, growing in popular appeal, has been to abandon the mechanistic worldview and revert to an organismic or even a divinistic concept of the natural world. The latter view can be traced to the 1960s.

Prompted by the apparently cavalier attitude of many scientists to the environment, Lynn White (1907–87) raised another doubt about current views of nature (White 1967). Was it, or was it not, something to be exploited for the benefit of all or some people? In the aftermath of Rachel Carson's *Silent Spring* (1962), and at the height of the antiscience movement of the 1960s, he argued that many of our present ills stem from the use (or misuse) of science and technology. He concluded that this approach is "at least partly to be explained . . . as a realization of the Christian dogma of man's transcendence of, and rightful mastery over, nature." If that is correct, then "Christianity bears a huge burden of guilt." By "Christianity" White meant orthodox belief, but he himself advocated a return to the rather heterodox naturalism of Francis of Assisi, in which animate and inanimate objects are seen as "brothers" to be cherished, rather than as objects to be manipulated.

Lynn White's thesis has been much discussed at both theological and historical levels. It seems clear in retrospect that its historical claim is much open to question, not least from an examination of the relevant literature over several centuries in both science and theology. The writings of Francis Bacon (1561–1626), John Calvin (1509–64) and his followers, William Derham (1657–1735), and others consistently disclose a concern for nature as a gift entrusted to their stewardship. To draw the conclusion that the church (or even part of it) taught unrestrained plunder of the earth's resources is to fall into the most elementary trap of selective reading.

Furthermore, the global ecological crisis has many elements that cannot possibly be attributed to any particular Christian view of nature: the rape of the forest on the Mediterranean seaboard in the centuries before Christ; the fetid pollution of many rivers in the Indian subcontinent; the endangered species in Buddhist lands; the appalling air pollution in inner-city Tokyo. Even if these examples are ignored, Lynn White's thesis suggests that reverence for nature could never be combined with a powerful desire to control and use it. Yet, there are many cases in which this has occurred. In fact, it was not Christianity but Marxism that in the past argued most forcefully for the subjugation of nature, seeking dominion, conquest, and mastery over it.

More recently, the alternative responses urged by White have often been associated with that very heterogeneous group called "New Age." One of its spokesmen, Sir George Trevelyan, founded the Wrekin Trust with this objective:

> We must learn to think wholeness, to realise the reality of the Earth mother and that our exploitation of the animal kingdom and the rest of nature is piling up for us an enormous karmic debt (Trevelyan 1987).

This statement reflects a worldview totally incompatible with that of science for at least the last two centuries and, in most respects, for far longer than that. It is, in fact, a return to the pre-Baconian organismic universe, and it offers another prospect of a postscientific era. Whether this is to be desired is debatable. It has been frequently observed that such a position is also diametrically opposed to that of orthodox Christianity.

The concept of "Mother Earth" has been widely used in such diverse circumstances as promotion of environmentalism and the advertising of "natural" food products. So strong has been the reaction against science and technology that some people regard all technical artifacts with suspicion, as when any noxious substance is called a "chemical" regardless of whether it is manmade or not. With this has gone a frequently uncritical faith in the desirability of "natural foodstuffs," "nature cures," and organic farming. In the West, a whole subculture has emerged based on the ancient organismic view of nature.

More remarkable is the way in which the "Mother Earth" myth became transformed into something like a scientific hypothesis. This process originated from a slow realization that the earth was involved in a number of systems showing at least some degree of self-regulation or feedback. As far back as 1788, the Scottish geologist James Hutton (1726–97) addressed the question of the virtually endless cycle of decay and repair undergone by the earth's surface. He suggested that the world is a kind of superorganism, not exactly alive but probably more than a machine:

> But is this world to be considered thus merely as a machine, to last no longer than the parts retain their present position, their proper forms and qualities? Or may it not also be considered as an organized body? Such as has a constitution in which the necessary decay of the machine is naturally repaired, in the exertion of those productive powers by which it has been formed? (Hutton 1788, 216).

In 1834 William Prout (1785–1850) wrote of a "grand conservation principle" in the atmosphere. Even in his day he was aware of something strange about the air, but he presumed that the "conservation" of air quality was intended to prevent uneven distributions of gases, through, for example, consumption of all of the local oxygen in a large conflagration. For Prout, such self-regulation in our environment was glowing testimony to design in the world. Later, the concept of a "biosphere" emerged in a book on Alpine geology by Eduard Suess (1831–1914), published in 1875. His "*selbstandige Biosphare*" implied a larger self–regulating system, extending to living as well as nonliving objects. His ideas were largely unnoticed at the time, though his term was taken up by the Roman Catholic philosopher Teilhard de Chardin (1881–1955).

The most dramatic return to something like an organismic nature came in the work of James Lovelock (1919–   ), whose hypothesis concerning the self-regulating process that the earth continuously undergoes was dignified by the Greek word for "Mother Earth," Gaia. Indeed, Lovelock has stated that "[t]he Gaia hypothesis supposes the earth to be alive." However, it is easy to show that the term has a multiplicity of meanings and does not necessarily convey the intention to reanimate the earth (or all of nature). Moreover, it has been employed for a range of purposes outside science, with rhetorical, political, and theological intentions.

In conclusion, it is perhaps worth repeating that science, like Christianity, has had strong reasons for retaining a mechanical worldview. To hold to an organismic nature is to revert to prescientific categories of thought and, thus, to undermine one of the important bases of the modern scientific enterprise. In our own era, once again an animate cosmos, pulsating with semidivine life, has gained a credibility not known for four centuries. It has become a central theme of postmodernism and New Age movements, so that it is possible to describe that era simultaneously as post-Christian *and* postscientific. As C. S. Lewis (1898–1963) observed: "[W]e may be living nearer than we suppose to the end of the Scientific Age" (Lewis 1982, 110). The human catastrophe attendant on the demise of science is hard to exaggerate, given a future demographic explosion. It is the author's opinion that neither of these two options is truly viable, and only a third possibility remains: That is to retain the ideological and practical bases for science (which means a largely mechanistic universe) and to couple them with a commitment to responsible stewardship. Only then will nature (and humanity) have a chance.

See also Cambridge Platonists; Ecology and the Environment; God, Nature, and Science; Macrocosm/ Microcosm; Mechanical Philosophy; Natural Theology; Postmodernism; Process Philosophy and Theology; Scientific Naturalism

BIBLIOGRAPHY

Boyle, Robert. *A Free Enquiry into the Vulgarly Received Notion of Nature.* Ed. by E. B. Davies and M. Hunter. 1686. Reprint. Cambridge: Cambridge University Press, 1996.

———. *A Disquisition About the Final Causes of Natural Things.* London: 1688.

Brooke, John Hedley. *Science and Religion: Some Historical Perspectives.* Cambridge: Cambridge University Press, 1991.

Collingwood, R. G. *The Idea of Nature.* Oxford: Clarendon, 1945.

Copernicus, Nicholas. Preface to *De Revolutionibus.* Trans. by C. G. Wallis. Great Books of the Western World. Vol. 16. 1543. Chicago: Encyclopedia Britannica, 1952, 506–9.

Dales, R. C. "The De-Animation of the Heavens in the Middle Ages." *Journal of the History of Ideas* 41 (1980): 531–50.

Dijksterhuis, E. J. *The Mechanization of the World-Picture.* Oxford: Clarendon, 1961.

Eliade, M. *The Forge and the Crucible.* Trans. by S. Corrin. New York: Harper, 1962.

Frankfort, H., and H. A. Frankfort. "The Emancipation of Thought from Myth." In *Before Philosophy,* ed. by H. Frankfort and H. A. Frankfort et al. Harmondsworth: Penguin, 1951.

Gilbert, William. *De Magnete.* Trans. by P. F. Mottelay. Great Books of the Western World. Vol. 28. 1600. Chicago: Encyclopedia Britannica, 1952, 1–121.

Godwin, J. *Robert Fludd: Hermetic Philosopher and Surveyor of Two Worlds.* Boulder, Colo.: Shambhala, 1979.

Greenwood, W. Osborne. *Christianity and the Mechanists.* London: Religious Book Club, 1942.

Grinevald, J. "Sketch for a History of the Idea of the Biosphere." In *Gaia, the Thesis, the Mechanisms, and the Implications,* ed. by P. Bunyard and E. Goldsmith. Camelford, U.K.: Wadebridge Ecological Centre, 1988, 1–32.

Hooykaas, R. *Religion and the Rise of Modern Science.* Edinburgh: Scottish Academic Press, 1972.

Hutton, J. "Theory of the Earth." *Transactions of the Royal Society of Edinburgh* 1 (1788): 216.

Kaiser, C. *Creation and the History of Science.* London: Marshall Pickering, 1991.

Lewis, C. S. *Miracles.* 1947. Reprint. London: Fontana, 1982.

Miller, H. *The Testimony of the Rocks.* Edinburgh: Nimmo, 1881.

Nasr, S. H. *Islamic Science: An Illustrated Study.* London: World of Islam Festival Publishing, 1976.

Russell, C. A. *Cross-Currents: Interactions Between Science and Faith.* 1985. Reprint. Grand Rapids, Mich.: Eerdmans, 1995.

———. *The Earth, Humanity, and God.* London: University College Press, 1994.

Russell, Robert J., Nancey Murphy, and Arthur R. Peacocke, eds. *Chaos and Complexity.* Vatican City: Vatican Observatory Publications, 1995.

Trevelyan, George. Advertisement for Wrekin Trust Conference, 1987.

Wallace-Hadrill, D. S. *The Greek Patristic View of Nature.* Manchester, U.K.: Manchester University Press, 1968.

Westman, R. S., and J. E. McGuire. *Hermeticism and the Scientific Revolution.* Los Angeles: Clark Memorial Library, University of California, 1977.

White, Lynn. "The Historic Roots of Our Ecologic Crisis." *Science* 155 (1967): 1203–7.

Wiman, I. M. B. "Expecting the Unexpected: Some Ancient Roots to Current Perceptions of Nature." *Ambio* 19 (1990): 62–9.

7. GOD, NATURE, AND SCIENCE

Stanley L. Jaki

Science deals with an external reality, usually taken for nature, writ large, that is equivalent to the totality of material things or the physical universe. Such a nature, or universe, has been taken either for an entity not to be reduced to something else or for something essentially dependent for its existence on a supernatural factor, usually called God. Viewing nature as a self-explaining entity can translate itself into either a materialistic or a pantheistic ideology. In the former, spiritual experiences are taken to be the result of the processes of matter. In pantheistic theology, both nature and mind (spirit) are considered to be manifestations of some divine principle, which pervades all nature but is ultimately not different from it. The view that nature depends on God can be either theistic or deistic. In theism (essentially Christian theism in the Western world), God is not only the Creator, but also the Sustainer, who can interfere with nature by, say, working miracles in support of an information (revelation), which is superadded to what man can deduce about God from a philosophical reflection on nature. In deism, God is thought to have removed himself from nature's workings and from human affairs after the moment of creation.

All of these ideological trends have one thing in common: They assume that nature is ordered and that the human mind is capable of tracing out that order. One could, therefore, try to unfold on an analytical basis the respective impacts of those various religious ideologies on the scientific enterprise. However, such an approach would, at almost every step, imply historical considerations about science, and all the more so as science has only gradually revealed itself as a strictly quantitative study of things in motion. It may, therefore, seem more logical to specify, from the start, those impacts in their historical context, because pantheism, theism, deism, and materialism represent also a historical sequence.

This sequence is not essentially affected by the fact that the Greeks, who are usually credited with the dawn of scientific thinking in the West, showed markedly materialistic tendencies. Although among the statements attributed to the Ionians, who stood at the beginning of Greek philosophical and scientific speculation, one finds remarks about nature as being full of gods, they usually put the emphasis on the exclusive role of matter and motion. That trend was even more marked in the case of Anaxagoras (fifth century B.C.) and the atomists.

It was in reaction to that dehumanizing trend that Socrates (469–399 B.C.) proposed the animation of all matter so that a defense of the existence of an immortal human soul (*anima*) could be argued. According to Socrates, all parts of matter move in order to achieve what is "best" for them, in strict analogy to man's striving for what is best for him. Such was Socrates's way of "saving the purpose," no matter what was the object of inquiry. In the concluding sections of his *Phaedo,* Plato (c. 427–347 B.C.) gives some glimpses of that new physics. Plato goes into details in the third part of his *Timaeus,* in which the living human body serves as the explanation of the physical world. This third part, largely neglected by Plato's interpreters, stands in marked contrast with the first part, in which Plato sets up a geometrical explanation of matter in terms of the five perfect geometrical bodies. The contrast is between two principles. One is called by Plato the principle of "saving the phenomena," or a science that is confined to the task of correlating purely quantitative data about things. The other is the Socratic program, which is left unnamed but which best deserves the label "saving the purpose."

Greek Pantheism

The full articulation of a new program for science, within which the concept of organism was the chief explanatory device, is contained in Aristotle's (384–322 B.C.) *On the Heavens* and *Meteorologica,* of which the first deals with celestial, and the second with atmospheric and terrestrial, physics. They do not contain, to recall a remark of E. T. Whittaker, a single acceptable page from the modern scientific viewpoint. This "scientific" debacle is the result of Aristotle's assumption of the radical animation of all nonliving matter, as initiated by Socrates, who claimed that man's soul (*anima*) is best manifested by his purposeful actions aiming at what is best for him. It was, however, in the writings of Aristotle that this trend of attributing a "soul" to everything was given a sweeping theological twist in a pantheistic sense. Since Aristotle deified the universe in that sense, he had to deny that the universe could have been created out of nothing. Consistent with this denial, he also rejected the view that the actual universe was only one of the infinitely many possibilities for physical existence.

The Prime Mover of Aristotle is a part, however subtly, of the sphere of the fixed stars, which obtains its motion through an emotive contact with the Prime Mover and directly shares, therefore, in its "divine" nature. This sharing is the source of all other motions in the Aristotelian universe, in both its superlunary and its sublunary parts. In both parts, things are animated to move naturally in order to achieve their purpose by reaching their natural places. This animation of nature, in a more or less pantheistic sense, which discouraged a quantitative (or geometrical) approach to nature, is everywhere noticeable in the discourse of post-Aristotelian Greek thinkers, especially when their extant writings are sufficiently extensive.

It should seem significant that not even the non-Aristotelians among the ancients took issue with Aristotle's patently wrong statement (*On the Heavens* 1.6) that the rate of fall is proportional to the mass of the body, a statement that logically follows from his "animation" of nature. The scientifically valuable (that is, quantitatively correct) achievements in Greek science seem to have been worked out mostly in isolation from broader views of nature. Among them are Eratosthenes's (c. 275–194 B.C.) geometrical method to ascertain the size of the earth and a similarly geometrical method by Aristarchus of Samos (c. 215–c. 145 B.C.) to deduce the dimensions of the earth-moon-sun system. These achievements form an indispensable basis on which all subsequent science rests. They made possible the Ptolemaic system as the culmination of Greek efforts, at the instigation of Plato, "to save the phenomena." This phrase expressed the methodological conviction that the complex and variable planetary motions could be reduced to, and explained by, a simple and harmonious geometrical model. Still, when the extant corpus is fairly large, one cannot help noticing the intrusion of traces of the Aristotelian, and at times worse, forms of animization into scientific discourse. There are traces of it even in the *Almagest* of Ptolemy of Alexandria (second century A.D.). His astrological compendium, *Tetrabiblos,* remains the "Bible" of that animistic preoccupation. In his "physical" astronomy, a work on planetary hypotheses, Ptolemy considers the coordination of planets in terms of human beings. Only Archimedes's (c. 287–212 B.C.) writings do not show any trace of this animization of nature.

The ancient Greeks certainly recognized something of the nonideological character of quantitative considerations about nature, but, owing to the pervasive presence of pantheistic considerations, they failed to make the most of that character. The pantheistic conviction that the superlunary matter is divine prompted opposition to Anaxagoras's idea that a large meteor, which hit Aegospotami in 421 B.C., could come from above the moon's orbit. The pantheistic animation of the world also lurked behind the opposition to the heliocentric system proposed by Aristarchus of Samos.

In pantheism, the human mind is in particular a sharer in the divine principle. Therefore, pantheism encourages the idea that the human mind has some innate insights into the overall structure and workings of nature. This idea fosters an a priori approach, as opposed to an a posteriori, or partly experimental and observational, approach. This is particularly clear in the case of Aristotle's dicta on the physical world. This aprioristic influence could be harmless when the subject matter of investigation was rather restricted. There is no trace of pantheism in Aristotle's valuable observational researches in biology. Of course, there the subject matter consisted of living organisms that, in all appearance, acted for a purpose, and, therefore, there was no special need to fall back on the broader perspective of a pantheistically colored animation of nature.

The animation of nature exerted its unscientific impact with particular force in respect to the study of motion. First, it was asserted that since only the superlunary region was totally divine, matter in that realm obeyed laws of motion different from those of ordinary, or sublunary, matter. Moreover, this dichotomy between superlunary and sublunary matter implied that the latter was not truly ordered in its motions and interactions. Again, it was one thing to predict planetary positions; it was another to work out a physics of the motion of planets together with the motion of bodies on the earth. Here pantheism, as codified by Aristotle, blocked any meaningful advance. For, in Aristotle's system, the motion of planets (and even of things on the earth) was but a derivative of the motion of the sphere of the fixed stars, which, in turn, had its source in a continuous contact, however refined, with the Prime Mover. And since the source of all motion was thought to reside in that kind of contact between the Mover and the moved, the logic of that starting point demanded that all motion be explained as a continuous contact between the Mover and the moved. This, however, meant a rejection of the idea of inertial motion, which, as will be seen, proved to be indispensable for the eventual birth of a science that could deal with that most universal aspect of inanimate material things, which is their being in motion.

Greek science, with its major achievements and stunning failures, represents a tantalizing case of the most crucial, and most neglected, aspect of the history of premodern science. That aspect consists of the invariable failure of all major ancient cultures to make a breakthrough toward the science of motion. The ultimate root of that systematic failure is theological, a point that will stand out sharply when we turn to the impact that theism had on science. That theism was Christian theism.

Christian Theism

The possibilities that a theistic conviction could hold for science first appeared in the writings of Athanasius (c. A.D. 296–373), a resolute defender of the strict divinity of the Logos (Christ), through whom God the Father created all. If, however, the Logos was divine, its work had to be fully logical or ordered and harmonious. This theological insistence on full rationality in the created realm inspired Augustine of Hippo (354–430) to lay down the principle that, if conclusions that science safely established about the physical world contradicted certain biblical passages, the latter should be reinterpreted accordingly. This is not

to say that this principle quickly or invariably found a praiseworthy implementation among Christian thinkers. But it acted as part of a broader perception within Christian theism wherever serious attention was paid to Paul's insistence that Christians should offer a well-reasoned worship (Romans 12:1). Hence, the rights of scientific reasoning were protected whenever the rationality of faith was defended against various champions of fideism or against the claim that faith in a supernatural mystery is the condition for the understanding of this or that plainly philosophical proposition.

More generic, though very powerful and still to be fully aired, was the impact that the Christian doctrine of the Incarnation had. According to that doctrine, a real human being, Jesus Christ, was the "only begotten" Son of God, in the sense of possessing a truly divine status. For those adhering to that doctrine, it was impossible to embrace the tenet, popular among Greek as well as Roman authors, that the universe was the "only begotten" emanation from the divine principle. Hence, Christian theism contained a built-in antidote against the ever-present lure of nature worship or pantheism.

Apart from these general principles, Christian theism also showed its potential usefulness for science in some particular matters, as can be seen in the writings of John Philoponus (d. c. 570). He was the first to argue that, since stars shine in different colors, they should be composed of ordinary matter. The argument had for its target the divine status ascribed throughout pagan antiquity to the heavens, a status that introduced a dichotomy in the physical universe and thereby set a limit to considering scientific laws as being truly universal.

The crucial impact of Christian theism on science came during the intellectual ferment brought about by the introduction of Aristotle's works to the medieval educational system during the latter part of the thirteenth century. Whatever the medieval enthusiasm for Aristotle, his pantheistic doctrine of the eternity and uncreated character of the world was uniformly opposed from the start as irreconcilable with the basic tenets of Christian theism. With John Buridan (c. 1295–c. 1358), the opposition took on a scientific aspect as well. For if it was true that the world, with its motions, had a beginning, then one could logically search for the manner—the *how?*—in which that beginning could be conceptualized. Buridan explained that *how?* was an eminently scientific question by saying that, in the first moment of creation, God imparted a certain quantity of impetus (or momentum, as it was called later) to all celestial bodies, which quantity they keep undiminished because they move in an area where there is no friction. Such a motion, insofar as it implied a physical separation between the Mover and the things moved, is the very core of the idea of inertial motion, to employ a term to be used later.

In the context of his commentaries on Aristotle's *On the Heavens,* Buridan carefully notes that "inertial" motion, insofar as it is a physical reality, does not mean absolute independence of things from the Creator. Anything, once created, remains in existence only through the Creator's general support, which is, however, distinct from the act of creation. In other words, Buridan is not a forerunner of deism. In deism, there is no room for such a support. Buridan's notion of a created world implies, in a genuinely Christian vein, the world's utter, continuous dependence on the Creator. The depth of createdness reveals, in turn, a Creator so superior to his creation that he can give his creation a measure of autonomy without any loss to his absolute and infinite supremacy. Similar is the theological background of Oresme (c. 1320–82), Buridan's successor at the Sorbonne, who looked at the world as a clockwork. While the world had already in ancient times been referred to as a clockwork, Oresme used that concept with an important theological surplus. This is why Oresme's clockwork universe is not an anticipation of Voltaire's and other eighteenth-century deists' celebration of the idea of a clockwork universe.

Buridan's step can be seen rather as an anticipation of the Cartesian or Newtonian idea of inertial motion as long as one focuses on that step's very essence. It lies deeper than the difference between a circular and a rectilinear motion. There is no question that Buridan retained the Aristotelian idea of a naturally circular motion for the celestial bodies. But he broke with Aristotle on the truly essential point—namely, that celestial motions were not caused by those bodies remaining in a quasi-physical contact with the divine power. This represented the crucial breakthrough toward the Cartesian formulation of linear inertia and of its incorporation into Newton's laws of motion.

That Buridan's and Oresme's teaching about motion was a genuine product of their Christian theistic thinking is shown by the eagerness with which it was espoused in the fast-growing late-medieval and early-Renaissance university system. Buridan's and Oresme's doctrine was carried by their many students at the Sorbonne to the far corners of Europe. Among the many universities with copies of Buridan's commentaries was Cracow in Poland. It was there that Copernicus (1473–1543) learned a doctrine that sustained him in his efforts to cope with the dynamic problems created by the earth's motion in his system. With his vast articulation of the heliocentric system, Copernicus forced the physics of motion to the center of scientific attention. There was, of course, plenty of room to improve on the medieval doctrine of impetus, but only because that doctrine opened the way for meaningful advances toward a fully developed science of motion, which came only with Isaac Newton's *Principia.* One cannot overestimate the support that Christian theism afforded Copernicus and the major early Copernicans, especially Johannes Kepler (1571–1630). It was becoming increasingly clear that data of measurements were to have the last word concerning the structure and measure of the physical world. While the rhapsodically pantheistic Giordano Bruno (1548–1600) merely promoted confusion, Baruch Spinoza (1632–77) was so consistent with his pantheism as to be unable to explain why there had to be finite things, if everything was part of the infinite God.

Separating Science and Religion

Nothing showed so much the methodological independence of a fully fledged science from theology as the complete absence of any reference to God in the first edition of Newton's *Principia* (1687). Newton (1642–1727) contradicted that independence when he invoked, in the General Scholium that he added to the second edition of the *Principia* (1713), the Pantokrator as the all-powerful, infinitely dynamic Creator described in the Bible. Moreover, that Pantokrator is pictured as intervening periodically in the workings of the solar system so that it may stay in equilibrium.

The opposition of Gottfried Wilhelm Leibniz (1646–1716), a convinced Christian, to belief in God's periodic interventions in nature created a celebrated dispute that distracted from the influence of the *Principia* in respect to the relation of religion (be it pantheism, deism, or theism) to science. While a theist may take comfort from the fact that the author of the *Principia* was a genuine theist, there is nothing in that work that could not be equally useful and valid within any religious or nonreligious framework. This is so because the *Principia,* to quote its full title, is an exposition of the "*mathematical* principles of natural philosophy" (emphasis added). This means that, as long as exact science is a quantitative study of the quantitative aspects of things in motion, it enjoys a full independence from all ideological, religious, and theological perspectives. And this holds true in respect both to the formulation of a major scientific theory and to its subsequent interpretation. Hence, the relation of pantheism, theism, and deism to science is a matter that is essentially different in its status before and after Newton's *Principia.* Before the appearance of that work, which preceded the robust emergence of deism in the Western world, pantheism and theism could play their respectively inhibitory and creative roles in science. After the *Principia,* exact science had a broadly articulated mathematical, or quantitative, structure that safely operated within its own set of methodical canons and retained a very large measure of independence from participating scientists' religious or antireligious motivations.

This was not fully understood during the eighteenth century, and certainly not by deists, who claimed to have a better perspective on science because of their freedom from the fetters of Christian dogma. No deist of the eighteenth century is known to have spurred a major advance in the physical sciences. Voltaire (1694–1778) was at best a popularizer of Newtonianism. Nor could he live easily with the proverbial piety of Leonhard Euler (1707–83), to whom goes the credit of unfolding a great many consequences of Newton's physics. Whatever Pierre Laplace's (1749–1827) personal philosophies (he changed them as a weathervane turns with the prevailing political winds), his claim that his cosmogonic theory did not need God as a hypothesis expressed concisely the true character of the mathematical investigation of matter in motion. It was enough for the physicist to assume, as a matter of commonsense truth, that matter and motion existed and were measurable. Hence, after the *Principia,* the religious or antireligious interpretations of science could touch only on the philosophies spun around an essentially quantitative, or mathematical, core. That core rested on Newton's three laws of motion, a point that is true regardless of the extent to which science increasingly dealt with mere energy transfers, as was especially the case with modern atomic and subatomic physics. Whether in classical or quantum mechanics, energy, it is well to recall, is but the work done by force over a given amount of distance.

In other branches of empirical science, one can observe an ever stronger tendency to achieve a degree of exactness comparable to that obtained in physics. This tendency has almost completely triumphed in chemistry,

at least in the sense that only the complexity of many processes sets practical limits to it. The rise and flourishing of biophysics and biochemistry witness the same trend in biology, whatever the merits of the claim that the art of classification remains indispensable. It should, however, be noted that, even in that art, quantitative considerations have remained implicit.

Such a classification is still of paramount importance in evolutionary theory, Darwinian or other. In Charles Darwin's (1809–82) case, materialistic motivations came to play a major part in his having worked with dogged resolve, over thirty years, on what became *Origin of Species* (1859) and *The Descent of Man* (1871). It should be noted that Alfred R. Wallace (1823–1913), who was a theist, could formulate the same theory but that he rejected, in terms of the theory, Darwin's derivation of the human mind as a mere random product of biological processes. For it still contradicts Darwinian logic to ascribe the growth of the brain to the needs of a mind that is still to manifest itself through language.

Darwin's theory owed its success to two factors, very different from each other. One was a unified picture of material nature (nonliving and living), which prompted a vast amount of research with, at times, spectacular results. This is a point to be genuinely appreciated by many theists, who might find in their very belief in a rational Creator the chief motivation in espousing evolutionary theory. Theists have, of course, some excuse for dragging their feet in the other factor that assured so much popularity to Darwin's theory. That factor was materialism, within which man is not subject to any transcendental reality, not even to a set of invariably valid ethical norms. This materialistic interpretation of evolution has, however, no connection with any major advance in biology insofar as the latter is carefully distinguished from the materialistic proclivities of the discoverers themselves. A case in point is the unabashed materialism of Francis Crick (b. 1916) and James Watson (b. 1928), codiscoverers of the double-helix structure of DNA molecules.

The more a scientific proposition or a branch of science is embedded in mathematics, the clearer becomes its ideological independence and neutrality. This facet of science is the standard against which one can make a reliable appraisal of its interrelation with various forms of religious views and of the perceived impact of these views on science. In light of this fact, generalizations such as that nineteenth-century science was materialistic seem quite unfounded. While some of it was, of course, the majority of scientists during that century still adhered to theism and, in fact, to Christian theism.

Pantheism, Materialism, and Modern Physics

Theists cannot be sufficiently attentive to the fact that, if their theism ascribes some specific quantitative parameter to this or that facet of physical existence (classic cases are the earth's shape and its alleged stationary position, and the age of the universe), the outcome depends entirely on quantitative verification and, if necessary, the reinterpretation of Scripture, according to the principle already laid down by Saint Augustine. Proper attention to this point might very well have prevented the Galileo case or the much less publicized opposition of some Protestant Reformers (like Martin Luther) to Copernicus's theory. The same attention also might have discouraged continued efforts to establish a concordance between scientific cosmology and the six-day story of Creation in Genesis.

The failure to separate the mathematical core of science from philosophical or ideological interpretations has invariably created confusion as to the manner in which religion can have an impact on science and vice versa. The ability to make that separation does not come naturally. In fact, the opposite is true. Thus, the big bang theory of the expansion of the universe was, from the first, eagerly espoused by those who held the idea of an erstwhile creation, although it should have been clear that no science can specify the truly first moment of physical existence, or say anything about the nothing that, logically, had to precede it, and even less about the infinite divine power needed to create it. In fact, it should have been clear that science cannot even demonstrate that there is a universe, simply because no scientist can get outside it in order to observe and measure it.

Conversely, the big bang theory found resolute opponents among scientists with pantheist or materialist (atheist) tendencies. His pantheism made Albert Einstein (1879–1955) first dislike the possibility that the universe was expanding, while atheism prompted Fred Hoyle (b. 1915) and his colleagues to formulate the idea of the perfect cosmological principle or the not-at-all scientific claim that the universe forever remains unchanged, at least in its major features. Materialism played a clear part in giving popularity to the idea of an eternally oscillating universe and to the search for the missing mass.

In some forms, quantum theory has remained closely united to the nonscientific proposition that things can happen without a cause. This proposition, which lies at the basis of the Copenhagen interpretation of quantum theory, was championed almost from the start by some of the chief architects of quantum theory, such as Niels Bohr (1885–1962) and Werner Heisenberg (1901–76). Their pragmatist pantheism was in full harmony with an outlook on existence in which chance or random or uncaused occurrences were the ultimate factors of reality. The justification of such an outlook invariably involves somersaults in logic. One such somersault brings to a close Heisenberg's famous paper of 1928, in which he enunciated the principle of indeterminacy. For no logic can justify his claim that his formula was equivalent to a "definitive disproof" of the principle of causality. The formula merely stated an operational impossibility of achieving perfectly accurate measurements. From an operational defect one cannot, however, infer an ontological defect. And even if absolutely precise measurements were possible, a mathematically perfect accuracy is not equivalent to ontologically full causation, a point that Einstein himself failed to recognize as he opposed quantum mechanics, or rather its Copenhagen interpretation.

Integrating Science and Religion

The only meeting ground of science and religion (whether theism, deism, pantheism, or materialism) depends on a methodically realist epistemology. A firm espousal of the mind's ability to know the external world is indispensable to giving rational respectability to one's religious views. By the same token, a scientist must formulate similar epistemological views in order to relate his or her quantitative data to physical reality. The working out of an epistemology that assures reality to the theologian as well as to the scientist, though for different purposes, is the basis of a meaningful discourse about the relation between theology and science. An epistemology (or its lack) is evident in all methodologies of science. It can, indeed, be shown that most great creative advances in science have been made in the context of an epistemology that occupies a middle ground between idealism and empiricism. The former invariably leads to solipsism, whereas the latter proves incapable of coping with generalizations, inferences, and induction. The epistemological middle ground is, moreover, the one that has always been used in philosophical reasoning that allows an inference to the existence of that transcendental factor, which, at the very start of this essay, was called God, or the Creator. It can also be shown that, whenever a scientist or a philosopher worked out a scientific methodology that made impossible the foregoing inference, the results were potentially disastrous for science. René Descartes (1596–1650), Baruch Spinoza (1632–77), Immanuel Kant (1724–1804), and Georg Hegel (1770–1831) represent the major instances from the idealist (rationalist) side, whereas Francis Bacon (1561–1626), John Locke (1632–1704), Étienne Condillac (1715–80), and Ernst Mach (1838–1916) illustrate the same from the empiricist (sensationist) side.

During the twentieth century, paradigmists threw a red herring, by turning the philosophy of science into the psychology and the sociology of science, within which any objective difference among theism, deism, pantheism, and materialism or plain agnosticism had to appear irrelevant. Again, there is no point in talking about the relation of science to theism (or even to deism) if the latter merely stand for a religiously colored aestheticism (which was the kind of religion articulated in great detail by Alfred North Whitehead [1861–1947] and espoused in usually inarticulate phrases by many scientists who did not want to appear to be materialists). The eternity of matter has, as its basic dogma, the uncreatedness of the universe. Hence, materialist scientists must either outline a scientific touchstone for this dogma or demonstrate, through scientific observation or experiment, that matter is, in fact, eternal, that is, without the possibility of a beginning or an end.

In this age of science, in which the acceptability and credibility of any proposition so heavily depends on its true or alleged connection with science, theists should be wary of resting their stance on vague philosophical discourses just because they have been used by prominent scientists. One such discourse is the philosophy of complementarity as popularized by Niels Bohr. The fact that, in atomic, nuclear, and fundamental-particle physics, wave and particle concepts, though quantitatively irreducible to one another, are equally indispensable does not legitimize the acceptance in philosophy of mutually exclusive basic starting points. Precisely because a theist (or a deist or an atheist) takes an essentially philosophical position, that position can integrate only what is of genuinely philosophical content in a scientific proposition. But, as argued above, the content is independent of that

mathematical, or quantitative, structure that is the very core of a scientific theory. Thus, for instance, James Clerk Maxwell's (1831–79) theory will forever remain only the system of his equations (to recall a famous remark of Heinrich Hertz [1857–94], the first to demonstrate experimentally results that are best interpreted as electromagnetic waves). For such theories never exist in a one-to-one correspondence to the physical reality that is tied to them more or less philosophically. Failure to recognize this fact has vitiated many fashionable programs of integrating science and theology.

Science and theology work with mutually irreducible sets of concepts. This does not mean that they are in opposition, but only that they are different. This is the gist of a memorable remark made by a prominent British physicist, Sir William Bragg (1862–1942), a Nobel laureate. He likened the relation of the two to the cooperation of the thumb and the fingers, whereby one can grasp things. Their cooperation is also a spatial and functional opposition: Only by remaining different are they helpful for grasping a large variety of propositions.

See also Aristotle and Aristotelianism; Augustine of Hippo; Demarcation of Science and Religion; Epistemology; Isaac Newton; Medieval Science and Religion; Twentieth-Century Cosmologies

BIBLIOGRAPHY

Brooke, John. *Science and Religion: Some Historical Perspectives.* Cambridge: Cambridge University Press, 1991.

Duhem, P. *Études sur Léonard de Vinci, ceux qu'il a lus et ceux qui l'ont lu.* 3 vols. Paris: Hermann, 1906–13.

———. *Le système du monde: Histoire des doctrines cosmologiques de Platon à Copernic.* 10 vols. Paris: Hermann, 1913–59.

Gershenson, D. E., and D. A. Greenberg. *Anaxagoras and the Birth of Physics.* New York: Blaisdell, 1964.

Hooykaas, R. *Religion and the Rise of Modern Science.* Grand Rapids, Mich.: Eerdmans, 1972.

Jaki, Stanley L. "The World as an Organism." In *The Relevance of Physics* by Stanley L. Jaki. Chicago: University of Chicago Press, 1966, 3–51.

———. *The Road of Science and the Ways to God.* Chicago: University of Chicago Press, 1978, especially Ch. 2.

———. *Uneasy Genius: The Life and Work of Pierre Duhem.* The Hague: Nijhoff, 1984.

———. "The Labyrinths of the Lonely Logos." In *Science and Creation: From Eternal Cycles to an Oscillating Universe* by Stanley L. Jaki. 1974. Reprint. Edinburgh: Scottish Academic Press, 1986, 102–37.

————. *The Savior of Science.* Edinburgh: Scottish Academic Press, 1988.

————. *God and the Cosmologists.* Edinburgh: Scottish Academic Press, 1989.

————. *Is There a Universe?* Edinburgh: Scottish Academic Press, 1992.

————. *Patterns and Principles and Other Essays.* Bryn Mawr, Penn.: Intercollegiate Studies Institute, 1995.

————. *Means to Message: A Treatise on Truth.* Grand Rapids, Mich.: Eerdmans, 1999.

Lindberg, David C., and Ronald L. Numbers, eds. *God and Nature: Historical Essays on the Encounter Between Christianity and Science.* Berkeley: University of California Press, 1986.

Sambursky, S. *The Physical World of the Greeks.* Trans. by Merton Dagut. London: Routledge and Kegan Paul, 1956.

————. *The Physical World of Late Antiquity.* London: Routledge and Kegan Paul, 1962.

Whitehead, Alfred North. *Science and the Modern World.* New York: Macmillan, 1925.

8. Varieties of Providentialism

Margaret J. Osler

When we speak of providence we mean God's foresight in designing and caring for the world he created. European ideas of providence were the offspring of the marriage between Greek philosophy and Judeo-Christian theology. Greek philosophy contributed the idea that nature contains principles of order, while biblical religion contributed the idea of an omnipotent God who governs the world he created. Various attempts to reconcile divine omnipotence with principles of order produced different theories about the nature of God's relationship to the Creation.

Background: Greek Philosophy and the Bible

According to the Old Testament tradition, God created the world ex nihilo (from nothing) by an act of his power and will. God is omnipotent, and his actions do not necessarily conform to human standards of rationality. God's wisdom and power are evident in the Creation: "The heavens declare the glory of God; and the firmament sheweth his handywork" (Psalm 19.1 AV). His interactions with his people and miraculous interventions in the world are signs of his continuing activity in the Creation.

Several Greek philosophers also contributed to the formation of the idea of providence. Plato (c. 427–347 B.C.) explained the orderliness of the world in the *Timaeus.* According to Plato, a godlike being, the Demiurge, molded preexisting matter into the world and its contents on the model of the perfect, eternal forms. The Demiurge is like a divine potter, using preexisting materials and modeling them to replicate the eternal forms, and thereby differs from the God of the Bible who creates everything ex nihilo. In a late dialogue, the *Laws,* Plato asserted that a World Soul guides the universe benevo-

lently. Aristotle (384–322 B.C.) agreed with Plato that the orderliness of nature flows from forms or essences, but he thought that these forms are intrinsic to individual beings, which are inseparable composites of matter and form. His philosophy of nature included a notion of finality but denied that finality was imposed by an external agent or god. The Stoic philosophers, following Zeno of Citium (334–262 B.C.), believed that the cosmos is one of divine and purposeful design, a view expressed in their concept of Logos, which at once refers to the interconnectedness and design of the cosmos and to its underlying rationality, which is accessible to human understanding. Opposed to any idea of providence, Epicurus (341–270 B.C.) claimed that the world originated from the random collisions of atoms in empty space. The Epicurean doctrine of chance became the perennial target for providentialist philosophers and theologians. Both Platonic and Stoic ideas appear in many early Christian writings and contributed to the formulation of a characteristically Christian conception of divine providence.

The Middle Ages

Augustine of Hippo (A.D. 354–430), by far the most influential of the church Fathers, held a providential view of the world. Deeply influenced by Platonism, he believed that God created the world and ordered it "by measure and number and weight" (Wisdom of Solomon 11.20). This order, which is universal, enables humans to see the design in the world and to understand it as God's handiwork. Disorder is extrinsic to the original Creation, arising only as a consequence of sin. Augustinian philosophy and theology dominated medieval thought until the translation of Aristotle's works from Arabic into Latin in the eleventh and twelfth centuries.

Medieval Christian theologians faced the difficult task of reconciling the omnipotent God of the Old Testament, who created the world and rules it freely, with Greek ideas about the self-sufficiency and inherent rationality of the world. The confrontation between Christian theology and Greek philosophy intensified in the thirteenth century as the recently translated works of Aristotle infiltrated the university curriculum. Fearing that Aristotelianism would lead to the idea of an autonomous nature, which exists independently of God and is ruled by necessary relations that would impede the action of divine will, Augustinian theologians like the Franciscan Saint Bonaventure (c. 1217–1274) opposed the teaching of Aristotle's works. This movement reached a crisis in 1277 when Étienne Tempier, the bishop of Paris, condemned 219 propositions, many of which seemed to restrict God's power and freedom. Many of the condemned propositions asserted the existence of necessity in the world (for example, the propositions that the world must be eternal or that there can be only one world). Theologians and philosophers responded to this crisis by formulating two different approaches to the relationship between divine power and the natural order. They used the terms *potentia Dei absoluta* (the absolute power of God) and *potentia Dei ordinata* (the ordained power of God) to explain this relationship. God's absolute power is his power considered from the standpoint of what it is theoretically possible for him to do, barring logical contradiction. His ordained power is his power in relation to the world he has actually created.

Although there were Christian Platonists like Augustine who believed that certain absolute principles exist independently of God, most Christian thinkers asserted that God created the world by his absolute power and, therefore, could have created the world in any way that he wanted. They differed, however, about his relationship to the created world. Intellectualists, like Thomas Aquinas (c. 1225–74), who emphasized God's intellect, accepted some elements of necessity in the world, some things that God had created freely but was not thereafter able to change. Because of the unity of God's will and intellect, any change in the essence of some created thing would imply that God's intellect was faulty, because something he knew to be true at one time would turn out to be false at another. After the Condemnations of 1277, philosophers tended to emphasize God's absolute power. Voluntarists, like William of Ockham (c. 1280–c. 1349), considered God's absolute freedom to be preeminent, concluding that the world is utterly contingent since it is completely dependent on God's power and free will. The differences between intellectualists and voluntarists on the nature of divine providence had important epistemological and metaphysical consequences. Because intellectualists accepted the possibility of some necessary relations in the world, they believed that some a priori knowledge of the world is possible. Voluntarists, however, emphasizing the contingency of the Creation, argued that all knowledge of the world must be a posteriori, or empirical. Moreover, since the contingency of everything in the world rules out the existence of essences, nominalism—the view that universals have no reality except as names that humans invent to denominate groups of things—is a concomitant of voluntarism. These theological positions, with their attendant philosophical implications, endured into the early-modern period, when they influenced attitudes toward scientific method.

Early-Modern Natural Philosophy

Traditionally, the concept of providence was divided into general providence (the order and foreknowledge that God implanted in the original Creation) and special providence (his particular concern for humankind). In the seventeenth century, thinkers also distinguished between ordinary providence (God's design of the Creation) and extraordinary providence (his miraculous intervention in the natural order). Early-modern natural philosophers had two primary concerns about divine providence: (1) to understand God's relationship with the creation; and (2) to ensure that God's care for, and interaction with, the Creation retained a central role in any new philosophy of nature. The first issue raised questions about the status of the laws of nature; the second was entangled with controversies about the nature of matter and its properties.

Considerations of providence were important in the formulation of new philosophies of nature in the sixteenth and seventeenth centuries. In the wake of the Copernican revolution, European natural philosophers sought a philosophy of nature to replace Aristotelianism, which had provided metaphysical foundations for natural philosophy at least since the thirteenth century. Two prominent candidates for such a philosophy of nature were the mechanical philosophy, articulated by Pierre Gassendi (1592–1655) and René Descartes (1596–1650), and the so-called chemical philosophy, which derived from the work of Paracelsus (Philippus Aureolus Theophrastus Bombastus von Hohenheim [1493–1541]). Both of these philosophies were perceived to challenge the traditional Christian doctrine of providence, largely because their respective theories of matter seemed—in different ways—to exclude God from having an active role in nature. The mechanical philosophers postulated a sharp demarcation between matter and spirit, which seemed to place the mechanical philosophy in danger of falling into materialism and deism, if not outright atheism. The chemical philosophy incorporated active and spiritual properties into matter, but it was also thought to pose the danger of excluding God from the natural world. Active matter was thought to be self-sufficient: It could account for all of the phenomena in the world without recourse to divine action.

The antiprovidential consequences of the mechanical philosophy became manifest in the philosophy of Thomas Hobbes (1588–1679), whose materialism and determinism were notorious. Fear of Hobbist materialism led other thinkers to insist on providential interpretations of the mechanical philosophy. Gassendi, who modified atomism to rid it of the materialistic and atheistic associations with Epicureanism, explicitly incorporated divine providence into his version of the mechanical philosophy. Appealing to the argument from design, he considered the world to be the product of intelligent design rather than the result of the chance collision of atoms. Denying both the Epicurean doctrine of chance or fortune and the Stoic doctrine of fate, Gassendi insisted that the world is ruled by divine decree. Adopting a voluntarist theology, he described a world that is utterly contingent on divine will. Consequently, he believed that empirical methods are the only way to acquire knowledge about the natural world. The laws of nature, according to Gassendi, are simply empirical generalizations. They are contingent truths because God can change them at will, a fact to which miracles attest. At the same time, Gassendi emphasized God's role as Creator and Governor of the world, a position he supported by lengthy appeals to the argument from design.

Descartes was effectively an intellectualist, who described a world in which God had embedded necessary relations, some of which enable us to have a priori knowledge of substantial parts of the natural world. Often interpreted as a voluntarist because of his claim that God could have created the world so that $2 + 2 = 5$,

Descartes was, in fact, a mitigated intellectualist who drew on the traditional rhetoric of the distinction between the absolute and the ordained power of God. According to Descartes, God created certain truths to be eternal, such as the mathematical truths and the laws of nature. He created them by his absolute power and, therefore, was free to have created different laws and eternal truths had he so willed. But he created them freely, and, by his absolute power, he freely created them to be necessary. This necessity, which provided the underpinnings for his claim to know the first principles of nature a priori, places him squarely in the intellectualist camp and provided the foundation for his rationalist philosophy.

The Cambridge Platonists Henry More (1614–87) and Ralph Cudworth (1617–88) adopted an even more extreme form of intellectualism. They upheld the existence of the Platonic form of absolute goodness, which limits God's freedom of action. More was initially attracted to Descartes's philosophy particularly because it gave spirit the same ontological status as matter. Eventually, More grew very critical of Cartesianism, fearing that it would easily lead to materialism. To avoid this danger, he added another entity, the Spirit of Nature, to the Cartesian world of mind and matter. More argued that all sorts of phenomena are impossible to explain simply in terms of "the jumbling together of the *Matter*." Such phenomena included the parallelism of the axis of the earth and the consequent sequence of the seasons, gravity, the results of Boyle's air-pump experiments, and the evidence of design in the parts and habits of living things, all of which resisted purely mechanical explanation. To explain them, More introduced the Spirit of Nature, which is incorporeal, extended, and indiscerpible (indivisible), a causal agent, carrying out God's providential plan for the Creation.

Robert Boyle (1627–91) rejected More's Spirit of Nature because he thought that God's wisdom, power, and goodness alone sufficed to explain the order observed in the world. Boyle's voluntarism is evident throughout his writings. "God," he declared in *The Reconcileableness of Reason and Religion,* is "the author of the universe, and the free establisher of the laws of motion." Boyle believed that God continues to have power over the laws he created freely and that he can override them at will, as the biblical miracles demonstrate. He rejected intermediate entities, like More's Spirit of Nature, as limiting divine freedom. Boyle believed that God created matter and then set it into motion in determinate ways so that it formed the great mechanism of the world. Boyle frequently employed the metaphor of a clock to explain how an orderly world could result from the principles of matter and motion. God, the divine clockmaker, created the world with foresight, and he governs it with care. For Boyle, general providence could be explained in terms of God's initial creation of matter and his setting it into motion. Special providence was manifest in the life of every person both at the moment when God implants a soul in the embryo and, in a more personal way, in the divine guidance he gives for making daily decisions.

Like More, Isaac Newton (1642–1727) found it necessary to modify the mechanical philosophy in ways that would ensure an important role for providence and divine activity in the world. Newton's early notebooks on natural philosophy, composed in the 1660s, indicate that he found that many phenomena resisted purely mechanical explanation. These "difficult" phenomena included gravitation, the reflection and refraction of light, the cohesion of bodies, and the processes of living bodies. Moreover, the mechanical philosophy posed dangers for a providential view of the world. As an Arian, Newton rejected the doctrine of the Trinity and held that Jesus was a created, although a divine, being; he also held a conception of an extremely transcendent God. Consequently, he felt some urgency to secure a central place for divine activity in the world. Newton preserved his providential worldview by supplementing the mechanical philosophy with a variety of active principles drawn from his extensive alchemical studies. These active principles enabled him to explain the recalcitrant phenomena and contributed to the development of his theory of universal gravitation. He explained the passive and active forces, with which he enriched the mechanical philosophy, as resulting directly from divine activity, thus ensuring a central role for providence in his cosmology, which became a massive argument from design. Newton was also a voluntarist. He believed that God is able to do anything that is not logically contradictory and that the Creation might have been different from what it is because its creation was the voluntary act of an omnipotent God. In an extended criticism of Descartes's philosophy and particularly of his theory of matter, Newton stated that the existence of matter and its observed properties are completely dependent upon divine will. According to Newton, God or his agent is everywhere in the universe,

directly responsible for the activity and order that are found in the world.

Gottfried Wilhelm Leibniz (1646–1716) proposed a theory of preestablished harmony to explain how God's wisdom could be manifest in the world. According to this theory, God created each individual thing so that whatever happens to it arises from its own, internal nature. Despite the apparent independence of each individual from every other and from God, the whole world proceeds in a harmonious pattern, preestablished by God. Leibniz claimed that preestablished harmony accounted for the relation of body to mind and for the production of miracles, which presupposed a harmony between the physical and the moral orders. Leibniz's theory can be understood as an extreme form of intellectualism, for, in it, God literally does not act on the world after his initial act of creation.

The difference between voluntarist and intellectualist interpretations of providence was a central issue in the famous controversy in 1715 and 1716 between Newton's spokesman, Samuel Clarke (1675–1729), and Leibniz. As an intellectualist, Leibniz criticized the Newtonian insistence on divine activity in the world as implying that God's workmanship is less than perfect, so that he must constantly intervene in nature and repair his work. A better workman, according to Leibniz, would create a world that would run smoothly forever, without the need for intervention. Replying as a voluntarist, Clarke argued that Leibniz's account entails the existence of limits on God's freedom and power.

Later Developments

The seventeenth-century discussions of providence continued to resonate in the styles of science that emerged in the eighteenth century and beyond. A style of science is the specific manifestation of the general epistemological and metaphysical assumptions that govern a particular scientific practice. To the extent that some scientists emphasize the necessity of the laws of nature and the use of abstract reasoning and mathematics to unlock the secrets of nature, they continue to practice a style that reflects an intellectualist interpretation of divine providence. Albert Einstein's (1879–1955) abstract, mathematical approach to theoretical physics reflects this tradition. To the extent that others emphasize contingency, probability, and the use of empirical methods, they are practicing science in a style deriving from a voluntarist understanding of providence. Stephen Jay Gould's insistence on the historical contingency of the processes of evolution has roots in the voluntarist theology of an earlier period. Modern science has dropped the explicitly theological language that was so central to early-modern discussions, but it is still historically linked to earlier concerns about the nature of God's relationship to the Creation.

See also Atomism; Cambridge Platonists; Cartesianism; Epicureanism; Isaac Newton; Mechanical Philosophy; Stoicism; Theodicy

BIBLIOGRAPHY

Alexander, H. G., ed. *The Leibniz-Clarke Correspondence.* Manchester, U.K.: Manchester University Press, 1956.

Armstrong, A. H., ed. *The Cambridge History of Later Greek and Early Medieval Philosophy.* Cambridge: Cambridge University Press, 1967.

Brooke, John Hedley. *Science and Religion: Some Historical Perspectives.* Cambridge: Cambridge University Press, 1991.

Debus, Allen G. *The Chemical Philosophy: Paracelsian Science and Medicine in the Sixteenth and Seventeenth Centuries.* 2 vols. New York: Neale Watson Academic Publications, 1977.

Dobbs, B. J. T. *The Janus Faces of Genius: The Role of Alchemy in Newton's Thought.* Cambridge: Cambridge University Press, 1991.

Funkenstein, Amos. *Theology and the Scientific Imagination from the Middle Ages to the Seventeenth Century.* Princeton, N.J.: Princeton University Press, 1986.

Gould, Stephen J. *Wonderful Life: The Burgess Shale and the Nature of History.* New York: Norton, 1989.

Hutton, Sarah, ed. *Henry More (1614–1687): Tercentenary Studies.* Dordrecht: Kluwer, 1990.

Lovejoy, Arthur O. *The Great Chain of Being: A Study of the History of an Idea.* 1936. Reprint. New York: Harper Torchbooks, 1960.

Oakley, Francis. *Omnipotence, Covenant, and Order: An Excursion in the History of Ideas from Abelard to Leibniz.* Ithaca, N.Y.: Cornell University Press, 1984.

Osler, Margaret J., ed. *Atoms,* Pneuma, *and Tranquillity: Epicurean and Stoic Themes in European Thought.* Cambridge: Cambridge University Press, 1991.

———. "The Intellectual Sources of Robert Boyle's Philosophy of Nature: Gassendi's Voluntarism, and Boyle's Physico-Theological Project." In *Philosophy, Science, and Religion in England, 1640–1700,* ed. by Richard Kroll, Richard Ashcraft, and Perez Zagorin. Cambridge: Cambridge University Press, 1992, 178–98.

———. *Divine Will and the Mechanical Philosophy: Gassendi and Descartes on Contingency and Necessity in the Created World.* Cambridge: Cambridge University Press, 1994.

Westfall, Richard S. *Science and Religion in Seventeenth-Century England.* New Haven, Conn.: Yale University Press, 1958.

9. Natural Theology

John Hedley Brooke

Natural theology is a type of theological discourse in which the existence and attributes of the deity are discussed in terms of what can be known through natural reason, in contradistinction (though not necessarily in opposition) to knowledge derived from special revelation. Routine, timeless definitions of natural theology are, however, simplistic because "natural reason" and "revelation" have been understood differently in different cultures and at different times. Since the Enlightenment, natural theology has often been characterized as the attempt to construct rational "proofs" for God's existence and attributes—a project drawing on the natural sciences but vulnerable both to philosophical critiques and to changes in scientific sensibility. By contrast, in premodern cultures, adherents of the monotheistic religions would scarcely have entertained a discourse of natural theology independent of that greater knowledge of God revealed in their sacred texts. Doctrinal disputes abounded but, within Jewish, Christian, and Islamic societies, the existence of God was rarely the issue. The psalmist had spoken of the manifold and wondrous works of God (for example, in Psalm 19:1–6), but as an affirmation of faith in, not an attempted proof of, divine wisdom. There are many comparable examples from the history of Christendom and Islam, suggesting that to abstract what may look like "proofs" of God's existence from their contexts misses the significance that such arguments had within specific religious communities.

Order and Design in Nature

A recurring goal of natural theology has been to show the incompleteness of philosophies of nature that purport to explain the appearance of order and design without reference to supernatural agency. This was the challenge faced by Thomas Aquinas (c. 1225–74) as he engaged the philosophy of Aristotle (384–322 B.C.), for whom the world was eternal, governed by causes entirely within the cosmos. The primary controlling cause, without which there would be no change, was the "final cause," the end or purpose of the process. Such control was most evident in the development of a seed or embryo, where the inference to a goal-directed process was irresistible. Regarding the natural world as if it were a living organism, Aristotle saw these final causes as immanent within nature itself. In response, Aquinas asked why the components of nature should behave in so orderly a way. Physical bodies surely lacked knowledge and yet regularly acted in concert with others to achieve certain ends. In his *Summa Theologiae,* Aquinas insisted that such ends must, therefore, be achieved not fortuitously but designedly: Whatever lacks knowledge cannot move toward an end unless directed by some being endowed with knowledge and intelligence. This was the fifth of the "five ways" by which Aquinas affirmed the rationality of belief in a transcendent deity. But it was not so much a demonstration of the existence of God as a demonstration that the Aristotelian philosophy of nature was harmless to Christian theism since it was not fully coherent without it.

The association of Aristotle's "final cause" with a doctrine of providence was not the only basis on which a natural theology might be constructed. It was possible to argue, as Plato (c. 427–347 B.C.) had, that the world resembles a work of craftsmanship, bearing the marks of intelligent design. Plato had ascribed the order in nature to the work of a Demiurge (Craftsman), which had molded preexisting matter according to intentions that were partly frustrated by the recalcitrance of the material at its disposal. This model of divine activity had the attraction of accounting for imperfections in nature but has often been judged defective by Christian theologians because of the restrictions it placed on the power of a God who, as Creator of all things, would not have been bound by preexisting matter.

With the increasing mechanization of nature during the seventeenth century, new images of the divine craftsman were introduced. René Descartes (1596–1650) and Robert Boyle (1627–91) compared the universe with the cathedral clock at Strasbourg, both stressing the freedom of the divine will rather than restrictions on its power. The conjunction of a corpuscular theory of matter with a voluntarist theology of Creation is often seen as propitious for the reformation of natural philosophy. It could legitimate the quest for the divinely ordained "rules" or "laws" by which the movement of passive matter was regulated; it also justified empirical methods as the only means of discovering which of the many mechanisms the deity might have chosen or that he had, in fact, employed.

Descartes himself had not developed arguments for design based on his mechanistic worldview, preferring instead variants of the ontological argument to establish beyond doubt the existence of the Perfect Being who had planted the idea of perfection in his mind. Descartes even warned against presumptuous attempts to know the designs of God. It was this prohibition that so worried Boyle who, in his *Disquisition About the Final Causes of Natural Things* (1688), accused the Frenchman of having discarded the strongest argument for a deity: that based on such wonderful contrivances as the human eye, which had so evidently been made to see with. Boyle conceded that many of God's intentions we could not presume to know; but, having marveled at the intricacies of nature recently disclosed by the microscope, he was convinced that scientific knowledge supported the Christian revelation. That the machinery necessary for life had been packed into the minutest mite was, for Boyle, more astounding evidence for a deity than the larger machinery of the macrocosm. Such a natural theology, in which evidence for divine wisdom was uncovered in scientific investigation, was to prove especially durable in the English-speaking world. It was epitomized by Boyle's self-presentation as priest in the temple of nature.

A Higher Profile for Natural Theology

Why did natural theology gain a higher profile during the second half of the seventeenth century? Scientific discoveries could evoke a sense of wonder, as they did for

Boyle. The microscope revealed finely wrought structures, vividly captured in Robert Hooke's (1635–1703) depiction of the compound eye of a fly. The microscope also provided a rhetoric for religious apologists who observed that, whereas human artifacts, when magnified, revealed all of their deformities, the works of nature, from the beauty of a snowflake to the proboscis of a flea, revealed a kind of perfection. In John Ray's (1627–1705) *Wisdom of God Manifested in the Works of Creation* (1691), this contrast was used to argue for the transcendence of nature's art over human art and, by implication, the transcendence of the Supreme Designer. Ray also expatiated on the aesthetic appeal of Copernican astronomy. A hidden beauty had been unveiled once the sun had become the focus of the planetary orbits.

Social pressures may help explain the recourse to natural theology among natural philosophers themselves. Those such as Marin Mersenne (1588–1648), Pierre Gassendi (1592–1655), Walter Charleton (1620–1707), and Robert Boyle who favored an atomic or corpuscularian theory of matter had to stress that they were not reviving the atheistic atomism of Lucretius (c. 99–55 B.C.). The craftsmanship discernible in nature rendered it inconceivable that a chaos of atoms, left to itself, could have produced an ordered world. The pressure to affirm an active providence was acute because mechanists such as Thomas Hobbes (1588–1679) were gaining notoriety by contending that the soul was corporeal. In England, an emphasis on the rationality of faith was also a way of dispelling the religious "enthusiasm" that had flourished during the Puritan domination (1649–60) and had led to such a proliferation of sects that Boyle had feared lest the Christian religion should destroy itself. Arguments for an intelligent Creator grounded in the realities of the natural world offered an anchor, even the prospect of consensus, amid the turbulence created by religious divisions.

It was, however, a less-than-orthodox Christian, Isaac Newton (1642–1727), who gave the most decisive impetus to the design arguments. Newton's views on the Trinity were heterodox, but his abiding interest in the fulfillment of biblical prophecy reflected his belief in a deity having dominion over both nature and history. From his correspondence with Richard Bentley (1662–1742), from the *General Scholium* that he wrote for the second (1713) edition of his *Principia,* and from the "Queries" appended to his *Opticks* (1704), it is clear that Newton saw evidence of design in the structure of the universe. Against Descartes, he argued that only an intelligent being, "very well versed in mechanics and geometry," could have calculated the correct tangential component of each planet's velocity to ensure that it went into a stable orbit.

A natural theology could even generate confidence in a providential deity whose activity had not been confined to an initial Creation. Newton was concerned about the long-term stability of the solar system, given that planets might slow down as they moved through an ether, or given the loss of mass from the sun through vaporization. The necessary "reformation" of the system did not necessarily involve God's direct intervention. Secondary causes, such as comets, could serve as instruments of the divine will. But, either way, the inference to an active deity seemed to have all of the authority of Newton's science behind it. The elegance of the inverse-square law of gravity pointed to a God who had chosen to rule the world not by incessant acts of absolute power (though Newton never denied the deity that power) but through the self-limiting mediation of laws. A parallel with the constitutional monarchy that England was developing after the Revolution of 1688 has often been noted.

The Presuppositions of Natural Theology and Their Exposure

In much of eighteenth-century natural theology, images of the divine craftsman, geometer, or architect were distinctly anthropomorphic and, therefore, vulnerable to the objection that the transcendence of God was being demeaned. Newton's spokesman, Samuel Clarke (1675–1729), encountered this criticism in his controversy with Gottfried Wilhelm Leibniz (1646–1716). When Newton had spoken of space as if it were the "sensorium" of God, this, for Leibniz, implied that Newton was thinking of the deity in human terms, even possessing a body. Newton had once suggested that our ability to move our limbs affords an analogy on the basis of which it may be presumed rational to believe that God, as spirit, can (even more easily) move matter. The danger, sensed by Leibniz, was that the physical universe might be identified with the body of God—a position closer to pantheism than to Christian theism. The Clarke-Leibniz controversy also shows how deep divisions could ensue in prioritizing divine attributes. Newton and Clarke emphasized the freedom and power of the divine will. If God had willed a world in which a "reformation" of the solar system was periodically required, so be it. It was not for natural

philosophers to dictate to God the kind of world that God should have made. Leibniz, however, appeared to be doing just that when he argued that a perfect, rational Being would have had the foresight to make a world that did not need correction. This shows how an understanding of God's relation to nature could be deeply affected according to whether God's freedom or foresight was accentuated.

Leibniz's description of the Newtonian world-machine as second-rate clockwork highlights another feature of the design argument—one that was to engage David Hume (1711–76) in his posthumously published *Dialogues Concerning Natural Religion* (1779). Clockwork metaphors expressed an analogy between human artifacts and the natural world. In a skeptical critique, Hume exposed the fragility of analogical argument. Even if the world resembled a human artifact, one could not conclude that it had a single maker. Many hands were routinely involved in the making of machines. Consequently, polytheism was as plausible an inference as monotheism.

According to Hume, analogies other than clockwork were equally apposite for the expression of natural order. Why not regard the universe as an animal or a vegetable, in which case its cause would be an egg or a seed? The uniqueness of the universe did not mean that it was uncaused. Hume simply argued that, without experience of the creation of worlds, we can know nothing of the cause. Newton had claimed that the natural philosopher was to reason from effects to their causes, until one would finally reach an original cause that was certainly not mechanical. Hume retaliated that it was illegitimate to stop the inquiry with the introduction of an uncaused cause. To posit mental order in a divine Being as the cause of an intelligible order in nature only invited the further question: How had that mental order originated? Hume also questioned the ascription of properties such as divine, omnipotent, or omniscient to the originating cause. Claiming that it was a cardinal principle of reasoning that causes should always be proportioned to their effects, Hume saw no grounds for conferring infinite powers on the cause of a universe that, in all of its workings, was finite. Striking at the heart of natural theology, Hume also raised the problem of theodicy. If it was legitimate to infer the benevolence of the deity from beneficent features of the world, surely it was just as legitimate to infer the maleficence or, at best, the indifference of the deity from a preponderance of pain and evil.

The gist of Hume's critique was that apologists were assuming the existence of a beneficent Creator, not proving it. The dependence of the design argument on a prior, but rationally undemonstrable, belief in a Creator was also recognized by Immanuel Kant (1724–1804) in a subtle analysis that exposed other deficiencies. For example, Kant insisted that the purposive causality associated with living organisms, which allowed one to say that they were both causes and effects of themselves, could not be explained by analogy with a work of art. Among other weaknesses, Kant pointed to one that was decisive: No matter how much ingenuity and artistry might be displayed in the world, it could never demonstrate the moral wisdom that had to be predicated of God.

The Survival and Diversification of Natural Theology

In France, where a more secular culture prevailed at the time of the Revolution, and in Germany, where the full force of the Kantian critique was felt, physico-theology lost much of its appeal. In the English-speaking world, however, it continued to be visible in popular scientific and religious culture. Thus, James Hutton's *Theory of the Earth* (1795), which reported "no vestige of a beginning" or "prospect of an end," was defended from the charge of atheism by the Rev. John Playfair (1748–1819), who could point to the author's references to the wisdom of the overall design. The earth sciences, especially through Georges Cuvier's (1769–1832) proofs of extinction, raised particularly sensitive issues, but the English clerical geologists could still turn to natural theology for assistance. In Cambridge, Adam Sedgwick (1785–1873) turned the fossil record into arguments against both deists and atheists. The appearance of living forms that had once not existed confirmed a Creator who, unlike the clockmaker God of the deists, had clearly been active in the world since creation. Similarly, atheists were deprived of their solace: No longer could living things be said to have existed from eternity. A progressive pattern in the fossil record could also be used to argue for providence. Clerical scientists in Britain, such as William Whewell (1794–1866), felt the need to reassure their congregations that French science was not as dangerous as it seemed. Pierre Laplace (1749–1827) might have corrected Newton by showing that the solar system could restabilize itself without the need for a divine initiative, but, for Whewell, this only confirmed the greater skill and foresight of the Creator.

Indeed, design arguments were remarkably resilient, diversifying to meet the challenge presented by religious dissidents and new scientific perspectives. Immediately preceding the publication of Charles Darwin's (1809–82) *Origin of Species* (1859), several different styles of natural theology coexisted. William Paley's (1743–1805) argument for a divine Contriver based on the utility of anatomical structures left an almost indelible impression on Darwin himself, who later admitted that, even on his theory of natural selection, it had been difficult to relinquish the belief that every detail of organic structure must have some use. But Paley's argument based on specific contrivances was far from the only model. James Hutton (1726–97) and Joseph Priestley (1733–1804) had focused attention on the system of nature as a whole, each drawing attention to processes of replenishment that implied divine foresight—Hutton to processes of mountain building and erosion that maintained the earth's fertile soils, Priestley to the role of vegetation in maintaining the respiratory quality of the air.

A celebration of nature as a beneficent system could also be sustained by observing the harmonious manner in which many "laws" of nature combined. Whewell took this line in his *Bridgewater Treatise* (1833), arguing that a law presupposed an agent, a supreme legislator. The young Darwin was not unsympathetic to this model of God's relationship to nature. The existence of laws of nature did not exclude the existence of higher purposes, of which the production of more complex organic beings was the obvious example. Arguments based on the laws of nature could cut both ways, in that the weight of naturalistic explanation could easily exclude a personal, caring God, as it eventually did for Darwin.

Yet another style of natural theology, having resonances with Plato, was exemplified by T. H. Huxley's (1825–95) adversary Richard Owen (1804–92). The concept of a unity of skeletal structure, common to all vertebrates, had been used, especially in France, to contest the primacy given by Cuvier to teleological considerations. In response to this secular program, Owen reinterpreted the skeletal archetype as an idea in the mind of the Creator who, in the unfolding of a plan, had adapted it differently to the different needs of successive species. Still other claims for design were possible. The prolific popularizer of geology Hugh Miller (1802–56) marveled at the beauty of fossil forms, which, because they presaged all human architecture, confirmed that the divine and the human mind shared the same aesthetic sensibilities. For

William Whewell, there was no way that the sciences could undermine a Christian faith, because every scientific advance pointed to the divine gift of a mind that could elicit truths about nature.

The Darwinian Challenge to Natural Theology

Darwin's theory of evolution by natural selection is seen as a watershed because it challenged so many facets of natural theology. Principally, it showed how nature could counterfeit design. In a competitive struggle for limited resources, those individual variants with advantageous characteristics would tend to survive at the expense of the norm and leave more offspring. Over innumerable generations, this process of natural selection would lead to the accumulation of favorable variations, giving rise to new and well-adapted species having all the appearance of design. No longer could finely honed organic structures constitute proof of a Designer in the manner suggested by Paley.

In Darwin's theory, the course of evolution was depicted in terms of successive branching, of divergent lines stemming from common ancestors. This jarred with the idea that *homo sapiens* was the intended product of a divinely planned progression. In correspondence with American botanist Asa Gray (1810–88), Darwin denied that the variations on which natural selection worked were under divine supervision. They were random, in the sense that some were beneficial but some detrimental; they did not appear as if designed for a prospective use. Darwin's mechanism also highlighted the theodicy problem. The presence of so much pain and suffering in the world Darwin considered a formidable argument against a beneficent God, but it was what one would expect on the basis of natural selection. If the human mind was itself the product of evolution, there was the additional question whether it was equipped to reason profitably about the existence and attributes of the deity. Darwin's own view was that the very enterprise of natural theology was arrogant and anthropocentric. That man was descended from earlier forms of animal life taught a necessary lesson in humility.

Popular modern writers on evolution, notably Richard Dawkins, sometimes give the impression that, once Darwin had pronounced, a rational case for theism became a lost cause. Images of the divine Craftsman and the divine Magician were certainly moribund. The suffi-

ciency of Darwin's mechanism of natural selection was, however, a contentious issue among scientists themselves. In his *Descent of Man* (1871), Darwin himself said that he had given it too great a scope in his *Origin*. Even his "bulldog," T. H. Huxley, introduced mutations to speed up the earliest stages of evolution. Consequently, despite such a considered rejection of Darwinism as that of the Princeton theologian Charles Hodge (1797–1878), models of theistic evolution were developed that preserved a natural theology. For Asa Gray, even natural selection was compatible with natural theology because it helped rationalize suffering. If it was a necessary concomitant of a long creative process, some of its sting might be removed. In Britain, Frederick Temple (1821–1902), destined to become archbishop of Canterbury, made a not dissimilar point when he suggested that the theodicy problem was greater for those who believed in separate acts of Creation than for those who accepted the integrity of an evolutionary process. By the end of the nineteenth century, it was even possible for Aubrey Moore (1848–90) to argue that Darwin had done Christianity a service. On the basis of an Incarnational theology, in which God was immanent in the world, Moore was grateful for Darwin's destruction of semideistic schemes in which God was totally absent except for the occasional intervention. The contours of the evolutionary process as Darwin described them, coupled with distressing natural disasters, made it increasingly difficult to see any single, overriding divine purpose in the history of life on Earth. But this did not prevent sophisticated thinkers such as the Jesuit modernist George Tyrrell (1861–1909) from arguing that the universe still teemed with aims and meanings even though they could not be subsumed under a collective effort.

Natural Theology in the Twentieth Century

For much of the twentieth century, disincentives to natural theology have tended to outweigh the incentives. Traditional distinctions between "natural" and "revealed" theology proved difficult to sustain in the wake of historical criticism of the sacred texts. The meaning of "natural" as in "the natural world" has also been compromised by science-based technologies that have insinuated so many artificial products into local and global environments. The concept of a "natural reason" in all humanity has proved simplistic in the light of psychoanalytical models of the unconscious mind. Theodicies based on the evolution and prospective improvement of "human nature" were shattered by two world wars. After the first, Karl Barth (1886–1968) issued a stentorian "No" to natural theology that has resounded through the corridors of Reformed theology. Reaffirming a God of judgment and redemption, Barth insisted that such was the gulf between creatures and their Creator that no autonomous creaturely reasoning could reach a knowledge of God, who is knowable only through himself.

An interest in revised forms of natural theology has, however, never completely waned, as evidenced by the various schemes of "process theology" that have taken their inspiration from Alfred North Whitehead's (1861–1947) *Process and Reality* (1929) and the appearance of eco-feminist theologies that have also stressed the persuasive rather than the coercive agency of God. The impetus to experiment with science-based theologies has not always come from scientists themselves. Relativity theory, quantum mechanics, and, more recently, chaos theory have been used (not always circumspectly) to argue for less mechanistic, less deterministic conceptions of nature in which there might be hints of an openness to divine influence. The disclosure that the emergence of intelligent life has been possible only because of what looks like an extraordinary "fine-tuning" of the physical processes involved in the earliest moments of the big bang has encouraged those who already believe in a designing intelligence, though the apologetic force of such anthropic coincidences remains controversial, given the rejoinder that our universe may be one of a myriad possible universes—the "lucky one" that just happened to have the right parameters. In this example, as in others in which the roles of contingency and necessity in biological evolution are discussed, there is a deep paradox, in that both contingency and necessity are invoked by theists and their critics to support their respective positions. This paradox provides additional evidence for what John Hick has called the religious ambiguity of the universe.

See also Anthropic Principle; Design Argument; Great Chain of Being; Macrocosm/Microcosm; Theodicy; Varieties of Providentialism

BIBLIOGRAPHY

Barrow, John D., and Frank J. Tipler. *The Anthropic Cosmological Principle.* Oxford: Oxford University Press, 1986.

Bowler, Peter J. *The Eclipse of Darwinism: Anti-Darwinian Evolution Theories in the Decades Around 1900.* Baltimore: Johns Hopkins University Press, 1983.

Brooke, John Hedley. "Indications of a Creator: Whewell as Apologist and Priest." In *William Whewell: A Composite Portrait,* ed. by Menachem Fisch and Simon Schaffer. Oxford: Oxford University Press, 1991, 149–73.

———. *Science and Religion: Some Historical Perspectives.* Cambridge: Cambridge University Press, 1991.

Brooke, John Hedley, and Geoffrey Cantor. *Reconstructing Nature: The Engagement of Science and Religion.* Edinburgh: T. and T. Clark, 1998.

Brunner, Emil. *Natural Theology.* Trans. by Peter Fraenkel, comprising Brunner's "Nature and Grace" and Karl Barth's reply, "No!" London: Bles, Centenary, 1946.

Buckley, Michael J. *At the Origins of Modern Atheism.* New Haven, Conn.: Yale University Press, 1987.

Burbridge, David. "William Paley Confronts Erasmus Darwin: Natural Theology and Evolutionism in the Eighteenth Century." *Science and Christian Belief* 10 (1998): 49–71.

Clayton, John. "Piety and the Proofs." *Religious Studies* 26 (1990): 19–42.

Funkenstein, Amos. *Theology and the Scientific Imagination from the Middle Ages to the Seventeenth Century.* Princeton, N.J.: Princeton University Press, 1986.

Gascoigne, John. "From Bentley to the Victorians: The Rise and Fall of British Newtonian Natural Theology." *Science in Context* 2 (1988): 219–56.

Gaskin, J. C. A. *Hume's Philosophy of Religion.* London: Macmillan, 1978.

Gillespie, Neal C. "Divine Design and the Industrial Revolution: William Paley's Abortive Reform of Natural Theology." *Isis* 81 (1990): 214–29.

Gillispie, Charles C. *Genesis and Geology.* New York: Harper, 1959.

Glacken, Clarence J. *Traces on the Rhodian Shore: Nature and Culture in Western Thought from Ancient Times to the End of the Eighteenth Century.* Berkeley: University of California Press, 1967.

Gregory, Frederick. *Nature Lost? Natural Science and the German Theological Traditions of the Nineteenth Century.* Cambridge, Mass.: Harvard University Press, 1992.

Harsthorne, Charles. *A Natural Theology for Our Time.* La Salle, Ill.: Open Court, 1967.

Hick, John. *An Interpretation of Religion.* London: Macmillan, 1989.

Hurlbutt, Robert H. *Hume, Newton, and the Design Argument.* Lincoln: University of Nebraska Press, 1965.

Kenny, Anthony. *The Five Ways: Saint Thomas Aquinas' Proofs of God's Existence.* London: Routledge, 1969.

Mackie, John L. *The Miracle of Theism: Arguments for and Against the Existence of God.* Oxford: Oxford University Press, 1982.

Moore, James R. *The Post-Darwinian Controversies: A Study of the Protestant Struggle to Come to Terms with Darwin in Great Britain and America.* Cambridge: Cambridge University Press, 1979.

Ospovat, Dov. *The Development of Darwin's Theory: Natural History, Natural Theology, and Natural Selection.* Cambridge: Cambridge University Press, 1981.

Roberts, Jon H. *Darwinism and the Divine in America: Protestant Intellectuals and Organic Evolution, 1859–1900.* Madison: University of Wisconsin Press, 1988.

Russell, Robert J., Nancey Murphy, and Arthur R. Peacocke, eds. *Chaos and Complexity: Scientific Perspectives on Divine Action.* Vatican City: Vatican Observatory Press, 1995.

Stenmark, Mikael. *Rationality in Science, Religion, and Everyday Life.* Notre Dame, Ind.: University of Notre Dame Press, 1995.

Young, Robert M. *Darwin's Metaphor: Nature's Place in Victorian Culture.* Cambridge: Cambridge University Press, 1985, 126–63.

10. THE DESIGN ARGUMENT

William A. Dembski

In its most general form, the design argument infers from features of the physical world an intelligent cause responsible for those features. Just what features signal an intelligent cause, what the nature of that intelligent cause is, and how convincingly those features establish an intelligent cause remain subjects for debate and account for the variety of design arguments over the centuries. The design argument is also called the teleological argument.

The design argument needs to be distinguished from a metaphysical commitment to design. For instance, in the *Timaeus,* Plato (c. 427–347 B.C.) proposed a Demiurge (Craftsman) who fashioned the physical world, but not because the physical world exhibits features that cannot be explained apart from the Demiurge. Plato knew of the work of the Greek atomists, who needed no such explanatory device. Rather, within Plato's philosophy, the world of intelligible forms constituted the ultimate reality, of which the physical world was but a dim reflection. Plato, therefore, posited the Demiurge to transmit the design inherent in the world of forms to the physical world.

Often the design argument and a metaphysical commitment to design have operated in tandem. This has especially been true in the Christian tradition, in which the design argument is used to establish an intelligent cause, and a metaphysical commitment to the Christian God then identifies this intelligent cause with the Christian God. Moreover, the design argument and a metaphysical commitment to design tend also to be conflated within the Christian tradition, so that the design argument often appears to move directly from features of the physical world to the triune God of Christianity.

Full-fledged design arguments have been available since classical times. Both Aristotle's (384–322 B.C.) final causes and the Stoics' seminal reason were types of intel-ligent causation inferred at least in part from the apparent order and purposiveness of the physical world. For example, in his *De Natura Deorum,* Cicero (106–43 B.C.) writes:

> When we see something moved by machinery, like an orrery or clock . . . we do not doubt that these contrivances are the work of reason; when therefore we behold the whole compass of heaven moving with revolutions of marvelous velocity and executing with perfect regularity the annual changes of the seasons with absolute safety and security for all things, how can we doubt that all this is effected not merely by reason, but by a reason that is transcendent and divine? (Cicero 1933, 217–9).

Throughout the Christian era, theologians have argued that nature exhibits features that nature itself cannot explain, but which instead require an intelligence beyond nature. Church Fathers like Minucius Felix (third century A.D.) and Gregory of Nazianzus (A.D. c. 329–89), medieval scholars like Moses Maimonides (1135–1204) and Saint Thomas Aquinas (c. 1225–74), and commonsense realists like Thomas Reid (1710–96) and Charles Hodge (1797–1878) were all theologians who made design arguments, arguing from the data of nature to an intelligence that transcends nature. Saint Thomas's fifth proof for the existence of God is perhaps the best known.

Since the seventeenth century, design arguments have focused especially on biology. The British physico-theologians of the seventeenth through the nineteenth centuries, starting with Robert Boyle (1627–91) and John Ray (1627–1705) and finding their culmination in William Paley (1743–1805), looked to biological systems for convincing evidence that a designer had acted in the physical world. Accordingly, it was thought incredible that organisms, with their astonishing complexity and superb adaptation of means to ends, could originate strictly through the blind forces of nature. Paley's *Natural Theology* (1802) is largely a catalog of biological systems he regarded as inexplicable apart from a superintending intelligence. Who was this designer of the British physico-theologians? For many it was the traditional Christian God, while for others it was a deistic God, who had created the world but played no ongoing role in governing his creation.

Criticisms of the design argument have never been in short supply. In classical times, Democritus (c. 460–c. 370 B.C.) and Lucretius (c. 99–55 B.C.) conceived the natural world as a whirl of particles in collision, which sometimes chanced to form stable configurations exhibiting order and complexity. David Hume (1711–76) referred to this critique of design as "the Epicurean Hypothesis":

A finite number of particles is only susceptible of finite transpositions: and it must happen, in an eternal duration, that every possible order or position must be tried an infinite number of times. This world, therefore, with all its events, even the most minute, has before been produced and destroyed, and will again be produced and destroyed, without any bounds and limitations. No one, who has a conception of the power of infinite, in comparison of finite, will ever scruple this determination (Hume 1779 [reprint], 67).

Modern variants of this critique are still with us in the form of inflationary cosmologies (for example, Guth and Steinhardt 1989).

Though Hume cited the Epicurean hypothesis, he never put great stock in it. In *Dialogues Concerning Natural Religion* (1779), Hume argued principally that the design argument fails as an argument from analogy and as an argument from induction. Though widely successful in discrediting the design argument, Hume's critique is no longer as convincing as it used to be. As Elliott Sober observes, Hume incorrectly analyzed the logic of the design argument, for the design argument is, properly speaking, neither an argument from analogy nor an argument from induction but an inference to the best explanation.

Whereas Hume attempted a blanket refutation of the design argument, Immanuel Kant (1724–1804) tried

rather to limit its scope. According to Kant: "The utmost . . . that the [design] argument can prove is an *architect* of the world who is [constrained] by the adaptability of the material in which he works, not a *creator* of the world to whose idea everything is subject" (Kant 1787 [reprint], 522). Far from rejecting the design argument, Kant objected to overextending it. For Kant, the design argument legitimately establishes an "architect" (that is, an intelligent cause whose contrivances are constrained by the materials that make up the world), but it can never establish a Creator who originates the very materials that the architect then molds and fashions.

Charles Darwin (1809–82) delivered the design argument its biggest blow. Darwin was ideally situated historically to do this. His *Origin of Species* (1859) fit perfectly with an emerging positivistic conception of science that was loath to invoke intelligent causes and sought as far as possible to assimilate scientific explanation to natural law. Hence, even though Darwin's selection mechanism remained much in dispute throughout the second half of the nineteenth century, the mere fact that Darwin had proposed a plausible naturalistic mechanism to account for biological systems was enough to convince the Anglo-American world that some naturalistic story or other had to be true.

Even more than cosmology, biology had, under the influence of British natural theology, become the design argument's most effective stronghold. It was here more than anywhere else that design could assuredly be found. To threaten this stronghold was, therefore, to threaten the legitimacy of the design argument as a creditable intellectual enterprise. Richard Dawkins summed up the matter thus: "Darwin made it possible to be an intellectually fulfilled atheist" (Dawkins 1987, 6). God might still exist, but the physical world no longer required God to exist.

Is the design argument dead? Certainly, cosmological design arguments that appeal to the fine-tuning of physical constants remain very much alive (for example, Barrow and Tipler 1986; Leslie 1989; Swinburne 1979). What's more, biological design arguments are experiencing a resurgence. In his *Philosophy of Biology* (1993), Elliott Sober concedes that biology has no intrinsic quarrel with the design argument and that the only thing keeping it from being reestablished in biology is the absence of empirically adequate criteria for design. Michael Behe's (1996) work on irreducibly complex biochemical systems and William Dembski's (1998) on the logical structure of design inferences attempt to meet Sober's concern.

See also Anthropic Principle; Natural Theology

BIBLIOGRAPHY

Barrow, John, and Frank Tipler. *The Anthropic Cosmological Principle.* Oxford: Oxford University Press, 1986.

Behe, Michael. *Darwin's Black Box.* New York: Free Press, 1996.

Cicero, Marcus Tullius. *De Natura Deorum.* Trans. by H. Rackham. Cambridge, Mass.: Harvard University Press, 1933.

Dawkins, Richard. *The Blind Watchmaker.* New York: Norton, 1987.

Dembski, William. *The Design Inference.* Cambridge: Cambridge University Press, 1998.

———, ed. *Mere Creation: Science, Faith, and Intelligent Design.* Downers Grove, Ill.: InterVarsity Press, 1998.

Guth, Alan, and Paul Steinhardt. "The Inflationary Universe." In *The New Physics,* ed. by Paul Davies. Cambridge: Cambridge University Press, 1989, 34–60.

Hume, David. *Dialogues Concerning Natural Religion.* 1779. Reprint. Buffalo, N.Y.: Prometheus Books, 1989.

Hurlbutt, Robert H. *Hume, Newton, and the Design Argument.* Lincoln: University of Nebraska Press, 1965.

Kant, Immanuel. *Critique of Pure Reason.* 1787. Reprint. Trans. by N. K. Smith. New York: St. Martin's Press, 1929.

Jeffner, Anders. *Butler and Hume on Religion.* Stockholm: Diakonistyrelsens Bokforlag, 1966.

Leslie, John. *Universes.* London: Routledge, 1989.

Mackie, J. L. *The Miracle of Theism: Arguments for and Against the Existence of God.* Oxford: Clarendon, 1982.

Paley, William. *Natural Theology.* 1802. Reprint. Boston: Gould and Lincoln, 1852.

Sober, Elliott. *Philosophy of Biology.* Boulder, Colo.: Westview, 1993.

Swinburne, Richard. *The Existence of God.* Oxford: Oxford University Press, 1979.

11. MIRACLES

Robert M. Burns

If "miracles" are defined as events that appear to depart from nature's normal course, and so are judged to have a supernatural cause, belief in them was almost universal prior to the rise of modern science. The tendency to explain events by supernatural rather than natural causes sometimes became so extreme as virtually to obliterate the distinction between a natural and a supernatural event (for instance, in early-medieval Christendom), but it is clear that most conceptions of the miraculous presuppose some such distinction. In surveying the many attempts that have been made in the past two millennia to grapple with a concept that straddles the boundary between natural science and religious belief, our attention will focus largely on attempts to clarify the natural/supernatural distinction and to show how an event could be judged to fall on one side or the other of the dichotomy. There have always been some, however (such as Plutarch, Friedrich Schleiermacher, R. F. Holland), who have been ready to argue that an event can be classified as both, and in almost every age some who have denied any intelligible application to the term "supernatural."

In the centuries surrounding the beginning of the Christian era, a few thinkers anticipated more modern skeptical attitudes to miracle stories. Polybius (c. 205–c. 125 B.C.) wrote that "every event whether probable or improbable must have some cause" (*Histories* 2.38), so that miracles are "not only utterly improbable but absolutely impossible" (16.12). Cicero (106–43 B.C.) insisted on the sole validity of a single explanatory principle (*una ratio*), which is "whatever comes in being, whatever it is, necessarily has a cause in nature, so that even if it should appear conspicuously contrary to what is customary yet it cannot actually be contrary to nature" (*On Divination* 2.38.60). Plutarch (c. A.D. 50–120), in

seeking to prove the compatibility of the natural and the supernatural, argued that physical and purposive explanations are distinct but complementary in both human and divine cases: "Those who say that the discovery of the cause is destruction of the miracle (*semeion*) do not perceive that along with the divine acts they are thus rejecting humanly contrived symbols," such as signal fires, clashings of gongs, or sundials (*Pericles* 6.2–4). Galen (A.D. 129–c. 210), appealing to the authority of "Plato and others of the Greeks who pursue in a correct way the principles of nature," declared that "some things . . . are impossible by nature" and criticized Moses for holding that "all things are possible for God, even should he wish to make ashes into a horse."

However, the notion of divine power over nature did not enter Greco-Roman culture with Judaism and Christianity: So deeply rooted was it that even the leading Stoic Posidonius (c. 135–c. 50 B.C.), despite making the usual Stoic identification of God with a rigidly determined natural order, maintained that "there is nothing which God cannot do" and that Zeus was higher than nature and fate. By the late Roman period, leaders of the dominant Neoplatonist school of philosophy had integrated demonology and magical theurgy into their doctrines and practices and encouraged belief in the reality of miracle-working gods.

Early Christian Theology

Among early Christian thinkers, Tertullian (c. 160–c. 220) maintained that nothing is impossible for God except that which he does not will. Origen (c. 185–c. 251), on the other hand, denied that God causes events "contrary to nature" (although he produces some "beyond nature"). He held that some miracle stories recorded in the Gospels are "impossible" fictions woven into the narratives deliberately in order to impel the reader to adopt allegorical interpretations. Augustine of Hippo (354–430), in an attempt to avoid the suggestion that God would disrupt the otherwise immutable order of nature that he himself had devised, postulated that miracles emerge from "seeds" implanted into matter at the first moment of creation (*De Trinitate* 3.8.13). But elsewhere he affirms the contrary view that God does *not* "pre-establish every cause but retained some in His own will . . . [which therefore] do not depend on the necessity of created causes" (*De Genesi ad Litteram* 6.18.29).

The Middle Ages and Renaissance

The reception into Western philosophy and theology of Arabic Neoplatonized Aristotelianism in the twelfth and thirteenth centuries provoked a major crisis in a thought world in which Augustine had long been the dominant authority. According to Avicenna (Ibn Sina [980–1037]), the material cosmos is an eternal system of substances, interacting according to necessary causal laws, produced necessarily by the "Agent Intellect," which is the lowest in a chain of ten "Intelligences" emanating necessarily one from another. Only the first emanates directly from God, who neither knows nor cares about the particular beings and events of this world and, therefore, would never intervene in it miraculously. Inevitably, Avicenna sought to provide naturalistic explanations of Muslim miracle stories. Against such views, Kalam theologians had argued that the created order manifests so many essentially arbitrary aspects that it could only be the design of an all-powerful creator God, who was able to make free choices between equipossibles. Thus, al-Ghazali (1058–1111) maintained that the motion of heavenly bodies from east to west rather than vice versa could only be the result of such an arbitrary divine decision. No causal relationships between substances in such a radically contingent cosmos can then be "necessary"; rather, all must express the arbitrary power of a God who is, therefore, the sole real cause of events. Thus, although men, observing that substances become hot when placed near fire, tend to conclude that fire "naturally" causes heat, the sequence is, in fact, merely a convention that God can "miraculously" suspend at any time.

Later medieval *Via Moderna* scholastics, such as Nicholas of Autrecourt (c. 1300–c. 1360), were to develop a comparable empiricist "occasionalism," but much thirteenth-century scholasticism (later termed the *Via Antiqua*) sought to reconcile Arabic-Aristotelian science and Christian theology. Thomas Aquinas (c. 1225–74) rejected the claim that "God alone is the immediate cause of everything wrought; for instance, that it is not fire that gives heat, but God in the fire" (*Summa Theologiae* 1a 105 art 5). Miracles are, therefore, properly defined as actions that lie beyond the power of any created cause (1a 110.4 and 114.4), occurring not because God is the sole cause of all events, but because he "can Himself produce all the determinate effects which are produced by any created cause" (1a 105 art 2). But Aquinas acknowledges the difficulty that no human being can know the limits of the powers of natural causes, which is why "one man believes and another does not when both have seen the same miracle" (1a IIae 111.4). Accordingly, it is not possible to prove by "demonstrative reasoning" even the resurrection of Christ (IIIa 55.5 ad 2), for the evidence requires supplementation by a "believing disposition." However, to a person granted the grace of such faith, "the individual arguments" for Christ's resurrection "taken alone are not a sufficient proof . . . [but] taken together in a cumulative way they manifest it perfectly" (IIIa 55.6).

The revival of interest in Hermetic magic in the Renaissance led some of its advocates to interpret biblical miracles as magical. Among the list of points for which Giordano Bruno (1548–1600) was condemned by the Inquisition were apparently the views that Moses wrought his miracles by magic and that Jesus was a Magus or magician.

Seventeenth-Century Rationalism

Wide differences concerning miracles emerged among thinkers closely associated with the development of post-Copernican natural science. Embarrassment concerning miracles is particularly evident in those philosophers traditionally classified as "Continental rationalists." René Descartes (1596–1650) remained deliberately silent about them, writing to warn one of his supporters to say "not a word about miracles." In his early unpublished work *The World,* he ventured the supposition that "God will never perform any miracle . . . just as intelligences or rational souls will not disrupt in any way the ordinary course of nature" in order not to undermine the "infallibility" of our knowledge of the physical world. Baruch

Spinoza (1632–77) published the first modern rejection of the entire concept of the miraculous in Chapter 6 of his *Tractatus Theologico-Politicus* (1670), arguing that a miracle, "whether contrary or beyond nature," is a "mere absurdity" since "whatever comes to pass, comes to pass according to laws and rules which involve eternal necessity and truth." His underlying presupposition is the pantheistic one that the "fixed and immutable order" of nature is, in fact, nothing other than a necessary expression of the divine substance, so that God is, in this sense, identical with nature and nature's laws.

It was the Oratorian priest Nicolas de Malebranche (1638–1715) who developed what is possibly the neatest argument from the divine nature for the regularity of physical events while maintaining a sense of divine transcendence of nature: Distinguishing in his *Dialogues on Metaphysics* between God's "ways" (*voies*)—that is, his methods, style, or manner of working—and his "works" (*ouvrages*), he argued that, while God wishes the perfection of all the latter, "he loves his wisdom more . . . invincibly . . . inviolably." Thus, the divine commitment to a rationality that operates through universal principle must override concern for individuals, leading God to work through a "general will" (*volonté générale*) rather than idiosyncratic *"volontés particulières."* However, Malebranche's need to conform to Roman Catholicism led him to affirm with apparent inconsistency, although without producing any argument, that God did, indeed, sometimes perform miracles through particular volitions.

Gottfried Wilhelm Leibniz (1646–1716) strove to make room for miracles while endorsing a consistent Malebranchism: "I would say that God never has a *particular will* such as this Father implies," he writes in his *Theodicy,* since in a miracle "God departs from one law only for another law more applicable" for "reasons of an order superior to that of nature." What, therefore, distinguishes miracles from ordinary events is not their irregularity but that "they cannot be accounted for by the natures of created things." In contrast to Aquinas, Leibniz confidently claims certain knowledge of the natures of created things, maintaining, for example, with Isaac Newton (1642–1727) in mind, that, "should God make a general law causing bodies to be attracted the one to the other, he could only achieve its operation by perpetual miracles." His opposition to Newton's views on miracles was a main topic of the celebrated Leibniz-Clarke correspondence, which was published in 1717. Newton was

ready to appeal to divine miraculous intervention to explain how the solar system continued to exist when, according to his calculations, it should have collapsed. Leibniz scoffed that this meant that "God Almighty meant to wind up his watch from time to time. . . . He had not it seems sufficient foresight to make it perpetual motion" (First Paper, 4). Explanation by miracles, he argued, undermined genuine natural science, since "nothing is easier than to account for things by bringing in the deity, *deum ex machina,* without minding the natures of things" (Fifth Paper, 105). In response, Newton's spokesman, Samuel Clarke (1675–1729), appealed to the occasionalist view that the "natural" is merely the humanly perceived regular operation of things, so that God, whether he acts with regularity or irregularity, can be "absolutely equal and indifferent" (Third Reply, 16).

English Empiricist Evidentialism

The positive attitude toward miracles of many English thinkers of the late seventeenth and early eighteenth centuries provides a striking contrast to the hostility of the rationalists. Though many of them were closely associated with the scientific revolution, the primary object of their interest in miracles was not to fill gaps in scientific explanation, but rather to provide indispensable empirical evidence of the truth of Christianity. Their notion that Jesus's miracles were manifestations of his divinity was, of course, not new. It is expressed not merely in the New Testament but throughout early Christian literature, for example, by Athanasius (c. 296–373) in *De Incarnatione* 18–19 and by Gregory of Nyssa (c. 330–c. 395) in his *Catechetical Oration* 12, although Origen had commented that "Christ's stupendous acts of power were able to bring to faith those of Christ's own time, but . . . they lost their demonstrative force with the lapse of years and began to be regarded as mythical" (*Comm. John* 2:4). The logic of evidentialism had been clearly expressed by Aquinas despite his insistence that the credibility of miracle stories is always less than absolutely certain. He writes that the content of Christ's revelation cannot be "proved by human reasoning" because it transcends the capacities of our intellect. But when a man does "works that God alone can do, we may believe that what he says comes from God, just as when a man delivers a letter sealed with the king's ring, we believe that what it contains expresses the king's will" (*Summa Theologiae* IIIa 43).

The English evidentialists stressed this function of miracles to a hitherto unparalleled degree. Nonetheless, they rarely claimed that events, however well attested, could with certainty be known to be miraculous because of the impossibility of knowing the extent of the powers of natural agents and the possibility of fraud or delusion. Only through a probability judgment in which many positive factors are combined, including above all a conjunction with a likely revelation, was it possible to achieve, at most, a practical certainty "beyond reasonable doubt" that a miracle had occurred. This judgment, as Joseph Butler (1692–1752) was to put it, was like "discerning the *effect* in architecture or other works of art; a result from a great number of things so and so disposed and taken into one view." Though critics were quick to object that it was viciously circular to prove the doctrine by the miracles and vice versa, this objection misses the point that, in judgments of moral probability, different pieces of evidence can mutually strengthen one another. One of many statements of this position is John Locke's (1632–1704) *Discourse on Miracles,* which was published posthumously in 1706.

Eighteenth-Century Skepticism Concerning Miracles

In 1748 David Hume (1711–76) published his "Of Miracles" as Section 10 of his *Enquiry Concerning Human Understanding,* a work that has remained one of the most widely read philosophical attacks on belief in miracles. Its five arguments, all of which had previously been presented by deists, gained force by being incorporated into Hume's general presentation of empiricism. His major argument, which had been developed earlier by William Wollaston (1660–1724), among others, in his *Religion of Nature Delineated* (1722), was that laws of nature are merely summaries of absolutely uniform past experience of constant conjunctions between phenomena. Since these are our only measures of probability and of their upper limit of practical certitude, Hume asserted, any story of a "violation of the laws of nature" (a definition of miracle that Hume had taken from Locke) is, by definition, minimally credible. Hume's argument fails to address the emphasis of the leading evidentialists on the holistic, and irreducibly qualitative, nature of judgments concerning laws of nature and of divine intervention in the established order. He struggles to deal with the

objection that to regard all reports of rarely experienced events as incredible is to rule out much scientific practice. Moreover, he ignores the usual evidentialist emphasis on a revelatory context except to try to reverse its implications by suggesting that a *religious* context reduces credibility to a minimum because of its invariable link with fraud and unhealthy credulity.

Virtually the centerpiece of the mature philosophy of Immanuel Kant (1724–1804) was his claim that, since the empirical ("phenomenal") world is half-constituted by the categories of our thought (*Critique of Pure Reason* [1710], A126–8), and since one such category is the relation of cause and effect, every empirical event must be an effect predetermined by an equally empirical cause. It nonetheless remains possible that in the world of things-in-themselves, though unknowably, human agents and God might act freely. However, this possibility still rules out miracles as possible historical facts, and, in his *Religion Within the Limits of Reason Alone* (1793), Kant treats miracles stories, along with all of the cardinal Christian doctrines, as of merely allegorical value.

Nineteenth and Twentieth Centuries

It would be impossible to survey the variety of views on miracles that have proliferated in the last two centuries. Despite the rapid marginalization of the belief in miracles in Western culture at large during this period, many competent modern thinkers have continued to defend it along essentially traditional lines, which others would regard as thoroughly outdated. For example, Richard Swinburne has provided a sophisticated updated expression of essentially the same position as eighteenth-century evidentialists. He has been countered by philosophers such as Antony Flew who likewise argue along lines not essentially dissimilar from eighteenth-century skeptics. A well-established tendency among writers on historical method, such as Francis Bradley (1846–1924), Ernst Troeltsch (1865–1923), or Van Harvey, has been to argue that the modern historian's criteria for the credibility of alleged events can be derived only from the assumptions of physical possibility embedded in our present culture. These presuppositions are so hostile to belief in miracles that, in practice, belief in them is impossible, whatever arguments might be adduced in their favor at an abstract philosophical or theological level.

It seems best to conclude this brief survey by referring to three German thinkers whose views on miracles have been exceptionally influential. First, Friedrich Schleiermacher (1768–1834), in his *On Religion: Speeches to Its Cultured Despisers* (1799), entirely rejected a supernatural concept of miracle because of its incompatibility with his brand of early Romantic pantheism. "Miracle," he writes, "is merely the religious name for event. To me everything is a miracle. . . . The more religious you would be the more you would see miracles everywhere," because every finite being is equally an expression of the divine Infinity, and if in individual events you cannot "intuit" or "feel" this expression, the explanation can only be that your "religious sense is poor and inadequate." His views do not fundamentally change in his more mature and conservative *The Christian Faith* (1821–2). Schleiermacher rejected entirely the evidentialist use of miracles because, in the New Testament itself, faith can be produced without miracles, while miracles sometimes fail to produce it. It is to be expected, however, that Jesus's transformative impact on the human spirit should be connected with "a working upon the physical side of human nature and upon external nature." But this impact would be "relatively" miraculous in that it followed from the "universal connection" but in ways that we do not understand. "Absolute miracles," which would simply "destroy the whole system of nature," were rejected by Schleiermacher, who argued, as did Leibniz, that true omnipotence would be manifest in a "nature mechanism" that fulfills God's purposes without ad hoc interference. Dispensing with the notion of the absolutely miraculous was, for Schleiermacher, "pure gain" from the interests of both natural science and religion.

An epoch-making book in biblical criticism was David Friedrich Strauss's (1808–74) *The Life of Jesus Critically Examined* (1836). In this work, Strauss took for granted the scientific incredibility of miracles, but, instead of explaining the New Testament miracles either as instances of fraud or superstitious delusion, as eighteenth-century skeptics typically did, or along naturalistic lines, as did the later Schleiermacher, he developed a view of them as "myths," produced in a stage of human development now passed, in which truths about the human predicament were expressed symbolically. It is "an important and luminous fact" that such mythmaking was not the product of individual poetic genius but occurred when stories were orally transmitted over long periods

within communities under the sway of leading "ideas" or ideals. These stories were thereby remolded by the collective imagination working "so powerfully that its illusions were believed in by the very minds that invented them." The continued relevance of the stories of Jesus is that they are "human nature conceived ideally," so that they exhibit "what man ought to be." Miracle stories, in particular, portray how "in the course of human history the spirit more and more completely subjugates nature, both within and around man, until it lies before him as the inert matter on which he exercises his active power." In the third edition (1838) of his *Life,* however, Strauss modified his account to acknowledge some plausibility in naturalistic explanations of the Gospel miracles.

Understanding miracle stories as "myths" has been attractive to liberal theologians in the twentieth century. Rudolf Bultmann (1894–1976) maintained, like Strauss, that miracle stories were the product of communal mythmaking processes operative in periods of oral transmission. He argued that, for this reason, the miracle stories of Jesus "have exactly the same style as . . . a great many miracles stories of Jewish and Hellenistic origin," such as those of the pagan Apollonius of Tyana (first century A.D.). (This judgment has been widely challenged by more recent scholars, who emphasize the many sui generis characteristics of the Gospel miracles stories.) "It is impossible to use electric light and the wireless," wrote Bultmann, and "at the same time believe in the New Testament world of spirit and miracle," because we are all now committed to understanding the world "as a self-subsistent unity immune from the agency of supernatural power." Hence, he rejected miracles as incredible and called for the "demythologization" of Christianity "to uncover the deeper meaning . . . concealed under the cover of mythology." The perennially valid core of the "myths" of the New Testament is not, however, according to Bultmann, Strauss's left-wing Hegelian Promethean humanism, but a christianized version of the existential analytic of Martin Heidegger's (1889–1976) *Being and Time:* the self-sufficient "authentic" man of the latter being replaced by the man who is liberated from moral paralysis into a "freedom for the future" by hearing "the proclamation inaugurated by Jesus Christ" in which "God encounters us."

Critics were quick to accuse Bultmann of retaining miraculous activity by his transcendent God. Against them, Bultmann argued that the "act of God" remains invariably "hidden," in contrast to "the conception of miracles . . . as ascertainable processes accessible to objective observation." Faith, for Bultmann, inhabits the realm of personal or existential experience, encounter, and decision. He insisted that "I myself, my real self" am "no more visible or ascertainable than the act of God" and claimed that "I deny the worldly connection of events when I speak of myself." At the same time, he denied that this world of inner experience is purely "subjective." He acknowledged that to interpret events that can also be explored "objectively" in scientific psychology as acts of God is "paradoxical," but he did not concede its illegitimacy. Certainly the Kantian phenomenal/noumenal distinction is implicitly at work in Bultmann's approach to miracles, as well as an openly avowed element of Lutheran fideism. From present-day perspectives, the rigidity of the insistence that the system of physical nature is closed and predetermined in Bultmann, or Schleiermacher and the tradition of liberal theology generally, seems obviously dated, and the time is perhaps ripe for a fresh appraisal of the issue.

See also Epistemology; Scientific Naturalism; Varieties of Providentialism

BIBLIOGRAPHY

Bradley, Francis H. *Presuppositions of Critical History.* Chicago: Quadrangle Books, 1968.

Brown, Colin. *Miracles and the Critical Mind.* Grand Rapids, Mich.: Eerdmans, 1984.

Bultmann, Rudolf. "The Problem of Miracles." *Religion in Life* 27 (1957–8): 63–75.

———. *Jesus Christ and Mythology.* New York: Charles Scribner's Sons, 1958.

Bultmann, Rudolf, and Five Critics. *Kerygma and Myth.* New York: Harper Torchbooks, 1961.

Burns, Robert M. *The Great Debate on Miracles: From Joseph Glanvill to David Hume.* Lewisburg: Bucknell University Press, 1981.

Clarke, Samuel. *The Leibniz-Clarke Correspondence.* 1717. Reprint. Ed. by H. G. Alexander. New York: Philosophical Library, 1956.

Dear, Peter. "Miracles, Experiments, and the Ordinary Course of Nature." *Isis* 81 (1990): 662–83.

Flew, Antony. *Hume's Philosophy of Belief.* London: Routledge and Kegan Paul, 1961.

Grant, Robert M. *Miracles and Natural Law in Graeco-Roman and Early Christian Thought.* Amsterdam: North Holland, 1952.

Harvey, Van A. *The Historian and the Believer.* New York: Macmillan, 1966.

Holland, R. F. "The Miraculous." *American Philosophical Quarterly* 2 (1965): 432–51.

Houston, Joseph. *Reported Miracles.* Cambridge: Cambridge University Press, 1994.

Levine, Michael P. *Hume and the Problem of Miracles: A Solution.* Dordrecht: Kluwer, 1989.

Mullin, Robert Bruce. *Miracles and the Modern Religious Imagination.* New Haven, Conn.: Yale University Press, 1996.

Remus, Harold. *Pagan-Christian Conflict over Miracle in the Second Century.* Cambridge, Mass.: Philadelphia Patristic Foundation, 1983.

Swinburne, Richard. *The Existence of God.* Oxford: Clarendon, 1979.

Troeltsch, Ernst. "Historiography." In *Encyclopedia of Religion and Ethics,* ed. by James Hastings. Vol. 6. New York: Charles Scribner's Sons, 1913, 716–23.

Ward, Benedicta. *Miracles and the Medieval Mind.* London: Scolar, 1982.

Yates, Frances A. *Giordano Bruno and the Hermetic Tradition.* 1964. Reprint. Chicago: University of Chicago Press, 1979.

12. THEODICY

Kenneth J. Howell

Theodicy (from the Greek *theos* [God] and *dike* [justice]) is the justification of the ways and actions of God in the world, especially in connection with the problem of evil. While the problem of evil has a long history, it can be simply stated: How can the existence of evil in the world be reconciled with the belief in an all-good and all-powerful God? Either God is all good, but not powerful enough to rectify evil, or he is all powerful, but not beneficent enough to will to rectify it. Within Western Christianity, the predominant defense of God against these objections comes from Augustine of Hippo (A.D. 354–430). Augustine defined evil as the privation of good rather than an independent substance, and he argued that evil was necessary to achieve a greater good of moral virtue and divine justice. However, the term "theodicy" first appeared in the title of a book by Gottfried Wilhelm Leibniz (1646–1716), in which he defended God's perfect goodness against the objections of Pierre Bayle (1647–1706). Leibniz's famous defense employed a best-of-all-possible-worlds argument that, like Augustine's, made evil a component of the world that was necessary to achieve a greater good. The problem of evil is only a specific example of an underlying difficulty that is relevant to the interaction of science and religion and that concerns God's actions in the world more generally. It begins with observing certain features of the world or particular theories of nature that seem inconsistent with a particular concept of God. These concepts of nature give rise to questions of how God can be at work in the world in a manner implied by the particular theory.

Leibniz himself addressed the underlying metaphysics of science in his correspondence with the Rev. Samuel Clarke (1675–1729) in 1715, most of which centered on which view of God was implied in the other correspondent's view of nature. Clarke, the voice and advocate of Sir Isaac Newton (1642–1727), argued that God constantly sustained and adjusted the world by his divine presence and providence. Leibniz, on the other hand, maintained that God, the most perfect of all beings, would not have created a world that was in need of such constant repair. The difference between these views arose from two essentially different conceptions of providence: The Newtonian implied providence by means of God's perpetual presence and sustenance, while the Leibnitzian required perfect foresight on God's part and clocklike precision in the world. The Newton-Clarke view of providence can be seen in the concept of gravity as an action operating at a distance. Leibniz, in his letters to Caroline, Princess of Wales, seized on this concept to underscore the inconsistencies between the Newtonians' natural philosophy and their theology. If such a force as gravity were real, Leibniz maintained, its operation would require a constant miracle, and the difference between the normal course of nature and miraculous exceptions of grace would be obliterated. To Leibniz, these Newtonians were highly inconsistent when they argued against the Lutheran doctrine of the real presence of the body and blood of Christ in the Eucharist, which for Leibniz implied a miracle. They had misplaced the proper locus of miracle by locating it in nature and removing it from grace. The Leibniz-Newton debate demonstrates the extent to which concepts of God imply specific views of nature and the way in which certain properties of nature can raise fundamental theological problems.

Divine action in the world became a problem again in the wake of Charles Darwin's (1809–82) theory of evolution, which raised the issue of whether God worked through a process of transmutation (speciation) or only when evolution failed to account for the data (the theory of the "God of the gaps"). Some scientists and theologians in the nineteenth century argued that evolution (within the framework of theism) was yet another sign of divine providence, while others, including Darwin himself, argued for the exclusion of design in evolutionary history. The exclusion of design implied a total exclusion of God's interaction with nature, a view that was embraced by materialists and rejected by orthodox Christian theologians. Among those who held to some form of interactionism, the theistic evolutionists emphasized the constant presence and providence of God in the natural process, while the "God-of-the-gaps" thinkers believed that natural explanations were sufficient for most purposes.

Ironically, the latter group, while intending to defend orthodox Christianity, fell unawares into a deistic mode of reasoning. Evolution also raised the thorny problem of evil in the world before the Fall into sin of the first human pair, which was regarded as the source of all evil in traditional Western Christian thought. One strategy denied evolution on the ground that death and other evils could not have taken place before the Fall of man; another reinterpreted the Fall as a nonhistorical type in order to account for the existence of death in the natural world before the appearance of human beings. Those who believed in the historical reality of the Fall and yet adopted evolution had the greatest difficulty, and they often maintained a distinction between physical and moral death. In this view, evidence of death before the appearance of humans in the fossil record could be accounted for by acknowledging that physical death existed before the Fall, while the death of Adam and Eve mentioned in Genesis could be interpreted as a moral or spiritual death. Still others (for example, Asa Gray [1810–88]) developed a kind of Christian Darwinism, which saw in evolution the basis for a new theodicy. They regarded suffering and pain as necessary and even productive features of a universe in which God employed creative evolution to accomplish his plan.

Twentieth-century cosmology, based on work in physics and astronomy, again raised issues of God's method of providence that seemed to grow naturally out of the appearance of finely tuned features in the universe. If the universe displays such precision as the value of the gravitational constant or a specific amount of background microwave radiation, it not only suggests the presence of a Designer, it also calls for an explanation of the Designer's method of creation. According to the anthropic principle, which was extensively discussed in the 1980s, the fundamental features of the universe made possible and, to some extent, necessitated human life on our planet. Such teleological arguments raised the issue of design in a way that seemed to place human beings again at the center of a cosmic drama, a conclusion that runs counter to the antiteleological orientation of modern biology. While these cosmological discussions do not directly address the problem of evil, they raise fundamental questions of how the obvious presence of evil fits into the web of necessity and chance that the anthropic principle and chaos theory study. Here again, a tension is evident between those who view nature as having necessary properties and those who see these properties as contingent.

See also Anthropic Principle; Design Argument; Natural Theology; Varieties of Providentialism

BIBLIOGRAPHY

Alexander, H. G., ed. *The Leibniz-Clarke Correspondence.* Manchester, U.K.: Manchester University Press, 1956.

Augustine. *Confessions.* Book 7. Chs. 3–5. Trans. by Henry Chadwick. Oxford: Oxford University Press, 1991.

Barrow, John, and Frank J. Tipler. *The Anthropic Cosmological Principle.* Oxford: Oxford University Press, 1988.

Hick, John. *Evil and the God of Love.* New York: Harper and Row, 1966.

———. "The Problem of Evil." In *The Encyclopedia of Philosophy,* ed. by Paul Edwards. Vol. 3. 1967. Reprint. New York and London: Macmillan and Free Press, 1972, 136–41.

Leibniz, G. W. *Theodicy; Essays on the Goodness of God, the Freedom of Man, and the Origin of Evil.* 1710. Reprint. Trans. by E. M. Huggard. LaSalle, Ill.: Open Court, 1997.

Moore, James R. *The Post-Darwinian Controversies: A Study of the Protestant Struggle to Come to Terms with Darwin in Great Britain and America, 1870–1900.* Cambridge: Cambridge University Press, 1979.

13. GENESIS AND SCIENCE

John Stenhouse

Genesis, the first book of the Bible, the authorship of which has been traditionally ascribed to the Hebrew prophet Moses (who is variously dated to the fifteenth or the thirteenth century B.C.), constitutes the foundation text of those biblical religions (Judaism and Christianity) that have deeply shaped Western culture. The relationship between the first two chapters of Genesis, which describe God's creation of the world and the first human beings (Adam and Eve) in six days, and scientific knowledge has constituted one of the most important and controversial sites of intersection between science and religion throughout the ages. Of particular concern has been the question of how literally the account should be taken by those who accept its authority as divine revelation.

Some of the church Fathers christianized Greek natural philosophy, especially that of Plato (c. 427–347 B.C.), in their attempts to interpret the Genesis account of Creation. The fourth-century A.D. theologian Augustine of Hippo (354–430), for example, attempted to reconcile the Genesis notion that God created everything in the beginning with the observation that living things grow and develop. Borrowing the Stoic idea that nature contains seedlike principles, Augustine argued that God created many living things potentially rather than actually, in the form of seminal principles that determined their subsequent development.

Some theologians in the early church saw layers of meaning in Genesis, which provided a space for scientific theory, an interpretive tradition that continued during the Middle Ages. Commentators on the Hexameron (six days of creation), such as Thierry of Chartres (c. 1100–c. 1156), restricted God's supernatural intervention to the initial act of Creation. Everything else, including Adam and Eve, appeared naturally, as the gradual unfolding of the developmental principles that God had implanted in nature. The Dominican theologian Thomas Aquinas (c. 1225–74) argued that Genesis might be compatible with a variety of scientific theories. The firmament created on the second day in Genesis 1:6–9, for example, might refer either to the sphere of the fixed stars or to that part of the atmosphere in which clouds condense. Wary of tying the authority of Scripture too closely to changing scientific knowledge, Aquinas left the options open. Protestants emphasized the plain meaning of Scripture during the turbulent years following the Reformation, without reading Genesis as a scientific text. John Calvin (1509–64), for example, argued that Moses wrote Genesis in a popular style for ordinary people, and he warned against treating it as an authoritative source of astronomical (as opposed to religious) knowledge.

Until late in the seventeenth century, few scholars saw any compelling evidence against the view that creation had occurred within the last six thousand years. In the mid-seventeenth century, the learned biblical scholar James Ussher (1581–1656), archbishop of Armagh, calculated an exact date, 4004 B.C., which began to appear in the margins of the Authorized or King James Version of the Bible beside Genesis 1:1. The view that the cosmos, Earth, and Adam had been created almost simultaneously was challenged only by the occasional freethinker, such as Isaac de la Peyrère (1596–1676), a French Calvinist, who argued that humans had existed on Earth before Adam, who was the first Jew, not the first man.

Toward the end of the seventeenth century, scholars began to stretch the initial creation back into the past. Thomas Burnet (c. 1635–1715), an English clergyman, argued in *Sacred Theory of the Earth* (1680–9) that the cosmos had been created long before the earth and its inhabitants. During the eighteenth century, a growing number of thinkers began to suspect that the earth, too, had a history long predating the appearance of humans and that its origin might be explained scientifically. Georges Leclerc, Comte de Buffon (1707–88), was perhaps the first seriously to challenge the view that Earth's history and human history were coextensive. The French astronomer Pierre Laplace (1749–1827) argued in 1796 that a rotating nebula left behind rings that, cooling and condensing, became the planets of our solar system. When asked by Napoleon about the role of God in his theory, Laplace replied: "Sire, I have no need of that hypothesis." Some naturalists began to doubt whether the Deluge accounted for the entire fossil record. In the work of the French zoologist Georges Cuvier (1769–1832), the Flood became simply one of a series of dramatic natural events that periodically entombed living creatures in the rocks. By the early nineteenth century, most naturalists had come to believe that the earth was extremely old and had been inhabited by a succession of creatures, many of them now extinct, ages before Adam and Eve first appeared. Many opted for a local rather than a universal Deluge. Liberal Protestants such as the geologist Charles Lyell (1797–1875) abandoned the attempt to harmonize Genesis and geology in detail, finding in Genesis religious truths, such as God's creation of all things, but no science.

Evangelical Christians preferred more conservative interpretations, such as the gap theory of Thomas Chalmers (1780–1847), the Scottish Free Church scholar, who in 1814 proposed allowing a gap of indefinite duration between the first two verses of Genesis, which provided unlimited time prior to the Creation week for earlier creations and extinctions. Clerical geologists such as Edward Hitchcock (1793–1864) in the United States popularized the gap theory, which influential fundamentalists such as C. I. Scofield (1843–1921), editor of the widely circulated *Scofield Reference Bible*, disseminated in the twentieth century. A second interpretation popular among evangelicals, the day-age theory, interpreted the days of Genesis not as twenty-four hour periods but as long geological epochs. The Scottish geologist and Free Churchman Hugh Miller (1802–56) popularized this view in the nineteenth century, as did Benjamin Silliman (1779–1864) of Yale University and James Dwight Dana (1813–95) in the United States and Sir John William Dawson (1820–99) in Canada. American fundamentalists such as William Jennings Bryan (1860–1925) transmitted it to the twentieth century.

The theory of evolution raised further problems in the second half of the nineteenth century. How could the Genesis doctrine of the creation of humanity in the image of God be reconciled with the notion that humans had evolved from apelike ancestors? On the left of the spectrum of opinion, a growing band of atheists, free-thinkers, and agnostics, such as Charles Darwin (1809–82) and T. H. Huxley (1825–95), dismissed Genesis as falsehood or primitive religious superstition. This group shaded into a broad category of religious believers, including liberal Protestants, Reform Jews, and a few Catholics, who were prepared to reinterpret Genesis in order to embrace evolution. They argued that Genesis used the language of myth, symbol, or poetry to teach a few simple, profound religious truths, such as God's creation of humans in his image. Adam came to symbolize humanity in general, not a real person. Some, such as the American Protestant minister Henry Ward Beecher (1813–87), eagerly abandoned what he regarded as obnoxious traditional doctrines, such as the Fall and Original Sin (Genesis 3), for an optimistic evolutionary anthropology, being confident of the ability of humans to build the kingdom of God.

Orthodox believers, such as the Princeton Presbyterian theologian Benjamin B. Warfield (1851–1921) and some Roman Catholics, argued that, though the human body might have evolved, the soul remained a supernatural creation. Such thinkers accommodated evolution without drastically reinterpreting Genesis, though not all insisted on a historical Adam. Some sanctified the old preadamite heresy to argue that near-humans existed before Adam, who was the first full human (that is, the first to be made in the image of God). Further to the right of the religious spectrum, many continued to read Genesis literally. Ellen G. White (1827–1915), for example, the American founder-prophetess of Seventh-day Adventism, declared that God had created Adam and Eve and all earthly life in six days of twenty-four hours between about six and ten thousand years ago. George McCready Price (1870–1963), an Adventist geologist, transmitted this view to the twentieth century and tried to give it scientific standing. The views of Price, which became known as "creation science," reached a large audience in the pages of *The Genesis Flood* (1961), a best-seller written by Henry Morris (b. 1918), an engineer, and John C. Whitcomb (b. 1924), a theologian. By the 1980s, millions of evangelical Christians, particularly in the United States, believed that God had created the earth, Adam, and Eve within the last ten thousand years and that Noah's Flood accounted for virtually the entire fossil record.

As the creation-science movement indicates, Western thinkers in the twentieth century became more divided than ever in their views of human origins. Atheist and agnostic scientists such as the astronomer Carl Sagan (1934–96), the sociobiologist E. O. Wilson (1929–), and Stephen Hawking (1947–), a physicist, articulated a variety of naturalistic origin myths that owed nothing to Genesis. Protestant neo-orthodox theologians, following Karl Barth (1886–1968), emphasized the radical difference between God the Creator and a radically fallen creation, and neither quarreled with, or cared much about, what science had to say about origins. The Roman Catholic Church officially embraced the evolution of the human body in the papal encyclical *Humani Generis* (1950). The Swiss Protestant theologian Emil Brunner (1899–1966) read Genesis existentially rather than historically, with Creation signifying the dependence of the creature on the Creator and the Fall representing human rejection of that dependence. Such interpretations signified the decision of more liberal theologians to leave questions of cosmogony and human origins to science, while religious thinkers were free to inject meaning, purpose, and values into the Genesis account of Creation.

See also Augustine of Hippo; Creationism Since 1859; Genesis Flood; Geology and Paleontology from 1700 to 1900; Nineteenth-Century Biblical Criticism; Origin and Unity of the Human Race; Theories of the Earth and Its Age Before Darwin

BIBLIOGRAPHY

Anderson, Bernhard W. *Creation versus Chaos: The Reinterpretation of Mythical Symbolism in the Bible.* Philadelphia: Fortress, 1987.

Brooke, John Hedley. *Science and Religion: Some Historical Perspectives.* Cambridge: Cambridge University Press, 1991.

Dillenberger, John. *Protestant Thought and Natural Science: A Historical Interpretation.* London: Collins, 1961.

Gillispie, Charles Coulston. *Genesis and Geology: A Study in the Relations of Scientific Thought, Natural Theology, and Social Opinion in Great Britain, 1790–1850.* Cambridge, Mass.: Harvard University Press, 1951.

Grant, Robert M., with David Tracy. *A Short History of the Interpretation of the Bible.* 1984. 2d ed. Philadelphia: Fortress, 1985.

Jaki, Stanley L. *Genesis 1 Through the Ages.* London: Thomas More Press, 1992.

Lindberg, David C. *The Beginnings of Western Science: The European Scientific Tradition in Philosophical, Religious, and Institutional Context, 600 B.C. to A.D. 1450.* Chicago: University of Chicago Press, 1992.

Lindberg, David C., and Ronald L. Numbers, eds. *God and Nature: Historical Essays on the Encounter Between Christianity and Science.* Berkeley: University of California Press, 1986.

Numbers, Ronald L. *The Creationists.* New York: Knopf, 1992.

Ramm, Bernard. *The Christian View of Science and Scripture.* 1955. Reprint. London: Paternoster, 1964.

Roberts, Jon H. *Darwinism and the Divine in America: Protestant Intellectuals and Organic Evolution, 1859–1900.* Madison: University of Wisconsin Press, 1988.

Rudwick, M. J. S. *The Meaning of Fossils: Episodes in the History of Paleontology.* New York: Science History Publications, 1976.

Rupke, Nicolaas. *The Great Chain of History: William Buckland and the English School of Geology, 1814–1849.* Oxford: Clarendon, 1983.

14. NINETEENTH-CENTURY BIBLICAL CRITICISM

D. G. Hart

Modern biblical criticism began in the eighteenth century in France and Germany. Criticism (that is, scholarly study) of the Bible was not new. Textual criticism (called "lower criticism"), the determination of the original text of Scripture, had been practiced since the Renaissance, when the first critical editions of the New Testament were produced. "Higher criticism" was the attempt to determine the context in which the ancient texts were created and involved the study of the authorship, date, place of origin, and cultural and religious background of the biblical books. What was different about the new criticism was that it was based on naturalistic principles derived from the Enlightenment, in which supernatural events like miracles and predictive prophecy were believed not to occur. Christians had always held Scripture to be the product of God's revelation to mankind, written by prophets and apostles under the influence of divine inspiration. Proponents of the new criticism viewed the Bible as a fully human product and began to study it as they would any ordinary ancient text, without recourse to explanations that invoked miracles or prophecy. They were influenced as well by evolutionary theories of the origin and development of religion as a natural phenomenon. Biblical scholars, influenced by the study of anthropology and comparative religion, were reluctant to regard the origin of Judaism among the Israelites or Christianity among the first followers of Jesus as the product of supernatural revelation or divine intervention. Instead, they contended that all religions, including Judaism and Christianity, evolved from, and adapted to, their surrounding environments.

Combined with this naturalistic explanation of the origins of religion was a conception of history that evolutionary ideas greatly abetted. Historical events, accordingly, were always conditioned by what had gone before, and religious consciousness, where it existed, was simply the reflection of a given time and place. This way of looking at history, which drew heavily upon Hegelian philosophy, not only stressed God's immanence in human consciousness and history to a pantheistic degree, but also posited a progressive development of human cultures, ideas, and institutions from inferior and barbaric to superior and civilized. This understanding of history and the development of culture provided the backdrop in the nineteenth century for newer interpretations of the Old Testament and was partly responsible for the controversies that such scholarship sparked.

The Criticism of the Pentateuch

In Pentateuchal criticism, the work of Julius Wellhausen (1844–1918) exhibited the close connection between biblical scholarship and evolutionary views. His work built upon the kind of literary and historical investigation of the Old Testament that had been practiced since the seventeenth century. Wellhausen believed that a careful reading of the first five books of the Old Testament (the Pentateuch) had shown discrepancies and inconsistencies in the narrative. As early as 1753, with Jean Astruc's (1684–1766) *Conjectures About the Original Documents Which Moses Appears to Have Used in the Composition of the Book of Genesis,* rationalizing students of the Bible began to argue that the Pentateuch was a collection of separate stories patched together in a larger whole. The use of divine names, whether Jahweh (the "J" source) or Elohim (the "E" source), according to this view, indicated different narratives that were penned by different authors. By the late nineteenth century, Wellhausen, building on the work of Karl Heinrich

Graf (1815–69), gave classic expression to the purported literary origins of the Pentateuch, which he divided into the J, E, D (Deuteronomic), and P (Priestly) sources, arranging them chronologically, from the earliest, J and E, to the latest, P.

The immediate controversy surrounding the literary origins of the Pentateuch concerned the argument that parts of the Old Testament's first five books were written after the life of Moses. This theory conflicted with the traditional view that Moses was the sole author of the Pentateuch, which seemed to be supported by the testimony of Scripture itself. But even more threatening to traditional Protestant orthodoxy was the reconstruction of Israel's history that Wellhausen's views countenanced. No longer did critical scholars consider God's giving of the Law to Moses as the beginning of Israel's religious history. Rather, the Law was seen as the product of priests who, while in exile, wanted to restore Israel to its preexilic standing. This dating of narrative strands in the Pentateuch, in turn, recast the history of Old Testament theology along evolutionary lines, with Israel developing from primitive forms of belief (such as animism, totemism, and polytheism) to the postexilic ethical monotheism of the prophets. Although highly speculative and ultimately unprovable, the theory fit into the spirit of the age and was widely accepted in academic circles.

Even though Wellhausen's views, or the "Graf-Wellhausen school," as it came to be called, upset traditional views about the authorship of the Pentateuch, just as damaging for Protestant orthodoxy was the theological underpinning that supported Wellhausen's argument. The new understanding of the Old Testament developed at a time when modern historical methods were taking shape. Historians believed that their discipline was "scientific" in the sense that, through careful investigation of the sources, they could know an event in itself, as it really happened. So, too, Wellhausen claimed to have used the best historical methods for his understanding of Israel's development. Still, liberal Protestant assumptions about what counted for authentic religion, which had grown out of the Enlightenment, lurked behind Pentateuchal criticism. Here Wellhausen contrasted the religion of the letter—the allegedly dead, ritualistic, and legalistic faith of postexilic Judaism—with the religion of the spirit— the fresh and vital belief of the prophets. Hence, as much as the newer understanding of the Old Testament and Israel's history worked itself out according to the standards of professional scholarship, it also possessed a specific theological and ecclesiastical agenda, one that pitted Protestant orthodoxy's seemingly lifeless ritual of creed and ceremony with the vibrant and simple faith of Jesus and the early church. Biblical criticism was not, it was claimed, a way to discredit the Bible but, rather, an argument against the conventions of the Protestant churches that employed the prestige of "science." In effect, however, Wellhausen's views gave academic legitimacy to calls for a new liberal theology within the church that was constructed along naturalistic lines and rejected the supernatural theology of Reformation orthodoxy. Those calls urged Christians to think more about their deeds in this world than to be overly burdened about life in the next.

The Reception of the New Criticism

Though biblical scholars in the northeastern United States had benefited from German research prior to the American Civil War, the newer approach to the Pentateuch made its widest mark in the United States indirectly through the controversy in Scotland over the teaching of William Robertson Smith (1846–94). A professor of Hebrew and the Old Testament at the Free (Presbyterian) Church College in Aberdeen, Scotland, and a friend of Wellhausen, Smith became a controversial figure by his contributions to the ninth edition of the *Encyclopedia Britannica.* In his article on the Bible, Smith questioned the traditional view of Deuteronomy's authorship and argued, like Wellhausen, that the book was not Moses's farewell address to Israel but, rather, the legislative program of postexilic priests. Conservatives in the Free Church brought charges against Smith for denying the authority and inspiration of the Bible. The accused appealed to the Westminster Confession of Faith, arguing that it taught nothing specifically regarding the date, authorship, and circumstances of the Pentateuch. In 1881, after five years of court proceedings, Smith was dismissed from his post at the Free Church College.

American Presbyterians, who still had fairly close connections to Presbyterians in Scotland, followed the Smith case carefully, and their coverage of the proceedings generated controversy within their own ranks about the date, authorship, and historical origins of the Pentateuch. These debates among Presbyterians were indicative of tensions that would divide Protestants into conservative and liberal camps. Scholars such as Charles Briggs (1841–1913) of Union Seminary in New York were sympathetic to the new views about the Old Testament and Israel's origins, and they defended their acceptance of certain conclusions by appealing to scientific method. Briggs thought it significant that the bulk of biblical scholars in Europe, like Smith in Scotland, had embraced Wellhausen's views, a sign that the new understanding of the Bible was true because it had been verified by the best means for ascertaining truth, namely, "the principles of Scientific Induction." Yet, just as Wellhausen had justified biblical criticism as a better and more spiritual understanding of Christianity, so the American proponents of the newer ideas believed that critical study of Scripture would result in a more accurate interpretation of the Bible and, hence, greater piety and faithfulness. In contrast, conservatives such as Princeton Seminary's Benjamin B. Warfield (1851–1921) and William Henry Green (1825–1900) were less convinced by the new views and were instead inclined to attribute critical conclusions to the naturalistic assumptions of those who held them. From the conservatives' perspective, the traditional understandings of the Pentateuch and Israel's history were still plausible and, more important, crucial to the truth of Christianity. They argued that acceptance of the new methods of criticism would, in time, result in a Christianity that would eliminate the basic biblical doctrines that had been accepted by the church for nearly two millennia, on the grounds that they were part of an outmoded supernatural worldview.

One of the manifestations of this debate between traditional and newer approaches to the Old Testament was a disagreement over the nature of the authority and inspiration of the Bible. Liberals like Briggs still insisted that the Bible was inspired and authoritative, but they often understood inspiration in terms similar to the kind of creative and intellectual genius that could be found in great works of fiction or poetry. Hence, the Bible was inspired in the sense that it taught great moral and spiritual truths, and part of the biblical scholar's task was to find these truths. But for those like Briggs, inspiration did not necessarily extend to the historical and cultural circumstances of the Bible, which meant that, while the text should be understood in its historical sense, the best way to appropriate the text's message for the present was to search for the figurative and symbolic truths that lay beneath the biblical writings. In contrast, traditionalists like Warfield articulated a view of inspiration that taught that the Bible was without error in all of the truths it intended to communicate, whether spiritual, moral, or historical. Only an inerrant Scripture was an authorita-

tive Scripture. Conservatives were less inclined to look for the figurative meanings of the text, especially in those stories and passages that pointed to the supernatural, either in accounts of miracles or expressions of God's direct communication to men. While this approach could result in a wooden literalism, Warfield and other traditionalists were sufficiently informed about the nature of ancient texts to distinguish historical narratives from poetic idiom and prophetic discourse.

Coinciding as it did with the growing prominence of new scientific methods and the rising acceptance of the authority of academic expertise, the conflict over how to interpret the Bible was sometimes caricatured as one between churchmen who defended dogma and scholars who embraced the new learning. And cheerleaders for the new research universities that were emerging in the late nineteenth century and who wanted to see science liberated from the "bonds of religion," like Andrew Dickson White (1832–1918), president of Cornell University and author of *A History of the Warfare of Science with Theology in Christendom* (1896), were quick to interpret the controversy in these terms. But, in fact, both sides could lay claim to the prestige of science. Liberals had the scholarly consensus, especially that of the European universities, behind them, and their work benefited from many of the advances in the various disciplines that contributed to the study of ancient texts. But the new liberal interpretations looked less intellectually cogent when they were applied to the lives of modern Christians. To see in Israel's sacred writings a justification for democracy, certain forms of capitalism, and specific plans for social reform was not, in hindsight, the best form of biblical scholarship.

For their part, conservatives did not hesitate to use the newer methods of studying ancient texts and were fully informed about many of the debates and discoveries in the new learning. Even if they did not agree with the conclusions of modern critical scholarship, they sometimes shared the same methods. Traditionalists were better, however, at finding continuity between the ancient and modern understandings of the text. Rather than spiritualize the biblical materials, conservatives accepted the text's supernaturalism from the perspective of its original audience and regarded that perspective as valid for modern believers. This method of understanding the Old Testament had the advantage in scientific terms of assenting to the original meaning of the text without having to perform the intellectual gymnastics that usually came with figurative or spiritual interpretations. Hence, while conservatives clearly had a bias toward received interpretations of the Bible, they also had the mental tenacity to accept them even when confronted with the arguments of those who rejected miracles and divine revelation.

Behind this disagreement over inspiration lay an even more significant difference, which concerned the nature of Christianity itself. Was the religion of the Bible that culminated in Christianity one that made religious experience and ethical imperatives central, or was it a plan of redemption that God initiated through supernatural acts? Critical biblical scholarship in the mainstream Protestant churches increasingly came down on the former side, defending the Bible as the best collection of writings about religious experience known to humankind and the surest guide to morality. On the other side, conservatives stressed the supernatural and soteriological aspects of biblical writings, believing that sinful men and women were without hope apart from the miraculous display of God's saving grace. In the early twentieth century, these tensions within the scholarly world would eventually influence the broader public (both clergy and laymen) within the major Protestant denominations, pitting modernists against fundamentalists, those who accepted the "assured results of modern criticism" and modified Christian teaching to accommodate it against those who resisted in varying degrees that accommodation.

The widespread acceptance of the new criticism within most mainline American Protestant seminaries and secular universities contributed greatly to the decline of Protestant orthodoxy. Like the new uniformitarian geology and the new evolutionary biology, the new biblical criticism was widely used to attack traditional Christian belief in special creation and the reliability of Genesis in providing a true account of human origins. The relatively rapid reception of Darwinism in the Anglo-American scientific community and the subsequent triumph of academic professionals and science over the clergy and theology made evolution the chief rival to the claims of the Bible in the minds of many. While some Christians were able to accept and absorb the new ideas about the origins of the Bible into the framework of their beliefs, others were not and abandoned traditional Christian faith altogether. Moreover, the Protestant belief that each Christian was competent to read and interpret the Bible for himself or herself seemed to be undercut by the liberals' claim that only highly trained academic specialists could interpret the Bible and that the ordinary layman must defer to the views of scholars better able to understand the Bible. In matters of faith, as in every other area of modern life, controverted issues were becoming too complex for ordinary men and women to master. However destructive the new criticism might be, and however questionable its Enlightenment assumptions, it ended, perhaps forever, the unqualified confidence that earlier generations of Christians had placed in their Bibles.

See also Genesis and Science; Genesis Flood; Miracles

BIBLIOGRAPHY

Blenkinsopp, Joseph. "Introduction to the Pentateuch." In *The New Interpreter's Bible*. Vol. 1. Nashville, Tenn.: Abingdon, 1994, 305–18.

Brown, Jerry Wayne. *The Rise of Biblical Criticism in America, 1800–1870: The New England Scholars*. Middletown, Conn.: Wesleyan University Press, 1969.

Harrisville, Roy A., and Walter Sundberg. *The Bible in Modern Culture: Theology and Historical Critical Method from Spinoza to Käsemann*. Grand Rapids, Mich.: Eerdmans, 1995.

Massa, Mark S. *Charles Augustus Briggs and the Crisis of Historical Criticism*. Minneapolis, Minn.: Fortress, 1990.

Morgan, Robert, and John Barton. *Biblical Interpretation*. New York: Oxford University Press, 1988.

Neil, W. "The Criticism and Theological Use of the Bible, 1700–1950." In *The Cambridge History of the Bible: The West from the Reformation to the Present Day*, ed. by S. L. Greenslade. Cambridge: Cambridge University Press, 1963, 238–93.

Noll, Mark A. *Between Faith and Criticism: Evangelicals, Scholarship, and the Bible in America*. San Francisco: Harper and Row, 1986.

Silva, Moisés. "Contemporary Theories of Biblical Interpretation." In *The New Interpreter's Bible*. Vol. 1. Nashville, Tenn.: Abingdon, 1994, 107–24.

Terrien, Samuel. "History of the Interpretation of the Bible, III. Modern Period." In *The Interpreter's Bible*. Vol. 1. New York: Abingdon, 1952, 127–41.

PART II

Biographical Studies

15. GALILEO GALILEI

Richard J. Blackwell

The classic case of conflict between Western science and religion is the confrontation between Galileo Galilei (1564–1642) and the Roman Catholic Church in the early decades of the seventeenth century. This episode involved four central issues: (1) the state of the scientific debate at the time over the comparative merits of the older Earth-centered astronomy of Claudius Ptolemy of Alexandria (second century A.D.) and of the relatively more recent but conflicting sun-centered theory of Nicholas Copernicus (1473–1543); (2) the question of what are the proper exegetical standards to be used for understanding the meaning and the truth of the Bible; (3) the historical events and their rationale that led the Roman Catholic Church in 1616 to condemn Copernicanism as false; and (4) the charges, the legal ground, and the course of events in Galileo's trial and condemnation in 1633.

The Scientific Dispute

For nearly two thousand years before the Galileo controversy, the almost universally accepted view of the heavens in Western culture was the geocentric theory initially proposed by Aristotle (384–322 B.C.) and later considerably refined mathematically by Ptolemy of Alexandria. This common view, which came to permeate the medieval scientific tradition, looked upon the earth as spherical, motionless, and fixed in the center of the entire universe. The moon, sun, five visible planets, and all of the fixed stars were conceived as rotating daily from east to west around the earth in complex patterns, which the early astronomers had succeeded in reducing to combinations of simple circular motions. All of the then-known observational evidence concerning the heavens was consistent with this astronomical model, especially when it was interpreted in the light of Aristotelian natural philosophy.

The publication in 1543 of Copernicus's *Revolutions of the Celestial Spheres* significantly modified the earlier view by locating the sun at the center of the universe, and the Earth and its moon in motion around the sun above Mercury and Venus. Copernicus had no new evidence to justify his theory; rather, he thought that his view had more internal coherence and greater explanatory power than Ptolemy's. As the generations passed, some evidence slowly accumulated that tended to make the new cosmic theory more likely to be true. In Galileo's day, conclusive proof of Copernicanism still had not been found, despite Galileo's own lifelong efforts to establish such a proof. To understand the Galileo controversy, it is essential to keep in mind that no one, including Galileo himself, was yet able to settle the scientific debate conclusively, although the accumulating evidence, much of it discovered by Galileo himself, spoke more and more in its favor.

While Galileo had become personally persuaded sometime before 1597 that Copernicanism was true, he did not publicly enter into the cosmological debate until early in 1610, when, in a book entitled *The Starry Messenger,* he published his first observations, mostly of the moon, with his newly improved version of the telescope. In the next three years, he published still further telescopic observations, along with his interpretations of them, culminating in two statements in his *Letters on Sunspots* that explicitly endorsed the Copernican theory. In the course of his observations, he had discovered many new features on the surface of the moon, four of the moons of Jupiter, what we now call the rings of Saturn, sunspots, and the fact that Venus undergoes a regular series of phases similar to the phases of the Earth's moon.

This latter fact was particularly important: Although it did not prove Copernicanism to be true, since still other models of the heavens were not only possible but were actively under consideration at the time, it did demonstrate that the original version of the Ptolemaic theory was false. At any rate, by 1613, Galileo was explicitly defending the Copernican theory of the heavens in his published writings.

The Biblical Dispute

At this point, Galileo began to come under attack by various opponents, some of whom were motivated by scientific rivalries, while others were moved by overly zealous concerns for religious orthodoxy. The latter cited such passages as Genesis 1, Ecclestiastes 1:4–6, Joshua 10:12, Psalms 19:4–6, 93, and 104 as evidence of the Bible's explicit assertion that the sun moves and the earth is at rest. In reply to such biblical objections, Galileo wrote a lengthy letter in 1613 addressed to his friend and scientific colleague, the Benedictine priest Benedetto Castelli (1578–1643). The letter outlined his views on the relations between science and the Bible and was subsequently widely circulated privately. Unbeknown to Galileo, his *Letter to Castelli,* in an adulterated version intended to compromise him, was denounced a year later to the Holy Office (the Roman Inquisition) as religiously unorthodox, although these charges were dismissed shortly thereafter. In 1615, Galileo considerably expanded his views into the much longer *Letter to the Grand Duchess Christina.* By then, the topic had become so controversial that this *Letter* was withheld from publication until 1636, three years after his trial.

In writing these letters, Galileo was partly motivated by a desire to protect his patronage position at the Tuscan court in Florence, where he had been appointed in 1610 as the ducal philosopher and mathematician. Nevertheless, he must also have seen the dangers in publicly entering into discussions about the interpretation of the Bible. Galileo was trained neither as a theologian nor as a biblical scholar and, hence, was vulnerable to charges of not being competent to judge in this field. More serious, the Council of Trent, Session IV (April 8, 1546), had explicitly limited the interpretation of the Bible to the bishops and the councils of the church. Hence, no matter how reliable Galileo's reading of the Bible may have been, as merely a lay member of the church he ran the risk of standing in violation of this restriction, which was an

important part of the Catholic reaction to the Protestant Reformation. Yet, despite these complications, Galileo's views in the *Letter to the Grand Duchess Christina* have since become commonplaces in biblical exegesis and were even accepted by the Roman Catholic Church in 1893.

Galileo's views on the relations between science and the Bible can be summarized as follows. God is the common and always truthful author of both the book of revelation (the Bible) and the book of nature (the natural world). As a result, it is not possible, in principle, for the truths of science and of the Bible to be genuinely in conflict, provided that we have correctly understood the language and the meaning of both books. This proviso is an especially difficult condition to meet in the case of the Bible, because God has chosen to reveal the highest spiritual truths in words accommodated to the understanding of the common, uneducated person. Hence, the Bible contains a wide use of metaphorical and figurative expressions as they occur in the commonsense idiom of the era of its human authors. One should, thus, be very careful not to attribute literal meanings to figurative expressions. According to Galileo, the notion of the daily motion of the sun and the heavens from east to west is precisely such a case in point. Further, the Bible's central purpose is religious and moral, and, hence, it is not primarily intended to serve as a source of knowledge about the natural world. Galileo invoked the now famous remark by Cardinal Cesare Baronius (1538–1607) that the Bible tells us how to go to heaven, not how the heavens go.

Cardinal Robert Bellarmine (1542–1621), who was the Church's main theological respondent to Galileo, would have agreed with most of Galileo's views. But he also insisted on a critically important modification. Since God is its author, not only must every statement in the Bible be true, when properly understood, but the loyal Christian believer is also required to accept it as true as a matter of religious faith. Therefore, all factual and historical knowledge contained in the Bible about the natural world falls within the scope of religious faith and, thus, is governed by the authority of the Church.

The biblical dispute between Galileo and Bellarmine came down to the following points. If the scientist could conclusively prove that the heliocentric theory is true (which Galileo persistently attempted, but was never able, to do), then both sides would agree that contrary remarks in the Bible would need to be reinterpreted as figurative and not literal in order to maintain the coherent unity of truth. Bellarmine explicitly granted that point. But what about a case (such as the Copernican theory at that time) in which a new scientific view was not yet conclusively proven but might become so in the future? Bellarmine's answer was that the traditional view should be retained in such a case, since it was supported by the higher truth standards of the Bible and by the common agreement of the Fathers of the Church, through whom the content of the faith had been handed down through the centuries. But for Galileo, Copernicanism, proven or not, was ultimately not a matter of religious faith; so, for him, it was an objectionable procedure to bring biblical passages to bear on the question.

To put the matter in the terms most frequently used by Bellarmine, Copernicanism as an astronomical theory could, without ecclesiastical objection, be adopted hypothetically but not realistically. In other words, it could be arbitrarily assumed for purposes of making calculations about the motions and positions of the heavenly bodies, but it could not be adopted as an actually true account of the structure of the physical world, since this stronger claim conflicted with the truth of the Bible. This dispute over the use of the Bible in relation to the main scientific debate of the day remained unresolved throughout the Galileo affair.

The Condemnation of Copernicanism

The entire issue reached its climax in the early months of 1616. Galileo had gone to Rome, apparently with the hope of persuading the Church to take no action on the matter. The actual results were precisely the opposite. In February, Pope Paul V (b. 1552; p. 1605–21) requested the opinion of a group of his theologians on the orthodoxy of heliocentrism. They advised him unanimously in a private report that Copernicanism was not only false, but was also formally heretical, since it explicitly contradicted the Scriptures in many places. The pope significantly modified this theological opinion. His decision was then publicly announced to the whole Church in a decree issued by the Congregation of the Index, dated March 5, 1616, in which Copernicanism was condemned not as heretical, but less forcefully as "false and completely contrary to the Divine Scriptures." Copernicus's *Revolutions of the Celestial Spheres* was placed on the Index and prohibited "until corrected." The corrections that were demanded, issued four years later, were not extensive in scope. They involved the removal of possibly one chapter (Book I, Chapter 8) and a few sentences throughout the book that assert that the earth moves.

This condemnation of Copernicanism, which closed the debate in the Roman Catholic Church on the scientific and biblical issues involved, proved to be a disaster, both then and since, for the relationship between science and religion. It was to be the centerpiece of the Galileo controversy.

Neither Galileo nor any of his writings were explicitly mentioned in the decree. A decision had been made to deal with him privately on the matter. The pope ordered Bellarmine to meet with Galileo, to explain to him the decision against Copernicanism, and to ask for his acceptance of the decision, with the threat of imprisonment to be held in reserve in case he refused. This meeting took place on February 26, 1616. Precisely what happened at that meeting is not known, since two inconsistent accounts of it have come down to us. First, in a letter that Galileo requested three months later, Bellarmine said that the only thing that happened was that Galileo was informed of the impending decree of March 5 to the effect that Copernicanism "cannot be defended or held." He did not report that Galileo resisted this decision. Second, however, a much stronger account of the meeting contained in the files of the Holy Office said that Galileo was served an injunction "not to hold, teach, or defend it [Copernicanism] in any way whatever, verbally or in writing." Some modern scholars have argued that this file memorandum is a forgery perpetrated in either 1616 or in 1632 to entrap Galileo. Although this interpretation has now been abandoned, there is still no general agreement regarding what occurred at the Galileo-Bellarmine meeting. This is unfortunate, since Galileo's later trial turned largely on the status of the supposed injunction.

The condemnation of Copernicanism in 1616 and Galileo's understanding with Bellarmine, whatever that may have been, brought the first half of the Galileo episode to an end. The die had now been cast, and there was no hope of recasting it. The issue that remained was how the decree and the injunction were to be observed in the years that immediately followed.

Galileo's Trial

For the next seven years, Galileo carefully avoided any dealings with the issue of Copernicanism. In 1623, however, he was delighted to learn that Maffeo Barberini

(1568–1644), an admiring personal acquaintance, a fellow Tuscan, and a man of letters in his own right, had been elected pope under the name of Urban VIII. The next year, Galileo went to Rome with high hopes that the censure of Copernicanism might be lifted. In a series of six conversations with the new pope (of which, unfortunately, no direct records have come down to us), Urban apparently told Galileo, among other things, that he could write again about Copernicanism, provided that he kept the discussion at the hypothetical level.

As a result, Galileo began to plan the writing of a long fictional dialogue, in the Platonic literary tradition, that would review and evaluate all of the evidence and arguments on both sides of the Copernican question. One spokesman, Salviati, would vigorously present the new ideas; another, Simplicio, would argue doggedly and in detail for the old tradition; and the third, Sagredo, would be an open-minded inquirer who would critically assess the issues from a neutral standpoint. Galileo hoped that the dialogue format itself would help place the entire discussion at the required hypothetical level. The result was the publication of the *Dialogue Concerning the Two Chief World Systems* (1632), Galileo's best-known scientific writing and an Italian literary masterpiece in its own right. The appearance of the book created sensational reactions, including discussion of whether it violated the decree of 1616 against Copernicanism. Most readers, now as well as then, have concluded that Salviati clearly won the debate, as Galileo intended he should, thereby making the *Dialogue* a plea for heliocentrism.

Pope Urban VIII appointed a special commission to investigate the entire matter. In the process, the commission uncovered in the files of the Holy Office the above-mentioned document, previously unknown even to Urban VIII, which stated that Galileo had been personally served with an injunction against future writings on Copernicanism at his ill-fated meeting with Cardinal Bellarmine in 1616. Their judgment was that Galileo had also exceeded the instructions to treat the matter only hypothetically.

At this point, the pope's friendship with Galileo was transformed into a feeling of betrayal and anger. A trial on the above charges became inevitable, and it took place in the spring of 1633. The two main legal questions at the trial were: (1) Had Galileo acted improperly in the three years before the book appeared in gaining the required approvals for publication from lower-level church officials? (2) More important, had he violated the injunction

supposedly served on him in 1616? The most dramatic moment of the trial occurred when Galileo produced Bellarmine's letter of 1616, previously unknown to the prosecution, which made no mention of any injunction and contained the weaker restriction on "defending and holding" Copernicanism. Not surprisingly, the court gave preference to the Holy Office's document, which Galileo had never seen before and which was legally inadmissible because it was not properly signed and notarized. The substantive questions of the scientific truth of Copernicanism and of the proper use of the Bible in relation to science did not arise at the trial itself, although they were the real issues behind it.

The final result, approved by Pope Urban VIII, was the judgment that Galileo was "vehemently suspected of heresy." On June 22, he was forced to read an oath, prepared by the court, in which he denounced his own teachings about Copernicanism. The old man was disgraced and his spirit broken. Galileo spent most of the remainder of his days under what we would now call house arrest at his villa at Arcetri near Florence. Although the Copernican question was now totally closed to him, he continued his work and writing in theoretical mechanics, resulting in the publication in 1638 of the *Discourse on Two New Sciences,* his major scientific contribution to physics.

During the intervening centuries, the Galileo affair has cast a long and disturbing shadow over the intersection of science and religion. As the best-known example of a conflictive relationship between the two, it has continued, perhaps unfairly, to dominate discussions of this issue, and the distrust it has caused on both sides is often not far beneath the surface.

See also Conflict of Science and Religion; Copernican Revolution; Roman Catholicism Since Trent

BIBLIOGRAPHY

Biagoli, Mario. *Galileo Courtier.* Chicago: University of Chicago Press, 1993.

Blackwell, Richard J. *Galileo, Bellarmine, and the Bible.* Notre Dame, Ind.: University of Notre Dame Press, 1991.

Coyne, G. V., et al., eds. *The Galileo Affair, A Meeting of Faith and Science: Proceedings of the Cracow Conference, May 24–27, 1984.* Vatican City: Specola Vaticana, 1985.

Drake, Stillman. *Galileo Studies: Personality, Tradition, and Revolution.* Ann Arbor: University of Michigan Press, 1970.

———. *Galileo at Work: His Scientific Biography.* Chicago: University of Chicago Press, 1978.

———. *Galileo: Pioneer Scientist.* Toronto: University of Toronto Press, 1990.

Fantoli, Annibale. *Galileo: For Copernicanism and for the Church.* Trans. by George V. Coyne, S.J. Vatican City: Vatican Observatory Press, 1994.

Finocchiaro, Maurice A., ed. *The Galileo Affair: A Documentary History.* Berkeley: University of California Press, 1989.

Geymonat, Ludovico. *Galileo Galilei.* Trans. by Stillman Drake. New York: McGraw-Hill, 1965.

Gingerich, Owen. "The Galileo Affair." *Scientific American* 247 (1982): 132–43.

———. *The Great Copernican Chase and Other Adventures in Astronomical History.* Cambridge, Mass.: Sky, 1992.

Koyré, Alexandre. *Galileo Studies.* Trans. by John Mepham. Atlantic Highlands, N.J.: Humanities, 1978.

Langford, Jerome J. *Galileo, Science, and the Church.* 1966. Rev. ed. Ann Arbor: University of Michigan Press, 1971.

McMullin, Ernan, ed. *Galileo: Man of Science.* New York: Basic Books, 1967.

Pedersen, Olaf. *Galileo and the Council of Trent.* Vatican City: Vatican Observatory Press, 1991.

Redondi, Pietro. *Galileo Heretic.* Trans. by R. Rosenthal. Princeton, N.J.: Princeton University Press, 1987.

Reston, Jr., James. *Galileo: A Life.* New York: HarperCollins, 1994.

Shea, William R. *Galileo's Intellectual Revolution: Middle Period, 1610–1632.* New York: Science History Publications, 1972.

Wallace, William A., ed. *Reinterpreting Galileo.* Princeton, N.J.: Princeton University Press, 1984.

Westfall, Richard S. *Essays on the Trial of Galileo.* Notre Dame, Ind.: University of Notre Dame Press, 1989.

16. BLAISE PASCAL

Douglas Groothuis

Although he was an infirm man who lacked formal education, never held an academic position, and failed to reach his fortieth year, Blaise Pascal (1623–62) was one of the foremost scientists of the mid-seventeenth century, and he left an indelible mark on science and its relationship to religious faith. While Pascal is most widely known today for his *Pensées (Thoughts),* an unfinished defense of the Christian faith consisting of variously sized fragments, during his lifetime he was recognized as a scientist and mathematician of great originality.

Pascal's Early Life

Pascal was born at Clermont (now Clermont-Ferrand) in Auvergne, France, on June 19, 1623. After his mother's death in 1626, Pascal and his two sisters were raised by his father, Etienne, a lawyer. An excellent mathematician, Etienne educated his son entirely at home, initially intending to teach him mathematics only after he had mastered Latin and Greek. The precocious Blaise, however, began to demonstrate proficiency in geometry even before receiving instruction in it. As a result, his father wisely abandoned his strategy and acquainted his son with Euclid. Shortly after, about 1639, father and son began regularly to attend the weekly mathematical meetings of Father Marin Mersenne (1588–1648), a friend of mathematician and philosopher René Descartes (1596–1650), whom Pascal would later meet and with whom he often disagreed. Pascal's first major work, *Essai pour les coniques (Essay on Conic Sections* [1640]), was an illustrated treatise that extended the innovatory projective geometry of Gérard Desargues (1593–1662) and treated conics as plane sections through a circular cone, or as perspectives of circles. Pascal continued to work intermittently in this area, and, in 1654, he indicated that he was close to finishing a major treatise on projective geometry, but this, in fact, was never completed. Although Pascal's mathematical skill enabled him to exploit the power of projective geometry, it was greatly overshadowed by the new analytic geometry developed by Descartes and failed to win adherents until the nineteenth century.

The Calculating Machine and the Vacuum

Although Pascal lacked physical strength, his extraordinary intellectual prowess continued to push him into previously uncharted scientific territories. In an effort to help expedite his father's tabulation of taxes for the French government, Pascal formulated his idea for a calculating machine in 1642. After two years of labor, a craftsman built the first working model in 1644 under Pascal's direction. Despite its cumbersome nature, the machine added, subtracted, multiplied, and divided numbers having as many as eight digits. Pascal worked intensely for approximately a decade on perfecting the machine, after which he developed an advertising strategy to advance his labor-saving invention. The difficulty of manufacture and its high price limited the machine's success, however, and only seven are now extant. Nevertheless, by building a mechanism to perform mathematical functions that were previously calculated only by the mind, Pascal can be credited with the invention of an early precursor of the modern calculator. Unlike modern materialists, however, he never countenanced the notion that the human mind was reducible to a sophisticated machine.

Always a good Catholic, early in 1646 Pascal became converted to the teachings of Jean Duvergier de Hauranne (1581–1643), abbot of Saint-Cyran and friend of the reforming Catholic theologian Cornelius Jansen

(1585–1638). His newfound reformist convictions were to have a profound effect on Pascal's life and thought, but they did not entirely divert him from his work in mathematics and natural philosophy. In October of the same year, Pascal repeated the barometric experiments of Evangelista Torricelli (1608–47), which were then attracting a great deal of intellectual attention. By inverting a long glass tube full of mercury in a bowl of mercury, Torricelli noticed that the mercury in the tube dropped down until it was about 76 cm above the level in the bowl. The aim of the experiment was to confirm Galileo's suspicions about the role of the atmosphere in the limitation of the height to which a pump could lift water, but it also suggested that the space remaining at the end of the tube when the mercury dropped down must be a vacuum. This contradicted not only the Aristotelian dictum that "nature abhors a vacuum," but also the Cartesian metaphysical claim that matter and extension are essentially identical and that, therefore, empty space is a contradiction in terms.

When Pascal published the results of his own barometric experiments in his *Expériences nouvelles touchant le vide* (*New Experiments Concerning the Vacuum*) [1647]), Etienne Noël (1581–1660), a Jesuit metaphysician and friend of Descartes, argued that some rarified substance existed in the seemingly empty space between the mercury and the end of tube. On the basis of a series of detailed experiments, however, Pascal maintained that the appeal to some esoteric matter was unsubstantiated. After explaining his various experiments, he concluded: "Having demonstrated that none of the substances perceived by our senses and known by us fills this apparently empty space, I shall think, until I am shown the existence of a substance filling it, that it is really empty and void of all matter" (Pascal, "New Experiments Concerning the Vacuum," 1952, 364). More generally, Pascal pointed out to his critic that, while a conformity of all of the facts with a hypothesis at best serves only to make the hypothesis probable, a single contrary phenomenon can prove the hypothesis false. Pascal's response to Noël is greatly admired by philosophers of science as an accomplished statement of correct scientific methodology. It is important to note, however, that the probabilism inherent in Pascal's account of scientific knowledge was later to play an important part in his defense of religion in the *Pensées*. According to Pascal, our reason and understanding can attain certainty only by logically deriving propositions from given axioms. Such supposed certainty is entirely dependent upon the assumption that the axioms are true, however. Yet, the truth of these axioms can never be independently established, since they must depend upon more fundamental presuppositions, which themselves must be taken on trust or acknowledged to depend on yet more fundamental unsupported assumptions. This leads Pascal to conclude that we can gain certain knowledge only through submission to God and acceptance of revelation.

Although he left notes and letters on his experiments, Pascal never finished his proposed treatise on the nature of the vacuum; but his preface to that intended work remains a lucid account of his pivotal contribution to the developing scientific method of the day. Matters of empirical investigation, Pascal averred, must be separated from the knowledge—such as history, geography, language, and theology—that justifiably rests on authority found in books. The ancients may have much to teach us in the areas of geometry, arithmetic, music, physics, and architecture, but their views are not beyond revision, given new knowledge derived through reliable scientific procedures. Challenging the deductivism of Cartesian physics and the Aristotelian tradition, Pascal maintained that, while nature "is always at work, her effects are not always discovered; time reveals them from generation to generation, and although always the same in herself, she is not always equally known. The experiments which give us knowledge of nature multiply continually" (Pascal, "Preface to the Treatise on the Vacuum," 1952, 357).

Pascal believed that the long-standing resistance to the notion of a vacuum rested on experimental deficiencies and the force of unjustified tradition. Better experimentation and an openness to new empirical discoveries challenge static opinion not adequately supported by evidence. "For in all matters whose proof is by experiment and not by demonstration, no universal assertion can be made except by the general enumeration of all the parts and all the different cases" (Pascal, "Preface to the Treatise on the Vacuum," 1952, 358). Despite the rigor of Pascal's experiments and arguments, he remained open to empirical refutation. His exacting empirical method, coupled with his penchant for detailed mathematical explanation, helped develop a more mechanical view of nature that would challenge both Aristotelian teleology and Cartesian rationalism concerning supposed natural laws.

Pascal deemed the discovery of objective truth to be the aim of scientific study: "Whatever the weight of antiquity, truth should always have the advantage, even when newly discovered, since it is always older than every opinion men have held about it, and only ignorance of its nature could imagine it began to be at the time it began to be known" (Pascal, "Preface to the Treatise on the Vacuum," 1952, 358). For Pascal, authority, reason, and observation all play distinctive, irreducible, and (ultimately) harmonious roles in acquiring objective scientific knowledge. In *Pensées,* Pascal later applied this basic insight regarding various ways of knowing to his analysis of religious rationality. In the case of Christianity, revelation, reason, and experience all contribute in different ways to justifying religious belief.

Christian Faith and Scientific Endeavor

After a mystical experience on November 23, 1654, Pascal turned most of his skills to defending the Christian faith. This transformative experience, sometimes called Pascal's "second conversion" because it intensified and focused his religious devotion, was recorded on a scrap of paper that Pascal had sewn into the lining of his coat. The short, elliptical, and poetic statement recounts a profound and direct awareness of God during a two-hour experience that night.

Although this experience impressed upon Pascal the importance of the "God of Abraham, God of Isaac, God of Jacob, not of the philosophers and of the learned," he by no means ceased to be a natural philosopher and mathematician. He had just completed a protracted correspondence with the mathematician Pierre Fermat (1601–65), in which they had both made great strides in the calculus of probability and which enabled Pascal to write his *Traité du triangle arithmétique (Treatise on the Arithmetical Triangle),* an important study of combinatorial analysis and mathematical probability, which has been seen by modern historians of mathematics as the beginnings of a theory of decision. This, in turn, led to work in 1658 and 1659 on the mathematical theory of indivisibles first developed by Bonaventura Cavalieri (1598–1647) in 1635. Pascal was able to extend this work and the subsequent work of Gilles Roberval (1602–75) and Fermat to develop his own method. His work was later exploited by other mathematicians, most notably, Gottfried Wilhelm Leibniz (1646–1716), who were involved in the elaboration of infinitesimal calculus.

Increasingly, however, Pascal became concerned with religion. A two-week retreat to the convent of Port-Royal des Champs, and subsequent frequent visits there and to the Port-Royal convent in Paris, mark the beginnings of increased identification with the Jansenism that Port-Royal represented. In collaboration with Antoine Arnauld (1612–94) and Pierre Nicole (1625–95), Pascal wrote the eighteen *Lettres provinciales (Provincial Letters)* that were printed as a collection in 1657. Highly regarded as a great literary masterpiece in France, the *Lettres* ridicule and condemn the casuistry and downright immorality of contemporary Jesuit theology. Unfortunately, the published collection was immediately placed on the Catholic Church's Index of Prohibited Books, and Jansenism, which taught that grace and not good works was the key to salvation and which has been seen as a kind of Catholic Calvinism, was condemned by the pope shortly after. In 1661, the schools at Port-Royal were closed, and the nuns, secular priests, pious laymen, and others in residence had to submit to the church. This prompted Pascal's *Écrit sur la signature du formulaire (Pamphlet on the Signing of the Formulary),* urging the Jansenists not to give in. He then withdrew from further controversy, perhaps because of a difference of opinion with the Jansenists, although he certainly did not sever his connection with them. By now, Pascal was scarcely capable of regular work owing to ill health, but he did come up with the idea of a large carriage with many seats and used it to set up, in Paris, the first public-transportation system. The aim of the enterprise was to raise money for the poor.

Pascal's greatest religious achievement, however, was his unfinished *Apologie de la religion chrétienne (Apology for the Christian Religion),* which had taken up much of his time from the summer of 1657 to the summer of the following year. It was the notes for this that were subsequently published as his *Pensées.* Pascal never renounced scientific endeavors as intrinsically unspiritual, nor did he see a conflict between scientific discoveries and revealed truths. Nevertheless, he warned of intellectual hubris, or "proud reason," which presumes to fathom mysteries beyond its ken. In a famous fragment in the *Pensées,* Pascal speaks of human knowers as stranded between the infinitely small and the infinitely great, such that absolute and comprehensive certainty is unattainable through unaided reason.

Pascal's knowledge of science, combined with his Christian commitment, kept him from succumbing to either an excessively ambitious positivism or a despairing skepticism. F. X. J. Coleman notes that "as a man of science Pascal is never anti-scientific; yet he is opposed to the attitude that can be expressed as, 'whatever is, is what science says'" (Coleman 1986, 152). Science discovers some truth, but it does not monopolize knowledge. Moreover, it is unable to speak to our deepest concerns. Under the heading "Vanity of science" in *Pensées,* Pascal observes: "Knowledge of physical science will not console me for ignorance of morality in time of affliction, but knowledge of morality will always console me for ignorance of physical science" (Pascal 1966, 36). Science is vain when it pretends to extend beyond its proper sphere or order.

Pascal believed that, because religious knowledge is situated within its own "order" of existence and is discerned by faith through "the heart," it does not contradict scientific discoveries. The heart, for Pascal, is not merely the faculty of emotion but the organ of intuitive knowledge—whether knowledge of the unprovable but certain, or of first principles of mathematics, or of logic, or of God. Although Pascal's unfinished apology appealed to many lines of reasoning to defend Christianity as existentially attractive and intellectually cogent, he gave primacy to divine revelation as the most significant source of knowledge. Without revelation, Pascal claimed, we remain mysteries to ourselves, oblivious to our origin, nature, and destiny.

Pascal's approach to divine revelation involved applying a kind of scientific method to its claims. Although one cannot directly test by empirical means the deliverances of revelation on many matters (such as the origin of the universe, the creation of humanity, and the Fall into sin), Pascal thought that key theological claims offer the best explanation for the perplexing phenomena of human nature. "Man's greatness and wretchedness are so evident," he writes, "that the true religion must necessarily teach us that there is in man some great principle of greatness and some great principle of wretchedness" (Pascal 1966, 76). By adducing evidence from a wide diversity of situations, Pascal argues that the Christian view of humans as "deposed kings"—made in God's image but now east of Eden—is the best way to account for the human condition. In so arguing, he employs an abductive method (that is, inference to the best explanation) similar to that used in much scientific endeavor.

Although Pascal has sometimes been described as a fideist, he did not deem the acceptance of revelation in Scripture or the exercise of religious faith to be irrational. "Faith certainly tells us what the senses do not, but not the contrary of what they see; it is above, not against them" (Pascal 1966, 85). Moreover, "[r]eason's last step is the recognition that there are an infinite number of things beyond it. It is merely feeble if it does not go as far as to realize that. If natural things are beyond it, what are we to say about supernatural things?" (Pascal 1966, 85). When Pascal wrote of faith being above reason, he was not advocating that the principles of logic or scientific experimentation be abandoned. For him, "reason" referred to that which can be known through the discursive faculty when unaugmented by divine revelation. Pascal's famous epigram, "The heart has reasons of which reason knows nothing; we know this in countless ways" (Pascal 1966, 154), emphasizes the diverse ways of knowing, not the primacy of emotion or imagination over rationality.

See also Cartesianism; Skepticism

BIBLIOGRAPHY

Ashworth, William B., Jr. "Catholicism and Early Modern Science." In *God and Nature: Historical Essays on the Encounter between Christianity and Science,* ed. by David C. Lindberg and Ronald L. Numbers. Berkeley: University of California Press, 1986, 136–66.

Calliet, Emile. *Pascal: The Emergence of Genius.* New York: Harper, 1945.

Coleman, F. X. J. *Neither Angel nor Beast.* New York: Routledge and Kegan Paul, 1986.

Dear, Peter. "Miracles, Experiments, and the Ordinary Course of Nature." *Isis* 81 (1990): 663–83.

Groothuis, Douglas. "Bacon and Pascal on Mastery over Nature." *Research in Philosophy and Technology* 14 (1994): 191–203.

Harrington, Thomas More. *Pascal philosophe: Une étude unitaire de la pensées de Pascal.* Paris: Societe d'Edition d'Enseignement Superieur, 1982.

Koyré, Alexandre. "Pascal Savant." In *Metaphysics and Measurement: Essays in Scientific Revolution,* ed. by Alexandre Koyré. Harvard University Press, 1968, 131–56.

Krailsheimer, Alban. *Pascal.* New York: Hill and Wang, 1980.

O'Connell, Marvin R. *Blaise Pascal: Reasons of the Heart.* Grand Rapids, Mich.: Eerdmans, 1997.

Pascal, Blaise. "New Experiments Concerning the Vacuum." In *Pascal.* Trans. by Richard Scofield. Great Books of the Western World. Vol. 33. Chicago: Encyclopedia Britannica, 1952, 359–81.

———. "Preface to the Treatise on the Vacuum." In *Pascal.* Trans. by Richard Scofield. Great Books of the Western

World. Vol. 33. Chicago: Encyclopedia Britannica, 1952, 355–8.

———. *Oeuvres Completes (l'Integrale)*. Paris: Editions du Seuil, 1963.

———. *Pensées*. Trans. by A. J. Krailsheimer. New York: Penguin, 1966.

Popkin, Richard. "Pascal." In *Encyclopedia of Philosophy,* ed. by Paul Edwards. Vol. 8. New York: Macmillan and Free Press, 1967, 51–5.

Taton, René. "Pascal, Blaise." In *Dictionary of Scientific Biography,* ed. by C. C. Gillispie. Vol. 10. New York: Charles Scribner's Sons, 1974, 330–42.

Wells, A. N. *Pascal's Recovery of Man's Wholeness.* Richmond, Va.: John Knox, 1965.

17. Isaac Newton

Richard S. Westfall†

Newton's Life

If the date of Isaac Newton's birth, Christmas Day 1642, suggests the important role that Christianity would play in his life, it does not even begin to hint at the heterodox opinions he would embrace as he struggled to bring his Christianity into harmony with his science.

The son of a prosperous yeoman farmer in Lincolnshire who died three months before his only child's birth, Newton (1642–1727) was educated at the grammar school in Grantham and admitted to Trinity College, Cambridge, in the summer of 1661. Trinity was his home for the following thirty-five years. Two years after commencing his B.A. he was elected to a fellowship in the college, and two years after that he received appointment as the university's Lucasian Professor of Mathematics. All of Newton's contributions to science belong to the years in Trinity. Already by the time of his B.A., his independent, untutored study of mathematics was beginning to lead him toward the calculus, and only a year later he composed what is known as the Tract of October 1666, in which he set its principles down. About the same time, he became interested in optics and phenomena of color and first entertained his insight into the heterogeneity of light. His initial series of lectures as Lucasian Professor devoted themselves to this topic, and in them he polished the theory that phenomena of colors arise from the analysis of heterogeneous light into its components. Although Newton published his *Opticks* only in 1704, virtually all of its content went back to the late 1660s. At this time, he also took up the science of mechanics and began to think about gravity. He was still a member of Trinity in the 1680s, when he returned to mechanics, addressed the problem of orbital dynamics, and composed *The Mathematical Principles of Natural Philosophy* (or *Principia,*

from the key word in its Latin title), which was published in 1687 and established his renown in science for all time. About a decade after the *Principia,* Newton moved from Cambridge to London, where he became first warden and then master of the Royal Mint. In 1703, the Royal Society elected him president. Both of these positions he held until his death on March 20, 1727.

Newton and Theology

It was also in Cambridge that Newton began seriously to study theology. There is, of course, no reason to doubt that he had been a normally pious young man in an age when normal young men tended to be pious, but his surviving manuscripts do not indicate any sustained study of theology until about 1672. Perhaps the statutory requirement of Trinity College that fellows be ordained to the Anglican clergy within seven years of commencing the M.A. initially stimulated his active concern with theology. He had received his M.A. in 1668. The required ordination would have to take place by 1675, and Newton was never one to take an obligation lightly. Whether or not the Trinity ordinance was the cause, the manuscript remains leave no doubt that he began to study theology intensely about 1672. He devoured the Scriptures. Years later, John Locke (1632–1704) would confess that he had never known anyone with a better command of Scripture. With equal gusto, he devoured the early Fathers of the church, making himself a master of that extensive literature as well. For the following decade and more, Newton devoted very little time to the scientific and mathematical topics we associate with his name. Along with alchemy, theology was the staple of his intellectual life in those years. The *Principia* interrupted this pattern, and, during the following twenty years, the quantity of theological manuscripts that he penned greatly diminished. He returned once more to theology during the first decade of the eighteenth century, however, and, from that time until his death, it was the focus of his attention. Newton never threw a paper away, so the record of his long immersion in theology survives. The manuscript remains can only be described as immense, at least several million words. In quantity, they far exceed those from any of his other fields of study.

At the time when Newton turned to theology, a tradition of natural theology was well established among English scientists. Books by scientists bearing such titles as *The Darknes of Atheism Dispelled by the Light of Nature* and *The Wisdom of God Manifested in the Works of the Creation* appeared in constant succession. Robert Boyle (1627–91), a prolific author, included arguments to this effect in nearly every one of the many books he published, and, toward the end of his life, he summarized the message in *The Christian Virtuoso* (a title that is not distorted if translated as *The Christian Scientist*). Newton also contributed to this literature. "When I wrote my treatise about our Systeme," he stated in a letter to the theologian Richard Bentley (1662–1742), "I had an eye upon such Principles as might work with considering men for the beleife of a Deity & nothing can rejoyce me more than to find it usefull for that purpose." A passage in Query 28 at the end of the *Opticks* asserted that the "main Business of natural Philosophy is . . . to deduce Causes from Effects, till we come to the very first Cause, which certainly is not Mechanical." In perhaps his most eloquent statement of this argument, the *General Scholium* appended to the second edition of the *Principia,* he described the solar system with planets and satellites moving in the same direction in the same plane while comets course among them. "This most beautiful system of the sun, planets, and comets," he argued, "could only proceed from the counsel and dominion of an intelligent and powerful Being."

These passages have been well known ever since Newton wrote them; there is no reason whatever to doubt their sincerity. Nevertheless, they are not what one finds in his many theological manuscripts. The quoted passages repeat an inherited piety, the deposit of centuries of Christianity, that part of Newton's religion not seriously touched by the new science, despite its seeming utilization of it. In the manuscripts, we find a different Newton, who brings a different attitude to bear on the established religion. The different attitude was intimately related to the new science, though not to its overt conclusions as it forged a new image of physical reality. The attitude was related, rather, to the questioning stance of science, as it rejected one received authority after another, to all that Basil Willey had in mind when he spoke (repeating a seventeenth-century phrase) of the "touch of cold philosophy" (Willey 1967, vii).

Newton's Arianism

Early in his theological reading, Newton become absorbed in the doctrine of the Trinity and in the fourth-century struggle between what became Christian orthodoxy and Arianism. He identified with Arius (250–336), who taught that Jesus was a created being and not coeternal with God the Father, and came to hate Athanasius (c. 296–373), the principal architect of trinitarian orthodoxy. Newton did not think of Athanasius and his cohorts in the fourth century merely as mistaken. Rather, he regarded them as criminals, who had seized Christianity by fraud and perverted it as they pursued selfish ends, even tampering with the Scriptures to insert trinitarian passages that he could not find in versions earlier than the fourth century. One of his papers, "Paradoxical Questions concerning the morals & actions of Athanasius & his followers," virtually stood Athanasius in the dock and prosecuted him for an extended litany of alleged sins, both doctrinal and moral.

Newton became either an Arian or something so close to an Arian that it is difficult to distinguish them. Arianism is similar to, but not identical with, early unitarianism. It considered Christ to be not an eternal person in a triune God, but a created intermediary between God and man. In his manuscripts, Newton insisted on a distinction between God, the omnipotent Pantocrator, and Christ the Lord, who was always subordinate to God and whom God elevated to sit at his right hand. From this position, which he adopted in the 1670s, Newton never retreated. In his old age, he was still writing Arian statements on the nature of Christ. Trinitarianism he always treated as more an abomination than a mere error. He referred to it as the "false infernal religion" and "the whole fornication." "Idolators, Blasphemers & spiritual fornicators," he thundered at the trinitarians in the isolation of his chamber. A shrill note of iconoclasm that one does not ordinarily associate with Newton rings through these pages as he denounced "vehement superstition" and "monstrous Legends, fals miracles, veneration of reliques, charmes, the doctrine of Ghosts or Daemons, & their intercession invocation & worship & such other heathen superstitions as were then brought in."

This was hardly a safe position to adopt in England in the late seventeenth century. For a man of Newton's rigid posture, it made ordination impossible, and in 1675 he was preparing to lay down his fellowship at Trinity. Perhaps the Lucasian chair could have been held separately, but questions would inevitably have been raised in an institution that explicitly considered orthodoxy a requirement for membership. The Lucasian chair also had orthodoxy written into its statutes. It is not too much to say that Newton's career hung in the balance in 1675. At the last minute, probably through the influence of Isaac Barrow (1630–77), master of Trinity College, a royal dispensation from the requirement of ordination was granted, not to Isaac Newton, but to the holder of the Lucasian chair in perpetuity, and the crisis passed. Newton understood that absolute secrecy had now become the condition of his continued presence in Cambridge, and there is no indication that he divulged the content of his theological papers to anyone there. Though unwilling to accept ordination, he was prepared to accommodate to silence. The need to shield this important dimension of his existence from public scrutiny became a permanent part of Newton's life. Even in the greater laxity of the capital city at the turn of the century, after Newton moved there in 1696, the need for secrecy remained. The law of the land explicitly set belief in the Trinity as a requirement for public servants. It does seem clear that, in London, Newton shared his views with a restricted circle of mostly younger men, who may, indeed, have learned their heresy from him. Because some of them were less cautious, a few rumors did spread, but only in the late twentieth century, when his theological manuscripts became accessible to the scholarly public, did the extent of his heretical views become known.

Newton's Interest in Biblical Prophecy

Along with Arian theology, Newton maintained a concern with biblical prophecy, initially with the Book of Revelation and later with Daniel as well. Newton's interest in prophecy is well known; shortly after his death, his heirs published *Observations on the Prophecies*. The manuscript they published, really two different manuscripts together with three other miscellaneous chapters

that they melded together, was a product of Newton's old age when, increasingly aware of his own prominence, he wanted to obscure his heterodoxy. It is quite impossible to find any point in the published book's meandering chronologies. This was not the case with the original interpretation of Revelation that Newton composed in the early 1670s. There he drew upon an established Puritan interpretation that centered on the "Great Apostasy." To the Puritan interpreters, the Great Apostasy was the Roman Church. For Newton, it was trinitarianism. The purpose of the Apocalypse was to foretell the rise of the Great Apostasy and God's response to it. At the end of the sixth Seal (the Seals represented periods of time to Newton), the first six trumpets and the vials of wrath associated with them (also periods of time) prophesied the barbarian invasions of the Roman Empire, punishments poured out on a stiff-necked people who had gone whoring after false gods. In pursuit of this interpretation, Newton, who had come to doubt the accuracy of the received text of the New Testament, collated some twenty different manuscript versions of the Book of Revelation to establish the correct text. An interpretation could be correct, in his view, only if the prophecy corresponded in detail to the facts of history as they later unfolded, and he was no less vigorous in pursuing those facts in the sources for the history of the early Christian era.

In the late 1670s, Newton's interpretation acquired a new dimension as he became convinced of the role of Jewish ceremony as a "type," or figure, in prophecy. With his characteristic thoroughness, Newton plunged into Jewish literature—Josephus (c. A.D. 37–c. 100), Philo (c. 30 B.C.–A.D. 45), Moses Maimonides (1135–1204), and the Talmudic scholars. In this context, the exact shape of the temple in Jerusalem became increasingly important to Newton. He was convinced that the tabernacle of Moses and the temples of Solomon and Ezekiel had followed the same plan, although the temples were bigger. He found the best description in chapters 40–43 of Ezekiel. On its basis, he drew a detailed plan of the temple, using the exigencies of the plan when necessary to correct the text.

Early in the 1680s, Newton began to work on a new theological treatise, which never even approached final form and which he called *Theologiae gentilis origines philosophicae* (*The Philosophical Origins of Gentile Theology*) in the manuscript that most approaches a finished form. The *Origines* was the most radical of Newton's theological writings. It was also his most important. Its ideas echoed through his scientific works during the following thirty years—in the first section of the original draft of the *Principia*'s concluding book, in the so-called *Classical Scholia* inserted in revisions of Book 3 during the 1690s but never published, in the final lines of Query 31, which he published initially in 1706, and in two footnotes to the *General Scholium* added to edition two of the *Principia* in 1713.

The *Origines* proposed a cyclical pattern of human history, in which the one true religion is continually perverted into idolatry. Newton argued that all of the ancient civilizations worshiped the same twelve gods, though under different names. The twelve corresponded to the seven planets, the four elements, and the quintessence, the noblest parts of nature, with which the ancient peoples had identified their divinized rulers and heroes. Kings who wanted to claim descent from divinities had every incentive to promote this religion. For Newton, gentile theology was rank idolatry. Mankind had started with the one true religion, manifest from the observation of nature, and Newton was convinced that he could see evidence of the true religion among early people before idolatry set in. Everywhere throughout the ancient world, he found, temples that he called "prytanea" had been built to a common plan. They had a central fire surrounded by seven candles, a representation of the universe—indeed, a heliocentric representation—for true philosophy had accompanied true religion. His primary evidence for the original true religion was the worship of Noah and his children. But mankind has an inherent tendency to idolatry. In fact, the common twelve gods were Noah, his children, and his grandchildren, the source of all of the ancient peoples, each of whom saw the twelve as their unique ancestors and divinized them. Egypt had led the way in idolatry; the other ancient peoples had learned it from the Egyptians.

In the twentieth century, it would be easy to overlook the radical thrust of the *Origines*. We smile at the quaint themes of Noah and his children and see in the special place the treatise seems to accord to the Judeo-Christian revelation a hallmark of Christian provincialism. We might miss the message that Newton clothed in the common idiom of the day, which was the only idiom available to him. However, he treated the historical records of the other ancient peoples as sources equal in validity to the Hebrew writings. For example, he found a universal story of a flood and of a line of ten patriarchs before Noah. "Noah" was only the name most familiar to

Newton's potential audience; in fact, in his view the man had been more Egyptian than Hebrew, more Hammon than Noah. Above all, the *Origines* deflated the Christian message by making Christianity another instance of a repetitive cycle. As he saw human history, God had continually sent prophets to recall mankind from idolatry. Christ was no different from the rest, and, in trinitarianism, the work of Athanasius, another Egyptian, mankind had slid again into idolatry, for what is trinitarianism but the worship of a man as God? "What was the true religion of the sons of Noah before it began to be corrupted by the worship of false Gods?" Newton set down as the title of a Chapter 11 that he never, in fact, composed. "And that the Christian religion was not more true and did not become less corrupt." In turn, "the true religion of the sons of Noah" appears to have been a naturalistic religion, restricted to the acknowledgment of God and our duties to one another, the common property of all of mankind who are willing carefully to study nature.

Newton was at work on the *Origines* when the visit of Edmond Halley (1656–1742) in 1684 set him in motion toward the *Principia*. The *Principia,* in turn, marked a break in his theological endeavors, as mentioned above, and, though he later returned and devoted reams of paper to them, he was by then an old man engaged largely in reshuffling earlier ideas. He did produce a sanitized version of the *Origines,* analogous to his late manuscript on prophecy. *The Chronology of Ancient Kingdoms Amended* appeared after his death; it gives no hint of its radical provenance.

Conclusion

Different interpretations of Newton's religious odyssey are possible. It seems to offer the record of a man seeking to reconcile a spiritual heritage that was precious in his sight with a new intellectual reality. Somewhat the same can be said of all of the scientists in their exercises in natural theology. Read in isolation, each one seems to offer testimony to an unshaken faith. Read one after another, each repeating essentially the argument of its predecessors, they begin to project an uneasiness that unbelief was not so readily banished. After a lifetime of refuting atheism, Boyle left an endowment for a series of lectures to refute atheism some more. When in the previous millennium had that seemed necessary? The scientists of the late seventeenth century sensed that the ground was moving under the inherited structure of Christianity, and they sought to shore it up with a new foundation. Newton felt the same movement, but his response went further. He attempted to purge Christianity of elements, centering on the doctrine of the Trinity, that he regarded as irrational. He wrote:

If it be said that we are not to determin what's scripture & what not by our private judgments [he wrote about the two trinitarian passages that he considered corruptions of Scripture], I confesse it in places not controverted: but in disputable places I love to take up with what I can best understand. Tis the temper of the hot and superstitious part of mankind in matters of religion ever to be fond of mysteries, & for that reason to like best what they understand least. Such men may use the Apostle John as they please: but I have that honour for him as to beleive he wrote good sense, & therefore take that sense to be his which is the best.

The *Origines* arrived at a vision of true religion not far different from deism except in one, perhaps all important, respect. Where the deists could not contain their animosity toward Christianity, Newton always believed that he was restoring true Christianity. In a tract from his old age called *Irenicum,* he reduced Christianity, or true religion, to two doctrines: love of God and love of neighbor. On his deathbed, after years of compromise for the sake of appearances, he refused the sacrament of the Anglican Church.

The deist storm had broken long before Newton's death, and, in the years following his death, religious radicalism reached positions he would have abhorred. He himself contributed almost nothing to this movement. Always secretive, he had communicated his doubts only to a very narrow circle, and there is no evidence to suggest that, through them, he played a role in fomenting the storm. On the contrary, there is every reason to think that the religious rebels of the eighteenth century responded on their own to the same influences that had moved Newton. Both alike testify that, with the rise of modern science, the age of unshaken faith was forever gone in the West.

See also Early-Modern Protestantism; Mechanical Philosophy; Natural Theology; Varieties of Providentialism

BIBLIOGRAPHY

Brooke, John H. *Science and Religion: Some Historical Perspectives.* Cambridge: Cambridge University Press, 1991.

Christianson, Gale. *In the Presence of the Creator: Isaac Newton and His Times.* New York: Free Press, 1984.

Cragg, Gerald R. *From Puritanism to the Age of Reason: A Study of Changes in Religious Thought Within the Church of England, 1660 to 1700.* Cambridge: Cambridge University Press, 1950.

Dobbs, Betty Jo. *The Foundations of Newton's Alchemy: The Hunting of the Greene Lyon.* Cambridge: Cambridge University Press, 1975.

———. *The Janus Faces of Genius: The Role of Alchemy in Newton's Thought.* Cambridge: Cambridge University Press, 1991.

Force, James E., and Richard H. Popkin. *Essays on the Context, Nature, and Influence of Isaac Newton's Theology.* International Archives for the History of Ideas. Vol. 129. Dordrecht: Kluwer, 1990.

Hazard, Paul. *The European Mind: The Critical Years, 1680–1715.* Trans. by J. Lewis May. 1935. Reprint. New Haven, Conn.: Yale University Press, 1953.

Hooykaas, R. *Religion and the Rise of Modern Science.* Edinburgh: Scottish Academic Press, 1972.

Jacob, Margaret C. *The Newtonians and the English Revolution, 1689–1720.* Hassocks, Sussex: Harvester, 1976.

Lindberg, David C., and Ronald L. Numbers, eds. *God and Nature: Historical Essays on the Encounter Between Christianity and Science.* Berkeley: University of California Press, 1986.

Manuel, Frank E. *Portrait of Isaac Newton.* Cambridge, Mass.: Harvard University Press, 1968.

———. *The Religion of Isaac Newton.* Oxford: Oxford University Press, 1974.

Popkin, Richard H. "Newton's Biblical Theology and His Theological Physics." In *Newton's Scientific and Philosophical Legacy,* ed. by P. B. Scheuer and G. Debrock. International Archives of the History of Ideas. Vol. 123. Dordrecht: Kluwer, 1988, 81–97.

Westfall, Richard S. *Science and Religion in Seventeenth Century England.* New Haven, Conn.: Yale University Press, 1958.

———. *Never at Rest: A Biography of Isaac Newton.* Cambridge: Cambridge University Press, 1980.

Willey, Basil. *Seventeenth Century Background: Studies in the Thought of the Age in Relation to Poetry and Religion.* 1934. Reprint. New York: Columbia University Press, 1967.

18. CHARLES DARWIN

James R. Moore

Each age fashions nature in its own image. In the nineteenth century, the English naturalist Charles Darwin (1809–82) recast the living world in the image of competitive, industrial Britain. He abandoned the Bible as a scientific authority and explained the origin of living things by divinely ordained natural laws. Once destined for the church, he became the high priest of a new secular order, proclaiming a struggling, progressive, and law-bound nature to a struggling, improving, and law-abiding society. For his devotion to science and his exemplary life, he received England's highest religious honor when scientists joined churchmen and politicians of all parties to inter his mortal remains in Westminster Abbey.

Darwin was born at Shrewsbury in 1809, the second son of a wealthy Whig household. His father was a freethinking physician; his mother, a conservative Unitarian. Upright and respectable, they had Charles christened in the local Anglican Church. As a boy, he attended chapel with his mother and was first educated by the minister. After her death in 1817, he sat under a future bishop at Shrewsbury School and learned to despise the classics. Chemistry was more to his taste, and his first experiments were conducted in a garden shed with his brother, Erasmus. Five years older, Erasmus followed their father into medicine at Edinburgh University, leaving Charles in the care of his sisters. He fretted and his lessons suffered, so, in 1825, his father sent him to study medicine with Erasmus.

Edinburgh was liberal and cosmopolitan, full of brash freethinkers. Charles struck up a friendship with one of them, Dr. Robert E. Grant (1793–1874), Britain's leading invertebrate zoologist. Together they scoured the coast for exotic sea life and attended the university's Plinian Society, in which students and staff debated hot topics in natural history. Grant was an atheist and evolutionist, following the French naturalist Jean Baptiste de Monet de Lamarck (1744–1829); the Plinian served as a platform for his and other members' radical, materialist ideas. Here Charles first saw scientific heresy punished when a fellow student's remarks on the identity of mind and brain were struck from the minutes.

Charles dropped out of medicine, unable to stomach surgery. To cure his indirection, his father prescribed a stint at Cambridge University to train for the Church of England. A country parish would make few demands on his son's faith; he would have a respectable social role, a guaranteed income, and, above all, the leisure to indulge his Edinburgh interest in natural history. Charles read a few divinity books and decided there was nothing in them he could not say he believed. In 1828, he went up to Christ's College to study for the B.A. and ordination.

Cambridge was strict and feudal, a market town dominated by a medieval university. Here the professors were untainted by French radicalism. They included clergymen like John Stevens Henslow (1796–1861), who taught Charles botany, and Adam Sedgwick (1785–1873), who introduced him to geology. These men believed that living species had been created miraculously and that species and society alike were kept stable by God's will. This was the reigning orthodoxy, enshrined in required textbooks by the Rev. William Paley (1743–1805). Everyone conformed to it, more or less. Unbelievers were unwelcome. In 1829, when a renegade Cambridge graduate, the Rev. Robert Taylor, attempted an "infidel mission" to the university, he was hounded out of town. Charles never forgot the example of this apostate priest, dubbed "the Devil's Chaplain."

In August 1831, after a geological fieldtrip with Sedgwick, Darwin found a letter at home from Henslow offering him a place as captain's companion aboard H. M. S. *Beagle*. This was the turning point of his life. The Church could wait. His path to a country parish was now diverted via a voyage around the world. For five years, Darwin collected specimens, kept a diary, and made countless notes. He dreamed of becoming a parson-naturalist, and his religious beliefs and practices remained conventional. Like his professors, he did not take Genesis to be a literal account of creation, but he quoted Scripture as a supreme moral authority. He carried a copy of Milton's *Paradise Lost* with him and, on Henslow's recommendation, the first volume of Charles Lyell's (1797–1875) *Principles of Geology* (1830–33). Lyell, a Unitarian, argued that the earth's crust had been laid down over countless ages according to natural law. Darwin was convinced. More and more, he saw himself as a geologist, and he began to theorize about the formation of islands and continents and the causes of extinction. The *Beagle*'s aristocratic captain, Robert FitzRoy (1805–65), disagreed. He held to the literal interpretation of Genesis, and his faith became a foil for Darwin's developing science. Equally, it was a reminder of Tory-Anglican prejudice. FitzRoy's defense of slave-owning colonial Catholics outraged Darwin's Whig abolitionist morals, although in 1836 they jointly published an article vindicating the moral influence of missionaries in Tahiti.

Nothing on the voyage prepared Charles for the political sea change at home. The ferment was palpable in March 1837, when he took lodgings in London near Erasmus to seek expert help with his *Beagle* collections. Successive Whig governments had tackled corruption, extended the franchise, and opened public offices to non-Anglicans. Angry radicals and nonconformists, unappeased, demanded further concessions, including the disestablishment of the Church of England. A national movement was already under way, leading to a general strike in August 1842. For Britain, these were the century's most turbulent years; for Darwin, they were the most formative.

He entered scientific society, his fame as the *Beagle*'s naturalist preceding him. Here materialism and evolution were debated as in Edinburgh, though, again, he had little to prepare him—only his copy of Lyell's *Principles,* with its refutation of Lamarck. Evolution had been taken up by radical naturalists and medical men, not just as a true theory of life but as a political weapon for attacking miracle-mongering creationists—Oxbridge professors and Tory placemen—who kept scientific insti-

tutions in a stranglehold. To the radicals, evolution meant material atoms moving themselves to ever higher states of organization, just as social atoms—humans—could. It was nature's legitimation of democracy in science and society alike.

Darwin himself was rising fast. Within months he had a huge government grant to publish his *Beagle* research. Lyell became his patron at the elite Geological Society and saw him on to the governing council. Here Darwin read papers before the Oxbridge dons, and one of them, the Rev. William Whewell (1794–1866), the president, asked him to become a secretary. All in all, the young man was a paragon of public respectability. But, in private, the voyage, the political ferment, and specialist reports on his collections had shattered his orthodoxy; he became a closet evolutionist. In a series of pocket notebooks, started in 1837, Darwin began working out a theory that would transform the study of life. His aim was to explain the origin of all plant and animal species, including the human mind and body, by divinely ordained natural laws. Such a theory was dangerous— "oh you Materialist!" he jotted half in jest (C. Darwin 1987, 291)—and it was sure to be damned as atheistic by those he least wished to offend. So secrecy was vital.

About this time, Darwin became unwell, with headaches and stomach troubles. Insomnia and nightmares plagued him, and once he even dreamed of public execution. He felt like a prisoner in London, tied down by his *Beagle* work, theorizing about evolution, and dreading the consequences. In his notebooks, he devised protective strategies lest he should ever publish. He would pitch his theory to Anglican creationists by emphasizing its superior theology. A world populated by natural law was "far grander" than one in which the Creator interferes with himself, "warring against those very laws he established in all organic nature." Just think— Almighty God personally lavishing on earth the "long succession of vile Molluscous animals!" "How beneath the dignity of him, who is supposed to have said let there be light & there was light" (C. Darwin 1987, 343).

In mid-1842, Darwin took up the theme again in a pencil sketch of his theory, which he now called "natural selection." It seemed so obvious: Nature alone "selects" the best-adapted organisms, those celebrated in Paley's *Natural Theology* (1802) as proofs of a designing Providence. They survive the constant struggle for food described in the Rev. Thomas Malthus's (1766–1834) *Essay on the Principle of Population* (1798), passing on their adaptive advantage to offspring. In this way, Darwin believed, the laws governing "death, famine, rapine, and the concealed war of nature" bring about "the highest good, which we can conceive, the creation of the higher animals." Good from evil, progress from pain: This was a boost for God. "The existence of such laws should exalt our notion of the power of the omniscient Creator" (C. Darwin 1909, 51–2).

Darwin might have sounded like a parson, but the Church was now the last thing on his mind. He knew that his theory undermined the "whole fabric" of Anglican orthodoxy. Let one species alter, he noted tartly, and the whole creationist edifice "totters & falls" (C. Darwin 1987, 263). With such ideas, he was plainly unfit to seek ordination, quite apart from his devotion to geology and his bad health. In 1838, Charles's father had opened the family purse to endow him as a gentleman naturalist. Months later, Charles married his first cousin Emma Wedgwood and began making plans to escape from London. In September 1842, they moved out fifteen miles to the Kentish village of Downe, where Charles fulfilled his old ambition to be a parish naturalist. His new home was the former parsonage, Down House. Here his clerical camouflage was complete.

Emma became his full-time nurse and the mother of ten. She was a sincere Christian, like all Wedgwoods of her generation: Unitarian by conviction, Anglican in practice. Charles differed from her painfully. Ever since their engagement, when he revealed his evolution heresy to her, she had feared that in death they would be separated, and he would suffer eternal torments. Emma's anxiety remained a sad undercurrent throughout the marriage, her heartache and prayers increasing with his illness.

Darwin's own feelings sometimes showed, as on the rare occasions he mooted his theory to friends. It was criminal, "like confessing a murder," he confided to a colleague, Joseph Hooker. In 1845, when Sedgwick damned the anonymous evolutionary potboiler *Vestiges of the Natural History of Creation* (1844) for being subversive and unscientific, Darwin read his old professor's review with "fear & trembling." He had just finished a draft of his own theory and given Emma instructions for publishing it "in case of my sudden death" (Burkhardt et al. 1985–97, 3:2, 43, 258).

Events came to a head when he had a serious breakdown after his father's death in 1848. For the first time, he felt sure that he himself was about to die. Four months at a spa worked wonders, but he returned home only to see his eldest daughter taken ill. When Annie died tragically in April 1851, at age ten, he found no comfort in Emma's faith. After years of backsliding, he finally broke with Christianity. His father's death had spiked the faith; Annie's clinched the point. Eternal punishment was immoral. He would speak out and be damned.

Down House was now his pulpit; evolution, the new "gospel." He pressed on through sickness and sorrow, polishing his theory, extending it, finding illustrations everywhere. Finally, in 1856, he was ready to write it up. His confidants—Lyell now, as well as Hooker and Thomas Henry Huxley (1825–95)—egged him on. Huxley, angry and anticlerical, baited him with juicy tidbits, like the "indecency" of jellyfish cross-fertilizing through the mouth. Darwin, about to start the *Origin of Species* (1859), shared the lewd jest with Hooker: Good grief, he spouted, "What a book a Devil's Chaplain might write on the clumsy, wasteful, blundering low & horridly cruel works of nature!" (Burkhardt et al. 1985–97, 4:140, 6:178).

But he was the apostate now, touting not treachery but a "grander" theology than Anglican creationism. His book would be a hymn to the Creator's immutable laws by which the "higher animals" had evolved. The *Origin of Species* did not once use the word "evolution," but "creation" and its cognate terms appeared more than one hundred times. At the front, opposite the title, stood a quotation from Francis Bacon (1561–1626) on studying God's works as well as his Word, and another from Whewell on "general laws" as God's way of working. On the last page, Darwin rhapsodized about the "grandeur" of viewing nature's "most beautiful and most wonderful" diversity as the product of the "several powers . . . originally breathed into a few forms or into one." From start to finish, the *Origin* was a pious work, "one long argument" against miraculous creationism but equally a reformer's case for creation by law (C. Darwin 1959, 719, 759).

There was doublethink in it and a certain subterfuge. The book was the man, after all—ambiguous, even contradictory. In the end, the *Origin* held multiple meanings; it could become all things to everyone. Radicals like brother Erasmus loved it, the theology notwithstanding. Anglican diehards loathed it, and some, like Sedgwick, muttered about Darwin's eternal destiny. Emma now worried more about her husband's present suffering, his anxiety and illness, as the *Origin* went into the world. But she still prayed that these pains would make him "look forward . . . to a future state" in which their love would go on forever (Burkhardt et al. 1985–97, 9:155).

Not all Anglicans damned Darwin. The "celebrated author and divine" quoted in later editions of the *Origin* was the Rev. Charles Kingsley (1819–75), novelist, amateur naturalist, and professor of history at Cambridge. His plug for Darwin's theology—it seemed "just as noble" as miraculous creationism (C. Darwin 1959, 748)—was timely but timid, a mere "yea" to the hearty "amen" from the Oxford geometry professor, the Rev. Baden Powell (1796–1860). Writing in the Broad Church manifesto *Essays and Reviews* (1860), he declared that the *Origin* "must soon bring about an entire revolution of opinion in favour of the grand principle of the self-evolving powers of nature" (Powell 1860, 139). For such remarks, Powell and his fellow authors were hounded for heresy and two of them eventually prosecuted. In 1861, when a private petition was got up in their defense, Darwin rallied to the cause, adding his signature. He welcomed the essayists' efforts to "establish religious teaching on a firmer and broader foundation" (Burkhardt et al. 1985–97, 9:419).

Worse heretics embarrassed the Church from without, and, during the 1860s and 1870s, Darwin was repeatedly asked to back them. But although the *Origin* became all things to everyone, he found this impossible. He steered clear of public support for religious heretics—in Great Britain. Only in the United States did he allow freethinkers to use his name. They called themselves the Free Religious Association, and their creed, printed as *Truths for the Times,* augured "the extinction of faith in the Christian Confession" and the development of a humanistic "Free Religion" (Abbot 1872, 7). Darwin wrote that he agreed with "almost *every word*" and allowed his remark to be published (Desmond and Moore 1991, 591).

Meanwhile, at Downe, his dual life went on. For years he had worked closely with the incumbent, the Rev. John Brodie Innes. Together they started a benefit society for the local laborers, with Darwin as guardian, and Innes made his friend treasurer of the parish charities and the village school. But in 1871, a boorish new vicar took over and soon fell out with the Darwins. Charles cut his ties with the charities; Emma left the church for one a few miles away. The neighbors hardly noticed their absence. The "great folks" in Down House continued to be parish paternalists, tending the social fabric. With Emma's help, Charles started a temperance reading room in an old hall, where, for a penny a week, working-

men could smoke, play games, and read "respectable" literature without resorting to the pub.

In 1871, his long-awaited *Descent of Man* came out bearing the imprimatur of his daughter Henrietta. Parts, he had feared, would read like an infidel sermon—"Who w[oul]d ever have thought I sh[oul]d turn parson"! (Burkhardt et al. 1994, 7124)—and he asked her to tone them down. Emma, too, had jogged the family censor, reminding her that, however "interesting" the book's treatment of morals and religion might be, she would still "dislike it very much as again putting God further off" (Litchfield 1915, 2:196). Henrietta dutifully preened the proofs, and the *Descent* caused few commotions. For her good work, she was given a free hand in Charles's biographical sketch of his grandfather. These proofs she pruned. *Erasmus Darwin* appeared in 1879 shorn of everything religiously risqué.

No one curbed Darwin's candor in his own biography, written between 1876 and 1881. But, then, it was intended for the family, not publication. Here he gave his fullest statement ever on religion (Darwin 1958, 85–96). At first he had been unwilling to abandon Christianity and had even tried to "invent evidence" to confirm the Gospels, which had prolonged his indecision. But just as his clerical career had died a slow "natural death," so his faith had withered gradually. There had been no turning back once the deathblow fell. His dithering had crystallized into a moral conviction so strict that he could not see how anyone—even Emma—"ought to wish Christianity to be true." If it were, "the plain language" of the New Testament "seems to show that the men who do not believe, and this would include my Father, Brother and almost all my best friends, will be everlastingly punished. And this is a damnable doctrine."

These hard, heartfelt words recalled the bitter months and years after his father's death. Since then, Darwin's residual theism had weakened, worn down by controversy. Now as one with "no assured and ever present belief in the existence of a personal God or of a future existence with retribution and reward," he confessed, "I . . . must be content to remain an Agnostic." An unbeliever, yes, but still an upright man, living without the threat of divine wrath. "I feel no remorse from having committed any great sin," he assured Emma and the children. "I believe that I have acted rightly in steadily following and devoting my life to science."

Charles entrusted the autobiography to Francis, the son who shared his biological interests. William, the

eldest, was asked to tackle a more sensitive matter. He
had married a relative of one of the Free Religious Association's founders, so was well placed to ask in 1880 for
his father's endorsement of *Truths for the Times* to be
stopped. He did not explain why this was necessary, but
the Americans complied.

William's intervention, like Henrietta's editing, served
to conceal Charles's identity and restore it to the family. As
his anxious life drew to a close, he was his own man again,
safe at Downe, guarded by loved ones. They knew him in
different ways, for he had shown them his separate sides.
To the daughters, he was the respectable evolutionist,
careful not to offend; to his sons, he was the radical unbeliever whose worst heresies were tucked away in the autobiography (as they once had been in pocket notebooks).
Only Emma knew him as he knew his own divided self,
and he was desperate that she should survive him. With
her guidance, the world would know only the "Darwin"
the family chose to reveal.

Not that no one pried. Within weeks of his brother
Erasmus's death in August 1881, Darwin was, it seems,
visited by the dowager Lady Hope, an evangelical temperance worker who read the Bible from door to door
among the poor, the sick, and the elderly. She later
claimed to have found Darwin himself reading the Bible,
and this story, first published in 1915, became the basis
of a deathbed-conversion legend.

About the same time, Edward Aveling (1851–98), a
young medical doctor and militant secularist, came to
lunch at Down House. It was he (not Karl Marx, as was
long believed) to whom Darwin had written, refusing
permission for an atheist primer, *The Student's Darwin*
(1881), to be dedicated to him. Books like Aveling's, and
current secularist agitation, had, in fact, probably made
Darwin cautious about his exposure in the United States,
and after lunch he remained coy. Aveling tried to extract
an atheistic confession. Darwin insisted on calling himself an agnostic. Only one subject could they agree on,
Christianity. Darwin admitted that it was not "supported
by evidence" but pointed out that he had reached this
conclusion very slowly. "I never gave up Christianity until
I was forty years of age" (Aveling 1883, 4–5). It had taken
his father's and Annie's deaths to make him shake off the
last shreds. And even then he had refused to speak out or
to assail people's faith. He never was a comrade at arms.

In this period, Darwin thought much on the eternal
questions—chance and design, providence and pain—
and struggled with despondency, feeling worn out. He
saw his last book, on earthworms, published and
resigned himself to joining them. On April 19, 1882, he
succumbed to a massive heart attack. Emma and the
daughters were present to hear him whisper, "I am not in
the least afraid to die" (F. Darwin 1887, 3:358). The family had planned for a funeral at Downe, but it was not to
be. In London, Darwin's scientific friends lobbied for a
public funeral in Westminster Abbey. Churchmen joined
in, heralding the event as a visible sign of "the reconciliation between Faith and Science" (Moore 1982, 103). On
April 26, at high noon, Darwin's body was borne up the
nave at Westminster as white-robed choristers sang: "I
am the resurrection." Behind them in the procession
came the Darwin children, followed by the elders of science, State, and Church. After the service, the coffin was
carried to the north end of the choir screen, where the
floor was draped with black cloth that dropped into the
grave. Anglican priests rubbed shoulders with agnostic
scientists; the Tory leaders closed ranks with Liberal
lords. The coffin was lowered, and the choristers sang:
"His body is buried in peace, but his name liveth evermore." Emma stayed at Downe.

See also Evolution; Evolutionary Ethics

BIBLIOGRAPHY

Abbot, Francis Ellingwood. *Truths for the Times.* Ramsgate,
   Kent: Scott, [1872].

Aveling, Edward B. *The Religious Views of Charles Darwin.*
   London: Freethought, 1883.

Brooke, John Hedley. "The Relations Between Darwin's Science
   and His Religion." In *Darwinism and Divinity: Essays on
   Evolution and Religious Belief,* ed. by John R. Durant.
   Oxford: Blackwell, 1985, 40–75.

Brown, Frank Burch. *The Evolution of Darwin's Religious
   Views.* Macon, Ga.: Mercer University Press, 1986.

Browne, Janet. "Missionaries and the Human Mind: Charles
   Darwin and Robert FitzRoy." In *Darwin's Laboratory: Evolutionary Theory and Natural History in the Pacific,* ed. by Roy
   MacLeod and Philip F. Rehbock. Honolulu: University of
   Hawaii Press, 1994, 263–82.

———. *Charles Darwin.* Vol. 1: *Voyaging.* London: Cape, 1995.

Burkhardt, Frederick et al., eds. *The Correspondence of Charles
   Darwin.* 10 vols. to date. Cambridge: Cambridge University
   Press, 1985–.

———. *A Calendar of the Correspondence of Charles Darwin,
   1821–1882, with Supplement.* Cambridge: Cambridge University Press, 1994.

Darwin, Charles. *The Foundations of the Origin of Species: Two
   Essays Written in 1842 and 1844.* Ed. by Francis Darwin.
   Cambridge: Cambridge University Press, 1909.

———. *The Autobiography of Charles Darwin, 1809–1882, with Original Omissions Restored.* Ed. by Nora Barlow. London: Collins, 1958.

———. *The Origin of Species by Charles Darwin: A Variorum Text.* Ed. by Morse Peckham. Philadelphia: University of Pennsylvania Press, 1959.

———. *Charles Darwin's Notebooks, 1836–1844: Geology, Transmutation of Species, Metaphysical Enquiries.* Ed. by Paul H. Barrett et al. Cambridge: Cambridge University Press and British Museum (Natural History), 1987.

Darwin, Francis, ed. *The Life and Letters of Charles Darwin, Including an Autobiographical Chapter.* 3 vols. London: John Murray, 1887.

Desmond, Adrian, and James Moore. *Darwin.* London: Michael Joseph, 1991.

Gillespie, Neal C. *Charles Darwin and the Problem of Creation.* Chicago: University of Chicago Press, 1979.

Kohn, David. "Darwin's Ambiguity: The Secularization of Biological Meaning." *British Journal for the History of Science* 22 (1989): 215–39.

Litchfield, Henrietta. *Emma Darwin: A Century of Family Letters, 1792–1896.* 2 vols. London: John Murray, 1915.

Moore, James. "Charles Darwin Lies in Westminster Abbey." *Biological Journal of the Linnean Society* 17 (1982): 97–113.

———. "Darwin of Down: The Evolutionist as Squarson-Naturalist." In *The Darwinian Heritage,* ed. by David Kohn. Princeton, N.J.: Princeton University Press, 1985, 435–81.

———. "Freethought, Secularism, Agnosticism: The Case of Charles Darwin." In *Religion in Victorian Britain.* Vol. 1: *Traditions,* ed. by Gerald Parsons. Manchester, U.K.: Manchester University Press, 1988, 274–319.

———. "Of Love and Death: Why Darwin 'Gave Up Christianity.'" In *History, Humanity, and Evolution: Essays for John C. Greene,* ed. by James Moore. New York: Cambridge University Press, 1989, 195–229.

———. *The Darwin Legend.* Grand Rapids, Mich.: Baker, 1994.

Ospovat, Dov. *The Development of Darwin's Theory: Natural History, Natural Theology, and Natural Selection, 1838–1859.* Cambridge: Cambridge University Press, 1981.

Powell, Baden. "On the Study of the Evidences of Christianity." In *Essays and Reviews.* Oxford: Parker, 1860, 94–144.

PART III

Intellectual Foundations and Philosophical Backgrounds

19. PLATO AND PLATONISM

Peter Losin

Plato's Life and Teachings

The written work of Plato (c. 427–347 B.C.) consists almost entirely of dialogues, all of which survive. He began writing soon after 399 B.C. (when Socrates was put to death); the latest dialogues, including the unfinished *Critias,* were probably written in the last years of his life.

The status of his influential Athenian family would have made a career as a statesman or a politician a natural one for Plato. Several events kept him from making this choice, however: the oligarchic revolt of 404 B.C., the trial and death of Socrates in 399 B.C., and three trips to Sicily (in 387, 367, and 361 B.C.), in which Plato's political naiveté nearly cost him his life. Plato showed no aptitude for, or personal interest in, active political life. The contrast between the political and the philosophical lives, and the stakes involved in choosing between them, are prominent themes in the dialogues (for example, *Gorgias, Republic, Theaetetus*).

Soon after Socrates's death, Plato apparently left Athens for Megara, where he visited Euclides (450–380 B.C.), founder of the Megarian school; Cyrene, where he visited the mathematician Theodorus (c. 460–390 B.C.); and Italy, where he visited the Pythagorean Philolaus (c. 470–390 B.C.). Some sources suggest that Plato traveled also to Egypt. The object of his travels appears to have been to establish contact with thriving philosophical and mathematical communities. Already in his late twenties, Plato showed an abiding interest in the science and mathematics of his day, and, perhaps as a result of his travels, he was able to draw accomplished scientists and mathematicians (notably, Theaetetus [414–369 B.C.], Eudoxus of Cnidus [390–340 B.C.], and Heraclides of Pontus [390–310 B.C.]) into his circle.

Of the intellectual influences on Plato, the most important was undoubtedly Socrates (469–399 B.C.), from whom Plato learned the importance of definitional questions and the value of dialectic (*dialektikê*). In addition, Plato showed himself to be well aware of the Sophists, especially their relativism and their teaching of the opposition between nature (*phusis*) and law (*nomos*). He drew on the pre-Socratic philosopher Heraclitus (540–480 B.C.) and his followers for the view that perceptible things are constantly changing. From Parmenides (515–440 B.C.) and the Eleatic school, Plato saw more clearly the problems attendant on the notion of change, the differences between "being" and "becoming," and the need to employ reasoning, not perception, in constructing adequate accounts of the world. This lesson Plato also learned from contemporary medical writers. Pythagorean mathematical discoveries confirmed the value of reasoning, the centrality of number and measure, and the importance of systematic organization of inquiry. Plato also drew on Pythagorean religious views such as the immortality of the soul and the limitations of the body. The views of other pre-Socratic writers such as Anaxagoras (500–428 B.C.), Empedocles (c. 492–432 B.C.), and the atomists are evident in Plato's work.

Plato founded the Academy sometime after his return to Athens from his travels abroad. It is impossible to date its beginning exactly, but the period 380–370 B.C. seems likely. It was not the first academy; Antisthenes (445–360 B.C.) and Isocrates (436–338 B.C.) had established schools in which rhetorical proficiency was the primary object. Unlike the practical emphasis of these schools, however, the purpose of Plato's Academy was, from the beginning, theoretical, and it is probably the first occurrence in the West of the sort of institution we now think of as academic. The curriculum was diverse, involving Plato's mathematical colleagues and natural philosophers and incorporating many of what we now regard as the liberal arts.

Most of the Platonic works with scientific or cosmological import were written while Plato was head of the Academy. Their object may have been less to convey Plato's settled views than to provoke discussion or to stimulate research. Whatever their object may have been, the fact that Plato wrote dialogues with consummate dramatic skill and that he was deeply suspicious of writing as a vehicle for conveying understanding must be noted at the outset. The probing tentativeness that is a hallmark of Plato's thought is missing from Platonism in most of its later incarnations.

In Book VII of the *Republic,* Plato outlines an educational program for the philosopher-rulers of his model city. From a young age, students are to study arithmetic, geometry, astronomy, and music. They must master these sciences before they are allowed to practice philosophy, much less to rule. What impressed Plato about these sciences is made clear in the central books of the *Republic.* Perception is of limited use in understanding the world. Perceptible things and qualities are constantly changing, and our accounts of them are confused and contradictory. Of such things, genuine knowledge (of the sort that can withstand Socratic examination) cannot be attained. So long as we rely on our senses and do not employ abstract and systematic reasoning (of which the supreme example is mathematics), the best we can hope for is opinion (*doxa*). Genuine knowledge or understanding (*nous* or *epistêmê*) requires a different kind of object, one that is stable and not susceptible to the sorts of confusing change that characterize perceptible things. These intelligible objects Plato calls Forms (*eidê*) or Ideas (*ideai*).

Throughout the dialogues, Plato treats the existence of Forms as relatively unproblematic. They are evidently distinct from perceptible things; to what degree and in what ways they are separate from such things, and just how they are related to them, are less obvious from Plato's writings, which contain differing accounts of such matters. For example, Plato frequently speaks of perceptibles as compounds or mixtures of Forms; this suggests that Forms literally constitute the perceptible things around us. (In this he is following Anaxagoras, Empedocles, and some of the philosophically inclined medical writers of his day.) In other places, Plato speaks of the Forms as paradigms or patterns and of perceptibles as

imperfect instances, shadows, or copies, or reflections of such paradigms. It is unclear whether this latter way of speaking about the Forms is intended to complement the former or to supplant it. In any case, these were matters of keen debate in the Academy. Plato's successor, Speusippus (407–339 B.C.), emphasized the transcendence of the Forms, assimilating them to Pythagorean numbers. Eudoxus emphasized the immanence of the Forms, treating them as physical ingredients in the perceptibles around us. Aristotle's (384–322 B.C.) influential criticisms of the Forms must have been honed in these debates.

What is clear is that Plato thought that the Forms could solve a number of philosophical and scientific problems bequeathed by his predecessors. For example, perceptible things *are* unstable and unknowable (as Heraclitus, Parmenides, and others held), but the Forms, which are intelligible and can be grasped securely by reasoning, are knowable and can serve as the basis of true accounts. Perceptible things *do* appear differently to different people (as the Sophist Protagoras [c. 485–411 B.C.] had noted), but, if one grasps the underlying Forms, one can both avoid being deceived by conflicting appearances and explain why the appearances conflict in the first place. The Forms are epistemically reliable because they are ontologically secure; perceptible things are neither. Clarity and understanding can be found only among intelligible things.

Plato's most notable ventures into science all follow this route. For example, in the *Timaeus,* Plato explains the apparently irregular wanderings of the planets as manifestations of underlying perfectly orderly circular motions. He reduces to order the apparently random transformations of earth, water, air, and fire by suggesting that the atoms of which everything is made are really combinations of right triangles. Equipped with such microlevel accounts, he can explain the susceptibility of our bodies to disease, the efficacy of treatment, and the processes of sensory perception, respiration, and digestion.

The influence of the *Timaeus* on later scientific and theological thought is hard to overstate. Before the systematic reintroduction of Greek philosophical works to the Latin West in the twelfth and thirteenth centuries, Chalcidius's (fourth century A.D.) Latin translation and commentary on the *Timaeus* (c. A.D. 360) was the only Platonic work widely known in the West. It is important to understand that Plato's ventures into science all serve a philosophical-ethical end. The universe is a *kosmos,* an organized and rationally accessible whole. It can be understood only because it is the product of intelligence, and intelligence always orders things for the best. This teleological emphasis is clear in very early dialogues (for example, *Gorgias*); in those of Plato's middle period, such as *Phaedo* and the *Republic*; and in those of his later years, including *Timaeus, Philebus,* and *Laws.* The presence in late dialogues of a divine Craftsman, or Demiurge, may or may not have been intended literally (this, too, was a matter hotly debated in the Academy), but the central point—that the universe is intelligible because, and to the degree that, it is the product of intelligence—is undeniably Platonic.

Plato's forays into arithmetic, geometry, astronomy, and music, as well as his metaphysical and epistemological views, provided his Academic colleagues with a productive research program. Aristotle, associated with the Academy for the last twenty years of Plato's life, contributed to this program, as did Menaechmus (fl. mid–fourth century B.C.), Heraclides, and Eudoxus. The last of these was a mathematician of great importance; in addition to inventing methods for approximating areas and volumes under curves and a theory of proportion applicable to incommensurable as well as commensurable magnitudes, Eudoxus developed an elegant model of the universe based on the idea of concentric spheres. This model, refined versions of which were visible in astronomy until the sixteenth century, may have been inspired by Plato (it is sketched in the *Timaeus*). According to an early source, Plato set his Academic colleagues this problem: "By the assumption of what uniform and orderly motions can the apparent motions of the planets be accounted for?" It is impossible to know how actively Plato contributed to Academic developments in astronomy, geometry, number theory, and the like; but his abiding interest and inspirational role in such developments is clear.

Platonism in Later Antiquity

In the decades after Plato's death, the Academy, under Arcesilaus (c. 315–241 B.C.) and later Carneades (c. 213–129 B.C.), changed its emphasis from mathematics and science to a kind of skepticism, apparently in reaction to trends in Hellenistic philosophy. Little is known about the Academy during these years. The first centuries of the common era, however, saw the development of "Middle" Platonism in Athens, Alexandria, and elsewhere. This was an uneasy synthesis of a variety of influences: Aristotelian, Stoic, Pythagorean, Hebrew, Zoroastrian, and Gnostic, among them. Plato's Forms were now conceived as Ideas in the mind of God, who was, in turn, an amalgam of Aristotle's Prime Mover and the God of the Hebrew and Christian Scriptures; matter and soul were opposed; several "grades" of reality were distinguished; and genuine knowledge or understanding was often taken to require a divine "spark" or illumination. Hints of all of these views can be found in Plato's writings, especially when one is equipped with techniques of allegorical interpretation. Such techniques, routinely practiced on the Homeric epics as well as on the scriptures, were now widely applied to philosophical texts.

The Alexandrian Jew Philo (c. 30 B.C.–A.D. 45) was heavily influenced by Middle Platonism, as were the early Christian apologists Justin Martyr (c. 100–165), Clement of Alexandria (c. 155–c. 220), and Origen (c. 185–c. 251). All four writers used Middle Platonism, especially the cosmology of the *Timaeus,* to reveal the mysteries of the Genesis account of Creation. Platonism, suitably understood, became an important ally of Jewish and Christian revelation. It is not hard to see why. Unlike Aristotle, who maintained the eternity of the world and the materiality of the soul, Plato's insistence on the immortality of the soul, the role of the Demiurge in crafting and sustaining the world, as well as the necessity of teleological explanation, could be harmonized with what had been revealed about the world in the Jewish and Christian scriptures.

The Neoplatonist movement of the third century A.D. represents a further step toward systematization and synthesis. It, too, incorporated aspects of current antimaterialist schools, especially of Platonism and Pythagoreanism. In the hands of Plotinus (A.D. 205–70), Porphyry (A.D. 232–305), and Iamblichus (A.D. 250–325), Platonic views exerted a powerful influence on early-medieval philosophy and theology, in spite of the fact that several Neoplatonists, especially in Athens, were bitterly opposed to Christianity. Plotinus, drawing on Platonic images and metaphors, posited an ineffable One as the basic constituent of the universe. From this One there arise, by a series of emanations, the Intellect, then the Soul, then Nature, and, finally, Matter. Corresponding to these emanations is a diminution in reality: Matter, which is inert unless acted on by mind, is hardly real at all. Adequate explanations even of material phenomena, then, must exhibit the workings of the nonmaterial world of mind.

The rise of Middle Platonism and Neoplatonism corresponds with the decline of Greek science, the displacement of original research by a tradition favoring commentary and compendia, and the growth of Christianity as an intellectually respectable alternative to paganism. Not all Fathers of the Church were sympathetic toward pagan (that is, Greek) philosophy, but most found ways to accommodate Plato and Platonism. Augustine (354–430) studied Neoplatonism before his conversion to Christianity, and many of his most important works attempt to reconcile the best insights of the Platonic tradition with the truths of Christianity.

Three Neoplatonist writers of late antiquity deserve special mention for their scientific contributions. Proclus (410–85), head of the Academy at Athens and critic of Christianity, wrote long commentaries on Euclid's *Elements* and on Plato's *Parmenides* and *Timaeus,* as well as an influential treatise, *Elements of Theology.* These works are among our most valuable sources of knowledge concerning ancient mathematical and scientific theory and practice. Simplicius (d. 540) wrote lengthy and learned commentaries on most of Aristotle's works, drawing on pre-Socratic and Hellenistic works in an attempt to reconcile the systems of Plato and Aristotle. John Philoponus (d. c. 570), an Alexandrian Christian and staunch anti-Aristotelian, also wrote commentaries on Aristotelian works, as well as other polemical treatises, including an attack on Proclus. His object was to show the defects of Aristotle's system and the superiority of the Christian-Neoplatonic one. His trenchant criticisms of Aristotelian dynamics are a striking anticipation of later medieval and early-modern attacks on Aristotle. Especially in the work of Simplicius and Philoponus, we see original scientific work of undeniable importance.

The Middle Ages

Soon after the Islamic conquest of western Asia in the seventh century A.D., Muslim scholars encountered Greek philosophy. By the ninth century, large numbers of Greek philosophical and scientific texts had been translated into Arabic, including works of Plato, Galen (129–c. 210), Hippocrates (c. 460–377/359 B.C.), Euclid (fl. c. 300 B.C.), and Ptolemy (second century A.D.). Plato's views, especially those of the *Timaeus,* attracted Islamic theologians for the same reasons they had attracted Christian ones. Since many of the Arabic writers whose philosophical views were most influential were also physicians or scientists, the *Timaeus* was especially important. Among those most clearly influenced by Pla-

tonism were the mathematician al-Kindi (800–70), the musical theorist al-Farabi (873–950), and (as a critic) Avicenna (Ibn Sina [980–1037]). Later Islamic philosophical and scientific developments, however, appear to owe more to Aristotelian traditions than to Platonic ones.

The revival of learning in the Latin West during the twelfth century kindled a renewed interest in Greek and Latin texts. Although attention was largely devoted to grammar and rhetoric, Plato's *Timaeus,* together with Chalcidius's commentary, inspired a number of significant and original thinkers. Two deserve special mention. In his *Treatise on the Six Days of Creation,* Thierry of Chartres (c. 1100–c. 1156) attempted a detailed accommodation of the biblical account of Creation to that given in the *Timaeus.* William of Conches (1080–1160) wrote long commentaries on the *Timaeus* and the Book of Genesis and an influential treatise, *The Philosophy of the World,* with a similar aim. Both thinkers offered and defended mechanisms by which God's creative purposes were achieved. They invoked processes such as heating and cooling, evaporation and condensation, together with the natural motion of the four elements, to account for the sequence of events following God's initial creative act in the Genesis story. Drawing on Platonic and Stoic views, these thinkers distinguished between what was created directly by God and what resulted from interactions among things God had endowed with causal properties of their own. These properties (the "natures" of things) can be studied on their own, without appeal to God's activity. And, because of the close relations between macrocosm (the universe) and microcosm (individual person), human beings, too, must be seen as part of this natural order and should be studied accordingly. This naturalistic perspective (which accounted for the efficacy of astrology and theurgy, as well as scientific inquiry) held obvious dangers for religious orthodoxy, but they were partly offset by the insistence that the natural order was itself a product of God's handiwork.

The value of Platonic stock fell considerably in the late twelfth and thirteenth centuries as a result of the systematic translation of the Aristotelian corpus into Latin. Among the earliest Aristotelian works translated were those with scientific ramifications: *Physics, On the Heavens, Meteorology,* and *On Generation and Corruption.* The "likely story" of Plato's *Timaeus* was no match for Aristotle's rigorous and detailed cosmological treatises. Further, the scope and interconnectedness of the Aristotelian corpus were well suited to the setting of the new universities.

The new interest in Aristotelian natural philosophy had its benefits for the study of Plato, however. Not only were the Aristotelian texts made available in translation; many of the ancient commentaries were as well. Some of them, such as those of Simplicius and Philoponus, contained valuable information about early Platonism as well as its pre-Socratic forerunners. The availability of these commentaries provided a much fuller picture of Platonic claims and arguments and their context than had previously been available. It became possible, for the first time in more than a thousand years, to begin to distinguish Plato's own opinions from those of the later traditions that grew up around them.

Plato's writings never disappeared from the curriculum altogether. In a famous remark, Petrarch (1304–74) writes: "More men praise Aristotle; the better ones, Plato." While the Platonic cosmology typically yielded to the Aristotelian when the two diverged, it had the virtues of affirming both God's role as Creator and the creation of the world in time and of not supporting a rigorously deterministic world. Of the thirteen propositions condemned in 1270 by the bishop of Paris, and the 219 condemned in 1277, the vast majority were of Aristotelian, not Platonic, provenance.

Platonic influences are not hard to find in thirteenth-century Oxford natural philosophy. Robert Grosseteste (c. 1168–1253), like the Chartres Platonists of the twelfth century, put Platonic and Neoplatonic metaphysical ideas to "scientific" use. Borrowing Neoplatonist images of light (which, in turn, drew on Platonic similes, such as the sun in *Republic* V), Grosseteste suggested that the propagation of light was the key to understanding God's creative activity. Both Grosseteste and Roger Bacon (1213–91) drew from Platonic and Aristotelian sources in developing their distinctive views on scientific methods, the place of mathematics in the study of nature, and the relations between scientific and theological inquiry.

The Renaissance and Early-Modern Period

Nevertheless, throughout the thirteenth and fourteenth centuries, Aristotle's importance waxed as Plato's waned. It was not until the Renaissance in the fifteenth century, and the growth of humanistic learning outside the university, that Plato's writings recovered some of their former currency. Among Italian humanists, Plato's writings were initially prized for their literary and dramatic qualities; it was not until the late fifteenth century, with the Christian Platonism of Nicholas of Cusa (1401–64) and Marsilio Ficino (1433–99), that the philosophical and cosmological richness of the Platonic tradition regained some of its former place. Nevertheless, Plato's works were repeatedly translated in the fifteenth century, and in 1484 Ficino published a complete edition of the Platonic dialogues in Latin. These translations and the lengthy commentaries Ficino wrote to accompany them were widely used in the early-modern period.

The new mechanistic philosophy of the early seventeenth century provoked a resurgence of interest in Platonism at Cambridge. Among the so-called Cambridge Platonists, Ralph Cudworth (1617–88) and Henry More (1614–87) invoked Platonic images and arguments against Hobbesian materialism and Cartesian mechanism. By emphasizing the need for contemplation and illumination, the Platonism of Cudworth and More contributed to an effort to unify an English Church riven by decades of bloody faction.

Of the major figures of the scientific revolution, the most clearly indebted to Plato was Johannes Kepler (1571–1630). Kepler's most important cosmological works owed their inspiration and many of their basic principles to the *Timaeus*. Kepler's underlying conviction that there must be elegant mathematical laws underlying the apparently anomalous planetary motions is certainly Platonic and Pythagorean. It gave rise to both Kepler's relatively sober three laws of planetary motion and his fanciful speculations about the arrangements of the planetary orbits.

From the early days of the Academy, Platonism has meant different things to different people, and it was frequently defined in opposition to other views. In part, this is because Plato articulated many of his own positions in the course of polemics against other views. Yet, the positive doctrines of Platonism—the emphasis on teleology and on nonmaterial aspects of explanation, the insistence on the inadequacy of perception and the connection between the intelligible and the real, and the faith that there is order and reason at the heart of things—have been, and continue to be, a vital force in the philosophical, scientific, and religious thought of the Western tradition.

See also Cambridge Platonists

BIBLIOGRAPHY

Anton, J. P., ed. *Science and the Sciences in Plato.* Delmar, N.Y.: Caravan Books, 1980.

Bowen, Alan C., ed. *Science and Philosophy in Classical Greece.* New York: Garland, 1991.

Cornford, F. M. *Plato's Cosmology.* London: Routledge and Kegan Paul, 1937.

Crombie, A. C. *Styles of Scientific Thinking in the European Tradition.* London: Duckworth, 1994.

Dillon, John R. *The Middle Platonists: A Study of Platonism, 80 B.C. to A.D. 120.* London: Duckworth, 1977.

Fowler, D. H. *The Mathematics of Plato's Academy: A New Reconstruction.* Oxford: Clarendon, 1987.

Gersh, Stephen. *Middle Platonism and Neoplatonism: The Latin Tradition.* 2 vols. Notre Dame, Ind.: University of Notre Dame Press, 1986.

Gerson, Lloyd P. *God and Greek Philosophy: Studies in the Early History of Natural Theology.* London: Routledge, 1990.

Gregory, Tullio. "The Platonic Inheritance." In *A History of Twelfth-Century Western Philosophy,* ed. by Peter Dronke. Cambridge: Cambridge University Press, 1988, 54–80.

Jaeger, Werner. *The Theology of the Early Greek Philosophers.* Oxford: Clarendon, 1947.

Lee, Edward N. "Reason and Rotation: Circular Movement as the Model of Mind (*Nous*) in Later Plato." In *Facets of Plato's Philosophy,* ed. by W. H. Werkmeister. Assen: Van Gorcum, 1976, 70–102.

Lindberg, David C. *The Beginnings of Western Science: The European Scientific Tradition in Philosophical, Religious, and Institutional Context, 600 B.C. to A.D. 1450.* Chicago: University of Chicago Press, 1992.

Lloyd, G. E. R. "Plato as Natural Scientist." *Journal of Hellenic Studies* 88 (1968): 78–92.

———. "Plato on Mathematics and Nature, Myth and Science." In Lloyd, G.E.R., *Methods and Problems in Greek Science.* Cambridge: Cambridge University Press, 1991, 333–51.

Mohr, Richard D. *The Platonic Cosmology.* Leiden: E. J. Brill, 1985.

Patrides, C. A. *The Cambridge Platonists.* London: Edward Arnold, 1969.

Robinson, T. M. "The World as Art-Object: Science and the Real in Plato's Timaeus." *Illinois Classical Studies* 18 (1993): 99–111.

Solmsen, Friedrich. *Plato's Theology.* Ithaca, N.Y.: Cornell University Press, 1942.

Southern, R. W. *Platonism, Scholastic Method, and the School of Chartres.* Reading, U.K.: Reading University Press, 1979.

Taylor, A. E. *A Commentary on Plato's Timaeus.* Oxford: Clarendon, 1928.

Vlastos, Gregory. "Disorderly Motion in the *Timaeus.*" *Classical Quarterly* 33 (1939): 71–83. Reprinted in Vlastos, Gregory, *Studies in Greek Philosophy.* Vol. 2: *Socrates, Plato, and Their Tradition,* ed. by Daniel W. Graham. Princeton, N.J.: Princeton University Press, 1995, 247–64.

———. "Creation in the Timaeus: Is It a Fiction?" In *Studies in Plato's Metaphysics,* ed. by R. E. Allen. London: Routledge and Kegan Paul, 1965. Reprinted in Vlastos, Gregory, *Studies in Greek Philosophy.* Vol.2: *Socrates, Plato, and Their Tradition,* ed. by Daniel W. Graham. Princeton, N.J.: Princeton University Press, 1995, 265–79.

———. *Plato's Universe.* Seattle: University of Washington Press, 1975.

Wetherbee, Winthrop. "Philosophy, Cosmology, and the Twelfth-Century Renaissance." In *A History of Twelfth-Century Western Philosophy,* ed. by Peter Dronke. Cambridge: Cambridge University Press, 1988, 21–53.

20. ARISTOTLE AND ARISTOTELIANISM

Edward Grant

No one in the history of civilization has shaped our understanding of science and natural philosophy more than the great Greek philosopher and scientist Aristotle (384–322 B.C.), who exerted a profound and pervasive influence for more than two thousand years, extending from the fourth century B.C. to the end of the seventeenth century A.D. During this long period, Aristotle's numerous Greek treatises were translated into a variety of languages, most notably Arabic and Latin. He was, thus, a dominant intellectual force in at least three great civilizations that ranged over a vast geographical area, embracing sequentially the Byzantine Empire (which succeeded the Roman Empire in the east), the civilization of Islam, and the Latin Christian civilization of western Europe in the late Middle Ages.

Aristotle's dazzling success is not difficult to understand. Early on, and before anyone else, he left treatises on a breathtaking variety of topics that included logic, natural philosophy, metaphysics, biology, ethics, psychology, politics, poetics, rhetoric, and economics (or household management). Because they seemed to embrace almost all knowledge worth having, Aristotle's works could readily serve as guides to an understanding of the structure and operation of the physical universe, as well as to human and animal behavior. Aristotle's collected works bulked so large in history because relatively little survived intact from the works of his predecessors on the subjects about which he wrote. In some of those subjects, logic and biology, for example, there is reason to believe that he may have written the first comprehensive treatises and been the first to define those disciplines. Moreover, until the sixteenth and seventeenth centuries, Aristotle's interpretation of the world had few significant rivals. He was usually regarded as the preeminent guide for understanding the material and immaterial worlds.

Aristotle covered such a wide range of learning that many subsequent scholars found it convenient to present their own ideas on those subjects by way of commentaries on one or more of his works. Over the centuries, many such commentaries were written, primarily in the Greek, Arabic, and Latin languages. Taken collectively, they form the phenomenon called Aristotelianism, although that phenomenon is much broader because Aristotle's ideas were also injected into other disciplines, most notably medicine and theology.

Although Aristotle's natural philosophy and metaphysics reveal an interest in the divine, they were written without regard for any of the religious concerns that subsequently proved critical to the civilizations of Christianity and Islam, in which Aristotle's philosophy was a major factor. Aristotle's treatises on natural philosophy and metaphysics form the basis of his interpretation of the material and immaterial entities that make up our world. His natural philosophy essentially comprises five treatises: the *Physics,* which treats of motion, matter and form, place, vacuum, time, the infinite, and the Prime Mover; *On the Heavens (De caelo),* which is devoted largely to cosmology; *On Generation and Corruption,* which is concerned with elements, compounds, and material change generally; *Meteorology,* which describes phenomena in the upper atmosphere just below the moon; and *On the Soul (De anima)*, in which Aristotle treats different levels of soul and discusses perception and the senses. Aristotle's metaphysics, or "first philosophy," or "theology," as it was sometimes called, is embodied in his work titled *Metaphysics*. In this basic work, Aristotle analyzes the nature of immaterial being wholly divorced from matter. Despite its problematic nature, Christian theologians found the *Metaphysics* an invaluable resource for confronting difficult problems about God's nature and existence.

Aristotle's Theology

Aristotle's metaphysics and natural philosophy had a profound, and often disquieting, effect on the theologians and religious guardians of the monotheistic religions of Christianity, Islam, and Judaism. Various elements in Aristotle's philosophy were relevant to theology, most notably his conviction that the world is eternal: that it had no beginning and would never have an end. Aristotle could find no convincing argument for supposing that our world could have come into being naturally from any prior state of material existence. For if the world came from a previously existing material thing, say B, we would then have to inquire from whence did B come, and so on through an infinite regression, since it was assumed that the world could not have come from nothing. To avoid this dilemma, Aristotle concluded that the world had no beginning and, therefore, that it could have no end, for if it could end, it could, necessarily, have had a beginning.

Despite his conviction that the world was uncreated, Aristotle did believe in a divine spirit, or God. But the attributes he assigned to his God, whom he called an "Unmoved Mover," would have been strange, and perhaps repugnant, to anyone raised in one of the three traditional monotheistic religions. Obviously, Aristotle's God was not the creator of our world, since it is uncreated. Indeed, he is not even aware of the world's existence and, therefore, does not, and could not, concern himself with anything in our world. Such a deity could not, therefore, be an object of worship. The only activity fit for such a God is pure thought. But the only thoughts worthy of his exalted status are thoughts about himself. Totally remote from the universe, Aristotle's God thinks only about himself.

Despite his total isolation from the world, the God of Aristotle unknowingly exerted a profound influence on it. He was its "Unmoved Mover," causing the orbs and the heavens to move around with eternal circular motions. The celestial orbs move around eternally because of their love for the Unmoved Mover. By virtue of these incessant motions, the celestial orbs cause all other motions in the world. Thus was Aristotle's Unmoved Mover, or God, the final cause of all cosmic motions.

Aristotle's view of the human soul also proved problematic. He regarded the soul as a principle of life that was inseparable from its body. Aristotle distinguished three levels of soul: (1) the nutritive, or vegetative, soul, which is found in both plants and animals and is solely concerned with the nutrition essential for the sustenance of the organism's life; (2) the sensitive soul, which is possessed only by animals and oversees motion, desire, and sense perception; and (3) the rational soul, which is found only in humans and subsumes the two lower levels of soul to form a single, unified soul in each human being. Each human soul contains an active and a passive intellect. Our thoughts are formed from images abstracted by the active intellect and implanted in the passive intellect as concepts. Except for the active intellect, which is immortal, the soul perishes with the body. Whether Aristotle regarded an individual's active intellect as personally immortal or whether he thought it loses its individuality when it rejoins the universal active intellect is unclear. Those who wished to "save" Aristotle and reconcile his view with the Christian conception of the soul opted for the first alternative, even though such an interpretation involved an elastic view of Christian doctrine.

Aristotle's strong sense of what was possible and impossible in natural philosophy posed serious problems for his Christian, Muslim, and Jewish followers. On a number of vital themes, he presented demonstrations to show that nature was necessarily constrained to operate in one particular way rather than another way. The question confronting Aristotle's followers, then, was whether God could have created our world to operate in ways that Aristotle regarded as impossible.

Later Antiquity, Byzantium, and Islam

Such difficulties were of little concern to the earliest commentators, who were pagans like Aristotle himself. Not until members of the great monotheistic religions began to comment on the works of Aristotle did problems arise. Although the names of the earliest commentators are unknown, commentaries on Aristotle's works were probably written in the Hellenistic period (323–30 B.C.), shortly after his death, and they continued on through the duration of the Roman Empire (30 B.C.–A.D. 476). The historical emergence of the Aristotelian commentary tradition took place in the Greek-speaking area that would become the Byzantine Empire in the eastern Mediterranean world. Here, beginning in the third century A.D., a group of commentators writing in Greek began the historical development of Aristotelianism (the tradition of commenting on the works of Aristotle). The most prominent of these were Alexander of Aphrodisias (fl. second or third century), Themistius (317–c. 388), Simplicius (d. 540), and, especially, the Christian Neoplatonic author John Philoponus (d. c. 570), who rejected many of Aristotle's basic concepts about the nature of the world. After the translation of some of their works into Arabic, these Greek commentators exercised a significant influence on Islam.

Because of religious hostility to Aristotle's natural philosophy, the number of Aristotelian commentators in Islam was not large. The most important of them—al-Kindi (800–70), al-Farabi (873–950), Avicenna (Ibn Sina [980–1037]), and Averroës (Ibn Rushd [1126–98])—were translated into Latin and exerted a major influence in the European Middle Ages—in some instances, playing a greater role in Christendom than in Islam. Three of the most important charges against Aristotle's natural philosophy were: (1) his advocacy of the eternity of the world; (2) the conviction that his natural philosophy was hostile to the basic Muslim belief in the resurrection of the body; and (3) his concept of secondary causation. In Islamic thought, the term "philosopher" (*faylasuf*) was often reserved for those who assumed, with Aristotle, that natural things were capable of causing effects, as when a magnet attracts iron and causes it to move or when a horse pulls a wagon and is seen as the direct cause of the wagon's motion. On this approach, God was not viewed as the immediate cause of every effect. Philosophers believed, with Aristotle, that natural objects could cause effects in other natural objects because things had natures that enabled them to act on other things and to be acted upon. By contrast, most Muslim theologians believed, on the basis of the Koran, that God caused everything directly and immediately and that natural things were incapable of acting directly on other natural things. Although secondary causation was usually assumed in scientific research, most Muslim theologians opposed it.

The European Middle Ages

Aristotle's ideas were destined to play a monumental role in western Europe. In the twelfth and thirteenth centuries, his works, along with much of Islamic science and natural philosophy, were translated from Arabic into Latin. The Arabic commentaries on Aristotle spoke favorably of the philosopher and, once translated, were often used in Europe as guides to his thought. Indeed, Averroës, who was probably the greatest of all Aristotelian commentators, was known to all simply as "the Commentator."

Until the thirteenth century, Aristotelian commentators were a disparate group scattered in time and place. All of this changed, however, with the emergence of universities around 1200. Aristotle's thought achieved a widespread prominence as his logic, natural philosophy, and metaphysics became the basis of the curriculum leading to the baccalaureate and master of arts degrees. As a result, universities in western Europe—and by 1500 there were approximately sixty of them in Europe, extending as far east as Poland—became the institutional base for Aristotelianism. A relatively large class of professional teachers developed who were specialists in Aristotelian thought, and a much larger class of nonteaching scholars emerged who had studied Aristotelian natural philosophy and metaphysics in depth. Nothing like this had ever been seen before. For the first time in history, natural philosophy, the exact sciences (primarily geometry, arithmetic, astronomy, and optics), and medicine were permanently rooted in an institution, the university, that has endured for approximately eight hundred years and has been established worldwide.

By the end of the thirteenth century, the method of teaching both theology and Aristotle's natural philosophy, which significantly influenced theology, was to proceed by way of a series of questions. Indeed, the very titles of many of the treatises indicate their pedagogical method. For example, in his *Questions on Aristotle's Book on the Heavens,* John Buridan (c. 1295–c. 1358), perhaps the greatest arts master of the Middle Ages, proposed and responded to the following questions: "whether there are several worlds"; "whether the sky is always moved regularly"; "whether the stars are self-moved or moved by the motion of their spheres"; "whether the earth always rests in the middle [or center] of the world"; and many others about the terrestrial and celestial regions. Similar questions were posed in various treatises on Aristotle's other works. Peter Lombard (c. 1100–c. 1160), for example, employed the questions format in his *Sentences.* Composed in the 1140s, *Sentences* was the great theological textbook of the late Middle Ages, an essential work on which all bachelors in theology lectured and commented. Many of the questions fused natural philosophy and theology, utilizing natural philosophy to resolve theological issues, especially in the second book, which considered the Creation. They covered such matters as "whether God could make a better universe"; "whether the empyrean heaven is luminous"; "whether light is a real form"; "whether the heaven is the cause of these inferior things"; "whether every spiritual substance is in a place"; "whether God could make something new"; and "whether God could make an actual infinite."

Logic, natural philosophy, and the exact sciences, along with the scholastic methods for treating these subjects, became permanent features of medieval universities. But the entry of natural philosophy into the curriculum of the University of Paris, the premier university of western Europe during the Middle Ages, differed markedly from its entry into other contemporary universities, such as Oxford and Bologna. While the exact sciences and medicine encountered little opposition, Aristotelian natural philosophy met a different fate. Christianity, during its first six centuries, had adjusted fairly easily to pagan Greek learning and had adopted the attitude that Greek philosophy and natural philosophy should be used as "handmaidens to theology" (that is, they should be studied for the light they shed on Scripture and theological problems and for any insights they might offer for a better understanding of God's Creation). Nevertheless, some influential theologians in Paris, specifically those at the university, were deeply concerned about the potential dangers that Aristotelian natural philosophy posed for the faith. During the first half of the thirteenth century, the Parisian authorities first banned the works of Aristotle, decreeing in 1210 and 1215 that they were not to be read in public or private. Subsequently, in 1231, they sought to expurgate his works, an intention that was apparently never carried out. By 1255, Aristotle's works had been adopted as the official curriculum at the University of Paris. Efforts to deny entry of Aristotelian natural philosophy into the University of Paris failed utterly. The reason is obvious: For Christians, the value of Aristotle's works, and the commentaries thereon, far outweighed any potential danger they might pose.

During the second half of the thirteenth century, a number of conservative theologians, who were still concerned about the impact of Aristotelian thought, changed their means of attack. Rather than attempt to ban or expurgate Aristotle's works, they now sought to identify and condemn specific ideas that they believed were dangerous to the faith. When it became apparent that repeated warnings about the perils of secular philosophy were to no avail, the traditional theologians appealed to the bishop of Paris, Etienne Tempier (d. 1279). In 1270, Tempier intervened and condemned 13 articles that were derived from the teachings of Aristotle or were upheld by his great commentator, Averroës. In 1272, the masters of arts at the University of Paris instituted an oath that compelled them to avoid consideration of theological questions. If, for any reason, an arts master found himself unable to avoid a theological issue, he was further sworn to resolve it in favor of the faith. The intensity of the controversy was underscored by Giles of Rome's (c. 1243–1316) *Errors of the Philosophers,* written sometime between 1270 and 1274, in which Giles compiled a list of errors drawn from the works of the non-Christian philosophers Aristotle, Averroës, Avicenna, al-Ghazali (1058–1111), al-Kindi, and Moses Maimonides (1135–1204). When these countermoves failed to resolve the turmoil or abate the controversy, a concerned Pope John XXI instructed the bishop of Paris, still Etienne Tempier, to initiate an investigation. Within three weeks, in March 1277, Tempier, acting on the advice of his theological advisers, issued a massive condemnation of 219 articles. Excommunication was the penalty for holding or defending any one of them. Although the condemned articles were drawn up in haste without apparent order and with little concern for consistency or repetition, many, if not most, of the 219 articles reflected issues that were directly associated with Aristotle's natural philosophy and, hence, form part of the history of the reception of Aristotelian learning. Some 27 of the articles—more than 10 percent—condemned the eternity of the world in a variety of guises. Numerous articles were condemned because they set limits on God's absolute power to do things that were deemed impossible in Aristotle's natural philosophy.

Scattered through the works of Aristotle were propositions and conclusions demonstrating the natural impossibility of certain phenomena. For example, Aristotle had shown that it was impossible for a vacuum to occur naturally inside or outside the world, and he had also demonstrated the impossibility that other worlds might exist naturally beyond ours. Theologians came to view these Aristotelian claims of natural impossibility as restrictions on God's absolute power to do as he pleased. Just because Aristotle had declared it impossible, why should an omnipotent God not be able to produce a vacuum inside or outside the world, if he chose to do so? Why could he not create other worlds, if he wished to do so? Why should he not be able to produce an accident without a subject? And why should he not be able to produce new things in the world that he had created long ago? A condemned article was issued for each of these restrictions on God's power. As if to reinforce all of the specific articles, the bishop of Paris and his colleagues included a separate article (147) that condemned the general opinion that God could not do what was judged impossible in natural philosophy.

By appeal to the concept of God's absolute power, medieval natural philosophers introduced subtle and imaginative questions that often generated novel responses. By conceding that God could create other worlds, they inquired about the nature of those worlds. By assuming that God could, if he wished, create vacuums anywhere in the universe, they were stimulated to pose questions about the behavior of bodies in such hypothetical vacuums. They asked, for example, whether bodies would move with finite or infinite speeds in such empty spaces. They posed similar questions about a variety of imaginary, hypothetical physical situations. Although these speculative questions and their responses did not cause the overthrow of the Aristotelian worldview, they did challenge some of its fundamental principles and assumptions. They made many aware that things might be quite otherwise than were dreamt of in Aristotle's philosophy.

Despite the adverse theological reaction to some of Aristotle's ideas and attitudes during the thirteenth century, it would be a serious error to suppose that medieval theologians in general opposed Aristotelian natural philosophy. If the majority of theologians had chosen to oppose Aristotelian learning as dangerous to the faith, it could not have become the focus of studies in the universities. But theologians had no compelling reason to oppose it. Western Christianity had a long-standing tradition of using pagan thought for its own benefit. As supporters of that tradition, medieval theologians treated the new Greco-Arabic learning in the same manner—as a welcome addition that would enhance their understanding of Scripture.

Indeed, we can justifiably characterize medieval theologians as theologian–natural philosophers, since almost all of them were thoroughly trained in natural philosophy, which was a virtual prerequisite for students entering the higher faculty of theology. So enthusiastically did these theologian–natural philosophers incorporate natural philosophy into their theological treatises that the Church had to admonish them, from time to time, to refrain from frivolously employing it in the resolution of theological questions. Some of the most significant contributors to science, mathematics, and natural philosophy came from the ranks of theologians, as is obvious from the illustrious names of Albertus Magnus (1193–1280), Robert Grosseteste (c. 1168–1253), John Pecham (d. 1292), Theodoric of Freiberg (d. c. 1310), Thomas Bradwardine (c. 1290–1349), Nicole Oresme (c. 1320–82), and Henry of Langenstein (fl. 1385–93). The positive attitude of medieval theologians toward Aristotelian natural philosophy, and their belief that it was a useful tool for the elucidation of theology, must be viewed as the end product of a long-standing attitude that was developed and nurtured during the first four or five centuries of Christianity and maintained thereafter in the Latin West.

The Early-Modern Period

Because Aristotle's works formed the basis of the medieval university curriculum, Aristotelianism emerged as the primary, and virtually unchallenged, intellectual system of western Europe during the thirteenth to fifteenth centuries. Not only did it provide the mechanisms of explanation for natural phenomena, it also served as a gigantic filter through which the world was viewed. Whatever opposition theologians may once have offered to it, by the thirteenth century that opposition had long ceased. Aristotelian physics and cosmology were triumphant and dominant. By the sixteenth and seventeenth centuries, however, rival natural philosophies had materialized following a wave of translations of new Greek philosophical texts previously unknown in the West. Opposition to Aristotelianism now became widespread. As a direct consequence of the new science that was emerging in the first half of the seventeenth century, the positive medieval attitude toward science and natural philosophy that prevailed in the late Middle Ages underwent significant change. In the aftermath of the Council of Trent (1545–63), the Roman Catholic Church came to link the defense of the faith with a literal interpretation of those biblical passages that clearly placed an immobile earth at the center of the cosmos. By this move, it aligned itself with the traditional Aristotelian-Ptolemaic geocentric universe in opposition to the Copernican heliocentric system. In 1633, the Church condemned Galileo (1564–1642) for upholding the truth of the Copernican heliocentric planetary theory. By condemning Galileo, the Church and its theologians came to be viewed as obscurantists who were hostile to science and natural philosophy. Instead of confining that opinion to Aristotelian scholasticism of the seventeenth century, when Aristotelian natural philosophy was under assault and nearing the end of its dominance in European intellectual life, the critics of Aristotle and Aristotelianism indiscriminately included the late Middle Ages in that judgment and viewed it as an equally unenlightened period.

In this way, medieval attitudes toward science and natural philosophy have been seriously distorted. The aftermath of Galileo's condemnation produced hostility and contempt toward the late Middle Ages. Not only was the attitude of theologians toward natural philosophy misrepresented, but the positive role that Aristotle and Aristotelian natural philosophers played in the history of science was ignored, as was the legacy they bequeathed to the seventeenth century. More than anyone else in the history of Western thought, it was Aristotle who molded and shaped the scientific temperament. He was the model for the Middle Ages. Gradually, medieval scholars reshaped and supplemented Aristotle's methods and insights by their own genius and fashioned a more sophisticated body of natural philosophy, which they passed on to the scientists and natural philosophers of the seventeenth century. This legacy included a variety of methodological approaches to nature that had been applied to a large body of important questions and problems about matter, motion, and vacuums. These questions were taken up by nonscholastic natural philosophers in the seventeenth century. Initially, the scientific revolution involved the formulation of successful responses to old questions that had been posed during the Middle Ages.

Embedded in the vast medieval Aristotelian commentary literature was a precious gift to early-modern science: an extensive and sophisticated body of terms that formed the basis of scientific discourse. Terms such as "potential," "actual," "substance," "property," "accident," "cause," "analogy," "matter," "form," "essence," "genus," "species," "relation," "quantity," "quality," "place," "vacuum," and "infinite" formed a significant component of scholastic natural philosophy. The language of medieval natural philosophy, however, did not consist solely of

translated Aristotelian terms. New concepts, terms, and definitions were added, most notably in the domains of change and motion, in which new definitions were fashioned for concepts like uniform motion, uniformly accelerated motion, and instantaneous motion.

The universities of the Middle Ages, in which natural philosophy and science were largely conducted, also conveyed a remarkable tradition of relatively free, rational inquiry. The medieval philosophical tradition was fashioned in the faculties of arts of medieval universities. Natural philosophy was their domain, and, almost from the outset, masters of arts struggled to establish as much academic freedom as possible. They sought to preserve and expand the study of philosophy. Arts masters regarded themselves as the guardians of natural philosophy, and they strove mightily for the right to apply reason to all problems concerning the physical world. By virtue of their independent status as a faculty with numerous rights and privileges, they achieved a surprising degree of freedom. During the Middle Ages, natural philosophy remained what Aristotle had made it: an essentially secular and rational enterprise. It remained so only because the arts faculty, whose members were the teachers and guardians of natural philosophy, struggled to preserve it. In the process, they transformed natural philosophy into an independent discipline that had as its objective the rational investigation of all problems relevant to the physical world. However, the success of the arts masters was dependent on the theological faculties, which were sympathetic to the development of natural philosophy. Despite the problems of the thirteenth century, medieval theologians were as eager to pursue that discipline as were the arts masters. If that had not been so, medieval natural philosophy would never have attained the heights it reached, nor would it have been so extensively employed. For not only was natural philosophy imported into theology, especially into theological commentaries on the *Sentences* of Peter Lombard, the textbook of the theological schools for five centuries, but it was also integrated into medicine, both in the standard textbooks of physicians such as Galen (129–c. 210), Avicenna, and Averroës and in the numerous medical commentaries by physicians who were thoroughly acquainted with Aristotle's natural philosophy and recognized its importance for medicine. Even music theorists occasionally found it convenient to introduce concepts from natural philosophy to elucidate musical themes and ideas.

Finally, the seventeenth century also inherited from the late Middle Ages the profound sense that all of these activities were legitimate and important; that discovering the way the world operated was a laudable undertaking. Without the crucial centuries of medieval Aristotelianism to serve as a foundation, the scientific revolution of the seventeenth century would have been long delayed or might still lie in the future.

See also Islam; Medieval Science and Religion; Natural History; Plurality of Worlds and Extraterrestrial Life; Thomas Aquinas and Thomism; Varieties of Providentialism

BIBLIOGRAPHY

Callus, D. A. "The Introduction of Aristotelian Learning to Oxford." *Proceedings of the British Academy* 29 (1943): 229–81.

Courtenay, W. J. "Theology and Theologians from Ockham to Wyclif." In *The History of the University of Oxford.* Vol. 2. Ed. by J. I. Catto and Ralph Evans. Oxford: Clarendon, 1992, 1–34.

Evans, Gillian R. *Philosophy and Theology in the Middle Ages.* London and New York: Routledge, 1993.

Fletcher, John M. "Some Considerations of the Role of the Teaching of Philosophy in the Medieval Universities." *British Journal for the History of Philosophy* 2(1) (1994): 3–18.

Gabriel, Astrik L. "Metaphysics in the Curriculum of Studies in the Mediaeval Universities." In *Die Metaphysik im Mittelalter,* ed. by P. Wilpert. Berlin: Walter de Gruyter, 1963, 92–102.

Grant, Edward. "Aristotelianism and the Longevity of the Medieval World View." *History of Science* 16 (1978): 93–106.

———. "The Condemnation of 1277, God's Absolute Power, and Physical Thought in the Late Middle Ages." *Viator* 10 (1979): 211–44.

———. "Science and the Medieval University." In *Rebirth, Reform, and Resilience: Universities in Transition, 1300–1700,* ed. by James M. Kittelson and Pamela J. Transue. Columbus: Ohio State University Press, 1984, 68–102.

———. "Science and Theology in the Middle Ages." In *God and Nature: Historical Essays on the Encounter Between Christianity and Science,* ed. by David C. Lindberg and Ronald L. Numbers. Berkeley: University of California Press, 1986, 49–75.

———. "Ways to Interpret the Terms 'Aristotelian' and 'Aristotelianism' in Medieval and Renaissance Natural Philosophy." *History of Science* 25 (1987): 335–58.

———. "Medieval Departures from Aristotelian Natural Philosophy." In *Studies in Medieval Natural Philosophy,* ed. by Stefano Caroti. Biblioteca di Nuncius. Florence: Olschki, 1989, 237–56.

———. *The Foundations of Modern Science in the Middle Ages: Their Religious, Institutional, and Intellectual Contexts.* Cambridge: Cambridge University Press, 1996.

Iorio, Dominick A. *The Aristotelians of Renaissance Italy.* Lewiston, N.Y.: Edwin Mellen, 1991.

McKeon, Richard P. "Aristotelianism in Western Christianity." In *Environmental Factors in Christian History,* ed. by John Thomas McNeill. Chicago: University of Chicago Press, 1939, 206–31.

Murdoch, John E. "The Analytic Character of Late Medieval Learning: Natural Philosophy Without Nature." In *Approaches to Nature in the Middle Ages,* ed. by L. D. Roberts. Binghamton, N.Y.: Center for Medieval and Early Renaissance Studies, 1982, 171–213. See also "Comment" by Norman Kretzmann, 214–20.

Murdoch, John E. "The Involvement of Logic in Late Medieval Natural Philosophy." In *Studies in Medieval Natural Philosophy,* ed. by Stefano Caroti. Biblioteca di Nuncius. Florence: Olschki, 1989, 3–28.

North, J. D. "Natural Philosophy in Late Medieval Oxford." In *The History of the University of Oxford.* Vol. 2. Ed. by J. I. Catto and Ralph Evans. Oxford: Clarendon, 1992, 65–102.

Sabra, Abdelhamid I. "Science and Philosophy in Medieval Islamic Theology: The Evidence of the Fourteenth Century." *Zeitschrift für Geschichte der Arabisch-Islamischen Wissenschaften* 9 (1994): 1–42.

Schmitt, Charles B. *Aristotle and the Renaissance.* Cambridge, Mass.: Published for Oberlin College by Harvard University Press, 1983.

Steenberghen, Fernand Van. *Aristotle in the West: The Origins of Latin Aristotelianism.* Trans. by L. Johnston. Louvain: Nauwelaerts, 1955.

———. *The Philosophical Movement in the Thirteenth Century.* Edinburgh: Nelson, 1955.

Sylla, Edith D. "Autonomous and Handmaiden Science: St. Thomas Aquinas and William of Ockham on the Physics of the Eucharist." In *The Cultural Context of Medieval Learning,* ed. by John E. Murdoch and Edith D. Sylla. Dordrecht and Boston: D. Reidel, 1975, 349–96.

———. "Physics." In *Dictionary of the Middle Ages.* Vol. 9. Ed. by Joseph R. Strayer. New York: Charles Scribner's Sons, 1987, 620–28.

Wallace, William A. "Aristotle in the Middle Ages." In *Dictionary of the Middle Ages.* Vol. 1. Ed. by Joseph R. Strayer. New York: Charles Scribner's Sons, 1982, 456–69.

21. Atomism

John Henry

Atomism originated in ancient Greece as a system of philosophy that explained all physical phenomena in terms of the behavior and interaction of vanishingly small indivisible particles. The emphasis on indivisibility (always a thorny philosophical issue) later gave way to a stress on the particulate nature of matter far below the level of sensory detection. These later manifestations of atomism should more correctly be referred to as, say, "corpuscularism" (to use a favored seventeenth-century term) since the very word "atomism" comes from the Greek word for "indivisible" (*atomos*). Nevertheless, the term will be used loosely here to refer to theories that explain qualitative differences between bodies and all other physical phenomena by means of the order and arrangement, orientations, shapes, and movements of submicroscopic particles. Although atomism has had immense success as an explanatory system of natural philosophy (even our own physical and chemical sciences are based on an atomic theory of matter), it has frequently clashed with Christianity. There are two main reasons for this. First, from its beginnings atomism included an account of world-building in which the multiplicity of things was explained by the richly varied coming together of atoms "by necessity" (we would say, "in accordance with laws of nature"), but which seemed to early Christians to be "by chance." Second, the major advocate of atomism was the Hellenistic Greek philosopher Epicurus (341–270 B.C.), whose closely associated moral philosophy and nonprovidential theology were vigorously condemned by Christians.

Pre-Christian Origins

Atomism was first propounded by Leucippus (fl. c. 400 B.C.) and Democritus (c. 460–c. 370 B.C.) in response to the claim of Parmenides (515–440 B.C.) and his followers, the so-called Eleatics, that change was impossible. Taking an extremely rationalist view and evidently constrained by what was possible to express in the language of his day, Parmenides concluded in his *Way of Truth* that, because change implied the coming into existence of something that did not exist before, it could not occur (since nothing could come into existence from nothing). Change was illusory, therefore, and reality consisted of the unchanging "One." The atomism of Leucippus and Democritus can be seen as a way of physicalizing Parmenides's conception. The atoms were envisaged as indivisible, indestructible, and unchangeable pieces of an ungenerated, homogeneous matter. The matter is the unchanging "One," but the particles of it come together in different ways to give rise to the phenomena we perceive around us. By insisting that atoms move in a surrounding void space, atomists were, in fact, extending contemporary ways of understanding the world. Constraints of vocabulary meant that they had to declare that "what is not" is just as real as "what is." Although this gave rise to fierce and protracted criticism, eventually the notion of empty space became distinguished from other senses of nothingness or nonexistence. The immediate cause of the atomists' conception of empty space, however, was the suggestion of the Eleatic philosopher Melissus of Samos (fl. 440 B.C.) that motion is impossible because there is no room for it. The packed "One" of Parmenides gave way to the fragmented matter of the atomists scattered through the surrounding void.

Atomism was controversial but influential. Plato's (c. 427–347 B.C.) only work of natural philosophy, the *Timaeus,* developed a form of atomism that accommodated the popular Empedoclean theory of change (developed by Empedocles [c. 492–432 B.C.] also in response to

Parmenides), based on the intermixing of the four elements of earth, water, air, and fire. Plato suggested that the elements existed in the form of characteristic atoms, each being the shape of one of the five regular Euclidean solids, which included the cube for Earth and the icosahedron for water; the unattributed fifth solid, the dodecahedron, was said to represent the cosmos.

Aristotle (384–322 B.C.), while admiring the genius of Democritus, developed a number of influential arguments against atomism. Most of them gain their force, however, by failing properly to present atomist theories. First, Aristotle tended to assume that the atomists believed in the mathematical indivisibility of their atoms (that is, that atoms are indivisible by definition, being dimensionless points), whereas it seems much more likely that they believed only in the *physical* indivisibility of their atoms. Second, Aristotle misapplied consequences that follow from his own concept of *place* to the atomists' concept of space. Aristotle, like many of his contemporaries, did not seem to have a concept of space in our sense, only a notion of place, and sometimes merely of room. In Aristotle's conception of things, an empty place really is a contradictory idea, but it evidently takes a non-Aristotelian to see that this is irrelevant to the atomists' differently conceived notion of space. Telling as Aristotle's objections were among the ranks of his followers, they did not deter Epicurus from developing the fullest and the most influential version of ancient atomism, whose physics was closely affiliated to an ethical and religious philosophy.

Atomism in the Middle Ages and the Renaissance

For the most part, Aristotle's strictures against the possibility of atomism held sway throughout the medieval period. There were rich and extensive discussions of the possibility of indivisible magnitudes, but they do not seem to have derived from interests in atomism. At least in part, they derived from a concern with the motion of angels (angels are moving indivisibles, a notion that, it was thought, demanded the indivisibility of time and space, too). Similarly, the possibility of void space was widely discussed, but the consensus was always against it. Interestingly, the only known supporter of atomism in the Middle Ages, Nicholas of Autrecourt (c. 1300–c. 1360), was inspired by theological considerations. A follower of William of Ockham (c. 1280–c. 1349),

Nicholas shared his disapproval of the restrictions placed upon God's power by Aristotelian philosophers. To undermine the philosophers, Nicholas wanted to show not only that Aristotle's conclusions were not demonstrable, but also that they were not as probable as some alternatives. Specifically, he argued that motion, condensation, rarefaction, and other changes could be explained more plausibly by the movements of invisible and indivisible particles in a void space than by Aristotle's more elaborate schemes. It seems safe to conclude, however, that Nicholas was without influence. We know of his ideas only from a few fragments of his writings that survived the public burning of his works in 1347 for error and heresy.

The details of Epicurean atomism became available to Renaissance scholars with the discovery (in 1473 and 1475, respectively) of its exposition in hexameter verse written by the Roman poet Lucretius (c. 99–55 B.C.), *De rerum natura* (*On the Nature of Things*), and of the account of Epicurus by Diogenes Laertius (fl. second century A.D.) in his *Lives of the Philosophers,* which included three letters by Epicurus himself. Together with an increasing dissatisfaction with the Aristotelianism of university scholars, their rediscovery led to a number of new versions of atomist philosophy. Some of them can be seen to be principally mathematical in inspiration, while others are more physicalist.

Galileo Galilei (1564–1642), after introducing physical atoms into some of his explanations in *The Assayer* (1623), was persuaded of the incompatibility of such atoms with his mathematical approach to the understanding of nature (geometry demands infinite divisibility) and, accordingly, developed a system in which every body is held to be composed of an infinite number of dimensionless atoms (that is, mathematical points). This mathematical atomism could lead nowhere in the explanation of physical phenomena, but, in the hands of his followers Bonaventure Cavalieri (1598–1647) and Evangelista Torricelli (1608–47), it led to innovations in the geometry of indivisibles that have been seen as contributions to the development of calculus.

One of the major concerns of Pierre Gassendi (1592–1655), principal reviver of Epicureanism, was to show how physical atomism was unaffected by arguments against mathematically conceived dimensionless indivisibles. In so doing, he showed the explanatory power of atoms of a finite size and determinate shape. This newly invigorated atomistic philosophy could be combined with a separate tradition, developing principally among medical writers, that emphasized the role of so-called *minima naturalia* (natural minimums) in chemical change. While accepting the Aristotelian arguments in support of the infinite divisibility of matter, the *minima* theorists were led by their knowledge of chemical interactions to assume that, in reality, different substances interact as particles of natural minimum sizes.

The revival of ancient atomism and its melding with the *minima naturalia* tradition culminated in the new mechanical philosophy of the seventeenth century. Like atomism, the mechanical philosophy sought to explain all physical phenomena in terms of invisibly small particles of matter in motion. It is important to note, however, that, while Gassendi and his followers accepted the physical indivisibility of the fundamental particles and the existence of surrounding void space, rival mechanical philosophers, notably René Descartes (1596–1650), upheld the infinite divisibility of matter and denied the possibility of void space. Others, like Robert Boyle (1627–91), dismissed dispute on both of these fundamental principles as merely metaphysical and emphasized a more pragmatic, experimentalist approach. These differences of approach certainly owe a great deal to the backgrounds of the individuals concerned. Gassendi had steeped himself in Epicureanism, while Descartes was much less able to discard his Aristotelian education and could not help thinking like a mathematician, and Boyle's experimental alchemical labors led him into the *minima naturalia* tradition. But there can be little doubt that religious differences also played a major role.

Atomism, Religion, and Irreligion

Gassendi and Boyle subscribed to a voluntarist theology in which all things are contingent upon God's arbitrary will. It followed for them that there are no necessary connections between one created thing and another; the nature of the world system cannot be understood by a process of rational reconstruction, only by empirical means. This view led Gassendi to defend the principles of atoms and the void only probabilistically. Boyle, acutely aware of the dangers of religious dispute as a result of the English Civil Wars, went further than Gassendi in his emphasis on empiricism, claiming to assert only indisputable matters of fact. Accordingly, he refused even to commit himself on the possibility of void space in spite of his extremely fruitful research with the newly invented air pump (the point being that the space in the air pump, even if empty of air, might be full of, for example, a subtle ether or light). Descartes, by contrast, took a more intellectualist approach in theology. God's reason, not his unconstrained will, played the dominant role in Descartes's conception of how things are. For Descartes, there was a greater tendency to believe that the world system could be understood by the power of reason. Descartes's reason led him to identify extension with matter and to conclude that matter is infinitely divisible and empty space a contradictory notion.

The voluntarism of Gassendi and Boyle also led them to differ from Descartes about the cause of motions in the world system. Both camps acknowledged that matter was a passive principle; there was no logical necessity that matter must be active. For Descartes, however, this view indicated that God, following logical dictates, created inert matter. The motions in the system, therefore, must be maintained directly by God. Gassendi, Boyle, and other voluntarist mechanical philosophers, however, drew upon empirical observation to conclude that matter was invested with its own activity and functioned as a secondary cause (that is, an independent cause of action established by the primary cause, God). They used this conclusion to point out that, since matter is a passive principle, its activity must have been bestowed upon it by God.

Disputes about theories of matter between different mechanical philosophers were frequently disputes about the nature of providence. For voluntarist theologians, therefore, even Cartesianism, which seems to rely directly upon the involvement of God, could look dangerously atheistic. Since Descartes had analyzed the behaviors of colliding bodies in terms of seven rules of impact, insisting that God always maintained motions in strict accordance with these rules, it was easy to suppose that God was not required and that the system could be explained in terms of the blind operation of laws of nature. Similarly, as far as the intellectualist was concerned, the voluntarist recourse to superadded activity in matter could be reinterpreted atheistically by assuming that matter simply is active by its nature. The only way to deny this support to atheism, intellectualist theologians insisted, was to insist that not even God could make matter active and must, therefore, be directly involved in the production of motions.

Differences in the other major versions of the mechanical philosophy, from Sir Kenelm Digby (1603–65) to Thomas Hobbes (1588–1679) and from Isaac Newton (1642–1727) to Gottfried Wilhelm Leibniz (1646–1716), can be seen to derive in large measure from fundamental religious differences. Digby's system dovetailed with his counterreforming Roman Catholic beliefs, while Hobbes's extremely materialistic philosophy was partly intended to reveal what he saw as the irremediable corruption of Roman Catholicism. The differences between Newton and Leibniz can be seen as the high-water mark of the opposing theologies of voluntarism and intellectualism.

Traditional Aristotelianism, as taught in the universities, had always been regarded as the handmaiden to the queen of the sciences, theology. Since the mechanical philosophies were intended completely to displace Aristotelianism, it is inevitable that they also tried to prove themselves suitable handmaidens to religion. One important aspect of this attempt can be seen in the various attempts to prove the immortality of the soul. Although the details were different, the basic argumentation was consistent from one mechanical philosopher to another. By insisting that all change, all generation and destruction, could be explained only in terms of the coming together and breaking apart of invisibly small particles of matter, it followed that the immaterial soul could not undergo change, much less destruction. On this issue, the mechanical philosophy could be presented as a surer support to religion than Aristotelianism.

Religious concerns clearly played an important role in the formulation of the new mechanical philosophies, but, for the majority of intellectuals, religious concerns militated against the acceptance of atomism. Gassendi labored long and hard to dispel the popularly perceived links between Epicureanism and atheism. For many in England, however, the extreme materialism and anticlericalism of Thomas Hobbes reinforced the association between atomism and atheism. Much remained to be done, therefore, if atomistic philosophies were to be made respectable.

The newly invented microscope proved to be a great help. Attempts to use the wonders of the natural world to prove the existence, omnipotence, and benevolence of God received a major stimulus from the revelation of previously unsuspected intricacies at the microscopic level. For the entomologist and microscopist Jan Swammerdam (1637–80), even the structure of the louse revealed "the Almighty Finger of God." Here was a new revelation, and one that the mechanical philosophers used simultaneously to support the claim that all bodies were built up from inconceivably small particles and that only God could have designed and built such tiny engines. Francis Bacon (1561–1626), in his essay "Of Atheism" (1612), had pointed out that atomism seemed to require a divine overseer more than other natural philosophies, in order to enable the atoms to produce such stable and complex forms. The microscope wonderfully confirmed this.

Another way to defend atomism against charges of atheism drew upon the highly respected humanist tradition of historical scholarship. Looking for the ancient origins of atomism, a number of natural philosophers claimed to trace it beyond the pagan Greeks to a more ancient philosophy in the Judeo-Christian tradition. A Phoenician by the name of Mochus was increasingly discussed in works of classical scholarship as the founder of atomism, and by some scholars he was identified with Moses himself. Even Newton, in Query 28 in the final book of his *Opticks* (1717 edition), referred to the authority of the Phoenicians "who made a vacuum, and atoms, and the gravity of atoms, the first principles of their philosophy."

For Roman Catholics, there was another major problem with atomism. The frequently performed miracle of the Eucharist was easily explained in Aristotelian terms. The substance of a particular body was always associated with a number of accidental (that is, nonessential, not part of the essence of the thing) properties. The transubstantiation of the Eucharist took place while leaving the accidental properties of the bread and wine unaffected; the substance changed, but the accidents remained the same, and, because of this, the elements of the Eucharist still seemed exactly like bread and wine. The accidental properties of taste, odor, color, and texture, according to atomistic accounts, however, depended only upon the arrangement of the constituent atoms. If bread becomes flesh, it does so by a rearrangement of the atoms and must be accompanied by a change of properties. The threat to Catholic orthodoxy presented by this aspect of atomism was noted by opponents of both Galileo and Descartes. Although Descartes himself tried to find ways around the difficulties, the issue did not become serious until after his death when his works were placed on the Index of Prohibited Books

(1663) and a royal ban was issued in France against teaching Cartesianism in the universities (1671).

After Newton

Isaac Newton's own natural philosophy, which assumed the existence of atoms endowed with attractive and repulsive forces, gave rise in the eighteenth century to a new turn in the relationship between atomism and theology. Ostensibly in reaction to charges of materialism leveled by Leibniz, but also reflecting earlier private speculations, Newton developed what has been called the "nutshell" theory of matter, which supposed that all the matter of the universe might be contained in a nutshell. In this theory, the immaterial, interparticulate forces took on a more prominent role than the matter from which they were supposed to emanate. Such speculations were taken up by a number of Newton's followers, but they were carried to their extreme by the Unitarian minister and chemist Joseph Priestley (1733–1804) in his *Disquisitions Relating to Matter and Spirit* (1777).

Insisting that the supposed solidity and impenetrability of atoms was merely another manifestation of their repulsive forces, Priestley rejected the separate categories of material and immaterial, or matter and spirit, developing instead a monistic philosophy of forces. Priestley's monism in natural philosophy enabled him to avoid the problem of explaining the connection and interaction of matter and spirit that was inherent in all dualistic philosophies and theologies. Whereas in dualism it is impossible, according to Priestley, to understand how an incorporeal God could act upon matter, in the new monistic philosophy God and matter are all manifestations of spiritual force. Unfortunately for Priestley, his monistic denial of the reality of matter was regarded by contemporaries as tantamount to a materialistic and, therefore, atheistic monism, and his ideas gave rise to a reaffirmation of more traditional, and more religiously orthodox, atomistic ideas.

The reaction to Priestley's radical interpretation of Newtonian ideas has been seen as part of the intellectual background to the Quaker John Dalton's (1766–1844) new version of atomism, published in his *New System of Chemical Philosophy* (1808–27). Certainly, Dalton's insistence upon qualitatively different atoms for each of the new elements proposed by Antoine Lavoisier (1743–94) entailed a rejection of the Newtonian belief in primordial atoms, which combine to give rise to higher-order par-

ticles that take part in chemical reactions. Newton was led by his assumption to suppose that, because water was sixteen times less dense than gold and yet completely incompressible, water must differ from gold by having its particles of primordial matter held farther apart by strong repulsive forces. Dalton, however, was at liberty to suppose that the different densities of gold and water bore no relation to the amounts of matter in their composition. Dalton's atomism did not lead, therefore, to "nutshell" theories of matter, much less to the monistic schemes of a radical like Priestley.

For others, however, Dalton's new version of atomism, with its large number of irreducibly different kinds of particles, seemed to introduce an unnecessary complication into natural theology. Humphry Davy (1778–1829) preferred to uphold a belief in the Newtonian notion of atoms all of one matter, which he regarded as more in keeping with the simplicity and intelligibility that he took to be characteristic of God's providence. For Davy, the principles of chemistry should be few in number. Davy's ideas were combined with Dalton's by William Prout (1785–1850) in 1815, when he thought he could show that all atomic weights were multiples of the atomic weight of hydrogen. "Prout's hypothesis" that hydrogen might be the primary matter from which all other substances were formed proved to be influential well into the twentieth century, and, for a while, J. J. Thomson (1856–1940), discoverer of the electron, believed that he had confirmed it. Prout himself was extremely religious and incorporated his views on hydrogen as the unifying factor in matter theory in his Bridgewater Treatise of 1834 (eighth in the series), *Chemistry, Meteorology, and the Function of Digestion*.

By the late nineteenth century, science and religion in Britain had finally begun to initiate divorce proceedings. Interestingly, as Frank Turner has shown, the atomistic theory of Lucretius played a minor role as a witness. Initiated by an essay in the *North British Review* in 1868 written by H. C. Fleeming Jenkin (1833–85), Regius Professor of Engineering at Edinburgh, and taken up in the famous "Belfast Address" of 1874 by John Tyndall (1820–93), Lucretius was presented to the Victorian public as a precursor of modern science and, what's more, as a pioneer in the struggle to liberate science from the ignorant strictures of religion. Representatives of Christian orthodoxy were not slow to respond. On the one hand, there were efforts to disparage modern scientific "materialism" for its lack of originality and progress, having come no further than the frequently absurd speculations of Epicurus and Lucretius. On the other hand, somewhat more subtly, there were efforts to show that Lucretius's critique of pagan polytheism and superstition had, in fact, been a noble and necessary contribution to the development of pure religion. Lucretius deserved praise, the argument went, for preparing the way for the higher faith of rational Christianity. In this rhetoric, the Roman poet became an intelligent and forceful critic of false religion, while the modern scientists who sang his praises as a materialist were shown to have missed the point of his criticisms and to have revealed their own inability to comprehend the value and truth of Christianity. The scientists, in turn, now began to distance themselves from Lucretius, pointing out that his speculative atomism was a long way from their experimentally determined and supported theories. On the links between ancient atomism and the rejection of religion, these later scientific commentators chose to remain silent. It seems true to say that, by the beginning of the twentieth century, the atomism of physical theory proceeded independently of religious concerns. But the seventeenth-century belief that atomism demonstrated the providence of an omniscient God evidently lingered on. When the newly developing science of quantum mechanics seemed to indicate that atomic motions could not be understood deterministically but only in terms of probabilities, Albert Einstein (1879–1955) felt he could hear "an inner voice" telling him that the theory was not correct. "The theory hardly brings us closer to the secret of the Old One," he wrote in 1926. "I am at all events convinced that *He* does not play dice."

See also Cartesianism; Chemistry; Epicureanism; Mechanical Philosophy

BIBLIOGRAPHY

Emerton, Norma E. *The Scientific Reinterpretation of Form.* Ithaca, N.Y.: Cornell University Press, 1984.

Guthrie, W. K. C. *A History of Greek Philosophy.* 6 vols. Cambridge: Cambridge University Press, 1962–81.

Harman, P. M. *Metaphysics and Natural Philosophy: The Problem of Substance in Classical Physics.* Totowa, N.J.: Barnes and Noble, 1982.

Henry, John. "Atomism and Eschatology: Catholicism and Natural Philosophy in the Interregnum." *British Journal for the History of Science* 15 (1982): 211–39.

Joy, Lynn Sumida. *Gassendi the Atomist: Advocate of History in an Age of Science.* Cambridge: Cambridge University Press, 1987.

Meinel, Christoph. "Early Seventeenth-Century Atomism: Theory, Epistemology, and the Insufficiency of Experiment." *Isis* 79 (1988): 68–103.

Mintz, Samuel I. *The Hunting of Leviathan: Seventeenth-Century Reactions to the Materialism and Moral Philosophy of Thomas Hobbes.* Cambridge: Cambridge University Press, 1962.

Murdoch, John E. "Infinity and Continuity." In *The Cambridge History of Later Medieval Philosophy: From the Rediscovery of Aristotle to the Disintegration of Scholasticism, 1100–1600,* ed. by N. Kretzmann, A. Kenny, and J. Pinborg. Cambridge: Cambridge University Press, 1982, 564–91.

Osler, Margaret J. *Divine Will and the Mechanical Philosophy: Gassendi and Descartes on Necessity and Contingency in the Created World.* Cambridge: Cambridge University Press, 1994.

Pais, Abraham. *'Subtle is the Lord': The Science and the Life of Albert Einstein.* Oxford: Clarendon, 1982.

Redondi, Pietro. *Galileo: Heretic.* Trans. by Raymond Rosenthal. Princeton, N.J.: Princeton University Press, 1987.

Sailor, Danton B. "Moses and Atomism." *Journal of the History of Ideas* 25 (1964): 3–16.

Segre, Michael. *In the Wake of Galileo.* New Brunswick, N.J.: Rutgers University Press, 1991.

Thackray, Arnold. "'Matter in a Nut-Shell': Newton's Opticks and Eighteenth-Century Chemistry." *Ambix* 15 (1968): 29–53.

———. *Atoms and Powers: An Essay on Newtonian Matter-Theory and the Development of Chemistry.* Cambridge, Mass.: Harvard University Press, 1970.

Turner, Frank M. "Ancient Materialism and Modern Science: Lucretius Among the Victorians." In Turner, Frank, M. *Contesting Cultural Authority: Essays in Victorian Intellectual Life.* Cambridge: Cambridge University Press, 1993, 262–83.

Van Melsen, Andrew G. *From Atomos to Atom: The History of the Concept Atom.* New York: Harper, 1960.

Vlastos, Gregory. *Plato's Universe.* Oxford: Clarendon, 1975.

Weinberg, Julius R. *Nicolaus of Autrecourt.* Princeton, N.J.: Princeton University Press, 1948.

Wilson, Catherine. *The Invisible World: Early Modern Philosophy and the Invention of the Microscope.* Princeton, N.J.: Princeton University Press, 1995.

22. Epicureanism

Lisa Sarasohn

Epicureanism is the philosophy first taught by the Hellenistic Greek philosopher Epicurus (341–270 B.C.). It is primarily an ethical doctrine, concerned with establishing the best means to ensure individual happiness and tranquility. Physics joins ethics in a unified cosmology devoted to teaching the way to achieve a pleasurable life.

As traditional values toppled during the Hellenistic age (323–30 B.C.), an anguished search for new meanings focused on the happiness of the individual. While some found comfort in the new mystery religions that emphasized human salvation, and others turned to the Stoic vision of a virtuous and rational life, Epicurus emphasized that pleasure is the *telos,* the highest good. Meeting in his Garden, or school, in Athens, Epicurus gathered a group of men and women, free and slave, into a community that sought the pleasurable life.

Epicurean Pleasure

Pleasure, according to Epicurus, is often misunderstood: "When, therefore, we maintain that pleasure is the end, we do not mean the pleasures of profligates and those that consist in sensuality . . . but freedom from pain in the body and from trouble in the mind" (Epicurus 1926, 89). Although throughout history Epicureanism has been confused with voluptuary hedonism, it was far from Epicurus's intention. The highest, or katastematic, pleasure is the passive or tranquil pleasure associated with the absence of anxiety and physical pain. It is the state of being satisfied and can exist indefinitely. But it is linked with the pleasures of motion, or kinetic pleasures, which fulfill physical needs and cease once the need is filled.

Epicurus taught that any person could achieve tranquility if he understood that the natural and necessary are all that matter. The only real necessities in life are those, such as food and shelter, that release us from pain. Epicurus ranked desires on a scale of self-sufficiency. Those things that are most easily obtainable leave the individual most self-sufficient, independent, and free. Freedom and self-sufficiency contribute to the possibility of finding happiness. The outward things rejected by Epicurus included most forms of social ties, notably marriage, children, and any sort of political involvement. He considered friendship the only bond that helped, rather than hindered, the life devoted to tranquil pleasure. But Epicurus realized that not all pleasures are ultimately beneficial, while some pains can eventually lead to greater pleasure. It is, therefore, necessary, in conducting our lives, to calculate what will lead to an excess of pleasure over pain in the long run and, on this basis, to make decisions about what to pursue and what to avoid. Such a calculation will lead the wise man to shun hedonism for ascetic virtue, clearly the better choice for tranquility and contentment. Ultimately, Epicurus equated pleasure with the absence of pain. This pleasure cannot be intensified either by duration or by additional pleasures of motion. Once obtained, it contains eternity within itself.

Epicurean Physics

Some people, however, are unable to feel tranquil and happy. Fear of death and of the arbitrary nature of the gods, explained Epicurus, are the two major sources of mental anguish. The only way to avoid these anxieties is to understand the true nature of the universe. This understanding will reveal that there is no suffering, nor indeed any form of consciousness, after death. Likewise, once the nature of the universe is explored, men will understand that gods are not necessary to explain its functioning. Thus, Epicurus developed a detailed naturalistic philosophy to support his ethical teachings.

The Epicurean universe is composed of atoms and void and of nothing else. Borrowing his system from the atomist Democritus (c. 460–c. 370 B.C.), Epicurus argued that experience shows there must be one first principle, the atoms, that is indestructible, imperishable, and eternal. The atoms are finite in number and identical in substance but extremely diverse in shape and form. Their combinations explain all that exists, including sensible qualities and human consciousness itself. The idea of divine providence is unnecessary and unthinkable in such a world. In fact, the Epicurean gods, living eternally in the cosmic spaces, are simply immortal beings uninvolved in external affairs who pursue only their own bliss on a cosmic level.

Just as Epicurus insulated his universe from divine intervention, he also attempted to free it from the subjugation of fate. Natural necessity would destroy man's self-sufficiency and control over his own destiny. To avoid any form of determinism, Epicurus introduced the concept of the swerve (*clinamen*). He rejected the eternal erratic motion of the atoms described by Democritus and, instead, postulated that atoms naturally fall downward in parallel lines, like rain, because of their weight. At some indeterminate time, for no particular reason, an atom swerves, a chain reaction ensues, and world-building commences.

Epicurus used the swerve to explain both the formation of the cosmos and human free will. Without the swerve, the individual atoms would never entwine in ever more complex forms, and the cosmos could never take shape. Likewise, this element of fortuitous behavior on the part of the atoms explains human free will, which also originates in the swerves of the atoms that compose the soul. Mind and matter are nothing but conglomerations of bits of matter, which after death simply decompose into atoms. Therefore, the wise man, knowing the nature of material existence, is impervious to the fear of the future and lives his life content and tranquil.

The Later History of Epicureanism

Epicurean ethical and natural philosophy was popular during the Roman Republic. Lucretius (c. 99–55 B.C.) immortalized Epicureanism in his philosophic poem *On the Nature of Things* (*De rerum natura*). But many pagan philosophers, led vehemently by Cicero (106–43 B.C.), attacked both the physical and the moral tenets of Epicureanism. Under the Roman Empire, as the popularity of Stoicism increased, Epicurus's social doctrines were especially denigrated.

For Christians, Epicurus's denial of divine providence and the immortality of the soul was intolerable. The Christian apologists Arnobius (d. c. 327) and Lactantius (c. 240–c. 320) were particularly determined to refute him. By the fourth century, Epicureanism had ceased to be a vital force in the Western world. Augustine noted that the ashes of Epicureans "are so cold that not a single spark can be struck from them" (Ep. 118. 12, quoted in Jones 1989, 94). The condemnation of the church Fathers resounded through the ages, even landing Epicurus in the sixth circle of Dante's Hell, the place reserved for those who denied the immortality of the soul. For the most part, Epicureanism lingered in the Middle Ages almost entirely as a synonym for debauchery, until Lucretius was rediscovered in the fifteenth century and Epicurus's own writings, exerpted in Book 10 of Diogenes Laertius's (fl. second century A.D.) *Lives of the Philosophers,* became available in the sixteenth.

Epicureanism was one of the many ancient schools reinvigorated by the Italian humanists. Lorenzo Valla (1407–57), for example, in his treatise *De vero bono* (*On the True Good* [1431]) argued that Epicurus was correct in considering pleasure to be the highest good, but he reinterpreted the meaning of pleasure for his own Christian purposes. Pleasure is, indeed, the highest good, says Valla, but only within the Christian system of grace and redemption, in which the highest pleasure is the beatific vision of God. Thus, divine love should be the aim, the *summum bonum,* for which human beings should strive.

In the sixteenth century, sympathetic accounts of Epicureanism became more common. Thomas More (1478–1535) and Desiderius Erasmus (1466–1536) both commended the Epicurean view of tranquil pleasure, and Erasmus thought, like Valla, that "[i]n plain truth, there are no people more Epicurean than godly Christians," because they understand that leading a virtuous life will result in the ultimate pleasure of the vision of God (Erasmus 1965, 538). Michel de Montaigne (1533–92) incorporated almost all of Lucretius's text into his *Essays* without, however, actually advocating Epicureanism.

Pierre Gassendi

The ultimate task of rehabilitating and christianizing Epicureanism was not achieved until the French philosopher and priest Pierre Gassendi (1592–1655) reconstructed the entire Epicurean corpus according to his own religious and scientific preferences in the *Syntagma philosophicum* (1658). Gassendi was one of the founders of the mechanical philosophy, adopting the Epicurean cosmos of moving atoms and void space. He made it acceptable to Christian consciences by insisting that the motion of the atoms was infused into them at the time of their creation by a providential God, who then uses their interactions as the vehicle for his divine plan. Gassendi rejected the Epicurean swerve and instead insisted that God's "general providence" both makes and maintains the world. Gassendi's God is in the voluntarist tradition and can do anything short of a contradiction, but normally he allows the universe to function according to the motions and meetings of the atoms.

Gassendi also wanted to preserve the Epicurean ideal of pleasure as the highest good. To do so, he suggested that God instilled the desire for pleasure into each individual at the time of his birth. The desire for pleasure motivates all human behavior up to, and including, the creation of the family, society, and the civil state. Gassendi used his understanding of the properties of motion as a prism to describe analogous human activity. Human motion is both the process of pursuing pleasure and a state of constant motion in which a wise man achieves tranquility and calm. Hence, the neo-Epicurean retained the close identification of the natural and the human realms postulated by Epicurus, but always within a Christian framework.

Humanity and nature are not, however, identical. God guides humans by means of his special providence, Gassendi argued, and also allows them to be free, a quality that the rest of the cosmos does not share. Human rationality and choice, as well as the ability to make epistemological mistakes, free humans from the kind of necessity God imposes on every other creation. Angels must love God, and rocks must fall, but humans create their own destinies by pursuing what they think will bring them pleasure.

Gassendi, as well as christianizing the Epicurean cosmos, also reclaimed Epicurus's own reputation in a biography of the ancient philosopher. In the late seventeenth and eighteenth centuries, the Epicurean notion of pleasure was no longer misunderstood, and Epicureanism became steadily more popular, especially in Britain. John Locke (1632–1704) embraced many aspects of Gassendi's christianized Epicureanism, and Isaac Newton (1642–1727) incorporated atomism into the new worldview. Epicureanism had become part of the mainstream European tradition of thought, where it would remain into modern times.

See also Atheism; Atomism; Varieties of Providentialism

BIBLIOGRAPHY

Primary Sources

Epicurus. *Epicurus: The Extant Remains.* Trans. by Cyril Bailey. Oxford: Clarendon, 1926.

Erasmus, Desiderius. *Colloquies.* Trans. and ed. by C. R. Thompson. Chicago: University of Chicago Press, 1965.

Gassendi, Pierre. *Opera Omnia.* 6 vols. 1658. Reprint. Stuttgard-Bad Cannstatt: Friedrich Frommann Verlag, 1964.

Long, A. A., and D. N. Sedley. *The Hellenistic Philosophers.* 2 vols. New York: Cambridge University Press, 1987.

Lucretius, Titus Carus. *De rerum natura.* Trans. by James H. Mantinband. New York: Ungar, 1965.

Secondary Sources

Festugière, A. J. *Epicurus and His Gods.* Trans. by C. W. Chilton. Oxford: Oxford University Press, 1955.

Jones, Howard. *The Epicurean Tradition.* London: Routledge, 1989.

Joy, Lynn Sumida. *Gassendi the Atomist: Advocate of History in an Age of Science.* Cambridge: Cambridge University Press, 1987.

———. "Epicureanism in Renaissance Philosophy." *Journal of the History of Ideas* 53 (1992): 573–83.

Lennon, Thomas M. *The Battle of the Gods and the Giants: The Legacies of Descartes and Gassendi.* Princeton, N.J.: Princeton University Press, 1993.

Lorch, Maristella de Panizza. *A Defense of Life: Lorenzo Valla's Theory of Pleasure.* Munich: W. Fink Verlag, 1985.

Mitsis, Phillip. *Epicurus' Ethical Theory: The Pleasures of Invulnerability.* Ithaca, N.Y.: Cornell University Press, 1988.

Osler, Margaret J., ed. *Atoms, Pneuma, and Tranquillity: Epicurean and Stoic Themes in European Thought.* Cambridge: Cambridge University Press, 1991.

———. *Divine Will and the Mechanical Philosophy: Gassendi and Descartes on Contingency and Necessity in the Created World.* Cambridge: Cambridge University Press, 1994.

Rist, John M. *Epicurus: An Introduction.* Cambridge: Cambridge University Press, 1969.

Rochot, Bernard. *Les travaux de Gassendi sur Epicure et sur l'atomisme, 1619–1658.* Paris: J. Vrin, 1944.

Sarasohn, Lisa T. *Freedom in a Deterministic Universe: Gassendi's Ethical Philosophy.* Ithaca, N.Y.: Cornell University Press, 1996.

Sedley, D. N. *Lucretius and the Transformation of Greek Wisdom.* New York: Cambridge University Press, 1998.

Striker, Gisela. "Ataraxia: Happiness as Tranquillity." *Monist* 73 (1990): 97–110.

Strozier, Robert M. *Epicurean and Hellenistic Philosophy.* Lanham, Md. University Press of America, 1985.

Trinkaus, Charles. *In Our Image and Likeness.* Chicago: University of Chicago Press, 1970.

23. STOICISM

Robert B. Todd

Stoicism was a philosophical school established at Athens in the third century B.C. It won adherents throughout the Greco-Roman world until about the end of the second century A.D. Although it went through various doctrinal developments, it assumed a fairly definitive form under its third head, Chrysippus (c. 280–207 B.C.). Since its physical theories represented the universe as a structure with an order and a purpose, it proved basically compatible with traditional religious ideas, in contrast with Epicureanism, in which the gods had no influence on the universe. Stoicism, in fact, created the most intimate relationship between science, in the sense of cosmology, and religious thought of any ancient philosophical system, and in later antiquity it inspired memorable responses from writers like Seneca (c. 4 B.C.–A.D. 65), Epictetus (c. A.D. 55–c. 135), and Marcus Aurelius (A.D. 121–80).

The Stoics saw the physical world as a single whole, in which a process of events occurred providentially in cycles. These originated with, and terminated in, a state in which a single primal element, Fire, constituted the whole of matter. Fire was both rational and divine; there was no distinction between its spiritual and material aspects; hence, physical theory was, in and of itself, religious doctrine. An active principle called *pneuma* maintained the fully developed universe. In Christianity, *pneuma* signified a principle of spiritual intervention in the world, but for the Stoics it identified a physical force composed of fire and air that imposed systematic order and structure on the universe. Its movement through the whole of matter created the "dynamic continuum" of the Stoic cosmos (as Sambursky has called it) and created a system of natural law in which everything within the universe was, in differing degrees, a modification of *pneuma*. This system included the human soul, which, as a part of

pneuma, derived its rationality from the common rationality of the universe. The survival of the individual soul (about which there were various Stoic theories) was thus unimportant. This system also excluded traditional polytheistic religion, since the single cosmos was the only god that the Stoics recognized. Yet, although they allegorized both the major deities and the minor demons and heroes as physical substances, such as the planets, these were not regarded as agents of astrological influence.

Stoic physical theories had clear implications for ethics. The list of epithets for the world order included not only Reason, God, and Providence, but also Fate. The Stoics recognized that their physical system was deterministic, yet they tried (though in the eyes of many ancient and modern critics they failed) to explain free action and, thus, to justify a system of morality based on their physical theories. The link between the two is expressed by the imperative, "Live according to Nature." This injunction meant that morality followed from a knowledge of the cosmic order, of which every moral agent was a part. But scientific description and moral prescription could be combined only if a moral agent could choose a course of action freely. Otherwise, the physical processes of the cosmos, as well as human behavior, would remain predictable and amount to a Golden Age in which, as Seneca saw (*Letter* 90), morality would not exist.

The Stoics tried to escape this consequence by arguing for what modern philosophers call "soft determinism," an explanation of physical causality that makes free action and, hence, moral and immoral behavior possible. Since the Stoics inherited from Socrates (469–399 B.C.) the idea that morality was based on knowledge, and vice was the result of ignorance, they thought that they could explain moral success or failure in terms of an agent's knowledge or ignorance of the world order. But both their attempt to evade determinism and their ideal of a wise person, or "sage," who would have such comprehensive knowledge, were widely criticized. In Roman Stoicism, as found, for example, in the works of Cicero (106–43 B.C.), there were efforts to prescribe moral duties in specific terms and to use the general idea of natural law as the basis for morality. This allowed Stoics to define a way of life without despairing over the unattainability of knowledge. In this compromise, the religious character of the Stoic cosmos became the background to an austere ethical system of duties.

The spiritual experience of being a Stoic was a private pursuit, shared with at most a few intimates, such as the Lucilius who received Seneca's protreptic letters. This privacy and sense of moral autonomy are found particularly in later Stoicism and involved a detachment from the contemporary world. The slave Epictetus gloried in the freedom he felt in living a life according to a natural order that could be known and valued independently of the oppressive conditions of his life. Seneca, a leading statesman and tutor to Nero (ruled A.D. 37–68), used Stoicism to insulate himself against intolerable political and social pressures and finally found in it justification for the suicide imposed on him by the emperor. (Stoicism provided the fullest ancient rationale for suicide as an act that maintained moral dignity in the context of a religious view of the universe.) Finally, in the second century A.D., the emperor Marcus Aurelius, in his intimate reflections (commonly called *Meditations,* but, in fact, "notes to himself"), was able to put his power and authority into perspective by maintaining his humility before the larger structure of the universe into which his identity would eventually submerge.

Stoic science was religious, and its religion scientific, in a way unparalleled in antiquity. Yet, its uniqueness led to its demise: Its determinism was unattractive, and its vision of the physical universe could not match the appeal of a transcendent reality provided in Christianity for the many and in Platonism for the elite.

See also Epicureanism; Views of Nature

BIBLIOGRAPHY

Primary Sources

Aurelius, Marcus. *Marcus Aurelius Antoninus: The Meditations.* Trans. by G. M. A. Grube. Indianapolis, Ind.: Hackett, 1983.

Cicero, Marcus Tullius. *Cicero: The Nature of the Gods.* Book 2. Trans. by H. C. P. McGregor. Harmondsworth: Penguin, 1972.

Long, A. A., and D. N. Sedley, *The Hellenistic Philosophers.* Sections 43–55. 2 vols. Cambridge: Cambridge University Press, 1987.

Seneca, Lucius Annaeus. *Seneca: Letters from a Stoic.* Trans. by R. Campbell. Harmondsworth: Penguin, 1969.

Secondary Sources

Colish, Marcia L. *The Stoic Tradition from Antiquity to the Early Middle Ages.* 2 vols. Leiden: Brill, 1985.

Dragona-Monachou, M. *The Stoic Arguments for the Existence and the Providence of the Gods.* Athens, Greece: National and Capodistrian University of Athens, 1976.

Hahm, David E. *The Origins of Stoic Cosmology.* Columbus: Ohio State University Press, 1977.

Long, A. A. "Astrology: Arguments Pro and Contra." In *Science and Speculation: Studies in Hellenistic Theory and Practice,* ed. by J. Barnes et al. Cambridge: Cambridge University Press, 1986, 165–92.

Rist, John M. *Stoic Philosophy.* London: Cambridge University Press, 1969.

———, ed. *The Stoics.* Berkeley: University of California Press, 1978.

Sambursky, S. *The Physics of the Stoics.* London: Routledge, 1959.

Sandbach, F. H. *The Stoics.* 1975. Reprint. London: Duckworth, 1994.

Schofield, M. "Perception, Argument, and God." In *Doubt and Dogmatism: Studies in Hellenistic Epistemology,* ed. by M. Schofield et al. Oxford: Clarendon, 1980, 283–308.

Todd, R. B. "The Stoics and Their Cosmology in the First and Second Centuries A.D." In *Aufstieg und Niedergang der Römischen Welt* II. 36. 3, ed. by Wolfgang Haase and Hildegard Temporini. Berlin: Walter de Gruyter, 1989, 1365–78.

24. Augustine of Hippo

Kenneth J. Howell

Augustine of Hippo (354–430) is unquestionably the most influential theologian in the history of western Christendom. Known as the "Doctor of Grace," this North African bishop articulated the teachings of Christianity so persuasively as to influence both theology and natural philosophy for centuries. It has only been with the increasing eclipse of antiquity in modern times that Augustine has lost his position as a force to contend with in philosophy. Influenced deeply by the Platonic tradition, especially by Plotinus (205–70), Augustine trusted the rational processes of the human mind as a guide to truth. This belief, however, was tempered by his Christian conviction regarding the effects of human sin and the necessity of divine grace.

Augustine was not particularly interested in what is now called science, since much of his thought centered on the principle of interiority, the belief that God and truth are found in the depths of the human heart. True knowledge of God required divine illumination that was not attainable by the usual means of human investigation. This illumination provided knowledge of all creatures as well, so that no true knowledge of anything was possible apart from God. Although his principle of interiority emphasized the relative insignificance of empirical investigation compared to the greater good of knowing God (an attitude that influenced some of his readers to devalue science), Augustine also stressed that all truth comes from God, whether through the Scriptures and the Church or by means of empirical study. He shared the assumption of most ancient philosophers that truth could be found both by rational means and through empirical investigation, a belief that gave him an openness to truth, no matter what the source. The human senses and intellect come from God, Augustine maintained, and, therefore, are capable of discovering truths that God has placed in nature. Hence, what is true in nature cannot contradict what is taught in the Bible or in the Christian religion. If something can be proven through empirical science, then it cannot be dismissed as contrary to faith, since any true fact or proposition ultimately comes from God. This openness to empirical truth allowed Augustine to give considerable credence to the demonstrated conclusions of natural philosophy.

Augustine was an accomplished orator who recognized the multiple functions and limitations of human language, a fact that deeply informed his views of natural truth and Scripture. He skeptically evaluated Manichean claims that purported to prove the Genesis account of Creation wrong. Augustine, who always distinguished between the reality behind words and the linguistic expression of that reality, viewed Manichean arguments as artful uses of rhetoric without legitimate foundation. On the other hand, he chided fellow Christians for their overly literal reading of Genesis, as if the sacred author wanted to give a full cosmology analogous to that of the philosophers. Five times during his life, Augustine wrote on the first chapters of Genesis, but each time he concluded his task with only very tentative proposals regarding their meaning. This tentativeness had lasting importance for the relation of scriptural interpretation to natural philosophy, for it meant that considerable latitude could be given to the exposition of Genesis and that Christian theologians would be hesitant to endorse only one system of natural philosophy as the authoritative one. Augustine's cautious approach to language seems to have set the tone within Western Christendom for an open-ended inquiry into nature.

Augustine's natural philosophy, though lacking systematization, has three recurrent and enduring features: (1) a high view of mathematics; (2) the belief in a hierarchically ordered universe; and (3) his theory of *rationes seminales* (seedlike principles). Because Augustine's natural philosophy was Platonic, he stressed the importance of mathematics in understanding nature. Mathematical truths were not generalizations of empirical experience like counting objects, or mental constructs (as in intuitionism), but truths of reason whose existence was independent of human knowledge. They could be known only through rational "seeing," a process by which humans could know God's mind in part. Augustine believed that the triune God created the world in accordance with these mathematical principles because of the inherent perfection of mathematical forms and because of the declaration of Scripture: "You have formed all things in measure (*mensura*), number (*numerus*), and weight (*pondus*)" (Wisdom 11: 20). The world was made in six days, for example, because six is a perfect number whose aliquot parts (1, 2, 3) were reflections of the Trinity.

Second, Augustine endorsed the Neoplatonic belief in an ontological continuum with graded levels of being, the apex of which was God. Both Platonic and Aristotelian natural philosophy posited a plenum and, consequently, denied the existence of a vacuum. Augustine took the filling motif of the Creation account in Genesis as evidence of the agreement of the Hebrew Scriptures with Neoplatonism. As the Creator filled the heavens and Earth with creatures, so he also filled the universe with divine presence so that all physical beings were sustained by that presence.

A third concept central to Augustine's thought was that of *rationes seminales* (sometimes called *rationes causales*), perhaps best translated as "root explanations" or "root causes," a notion that had wide-ranging consequences for his view of nature and God's relation to it. Augustine argued that God created everything simultaneously at the first moment of Creation, an implication he saw in the opening words of Genesis that was supported by Ecclesiasticus 18:1 ("He who lives for ever created the whole universe" [Revised Standard Version]). The subsequent days of Creation were merely an unfolding of the original seeds placed in the visible world by God. These seeds (*semina*) function as God's agents for the growth of natural creatures, and, methodologically speaking, they explain how species that appear only after the original Creation can still be said to be created by

God. God's instantaneous creation of all things in seminal form implies that he is both the original cause of the universe, with no demiurge (intermediate divine craftsman) or contender, and that he providentially guides the developmental growth of nature.

In theology, the Augustinian tradition has remained unbroken since the fifth century. Augustine's ideas continued to be the predominant theological influence in the West until the incorporation of Aristotelian philosophy in the works of Albertus Magnus (1193–1280) and Thomas Aquinas (c. 1225–74) in the thirteenth century. Even then, Thomistic theologians of the late Middle Ages relied heavily on Augustine's biblical exegesis, while they jettisoned his Neoplatonism. The Catholic doctrines that Augustine helped formulate, such as the Trinity, sacramental objectivity, and predestination, were also embraced by those who disagreed with the philosophical underpinnings he espoused. And even the strictest followers of Augustine also considerably modified his approach to philosophy. Thus, the prominent theologian Bonaventure (c. 1217–74) sought to demonstrate rational grounds for belief in the Trinity, an exercise that Augustine himself would have thought pointless. He also modified Augustine's doctrine of *rationes seminales* by speaking of Creation as according to *rationes exemplares* (rational models), which existed in the Word, the second person of the Trinity. Like virtually all medieval theologians, however, Bonaventure also viewed the created order in Augustinian terms, as a reflection of the nature of God.

During the early-modern era, Augustine's influence was enormous, in both theology and natural philosophy. The revival of Platonism in the Renaissance naturally made Christian thinkers like Marsilio Ficino (1433–99) look to the greatest of the church Fathers, who was also an exponent of Plato's (c. 427–347 B.C.) worldview, since Augustine could strengthen their reform of philosophy with unassailable authority. Similarly, Augustinian themes reverberate through the work of Johannes Kepler (1571–1630), who stressed mathematical harmonies of the universe as reflections of the divine light. Roman Catholics and Protestants alike claimed Augustine as their father in faith in order to justify their competing theological positions. Martin Luther (1483–1546), himself an Augustinian monk, believed that he had rediscovered the central message of the Christian faith in Augustine's writings. The Calvinists also drew on his anti-Pelagian writings to argue for their own interpretation of grace and predestination. On the Catholic side, the polemic of Robert Bellarmine (1542–1621) against John Calvin (1509–64) argued vigorously that Augustine's views did not in any way support distinctively Protestant doctrines.

Some Catholic philosophers also employed Augustinian notions in their work. Both Augustine's high view of mathematics and his doctrine of interior illumination found their way into the thought of Blaise Pascal (1623–62), in both his philosophy of mathematics and his famous *Pensées*. The *Meditations* of René Descartes (1596–1650) can be viewed as modeled on the *Confessions,* and his *"Cogito ergo sum"* ("I think, therefore I am") has discernible affinities with Augustine's principle of interiority. In astronomy, the debates over the meaning of scriptural texts regarding the motion of the earth often invoked Augustine's handling of texts as a precedent for accommodation, the notion that the Bible employed phenomenal language in speaking of nature and was not intended to give a theoretical account of the heavens.

Augustine's influence continued in Christian theology into the twentieth century, but his developmentalism also became a focal point of discussion in the wake of Roman Catholic attempts to come to grips with Darwinian evolution in the nineteenth century. Some interpreted his *rationes seminales* as an ancient precursor of, and justification for, the theological compatibility of evolution and the Christian doctrine of Creation; others saw evolution as inherently naturalistic and, therefore, incompatible with Augustine's doctrine. In both cases, however, Augustine's approach to Christian doctrine and natural philosophy has remained a source of inspiration for the reconciliation of theology and natural science, especially his attempt to incorporate non-Christian philosophy into a Christian worldview and his openness to divergent interpretations of the Bible.

See also Plato and Platonism; Theodicy; Thomas Aquinas and Thomism

BIBLIOGRAPHY

Primary Sources

Augustine. *The Trinity*. Trans. by Stephen McKenna. Washington, D.C.: Catholic University of America Press, 1963.

——. *On the Literal Interpretation of Genesis: An Unfinished Book*. Trans. by Roland J. Teske. Washington, D.C.: Catholic University of America Press, 1980.

——. *Two Books on Genesis Against the Manichees*. Trans. by Roland J. Teske. Washington, D.C.: Catholic University of America Press, 1980.

——. *The Literal Meaning of Genesis*. Trans. by John Hammond Taylor. Ancient Christian Writers. Nos. 41–42. New York: Newman, 1982.

——. *Confessions*. Trans. by Henry Chadwick. Oxford: Oxford University Press, 1991.

Secondary Sources

Bubacz, Bruce. *St. Augustine's Theory of Knowledge: A Contemporary Analysis*. New York: Mellen, 1981.

Bonnardière, Anne-Marie de la. *Saint Augustin et la Bible*. Paris: Éditions Beuchesne, 1986.

Brown, Peter. *Augustine of Hippo*. London: Faber, 1967.

Gilson, Etienne H. *The Christian Philosophy of St. Augustine*. New York: Random House, 1960.

Heil, John. "Augustine's Attack on Skepticism: The *Contra Academicos*." *Harvard Theological Review* 65 (1972): 99–116.

Henseliek, Werner. *Sprachstudien an Augustins "De vera religione."* Vienna: Osterreichischen Akademie der Wissenschaften, 1981.

Maher, John P. "St. Augustine's Defense of the Hexaemeron." *Catholic Biblical Quarterly* 7 (1945): 76–90; 306–25.

Marrou, Henri-Irénée. *Saint Augustine and His Influence Throughout the Middle Ages*. New York: Harper and Row, 1954.

McWilliam, Joanne. *Augustine: From Rhetor to Theologian*. Waterloo, Ontario: Wilfrid Laurier University Press, 1992.

O'Connell, Robert. *St. Augustine's Confessions: The Odyssey of the Soul*. New York: Fordham University Press, 1989.

O'Meara, John J. *The Creation of Man in De Genesi ad Litteram*. Villanova, Penn.: Villanova University Press, 1980.

Pagels, Elaine. "The Politics of Paradise: Augustine's Exegesis of Genesis 1–3 versus that of John Chrysostom." *Harvard Theological Review* 78 (1985): 67–99.

Rist, John M. *Augustine: Ancient Thought Baptized*. New York: Cambridge University Press, 1994.

Ruef, Hans. *Augustin über Semiotik und Sprache: Sprachtheoretische Analysen zu Augustins Schrift "De Dialectica" mit einer deutschen Übersetzung*. Bern: Wyss, 1981.

Scott, Kermit. *Augustine: His Thought in Context*. New York: Paulist Press, 1995.

Sellier, Philippe. *Pascal et Saint Augustin*. Paris: Colin, 1970.

Steenberghen, Ferdnand van. *The Philosophical Movement of the Thirteenth Century*. Edinburgh: Nilson, 1955.

TeSelle, Eugene. *Augustine the Theologian*. London: Burns and Oates, 1970.

Trapp, D. A. "Augustinian Theology of the 14th Century." *Augustiniana* 6 (1956): 146–274.

25. THOMAS AQUINAS AND THOMISM

William A. Wallace

Thomas Aquinas (c. 1225–74) was an Italian Dominican philosopher and theologian, whose synthesis of the Christian faith with Aristotelian science was a major achievement of the high Middle Ages. The synthesis itself is sometimes called "Thomism," but this term is better applied to what others have made of that teaching in their attempts to comprehend it and relate it to the problems and needs of later centuries.

Life and Writings

After studies at the abbey of Monte Cassino and the University of Naples, Aquinas entered the Dominican Order in 1244. He was sent to complete his education at the University of Paris and at the Studium Generale in Cologne, newly founded and under the direction of Albertus Magnus (1193–1280). He held two professorships in theology at Paris, 1256–59 and 1269–72. In the intervening period, he was in Italy, serving with the papal curia in Anagni, Orvieto, and Viterbo and, in between, erecting a Dominican studium at Santa Sabina in Rome. Thomas wrote voluminously throughout his life. During his second professorship at Paris, he composed his highly original *Summa theologiae,* along with detailed expositions of Aristotle's logic, natural philosophy, metaphysics, and ethics.

Science and Religion

The juxtaposition of science and religion in the modern mind, with the connotation that the two must be either opposed or linked in some way, does not resonate significantly with Aquinas's thought. Much of what is now discussed under the category of science and religion he would have seen as part of a larger problem of the rela-

tionships between faith and reason. Once the respective spheres of these two types of knowing are made clear, most of the difficulties arising in debates over science and religion dissolve.

In brief, faith is taken by Thomas to mean belief in God and acceptance of divine revelation as true. He would differentiate faith from reason on the basis that reason refers to the way humans acquire knowledge through their natural powers of sense and intellect alone, without relying on God or supernatural revelation. His distinction focuses more on the mode of acquisition of knowledge than on the knowledge acquired. A person whose reason is complemented by faith might thus be capable of knowing more truths than one who knows through reason unaided. But, if contradictory truths seem to derive from the two sources, then the competing claims of faith and reason have to be resolved, and one is faced with the typical controversy between science and religion.

To be more precise, faith for Aquinas is a supernatural virtue (along with charity and hope) that accompanies grace in the soul of the Christian and that disposes him or her to believe in truths revealed by God. Such truths are not self-evident to human reason, and assent to them must be determined by a voluntary choice. If such a choice is made tentatively, it is called opinion; if it is made with certainty and without doubt, it is called faith. The objects of divine faith are formulated in creeds that are made up of articles (that is, of connected parts). Believing in such articles means putting faith in them, and this resembles knowing in its giving firm assent; it also resembles doubting or holding an opinion in that it does not entail a complete vision of the truth. Faith's assent is an act of the mind that is voluntary; it is determined not by reason but by the will. But since its object is truth, which is the proper object of the intellect, it is more proximately an act of the intellect and so is regarded as an intellectual virtue.

Religion, like faith, is a virtue for Aquinas, but it resides not in the intellect but in the will. It is allied to the virtue of justice, which disposes a person to render to others their due. Since humans owe their entire being to God, they owe him a special kind of honor. Obviously, they can never repay him for what he has given them, nor can they give him as much honor as they ought, but only as much as is possible for them and is deemed acceptable to him. Those who are sensitive to this obligation are, in fact, religious persons. Being religious in this sense does not involve their having any special scientific knowledge and, thus, does not bear directly on science-versus-religion controversies.

Science is also a virtue for Aquinas, but it is a natural virtue of the human intellect. It may be characterized as a type of perfect knowing wherein one understands an object in terms of the causes that make it be what it is. It is attained by demonstration that meets the norms of Aristotle's *Posterior Analytics* and, as such, is certain and not revisable. In no way dependent on divine faith, it falls completely outside the sphere of religious assent. Most of what passes under the name of science in the present day is fallible and revisable and, as such, would classify as opinion and not as science in Aquinas's sense.

Thomism and Medieval Science

With the element of religiosity removed, Thomism, as exemplified in the works of both Aquinas and his followers, can be characterized as an intellectual movement within medieval Aristotelianism. As such, its major characteristics may be seen by contrasting it with four other varieties of Aristotelianism that flourished in the medieval period: Augustinian, Averroist, Scotistic, and nominalist. Thomistic Aristotelianism differs from the first, which generally rejected any attempts to separate reason from faith and approached the study of nature in an ambience dominated by faith. It differs from the second, that held by Averroës (1126–98), which professed an extreme rationalism and saw all of truth as contained in the writings of Aristotle (384–322 B.C.), thus leaving no room for faith. Steering a middle path between the two, Saint Thomas granted autonomy to reason in the study of nature but allowed for reason's being complemented by faith in the realm of supernature. So great was his commitment to reason that his thought fell under

ecclesiastical condemnation in 1277 at both Paris and Oxford. The remaining two varieties of Aristotelianism developed in reaction to the condemnations. That of Duns Scotus (c. 1265–c. 1308) questioned the primacy Aquinas accorded to the intellect and placed emphasis instead on the will; his synthesis can be seen as articulating a position intermediate between Augustinianism and Thomism, though closer to the former. Nominalist Aristotelianism, as seen in the works of William of Ockham (c. 1280–c. 1349), reacted against the Scotistic version and further attenuated its knowledge claims by making singulars the object of the intellect and reducing demonstration to the level of hypothetical reasoning. The medieval mendicant orders institutionalized these teachings, with Dominicans being the main, but not exclusive, proponents of Thomism and the Franciscans of Scotism and Ockhamism.

Though not a scientist, Aquinas addressed many problems that arose in the medieval Aristotelian-Ptolemaic-Galenic counterparts of what are today called physics, astronomy, chemistry, and the life sciences. Most of the contributions of Thomists to medieval science consist of defenses and developments of his thought; they are contained in commentaries on his writings, the *Sentences* of Peter Lombard (c. 1100–c. 1160), and the works of Aristotle. In England, the foremost Thomists were William of Hothum, Richard Knapwell, Thomas Sutton, William of Macclesfield, Robert of Orford, and Thomas of Claxton; some might include Robert Holkot in this group, but there are strong nominalist leanings in his writing. In France, the principal Thomists were Hervaeus Natalis and John Capreolus; of lesser stature were Bernard of Trille, Giles of Lessines, Bernard of Auvergne, and William Peter Godin. Among early German Thomists, one might name John of Sterngasse, Nicholas of Strassburg, and John of Lichtenberg; more important later expositors include John Versor and Petrus Nigri (Schwarz). In Italy, the early group included Rambert of Bologna, John of Naples, and Remigio de' Girolami; fifteenth-century expositors were Dominic of Flanders and Tommaso de Vio Cajetan, the latter important for his disputes with Averroists at the University of Padua over the immortality of the human soul.

Thomism and Later Science

Cajetan (1469–1534) was largely responsible for a revival of Thomism, sometimes called "Second Thomism," which played a significant role in early-modern science, that of the sixteenth and seventeenth centuries. Here the locus of activity shifted to the Iberian peninsula, where the principal Dominicans were Francisco Vittoria, Domingo de Soto, Melchior Cano, and Domingo Bañez. Of this group, Soto (1491–1560) is of particular significance for his *Questions on the Physics of Aristotle* (1551–52), in which he adumbrated the concept of uniform acceleration in free fall. The Jesuit order, newly founded by Ignatius Loyola (1491/5–1556), also contributed to this development, since Loyola's constitution enjoined Thomism on the order in their teaching of theology, while it allowed them to be eclectic Aristotelians in their work in philosophy. Early professors at the Collegio Romano, the principal Jesuit institution of learning, founded by Loyola himself, relied heavily on Thomistic authors, but, as the order grew, it developed its own distinctive teachings. These are seen mainly in the writings of Francisco Suarez (1548–1617) and Luis de Molina (1535–1600), who incorporated Scotistic and nominalist strains in their thought. Their departures from Saint Thomas were combated by Bañez, giving rise to movements known as Suarezianism, Molinism, and Bañezianism—all of which were Thomistic in the broad sense, yet provided different accounts of how human freedom can be reconciled with divine grace and predestination.

One of Soto's students at the University of Salamanca, Francisco de Toledo (1532–96), joined the Jesuit order and was sent to the Collegio Romano as a professor of philosophy. By the end of the sixteenth century, the courses he inaugurated in logic and natural philosophy had become highly developed. It has been discovered that Galileo Galilei (1564–1642) obtained lecture notes from this period at the Collegio that are Thomistic in orientation (notably those of Paolo della Valle [1561–1622]) and, between 1589 and 1591, appropriated materials from them that are still extant in his Latin notebooks. The influence of the notebooks dealing with physical questions and with motion on Galileo's later work is disputed among scholars, but it seems indisputable that the notebook dealing with logical questions guided his investigations throughout his life.

Both Jesuits and Dominicans played an important part in Galileo's trial in 1633. Despite their differences, both groups subscribed to a Thomistic theory of knowledge and of demonstrative proof. In their eyes, it was Galileo's inability to provide a demonstration of the earth's motion that brought about his downfall. Records have been discovered showing that the Dominican Benedetto Olivieri (1769–1845) recognized by 1820 that empirical proofs of the earth's motion (stellar parallax and the deflection of falling bodies toward the east) had by then been given. By invoking such proofs, Olivieri was instrumental in having the Church finally remove its long-standing sanctions against Copernicanism and Galileo.

Thomism entered a third phase of development during the late nineteenth century and into the twentieth in a movement known as the Thomistic Revival or Neo-Thomism. Impetus for this revival came from Pope Leo XIII (b. 1810, p. 1878–1903), whose encyclical *Aeterni Patris* (1879) called for a return to the thought of Saint Thomas as a means of solving contemporary problems. This papal endorsement stimulated much historical research, including that bearing on the history of science. Though not a Thomist himself, the Catholic Pierre Duhem (1861–1916) used history to develop a positivist philosophy of science that restricted science's epistemic claims and so protected the Church's metaphysics against encroachments from science. Twentieth-century Thomists have generally shown little interest in science, being concerned mainly with metaphysics and social and political thought. Notable exceptions are Jacques Maritain (1882–1973) and Vincent Edward Smith (1915–72), both of whom developed philosophies of science, influenced by Duhem, that deny modern science the possibility of attaining demonstrations about the world of nature. A moderate realist position that allows such a possibility seems more in accord with Aquinas's own thought.

See also Aristotle and Aristotelianism; Augustine of Hippo; Galileo Galilei; Medieval Science and Religion; Roman Catholicism Since Trent

BIBLIOGRAPHY

Aquinas, St. Thomas. *Cosmogony* (*Summa theologiae,* First Part, Questions 65–74). Trans. by William A. Wallace. Latin text and English translation, Introduction, Notes, Appendices, and Glossary, 1967. Vol. 10 of 60 vols., ed. by Thomas Gilby. New York and London: Blackfriars, in conjunction with McGraw-Hill and Eyre and Spottiswoode, 1967.

Feldhay, Rivka. *Galileo and the Church: Political Inquisition or Critical Dialogue?* Cambridge: Cambridge University Press, 1995.

Roensch, Frederick J. *Early Thomistic School.* Dubuque, Ia: Priory, 1964.

Simon, Yves. "Maritain's Philosophy of the Sciences." *Thomist* 5 (1943): 85–102.

Smith, Vincent E. *Philosophical Physics.* New York: Harpers, 1950.

Wallace, William A. "The Enigma of Domingo de Soto: *Uniformiter difformis* and Falling Bodies in Late Medieval Physics." *Isis* 59 (1968): 384–401.

———. "Aquinas, Saint Thomas." In *Dictionary of Scientific Biography,* ed. by Charles Gillispie. Vol. 1. New York: Scribners, 1970, 196–200.

———. *Galileo's Early Notebooks: The Physical Questions. A Translation from the Latin, with Historical and Paleographical Commentary.* Notre Dame, Ind.: University of Notre Dame Press, 1977.

———. "The Philosophical Setting of Medieval Science." In *Science in the Middle Ages,* ed. by David C. Lindberg. Chicago and London: University of Chicago Press, 1978, 87–138.

———. "Thomism." In *The New Catholic Encyclopedia,* ed. by Thomas C. O'Brien. Vol. 17. New York: McGraw-Hill, 1979, 665–6.

———. "Aristotle in the Middle Ages." In *Dictionary of the Middle Ages,* ed. by Joseph R. Strayer. Vol. 1. New York: Scribners, 1982, 456–69.

———. "Galileo's Science and the Trial of 1633." *Wilson Quarterly* 7 (1983): 154–64.

———. *Galileo and His Sources: The Heritage of the Collegio Romano in Galileo's Science.* Princeton, N.J.: Princeton University Press, 1984.

———. "Thomism and Its Opponents." In *Dictionary of the Middle Ages,* ed. by Joseph R. Strayer. Vol. 2. New York: Scribners, 1989, 38–45.

———. *Galileo, the Jesuits, and the Medieval Aristotle.* Collected Studies Series CS346. Aldershot, U.K.: Variorum, 1991.

———. *Galileo's Logic of Discovery and Proof: The Background, Content, and Use of His Appropriated Treatises on Aristotle's Posterior Analytics.* Dordrecht and Boston: Kluwer, 1992.

———. "Galileo's Trial and Proof of the Earth's Motion." *Catholic Dossier* 1(2) (1995): 7–13.

———. *The Modeling of Nature: Philosophy of Science and Philosophy of Nature in Synthesis.* Washington, D.C.: The Catholic University of America Press, 1996.

Wallace, William A., and James A. Weisheipl. "Thomas Aquinas, St." In *The New Catholic Encyclopedia,* ed. by Thomas C. O'Brien. Vol. 1. New York: McGraw-Hill, 1967, 102–15.

Weisheipl, James A. "Thomism." In *The New Catholic Encyclopedia,* ed. by Thomas C. O'Brien. Vol. 14. New York: McGraw-Hill, 1967, 126–35.

———. *Friar Thomas d'Aquino: His Life, Thought, and Works.* 1974. Reprint. Washington, D.C.: The Catholic University of America Press, 1983.

———. *Nature and Motion in the Middle Ages,* ed. by William E. Carroll. Washington, D.C.: The Catholic University of America Press, 1985.

Wippel, John F. "The Condemnations of 1270 and 1277 at Paris." *Journal of Medieval and Renaissance Studies* 7 (1977): 169–201.

26. SKEPTICISM

Margaret J. Osler

Skepticism is a philosophical attitude that questions the reliability of, or even the possibility of acquiring, knowledge about the world. Tracing their origins to ancient Greek philosophy, skeptics argue that neither the senses nor a priori reasoning are reliable sources of knowledge about the world. In the classical world, Academic skeptics concluded that we can know nothing, while Pyrrhonian skeptics questioned whether we can even know whether we know anything. Both schools argued that knowledge about the world can never be certain.

Although some of the Church Fathers were acquainted with skepticism, this philosophy had little impact on medieval philosophy. It was only with the recovery of classical texts during the Renaissance, particularly Cicero's *Academica* and Sextus Empiricus's *Outlines of Pyrrhonism,* that skepticism played an important role in philosophical discourse. Coupled with the religious debates following the Reformation, the recovery of these texts produced a skeptical crisis during the second half of the sixteenth century. In the wake of the Copernican revolution and the decline of Aristotelianism, this crisis led natural philosophers to question the grounds for knowledge about the world. Consequently, discussions of method became an important feature of seventeenth-century natural philosophy. Skepticism reached its height in the philosophy of David Hume, who used it to criticize the traditional arguments for the existence of God.

Ancient Skepticism

In the Western tradition, skepticism has its roots in Greek philosophy. There were two schools of Greek skepticism, Academic skepticism, which developed within Plato's Academy, and Pyrrhonian skepticism, formulated by Pyrrho of Elis (c. 360–275 B.C.) and further developed in Alexandria during the first century B.C.

The Platonic philosophers Arcesilaus (c. 315–241 B.C.) and Carneades (c. 213–129 B.C.) argued against the "dogmatists," who believed in the possibility of attaining certain knowledge about the real nature of things, that nothing could be known. Their primary targets were the philosophies of the Stoics and the Epicureans. The Academic skeptics developed a series of arguments to show that the senses are unreliable sources of knowledge about anything beyond our immediate sensations, that, equally, reasoning cannot be trusted and, therefore, that there is no way of knowing which of our statements is true and which false. The *Academica* and *De natura deorum* (On the Nature of the Gods) of Marcus Tullius Cicero (106–43 B.C.) are important sources for knowledge and transmission of Academic skepticism.

Pyrrhonian skepticism received its fullest development in the writings of Sextus Empiricus (fl. c. 200 A.D.). He criticized the Academic skeptics for holding the negative dogmatic view that we can know nothing. Instead, he believed that the limitations of our knowledge should lead us to suspend belief, either positively or negatively. In *Outlines of Pyrrhonism* and *Against the Mathematicians,* Sextus Empiricus laid out the Pyrrhonian arguments, known as tropes, in a systematic attack on dogmatic claims to knowledge. These tropes questioned the possibility of acquiring reliable knowledge about the real natures of things on the following grounds: (1) the differences between different kinds of animals; (2) the differences among human beings; (3) the different structures of the organs of sense; (4) the relevance of circumstantial conditions, as well as positions and intervals and locations; (5) the effect of intermixtures of real objects with each other; (6) the relevance of quantities and formations of the underlying objects; (7) the fact of relativity; (8) the frequency or rarity of the occurrence; and (9) the impact of disciplines and customs and laws, the legendary beliefs, and the dogmatic convictions. Each of these modes, or tropes, was designed to show that evidence from the senses is an unreliable source of knowledge about the real natures of things because it leads to contradictory conclusions about the observed object.

Sextus Empiricus applied these skeptical arguments to all areas of knowledge, including physics, medicine, logic, and mathematics, all of which, he argued, were based on unjustified, dogmatic claims. He believed that the skeptical suspension of judgment produces a state of tranquility, or *ataraxia,* a goal he shared with the Epicureans. He did not doubt our knowledge of the way things appear and regarded such knowledge as adequate for life in the world.

Among the few early Christian writers who considered the skeptical arguments, two different approaches to skepticism emerged. Lactantius (c. 240–c. 320) moved toward fideism (the belief that all knowledge is based on premises accepted by faith), utilizing Academic skepticism to undermine the claims of the philosophers and thereby preparing the way for genuine knowledge, which, he maintained, comes only from God. For him, skepticism was a useful preparation, though not a necessary prerequisite, for Christian faith. Augustine of Hippo (354–430), who attempted to combine Christian theology with Neoplatonic philosophy, struggled with the problems posed by Academic skepticism as presented by Cicero. Rather than view skepticism as propaedeutic to faith, Augustine came to see it as an obstacle that must be overcome. In his early work, *Contra academicos,* he concluded that revelation is the only way to defeat the skeptical arguments. The views of Lactantius and Augustine were the earliest articulations of two divergent, but equally influential, ways of deploying skepticism in the name of Christianity. Discussion of skepticism was not widespread during the Middle Ages, although Augustine's approach to Academic Skepticism did receive some attention. While Cicero's writings were widely circulated, the *Academica* was not one of the most frequently copied of his works.

Sources of Early-Modern Skepticism

Serious consideration of skepticism revived during the Renaissance with the recovery of the writings of the ancient skeptical writers. Coupled with the intellectual crisis of the Reformation, this revival led to a general skeptical crisis in European thought.

Both Academic skepticism and Pyrrhonian skepticism were revived in the sixteenth century. The humanists' interest in the writings of Cicero produced a greater awareness of the ideas developed in his *Academica.* Around midcentury, several works were published that dealt with the arguments of the Academic skeptics in detail. These included the works of Omer Talon (1510–62), who published a commentary on the *Academica,* Giulio Castellani (1528–86), who rejected the skepticism of the *Academica* in his defense of Aristotle, and Joannes Rosa (1532–71), who wrote the most lengthy and detailed commentary on Cicero's work to date.

While the works of Sextus Empiricus were practically unknown during the Middle Ages, Greek manuscripts of his work became known in Italy during the fifteenth century and were gradually disseminated throughout Europe. *Outlines of Pyrrhonism* was published in 1562, and all of his works were published in Latin in 1569. From that time on, his works were frequently published, and skeptical ideas were in general circulation. The French essayist Michel de Montaigne (1533–92), who considered suspension of belief superior to the religious dogmatism that had led to the French wars of religion, popularized Pyrrhonian ideas.

Interest in skepticism was sparked by the Reformation debates concerning the rule of faith. Martin Luther's (1483–1546) challenge to the authority of the Roman Catholic Church concerning matters of the interpretation of Scripture presented philosophers and theologians with the problem of determining a rule of faith. Rejecting the traditional authority of the Catholic Church, Protestant thinkers argued that the only authority in questions of religion is the word of God as revealed in Scripture. Catholics, appealing to skeptical arguments, noted that such a view would lead to fragmentation of the Church and, hence, to religious anarchy. To avoid these dangers, they fell back on the traditional authority of the Catholic Church. This debate led to the broader questions of determining a proper criterion for judging among rival claims to authority and then to the metaquestion of how to decide which criterion to choose. Thinkers on both sides of confessional lines appealed to skeptical arguments to discredit the positions of their opponents.

Skepticism and Scientific Method in the Seventeenth Century

The skeptical crisis prompted many natural philosophers to question the foundations of knowledge about the world and traditional methods for seeking it. Ever since the translation of Arabic works in the twelfth and thirteenth centuries had reintroduced Aristotelianism into the mainstream of European philosophy, Aristotle's prescriptions about method had provided an important model for natural philosophy. Aristotle (384–322 B.C.) had described the goal of natural philosophy to be the discovery of demonstrative truths about the real essences of things. In the *Posterior Analytics,* he had spelled out the method by which to distinguish essential from accidental properties of things. Knowledge of essential properties, based on observation, provided the premises on which Aristotle's demonstrations were to be based. In the seventeenth century, natural philosophers, already critical of Aristotelianism in the wake of the Copernican challenge, used the skeptical arguments to undermine Aristotle's method as the first step in formulating new approaches to the investigation of the world.

Skepticism served a dual role for seventeenth-century natural philosophers: It provided them with a powerful tool for criticizing traditional Aristotelian methods, and it led to the formulation of new approaches to method. Many of the discussions of method opened by invoking the skeptical arguments to undermine the Aristotelian approach. Two different paths to skepticism led to the formulation of two very different approaches to the epistemological foundations of natural philosophy. Acquainted with the philosophy of the skeptics, René Descartes (1596–1650) began his search for a new method by employing "systematic doubt," a thorough application of the skeptical arguments to all forms of knowledge. He argued that traditional methods did not provide any kind of epistemological warrant for claiming that their results could be known to be certain. Descartes used this systematic application of skepticism to root out all dubitable claims in his search for an indubitable foundation upon which to build natural philosophy. In his *Discourse on Method* (1637) and *Meditations* (1641), Descartes showed how claims based on sensory knowledge and even the results of mathematical demonstration were dubitable in light of a skeptical critique. One important consequence of this critique was to show that there was no sound basis for Aristotle's method. A demonstrative science of nature could not be built on dubitable foundations.

Descartes was no skeptic, however. He believed that his new method could defeat skepticism. Having employed skeptical arguments to criticize the traditional Aristotelian approach to science, he set out to find some indubitable proposition that he could use to erect a natural philosophy that would provide demonstrative knowledge about the real essences of things. Descartes thought that he had found such a foundation in the famous proposition, *"Cogito ergo sum"* ("I think, therefore I am"), on which he based his new approach to knowledge and natural philosophy. Starting from the indubitable *"cogito,"* he attempted to prove the existence of God, who, in turn, provided him with his warrant for reasoning a priori from ideas in his mind to the nature of things in the world. Using this warrant, his claim that anything we perceive clearly and distinctly exists in the world precisely in the way that we perceive it, Descartes believed that he could proceed to certain conclusions by means of geometrical demonstration. Although he rejected Aristotle's method, he retained his epistemological goal. He described his natural philosophy in detail in the *Meditations* and *The Principles of Philosophy* (1644). Descartes's philosophy did not go unchallenged. In the *Objections and Replies* that followed the publication of the *Meditations,* a number of philosophers, including Pierre Gassendi (1592–1655), Thomas Hobbes (1588–1679), Pierre-Daniel Huet (1630–1721), and Antoine Arnauld (1612–94), criticized Descartes's arguments by showing that he had by no means succeeded in defeating skepticism.

Pierre Gassendi and Marin Mersenne (1588–1648) also employed skepticism to formulate a very different approach to natural philosophy. Like Descartes, Gassendi subjected the Aristotelian approach to philosophy to a skeptical critique. In his first published work, *Exercitationes paradoxicae adversus Aristoteleos (Paradoxical Exercises Against the Aristotelians* [1624]), Gassendi used the skeptical arguments, closely following the tropes of Sextus Empiricus, to prove that science in the Aristotelian sense is impossible. Skeptical criticism of sensory knowledge attacked the Aristotelian method at its root. Without the ability to reason from observations to the essential attributes of things, he thought the method of the *Posterior Analytics* was worthless.

In contrast to Descartes, who sought to defeat skepticism by means of some unassailable kernel of certainty, Gassendi—along with Mersenne and others—advocated redefining the epistemic goal of science. Replacing certainty with probability, he argued that knowledge consists of probable statements based on our experience of the phenomena. He also denied the possibility of acquiring knowledge of the essences of things. In making these moves, he rejected the traditional Aristotelian and Scholastic conception of *scientia* as demonstrative knowledge of real essences, replacing it with what he called a "science of appearances" (that is, probable knowledge of the appearances of things). While such knowledge is neither as certain nor as deep as traditional *scientia*, it suffices for our needs. Richard Popkin has called Gassendi's approach "mitigated skepticism."

During the second half of the seventeenth century, a group of natural philosophers elaborated the epistemology of mitigated skepticism into a nuanced account of the degrees of certainty of empirical knowledge. This group of thinkers included John Wilkins (1614–72), Seth Ward (1617–89), Walter Charleton (1620–1707), Joseph Glanvill (1636–80), Robert Boyle (1627–91), and John Locke (1632–1704). They argued that different kinds of knowledge require different kinds of proof, thus denying that all knowledge can attain the certainty of mathematical demonstration. Accordingly, they claimed that only God possesses knowledge that is absolutely and infallibly certain. Mathematics and the parts of metaphysics that can be established by logic and mathematical demonstration compel assent. A step below mathematical certainty is moral certainty, which characterizes knowledge that is based on immediate sense experience or introspection. A slightly weaker kind of moral certainty characterizes belief, religious belief, and conclusions about everyday life that are based on observation and the reports of others about their observations. Finally, opinions based on secondhand reports of sense observations can be known only as probable or perhaps just plausible.

Robert Boyle elaborated the theory of degrees of certainty into an epistemology for natural philosophy, advocating an empiricist method. He said that theories should be evaluated in terms of their intelligibility, simplicity, explanatory scope, and predictive power and that they are confirmed to the degree that they successfully explain different kinds of observed facts. Just as he argued in his *Discourse of Things Above Reason* (1681)

that many of the mysteries of Christianity lie beyond the limits of human understanding, so he noted that, in natural philosophy, intelligibility to human understanding is not necessary to the truth or existence of a thing. Hence, he believed that the results of natural philosophy could at best attain physical certainty (that is, a high degree of probability).

John Locke, whose *Essay Concerning Human Understanding* (1690) drew on the tradition of mitigated skepticism and degrees of certainty, articulated a fully developed empiricist epistemology. He claimed that all of our ideas are derived from either the senses or reflection on ideas drawn from the senses. He argued that we cannot attain certainty about things in the world and that we can acquire no knowledge of the real essences of things. Acknowledging that this approach represented a major departure from the epistemic goals of both the Aristotelian and Cartesian approaches to natural philosophy, he asserted that "natural philosophy is not capable of being made a science."

Later Developments

If the sixteenth-century revival of skepticism in the context of post-Reformation debates about the rule of faith had a formative influence on the development of empirical and probabilistic methods in natural philosophy, in the eighteenth century these methods were turned on the foundations of religion. This reversal of priorities in the relationship between reason and religion was one of the defining characteristics of the philosophy of the Enlightenment.

At the very end of the seventeenth century, Pierre Bayle (1647–1706) adopted a skeptical approach to all areas of knowledge. In his *Dictionnaire historique et critique* (*Historical and Critical Dictionary* [1697–1702]), he applied skeptical techniques to challenge the claims of theology, philosophy, mathematics, and the sciences. He argued that the Cartesian attempt to defeat skepticism had failed and that philosophy could lead only to doubts. Since any attempt to provide rational grounds for knowledge is bound to fail, he believed that the only recourse we have is to faith. Whether Bayle was truly a fideist or whether he was a skeptic trying to pass the censors remains a matter of controversy.

David Hume (1711–76) used empiricist and skeptical arguments to question our ability to know anything beyond immediate sensations. In particular, he argued that claims about causes are based only on the psychological expectation that events that have been constantly conjoined in the past will continue to be conjoined in the future. He applied this analysis of cause to the traditional arguments for belief in God and religion to demonstrate that those arguments have no foundation. In his *Treatise of Human Nature* (1739 and 1740), *Enquiry Concerning Human Understanding* (1748), and the posthumous *Dialogues Concerning Natural Religion* (1779), Hume showed how each of the standard arguments violated empiricist criteria for knowledge and thereby failed to accomplish what it set out to prove. Since the statement that God exists is a factual claim, it cannot be proven by a priori means. Consequently, the ontological argument that attempts to prove God's existence from the concept of God is impossible. The other two arguments, the argument from design and the argument from miracles, are subject to the same strictures as any empirical argument. According to Hume, the argument from design fails because if all we know about God is that he could create the world, and if we can have no empirical knowledge of creation, we can infer nothing about God except what we already know about the world from experience. Hence, the argument from design is empty. As for the argument from miracles, it asks us to violate the basic empiricist rule that knowledge claims are justified in proportion to the evidence we have for them. Since miracles are, by definition, unusual or singular events that violate the usual course of nature, we can never accumulate enough evidence to support a claim for a miracle in the face of all of our ordinary experience. Hence, a miracle can never provide a justifiable foundation for religion.

In its relationship to the history of science, skepticism played a critical role. Differing responses to the challenge of the skeptics forced natural philosophers to refine their ideas about method. While few philosophers or scientists ever adopted skepticism as a philosophy, many have used it to question the epistemological grounds for knowledge and the basis for religious belief.

See also Atomism; Cartesianism; Enlightenment; Epistemology; Materialism; Mechanical Philosophy; Miracles

BIBLIOGRAPHY

Ariew, Roger, and Marjorie Grene, eds. *Descartes and His Contemporaries: Objections and Replies.* Chicago: University of Chicago Press, 1995.

Buckley, Michael J., S.J. *At the Origins of Modern Atheism.* New Haven, Conn.: Yale University Press, 1987.

Burnyeat, Myles, ed. *The Skeptical Tradition.* Berkeley: University of California Press, 1983.

Curley, Edwin. *Descartes Against the Skeptics.* Cambridge, Mass.: Harvard University Press, 1978.

Dear, Peter. "Marin Mersenne and the Probabilistic Roots of 'Mitigated Skepticism.'" *Journal of the History of Philosophy* 22 (1984): 173–205.

Hurlbutt, Robert H. *Hume, Newton, and the Design Argument.* 1965. Rev. ed. Lincoln: University of Nebraska Press, 1985.

Kors, Charles Alan. *Atheism in France, 1650–1729.* Vol. I: *The Orthodox Sources of Disbelief.* Princeton, N.J.: Princeton University Press, 1990.

Larmore, Charles. "Scepticism." In *The Cambridge History of Seventeenth-Century Philosophy,* ed. by Daniel Garber and Michael Ayers. Vol. 2. Cambridge: Cambridge University Press, 1998, 1145–92.

Osler, Margaret J. "John Locke and the Changing Ideal of Scientific Knowledge." *Journal of the History of Ideas* 31 (1970): 1–16. Reprinted in *Philosophy, Religion, and Science in the 17th and 18th Centuries,* ed. by John W. Yolton. Rochester, N.Y.: University of Rochester Press, 1990, 325–38.

———. "Certainty, Skepticism, and Scientific Optimism: The Roots of Eighteenth-Century Attitudes Towards Scientific Knowledge." In *Probability, Time, and Space in Eighteenth-Century Literature,* ed. by Paul R. Backscheider. New York: AMS, 1979, 3–28.

Popkin, Richard H. *The History of Skepticism from Erasmus to Spinoza.* 1960. Rev. ed. Berkeley: University of California Press, 1979.

Redwood, John. *Reason, Ridicule, and Religion: The Age of Enlightenment in England, 1660–1750.* Cambridge, Mass.: Harvard University Press, 1976.

Schmitt, Charles B. *Cicero Scepticus: A Study of the Influence of the Academica in the Renaissance.* The Hague: Martinus Nijhoff, 1972.

Shapiro, Barbara J. *Probability and Certainty in Seventeenth-Century England: A Study of the Relationships Between Natural Science, Religion, History, Law, and Literature.* Princeton, N.J.: Princeton University Press, 1983.

van Leeuwen, Henry. *The Problem of Certainty in English Thought, 1630–1680.* The Hague: Martinus Nijhoff, 1963.

27. CARTESIANISM

Thomas M. Lennon

Cartesianism refers to the scientific and, especially, the philosophical doctrines originating with René Descartes (1596–1650). Scientifically, the most prominent doctrine was mechanism, according to which all change is change of motion, and motion changes only upon contact. The distinctively Cartesian version of this doctrine gave it a mathematical cast. Material nature was fundamentally mathematical, not only in the sense that its laws were mathematical, but also that its essence was the extension thought to be the object of geometry. Indeed, Descartes boasted that his "physics is nothing but geometry" and that with extension and motion alone he could re-create the universe. The most prominent philosophical doctrines of Cartesianism are radical dualism, according to which mind and body are distinct substances, and foundationalism, according to which human knowledge must have an unshakable basis that is immune to skeptical doubt. Unlike Descartes's scientific views, which have been largely either modified beyond recognition or rejected outright, his philosophical views continue to be debated.

The place of Cartesianism in the history of science and religion is, to say the least, ambiguous. With respect to its philosophical structure, the intentions of its proponents, and its historical influence, there is little agreement whether, and in what sense, Cartesianism was a negative or a positive factor for religion. Cartesianism itself was, in many respects, like a religion. Like many religions, it had canonical texts that have proven to be very difficult to interpret, most notably, Descartes's statement *"Cogito ergo sum"* ("I think, therefore I am") from the *Meditations*. Descartes thought that he could refute the most extreme version of skepticism merely by asserting his own existence, which would give him at least one instance of certain knowledge. But just how he connected his thought that he existed with the knowledge that he existed has never been clear. To the extent that this refutation of skepticism has been problematic, the grounds that Descartes cited for religious belief were also seen by many to be problematic.

Cartesianism resembled a religion in other respects as well. It also had would-be adherents who claimed an orthodoxy that excluded as heretical other would-be adherents. Thus, when Robert Desgabets (1610–78) was presented with Géraud de Cordemoy's (1626–84) atomism in *Le discernement* (1666), he wrote to Claude Clersellier that its author "thoughtlessly causes a schism." On the other hand, part of the vitality of Cartesianism for the half-century beyond the death of Descartes may be attributable to efforts made by Descartes's followers to deal with problems of interpretation and orthodoxy. It is also interesting to note that the death and disposition of the body of Descartes himself became part of the cult of the eponymous founder of Cartesianism. The skeptic Pierre-Daniel Huet's (1630–1721) hilarious send-up of Descartes's exceedingly optimistic life expectancy and the protracted debate whether his mortal remains were to be buried in the secular Pantheon or the religious Saint Germain des Prés are only two chapters in this fascinating story.

Descartes's *Meditations* (1641) was dedicated to "those most learned and illustrious men, the Dean and Doctors of the Sacred Faculty of Theology at Paris." In his dedicatory letter, Descartes pointed to two topics, the existence of God and the immortality of the soul, on which he claimed to have demonstrative proofs. He was responding to the Fifth Lateran Council (1512–17), which a century earlier had instructed philosophers to refute Averroism, the interpretation of Aristotle (384–322 B.C.) according to which only a universal human soul survives separation from the body. Descartes tried to show that, because the human body and soul are really distinct, the immortality of individual human souls can be demonstrated.

In the *Meditations* themselves, however, Descartes's proofs for the immortality of the soul and even for the existence of God pale in significance beside his attempt to give a non-Aristotelian account of knowledge and the world. Moreover, Descartes's attempt to refute skepticism as part of this account was generally taken to be a failure. One result of this failure has been the "epistemological turn" that he gave to subsequent philosophy with its generally negative implications for religious belief. Such, at least, is the argument advanced by Pope John Paul II (b. 1920, p. 1978–) in his *Crossing the Threshold of Hope* (1994).

Descartes himself tried to steer clear of religious and theological controversy lest other parts of his philosophy come under suspicion. Silence was one response to theological controversy. Thus, for example, Descartes never directly mentioned a doctrine that he very early came to believe was at the basis of his philosophical thinking. This was the doctrine that all truth, including eternal truth such as is found in mathematics, depends on the will of God and, in that sense, is created. In early correspondence, Descartes was willing to have this doctrine "broadcast everywhere." But once apprised of its controversial status among theologians, he later referred to it in his published work only twice, and then incidentally.

Theological conservatism led Descartes to suppress a treatise that he was preparing for publication. When, in 1633, he heard of the Catholic Church's condemnation of Galileo (1564–1642), Descartes left off the work that was posthumously published as *The World* and the *Treatise on Man,* lest he publish anything the "least word of which the Church would disapprove." Later, in one of his most important works, *Principles of Philosophy* (1644), he would publish a textbook version of much of this work. The last of the principles is that "I submit all my views to the authority of the Church." Descartes's caution was part of his campaign on behalf of the new worldview: He hoped not only to overthrow Aristotle, but to replace him, not merely in the secular sphere of science and philosophy, but also in the religious sphere, as the philosopher best in a position to explicate the truths of faith. The caution was for naught. Far from convincing his former teachers, the Jesuits, to take up his cause, Descartes, in 1663, was placed on the Church's Index of Prohibited Books "until corrected."

One theological topic that Descartes and his followers could not avoid—precisely because of the overthrow of Aristotle—was transubstantiation, the doctrine that the bread and wine of the Eucharist are miraculously changed into the body and blood of Christ. According to the Cartesian version of mechanism, matter, the stuff whose motion explained all natural phenomena, had as its essence extension. A material thing was merely tridimensional. It was identical to the space it occupied and nothing more. With this dramatic doctrine, the Aristotelian distinction between matter and form was swept away and, with it, the hitherto accepted way of understanding the doctrine of the Eucharist. If there were no substantial forms, then consecration could not convert the host into the body of Christ by means of transubstantiation. Descartes and his followers tried to account for the phenomenon by focusing on the surface of the host, which as either bread or the body of Christ would have the same mechanical effects on the sensory apparatus.

The Cartesian effort to account for the Eucharist was resisted by many, and great debates over it ensued, most notably with the Jesuit Louis LeValois (1639–1700), who, under the pseudonym of Louis de La Ville, argued the incompatibility of the Cartesian and the Roman Catholic doctrines. Pierre Bayle (1647–1706) was one important thinker who agreed with LeValois, but, as a Calvinist, he concluded that it was the Catholic doctrine that was mistaken. The Catholic fideist Blaise Pascal (1623–62) passed a judgment on Descartes that may have been extended to all who took part in these debates: They "probe too deeply into the sciences."

The other of the two main Cartesian doctrines also led to religious and theological problems. As extension was taken to be the essence of matter, so thought was regarded as the essence of mind. Mind and matter were the only two kinds of substance in the world, according to Descartes, who cited this dualism as a key premise in his argument for the soul's immortality. But he developed his conception of the mind in such a way that it appeared to be cognitively self-sufficient and, hence, independent of any divine or supernatural illumination. This issue was investigated at great length by the two most important followers of Descartes, Antoine Arnauld (1612–94) and

Nicolas de Malebranche (1638–1715), when they argued over the nature of ideas. There is a rationalist trajectory, in any case, that moves from Descartes to the crowning, at the French Revolution, of a naked woman as Reason in Paris's Cathedral of Notre Dame.

The ambiguous place of Cartesianism might be epitomized by its relation to Augustinianism, a seventeenth-century touchstone of orthodoxy. Although Descartes seems to have denied the need of human beings for divine illumination, he was perceived to share much with Augustine (354–430). In fact, when Cartesianism fell upon politically hard times in the 1670s and its teaching was forbidden in the schools, Cartesians went on teaching as before but used texts from Augustine. Even this advantage had its peril, however, for it served to underline a perceived connection between the Cartesians and Port-Royal, the center of the Jansenist movement, which emphasized Augustinian theology within French Catholicism. Madame de Sevigny's (1626–96) epithet for René LeBossu (1631–80) says it all: "Jansenist, that is, Cartesian." Typically, then, it was difficult to say where Cartesianism stood, or, given any stance, what its significance might be, or, given any interpretation, what its orthodoxy might be.

See also Blaise Pascal; Mechanical Philosophy; Skepticism

BIBLIOGRAPHY

Armogathe, J.-R. *Theologia Cartesiana: L'explication de l'Eucharistie chez Descartes et dom Desgabets.* The Hague: Martinus Nijhoff, 1977.

Cottingham, John. *The Cambridge Companion to Descartes.* Cambridge: Cambridge University Press, 1992.

Gaukroger, Stephen. *Descartes: An Intellectual Biography.* New York: Oxford University Press, 1995.

Gouhier, Henri. *La pensée religieuse de Descartes.* Paris: Vrin, 1924.

Rorty, Amelie O. *Essays on Descartes' Meditations.* Berkeley: University of California Press, 1986.

Shea, William R. *The Magic of Numbers and Motion: The Scientific Career of René Descartes.* Canton, Mass.: Science History Publications, 1991.

28. Mechanical Philosophy

Margaret J. Osler

Mechanical philosophy was a philosophy of nature, popular in the seventeenth century, that sought to explain all natural phenomena in terms of matter and motion without recourse to any kind of action-at-a-distance. During the sixteenth and seventeenth centuries, many natural philosophers rejected Aristotelianism, which had provided metaphysical and epistemological foundations for both science and theology at least since the thirteenth century. One candidate for a replacement was the mechanical philosophy, which had its roots in classical Epicureanism. Mechanical philosophers attempted to explain all natural phenomena in terms of the configurations, motions, and collisions of small, unobservable particles of matter. For example, to explain the fact that lead is denser than water, a mechanical philosopher would say that the lead has more particles of matter per cubic measure than water. The mechanical explanation differed from Aristotelian explanations, which endowed matter with real qualities and used them to explain the differences in density by appealing to the fact that lead has more absolute heaviness than the water. A hallmark of the mechanical philosophy was the doctrine of primary and secondary qualities, according to which matter is really endowed with only a few "primary" qualities, and all others (such as color, taste, or odor) are the result of the impact of the primary qualities on our sense organs. Nature was thus mechanized, and most qualities were considered subjective. This approach enhanced the mathematization of nature at the same time that it provided an answer to the skeptical critique of sensory knowledge.

While the mechanical philosophy was attractive to thinkers working in the tradition of Galileo Galilei (1564–1642) and William Harvey (1578–1657), it posed serious problems for those holding a Christian worldview. Orthodox natural philosophers feared that the mechanical philosophy would lead to materialism or deism, resulting in the denial of Creation and divine providence. The fact that the Thomist synthesis of theology and Aristotelian philosophy had become dominant in the Catholic world, especially after the Council of Trent (1545–63), also meant that the rejection of Aristotelianism seemed to challenge the doctrine of transubstantiation (the doctrine that the bread and wine in the Eucharist were miraculously transformed into the body and blood of Christ).

Christian mechanical philosophers adopted a variety of strategies to stave off these perceived threats, including frequent appeal to the argument from design as a way of establishing God's providential relationship to the world he created, special attention to proving the existence of an immaterial, immortal human soul, and attempts to explain the real presence in the Eucharist in mechanical terms.

Background

The mechanical philosophy originated in classical times with the Greek philosopher Epicurus (341–270 B.C.), who sought to explain all natural phenomena in terms of the chance collisions of material atoms in empty space. He even claimed that the human soul is material, composed of atoms that are exceedingly small and swift. Epicurus believed that atoms have always existed and that they are infinite in number. Epicureanism, while not strictly atheistic, denied that the gods play a role in the natural or human worlds, thus ruling out any kind of providential explanation. Because of its reputation as atheistic and materialistic, Epicureanism fell into disrepute during the Middle Ages. The writings of Epicurus and his Roman disciple Lucretius (c. 99–55 B.C.) were published during the Renaissance, along with a host of other classical writings.

Following the development of heliocentric astronomy in the late sixteenth and early seventeenth centuries, many natural philosophers believed that Aristotelianism, which rests on geocentric assumptions, could no longer provide adequate foundations for natural philosophy. Among the many ancient philosophies that had been recovered by the Renaissance humanists, the atomism of Epicurus seemed particularly compatible with the spirit of the new astronomy and physics. Moreover, the mechanical philosophy often seemed easier to reconcile with Christian theology than the alternatives—Stoicism, Neoplatonism, and Paracelsianism—all of which appeared to limit the scope or freedom of God's action in the world. Early advocates of the mechanical philosophy included David van Goorle (d. 1612), Sebastian Basso (fl. 1550–1600), and various members of the Northumberland Circle, of which Walter Warner (c. 1570–c. 1642), Thomas Hariot (1560–1621), and Nicholas Hill (c. 1570–1610) were members. Although each of these men favored some version of atomism, none of them developed a systematic philosophy or addressed the theological problems associated with atomism. Isaac Beeckman (1588–1637), a Dutch schoolmaster, advocated a mechanical view of nature and wrote about it extensively in his private journal, which was not published until the twentieth century. Beeckman's personal influence was enormous, however, and he was instrumental in encouraging both Pierre Gassendi (1592–1655) and René Descartes (1596–1650) to adopt the mechanical philosophy.

Major Advocates

A number of the major figures whose names are associated with the scientific revolution adopted some version of the mechanical philosophy. Although Galileo did not write a fully articulated account of it, he implicitly adopted its major tenets. In *Il Saggiatore* (*The Assayer* [1623]), he employed the doctrine of primary and secondary qualities to explain perception.

Gassendi and Descartes published the first systematic, and the most influential, accounts of the mechanical philosophy. Their treatises were not detailed accounts of particular subjects. Rather, they spelled out the fundamental terms of a mechanical philosophy and functioned as programmatic statements, describing what such a phi-

losophy would look like in practice. While both men agreed that all physical phenomena should be explained in terms of matter and motion, they differed about the details of those explanations. Gassendi, writing in the manner of a Renaissance humanist, saw himself as the restorer of the philosophy of Epicurus. Deeply concerned with Epicurus's heterodox ideas, Gassendi, a Catholic priest, sought to modify ancient atomism so that it would be acceptable to seventeenth-century Christians. Accordingly, he insisted on God's creation of a finite number of atoms, on God's continuing providential relationship to the Creation, on free will (both human and divine), and on the existence of an immaterial, immortal human soul that God infused into each individual at the moment of conception.

Gassendi believed that God had created indivisible atoms and endowed them with motion. The atoms, colliding in empty space, are the constituents of the physical world. In his massive *Syntagma philosophicum* (published posthumously in 1658), Gassendi set out to explain all of the qualities of matter and all of the phenomena in the world in terms of atoms and the void. He argued for the existence of the void—a controversial claim at the time—on both conceptual and empirical grounds, appealing to the recent barometric experiments of Evangelista Torricelli (1608–47) and Blaise Pascal (1623–62). The primary qualities of Gassendi's atoms were size, shape, and mass. He advocated an empiricist theory of scientific method and considered the results of this method to be, at best, probable.

Gassendi insisted that God has complete freedom of action in the universe that he freely created. Indeed, God can, if he wishes, violate or overturn the laws of nature that he established. The only constraint on divine freedom is the law of noncontradiction. One consequence of divine freedom is that humans must have free will, too, for, if human actions were necessarily determined, that necessity would be a restriction on God's freedom to act. Gassendi rejected as question begging Epicurus's explanation of human freedom as a consequence of unpredictable, random swerves of the atoms composing the human. Instead, he argued for the existence of an immaterial and immortal human soul, which is the seat of the higher mental faculties. In addition to the immaterial, immortal soul, Gassendi claimed that there exists a material, sensible soul, composed of very fine and swiftly moving particles. This material soul (which animals also possess) is responsible for vitality, perception, and the less abstract aspects of understanding. The material soul is transmitted from one generation to the next in the process of biological reproduction. Gassendi's ideas were brought to England by Walter Charleton (1620–1707) and popularized in France by François Bernier (1620–88).

Although Descartes also articulated a full-fledged mechanical philosophy in his *Principia philosophiae* (*Principles of Philosophy* [1644]), his ideas were quite different from those of Epicurus. In contrast to Gassendi's atomic view of matter, Descartes claimed that matter fills all space and is infinitely divisible, thus denying the existence of both atoms and the void. He believed that matter possesses only one primary quality, geometrical extension. This belief provided foundations for his attempted mathematization of nature. Descartes drew a sharp distinction between matter and mind, considering thinking to be the essential characteristic of the mind. Like Gassendi's doctrine of the immortal soul, Descartes's concept of mind established the boundaries of mechanization in the world.

Descartes derived his mechanical philosophy directly from theological considerations. His rationalist epistemology was grounded in the conviction that, since God is not a deceiver, his existence provides a warrant for reasoning from clear and distinct ideas in our minds to knowledge about the created world. Since geometrical concepts are paradigmatic of clear and distinct ideas, we can conclude that the physical world has geometrical properties. It is on such grounds that Descartes justified the claim that matter is infinitely divisible. The divine attributes also lie at the base of Descartes's attempts to prove the laws of motion. He appealed to God's immutability to justify his law of the conservation of motion and his version of the principle of inertia, the foundations of his physics.

Like Gassendi, Descartes intended his philosophy to replace Aristotelianism. He hoped that the Jesuit colleges would adopt the *Principia philosophiae* as a physics textbook to replace the Aristotelian texts still in use. His hopes were dashed, however, when his book was condemned in 1662 and placed on the Index of Prohibited Books in 1663 in response to his attempt to give a mechanical explanation of the real presence in the Eucharist.

The differences between the mechanical philosophies of Gassendi and Descartes reflect their theological differences concerning providence, or God's relationship to the creation. Gassendi was a voluntarist, believ-

ing that the created world is utterly contingent on God's will, which is constrained only by the law of noncontradiction. The contingency of the world rules out the possibility of any kind of rationalist epistemology because it would embody some kind of necessity, such as the relationship between ideas in our minds and the world. Gassendi's empiricism and probabilism, and the fact that he believed that matter possesses some properties that can be known only by empirical methods, reflect his voluntarist theology. In contrast to Gassendi, Descartes believed that, although God was entirely free in his creation of the world, he freely created some things to be necessary (for example, the eternal truths), which we are capable of knowing a priori and with certainty. Descartes's theory of matter, according to which matter possesses only geometrical properties that can be known a priori, follows from his rationalist epistemology. Both his theory of knowledge and his theory of matter are closely associated with his theological presuppositions.

Another mechanical philosopher, Thomas Hobbes (1588–1679), was the specter haunting more orthodox mechanical philosophers. Whatever the state of his religious beliefs, Hobbes's philosophy seemed—to the seventeenth-century reader—to be materialistic, deterministic, and possibly even atheistic. In *The Elements of Philosophy* (1655), Hobbes propounded a complete philosophy—of matter, of man, and of the state—according to mechanistic principles. Although the details of his mechanical philosophy were not very influential among natural philosophers, his mechanical account of the human soul and his thoroughly deterministic account of the natural world alarmed the more orthodox thinkers of his day.

Later Developments

Gassendi and Descartes were founding fathers of the mechanical philosophy in the sense that the next generation of natural philosophers, who accepted mechanical principles in general, believed that they had to choose between Gassendi's atomism and Descartes's corpuscularism. Robert Boyle (1627–91) and Isaac Newton (1642–1727), among the most prominent natural philosophers of the second half of the seventeenth century who developed their philosophies of nature in this context, were both deeply concerned with the theological implications of their views.

Boyle is best known for his attempt to incorporate

chemistry within a mechanical framework. His corpuscular philosophy—which remained noncommittal on the question of whether matter is infinitely divisible or composed of indivisible atoms—was founded on a mechanical conception of matter. His reluctance to commit himself to a position on the ultimate nature of matter reflected his concern about the atheism still associated with Epicureanism, as well as his recognition that some questions lie beyond the ability of human reason to resolve. Material bodies are, according to Boyle, composed of extremely small particles, which combine to form clusters of various sizes and configurations. The configurations, motions, and collisions of these clusters produce secondary qualities, including the chemical properties of matter. Boyle conducted many observations and experiments with the aim of demonstrating that various chemical properties can be explained mechanically. He performed an extensive series of experiments with the newly fabricated air pump to prove that the properties of air—most notably its "spring"—could be explained in mechanical terms.

Boyle was a deeply religious man and discussed the theological implications of his corpuscularianism at great length. He believed that God had created matter and had endowed it with motion. God had created laws of nature but could violate those laws at will; biblical miracles provided evidence for that claim. In addition to matter, God creates human souls, which he imparts to each embryo individually. He also created angels and demons, which are spiritual, not material entities.

For Boyle—and many other natural philosophers of his day—the practice of natural philosophy was an act of worship, since it led to greater knowledge of the Creator by directly acquainting the careful observer with God's wisdom and benevolence in designing the world. God's purposes are everywhere evident to the astute observer. God is not entirely knowable, however, and neither are his purposes. Boyle was careful to acknowledge the limits of human reason in theology, and those limits extend as well to natural philosophy, in which human knowledge is limited in scope and is never certain. Boyle's ideal was that of "the Christian Virtuoso," who discovered the deep connections between natural philosophy and Christian theology.

Newton, whose reputation rests on his achievements in mathematical physics and optics, accepted the mechanical philosophy from his student days in Cambridge. A notebook written in the mid-1660s shows him thinking about natural phenomena in mechanical terms and designing thought experiments for choosing between Cartesian and Gassendist explanations of particular phenomena. A number of phenomena—gravitation, the reflection and refraction of light, surface tension, capillary action, certain chemical reactions—persistently resisted explanation in purely mechanical terms. Failing in the attempt to explain them by appeal to hypotheses about submicroscopic ethers, Newton was led to the view that there exist attractive and repulsive forces between the particles composing bodies. This idea came to him from his alchemical studies. Newton's most notable discovery, the principle of universal gravitation, which provided a unified foundation for both terrestrial and celestial mechanics and which marks the culmination of developments started by Copernicus (1473–1543) in the mid-sixteenth century, demanded a concept of attractive force. The concept of force, which seemed to some contemporaries to be a return to older theories of action-at-a-distance banished by the mechanical philosophy, enabled Newton to accomplish his stunning mathematization of physics.

In addition to physics and mathematics, Newton devoted years of intellectual labor throughout his life to the study of alchemy and theology. Recent scholarship has suggested that Newton's primary motive in all three areas was theological: to establish God's activity in the world. Theologically, Newton was an Arian, believing that Christ, while divine, was a created being and denying the doctrine of the Trinity. The transcendence of the Arian God suggested the possibility of deism, a doctrine Newton rejected. Consequently, Newton devoted himself to discovering evidence of divine activity in the world, something he found in the active matter of the alchemists, in the fulfillment of the biblical prophecies in history, and in the gravitation of matter. Because matter itself is inert, it cannot generate any motion, and it cannot deviate from uniform rectilinear motion without the action of some external mover. The orbital motions of the planets are a departure from inertial motion, which Newton explained in terms of gravitational force. Explaining gravitation had been a challenge to Newton throughout his life. Denying that it is an innate property of matter, Newton sought to explain this force in some way that was consistent with both his theology and his philosophy of nature. Early in his career, he attempted to explain gravity, along with other recalcitrant phenomena, such as surface tension, capillary action, and the reflection and refraction of light, in terms of such mechanical devices as density gradients in the ether. In the 1670s, he abandoned attempts to explain gravity in purely mechanical terms, recognizing that such explanations led to an infinite regress. Moreover, as he proved in the *Principia,* the presence of even the most subtle mechanical ether in space would resist the motions of the planets, causing the solar system to run down. Newton speculated further in several of the "Queries" to his *Opticks* (1704). At one stage, he proposed the existence of an ether that would not resist the motions of the planets and that was composed of particles endowed with both attractive and repulsive forces. At another stage, he proposed that gravitation results from God's direct action on matter. On this account, he regarded his physics and his cosmology as part of a grand argument from design, leading to knowledge of the intelligent and all-powerful Creator.

In the decades after Newton's death, the worst fears of the Christian mechanical philosophers of the seventeenth century came true. John Locke (1632–1704) argued for the reasonableness of Christianity, and his environmentalist analysis of the human mind—which grew directly from the ideas of the mechanical philosophers—implied the denial of the Christian doctrine of original sin. Deism and natural religion flourished both in England and on the Continent. Some of the French philosophes, notably Julien Offray de La Mettrie (1709–51) and Paul Henry Thiry, Baron d'Holbach (1723–89), espoused atheistic materialism and adopted vigorously anticlerical and antiecclesiastical views. David Hume (1711–76) undermined the possibility of natural religion and a providential understanding of the world by purporting to demonstrate the invalidity of the standard arguments for the existence of God, particularly the argument from design, which had played such a crucial role for the seventeenth-century mechanical philosophers. Newtonian mechanics rose to great heights, having shed the theological preoccupations of its creator. These developments culminated in the work of Pierre Laplace (1749–1827), who articulated a clear statement of classical determinism and was able to demonstrate that the solar system is a gravitationally stable Newtonian system. When asked by Napoleon what role God played in his system, Laplace is reputed to have replied: "Sire, I have no need for that hypothesis."

See also Atomism; Cartesianism; Early-Modern Protestantism; Isaac Newton; Varieties of Providentialism

BIBLIOGRAPHY

Boas, Marie. "The Establishment of the Mechanical Philosophy." *Osiris* 10 (1952): 412–541.

Brandt, Frithiof. *Thomas Hobbes' Mechanical Conception of Nature.* Trans. by Vaughan Maxwell and Annie Fausball. Copenhagen and London: Levin and Munksgaard/Librairie Hachette, 1928.

Dijksterhuis, E. J. *The Mechanization of the World Picture.* Trans. by C. Dikshoorn. Oxford: Oxford University Press, 1961.

Dobbs, Betty Jo Teeter. *The Janus Faces of Genius: The Role of Alchemy in Newton's Thought.* Cambridge: Cambridge University Press, 1991.

Funkenstein, Amos. *Theology and the Scientific Imagination from the Middle Ages to the Seventeenth Century.* Princeton, N.J.: Princeton University Press, 1986.

Gabbey, Alan. "Henry More and the Limits of Mechanism." In *Henry More (1614–1687): Tercentenary Studies,* ed. by Sarah Hutton. Dordrecht: Kluwer, 1990, 19–35.

Garber, Daniel. *Descartes' Metaphysical Physics.* Chicago: University of Chicago Press, 1992.

Garber, Daniel, and Michael Ayers. *The Cambridge History of Seventeenth-Century Philosophy.* 2 vols. Cambridge: Cambridge University Press, 1998.

Hutchison, Keith. "Supernaturalism and the Mechanical Philosophy." *History of Science* 21 (1983): 297–333.

Kargon, Robert. *Atomism in England from Hariot to Newton.* Oxford: Oxford University Press, 1966.

MacIntosh, J. J. "Robert Boyle on Epicurean Atheism and Atomism." In *Atoms, Pneuma, and Tranquillity: Epicurean and Stoic Themes in European Thought,* ed. by Margaret J. Osler. Cambridge: Cambridge University Press, 1991, 197–219.

McGuire, J. E. "Boyle's Conception of Nature." *Journal of the History of Ideas* 33 (1972): 523–43.

Mintz, Samuel I. *The Hunting of Leviathan: Seventeenth-Century Reactions to the Materialism and Moral Philosophy of Thomas Hobbes.* Cambridge: Cambridge University Press, 1962.

Nadler, Steven M. "Arnauld, Descartes, and Transubstantiation: Reconciling Cartesian Metaphysics and Real Presence." *Journal of the History of Ideas* 49 (1988): 229–46.

Osler, Margaret J. "The Intellectual Sources of Robert Boyle's Philosophy of Nature: Gassendi's Voluntarism and Boyle's Physico-Theological Project." In *Philosophy, Science, and Religion, 1640–1700,* ed. by Richard Ashcraft, Richard Kroll, and Perez Zagorin. Cambridge: Cambridge University Press, 1991, 178–98.

———. *Divine Will and the Mechanical Philosophy: Gassendi and Descartes on Contingency and Necessity in the Created World.* Cambridge: Cambridge University Press, 1994.

Redondi, Pietro. *Galileo: Heretic.* Trans. by Raymond Rosenthal. Princeton, N.J.: Princeton University Press, 1987.

Schaffer, Simon. "Godly Men and Mechanical Philosophers: Souls and Spirits in Restoration Natural Philosophy." *Science in Context* 1 (1987): 55–86.

Shanahan, Timothy. "God and Nature in the Thought of Robert Boyle." *Journal of the History of Philosophy* 26 (1988): 547–69.

Westfall, Richard S. *Force in Newton's Physics: The Science of Dynamics in the Seventeenth Century.* London and New York: MacDonald/American Elsevier, 1971.

Wojcik, Jan W. *Robert Boyle and the Limits of Reason.* Cambridge: Cambridge University Press, 1997.

29. The Cambridge Platonists

Sarah Hutton

The Cambridge Platonists were a group of seventeenth-century thinkers, all of whom were associated with the University of Cambridge, England, whose writings are distinguished by a marked admiration for the philosophy of Plato (c. 427–347 B.C.) and his followers. The chief members of this group were Ralph Cudworth (1617–88) and Henry More (1614–87). The group also included Nathaniel Culverwell (1619–51), Peter Sterry (1613–72), and John Smith (1618–52). The younger generation associated with them included Joseph Glanvill (1636–80) and Anne Conway (c. 1630–79). They are characterized by a liberal religious temper rather than a specific set of common doctrines. In their emphasis on free will and their opposition to predestinarian Calvinism, they can be placed in the Erasmian tradition. Most of them expressed open admiration for Origen (c. 185–c. 251). In philosophy, they were distinguished by a broad receptivity to ideas modern as well as ancient. In addition to Platonism, they drew on Stoicism and the new philosophy and science of the seventeenth century, and, in particular, on the mechanical philosophy of René Descartes (1596–1650) and the new astronomy of Copernicus (1473–1543) and Galileo (1564–1642). This interest in new ideas was accompanied by a repudiation of the authority of Aristotle (384–322 B.C.) and scholastic thought. They were also hostile to some contemporary thought, especially to the philosophy of Thomas Hobbes (1588–1679) and Baruch Spinoza (1632–77), which they attacked on religious grounds as materialist and, therefore, atheistic.

The Cambridge Platonists were all theologians, albeit of a philosophical bent, who stressed the importance of the role of reason in religious matters. They defended religion using arguments drawn from philosophy, in particular from natural philosophy (or what is now called science). Four aspects of their apologetic might be singled out for mention: (1) their support for new scientific theories; (2) their reception of experimentalism; (3) their critique of some aspects of the new theories they encountered; and (4) their contribution to the formulation of new concepts.

More's enthusiasm for Copernicus and Galileo is first registered in his *Philosophical Poems* (1647). More was also one of the first promoters of Cartesianism in England, especially of Descartes's natural philosophy, which, according to the preface of his *Immortality of the Soul* (1659), he thought ought to be part of the university curriculum. Initially, for both More and Cudworth, the appeal of the mechanical philosophy as proposed by Descartes lay not just in the fact that it appeared to offer a satisfactory account of the phenomena of nature, but that it implied the need for some kind of immaterial agency to set inert matter in motion. It thus presupposed the existence of spiritual substance and, ultimately, of God. Cudworth, in particular, took up new corpuscularian hypotheses about the structure of matter, which he promoted in his only published work, *True Intellectual System of the Universe* (1678), as a hypothesis that was both philosophically sound and theologically respectable. He argued, on both philosophical and historical grounds, for its compatibility with theism, regarding Descartes as a reviver of the ancient atomism of Democritus (c. 460–c. 370 B.C.).

More also sought to elaborate the argument for the existence of God from the design of the universe—that the organization of the observable world implies that it must be the product of a wise and beneficent deity. In Book 2 of his *Antidote Against Atheism* (1653), he cites a whole variety of natural phenomena, from gravity and "the Elastick power of the Aire" to human anatomy, to support the argument from design. More, Cudworth, and Culverwell were all conversant with the works of William Harvey (1578–1657) and Francis Bacon (1561–1626). Cudworth's *True Intellectual System* is a vast compendium of ancient learning, which provides a historical taxonomy of theories and doctrines with the aim of distinguishing true from false philosophy. More used inductive methods as part of his project to provide unshakable proof of the existence of God. He sought to demonstrate the existence of spirits of all kinds, including ghosts and diabolic manifestations, by collecting data from reliable witnesses, which he presented in his *Antidote* and in his *Immortality of the Soul*. This project was continued by Joseph Glanvill in his *Sadducismus triumphatus* (1681).

As this last example suggests, More's application of observational techniques (in this case, to examining the spirit world) would hardly be considered scientifically orthodox today. Nor were his excursions into experimentation particularly productive. His own inclination was toward an a priori approach. He upset Robert Boyle (1627–91) when he used the experiments described in Boyle's *New Experiments Physico-Mechanical* (1660) as support for his own theory of the existence of a Spirit of Nature. More's overhasty metaphysical interpretation of Boyle's experiments should not, however, obscure the fact that he was a well-meant enthusiast for the new science of the Royal Society.

It was metaphysical concerns, again, that eventually led More to revise his view of Descartes's philosophy because it did not give a satisfactory account of spiritual substance. His critique of Cartesianism is most fully set out in *Enchiridion metaphysicum* (1671). Here he attempts to expose the shortcomings of the mechanical philosophy by adducing a plethora of natural phenomena—such as the sympathetic vibration of strings, the shape of the planetary bodies, the inclination of the axis of the earth, and gravity—that either could not be satisfactorily explained in mechanical terms or that plainly contradicted Cartesian theory. In place of the mechanical explanation of natural phenomena in terms of the impact of matter in motion, More proposed his concept of the Spirit of Nature, or the Hylarchic Principle, which directs the operations of nature. Cudworth proposed an analogous concept, that of Plastic Nature, an immaterial regulatory principle supervising all of the operations of nature and executing God's designs in the world. Both Plastic Nature and the Hylarchic Principle were vitalistic

hypotheses framed to account for phenomena otherwise inexplicable in merely mechanical terms. Each could be justified in terms of observable phenomena, but neither could, in modern terms, be verifiable except in negative relation to mechanism. Nonetheless, it has been argued that they contributed to the concept of force as framed by Isaac Newton (1642–1727). An alternative solution to the problem of how motion is transmitted between bodies was that made by More's pupil Anne Conway, who dispensed with the dualism of immaterial spirit and material body, on which More and Cudworth relied, and proposed instead a monistic theory of substance, which, in effect, ascribed the properties of spirit (life and motion) to bodies, which she conceived as comprising infinite particles, or monads. Lady Conway's system anticipates that of Gottfried Wilhelm Leibniz (1646–1716). More's concept of infinite space, formulated as part of his argument for the existence of incorporeal substance (spirit), derived from his concept of spirit as immaterial extension (that is, the immaterial equivalent of material extension as conceived by Descartes). Space is, for More, a kind of shadow of God himself, whom More conceives as an infinitely extended incorporeal being.

The philosophical influence of the Cambridge Platonists in Britain extends to Lord Shaftesbury (1671–1713), Richard Price (1723–91), Thomas Reid (1710–96), and Samuel Taylor Coleridge (1772–1834). The writings of Cudworth and More were known in Europe in Latin translation. In particular, Cudworth's doctrine of Plastic Nature attracted interest as an explanatory hypothesis in the Enlightenment. In theology, their tolerant outlook had a lasting impact on the Church of England, in which they became known as the fathers of the Latitudinarian movement, which attached little importance to doctrine and appealed to reason as a source of religious authority.

See also Cartesianism; Mechanical Philosophy; Plato and Platonism

BIBLIOGRAPHY

Cassirer, Ernst. *The Platonic Renaissance in England*. Trans. by J. P. Pettigrove. Edinburgh: Nelson, 1953.

Colie, R. *Light and Enlightenment*. Cambridge: Cambridge University Press, 1957.

Copenhaver, B. P. "Jewish Theologies of Space in the Scientific Revolution: Henry More, Joseph Raphson, Isaac Newton, and Their Predecessors." *Annals of Science* 37 (1980): 489–548.

Hall, A. Rupert. *Henry More: Magic, Religion, and Experiment.* Oxford: Blackwell, 1990.

Henry, John. "Henry More, Richard Baxter, and Francis Glisson's Treatise on the Energetic Nature of Substance." *Medical History* 31 (1987): 15–40.

Hutton, Sarah, ed. *Henry More (1618–1687): Tercentenary Studies.* Dordrecht: Kluwer, 1987.

Koyré, Alexandre. *From the Closed World to the Infinite Universe.* Baltimore: Johns Hopkins University Press, 1957.

McAdoo, H. R. *The Spirit of Anglicanism: A Survey of Anglican Method in the Seventeenth Century.* London: A. and C. Black, 1965.

Mintz, S. *The Hunting of Leviathan: Seventeenth-Century Reactions to the Materialism and Moral Philosophy of Thomas Hobbes.* Cambridge: Cambridge University Press, 1962.

Passmore, J. A. *Ralph Cudworth: An Interpretation.* Cambridge: Cambridge University Press, 1951.

Patrides, C. A. *The Cambridge Platonists.* Cambridge: Cambridge University Press, 1969.

Power, J. E. "Henry More and Isaac Newton on Absolute Space." *Journal of the History of Ideas* 31 (1970): 289–96.

Rogers, G. A. J. "Die Cambridge Platoniker." In *Ueberwegs Grundriss der Geschichte der Philosophie: die Philosophie des 17. Jahrhunderts*, ed. by J.–P. Schobinger. Vol. 3. Basle: Schwabe, 1988, 240–90.

Shapin, S., and S. Schaffer. *Leviathan and the Air Pump.* Princeton, N.J.: Princeton University Press, 1985.

Stewart, J. A. "The Cambridge Platonists." In *The Encyclopedia of Religion and Ethics,* ed. by James Hastings. Vol. 3. New York: Charles Scribner's Sons, 1911, 167–73.

Tulloch, J. H. *Rational Theology and Christian Philosophy in England in the Seventeenth Century.* Edinburgh: Blackwood, 1872.

Webster, C. "Henry More and Descartes: Some New Sources." *British Journal for the History of Science* (1969): 359–77.

30. DEISM

Stephen P. Weldon

Deism is a religious position that was common among European and American intellectuals during the late seventeenth and eighteenth centuries. It extolled the virtues of a universalistic natural religion and condemned revealed religion—especially Christianity—for its alleged parochialism and irrationality. Deists believed that the universe was governed by mathematically perfect natural laws, that it was created by a benevolent and rational Deity, that all people, past and present, had an equal capacity for rational thought, and that the true religion was a "natural religion," accessible to all through the rational intellect and the empirical study of nature. The moral agenda of the deists often played a greater part in their anti-Christian polemics than did their views on nature and philosophy, but both the moral and the scientific issues were important components of their worldview. In essence, deism arose out of an intersection of the new science and an anti-Christian moral sensibility.

The word *"déistes"* describing a type of irreligious freethinker is first attested in France as early as 1563, but not until the 1620s do we find a published, fully developed position similar to that discussed in this essay. In 1624, the English Lord Herbert of Cherbury (1583–1648) published a description of what he considered the five articles upon which all religions were based. But even Lord Herbert's exposition falls short of a mature deism in that it does not exhibit the same anticlerical critical stance that most later deists embraced. As a result, one might do best to consider mainstream deism as dating from late-seventeenth-century England and reaching a culmination with the publication of Matthew Tindal's *Christianity as Old as the Creation* in 1730. In this work, Tindal (1657–1733) argued that Christian doctrine was correct only insofar as it reiterated the tenets of a rational, universal religion discoverable through unclouded mental faculties of all human beings. Although deism declined precipitously in England after Tindal, it found strong advocates in France and Germany. The French philosophe Voltaire (François Marie Arouet [1694–1778]), in particular, took up its defense in numerous books and writings in the latter part of the eighteenth century. The movement spread as well to North America, where some of the most noted intellectuals, including Thomas Jefferson (1743–1826) and Benjamin Franklin (1706–90), espoused forms of deism. Thomas Paine (1737–1809) wrote one of the last and most widely popular deist tracts, *The Age of Reason,* in the 1790s.

Some scholars have depicted deism as the logical outgrowth of the scientific revolution because of its oft-repeated reliance on Newtonian arguments for design in nature. By and large, deists did affirm a distinctly Newtonesque God with an affinity for mathematical perfection and cosmic order. This God was the reification of the natural-philosophers' ideals of a lawlike and perfect universe. Yet, the deists held only one particular interpretation of that God, and—as Isaac Newton (1642–1727) and his closest Anglican supporters themselves showed—a person could as easily use Newtonian ideas to attack deism as to advance it. Newton thought that God must periodically intervene in the creation, and, in his scientific work, he made a place for that intervention. The Boyle lectures, a series of liberal Anglican sermons established in 1692 to defend Christianity against atheism and other heretical religious positions, utilized a Newtonian framework in their attack on the God of the deists. That God, a being wholly apart from the world, stood in direct opposition to the active God of Christianity in which the

Anglican lecturers believed. The situation is quite complex, however. Although many Newtonians opposed deism, they were often denounced by more conservative Anglicans as being virtual deists themselves. These conservatives feared that the theology derived from Newtonian natural philosophy would lead down the slippery slope toward deism and atheism.

Part of the problem in defining deism precisely with respect to liberal Christianity arises from its diversity; many early deists believed that they were merely purifying Christianity, while others felt quite antagonistic toward it. Perhaps the best that can be said is that deism appears at the extreme end of a spectrum of liberal religious opinions, all spawned by the desire to reconcile the new scientific outlook with an understanding of God and religion, whether that religion be Christian or non-Christian.

Part and parcel of this scientific worldview was the belief in unchanging laws of nature. Deists went further than most Christians in extending this notion to religion itself. They contended that, in a world governed by perfect natural laws, religion in its essence did not change, only the superstitions and rituals did. Thus, the historical elements of Christianity that differentiated it from other religions had little real value and, in fact, were often considered detrimental. The original religion of mankind was the true religion, and all changes since then had negative effects by invoking unfounded myths and by establishing religious hierarchies artificially invested with authority.

Most deists did draw radical, un-Christian conclusions from the new sciences. The way that John Toland (1670–1722) used the empirical philosophy of John Locke (1632–1704) to argue for a deist position provides one of the best examples of this radicalizing spirit. Locke believed that he had given a firm philosophical foundation to empiricism, claiming that all knowledge came from the senses and that there were no innate ideas. Such a theory had significant—and potentially dangerous—ramifications for understanding Christian doctrine, ramifications that Locke himself sought to mitigate in a book-length defense of a simplified Christian faith. In *The Reasonableness of Christianity* (1695), Locke defended the Christian religion by claiming that both reason and revelation arrived at the same answers; his arguments, however, distilled Christianity to the point that he verged on deism himself. Toland's *Christianity Not Mysterious,* published a year later, drew out those deist implications by eschewing the need for mystery and establishing an entirely rational account of the Christian religion. This empirical and rationalistic temper set the direction for later deists, who proceeded to remove nearly all aspects of supernaturalism from religion. Toland himself ended up proclaiming a pantheistic faith, while his deist successors destroyed all foundation for belief in Christian miracles. And Voltaire in Catholic France drew unending material for his anti-Christian polemics by ridiculing the miraculous events of the Bible.

Although the scientific arguments played an indispensable role in the formulation of deism, they often held only a secondary place in deist polemics, the primary thrust of which was to establish the moral insufficiency of Christianity. Since deists embraced a faith in a rational and benevolent God, they delighted in exposing what they found to be the pernicious doctrines of traditional Christianity. The doctrine of salvation was one of their favorite targets. According to the traditional interpretation, salvation was given only to those people who had consciously accepted Christ; as a result, the Christian God condemned to damnation the vast majority of the world's people throughout history who had never had the opportunity to hear of Christ and his work. For the deists, this doctrine merely illustrated the provincialism and depravity of Christianity. A God who behaved in so arbitrary a manner could not be an all-wise and all-good Being. Christian doctrines of this sort, concerning both the moral nature of the Deity and the ethical doctrines of the Church, formed a focal point for deist polemics.

Historians differ in their interpretations of the relationship between deism and science. Some historians are inclined to see natural science as the key to the whole deist program. For them, the philosophical ideas that came out of the scientific revolution have a certain amount of inevitability, guiding thought toward a deistic reconciliation of science and religion. Other historians have pointed to the nonphilosophical issues that drove deistic thought. They have tended to focus on struggles over political and religious authority as having primary importance in the origin of deism. However one sees the relationship between deism and science, one cannot understand deism without understanding how contemporary scientific and cosmological arguments complemented and gave force to the deists' broadly universalistic vision.

See also Isaac Newton; Mechanical Philosophy; Natural Theology; Scientific Naturalism; Skepticism

BIBLIOGRAPHY

Betts, C. J. *Early Deism in France: From the So-Called "Déistes" of Lyon (1564) to Voltaire's "Lettres philosophiques" (1734).* Boston: Martinus Nijhoff, 1984.

Brooke, John Hedley. *Science and Religion: Some Historical Perspectives.* New York: Cambridge University Press, 1991.

Byrne, Peter. *Natural Religion and the Nature of Religion: The Legacy of Deism.* New York: Routledge, 1989.

Champion, J. A. I. *The Pillars of Priestcraft Shaken: The Church of England and Its Enemies, 1660–1730.* New York: Cambridge University Press, 1992.

Emerson, Roger L. "Latitudinarianism and the English Deists." In *Deism, Masonry, and the Enlightenment: Essays Honoring Alfred Owen Aldridge,* ed. by J. A. Leo Lemay. Newark: University of Delaware Press, 1987, 19–48.

Force, James E. "Science, Deism, and William Whiston's 'Third Way.'" *Ideas and Production: A Journal in the History of Ideas* 7 (1987): 18–33.

———. "The Newtonians and Deism." In *Essays on the Context, Nature, and Influence of Isaac Newton's Theology,* ed. by James E. Force and Richard W. Popkin. Boston: Kluwer, 1990, 43–73.

Gay, Peter. "Beyond the Holy Circle." In *The Enlightenment: An Interpretation,* ed. by Peter Gay. 2 vols. Vol. 1: *The Rise of Modern Paganism.* New York: Norton, 1966, 358–419.

Hazard, Paul. *European Thought in the Eighteenth Century: From Montesquieu to Lessing.* New Haven, Conn.: Yale University Press, 1954.

Jacob, Margaret C. *The Newtonians and the English Revolution, 1689–1702.* Ithaca, N.Y.: Cornell University Press, 1976.

———. "Christianity and the Newtonian Worldview." In *God and Nature: Historical Essays on the Encounter Between Christianity and Science,* ed. by David C. Lindberg and Ronald L. Numbers. Berkeley: University of California Press, 1986, 238–55.

Manuel, Frank E. *The Changing of the Gods.* Hanover: Brown University Press, 1983.

Morais, Herbert M. *Deism in Eighteenth Century America.* New York: Russell and Russell, 1960.

Redwood, John A. "Charles Blount (1654–93), Deism, and English Free Thought." *Journal of the History of Ideas* 35 (1974): 490–8.

———. *Reason, Ridicule, and Religion: The Age of Enlightenment in England, 1660–1750.* Cambridge, Mass.: Harvard University Press, 1976.

Shoaf, Richard. "Science, Sect, and Certainty in Voltaire's *Dictionnaire Philosophique.*" *Journal of the History of Ideas* 46 (1985): 121–6.

Sullivan, Robert E. *John Toland and the Deist Controversy: A Study in Adaptations.* Cambridge, Mass.: Harvard University Press, 1982.

Walters, Kerry S. *The American Deists: Voices of Reason and Dissent in the Early Republic.* Lawrence: University Press of Kansas, 1992.

Westfall, Richard S. *Science and Religion in Seventeenth-Century England.* New Haven, Conn.: Yale University Press, 1958.

———. *Deism: An Anthology.* Princeton: Van Nostrand, 1968.

Paine, Thomas. *The Age of Reason: Being an Investigation of True and Fabulous Theology.* 1794–96. Reprint. New York: G. P. Putnam's Sons, 1896.

Stephen, Leslie. *History of English Thought in the Eighteenth Century.* 3d ed. 2 vols. Vol. 1. New York: Peter Smith, 1902.

Tindal, Matthew. *Christianity as Old as the Creation.* 1730. Reprint. Stuttgart-Bad Cannstatt: Frommann-Holzboog, 1967.

31. THE ENLIGHTENMENT

Thomas Broman

For most people, the diatribe of Antoine-Nicolas de Caritat, Marquis de Condorcet (1743–94), against the evils of Christianity aptly represents the eighteenth-century Enlightenment's view of religion, a view that has become the touchstone of the period's historical identity. Condorcet wrote:

> Disdain for the humane sciences was one of the first characteristics of Christianity. It had to avenge itself against the outrages of philosophy, and it feared that spirit of doubt and inquiry, that confidence in one's own reason which is the bane of all religious beliefs.... So the triumph of Christianity was the signal for the complete decadence of philosophy and the sciences [*Sketch for an Historical Picture of the Progress of the Human Mind,* 1794].

For conservative Christians, the Enlightenment started Western culture on a secularizing path that has brought social chaos and spiritual misery. Nonbelievers, too, see the Enlightenment as the beginning of a path, but one leading to the liberation of the human spirit from the shackles of intolerance and ignorance. For both groups, the Enlightenment touched off that interminable "war" between science and religion for the sake of which so many innocent trees have sacrificed their lives.

Yet, as enduring and deeply held as such perceptions are, they can mislead us both about Enlightenment attitudes toward religious belief and about the Enlightenment's place in European cultural history. Condorcet's extreme hostility toward Christianity was one that few eighteenth-century intellectuals shared. Voltaire (François Marie Arouet [1694–1778]) and David Hume (1711–76) may have railed against the clergy and lampooned its pretensions and institutions, but their criticisms of religious belief were more muted, and, in Hume's case, published only posthumously. Moreover, the conviction that the Enlightenment represented a decisive liberating moment in Western cultural history must itself be called into question. The bald citation of Condorcet's views out of their historical context masks the fact that they were formulated at a moment when this most ardent propagandist for enlightenment was being hunted down by the French revolutionary government. The irony of Condorcet's position arises not because the radicalism of the French Revolution was in any obvious way either the realization or the perversion of Enlightenment ideology—the transformative experience of political revolution belies any such direct linkage—but because both enlightenment and political repression are more deeply linked in the historical trajectory of Western culture, a point made so brilliantly by Max Horkheimer and Theodor Adorno half a century ago.

The same ironies underlay the confrontation between the Enlightenment and religious belief as well and mirror the link between liberation and repression. If enlightenment represents, as Horkheimer and Adorno put it, "the disenchantment of the world," the attack on religious belief implied therein did not begin in the eighteenth century; indeed, it might reliably be located at that moment in Genesis when God gave Adam dominion over the earth. Enchantment and disenchantment, religious belief and enlightenment were simultaneously implicated in the apprehension of the world, it seems, almost from the moment human beings began recording their reflections about their place in it.

If such is the case, what then allowed eighteenth-century intellectuals to perceive themselves as men of enlightenment? What self-consciousness permitted Jean d'Alembert (1717–83), in his "Preliminary Discourse" to

Denis Diderot's (1713–84) *Encyclopédie* (1751–72), to present the history of European thought as a series of increasingly urgent anticipations to the full flowering of philosophy, as d'Alembert believed had been recently achieved in the writings of Isaac Newton (1642–1727) and John Locke (1632–1704)? The answer might be found in an observation made by Immanuel Kant (1724–1804) in the preface to his *Critique of Pure Reason* (1781):

> Our age is, in especial degree, the age of criticism, and to criticism everything must submit. Religion through its sanctity, and law-giving through its majesty, may seek to exempt themselves from it. But they awaken just suspicion, and cannot claim the sincere respect which reason accords only to that which has been able to sustain the test of free and open examination.

By naming his age one of criticism, Kant understood the act of criticism as a systematic and, most of all, a *public* examination of beliefs of all kinds. The publicity of criticism suggests that it was intended not as a series of specialized debates among experts but as a broad and searching discussion by the members of society of their own values, aspirations, and knowledge. It was, of course, no small matter to Christian churches that the advocates of Enlightenment were elevating public criticism to the authoritative status once reserved for religious dogma. And, not surprisingly, to the extent that religion came under public criticism, it was often because religious institutions attempted to limit or suppress criticism. Furthermore, there can be no denying that the same critical impulses also brought religious faith under direct attack. Materialist views that denied a transcendent spirituality to humanity were represented by Paul Henri Thiry, Baron d'Holbach's (1723–89) *System of Nature* (1707) and Julien Offray de La Mettrie's (1709–51) *Man a Machine* (1747), while traditional Christian morality was attacked in Diderot's posthumous *Supplement to the Voyage of Bougainville*. But these works mark the extreme boundary of the Enlightenment sensibility toward religion, not its dominant contours.

Just as the Enlightenment as a cultural movement was not implacably or even largely inimical to religion, the science produced during the eighteenth century was anything but secular in character. Quite to the contrary, as will be explained below, perhaps the most significant strand of scientific work during the century was directly and explicitly tied to metaphysical and religious issues. That strand of science, which united problem domains as diverse as chemistry, mechanics, and animal reproduction, was the question of whether physical matter was endowed with inherent forces or whether forces acted on matter externally. The question of the physical reality of forces and the metaphysical and religious implications presented by this question exercised most of the leading natural philosophers of the century. In what follows, I discuss this problem from three distinct perspectives: (1) the problems of *vis viva* (living force) and least action in physics; (2) the debates over animal reproduction and spontaneous generation; and (3) the public fascination with electricity and magnetism. In all of these instances, we will see how deeply embedded were the scientific issues of the period in metaphysical and religious contexts.

Force and Matter

How does matter exert the effects we perceive in it? Does it possess an inherent capacity for action that is transferred, for example, when one body collides with another, or is matter fundamentally inert, requiring an external agency for it to produce its effects? On such simple questions turned some of the most contentious and metaphysically charged disputes in the natural philosophy of the seventeenth and eighteenth centuries. The problem of motion and other powers of matter had attracted the attention of ancient and medieval philosophers, of course, but for the purposes of eighteenth-century science it was given a distinctive formulation by Newton, who described gravity as the capacity of bodies to attract each other. The mathematical description presented by Newton's laws of motion, in which gravity played an important role, offered an accurate and unified description of celestial and terrestrial motion. But the concept of gravity itself was incomprehensible. How, asked Gottfried Wilhelm Leibniz (1646–1716) and numerous others, could bodies act on each other at a distance? Leibniz accused Newton of conjuring up a secret power or virtue in matter to justify gravity, while Newton, for his part, attempted at first to avoid the metaphysical implications of his theory by claiming that it was only a mathematical description, not a theory of nature. This satisfied virtually no one: not Leibniz, who entered into a protracted polemical exchange over the question with Samuel Clarke (1675–1729), one of Newton's champions, and not even Newton, whose later writings pondered the possibility that motion was communicated by means of contact through a subtle, but very material, medium.

At issue between Newton and Leibniz was more than the question of whether forces could be transmitted through empty space without contact between bodies. Newton's view of action at a distance depended on a metaphysics that held the world to be composed of inert matter contained in empty space, which was then acted upon by forces from without. It must be recalled here that these "forces" seem originally to have been understood by Newton not as real entities but in an epistemological sense as the linking term between cause and effect. This allowed the world to be portrayed by Newton and his followers as being actively and continually sustained and, indeed, modified by God's intervention. It stressed the absolute freedom of will that belongs to God. Leibniz's own position derived in part from his conviction that Newton's system reduced God's majesty (not to mention his intelligence) by supposing him to have created a world that needed continual maintenance. In contrast, Leibniz supposed God to have created a perfect world system animated by a real force in matter. He named this force *vis viva* (living force) and calculated it as equivalent to a moving body's mass times the square of its velocity. This quantity, Leibniz argued, was a constant; it could be transferred between bodies but never created or destroyed.

The argument over *vis viva* and whether it represented a real force or just a convenient mathematical device carried over with undiminished vigor into the eighteenth century. One school of thought, represented by d'Alembert, held the debate over *vis viva* to be an empty one. While in certain contexts it was quite appropriate to use *vis viva* to describe physical motion, d'Alembert argued, its status as a "real" force was irrelevant to its utility in physics. D'Alembert's approach to problems of motion attempted to treat them analytically as cases of equilibrium—essentially, dynamics was transformed into statics, with the world being rendered as an elaborate balance. For the purposes of this method, it was not necessary to invest anything in the reality of force, because "force" as a concept virtually dropped out of the picture. Not surprisingly, d'Alembert derided forces as "obscure and metaphysical entities," which only obfuscate a science which is otherwise "full of clarity."

The other position was held by Leonhard Euler (1707–83) and Pierre-Louis de Maupertuis (1698–1759), who argued that metaphysical commitments were, indeed, appropriate and even essential for a proper understanding of physics. In particular, Maupertuis and Euler advanced the principle of least action, which argued that nature (and God) acted in the most economical manner possible. Following upon such commitments, Euler developed the calculus of variations as a mathematical technique for describing the motion of a body or system of bodies under prescribed conditions. The conditions of greatest interest, given Euler's and Maupertuis's assumptions, were those involving the minimum amount of "action," which Maupertuis defined as the product of a body's mass, velocity, and distance traveled. In contrast to d'Alembert, therefore, for whom mechanics amounted to an instantaneous snapshot of physical systems, Maupertuis and Euler intended the principle of least action as an account of motion under the causal influence of forces acting on bodies.

The divergent treatments of force and matter supported by d'Alembert, Maupertuis, Euler, and a host of other physicists and mathematicians would remain a contentious issue throughout much of the century. In response to these debates, a great deal of experimental work was devoted to measuring quantities such as *vis viva* in elastic and inelastic collisions, to determine, in part, whether *vis viva* had any relevance for observed physical phenomena. But no amount of experimentation could resolve larger questions concerning the metaphysical status of forces, issues of such unmistakable urgency that it took virtually no time at all for them to be taken up outside the domain of physical mechanics.

The Forces of Living Matter

In the late summer of 1740, a Swiss naturalist by the name of Abraham Trembley (1710–84) began studying an unusual organism. Collected in a jar along with a number of aquatic insects that were his primary focus of interest, Trembley paid scant attention at first to the little "plants" that clung to the jar's glass sides. But gradually he became intrigued by some odd characteristics: The little plants had tiny "arms" that would wave in the water and contract suddenly when the jar was shaken. They also seemed to be able to migrate toward the light, for, if Trembley rotated the jar one-half turn, the little beings would begin walking head over foot toward the other side. These and other traits led Trembley to rethink his previous assumption that he was studying a plant. But, most amazing of all, Trembley discovered that when he cut one of the little critters in two, the parts grew back into two complete forms. "I first thought of the feet and antennae of crayfish which grow back," he wrote to the French naturalist René-Antoine de Réaumur (1683–1757), "but the difference is that the two portions . . . seem actually two complete animals; in such a manner that one could say that from one animal, two have been produced."

Trembley's description of the little polyp (*Hydra*) was perhaps the most notorious scientific novelty of the century, for it dramatically cast doubt on widespread assumptions about how animals reproduce and, more generally, on the nature of life itself. By the end of the seventeenth century, European naturalists had reached agreement that sexual reproduction involved the growth of individuals that exist preformed in the maternal parent's egg, with the male sperm serving to activate the egg. This doctrine of preformation coexisted easily with orthodox religious beliefs on both Catholic and Protestant sides, since it held that God had laid down the framework for all future generations of living beings at the moment of Creation. Yet, Trembley's discovery, by showing that animal reproduction was possible without sexual union—he later described the *Hydra*'s ability to reproduce by budding—appeared to undercut the divine wisdom "encapsulated" in preformation.

Other unsettling discoveries began receiving attention, too. Even before Trembley published the results of his work on *Hydra*, a fellow Swiss naturalist, Charles Bonnet (1720–93), found that female aphids isolated at birth from any contact with males could nevertheless bear young. While this did not directly undercut the idea of preformation (indeed, Bonnet took his results as confirmation of it), the work did cast doubt on the conventional wisdom about sexual reproduction. After Trembley's discovery, Bonnet commenced a series of experiments on worms and snails, in which he found that snails could grow new heads after decapitation and certain worms, when chopped into several dozen pieces, could grow into entirely new individuals. The results of these experiments attracted considerable debate, although Bonnet himself interpreted them in line with his preformationist beliefs. Accordingly, he suggested the possibility that every part of certain animals contains preformed germs capable of generating a complete individual.

While Bonnet refused to let the new discoveries shake his faith in preformation, others permitted themselves to draw more materialist and radical conclusions. In France, Georges Louis Leclerc, Comte de Buffon (1707–88), and John Needham (1713–81) performed a series of experiments using various kinds of organic matter, including wheat seeds and gravy made from roast mutton, in tightly closed vessels to demonstrate the spontaneous generation of tiny "animicules" from that matter. When Needham examined the black powdery material from blighted wheat under the microscope, for example, he observed that it consisted of white fibers that appeared to become animated when water was added. Even more directly than the evidence from Trembley's *Hydra*, the experiments of Needham and Buffon suggested the potential for living matter to organize itself seemingly without the participation of divine influence or even the presence of a "soul" (*anima*) commonly believed to separate animals from plants.

It was such atheistic implications that made the issue of spontaneous generation so contentious and unsettling. Those implications, it should be remarked, did not follow by logical necessity; the link between atheism, materialism, and spontaneous generation arose more out of their historical juxtaposition than because materialist doctrines like spontaneous generation demanded or necessarily implied atheism. Needham himself, an English Catholic in holy orders, refused to accept spontaneous generation as providing support for atheism, attempting valiantly to argue that spontaneous generation could be taken to be just as much evidence for God's divine plan as could doctrines of preformation. But Needham's voice went unheeded. Before the eighteenth century, the association between materialism and atheism had already been solidified by Lucretius (c. 99–55 B.C.) and Thomas Hobbes (1588–1679), not to mention the socially threatening materialist doctrines espoused by various radical movements during the English Civil War of the seventeenth century. In light of this tradition, the more typical position was held by the Italian cleric and naturalist Lazzaro Spallanzani (1729–99), whose furious reaction against spontaneous generation prompted him to undertake a lengthy series of experiments that attempted to refute Buffon's and Needham's findings. Spallanzani demonstrated to his own satisfaction that what Buffon and Needham had observed had resulted from the contamination of eggs present in the specimens. But, as events during the subsequent century would show, spontaneous generation and its attendant stain of radicalism and atheism would not go away.

As sprawling and contentious as these debates over spontaneous generation and animal reproduction were, they formed but one arena for a still larger debate over the forces that characterize living matter. And just as Newton's *Principia* (1687) crystallized the issue for physical matter, the publication of *De partibus corporis humani sensibilibus et irritabilibus* (*On the Sensible and Irritable Parts of the Human Body*) in 1752 by the Swiss physician Albrecht von Haller (1708–77) placed the issue of organic forces squarely before the scholarly community. In this relatively brief publication, Haller identified two fundamental properties of the human body: The first, irritability, is displayed by those structures, such as muscles, that contract upon being stimulated via touch or electrical shock; by contrast, the second, sensibility, is the property of organic structures such as the nerves to communicate impressions to the brain. Haller's point in making this distinction was to isolate those parts displaying irritability from any involvement with the soul; insofar as the animal displays properties such as irritability, he argued, it is not because of the action of any inherent vivifying principle or soul. Instead, Haller deliberately likened irritability to Newton's gravity—whatever its ultimate ontological status, irritability, like gravity, could best be understood in terms of the effects it produces under specified conditions.

Unfortunately for Haller, his contemporaries refused to follow him down this antimetaphysical path. On one side, critics such as Robert Whytt (1714–66) and Théophile de Bordeu (1722–76) attacked the distinction between sensibility and irritability. Whytt believed that a soul or other animating principle is necessarily implicated in irritability and other vital processes. Bordeu likewise criticized Haller's attempt to restrict sensibility to certain parts of the body. All living matter is sensible, Bordeu claimed, and what Haller defined as "irritability" was only a special case of this more general situation. On the other side, La Mettrie read Haller's early comments on irritability (La Mettrie was already dead by the time Haller published his dissertation on the sensible and irritable parts in 1752) as confirmation of his own materialist beliefs. There was no need, La Mettrie argued in *Man a Machine,* to invoke any immaterial principle or soul to explain the seeming purposiveness of human life. Functions such as irritability prove that the human body can act as a self-moving machine. In acknowledgment of what he perceived was his debt to Haller, La Mettrie dedicated *Man a Machine* to him. The pious Haller, for his part, was horrified to have so scandalous a work associated with his name, and he entered into a polemical exchange with La Mettrie over the doctrine of irritability.

Despite his best intentions, therefore, Haller ultimately found himself caught in the same metaphysical and religious trap that had snared Newton as well. In the context of eighteenth-century metaphysics, it appeared nearly impossible to attribute forces and properties to matter (be they "gravity," "generation," or "irritability") in such a way that one could use those forces to describe real agencies without, at the same time, making the forces themselves material. Haller hoped to escape the trap by distinguishing between sensibility, as the sensate soul's extension in the body, and irritability, the latter understood as a vital property entirely distinct from the action or participation of the soul. His point in making the distinction was to preserve both the soul and irritable vitality as separate components of animal life. In this way, Haller hoped to have it both ways, with the soul being immanent in the animal without being coextensive with living matter. But the idea of an immaterial soul somehow "extended" through sensible parts of the body was no more easily digested by most of Haller's contemporaries than was Newton's idea of gravity as action at a distance.

The Subtle Fluids

If accounting for the forces affecting ordinary matter proved a vexatious task, and if living matter acted in ways that made the interaction between material and immaterial principles appear especially intimate, there was a third class of phenomena that made the relationship between force and matter still more troublesome. This class comprised what were believed to be the subtle fluids, substances that lacked the mass and extension of ordinary matter, yet whose effects could be readily studied and manipulated. A number of such fluids were thought to exist, including light and fire. But, for eighteenth-century intellectuals, two stood out as particularly interesting: magnetism and, above all, electricity. Although controversies over the nature of electricity during the Enlightenment mostly lacked the obvious theological implications that attended the debates discussed above, a full appreciation of the theological and metaphysical debates requires a brief look at the subtle fluids because they drew so much scholarly and popular attention.

The ability of amber and certain other substances to attract bits of stuff after being rubbed with a cloth had been known in antiquity, but it became an object of serious inquiry only after publication of William Gilbert's (1544–1603) treatise *On the Magnet* in 1600. Gilbert's book, which, as its title suggests, was primarily concerned with the phenomenon of magnetism, advanced the study of electricity in two ways. First, it distinguished electricity from magnetism, describing the former as an "effluvium" that flows from one body to another. Second, Gilbert classified substances as either "electric" or "nonelectric" on the basis of their ability to attract other substances after rubbing.

For eighteenth-century scholars, electricity resembled gravity in its ability to attract and repel bodies, but with one hugely important difference. Unlike gravity, which stoutly resisted experimental manipulation, electricity could easily be produced, transferred, stored, and released, often with dramatic consequences. The ease of manipulation of electricity made it an immensely entertaining diversion, and it rapidly became a stock item in scientific demonstrations aimed at both the high born and the commoner. In one case, a charged electrical machine was discharged into a line of two hundred Carthusian monks. Needham, who happened to be present at that demonstration, remarked how, at the moment of discharge, all of the monks "gave a sudden spring." No mention was made by Needham or anyone else there of whether after the demonstration the monks gave thanks that they were still alive.

In any case, electricity seized the imaginations of Europeans, and of Americans such as Benjamin Franklin (1706–90) as well, in ways both serious and frivolous. Its varied phenomena, including the ways it could be "stored" in enormous and sometimes dangerous quantities, the way it could be transmitted through metal wires to places quite distant from its point of generation, and the visible sparks it could produce all suggested that electricity was some kind of fluid, or perhaps two fluids, flowing between substances. The apparent ubiquity of electrical phenomena in nature gave rise to speculation that electricity might, indeed, be the universal principle of action. To take just one among many such conjectures, John Wesley (1703–91), the founder of Methodism, offered the following observation in 1759:

> It is highly probable [electricity] is the general instrument of all the motion in the universe; from this pure fire (which is properly so called) the vulgar culinary fire is kindled. For in truth there is but one kind of fire in nature, which exists in all places and in all bodies. And this is subtle and active enough, not only to be, under the Great

Cause, the secondary cause of motion, but to produce and sustain life throughout all nature, as well in animals as in vegetables.

Wesley's connection of electricity to life was no idle or ignorant remark, for it became common currency to believe that subtle fluids such as electricity or magnetism underlay life. Such beliefs received powerful empirical support late in the century from the Italian anatomist Luigi Galvani (1737–98), who observed in 1791 that a frog leg could be made to contract spontaneously when the leg was hung from a brass hook, and the hook touched to an iron beam or railing. Since a similar contraction could be observed when the leg was jolted with an electrical discharge, Galvani concluded not unreasonably that he had discovered a form of "animal electricity" produced inside the frog. It took but little imagination on the part of those hearing of Galvani's findings to conclude that he had discovered the active principle of life itself. Although Galvani would soon find himself embroiled in a dispute with Allessandro Volta (1745–1827) over the cause of the contraction—Volta claimed that it was the junction of two dissimilar metals that caused the observed electricity—nothing could dampen the intriguing suggestiveness of electricity as the force of life.

Similar claims were advanced for magnetism as well, although the interest in the magnetic subtle fluid was not as widespread as in electricity. One prominent advocate for the role of magnetism in life was Franz Mesmer (1734–1815), a physician from southern Germany who made a name for himself in Vienna in 1774 by treating a woman suffering from convulsions and headaches with magnets laid upon her stomach and legs. The symptoms abated, and, according to Mesmer, the woman claimed to feel "some painful currents of a subtle material" in her body. On the basis of these treatments, Mesmer developed a general doctrine of animal magnetism as a vital force that could be directed by himself as therapist. He opened a magnetic clinic in Vienna that soon overflowed with patients, the large majority of them women. Mesmer was forced to leave Vienna late in 1777, following a dispute with the University of Vienna's medical faculty. He then migrated to Paris, where he again established a lucrative practice with his magnetic cures and developed his ideas about animal magnetism into a doctrine of a universal fluid that was responsible for sustaining all life. Despite—or perhaps because of—the disapproval of his therapies registered by the official Royal Academy of Sciences, Mesmer's practice thrived. So popular did he become, in fact, that the mere intimation that he might depart the "unfriendly" environs of Paris for Holland prompted Queen Marie-Antoinette (1755–93) to implore the government's senior ministers to drop whatever trivial matters they were engaged with and find a way to keep Mesmer in the capital.

The popularity of Mesmerism and animal magnetism, which endured well beyond Mesmer's own lifetime, testifies to the phenomenal fascination that subtle fluids of all kinds held for Europeans during the Enlightenment. Like the subtle fluids themselves, that interest was pervasive, permeating all areas of cultural life and every social stratum. But beyond mere spectacle and the trendiness of medical practices such as Mesmer's, the engagement with subtle fluids betrayed a more deep-seated concern with the relation between matter and force, a duality readily capable of juxtaposition onto the traditional Christian duality of body and spirit. In a sense, debates over the nature of electricity and other subtle fluids merely replayed in other language older debates between Christians, Gnostics, and Neoplatonists over the distinctive natures of matter and spirit. In some cases, as in the writings of the chemist and Unitarian Joseph Priestley (1733–1804), the religious implications of the continuity between force and matter could be made startlingly explicit. In physics, Priestley argued in his *Disquisitions Relating to Matter and Spirit* (1777), there was no meaningful distinction to be made between matter and force, since every "solid" body was, in fact, the product of the forces that bound its parts together. But the continuity between matter and force, Priestley continued, undermines the absolute distinctions that can be made between matter and spirit as well. The consequences drawn by Priestley from this line of argument were breathtaking: denial of Creation as a temporal act, denial of Jesus's divine nature, and affirmation of an unbroken and eternal continuity of being between matter and spirit.

With the introduction of Priestley's views on matter and spirit, we have come full circle in our discussion, for the radicalism of Priestley's version of the Enlightenment was fully a match for Condorcet's. Like Condorcet, Priestley believed in the infinite perfectibility of humanity. Like Condorcet, too, Priestley believed that his own age had advanced the cause of perfection in no small measure. Yet, unlike Condorcet, Priestley held fervently to an essentially millennialist and, so he proclaimed

loudly and repeatedly, *Christian* view of history. As things turned out, Priestley's religious and political radicalism proved no more palatable to his contemporaries than did Condorcet's; his house was burned by a London mob in 1790, and Priestley sought refuge in the new United States, where he was first feted and then ignored.

If, therefore, the Enlightenment did introduce those notions of social progress and human perfectibility with which it is so often either credited or blamed, it was not necessarily religious belief in general, or Christian belief in particular, that was destined to be the loser in the process. The examples of Condorcet and Priestley, along with those of Haller, Newton, and scores of others, suggest that the study of nature and man in the eighteenth century proved fertile ground for a variety of religious and metaphysical positions, some of which, to be sure, emphatically denounced orthodox belief, but others of which renewed religious debates as old as the Christian church itself.

See also Deism; Electricity; Isaac Newton; Premodern Theories of Generation; Skepticism

BIBLIOGRAPHY

Brooke, John Hedley. *Science and Religion: Some Historical Perspectives.* Cambridge: Cambridge University Press, 1991.

Darnton, Robert. *Mesmerism and the End of the Enlightenment in France.* Cambridge, Mass.: Harvard University Press, 1968.

Dawson, Virginia. *Nature's Enigma: The Problem of the Polyp in the Letters of Bonnet, Trembley, and Réaumur.* Philadelphia: American Philosophical Society, 1987.

Hankins, Thomas. *Science and the Enlightenment.* Cambridge: Cambridge University Press, 1985.

Heilbronn, John L. *Electricity in the Seventeenth and Eighteenth Centuries: A Study of Early Modern Physics.* Berkeley: University of California Press, 1979.

Jacob, Margaret. *The Newtonians and the English Revolution, 1689–1720.* Ithaca, N.Y.: Cornell University Press, 1976.

Mazzolini, Renato G., and Shirey A. Roe. *Science Against the Unbelievers: The Correspondence of Bonnet and Needham, 1760–1780.* Studies on Voltaire and the Eighteenth Century. Vol. 243. Oxford: Voltaire Foundation, 1986.

McEvoy, J., and J. E. McGuire. "God and Nature: Priestley's Way of Rational Dissent." *Historical Studies in the Physical Sciences* 6 (1975): 325–404.

Roe, Shirley A. *Matter, Life, and Generation: Eighteenth-Century Embryology and the Haller-Wolff Debate.* Cambridge: Cambridge University Press, 1981.

Roger, Jacques. "The Mechanistic Conception of Life." In *God and Nature: Historical Essays on the Encounter Between Christianity and Science,* ed. by David C. Lindberg and

Ronald L. Numbers. Berkeley: University of California Press, 1986, 277–95.

Shapin, Steven. "Of Gods and Kings: Natural Philosophy and Politics in the Leibniz-Clarke Disputes." *Isis* 72 (1981): 187–215.

Terrall, Mary. "The Culture of Science in Frederick the Great's Berlin." *History of Science* 28 (1990): 333–64.

Wilde, C. B. "Hutchinsonianism, Natural Philosophy, and Religious Controversy in Eighteenth Century Britain." *History of Science* 18 (1980): 1–24.

32. BACONIANISM

Walter H. Conser Jr.

Baconianism is a model of science and a pattern of thought suggestive of the compatibility of science and religion that had an important influence among Protestant Americans in the eighteenth and nineteenth centuries. Named after the philosophical reflections of Sir Francis Bacon (1561–1626), the English thinker and scientist, Baconianism championed an experimentally based inductive method of analysis. Against the deductive categories of Aristotelian logic, Bacon emphasized a new approach to, and foundation for, scientific method. For Bacon, the proper scientist made empirical observations, which resulted inferentially in hypotheses, which were, in turn, verified through continued observation and experimentation. Slow and patient examination, careful and cautious inquiry, with provisional results subject always to additional testing and possible disconfirmation: This was the Baconian ideal of induction. Moreover, just as this empirical method was available to anyone who properly understood its experimental procedures (a revolutionary step in the context of the older medieval scholastic tradition, with its habitual deference to the authority of received teachings), so, too, did Bacon envision science and its findings as ideally useful for all.

Scottish Common Sense Realism

This Baconian model of science was taken over in the eighteenth century by a group of Scottish philosophers who reworked it into the tradition of Scottish Common Sense philosophy. These Scottish philosophers included Thomas Reid (1710–96), Dugald Stewart (1753–1828), James Oswald (1703–93), James Beattie (1735–1803), and others. In their writings, as well as in those of John Witherspoon (1723–94), president of Princeton College,

Scottish Common Sense entered into American intellectual life. Common Sense philosophy prided itself on its empirical and inductive premises. In large part a response to the skepticism of David Hume's (1711–76) philosophy, with its radical challenge to epistemology and morality, Scottish Common Sense philosophy countered Hume's conclusions about the uncertainty of truth and morals with a defense of the possibility of human knowledge built upon inductive foundations. The Common Sense philosophers argued that there were categories in human consciousness, such as personal identity, cause and effect, and the existence of moral principles that were known intuitively, or through "common sense," by anyone who took the time to examine properly and thoroughly his or her own self-consciousness. And a "proper" examination for these Common Sense philosophers was an inductive one, which began with the "facts" of self-consciousness (such as personal identity, cause and effect) and, from that basis, developed an account of the individual, society, and the world.

Influence on American Protestantism

This reaffirmation of the accuracy and validity of sense perceptions of the world, as well as the insistence on the existence of a moral sense that could correctly distinguish right and wrong, was immensely attractive to many nineteenth-century American Protestant leaders. For example, David Tappan (1752–1803) at Harvard Divinity School, Nathaniel William Taylor (1786–1858) at Yale, and Edwards Amasa Park (1808–1900) at Andover invoked Scottish Common Sense themes and reasoning. Nor was this attraction to Scottish principles exclusively a New England phenomenon. Archibald Alexander (1772–1851) and Charles Hodge (1797–1878) at Princeton

Seminary and James Henley Thornwell (1812–62) at Columbia Theological Seminary in South Carolina likewise proffered Common Sense conclusions in their classes. Hence, from the late eighteenth century through the middle of the nineteenth, Scottish Common Sense philosophy, with its roots in the thought of Francis Bacon, was influential not only among Presbyterians and Congregationalists, but also among Unitarians, Episcopalians, Disciples of Christ, and even among some Baptists and Methodists as well.

Beyond their use of Common Sense philosophy to shore up claims for knowledge and morality, American Protestant theologians found a use for Baconianism in their attempts to reconcile science and religion. Here invocations of Baconianism became emblematic of the harmony between the scientific and the theological enterprises, for to study nature properly was to reveal the work of God. The crux, of course, was to establish the proper method, and here the resounding, if not surprising, response was an endorsement of the inductive method of Francis Bacon. Charles Hodge and James Henley Thornwell, for example, both insisted that the inductive method was the correct method of scientific inquiry. For them, no radical disjunction existed between the scientist and the theologian, as all true scientists proceeded inductively. Where the student of nature investigated the facts of biological life, the Christian theologian, as the exegete of faith, investigated the Bible for its materials. In this way, Hodge maintained, true religion was not opposed to true science, for any discrepancies were due to careless procedures and hasty generalizations. For his part, Thornwell found in the emphasis on inductive observation of the natural world a clear reaffirmation of the task and validity of natural theology. Confidence in inductive method reinforced confidence in natural theology. And, as Thornwell contended that natural theology conformed to revealed theology, the link from investigation of the natural world to interpretation of that investigation and its reconciliation with biblical revelation appeared unbroken. For Hodge and Thornwell, as for many Protestant theologians in the Antebellum era, these lines of argument, so deeply tinctured with the imprint of Scottish Common Sense and the legacy of Francis Bacon, forged a holy alliance between science and religion and led many to anticipate in the findings of the scientist praise for the work of God.

This argument for the methodological unity of science in the procedures of induction was a powerful one

in nineteenth-century America. However, both at that time and subsequently, problems with the Baconian position were raised. First, the parallel between students of nature and students of the Bible broke down to the extent that the Bible was considered infallible, and, hence, its statements were impossible to falsify. If any disagreements between religious and scientific claims were dismissed as faulty deductions and a priori thinking on the part of scientists, as Hodge and Thornwell often suggested, then the alliance between science and religion appeared to come at a high price. Beyond that, statements indicating unmediated individual access to facts, oblivious to the restrictions of the sociological character of knowledge, the relevance of paradigms of inquiry, or even the existence of unconscious motivations about which the individual was unaware made the claims of these nineteenth-century religious thinkers appear naive to many commentators. Finally, while the epistemological and moral intuitionalism of Common Sense philosophy placed limits on its real grounding in empiricism, a larger attack came from the Romantic movement of the nineteenth century, which castigated the Common Sense philosophy as ahistorical and static in its outlook and analysis, rather than developmental and organic, as the Romantics preferred.

While Baconianism reached its apogee in American culture during the first half of the nineteenth century, echoes of the movement can be identified in the twentieth century. In evangelical Protestant (especially dispensationalist) circles, continued allegiance to, and invocation of, Baconianism was evident. Unconcerned with sociological or psychological strictures regarding the character of knowledge, reassured by the insistence on an innate sense of right and wrong, and convinced of the superiority of inductive empirical analysis over what they dismissed as theoretical hypotheses, conservative Christians in the twentieth century attested to the persistence of the Baconian ideal in American religion.

See also Early-Modern Protestantism; Evangelicalism and Fundamentalism; Modern American Mainline Protestantism

BIBLIOGRAPHY

Ahlstrom, Sydney E. "The Scottish Philosophy and American Philosophy." *Church History* 24 (1955): 257–72.

Bozeman, Theodore Dwight. *Protestants in an Age of Science: The Baconian Ideal and Antebellum American Religious*

Thought. Chapel Hill: University of North Carolina Press, 1977.

Cohen, I. Bernard. *Revolution in Science*. Cambridge, Mass.: Harvard University Press, 1985.

Conser, Walter H., Jr., *God and the Natural World: Religion and Science in Antebellum America*. Columbia: University of South Carolina Press, 1993.

Daniels, George H. *American Science in the Age of Jackson*. New York: Columbia University Press, 1968.

Dillenberger, John. *Protestant Thought and Natural Science*. Nashville: Abingdon, 1960.

Hovenkamp, Herbert. *Science and Religion in America, 1800–1860*. Philadelphia: University of Pennsylvania Press, 1978.

Lindberg, David C., and Ronald L. Numbers, eds. *God and Nature: Historical Essays on the Encounter Between Christianity and Science*. Berkeley: University of California Press, 1986.

Marsden, George. *Fundamentalism and American Culture*. New York: Oxford University Press, 1980.

Noll, Mark. "Common Sense Traditions and American Evangelical Thought." *American Quarterly* 37 (1985): 217–38.

33. GERMAN NATURE PHILOSOPHY

Nicolaas A. Rupke

Nature philosophy (*Naturphilosophie*) was a theory of knowledge, briefly popular in the early nineteenth century, in which speculative thought, especially intuition, more than observation and experiment, were put forward as a reliable means to understanding the physical world. Because of its metaphysical tenets, nature philosophy could give shelter to a wide range of religious beliefs. It was commonly associated with mysticism and a latitudinarian attitude toward the Bible and religious confessional statements.

The term *Naturphilosophie* became familiar through the titles of several books, such as *Ideen zu einer Philosophie der Natur* (*Ideas Concerning a Philosophy of Nature* [1797]), written by the German philosopher Friedrich Wilhelm Joseph von Schelling (1775–1854). Other influential philosophers associated with the nature-philosophical movement in science were Johann Gottlieb Fichte (1762–1814) and Georg Wilhelm Friedrich Hegel (1770–1831), who, like Schelling, advocated a type of philosophical idealism. *Naturphilosophie* was anything but a monolithic system of thought, and its various advocates were more than commonly individualistic.

In the course of the second quarter of the nineteenth century, nature philosophy wilted under the onslaught of materialism, positivism, and scientific naturalism. Ever since then it has had a bad press. In the late twentieth century, however, the possibility that the approach of nature philosophy had a certain scientific validity has been seriously and sympathetically considered. Historians are divided over its scientific success, but some believe that the theory of electromagnetism owes much to its teachings. In the nonorganic sciences, the Danish physicist Hans Christian Oersted (1777–1851) and the English chemist Humphry Davy (1778–1829) were influenced by nature philosophy. Moreover, it has been argued that the Romantic, or nature-philosophy, program constituted a viable research tradition, especially in comparative anatomy and physiology. The cell theory, for example, has been regarded as one of its fruits.

Nature Philosophy's Antirationalism

Nature philosophy was an integral part of the wider cultural fashion of Romanticism that flourished during the period 1780–1830, especially in Germany and, to a significant extent, also in such Nordic regions as Scotland and Scandinavia. During this period, a new, anti-Enlightenment *Weltbild* (world picture) originated that turned its back on the rationalism of the French philosophes. The *Encyclopédie* lost its attraction, and the pendulum of fashion swung in the opposite direction, to an interest in the metaphysical and the religious. The new world picture emphasized feeling and intuition, the mystery of unseen forces, what was old, simple, and indigenous, and the veneration of those times when man had been in harmony with nature and reflective reason had not yet spoiled his primeval innocence and discarded the wisdom of priests and prophets.

The new nature philosophy was an integral part of this antirationalistic world picture. It represented an attempt to counter the mechanization of our understanding of the world, such as that proposed by the French philosopher René Descartes (1596–1650), who not only had taught that both terrestrial and celestial movement can be subsumed under a single, mechanistic point of view, but had gone as far as to interpret animals as machines. Physico-theology had managed to reconcile the mechanical worldview with traditional teleology by depicting the relationship of God to his creation as that of a watchmaker to a watch, using the functional contrivances of the clockwork universe as proofs of divine design. The advocates of nature philosophy turned their back on this form of rationalist apologetics and moved to the opposite extreme of repudiating the dualism of a mechanical universe with a transcendent God and of postulating that the world is an organism, animated by an immanent God, or *Weltseele* (universal mind or soul). God is revealed in nature through analogies, correspondences, and harmony.

Organic Unity and Archetypes

The impact of nature philosophy on the sciences was greatest in biology and medicine. Whereas the generation of the French naturalist Georges Louis Leclerc, Comte de Buffon (1707–88), and the Swedish botanist Carolus Linnaeus (1707–78) had been primarily concerned with the description and classification of individual species, the Romantic naturalists were interested in establishing the relatedness of organic forms. They shared a belief in the importance of mind and mental ideas that transcend empirical reality and constitute the unifying principles of logic behind nature's phenomena. The merger of Romantic and idealist thought with the study of early-nineteenth-century biology produced what has been called "transcendental morphology." Simply put, it was the notion that organic diversity, as present in the myriad of different species, can be subsumed under one or a few ideal types. Characteristic was an interest in prototypes or archetypes, exemplified by Goethe's *Urpflanze* (primeval plant) and Carl Gustav Carus's (1789–1869) generalized vertebrate skeleton. *Von den Ur-Theilen des Knochen und Schalengerüstes (On the Principal Elements of the Endo- and Exo-Skeleton* [1828]) by Carus is a classic example of nature-philosophical osteology.

In Jena, the major center of German nature philosophy, Schelling's philosophy was applied to the study of nature by the idiosyncratic Lorenz Oken (1779–1851), for example, in his *Lehrbuch der Naturphilosophie (Textbook on Nature Philosophy* [1809–11]). A typical instance of nature-philosophical biology was the vertebral theory of the skull, which states that the skeleton of the head can be understood as a series of metamorphosed vertebrae. In other words, the fact that the fetal skull of humans (and of vertebrates in general) consists of a number of uncoalesced, separate pieces does not serve the functional purpose of making the cranium supple, thereby facilitating childbirth. Rather, the cranial

elements fit a numerical and geometric logic derived from their consideration as vertebrae. Oken believed that the head was a recapitulation of the rest of the body; others, more moderately, interpreted the skull merely as a modified segment of the vertebral column, the cranial counterpart to the caudal coccyx. More generally, Oken interpreted higher levels of organization in nature as repetitions of lower levels, producing an integral totality of "all in everything." Man, the highest form of organization, summarizes the entire animal kingdom, a "microzoon" of the "macrozoon."

The notion of recapitulation, present in an all-encompassing form in Oken's philosophy, was one of the most pervasive of the holistic concepts that were popular among the nature-philosophical Romantics. It was developed in embryology, among others, by the Halle anatomist Johann Friedrich Meckel (1781–1833), who argued, as had the Tübingen physiologist Carl Friedrich Kielmeyer (1765–1844), that the successive stages of embryonal development in the higher animals are a recapitulation of the adult forms of the lower animals. Other popular concepts, in addition to that of recapitulation, were those of analogy and polarity.

Pantheistic Tenets

The Romantic, nature-philosophical preoccupation with "unity" concerned not only "God and the universe" and, as one of the manifestations of this oneness, the morphological harmony of organic species, but also the unity of "mind and matter" and of "God and man." To Carus, real understanding is a function of our becoming conscious of the universal unconscious. Oken believed that in man God has become self-conscious and that we are the self-manifestation of God. *Homo sapiens* represents the finite or corporeal God who is becoming self-aware in our minds. True knowledge could, therefore, be a matter of inner knowledge and experience: Not only rational thought, but also faith, feeling, mystical experience, and even dreams contribute to an understanding of nature.

A link existed here with the pietistic movement. The leading theologian of the Romantic era was Friedrich Daniel Ernst Schleiermacher (1768–1834). The pietistic doctrine of the primacy of inner religious experience merged seamlessly with the Romantic emphasis on intuition as a pure source of the knowledge of nature. Oken recounted that he had hit upon the vertebral interpretation of the skull in a flash of inspiration.

The Romantic distaste for intellectualized, scholarly systems of theology led away from confessional polemics and also from a biblical literalism that in contemporaneous England fed the "Genesis and geology" debates. Several of the nature philosophers, however, were devoutly religious, such as Gotthilf Heinrich von Schubert (1780–1860), who connected Romantic nature philosophy with simple biblical piety. Yet, they did not show nearly the same concern as did their British colleagues for the question of divine design in nature. Nothing equivalent to William Paley's (1743–1805) *Natural Theology* (1802) or to the Bridgewater Treatises "on the power, wisdom and goodness of God as manifested in the creation" was produced by Schelling and his followers. After all, the argument from design was tainted with the tarbrush of a Cartesian, mechanistic worldview.

An issue of science and religion that was shared by British, French, and German naturalists of the period was that of vitalism and the related question of the nature of the human mind/soul. The Romantic naturalists wrote fervently in the affirmative with respect to matters of spirit. Much debate was generated from the time that the comparative and human anatomist Samuel Thomas Soemmerring (1755–1830), in his famous booklet *Über das Organ der Seele* (*On the Organ of the Soul* [1796]), localized the soul in the intraventricular cerebrospinal fluid, to the appearance of the popular *Menschenschöpfung und Seelensubstanz* (*The Creation of Mankind and the Soul's Substance* [1854]), written by Göttingen's Rudolph Wagner (1805–64). With the latter's defense of the independent existence of the human soul, Wagner laid himself open to fierce criticism by the materialist thinker and naturalist Carl Vogt (1817–95).

National Context and the English Reaction

While Germany formed the heartland of nature philosophy, positivistic criticism of its doctrines was not uncommon even there. Nature philosophy never gained much ground in France, where Georges Cuvier (1769–1832) was one of its powerful detractors. Yet, some of the notions of nature philosophy were propagated also in Paris, among others by Cuvier's rival at the Muséum d'histoire naturelle, the zoologist Étienne Geoffroy Saint-Hilaire (1772–1844).

In the United States, émigré scientists from the European Continent brought with them elements of Romantic nature philosophy. Prominent among them were two Swiss friends, both educated in the German idealist tradition, namely Harvard zoologist Jean Louis Rodolphe Agassiz (1807–73) and Princeton geographer Arnold Henri Guyot (1807–84), who saw in the progressive development of the earth and its inhabitants the unfolding of a divine plan.

In Britain, too, the nature-philosophical movement never acquired a major following; yet, it had a number of influential representatives, both in Edinburgh and in London, and ironically, as in the United States, survived longer than it did in Germany. The poet Samuel Taylor Coleridge (1772–1834) was an early adherent. London's Royal Institution, in particular, where Humphry Davy worked, and later Michael Faraday (1791–1867), provided a platform for German idealist thought. Nature philosophy was also admitted into the Royal College of Surgeons, where Joseph Henry Green (1781–1863) propagated Coleridgean views.

The most accomplished English proponent of German idealism was Richard Owen (1804–92), who instigated a translation into English of Oken's *Lehrbuch* (3d ed., 1843) under the title *Elements of Physiophilosophy* (1847). Owen's own major contribution was *On the Archetype and Homologies of the Vertebrate Skeleton* (1848), in which he developed the concept of a vertebrate archetype, initially understood as the reflection of an immanent, polarizing force. In a subsequent book, *On the Nature of Limbs* (1849), Owen gave a new, Platonist twist to his vertebrate archetype by defining it as a transcendent entity, an idea in the divine mind that had functioned as a blueprint for the morphological diversity of vertebrate species. The organicist, developmental language of nature philosophy—and, in particular, Oken's—sounded much like the phraseology of evolutionary ideas, and Owen, for one, was a closet evolutionist, while his colleague and rival, University College's Robert Edmond Grant (1793–1874), openly advocated the transformism of Geoffroy Saint-Hilaire.

Idealist science provided a philosophical space for those who held religious beliefs, yet wanted to distance themselves from the traditional natural theology of the Anglican Church, cultivated at the ancient universities of Oxford and Cambridge. To the traditionalists, it seemed that, with the advocacy of German idealism, a door was opened for pantheism to enter England. Owen's initial definition of his vertebrate archetype must have added fuel to this fear. By defining the archetype as a reflection of the all-pervading polarizing force, he implicitly attributed the origin of species, constructed upon the archetypal plan, to natural causes and made it part of the theory of pantheistic, self-developing energy of nature, of which Oken spoke in his *Lehrbuch*. To various traditionalist Oxbridge scientists, such as the geologist Adam Sedgwick (1785–1873) and the polymath William Whewell (1794–1866), these theories appeared to amount to a form of pantheistic organic evolution, in essence no better than the evolution of the *Vestiges of the Natural History of Creation* (1844), anonymously issued by the Scottish publisher Robert Chambers (1802–71). A furious condemnation of Oken followed, especially in the new preface to the fifth edition of Sedgwick's *A Discourse on the Studies of the University of Cambridge* (1850).

Like Sedgwick, later historians have seen in the work of Oken and other Romantic naturalists notions of organic evolution. The developmental language of nature philosophy about taxonomic systems, however, is ambiguous in its meaning with respect to the origin of species: On the one hand, this language can be read to express a Darwinian descent; on the other hand, it can equally well be interpreted in terms of an ideal progression, like numbers in an arithmetic sequence. What is certain is that the origin of species was not a central issue on the research agenda of the nature philosophers.

See also Enlightenment; Mechanical Philosophy

BIBLIOGRAPHY

Cunningham, Andrew, and Nicholas Jardine, eds. *Romanticism and the Sciences.* Cambridge: Cambridge University Press, 1990.

Engelhardt, Dietrich von. *Historisches Bewusstsein in der Naturwissenschaft von der Aufklärung bis zum Positivismus.* Freiburg and Munich: Verlag Karl Alber, 1979.

———. "Natural Science in the Age of Romanticism." In *Modern Esoteric Spirituality,* ed. by Antoine Faivre and Jacob Needham. New York: Crossroad, 1992, 101–31.

Gode-von Aesch, Alexander. *Natural Science in German Romanticism.* New York: Columbia University Press, 1941.

Gregory, Frederick. "Theology and the Sciences in the German Romantic Period." In *Romanticism and the Sciences,* ed. by Andrew Cunningham and Nicholas Jardine. Cambridge: Cambridge University Press, 1990, 69–81.

Jacyna, L. S. "Romantic Thought and the Origins of Cell Theory." In *Romanticism and the Sciences,* ed. by Andrew Cunningham and Nicholas Jardine. Cambridge: Cambridge University Press, 1990, 161–8.

Knight, David. "Romanticism and the Sciences." In *Romanticism and the Sciences,* ed. by Andrew Cunningham and Nicholas Jardine. Cambridge: Cambridge University Press, 1990, 13–24.

Levere, Trevor H. *Poetry Realized in Nature: Samuel Taylor Coleridge and Early Nineteenth-Century Science.* Cambridge: Cambridge University Press, 1981.

Lenoir, Timothy. "The Göttingen School and the Development of Transcendental Naturphilosophie in the Romantic Era." *Studies in History of Biology* 5 (1981): 111–205.

Poggi, S., and M. Bossi, eds. *Romanticism in Science: Science in Europe, 1790–1840.* Dordrecht: Kluwer, 1994.

Rehbock, Philip F. "Transcendental Anatomy." In *Romanticism and the Sciences,* ed. by Andrew Cunningham and Nicholas Jardine. Cambridge: Cambridge University Press, 1990, 130–43.

Rupke, Nicolaas A. "The Study of Fossils in the Romantic Philosophy of History and Nature." *History of Science* 21 (1983): 389–413.

———. "Richard Owen's Vertebrate Archetype." *Isis* 84 (1993): 231–51.

———. *Richard Owen: Victorian Naturalist.* London and New Haven, Conn.: Yale University Press, 1994.

Russell, E. S. *Form and Function: A Contribution to the History of Animal Morphology.* London: Murray, 1916.

Snelders, H. A. M. "Romanticism and Naturphilosophie and the Inorganic Natural Sciences, 1797–1840: An Introductory Survey." *Studies in Romanticism* 9 (1970): 193–215.

———. "Oersted's Discovery of Electromagnetism." In *Romanticism and the Sciences,* ed. by Andrew Cunningham and Nicholas Jardine. Cambridge: Cambridge University Press, 1990, 228–40.

———. *Wetenschap en Intuitie: Het Duitse Romantisch-Speculatief Natuuronderzoek Rond 1800.* Baarn: Ambo, 1994.

34. MATERIALISM

Frederick Gregory

"Is the Person or is matter in motion the ultimate metaphysical category? There really is no third." This terse declaration from a late-twentieth-century philosopher (Kohak 1984, 126) bears testimony to the age-old tension between materialism and religion. From the time of the ancient Greeks to the modern era, the response to the human need for a foundational belief upon which to base a worldview has swayed back and forth between the poles of matter and spirit. Depending upon which pole one chooses as a starting point, of course, the worlds that result turn out to be very different places.

The Classical Period

The mythopoeic conceptions of the ancient Middle East understood the world in personal terms; nature behaved as it did because of the deities that constituted it. Nothing like materialism was possible in a world so pervasively religious. Not until the Greek invention of "natural" processes, which were created by removing divine agency as the explanation of nature's course, did the earliest version of a materialistic view make its appearance. It should be understood that, when the Greeks removed the gods from their explanations of nature, they created neither a completely impersonal nor even an antireligious view as a replacement. On the contrary, the Greeks assumed that nature's behavior could be described according to qualities possessed by human beings, particularly Greek human beings. Known for their cultivation of rational analysis, the Greeks assumed that nature, too, was rational. They likewise presumed that another quality important to humans, purpose, was to be found in nature. As a result, the Greek explanation of nature employed rational analysis, epitomized in mathematical description and the identification of nature's purposeful goals. As long as one's God was regarded as rational and purposeful, there was nothing about the Greek conception of nature that was inconsistent with religion.

Were one to deny either nature's rationality or nature's purposefulness, however, there would be a challenge to religion. While the view that would come to be known as materialism continued to accept the rationality of nature, in its purest forms it denied that a purpose sympathetic to human goals was anywhere to be found in the physical world. Everything that occurred did so in accordance with natural necessity. Personal wishes were irrelevant to the patterns of natural things. The pre-Socratic philosopher Democritus (c. 460–c. 370 B.C.) taught that the basic elements of reality were atoms and the void. In one of the characteristic claims of materialism, Democritus asserted that atoms had no intrinsic qualities; rather, the endless variety of form, size, and number in which atoms existed accounted for the diversity that one encountered. By the same token, it was the natural motion of atoms through the infinite void that determined all events. In such a world, nothing happened spontaneously or in accordance with an existing purpose, since everything happened by necessity in conjunction with the motion of uncontrolled atoms.

The ideas of Aristotle (384–322 B.C.), one of the greatest of the ancient Greek philosophers, ran counter to these materialistic tenets. He insisted that form, which comprised the properties of a corporeal object, was as basic a category as matter, which serves as the subject of these properties. Further, Aristotle included an effect's function or purpose among the causes that produced it; hence, he objected to the exclusion of purpose from the natural world that characterized the materialistic viewpoint of Democritus.

The fourth-century Greek materialist Epicurus (341–270 B.C.) and his Roman follower Lucretius two centuries later (c. 99–55 B.C.) deliberately opposed Aristotle. They attempted to develop the implications of a system based on atoms and an infinite void, asserting that the soul must be a material entity that does not survive the body, since, by definition, only the void was bereft of matter. Further, atoms "fell" though the infinite void eternally. While in none of his extant works did Epicurus explicitly discuss the doctrine of a deviation or swerve from the fall, we learn from Lucretius that he believed that atoms could collide and even maintain a constant vibratory motion. Lucretius, in particular, associated the lateral motion of atoms with the nonmechanical action of the will in what most regard as an inconsistent attempt to incorporate human freedom into his system.

From these two Epicurean materialists emerged an emphasis that has been a familiar feature of materialism ever since: the rejection of religion because of its tendency to inspire unnecessary fear and superstition. Both men taught that, if one could discover the causes of terrifying natural phenomena like thunder and lightning, one could embrace the necessity governing human actions without fear. Epicurus, for example, in his *Letter to Pythocles,* set out four conditions capable of producing thunder, while Lucretius, in his famous poem, *De rerum natura* (*On the Nature of Things*), listed twelve. If one could come to believe that all things resulted from natural necessity, one could submit without anxiety to the course of events that impinged on human life. This implied, of course, that the gods did not intervene in the affairs of the physical world or of mortals. For Epicurus and Lucretius, who believed in the existence of the gods, the lack of involvement was due to the gods' complete lack of interest in natural or human affairs.

While it is perhaps easy to see why later Christian writers regarded Epicurean materialism as atheistic, Stoic materialism from the time of Epicurus presented a different challenge. Although Stoics agreed that nothing existed other than matter, they attributed to a subtle material called *pneuma* an active principle that united passive material components into the wholes that gave objects their unique natures. *Pneuma* was, in fact, associated with divine rationality to the extent that the Stoics effectively materialized deity. What resulted was a world both purposeful and deterministic.

These options established materialism's legacy for the future development of religion. The central issue would contrast the determinism of natural events with their possible spontaneity. Associated with this issue were variations on the theme. Was the universe governed by purpose or was it wholly subject to chance, and, if the former, was the purpose preestablished and determined or an emergent expression of will? Did God exist, and, if so, was God immanently involved in his creation or removed from it? Did humans possess an immaterial soul, and, if not, to what extent were they free and responsible for their moral choices and eternal destiny?

The Early-Modern Period

From a monotheistic religious perspective, in which God's relationship to human beings was central, anything that rendered problematic the relationship of God to the world would be regarded with suspicion. Aristotle's antipathy to the deterministic dimension of materialism, with its exclusion of purpose from the worlds of nature and human beings, was among the reasons his philosophy eventually proved attractive and amenable to theologians in the late Middle Ages. Jewish and Christian conceptions of providence resisted acceptance of a belief in the unavoidable necessity of events; however, Aristotle's ideas, especially as they were appropriated by medieval Christian theologians, accounted for the dominance of a nonmaterialistic perspective in the West until the sixteenth century, when Aristotle's philosophy was fundamentally challenged.

This challenge to Aristotle's physics and cosmology from humanist quarters and from Galileo (1564–1642) and others contributed to the growth of a thoroughgoing criticism of the Aristotelian canon of philosophy. Among those opposed to Aristotle was the Roman Catholic priest Pierre Gassendi (1592–1655) in France, whose first work, in 1624, was a skeptical attack on Aristotelian philosophy. Prominent among multiple hypotheses to account for Gassendi's eventual attraction to Epicureanism was his wish to find an alternative to Aristotle's thought that would be more compatible with the new knowledge of nature that was emerging in the first half of the seventeenth century. Gassendi became acquainted with Epicureanism in the 1620s and devoted himself to a revision of Epicurus's philosophy that was completed in several works of the 1640s.

Gassendi's challenge as a priest lay in showing how acceptance of Epicurean atoms and the void could be made compatible with a Christian worldview. In general, he accomplished this task by declaring God the first cause of everything (thereby registering God's superintendence of the world) but focused his attention on the so-called secondary causes of natural phenomena. Here it was the motion of atoms through the void that accounted for observed reality. Human explanations of the properties of a corporeal body and its behavior should derive from the divinely imposed motions of indivisible atoms. Gassendi's was a voluntarist theology, according to which the continuing free exercise of God's will took precedence over what others, embracing an intellectualist theology, argued were constraints self-imposed by God in the original creative decree. Gassendi consequently rejected the notion that permanent forms, whether Platonic or Aristotelian, existed outside the mind. What resulted was a reverence for the foundational role of *materia prima* (prime matter). Since God was not constrained always to act in the same way, Gassendi urged that we must rely on what we learn through the senses more than on what reason dictated. His stance was a thoroughgoing empiricism, a "science of appearances," quite supportive of practical science.

Gassendi's retention of a providential God and an immaterial and immortal human intellect proved sufficient for some of his contemporaries to remove him from the ranks of true materialists. The same cannot be said for Thomas Hobbes (1588–1679), Gassendi's acquaintance from England, whose countrymen regularly denounced him as a materialist and an atheist. In his best-known work, *Leviathan* (1651), Hobbes wrote that "every part of the universe is body, and that which is not body is not part of the universe: and because the universe is all, that which is no part of it is nothing." While he was loath to regard motion as an inherent property of matter, Hobbes nevertheless contended that God, whom he regarded also as a material entity, had initiated the universe's present motion.

In the eighteenth century, the antireligious agenda of materialism came again to the fore in the works of several figures whose focus was a materialistic account of the human soul. In seventeenth-century France, René Descartes (1596–1650) had conceded that materialism and mechanism reigned everywhere except over *res cogitans* (thinking substance). Now his countrymen, particularly physicians involved in the growth of physiological science, wished to dispute his exception of the human soul by rendering a materialistic account of it. Of several attempts from the first half of the eighteenth century, the

most famous is that of Julien Offray de La Mettrie (1709–51).

La Mettrie's first defense of the material soul appeared in his *Natural History of the Soul,* published in the midst of his military service (1743–6) as an army physician during the war with Austria, but it was for his *Man a Machine* (1747) that he is best remembered. In *Man a Machine,* La Mettrie marshaled evidence for the physical basis of mental activity, including facts (he argued) that everyone knew from daily experience about the effect of the body's condition (owing to sickness, hunger, age, fatigue, and the like) on cognitive ability. Drawing on recent work on the irritability of muscle tissue, he likened the body to a machine that responded to stimuli supplied to it. La Mettrie wished to utilize new discoveries and the empirical methodology of natural science to discredit and undermine what he regarded as the dogma of the immaterial and immortal soul.

The anticlerical spirit of the Enlightenment philosophes was nowhere more evident than in the work of the French materialist Paul Henri Thiry, Baron d'Holbach (1723–89). His famous *System of Nature* appeared anonymously in 1770 on the heels of numerous antireligious tracts whose writing and illegal circulation in France he had supervised in the 1760s. D'Holbach's account of a nature produced by matter moving in accordance with mechanical laws rendered obsolete, in his view, all notions of God and the immortal soul. Gone was any attempt to dissociate materialism from atheism. Through his association with other philosophes, especially Denis Diderot (1713–84), an editor of the *Encyclopédie* sympathetic to his views, d'Holbach promoted the regular exchange of radical ideas through what came to be known as the *côterie holbachique* (d'Holbach's Coterie).

Eighteenth-century England produced something of a counterpart to the Christian materialism of Gassendi in the experimentalist-clergyman-materialist Joseph Priestley (1733–1804), although his theological starting point was quite different from Gassendi's. Priestley was ordained outside the Church of England, and his views eventually began to appear unorthodox even to the dissenting sects to which he ministered. He could not, for example, find justification in Scripture, when read with the eye of reason like any other record, that the soul survived the body after death. In two works from the 1770s, *Disquisitions Relating to Matter and Spirit* (1777) and *A Free Discussion of the Doctrines of Materialism and Philosophical Necessity* (1778), Priestley argued that what we call mind was not a substance distinct from the body but the result of corporeal organization. While he held to a belief in the resurrection of believers, it would be solely a resurrection of the body brought about not by a miracle but through an unknown law.

Priestley believed that he had to follow reason wherever it led him; moreover, he believed that, because God also acted in accordance with reason, God had effectively imposed constraints upon himself that could not be violated. Unlike Gassendi, who understood divine nature in a manner that favored God's will over reason, Priestley held that Creation itself was the necessary result of God's nature, which was unchangeable and, therefore, not subject to volitional alteration. What resulted, curiously, was as sincere an attempt to create a Christian materialism as that stemming from Gassendi's voluntarist emphasis. That materialism could emerge from the different assumptions of both men is a testimony to its pervasive and enduring attraction.

The Nineteenth Century

Not until the waning of the Romantic period in the third and fourth decades of the nineteenth century did materialism make its appearance in Germany. In his early philosophical writings, Ludwig Feuerbach (1804–72) embraced the idealistic philosophy of his mentor, Georg Wilhelm Friedrich Hegel (1770–1831). But in 1839 he abruptly changed course with a critique of the master's thought. Feuerbach had become impressed with the need to take account of the immediacy of sense experience. In his *Critique of Hegelian Philosophy* (1839), Feuerbach concluded that he could no longer defend Hegel's subordination of sensation to mind and thought; he could not, in other words, continue to accept Hegel's assumption that consciousness determined being. Feuerbach came to believe that sense experience, as it came to the mind, accurately reflected real pieces of nature and their relations to one another. Thought then further amplified this determinative raw material. Anything that was a product of the mind alone—anything, that is, that could not be traced directly back to the material world—was empty of true reality.

Feuerbach regarded his most famous work, *The Essence of Christianity* (1841), as an application of his new perspective. He now saw himself as a "natural scientist of the mind," by which he meant that he preferred, as he put it, to "unveil existence," not to invent, but to dis-

cover. What he claimed to have discovered about the doctrines of the Christian religion was that their origin lay in the world humans experienced immediately, a material and social realm that theologians were ignoring. Christian doctrines, including acceptance of the very existence of God, had been born of human needs. God was a magnified projection of human abilities, values, and hopes. Because humans possessed knowledge, they made God omniscient; because they had power, God was omnipotent; because they needed love, God was all loving; because they revered life, God granted it eternally. In inventing a domain of divine existence that they claimed transcended their ordinary experience of the material world, humans had created an illusory realm that they mistook for reality. Religion was, then, one grand anthropomorphism.

In the wake of Feuerbach's achievement in the 1840s, two materialistic movements took hold. The dialectical materialism of Karl Marx (1818–83) and Friedrich Engels (1820–95) built upon Feuerbach's critique of Hegelian philosophy with an extended analysis of its own. And in the 1850s, the so-called scientific materialists (called vulgar materialists by Marx) proclaimed a new gospel of realism based on natural science. In both programs, religion faced substantial criticism.

The senior member of what one of them called "a kind of underground trinity" of scientific materialists in the 1850s, which included Ludwig Büchner (1824–99) and Jakob Moleschott (1822–93), was the zoologist Karl Vogt (1817–95), whose materialistic writings in the late 1840s sounded the alarm for the coming movement. In his *Physiological Letters* (1847), Vogt declared that the mental activities commonly attributed to the soul should rather be understood as functions of the brain. It was here that he uttered his famous claim that "thoughts stand in the same relation to the brain as gall does to the liver or urine to the kidney." As a delegate to the Frankfurt Parliament a year later, Vogt campaigned aggressively for the separation of church and state because he believed that all churches restricted freedom.

Most famous of the scientific materialists was Büchner, whose *Force and Matter* originally appeared in 1855 and went through twenty-one editions and translation into seventeen foreign languages. As a young physician working in a clinic in Tübingen, Büchner wrote his book with a nontechnical approach that summarized the general philosophical conclusions of the new materialism of natural science. Büchner's overriding theme was that we must go where the truth (of science) leads us, whether we like it or not. Supernatural knowledge was impossible because it was inaccessible to the senses. There was no force without matter and no matter without force. Immaterial entities like the human soul simply did not exist.

Echoes of this line of thinking continued to be heard as the century wore on. Charles Darwin's (1809–82) *Origin of Species* (1859) reinforced in the minds of writers like Ernst Haeckel (1834–1919) and the theologian David Friedrich Strauss (1808–74) the priority of the material realm and the mechanical processes that regulated it. Naturally, these writers and others exploited natural selection to oppose the relationship between Creator and creation supported by traditional religious perspectives. They contested, for example, the assumption that God superintended nature, and they disputed the argument from design so treasured by the orthodox, contending all the while that scientific explanation should be confined to the categories of the senses and permitting no appeal to supernatural categories with no tie to the material world. Variations of these arguments have persisted since Darwin and continue to represent the point of departure for many materialists today when formulating the relationship between science and religion.

The other materialism to emerge in the wake of Feuerbach's critique of Hegel was the dialectical version of Marx and Engels. Marx appreciated Feuerbach's "correction" of the Hegelian emphasis on the primacy of mind. He regarded Feuerbach's "exposure" of religion as rooted in the material as well as the social world of human beings to be a crucial insight. In general, he recognized, as he and Engels wrote in *The German Ideology* (1845), that "the nature of individuals depends on the material conditions determining their production." But Marx's famous materialist conception of history was far more subtle than the straightforward determinism it has frequently been presented to be. Having rejected the conventional logic of being in favor of Friedrich Schelling's (1775–1854) and Hegel's logic of becoming, Marx moved beyond the mere demand that what the mind envisioned was ultimately tied to a foundation in the material realm. He argued that both the material and the mental world influenced each other as both developed in a mutual embrace. Reality and consciousness, bound up with each other, could not be separated.

Marx thus took Feuerbach one step further. Not only, he argued, must we privilege sensations derived from the material world to the same degree that we have revered thought, but, because the worlds of matter and mind are in process and interlinked, we must also view our practical experience of the world as no less significant than our understanding of it. In this view, epistemology was less a mere theory of cognition than a means of shaping the very reality one is trying to get to know. Feuerbach's critique of Hegel did not go far enough, according to Marx, for, in taking the master to task for holding that consciousness determined being, Feuerbach had assumed (as in his critique of Christianity) that the mere *awareness* of neglecting the equivalence of being and consciousness would be a sufficient corrective. But, to Marx, this judgment remained in the end a passive conclusion of the intellect. Feuerbach's position, in essence, retained the very assumption he criticized in Hegel, that consciousness determined being. The final step, a materialist conception of history that allowed for the dialectical interaction between humankind and the material world, must be taken. As Marx said in his eleventh thesis on Feuerbach: "Philosophers have only *interpreted* the world, in various ways; the point, however, is to *change* it."

In Marx's view, the action of nature and humankind formed the stuff of history. Religion, for its part, had to be regarded purely as a social and political phenomenon. Marx sought its social function, finding it (as is well known) in the class structure of Western society. Religion was a vehicle by means of which the powerful kept the powerless in their place. Its illusory promises for the future acted like a drug to deaden the masses to the miseries of poverty and injustice.

The Twentieth Century

Marxist materialism, as it persisted into the twentieth century, developed in several directions, all opposed to a religious worldview. In V. I. Lenin's (1870–1924) writings, materialism was held up as the commonsense response to critiques of scientific realism developed by Ernst Mach (1838–1916) and others. Later, Georg Lukács (1885–1971) explored the meaning and implications of a "materialized" consciousness for Western philosophy and sociology, while the Frankfurt School investigated the materialization of Western social and cultural life.

Non-Marxist materialists in the twentieth century found some historical debates, such as that over vitalism as an explanation of living things, no longer interesting. They have preferred to concentrate their attention on a materialist theory of mind. Behaviorists like Gilbert Ryle (1900–1976) and physicalists such as David Armstrong (1926–) employ various arguments to establish that human capabilities to intend, to choose, and the like ultimately reduce to a state of the body. Others object to the notion that there is nothing over and above the physical. A central feature of the disagreements among philosophers like John Searle (1984), Daniel Dennett (1991), and David Chalmers (1996), and among scientists like John Eccles (1903–), Francis Crick (1993), and Roger Penrose (1994), is the question of whether and how one might provide a materialistic explanation of qualia, inner states of awareness that are, in some sense, unique and private to the one experiencing them. Throughout the debate, the language and the categories associated with computer technology have proven useful and have been prominently employed.

The many systems of materialism that have existed throughout Western history demonstrate that there is no single agreed-upon position on religion among materialists. One can say that materialists tend to be critical of religious doctrines that appear to have no bearing on, or relation to, the material world, but not all materialists regard themselves as irreligious or antireligious. However, materialists insist on acknowledging the impact upon human experience of our dependence on the material world when they attempt to address the classical questions of religion, philosophy, and politics.

See also Atheism; Atomism; Enlightenment; Epicureanism; Mechanical Philosophy; Positivism; Scientific Naturalism

BIBLIOGRAPHY

Chalmers, David J. *The Conscious Mind: In Search of a Fundamental Theory.* New York: Oxford University Press, 1996.

Clay, Diskin. *Lucretius and Epicurus.* Ithaca, N.Y.: Cornell University Press, 1983.

Crick, Francis. *The Astonishing Hypothesis: The Scientific Search for the Soul.* New York: Scribner, 1993.

Dennett, Daniel C. *Consciousness Explained.* Boston: Little, Brown, 1991.

Gregory, Frederick. *Scientific Materialism in Nineteenth Century Germany.* Dordrecht: D. Reidel, 1977.

———. "Scientific versus Dialectical Materialism in Nineteenth Century German Radicalism." *Isis* 68 (1977): 206–23.

Hiebert, Erwin N. "The Integration of Revealed Religion and Scientific Materialism in the Thought of Joseph Priestley." In *Joseph Priestley: Scientist, Theologian, and Metaphysician,* ed. by Lester Kieft and Bennet R. Willeford. Lewisberg, Pa.: Bucknell University Press, 1980.

Joy, Lynn Sumida. *Gassendi the Atomist: Advocate of History in an Age of Science.* Cambridge: Cambridge University Press, 1987.

Kohak, Erazim. *The Embers and the Stars: A Philosophical Inquiry into the Moral Sense of Nature.* Chicago: University of Chicago Press, 1984.

Kors, Alan. *D'Holbach's Coterie: An Enlightenment in Paris.* Princeton, N.J.: Princeton University Press, 1976.

Lange, Friedrich Albert. *The History of Materialism.* Trans. by Ernest Chester Thomas. 3d ed. 3 vols. in one. New York: Harcourt, Brace, 1925.

Lindberg, David C. *The Beginnings of Western Science: The European Scientific Tradition in Philosophical, Religious, and Institutional Context, 600 B.C. to A.D. 1450.* Chicago: University of Chicago Press, 1992.

McLellan, David. *Karl Marx: His Life and Thought.* New York: Harper and Row, 1973.

Osler, Margaret. *Divine Will and the Mechanical Philosophy: Gassendi and Descartes on Contingency and Necessity in the Created World.* Cambridge: Cambridge University Press, 1994.

Penrose, Roger. *Shadows of the Mind: A Search for the Missing Science of Consciousness.* New York: Oxford University Press, 1994.

Sarasohn, Lisa T. "Motion and Morality: Pierre Gassendi, Thomas Hobbes, and the Mechanical World View." *Journal of the History of Ideas* 46 (1985): 363–79.

Schofield, Robert E. *Mechanism and Materialism: British Natural Philosophy in an Age of Reason.* Princeton, N.J.: Princeton University Press, 1970.

Searle, John R. *Minds, Brains, and Science.* Cambridge, Mass: Harvard University Press, 1984.

Shapin, Steven, and Simon Schaffer. *Leviathan and the Air-Pump: Hobbes, Boyle, and the Experimental Life.* Princeton, N.J.: Princeton University Press, 1985.

Staum, Martin S. *Cabanis: Enlightenment and Medical Philosophy in the French Revolution.* Princeton, N.J.: Princeton University Press, 1980.

Wellman, Kathleen. *La Mettrie: Medicine, Philosophy, and Enlightenment.* Durham, N.C.: Duke University Press, 1992.

35. ATHEISM

John Henry

Introduction

The rise of religious unbelief marks one of the most significant transformations of Western culture. Although few historians would now go so far as fully to endorse Lucien Febvre's famous claim that disbelief in God was a cultural impossibility before the seventeenth century, there can be no doubt that belief in God and the validity of religion were once characterizing aspects of the culture in a way that they are no longer. From the closing decades of the nineteenth century, belief in God became (for the majority, at least) a question of individual choice and was regarded as a private and personal matter. Until the early-modern period and even beyond, however, it was so pervasive in social, political, and intellectual life that systematic disbelief was, to a very large extent, practically impossible.

The reasons for this cultural sea change are debated by historians, but there is no doubt that many factors were involved. Religious pluralism after the Reformation, together with a growing awareness of the cultural relativism that resulted from increased contact with non-European civilizations, made it easier to see religion as a human institution shaped by local customs and interests. This, in turn, made it possible to believe that a society could function well even though the individual members were not constrained to behave by the promise of heaven or the threat of hell. Although Jesuit missionaries to China in the seventeenth century tried to present Confucianism as a theistic philosophy, in order to maintain the validity of claims that the universality of theism testified to the existence of God, other early China watchers insisted that Confucianism was essentially an atheistic system. When it became possible to argue, as Pierre Bayle (1647–1706) did in his *Pensées diverses sur la*

comète (1682), that individual self-interests might guarantee the cooperative interactions required to maintain social order, moral philosophy became secularized and the influence of religion was weakened.

The growth of moral and cultural relativism, together with both the increasing awareness of alternatives to Aristotelian philosophy and the acceptance of ancient skepticism, gave rise to the so-called skeptical crisis of the late Renaissance. Although for some believers a skeptical epistemology led to a fideistic insistence that religious belief lay beyond the realm of reason, many others, it seems, tried to combat skepticism by reasserting the extent to which sound reasoning might be assumed to be reliable. The efforts of rival churches to lay claim to the true primitive faith of the early Church, for example, led to concerns with epistemology and intellectual authority that tended to emphasize the use of reason. This new emphasis on reason within Christian belief has been seen as leading to the unintended consequence of increased unbelief. For instance, differences about the significance and nature of the Eucharist led Protestants to insist that the age of miracles was past and to emphasize the reasonableness of their interpretation of the Eucharist compared to the allegedly superstitious belief of Roman Catholics in transubstantiation. Philological and other scholarly investigations of the biblical texts, yet another development in the efforts to establish authoritatively the principles of the true faith, led to increasingly critical, rationally based, assessments of the status of Scripture and again made unbelief easier to sustain. Here developments within the churches themselves contributed to secularization, but there were, of course, parallel developments. Anticlerical feeling flourished in Italy, for example, in the sixteenth and seventeenth centuries, in France in the seventeenth and eighteenth centuries, and in Germany in the nineteenth century. The separation of church and state, which in some cases led to the secularization of various aspects of public life, notably education, also diminished the previously all-pervasive influence of religion.

Discussion of the causative factors involved in the rise of atheism could easily be extended. The rise of literacy has even been advanced, although it is an argument that seems to depend upon the question-begging assumption that a better-educated populace will be a less religious one. Alternatively, some suggest that the class consciousness that arose out of the massive social changes brought about by industrialization enabled the working classes to recognize the churches as middle-class institutions of social control and so led to an increase in religious skepticism. Our concern here, however, is with the interaction between religion and science. In every account of secularization and the decline of religious belief, the rise of science plays a prominent role. In what follows, therefore, we will concentrate exclusively upon this aspect of the background to modern atheism. The aim of this essay is to assess how important science or natural philosophy was to the rise of irreligion. We will not consider a number of issues that have figured prominently in the historiography of atheism, such as the issue of popular unbelief, which, at least until most recent times, had little to do with scientific considerations, and the historiographical difficulty of deciding the extent of atheism in the premodern and early-modern periods.

The Premodern Period

Although the charge of atheism or the denial of belief in the gods worshiped by the state was leveled against certain individuals among the ancient Greeks, most famously against Socrates (469–399 B.C.), it was both rare and equivocal. Anaxagoras of Clazomenae (500–428 B.C.), for example, was forced out of Athens because he taught that the sun was a red hot mass, the moon a body like the earth, and the other heavenly bodies similarly natural objects. It is significant that he was not immediately charged with atheism as a result of such doctrines, but a public resolution was first carried to proscribe the doctrines themselves. There is no real evidence, therefore, that Anaxagoras explicitly denied the existence of the gods, and the same could be said of other accused atheists, such as Protagoras of Abdera (c. 485–411 B.C.) and Socrates himself. It is hard to

know, therefore, to what extent, if any, naturalistic thinking among the ancient Greek philosophers might have contributed to the rise of atheism (in popular awareness, if not in acceptance). The thinkers with the greatest reputation for radical freethinking were the Sophists, but their arguments were seldom derived from natural philosophy. It is clear also that Socrates was not accused of atheism as a result of a perceived naturalism in his philosophy. Nevertheless, when Aristophanes (c. 448–388 B.C.), in his play *The Clouds* used Socrates as the chief representative of what he took to be the latest pernicious freethinking, he had him utter a number of naturalistic claims. This suggests that, in the popular mind, naturalism was associated with atheism.

Generally, within a polytheistic system of belief it is easy to acknowledge, and even to participate in, the established public worship of new and foreign gods. Hence, imperial Rome was able to be highly tolerant of other religions, effectively allowing a wide degree of freedom of worship. Such tolerance was not extended to Christians, however, who denied the Roman gods and refused to take part in public worship. Christians were thus subject to capital punishment as a result of their allegedly subversive "atheism." But when Christianity became the official religion of the Roman Empire in A.D. 393, the definition of atheism necessarily changed. It is now that we enter into the period that was so thoroughly dominated by Christian belief that anti-Christian atheism became a practical impossibility. During the centuries of the early Church and into the high Middle Ages, heresy was recognized as a threat to sound religion, while atheism, for the most part, was not. Nevertheless, one or two aspects of naturalistic thought in the Middle Ages seemed to contemporaries to suggest a lack, rather than a perversion, of faith.

One of the earliest associations of naturalism with atheism is to be found in the realm of medicine. Where there are three medical practitioners (*medici*), a medieval proverb suggested, there are two atheists. Medieval literature abounds with intimations that doctors are "nulla fidians," nonbelievers who know little and care less about Christian teachings. These sentiments seem to derive from a general conviction that doctors were too materialistic in their approach to health and disease and failed to acknowledge the role of God and the state of the patient's soul in illness. This was exacerbated by the fact that the principal ancient medical authority, Galen (A.D. 129–c. 210), doubted the immortality of the soul and rejected Christianity. It is no longer possible to ascertain how fair such accusations against the medical profession were, much less to assess the degree of unbelief alluded to in the medieval proverb. In defense of doctors, it is certainly true to say that most medical literature is extremely pious in tone (although atheists would not have been so foolish as to publish their views, and dissembling was easy). The charge of atheism was persistent, but it was by no means the most prominent accusation against doctors; their general incompetence, covetousness, and immorality figured much more highly. Furthermore, Galen's reputation for profanity and irreligion made him a frequently cited figure in antiatheist literature because it was also well known that he was moved by the wonderful contrivance of the human body to acknowledge the existence of a divine architect. If even someone like Galen accepted the existence of God, the argument went, who could deny it? Doctors could lay claim to being more familiar with the intricate design of nature and, therefore, more deeply theistic. So, while for some the doctor might seem an atheist, doctors frequently presented themselves as God's emissaries, priests of the book of nature, taking care of bodies just as priests of God's other book took care of souls.

The dominant natural philosophy of Aristotelianism was also occasionally associated with atheism. In 1277, the bishop of Paris condemned 219 propositions drawn from various Aristotelian sources, including the works of Thomas Aquinas (c. 1225–74). Some of them were merely scurrilous attacks on religion, such as the proposition that theological discussions are based on fables, but others were irreligious claims drawn from Aristotle's teachings: denial of the Creation and affirmation of the eternity of the world, denial of a first man and insistence upon the eternity of human generation, denial of the immortality of the soul and of God's providence. Underlying these religiously subversive positions, it seems, was a doctrine of "double truth," a claim that contrary truths could be simultaneously upheld if it were assumed that one truth was demonstrated by natural reason, even though it was contrary to faith, and the other was based upon faith and dogma, even though it was contrary to reason. Threatening though all of this looks to religious belief, it is well known that Aristotelianism soon became a faithful handmaiden to Roman Catholic theology, as it subsequently came to be used as a reliable handmaiden to theology by the Reformed churches.

The Early-Modern Period

To be sure, the denial of God's providence on Aristotelian grounds was revived early in the sixteenth century by Alessandro Achillini (1463–1512) and Pietro Pomponazzi (1462–1525) and maintained into the seventeenth century by Cesare Cremonini (1550–1631) and Giulio Cesare Vanini (1585–1619). Similarly, the notion of the eternity of the world and of humankind was revived by Girolamo Cardano (1501–76), Agostino Steuco (1497/8–1548), and others, while the Aristotelian rejection of the immortal soul was once again defended upon rationalist grounds by Cardano, Pomponazzi, Andrea Cesalpino (1519–1603), and Vanini. But they must be seen as radical and untypical manifestations of Renaissance Aristotelianism. It is not Aristotelianism per se that contributed to the origins of modern atheism, but only some Aristotelians.

The natural philosophy most closely associated with atheism was atomism, which was revived in the late fifteenth century after the publication in 1473 of the recently discovered *De rerum natura* (*On the Nature of Things*) of Lucretius (c. 99–55 B.C.) and, two years later, of three letters by Epicurus (341–270 B.C.) in Diogenes Laertius's (fl. second century A.D.) *Lives of the Philosophers*. Ample evidence suggests that Epicureanism, with its denial of providence and its insistence that all of the phenomena of the natural world might arise as the result of the motions and interactions of atoms acting "by necessity," provided a major stimulus to atheism. Certainly, Epicureanism was vigorously attacked by the devout in terms that suggest that it was becoming increasingly popular in circles that were deemed irreligious and immoral. It was possible, however, to accept the natural philosophy of atomism without being an atheist. All of the major writers involved in the promotion of the mechanical philosophy (which was based on an essentially atomist theory of matter), with the notable exception of Thomas Hobbes (1588–1679), evidently were devout believers, concerned to rescue atomism and, in some cases, Epicureanism from the taint of atheism. Although there has been some controversy over the religious sincerity of Pierre Gassendi (1592–1655), the leading advocate of Epicureanism, the prevalent consensus among historians is that he was a true son of his church. But even a writer like Francis Bacon (1561–1626), who was by no means a confirmed atomist, could deny the supposed atheistic import of atomism. In his essay "Of Atheism," Bacon argued that it was far easier for an atheist to suggest that the world came together by chance from the assumption that there were only four principles in the world—earth, water, air, and fire—than from the assumption that all things were made from countless rapidly moving, invisibly small atoms. This argument, repeated in many forms, was an underlying premise of the natural theology that came to be built upon the new mechanical philosophies of the seventeenth century, with their essentially atomist theories of matter. Atomism, in short, seemed to the overwhelming majority of natural philosophers to demand, and therefore to testify to, the supervision of God. If Scripture declared that only a fool could deny God, atomistic natural philosophy could easily be made to show why. So, as with medical naturalism and Aristotelian rationalism, atomism might lead some to atheism, but for many others it not only did not point to impiety but even reinforced religious belief.

Nevertheless, early-modern commentators on atheism invariably attributed its growth, at least in part, to natural philosophy. Ralph Cudworth's (1617–88) extended typology of atheism, for example, *The True Intellectual System of the Universe* (1678), was based entirely upon theories of matter, including mechanistic atomism and Aristotelian hylomorphism (the theory that a body is an inseparable combination of a portion of passive matter and a specific substantial form responsible for the body's properties). Although few other commentators were to see the causes of atheism in quite such naturalistic terms, most placing greater emphasis on immorality and skepticism, natural philosophy was seldom entirely exonerated. One major reason for the failure of devout natural philosophers, such as Gassendi, René Descartes (1596–1650), Robert Boyle (1627–91), and Isaac Newton (1642–1727), to convince contemporary churchmen that the mechanical philosophy was not irreligious was the fact that it clearly promoted deism, in which religious sentiment was essentially confined to acknowledging the existence of a divine architect of the intricacies of the natural world. Although from a modern point of view deism is easily distinguishable from atheism, for early-modern thinkers the denial of revealed religion and many of the doctrines of Christianity, which was implicit, if not explicit, in deism, made it tantamount to atheism.

The general picture seems to remain pretty much the same throughout the eighteenth century and into the nineteenth. Natural philosophy continued to be used to support religion, though for many, including, for example, readers of the published Boyle Lectures (annual lectures, from 1692 to 1714, established by the terms of Boyle's will to combat, among other forms of anti-Christian infidelity, atheism and deism), it was deism, not Christianity, that captivated them. In addition, by the eighteenth century it is certainly possible to point to individual skeptics who might be described as practical rather than dogmatic atheists, such as Jean Meslier (1664–1729), Julien Offray de La Mettrie (1709–51), David Hume (1711–76), Denis Diderot (1713–84), and Paul Henri Thiry, Baron d'Holbach (1723–89), as well as to others whom it is perhaps safer to call vigorously anti-Christian deists, such as John Toland (1670–1722) and Matthew Tindal (1657–1733). All of them drew some of their inspiration and argument from contemporary natural philosophy, but it was by no means their only source of antireligious sentiment. Indeed, it seems fair to say that they had to develop interpretations of natural phenomena that differed markedly from the leading natural philosophers to promote their own ideas. La Mettrie's *L'Homme machine* (*Man a Machine* [1747]), for example, was derived from Descartes's *bête machine* (machine brute) but only after rejecting Descartes's dualism and his arguments for the immateriality of the *res cogitans* (thinking substance). Similarly, John Toland's philosophy was essentially Newtonian but with a theologically crucial difference: Rejecting Newton's concept of divinely superadded active principles in matter, Toland held matter to be innately active by its own nature.

Three developments in eighteenth-century natural philosophy were especially conducive to atheistic interpretations. John Turbeville Needham's (1713–81) new evidence for the spontaneous generation of life, Albrecht von Haller's (1708–77) discovery of the innate irritability of muscle tissue, and Abraham Trembley's (1710–84) revelation of the ability of the *Hydra* to regenerate itself when cut into pieces could all be presented as evidence of the innate ability of matter to organize itself. Materialist atheists could certainly draw upon these developments to support their positions, but it was equally possible to interpret them, as Needham and Haller did, theistically.

Atheistic tendencies in eighteenth-century physical science are perhaps most famously represented by Pierre

Simon Laplace (1749–1827), who demonstrated in 1786 that the observed gradual acceleration of Jupiter and deceleration of Saturn were an oscillatory system that would reverse itself after about nine hundred years. Laplace's proof that the solar system was self-regulating was a triumph of Newtonian mathematical physics. Subsequent work, in which he showed how the solar system might have come into existence in its precise form as a result of the operations of Newton's laws on a nebula of hot gaseous matter, enhanced his reputation. It was subsequently said that when Napoleon Bonaparte remarked that God was not mentioned in Laplace's *Traité de mécanique céleste* (*Treatise on Celestial Mechanics* [1799–1825]), the author replied that he had no need of that hypothesis. If the story is true, Laplace was clearly distancing himself from his precursor, Isaac Newton (for whom God always had an important place in natural philosophy), but he would not have been alone among his scientific contemporaries in wishing to avoid recourse to a "God of the gaps." Nevertheless, he acquired a reputation as a notorious atheist in a way that others did not. This did not mean, however, that his work was taken to undermine faith in God. On the contrary, as John Robison (1739–1805) and William Whewell (1794–1866) took pains to point out, extending an argument raised by Gottfried Wilhelm Leibniz (1646–1716) against Newton in 1715, a self-developing and self-correcting universe must be even more perfectly designed than one that requires repeated interventions by its Creator.

The Nineteenth Century

It is true to say, however, that, by the nineteenth century, the sciences were being pursued by increasing numbers of practitioners in a way that demarcated them from religious issues. Scientists, newly emerging as a profession in the early decades of the nineteenth century, tried to exclude reference to God and to theological concerns from their work. As Frank M. Turner has shown with regard to science in Victorian Britain, this exclusion was, to a large extent, a professionalizing strategy, enabling lay scientists to oust clergymen amateurs from paid posts or positions of authority, but it should also be seen as another example of the spread of secularization. Far from being the predominant driving force in secularization, the practice of science itself was secularized as a result of influence from the wider culture. This secularization of science did not in itself directly promote atheism, of course, but it did

result in a marked weakening of the support that science had traditionally provided for religion. Hence, the balance between science as support for religion and science as a force for irreligion began to shift, once again making it easier to maintain an atheist position.

The clearest example of this new development in the practice of science can be seen in the emerging science of geology. Concerning themselves with discovering the order of deposition of the rocks and the physical processes that resulted in the observed complexities of the earth's topography, geologists eschewed speculations about the origin of the earth, the origin of the creatures in the fossil record, and the origins and early history of humankind as unscientific. In Britain and the United States, there was some resistance to the social and intellectual exclusiveness of scientific geology. A number of mostly popular writers continued to maintain earlier traditions of what was called Mosaic or scriptural geology, which took it for granted that the geological record could be shown to support a literal reading of the Creation account in Genesis, provided that both the rocks and Scripture were interpreted correctly.

Scientific geologists were certainly dismissive of the Mosaic geologists' enterprise, but even they were not opposed to the use of geology in traditional natural theology, for instance, in extending the design argument to embrace both the implications of the fossil record and the vast age of the earth before humankind appeared. If this was a compromise with their otherwise nonreligious position, they were soon forced to make another, although the pressure here came from another newly emerging science—biology. Unlike the earlier classificatory tradition of natural history, biology sought to explain life, its emergence, historical development, and diversity in terms of scientific "laws." The fossil record seemed to imply a progression of living forms from simple to increasingly complex throughout the geological ages. Geologists and paleontologists confined themselves to explaining this progression by the changing habitat of the earth, as it cooled from its supposedly original molten state to successive states capable of supporting richer diversities of life. The assumption was, in keeping with the design argument, that the creatures in any given habitat were providentially adapted to their environmental conditions. The question of the actual origin of the new species that, according to the fossil record, suddenly appeared at specific times, was excluded from scientific geology.

One obvious answer to the problem was evolution. But this was a theory, firmly based on the self-organizing powers of matter, with a distinctly atheistic pedigree. First suggested by Diderot, Benoît de Maillet (1656–1738), Georges Louis Leclerc, Comte de Buffon (1707–88), and Erasmus Darwin (1731–1802), all of whom had a reputation for atheism, it was systematically developed by Jean Baptiste Lamarck (1744–1829) in his *Philosophie zoologique* (Zoological Philosophy [1809]). It is hardly surprising that biological evolutionism was first taken up in Britain by various radical groups, including working-class socialists, democratic republicans, phrenologists, and other materialists, all of whom used Lamarckism in their attacks on religion, "priestcraft," and other aspects of the old order.

Evolution did not win scientific credibility until after the appearance of Charles Darwin's (1809–82) *Origin of Species* (1859). Somewhat ironically, Darwin's mechanism for evolution, natural selection, was seen as too negative a process to account for the widely perceived progression of animal forms through time. Consequently, the majority of post-Darwinian evolutionists took up theories of evolution that, like Lamarck's, implied some more positive law of progress at work. This, in turn, made it possible to present evolution, in a "grander view" of the Creator, as God's way of bringing about his designs. The natural-theological accommodation of evolution in this way was particularly easy within Anglicanism, since Darwin himself acknowledged the influence upon his ideas of two Anglican clergymen, William Paley (1743–1805) and Thomas Malthus (1766–1834). Both Paley and Malthus contributed to their church's tradition of theodicy by defending the seeming viciousness and amorality of the status quo in terms of an intellectualist theology and God's higher purposes. It is surely significant also that Darwin, erstwhile trainee for the Church, clearly saw his theory as a contribution to natural theology for a number of years after he first thought of natural selection in 1838. When he did give up his faith, in about 1851, he seems to have done so on moral and emotional grounds (brought to a head by the death of his ten-year-old daughter, Annie), rather than as a result of his detailed awareness of the apparent cruelty and wastefulness of nature or of his commitment to scientific naturalism. Darwin once said, however, that he had never been an atheist, and he preferred in his later years to describe himself as an agnostic.

Darwinism perhaps marks the final removal of God and religion from the scientific enterprise. Just as physicists after Newton tried to explain everything without recourse to God, just as geologists tried to define their science as lying outside biblical and religious concerns, so biologists declared themselves to be concerned only with natural laws. Scientists sought explanations of nature only in naturalistic terms. Darwinism, therefore, as T. H. Huxley (1825–95) insisted, was neither for religion nor against it—it was irrelevant to it. By the end of the century, science and religion were entirely separate spheres with their own points of view and their own territories. Of course, it was (and still is) possible to use science either for or against religious belief, but such arguments no longer seem so obviously relevant to belief, and, within the scientific community, religious doctrines seldom seem germane to judgments about the validity of scientific theories.

Atheism is now a significant aspect of Western, previously Christian, culture, but the reasons for this are many. The role of science, as we have seen, has never been clearcut. For every atheistic use of science, there have always been corresponding theistic uses. From the historian's point of view, the story seems to be one of historical contingency. Had things been different and our culture had remained predominantly religious, it seems reasonable to suppose that science would have continued to be seen as a major supporter of faith. There is, after all, nothing about science that logically entails atheism. But perhaps this is a view that seems more plausible within the British and North American tradition, in which natural theology thrived the longest and still is not entirely dead. From the perspective of Continental Europe, with its stronger Enlightenment heritage, it may be easier to believe, with Pierre Bayle, that the application of reason must lead to unbelief, or with Auguste Comte (1798–1857), that the "positive" or scientific way of thinking must repudiate and supersede the theological way. Blaise Pascal (1623–62) may not have been mistaken when he discerned only an eternal silence in the infinite space revealed to him by contemporary science, and perhaps, as a devout Christian believer, he was right to be afraid.

See also Atomism; Deism; Enlightenment; Epicureanism; Evolutionary Ethics; Materialism; Positivism; Scientific Naturalism; Secular Humanism

BIBLIOGRAPHY

Allen, D. C. *Doubt's Boundless Sea: Skepticism and Faith in the Renaissance.* Baltimore: Johns Hopkins University Press, 1964.

Berman, David. *A History of Atheism in Britain: From Hobbes to Russell.* London and New York: Routledge, 1990.

Betts, C. J. *Early Deism in France: From the So-Called "Deistes" of Lyon (1564) to Voltaire's Lettres Philosophiques (1734).* The Hague: Nijhoff, 1984.

Buckley, Michael J., S.J. *At the Origins of Modern Atheism.* New Haven, Conn.: Yale University Press, 1987.

Budd, Susan. *Varieties of Unbelief: Atheists and Agnostics in English Society, 1850–1960.* London: Heinemann, 1977.

Chadwick, Owen. *The Secularization of the European Mind in the Nineteenth Century.* Cambridge: Cambridge University Press, 1975.

Desmond, Adrian. *The Politics of Evolution: Morphology, Medicine, and Reform in Radical London.* Chicago: University of Chicago Press, 1989.

Drachmann, A. B. *Atheism in Pagan Antiquity.* London and Copenhagen: Gyldendal, 1922.

Febvre, Lucien. *The Problem of Unbelief in the Sixteenth Century: The Religion of Rabelais.* Trans. by Beatrice Gottlieb. Cambridge, Mass.: Harvard University Press, 1982.

Ginzburg, Carlo. *The Cheese and the Worms: The Cosmos of a Sixteenth-Century Miller.* Trans. by J. Tedeschi and A. Tedeschi. Baltimore: Johns Hopkins University Press, 1980.

Hunter, Michael. "Science and Heterodoxy: An Early Modern Problem Reconsidered." In *Reappraisals of the Scientific Revolution,* ed. by D. C. Lindberg and R. S. Westman. Cambridge: Cambridge University Press, 1990, 437–60.

Hunter, Michael, and David Wooton, eds. *Atheism from the Reformation to the Enlightenment.* Oxford: Clarendon, 1992.

Kocher, Paul H. *Science and Religion in Elizabethan England.* San Marino, Calif.: Huntington Library, 1953.

Kors, Alan Charles. *Atheism in France, 1650–1729.* Vol. 1: *The Orthodox Sources of Disbelief.* Princeton, N.J.: Princeton University Press, 1990.

Mintz, Samuel I. *The Hunting of Leviathan: Seventeenth-Century Reactions to the Materialism and Moral Philosophy of Thomas Hobbes.* Cambridge: Cambridge University Press, 1962.

Moore, James R. "Of Love and Death: Why Darwin 'Gave up Christianity.'" In *History, Humanity and Evolution: Essays for John C. Greene,* ed. by J. R. Moore. Cambridge: Cambridge University Press, 1989, 195–229.

Roe, Shirley A. "Voltaire Versus Needham: Atheism, Materialism, and the Generation of Life." *Journal of the History of Ideas* 46 (1985): 65–87.

Rudwick, Martin. "The Shape and Meaning of Earth History." In *God and Nature: Historical Essays on the Encounter Between Christianity and Science,* ed. by D. C. Lindberg and R. L. Numbers. Berkeley: University of California Press, 1986, 296–321.

Spink, J. S. *French Free Thought from Gassendi to Voltaire.* London: Athlone, 1960.

Thrower, James. *The Alternative Tradition: Religion and the Rejection of Religion in the Ancient World.* The Hague and New York: Mouton, 1980.

Turner, Frank M. "The Victorian Conflict Between Science and Religion: A Professional Dimension." In *Contesting Cultural Authority: Essays in Victorian Intellectual Life,* ed. by Frank M. Turner. Cambridge: Cambridge University Press, 1993, 171–200.

Turner, James. *Without God, Without Creed: The Origins of Unbelief in America.* Baltimore: Johns Hopkins University Press, 1985.

Wootton, David. *Paolo Sarpi: Between Renaissance and Enlightenment.* Cambridge: Cambridge University Press, 1983.

———. "Lucien Febvre and the Problem of Unbelief in the Early Modern Period." *Journal of Modern History* 60 (1988): 695–730.

36. POSITIVISM

Charles D. Cashdollar

Positivism is a movement in philosophy that grew out of the theories of Auguste Comte (1798–1857), especially the limitation of knowledge to an empirical study of phenomena and their relationships and the commitment to an altruistic ethics and a "Religion of Humanity." Comte's theories had an important influence on Christian thought during the second half of the nineteenth century. Very few religious leaders became devoted believers in positivism, and many rejected it outright. But between those extremes there was a large number of thinkers who adjusted their theology in response to positivism. A few radicals abandoned tradition for humanistic theism, but most remained within the churches, where they made modest to significant changes. Positivism affected mainstream religion in two primary ways: Its epistemological challenge forced theologians to reconsider how and what humans could know of God, and its ethical challenge pushed them toward a stronger commitment to social reform in what became the social gospel.

Comtean Positivism

Auguste Comte was born in Montpellier, France, where he was raised in a Roman Catholic home. After studying at the École Polytechnique in Paris, he spent several years as a secretary to the utopian socialist Henri de Saint-Simon (1760–1825). He held minor academic positions from 1832 to 1844, but for most of his life he existed on income from private pupils and the generosity of his supporters.

Comte articulated his philosophical system in the six-volume *System of Positive Philosophy* (1830–42) and the four-volume *System of Positive Polity* (1851–54). Comte was convinced that nineteenth-century society had lost the ability to act decisively and that it was over-whelmed by, rather than in control of, social problems. He considered this impasse fundamentally intellectual and spiritual: The old ways of viewing the world were no longer relevant, and, until a new foundation for analysis and decision making was instituted, there could be no progress. Comte's prescription was positivism—an interpretation of history, a theory of knowledge, a classification of the sciences, the creation of a new science called sociology, and the establishment of a new ethics and a new religion based on service to humanity.

Comte argued that human history had progressed through three stages, which he termed the theological, the metaphysical, and the positive. In the first stage, humans attributed events to gods and, eventually, to a single God. In the second, they explained events by metaphysical abstractions, such as nature. These two stages shared an appeal to supernatural causation—in one case, personal and theological; in the other, impersonal and metaphysical. In the third, or positive, stage, humans relied on the empirical methods of science.

Comte's argument for the positive stage was based upon his system's epistemology, or theory of knowledge. He contended that humans were capable of knowing only natural phenomena and their relationships; the human mind had no ability to reach beyond phenomena into the realm of the theological or the metaphysical. Yet, for most of human history, people had tried to explain occurrences by relating them not to each other but to someone or something beyond; they made a similar mistake when they sought a supernatural basis for their ethical and religious obligations. But at last humanity had reached the positive stage, abandoned these barren searches, and achieved progress through science.

Despite Comte's sharp criticism of the two prepositivist stages, he was envious of the cultural coherence that the final monotheistic phase of the theological era had been able to create. He particularly admired medieval Catholicism's unification of Western culture. In contrast, the Protestant Reformation was a destructive, centrifugal force, and the intellectual disintegration that it started had only been made worse by the ensuing negations of the Enlightenment metaphysicians. Cultural cohesion mattered a great deal to Comte, and he expected the emerging positive stage to usher in a new age of unity.

Comte recognized that different aspects of human life had achieved the ultimate positive stage earlier than others, and, based on this recognition, he laid out a classification of the sciences. Mathematics had been the first to abandon theological and metaphysical speculation; it was followed, in turn, by astronomy, physics, chemistry, and biology. Now in the nineteenth century, Comte thought that humanity was ready to extend this progress by applying scientific rigor to social phenomena, too. Therefore, he proposed and named a new science of society, "sociology." Henceforth, social questions such as the causes of poverty or crime would be examined on a scientific, rather than on a theological or philosophical, basis.

Comte's examination of social relationships impressed upon him the interconnectedness of human life—"the solidarity of the human race," as he called it. This insight became the basis for his ethical and religious recommendations. Since theology and metaphysics had already been ruled out, Collective Humanity became, in effect, Comte's absolute, or deity. It was to Collective Humanity that humans owed their ultimate ethical obligation, and Comte invented the word "altruism" to express his ethical ideal of totally selfless service to other people. He claimed that his new ethics stood in sharp contrast to Christianity, which was characterized by its selfish pursuit of personal salvation in a future life and its abandonment of ethical responsibility in this pursuit.

During his last years, Comte, to the consternation of his more strictly scientific admirers, designed an elaborate "Religion of Humanity," complete with priests, sacraments, and saints, to organize his followers' worship of Collective Humanity. The new religion attracted a number of followers who met regularly for worship and prayer and dedicated their lives to altruism. Many more, however, were scathing in their rejection of Comte's Religion of Humanity. The criticisms were not confined to the religiously faithful. The skeptic Thomas Henry Huxley (1825–95) quipped that it was nothing but "Catholicism minus Christianity." Some, such as Émile Littré (1801–81) and John Stuart Mill (1806–73), who had been among the most vocal supporters and popularizers of positivism, lamented what they considered Comte's wrong turn.

In his personal life as well as his philosophy, Comte did not tolerate dissent well, and there were frequent fallings out with disciples; at its most rigid, Comte's system could be dogmatic, even authoritarian. Mill, for one, cared too much about individualism and liberty to accept all of what Comte wrote, and, as their differences became apparent, their exchange of letters stopped. Nevertheless, Mill's volume *Auguste Comte and Positivism* (1865) was important in helping English-speaking intellectuals decide how much of Comte they would accept.

While nineteenth-century participants were divided over whether Comte's ethical and religious writings were consistent with, or a betrayal of, his scientific side, modern biographers of Comte emphasize the continuity. From the beginning, Comte had diagnosed the nineteenth-century's crisis as a spiritual one that could not be resolved by dispassionate science alone. So while he required a science of society, he demanded that it be invigorated with an ethics of service. Sociology and religion were inseparable partners.

The fact that nineteenth-century readers could pick and choose which parts of Comte they would accept created some confusion about the definition of positivism. Comte, of course, hoped that positivism would mean nothing more, and nothing less, than all he advocated; positivism meant Comtism. Such a strict Comtean definition was soon overwhelmed, however, by a second, more expansive, usage. The broader, more generic, definition of positivism was still linked to Comte, but it allowed people to ignore whatever specific details of his system they disliked—such as the ritualistic aspects of the "Religion of Humanity" or the precise order of the classified sciences or the preference for social solidarity over individualism. People often integrated Comte's epistemology into the longer Western empirical tradition that stretched back to David Hume (1711–76). In a few, very loose, applications, positivism was not much more than a convenient label for the whole scientific and empirical tendency of the century. But most writers, when they spoke of positivism, meant something more specific than that, and, for them, two Comtean themes remained central: Positivism was, on the negative side, a rejection of any tenet that could not be empirically grounded; on the positive side, it was a commitment to religion centered on altruistic service to others.

Certain historians, rejecting the broader definition as meaningless, have argued that positivism, if limited to a strict Comtean purity, had little religious influence outside a tiny, if articulate, band of Comtists. Historians willing to accept a broader definition have claimed a greater influence for positivism. Late-twentieth-century historians of religion have followed the second course; by tracing the diffusion of positivism from Comte outward through prominent intermediaries such as Mill, Harriet Martineau (1802–76), and Herbert Spencer (1820–1903), as well as a host of lesser-known essayists and popularizers, they have identified distinct and important influences on religious thought.

Religious Responses

The most easily recognized Comtean influence is upon the orthodox Comtists, those true believers who became active participants in the "Religion of Humanity" and who worshiped according to the strict regimen prescribed in Comte's *Catechism of Positive Religion* (1852). The numbers were not large, but members typically were attracted to the "Religion of Humanity" because of its uncompromising ethical intensity or its promised reconciliation of science and religion. Pierre Laffitte (1823–93) was the head of organized Comtism in France; Richard Congreve (1818–99) and Frederic Harrison (1831–1923) were key leaders in London. Mary Ann Evans (1819–80), the novelist who wrote as George Eliot, frequented Comtist meetings in London and infused her fiction with Comtean ethics. Small associations of worshiping Comtists existed in English provincial cities and in New York City and Philadelphia.

In sharp contrast, the most conservative church leaders repudiated outright positivism in any and all of its forms. These opponents could not see beyond Comte's rejection of revealed religion and, indeed, his dismissal of all possibility of theological knowledge, and they quickly hurled charges of atheism at him. Protestants especially found his ritualistic Religion of Humanity offensive. Such unequivocal rejection had implications, however. Because these uncompromising conservatives had such a visceral disgust for Comtism, they spurned, or were at least slower to accept, other potentially discrete ideas such as Dar-

winism or biblical criticism, which they associated with positivism. Moreover, as positivist-inspired skepticism gained ground in secular circles, the conservatives who felt most insecure sought protection in church authority, papal infallibility, and biblical literalism. Fear that there was no sustainable middle ground between positivistic science and Roman Catholicism spurred Anglicans who were members of the Oxford Movement, such as William George Ward (1812–82), to become Catholics. Similar concerns propelled American journalist Orestes Brownson (1803–76) to convert to the Roman Catholic faith. Threatened Protestants, for whom Church authority held no appeal, turned increasingly toward biblical literalism as a safe harbor in the sea of scientific doubt that they attributed to positivism.

Ironically, these conservative religious leaders shared with the orthodox, worshiping Comtists an admiration for authority and social order and an intolerance of dissent. For a time in France, in the wake of the Dreyfus Affair (1899), Charles Maurras (1868–1952) was able to manage a right-wing alliance, known as Action Française, between orthodox Comtists and conservative Catholics. Papal condemnation in 1926 and the movement's subsequent support of the fascist Vichy Régime in the 1940s ultimately discredited and ended the union.

Positivism had a much greater influence on the left wing of Christianity. The most impatient and radical response was the severing of previous ties to organized Christianity in preference for humanistic theism. This theism took several forms. In America, John Fiske (1842–1901) pursued meaning through philosophy and evolution; in England, Leslie Stephen (1832–1904) proposed a "science of ethics"; and in France, Ernest Renan (1823–92) turned to historical and philological research. Radical Unitarians, such as Octavius Brooks Frothingham (1822–95), author of *The Religion of Humanity* (1873), and Francis E. Abbot (1836–1903), author of *Scientific Theism* (1885), hovered on the boundary between Christianity and theism in the newly organized Free Religious Association.

Most religious thinkers did not reject tradition so completely. Judicious conservatives made only modest adjustments to their theology. These thinkers—academic theologians such as Edinburgh's Robert Flint (1834–1910) and Princeton's James McCosh (1811–94)—were conservative at heart, but they believed that Christians had to change their line of defense and rethink those tenets of faith that had been left vulnerable by the positivist critique.

The most innovative responses to positivism came from theological liberals. Positivism was one important factor in the reconstructions of theology undertaken by three Oxford professors, Benjamin Jowett (1817–93), Andrew Martin Fairbairn (1838–1912), and Edward Caird (1835–1908), the author of *The Social Philosophy and Religion of Comte* (1885). Cambridge professors Brooke Foss Westcott (1825–1901) and Frederick Denison Maurice (1805–72) were pushed along the road toward Christian socialism. Among the many other liberals who wrestled with, and borrowed from, positivism were Scotland's John Tulloch (1823–86) and America's John Bascom (1827–1911) and Bordon Bowne (1847–1910). Catholic modernists, Alfred Loisy (1857–1940) and George Tyrrell (1861–1909) at least shared common tendencies with positivism and, in Tyrrell's case, openly admitted an admiration for aspects of it.

The Larger Influence of Positivism

Although these thinkers—theists, judicious conservatives, and liberals—differed significantly in the magnitude of their theological response, all of them reformulated traditional Christian thinking about the admissibility of evidence, the philosophical basis for religion, the nature of God, the role of Jesus Christ, and ethics and social responsibility.

In the first place, positivism instilled doubts in the minds of theologians about the validity of the dogmatic, biblical, and metaphysical evidence that traditionally had been used to validate religious belief. Even theologians who did not personally question old methods knew that such arguments could no longer convince skeptics. As a result, they began to emphasize factual, phenomenal evidence that was more in keeping with the demands of positivism. One source of such data was history, especially the history of the church. Advocates for history as a theological method argued that, even if humans could not approach God in the abstract, they could search successfully for evidence of divine action in history. Ethnography was a second new source of data. Proponents of this approach hoped to strengthen the case for religion by using comparative cultural studies to demonstrate that belief was a universal aspect of human culture. Sensing that the reports of returning missionaries would be

too easily dismissed as partisan pleading, they turned to the work of social scientists, especially anthropologists such as E. B. Tylor (1832–1917) and Friedrich Max Müller (1823–1900), to find support for their case. In addition to history and ethnography, a third form of evidence gained prominence—stories of the practical results of belief in contemporary lives. When theologians sought to buttress the claim that religion promoted morality and personal well-being, they bypassed traditional biblical and dogmatic arguments for examples of real people in real situations.

In the second place, the encounter with positivism caused theologians to shift the philosophical base upon which their religious thought rested. When positivism first thrust its epistemological challenge at religion, British and American Protestants worked from a philosophical position known as Scottish Common Sense realism. Suspicion soon arose, however, that the Scottish thought, which itself placed great trust in factual evidence, conceded too much and could not provide a sustainable alternative to positivism. Consequently, theologians turned increasingly to the less empirically based German systems of Immanuel Kant (1724–1804) or Georg Wilhelm Friedrich Hegel (1770–1831).

Third, theologians reconsidered their understanding of God. Comte had asserted that "God" was created by humans in a human image to explain those things that science could not yet explain, and perceptive theologians recognized that the pervasive use of anthropomorphic language to describe God left them vulnerable to Comte's attack. Few followed Fiske's radical "deanthropomorphization" and redefinition of God as the "Unknowable," but many grew more cautious about their language and tried to eliminate what they regarded as the most extreme and offensive forms of anthropomorphism.

At the same time, theologians had to answer Comte's charge that knowledge of God was beyond the capability of the human mind. A stronger emphasis on divine immanence was one way to counter the epistemological limits that positivism set; humans might not be able to know the totality of God, but they could know something of a God who was immanent and present among them. A strong Christocentric focus followed: If positivists wanted to find God in humanity, then Christians could point to Jesus.

Finally, positivism helped promote the social gospel, the movement that called for the church to become more involved in social reform. Comte had claimed that his altruism was preferable to Christianity's selfish other-worldliness. Most religious leaders disagreed with his characterization and argued that concern for humanity was not only central to Christianity, but had, indeed, been started by Jesus. However, they knew that if they were going to make their counterargument stick, they had to demonstrate it by their actions as well as by their words. Some writers, like Westcott, said that Comte had forced Christianity to reclaim its heritage of social service. For Christian socialists in particular, but for some others also, Comte's vision of the solidarity of the human race was a more compelling metaphor than the survival of the fittest.

Positivism played a significant and special role in Latin American thought. During the nineteenth century, Comte's ideas, together with those of English positivists such as Spencer, replaced Catholic scholasticism as the primary postcolonial ideology. Positivism was appealing because it promised both an end to the colonial (theological) spirit and the basis for a new national (positivist, scientific) order. Although Comte's "Religion of Humanity" found virtually no support in Hispanic America, it did gain popularity in Brazil. Positivism has remained particularly influential in twentieth-century Latin American education, political theory, and ethics.

In contrast, by the end of the nineteenth century, positivism as a distinguishable system of thought had largely ceased to command the attention of important thinkers in North America and Europe. In religious thought, this was because theological liberals, or modernists, had settled or answered Comte's challenges to their satisfaction and had made their peace with modern science. Those on the other side—high-church traditionalists and fundamentalists—had made their decisions, too, and increasingly closed themselves off from modern scientific thought.

Logical Positivism

After World War I, a new form of positivism challenged religious thinkers. Logical positivism, or logical empiricism, emerged during the 1920s, most notably in the work of the Vienna Circle, which was led by Moritz Schlick (1882–1936) and articulated most fully by Rudolf Carnap (1891–1970). A second group in Berlin was led by Hans Reichenbach (1891–1953), and A. J.

Ayer (1910–89) became the preeminent advocate in the English-speaking world. As logical positivism's popularity spread, Bertrand Russell (1872–1970) and Ludwig Wittgenstein (1889–1951) were often identified with the movement, but, while it is true that their ideas overlapped and that Wittgenstein's *Tractatus Logico-Philosophicus* (1921) influenced the Vienna Circle, there were important differences as well.

Logical positivism's most distinguishing characteristic was its claim to have eliminated metaphysics. Whereas Comte and earlier empiricists had argued that metaphysical certainty was beyond human capability and its pursuit futile, logical positivists now insisted that, with a proper application of logical method, metaphysics turned out to be meaningless. It was not merely that metaphysical questions were too difficult; they were linguistic nonsense. The tool by which the logical positivists carried out this excision of metaphysical language was the verification principle: A statement had descriptive validity only if it could be verified, or falsified, by factual evidence. Wittgenstein, less radical, allowed the existence of metaphysical mystery but deemed it unutterable, inexpressible in language. Either way, theology and religious language were called into question.

The impact of logical positivism differed in two ways from that of nineteenth-century positivism. First, Comte's strong commitment to altruism was gone. Logical positivists considered ethical principles no more than expressions of emotion. To say that "theft is wrong" expressed an abhorrence of stealing but nothing more. Thus, although some empiricists like R. B. Braithwaite sought to maintain a legitimate sphere for religion as an affirmation of ethical intent, the religious community received no great ethical stimulus from logical positivism as it had from Comtean positivism.

Second and more important, logical positivism focused attention on the nature and function of religious language. Some thinkers used the tools of linguistic analysis to sharpen or purify religious language, and calls went forth for the demythologizing of religion and for a moratorium on "God-talk" while attention turned to religious practice. A second group sought in various ways to reestablish the independent legitimacy of religious language. There were efforts to locate verifiable religious experience within the natural realm and to establish credence for private, personal forms of verification. More typical, theologians argued for linguistic pluralism:

Language took many forms, and religious language was simply different and had its own set of rules, but it was not less legitimate than the cognitive or descriptive language examined by logical positivism. Paul Tillich (1886–1965), for example, explored the symbolic, or analogical, character of religious language. By the 1960s and 1970s, as logical positivism's popularity waned, theologians began to extend their linguistic interests in other, postpositivist, directions.

See also Materialism; Secular Humanism

BIBLIOGRAPHY

Annan, Noel. *The Curious Strength of Positivism in English Political Thought.* Oxford: Oxford University Press, 1959.

Ayer, A. J., ed. *Logical Positivism.* New York: Free Press, 1959.

Cashdollar, Charles D. *The Transformation of Theology, 1830–1890: Positivism and Protestant Thought in Britain and America.* Princeton, N.J.: Princeton University Press, 1989.

Charlton, Donald Geoffrey. *Positivist Thought in France During the Second Empire, 1852–1870.* Oxford: Clarendon, 1959.

Grant, Colin. "The Theological Significance of Hartshorne's Response to Positivism." *Religious Studies* 21 (1985): 573–88.

Harp, Gillis. *The Positivist Republic: Auguste Comte and the Reconstruction of American Liberalism, 1865–1920.* University Park: Pennsylvania State University Press, 1994.

Hughes, H. Stuart. *Consciousness and Society: The Reorientation of European Social Thought, 1890–1930.* New York: Knopf, 1958.

Kent, Christopher. *Brains and Numbers: Elitism, Comtism, and Democracy in Mid-Victorian Britain.* Toronto: University of Toronto Press, 1978.

Klein, Kenneth H. *Positivism and Christianity: A Study of Theism and Verifiability.* The Hague: Nijhoff, 1974.

Lenzer, Gertrude, ed. *Auguste Comte and Positivism: The Essential Writings.* New York: Harper, 1975.

Lints, Richard. "The Postpositivist Choice: Tracy or Lindbeck?" *Journal of the American Academy of Religion* 61 (1993): 655–77.

Manuel, Frank. *The Prophets of Paris.* Cambridge, Mass.: Harvard University Press, 1962.

Pickering, Mary. *Auguste Comte: An Intellectual Biography.* Vol. 1. Cambridge: Cambridge University Press, 1993.

Reardon, Bernard. *Religion in the Age of Romanticism.* Cambridge: Cambridge University Press, 1985.

Santoni, Ronald E., ed. *Religious Language and the Problem of Religious Knowledge.* Bloomington: Indiana University Press, 1968.

Simon, W. M. *European Positivism in the Nineteenth Century: An Essay in Intellectual History.* Ithaca, N.Y.: Cornell University Press, 1963.

Standley, Arline Reilein. *Auguste Comte.* Boston: Twayne, 1981.

Sutton, Michael. *Nationalism, Positivism, and Catholicism: The Politics of Charles Maurras and French Catholics, 1890–1914.* Cambridge: Cambridge University Press, 1983.

Vogeler, Martha. *Frederic Harrison: The Vocations of a Positivist.* Oxford: Clarendon, 1984.

Wright, T. R. *The Religion of Humanity: The Impact of Comtean Positivism on Victorian Britain.* Cambridge: Cambridge University Press, 1986.

Zea, Leopoldo. *The Latin American Mind.* Trans. by James H. Abbott and Lowell Dunham. Norman: University of Oklahoma Press, 1963.

———. *Positivism in Mexico.* Trans. by Josephine H. Schulte. Austin: University of Texas Press, 1974.

37. PRAGMATISM

Deborah J. Coon

Pragmatism is widely regarded as America's leading contribution to Western philosophy. Far from being a unified theory, pragmatism stood for a number of loosely connected theories of meaning, knowledge, and conduct formulated by its proponents. Some generalities can be made, however. Pragmatists held that the meaning/truth of ideas and concepts was not absolute but was determined by how they were used in practice, by the functions they served, and by the results they achieved. This differed from the tradition of Cartesian rationalism, for example, which held that certain truths are eternal and are known to be self-evident through reason alone. Pragmatists, instead, extended the empirical methods of scientific inquiry to philosophy, arguing that humans ascribed truth and meaning to concepts and beliefs by testing them out in practice and noting their results. Leading American pragmatists were William James (1842–1910), Charles Sanders Peirce (1839–1914), John Dewey (1859–1952), George Herbert Mead (1862–1931), and Clarence Irving Lewis (1883–1964). While pragmatism was an American-based philosophy, it was influential in Europe as well; among the most notable to ally themselves with the movement were philosophers such as F. C. S. Schiller (1864–1937) in England and a school of young philosophers in Italy headed by Giovanni Papini (1881–1956).

All of the early pragmatists were, to a greater or lesser extent, concerned with mediating between the realms of science and human values. For Dewey and James, this concern was predominant. Dewey wrote in *The Quest for Certainty*: "The problem of restoring integration and co-operation between man's beliefs about the world in which he lives and his beliefs about values and purposes that should direct his conduct is the deepest problem of modern life. It is the problem of any philosophy that is not isolated from that life" (Dewey 1929, 255).

Background

It is generally agreed that the origins of pragmatism lay in the meetings in the early 1870s of a group of young intellectuals in Cambridge, Massachusetts, who called themselves the Metaphysical Club. Among the club's members were James, Peirce, Oliver Wendell Holmes Jr. (1841–1935), Chauncey Wright (1830–75), John Fiske (1842–1901), and Nicholas St. John Green (1830–76). They met to read and discuss each other's work, as well as to discuss the new scientific ideas that were percolating throughout the intellectual world, including thermodynamics, the kinetic theory of gases, and, perhaps most important, Darwinian evolutionary theory. Fascinated by issues of growth, change, continuity, chance, and probability, they explored how these new scientific principles might be applied outside the biological and physical world to philosophical, psychological, social, and historical questions.

The first published works to expound pragmatist views, although they did not use the term, were Peirce's two essays "The Fixation of Belief" and "How to Make Our Ideas Clear," published in *Popular Science Monthly* (1877 and 1878, respectively), and James's essay "Spencer's Definition of Mind as Correspondence," published in the *Journal of Speculative Philosophy* (1878). The term "pragmatism" was first publicly used by James in a lecture delivered in 1898 at the University of California, "Philosophical Conceptions and Practical Results." However, it was not until James's Lowell Lectures of 1906 were published as *Pragmatism* in 1907 that pragmatism became a widespread intellectual movement.

Views on Science and Religion

Darwinian evolutionary theory was seen by many in the late nineteenth century as having rendered religion irrelevant at best. If the development of species was due to natural forces working over time, then there was no need for a Creator. Religious belief was outmoded and possibly even dangerous if it stood in the way of scientific progress. While Charles Darwin (1809–82) was reluctant to draw these conclusions himself, some of his most vocal followers, such as T. H. Huxley (1825–95) and William K. Clifford (1845–79), were not.

Peirce and Dewey both addressed, at least briefly, the issue of the relationship between science and religion and argued against their contemporaries' view that science had dealt the deathblow to religion. Peirce, for example, argued that religion was essentially different from science because religious belief was fundamentally rooted in human sentiment and instinct, while science was rooted in rational processes. Religion was valuable for the ethical and spiritual life it provided people; it found its full fruition in its social institutions, the churches. Peirce argued for a reconciliation between science and religion based on the separate spheres to which they pertained; science was needed in the pursuit of truth and empirical fact, while religion was necessary in fulfilling the human spirit.

Dewey agreed with Peirce that religion seemed to be a fundamental part of human sensibility. He thought that religious belief was particularly valuable in contributing to our sense that there is a whole existing beyond us as individuals. This sense of a transcendent wholeness was the reason that humans crave community, for community represents that wholeness beyond ourselves that our religious sentiment tells us must exist. Dewey, unlike Peirce, was critical of organized religion as it had evolved historically. In *Human Nature and Conduct* (1922), Dewey argued that institutionalized religion had historically promoted intolerance and division rather than promoted the wholeness that the religious spirit sought. While Dewey and Peirce each had something to say about science and religion, the topic was not a central concern for them as it was for William James. James attempted to heal the rift between science and religion by making religious belief an explicit object of investigation and writing extensively about the value of religious belief. James had suffered a severe depression in the late 1860s and early 1870s, owing at least in part to his concern that

Darwinian theory implied a deterministic universe in which there was no place for belief in free will. Without free will, what was the point of human existence and wherein lay the basis of moral behavior? James eventually answered the question of free will for himself with the statement: "My first act of free will shall be to believe in free will" (quoted in Richards 1987, 418). Related to the question of free will for James was the question of whether it made sense to believe in God in a post-Darwinian era. James answered the antireligious scientists of his day in his 1897 essay "The Will to Believe," arguing that, if belief in God helped one live a better, more fulfilling or rewarding life, then that belief was valid and useful in spite of insufficient scientific evidence for God's existence. James went still further to argue that even the truth of scientific facts was a matter of belief at some level.

In 1902, James published *The Varieties of Religious Experience*. While nominally a psychological study of religious experience and not an explicit statement of pragmatism, it was a distinctly pragmatic analysis of the value of religious experience. James viewed faith as a crucial quality of human life that was useful (the ultimate pragmatic test) to the world because many passionately religious people devoted themselves to social action. They improved the world and set an example for others. Arguing against scientists who maintained that religiosity was a throwback to more primitive forms of human thought, James urged that religion was still vital and useful for many people and was not merely an atavism.

A few years after publishing *The Varieties of Religious Experience,* James published his essays on pragmatism. For him, pragmatism was both a theory of truth and a method for weighing truths and values. James opposed the rationalist notion of truth as something that inheres in ideas. Rather, he argued that truth "*happens* to an idea. It *becomes* true, is *made* true by events" (James 1907, 97). That is, only as we implement ideas or hypotheses in the real world can we tell whether or not they are true. Furthermore, he argued against the notion of absolute truth. Even if we find ideas or beliefs to be true when we try them out on one occasion, their truth is provisional, awaiting further evidence from future use. Under changed circumstances or a different setting, we may no longer find them true or useful.

These connected notions of truth as dynamic and functional were Darwinian in origin. Just as Darwin had overthrown the notion of fixed species in favor of a theory of evolving species, so James abandoned the notion of absolute truth and substituted his pragmatic conception of dynamically changing truths. Similarly, just as for Darwin the "success" of an anatomical characteristic was not something absolute but was contingent on its usefulness in survival under particular environmental circumstances, so the "truth" of an idea was not determined a priori but was a function of its usefulness in helping the organism survive in its natural, social, and intellectual environments.

As mentioned, James also intended pragmatism to be a philosophical method that would help people judge the value of particular actions, concepts, and worldviews. Hence, pragmatism provided a secular basis for ethical decision making. However, James still held that religion was important to many people as a source of values and morals. Indeed, James proposed pragmatism as a mediator between the "tough-minded" world of scientific facts and the "tender-minded" realm of religious and moral values, and he viewed pragmatism as providing the philosophical justification for holding religious beliefs or other ideals that went against the grain of scientific thinking. As in his earlier work, James judged religious ideals to be extremely valuable to those who held them. What James praised in religion was the personal religious impulse. He was critical of institutionalized religions, as was Dewey, for having become dogmatic and rigid in their views. Above all, James's pragmatism promoted pluralism and tolerance of all differences, religious and otherwise.

Neopragmatism

For a few decades following World War II, pragmatism was out of fashion within philosophical circles, while logical positivism and analytic philosophy predominated, but since then a resurgence of interest in pragmatism has occurred. Richard J. Bernstein (1932–), Donald Davidson (1917–), Stanley Fish (1938–), Hilary Putnam (1926–), and Richard Rorty (1931–) are some of the leading proponents of varieties of neopragmatism in contemporary philosophy. In their hands, however, pragmatism has taken a "linguistic turn" (a phrase coined by Rorty in his 1967 book of the same title) that is in keeping with the linguistic emphasis of much twentieth-century philosophy. Emphasizing only particular aspects of earlier forms of pragmatism, the neopragmatists' focus is primarily on language and the contingent status of truth claims and less on the aesthetic and religious dimensions

of experience that were also important concerns for the earlier pragmatists.

See also Evolutionary Ethics; Positivism

BIBLIOGRAPHY

Ayer, A. J. *The Origins of Pragmatism: Studies in the Philosophy of Charles Sanders Peirce and William James.* San Francisco: Freeman, Cooper, 1968.

Brent, Joseph. *Charles Sanders Peirce: A Life.* Bloomington: Indiana University Press, 1993.

Conkin, Paul K. *Puritans and Pragmatists: Eight Eminent American Thinkers.* New York: Dodd, Mead, 1968.

Coon, Deborah J. "'One Moment in the World's Salvation': Anarchism and the Radicalization of William James." *Journal of American History* 83(1) (1996): 70–99.

Cotkin, George. *William James: Public Philosopher.* Baltimore: Johns Hopkins University Press, 1990.

Croce, Paul Jerome. *Science and Religion in the Era of William James: Eclipse of Certainty, 1820–1880.* Chapel Hill and London: University of North Carolina Press, 1995.

Dewey, John. *The Quest for Certainty.* New York: Minton, Balch, 1929.

Diggins, John Patrick. *The Promise of Pragmatism: Modernism and the Crisis of Knowledge and Authority.* Chicago: University of Chicago Press, 1994.

Fisch, Max H. *Peirce, Semeiotic, and Pragmatism: Essays by Max H. Fisch.* Ed. by Kenneth Laine Ketner and Christian J. W. Kloesel. Bloomington: Indiana University Press, 1986.

Gunn, Giles. *Thinking Across the American Grain: Ideology, Intellect, and the New Pragmatism.* Chicago: University of Chicago Press, 1992.

Hausman, Carl R. *Charles S. Peirce's Evolutionary Philosophy.* New York: Cambridge University Press, 1993.

Hollinger, David A. *In the American Province: Studies in the History and Historiography of Ideas.* Bloomington: Indiana University Press, 1985.

James, William. *Pragmatism: A New Name for Some Old Ways of Thinking.* 1907. Reprint. In *The Works of William James,* ed. by Frederick H. Burkhardt, Fredson Bowers, and Ignas K. Skrupskelis. Cambridge, Mass., and London: Harvard University Press, 1975.

Kloppenberg, James T. *Uncertain Victory: Social Democracy and Progressivism in European and American Thought, 1870–1920.* Oxford and New York: Oxford University Press, 1986.

———. "Pragmatism: An Old Name for Some New Ways of Thinking?" *Journal of American History* 83(1) (1996): 100–38.

Kuklick, Bruce. *The Rise of American Philosophy: Cambridge, Massachusetts, 1860–1930.* New Haven, Conn.: Yale University Press, 1977.

Levinson, Henry S. *The Religious Investigations of William James.* Chapel Hill: University of North Carolina Press, 1981.

Murphy, John P. *Pragmatism: From Peirce to Davidson.* Boulder, Colo.: Westview, 1990.

Myers, Gerald E. *William James, His Life and Thought.* New Haven, Conn.: Yale University Press, 1986.

Ramsey, Bennett. *Submitting to Freedom: The Religious Vision of William James.* New York: Oxford University Press, 1993.

Richards, Robert J. *Darwin and the Emergence of Evolutionary Theories of Mind and Behavior.* Chicago and London: University of Chicago Press, 1987.

Scheffler, Israel. *Four Pragmatists: A Critical Introduction to Peirce, James, Mead, and Dewey.* New York: Humanities Press, 1974.

Smith, John Edwin. *Purpose and Thought: The Meaning of Pragmatism.* New Haven, Conn.: Yale University Press, 1978.

West, Cornel. *The American Evasion of Philosophy: A Genealogy of Pragmatism.* Madison: University of Wisconsin Press, 1989.

Westbrook, Robert B. *John Dewey and American Democracy.* Ithaca, N.Y.: Cornell University Press, 1991.

Wiener, Philip P. *Evolution and the Founders of Pragmatism.* Philadelphia: University of Pennsylvania Press, 1972.

38. EVOLUTIONARY ETHICS

Paul Farber

Evolutionary ethics attempts to use theories of biological evolution as a foundation for establishing normative standards of human behavior. The approach was especially popular in the Anglo-American intellectual community during three distinct periods: the Darwin-Spencer period; the post–World War I period; and the sociobiology period.

The Development of Evolutionary Ethics

Intellectuals in the Anglo-American community experienced a "crisis of consciousness" during the second half of the nineteenth century. Industrialization, German biblical criticism, and the growth of science all contributed to an increased secularism that, for many, eroded confidence in traditional religious beliefs. The search for an alternative to religion as a foundation for ethics led some to consider science as a possibility.

Charles Darwin (1809–82) attempted a naturalistic explanation for the origins of ethics. According to his view, ethics arose as an adaptation of human societies: Those groups whose members valued such traits as honesty were more cohesive and better fit to survive. Darwin did not attempt to derive specific moral values, but he believed that they could be explained by their social utility. Of greater importance to the first period of evolutionary ethics was Herbert Spencer (1820–1903), who, like Darwin, believed that ethics had arisen in the course of human evolution. Unlike Darwin, however, he believed that he could use evolution to justify specific moral positions. In his writings, he attempted to show how the middle-class values of his contemporaries had social value and contributed to survival. He further argued that evolution had an overall direction and that

certain qualities, such as altruism, would contribute to the cosmic plan. Darwin and Spencer provided the basis for a number of popularizers who attempted to elaborate a complete system of evolutionary ethics. Leslie Stephen (1832–1904), Benjamin Kidd (1858–1916), and Samuel Alexander (1859–1938) in Britain and John Fiske (1842–1901) and Woods Hutchinson (1862–1930) in the United States were the most famous and widely read.

The interwar period was a fertile time for new ideas. The collapse of the Victorian worldview stimulated many intellectuals to create alternative visions in politics, economics, and moral philosophy. Among the competing perspectives were naturalistic and progressive views of human society that are sometimes called scientific humanism. Particularly active were Julian Huxley (1887–1975) and C. H. Waddington (1905–75), each of whom elaborated a new system of evolutionary ethics that was based on the latest biology and the psychology of the day. Huxley and Waddington claimed that evolution was a general process that was now capable of human direction. Humans had the responsibility to guide evolution toward greater human fulfillment and the realization of higher values.

The synthesis of animal behavior, population biology, genetics, and evolutionary theory, as exemplified by the work of Harvard biologist E. O. Wilson (1929–) in his book *Sociobiology* (1975), provided another invitation to elaborate an evolutionary perspective on ethics. For Wilson and his followers, the understanding gained through sociobiology made possible a new appreciation of the biological significance of morality. According to this view, actions that contribute to the survival of the gene pool are intrinsically good, whereas actions that harm or threaten it are bad. At issue has been how cultural systems have coevolved with biological systems, and anthropologists, ethologists, geneticists, naturalists, and philosophers have for the last two decades of the twentieth century debated the significance of sociobiology for ethics.

Critiques of Evolutionary Ethics

Evolutionary ethics has not been well received by the philosophical community or by the general public. Henry Sidgwick (1838–1900), whose writings dominated British moral philosophy at the end of the nineteenth century, wrote several highly damaging critiques that set out the major objections to evolutionary ethics. He questioned the logic of attempting to derive how one "ought" to act from beliefs in what the natural state of humans (or society) is. Even if human societies had evolved ethical patterns, the ethical systems produced were not justified simply because they had come into existence. According to Sidgwick, the question was not whether any impulse, tendency, desire, or belief that was held by humans was "natural." Rather, the issue was to produce a convincing argument that a particular action was or was not ethically justified. Even showing that certain actions would benefit survival was not adequate unless one first demonstrated that survival was ethically valuable. As for Spencer's belief that we should act in a manner that would contribute to a more perfect state in the future, Sidgwick pointed out that such visions needed to be justified, not merely appealed to.

Sidgwick was not alone in criticizing evolutionary ethics. Other philosophers of the period, such as Thomas Hill Green (1836–82) at Oxford, were equally critical. Even leading philosophers who stressed the importance of an evolutionary perspective, such as William James (1842–1910) and John Dewey (1859–1952) in the United States, did not support evolutionary ethics. G. E. Moore (1873–1958) of Cambridge, whose writings on ethics were central to the Anglo-American tradition, repeated Sidgwick's critique and added a broader criticism of all naturalistic ethical systems in his *Principia Ethica* (1903). He argued that such systems were based on the naturalist fallacy and, therefore, invalid. Few philosophers have ventured onto the path of evolutionary ethics since then. More recently, philosophers such as Mary Midgley (1919–) have renewed the

criticism of evolutionary ethics in their critiques of theories inspired by sociobiology. She argues that reducing ethics to an understanding of contributions to the gene pool is an inadequate approach to the subject.

Current Status

Given the dismal history of evolutionary ethics, it is not surprising that, at the end of the twentieth century, this position was not widely held among philosophers. Although a few philosophers have argued for an evolutionary philosophy that includes evolutionary ethics, for the most part that position is ignored. Philosophers are not agreed regarding what constitute a proper foundation for ethics or whether a foundation is even possible. This ambivalence has encouraged intellectuals in other fields to explore the possibility of an evolutionary ethics. Scientists like E. O. Wilson continue to emphasize the value of a Darwinian perspective on life, and their writings are popularized by those who seek a unified but naturalistic worldview.

See also Evolution; Scientific Naturalism

BIBLIOGRAPHY

Farber, Paul Lawrence. *The Temptations of Evolutionary Ethics.* Berkeley: University of California Press, 1994.

Flew, Anthony. *Evolutionary Ethics.* London: Macmillan, 1967.

Huxley, Julian. *Evolutionary Ethics.* Oxford: Oxford University Press, 1943.

Midgley, Mary. *Evolution as a Religion: Strange Hopes and Stranger Fears.* London: Methuen, 1985.

Murphy, Jeffrie. *Evolution, Morality, and the Meaning of Life.* Totowa, N.J.: Rowman and Littlefield, 1982.

Quillian, William, Jr. *The Moral Theory of Evolutionary Naturalism.* New Haven, Conn.: Yale University Press, 1945.

Richards, Robert. *Darwin and the Emergence of Evolutionary Theories of Mind and Behavior.* Chicago: University of Chicago Press, 1987.

Ruse, Michael. *Taking Darwin Seriously: A Naturalistic Approach to Philosophy.* Oxford: Blackwell, 1986.

Schilcher, Florian von, and Neil Tennant. *Philosophy, Evolution, and Human Nature.* London: Routledge and Kegan Paul, 1984.

Williams, Cora. *A Review of the Systems of Ethics Founded on the Theory of Evolution.* London: Macmillan, 1893.

Wilson, Edward O. *On Human Nature.* Cambridge, Mass.: Harvard University Press, 1978.

39. SCIENTIFIC NATURALISM

Edward B. Davis and Robin Collins

Scientific naturalism is the conjunction of naturalism—the claim that nature is all that there is and, hence, that there is no supernatural order above nature—with the claim that all objects, processes, truths, and facts about nature fall within the scope of the scientific method. This ontological naturalism implies weaker forms of naturalism, such as the belief that humans are wholly a part of nature (anthropological naturalism); the belief that nothing can be known of any entities other than nature (epistemological naturalism); and the belief that science should explain phenomena only in terms of entities and properties that fall within the category of the natural, such as by natural laws acting either through known causes or by chance (methodological naturalism). Before the late nineteenth century, scientific naturalism was not the dominant way of understanding the world, nor is it in the late twentieth century the only metaphysical position consistent with modern science. Technically, scientific naturalism is not the same thing as philosophical materialism, which is the belief that everything is ultimately material, but it is closely related, and today they are usually conflated. Traditional theists do not accept scientific naturalism, although they may agree with anthropological naturalism and/or methodological naturalism.

Naturalism Before 1900

The first naturalists in the Western tradition were certain pre-Socratic philosophers who sought to explain all things as natural events rather than as the result of divine action. For example, Thales of Miletus (fl. c. 585 B.C.) attributed earthquakes to tremors in the water on which the disk of the earth floated. This was a naturalistic rendering of the older Greek view that the god of the sea, Poseidon, was responsible for causing them. Similarly,

the author of the Hippocratic treatise *On the Sacred Disease* (which deals with epilepsy), written about 400 B.C., opens the work by rebuking those who attribute the cause of the disease to the gods. In his opinion, they are simply hiding their own ignorance of the real cause, like "quacks and charlatans." The atomist Empedocles (c. 492–432 B.C.) assigned the origin of all living things to a crude forerunner of evolution by survival of the fittest, an idea later developed by the Roman Epicurean poet Lucretius (c. 99–55 B.C.). The parts of animals would form by chance and then come together; only those combinations of parts that fit the right pattern were viable. Two other atomists of the fifth century B.C., Leucippus and Democritus, viewed the world as an infinite number of uncreated atoms moving eternally in an infinite, uncreated void, colliding by chance to form larger bodies. Epicurus (341–270 B.C.) extended this description to the gods themselves, holding that they were composed of atoms and situated in the spaces between the infinite number of universes that coexisted at any one time. In this way, atomists sought to combat superstition and bondage to irrational fears of capricious gods who needed to be appeased.

Although Plato (c. 427–347 B.C.) shared the atomists' opposition to Greek polytheism, he rejected their purely natural and nonteleological mode of explanation. In the dialogue *Timaeus,* Plato accounted for the origin of order in the world by means of a godlike figure, the Demiurge, who imposed form on undifferentiated matter. Plato asserted the impossibility of attaining real "knowledge" of the material world, about which one could have only "opinions." A true science of nature was possible only insofar as the human mind could grasp the essences of the eternal Forms or Ideas of things, especially the axioms of logic and mathematics. This was the basis of an important kind of idealism (not naturalism), according to which the rational soul has been "imprisoned" in the flesh, and true freedom is found in contemplation of the Forms.

Like his teacher Plato, Aristotle (384–322 B.C.) rejected the atomists' assumption that the world was a mindless chaos rather than an intelligently ordered cosmos. Unlike Plato, however, he made the Forms and the teleology deriving from them immanent within nature rather than the result of an external intelligence. In doing this, Aristotle naturalized Plato's account of knowledge by emphasizing that knowledge of the Forms arises out of studying matter itself. For Aristotle, scientific explanations required the identification of four causes to be complete. They included not only the secondary (or efficient) and material causes (corresponding to the mechanistic explanations of the atomists), but also the formal and final causes, containing the immediate plan and ultimate purpose of the thing or event. As Aristotle understood them, all four causes were entirely natural, but the final and formal causes would later be associated with the divine design for the creation, especially the organic creation. Aristotle also distinguished three levels of soul (vegetative, animal, and rational), understanding them, too, in natural terms, as principles of vitality and organization.

During the first millennium of Christianity, thinkers in the Latin West had limited access to Greek scientific literature, especially the works of Aristotle. In the absence of a sophisticated form of naturalism, Plato's idealism provided the philosophical framework for most Christian thought. The most influential early Christian author was undoubtedly Augustine (354–430), who followed Plato in granting little importance to the study of the material world. Throughout this early period, Christian thinkers typically thought of science as a "handmaiden" to theology, which was the "queen of the sciences": science might serve theology by assisting in understanding biblical references to nature, but it ought never challenge the sole authority of theology to define reality.

That situation changed dramatically with the recovery of a large body of Greek scientific and medical works previously unavailable in the Latin West, a process that began in the eleventh century and culminated in the twelfth and thirteenth centuries with the appearance in Europe of universities dominated by Aristotelian natural philosophy. Thomas Aquinas (c. 1225–74), a Dominican who taught theology at Paris, undertook an ambitious project to integrate Aristotle with Christian theology. Thomas was careful to limit the scope of reason and to reject those Aristotelian tenets that seemed most threatening to the faith, especially the claim that the world is eternal. He also modified Aristotle's view that the order in nature is rationally necessary, claiming that God is free to establish any particular order in the world, although, once established, it would apply necessarily except for miracles and the free actions of humans. A fundamental problem for Thomas and other monotheistic scholars, such as the Jewish physician and philosopher Rambam (also called Moses Maimonides [1135–1204]), is still central to theology: how to relate God to nature in a manner that acknowledges his sovereignty and ongoing involvement in the world, while affirming the integrity of the world as a creation with a measure of independence. Ultimately, Thomas succeeded in creating a synthesis that would become the most widely accepted form of Christian philosophy until modern times, but his efforts were controversial at the time. Indeed, many ideas of Aristotle and certain Arabic commentators were formally banned from being taught at Paris, the last and largest ban coming in 1277, when 219 specific propositions were condemned as contrary to the faith. The thrust of this condemnation was boldly to assert God's absolute power to do things contrary to the tenets of Aristotelian naturalism.

Although the condemnation did not give birth to modern science—a claim that has sometimes been advanced—it did contribute to the appearance of a vigorous new supernaturalism in the form of medieval nominalism. According to its outstanding exponent, William of Ockham (c. 1280–c. 1349), God's absolute power can do anything short of a logical contradiction, so the laws of nature are not necessary truths. The order of nature is, therefore, contingent, with observed regularities reflecting God's faithfulness in upholding the creation as expressed through his ordinary power rather than through any rational necessity arising from the nature of things.

This belief in the ongoing supernatural activity of the Creator became even stronger in the sixteenth century with the spread of the doctrines of the Protestant Reformation about God's absolute sovereignty, which encouraged many early-modern natural philosophers to downplay the independence of nature from God and to advocate an unambiguously empirical approach to scientific knowledge. As tools of the divine will, matter and its properties had to be understood from the phenomena, not from metaphysical first principles, giving empiricism a clear theological foundation. For example, Robert

Boyle (1627–91), the most influential publicist of mechanistic science, held that the laws by which God governed matter were freely chosen, ruling out the possibility of an a priori science of nature.

Boyle's critique of the very ideas of nature and natural law in *A Free Enquiry into the Vulgarly Receiv'd Notion of Nature* (1686) underscores the general historical truth that the concept of natural law is metaphysically ambivalent: Either God or nature can be seen as the ultimate agent behind the laws we observe in operation. Thus, for supernaturalists like Boyle, Isaac Newton (1642–1727), and Marin Mersenne (1588–1648), miracles were defined as extraordinary acts of God outside the ordinary course of nature, but the ordinary course of nature itself was understood to be nothing other than the ordinary acts of God. Newton's belief that God occasionally adjusts the motions of the planets is often misunderstood as involving a "God of the gaps," in which God is conceived to be a "clockmaker" active only in extraordinary events that are inexplicable by natural law. Rather, Newton believed that all natural events were divinely caused, and he never endorsed the clock metaphor with which he is wrongly associated. If supernaturalists emphasized the miraculous character of the ordinary, Thomas Hobbes (1588–1679) took the opposite track, making God a material being and endowing matter with activity and thought. In another materialistic step, physicians such as William Harvey (1578–1657) and Francis Glisson (1597–1677) endowed matter with sensation and treated diseases as wholly natural disorders, in keeping with the tradition of a profession that was often thought by contemporary commentators to exude the faint odor of atheism.

Toward the end of the seventeenth century, the plausibility of miracles came under increasing attack. At the same time, critical approaches to Scripture began to take hold. In the next century, both of these currents tore into the biblical testimony concerning miracles. "Rational" religion, ultimately rooted in the crisis of religious authority that resulted from the Reformation, appealed widely to intellectuals of the eighteenth century.

By 1800, appeals to direct divine agency were increasingly rare in science, even in natural history. As the nineteenth century progressed, natural historians tended increasingly to admire and to imitate the lawlikeness of physics and to divorce their discipline from theology by finding ways to explain nature without miracles. An obvious example is the enormous influence of the

nebular hypothesis of Pierre Simon Laplace (1749–1827), a naturalistic account of the origin of the solar system. This was consistent with a general trend among theologically inclined scientists, such as William Whewell (1794–1866) and Charles Babbage (1792–1871), to locate evidence of divine governance more in the regularity of nature (God as lawgiver) than in exceptions to it. Several attempts to give a naturalistic account of all living creatures culminated in Charles Darwin's (1809–82) *Origin of Species* (1859) and *The Descent of Man and Selection in Relation to Sex* (1871), the tenets of which are still regarded as essentially correct by most scientists today.

Twentieth-Century Naturalism

Darwin's theory spawned the widespread use of the concept of evolution to justify various social, political, and religious agendas, claiming for them a scientific basis. But, more important, it played a pivotal role in scientific naturalism's becoming the dominant worldview of the academy by the middle of the twentieth century. Indeed, in every discipline today, except in some schools of theology, a strict methodological naturalism is observed, and typically an ontological naturalism is presupposed by most of the practitioners of these disciplines. For example, a largely unspoken rule in both the sciences and the humanities is that, insofar as one attempts to explain human behavior or beliefs, they must be explained by natural causes, not by appealing to such things as an immaterial soul or a transcendent ethical or supernatural order, as previous thinkers had done.

Although Darwinism largely set the stage for the dominance of scientific naturalism, it was not until the twentieth century that serious attempts were made to work out and defend it as a comprehensive philosophy, especially with regard to ethics and our understanding of the human mind, two areas that have presented particularly difficult problems for naturalism. Two major approaches have been used by naturalists in response to these difficulties: reductionism and eliminativism. (Since the 1980s, however, a third alternative has gained some adherents in the philosophy of mind, in which a naturalism concerning the mind is affirmed, but the metaphysical nature of the mind and its metaphysical relation to the body are claimed to be largely intrinsically incomprehensible by us. We do not discuss this alternative here, however.) *Reductionism* affirms the validity of the area of discourse in question but interprets it as really being about the natural world, even though the discourse might appear to be about some other realm. In ethics, for example, this approach takes the form of attempting to reduce all terms of ethical appraisal—terms such as good, bad, right, and wrong—to statements about social customs or human happiness, or to expressions of emotions or approval, all of which are subject to scientific investigation. So, for instance, under one commonly held version of ethical naturalism, to say something is wrong is merely to say that it is contrary to the customs of one's culture.

In philosophy of mind and related fields, such as cognitive science and artificial intelligence, reductionism takes the form of attempting to reduce everyday statements about the mind—statements such as that John is in pain or that Sally believes that Jim likes her—to statements about natural processes or interrelations between natural processes. For example, behaviorism, one of the first proposals along these lines, argues that statements about beliefs, feelings, and other mental states are ultimately merely statements about our physical behavior. Similarly, functionalism, a successor to behaviorism and the dominant view, claims that statements about human mental states are analogous to statements ascribing human mental characteristics to a computer running a piece of software. To say, for instance, that a computer is figuring out its next move in a chess game is to say something about a complex functional interrelationship between elements of the computer's hardware and the environment. Similarly, functionalists hold that statements about human mental states are really disguised statements about "functional" interrelations both between brain states themselves and between these states and the environment.

Most philosophers agree that reductionism has not succeeded in ethics and the philosophy of mind. This, among other things, has led many naturalists to adopt the second major approach, that of *eliminativism.* To be an eliminativist about a certain domain of discourse is to claim that the primary terms or concepts of the discourse fail to correspond to anything in the world, and, hence, statements using these terms are, strictly speaking, false. For example, ethical eliminativists, such as J. L. Mackie, claim that nothing is really morally right or morally wrong, or good or bad, since there are no properties such as rightness or wrongness existing out in the world. Similarly, eliminativists in neuroscience and philosophy of mind, such as Paul Churchland, claim that most mental items such as beliefs do not really exist, and, hence,

statements referring to these items, such as that John *believes* that Sue loves him, are always false.

Eliminativism is still largely a minority position among naturalists, especially in the philosophy of mind, mostly because it is widely thought either to contradict what is obvious or to be self-refuting. For example, many philosophers, such as Lynn Rudder Baker, argue that the mind/body eliminativist's denial of the existence of beliefs—especially the more radical eliminativist denial that anyone is conscious—not only runs against what is absolutely obvious from experience, but also is self-refuting since, if we do not have beliefs, then the eliminativists themselves cannot really believe in eliminativism.

Even though both reductionism and eliminativism have encountered serious problems, many naturalists reject nonnaturalism as a serious option, largely for the following reasons. First, they cite the success of the physical sciences in support of their position, claiming that, in case after case, science has been able to take events and processes that were once thought mysterious or ascribed to supernatural agencies (such as diseases, earthquakes, and psychological disorders) and has offered well-supported naturalistic explanations of them. Hence, they argue, we have every reason to believe that mysteries such as human consciousness will one day be explained by physical science, even though we cannot at present see how. More implicit, naturalists often assume that the modes of explanation adopted in the physical sciences, with their requirement that explanations be given solely in terms of natural causes, are paradigmatic of what it is to explain or even to understand a phenomenon. Thus, for instance, Colin McGinn, a leading naturalist in the philosophy of mind, states that "naturalism about consciousness is not merely an option; it is a condition of understanding" (McGinn 1991, 47), a view echoed by other leading workers in the field such as Daniel Dennett.

Second, naturalists have associated nonnaturalism with superstition, antiscience, and traditional religious worldviews, all of which, they claim, are ultimately harmful to human progress. Thus, in the words of Bertrand Russell (1872–1970), many adopt materialism (today the most common form of naturalism) not so much from an independent conviction of its truth, but "as a system of dogma set up to combat orthodox dogma" (Russell 1925, xi), particularly religious dogma and superstition. Indeed, according to John Searle, himself a prominent materialist, the "unstated assumption behind the current batch of [materialist] views is that they represent the only scientifically acceptable alternatives to the antiscientism that went with traditional dualism, the belief in the immortality of the soul, spiritualism, and so on" (Searle 1992, 3).

Third, in support of their position, naturalists have pointed to the purportedly intractable problem of relating a hypothesized nonnatural order—whether it be transcendent ethical principles, an immaterial soul, or God—to the natural order. For instance, since the time of René Descartes (1596–1650), naturalists have persistently criticized Cartesian dualism for supposedly being unable to explain how an immaterial mind could causally interact with the material brain.

Finally, naturalists have often blamed traditional Western forms of dualism, along with the attendant claim going back to Plato, that the nonnatural order is superior, for the denigration and neglect of the natural order and, hence, the denigration of the body, the denigration of women (who have been traditionally associated with the body), and the oppression of non-Western cultures (especially cultures that have often been thought of as primitive, that is, close to a state of nature). Similarly, thinkers such as Karl Marx (1818–83), Sigmund Freud (1856–1939), Bertrand Russell, and many modern secular humanists have blamed nonnaturalism, particularly in the form of traditional religious worldviews, for not only oppressing human freedom and creating various psychological and sociological disorders, but also for impeding human progress by diverting our attention to some putative supernatural order instead of helping us scientifically deal with our problems.

More than any other group, those who value religion (whether or not they are believers) have been particularly concerned with scientific naturalism and have offered a variety of responses both to it and to the arguments offered in its favor. One extreme response has been to reinterpret religious beliefs naturalistically. Gordon Kaufman, for example, claims that the word "God" should be interpreted as referring to those cosmic evolutionary forces that gave rise to our existence (Kaufman 1981, 54–6). Another extreme response in the opposite direction has been vigorously to reject any form of naturalism, such as the young-earth creationists have done with regard to human and animal origins. The majority of religious believers in the academy, however, have attempted to accommodate and incorporate as much as possible the generally accepted insights of naturalists, even as they retain what they believe is essential to their religion. Today, for example, most religious believers

working in psychology and psychiatry would first attempt to explain a mental disorder naturalistically, instead of appealing to supernatural causes as in times past, and many religious people accept some type of theistic evolution. Similarly, most biblical scholars, even many of those who are quite theologically conservative, attempt to account for the origin, genre, and meaning of biblical texts largely by appealing to natural causes.

Of course, this adaptation takes different forms, largely depending on what is regarded as essential to a particular religion. For instance, some Christians philosophers (including some who are otherwise quite orthodox) have rejected the idea of an immaterial soul, claiming that it is not essential to Christianity, while on similar grounds many Christian biblical scholars have denied the occurrence of a bodily resurrection. On the other hand, many religious believers think that a fully supernatural understanding of the inspiration of their scriptures is essential to their religion: For instance, some Christians believe in the inerrancy of the Bible, while some Jews and almost all Muslims believe that every individual letter of their scriptures was dictated by God.

Along with the appropriation of the insights of scientific naturalism, religious believers and other nonnaturalists have also offered a systematic critique of scientific naturalism as a comprehensive philosophy. They have both critiqued the arguments offered in favor of it and pointed out its current lack of success in adequately accounting for such things as ethics, rationality, and the human mind, despite decades of effort, something that most naturalists concede. Moreover, nonnaturalists have begun to pursue more positive programs of their own ranging over a wide variety of issues. For example, philosopher Richard Swinburne has argued for a model of explanation based on reasons and actions of a personal agent (Swinburne 1979); physicist John Polkinghorne has attempted to develop models of God's providential control over creation that respect the internal integrity of the created order (Polkinghorne 1989); Nobel Prize–winning physiologist John Eccles (1903–) has attempted to develop a nonphysicalist account of the mind (Eccles and Popper 1981); and a wide range of authors are engaged in exploring the hypothesis of an intelligent designer as the ultimate explanation for the so-called fine-tuning of the basic structure of the universe and/or the evolution of life.

In addition, some theists, such as philosopher Alvin Plantinga and professor of law Phillip Johnson, have challenged the hegemony of methodological naturalism in all areas of the academy (Johnson 1995; Plantinga 1996). Instead, these thinkers have advocated the acceptance of a pluralism of research methodologies, each with its own assumptions. Under their proposal, for example, some groups of biologists would construct theories and research programs under the assumption that life is ultimately a result of divine design, whereas others (perhaps the majority) would continue to operate under methodological naturalism. Other theists, however, such as philosopher of science Ernan McMullin and physicist Howard van Till, accept the general validity of methodological naturalism for scientific inquiry, while they reject its extrapolation into a broader, ontological naturalism.

Finally, a highly diverse, largely popular movement has developed that seeks to find an alternative paradigm to mechanistic naturalism and that proposes ideas that tend to fall outside current mainstream Western forms of thought. Thinkers in this movement typically stress ideas such as holism, vitalism, the primacy of consciousness, and various ideas from Eastern philosophies and religions, which they often attempt to relate to certain interpretations of modern physics. Although this sort of movement is frequently called "New Age," such a label is inadequate, since it tends to leave the false impression that the movement forms some homogeneous whole, when actually it is simply a loosely related set of dissatisfactions with current reductionistic and dualistic worldviews. Moreover, this label implies that these ideas are new, when many of them are actually ancient. Finally, it is often unclear whether the conclusions of a specific thinker in this movement fall outside the confines of scientific naturalism, or whether he or she is merely advocating a new, nonmechanistic form of it. Thinkers who postulate such things as telepathy or advocate the virtues of acupuncture, for instance, typically consider them to be part of the natural, scientifically explicable world, whereas authors who believe in the existence of ghosts, spirit guides, reincarnation, and the like usually think that they fall outside the confines of scientific naturalism.

Although scientific naturalism, particularly in its methodological and mechanistic varieties, dominates in the academy, it is increasingly being challenged both inside and outside academic circles. Whether naturalism in any variety can ultimately meet these challenges is uncertain. But one thing seems clear. As philosopher Thomas Nagel and others have stressed with regard to

human consciousness, scientific naturalism in its current form will need to undergo radical conceptual revision to account for important features of the world and human experience.

See also Atheism; Evolutionary Ethics; Materialism; Mechanical Philosophy; Secular Humanism; Varieties of Providentialism

BIBLIOGRAPHY

Baker, Lynn Rudder. *Saving Belief: A Critique of Physicalism.* Princeton, N.J.: Princeton University Press, 1987.

Brooke, John H. "Natural Law in the Natural Sciences: The Origins of Modern Atheism?" *Science and Christian Belief* 4 (1992): 83–103.

Cannon, Walter F. "The Problem of Miracles in the 1830s." *Victorian Studies* 4 (1960): 5–32.

Churchland, Paul M. *Matter and Consciousness.* Rev. ed. Cambridge, Mass.: MIT Press, 1988.

Davis, Edward B. "Newton's Rejection of the 'Newtonian World View': The Role of Divine Will in Newton's Natural Philosophy." *Science and Christian Belief* 3 (1991): 103–17.

Dear, Peter. "Miracles, Experiments, and the Ordinary Course of Nature." *Isis* 81 (1990): 663–83.

Eccles, John, and Karl R. Popper. *The Self and Its Brain.* New York: Springer International, 1981.

Grant, Edward. "The Condemnation of 1277, God's Absolute Power, and Physical Thought in the Late Middle Ages." *Viator* 10 (1979): 211–44.

Henry, John. "The Matter of Souls: Medical Theory and Theology in Seventeenth-Century England." In *The Medical Revolution of the Seventeenth Century,* ed. by Roger French and Andrew Wear. Cambridge: Cambridge University Press, 1989, 87–113.

Hooykaas, R. "Science and Theology in the Middle Ages." *Free University Quarterly* 3 (1954): 77–163.

Hutchison, Keith. "Supernaturalism and the Mechanical Philosophy." *History of Science* 21 (1983): 297–333.

Johnson, Philip. *Reason in the Balance: The Case Against Naturalism in Science, Law, and Education.* Downers Grove, Ill.: InterVarsity, 1995.

Kaufman, Gordon D. *Constructing the Concept of God.* Philadelphia: Westminister, 1981.

Krikorian, Yervant H. *Naturalism and the Human Spirit.* New York: Columbia University Press, 1987.

Mackie, J. L. *Ethics: Inventing Right and Wrong.* New York: Penguin, 1983.

McGinn, Colin. *The Problem of Consciousness.* Cambridge, Mass.: Blackwell, 1991.

McMullin, Ernan. "Plantinga's Defense of Special Creation." *Christian Scholar's Review* 21 (1991): 55–79.

Nagel, Thomas. "What Is It Like to Be a Bat?" *Philosophical Review* 83 (1974): 435–50.

Numbers, Ronald L. *Creation by Natural Law: Laplace's Nebular Hypothesis in American Thought.* Seattle: University of Washington Press, 1977.

Oakley, Francis. *Omnipotence, Covenant, and Order: An Excursion in the History of Ideas from Abelard to Leibniz.* Ithaca, N.Y.: Cornell University Press, 1984.

Plantinga, Alvin. "Methodological Naturalism?" In *Facets of Faith and Science.* Vol. 1: *Historiography and Modes of Interaction,* ed. by J. van der Meer. Lanham, Md.: University Press of America, 1996, 177–221.

Polkinghorne, John. *Science and Providence: God's Interaction with the World.* London: SPCK, 1989.

Robinson, Howard. *Matter and Sense: A Critique of Contemporary Materialism.* New York: Cambridge University Press, 1982.

Russell, Bertrand. "Introduction: Materialism, Past and Present." In *The History of Materialism,* by Frederick Albert Lange. London: Routledge and Kegan Paul, 1925. Reprint. 1950, 1957.

Searle, John R. *The Rediscovery of the Mind.* Cambridge, Mass: MIT Press, 1992.

Swinburne, Richard. *The Existence of God.* Oxford: Clarendon, 1979.

40. Secular Humanism

Stephen P. Weldon

Secular humanism is a nontheistic belief system based on a faith in rationality, human autonomy, and democracy. Originating properly in the twentieth century, secular humanism finds its roots in earlier anticlerical and anti-Christian movements and is closely akin to a number of radical religious positions espoused during and after the Enlightenment. Its institutional embodiment varies from country to country, but Unitarianism and Ethical Culture have been particularly important in its history. Secular humanism has an ambiguous relationship to religion. On the one hand, it asserts that religion per se is an outmoded, antimodern way of relating human beings to the cosmos, but, on the other hand, its totalistic worldview makes it a functional equivalent of traditional religions.

Broadly, humanism can be categorized as a phenomenon of the modern era that has attracted the attention and interest primarily of intellectuals in the West. When considered solely as an intellectual worldview, it encompasses the general scientific, philosophical, and religious perspectives of modern secular thought. In fact, some commentators have considered it to be the ideology of modernity. Others have equated it with a generalized "religion of democracy" or the American civil religion. This essay treats humanism more narrowly, as a social movement tied to liberal Protestantism and iconoclastic freethought. It should not be confused with Renaissance humanism, literary humanism, or Christian humanism, all of which have some points in common with it but, by and large, stem from entirely different roots and hold quite different assumptions about the nature of human beings and the world. The humanists discussed here rejected theism and supernaturalism and emphasized humankind's responsibility for its own well-being.

Science holds a central place in humanism. Both the cosmological perspective furnished by the discoveries of science and the epistemological foundations provided by the scientific method have shaped humanist thought. One of the characteristics of secular humanism has been the continued insistence that science, by its very nature, invalidates the authority of traditional religion, a view that leads humanists to see science unambiguously allied with nontheism.

The Eighteenth and Nineteenth Centuries

Humanists have traced their history as far back as ancient Greece and the Sophists. "Man is the measure of all things," proclaimed the Sophist Protagoras (c. 485–411 B.C.). But the twentieth-century movement originated in the rationalism of the Enlightenment. In the eighteenth century, several political, ethical, and religious currents coalesced into a bellicose anticlericalism. The resulting ideology emphasized the unity of man and advanced the cause of civil liberty. The ideology of civil liberty, especially liberty of thought, was probably the Enlightenment's main contribution to humanism and freethought. Many Enlightenment intellectuals espoused some form of deism and attacked what they regarded as the hypocrisy and irrationality of Christianity. Thomas Paine (1737–1809) was perhaps the most widely read of these deists as a result of his enormously popular book, *The Age of Reason* (1794–96). Christianity, the deists contended, merely placed shackles on the mind and was not consonant with what they termed "natural religion," a universal religion that could be deduced from the "book of nature" and lacked the provincialism of Christianity. The deists emphatically affirmed the existence of a Creator-God even as they found contemporary religion muddled with ancient superstitions. They sought to discover a religion that conformed to the universal truths of science. This spirit of revolution (the abandonment of Christianity and the rationalistic reformulation of religion) most directly links deism to the humanist tradition. Religion purified of its hypocrisies, the deists contended, could serve the needs of mankind.

August Comte's (1798–1857) Religion of Humanity exemplifies one extreme of religious nontheism. This French philosopher advanced, as part of his progressive view of history, a suggestion for a new religion, one that eliminated all supernaturalism and emphasized science and human achievement. His religion was modeled closely on Roman Catholic ritual and observances, substituting, for example, a pantheon of great scientists for the traditional Catholic saints. Comtianism found enthusiasts among French and British intellectuals who sought to reconstitute the state church (Roman Catholic in France and Anglican in England) along nontheistic lines, but, as a religious movement, it failed to win popular support in the United States, with its predominant anti-Catholic bias.

The distinctiveness of American religious radicalism was its unwavering opposition to creedalism of all forms, a position that united a motley group of non-Christians shortly after the Civil War. This group, the Free Religious Association, was founded and led by a core of radical Unitarians. One of them, Francis Ellingwood Abbot (1836–1903), recognized the diversity in the organization and distinguished two main schools of thought: the intuitional and the scientific. The intuitional school harbored transcendentalists, who found scientific empiricism unconvincing or inadequate. Abbot, in contrast, favored the scientific school and advanced what he called "scientific theism," which he based on the idea that the existence and nature of an immanent God could be discovered through the scientific study of the natural world. It was a teleological position, consonant with the theological doctrines of many Protestant modernists in the early twentieth century. Scientific theism rested on the faith that science could and did justify teleology in some form.

A second group of radical religionists, Ethical Culture, was an offshoot of Reform Judaism, which spread to many major cities in the late nineteenth century, both in America and abroad. The founder, Felix Adler (1851–1933), emphasized social activism over belief—"deed, not creed," he stated. Adler, an agnostic, espoused Kantian idealism and opposed scientific materialism. Ethical Culture groups generally deemphasized science and found more profit in social work and ethical dialogue than in philosophical disputes over a particular worldview.

New developments in science brought about changes in the content of freethought. Enlightenment thought on science had largely stemmed from the fundamental discoveries and proofs of Isaac Newton (1642–1727). Based on the logically rigorous disciplines of mathematics, astronomy, and physics, the model of science that Newton left to posterity was precise, empirical, and objective. The deistic ideal of natural religion, which arose out of the Enlightenment, reflected the optimism of a culture that believed that all knowledge could be derived through Newtonian-like scientific investigation. Newtonianism brought with it a faith in a universal and rational order that underlay the world, an order that could only be the result of a completely rational Creator. Hence, the religion of the deists was a reaction against the seeming provincialism and arbitrariness of Christianity. The Enlightenment promoted a faith in rational thought and in nature's underlying perfection. That view would change.

The nineteenth century witnessed a revolution in biology that directly affected freethinking religionists: As an increasing number of scientists adopted one or another form of evolutionism, freethinkers adjusted their worldviews accordingly. Biology superseded physics and astronomy as the scientific paradigm for religious iconoclasts. The evolving universe had no need of a separate and distinct Creator, as postulated by the deists. Instead, if a Creator was postulated, it was an immanent being or force, part of the evolving universe itself. Human beings in this system might continue to remain at the pinnacle of creation, but not necessarily. More pessimistic views of the relationship between humans and nature became justifiable and more widely accepted. Popular freethought came to embrace a variety of views: belief in an immanent God, ethical agnosticism, and even outright atheism. The assertion of absolute human autonomy, together with an explicit rejection of otherworldly belief systems, marked a transition in freethought and, indeed, in much of the secular scholarship at the end of the nineteenth century. Some parts of the Enlightenment heritage remained unaltered, however; the view of the common humanity of mankind did not disappear, nor did the belief in the ultimate efficacy of science to uncover universal truths.

Twentieth-Century Humanism

Bringing with it new conditions and new scientific and philosophical premises, the twentieth century saw the rise of humanism proper. The developments in the United States proved to be of singular importance. In the 1910s, several Unitarian ministers, all of whom had left the more conservative denominations of their youth, began to preach what they specifically called humanism, which they defined as a "religion without God." Fighting considerable opposition from fellow Unitarians, these humanists eventually established themselves within the denomination. A small group of them in 1933 published "A Humanist Manifesto," fifteen terse affirmations that presented the basic thrust of humanism. The thirty-four signatories included liberal clergymen (Unitarian, Ethical Culture, and Reform Jewish) and well-known intellectuals, most notably John Dewey (1859–1952).

The humanists' views of science were largely determined by their philosophical commitment to naturalism and pragmatism. Nontheistic naturalism had flourished in the previous century, promoted by such men as Comte, Herbert Spencer (1820–1903), and Ernst Haeckel (1834–1919). Twentieth-century naturalists, however, repudiated the deterministic and reductionistic elements of these earlier men's views and sought to provide a more satisfactory way of explaining human experience, which respected the holistic quality of human values and human wisdom. In the wake of the pragmatic movement in American philosophy, naturalists came to emphasize the method of science over the subject matter of science. Where the earlier naturalism had understood science to be confined to the natural world and the study of material objects, the new naturalism allowed that any object (material or immaterial) could be studied as long as it was done in a detailed, rigorous, and empirical manner. Using the rhetoric of the scientific method, humanists attacked traditional religious authorities (for example, biblical revelation and mystical insight) and defended democratic ideals. The method of science gave public access to all knowledge claims, making it the epistemological arm of democracy.

Religious humanism was an obvious outgrowth of this point of view, for one could even apply the scientific method to the study of religion and religiosity without sacrificing their human significance or reducing them to some physiochemical mechanism or biological urge. The significance of religion, claimed the humanists, lay in the ability of the human religious experience to integrate the world for each person, providing a sense of unity and coherence to life and a foundation for moral values. Humanists retained a place for religion by separating the private religious experience from the public knowledge of science. In the modern world, religion would have to yield to science in all instances in which empirical facts were important. Where science provided no information about factual claims (as regards the existence of God or immortality, for instance), religion must also remain mute. Humankind in the scientific age had to learn to live without certainty. Humanists insisted on this last point, reiterating over and over the need for people to internalize the methods of modern science and resist seeking answers where there were none. Hence, science came to be seen as the locus of certain especially important modern values, namely tentativeness and open-mindedness.

During the late 1920s, a number of like-minded intellectuals wrote books espousing the humanist point of view. The young British biologist Julian Huxley (1887–1975), grandson of T. H. Huxley (1825–95), published his personal expression of a humanistic faith, *Religion Without Revelation* (1927). In America, social commentator Walter Lippmann (1889–1974) wrote *A Preface to Morals* (1929), a long portrait of an age transformed by "the acids of modernity." Similar views were presented in E. A. Burtt's (1892–1989) *Religion in an Age of Science* (1929), J. H. Randall Sr. and Jr.'s (1871–1946 and 1899–1980) *Religion and the Modern World* (1929), and John Dewey's *A Common Faith* (1934). These men believed that the demise of traditional religion left a spiritual vacuum. Men and women were left aimless in the modern world and needed some way to integrate personal and cosmic elements of life. Humanism was that way.

Early British humanism was generally less sympathetic to the idea of religion than its American counterpart. Although the British Ethical Culture societies retained a distinctly religious form of freethought—with congregations and rituals, like traditional churches—other freethought groups counterbalanced these societies. The Rationalist Press Association, in particular, expressed a strident antisupernaturalism that appealed to many well-known intellectuals, including Bertrand Russell (1872–

1970), Gilbert Murray (1866–1957), Jacob Bronowski (1908–1974), Julian Huxley, and A. J. Ayer (1910–89).

Humanism became an international movement at midcentury. The American Humanist Association (AHA) was formed in 1940, and groups in other countries soon followed suit. Ethical Culturists slowly came to see themselves as essentially humanistic and joined more and more with humanists on common causes. In 1952, humanist groups in Western Europe, America, and India formed the International Humanist and Ethical Union. At the same time, a number of prominent humanists became influential members of the United Nations, an organization that seemed, to the humanists, to embody many of the ideals of humanistic thought. Democracy and science defined the humanist outlook in this period, providing it with the fundamental assumptions upon which specific religious, social, and political issues were considered.

The Emergence of Skepticism and Secular Humanism

The 1960s counterculture brought with it a challenge to the intellectualism that had until then dominated humanism. Abraham Maslow and other self-proclaimed humanistic psychologists were acclaimed by the humanists for their work in psychology. Maslow, in particular, opened the way for an understanding of religion divorced from supernatural belief. His work on "peak experiences" located the essence of religious feeling in one's own personal psychological experiences. As Maslow's followers became ever more drawn into the counterculture scene, the more rationalistic humanists reacted against what they saw as narcissism and subjectivism, which they regarded as the most insidious qualities of traditional religion. Religious humanism along these lines was not at all what the earlier humanists had had in mind, and Maslow's followers parted ways with the mainstream humanists. Shortly thereafter, a number of humanists began to recognize strong humanistic qualities in the behaviorism of B. F. Skinner (1904–90), despite its determinism. Skinner's presence provided an unambiguous counterpoint to the humanistic psychologists. Even though Skinner's work was controversial among humanists, the favorable recognition it received indicates a general turn toward a more rationalistic perspective.

This rationalistic temper came to be embodied in a surprisingly popular skeptical movement that took explicit aim at countercultural "irrationalism." This skepticism came out of a narrowly defined educational and scientific project. Its organizational center, the Committee for the Scientific Investigation of Claims of the Paranormal (CSICOP), arose during the mid-1970s after the AHA published "Objections to Astrology," a statement signed by noted scientists around the world that received wide publicity. Following the general line of argument expressed in David Hume's (1711–76) essay "Of Miracles" (1748), these skeptics demanded extraordinary proof for extraordinary claims and devoted themselves to the rigorous examination of paranormal and occult phenomena of all kinds. A number of prominent scientists, including the science writer Isaac Asimov (1920–92) and the astronomer Carl Sagan (1934–96), gave their support to CSICOP and its agenda. The public must be warned against widespread pseudoscientific claims, they argued, because irrationalism masquerading as science endangers both individuals and societies. Claiming that democratic government can function only when people act rationally and knowledgeably, the skeptics defended science in order to defend democracy.

The skeptics understood science to be both empirical and nonexclusive. One need not be a scientist, they maintained, to understand the methods of science or to investigate phenomena scientifically. On the whole, the skeptics reiterated the twentieth-century philosophical naturalists' understanding of science, emphasizing method over substance. They presented themselves as open-minded investigators willing to give a hearing to all claims of unusual phenomena, but their detractors argued that they were merely debunkers and apologists for a dogmatic scientific orthodoxy. One of the most common criticisms, in fact, was that they were not empirical at all but, rather, prone to prejudge cases and to rationalize unusual phenomena. The skeptics often equated belief in the paranormal with religious "overbeliefs," and a significant part of their work explored the psychology of belief and credulity, as well as the related art of tricksterism.

A group of self-declared secular humanists continued this aggressive rationalism of the skeptics, but in a broader, more comprehensive manner. The notion of a *secular* humanism arose by way of contrast with the earlier explicitly religious humanism espoused by the American Unitarians in the 1920s and 1930s, and the name seems to be of American origin. The secular humanists denied that humanism was a religion. Apart from that denial, secular humanism signified less a change in ideology than a change in name. Religion, they argued, most properly referred to belief systems that contain unverifiable supernaturalistic assumptions.

Ironically, however, the term "secular humanism" became popularized through its use by Christian fundamentalists, who sought to emphasize the very point that the secular humanists objected to: the religious nature of humanism. To support their argument, fundamentalists often referred to a footnote in a 1961 Supreme Court decision, *Torcaso v. Watkins,* that stated that "among religions in this country which do not teach what would generally be considered a belief in God are Buddhism, Taoism, Ethical Culture, Secular Humanism and others." Some fundamentalists purported to expose a worldwide conspiracy of humanists who controlled political and media organizations and were bent on eliminating morality and religious belief. They maintained that humanism, the worship of man, led to hedonism and anarchy. Although the fundamentalist attack on humanism took various forms, it was in the arena of public-school education that the battle was most vociferously fought. Sex education and evolutionism became the focus of their criticism. Both subjects, they asserted, were part of the humanist religion and, hence, could not be taught in public schools without infringing on the establishment clause of the First Amendment. (Equal-time arguments tended to moderate this stark position, but the identification of evolutionism with secular religion remained.)

Humanists played a prominent role in the defense of evolutionism. Since the early twentieth century, the theory of evolution had proven to be an integral element in most battles between fundamentalists and freethinkers. Humanists, too, naturally identified with the theory because of its comprehensive explanation of human origins and man's relation to the natural world. When both humanism and evolutionism came under attack, the AHA was one of the first organizations publicly to take notice and respond. During the early 1980s, the AHA had close ties with the anticreationist movement. It later distanced itself from that movement, in part to avoid the charge that evolutionism was merely a religious stance promoted by "the religion of humanism." Humanist sympathies with anticreationism did not change, however.

Increasingly vocal religious conservatism spawned a new, explicitly secular, humanist group. Eschewing the nominally religious status of the AHA, this group, the Council for Democratic and Secular Humanism (CODESH), issued "A Secular Humanist Declaration" (1980/81). The strident tone of CODESH reflected the influence of the rationalist antireligious tradition but did not alter the substance of the humanist worldview. The philosopher Paul Kurtz, one of the leading exponents of both skepticism and secular humanism, sought firmly to end any ambiguity regarding secular humanism's religious status by coining a new word, *eupraxophy,* to describe a nontheistic life stance (Kurtz 1973). In all, secular humanism can be seen as a reactionary movement within humanism, one that sought to maintain the original spirit of Enlightenment rationalism and anticlerical freethinking.

The last decades of the twentieth century brought one other attack on humanism, this time from postmodern scholars. On the whole, humanists have found postmodernism's anarchic approach to knowledge unsettling and dangerous. Some humanists have acceded to the postmodernists' claim that there are sharp limits on the power of reason and human autonomy; these humanists have adopted a radical pragmatism that divorces ultimate knowledge from practical control. Other humanists, however, have replied that science already includes a tentativeness and an awareness of limitations. Humanists' varying receptivity to postmodern arguments indicates yet one more division between the rationalist wing and other more moderate positions.

Humanism in the late twentieth century is an antisupernaturalistic worldview that claims to rely on both the findings and the methods of science. Its ethical system is based on assumptions about individual worth and the ability of human beings to take control of their own lives for the betterment of themselves and those of the rest of humanity. In the humanist worldview, science comes to the aid of humankind, helping answer fundamental questions about the place of human beings in the world by providing nonreligious answers to age-old religious questions. In the same way that Newton and Darwin became exemplars of the scientific ideal, so, too, have contemporary scientists such as Skinner, Sagan, and the sociobiologist Edward O. Wilson (1929–) often become exemplars for the humanists precisely because their work provides a cogent reply to traditional religious explanations of the world. Humanists have praised the utility of science for its ability to provide people with both knowledge and control. With these two possessions, they have repeatedly argued, humankind can take responsibility for its own future.

See also Atheism; Deism; Evolutionary Ethics; Materialism; Positivism; Postmodernism; Pragmatism; Scientific Naturalism; Skepticism

BIBLIOGRAPHY

Primary Works and Programmatic Statements

Dewey, John. *A Common Faith.* New Haven, Conn.: Yale University Press, 1934.

"A Humanist Manifesto." *New Humanist* 6 (May/June 1933): 1–5.

"Humanist Manifesto II." *Humanist* 33 (September/October 1973): 4–9.

Huxley, J. S. *Religion Without Revelation.* New York: Harper, 1927.

Kurtz, Paul, ed. *The Humanist Alternative: Some Definitions of Humanism.* Buffalo, N.Y.: Prometheus Books, 1973.

Lamont, Corliss. *The Philosophy of Humanism.* 7th ed. New York: Continuum, 1993.

Lippmann, Walter. *A Preface to Morals.* New York: MacMillan, 1929.

Reese, Curtis W., ed. *Humanist Sermons.* Chicago: Open Court, 1927.

"A Secular Humanist Declaration." *Free Inquiry* 1 (Winter 1980/81): 3–7.

Sellars, R. W. *Religion Coming of Age.* New York: MacMillan, 1928.

General Works on Freethought, Unbelief, and Irreligion

Brown, Marshall G., and Gordon Stein. *Freethought in the United States: A Descriptive Bibliography.* Westport, Conn.: Greenwood, 1978.

Budd, Susan. *Varieties of Unbelief: Atheists and Agnostics in English Society, 1850–1960.* London: Heinemann, 1977.

Chadwick, Owen. *The Secularization of the European Mind in the Nineteenth Century.* New York: Cambridge University Press, 1975.

Persons, Stow. *Free Religion: An American Faith.* New Haven, Conn.: Yale University Press, 1947.

Robinson, David. *The Unitarians and the Universalists.* Denominations in America Series. Vol. 1. Westport, Conn.: Greenwood, 1985.

Turner, James. *Without God, Without Creed: The Origins of Unbelief in America.* Baltimore: Johns Hopkins University Press, 1985.

White, Edward A. *Science and Religion in American Thought: The Impact of Naturalism.* Stanford, Calif.: Stanford University Press, 1952.

Secondary Works and Critiques of Humanism and Skepticism

Ehrenfeld, David W. *The Arrogance of Humanism.* New York: Oxford University Press, 1978.

Hess, David J. *Science in the New Age: The Paranormal, Its Defenders and Debunkers, and American Culture.* Madison: University of Wisconsin Press, 1993.

LaHaye, Tim. *The Battle for the Mind.* Old Tappan, N.J.: Fleming H. Revell, 1980.

Meyer, Donald H. "Secular Transcendence: The American Religious Humanists." *American Quarterly* 5 (Winter 1982): 524–42.

North American Committee for Humanism. *Humanism Today: Humanism and Postmodernism.* Ed. by Deborah Shepherd and Khoren Arisian. Vol. 8. 1993.

Olds, Mason. *Religious Humanism in America: Dietrich, Reese, and Potter.* Washington, D.C.: University Press of America, 1978.

Radest, Howard B. *The Devil and Secular Humanism: The Children of the Enlightenment.* New York: Praeger, 1990.

Schuler, Michael Anthony. "Religious Humanism in Twentieth-Century American Thought." Ph.D. diss., Florida State University, 1982.

Shermer, Michael Brant. "Science Defended, Science Defined: The Louisiana Creationism Case." *Science, Technology, and Human Values* 16 (Autumn 1991): 517–39.

Toumey, Christopher P. "Evolution and Secular Humanism." *Journal of the American Academy of Religion* 61 (1993): 275–301.

Truzzi, Marcello. "Editorial [on CSICOP and the Mars Effect]." *Zetetic Scholar* 9 (March 1982): 3–5.

Weldon, Stephen Prugh. "The Humanist Enterprise from John Dewey to Carl Sagan: A Study of Science and Religion in American Culture." Ph.D. diss., University of Wisconsin, Madison, 1997.

41. Process Philosophy and Theology

David Ray Griffin

Process theology is a movement based primarily on the philosophy of Alfred North Whitehead (1861–1947), whose major work was *Process and Reality* (1929), and secondarily on that of Charles Hartshorne (1897–). Whereas the term "process theology" can refer to their philosophies in that they are philosophical (or natural) theologies, it also refers more narrowly to the work of a number of theologians, thus far primarily Christian, who have employed these philosophies to interpret the doctrines of their religious traditions.

Whitehead's convictions regarding the importance of this issue were based on his view that religion and science are the two strongest general forces, aside from bodily impulses, that influence us. The basic intellectual problem of modernity is that these two forces—"the force of our religious intuitions, and the force of our impulse to accurate observation and logical deduction"—now seem opposed to each other. The future course of history, Whitehead suggested, depends upon our decision regarding the relations between them (Whitehead 1967a, 181–2).

The idea that science and religion have primarily been involved in "conflict" and "warfare" has been widespread since those terms were used in titles of books by John William Draper (1811–82) and Andrew Dickson White (1832–1918) in the late nineteenth century. Later historians have shown that this idea is an exaggeration. The conflicts, nevertheless, have been significant.

Kinds of Conflict Between Science and Religion

The conflicts between religion and science have been of three basic kinds. Most obvious are conflicts in which science has suggested the falsity of beliefs about particu-lar facts to which religious belief had become attached, such as God's creation of the world a few thousand years ago and the inerrant inspiration of the Bible. Conflicts of this kind have been resolved in liberal religious circles by simply saying that the traditional religious beliefs were wrong, but they remain vital in some conservative religious circles.

The other kinds of conflict are more general, involving the issue of overall worldview. Conflict of the second kind results from the fact that the scientific community has accepted a naturalistic worldview, while much religious thought still accepts a supernaturalistic one. "Naturalism" here does not necessarily mean philosophical materialism or even atheism but only that the universal nexus of natural causal relations is never interrupted. Theistic religious thought, by contrast, has widely understood God as a supernatural being who does occasionally interrupt these relations. This second kind of conflict lies behind the first. Belief in a supernatural deity is generally presupposed in the acceptance of particular religious ideas, such as infallible inspiration and an antievolutionary creationism, which conflict with current scientific views. This second kind of conflict, however, goes deeper. Many religious thinkers who side with science on at least most of the conflicts of the first kind would be loath to accept a fully naturalistic worldview, as that would seem tantamount to relinquishing theism altogether.

Even more serious is conflict of the third kind, which results from the fact that the scientific community has, since the latter part of the nineteenth century, increasingly associated science with a worldview that is not only naturalistic, as just defined, but also materialistic, atheistic, and sensationistic. Sensationism, which limits perception to the physical senses, rules out religious (and even moral and aesthetic) experience. Atheism rules out not only a supernatural, interventionist deity but any divine reality whatever (unless matter or energy be divinized). Materialism rules out what most philosophers of religion, such as Immanuel Kant (1724–1804), have identified as further presuppositions of a religious attitude: freedom, the objectivity of values, and immortality.

Whitehead's Approach

Whitehead's response to these conflicts stands in contrast to the three most prevalent responses: religious fundamentalism, scientific materialism, and a two-truth resolution. Religious fundamentalism, which simply rejects science insofar as it conflicts with what it considers revealed truth, was never an option for Whitehead. But he also could not accept scientific materialism's essential rejection of religion, as he considered religious experience to be genuine and religious intuition to point to important truths.

Among those who could not countenance a simple rejection of either science or religion, the most popular response has been a two-truth resolution, according to which science and religion cannot conflict because they belong to autonomous spheres. For Whitehead, this position contained an element of truth, in that religious assertions are based primarily on values derived from nonsensory intuitions, while science is primarily the attempt to systematize the data of sensory perception. This position could not be a complete solution, however, because the two kinds of assertions inevitably overlap. For example, the early-modern division based upon the distinction by René Descartes (1596–1650) between mind and matter, according to which religion has authority with regard to the human mind and science with regard to the body and the rest of the physical world, is destroyed by the fact that mind and body interact. Whitehead also rejected the solution based upon Kant's philosophy, according to which science, in presenting a wholly deterministic world, tells us merely about appearances, while religion, in speaking of freedom, values, and immortality, is pointing to reality. We cannot help believing that the world studied by the natural sciences is real. Finally, in contrast to those who, without appeal to either a Cartesian or a Kantian dualism, simply affirmed both scientific and religious beliefs without any attempt to show how they are compatible, Whitehead insisted that we need "a vision of the harmony of truth" (Whitehead 1967a, 185).

Whitehead's own procedure formally echoed the approach taken in medieval times: reconciling the claims of science and religion by means of metaphysical philosophy. He said, indeed, that philosophy "attains its chief importance by fusing the two, namely, religion and science, into one rational scheme of thought" (Whitehead 1978, 15). To perform this role, a philosophy must provide an overall view of the world, a cosmology. Unlike the dominant cosmology of the modern period, which has been based almost exclusively upon science, he believed that this cosmology must draw equally upon the other human interests that have traditionally suggested cosmologies: religion, ethics, and aesthetics. This point, that philosophy must draw upon "the whole of the evidence" (Whitehead 1967a, vii), is a constant refrain in Whitehead's writing. Philosophy must, in particular, draw upon nonsensory intuitions as well as sensory experience, thereby allowing religious experience to make its own contribution to metaphysics.

Given such a philosophy, the task was to overcome the various contradictions between assertions made in the name of science and religion, respectively. Whitehead's general approach was to assume that each side is expressing important truths, but that each is exaggerating its own claims, expressing them in doctrines that exclude the truths seen by the other side. To think is to abstract, he maintained, "and the intolerant use of abstractions is the major vice of the intellect" (Whitehead 1967a, 18), which applies whether the intellectuals be theologians or scientists. The task of philosophy is to show that this "clash of doctrines is not a disaster—it is an opportunity." The opportunity is to seek a wider perspective "within which a reconciliation of a deeper religion and a more subtle science will be found" (Whitehead 1967a, 186, 185).

Overcoming Conflicts of the First and Second Kinds

With regard to theistic religion, Whitehead argued that the central overstatement involves the idea of divine power. Theists have been correct to say that the order of the world presupposes an Orderer and to identify the source of order in the physical world with the source of values and ideals in human experience. But he believed that theism has generally exaggerated divine power, regarding the divine agency as coercive and even attributing omnipotence to it. Included in this perceived exaggeration is the idea that God created the world *ex nihilo* (from nothing), so that God's relation to the world is entirely voluntary, involving no element of necessity. God thereby exists beyond all the principles that otherwise appear necessary or metaphysical, so that God can interrupt them at will. This idea has been useful, as God could be appealed to as a "*deus ex machina . . .* capable of rising superior to the difficulties of metaphysics," such as the mind-body problem created by Cartesian dualism (Whitehead 1967a, 156). But, besides the fact that this approach is "repugnant to a consistent rationality" (Whitehead 1978, 190), the doctrine of unqualified omnipotence, by assigning to God "responsibility for every detail of every happening" (Whitehead 1967b, 169), creates an insoluble problem of evil. Finally, it is this idea of divine power that creates the first and second kinds of conflict between science and religion.

Whitehead emphatically rejected a supernatural, omnipotent God. In so doing, he followed an approach to the conflict between science and religion (as well as to the problem of evil) that has been taken by a large number of philosophers and theologians. In rejecting supernaturalism, however, many of them have rejected theism, the belief in a personal divine reality who influences the world. During most of Whitehead's professional life, he, too, had rejected theism of all sorts. However, after he began developing his metaphysical philosophy (upon coming to Harvard University in the 1920s), he quickly concluded that no adequate, coherent system was possible without speaking of God. At first (in *Science and the Modern World* [1925]), this "God" was merely an impersonal principle. Shortly thereafter, however (in *Religion in the Making* [1926] and *Process and Reality* [1929]), he described God as an actual entity, consciously responsive to the world and influencing it by means of values.

Whitehead's theism, nevertheless, is a *naturalistic* theism. God created our world not out of nothing, but out of chaos, by inducing new forms of order. The nature of the world, being eternal, is as necessary as the nature of God, which means that the relationship between God and the world is necessary, not arbitrary. Rather than being "an exception to all metaphysical principles," God is "their chief exemplification" (Whitehead 1978, 343). It does not belong to divine power, accordingly, to interrupt the normal causal relations of nature. God does exert influence in the world—in fact, in every event, from subatomic particles to human experience. But this divine influence is a regular aspect of the normal pattern of causality, not an exception thereto.

Overcoming Conflict of the Third Kind

"Process theology" is known primarily for the doctrine that divine power is persuasive rather than coercive, through which its proponents believe that conflicts between science and religion of the first and second kinds (as well as the problem of evil) are overcome. Much more of Whitehead's attention, however, was devoted to overcoming the association of science with a materialistic worldview and thereby conflict of the third kind. This conflict results from the same tendency of human nature. "Science has always suffered from the vice of overstatement" (Whitehead 1958, 27). Indeed, whereas in earlier times theologians were the chief sinners, today scientists are especially guilty of exaggerating their truths, thereby excluding truths arising from other intuitions. A central aim of Whitehead's philosophy, accordingly, was "to challenge the half-truths constituting the scientific first principles" (Whitehead 1978, 10).

At the root of these half-truths is scientific materialism's view of the ultimate units of the physical world. According to this view, these units are actual but "vacuous," meaning completely void of any experience and, therefore, of internal values. These actualities must be considered vacuous, as having no inner reality, because they are purely spatial. Although they endure through time, their existence, unlike that of a moment of human experience, involves no inner duration. A bit of matter can exist at an "instant," in the technical sense of a slice of time with no duration. In matter thus conceived, accordingly, there can be no experience, no value, no aim, and no self-determination.

This idea of matter was at first, in the philosophy of Descartes and most other seventeenth-century thinkers, part of a dualistic cosmology, according to which these vacuous actualities interacted with experiencing actualities, or minds. The question of how these completely different kinds of actualities could interact, however, proved unanswerable (especially after thinkers were no longer inclined to explain it by appeal to God). Although some thinkers rejected dualism in favor of idealism, according to which matter is mere appearance, the dominant move, especially in scientific circles, was to reject the idea that the mind is a full-fledged actuality, regarding it instead as an epiphenomenal by-product of matter with no causal power of its own. The result is the wholly materialistic philosophy, in which self-determination, values, and deity can play no role.

Whereas many have thought that room could be made for religion and morality only by returning to dualism, Whitehead agreed with materialists that interaction between vacuous and experiencing actualities is inconceivable. The solution was to criticize the idea of matter as vacuous actuality, showing it to be based on "the fallacy of misplaced concreteness," which involves "mistaking an abstraction for a final concrete fact" (Whitehead 1967b, 190). The ultimate units of nature, in their concreteness, are not devoid of duration, experience, intrinsic value, and self-determination. Rather, they are "actual occasions," each of which is temporally, as well as spatially, extensive. Their temporal extensiveness, or duration, is constituted by experience. Actual occasions, accordingly, are "occasions of experience." Each occasion has a physical aspect, insofar as it is determined by antecedent occasions, and a mental aspect, insofar as it is partly self-determining. Enduring individuals, such as electrons, atoms, and molecules, are temporal societies of occasions in which each occasion virtually repeats the form of its predecessors. The scientific description of these entities as vacuous bits of matter moving through space and interacting deterministically involves a great abstraction from their concrete existence as routes of experiencing, partly self-determining events. Materialism involves the confusion of this abstraction with the concrete events.

This doctrine can be called "panexperientialism" (although Whitehead himself used neither this term nor the more common "panpsychism," which Hartshorne used). But it does not mean that all identifiable objects have experience and spontaneity. Rather, the doctrine involves a distinction between two basic ways in which a myriad of enduring individuals can be organized: aggregational societies, such as rocks and stars, and "compound individuals" (Hartshorne's term), such as living cells and multicelled animals, including humans. In the latter, the organization of the parts gives rise to the emergence of a higher-level individual, which incorporates the experiences of all of the others and, in turn, exercises an organizing power over them, thereby giving the whole society a unity of response and action. This temporal society of "dominant occasions" is what is commonly called the mind. In aggregational societies, by contrast, there is no dominant member to give the total society, such as a rock, any unity of experience or action. Although there is spontaneity in the individual members, such as the subatomic particles, the spontaneous movements of the various members "thwart each other, and average out so as to produce a negligible total effect" (Whitehead 1967b, 207). The rock stays put.

The image of what "science" is has been based on the study of these aggregational societies, such as Galileo's (1564–1642) metal balls and Isaac Newton's (1642–1727) stellar masses. With such things, the reductionistic, deterministic approach has had remarkable success. A problem arises only when this method, which is really a science of averages, is applied to the study of compound individuals, especially humans and other higher animals. In such beings, the functioning is not analogous to the functioning of rocks and billiard balls. The dogmatic claim that it must be analogous is the central overstatement of modern science. In compound individuals, the spontaneities of the members, rather than being cancelled out by the "law of large numbers," are coordinated by the dominant member, the mind. A science of the average does not suffice. To understand the behavior of a person, one must understand that person's beliefs, emotions, and self-determining decisions. The need to account for individual self-determination applies, to lesser degrees, all the way down the hierarchy of individuals—an idea that is consistent with the lack of full determinism at the lowest level suggested by quantum physics.

This position is like dualism in regarding the mind as a fully actual individual, capable of exercising self-determination and efficient causation. But it is not bedeviled by the problem of dualist interaction, because the mind, as a temporal society of spatio-temporal occasions of experience, is different only in degree, not in kind, from the brain cells. Whitehead thereby provides a nondualistic interactionism. Through this combination of ideas—that all individuals exercise at least an iota of self-determination, that evolution has produced compound individuals whose dominant members exercise greater degrees of self-determination, and that these dominant members exercise "downward causation" upon the subordinate members—Whitehead suggested a way to reconcile the determinism verified by humans as scientists with the freedom presupposed by humans as moral and religious beings.

Implicit in this position is a reconciliation of the importance of sensory perception with the assumption, implicit in ethical, aesthetic, and religious judgments, that we also have nonsensory perceptions, through which we are aware of normative values or ideals. Through sensory perception, we gain precise information about physical objects that are capable of activating our sensory organs, and our perception of such objects is prominent in our conscious experience. The primacy of sensory perception in consciousness, however, does not mean that sensory perception is our only, or even basic, mode of perception. Sensory perception can occur only because the mind directly perceives those brain cells that convey the information from the various sensory organs. This direct perception of the brain, which Whitehead calls "prehension," is an example of nonsensory perception. Another example is telepathy, in which one mind directly prehends another. Although most of our prehensions do not rise to consciousness, we at some level prehend everything in our environment. Because our environment includes God as envisaging ideal values, every moment of experience prehends God. This prehension of God is generally not conscious, but it is not thereby without effect. It results in that vague but persistent awareness of normative ideals that we all presuppose in practice. Furthermore, just as telepathic prehensions, which are occurring all the time, may occasionally rise to consciousness, leading us to speak of "extrasensory perception," our prehensions of God may sometimes rise to consciousness, leading us to speak of "religious experience" or the "experience of the holy."

Although Whitehead's alternative philosophical framework for science was offered "in the interest of science itself" (Whitehead 1967a, 83), it was also offered to overcome conflicts between science and religion of the third kind. Science reconceived within Whitehead's ontology and epistemology no longer rules out the reality of freedom, values, God, and religious experience. Whitehead's process philosophy even allows for immortality in a twofold sense. The distinction between mind and brain allows for the possibility of life after bodily death, leaving the issue to be settled by empirical evidence. Whitehead, however, devoted more attention to the question of immortality in a second sense: whether our lives have any permanent significance. Because Whitehead regarded God as exemplifying the general metaphysical principles, thereby regarding God as well as the world to be in process, he rejected the traditional notion of God as an immutable, impassible being to which the world could make no contribution. Besides a "primordial nature," through which God influences the world by means of ideal values, God also has a "consequent nature," in which the world's experiences are taken up into God. The fact that "conscious, rational life refuses to conceive itself as a transient enjoyment, transiently useful" is answered by our "objective immortality" in God, which guarantees the "unfading importance of our immediate actions, which perish and yet live for evermore" (Whitehead 1978, 340, 351).

Later Developments

Whitehead's writing career effectively ended in 1941. During the 1940s and 1950s, his vision of a positive relation between "a deeper religion and a more subtle science" was embodied primarily at the University of Chicago, especially in the theologian of culture Bernard Meland (1899–1993) and the philosopher Charles Hartshorne, who, in fact, had written some of his most important works on this topic in the 1930s. Since the 1960s, however, there has been a wider interest in Whitehead's position, thanks to a spate of books clustered around 1960 on his metaphysics and his philosophy of science, followed shortly thereafter by books articulating Whitehead's and Hartshorne's philosophical theologies. With regard to the relation of science to religion in particular, a number of process thinkers have articulated a Whiteheadian position, but the major figure has been Ian Barbour (1923–), whose first book on the topic (*Issues in Science and Religion* [1966]) has become a standard in the field, and who has given the Gifford Lectures on natural theology.

Process thinkers have given special attention to the issue of evolution, both in itself and in relation to the idea of divine creation. In the 1980s and 1990s, further studies of Whitehead's philosophy of science appeared, and the contrast between modern and postmodern views of science that was implicit in Whitehead's *Science and the Modern World* has been explicated by several authors in a way that emphasizes the Whiteheadian reconciliation between science and religion. A central dimension of the recent discussion is an emphasis on the possibilities inherent in process philosophy for theologies that are distinctively feminist and ecological.

Whitehead's understanding of the relation between science and religion will become the dominant understanding only if his view of science itself comes to prevail in the scientific community. Although this possibility is not yet imminent, the ideas of several important scientific thinkers have been decisively influenced by Whitehead's view.

See also Conflict of Science and Religion; Postmodernism; Varieties of Providentialism

BIBLIOGRAPHY

Barbour, Ian G. Issues in Science and Religion. Englewood Cliffs, N.J.: Prentice-Hall, 1966.

———. Religion in an Age of Science. San Francisco: Harper, 1990.

Birch, Charles, and John B. Cobb, Jr. The Liberation of Life: From the Cell to the Community. 1981. Reprint. Denton, Tex.: Environmental Ethics Books, 1990.

Cobb, John B., Jr. A Christian Natural Theology: Based on the Thought of Alfred North Whitehead. Philadelphia: Westminster, 1965.

Cobb, John B., Jr., and David Ray Griffin, eds. Mind in Nature: Essays on the Interface of Science and Philosophy. Washington, D.C.: University Press of America, 1977.

Griffin, David Ray, ed. Physics and the Ultimate Significance of Time: Bohm, Prigogine, and Process Philosophy. Albany: State University of New York Press, 1986.

———, ed. The Reenchantment of Science: Postmodern Proposals. Albany: State University of New York Press, 1988.

Hahn, Lewis Edwin. Beyond Humanism: Essays in the New Philosophy of Nature. 1937. Reprint. Lincoln: University of Nebraska Press, 1968.

———. Whitehead's Philosophy: Selected Essays, 1935–1970. Lincoln: University of Nebraska Press, 1972.

———. The Philosophy of Charles Hartshorne. The Library of Living Philosophers. Vol. 20. LaSalle, Ill.: Open Court, 1991.

Haught, John F. The Cosmic Adventure: Science, Religion, and the Quest for Purpose. New York: Paulist, 1984.

Keller, Catherine. From a Broken Web: Separation, Sexism, and Self. Boston: Beacon, 1986.

Lawrence, Nathaniel. Whitehead's Philosophical Development: A Critical History of the Background of Process and Reality. Berkeley: University of California Press, 1956.

Lowe, Victor. Understanding Whitehead. Baltimore: Johns Hopkins University Press, 1962.

Meland, Bernard E. Faith and Culture. Carbondale: Southern Illinois University Press, 1953.

Overman, Richard H. Evolution and the Christian Doctrine of Creation: A Whiteheadian Interpretation. Philadelphia: Westminster, 1967.

Palter, Robert M. Whitehead's Philosophy of Science. Chicago: University of Chicago Press, 1960.

Schilpp, Paul Arthur. The Philosophy of Alfred North Whitehead. The Library of Living Philosophers. Vol. 3. Evanston, Ill.: Northwestern University Press, 1941.

Whitehead, Alfred North. Science and the Modern World. 1925. Reprint. New York: Free Press, 1967a.

———. Religion in the Making. 1926. Reprint. Cleveland: World, 1960.

———. The Function of Reason. 1929. Reprint. Boston: Beacon, 1958.

———. Process and Reality: An Essay in Cosmology. 1929. Corrected ed., ed. by David Ray Griffin and Donald W. Sherburne. New York: Free Press, 1978.

———. Adventures of Ideas. 1933. Reprint. New York: Free Press, 1967b.

———. Modes of Thought. 1938. Reprint. New York: Free Press, 1968.

———. Essays in Science and Philosophy. New York: Philosophical Library, 1947.

Waddington, C.H., ed. Towards a Theoretical Biology. 3 vols. Edinburgh: Edinburgh University Press/Chicago: Aldine, 1968–70.

42. THE SOCIAL CONSTRUCTION OF SCIENCE

Stephen P. Weldon

The phrase "social construction of science" denotes the view that scientific knowledge is not autonomous or based on universal principles of rationality but, rather, tied directly to social interests and conditions. Science, in this view, is seen to be solely a human production that does not differ fundamentally from other human endeavors. By relativizing scientific knowledge in this way, social constructionism has had direct implications for the way in which one approaches the study of the relationship between science and religion in that it has forced scholars to stop privileging the scientific point of view over the religious.

The methodological orientation of social constructionism was spawned by Thomas Kuhn's classic analysis of the scientific enterprise, *The Structure of Scientific Revolutions* (1962). In it Kuhn (1922–96) argued that fundamental changes in scientific theories occurred through gestalt shifts in the way that communities of scientists perceived central problems of their field. By explaining certain basic theoretical transformations in terms of social and psychological factors, Kuhn deemphasized the role of rational thought in the establishment of scientific knowledge. This way of describing science ran counter to most prevailing conceptions of science that placed great weight on the autonomy of the scientific method. When Kuhn concluded that scientific theories were not independent of the social realm, he unleashed a theoretical current that radically redirected studies in the history of science.

Convinced by Kuhn's thesis, many scholars pursuing the sociology of knowledge undertook a research program to explore the socially contingent nature of scientific knowledge. Contrasting their position with the older sociology of science in the Mertonian tradition, they argued that, instead of correlating social factors with transformations in the institutional structures of scientific communi-

ties, the new sociology should investigate how social factors influenced the very content of scientific discovery. Termed the "strong programme" by its leaders at the University of Edinburgh, this new line of research held to a number of strict criteria for the investigation of science. David Bloor's treatise *Knowledge and Social Imagery* (1976, 2d ed. 1991) canonized this school of thought and proposed that research into science be highly empirical and avoid all attempts at what he called a teleological view of scientific developments. In essence, Bloor argued for the need to approach the study of science without any preconceptions regarding the truth or falsity of the knowledge itself. Methodological relativism thus formed the heart of his research proposals, which meant that sociologists studying knowledge would treat "accepted" knowledge and "rejected" knowledge symmetrically.

Previously, argued Bloor and his colleagues, students of scientific knowledge had treated what they knew to be false ideas quite differently from those they knew to be correct. The false ones were explained by sociological and psychological factors, whereas the true ones were seen to be merely the result of the unproblematic application of scientific method. For the new sociologists of knowledge who were influenced by Kuhn, this procedure was no longer considered to be viable because the very nature of rationality was the object under investigation. Their central project was to determine what caused people to think that a particular assertion was right.

The major premises outlined by the "strong programme" have been reiterated, expanded, and revised by a number of other social constructionists. One alternative point of view comes from scholars who have used the methods of literary criticism in their study of the production of scientific knowledge. This group, led by Steven Woolgar, Bruno Latour, and others, believes that the best way to understand how knowledge comes into being is to pay attention to the rhetoric of scientists. Another group of researchers, who call themselves eth-nomethodologists, have avoided such purely textual studies and attempted, instead, to learn about science's social features through participant observation in the laboratory. Finally, the philosopher Paul Feyerabend (1924–94) has likened scientific rationality to a performance. Science, he has contended, does not have any set methodology. Somewhat facetiously, he has claimed that scientific method is a method in which "anything goes": In essence, scientists do whatever they can in order to make their ideas convincing to others.

Out of this plethora of scholarship has come a substantially different picture of the nature and operation of scientific practice. Where science once appeared to be a universal source of knowledge about the world, the social constructionists see it as highly contextual and contingent upon local circumstances. According to these scholars, there is no single entity called "science." Rather, each scientific discipline has its own methodologies, rules, and procedures that differentiate it from other fields. Furthermore, the line between science and other human endeavors threatens to disappear.

Theoretical principles that so clearly challenge the autonomy and rationality of science have had a pronounced effect on the understanding of the science-religion interaction. The relationship between social constructionism and the study of this interaction, however, varies considerably from case to case. Part of the reason for this is that, by and large, the major developments in social constructionism have subordinated the science-religion relationship to a secondary concern. By placing so much emphasis on the understanding of scientific knowledge, many social constructionists tend to regard religion as merely one social influence among many that affect the production of scientific knowledge. Hence, religion and science are no longer a focal point for analysis; instead, elements perceived to underlie both categories (such as linguistic factors, power relationships, and social hierarchies) have taken center stage.

New studies by social constructionists have shed light on the relationship between religion and science during the scientific revolution. When studying topics such as the origin of the mechanical philosophy or Robert Boyle's (1627–91) conception of science, scholars have shown that it is no longer clear where religion or irrationalism end and "pure science" begins. This is in marked contrast to

earlier works by people like Robert Merton (1910–), who assumed a clear distinction between the two and sought to show the effect of one side upon the other. In other revisionist histories, political and cultural questions intrude on the standard story (as, for example, in discussions of Galileo [1564–1642] and the Church), thereby making the religion-science controversy of secondary importance.

In an important article published in 1981, the historian Martin Rudwick pointed out an asymmetry in the treatment of religious knowledge and scientific knowledge. Even among social constructionists, he contended, when the subject turned to modern religious views, far too many scholars still tended to depict a triumphant science and a defeated religion. Rudwick spelled out the implications of strictly adhering to the principles of the "strong programme" when treating religion-science interactions: The two ways of thinking, he argued, must be treated symmetrically. The study of Christian creationism has posed problems for the historian for this very reason. At times, creationists have presented their theory as a science and, at other times, as a religious position. All the while, however, they have argued their position using both physical and biblical evidences. Referring to Rudwick's article, the historian Ronald Numbers has explicitly used social constructionism to justify an even-handed, unbiased treatment of creationist ideas, calling for the need to treat them with the same seriousness and rigor as other historians of science have treated the views of evolutionists.

Social constructionism has not gone unchallenged among science-studies scholars. One of the most damning criticisms asserts that the insights of social construction are, in fact, not new. The notion that science is a social enterprise and that the knowledge it produces is prone to the same errors and problems as any other human activity should not, argue some, surprise scientists themselves. Furthermore, one need not invoke social constructionism merely to justify a rigorously historicist perspective, one that treats discoveries and failures according to local and historical contexts. The fact that many historians uninterested in questions about the contingent nature of rationality have produced thoughtful and fair-minded studies of science and religion suggests that social constructionism is not as influential in this regard as some suppose. The discipline of the history of ideas has long demonstrated the fluidity with which beliefs move between scientific and religious contexts.

One recent work that has (perhaps inadvertently) tested the limits of social constructionism insofar as it relates to the science-and-religion question is John Brooke's monumental synthesis, *Science and Religion: Some Historical Perspectives* (1991). In this book, Brooke invokes a "complexity thesis" to replace the old conflict and harmony models of the relationship between the two enterprises. This complexity thesis stemmed, in part, from Brooke's view that religion and science can no longer be viewed in broad universal terms. Much of the recent literature in the history of science upon which Brooke has drawn has demonstrated the need to understand both science and religion according to locally contingent factors. In this sense, Brooke's thesis finds much in common with social construction. Nevertheless, one social constructionist has taken Brooke to task for not going far enough in this direction because the very terms "science" and "religion" work against the constructionist enterprise. Any historian who uses those terms, claims Brooke's critic, needs to be aware that the meanings of the words are themselves constructed and may not be useful in understanding a particular situation. In other words, the late-twentieth-century categories of the historian interfere with our understanding of the social and intellectual categories of the period being studied.

Interestingly, David Bloor's 1991 afterward to the second edition of his *Knowledge and Social Imagery* makes explicit mention of the historical study of religion, pointing out that the same kinds of arguments currently being waged over the social construction of science were, a century before, waged over the study of religion—namely, could religious dogma still be maintained even when beliefs were subject to a probing analysis that deprivileged them? The revelation of this parallel between nineteenth-century religious studies and twentieth-century science studies illustrates something not only about the changing relationship between science and religion in Western culture, but also about the role of the investigator who studies science and religion. Bloor's point seems to be that the debate over the more radical claims of social constructionism will not vanish quietly but will continue to inform all areas of science studies, including the history of science and religion.

See also Demarcation of Science and Religion; Historiography of Science and Religion; Postmodernism

BIBLIOGRAPHY

Berger, Peter L. *The Sacred Canopy: Elements of a Sociological Theory of Religion.* New York: Doubleday, 1967.

Bloor, David. *Knowledge and Social Imagery.* 2d ed. Chicago: University of Chicago Press, 1991.

Brooke, John Hedley. *Science and Religion: Some Historical Perspectives.* New York: Cambridge University Press, 1991.

Cole, Stephen. *Making Science: Between Nature and Society.* Cambridge, Mass.: Harvard University Press, 1992.

Collins, H. M., and T. J. Pinch. *Frames of Meaning: The Social Construction of Extraordinary Science.* Boston: Routledge and Kegan Paul, 1982.

Desmond, Adrian. *The Politics of Evolution: Morphology, Medicine, and Reform in Radical London.* Chicago: University of Chicago Press, 1989.

Feyerabend, Paul K. *Against Method.* New York: Verso, 1993.

Gieryn, Thomas F. "Relativist/Constructivist Programmes in the Sociology of Science: Redundance and Retreat." *Social Studies of Science* 12 (1982): 279–97.

Hess, David J. *Science in the New Age: The Paranormal, Its Defenders and Debunkers, and American Culture.* Madison: University of Wisconsin Press, 1993.

Lindberg, David C., and Ronald L. Numbers, eds. "Introduction." In *God and Nature: Historical Essays on the Encounter Between Christianity and Science.* Berkeley: University of California Press, 1986, 1–18.

Kaye, Howard L. *The Social Meaning of Modern Biology: From Social Darwinism to Sociobiology.* New Haven, Conn.: Yale University Press, 1986.

Kuhn, Thomas S. *The Structure of Scientific Revolutions.* Chicago: University of Chicago Press, 1962.

Latour, Bruno, and Steve Woolgar. *Laboratory Life: The Social Construction of Scientific Facts.* Beverly Hills, Calif.: Sage, 1979.

Moore, James. "Speaking of 'Science and Religion'—Then and Now." Review of *Science and Religion* by John Hedley Brooke. *History of Science* 30 (1992): 311–23.

Myers, Greg. *Writing Biology: Texts in the Social Construction of Scientific Knowledge.* Madison: University of Wisconsin Press, 1990.

Numbers, Ronald L. *The Creationists.* New York: Knopf, 1992.

Pickering, Andrew, ed. *Science as Practice and Culture.* Chicago: University of Chicago Press, 1992.

Rudwick, Martin. "Senses of the Natural World and Senses of God: Another Look at the Historical Relation of Science and Religion." In *The Sciences and Theology in the Twentieth Century,* ed. by A. R. Peacocke. Notre Dame, Ind.: University of Notre Dame Press, 1981, 241–61.

Shapin, Steven. "History of Science and Its Sociological Reconstructions." *History of Science* 20 (1982): 157–211.

Shapin, Steven, and Simon Schaffer. *Leviathan and the Air-Pump: Hobbes, Boyle, and the Experimental Life.* Princeton, N.J.: Princeton University Press, 1985.

Slezak, Peter. "The Social Construction of Social Constructionism." *Inquiry* 37 (1994): 139–57.

Wallis, Roy, ed. *On the Margins of Science: The Social Construction of Rejected Knowledge.* Keele: University of Keele, 1979.

43. GENDER

Sara Miles and John Henry

The term "gender" is used in this essay in accordance with the way late-twentieth-century feminists have borrowed the word, to differentiate those socially and politically variable meanings of "masculine" and "feminine" from the more fixed biological meanings. In this sense, the notion of gender is intended, as Donna Haraway (a leading feminist thinker) has suggested, "to contest the naturalization of sexual difference." Her point is that a wide range of supposed differences between the sexes have been invoked and exploited to support different attitudes toward, and treatment of, the sexes in various social and political contexts. To talk of gender differences in these contexts, rather than differences of sex, is to alert readers to the all too real possibility that such differences may have been socially constructed to serve particular interests.

Consideration of gender issues arising from, or occurring within, the natural sciences and its various forms of institutional organization was first explicitly signaled in an article called simply "Gender and Science" by Evelyn Fox Keller that appeared in 1978. Although it is possible to find earlier studies concerned with different aspects of relationships between women and the sciences, the subject has become a growth area in feminist scholarship since the publication of Keller's article. Essentially, there are three major aspects of gender and science that have attracted feminist attention: (1) the study of women by science; (2) the role of women in science; and (3) the "gendered" nature of science itself, which (it is alleged) traditionally excluded women and their experiences from any association with, or relevance to, scientific development. There is now a considerable literature in each of these areas. An increasing number of historical studies seek to show, on the one hand, the changing ways in which women, their sexuality, their anatomy, and their mentality have been viewed by almost exclusively male scientists and, on the other hand, the previously unacknowledged contributions that women themselves have made to scientific development. Meanwhile, there is an equally burgeoning area of feminist studies that addresses Keller's original concern that there exists a "pervasive association between masculine and objective, [and] more specifically between masculine and scientific." In what follows, each of these areas of feminist focus is considered in turn, but no attempt is made to give a comprehensive coverage of all of the issues. Our concern is to consider primarily how these different aspects of gender and science relate to religious or theological matters.

Women According to Science

Since ancient times, Western culture has viewed women as inferior to men, offering a justification for this view that has typically been religious, philosophical, or scientific in nature. In the *Republic* (5.25), Plato (c. 427–347 B.C.) accepted the theoretical possibility that women could be equal to men in abilities, differing only in reproductive functions. For Plato, it was important and just, therefore, to provide both sexes with a common education to allow individual differences to appear. Aristotle (384–322 B.C.), however, differed from his mentor and established the scientific basis for many of the standard arguments for women's inferiority. For Aristotle, biology was destiny. Defining a female as a "mutilated male," he developed a biological/philosophical theory that dichotomized traits hierarchically, with male traits being superior to female traits. Hence, men were hot, dry, active, rational, powerful, and spiritual, whereas women were cold, wet, passive, emotional, weak, and material, and no amount of education could overcome women's inherent inferiority. Aristotle's theory provided a scientific explanation for his society's views concerning women and men and justified its cultural rules and practices regarding the sexes.

Aristotle was to be immensely influential in the tradition of natural philosophy, particularly during the Western European Middle Ages, but there was a rival theory in the biological tradition, developed by the supremely influential Greek medical writer Galen (A.D. 129–c. 210). For both Aristotle and Galen, women were underdeveloped males, whose sexual organs remained inside their bodies instead of descending to form the penis, scrotum, and testicles. The ovaries received no name of their own until the seventeenth century, being referred to by medical writers as the female testicles, while the vagina was seen as homologous with the penis. But, while Aristotle believed that the female testicles must be useless on account of their lack of development, Galen insisted that they were fully functional. So while Aristotle was able to see women as mutilated or deformed males, Galen saw them as "perfect in their sex." This difference reflected the two thinkers' opposed views of procreation. For Aristotle, women were like the ground into which the sower plants his seed. They provided only the material from which the embryo was formed, while the man's sperm performed the act of shaping and organizing the matter into a human being. Galen, taking seriously the fact that children often resemble their mothers more than their fathers, believed that both partners contributed equally and that children were formed from a mixture of spermatic fluid from father and mother. (A corollary of this view was that women must achieve orgasm to conceive—another notion that ran counter to the influential Aristotelian view that women are passive in the sexual act.) It should be noted, however, that, while Galen regarded women as "perfect in their sex," there was no question that their sex was inferior to the male sex. Here Galen was in complete agreement with Aristotle.

While Hebrew attitudes toward women led to the same kinds of conclusions as did the Greek, they were justified on religious premises rather than the scientific and philosophical reasoning of Greek thought. Eve was tempted by the serpent and caused Adam to sin; as punishment, God placed women in a subordinate position, to be ruled over by men (Genesis 3). The author of the apocryphal Ecclesiasticus writes: "From a woman sin had its beginning, and because of her we all die" (25:24). Etymologically, the word "wife" in the Pentateuch often means "woman belonging to a man" (for example, Genesis 2:24–5, 3:8, 17). A woman's mind and spirit were especially weak and susceptible to false teachings and deceptions. She therefore needed the protective authority of a male—father, brother, or husband. The Hebrew tradition nonetheless placed a positive value on many of the emotional characteristics viewed as feminine, such as compassion, love, and pity. Since the Jews believed that both men and women were created in the image of God and so reflect his rational, spiritual, and moral attributes, some of the feminine attributes were believed to belong to God as well. Hence, the prophet Isaiah taught that God will act in a "motherly" fashion as he comforts his people (Isaiah 66:13). The Greeks, by contrast, viewed such characteristics as weak because they were opposed to the rational attributes of the male.

The early Christian view of women in some ways challenged traditional attitudes toward women in both Hebrew and Greek thinking. The Apostle Paul (d. A.D. c. 67) wrote to the church at Galatia that, in Jesus Christ, the old divisions based on human understanding had been overcome and that "there is neither male nor female; for you are all one in Christ Jesus" (Gal. 3:28 New International Version). Early Christians were careful, however, not to upset traditional cultural norms. Women carried on active charitable work in local churches, but did not participate in the ministry as elders or presbyters. With the growth of the monastic movement in the fourth century, women were active in forming convents. During the High Middle Ages (c. 1000–c. 1400), the influence of Greek ideas became more dominant after the establishment of Galenism in the medical faculties and Aristotelianism in the arts faculties of the medieval universities. The synthesis of Aristotelianism with Christian theology, initiated by Thomas Aquinas (c. 1225–74) and consolidated in subsequent university scholasticism, ensured that theories of the inferiority of women were fully endorsed by natural philosophy. The coupling of rationality with maleness and passion with femaleness was perhaps the most significant way that this Christian-Aristotelian synthesis influenced attitudes toward women. On the one hand, women's supposed inferior rational powers—and, hence, their inability to control their emotions—became the explanation for Eve's inability to withstand the serpent's wiles. For the Dominican authors of the highly influential fifteenth-century work on witchcraft, *Malleus maleficarum,* this rational inferiority explained why such a high proportion of witches were women. It made them more susceptible to the devil's deceptions and, combined with their unruly, passionate natures, prompted them to unnatural demonic alliances and to inappropriate emotional responses in human relationships. At the same time, the belief in the intellectual inferiority of women provided the basis for their exclusion from scientific and medical education and later even from those practices with which they had been traditionally involved, such as midwifery.

The period known as the scientific revolution did nothing to redress the balance. On the contrary, as a number of feminist scholars have pointed out, it saw a renewed emphasis on sexual metaphors of male dominance over the passive female. As the standard view of sexual politics was increasingly applied to Mother Nature, so the natural philosopher increasingly saw himself as ravishing and enslaving her. Francis Bacon (1561–1626), a leading spokesman for both the new empirical science and the usefulness of natural knowledge, said that nature must be captured and enslaved, and her secrets, like her inner chambers, penetrated. Concomitant with such views was an increased emphasis on natural philosophy, not merely as a way of understanding the physical world (as it had been previously) but as a means of controlling, manipulating, and exploiting it for the benefit of mankind. Feminist historians have also suggested that the mechanistic natural philosophy developed during the scientific revolution, and in many ways characteristic of it, was a masculine kind of natural philosophy that replaced the more feminine holistic, vitalistic, and magical worldviews that had preceded it. It should be noticed, however, that the justification for attributing gender to these differing approaches to nature is itself open to dispute. Magic, for example, was always an exploitative endeavor and was, for example, a major influence upon Francis Bacon's ideas about the reform of natural philosophy. Even so, feminist historical analyses of the gendered nature of the scientific revolution seem hard to deny. After all, if the magical tradition did, indeed, influence modern science, it did not survive the experience. As seventeenth-century natural philosophers took what they wanted from the magical worldview and turned it into the new philosophy, they vigorously denounced what was left of that tradition as superstition. Moreover, the branch of magic known as witchcraft became, during the period of the European

witch craze, a major means of discrediting magic as blasphemous, heretical, or superstitious.

If the scientific revolution saw a renewed emphasis upon the biological and, therefore, sociopolitical inferiority of women, a further change in sexual politics was required during the eighteenth century. The replacement of absolutist political systems, with their belief in the divine right of kings and a rigid hierarchical organization, by social-contract theories of politics, which held that monarchy or other forms of government were based upon the delegation of political power by the people to the government to act on their behalf, gave rise to more egalitarian notions of social organization. Thomas Laqueur, Londa Schiebinger, and others have argued that, with the newly pervading political theory of liberal egalitarianism, it no longer seemed acceptable to maintain the old hierarchical positioning of men over women. Some thinkers, accordingly, argued for equality of the sexes, but, for most, this notion was unacceptable. Hence, the authority of science began to develop new theories of women that reestablished the age-old claims that they were biologically unsuited for public and political life, but without having to rely on crude notions of inferiority and superiority.

From now on, the notion that women were inferior to men was replaced by the view that women were so completely different from men in all respects, and so obviously intended for childbearing and childrearing, that they could legitimately be excluded from ongoing political deliberations about who was entitled to vote or to take part in government. It is no coincidence that at just this time we see books appearing with titles such as Edward Thomas Moreau's *A medical question: Whether apart from genitalia there is a difference between the Sexes?* (1750) and Jakob Ackermann's *On the discrimination of sex beyond the genitalia* (1788). Numerous other medical writers begin to insist that women are different not just with respect to their genital organs but in their bone structure, their hair, their eyes, their sweat, their brains, and, indeed, as one writer insisted, "in every conceivable respect of body and mind." As Pierre Roussel put it in 1775: "the essence of sex is not confined to a single organ but extends through more or less perceptible nuances into every part." Ideas like this form the scientific background to Jean Jacques Rousseau's (1712–78) insistence in *Emile* (1762) that "once it is demonstrated that man and woman are not and ought not to be constituted in the same way in either their character or their temperament, it follows that they ought not to have the same education" and, by a facile implication, that they ought not to be included in discussions of the political rights of man.

Philosophers such as Rousseau and Immanuel Kant (1724–1804) argued that moral action required the ability to reason abstractly: Since, they posited, women lacked this ability, their inferior moral sense was confirmed. Whereas women acted morally on the basis of emotion, men relied on reason to determine the appropriate moral response in a given situation. It was the heart that led women to acts of compassion, to tender nurturing, and loving sacrifice. It was the mind that enabled men to develop just laws and a sense of social duty. Therefore, if the political sphere was to be rationally and scientifically constructed, women must continue to be excluded.

However, a somewhat contradictory view was simultaneously developing that posited the moral superiority of women. Since Englightenment thinkers increasingly came to view religion as a nonrational (if not *ir*rational) endeavor, faith, revelation, and spiritual sensitivities were evidently more appropriate for women. Women were, therefore, more likely to acknowledge and obey the moral obligations arising from religious devotion than were men. Beginning in the eighteenth century and continuing into the nineteenth, society expected women to provide some kind of moral leadership on authority founded in religious experience. Thus, women established, organized, and led reform-oriented, benevolent associations, such as the Women's Christian Temperance Union and the British Society of Ladies for Promoting the Reformation of Female Prisoners. Those denying any moral superiority to women explained these forms of moral leadership as merely the extension of maternal feelings to those beyond the family circle. Both sides agreed that *real* institutional reform still necessitated the rational intervention of men using a scientific approach to the political, legal, and economic spheres.

Given the importance of the interests that ensured the perpetuation of this kind of sexual politics, it is hardly surprising that the new developments in the biological sciences of the nineteenth century were interpreted in such a way as to confirm these ideas. Charles Darwin's (1809–82) evolutionary theory, especially as extended and applied to humans in *The Descent of Man* (1871), seemed to corroborate earlier theories concerning the lower standing of women. All differences between males and females demonstrated for Darwin that the former were closer to perfection than the latter. Female traits resembled more closely those either of a child or of a lower species. The formation of the skull and the lack of facial hair, for example, placed women between the rank of children and the level of adult males—higher than the one but lower than the other. The emotional proclivities of women placed them lower than rational men but higher than the animals, which acted by instinct rather than by reason. Whereas in all races the female members were not as fully evolved as the males, Darwin was clear to point out that white women, while not as evolved as white men, were more highly evolved than men of other races.

The newly emerging science of psychology was also used to bolster traditional gender differences. In Greek Hippocratic medicine, hysteria had been defined as a woman's disease that resulted from a wandering uterus (the word "hysteria" is derived from the Greek word for uterus). Seventeenth- and eighteenth-century physicians had theorized that women's reproductive organs in general made women more susceptible to illness, and hysteria and many other mental conditions were classified as resulting primarily from their uterine condition. By the nineteenth century, the notion of nervous or psychological conditions was accepted, but women's vulnerability to these problems was still believed to be related to connections between the organs of reproduction and the central nervous system. The menstrual cycle was perceived to create an unstable condition in women, making them more easily overcome by internal and external stimuli that would leave men unaffected. Treatises on the prevention of nervous conditions in women, therefore, emphasized the need to eliminate excessive stimulation and to economize mental and physical energy in order to have sufficient resources to respond to the assaults in and on the person, including the rigors of childbearing.

Thus, advanced education was deemed acceptable for only single women, who, in choosing education over marriage, were thought to have picked the lesser alternative. For health reasons, therefore, women should not study too hard (especially at subjects that required a great deal of reasoning), try to perform masculine activities (such as working outside of the home or filling leadership roles), or exercise too much (for instance, by running rather than walking sedately). Using energy to perform such tasks put the woman at risk, since that energy was also needed to maintain stability and to respond to normal stimuli because of their innate weakness. Even when psychological theories changed with Sigmund Freud (1856–1939) and the introduction of psychoanalysis, cultural opinions reflected many of the earlier views. Moreover, the newer psychological theories still posited males as the norm. Freud's concept of penis envy assumed that females would recognize that the male anatomy was "normal" and that their own anatomy was, therefore, "abnormal." Such theories also reinforced traditional societal spheres for women as the natural spheres, limited, according to Freud, to *Kinder, Küche,* and *Kirche* (children, kitchen, and church).

In spite of the various changes in intellectual outlook from the Greeks to the scientific revolution, through the Enlightenment, and on to the establishment of evolutionary biology and the major scientific achievements of the early twentieth century, the alleged incapacity of women for public life and high achievement remained so persistent as to be scarcely credible. The fact that the situation has changed so considerably in the last two decades of the twentieth century undoubtedly owes more to the consciousness-raising efforts of recent feminism than it does to new developments in science. Furthermore, given the close alliance between science and religion through most of the period under discussion and the patriarchal nature of much traditional faith and practice (which merely reflected its cultural framework), it seems safe to say that religion played little or no significant part in the improved *scientific* understanding of female nature.

Women in Science

Scientific claims about the mental and physical inability of women to excel beyond the domestic sphere have been seen as one reason that women have been excluded from science and medicine and have, therefore, made only minor contributions to the history of science. But this is not the only reason behind women's lack of success in the history of science. The very fact that science has come to be seen in our culture as a masculine pursuit is another major factor, but even this does not cover all of the ground. Women's traditional absence from the history of science must be seen as one more example of the traditional exclusion of women from all but a few circumscribed aspects of social life. Until comparatively recently, women have been systematically excluded from the institutions of science and medicine, while their individual achievements have rarely been taken seriously.

Here again, however, the situation has begun to change. Recent work by feminist historians has done much to uncover the previously unnoticed history of women in science. In spite of a few pioneering efforts, beginning during the first feminist movement of the late nineteenth century, it is only since the 1980s that a feminist historiography, detailing women's contributions to science, has impinged in a significant way upon the consciousness of other historians. A major proportion of this work focuses upon individual heroines, women whose achievements are remarkable by any standards and all the more so given the barriers laid in their way by their own society. Sneers against women's achievements in science on the grounds that they are a long way from a Galileo, a Newton, or a Leibniz are silenced by the incidental details in the histories of women like Margaret Cavendish, Duchess of Newcastle (1623–73), and Anne, Viscountess Conway (c. 1630–79), in the seventeenth century; Émilie du Châtelet (1706–49) in the eighteenth; and Mary Somerville (1780–1872), Sofya Kovalevski (1840–1901), and Marie Curie (1867–1934) in the nineteenth. On reading their and other women's stories, one cannot help wondering what these women might have achieved had their society viewed them and their work differently or had their circumstances allowed them to pursue their work more single-mindedly. It cannot be denied, however, that such heroines are few. Accordingly, other feminist historians have preferred to look at the social history of women in science, the nature of the work they are allowed to do, the way they work and interact with male colleagues, and other patterns of their participation in science. This aspect of the feminist historiography of science also includes studies of the institutional context against which women all too often had to fight, such as a system of higher education that excluded women or provided them with a separate, more "suitable," education, or a system of scientific societies that excluded women, no matter what their achievements.

Some patterns are beginning to emerge from this historical research. Women have occasionally been able to colonize particular areas of science, such as botany in the eighteenth and nineteenth centuries or primatology in the twentieth century, but much work remains to be done before we can fully understand these unusual formations in the structure of science. It is also clear from contemporary research by historians and sociologists of science that women are increasingly entering science as a profession. In the last several decades of the twentieth century, women have entered scientific careers at an unprecedented rate.

The inextricability of science and religion in the history of Western culture makes it inevitable that both must be considered together to understand the historical absence of women from science. David Noble has argued that Western science, because of its links to natural theology, "was always in essence a religious calling," and he has seen it as a "clerical culture." Margaret Wertheim, similarly, has suggested that "the priestly conception of the physicist continues to serve as a powerful cultural obstacle to women." Just as women were not permitted into the priesthood, so they were hindered from being priests of God's other book, the book of nature. It is easy to see, however, that, like their male counterparts, female scientists could have religious motivations for their interests. Anne Conway, for example, developed a vitalistic and monistic natural philosophy and used it to dismiss the traditional dichotomy between matter and spirit in order to counter the perceived atheism of dualistic mechanical philosophies. It seems safe to conclude, therefore, that religion, both in its alliance with science and in accordance with its own generally nonfeminist agenda, usually tended to accept the exclusion of women from science as much as from other areas of public life. In this respect, it merely reflected the broader culture.

Women and Science

A final and highly important aspect of feminist critiques of science has arisen in response to the perception that science itself is gendered and that its gender is masculine. Evelyn Fox Keller's 1978 article was primarily concerned with this "unexamined myth," which she saw as familiar and deeply entrenched in Western culture. Similarly, Carolyn Merchant's historical study of the Scientific Revolution, *The Death of Nature* (1980), was, in part, an attempt to understand the roots of the belief that science is a masculine pursuit. A number of other feminists have taken up this theme, pointing out that there was a prevailing assumption that women did not, indeed could not, think scientifically (notable exceptions being tacitly presumed to think like men). It is undoubtedly the feminist awareness of these claims that has led to the proliferation of historical studies of women's role in science, both as practitioners and as scientific subjects, but this awareness

also has led to a profound reexamination of scientific epistemology. Rejecting the allegedly inherent sexism of current epistemologies propagated by men and believing that their own philosophies should bring some benefit to women, feminist philosophers have sought to develop new and more appropriate ways of knowing the world.

Some feminists simply believed that allegedly sexist and androcentric conclusions in science were merely the result of ideological distortion. The resulting errors arose because the truly "objective" scientific method had been insufficiently rigorously applied. It was their belief that proper vigilance against cultural bias and a more careful pursuit of the scientific method would lead to improved scientific knowledge. Implicit in these beliefs was a conviction that there was nothing innately masculine about science and its methodology, that science was not, in fact, gendered, but that scientists, predominantly male, were all too easily led astray by cultural pressures. This position was called "feminist empiricism" by Sandra Harding, a leading feminist philosopher of science.

Harding herself rejected this position and has tried to advocate a more ambitious approach, first signaled by Georg Wilhelm Friedrich Hegel (1770–1831) and, subsequently, by Marxist philosophers, called "standpoint epistemology." Originally developed in the social sciences, in which feminist practitioners became aware of the cultural biases in their questionnaires and other testing procedures, the standpoint approach takes it for granted that there is no one, privileged position from which value-free knowledge can be established. Assuming this, the standpoint theorist seeks to determine the best position for understanding the particular phenomena under investigation. Feminist sociologists, therefore, would valorize the perspective of the socially disadvantaged in the hope of learning something new about the social conditions of that group. Harding has tried to promote this approach in science, suggesting that women's perspectives may lead to an improved science.

The difficulty with this position, of course, is that it is not clear which women's perspectives would provide the best perspective. There are many different women, from different social, religious, or racial backgrounds, for example, who are all likely to have different standpoints on scientific issues. Similarly, should we take the standpoint of a female scientist, who nonfeminist critics might well claim has a rather masculine standpoint, or the standpoint of a woman far removed from scientific concerns, in which case it might legitimately be argued that her standpoint can hardly be considered the best available for understanding science? In spite of the formal difficulty of deciding upon this issue, feminist scholars have provided some excellent case studies to show just how women's perspectives have made major contributions to the improvement of our scientific understanding. Notable among them are studies of menopause related by Anne Fausto-Sterling and studies of primatology analyzed by Donna Haraway. There has, however, been a tendency among less careful feminist thinkers to suggest that women's "standpoint" allows greater recognition of nonrational, creative, and "intuitive" ways of thinking than masculine standpoints. But this, as other feminists have been quick to point out, is merely to accept the traditional male view of what women are supposed to be like (according to masculine science).

Another leading feminist philosopher, Helen Longino, has drawn upon recent work in the sociology of scientific knowledge to propose an alternative epistemology. Beginning from the traditional view that scientific objectivity, purged of cultural or political biases, is guaranteed by science's unique method (which relies upon repeated observations of the phenomena by different researchers and a thoroughly rational, even mathematical, analysis of the results), Longino reminds her readers of the work of N. R. Hanson (1924–67) and Thomas S. Kuhn (1922–96), who suggested that observations are theory laden, and Pierre Duhem (1861–1916) and W. V. O. Quine (1908–), who suggested that all theories are underdetermined by the data (that is, not sufficiently grounded upon the data to ensure that no alternative theory is possible). She then goes on to develop, as nonfeminist sociologists of scientific knowledge had before her, a theory of scientific knowledge based on the consensus of scientific practitioners. "Scientific knowledge, on this view," she writes, "is an outcome of the critical dialogue in which individuals and groups holding different points of view engage with each other. It is constructed not by individuals but by an interactive dialogic community" (Longino 1993, 112). Longino calls this position "contextual empiricism." It is "contextual" because it acknowledges that scientific knowledge can be understood only by considering the context from which it emerged. It is "empiricist" in the same way as the feminist empiricists because it implies that there is nothing inherently masculine in scientific thinking, or method, merely that women's voices have thus far been excluded from the critical dialogue of scientific-consensus formation.

Debates about feminist epistemologies in science are continuing, but the literature on these matters so far has paid no attention to religious or theological concerns. Similarly, in the ongoing debates about feminist theology, the major concern is to link feminist theology to other theories of liberation theology, and scant attention has been paid to scientific issues. It seems clear, however, that feminist theologians have as much right as anyone else to look at science from their particular standpoint (if it can be said that they have a single standpoint) or that female scientists who are theists have as much right to engage in the consensus formation of science as male theistic scientists or, for that matter, nontheistic scientists. Until a literature begins to emerge that specifically discusses these three related issues, it is worth noting the similarities between the treatment of women in science and Christianity. The Christian churches, like scientific theory and institutions, have often reflected cultural norms by depicting women as inferior to men. On the other hand, they have, on other occasions, elevated the status of women above conventional societal patterns (witness the medieval cult of the Virgin Mary or the idea of companionate marriage in the Protestant Reformation). While it is hardly surprising that feminist theologians have found Christian theology to be masculine in the way it has been gendered, just as feminist historians and philosophers have found science to be, perhaps one ought to caution against drawing facile generalizations that ignore the theological complexities of what is hardly a monolithic tradition, as well as the cultural conditioning of time and place. Essentialist and presentist approaches are as out of place here as they are in any historical endeavor.

See also Epistemology; Premodern Theories of Generation; Social Construction of Science

BIBLIOGRAPHY

Bem, Sandra Lapses. *The Lenses of Gender: Transforming the Debate on Sexual Inequality.* New Haven, Conn.: Yale University Press, 1993.

Borresen, Kari E., ed. *Image of God and Gender Models in Judaeo-Christian Tradition.* Oslo: Solum Fodag, 1991.

Cadden, Joan. *Meanings of Sex Difference in the Middle Ages: Medicine, Science, and Culture.* Cambridge: Cambridge University Press, 1993.

Clatterbaugh, Kenneth. *Perspectives on Masculinity: Men, Women, and Politics in Modern Society.* Boulder, Colo.: Westview, 1990.

Fausto-Sterling, Anne. *Myths of Gender: Biological Theories About Women and Men.* New York: Basic Books, 1985.

Fox, Mary Frank. "Women and Scientific Careers." In *Handbook of Science and Technological Studies,* ed. by Sheila Jasanoff, Gerald E. Markle, James C. Petersen, and Trevor Pinch. Thousand Oaks, Calif.: Sage, 1995, 205–23.

Harding, Sandra. *Whose Science? Whose Knowledge? Thinking from Women's Lives.* Ithaca, N.Y.: Cornell University Press, 1991.

Haraway, Donna J. *Primate Visions: Gender, Race, and Nature in the World of Modern Science.* New York: Routledge, 1989.

———. *Simians, Cyborgs, and Women.* New York: Routledge, 1991.

Keller, Evelyn Fox. *Reflections on Gender and Science.* New Haven, Conn.: Yale University Press, 1985.

———. "Gender and Science: Origin, History, and Politics." *Osiris* 10 (1995): 27–38.

Keller, Evelyn Fox, and Helen E. Longino, eds. *Feminism and Science.* Oxford: Oxford University Press, 1996.

Laqueur, Thomas. *Making Sex: Body and Gender from the Greeks to Freud.* Cambridge, Mass.: Harvard University Press, 1990.

Longino, Helen E. *Science as Social Knowledge: Values and Objectivity in Scientific Inquiry.* Princeton, N.J.: Princeton University Press, 1990.

———. "Subjects, Power, and Knowledge: Description and Prescription in Feminist Philosophies of Science." In *Feminist Epistemologies,* ed. by L. Alcoff and E. Potter. New York: Routledge, 1993.

Merchant, Carolyn. *The Death of Nature: Women, Ecology, and the Scientific Revolution.* New York: Harper and Row, 1980.

Noble, David F. *A World Without Women: The Christian Clerical Culture of Western Science.* New York: Oxford University Press, 1992.

Porter, Roy, and Mikulas Teich, eds. *Sexual Knowledge, Sexual Science: The History of Attitudes to Sexuality.* Cambridge: Cambridge University Press, 1994.

Rossiter, Margaret. *Women Scientists in America: Struggles and Strategies to 1940.* Baltimore: Johns Hopkins University Press, 1982.

———. *Women Scientists in America: Before Affirmative Action, 1940–1972.* Baltimore: Johns Hopkins University Press, 1995.

Schiebinger, Londa. *The Mind Has No Sex? Women in the Origins of Modem Science.* Cambridge, Mass.: Harvard University Press, 1989.

———. *"Nature's Body": Gender in the Making of Modern Science.* Boston: Beacon, 1993.

Scully, Diana, and Pauline Bart. "A Funny Thing Happened on the Way to the Orifice: Women in Gynecology Textbooks." *American Journal of Sociology* 78 (1974): 1045–9.

Tuana, Nancy. *The Less Noble Sex: Scientific, Religious, and Philosophical Conceptions of Woman's Nature.* Bloomington: Indiana University Press, 1993.

Wertheim, Margaret. *Pythagoras' Trousers: God, Physics, and the Gender Wars.* New York: Random House, 1995.

44. POSTMODERNISM

Stephen P. Weldon

Postmodernism is a chameleonlike word that refers variously to the artistic and cultural production of the late twentieth century, to the philosophical or critical orientation of Western scholars in this period, or to specifically Christian theological positions that distinguish themselves from religious modernism and that may or may not draw on the views of secular critical theorists. This essay discusses the philosophical and theological postmodernisms. As a critical orientation to philosophical problems, postmodernism has no single school or line of thought. Instead, its perspective surfaces in numerous areas of modern scholarship. The orientation is explicitly antagonistic toward several principles deemed to have dominated Western philosophy since René Descartes (1596–1650) and, according to some scholars, since the emergence of metaphysics in ancient Greece.

Postmodernist Theory

In general, postmodernist intellectuals have waged a war against "totalizing" systems or perspectives. Reacting to conditions of modernity that they find inimical to freedom—namely the bureaucracy, technocracy, and rationalism of twentieth-century capitalist societies—the postmodernists have developed methods of analysis and discourse aimed at breaking down those monolithic systems and have done so in the cause of heterogeneity and pluralism. They offer what often turns out to be a despairing view of the human condition, one that depicts people as trapped in webs of language, social structures, cultural conventions, and economic forces so constraining that individual freedom and autonomy become virtually impossible. Language, in particular, has drawn the attention of postmodernists because of the extreme dependence of people on it. Hence, understanding the limitations of language is essential for comprehending the ineluctability of the human condition.

A survey of a few key tenets espoused by a majority of postmodern scholars provides an insight into the nature of their understanding of the world. First of all, postmodernism claims that there are no foundations for ethical principles or knowledge claims and that morality and knowledge are grounded only in particular circumstances of history and culture. This means that, for all human endeavors (including religion and science), there can be no transcendental or transcultural truths. Language and culture constrain behavior and thought, making the world appear differently to people in different times and places. However cogent these appearances, postmodernists warn, they must not be mistaken for universal truths, since such universals do not exist.

Second, postmodernists have generally repudiated all representational theories of language, which means that words do not derive their meaning by referring to objects in the world but, rather, take their meanings from specific contexts in which they are found. Focusing on the relationships between texts, linguistic theorists, using a method called deconstruction, have turned their attention to the act of reading a text, because it is only in that act itself that the meanings of the words take shape. Deconstruction completely undermines the idea that there is any stability in language. There are no permanent structures or rules governing language use; everything is in constant flux. As a result, meaning becomes so slippery that no specific text can be said to have a single correct interpretation. Furthermore, deconstructionists have claimed that any text can be shown to exhibit radical discontinuities; every text contains elements that undermine its basic assumptions, thereby rendering meaning completely fragmentary and ephemeral. Drawing out the implications for human beings, deconstructionists have posited that individuals are products of the language they use; even thoughts about one's self are constrained by language. This means that, given the fragmented nature of language, human self-conceptions cease to have any unity or coherence. The individual becomes "de-centered."

All of this theorizing has significant implications for the understanding of rationalism, which postmodernists also attack. In a word, they deny its autonomy and, hence, its legitimacy as a privileged mode of finding knowledge and solving problems. One of the principal expositors of this view, Michel Foucault (1926–84), has argued that knowledge and power are inextricably interrelated to the extent that knowledge is impossible without power. By describing knowledge in this way, Foucault radically undermined the notion that rational thought produces any privileged perspective. That which is called rational, Foucault asserted, is as socially mediated as any other claim to knowledge.

Science and Religion

Perceptions of the relationship between religion and science have been substantially affected by postmodernism. In the first place, many religious apologists have embraced the academic attacks on rationalism and humanism, finding common cause with the postmodernists in fighting the hegemony of contemporary secular culture. Postmodernists have denounced humanism for its misguided view of human beings and its naively optimistic ideas about the capability of human control over the natural and social worlds. Humanism is not warranted, according to postmodernists, because the constraints imposed by society, language, and culture limit the ability of people actually to achieve any real measure of freedom. Religionists, too, have often upbraided humanism for precisely this reason: its arrogant appraisal of mankind's status on this earth. Even Pope John Paul II (b. 1920, p. 1978–) has expressed himself as being in agreement with critical postmodern scholarship on certain points. On the whole, however, most traditional religionists have only limited use for postmodern theory, since postmodernism can as equally undermine the foundations of traditional religion as it can scientific humanism. For their part, the humanists, with their strong faith in the power of science and the scientific method, find postmodernism dangerous because it provides a legiti-

mation of irrationality. Although some humanists have found a way to incorporate the postmodern critique, as a group they tend to distrust it and decry it as a serious threat to human progress.

Despite the wide differences between traditional religion and academic postmodernism, a number of theologians have designed theologies that they explicitly label postmodern. Of these various theologies, two are especially important with regard to perceptions of the science-religion relationship. First, a number of theologians like David Griffin have asserted that transformations in science and culture necessitate a transformation in theology. In particular, developments in ecology, quantum mechanics, and psychology have altered the face of Western science so that it is no longer the mechanistic and positivistic study that it once was. In fact, Griffin's reading of science now admits a place for spiritual values. In this account, then, postmodern theology has less to do with rejecting the scientific worldview than with recognizing a new renaissance in which science and religion can once again be found compatible partners. For Griffin, this reconciliation takes the form of a Whiteheadian or Hartshornian process theology. Theologians of this sort use the adjective "postmodern" primarily to contrast their theology with early-twentieth-century religious modernism, as their postmodern theology has little to do with the academic version of postmodernism discussed above. In fact, in some respects, it differs little from its modernist precursor in the basic notion that religion must be made compatible with a scientific understanding of the world; the difference lies in the nature of what each considers scientific and the way in which the reconciliation takes place.

Following an altogether different direction, Mark C. Taylor's postmodern theology derives its insights directly from the deconstructionist wing of academic postmodernism. Like the secular academics, Taylor has called into question all forms of foundationalism (the idea that human knowledge must rest on a foundation of axiomatic beliefs). His attempt to create a new religious system has led him to what he calls an "a/theology," in which he explores the space between atheism and theism. He has endeavored to read the Bible in a deconstructive mode that reveals, in a surprising fashion, basic Christian moral tenets. His practice of deconstruction has led him to establish a religious outlook that comes close to the negative mystical tradition in which God is defined only by that which he is not. Indeed, this parallelism is even indicated in the writings of Jacques Derrida (1930–), one of the founders of deconstructive criticism.

Critiques of Postmodernism

Aspects of secular postmodernism have come under heavy scrutiny by many scholars who vehemently disagree with its assumptions and use, as well as by partisans of one or another school of postmodern thought itself. Some scholars have asserted that postmodernism actually sets up a straw man, attacking an antiquated idea of modernism. This positivistic and reductionistic view of modernism, these critics argue, is more or less a caricature of eighteenth-century Enlightenment views and not a serious twentieth-century standpoint. This critique often raises the question of whether postmodernism is really a radical departure from modernist thought or merely an extension of it.

In defending the latter interpretation, analysts have pointed to the fact that postmodern theory has deep roots in the literary modernist tradition and has been strongly influenced by Karl Marx (1818–83), Friedrich Nietzsche (1844–1900), and Martin Heidegger (1889–1976), among others. These roots demonstrate continuity in terms of both a general Romantic sentiment against antihuman social conditions and a similarity of ideas. On a political level, postmodernists are seen by some to be making unjustified claims about the subversiveness of their radicalism when they are, in fact, merely playing meaningless intellectual games. Critics have also pointed out logical inconsistencies in postmodernist views: The statement, for example, that there can be no truth claims is itself a truth claim. In essence, there seem to be certain foundational elements hidden beneath all of the rhetoric of antifoundationalism. Whether or not the postmodernists have adequately addressed these apparent contradictions in their work is a matter of great debate. Regardless of the outcome, the relationship between religion and science in late-twentieth-century thought cannot be fully understood without accounting for the postmodernist point of view.

See also Process Philosophy and Theology; Social Construction of Science

BIBLIOGRAPHY

Allen, Diogenes. "The End of the Modern World." *Christian Scholars Review* 22 (4) (1993): 339–47.

Berry, Philippa, and Andrew Wernick, eds. *Shadow of Spirit: Postmodernism and Religion.* New York: Routledge, 1992.

Eagleton, Terry. *Literary Theory: An Introduction.* Minneapolis: University of Minnesota Press, 1983.

Ferry, Luc, and Alain Renaut. *Heidegger and Modernity.* Trans. by Franklin Philip. Chicago: University of Chicago Press, 1990.

Feyerabend, Paul K. *Against Method.* New York: Verso, 1993.

Foucault, Michel. *The Order of Things: An Archaeology of the Human Sciences.* New York: Vintage Books, 1970.

Griffin, David Ray. *God and Religion in the Postmodern World: Essays in Postmodern Theology.* Albany: State University of New York Press, 1989.

———. "Green Spirituality: A Postmodern Convergence of Science and Religion." *Journal of Theology* 96 (1992): 5–20.

Griffin, David Ray, William A. Beardslee, and Joe Holland. *Varieties of Postmodern Theology.* Albany: State University of New York Press, 1989.

Habermas, Jürgen. *The Philosophical Discourse of Modernity: Twelve Lectures.* Cambridge, Mass.: MIT Press, 1987.

Harvey, David. *The Condition of Postmodernity: An Enquiry into the Origins of Cultural Change.* Cambridge, Mass.: Blackwell, 1989.

Hollinger, David A. "The Knower and the Artificer, with Postscript 1993." In *Modernist Impulses in the Human Sciences, 1870–1930,* ed. by Dorothy Ross. Baltimore: Johns Hopkins University Press, 1994, 26–53.

Jameson, Fredric. "Postmodernism, or the Cultural Logic of Late Capitalism." *New Left Review,* 146 (1984): 53–92.

Kuhn, Thomas S. *The Structure of Scientific Revolutions.* Chicago: University of Chicago Press, 1962.

Lyotard, Jean-François. *The Postmodern Condition: A Report on Knowledge.* Trans. by Geoff Bennington and Brian Massumi. Minneapolis: University of Minnesota Press, 1984.

McGowan, John. *Postmodernism and Its Critics.* Ithaca, N.Y.: Cornell University Press, 1991.

Murphy, Nancey, and James Wm. McClendon Jr. "Distinguishing Modern and Postmodern Theologies." *Modern Theology* 5(3) (April 1989): 191–214.

Norris, Christopher. *What's Wrong with Postmodernism: Critical Theory and the Ends of Philosophy.* Baltimore: Johns Hopkins University Press, 1990.

Nuyen, A. T. "Postmodern Theology and Postmodern Philosophy." *Philosophy of Religion* 30 (1991): 65–76.

Rorty, Richard. *Philosophy and the Mirror of Nature.* Princeton, N.J.: Princeton University Press, 1979.

Tilley, Terrence W. *Postmodern Theologies: The Challenge of Religious Diversity.* New York: Orbis Books, 1995.

PART IV

Specific Religious Traditions and Chronological Periods

45. Judaism to 1700

David B. Ruderman

Despite its historical significance, no comprehensive account yet exists of the encounter between Judaism and scientific thought and activity, especially before the modern era. The reasons for this are probably varied. Jewish historiography has focused primarily on matters of Jewish religious thought, law and mysticism, intercommunal and interfaith relations, and, more recently, on the social and economic foundations of Jewish communal life. Isolating Jewish "scientific" concerns imbedded in theological, philosophical, and legal discourses is not always an easy matter. Most historians of Judaism lack the particular expertise or interest to comprehend fully the import of scientific discussions among Jewish thinkers, while most historians of science usually do not possess a proper linguistic and cultural understanding to assess the place of scientific concerns within the intellectual and spiritual lives of premodern Jews.

In recent years, however, a considerable amount of new research has emerged on several key dimensions of this larger subject: on ancient Jewish magic and medicine; on the Jewish medical profession in the Middle Ages; on medieval astrology and astronomy; on Jewish translators of scientific texts; and on early-modern medical and scientific thought, to name only a few subjects. We are in a better position to offer a provisional overview of a vast and fruitful field of inquiry, one that needs to be incorporated into the larger history of interactions between science and religion in Western civilization as a whole.

The Study of Nature in Ancient Judaism

A systematic presentation of ancient Jewish attitudes toward nature has yet to be written. The cultures of ancient Israelite religion and Hellenistic and rabbinic Judaism before the tenth century of the Christian era, sprawling over centuries and subject to variegated social and intellectual influences in Palestine, Babylonia, and elsewhere, are notoriously difficult to reconstruct historically. The narrative, legal, exegetical, and homiletical literatures produced by these cultures are extremely slippery to situate within a specific historical context. In the case of the study of nature, one must also examine and evaluate the cultural significance of materials generally outside the documents preserved by "official" rabbinic circles, such as mystical literature, magical handbooks, amulets, and magic bowls. There is also the problem of considering the organic relations among such disciplines as astronomy and astrology, geography, biology and botany, medicine and magic, as well as the religious, spiritual, and intellectual motivations of persons engaged in these disciplines. For the most part, modern scholarship has studied each of these areas in isolation from the other, nor has it considered these special areas within a more comprehensive religious and social matrix.

Despite the dangers of broad generalization, at the outset at least three observations might be stated with reasonable confidence when considering the place of nature in the cultures of ancient Judaism. In the first place, most rabbis viewed the study of the natural world positively, especially when integrated with, and subordinated to, their primary mandate of elucidating Jewish law. Taking as their inspiration the large number of biblical verses extolling nature, they were enthralled with natural operations; they tried to understand and master them; and they viewed information about the natural world as a prerequisite for knowing and appreciating God, particularly for better comprehending his divine dictates. One can find isolated voices within the rabbinic tradition opposing nature study when it interfered with the study of Torah such as the following: "He who walks by the way and interrupts his study by saying: 'How pleasant is this tree!,' it is as if he is deserving of death" (Avot 3:9). But even so strong a formulation would not negate its generally positive mandate of the study of nature, especially when appreciated as an enhancement and aid to Torah study rather than a mere distraction.

Second, most rabbis endorsed without reservation the practice of medicine and demanded that the ill person seek out medical expertise. They generally refused to interpret the biblical verse "For I the Lord am your healer" (Ex. 15:26) to mean that God alone should heal the sick; on the contrary, they consistently valued medical expertise and the advice of physicians. The rabbis considered medical and naturalistic knowledge, including knowledge of the stars, among their self-proclaimed skills and fully integrated them with their ritualistic and legal ones. They established a close connection between rabbinic knowledge and medicine and, thus, already in antiquity, underscored the notion that medicine and spiritual healing constituted a special Jewish skill.

Finally, they not only endorsed the acquisition of naturalistic knowledge; they were receptive to improving nature, to mastering its forces, and even to replicating it. Despite the explicit biblical prohibitions against most forms of magical activity, individual rabbis either ignored, camouflaged, rationalized, or encouraged the pursuit of magic among Jews. Some rabbis took special pride in their "wonder working" accomplishments. Others complained about the dangers of the occult but ignored its practitioners. And judging from the material remains of magical activities, such as amulets and magic bowls, a widespread belief in the efficacy of, and critical need for, such operations to ensure the physical and social well-being of both the individual and the community seemed to represent the continuous norm within Jewish societies in Palestine and throughout the diaspora from antiquity and throughout the Middle Ages.

The Sciences and Medieval Jewish Culture

The dramatic stimulus afforded Jewish life by the dynamic intellectual centers of medieval Islam such as Baghdad, Cordoba, and Cairo, as well as those in the Christian West in Spain, Sicily, Italy, and Provence, perpetuated the rabbinic approaches to the study of nature while deepening their religious and intellectual significance. Spurred by the Islamic renaissance of classical philosophy, several Jewish thinkers recast the Jewish tradition into a philosophic key, elevating the quest for knowing God and his divine creation to the ultimate ideal of Jewish religiosity. Bahya Ibn Pakuda (second half of the eleventh century) and Moses Maimonides (1135–1204), in particular, stressed the religious obligation of studying nature. For others, knowing God's handiwork not only enhanced both the mind and the heart, it could also facilitate the complete observance of Jewish law, which relied on information about the natural world, and it had pragmatic value in enhancing the social and economic status for those versed in astronomy and medicine.

With the decline of the Islamic centers in Spain by the twelfth century, a conspicuous group of Jewish scholars who immigrated to northern Spain, Provence, Sicily, and Italy found themselves in advantageous positions as translators and cultural intermediaries between Muslim and Christian cultures. These individuals not only created a new library of accessible scientific texts in Hebrew and Latin for their Christian patrons, they also stimulated among their own coreligionists an enlargement of intellectual interests, a rethinking of religious traditions in the light of new philosophical ideas, and even an acrimonious debate, especially in the generation following the death of Moses Maimonides, regarding the alleged pernicious effect of such ideas on Jewish religious sensibilities.

In both Muslim and Christian societies, Jewish physicians benefited from the increased social status and economic success that their intellectual attainments often brought them. Their patients were both Jews and non-Jews; in some cases, their medical careers assured them political influence, as the cases of Hasdai Ibn Shaprut (c. 915–c. 970) and Moses Maimonides amply demonstrate. In the Christian environments of Spain, Italy, and especially Provence, a significant number of Jews practiced medicine and were licensed to do so despite the fact that they were barred from attending the medical schools of the universities. Other exceptional Jews derived social and political status as astronomers and astrologers, and, while their numbers were small, their influence on the intellectual and religious life of their communities was far from negligible, as the careers of Abraham bar Hiyya (beginning of the twelfth century), Abraham Ibn Ezra (1089–1164), Levi ben Gerson (1288–1344), Isaac Ibn Sid (second half of the thirteenth century), Abraham Zacuto (1452–c. 1515), and others testify. Maimonides had emphatically maintained that the more recent knowledge of the astronomers could override the outdated scientific assumptions of the rabbis, who, in astronomical matters, "did not speak . . . as transmitters of dicta of the prophets" (*Guide of the Perplexed* 3:14). In the view of Ibn Ezra and especially a group of his commentators in the fourteenth century, even the biblical text and religious concepts and rituals were not immune to explanations based on astrology and astral magic.

By the thirteenth century, the study of the cabala (the mystical and theosophic teachings of Judaism) had established a significant place within the same Jewish cultures in which philosophy and the sciences had previously dominated. The cabalists objected to the intrusion of Aristotelian notions into the sacred space of Jewish texts and exegesis, but they were not necessarily hostile to, or unappreciative of, nature and its mysterious forces. Their own traditions of magic and theurgy attuned them to the powers of nature and encouraged them to gain mastery of the latter in spite of their repudiation of the metaphysics of Greek philosophy. They recalled a tradition of ancient magical-medical wisdom among the Jews, a book of medicine lost but still faintly recalled, transmitted by angels, that underscored the still unique curative and occult talents of Jews. Some Jewish thinkers, such as Moses Nahmanides (1194–1270), stimulated by the cabala and the ancient traditions of magic, deemed the occult the highest form of "a Jewish spiritual science" and advocated its practice in opposition to the regnant physics based on the "false" philosophical assumptions of Aristotle (384–322 B.C.) and his disciples. In the thirteenth and fourteenth centuries, a circle of German pietists, unaffected by the philosophical assumptions of some of their coreligionists in the south, displayed a remarkable interest in the oddities of nature despite their alienation from the cultural orientation of Aristotelian natural philosophy.

As one might expect, medieval Jewish reflections on nature often resembled those of their Muslim and Christian neighbors, especially given their shared commitments to the study of classical philosophy and science. The permeability of boundaries between magic and experimental science was also not uncommon within the other communities as well. Nevertheless, a variety of forms of magic, astrology, and astral magic seem to have flourished especially in Jewish culture, particularly when introduced as an assertion of Jewish superiority or self-

differentiation from the dominant culture. But, despite the scientific achievements of individuals within the Jewish community, accomplished scientific figures like Levi ben Gerson were exceptional. Since Jews were barred from attending the universities, the overwhelming majority of Jews could not pursue autonomous research in philosophy and the sciences. They studied the sciences and the natural world within the framework of the traditional rabbinic curriculum or as a supplement to it; they absorbed scientific notions through popular handbooks of scientific knowledge disseminated within their communities; and they reflected on nature primarily in the course of their exegetical, legal, and theological studies.

Jewish Responses to Early-Modern Science

Medieval Jewish attitudes toward nature and scientific activity left their imprint on the early-modern period as well. Jews living at the end of the Middle Ages continued to see their scientific studies as a cultural legacy and a badge of honor. As proud heirs of Maimonides, Ibn Ezra, and Levi ben Gerson, they continued to appreciate the study of nature as a religious ideal and reveled in the notion of an ancient Jewish provenance for magic and medicine, astrology, and astronomy. But important differences are also noticeable, especially by the sixteenth century and beyond. In this later period, the interaction of medicine and science with Jewish culture was more substantial and repercussive than earlier, and this enhanced encounter had a profound impact in shaping a new Jewish discourse on science.

Larger numbers of Jews were drawn to medicine and science in this later period for several reasons. In the first place, science and technology, catapulted by their revolutionary and dramatic successes, became more prominent in the political culture of Europe in general. Second, all Europeans, including Jews, were profoundly affected by the formidable impact of the printing press in publicizing and disseminating the new scientific discoveries. Third, in contrast to their medieval ancestors, large numbers of Jews were allowed entrance into the university medical schools, first in Italy and eventually in the rest of Europe. Accompanying this change was the integration of a highly educated and scientifically sophisticated Converso (Marrano) population of Jews who had converted to Christianity but had been expelled from Spain and Portugal and settled in Jewish communities in western and, to a lesser extent, eastern Europe. Finally, a general ideological transformation affected Jewish religious sensibilities regarding scientific study, one not unlike that affecting the Christian community. Beginning as early as the fifteenth century, Jewish thinkers increasingly displayed a crisis of confidence regarding the still dominant place of philosophy in Jewish intellectual life. They criticized philosophy without disparaging the study of nature, divorcing philosophical metaphysics from science, and, consequently, liberating and elevating scientific activity within the Jewish community. When science was no longer linked to an ideology that made claims to truths challenging those of the Jewish faith but, rather, was viewed as a hypothetical and contingent way of describing the physical world, a new coexistence between the secular and the sacred, between scientific pursuits and Jewish religious thought, even Jewish mystical thought, could successfully emerge.

As early as the second half of the sixteenth century, certain circles of Jewish scholars in central and eastern Europe pursued scientific learning, especially astronomy, as a desirable supplement to their primary curriculum of rabbinics. Jewish cultural centers such as Prague and Krakow appear to have been especially hospitable to such learning. Two rabbinic luminaries, Moses Isserles (1525–72) and Judah Loew ben Bezalel (the Maharal [c. 1525–1609]), openly encouraged the acquisition of scientific knowledge. Isserles integrated it into his rabbinic exegesis and even introduced a Hebrew textbook of astronomy for the use of his students. The Maharal explicitly demarcated the study of theology from physics, arguing for the legitimacy and the autonomy of the latter within the culture of traditional Judaism. Their student David Gans (1541–1613) accepted their religious mandate in composing his own Hebrew compendium of geographical and astronomical information, far surpassing that of Isserles, and even offering his readers a glimpse of the more current discoveries of Johannes Kepler (1571–1630) and Tycho Brahe (1546–1601) based on his own personal contact with them in Prague.

In the West, the impact of the new scientific learning on Jewish culture was more profound and more sustained through the regularized attendance of hundreds of Jews at the medical schools of Italy, especially at the University of Padua, from the late sixteenth through the eighteenth centuries. For the first time, a relatively large number of Jews were graduated from major medical schools and went on to practice medicine throughout Europe. During their studies they were afforded the opportunity for intense socialization among other Jews of remarkably diverse backgrounds—former Conversos from Spain and Portugal, together with those stemming from Italy, Germany, Poland, and the Ottoman Empire. University graduates often maintained social and intellectual ties with one another and constituted a significant cultural force within their widely scattered communities. Moreover, the new university setting invariably allowed Jewish students constant social and intellectual contact, both casual and formal, with non-Jewish students and faculty. Above all, the university offered talented Jewish students a prolonged exposure to the study of the liberal arts, to Latin studies, to classical scientific texts, as well as to the more recent scientific advances in botany, anatomy, chemistry, clinical medicine, physics, and astronomy.

The writing of several illustrious graduates of Padua illustrates quite dramatically the impact the new medical education could have on Jewish religious and cultural sensibilities. Joseph Delmedigo (1591–1655) produced a highly technical and sophisticated compendium of current physics, mathematics, and astronomy while, at the same time, delineating the latest cosmological theories of the cabala and even attempting to integrate them with those of contemporary science. Tobias Cohen (1652–1729) produced an up-to-date and comprehensive textbook of medicine, revealing an impressive familiarity with both classical medical texts and the more recent theories of the new chemical philosophers of the seventeenth century. Isaac Lampronti (1679–1756) devoted a lifetime to the composition of the first Talmudic encyclopedia, displaying throughout his medical expertise as well as his new intellectual orientation to reorganize rabbinic knowledge in conformity with the norms of current scientific practice. Simone Luzzatto (1583–1663), the rabbi of Venice, although not a graduate of Padua, nevertheless obtained a vast knowledge of mathematics and the sciences worthy of a university graduate. His Italian book on the trial of Socrates (469–399 B.C.) was totally unrelated to Jewish religious concerns and was directed to readers not exclusively Jewish. In fact, it espoused a skeptical view of knowledge seemingly inappropriate to one entrusted with the safeguarding of traditional Jewish belief and praxis. And David Nieto (1654–1728) utilized his impressive knowledge of current scientific theories and discoveries to defend rabbinic Judaism before a highly assimilated and secularized community of Jewish merchants recently settled in London.

The graduates of Padua and other Italian universities were not the only group within the Jewish communities of early-modern Europe conversant in medicine and natural philosophy. They were joined by hundreds of university-trained Converso physicians who fled Spain and Portugal in the seventeenth century and settled in Holland, Italy, Germany, England, and even eastern Europe, serving as physicians and purveyors of scientific learning within the Jewish community while often wielding considerable political and economic power. Among these recent converts to Judaism, their allegiance to traditional Jewish beliefs and practices varied from enthusiastic orthodoxy to conspicuous indifference or even antipathy. Nevertheless, it would be fair to say that these physicians of Spanish and Portuguese origin shared a common professional and cultural agenda with the other Jewish medical graduates from Italy and elsewhere in Europe and, like them, projected themselves as a kind of intellectual elite within their own communities. Having been exposed to the shame and racial stigma attached to the medical profession in their countries of origin, they increasingly associated their professional status with their newly evolving cultural and social identities. In other words, their professional identity, belonging to a highly successful, albeit maligned, group of clinical physicians, was directly linked with their own personal quest to define and understand their newly found place within the Jewish communities in which they now settled. The personal biographies of such illustrious Converso physicians as Amatus Lusitanus (1511–68), Zacutus Lusitanus (1575–1642), Rodrigo de Castro (1550–1627), and his son Benedict (1597–1684) reveal such linkages clearly and, to a great extent, exemplify the shared convictions of many others stemming from the same professional and ethnic background.

The study of attitudes toward medicine, astronomy, and the other sciences among Jews living in early-modern Europe, especially among these three subcommunities—rabbinic scholars in Prague and Krakow, graduates of Padua and other Italian medical schools, and Converso physicians—suggests at least a tolerance and sometimes an enthusiastic endorsement of the study of the sciences within Jewish culture, one even greater than in previous eras of Jewish history. Jewish religious thinkers in this period were increasingly willing to disentangle physics from metaphysics, the secular from the sacred, science from theology and, thus, in a manner similar to many of their Christian counterparts, to view scientific advances as positive resources to be enlisted in the cause of perpetuating their ancestral faith. Opposition or sheer indifference to the study of nature could still be located among certain Jewish intellectuals, especially those living in eastern Europe in the era after Isserles, the Maharal, and Gans. Yet, there was never an ideological struggle over the study of the sciences similar in magnitude to the struggle over the philosophical writings of Maimonides within the thirteenth-century Jewish community. While Aristotelian metaphysical assumptions about God and the universe appeared to threaten the very foundations of the Jewish faith, mere inquiry into the physical universe was deemed to be generally benign and neutral. In the main, Jews in early-modern Europe erected carefully drawn boundaries between the domains of scientific activity and religious faith so that the two could live peacefully and harmoniously with each other, avoiding the bitter consequences of their commingling, the troubled legacy of the medieval period. With the increasing dissonance between traditional faith and modern secularism by the end of the eighteenth century, however, the seeming alliance between science and Jewish faith would become more tenuous and difficult to maintain.

Reflections on scientific activity among early-modern Jewish thinkers, to be sure, are not the same as actual scientific performance itself. For the most part, the achievements of Jewish practitioners of science in both the medieval and the early-modern periods were unimpressive in comparison with those of more recent times. The lack of such achievements, however, should not be attributed to any religious or theological inhibitions on the part of Jewish religious thinkers. More critical is the fact that Jews conspicuously lacked the institutional support of churches, courts, and especially scientific academies and, thus, had little opportunity to "do" science other than medicine. The only avenues available to them to keep abreast of the latest discoveries in all of the sciences were the medical education offered by some universities and their own reading. They subsequently remained outside the scientific laboratory primarily because of social, not religious, constraints.

See also Cabala; Judaism Since 1700

BIBLIOGRAPHY

Alexander, Philip. "Incantations and Books of Magic." In the revised and expanded version of Emil Shürer, *The History of the Jewish People in the Age of Jesus Christ (175 B.C.–A.D. 135).*

Ed. by Geza Vermes, Fergus Millar, and Martin Goodman. Vol. 3, pt. 1, sec. 32. Edinburgh: T. and T. Clark, 1986, 342–79.

Charlesworth, James. H. "Jewish Astrology in the Talmud, Pseudepigrapha, and Dead Sea Scrolls, and Early Palestinian Synagogues." *Harvard Theological Review* 70 (1977): 183–200.

Fisch, Menachem. *Rational Rabbis: Science and Talmudic Culture.* Bloomington: Indiana University Press, 1997.

Freudenthal, Gad. "Science in the Medieval Jewish Culture of Southern France." *History of Science* 33 (1995): 23–58.

———, ed. *Studies on Gersonides: A Fourteenth-Century Jewish Philosopher-Scientist.* Leiden: Brill, 1992.

Friedenwald, Harry. *The Jews and Medicine.* 2 vols. 1944. Reprint. New York: Ktav, 1962.

Gandz, Solomon. *Studies in Hebrew Mathematics and Astronomy.* New York: Ktav, 1970.

Goitein, S. D. "The Medical Profession in the Light of the Cairo Genizah Documents." *Hebrew Union College Annual* 34 (1963): 177–94.

Goldstein, Bernard. "The Hebrew Astronomical Tradition: New Sources." *Isis* 72 (1981): 237–51.

———. *The Astronomy of Levi ben Gerson (1288–1344).* Berlin: Springer-Verlag, 1985.

Idel, Moshe. "Hermeticism and Judaism." In *Hermeticism and the Renaissance,* ed. by Inid Merkel and Alan Debus. Washington, D.C.: Associated University Presses, 1988.

———. *Golem: Jewish Magical and Mystical Traditions on the Artificial Anthropoid.* Albany: State University of New York Press, 1990.

Langermann, Y. Tzvi. "Science, Jewish." In *Dictionary of the Middle Ages,* ed. by J. Strayer et al. Vol. 11. New York: Scribners, 1989, 89–94.

———. "The Astronomy of Rabbi Moses Isserles." In *Physics, Cosmology, and Astronomy, 1300–1700,* ed. by Shabbetai Unguru. Dordrecht: Kluwer, 1991, 83–98.

———. "Some Astrological Themes in the Thought of Abraham Ibn Ezra." In *Rabbi Abraham Ibn Ezra: Studies in the Writings of a Twelfth-Century Jewish Polymath,* ed. by Jay Harris and Isadore Twersky. Cambridge, Mass.: Harvard Center for Jewish Studies, 1993.

Levine, Hillel. "Paradise not Surrendered: Jewish Reactions to Copernicus and the Growth of Modern Science." In *Epistemology, Methodology, and the Social Sciences,* ed. by Robert S. Cohen and M. W. Wartofsky. Dordrecht: Reidel, 1983, 203–25.

Lieber, Eleanor. "Asaf's Book of Medicines: A Hebrew Encyclopedia of Greek and Jewish Medicine, Possibly Compiled in Byzantium on an Indian Model." In *Symposium on Byzantine Medicine,* ed. by John Scarborough. *Dumbarton Oaks Papers* 38 (1984): 233–49.

Lieberman, Saul. "The Natural Sciences of the Rabbis." In *Hellenism in Jewish Palestine.* 1950. Reprint. New York: Jewish Theological Seminary of America, 1963, 1994.

Neher, Andre. *Jewish Thought and the Scientific Revolution of the Sixteenth Century: David Gans (1541–1613) and His Times.* Trans. by David Maisel. Oxford: Oxford University Press, 1986.

Rosner, Fred. *Julius Preuss's Biblical and Talmudic Medicine.* New York: Sanhedrin, 1978.

Rosner, Fred, and Samuel Kottek, eds. *Moses Maimonides: Physician, Scientist, and Philosopher.* Northvale, N.J.: Jason Aronson, 1993.

Ruderman, David. *Kabbalah, Magic, and Science: The Cultural Universe of a Sixteenth-Century Jewish Physician.* Cambridge, Mass.: Harvard University Press, 1988.

———. *Jewish Thought and Scientific Discovery in Early Modern Europe.* New Haven, Conn., and London: Yale University Press, 1995.

Schäfer, Peter. "Jewish Magic Literature in Late Antiquity and Early Middle Ages." *Journal of Jewish Studies* 41 (1990): 75–91.

Shatzmiller, Joseph. *Jews, Medicine, and Medieval Society.* Berkeley: University of California Press, 1994.

Trachtenberg, Joshua. *Jewish Magic and Superstition: A Study in Folk Religion.* 1939. Reprint. New York: Atheneum, 1974.

46. Early Christian Attitudes Toward Nature

David C. Lindberg

The Christian Intellectual Tradition

When we refer to Christian attitudes toward nature, we are referring to the attitudes of a small, highly educated Christian elite. This elite emerged during the second and third centuries of the Christian era as educated Christians, attempting to come to terms with Greco-Roman intellectual culture and entering into dialogue with pagans on critical philosophical and theological issues. In the course of this dialogue, they took important steps toward the definition, refinement, and defense of the fundamentals of Christian belief and practice. Many who belonged to this Christian intelligentsia had been the recipients of a pagan literary, rhetorical, and philosophical education before their conversion to Christianity, and inevitably they brought with them attitudes and ideals acquired in the Greco-Roman schools. Although they frequently turned against significant portions of the content learned in this prior educational experience, especially where it touched upon theological issues, the broad intellectual values and methodology of this pagan schooling had been absorbed too deeply to be easily abandoned.

The early Church has often been portrayed as a haven of anti-intellectualism, and evidence apparently favorable to this opinion is not hard to find. The Apostle Paul (whose influence in shaping Christian attitudes was enormous) warned the Colossians: "Be on your guard; do not let your minds be captured by hollow and delusive speculations, based on traditions of man-made teaching centered on the elements of the natural world and not on Christ" (Col. 2:8 New English Bible, substituting an alternative translation provided by the translators for one phrase). In his first letter to the Corinthians, he admonished: "Make no mistake about this: if there is anyone among you who fancies himself wise . . . he must become a fool to gain true wisdom. For the wisdom of this world is folly in God's sight" (I Cor. 3:18–19 New English Bible). Tertullian (c. 160–c. 220), who frequently expressed similar sentiments, elaborated these thoughts in a celebrated passage:

> What indeed has Athens to do with Jerusalem? What concord is there between the Academy and the Church? What between heretics and Christians? . . . Away with all attempts to produce a mottled Christianity of Stoic, Platonic, and dialectic composition! We want no curious disputation after possessing Christ Jesus, no inquisition after enjoying the gospel! With our faith, we desire no further belief. For once we believe this, there is nothing else that we ought to believe (Tertullian 1986, 246b, with minor revision).

Denunciations of Greek philosophy for its vanity, its contradictions, its occupation with the trivial and disregard for the consequential, and its instigation of heresy became standard, almost formulaic, elements in the works of Tertullian and other early Christian writers.

But to stop here would be to present an incomplete and highly misleading picture. The very writers who denounced Greek philosophy also employed its methodology and incorporated parts of its content into their own systems of thought. In the battle for the minds of the educated, Christian apologists had no alternative but to meet pagan intellectuals on their own ground. From Justin Martyr (c. 100–165) to Saint Augustine (354–430) and beyond, Christian scholars allied themselves with Greek philosophical traditions that they considered congenial to Christian thought. Chief of these traditions was Platonism or Neoplatonism, but borrowing from Stoic, Aristotelian, and Neo-Pythagorean philosophy was also common. Even the denunciations issuing from Christian pens, whether of specific philosophical positions or of philosophy generally, often reflected an impressive command of the philosophical tradition.

The Church Fathers and Natural Philosophy

But where and how did science enter the picture? In the first place, we must understand that there was no activity and no body of knowledge during the patristic period that bore a close resemblance to modern science. However, there *were* beliefs about nature: about the origins and structure of the cosmos, the motions of celestial bodies, the elements, sickness and health, the explanation of dramatic natural phenomena (thunder, lightning, eclipses, and the like), and the relationship between the cosmos and the gods. These are the ingredients of what would develop centuries later into modern science, and, if we are interested in the origins of Western science, they are what we must investigate. The best way of denoting these ingredients is by the expression "natural philosophy." The term is useful because it calls attention to the relationship between the philosophy of nature and the larger philosophical enterprise (although the expressions "science" and "natural science" will also be used occasionally in the remainder of this essay). As an integral part of philosophy, natural philosophy shared the latter's methods and its fate, and it became a concern of Christians and entered into their sermons, debates, and writings insofar as it impinged on Christian doctrine and Christian worldview, as it frequently did. After all, Christians had as much need of a cosmology as did pagans.

Among Christian writers, we find expressions of hostility toward natural philosophy, just as we do toward philosophy in general. Tertullian, for example, attacked the pagan philosophers for their assignment of divinity to the elements and the sun, moon, other planets, and stars. In the course of his argument, he vented his wrath on the vanity of the ancient philosophers:

Now pray tell me, what wisdom is there in this hankering after conjectural speculations? What proof is afforded to us . . . by the useless affectation of a scrupulous curiosity, which is tricked out with an artful show of language? It therefore served Thales of Miletus quite right, when, stargazing as he walked, . . . he had the mortification

of falling into a well. . . . His fall, therefore, is a figurative picture of the philosophers; of those, I mean, who persist in applying their studies to a vain purpose, since they indulge a stupid curiosity on natural objects (Tertullian 1986, 133).

But it *is* an argument that Tertullian presents, and, to a very significant degree, he builds it out of materials and by the use of methods drawn from the Greco-Roman philosophical tradition. He argues, for example, that the precise regularity of the orbital motions of the celestial bodies (a clear reference to the findings of the Greek astronomical tradition) bespeaks a "governing power" that rules over them, and, if they are ruled over, they surely cannot be gods. He also introduces the "enlightened view of Plato" in support of the claim that the universe must have had a beginning and, therefore, cannot partake of divinity. In this and other works, he "triumphantly parades" his learning (as one of his biographers puts it) by naming a long list of other ancient authorities (Barnes 1985, 196).

Basil of Caesarea (c. 330–79), representing a different century and a different region of the Christian world, reveals similar attitudes toward Greek natural philosophy. He sharply attacked philosophers and astronomers who "have wilfully and voluntarily blinded themselves to the knowledge of the truth." These men, he continued, have "discovered everything, except one thing: they have not discovered the fact that God is the creator of the universe." Elsewhere he inquired why we should "torment ourselves by refuting the errors or rather the lies of the Greek philosophers, when it is sufficient to produce and compare their mutually contradictory books." And he attacked belief in the transmigration of souls by admonishing his listeners to "avoid the nonsense of those arrogant philosophers who do not blush to liken their own soul to the soul of a dog" (Amand de Mendieta 1976, 38, 31, 37).

But, while attacking the errors of Greek natural philosophy—and what he didn't find erroneous, he generally found useless—Basil also revealed a solid mastery of its content. He argued against Aristotle's (384–322 B.C.) fifth element, the quintessence; he recounted the Stoic theory of cyclic conflagration and regeneration; he ridiculed theories of the eternity and divinity of the cosmos; he applauded those who employ the laws of geometry to refute the possibility of multiple worlds (a clear reference to Aristotle's argument for the uniqueness of the cosmos); he derided the Pythagorean notion of music of the planetary spheres; he proclaimed the vanity of mathematical astronomy; and he revealed familiarity with various opinions about the shape of the earth and (for those who believed it to be spherical) calculations of its circumference.

Tertullian and Basil have generally been portrayed as outsiders to the philosophical tradition, attempting to discredit and destroy what they regarded as a menace to the Christian faith. Certainly, much of their rhetoric supports such an interpretation, as when they appealed for simple faith as an alternative to philosophical reasoning. But we need to look beyond rhetoric to actual practice: It is one thing to deride natural philosophy or declare it useless, another to abandon it. Despite their derision, Tertullian, Basil, and others like them were continuously engaged in serious philosophical argumentation. It is no distortion of the evidence to see them as insiders, attempting to formulate an alternative natural philosophy based on Christian principles and opposed, not to the enterprise of natural philosophy, but to specific principles of natural philosophy that they considered both erroneous and dangerous.

The most influential of the church Fathers and the one who codified Christian attitudes toward nature was Saint Augustine, bishop of Hippo in North Africa. Like his predecessors, Augustine had deep reservations about the value of natural philosophy. But his criticism was more muted and qualified by an acknowledgment, in both word and deed, of legitimate uses to which natural knowledge might be put and a recognition that it may even be of religious utility. In short, Augustine certainly did not devote himself to the promotion of natural science, but neither did he fear pagan versions of it to the degree that some of his predecessors had.

Scattered throughout Augustine's voluminous writings are worries about pagan philosophy (including natural philosophy) and admonitions for Christians not to overvalue it. In his *Enchiridion,* he assured his readers that there is no need to be

dismayed if Christians are ignorant about the properties and the number of the basic elements of nature, or about the motion, order, and deviations of the stars, the map of the heavens, the kinds and nature of animals, plants, stones, springs, rivers, and mountains. . . . For the Christian, it is enough to believe that the cause of all created things . . . is . . . the goodness of the Creator (Augustine 1955, 341–2).

In his *On Christian Doctrine,* he commented on the uselessness of astronomical knowledge:

Although the course of the moon . . . is known to many, there are only a few who know well the rising or setting or other movements of the rest of the stars without error. Knowledge of this kind in itself, although it is not allied with any superstition, is of very little use in the treatment of the Divine Scriptures and even impedes it through fruitless study; and since it is associated with the most pernicious error of vain [astrological] prediction it is more appropriate and virtuous to condemn it (Augustine 1976, 65–6).

And, in his *Confessions,* he argued that "because of this disease of curiosity . . . men proceed to investigate the phenomena of nature, . . . though this knowledge is of no value to them: for they wish to know simply for the sake of knowing" (Augustine 1942, 201, slightly edited). Knowledge for the sake of knowing is without value and, therefore, illegitimate.

But, once again, this is not the whole story. Natural philosophy may be without value for its own sake, but from this we are not entitled to conclude that it is entirely without value. Knowledge of natural phenomena acquires value and legitimacy insofar as it serves other, higher purposes. One such purpose is biblical exegesis, since ignorance of mathematics, music (conceived as a mathematical art in Augustine's day), and natural history renders us incapable of grasping the literal sense of Scripture. For example, only if we are familiar with serpents will we grasp the meaning of the biblical admonition to "be as wise as serpents and as innocent as doves" (Matt. 10:16). Augustine also conceded that portions of pagan knowledge, such as history, dialectic, mathematics, the mechanical arts, and "teachings that concern the corporeal senses," contribute to the necessities of life (Augustine 1976, 74).

In his *Literal Meaning of Genesis,* in which he put his own superb grasp of Greek cosmology and natural philosophy to good use, Augustine expressed dismay at the ignorance of some Christians:

Even a non-Christian knows something about the earth, the heavens, and the other elements of this world, about the motion and orbit of the stars and even their size and relative positions, about the predictable eclipses of the sun and moon, the cycles of the years and the seasons, about the kinds of animals, shrubs, stones, and so forth, and this knowledge he holds to as being certain from reason and experience. Now it is a disgraceful and dangerous thing for an infidel to hear a Christian . . . talking nonsense on these topics; and we should take all means to prevent such an embarrassing situation, in which people show up vast ignorance in a Christian and laugh it to scorn (Augustine 1982, I, 42–3).

Insofar as we require knowledge of natural phenomena—and Augustine is certain that we do—we must take it from those who possess it: "If those who are called philosophers, especially the Platonists, have said things which are indeed true and are well accommodated to our faith, they should not be feared; rather, what they have said should be taken from them as from unjust possessors and converted to our use" (Augustine 1976, 75). All truth is ultimately God's truth, even if found in the books of pagan authors; we should seize it and use it without hesitation.

In Augustine's view, then, knowledge of the things of this world is not a legitimate end in itself, but, as a means to other ends, it is indispensable. Natural philosophy must accept a subordinate position as the handmaiden of theology and religion: The temporal must be made to serve the eternal. Natural philosophy is not to be loved, but it may be legitimately used. This attitude toward scientific knowledge was to flourish throughout the Middle Ages and well into the modern period.

But does endowing natural philosophy with handmaiden status constitute a blow against scientific progress? Are the critics of the early Church right in viewing it as the opponent of genuine science? We need to make three points here. First, it is certainly true that the early Church was no great patron of the natural sciences. These had low priority for the church Fathers, for whom the major concerns were establishment of Christian doctrine, defense of the faith, and the edification of believers. Second, low priority was far from no priority. Throughout the Middle Ages and well into the modern period, the handmaiden formula was employed countless times to justify the investigation of nature. Indeed, some of the most celebrated achievements of the Western scientific tradition were made by scholars who justified their labors by appeal to the handmaiden formula.

Third, there were no institutions or cultural forces during the patristic period that offered more encouragement for the investigation of nature than did the Christian Church. Contemporary pagan culture was no more favorable to disinterested speculation about the cosmos than was Christian culture. It is at least arguable that the presence of the Christian Church enhanced, rather than damaged, the prospects for the natural sciences.

Three Illustrative Examples

We cannot end this account without touching briefly on a trio of examples that illustrate how Christian attitudes toward natural philosophy worked themselves out in actual practice: First, Augustine on Creation; second, the shape of the earth; third, medicine and the supernatural.

Augustine not only authorized the use of natural philosophy in biblical exegesis, he also practiced what he preached. In his *Literal Meaning of Genesis,* Augustine produced a verse-by-verse exposition of the biblical account of Creation as it appears in the first three chapters of Genesis. In the course of this work of his mature years, he brought to bear all knowledge that would help elucidate the meaning of the biblical text, including the pagan tradition of natural philosophy. In so doing, he transmitted to medieval scholars (before the thirteenth century) one of their richest sources of cosmological, physical, and biological knowledge.

It is almost universally held that Europeans of the Roman and medieval periods believed in a flat earth and that biblical literalism had something to do with this belief. The truth is quite otherwise. The sphericity of the earth was proposed by Pythagorean philosophers no later than the fifth century B.C. The sphericity of the earth was never seriously doubted after Aristotle, and the earth's circumference was satisfactorily calculated by Eratosthenes (c. 275–194 B.C.). But what about Christian opinion? Did the literal interpretation of certain biblical passages compel Christians to deny the earth's sphericity? The shape of the earth was not a source of controversy during the patristic period, and the evidence is, therefore, thin. Scholars have been able to discover only two Christian writers of the patristic period who denied the sphericity of the earth: the Latin church Father Lactantius (c. 240–320) and the Byzantine merchant Cosmas Indicopleustes (fl. 540). Evidently, early Christians did *not* reject the powerful arguments of Greek cosmologists for a spherical earth in favor of a literal interpretation of biblical passages that seemed to suggest otherwise.

Finally, can we learn anything by exchanging the purely theoretical subjects of cosmology and mathematical geography for the far more practical realm of medicine? Much has been made of Christian supernaturalism and its incompatibility with aspects of Greco-Roman medical theory and practice. But, in fact, the tension, though not totally absent, was not as serious as alleged. In the first place, religious elements (including miracle cures) were also an important part of Greco-Roman medicine. Second, belief in sickness as a divine visitation did not rule out simultaneous belief in natural causes. When Christians maintained that disease could be both natural and divine, conceiving natural causes as instruments of divine purpose, they were not breaking new ground, for this was a commonplace of the Hippocratic tradition. Third, belief in the existence of supernatural medicine and active pursuit of supernatural cures did not prevent Christians from availing themselves simultaneously of secular, naturalistic medicine—just as many of the sick in our own day participate simultaneously in conventional and nonconventional medical therapies.

See also Augustine of Hippo; Medieval Science and Religion

BIBLIOGRAPHY

Amand de Mendieta, Emmanuel. "The Official Attitude of Basil of Caesarea as a Christian Bishop Towards Greek Philosophy and Science." In *The Orthodox Churches and the West,* ed. by Derek Baker. Oxford: Blackwell, 1976, 25–49.

Amundsen, Darrel W. "Medicine and Faith in Early Christianity." *Bulletin of the History of Medicine* 56 (1982): 326–50.

Armstrong, A. H., ed. *The Cambridge History of Later Greek and Early Medieval Philosophy.* Cambridge: Cambridge University Press, 1970.

Armstrong, A. H., and R. A. Markus. *Christian Faith and Greek Philosophy.* London: Darton, Longman, and Todd, 1960.

Augustine St. of Hippo. *Confessions.* Trans. by F. J. Sheed. New York: Sheed and Ward, 1942.

———. *Confessions and Enchiridion.* Trans. by Albert C. Outler. Philadelphia: Westminster, 1955.

———. *On Christian Doctrine.* Trans. by D. W. Robertson Jr. 1958. Reprint. Indianapolis: Bobbs-Merrill, 1976.

———. *The Literal Meaning of Genesis.* Trans. by John Hammond Taylor, S.J. In *Ancient Christian Writers: The Works of the Fathers in Translation,* ed. by Johannes Quasten et al. Vols. 41–2. New York: Newman, 1982.

Barnes, Timothy David. *Tertullian: A Historical and Literary Study.* Rev. ed. Oxford: Clarendon, 1985.

Cochrane, Charles N. *Christianity and Classical Culture.* Oxford: Clarendon, 1940.

Ferngren, Gary B. "Early Christianity as a Religion of Healing." *Bulletin of the History of Medicine* 66 (1992): 1–15.

———. "Early Christian Views of the Demonic Etiology of Disease." In From *Athens to Jerusalem: Medicine in Hellenized Jewish Lore and Early Christian Literature,* ed. by Samuel Kottek, Gerhard Baader, Gary B. Ferngren, and Manfred Horstmanshoff. Rotterdam: Erasmus, 2000, 195–213.

Grant, Robert M. *Miracle and Natural Law in Graeco-Roman and Early Christian Thought.* Amsterdam: North-Holland, 1952.

Lindberg, David C. "Science and the Early Church." In *God and Nature: Historical Essays on the Encounter Between Christianity and Science,* ed. by David C. Lindberg and Ronald L. Numbers. Berkeley: University of California Press, 1986, 19–48.

———. "Science as Handmaiden: Roger Bacon and the Patristic Tradition." *Isis* 78 (1987): 518–36.

———. *The Beginnings of Western Science: The European Scientific Tradition in Philosophical, Religious, and Institutional Context, 600 B.C. to A.D. 1450.* Chicago: University of Chicago Press, 1992.

Pelikan, Jaroslav. *Christianity and Classical Culture: The Metamorphosis of Natural Theology in the Christian Encounter with Hellenism.* New Haven, Conn. and London: Yale University Press, 1993.

Scott, Alan. *Origen and the Life of the Stars: A History of an Idea.* Oxford: Clarendon, 1991.

Tertullian. *Writings,* in *The Ante-Nicene Fathers.* Ed. by Alexander Roberts and James Donaldson, rev. by A. Cleveland Coxe. Vol. 3. Reprint. Grand Rapids: Eerdmans, 1986.

47. ISLAM

Alnoor Dhanani

Primarily, "Islam" denotes the monotheistic religion established in the seventh century by the Arabian prophet Muhammad. Secondarily, it denotes the world-historical consequences of this religion, namely, the empire founded by Muslim rulers that, in the ninth century, extended from the Atlantic to the borders of China. "Islam" also denotes a distinct world civilization—Islamic civilization—that first emerged within the heartland of this empire but continued within successor states well into the eighteenth and nineteenth centuries. Any discussion of science and religion in Islam must take into account these three interrelated aspects of Islam: as religion, empire, and civilization.

Background: Religion, Empire, and Civilization

The religion of Islam was established by the Prophet Muhammad, born in A.D. 570 in the Arabian pilgrimage center and commercial town of Mecca. Deeply distressed by the decline in social values in this predominantly pagan milieu, Muhammad would retreat to the surrounding mountains to reflect and meditate. During one such retreat, the angel Gabriel appeared to Muhammad with the first of many revelations from Allah, the one true God (which were collected into the Qur'an), declaring to Muhammad that he was the chosen messenger of Allah. Soon thereafter, Muhammad began preaching monotheism—belief in Allah—and declared himself to be his prophet in the tradition of earlier Semitic prophets, warning of the impending day of judgment, when individuals would have to account for their actions and enter paradise or be banished to hell. He was particularly critical of social injustices resulting from the breakdown of traditional values of charity and hospitality and of the accumulation of wealth without regard to the needy. Not surprising, the Meccan elite rejected Muhammad's message; the handful who answered his call were slaves and others of low socioeconomic status. In A.D. 622, deteriorating relations forced Muhammad to flee to the northern oasis town of Yathrib (thereafter renamed Madina, the city of the Prophet). Here he established the first Muslim community and built its first mosque. Muhammad became the spiritual leader of the Muslims as well as ruler of the multifaith community of Madina. Ten years later, after a series of skirmishes, Muhammad triumphantly reentered Mecca. Thereafter, so many Arabian tribes acknowledged Muhammad's political supremacy and religious mission that the Arabian peninsula was almost united by the time of Muhammad's death in A.D. 632.

Muhammad's death was the first of many crises for the nascent community. Who was to succeed Muhammad? What was to be the basis of authority? These questions were critical to the historical development of the political and religious institutions of Islam. At this early juncture, two tendencies were manifested: One favored continuing Muhammad's religious and political authority under the leadership of his cousin and son-in-law 'Ali (it would later crystallize into the Shia interpretation of Islam); the other held that religious authority had ended (it would crystallize into the majority Sunni interpretation of Islam) but favored political leadership under the first caliph, Abu Bakr (ruled 632–634), a close companion to Muhammad. Abu Bakr's immediate task was to reintegrate the Arabian peninsula under the Islamic banner, preparing the way for his successors' conquests of Palestine, Syria, Egypt, and Iran within two decades of Muhammad's death. Internal division caused by conflict over the distribution of wealth and booty, as well as charges of nepotism, characterized the reign of the third caliph, Uthman (ruled 644–656), leading to a civil war during the reign of the fourth caliph, 'Ali (ruled 656–661). Thereupon the "rightly guided Caliphate" of Muhammad's close companions came to an end, and political control passed on to the Ummayad dynasty (661–750).

The Ummayad dynasty established many of the normative features of Muslim polity, including dynastic political succession and conflict between political and religious elites (despite the nominal title of the caliph as "commander of the faithful"). The latter is significant, as the dialectic of frequent opposition and infrequent cooperation between Muslim political rulers and religious scholars forms the backdrop for the relationship of science and religion in Islam. Thus, pious religious scholars declined Ummayad appointment to judicial positions. However, the Ummayads continued the conquests, pressing east to the Indus Valley and west over the Straits of Gibraltar into Spain, incorporating established centers of science and learning within a single empire. This large empire, with its multiethnic, multifaith, and multinational populations and retaining preconquest administrative structures, was becoming increasingly fractious and ungovernable. In A.D. 696, 'Abd al-Malik (ruled 692–705) adopted measures to unify the empire by introducing Arabic coinage and making Arabic the language of administration. But the significance of these measures was greater, for Arabic was to extend beyond being the language of revelation and now the language of administration to become the language of literature, art, and science. However, opposition to the Ummayads did not subside and culminated in the Abbasid revolution in A.D. 750.

The Abbasids had harnessed several strands of anti-Ummayad sentiment arising from the dynasty's alleged impiety, disregard of religious scholars, and blatant Arabism. While the Abbasids successfully draped themselves with the banner of Islam, they quickly adopted policies, once they were in power, that were opposed by many religious scholars. Divisive tendencies also continued to plague the empire so that, by the mid-ninth century, it was no longer unitary but consisted of semi-independent kingdoms that paid nominal allegiance to the caliph but retained tax revenues. Nevertheless, a unitary vision of Islamic civilization—united by language, common political and religious institutions, burgeoning trade and commerce within the market of a vast empire and beyond, shared aesthetic sensibilities, and rooted in an emerging sense of "Islamic" values—began to take hold. It is

within such a milieu that religion and science, to say nothing of literature and the arts, which had hitherto undergone modest development, were to blossom and reach the remarkable level that was to become the hallmark of Islamic civilization.

The Appropriation and Naturalization of Science

Within the milieu of Islamic civilization, science and philosophy came to be denoted by several Arabic terms, including 'ulum al-aw'ail or 'ulum al-qudama' (the sciences of the ancients), al-'ulum al-qadima (ancient sciences), al-'ulum al-nazariyya (rational sciences), al-'ulum al-'aqliyya (intellectual sciences), and al-'ulum al-falsafiyya (philosophical sciences). These terms emphasized the pre-Islamic origins of science and philosophy, their rational character, and their universality, as was well known even in the fourteenth century to the famous historian and judge Ibn Khaldun (1332–1406), who, in his *Introduction to History* (1377), states: "The intellectual sciences are natural to man, in as much as he is a thinking being. They are not restricted to any particular religious group. They are studied by the people of all religious groups who are equally qualified to learn them and to do research in them. They have existed (and been known) to the human species since civilization had its beginning in the world." On the other hand, terms like 'ulum al-'arab (the sciences of the Arabs), al-'ulum al-naqliyya (transmitted science), and 'ulum al-din (religious sciences) were used for linguistic and religious disciplines, such as grammar, lexicography, religious law, Qur'anic commentary, and philosophical theology. These sciences were considered to be particular insofar as they were practiced only by Arabs or Muslims.

The stage for the process of the appropriation and naturalization of these intellectual sciences was set as a result of the Muslim conquests of the seventh century, when several pre-Islamic centers of science and learning were incorporated into the nascent Islamic Empire. Initially, intellectual activity at these centers continued with little disruption despite the change of rulers. As before, they continued to provide skilled practitioners to the court and wealthy patrons. Ummayad rulers availed themselves of physicians and astrologers, and the Ummayad prince Khalid Ibn al-Walid (d. c. 704), who was interested in alchemy, sponsored the translation of some alchemical texts into Arabic. Such mostly utilitarian Ummayad interest in science pales when compared to the interest of early Abbasid rulers, particularly Harun al-Rashid (ruled 786–809) and al-Ma'mun (ruled 813–33), who established and generously funded the institution of the House of Wisdom (*Bayt al-Hikma*). The primary function of this institution was to appropriate past "wisdom" and learning and to enhance it. Apart from its director, the House of Wisdom included translators, copyists, and binders, as well as scientists. It was the royal institution for the translation of Greek, Syriac, Pahlavi, and even Sanskrit scientific and philosophical texts into Arabic. Al-Ma'mun's keen interest is evident in the report that he would attend the weekly salons at the House of Wisdom. Astronomy was of particular interest: Ptolemy's (second century A.D.) *Almagest* was translated into Arabic, as were Sanskrit astronomical texts. In addition, programs of solar observation and terrestrial measurement were conducted at observatories in Baghdad and Damascus, some of whose personnel were also affiliated with the House of Wisdom, followed by the publication of revised astronomical tables. Significantly, al-Ma'mun was also a keen supporter of the nascent discipline of Islamic philosophical theology (*kalam*).

The House of Wisdom, albeit a royal institution, was one among several sponsors of scientific research and translation. The attitude of these patrons toward earlier civilizations is reflected in the statement of the scientist and philosopher Abu Ya'qub al-Kindi (800–870): "We ought not to be ashamed of appreciating truth and of acquiring it wherever it comes from, even if it comes from races distant and nations different from us." Significantly, al-Kindi's remark demonstrates a conscious commitment to appropriating learning and knowledge. We may surmise that this commitment was shared by al-Kindi's royal patrons, al-Ma'mun and al-Mu'tasim (ruled 833–42). True to his dictum, al-Kindi sponsored an early Arabic translation of Aristotle's (384–322 B.C.) *Metaphysics*. The active sponsorship of translation led to Arabic versions of the available Greek scientific and philosophical corpus, as well as some Syriac, Pahlavi, and Sanskrit texts.

Constant efforts to improve translations of texts laid the basis for Arabic "naturalization" of the pre-Islamic scientific and philosophical heritage. Knowledge of Greek or other languages was no longer a requisite for scientific activity. Rather, from Spain to the borders of China, scientific activity was conducted in Arabic, utilizing a vocabulary coined by the translators but naturalized in subsequent scientific works. The ready availability of cheap paper since the end of the seventh century allowed booksellers, even in smaller provincial towns, to stock their shelves with translated, as well as a growing corpus of original Arabic, scientific texts. Moreover, royal and provincial courts and wealthy patrons vied to sponsor scientific work and establish public and private libraries. The education of Abu 'Ali Ibn Sina (980–1037), known in Latin as Avicenna, is illustrative in this regard. Born in a village in Turkistan, at a very young age he moved with his family to the provincial capital of Bukhara, where his formal learning started with the Qur'an and literature. His father then sent him to a vegetable seller to learn arithmetic. Later, when someone who claimed to be a philosopher came to Bukhara, his father had him stay in their house and tutor the young Ibn Sina, who soon surpassed his teacher. He began to study on his own, reading Euclid's (fl.c. 300 B.C.) *Elements,* Ptolemy's *Almagest,* and Aristotle's logical, physical, and metaphysical works and their commentators. He then taught himself medicine and became so proficient that distinguished physicians began to read medicine with him. Aristotle's *Metaphysics* raised difficulties. Rereading this work forty times, he despaired until he was persuaded in the booksellers' quarter to purchase al-Farabi's (873–950) *On the Purposes of Metaphysics* for the cheap price of three dirhams. With the aid of this text, he overcame his difficulties. At this time, the ruler of Bukhara was ill, and the young Ibn Sina was summoned to participate in his treatment. Here Ibn Sina entered the royal library, "a building with many rooms . . . in one room were books on the Arabic language and poetry, in another jurisprudence, and so on in each room a separate science. I looked through the catalogue of books by the ancients and requested those which I needed."

Ibn Sina's account illustrates the fact that scientific education was not imparted through formal institutions but, rather, via informal, personal contacts. Notable exceptions include hospitals, where medicine was taught in a master-apprentice setting, and possibly astronomical observatories and academies like the House of Wisdom of Baghdad or the House of Knowledge founded by the Fatimid caliphs of Cairo in the tenth and eleventh centuries, as well as Christian theological schools where Aristotelian texts were studied within a centuries-old curriculum. (That these Christian theological schools had survived into the eleventh century is evident in Ibn

Sina's disparaging and acerbic critique of their dogmatic and rigid philosophical views.) The lack of formal educational institutions does not, however, entail the absence of a curriculum. There was an established order of study and of texts. Moreover, scientific texts were available both in private and public libraries and for purchase in thriving booksellers' markets. Courts patronized scientists in their practical roles as engineers, astronomers, astrologers, and physicians, thereby providing them with the wherewithal to pursue their research interests. Hence, despite the lack of formal educational institutions for the study of science, the environment of Islamic civilization was conducive to the pursuit of science and philosophy, as is obvious from its scientific and philosophical legacy. Individuals from diverse religious communities, spread over a vast geographical span, participated in this enterprise. They were critical of the scientific theories of predecessors and contemporaries and made substantial advances in their chosen fields.

In addition to critical evaluation of previous theories and continuing research programs, several peculiar problems occupied scientists in an enterprise that has been termed "science in the service of Islam." These problems, which arose from the requirements of religious practice, included the determination of inheritance shares, the determination of the direction of Mecca from any locality so that the faithful might know in which direction to face for prayer, and the determination of times of prayer, some of which were formulated in terms of shadow lengths. In his foundational work on algebra, the mathematician and astronomer al-Khwarizmi (d. c. 847) shows how arithmetic and algebra can be applied to solve problems of Muslim inheritance law. The other two problems of determining the direction of prayer and its times occupied many of the mathematicians of Islamic civilization, who, using novel trigonometric approaches, proposed several solutions.

However, despite the engagement of scientists in such uniquely Muslim problems, the close links between science and Hellenistic philosophy established in Greek antiquity continued to be maintained in the Islamic milieu, as, indeed, in western Europe until the scientific revolution. Thus, the scientific worldview was the predominant Neoplatonized version of Aristotelianism formulated in late antiquity. While God was the ultimate cause and Creator of the cosmos, he played no direct role in its activity. Rather, creation was an eternal process of

emanation, from God to celestial intellects, celestial souls, and thence to entities lower in the chain of being. The eternal cosmos consisted of the incorruptible celestial and the corruptible terrestrial realms. In the celestial realm, planets, which were intelligent living beings, revolved around the earth, their motion caused by their souls. Planets influenced events on the earth, though there were different views about whether this influence was predictable, as claimed by astrology. In the terrestrial realm, combinations of the four elements of air, water, earth, and fire gave rise to inanimate minerals and animate plants, animals, and man. Animation was the result of vegetative, animal, and rational souls, which were susceptible to the influence of planetary souls. There were differing views on the nature of soul, whether it was immaterial or whether it was produced by an equilibrium of the combination of elements. The philosophical worldview also incorporated a modified version of Platonic political philosophy, deriving from the *Republic.* The phenomena of prophecy and religion were understood within the political and psychological perspectives of this system. There was great emphasis on the role of celestial planetary beings in producing and sustaining these phenomena. Such a worldview was far removed from the literal text of revelation. Hence, scientists and philosophers were, to varying degrees, proponents of an allegorical and interpretive reading of the Qur'an.

Not surprising, religious groups and scholars sympathetic to an allegorical interpretation of revelation were quick to adopt this worldview, with some modification to bring it into conformity with their specific doctrines. One such group were the Isma'ilis, a branch of the Shia, who founded the Fatimid state in North Africa in the tenth century. Later, in their new capital of Cairo, they established institutions like the House of Science (*Dar al-'Ilm*) and the university-mosque of al-Azhar and patronized the activities of several scientists. An anonymous group sympathetic to the Isma'ilis was responsible for the encyclopedic *Treatises of the Brothers of Sincerity,* written in the tenth century. These treatises present a popular account of the Neoplatonic-Aristotelian worldview within a pietistic, Muslim framework. The popularity of these treatises, which were even read by Ibn Sina and the religious scholar al-Ghazali (1058–1111), among others, attests to the widespread naturalization of this worldview within the milieu of medieval Islamic civilization among nonscientists, particularly, belletrists, poets, and others.

Attitudes toward the "Foreign" Sciences

The relationship of religion to science in Islamic civilization is complex. The roots of such complexity lie in the long-drawn and sustained dynamic between local context, political power, religious authority, patronage, and competition among elites, as well as individual epistemological commitments. Attitudes expressed by proponents and opponents of the "foreign" sciences do not reveal this larger setting. Rather, the participants in this discourse formulated their positions within distinctive analytical frameworks and categories. From our perspective, this discourse can be framed by asking certain questions. How, from a religious point of view, should science be evaluated? By which religious disciplines? What is to be the analytic framework of evaluation? What was the reaction of the proponents to their opponents' views?

The disciplines of religious law (*shar'ia*) and philosophical theology (*kalam*) are paramount to understanding the attitudes of religious scholars regarding the relationship of religion to science. The status and roles of these two disciplines varied over the course of Islamic history and were quite different from those in the medieval West. While the origins of these disciplines lie in the seventh century, their mature formulation and formalization were achieved later. Their formative period was contemporaneous with the translation movement to appropriate the scientific and philosophical heritage of earlier civilizations. Interpretive differences, made evident in sectarianism but also arising from differences in local contexts, played a substantial role in the formation of competing schools of religious law and philosophical theology. In the case of the former, pressure to normatize was manifested in the quest to establish a methodology that would restrict the derivation of religious law to "valid" sources only. According to the ninth-century formalization by the Sunni religious scholar al-Shafi'i (d. 820), these sources must consist of only prescriptions of the Qur'an, the tradition of the prophet Muhammad, and the consensus of religious scholars. Earlier Sunni authorities had allowed reasoning by analogy and judicial personal opinion as legitimate sources, thereby incorporating local customary practices into their formulation of law. On the other hand, Shia scholars maintained that the continuity of the Prophet's religious authority in the *imam* meant that the *imam* was the primary source of religious law and Qur'anic interpretation.

Despite some convergence with the passage of time, such differences over the sources of law and over legal prescriptions manifested themselves in opposing schools of law and in competition between scholars even within the same school. (Only four Sunni schools, Hanafi, Maliki, Shafi'i, and Hanbali, survive today; several Shia schools also survive.) Proponents of religious law insisted that it should govern all spheres of life: personal conduct, the activities of state, religious affairs, and commercial transactions, as well as intellectual pursuits.

Diversity notwithstanding, scholars of religious law had developed a system of categories whereby any activity was either required, recommended, neutral, abhorred, or prohibited. Within this scheme, some early religious scholars had advocated the pursuit of only those sciences that had practical utility, whether religious or social. A mature exposition of this is found in the section on knowledge in the *Revival of the Religious Sciences* by the influential Sunni religious thinker Abu Hamid al-Ghazali, who belonged to the Shafi'i school of religious law. After extolling the virtues of knowledge on the basis of Qur'anic references and prophetic traditions, al-Ghazali classifies the sciences as sacred or profane. Sacred sciences are acquired through prophets, not (like arithmetic) through reason, or (like medicine) through experience, or (like language), through "hearing" (that is, social discourse). Profane sciences, whether acquired through reason, experience, or social discourse, may, from the point of view of religious law, be praiseworthy, blameworthy, or tolerated. Praiseworthy profane sciences are those upon which everyday worldly activities depend, such as arithmetic and medicine. Blameworthy profane sciences include magic, talismanic sciences, and trickery. After discussing the sacred sciences, al-Ghazali has an imaginary interlocutor state: "In your classification, you have mentioned neither philosophy nor philosophical theology, nor have you clarified whether they are praiseworthy or blameworthy." In response, al-Ghazali states that, as for philosophical theology, whatever is of utility in it is already covered in the Qur'an and the prophetic tradition. As for philosophy, it consists of four types of sciences: mathematical sciences, logic, metaphysics, and physical sciences. Mathematical sciences are permissible as long as the mathematician is not led to the blameworthy sciences (al-Ghazali believed that most mathematicians eventually are enticed). Logic studies proofs and definitions, subjects also covered in philosophical theology. Metaphysics studies God and his attributes (also covered by philosophical theology), but here philosophers have branched into schools, some of which are characterized by outright unbelief, while others are heretical. As such, metaphysics is clearly blameworthy. As for the physical sciences, some of them are opposed to religion and truth, while others study bodies, their properties, and their changes. Unlike medicine, which studies human bodies, the latter do not have any utility. Al-Ghazali thus endorses a utilitarian position, which is approving of "practical" sciences such as arithmetic and medicine, skeptical of "theoretical" sciences, and disapproving of metaphysics and some physical sciences.

A proponent's attitude toward the foreign scientists is provided by the famous mathematician and scientist al-Biruni (d. 1050). He frames his attitude within a critique of religious scholars who, lacking the nuanced position of al-Ghazali, considered the pursuit of all science and philosophy to be a blameworthy activity. Al-Biruni was patronized by Sultan Mahmud of Ghazna (ruled 998–1030), the ruler of the eastern edge of the Islamic Empire and the conqueror of India. Al-Biruni characterizes these religious scholars as

> the people of our times . . . who oppose the virtuous and attack those who bear the mark of knowledge. . . . they have settled on the worst of morals. . . . You always see them unashamedly begging with outstretched hands . . . seizing opportunities to grab more and more leading them to reject the sciences and despise its practitioners. The extremist among them relates sciences to the path which leads astray thus making like-minded ignoramuses detest the sciences. He labels sciences as heretical so as to allow himself to destroy their practitioners.

Al-Biruni goes on to state that such religious scholars feign wisdom by questioning the utility of the sciences, ignoring the fact that man's virtue over other animals lies in pursuing knowledge and that good can arise, or evil be avoided, only by means of knowledge. Neither in spiritual nor in worldly affairs can we be sure without knowledge. Al-Biruni reiterates the scientists' view that a believer seeking real truth (which, to al-Biruni, is obviously not found in competing religious dogmas) must study creation in order to know the Creator and his attributes. Significantly, the context for these remarks is al-Biruni's work on *The Determination of Coordinates of . . . Cities,* in which he presents methods for determin-

ing latitude and longitude of localities, as well as methods to determine the direction of Mecca, toward which Muslims must turn for their daily prayers. As he tells us: "What we have discussed regarding the correction of longitudes and latitudes of towns is beneficial to the majority of Muslims in determining the direction of prayer and hence its performance free of the errors of the unfounded legal determination [by religious scholars]." In his *Exhaustive Treatise on Shadows,* al-Biruni defends the study of astronomy: "The learned in religion who are deeply versed in science know that religious law does not forbid what astronomers practice except [the visibility] of the lunar crescent." (Here al-Biruni accepts the prevalent social attitude based on religious law that the beginning of a lunar month is to be established by the actual observation of the lunar crescent by qualified witnesses rather than by astronomical calculation. The importance of this to religious ritual is evident, for example, in determining the beginning and end of Ramadan, the month of fasting.) In this interesting work, al-Biruni presents several views about Muslim times of prayer, demonstrating his mastery of the religious sciences, and then shows how trigonometrical methods may be used to determine times of prayer.

The discipline of philosophical theology, like religious law, also played a substantial role in the relationship between religion and science in Islam. It had emerged in the early Islamic milieu of intense debate with proponents of other religious traditions and cosmologies, especially in natural philosophy. Characterized by rationalism (insofar as it subscribes to a rationalist epistemology rather than the faith-based epistemology of some Christian theology), it sought to explicate Islamic beliefs regarding God, Creation, prophecy, and human religious obligation. By the mid-ninth century, the Mu'tazili school of philosophical theology reached consensus on several aspects of its concerns: The eternal God was the direct Creator and Sustainer of a created world whose ultimate constituents were atoms and the inherent qualities (like color and taste). They combine to form bodies that we perceive. A particular combination of atoms and qualities constituted in a specific manner, namely the shape of a human being, allowed for the further inherence of qualities of life, will, knowledge, and the capacity for action. Human beings were obligated to God, who had provided them with material sustenance and natural intellect, as well as religious guidance mediated through revelation via prophets, to live in a manner consistent with God's law—a manner that was for the benefit of mankind. Conforming to these obligations would enable man to achieve the felicity of paradise; disregarding them would lead to harm in hell. Causal agency was restricted to direct and indirect action by living agents, namely God and human beings; the concept of natural causation as a result of "natural properties" was unintelligible. Planets were not living beings but inanimate stones with no causal influence whatsoever. This brief summary demonstrates the radically different, non-Aristotelian character of the worldview of philosophical theology compared to the philosophical worldview.

However, philosophical theology was not, as is evident in al-Ghazali's account in the *Revival of the Religious Sciences,* without its detractors from within, who, critical of its rationalist methods, insisted on a conformist adherence to religious tenets as propounded by orthodox schools of religious law. These schools defined themselves as "followers of the pious ancestors," rejecting any deviation from their views as a heretical innovation and, therefore, against religious law. The attempt by the Abbasid caliph al-Ma'mun to impose Mu'tazili philosophical theology on religious scholars was met with stiff resistance by opponents of this view, forcing his successors to abandon the enterprise. Subsequently, a school of philosophical theology that was more in alignment with the traditionalists but maintained the rationalist stance characteristic of this discipline, was founded by al-Ash'ari (d. 935). It became the predominant school of theological philosophy after the eleventh century. Significantly, al-Ash'ari's school restricted causal agency further, holding that God was the only and direct cause of all events, even of human actions.

Despite al-Ghazali's later misgivings about philosophical theology, he had, in his earlier years, embraced al-Ash'ari's critique of the Neoplatonic-Aristotelian worldview of the scientists and philosophers. His thorough acquaintance with the philosophers' worldview, in particular, as explicated by Ibn Sina, is reflected in his work *On the Aims of the Philosophers,* which is a summary of the doctrines of the Islamic philosophers. (In the Latin West, al-Ghazali was erroneously considered to be one of the principal Islamic philosophers primarily through the translation of this work.) Al-Ghazali followed this preliminary study with a masterful critique, *The Incoherence of the Philosophers,* which argued against key elements of the philosophical worldview that were contrary to the literal meaning of revelation and to

philosophical theology, such as the doctrines of the eternity of the world, God's lack of knowledge of particular events in the world, and the impossibility of physical resurrection. On this basis, he accused the philosophers of unbelief. Moreover, he rejected the philosophers' theory of natural causation, which was fundamental to their physical doctrines. In conformity with al-Ash'ari's philosophical theology, he denied any connection between causes and effects. Rather, God is the only cause of all events, and, as a free agent, he can alter habitual patterns of presumed effects following their presumed causes (for example, burning when fire and cotton are brought together) because their connection is arbitrary. Such observed patterns are entirely within God's causal activity, which is wholly volitional, for God can choose to alter such patterns at any juncture.

A direct answer to al-Ghazali's critique was made in the westernmost part of the Islamic Empire by the famous Spanish Muslim philosopher and judge Ibn Rushd (1126–98), known to the Latin West as Averroës. A biographical account tells how Ibn Rushd was introduced by the philosopher and royal physician Ibn Tufayl (d. 1186) to the Almohad ruler Abu Ya'qub Ibn Yusuf (ruled 1163–84). Prompted by the ruler to discuss the controversial question of the eternity of the world, Ibn Rushd hesitated. But the ruler displayed his familiarity with philosophy by discussing the question with Ibn Tufayl, easing the young Ibn Rushd's anxieties. Abu Ya'qub then commissioned Ibn Rushd to write the Aristotelian commentaries that earned him the epithet of "The Commentator" in the Latin West. Ibn Rushd was also appointed judge of Seville and later chief judge of Cordoba, continuing the family tradition of engagement with religious law. Within this context, Ibn Rushd was also the author of a major Maliki treatise on religious law. Ibn Rushd adopted a legal framework in his work *The Decisive Treatise on the Harmony Between Religion and Philosophy,* in which he reexamined al-Ghazali's question of the validity of the pursuit of science and philosophy. Rather than discuss this question in terms of whether the science is blameworthy, praiseworthy, or tolerated, as al-Ghazali had, Ibn Rushd examined whether, from the perspective of religious law, philosophical inquiry and logic are permissible, prohibited, or required. Ibn Rushd argued that philosophy studies creation and reflects upon the Creator. Since revelation commands believers to recognize the Creator, he concluded that philosophy provides the best method for this, for it is a demonstrative science. However, not everyone is suited to pursue demonstrative science, and, for the masses of believers, Islam allows rhetorical and dialectical knowledge provided by the religious sciences, including theological philosophy. Philosophy does not conflict with revelation. Rather, the true intent of revelation is accessible only to the philosopher, who, grounded in demonstrative science, is best suited to undertake the interpretive task. Such interpretation is necessary, for, in its apparent form, revelation must be couched in symbols to be accessible to the masses so that they may be persuaded to believe, perform religious acts, and maintain social order. Conflicts arise only when unqualified masses are provided access to metaphorical meanings of revelation and the results of demonstrative science by religious scholars like al-Ghazali.

Ibn Rushd also responded to al-Ghazali's critique of philosophical doctrines in his *The Incoherence of the Incoherence of the Philosophers* with a point-by-point rebuttal of the doctrines of Ash'ari philosophical theology that al-Ghazali had championed. Ibn Rushd and other scientist-philosophers were put in a precarious position when, in 1190, they lost the support of the Almohad ruler Abu Yusuf (ruled 1184–99), who, under the pressure of a growing Reconquista threat by the Portuguese, acquiesced in the antagonism of Maliki legal scholars toward scientists and philosophers. Ibn Rushd was rehabilitated a few months before his death, no doubt because of improvement in Abu Yusuf's political position.

Ibn Rushd's case illustrates the complexity of the relationship between religion and science in Islam, but it would be inappropriate to draw general conclusions about this relationship on the basis of such cases. This is because diversity is a characteristic of Islamic religious doctrines and institutions, as is evident from differing views of religious law. As such, the case of Ibn Rushd is not as representative as it is sometimes made out to be. This is not surprising. Islamic doctrines and institutions developed across a vast geographical area and over a long temporal period, sometimes in the context of opposition to political authority and almost always within localized milieus that had retained pre-Islamic concepts and institutions and even naturalized them within "Islamic" terms. Moreover, like other world religions, Islam has also been engaged in a continual dialectic with competing worldviews (for example, Hellenism in the past and secularism in the present), which has given rise

to movements that have sought to accommodate, adapt, or reject such worldviews. Such movements and their doctrines, influence, and impact on the relationship of religion to science need to be placed in their historical context.

In the case of Ibn Rushd, the local Andalusian milieu, where predominantly Maliki religious scholars opposed the theological and legal views of their Almohad rulers, the anti-Ash'arism, both of Almohad theology and Andalusian Malikism, Almohad literalist legal theory, and the pressure of the Reconquista movement are all local factors that need to be considered to understand the environment that, in good times, sustained a substantial number of scientists and philosophers but, in bad times, led to their persecution. Even al-Ghazali's opposition to science and philosophy needs to be placed in the context of the ongoing pro-Shia Fatimid military and intellectual challenge to the Abbasids; the growing strength of the Sunni Seljuqs, who were the principal backers of the Abbasids; and the establishment by the Seljuq vizier Nizam al-Mulk (1018–92) of a state-sponsored system of colleges of religious law (*madrasas*), in which Shafi'i religious law and Ash'ari philosophical theology were primarily taught (al-Ghazali was a professor in such a college in Baghdad). Moreover, due consideration needs to be given to al-Ghazali's positive attitude to logic, resulting in his wholesale appropriation of it into religious law. For this reason, al-Ghazali was viewed with suspicion by some religious scholars and even condemned by others.

Clearly, the lack of a central hierarchical religious institution in Islam, analogous to the Church, inhibited uniformity of doctrine and religious law. Rather, uniformity was possible only through the widespread consensus of religious scholars, which was hard to achieve. When it was achieved, it was largely the result of the decline of opposing views or of the domination of one group through its alliance with political authority. As a result, political power and religious authority were neither allied nor concentrated in the same manner as in the medieval West but relied much more on local factors, particularly the political ambitions of local elites, which so infuriated al-Biruni. However, when faced with a united and powerful opposition, which in normal circumstances tended to be fractious, political authority was under great pressure to conform, as was the case in Ibn Rushd's Andalusia. Yet, the fact that Ibn Rushd himself was a legal scholar and that biographical accounts mention other examples of legal scholars who were well versed in science reveals the complexity of the actual situation and the difficulty of maintaining the view of a simple dichotomy between scientists on one side and religious scholars on the other.

The Decline of Science in Islam

What was the impact of the opposition to scientific activity described above? Some scholars maintain that science and philosophy were "marginal" to Islamic civilization, while others have suggested that such opposition caused the decline of scientific activity in Islamic civilization and explains the absence of a scientific revolution. The marginality thesis suffers from an obvious flaw. It underrates the geographical breadth and the temporal duration of the scientific enterprise, the large number of people who were engaged in it despite the lack of formal educational institutions, the patronage of the court and other wealthy citizens, and, finally, its achievements.

That scientific activity declined is indisputable. The scientific activity of later centuries was not qualitatively at the same level as that of the earlier period. But when it declined, where it declined, why it declined, and whether it declined as a result of opposition to science are questions requiring detailed study. The thesis that al-Ghazali's critique was responsible for the decline of science in the twelfth and later centuries can no longer be maintained, for substantial progress was made in astronomy and mathematics in the thirteenth and fourteenth centuries as a result of the research program of the Maragha observatory, initially sponsored by the Mongols. Moreover, there were also important developments in medicine and optics during this period.

Even in the case of philosophy, al-Ghazali's impact has been exaggerated. The case of Nasir al-din al-Tusi (d. 1274), the famous mathematician, astronomer, director of the Maragha observatory, and Ibn Sina commentator, is illustrative. Al-Tusi is also the author of several religious texts, including a very influential Twelver Shia text on religious philosophy in which he presented Twelver philosophical theology within the framework of Ibn Sina's philosophy (earlier Twelver works on philosophical theology were under the influence of Mu'tazilism). Within Twelver intellectual circles, the pursuit of philosophy continued, reaching its peak in the "School of Isfahan." The representatives of this school, including Mir Damad (d. 1630) and Mulla Sadra (d. 1640), were

part of a broad cultural and intellectual renaissance initiated by the founding of the Safavid state in Iran in 1501. In Sunni circles, too, the impact of al-Ghazali's critique of philosophy and philosophical theology was not definitive. The pursuit of theological philosophy continued in the centuries after his death, producing some of its classic texts. However, Sunni theological philosophy had also undergone transformation, for, while remaining true to al-Ash'ari's central tenet of an absolutely free Creator, it appropriated many elements of philosophy. (Many features of late Ash'ari philosophical theology find resonance with the ideas of seventeenth-century European philosophy. They include a determined anti-Aristotelianism and the concept of an omnipotent and absolutely free God, features that are usually regarded as being fundamental to the seventeenth-century reorientation of science and philosophy.) Hence, without substantive direct evidence, it is difficult to maintain that al-Ghazali's critique of science and philosophy entailed the decline of scientific activity in the world of Islam.

However, historical factors of the disintegrating Islamic Empire of the twelfth and thirteenth centuries, such as the rise of regional nationalisms (particularly Iranian), the gradual displacement of Arabic, which was the language of science, by "vernacular" languages like Persian and Turkish, and the economic and social havoc wreaked by the Mongol conquest, bear further examination. So do changes in patronage patterns that began in the late eleventh century when the Seljuq vizier Nizam al-Mulk diverted substantial public resources into a state system of religious colleges. Such a change in patronage is even found in the case of private donors who now patronized religious colleges as well as Sufi centers. Funds that previously may have been used to support scientific activity were now diverted into these kinds of activities. Nevertheless, several accounts suggest that sciences continued to be taught privately despite being excluded from the official curriculum of most religious colleges. Clearly, where hospitals were allied to religious colleges, allowances must have been made for the study of natural sciences as a prerequisite for those pursuing medical careers.

Regional factors must also be explored. In Syria and Egypt, the position of mosque timekeeper was established in the fourteenth century. His function was to determine times of prayer and times of religious festivals. Most appointees to this position were very skilled astronomers, such as Ibn al-Shatir (fl. c. 1360), who completed the project of reforming astronomy, or al-Khalili (fl. c. 1360), who compiled an extremely accurate set of astronomical tables based on the astronomical work of the Maragha school. In Safavid Iran, there was renewed interest in philosophy, evident in the sixteenth-century School of Isfahan. Evidence from post-fifteenth-century Ottoman religious colleges shows the incorporation of the sciences into the curriculum. Only such continued study of science can explain the proliferation of commentaries on established scientific texts and, indeed, the existence of manuscript copies of the texts themselves from later periods when science is thought to have declined, to say nothing of the continued, albeit less prolific, production of new texts.

The decline of scientific activity is thus a complex phenomenon, but it is usually seen by historians through the lens of the seventeenth-century scientific revolution in Europe. The question has been raised whether religious opposition to science inhibited such a scientific revolution in Islam, given the otherwise high level of scientific achievement. But the premise of this question—that successful scientific activity must lead to a scientific revolution like that of the seventeenth century in Europe—is invalid and introduces misleading hypothetical conjectures.

The relationship of religion and science in the Islamic milieu is complex. That the scientific enterprise in Islam reached the remarkable level of achievement it did shows that science was a valued endeavor. On the other hand, it is also clear that there was opposition to science and that science did, indeed, subsequently decline. But these features, in their more detailed manifestations of the appropriation of science, its subsequent naturalization, its efflorescence, the opposition to it, and its decline, are historical phenomena, and, as subjects for historical investigation, they require detailed study of the local social, political, and epistemic contexts in which they occurred. The need to reiterate such a basic methodological norm of historical study reflects the continued domination of general universalistic explanations grounded in essentialist and ahistorical notions—explanations that have rightfully been abandoned elsewhere—in studies investigating the relationship of religion to science in the Islamic milieu.

See also Calendar; Causation

BIBLIOGRAPHY

al-Biruni, Abu al-Rayhan. *The Determination of the Coordinates of Positions for the Correction of Distances Between Cities.*

Trans. by Jamil Ali. Beirut: American University of Beirut, 1967.

———. *The Exhaustive Treatise on Shadows.* Trans. by E. S. Kennedy. Allepo: Institute for the History of Arabic Science, 1976.

al-Ghazali, Abu Hamid. "Autobiography." In *Freedom and Fulfillment: An Annotated Translation of al-Ghazali's Muqidh min al-Dalal and Other Relevant Works of al-Ghazali.* Trans. by R. McCarthy. Boston: Twayne, 1980, 61–143.

———. "The Clear Criterion for Distinguishing Between Islam and Heresy." In *Freedom and Fulfillment: An Annotated Translation of al-Ghazali's Muqidh min al-Dalal and Other Relevant Works of al-Ghazali.* Trans. by R. McCarthy. Boston: Twayne, 1980, 145–74.

———. *The Book of Knowledge, Being a Translation with Notes of the Kitab al-'ilm of al-Ghazali's Ihya 'ulum al-din.* Trans. by N. Faris. Delhi: International Islamic Publishers, 1988.

———. *The Incoherence of the Philosophers.* Trans. by M. Marmura. Provo, Utah: Brigham Young University Press, 1997.

al-Kindi, Abu Ya'qub. *Al-Kindi's Metaphysics.* Trans. by A. Ivry. Albany: State University of New York Press, 1974.

Averroës. *On the Harmony of Religion and Philosophy.* Trans. by George Hourani. London: Luzac, 1967.

———. *The Incoherence of the Incoherence of the Philosophers.* Trans. by Simon van den Bergh. London: Luzac, 1978.

Avicenna. *The Life of Ibn Sina.* Trans. by William Gohlman. New York: State University of New York Press, 1974.

Gimaret, D. *La doctrine d'al-Ash'ari.* Paris: Les éditions du Cerf, 1990.

Goldziher, Ignaz. "The Attitude of Orthodox Islam Towards the 'Ancient Sciences.'" In *Studies in Islam.* Trans. by M. Schwartz. New York: Oxford University Press, 1981, 185–215.

Grunebaum, Gustav von. "Muslim World View and Muslim Science." In *Islam: Essays in the Nature and Growth of a Cultural Tradition.* London: Routledge and Kegan Paul, 1964, 111–26.

Gutas, Dimitri. *Avicenna and the Aristotelian Tradition.* Leiden: Brill, 1988.

Halm, Heinz. *The Fatimids and Their Traditions of Learning.* London and New York: I. B. Tauris, in conjunction with the Institute of Ismaili Studies, 1997.

Huff, Toby. *The Rise of Early Modern Science: Islam, China, and the West.* Cambridge: Cambridge University Press, 1993.

Ibn Khaldun. *The Muqadimmah: An Introduction to History.* Trans. by F. Rosenthal. Princeton, N.J.: Princeton University Press, 1958.

Khadduri, Majid. *Islamic Jurisprudence: Shafi'i's Risala.* Baltimore: John Hopkins University Press, 1961.

King, David. *Astronomy in the Service of Islam.* Aldershot, U.K.: Variorum, 1993.

Marmura, Michael. "Al-Ghazali's Attitude Towards the Secular Sciences and Logic." In *Essays on Islamic Philosophy and Science,* ed. by G. Hourani. Albany: State University of New York Press, 1975, 100–11.

Puig, J. "Materials on Averroës' Circle." *Journal of Near Eastern Studies* 51 (1992): 241–61.

Sabra, A.I. "The Appropriation and Subsequent Naturalization of Greek Science in Medieval Islam: A Preliminary Statement." *History of Science* 25 (1987): 223–43.

———. "Philosophy and Science in Medieval Islamic Theology: The Evidence of the Fourteenth Century." *Zeitschrift für Geschichte der arabisch-islamischen Wissenschaften* 9 (1994): 1–42.

———. "Situating Arabic Science: Locality Versus Essence." *Isis* 87 (1996): 654–70.

Saliba, George. *A History of Arabic Astronomy.* New York: New York University Press, 1994.

Sayili, Aydin. *The Observatory in Islam.* Ankara: Türk Tarih Kurumu Basimevi., 1960.

48. MEDIEVAL SCIENCE AND RELIGION

David C. Lindberg

Methodological Remarks

Discussions of the relationship between science and religion in the Middle Ages have long been dominated by a bitter debate between the defenders of two extreme positions. At one extreme are the nineteenth-century popularizers and polemicists John William Draper (1811–82) and Andrew Dickson White (1832–1918), who formulated what has come to be called the "warfare thesis," according to which the Christian Church set itself up as the arbiter of truth and the opponent of the natural sciences, thereby retarding the development of genuine science for a thousand years.

The warfare thesis has retained a following throughout the twentieth century, at both a scholarly and a popular level, but it has also elicited strong opposition from scholars (some with a religious agenda) who have attempted to demonstrate that the Christian Church was not the opponent of science but its ally—that Christian theology was not an obstacle to the development of modern science but its necessary condition. Pierre Duhem (1861–1916) pioneered this line of argument early in the twentieth century. Stanley Jaki is its most notable contemporary champion.

It seems quite possible that the debate between defenders of the warfare thesis and their opponents will never entirely disappear, but it has been pushed off the center of the scholarly stage by a determined effort to gain a more dispassionate, balanced, and nuanced understanding. There are several definitions and methodological precepts prerequisite to the success of this venture. First, we must continually remind ourselves that "science," "Christianity," "theology," and "the Church" are abstractions rather than really existing things, and it is a serious mistake to reify them. What existed during the Middle Ages were highly educated scholars who held beliefs about both scientific and theological (and, of course, many other) matters. Science and theology cannot interact, but scientists and theologians can. Therefore, when the words "science," "theology," and "the Church" are employed in the following pages, the reader should understand that such locutions are shorthand references to beliefs and practices of scientists, theologians, and the people who populated the institutions of organized Christianity.

Second, scholars who made scientific beliefs their business and scholars who made religious or theological beliefs their business were not rigidly separated from one another by disciplinary boundaries. It is true that the nontheologian who encroached on theological territory ran certain risks (which varied radically with time and place), but all medieval scholars were both theologically and scientifically informed, and all understood that theological beliefs necessarily entailed scientific consequences *and conversely*. Indeed, the scientist and the theologian were often the very same person, educated in the full range of medieval disciplines—capable of dealing with both scientific and theological matters and generally eager to find ways of integrating theological and scientific belief.

Third, we need to agree on what is meant when we talk about medieval "science." There was nothing in the medieval period corresponding even approximately to modern science. What we do find in the Middle Ages are the roots, the sources, of modern scientific disciplines and practices—ancestors of many of the pieces of modern science, which bear a family resemblance to their offspring without being identical to them. In short, medieval scholars had ideas about nature, methods for exploring it, and languages for describing it. Many of these ideas, methods, and languages were drawn from the "classical tradition," the corpus of philosophical thought that originated in ancient Greece and was transmitted by various complicated processes to medieval Europe, where it became the object of intense scholarly discussion and dispute. Within the classical tradition, thought about nature was not sharply separated from thought about other subjects; all belonged to the general enterprise known as "philosophy," within which there was considerable methodological unity and interlocking content. If one wished to refer specifically to the aspects of philosophy concerned with nature, the expression "natural philosophy" was readily available. In the account that follows, the expressions "natural philosophy," "science," and "natural science" are employed as approximate synonyms, with the context being relied upon to make clear any shades of meaning. Furthermore, because natural philosophy interacted with Christianity not as a distinct enterprise but as one aspect of philosophy more generally, it will frequently prove useful to refer to "philosophy" (without qualification); it is to be understood, in such cases, that philosophy and natural philosophy shared approximately the same fate.

Fourth, medieval natural philosophy as a collection of theories was not uniform or monolithic; as an activity, its pursuit was as varied as the scholars who pursued it. The relations between medieval natural philosophy and medieval Christianity, therefore, varied radically over time, from place to place, from one scholar to another, and with regard to different issues, and it will never be possible to characterize those relations in a catchy slogan, such as that old stand-by, "the warfare of science and theology." A useful historical account must take the variations seriously, make distinctions, and reveal nuance. In short, the interaction between science and religion in the Middle Ages was not an abstract encounter between bodies of fixed ideas but part of the human quest for understanding. As such, it was characterized by the same vicissitudes and the same rich variety that mark all human endeavor.

The Patristic Period and the Early Middle Ages

The church Father who has most often been taken to represent the attitude of the early Christian church toward Greco-Roman philosophy is Tertullian (c. 160–c. 220), a North African, born of pagan parents, knowledgeable in

philosophy, medicine, and law. Though superbly educated, Tertullian has been presented (through selective quotation) as radically anti-intellectual, preferring blind faith to reasoned argument. The truth is that Tertullian had considerable respect for philosophical argument and frequently demonstrated argumentative prowess on behalf of his religious beliefs. But it is also true that he was no great friend of pagan philosophical systems, including systems of natural philosophy.

A wider examination of attitudes within the early church reveals a range of reactions to pagan philosophy, most of them more favorable than that of Tertullian. The first serious encounter between Christianity and Greco-Roman philosophical culture occurred in the second century of the Christian era. Plagued by internal doctrinal disputes and external persecution, the Christian church turned to Greek philosophy for help. The result was the emergence of a Christian intellectual tradition, which employed Greek philosophy for apologetic purposes, attempting to demonstrate not merely that Christian doctrine was true, but also that Christianity measured up to the highest aspirations of the Greek philosophical tradition. Thus, Justin Martyr (c. 100–165), Clement of Alexandria (c. 155–c. 220), and Origen of Alexandria (c. 185–c. 251) adopted an eclectic mixture of Greek philosophies, dominated by Platonism or Neoplatonism, but with an admixture of influences from Stoic, Aristotelian, and Neo-Pythagorean sources.

But if Justin, Clement, and Origen appear to have been generally receptive to influences coming from Greek philosophy, others were less welcoming. Justin's student Tatian (second century A.D.) deeply disapproved of Greek philosophy and issued a strong condemnation of its errors and perversions. And, of course, there was Tertullian, lashing out against philosophical conclusions that ran counter to Christian doctrine. Indeed, Justin, Clement, and Origen themselves understood the problematic character of Greek philosophy and frequently expressed ambivalent feelings toward it. For example, all three had cosmological interests, and all incorporated elements of Greek cosmology into their own cosmologies; at the same time, all perceived the dangers of uncritical acceptance of Greek cosmological doctrine and the difficulties of reconciling portions of it with the teachings of Christian theology.

Similar ambivalence is apparent in the writings of Augustine of Hippo (354–430), the most influential of all of the early Fathers and codifier of early Christian attitudes toward Greek philosophy and science. Augustine made no attempt to conceal his worries about the Greek philosophical tradition, firmly elevating divine wisdom, as revealed in Scripture, over the results of human rational activity. As for nature, Augustine maintained that there is nothing to worry about if Christians are ignorant of its workings; it is sufficient for them to understand that all things issue from the Creator.

But this is only part of the story. In other contexts, Augustine admitted that knowledge of the natural world is mandatory for the assistance it can provide in the task of biblical exegesis. And he rebuked Christians for opening themselves to ridicule by refusing to accept knowledge about nature from the Greek philosophers who possessed it. Insofar as the philosophical tradition contains truth (and there was no question in Augustine's mind that the truth it contained was substantial), and insofar as this truth is of religious or theological importance, it is to be seized upon and put to use by Christians. This is a clear statement of what has come to be known as the "handmaiden formula": the acknowledgment that science or natural philosophy is not an end in itself but a means to an end. It is to be cultivated by Christians insofar as it contributes to the interpretation of Scripture or other manifestly religious ends. Augustine did not repudiate the natural sciences; he christianized them and subordinated them to theological or other religious purposes. Science became the handmaiden of theology.

It was largely this attitude that motivated pursuit of the natural sciences through the early Middle Ages (c. A.D. 500–1000). During this period of political disintegration, social turmoil, and intellectual decline that came after the barbarian conquest of the western Roman Empire in the fifth century A.D., natural philosophy was an item of low priority. But when it was cultivated, as it sometimes was, it was cultivated by people in positions of religious authority or with a religious purpose, motivated by its perceived religious or theological utility. A sketch of the lives of five leading scholars, one each from the sixth through the tenth centuries and all interested in natural philosophy, may illuminate this claim.

Cassiodorus (c. 485–c. 580), a Christian member of the Roman senatorial class, founded the monastery of Vivarium, to which he retreated after his departure from public life. There he established a scriptorium, where secular Greek authors in substantial numbers were translated into Latin for use by the monastic community. Cassiodorus also wrote a manual of the liberal arts, the

Institutiones, in which he discussed mathematics, astronomy, and other scientific subjects.

Isidore (c. 560–636), bishop of Seville, was the outstanding scholar of the seventh century. Recipient (probably) of a monastic education, Isidore found time in his busy ecclesiastical career to write books, one of which, the *Etymologiae* (or *Origines*), became extraordinarily influential. In it he surveyed contemporary knowledge in biblical studies, theology, liturgy, history, law, medicine, and natural history.

In the eighth century, the Venerable Bede (c. 673–735), a monk from Northumbria in England, wrote a series of books for his fellow monks, including one on natural philosophy, entitled *On the Nature of Things,* and two on timekeeping and the calendar (which dealt largely with astronomical matters). In the ninth century, John Scotus Erigena (c. 810–c. 877), a product (in all likelihood) of Irish monastic schools, composed a sophisticated synthesis of Christian theology and Neoplatonic philosophy, including a well-articulated natural philosophy.

Finally, in the tenth century, a monk named Gerbert (945–1003), from the monastery at Aurillac in south-central France, crossed the Pyrenees to study the mathematical sciences in Catalonia with Atto, bishop of Vich. Gerbert occupied a number of teaching and administrative posts after his return from Catalonia and ended his career as Pope Sylvester II (999–1003). What is particularly noteworthy is the extent to which Gerbert, throughout a busy career, consistently advanced the cause of the mathematical sciences.

Several striking characteristics are shared by these five scholars. First, all had religious vocations: One was a bishop, another a pope, and a third a monk; one of the remaining two founded a monastery, to which he then belonged; another (Erigena), though apparently associated primarily with the court of Charles the Bald (823–77), emerged as an important theologian. Second, all evidently had monastic educations, except Cassiodorus, who became a monastic educator, and it was out of the educational experience in the monastery, rather than in repudiation of it, that their interest in the natural sciences grew. Third, all wrote treatises that revealed their interest in the natural sciences and helped enlarge the role of the sciences in European culture. And, finally, it can be plausibly argued in each case that the handmaiden formula supplied the motivation for writing about the natural sciences: The natural sciences are worth pursuing because ultimately they are a religious necessity. The Christian scholar cannot fulfill his calling without them.

But there is an important question that we must face: Can such studies, pursued as handmaidens of theology, count as genuine science? First, can science be a handmaiden of anything and remain science? Of course! Who would deny the status of genuine science to research on the atomic bomb during World War II (as handmaiden of the war effort) or to pharmacological research pursued by modern pharmaceutical corporations (as handmaiden of commerce)? Indeed, it is not easy to find scientific research during any period of Western history that was not the handmaiden of some ideology, social program, practical end, or profitmaking venture.

Second, it must be understood that an important aspect of every scientific tradition is the preservation and transmission of accumulated scientific knowledge; it is primarily to these functions that the early Middle Ages contributed. The church played a crucial positive role in the process, principally as the patron of European education, and its patronage extended to all aspects of learning, including the natural sciences. There can be no question about where the church placed priority. The natural sciences were not its primary interest, but they were given a small place in the curriculum of the schools and the writings of the leading scholars. Most assuredly, the early medieval church did not mobilize the resources of European society in support of the natural sciences, but no element in the European social or cultural fabric contributed more than did the church to the preservation of scientific knowledge during this intellectually precarious period.

Eleventh- and Twelfth-Century Renewal

Europe saw dramatic political, social, and economic renewal in the eleventh and twelfth centuries. The causes are complex, involving the restoration of centralized monarchies, reduction of the ravages of warfare, and the revival of trade and commerce. They led to rapid urbanization, the multiplication and enlargement of schools, and the growth of intellectual culture. Education shifted from the countryside to the cities, as cathedral and municipal schools replaced the monasteries as the principal educational institutions. Although cathedral schools shared the monastic commitment to education that was

exclusively religious in its aims, the curriculum of the cathedral schools reflected a far broader conception of the range of studies that were religiously beneficial and might, therefore, be legitimately taught and learned.

This broader curriculum of the schools had important consequences. In the first place, new emphasis was placed on the Latin classics (including Greek works available in Latin translation), which had long been available but had been little studied during the early Middle Ages. The most important of these for natural philosophy was Plato's (c. 427–347 B.C.) *Timaeus,* which became the principal source for cosmological instruction and speculation in the twelfth-century schools. A major preoccupation of twelfth-century natural philosophers became the task of harmonizing Plato's account of the construction of the cosmos by the Demiurge (Plato's divine craftsman) with the account of Creation in Genesis. An associated development was increasing insistence on the principle that natural phenomena were to be explained exclusively in naturalistic terms. This was not a result of skepticism about the divine origins of the universe, but the product of a growing conviction that investigation of the secondary causes established by the Creator was a legitimate (and perhaps the only legitimate) means of studying natural philosophy.

A second development associated with the schools was a rationalistic turn: the attempt to extend the application of reason or philosophical method to all realms of human activity, including theology. Much of the impetus came from Aristotle's (384–322 B.C.) logic and commentators on it (especially Boethius [c. 475–c. 525]). Illustrative of this movement and its potential dangers was the attempt by Anselm of Bec and Canterbury (1033–1109) to extend rational methodology into the theological realm by proving God's existence without any reliance on biblical authority or the data of revelation. While this does not appear, on the face of it, to be a perilous activity, what would happen if, having made reason our guide, we found that it led us to the wrong answer?

Third, a development that was certainly stimulated by educational developments and that was, in turn, to have momentous consequences for the schools was the translation movement of the eleventh and twelfth centuries. Through an intricate process spread over about two centuries, an enormous body of new learning became available in Latin through translation from Greek and Arabic. The classical tradition of natural philosophy became available virtually in its entirety, including almost the entire Aristotelian corpus, the medical writings of the Galenic tradition, and the mathematical works produced in ancient Greece and the world of medieval Islam. As this new learning was assimilated by Europeans in the thirteenth century, it enormously complicated the relations of science and Christianity.

Finally, as the schools grew in size and sophistication, some of them were transformed into universities, offering a higher level of learning, including graduate education in one or more of three advanced subjects: theology, medicine, and law. From the thirteenth century onward, these universities were the scene of much scientific activity and corresponding tension between scientific and theological doctrine.

The Later Middle Ages

The project that dominated the intellectual life of the thirteenth century was the organization and assimilation of the new learning, Greek and Arabic in origin, made available through the activity of the translators. Tensions between this new learning and the blend of Platonic philosophy and Christian theology that had come to dominate European thought over the previous millennium set an agenda that would challenge many of the best European minds. On the one hand, the new literature was enormously exciting because of its breadth and explanatory power. In almost every area, the new treatises surpassed in scope and sophistication anything the West had hitherto known. Moreover, they exhibited methodological principles that held the promise of future intellectual gains for those who would take the trouble to master them. On the other hand, substantial portions of the new literature impinged on Christian doctrine and not always benignly. If the Platonism of the early Middle Ages proved itself relatively congenial to developing Christian theology, the Aristotelianism that arrived with the translations would prove itself far more troublesome.

Aristotle was known during the early Middle Ages mainly through a group of logical works called the "old logic." Now, as a result of the translations, scholars had access to practically the entire Aristotelian corpus, including the works of important Muslim commentators (especially Avicenna [980–1037] and, by the middle of the thirteenth century, Averroës [1126–98]). There was much in Aristotelian philosophy that could be immediately put to use, and it is this (rather than coercion from some source of authority in medieval culture) that

explains the overwhelming popularity and influence of the Aristotelian system. But Aristotelian philosophy also had theological implications that threatened central Christian doctrines and posed a serious challenge for scholars who were unwilling either to abandon the theology to which they were firmly committed or to ignore the enormous promise of the new Aristotle.

What were the major problems? Perhaps the most obvious and one of the most contentious was Aristotle's claim that the world is eternal—that the cosmos had no beginning and will have no end. This belief obviously clashed with the Christian doctrine of Creation. The nature of the soul also posed problems, for it was not easy, within an Aristotelian framework, to view individual souls as separable from the body and eternal. The determinism and naturalism of the Aristotelian system presented further difficulties. The Aristotelian cosmos was a network of natural causes (associated with the natures of things) operating deterministically. Such a cosmos threatened the Christian doctrines of divine omnipotence and providence and, especially, of miracles. Before the end of the century, some philosophers at Paris, inspired by Aristotelian naturalism and determinism, went so far as to explain biblical miracles in naturalistic terms—and, thus, in the opinion of the theological authorities, to explain them away.

Finally, these troublesome Aristotelian doctrines were manifestations of a general outlook that pervaded the Aristotelian corpus, namely the view that Aristotelian demonstration, with its exclusive reliance on sense perception and rational inference, was the only way of achieving truth or of testing truth claims. Aristotelian philosophy thus arrived under the banner of extreme rationalism, which, if taken seriously, excluded biblical revelation and church tradition as sources of truth and made human reason the measure not only of philosophical claims but of theological ones as well.

The trouble was first felt at Paris (the leading theological center in Europe) early in the thirteenth century. In 1210 and again in 1215, the teaching of Aristotle's natural philosophy in the faculty of arts was banned, first by a council of bishops and subsequently by the papal legate. A papal bull (and subsequent letter) issued by Gregory IX (b. 1147, p. 1227–41) in 1231 acknowledged both the value and the dangers of Aristotelian philosophy, mandating that Aristotle's writings on natural philosophy be "purged of all suspected error" (Thorndike 1944, 38) so that, once erroneous matter had been removed, the remainder could be studied by Parisian undergraduates. (There is no evidence that the commission appointed by the pope ever met or that a purged version of Aristotle was ever produced.)

Within a decade of the papal bull of 1231, these early bans had lost their effectiveness. By the late 1230s or early 1240s, lectures on Aristotle's natural philosophy began to make their appearance in the faculty of arts at Paris. One of the first to give such lectures was the English friar Roger Bacon (1213–91). By 1255, all restrictions on the use of Aristotle had either been rescinded or were being ignored, for in that year the faculty of arts passed new statutes mandating lectures on all known Aristotelian works. In a remarkable turning of the tables, Aristotelian philosophy had moved from a position of marginality, if not outright exclusion, to centrality within the arts curriculum.

It is clear why this occurred. The Aristotelian corpus offered a convincing framework and a powerful methodology for thinking and writing about cosmology, meteorology, psychology, matter theory, motion, light, sensation, and biological phenomena of all kinds. The persuasive power of Aristotelian philosophy was so great as to preclude its repudiation. Traditionalists might be terrified by its theological implications, but Aristotelian philosophy was simply too valuable to relinquish. The task confronting those who wrestled with this problem would be the domestication, rather than the eradication, of Aristotle.

How was the domestication of Aristotle to be accomplished? Robert Grosseteste (c. 1168–1253), first chancellor of the University of Oxford, made an early and influential attempt to understand and explain Aristotle's method and some of his physical doctrines, while reconciling them with certain aspects of Plato's philosophy and a variety of other non-Aristotelian teachings. A generation later, Roger Bacon, a great admirer of Grosseteste but equipped with a much fuller knowledge of the newly translated learning, wrote an impassioned plea for papal support of the new learning (not only of Aristotle and his commentators, but also of the mathematical, and what Bacon called the "experimental," sciences). Bacon's case was based on claims of the utility of the new learning: for biblical exegesis, for proving the articles of the Christian faith, for establishing the religious calendar, for prolonging life, for producing devices that would terrorize unbelievers and lead to their conversion, and much more. This was Augustine's handmaiden formula, skillfully applied

by Bacon to fresh circumstances in which the quantity and variety of knowledge available to be enlisted as handmaiden was far larger and more problematic.

But perhaps the most influential actors in this drama were a pair of theologians (both with Parisian connections) writing after midcentury. Albert the Great (Albertus Magnus [1193–1280]) and Thomas Aquinas (c. 1225–74), both Dominican friars, undertook to interpret the whole of Aristotelian philosophy, correcting it where necessary, supplementing it from other sources where possible, and, in the process, attempting to define the proper relationship between the new learning and Christian theology. To offer a single example, both Albert and Thomas took up the question of the eternity of the world. Albert's early opinion was that philosophy can offer no definitive answer to this question, so that one is obliged to accept biblical teaching. Later, he concluded that Aristotle's opinion was *philosophically* absurd and must be rejected. Thomas argued that philosophy is incapable of resolving the question but that there is no philosophical reason why the universe could not be both eternal (having no beginning or end) and created (dependent on God for its existence).

What Albert and Thomas accomplished (assisted, of course, by Grosseteste, Bacon, and many others) was to find a solution to the problem of faith and reason—perhaps not a permanent solution but one that proved satisfactory to many in the Middle Ages and that continues to attract a significant following at the end of the twentieth century. They produced an accommodation between Aristotelian philosophy and Christian theology by christianizing Aristotle (correcting Aristotle where he was theologically unacceptable or had otherwise gone astray), and "Aristotelianizing" Christianity (importing major pieces of Aristotelian metaphysics and natural philosophy into Christian theology).

But not everybody was interested in accommodation. The freedom at the University of Paris and elsewhere that allowed Albert and Thomas to think creatively about the reconciliation of Aristotelian philosophy and Christian theology allowed others to promote Aristotle's philosophical program with little regard for its theological risks. In short, where there were those of liberal outlook, like Albert and Thomas, there would be others with more radical purposes. The radical faction at the University of Paris, led by Siger of Brabant (c. 1240–84), adopted Aristotle's rationalistic and naturalistic agenda, setting aside theological concerns or constraints in order to engage in the single-minded application of philosophical method to philosophical problems. Moreover, these "radical Aristotelians" were apparently teaching dangerous Aristotelian doctrines, such as the eternity of the world and denial of divine providence, in the faculty of arts. They attempted to protect themselves from anticipated criticism by noting that, although such conclusions are the proper and necessary conclusions of philosophy, truth lay on the side of theology. In short, philosophical and theological inquiry, each properly pursued, may lead in different directions, which is, of course, to free philosophy from servitude as the handmaiden of theology.

It should come as no surprise that scholars and ecclesiastical authorities of more conservative outlook should come to regard Siger and his group as a threat that required decisive action. The decisive action came in 1270, when the bishop of Paris, Etienne Tempier, condemned thirteen philosophical propositions allegedly taught by Siger and his fellow radicals in the faculty of arts. The decree was renewed, with an enlarged list of propositions, now numbering 219, in 1277. The Aristotelian claims identified above as dangerous are all represented on the latter list: the eternity of the world, rationalism, naturalism, and determinism. But a miscellaneous collection of other propositions impinging on natural philosophy was also included. Among them were several astrological propositions that were apparently perceived as dangerous because of the risk of astrological determinism. But the most interesting of the propositions condemned in 1277, from the standpoint of science and religion, were several that described what God could not do (for example, move the universe in a straight line, create multiple universes, or create accidents without subjects), because these things were judged impossibilities within the framework of Aristotelian metaphysics and natural philosophy. Tempier's point in condemning them was to remind Parisian scholars that divine freedom and omnipotence were not to be compromised by the dictates of Aristotelian philosophy—that God can do anything that involves no self-contradiction and, therefore, could have created, had he wished, a world that violates the principles of Aristotelian metaphysics and natural philosophy.

A great deal of ink has been spilled over the significance of the condemnations of 1270 and 1277. Pierre Duhem, who regarded them as the "birth certificate" of modern science, argued that Tempier's attack on entrenched Aristotelianism provided scholars with the freedom and the incentive to explore non-Aristotelian alternatives and that this theologically sanctioned exploration led ultimately to the emergence of modern science. Most historians of science would now judge Duhem's position to be overblown. A more modest assessment of the condemnations might look like this. In the first place, the condemnations were clearly the product of a conservative backlash against liberal attempts to extend the application of philosophy into the theological realm. They reveal the strength of the opposition and must surely be judged a victory—not for modern science but for theological conservatives at the University of Paris. Their purpose and their effect were to impose limits on philosophical freedom. That they achieved their intended effect is nicely illustrated by the extreme caution exercised by the Parisian master of arts Jean Buridan (c. 1295–c. 1358), writing at the University of Paris about the middle of the fourteenth century. Having strayed into theological territory by arguing against the existence of angelic movers of celestial spheres, Buridan adds that he makes these assertions tentatively, seeking "from the theological masters what they might teach me in these matters as to how these things take place" (Clagett 1959, 536).

But, in the second place, historical reality is not orderly. While inhibiting philosophical speculation in some directions, the condemnations encouraged it in others. There can be no question that the condemnations' stress on God's absolute freedom and power to have made any sort of world he wished, including a non-Aristotelian one, sanctioned the exploration of non-Aristotelian cosmological and physical possibilities. Within the framework of Aristotelian natural philosophy, there was no possibility that the universe (conceived as a single mass) could be put in motion. But scholars committed to the proposition that God could have put it in motion, had he so wished, felt compelled to develop new theories of motion consistent with such an imaginary, but (in view of God's absolute power) possible, state of affairs. Likewise, no good Aristotelian believed in void space, but stress on God's ability to have created void within or outside the universe led to important speculations about what such a world would have been like, and these speculations contributed, in the long run, to belief in the actual existence of void space. A concrete example may again be useful. In 1377, a full century after the condemnations, the Parisian theologian Nicole Oresme (c. 1320–82) defended the opinion that the cosmos is surrounded by void space and that it is not logically impossible for the universe to be moved in a straight line through this void space, reminding his reader that "the contrary is an article condemned at Paris" (Oresme 1968, 369).

Third, and finally, we need to take the long view. The condemnations of 1270 and 1277 represent a victory for conservatives wishing to restrict the range of philosophical speculation, but surely an ephemeral victory. As the thirteenth century yielded to the fourteenth and the fourteenth to the fifteenth, it became clear that the administrators and scholars who staffed the church bureaucracy and the universities had neither the power nor the desire to place philosophy (especially natural philosophy) on a short leash. Compromises were made, working arrangements were developed, and the church found itself in the role of the great patron of natural philosophy through its support of the universities. Certainly, there were theological boundaries that scholars trespassed at great risk, and there would continue to be skirmishes on specific, sensitive issues. But the late-medieval scholar rarely experienced the coercive power of the church and would have regarded himself as free (particularly in the natural sciences) to follow reason and observation wherever they led. There was no warfare between science and the church. The story of science and Christianity in the Middle Ages is not a story of suppression nor one of its polar opposite, support and encouragement. What we find is an interaction exhibiting all of the variety and complexity that we are familiar with in other realms of human endeavor: conflict, compromise, understanding, misunderstanding, accommodation, dialogue, alienation, the making of common cause, and the going of separate ways. Out of this complex interaction (rather than by repudiation of it) emerged the science of the Renaissance and the early-modern period.

See also Aristotle and Aristotelianism; Augustine of Hippo; Early Christian Attitudes Toward Nature; Eternity of the World; God, Nature, and Science; Islam; Pre-Copernican Astronomy; Thomas Aquinas and Thomism; Varieties of Providentialism

BIBLIOGRAPHY

Amundsen, Darrel W. "The Medieval Catholic Tradition." In *Caring and Curing: Health and Medicine in the Western Religious Traditions,* ed. by Ronald L. Numbers and Darrel W. Amundsen. 1986. Reprint. Baltimore: Johns Hopkins University Press, 1998, 65–107.

Amundsen, Darrel W., and Gary B. Ferngren. "The Early Christian Tradition." In *Caring and Curing: Health and Medicine in the Western Religious Traditions,* ed. by Ronald L. Numbers and Darrel W. Amundsen. 1986. Reprint. Baltimore: Johns Hopkins University Press, 1998, 40–64.

Armstrong, A. H., and R. A. Markus. *Christian Faith and Greek Philosophy.* London: Darton, Longman, and Todd, 1960.

Chenu, M.-D. *Nature, Man, and Society in the Twelfth Century: Essays on New Theological Perspectives in the Latin West.* Ed. and trans. by Jerome Taylor and Lester K. Little. Chicago: University of Chicago Press, 1968.

Clagett, Marshall. *The Science of Mechanics in the Middle Ages.* Madison: University of Wisconsin Press, 1959.

Cochrane, Charles N. *Christianity and Classical Culture.* Oxford: Clarendon, 1940.

Dales, Richard C. *Medieval Discussions of the Eternity of the World.* Leiden: Brill, 1990.

Draper, John William. *History of the Conflict Between Religion and Science.* 1874. 7th ed. London: King, 1876.

Duhem, Pierre. *Medieval Cosmology: Theories of Infinity, Place, Time, Void, and the Plurality of Worlds.* Ed. and trans. by Roger Ariew. Chicago: University of Chicago Press, 1985.

Funkenstein, Amos. *Theology and the Scientific Imagination from the Middle Ages to the Seventeenth Century.* Princeton, N.J.: Princeton University Press, 1986.

Grant, Edward. "Science and Theology in the Middle Ages." In *God and Nature: Historical Essays on the Encounter Between Christianity and Science,* ed. by David C. Lindberg and Ronald L. Numbers. Berkeley: University of California Press, 1986, 49–75.

———. *Planets, Stars, and Orbs: The Medieval Cosmos, 1200–1687.* Cambridge: Cambridge University Press, 1994.

Hooykaas, Reijer. "Science and Theology in the Middle Ages." *Free University [of Amsterdam] Quarterly* 3 (1954): 77–163.

Jaki, Stanley L. *The Road of Science and the Ways to God.* Chicago: University of Chicago Press, 1978.

Knowles, David. *The Evolution of Medieval Thought.* New York: Vintage, 1962.

Lindberg, David C. "Science and the Early Church." In *God and Nature: Historical Essays on the Encounter Between Christianity and Science,* ed. by David C. Lindberg and Ronald L. Numbers. Berkeley: University of California Press, 1986, 19–48.

———. "Science as Handmaiden: Roger Bacon and the Patristic Tradition," *Isis* 78 (1987): 518–36.

———. *The Beginnings of Western Science: The European Scientific Tradition in Philosophical, Religious, and Institutional Context, 600 B.C. to A.D. 1450.* Chicago: University of Chicago Press, 1992.

———. "Medieval Science and Its Religious Context." *Osiris* n.s. 10 (1995): 61–79.

Oresme, Nicole. *Le livre du ciel et du monde.* Ed. and trans. by A.D. Menut and A. J. Denomy. Madison: University of Wisconsin Press, 1968.

Southern, Richard W. *Robert Grosseteste: The Growth of an English Mind in Medieval Europe.* Oxford: Clarendon, 1986.

Steneck, Nicholas H. *Science and Creation in the Middle Ages: Henry of Langenstein (d. 1397) on Genesis.* Notre Dame, Ind.: University of Notre Dame Press, 1976.

Sylla, Edith D. "Autonomous and Handmaiden Science: St. Thomas Aquinas and William of Ockham on the Physics of the Eucharist." In *The Cultural Context of Medieval Learning,* ed. by John E. Murdoch and Edith D. Sylla. Dordrecht: Reidel, 1975, 349–96.

Thorndike, Lynn, ed. and trans. *University Records and Life in the Middle Ages.* New York: Columbia University Press, 1944.

Van Steenberghen, Fernand. *Thomas Aquinas and Radical Aristotelianism.* Washington, D.C.: Catholic University of America Press, 1980.

White, Andrew Dickson. *A History of the Warfare of Science with Theology in Christendom.* 2 vols. New York: Appleton, 1896.

Wippel, John F. "The Condemnations of 1270 and 1277 at Paris." *Journal of Medieval and Renaissance Studies* 7 (1977): 169–201.

49. ORTHODOXY

Allyne L. Smith Jr., H. Tristram Engelhardt Jr.,

Edward W. Hughes, and John Henry

When Constantine (ruled 312–337), the first Roman emperor to profess Christianity, turned his back on Rome (after 326) and founded the great city of Constantinople as the "New Rome" and capital of the Roman Empire, he also effectively initiated what has come to be known in the West as the Eastern Orthodox Church and in the East became the church of the first seven councils. In 395, the Roman Empire was permanently divided into Eastern and Western empires. While Germanic rulers gradually took control of the Western Roman Empire during the fifth century, the Eastern Empire, which over time came to be known as the Byzantine Empire, struggled to maintain its identity, until it was finally captured by the Ottoman Turks in 1453. The Christian Church proved essential to these efforts, and Byzantium became the major stronghold of Christian civilization from the fourth to the tenth centuries. The patriarch of Constantinople, so-called bishop of the "New Rome," was technically supposed to hold second rank after the bishop of Rome in a hierarchy of the major primates of the Church, who were as bishops equal. However, the decadence of the Roman papacy increasingly led to a severance of relations. Eventually, this severance resulted in the Great Schism between the Western and Eastern churches, which became respectively the Roman Catholic and Orthodox churches. The date of 1054, which is often said to mark the beginning of the schism, was actually the occasion of an attempted reconciliation between what were already divided churches. In fact, the papal legates and the patriarch of Constantinople disagreed over points of doctrine and ritual and ended up by excommunicating one another. So began a protracted period of increasingly obvious schism.

Over the centuries during which the Byzantine Empire attempted to maintain or extend its boundaries, the Orthodox Church engaged in parallel missionary efforts. As a result, it is now made up of a number of so-called autocephalous churches, each with its own head, or patriarch. The largest is the Russian Orthodox Church, but it also includes the Greek, Bulgarian, Romanian, and Serbian Orthodox churches, among others. The Ecumenical Patriarch of Constantinople is recognized as the honorary primate of all of the Orthodox churches and stands as a living symbol of their unity and cooperation.

The Orthodox Theological Tradition

Unlike the other major Christian churches, Orthodoxy has had little significant conflict with empirical science. While Roman Catholicism carries with it the memory of its disputes regarding heliocentrism, and contemporary Protestantism its concerns regarding the process of Creation, Orthodoxy has been relatively untouched by such controversies. There are at least three reasons for this lack of conflict that derive from characteristics of the Orthodox theological tradition and that distinguish it from the West.

First, unlike the Roman Catholic tradition subsequent to the Great Schism between East and West (a separation that occurred over a period of time, roughly from 867 to 1204), Orthodoxy maintained the Greek patristic view of theology as a union with God and not as an academic enterprise. While recognizing a role for discursive theological reflection, it regards such reflection as derivative of the primary theological transaction, liturgical worship of, and union with, God. In the Orthodox tradition, theology is first and foremost grounded in mystical experience. The well-known saying of the monk Evagrius of Pontus (346–99) is often taken by those within the Orthodox tradition as expressing the epitome of its understanding of theology: "If you are a theologian, you will pray truly. And if you pray truly, you are a theologian" (Palmer 1979, 62). The exemplar of this theology "is not the scholar in his study but the ascetic in his cell, and the *theoria* implied is not secondary theological reasoning but contemplation on the highest level, the roots of which are sunk deep in the ascetic's own fasting and prayer, particularly in the recitation of the psalter" (Kavanagh 1984, 124). Hence, the Orthodox tradition has not typically understood theology as a science that can potentially conflict with empirical sciences.

Second, unlike the Protestant traditions, Orthodoxy has viewed Scripture primarily as a liturgical text. Rather than regard the Bible as a text over and against the church, Orthodoxy has understood the biblical canon as representing the texts that may be read in the church's liturgy. This view of Scripture has informed Orthodox biblical hermeneutics: The Bible may be properly understood only in context—when it is proclaimed in the Eucharistic assembly. To take the Bible out of its proper context (that is, as the proclamation of the Gospel within the church) and to use it as a text with import for astronomy or evolutionary biology is radically to mistake its very character. So while Orthodox theology is, indeed, scriptural, it is so within its theology's doxological character. This liturgical centering of the Scriptures has been inhospitable to any scriptural scientific realism.

This is not to say that Orthodoxy does not make historical claims that might seem to conflict with the received opinion of natural scientists. For example, it regards Adam and Eve as real persons, and some liturgical calendars place the creation of the world 7,507 years before the year 1999. Yet, Orthodoxy has recognized human freedom; its theology, following Maximus the Confessor (580–662), has generally regarded even the past as, in some sense, changed by the Fall, such that it is not possible easily to move from biblical descriptions of reality to empirical claims. For example, Orthodoxy would generally not find any contradiction between the notion of evolution and the Creation account in Genesis, including the existence of Adam and Eve.

Finally, there has been a tendency in Orthodoxy to consider science and technology as involving realities radically different from those of religion: Orthodoxy affirms an absolute gulf between created being and Uncreated Being. Because God is fully transcendent, no analogy holds between him and created beings. Ortho-

dox theologians have not generally considered the findings of science as likely to conflict with theological commitments. This reflects the apophatic character of Orthodox theology, the recognition that the transcendent God can be known only via the path of unknowing. The insistence that the Godhead can be defined only in terms of "what it is *not*" originates in Eastern theological experience. Thus, true knowledge is acquired not through theological or metaphysical reasoning or through a literal interpretation of the Bible but through a life of worship that centers the Scriptures in the liturgy and aims the inquirer's mind beyond natural knowledge to union with a fully transcendent God.

Historical Overview

It seems hard to resist the conclusion that Orthodoxy has experienced little significant conflict with science simply because it has failed to pay sufficient attention to science's intellectual claims. This certainly seems to be borne out by the historical development of the Orthodox Church in the civilization of Byzantium. Church and state in the Byzantine Empire (395–1453) were always inextricably linked; they have even been described as two aspects of the same entity. Accordingly, higher education was directed toward the production of servants of state or church. Intellectuals, particularly if they held official appointments, could easily find themselves involved in political or ecclesiastical disputes. This was especially true during the unstable times that prevailed in Byzantium throughout the twelfth century, when the Empire was threatened in the Balkan territories by Pechenegs, in southern Italy by the Normans, and in Asia Minor by the Seljuk Turks.

There is little evidence during this period that natural philosophy, or what we would think of as a concern with the natural world and its workings, was regarded as a central intellectual pursuit. In his inaugural lecture of about 1165, Michael Anchialos (Patriarch of Constantinople, 1170–78), newly appointed "Consul of the Philosophers," or head of the School of Philosophy in Constantinople, tells us that it is the intention of his emperor, Manuel Comnenus (c. 1120–80), to use the study of the visible world to lead to knowledge of the invisible world. Michael himself suggests that he intends to do this by teaching astronomy, optics, and meteorology and will draw upon Aristotle (384–322 B.C.) rather than Plato (c. 427–347 B.C.) and the Neoplatonists, whose philosophies were clearly associated with various heretical positions. If his lecture suggests an acknowledgment of the potential importance of natural philosophy, even if only as an innocuous support for Orthodox theology, it was evidently to have little real impact upon Byzantine intellectual life. For the most part, Byzantine philosophers seem to have been much more directly concerned with issues of philosophical theology than with the workings of nature. From the early centuries, the life of philosophy had been identified with the life of monastic asceticism.

The association of philosophy with traditional theology became even more marked after the conquest and sack of Constantinople by Latin Crusader armies in 1204. Rejection of the Latin forms of worship and belief and, eventually, scholastic reflection, along with an affirmation of Orthodoxy, became important elements in establishing one's identity as a Byzantine. This holds as well for the Palaeologan Renaissance of Byzantine culture, which took place after Michael Palaeologus (1234–82) recaptured Constantinople in 1261 and after the rejection of the union with the Latins proposed at the Second Council of Lyons (1274). Byzantines were trying to reassert their religious and cultural traditions to maintain their own national identity and survival as a people against the twin threats of Latin Christianity from the West and the Ottoman Turks from the East. It seems to have been generally assumed that Byzantine cultural values could best be maintained by reasserting the teachings of the Greek Fathers and the early ecumenical councils of the Eastern Church. At a time when intellectuals in western Europe were engaging the secular concerns of Aristotelian philosophy, seeking to accommodate it to Christian teaching (not without some reciprocal influence upon the nature of their theology), the Byzantines were concentrating much more on their traditional theology.

One major aspect of this religious tendency in the Palaeologan Renaissance was a mystical, antischolastic movement known as Hesychasm. Based on the writings and practices of the Fathers, at least according to its chief proponents, the monks of Mt. Athos, Hesychasm continued the attempt to achieve mystical union with God through prayer and various ascetic practices. Although a revival of the glories of ancient Greek philosophy was another element in this attempt to reassert old traditions, the emphasis was never on natural philosophy. Late-thirteenth-century interest in Aristotle and Thomas Aquinas's (c. 1225–74) Aristotelian commentaries was

motivated by a desire not to understand the natural world but to enable Byzantine theologians to respond adequately to the scholastic arguments used by Western theologians in the various ecclesiastical negotiations with Rome that were taking place at that time.

While Aristotelian natural philosophy, by the end of the thirteenth century, had carved a niche for itself in western Europe as a handmaiden to religion, there was no corresponding place for it in the intellectual life of eastern Europe. This situation did not change until the seventeenth century, when Theophilus Corydaleus (1570–1646), the greatest Greek philosopher since the fall of Constantinople (1453), established the neo-Aristotelianism of the School of Padua (where he had been a student of the Aristotelian philosopher Cesare Cremonini [1550–1631]) as the dominant philosophy in the territories of the Eastern Church. Just as western Europe was beginning to throw off the yoke of Aristotelianism, eastern Europe came under its thrall.

During the Enlightenment of the eighteenth century, Western scientific ideas became known in the East but were adopted slowly and only in a piecemeal fashion. Copernican astronomical theory was first introduced to Greek readers by Chrysanthos Notaras (1663–1731) in 1716, but he noted the scriptural arguments against the theory and continued to affirm Ptolemaic theory. It was not until 1766 that Nikiphoros Theotokis (1731–1800) declared the Copernican-Newtonian account of the solar system to be true. One of the leading figures in the Greek Enlightenment, Eugenios Voulgaris (1716–1806), accepted and taught many of the innovations of Western science even as he continued to see them either as compatible with, or subordinate to, traditional Orthodox thought. He seems to have been content to treat opposed views of nature eclectically, seeing ancient and modern views as having equal epistemological validity. It was a student of Voulgaris, Iossipos Moisiodax (c. 1725–1800), who made the first public commitment to the new science in works published in the 1780s. Moisiodax felt obliged to insist upon the separation of science from religion: "The Holy Spirit imparts mystical knowledge of the Holy Scriptures and of our supernatural religion but it does not instruct either builders, or goldsmiths, or stone-sculptors and therefore neither does it instruct mathematicians." Contrary to Byzantine tradition, his work came in for heavy criticism by his contemporaries in the Orthodox Church as heretical and atheistic. Similar criticisms were leveled at Veniamin Lesvios (1759–

1824), the leading proponent of the new science in the decade just before the Greek War of Independence (1821), although his work has been seen as marking the beginning of the acceptance of Western science into modern Greek culture. The subsequent development of science in the territories of the Orthodox Church still failed to rouse any serious opposition from church leaders. Although liberal and radical intellectuals in Russia in the late nineteenth century believed that evolutionary theory contradicted religious doctrines, the Orthodox Church did not join the debate. It continued to concern itself with the pastoral and mystical experiences of the faithful.

Orthodox Epistemology

Underlying Orthodoxy's largely disengaged attitude from empirical science has been its understanding of epistemology. The traditional view of knowledge is reflected in the threefold division articulated by Isaac of Syria (613–c. 700), bishop of Nineveh, who left the episcopate to become a hermit and whose subsequent writings have deeply influenced Orthodoxy. According to Isaac, there are three degrees, or orders, of knowledge that correspond to the three aspects of the human person—body, soul, and spirit (Isaac 1984, 258). Bodily, or "shallow," knowledge is directed to the world and not God. The second degree, soul knowledge, comes about "when a man renounces the first degree and turns toward deep reflections and the love of the soul" (Isaac 1984, 260). Although this order of knowledge is made perfect by the Holy Spirit, it "is still corporeal and composite" (Isaac 1984, 260). Only at the third degree of knowledge is there knowledge fully in the Spirit. These stages, which Isaac also terms natural, supranatural, and contra-natural knowledge, he summarizes thusly: "The first degree of knowledge renders the soul cold to works that go in pursuit of God. The second makes her fervent in the swift course on the level of faith. But the third is rest from labour, which is the type of the age to come, for the soul takes delight solely in the mind's meditation upon the mysteries of the good things to come" (Isaac 1984, 261–2).

The first two stages are neutral, gifts that may be used rightly to lead toward God or wrongly to lead away from him (Isaac 1984, 258). This theology was directed toward developing a spiritual openness to God rather than discovering theological propositions that may have empirical implications. It went along with an attitude toward philosophy that differed from that which emerged in the West. In the East, Orthodox theologians regarded philosophy in the sense of natural philosophy and independent of faith as radically incomplete. It was not expected that discursive philosophy, including natural philosophy, could demonstrate what faith disclosed as an article of belief (for example, that the world was created). The Orthodox have not given a theological standing to the many scientific reflections engaged in by theologians over the centuries. Rather, they have received them as historically conditioned attempts to understand the empirical character of the world. The failure of such musings to deliver empirical truth found an explanation in the general disregard of philosophical reasoning as a means of discovering ultimate truth. Exclusive attention to the science of secular philosophy was criticized by many of the Fathers, such as John Chrysostom (349–407), exactly because of its disengagement from faith.

Orthodoxy and Science

Given Orthodoxy's attitude toward discursive knowledge, it is not surprising that it has generally been at peace with the findings of natural science, medicine, and technology. The Orthodox have considered scientific endeavors as undertaken on an ontological plane quite different from that of theology. Because science and theology involve different orders of knowledge and being, the first, creation, and the second, the transcendent Creator, the methods and ends of science and theology are distinct. In that Orthodoxy has seen scientific knowledge and theology as radically distinct rather than conflicting, there is a long tradition of Orthodox theologians employing science without any commitment to the theological truth of the science. An early example of using science in concert with theological discourse is the *Hexaemeron* of Basil the Great (c. 330–79), a commentary on the six days of Creation. Although Basil accepts "spontaneous generation" as a scientific truth, subsequent theologians have not been concerned by the fact that this view seems to conflict with God's role as the Creator. More recently, one finds in the work of Nicodemus of the Holy Mountain (c. 1749–1809) the incorporation of the science of his day regarding the human heart. The subsequent disconfirmation of the scientific accounts that Nicodemus borrowed for purposes of illustrating theological concerns has engendered no embarrassment among Orthodox churchmen. Theologians appear to have recognized that his accounts of reality taken from science were drawn from a source of knowledge open to error and, therefore, in need of constant scientific revision. Empirical science cannot compete directly with theology. Disputes have generally involved particular misuses of science, as in the condemnation of the use of medicines for abortion.

In spite of the recognition that science and theology have a very different character, applied science has played a positive role within Orthodox cultures, particularly within a philanthropic context. The Byzantine Empire maintained, for example, a sophisticated level of medical practice. Perhaps the greatest contribution of Orthodoxy to medicine was the birth of the hospital in the fourth century. It has been argued that, unlike hospices in the West, which existed primarily to give comfort and care to the ill and dying, Byzantine *xenones* were "medical centers controlled by trained physicians and designed to cure the sick" (Miller 1997, xxviii). From the third-century saint and mathematician Catherine the Wise, to the various saint-physicians who practiced without charging for their services (the holy and unmercenary physicians), to "scientist-saints" of the twentieth century, the Orthodox Church has often (but not always) regarded science and technology as nonthreatening undertakings. A recent example is that of the Russian Orthodox priest and mathematician Pavel A. Florensky (1882–c. 1946), who made a number of contributions to science and technology before he was put to death under Stalin. Similarly, the great physiological psychologist Ivan Pavlov (1849–1936), who was educated at a religious seminary, never lost his interest in the Orthodox faith.

When conflicts have arisen between Orthodox theology and science, they have generally involved what, from an Orthodox theological perspective, should be considered a category mistake: confusing concerns about created being vs. Uncreated Being. When such conflict has occurred, it has usually, in retrospect, been attributed in Orthodoxy to the introduction of Western theological perspectives that disregard the Orthodox principle of a gulf between nature and God. Over the past two centuries, there has been a particular reaction within Orthodoxy against such confusions in favor of the earlier patristic and monastic understanding of theology as an experience of God and a recognition that no analogy exists between the Being of God and the being of nature. A climate has been created that favors the pursuit of science, technology, and medicine independently of theology.

In the modern age, the Orthodox community has objected to scientists attempting to speak authoritatively *qua* scientists on theological and metaphysical matters. This kind of category mistake has been understood within Orthodoxy to result in both the dehumanization of man and the desanctification of nature. Finally, as with the use of medicine for abortion, so, too, particular uses of science and technology have been brought into question in the Orthodox tradition when they have set human life and interests at jeopardy.

See also Early Christian Attitudes Toward Nature; Medieval Science and Religion

BIBLIOGRAPHY

Browning, Robert. "A New Source on Byzantine-Hungarian Relations in the Twelfth Century: The Inaugural Lecture of Michael Anchialos." *Balkan Studies* 2 (1961): 173–214.

———. "Enlightenment and Repression in Byzantium in the Eleventh and Twelfth Centuries." *Past and Present* 69 (1975): 3–23.

———. "Church, State, and Learning in Twelfth-Century Byzantium." In *History, Language, and Literacy in the Byzantine World*, ed. by Robert Browning. Northampton: Variorum Reprints, 1989, VI, 5–24.

Cavarnos, Constantine. *Modern Greek Thought*. 1969. Reprint. Belmont, Mass.: Institute for Byzantine and Modern Greek Studies, 1986.

Geanakoplos, Deno John. *Interaction of the "Sibling" Byzantine and Western Cultures in the Middle Ages and Italian Renaissance (330–1600)*. New Haven, Conn.: Yale University Press, 1976.

Graham, Loren R. *Science in Russia and the Soviet Union: A Short History*. Cambridge: Cambridge University Press, 1993.

Harakas, Stanley S. *Health and Medicine in the Eastern Orthodox Tradition: Faith, Liturgy, and Wholeness*. New York: Crossroad, 1990.

Henderson, G. P. *The Revival of Greek Thought, 1620–1830*. Albany: State University of New York Press, 1970.

Hussey, J. M. *The Orthodox Church in the Byzantine Empire*. Oxford: Clarendon, 1986.

Isaac the Syrian. *Ascetical Homilies*. Boston: Holy Transfiguration Monastery, 1984.

Kalomiros, Alexandre. "The Eternal Will: Some Thoughts Concerning Scriptural and Patristic Understanding of the Creation of Man and the World." *Christian Activist* 11 (Fall/Winter 1997).

Kavanagh, Aidan. *On Liturgical Theology*. New York: Pueblo, 1984.

Kitromilides, Paschalis M. "The Idea of Science in the Modern Greek Enlightenment." In *Greek Studies in the Philosophy and History of Science,* ed. by Pantelis Nicolacopoulos. Dordrecht: Kluwer, 1990, 187–200.

Lossky, Vladimir. *The Mystical Theology of the Eastern Church.* Crestwood, N.Y.: St. Vladimir's Seminary Press, 1976.

Miller, Timothy S. *The Birth of the Hospital in the Byzantine Empire.* 1985. Reprint. Baltimore: Johns Hopkins University Press, 1997.

Palmer, G. E. H., Philip Sherrard, Kallistos Ware, trans. and eds. *The Philokalia: The Complete Text.* Vol. 1. 1979. Reprint. Boston: Faber and Faber, 1986.

Pelikan, Jaroslav. *Christianity and Classical Culture: The Metamorphosis of Natural Theology in the Christian Encounter with Hellenism.* New Haven, Conn. and London: Yale University Press, 1993.

Popovich, Justin. "The Theory of Knowledge of Saint Isaac the Syrian." In *Orthodox Faith and Life in Christ.* Trans. by Asterios Gerostergios et al. Belmont, Mass.: Institute for Byzantine and Modern Greek Studies, 1994.

Scarborough, John, ed. *Symposium on Byzantine Medicine.* Dumbarton Oaks Papers 38. Washington, D.C.: Dumbarton Oaks, 1985.

Sherrard, Philip. *The Eclipse of Man and Nature: An Enquiry into the Origins and Consequences of Modern Science.* West Stockbridge, Mass.: Lindisfarne, 1987.

Vlachos, Hierotheos. *Orthodox Psychotherapy: The Science of the Fathers.* Levadia, Greece: Birth of the Theotokos Monastery, 1994.

Yannaras, Christos. *Elements of Faith: An Introduction to Orthodox Theology.* Edinburgh: T. and T. Clark, 1991.

50. ROMAN CATHOLICISM SINCE TRENT

Steven J. Harris

The attempt to characterize the relationship between the Roman Catholic Church and science has often suffered from two broad assumptions: first, that the Roman Catholic Church has been monolithic in regard to its institutions and opinions; and second, that there has existed a fundamental—perhaps inevitable—conflict between the aims and methods of the Catholic faith and those of modern science. These assumptions are nowhere more strongly in evidence than in the literature on the trial and condemnation of Galileo Galilei (1564–1642), in which the Church is portrayed as a univocal, authoritarian, and dogma-bound institution that invoked the inviolability of Scripture to suppress an essentially correct theory of the world (heliocentrism) and the mathematical and empirical methods upon which it rested. Although this reading of the Galileo affair has gained wide acceptance, there are several difficulties with the conflict thesis as a general characterization of the last four hundred years of Roman Catholic interaction with science. First, the Catholic hierarchy has rarely been of one mind regarding controversial scientific theories. Second, the Church's strong tradition of conservatism has not precluded accommodation to novel astronomical, evolutionary, and cosmological theories. Third, despite the implication of a "fundamental conflict" found in the Galileo affair, post-Galilean episodes fail to reveal evidence of a uniform, deliberate, and sustained attack on the methods of modern science. And, finally, an unqualified conflict thesis is difficult to reconcile with the long tradition of support of scientific activity within the Church itself. Perhaps most surprising in this regard is the fact that the greatest levels of clerical activity in science are to be found in the two hundred years following the Council of Trent.

The Council of Trent, an ecumenical gathering of bishops, cardinals, and prominent theologians who met in three sessions between 1545 and 1563, marked the beginning of a concerted effort on the part of the Roman Catholic Church to counter the advances made in the previous fifty years by the breakaway reform churches of the Lutherans, Calvinists, and Anglicans. Protestant challenges to papal authority, profound theological disagreement regarding matters of doctrine and faith, and an acknowledgment by the Church hierarchy of indiscipline within its own ranks led the Council to issue a series of decrees and institutional reforms that initiated what came to be called the Catholic Counter-Reformation. It was within this "era of restrictive orthodoxies" (both Protestant and Catholic) that the so-called Copernican revolution unfolded, a revolution that would result in the abandonment of the earth-centered worldview and the beginnings of modern astronomy and cosmology.

Attitudes toward Heliocentrism

While neither the Catholic nor Protestant churches had elevated geocentrism to the level of dogma, it rested on the seemingly unshakable foundations of received philosophical principles, scriptural corroboration, and plain common sense. The virtual sanctification of geocentric cosmology meant that the sun-centered (or heliocentric) planetary theory of Nicholas Copernicus (1473–1543) raised problems not only in theoretical astronomy, but also in philosophy and theology. Galileo's efforts to convince the world of the truth of the Copernican theory thus took place at a time when the Church sought to reaffirm its religious authority and when that authority seemed also to embrace questions in mathematical astronomy as well as theology. The publication of his *On the Two Chief World Systems* in 1632, sixteen years after Copernicus's work on the heliocentric system was placed on the Index of Prohibited Books, elicited a swift and punitive response from Rome. Sale of Galileo's book was immediately suspended, and Galileo was brought before the Inquisition. At the conclusion of his trial in 1633, heliocentrism was condemned as heretical, Galileo's works were placed on the Index, and Galileo was forced to recant his errors and sentenced to lifelong house arrest.

The startling vehemence of the Roman hierarchy in prosecuting Galileo has tended to mask the diversity of opinions found within the Church itself. Dominican inquisitors argued that the Copernican theory cannot, in principle, be true because its claims rested on mathematical demonstrations. The problem with Galileo's mathematical argument in favor of heliocentrism was, therefore, not the insufficiency of evidence but the inherent limitations of his mode of reasoning. Some Jesuits, on the other hand, believed in the validity of mathematically based demonstrations but thought that Galileo's proofs were incomplete and, therefore, that he should not argue for the physical truth of heliocentrism. Still other clerics argued that Galileo had presented compelling arguments and that, as a result, a reinterpretation of certain passages of the Bible was necessary.

Diversity of clerical opinion notwithstanding, the Inquisition declared that heliocentrism was "philosophically absurd and false, and formally heretical." Despite the fact that this condemnation came from the highest levels of the Roman Curia, practical constraints limited both the scope and the execution of its decrees. Both the Roman Inquisition and the Index depended largely upon secular rulers to enforce their decrees in Catholic lands, and so their authority was limited to the obedient and like-minded. Protestants, of course, ignored them completely. France, for example, failed to promulgate the decrees of 1633 (though the faculty of the Sorbonne in Paris would issue its own condemnation of heliocentrism), and fewer than ten percent of all surviving copies of Copernicus's book show signs of actually having been "corrected." The Spanish Inquisition operated independently of the one in Rome and neither endorsed Rome's injunctions against Copernicanism nor issued any of its own. Eventually, the vexed issue of heliocentrism achieved a belated, if incomplete, resolution in the mid-eighteenth century. In 1741, thirteen years after the discovery of the aberration of star light (a phenomenon understood to arise from the motion of the earth around the sun) and one year into his papacy, Pope Benedict XIV (b. 1675, p. 1740–58) effectively lifted the injunction against the heliocentric theory by having the Holy Office grant the first edition of *The Complete Works of Galileo* an imprimatur. In 1757, one year before the end of his papacy, Benedict ordered that all works espousing the heliocentric theory be removed from the Index.

Clerical Science, 1600–1800

Despite the Church's disastrous condemnation of Copernicanism, it retained an important role as patron of a wide range of scientific activity. Members of Catholic religious orders, especially the Jesuits, continued to pursue research in observational and practical astronomy. Jesuit astronomers in Rome were the first to confirm Galileo's telescopic observations, while confreres in Germany discovered sunspots independently of Galileo, made important improvements in telescope design, and undertook extensive telescopic observations of the sun, comets, moon, and planets. In several Italian cities, Catholic cathedrals were used as solar observatories by clerics who had obtained permission to have holes drilled in the walls and brass meridian lines embedded in the floors so that the motion of the sun could be studied with precision. Moreover, the Jesuit, Benedictine, and Oratorian religious orders operated a number of conventional observatories and collectively made important contributions not only to observational astronomy, but also to meteorology, geography, and geodesy. Closely allied with astronomy was the teaching of mathematics, and, by 1700, the Jesuit order alone controlled more than one hundred chairs of mathematics, making it the single largest purveyor of mathematical education in Europe.

In addition to their contributions to observational astronomy and mathematics, churchmen were also active in the newly emerging experimental and empirical sciences. And while clerics tended to adopt a conservative stance in regard to interpretation, often seeking to preserve Aristotelian notions (for example, arguing against the existence of the vacuum), they did so while insisting upon the importance of experiment in ascertaining the properties of physical reality and its validity as a means of testing theoretical claims. Because of their participation in overseas missions, Catholic clerics were well situated to engage in a wide range of empirical field sciences. In the period before the French Revolution, Dominican, Benedictine, Franciscan, and Jesuit missionaries together formed a loose but extensive network of amateur naturalists that literally spanned the globe. Their published reports of novel lands and peoples and their knowledge of indigenous herbal remedies added significantly to the fields of geography, natural history, botany, and medicine. Only in the eighteenth century, with the rise of large scientific societies and stable overseas trading companies, were networks of lay observers able to supplant missionary-naturalists.

Although clerical science continued to thrive well into the eighteenth century, the priest-scientist was brought to near extinction by 1800. Factors contributing to this demise were the Papal States' gradual loss of temporal wealth and political authority, the consolidation of state power under absolutist monarchies, and the pervasive anticlericalism of the Enlightenment. Perhaps the most severe blows were the suppression of the Jesuit order in 1773, which terminated what had been the richest scientific tradition within the post-tridentine Church, and the sequestration of monastic properties in the wake of the French Revolution. Despite various papal initiatives in the nineteenth and twentieth centuries, the Church has never recovered its prerevolutionary levels of scientific support and productivity.

Papal Patronage of Science

Modest recovery of the Church's patronage of science came with the reestablishment in the mid-nineteenth century of two post-tridentine institutions, the Vatican Observatory and the Pontifical Academy of Sciences. Though founded in 1576 by Pope Gregory XIII (b. 1502, p. 1572–85) to facilitate the calendar reform that bears his name, the Vatican Observatory fell into disuse even before 1600. Reestablished in 1839, the Pontifical Observatory (as it was then called) flourished under the patronage of Pius IX (b. 1792, p. 1846–78) and the directorship of the capable Jesuit astronomer Pietro Angelo Secchi (1818–78). In 1879, the Italian government confiscated the Pontifical Observatory and began operating it as a state-run institution. In 1888, Pope Leo XIII (b. 1810, p. 1878–1903) reopened the Vatican Observatory; it has operated without interruption ever since, largely under the direction of Jesuit astronomers.

The Pontifical Academy of Sciences, like the Vatican Observatory, claims descent from a much earlier institution, in this case the Academia Linceorum (Academy of the Lynx). Founded in 1603 by Prince Frederico Cesi (1585–1630), the Lincei flourished briefly in the 1610s and 1620s (when it could claim Galileo as its most illustrious member), but its activities came to a halt with the death of its founder in 1630. In 1847, Pius IX, invoking—and perhaps exploiting—the memory of the Lincei, founded the Pontificia Accademiae dei Nuovi Lincei as an official body of the Pontifical States. After a brief moment of reflected prestige under the astronomer Secchi, who served as the president from 1874 until his death in 1878, the New Lincei slowly slipped into invisibility. Under the initiative of Pius XI (b. 1857, p. 1922–39), the academy was reestablished in 1936 and rechristened the Pontifical Academy of Sciences. According to its charter, its membership was to be drawn from all nations and creeds, and its goal was "to honor pure science wherever it is found, assure its freedom and promote its researches."

Mendel, Teilhard, Lemaître

The renewal of the Vatican's direct patronage of scientific institutions since the mid-nineteenth century has been accompanied by a revival of scientific practice among Roman Catholic clerics. Although modest in comparison to former days, the modern tradition of clerical science has not been without its significant episodes. The work of three of its most prominent—though perhaps not most representative—members, Gregor Mendel (1822–84) in genetics, Pierre Teilhard de Chardin (1881–1955) in paleontology, and Georges Lemaître (1894–1966) in cosmology, suggests not only the disciplinary breadth of the modern tradition, but also the Church's direct, if sometimes strained, engagement with one of the central themes of modern science, namely the evolutionary worldview.

Gregor Mendel was born into a poor peasant family near Oldlau, Moravia (then part of the Austro-Hungarian Empire, now part of the Czech Republic); his only opportunity for an education was at the local school run by Piarist clerics. He went on to study at the university in Olomouc (Olmütz). After two years of extreme privation, he followed the recommendation of his physics professor and entered the Augustinian monastery of Saint

Thomas in Brno (Brünn)—though, as he himself admitted, "out of necessity and without feeling in himself a vocation for holy orders." The monastery, however, proved to be well-suited to his quiet, studious ways and an ideal place for his work on plant hybridization.

As well known as Mendel's contributions to genetics have since become, what remains less well known is the fact that his plant-breeding experiments were part of an ongoing program of agricultural research within the monastery. For twenty years prior to Mendel's arrival, the monks of Saint Thomas had engaged in plant-breeding experiments and had disseminated their results through teaching, publication, and participation in local agricultural and scientific societies. Mendel's initial work on plant heredity was conducted under Matthew Klácel (1802–82), director of the monastery's research gardens (an office that Mendel later held). Klácel's speculations on evolution, inspired in part by Hegelian philosophy (an intellectual allegiance that contributed to his eventual dismissal from the Augustinian order), deeply influenced Mendel's own work. During the period of Mendel's most important experimental work (c. 1853–68), scientific discussions within the monastery frequently touched upon the role of variation in the evolution of plants. Mendel had read the German translation of Charles Darwin's (1809–82) *Origin of Species* (1859) and fully accepted the theory of evolution by means of natural selection. Thus, his most important discoveries, the law of segregation (that the paired genes of body cells separate during the production of sex cells, or gametes) and the law of independent assortment (that the genes responsible for an organism's characteristics are inherited independently of each other), arose from a milieu of evolutionary speculation and a local monastic tradition of controlled experiments in plant hybridization. Although Mendel ceased his plant experiments in 1869 when he was elected abbot of Saint Thomas and his laws of heredity were ignored for the next thirty years, his work has since become foundational for modern genetics and a central component of modern evolutionary theory.

The question of evolution, especially human evolution, was most controversial in the work of Pierre Teilhard de Chardin. Teilhard, who entered the Society of Jesus in 1898 at the age of seventeen, studied in France and England before completing his doctorate in paleontology at the Sorbonne in 1922. During his studies, he was deeply influenced by the speculative evolutionary philosophy of Henri Bergson (1859–1941). While teaching at the Catholic Institute in Paris in the early 1920s, Teilhard lectured on the theological doctrine of original sin within the framework of (directed) human evolution. His ideas drew severe complaints from conservative theologians, and Teilhard's Jesuit superiors forbade him to lecture on these topics. In April 1926, he was transferred (some say "exiled") to China. There he continued his work in paleontology and geology, making significant contributions to both fields. In 1929, for example, he was part of the team that discovered the celebrated "Peking man" (or *Sinanthropus,* later assigned to *Homo erectus*) near Chou-k'ou-tien.

Teilhard remained in China until shortly after the end of World War II. During his last years in Asia, he continued to develop his philosophical speculations regarding human evolution. His central idea was one of a thoroughgoing cosmic evolution that embraced both inorganic and organic matter, as well as all organisms and human consciousness. According to Teilhard, evolution unfolds along an axis of increasing organizational complexity, including several levels of "consciousness." Hominid evolution—or the "hominization of matter," as he called it—marks the emergence of the noösphere on Earth (a "sphere" of thinking matter analogous to the biosphere of living matter) and points toward the next stage, "planetization," before culminating in the final stage of the complete self-consciousness of creation, which he called the "Omega Point." Grand in conception, often poetic in its expression, and mystical in tone, Teilhard's writings moved him into a new and untested territory situated between evolutionary theory and Catholic theology.

Once he was back in Paris, Teilhard found it difficult to present his ideas for public discussion, the resistance initially coming largely from within his own order. Not only did he fail to find a publisher for this work, but his Jesuit superiors forbade him in 1947 to write on philosophical topics and denied him permission to assume the prestigious chair in paleontology at the Collège de France when it was offered to him in 1949. The maneuvers on the part of Teilhard's Jesuit superiors to block or limit the public exposure of his ideas were undoubtedly bound up with developments in Rome—though not always in ways that help explain their decisions. In 1948, the Pontifical Biblical Commission reaffirmed earlier declarations of 1909 regarding Genesis and human evolution but also claimed that these pronouncements were "in no way a hindrance to further truly scientific examination of the problems [of human evolution]." This implicit loosening of the strictures of 1909 should have, at the very least, encouraged the placement of Teilhard in the most prestigious chair in paleontology in all of France, but it did not.

In 1950, Pope Pius XII (b. 1876, p. 1939–58) issued the encyclical *Humani generis,* in which questions of evolution and theology took center stage. The encyclical opened with a condemnation of both pantheism and philosophical materialism and went on to declare the philosophies of "evolutionism" and historicism suspect because of their complicity in "relativistic conceptions of Catholic dogma." The encyclical stated that "the evolution of the human body from preexisting and living matter . . . is not yet a certain conclusion from the facts and that revelation demands moderation and caution." Hesitations notwithstanding, the encyclical went on to offer—for the first time—a restrained acceptance of evolution: "the teaching authority of the Church does not forbid that, in conformity with the present state of human sciences and sacred theology, research and discussion on the part of men experienced in both fields take place with regard to the doctrine of evolution." While such words could have been read as encouragement for just the sort of public discussion Teilhard was hoping to pursue in Paris, his Jesuit superiors thought otherwise. In 1951, his order transferred (again, some say exiled) him to New York, thus removing him entirely from the French intellectual scene for a second time. In New York, Teilhard continued his paleontological research and his philosophical writings, though none of his nonscientific work was published before his death in 1955.

With the publication of *Le phénemène humain* (*The Phenomenon of Man*) in 1955 and several other of his philosophical works, the controversy intensified. In 1957, Rome sought to remove his published works from the shelves of Catholic libraries and bookshops, and in 1962 (as his works continued to gain in popularity), Pope John XXIII (b. 1881, p. 1958–63) issued a *monitum* or warning to readers against the uncertainties of Teilhard's theology. Neither step, however, slowed the international enthusiasm for "Teilhardism." Since the *monitum* of 1962, Rome has placed no further restrictions on his works, and he has become one of the most widely read and discussed Catholic intellectuals of the twentieth century.

Despite the controversies surrounding Teilhard's speculations concerning human evolution, Georges Lemaître's theoretical work on cosmic evolution met with immediate approbation. Four years after his ordination as a priest and in the same year that he completed his second doctoral thesis (1927), Lemaître published a short paper in which he laid out the basic framework of big bang cosmology. By combining the mathematical formalism of Albert Einstein's (1879 –1955) theory of general relativity with Edwin Hubble's (1889–1953) empirical evidence indicating a general outward motion of distant galaxies, Lemaître postulated a dynamic model of an expanding universe of finite age. He was the first to understand that the recessional velocities of galaxies observed at present meant that, at some time in the distant past (Lemaître's initial estimate was between twenty and sixty billion years ago), all of the matter in the universe must have been confined to a sphere of small volume and enormous density. Lemaître postulated further that this "primeval atom" would break apart through spontaneous radioactive decay, and, as the fragments dispersed, lower densities would allow for the formation of conventional atoms and, eventually, of stars, planets, and galaxies. Although Lemaître's model has since been modified in several of its details, his was the first rigorously scientific theory of the origin and evolution of the cosmos, and his assumptions regarding a physically definable beginning point in space-time and cosmic expansion still form the basis of all modern theories in big bang cosmology.

Lemaître's recognition within the Church came swiftly and from the highest levels. In 1936, he was elected as a lifelong member of the newly reorganized Pontifical Academy of Sciences. The first international symposium sponsored by the academy was to be on "The Problem of the Age of the Universe" (scheduled for December 1939, it was canceled because of the outbreak of World War II). Later symposia were on such topics as stellar evolution, cosmic radiation (organized by Lemaître), the nuclei of galaxies, and the relationship between cosmology and fundamental physics. Lemaître played an active role in the academy throughout his life and served as its president from 1960 until his death in 1966. At his request, the academy in 1961 began awarding annually the Pius XI Gold Medal to outstanding young researchers in the natural sciences.

Catholicism and Modern Science

The apparent contradiction in the Church's responses to Teilhard and Lemaître may be explained, in part, in terms of the particular brand of philosophy of science it has chosen to adopt, a philosophy perhaps best summarized under the notions of "autonomy" and "separation." Almost every pope since Pius XI has taken pains to reaffirm the autonomy of science. This autonomy, they have argued, is guaranteed on the one side by adherence to the methods of science and on the other by a theological view grounded in Saint Augustine (354–430), who taught that Scripture was not to be read as a textbook on nature but as a guidebook to salvation. Moreover, they have repeatedly invoked the traditional Catholic doctrine of the "two truths" (that is, natural or scientific knowledge can never contradict revealed or supernatural knowledge since both issue from the same source) to maintain the separation between the domain of science and the domain of religion.

Lemaître drew upon these very principles in his discussions of his own work. In a lecture before the Solvay Conference in 1958, he stated that, "as far as I can see, [the primeval atom hypothesis] remains entirely outside any metaphysical or religious question. It leaves the materialist free to deny any transcendental Being [while] for the believer, it removes any attempt at familiarity with God." And despite the self-evident resonance between Lemaître's cosmogony and the story of Creation as related in Genesis, he never pursued such a connection in his technical or philosophical writings. Teilhard, on the other hand, consciously sought to blend together in his philosophical works scientific evidence of human evolution with the theological issues of original sin and salvation. His attempted synthesis thus brought him into conflict with the principle of separation between science and theology—a principle that had enabled the modern Church to distance itself from the mistakes of the Galileo affair. At the same time, Teilhard chose to write in a domain (speculative philosophy) unprotected by the claims of autonomy and ungoverned by the methods and norms of scientific investigation.

The principles of autonomy and separation have also been invoked retrospectively in the case of Galileo. In 1981, Pope John Paul II (b. 1920, p. 1978–) appointed a commission of historians, theologians, and scientists to reexamine the trial and condemnation of

Galileo and to "rethink the whole question" of the relationship between science and religion. After reviewing the commission's finding, John Paul announced in 1992—some three hundred sixty years after the fact—that the Church had, indeed, erred in its condemnation of heliocentrism and its censure of Galileo. Furthermore, he pointed to the lessons to be learned from that affair:

> The error of the theologians of the time . . . was to think that our understanding of the physical world's structure was in some way imposed by the literal sense of Sacred Scripture. . . . In fact, the Bible does not concern itself with the details of the physical world. . . . There exist two realms of knowledge, one that has its source in revelation and one that reason can discover by its own power. . . . The methodologies proper to each make it possible to bring out different aspects of reality (John Paul II 1992, 373).

More recently still, John Paul has directly confronted the question of the relationship between Roman Catholic doctrine and human evolution—a question that has the potential of becoming as vexed as the question of heliocentrism in the seventeenth century. Evidently not wishing to repeat the mistakes of the past, the pope has made what have been seen as additional gestures of reconciliation and accommodation. In his welcoming address to participants in a symposium on "Evolution and the Origins of Life" sponsored by the Pontifical Academy of Sciences in October 1996 (the sixtieth anniversary of its refoundation), the pope forthrightly acknowledged the compelling advances that had been made in evolutionary theory:

> Today, almost half a century after the publication of the encyclical [*Humani generis,* 1950], new knowledge has led to the recognition of the theory of evolution as more than a hypothesis. It is indeed remarkable that this theory has been progressively accepted by researchers, following a series of discoveries in various fields of knowledge. The convergence, neither sought nor fabricated, of the results of the work that was conducted independently is in itself a significant argument in favor of this theory (John Paul II 1996).

Choosing neither to relinquish the matter of human evolution to scientists ("the Church's magisterium is directly concerned with the question of evolution, for it involves the conception of man") nor to abandon the long-held belief in the fundamental compatibility between science and theology ("truth cannot contradict truth"), the pope sought to reaffirm the Church's authority "within the framework of her own competence" by pronouncing upon the allowable philosophical interpretations of human evolution. Thus, as Pius XII had done before, John Paul II reiterated that "theories of evolution which . . . consider the [human] spirit as emerging from the forces of living matter or as a mere epiphenomenon of this matter, are incompatible with the truth about man." Despite such insistence upon interpretative restrictions, the pope's remarks were in general more scientifically informed, more nuanced in regard to the relationship between science and philosophy (as well as between philosophy and theology), and more conciliatory in tone than the encyclical from 1950. (It must be kept in mind, however, that John Paul's address was to a lay audience and, thus, did not carry the same ecclesiastical authority as an encyclical.)

Conclusion

What this broader perspective on the relationship between Roman Catholicism and science reveals is scarcely the unrelieved high drama of confrontation implied by the conflict thesis. Rather, it is a story characterized by long periods of support for certain branches of science and indifference toward others, punctuated by occasional instances of controversy (chiefly heliocentrism in the seventeenth century and evolutionary theory in the twentieth). While the Church's responses to controversial scientific innovations have been marked by a cautious conservatism, they have been monolithic neither across time nor even across a given generation. The complex and historically contingent relationship between Roman Catholicism and science since the Council of Trent cannot, therefore, be easily reduced to a single, all-embracing thesis.

See also Copernican Revolution; Evolution; Galileo Galilei

BIBLIOGRAPHY

Ashworth, William B. "Catholicism and Early Modern Science." In *God and Nature: Historical Essays on the Encounter Between Christianity and Science,* ed. by David C. Lindberg

and Ronald L. Numbers. Berkeley: University of California Press, 1986, 136–66.

Bowler, Peter J. *The Mendelian Revolution: The Emergence of Hereditarian Concepts in Modern Science and Society.* Baltimore: Johns Hopkins University Press, 1989.

Delfgaauw, Bernard. *Evolution: The Theory of Teilhard de Chardin.* New York: Harper and Row, 1969.

Feldhay, Rivka. *Galileo and the Church: Political Inquisition or Critical Dialogue?* Cambridge: Cambridge University Press, 1995.

Finocchiaro, Maurice A., ed. and trans. *The Galileo Affair: A Documentary History.* Berkeley: University of California Press, 1989.

Glick, Thomas F. "Teilhard de Chardin, Pierre." In *Dictionary of Scientific Biography,* ed. by Charles Gillispie. Vol. 13. New York: Scribners, 1976, 274–7.

Godart, O., and M. Heller. *Cosmology of Lemaître.* Tucson, Ariz.: Pachart, 1985.

Gould, Stephen Jay. "Nonoverlapping [sic] Magisteria." *Natural History* 3 (1997): 16–22, 60–2.

Heilbron, John. *Elements of Early Modern Physics.* Berkeley: University of California Press, 1982.

———. "Science in the Church." *Science in Context* 3 (1989): 9–28.

John Paul II. "Lessons of the Galileo Case." *Origins* (CNS Documentary Service) 22 (22) (1992): 371–3.

———. "Truth Cannot Contradict Truth." Address to the Pontifical Academy of Sciences, October 22, 1996.

Kragh, Helge. "The Beginning of the World: Georges Lemaître and the Expanding Universe." *Centaurus* 32 (1987): 114–39.

Kruta, V., and V. Orel. "Mendel, Gregor." *Dictionary of Scientific Biography,* ed. by Charles Gillispie. Vol. 9. New York: Scribners, 1974, 277–83.

Lemaître, Georges. "La culture catholique et les sciences positives." *Actes du VIᵉ Congres Catholique de Malines* 5 (1936): 65–70.

———. *The Primeval Atom.* New York: Van Nostrand, 1950.

Marini-Bettòlo, G. B. *The Activity of the Pontifical Academy of Sciences, 1936–1986.* Vatican City: Pontificiae Academiae Scientiarum Scripta Varia, 1987.

Olby, Robert C. *Origins of Mendelism.* 2d ed. Chicago: University of Chicago Press, 1985.

Pius XII. "*Humani Generis*: Encyclical Letter Concerning Some False Opinions Which Threaten to Undermine the Foundations of Catholic Doctrine," August 12, 1950.

Poupard, Cardinal Paul. "Galileo: Report on Papal Commission Findings." *Origins* (CNS Documentary Service) 22(22) (1992): 374–5.

Shea, William R. "Galileo and the Church." In *God and Nature: Historical Essays on the Encounter Between Christianity and Science,* ed. by David C. Lindberg and Ronald L. Numbers. Berkeley: University of California Press, 1986, 114–35.

Teilhard de Chardin, Pierre. *The Phenomenon of Man.* New York: Harper, 1959.

51. Early-Modern Protestantism

Edward B. Davis and Michael P. Winship

The relation between Protestantism and science in the first two centuries after the Reformation involved a creative tension, with important insights in theology coming from the new science and important elements of the new science being shaped by theological assumptions. The salient features of the new science—a new world picture, a new worldview, and new knowledge coupled with a new view of knowledge and its sources—interacted with Christian beliefs in a variety of ways.

The Protestant Reformation

The Protestant Reformation, a wholesale change in the European religious landscape precipitated by Martin Luther's (1483–1546) challenge to the sale of indulgences in 1517, actually involved several reformations by diverse groups of people with different goals and beliefs. They included the Reformed churches that followed John Calvin (1509–64), the Anglicans, the Anabaptists and other radical reformers, and even the Roman Catholics themselves, who sought a renewed spirituality within their own church. However, Luther and Calvin were the two leading architects of the Reformation, and we focus on them here. In response to various Roman Catholic practices that stressed that humans must cooperate with God to be saved, Luther and Calvin began with the proposition that salvation depends wholly on the sovereignty of God, who elects to save sinners based solely on his own mercy, not upon any intrinsic merits that sinners might have or any good works they might perform, not even upon a human standard of justice. The just, Luther taught, are saved by faith alone (*sola fide*), where even faith itself is understood as originating in God rather than in ourselves. This particular view of

God as utterly sovereign and radically free helped determine how the new science was interpreted and received.

This is not to say that the Protestant mainstream failed to value good works. Quite the contrary; though works themselves could not lead to salvation, Christians were, nevertheless, expected to evidence the presence of saving faith and thus to glorify God by their piety and by the righteousness of their lives. Many Protestants stressed the dignity of labor, and some even saw material success as a sign of God's blessing. Whether beliefs like these encouraged the pursuit of science in Protestant countries has been hotly debated.

Most Protestants also shared a commitment to the primacy of the Bible (*sola scriptura*) as a source of truth over tradition, reason, and experience. The Roman Catholic Church, in their opinion, had developed an erroneous theology by straying too far from the plain words of Scripture. This view was related to another Protestant belief, that individual believers have direct access to God through prayer and the reading of Scripture, apart from the clergy. Hence, believers can read and interpret the Bible profitably, under the guidance of the Holy Spirit, in some cases drawing conclusions contrary to those reached by Roman Catholic clergy. This cluster of beliefs about the Bible affected how Protestants responded to the new world picture.

The Scientific Revolution

The period from 1543 until about 1750, during which early-modern science replaced medieval and Renaissance versions of ancient Greek science, is still commonly (though hardly universally) called the scientific revolution. This phrase is derived from the philosophes of the eighteenth century, for whom the recent upheavals in science were loaded with ideological overtones, representing not only the triumph of reason over nature, but also the triumph of secular rationalism over the essentially religious (and, therefore, false) worldview of the Middle Ages. Although that interpretation is no longer tenable, the label "scientific revolution" is still appropriate for the period as a whole, not because the changes were rapid but because they were fundamental.

The most famous change was the eventual acceptance of the new heliocentric world picture of Nicholas Copernicus (1473–1543). A series of discoveries and new ideas led most astronomers by 1700 to reject celestial perfection and the circular motion it implied in favor of the heliocentric system, with the sun's powerful gravitational attraction for the planets as the cause of celestial motion. Isaac Newton's (1642–1727) elegant mathematical theory of motion replaced Aristotelian physics in the process. Some Copernicans also accepted an essentially infinite universe, which was often linked with a belief in the existence of other solar systems populated by intelligent beings.

But a change in worldview was actually more fundamental. In the late Renaissance, as the works of Lucretius (c. 99–55 B.C.) and other ancient atomists freshly rediscovered began to be read widely in Europe, the conception of nature as a great concourse of particles moving through an infinite void was revived, leading many early-modern natural philosophers to give mechanistic explanations to natural phenomena. Medievals had accepted the organic worldview of Aristotle, according to which motion was to be understood as a process of change from potentiality to actuality, governed by a functional teleology immanent within nature. Mechanical philosophers, by contrast, described motion in mathematical terms without reference to any principles of intelligence or purpose in bodies themselves. Most followed René Descartes (1596–1650) in dividing all things into two kinds of substance: mind (or soul) and matter (or body). Only humans, angels, and God had intelligence and will; animals were just complicated engines like the automatons of master clockmakers and hydraulic engineers, and the world itself was a vast vortex of particles in motion. Although this approach has often been criticized for "dehumanizing" nature, it was also a bold attempt to preserve the transcendence of God, the dignity of humans, and the autonomy of values by placing them all beyond the scope of mechanical explanation.

Just when Europeans were revising their notion of nature, they were also discovering an astonishing variety of new facts about nature. Many came from the numerous voyages of discovery undertaken since the fifteenth century, resulting in a complete reevaluation of the reliability of traditional natural histories and a veritable explosion of botanical and zoological knowledge. Equally important were two new optical instruments, the telescope and the microscope, which opened up wholly new worlds far away and close at hand. Other technical advances, such as the air pump, made possible new types of experiments that led many to question the veracity of older ways of understanding nature.

Rapidly advancing knowledge spurred a recognition that facts themselves must take priority over tradition, leading to a new view of the sources of knowledge. Where medieval scholars had tended to see scientific truth as something to be sought in human books, the older the better, early-modern thinkers looked to the book of nature. This renewed emphasis on empiricism (the importance of making systematic observations and experiments) is one of the outstanding features of the scientific revolution. In England, it became the defining characteristic of the new program of learning advocated by Francis Bacon (1561–1626), a lawyer and statesman who served as a prophet of scientific progress, advocating the use of science to alleviate the consequences of the Fall and to improve the human condition. Sometimes empiricism was allied with Hermeticism, a mystical philosophy based on writings attributed to Hermes Trismegistus, a legendary Egyptian sage once believed to have been a contemporary of Moses. It attracted many, including Newton, with its promise of holding the alchemical key to the deep secrets God had hidden in the creation.

Two varieties of rationalism also competed to replace scholasticism during the scientific revolution. One sought scientific truth in mathematical demonstration. Galileo Galilei (1564–1642) held that the kind of knowledge thus obtained was absolutely certain, for it had been arrived at deductively from an analysis of pure forms and was, therefore, superior to any knowledge we might gain from experience alone. The other followed Descartes in seeking certainty from self-evident metaphysical principles rather than from geometrical axioms.

Protestant Beliefs and the Substance of Science

Protestants interacted with the new science in a variety of ways that show both scientific influences on religious beliefs and religious influences on scientific beliefs. The reception of heliocentrism provides one of the clearest examples. Even before Copernicus had published his famous treatise, Luther was quoted by one his students as saying (around the dinner table one evening) that the new astronomy contradicted the tenth chapter of Joshua by placing the earth in motion rather than the sun; but this informal remark has probably been given more attention than it deserves. (Calvin is often said to have made an anti-Copernican statement of his own, but this report has no basis in fact.) Far more significant was the influence of Luther's leading associate, Philip Melanchthon (1497–1560), who viewed Copernicus as a moderate reformer (like himself) because he had sought to purify astronomy by replacing equants with uniform circular motions. Although Melanchthon never accepted the hypothesis of the earth's motion, he positively encouraged the teaching of mathematics (and its subdiscipline, astronomy) at Lutheran universities in Germany.

Three Lutheran astronomers were crucial to the spread of Copernican views. Georg Joachim Rheticus (1514–74), a mathematician from Wittenburg, visited the elderly Copernicus a few years before his death, urged him to publish the details of his cosmology, and received his permission to publish a digest of the new theory under his (Rheticus's) own name; a few years later, the full theory was published at Nuremburg with Rheticus's assistance. He returned to Germany a convinced Copernican. Another Copernican, Michael Mästlin (1550–1631), taught mathematics at Tübingen, where one of his pupils was Johannes Kepler (1571–1630). It was Kepler who showed his fellow Protestants how to reconcile Copernicanism with the Bible. In the preface to his most important book, *The New Astronomy* (1609), Kepler used the Augustinian principle of accommodation to justify the figurative interpretation of biblical references to the motion of the sun. The Bible, he noted, speaks about ordinary matters in a way that can be understood, using common speech to make understandable loftier theological truths. Thus, the literal sense of texts making reference to nature should not be mistaken for accurate scientific statements. Galileo made an identical argument just a few years later in his *Letter to the Grand Duchess Christina,* written privately in Italian in 1615 but later published in Latin and English. Clearly, Galileo behaved rather like a Protestant (as a layman interpreting the Bible for himself in ways contrary to tradition), and the Church soon ruled that heliocentrism

was heretical. Unfortunately for Catholic scientists, in 1616 Copernicus's book was placed on the Index of Prohibited Books "until corrected," where it remained until 1820. It is not clear, however, how much impact this ban really had, especially outside Italy. Since there was no similar ruling that was binding on Protestants, Protestant scientists generally accepted the arguments of Kepler and Galileo. By the end of the seventeenth century, many Protestant scientists were Copernicans, and many Protestant theologians seemed indifferent to the issue. Indeed, the principle of accommodation, which had made heliocentrism theologically acceptable, henceforth was widely used by theologians and scientists alike for understanding scriptural passages about nature, and it helped immensely to clarify the real purpose of biblical revelation.

The challenge of mechanical philosophies was not so easy to meet. Throughout the scientific revolution, one sees a growing tension with theology over the reality of special providence and the possibility of miracles in a mechanistic universe. In general, scientists and philosophers became increasingly skeptical about reports of miraculous events, including those in the Bible. In part, this skepticism was encouraged by Protestant attacks on Roman Catholic claims that saints had worked miracles. Protestants usually maintained that genuine miracles had ceased with the close of the apostolic age. Skepticism also resulted from repeated failures to demonstrate unambiguously the existence of a supernatural realm in cases of witchcraft and other events thought to involve occult powers. Furthermore, the dualism of soul and body (which ultimately owes more to pagan Greek views than to the Bible), which was commonly invoked by mechanical philosophers, was beset with difficulties, particularly for theologians who were obligated to tackle thorny problems about the origin, nature, and immortality of the human soul.

From these issues alone, one might tend to conclude that theology and mechanistic science have been engaged in a hard-fought battle for cultural supremacy since the seventeenth century. But closer examination reveals a far more complex relationship. In at least two very significant ways, theological assumptions affected the content of the new science. The Reformation emphasis on the saving activity of God alone and the total passivity of sinners was mirrored in the way in which several mechanical philosophers understood matter as utterly passive, possessing no powers or forces of its own, and under the direct manipulation of an ever-active God. This is certainly the way in which Newton understood nature; he actually disowned the clockwork metaphor with which he is so often, and so wrongly, associated. (Some Roman Catholic scientists, such as Nicolas de Malebranche [1638–1715], held similar views of God's relationship to passive matter. Reformation theology was essentially Augustinian and, thus, not the exclusive property of Protestants.)

The emphasis on divine sovereignty had an even more important consequence for the new science. Some of the leading mechanical philosophers believed that, whether or not matter was passive mechanically, it was passive ontologically (that is, its properties and powers were imposed on it by a free creative act of God, beyond the power of human reason to penetrate). Although Reformation theology similarly stressed the inscrutability of God's will in the central matter of election, in that God's reasons for saving some and not others could not be discovered, seventeenth-century discussions of divine action are linked no less strongly with pre-Reformation theological debates about the relative amount of emphasis to place upon God's will vis-à-vis God's reason. Theological rationalists emphasized divine reason and often viewed human reason as the image of the divine. They tended to have great confidence in our ability to understand the works of God with our reason alone, unaided by experience. Theological voluntarists, on the other hand, emphasized the freedom of the divine will, unfettered by divine or human reason, to do whatever God wished— not only in the original creation of the world, but also in its ongoing operations. Thus, reason alone was not sufficient to understand the freely created world; significant data from experience were needed to show us what God has actually done rather than what we think God's reason compelled him to do. And because the world was, at every moment, under the sovereignty of a radically free Creator, the laws of nature were not wholly binding on God's activity, so miracles could not be ruled out.

This dialogue of divine will and reason actually shaped conceptions of science, including notions of proper scientific method, in the seventeenth century. Galileo, for example, held to a rationalist theology and, with it, a rationalist philosophy of science. This is not to say that he did not perform experiments; we know that he did, and they were some of the most clever ever performed. But, in his heart of hearts, he believed that the word "science," or knowledge, was properly applied only to knowledge that was absolutely certain and could not be otherwise, the kind that only mathematics and logic could provide. This is precisely why he communicated his results in the form of Platonic dialogues and why he repeatedly emphasized the power of mathematics to persuade. Robert Boyle (1627–91), by contrast, viewed the laws of nature as free creations of an omnipotent God, who could just as easily have made a world of a different kind from that which God actually did create. Consequently, unaided human reason was incapable of telling us anything true about the created order; it was capable merely of comprehending to a limited degree the order revealed to us by our senses. The world, for Boyle, was full of "data" and "facts," things given and things made by a power outside ourselves and, therefore, unknowable by our minds alone. This is why he placed so much emphasis on the experimental life: It was the only way to understand a freely created universe. Newton's view of the inadequacy of pure reason in both science and theology was essentially the same.

Their voluntarist theology, therefore, made it possible for many early-modern natural philosophers to baptize mechanical explanations, which surely aided reception of the new ideas. It was easy for them to see how an omnipotent Creator might, by an act of sheer will, endow created matter with any desired properties and powers, which the human investigator then had to discover from the phenomena produced by those properties and powers. Seeing nature in this way encouraged both theologians and scientists to find within nature abundant evidence of God's wisdom, power, and benevolence. As Newton stated in the second edition of his book on *Opticks* (1717), "the main business of natural philosophy" was to arrive at convincing arguments for the existence of God. Many leading scientists of the seventeenth century were convinced that discoveries in science made philosophical atheism literally incredible. What Henry More (1614–87) called "practical atheism" (living a licentious life) was less difficult to understand; yet, many scientists took pains to attack it repeatedly and to enlist science as an ally in the religious controversies of the day. Boyle's enthusiasm for the argument from design, especially as seen in the organic world, derived from his conviction that it was the best argument available for producing in people a profound sense of God's existence, the kind of feeling that would move them to repentance. In his will, Boyle endowed a perpetual lectureship to prove the truth of Christianity against "notorious infidels, *viz.*, atheists, theists [that is, deists], pagans, Jews, and Mahometans," though he stopped short of entering into "any controversies that are among Christians themselves." The first Boyle lecturer, the Anglican cleric Richard Bentley (1662–1742), corresponded with Newton about the details of his physics and, clearly with Newton's approval, proceeded to use the motions of the planets about the sun to argue for the necessity of divine wisdom in making them move as they do.

In time, both scientists and theologians would come increasingly to rely on this kind of natural theology rather than upon the revealed theology of the Bible for propagating and defending the Christian faith. This tendency contributed in the eighteenth century to the popularity of deism, which accepted the doctrine of creation as evident from nature but rejected the doctrine of redemption. Deists saw God as a distant Creator who had made the world with wisdom but was no longer concerned with its day-to-day operation. They had grave doubts about miracles and rejected the Christian message of sin and salvation. Ironically, deists such as Voltaire (François Marie Arouet [1694–1778]) canonized the deceased Newton as their patron saint, yet Newton's own view of God's relation to the world was irreconcilably different from theirs.

The "Merton Thesis"

While some scholars have found a correlation between voluntaristic theology and science, others have sought links between science and a more broadly conceived Protestant religiosity. In 1938, Robert Merton introduced the "Merton thesis," the best-known example of this approach. Merton asserted that the Reformed Protestant movement known as puritanism shaped and encouraged English science. It did this through what Merton identified as its underlying "sentiments": diligence and industry, worldly vocation, "empirico-rationalism," a valuing of education, and the glorification of God through good works of a utilitarian sort and through studying nature. As a pioneering effort to move away from an internalist study of science to a sociological one and to explore the relationship of religion to science in a positive fashion, Merton's thesis was important. As a contribution to understanding seventeenth-century religion and science, however, it was seriously flawed.

The first flaw lay in Merton's definition of puritanism. In sixteenth- and seventeenth-century England,

the term was employed primarily as an insult in intra-Protestant religious quarrels. Scholars in the late twentieth century tend to use the term to refer to a zealous style of experiential Calvinist piety that also aimed to purge the Church of England of its remains of Catholicism and the English social order of its sins, this being the sort of posture that was most likely to attract the label "puritanism" from hostile contemporaries. The heuristic value of the term "puritanism" drops off sharply by the middle of the century, although it can be used, with ever-increasing care and ever-diminishing returns, into the beginning of the eighteenth century. Merton sometimes showed awareness that puritanism was a factional impulse within the Church of England, but far more often he made it roughly analogous with a generically conceived, historically flattened out Calvinism that, he asserted, underlay the religiosity of almost everyone in seventeenth-century England. Merton's use of the term bore little relationship to contemporary realities or common scholarly usage.

Besides its vastly overgeneralized and ahistorical definition of puritanism, Merton's thesis had other flaws. It was sloppy in its use of critical theological concepts, introducing, for example, incautious claims about the positive role of good works in salvation that would have appalled seventeenth-century Protestants who accepted the Reformation doctrine of justification by faith alone (*sola fide*). It took specific forms of late-seventeenth-century religious apologetics that stressed the value of reason and scientific endeavors to be representative of Reformed Protestantism in general, and it justified this chronological casualness by relying on dubious teleological assumptions about gradually emerging inherent tendencies in Protestantism. It sometimes made puritanism crucial to the emergence of modern science (which is how the thesis has usually been read), while at other times it made it only one of many factors of an indeterminable importance. This slipperiness allowed fudging on critical comparative questions, such as why, if Protestantism had an inherent bias toward the production of science that Roman Catholicism lacked, for more than one hundred years after the beginning of the Reformation, Roman Catholicism was generating scientific work that was as good if not better; and why, if Calvinism offered such stimulus to science, Calvin's Geneva produced so little.

Merton's thesis in itself was a blind alley; where it was not simply incorrect, it was too amorphous definitionally, chronologically, and causally to have much explanatory value. Later historians made far more historically informed efforts to link puritanism to science, but they have been criticized (like Merton) for using the term "puritan" arbitrarily and with excessive freedom or else for ascribing specifically to puritans tendencies that they shared with broader English religious streams.

Despite its many problems, Merton's thesis gave a spur to continuing research into the links between science and religion in seventeenth-century England. Recently, that research has tended to focus on what was in Merton's thesis an acknowledged but unresolved paradox: Science flourished only after the Restoration of Charles II (ruled 1660–85) in 1660 and the decline of puritanism as a political and cultural force. The two decades of puritan rule preceding the Restoration produced wild sectarian experimentation, religious "enthusiasm," and challenges to traditional hierarchies of authority. Those experiments and challenges claimed ancestry in the puritan movement's strains of illuminist theology and radical ecclesiology, and they shocked conservatives committed both to a traditional social order and to the idea of a unified national church. In response, many Anglicans attempted to deny legitimacy to the uncontrolled private religious interpretations that had shattered the national church and to recreate consensus in a deeply torn society. Their means, besides retreating from Calvinism, often included emphasizing reasonableness, freedom from dogmatism, and a probabilistic approach to truth. Those emphases could support a wide range of specific political stances, but they would not have had too much purchase with anyone recognizably a puritan in the first half of the century. People still committed to puritanism found themselves, often reluctantly, in the role of Dissenters, outside the national church altogether, although Dissent slowly assimilated much of the Anglican attack on its values.

Restoration scientists, no less than Anglican apologists, proclaimed the value of reasonableness, freedom from dogmatism, and a probabilistic approach to truth. A number of historians have recently argued from various perspectives that Restoration scientists self-consciously constructed their conceptual frameworks and research protocols out of a desire to avoid the instability of the previous period. Other historians have vigorously disputed these sociologically driven interpretations of Restoration science. But even historians inclined to stress the ideological neutrality of science acknowledge that experimental practices like alchemy and astrology were looked on as potentially subversive and "enthusiastic" in Restoration

England. They clashed with the dominant culture's standards of reasonableness and clarity, which attempted to restrict uncontrolled private interpretation in science no less than in religion, and to which people attempting to engage in "normative" science adhered. The newly stable, orderly, and benevolent providential world order increasingly evoked by late-seventeenth-century scientific apologists had a great deal in common with that evoked by Anglican apologists. It is hard to imagine that the coeval births of Restoration science and this specific form of early-modern Protestantism were coincidental and that they did not mutually reinforce each other and rest on similar "sentiments."

While interactions between Protestantism and early-modern science were both complex and uneasy, they hardly warrant a description in terms of conflict. Their complexity arose from the subtlety of both science and Protestantism and their uneasiness from the different goals and methods of two enterprises that both claimed the right to define the world. Above all, because early-modern thinkers rarely separated their science sharply from their religiosity, in spite of statements to the contrary, the interactions were as extensive as they were rich and varied.

See also Baconianism; Isaac Newton; Mechanical Philosophy; Varieties of Providentialism

BIBLIOGRAPHY

Brooke, John H. *Science and Religion: Some Historical Perspectives.* Cambridge: Cambridge University Press, 1991.

Davis, Edward B. "Newton's Rejection of the 'Newtonian World View': The Role of Divine Will in Newton's Natural Philosophy." *Science and Christian Belief* 3 (1991): 103–17.

———. "Rationalism, Voluntarism, and Seventeenth-Century Science." In *Facets of Faith and Science.* Vol. 3. *The Role of Beliefs in the Natural Sciences,* ed. by Jitse M. van der Meer. Lanham, Md.: Pascal Centre for Advanced Studies in Faith and Science/University Press of America, 1996, 135–54.

Debus, Allen G. *Man and Nature in the Renaissance.* Cambridge: Cambridge University Press, 1978.

Henry, John. "The Matter of Souls: Medical Theory and Theology in Seventeenth-Century England." In *The Medical Revolution of the Seventeenth Century,* ed. by Roger French and Andrew Wear. Cambridge: Cambridge University Press, 1989, 87–113.

Hooykaas, R. *Religion and the Rise of Modern Science.* Grand Rapids, Mich.: Eerdmans, 1972.

Jacob, James R. *Robert Boyle and the English Revolution: A Study in Social and Intellectual Change.* New York: Burt Franklin, 1977.

Jacob, James R., and Margaret C. Jacob. "The Anglican Origins of Modern Science: The Metaphysical Foundations of the Whig Constitution." *Isis* 71 (1980): 251–67.

Lindberg, David C., and Ronald L. Numbers. "Beyond War and Peace: A Reappraisal of the Encounter Between Christianity and Science." *Church History* 55 (1986): 338–54.

Merton, Robert K. "Science, Technology, and Society in Seventeenth-Century England." *Osiris* 4 (1938): 360–632. Reprint with new introduction. New York: Harper and Row, 1970.

Mulligan, Lotte. "Puritans and English Science: A Critique of Webster." *Isis* 71 (1980): 456–69.

Popkin, Richard. *A History of Scepticism, from Erasmus to Spinoza.* Rev. ed. Berkeley: University of California Press, 1979.

Webster, Charles, ed. *The Intellectual Revolution of the Seventeenth Century.* London: Routledge, 1974.

———. *The Great Instauration: Science, Medicine, and Reform, 1626–1660.* London: Duckworth, 1975.

Westfall, Richard S. *Science and Religion in Seventeenth-Century England.* 1931. Reprint. New Haven, Conn.: Yale University Press, 1973.

Westman, Robert S. "The Copernicans and the Churches." In *God and Nature: Historical Essays on the Encounter Between Christianity and Science,* ed. by David C. Lindberg and Ronald L. Numbers. Berkeley: University of California Press, 1986, 76–113.

Winship, Michael P. *Seers of God: Puritan Providentialism in the Restoration and Early Enlightenment.* Baltimore: Johns Hopkins University Press, 1996.

52. JUDAISM SINCE 1700

Ira Robinson

Since the eighteenth century, Judaism has been characterized by its confrontation with, and adaptation to, the varying political, social, and intellectual demands of modernity. Judaic responses to the challenges of modernity have varied from a relative resistance to a wholehearted acceptance of them. Judaism's attitude toward science is an important component of this process.

A feature of eighteenth-century Jewish intellectual history is its basic continuity with premodern Judaism with respect to its attitude toward science. The legacy of premodern Judaism included, on the one hand, a tradition of attempts on the part of Jews to reconcile Judaism with a rationalistic, essentially Aristotelian, worldview. Like Moses Maimonides (1135–1204), these Jews posited a religious system that was essentially in harmony with the realities of the natural world as understood by contemporary natural philosophers. Despite a systematic exclusion of Jews from almost all non-Jewish educational establishments in the early-modern period, which was an era of widespread ghettoization of Jews, Jewish interest in contemporary developments in science and philosophy persisted, most particularly, though not exclusively, in Italy. However, adherents of this group, many of whom were physicians, constituted a minority in comparison with those Jews informed by a cabalistic worldview. The cabala was an esoteric and theosophical body of knowledge that included the art of finding hidden meanings in the text of the Torah. Between the sixteenth and eighteenth centuries, it is fair to say that the Jewish mystical tradition of cabala achieved a place of prominence among the intellectual pursuits of Jews. It is not the case, however, that cabalists were necessarily antagonistic to scientific knowledge, as their opponents often portrayed them. On the contrary, several influential

eighteenth-century Jewish thinkers with a basically cabalistic formation exhibited keen interest in the scientific study of nature. These included Pinhas Elijah Hurwitz (1765–1821), author of a widely influential survey of scientific knowledge in Hebrew entitled *Sefer ha-Berit* (*The Book of the Coveneant,* 1797); Elijah Ben Solomon Zalman of Vilna (1720–97), the most famous talmudist and one of the greatest cabalists of his time; and Jonathan Eybeschuetz (1690–1764), another prominent rabbi who commented that "all the sciences are . . . necessary for [a proper understanding of] our Torah."

Political and social trends within western Europe in the eighteenth century spawned a movement for the Westernization of Jews and Judaism called *haskalah* (enlightenment). This movement, centered in Berlin, called for basic changes in the social, economic, and educational structures of the Jewish community. Its leaders, such as Moses Mendelssohn (1729–86) and Naftali Herz Wessely (1725–1805), while seeking to retain as much as possible of the Judaic tradition that was consistent with the rationalistic worldview of the eighteenth-century Enlightenment, called for a thoroughgoing Europeanization of Judaism. The program of the *haskalah* involved a basic shift in Jewish educational priorities from a predominant emphasis on the study of the Hebrew Bible and rabbinic literature to European languages, mathematics, and other secular subjects that would enable Jews to participate fully in European society and culture. The *haskalah* in particular embraced Enlightenment rationalism, with its attendant emphasis on philosophy and science. In the ideological battle within eighteenth- and nineteenth-century Judaism, which was spawned by the *haskalah,* and the attendant movement for civil and political rights for Jews in numerous countries, the status of natural science per se was never an issue, except insofar as it and other "secular" studies figured in the educational priorities of one side or the other.

The nineteenth century saw the beginning of a mass acculturation of western European Jews. Moreover, it marked the beginning of the entrance of a large contingent of Jews into the scientific professions, a trend that continued into the twentieth century. As a rule, however, until the twentieth century, these professions were not welcoming to non-Christians whose acculturation to Western Christian civilization was less than total. Hence, the vast majority of these people, while of Jewish origins, had little or nothing to do with the practice of Judaism as a religion, and a number of them took the step of formally converting to Christianity. Most nineteenth-century European scientific institutions were, at best, unaccommodating to the specific requirements and practices of Jews and Judaism and, at worst, openly hostile. In such a situation, many of the best and brightest among Jews abandoned the practice of Judaism, seeing it, in the light of contemporary Hegelian philosophy, as a fossil religion, not conducive to the objective pursuit of the truth.

The religious movements within western European Jewry, which were spawned by the social, intellectual, and political trends of the eighteenth century and which sought to demonstrate the relevance of Judaism in the contemporary world, included Reform, Neo-Orthodoxy, and Historical Judaism (which would inspire North American Conservative Judaism). All of these movements, despite their differences in interpreting the way in which the Jewish tradition was to be observed in contemporary times, more or less embraced the positivist scientific point of view of the Enlightenment, with its belief that knowledge is based on natural phenomena as verified by empirical investigation, and were at pains to declare their acceptance of the conclusions of contemporary science. Their battle with European thought was fought not over issues related to the scientific enterprise per se but over acceptance of new trends in critical biblical scholarship and the consignment of Judaism to the past by Hegelian philosophy. The Jews were, of course, vulnerable to the same challenges that confronted other Western religious traditions—those resulting from nineteenth-century advances in scientific discovery and theory—and they demonstrated the same range of varied responses. Thus, Jewish attitudes toward scientific theories of evolution in the nineteenth century ranged from fierce opposition to unqualified acceptance. While this acceptance represented the entire span of religious ideologies, from Orthodoxy to Reform, Jewish proponents of evolution tended to adopt a theistic, teleological interpretation that allowed for the preservation of human preeminence.

In eastern European Jewry, ideological lines were drawn somewhat differently than in the West: The challenge of modernization led some to maintain an ideology of acculturation, while others sought to create a modern society based on a Jewish ethnic nationalism. The traditional Orthodox community included some rabbis, such as Moses Sofer (1762–1830) of Hungary, who demonstrated a marked reluctance to accept science, though they did not seek a direct confrontation with its findings. However, others in the Orthodox community, such as Meir Leibush Malbim (1809–79), in the tradition of the eighteenth-century rabbis mentioned above, taught that science was indispensable to understanding the Torah. Similar in attitude among the Orthodox were Israel Lipschutz (1782–1860) of Danzig, who thought that the evidence of geology and fossils did not constitute a real problem for believing Jews. This division in the Orthodox community continued into the twentieth century among such prominent rabbis as Abraham Isaac Kook (1865–1935), who saw no essential problem with evolution and its reconciliation with Scripture, and Menahem Mendel Schneersohn (1902–94), who remained opposed to current theories concerning the age of the earth and the evolution of species.

Adherents of the eastern European *haskalah* made scientific and technological education among the Jews one of their great causes. The inventor and writer Hayyim Zelig Slonimsky (1810–1904) endeavored to spread knowledge of scientific and technical matters among eastern European Jewry through periodicals and other publications in Hebrew and Yiddish. One result of this effort was that a cadre of eastern European Jews entered the scientific professions in the late nineteenth and early twentieth centuries, the most prominent of whom was the chemist and Zionist leader Chaim Weizmann (1874–1952).

The event of the twentieth century that had the greatest impact on Judaism was the systematic destruction of European Jewry by Nazi Germany, known to Jews as the Holocaust. The perpetration of this crime involved the employment of the full resources of the German state's scientific and technological establishment. German National Socialist ideology, in the context of its campaign against Jewry, used science as one of its battlegrounds and spoke disparagingly of "Jewish" versus "Aryan" science. The Nazis attempted thus to discredit the scientific work of, among others, Albert Einstein (1879–1955) and Sigmund Freud (1856–1939), both of whom were identified as Jews and worked for some Jewish causes, though neither could be considered Jewish in any classically religious sense. The Nazi experience has raised moral and ethical questions concerning the supremacy of a Western scientific culture that could produce an event as malevolent as the Holocaust.

For twentieth-century Jews, other than a segment of the Orthodox, any perceived conflict between science and religion has to do not with natural science but with the humanities (for example, biblical criticism) and, to a lesser extent, the social sciences. For most twentieth-century Jewish thinkers and theologians, such as Martin Buber (1878–1965), Franz Rosenzweig (1886–1929), and Louis Jacobs (1920–), contemporary Jewish theology has remained essentially unaffected by modern scientific theories in that the major areas of Judaism's intellectual and ethical concerns do not conflict with modern science. Rosenzweig, who especially sought to dissociate Judaism and science, argued that scientists were not always aware of their own presuppositions and methods, and, hence that science had a tendency to distort what it purported to represent. Another prominent German-Jewish thinker, Hermann Cohen (1842–1918), believed that any perceived contradiction between science and ethics could be reconciled through a proper conception of God.

An interesting phenomenon of the twentieth century is that, for the first time, Jews have been able to enter the scientific professions while retaining their full allegiance to the rites and practices of Orthodox Judaism. A number of them have established the Association of Orthodox Jewish Scientists, which has attempted to formulate a rationally defensible synthesis between their scholarly concerns as scientists and their religious ideology.

See also Cabala; Judaism to 1700

BIBLIOGRAPHY

Aviezer, Nathan. *In the Beginning . . . Biblical Creation and Science.* Hoboken, N.J.: Ktav, 1990.

Barth, Aaron. *Creation in the Light of Modern Science.* Jerusalem: Jewish Agency, 1968.

Bemporad, Jack, Abraham Segal, Jack Spiro, and Robert Widom, eds. *Focus on Judaism, Science, and Technology.* New York: Union of American Hebrew Congregations, 1970.

Carmell, Aryeh, and Cyril Domb, eds. *Challenge: Torah Views on Science and Its Problems.* Jerusalem and New York: Feldheim, 1978.

Cohen, Naomi. "The Challenges of Darwinism and Biblical Criticism to American Judaism." *Modern Judaism* 4 (1984): 121–57.

Hollinger, David. *Science, Jews, and Secular Culture: Studies in Mid-Twentieth-Century Intellectual History.* Princeton, N.J.: Princeton University Press, 1996.

Katz, Stephen. "Judaism, God, and the Astronomers." In *God and the Astronomers,* ed. by Robert Jastrow. New York: Warner, 1978, 147–61.

Levi, Leo. *Torah and Science: Their Interplay in the World Scheme.* New York: Feldheim, 1983.

Levine, Hillel. "Paradise Not Surrendered: Jewish Reactions to Copernicus and the Growth of Modern Science." In *Epistemology, Methodology, and the Social Sciences,* ed. by Robert Cohen and Max Wartkowsky. Dordrecht: Reidel, 1983, 203–25.

Novak, David, and Norbert Samuelson, eds. *Creation and the End of Days: Judaism and Scientific Cosmology.* Lanham, Md.: University Press of America, 1986.

Rabkin, Yakov, and Ira Robinson, eds. *The Interaction of Scientific and Jewish Cultures in Modern Times.* Lewiston: Edwin Mellen, 1994.

Robinson, Ira. "Kabbala and Science in Sefer ha-Berit: A Modernization Strategy for Orthodox Jews." *Modern Judaism* 9 (1989): 275–89.

Ruderman, David B. *Jewish Thought and Scientific Discovery in Early Modern Europe.* New Haven, Conn.: Yale University Press, 1995.

Samuelson, Norbert. *An Introduction to Modern Jewish Philosophy.* Albany: State University of New York Press, 1989.

53. MODERN AMERICAN MAINLINE PROTESTANTISM

Ferenc M. Szasz

Episcopalians, Congregationalists, Presbyterians, Lutherans, Methodists, and Baptists were the major groups that dominated American cultural and scientific life from the early nineteenth century until the era of World War I. While these denominations lost their cultural hegemony in the decades after World War I, they still reflected the opinions of the majority of the nation's Protestants. Their relationships with the worlds of science shifted over time and reflected various factors.

The American mainline Protestant churches have a unique history. Unlike France, England, or Scotland, the United States never produced a national, established church. Religion in American life flowed through separate denominations, and these often reflected theological, regional, ethnic, and social-class differences. Hence, proclamations issued by one denomination would affect only that particular group and sometimes not even the entire body. To this must be added the central Protestant theological assumption: Religious faith is a matter of individual conscience. Consequently, the Protestant churches in America never spoke with a single voice.

Second, the Protestant denominations all viewed the Bible (until the twentieth century, usually in the Authorized or King James Version) as God's revelation to humankind. But regional and educational distinctions meant that interpretations of Scripture differed dramatically. Episcopalians, Congregationalists, most Presbyterians, and Lutherans stressed the role of an educated ministry in interpreting Scripture, whereas nineteenth-century Methodists and Baptists and some twentieth-century conservative evangelicals placed more emphasis on sincere professions of faith as fundamental. Still, most Protestant laypeople believed Scripture to be eminently understandable by believing Christians, addressed to the "common sense" of humankind.

Third, the majority of the Protestant churches made no distinction between science and its technical applications. Thus, railroads, steamboats, anesthesia, electricity, telegraph, telephone, radio, gas warfare, computers, space travel, nuclear power, interferon, and DNA were lumped together with biology, chemistry, geology, astronomy, and physics as "science." Any discussion of the Protestant response to science must include the technological dimension.

Finally, with exceptions to be noted later, the mainline American Protestant churches usually moved in harmony with science and technology, hoping to use contemporary scientific discoveries to help create "the Kingdom of God." With these generalizations in mind, one can chart two centuries of Protestant-scientific interaction in the United States through four overlapping periods.

The Period from 1800 to 1860

Despite their differences, the early-nineteenth-century Protestant churches agreed that God's word as revealed in the Bible ("Volume I," as it were) harmonized with God's word as revealed in the realm of nature ("Volume II"). Unlike German pietistic groups or twentieth-century fundamentalists, the mainline churches never drew a clear line between "the church" and "the world." On the contrary, they sought to guide the new American republic by shaping it in their own image. Early-nineteenth-century American scientists expanded scientific knowledge by exploring and mapping the land, collecting and classifying flora and fauna, and attempting to comprehend American Indians and African Americans. Hence, American science, technology, and the Protestant churches essentially grew up together.

For the most part, the Antebellum sciences of astronomy, biology, geology, and anthropology were seen by church leaders as compatible with a proper, "democratic" interpretation of Scripture. The arrival of Frenchman Pierre Laplace's (1749–1827) nebular hypothesis, a mechanistic interpretation of the origins of the universe, was easily countered by the popularity of the various British Bridgewater Treatises, which argued for the unity of theology and the sciences. The president of Williams College (Congregational) thought the Bridgewater Treatise on design in astronomy a perfect answer to the "deplorable atheism" of Laplace. Antebellum astronomy had a dual purpose. On the one hand, it could aid in such practical matters as establishing latitude and longitude; on the other, it could reveal the majesty of God's universe. As a popular saying phrased it, "an undevout astronomer is mad." Similarly, when amateur or professional biologists discovered previously unknown species, they were seen as cataloging the variety of God's creation. Upper-class clergymen were virtually expected to become experts on the natural history of their parishes.

Protestant responses to other Antebellum sciences, however, became a bit more problematic. Several fields held the potential for conflict: geology (the idea that the earth needed eons for creation rather than the six days of Genesis); paleontology (neither dinosaurs nor extinction are mentioned in Scripture); and anthropology (did people arrive through polygenesis—that is, separate creations for the various races?). But even here the responses varied.

The writings of William Buckland (1784–1856) and the English school of geology, as well as Scotsman Charles Lyell's (1797–1875) *Principles of Geology* (1830–33), argued for a greatly expanded time frame for Creation. Since the Bible was a religious document as well as a source of evidence for human and natural history, one might have expected considerable public reaction to these new geological assertions. Quickly, however, several Protestant theologians offered metaphorical readings of Genesis that obviated any difficulties. Congregational theologian Moses Stuart (1780–1852) maintained that the Bible concerned itself with religious truth, not the truths of geography, physics, astronomy, or chemistry. Similarly, Congregationalist Horace Bushnell (1802–76) reasoned that science and religion were complementary knowledge systems, with the truth of the latter verified by the heart rather than the head.

In the South, conservative Presbyterians, Methodists, and Baptists rejected the popular theory of polygenesis, acceptance of which would have supported slavery, because it contradicted the Genesis account of a single Adam and Eve; instead, they pointed to the biblical story of Ham as one justification for slavery. Nonetheless, most Antebellum Protestant theologians, North or South, were "mediation theologians," determined to reconcile Christianity with the changing world. There is even some evidence that trained biblical scholars united with trained paleontologists and geologists in their scorn of eccentric amateur interpretations of earth history; this alliance points to a crisis of "social authority" rather than conflict between science and religion.

Consequently, in the Antebellum era, Americans viewed the term "science" as an eminently flexible concept. Andover Seminary scholar W. G. T. Shedd (1820–94) spoke of "historical science," while Presbyterian Charles Hodge (1797–1878) argued that theology itself was a "science." For these Protestants, science generally meant a method of approach to all forms of knowledge, chiefly the careful collection and compilation of verifiable "facts." Rightly interpreted, this generation maintained, the story found in Scripture would be congruent with anything that biology, geology, or astronomy could discover. This flexibility would soon change.

The Period from 1860 to 1914

The driving force behind the shift was Charles Darwin's (1809–82) *Origin of Species* (1859), which offered a naturalistic, eon-long theory of Creation, and later his *Descent of Man* (1871), which linked humankind with the animal kingdom. Protestant thinkers were not long in responding. George F. Wright (1838–1921), later appointed professor of the harmony of science and revelation at Oberlin College (Congregational), argued that Darwin provided scientific support for a Calvinistic view of the world. The Rev. James McCosh (1811–94), president of Princeton (Presbyterian), supported evolution in his *Religious Aspects of Evolution* (1888). The Presbyterian Church, which was divided by the American Civil War into Northern and Southern branches, produced the most vigorous Gilded Age critiques of evolution. Theologian Charles Hodge responded to the question posed in his *What Is Darwinism?* (1874) with the judgment, "it is atheism." A decade later, Southern Presbyterian James Woodrow (1828–1907) defended evolution at Columbia Seminary in South Carolina and found himself convicted of heresy. During this uproar, debates over evolution filled the pages of Southern Presbyterian periodicals, which introduced the public to the notion that evolution was "atheistic." Hence, the Southern Presbyterians became the first mainline denomination officially to condemn the theory of human evolution. Still, the issue remained primarily a regional, denominational concern.

Responses to evolution outside the South proved more muted. Northern Methodist Luther T. Townsend (1838–1922) became a prominent clerical opponent of evolution, but Northern Presbyterian pulpit orator T. DeWitt Talmage (1832–1902) probably engendered the greatest popular controversy. Through his sermons, lyceum appearances, and, especially, his extensive newspaper columns—fifty million Americans read him weekly—Talmage ridiculed evolution: Evolution was "false science" and "atheism"; although others might claim possums or kangaroos as ancestors, "[his] father was God." Talmage also popularized the idea that the "logical outcome" of teaching evolution could be seen in mechanical atheism, unsettled morals, denial of immortality, and decline of respect for biblical authority. Despite Talmage's crusade, the mainline Northern Protestant churches were not seriously disrupted by the issue of evolution during the fin de siècle years.

The efforts of the reconcilers were largely responsible for this relative tranquility. Congregational minister Lyman Abbott (1835–1922) argued for harmony in *The Evolution of Christianity* (1897) and also in the pages of the popular *Outlook* magazine, which he edited for years. Probably the foremost clerical reconciler was Congregationalist Henry Ward Beecher (1813–87), a Victorian pulpiteer whose reputation rivaled Talmage's. Beecher's two-volume *Evolution and Religion* (1885) essentially declared the controversy between Christianity and Darwin closed, arguing that evolution was simply "God's way of doing things."

But controversy has a way of sustaining itself, and the late nineteenth century produced two works that proved to have considerable staying power. In 1874, scientist John William Draper (1811–82) penned his *History of the Conflict Between Religion and Science,* which was really an attack on the Roman Catholic Church rather than on American Protestantism. Twenty-two years later, Cornell President Andrew Dickson White

(1832–1918) wrote his two-volume study, *History of the Warfare of Science and Theology in Christendom.* Together, these books created a pervasive "metaphor of conflict." In spite of serious criticism, this metaphor has dominated public perception ever since.

Still, the absence of any wholesale Protestant reaction to evolution suggests that the reconcilers had won the first round. From the reconcilers, the Protestant lay public learned that, while the theory of evolution might be viewed atheistically, it might also be understood in a theistic or Christian framework. Moreover, the term "evolution" merged easily with Victorian ideas of "progress," as reflected in railroads, steam travel, telegraph, telephone, electricity, steel production, and advances in medicine. At the centenary of Darwin's birth in 1909, journalists agreed that the earlier polemics had forever passed.

During the fin de siècle years, Protestantism and science also forged a distinct alliance in the arena of the Social Gospel, or "practical Christianity." From the 1890s to World War I, all mainline denominations established institutional churches in the nation's major cities to provide a variety of social services. Simultaneously, the churches joined with physicians, civic chemists, biologists, and social scientists in a campaign directed toward urban water purification, disease and pollution control, improved sewage disposal, and modified social behavior. The Lutherans, Episcopalians, Methodists, and Presbyterians teamed with physicians to establish numerous denominational hospitals in the country's Western cities. Church periodicals that praised this alliance saw it as a fruitful combination of the discoveries of modern science and the ancient wisdom of Scripture.

At the same time, however, the professionalization of science began to usher in a new age. From 1870 to 1920, more than two hundred professional societies were created; gradually these groups began to exclude amateurs from their organizations. The Episcopal bishop of western Nebraska might still gather and classify regional plants and birds until the early 1930s, but he represented a dying breed. By about 1915, the field of biology had evolved into a laboratory discipline, with numerous subspecialties—botany, zoology, genetics, and forestry, just to name a few. This sophistication left little room for the amateur. In the parallel field of subatomic physics, the conclusions proved so complex that Protestant spokesmen said relatively little about them. At the onset of

World War I, the sciences had become specialized disciplines.

The Period from 1914 to the 1990s

The horrors of World War I, together with the emergence of new scientific concepts such as relativity, probability, complementarity, the uncertainty principle, and Freudian psychology, brought the Protestant-scientific alliance of the Social Gospel era to an end. In 1929, Congregational theologian John Wright Buckham (1864–1945) publicly attacked science for failing to shed real light upon the meaning of existence. Buckham also blamed science for not providing the moral and spiritual certainties essential for social or individual integrity. A study by psychologist James Leuba (1867–1946) concluded that most scientists were nonbelievers.

Although some interpretations of the Protestant-science interaction depict the relationship as an "armed standoff" or an "uneasy truce," for much of the century the two entities seemed to be moving on "parallel tracks." The foremost Protestant theologians of the twentieth century, such as Karl Barth (1886–1968), Emil Brunner (1899–1966), Rudolph Bultmann (1894–1976), Paul Tillich (1886–1965), and Reinhold Niebuhr (1892–1971), simply did not concern themselves with scientific questions. This division may be illustrated in the famous encounter between Albert Einstein (1879–1959) and the archbishop of Canterbury. When asked what impact the theory of relativity might have on the church, Einstein replied that it had none: Relativity was a purely scientific matter that had nothing to do with religion.

Changes in the American educational system also led to the rise of Protestant-science parallelism. As the sciences were professionalized and subdivided into specialties, the state-university curricula expanded accordingly. At the same time, most state-funded universities virtually eliminated the formal study of religion. When the discipline of theology became confined to denominational seminaries, it restricted accessibility, thereby leading to widespread popular illiteracy on religious matters.

From the 1920s forward, the scientific interpreters, aided by the onset of mass media, became crucial figures of the science-religion encounter. Some interpreters were trained as journalists, but many came from scientific or technical backgrounds. Their views covered a wide spectrum. After the Great War, botanist Luther Burbank (1849–1926) publicly expressed his skepticism about

any religion. Zoologist E. L. Rice took another tack, arguing that, since laypeople had no time to study science for themselves, they should accept the authority of the scientific specialist just as they accepted the medicine prescribed by their physician. Still others were reconcilers. Physicist Robert A. Millikan (1868–1953) and geologist Kirtley F. Mather (1888–1978), two of the foremost reconcilers of the mid-twentieth century, assured Protestants that science and religion were not in conflict.

A second wave of science interpreters emerged in the 1960s. Those who leaned toward the skeptical tradition included paleontologist Stephen Jay Gould (1941–), astronomer Carl Sagan (1934–96), physician Lewis Thomas (1913–93), and astrophysicist Stephen Hawking (1942–). Yet others, such as physicists Paul Davies and Robert Russell, have emphasized the harmony of faith and reason. There also exists a Society of Ordained Scientists, an international group begun by a British biologist who served as an Anglican priest. Hence, the average churchgoer could select the most appealing position within the wide spectrum of views.

Protestantism and science continued to move in "parallel tracks" from the 1920s through the 1960s. Major issues within Protestantism, such as the fundamentalist-modernist controversy, higher criticism of the Scriptures, Prohibition, the ordination of women, racial equality, abortion, and homosexuality, seldom concerned the world of science. Similarly, the changes in the scientific community—such as the discovery of DNA in the 1950s, which revolutionized biology; the acceptance of plate tectonics or continental drift in the 1960s, which revolutionized geology; and the discovery of quarks and other subnuclear particles from the 1950s through the 1970s, which kept physics in turmoil—evoked little interest in the churches.

After World War II, however, several groups tried to close the gap between the two communities. The Chicago Center for Religion and Science, which began in the early 1950s, soon housed *Zygon* (founded 1966), a refereed journal of religion and science. In 1979, the World Council of Churches hosted a conference at the Massachusetts Institute of Technology on "Faith, Science, and the Future." The 1989–91 Gifford lectures delivered in Aberdeen, Scotland, by physicist-theologian Ian Barbour (1923–) explored the themes of "Religion in an Age of Science" and "Ethics in an Age of Technology." A handful of academic conferences also renewed the dialogue, but the scholars most often represented the

United Kingdom or the Commonwealth, where one might still read theology at a university level.

The Clashes of the Modern Era, 1914–1990s

In two areas, however, popular Protestant reaction launched distinct attacks on science. The first attack was directed toward the field of weapons technology, especially nuclear weapons. The second was directed toward two aspects of biology: the teaching of evolution in public schools and the ethical questions of recombinant DNA. In the field of astronomy, the Protestant public failed to react to publicity over largely naturalistic theories concerning the origin of the universe, such as the Big Bang theory, perhaps because people could conflate the Big Bang with the idea of original creation.

The question of science and ethics evoked strong response. Prior to World War I, few mainline Protestants believed that science, which promised to produce "objective truths," could cause major ethical dilemmas. But the common weapons of World War I, mustard gas, the machine gun, tanks, submarines, aircraft, and gigantic canons, produced intense reaction by the churches against "military science." Led by Charles C. Morrison, long-term editor of *Christian Century* (founded 1908 as the voice of liberal Protestantism), many Protestant ministers and a number of laypeople in the interwar period became pacifists. This position faded with the onset of World War II, but it revived after disclosure of the Nazi concentration camps, the Japanese atrocities, and the Allied atomic bombings of Hiroshima and Nagasaki. America's involvement in Vietnam also called forth a renewed Protestant pacifism. During the 1980s, an antinuclear stance became the chief means by which the mainline Protestant churches opposed the defense program of Presidents Ronald Reagan and George Bush. The National Council of Churches (founded 1908) provided strong moral leadership in the nuclear-disarmament movement. Most major denominations passed resolutions opposing further weapons development, with perhaps the strongest statement emerging from the United Methodist Bishops' *In Defense of Creation: The Nuclear Crisis and a Just Peace* (1986). During the Cold War decades, the mainline Protestant churches came to believe that science and technology were ethically "neutral" and, if left to themselves, might bring about global destruction.

The second popular Protestant reaction to science, confrontation with the theory of evolution, also flourished after World War I. The irenic compromise of the first decade of the century ended when three-time presidential candidate and Presbyterian layman William Jennings Bryan (1860–1925) began to denounce Darwinism on the lecture platform in the late teens. Bryan blamed the Great War on the "false philosophy" of evolution that taught "might makes right." Although liberal clergymen such as the Rev. Harry Emerson Fosdick (1878–1969) defended evolution, the national press seized on Bryan's comments, thrusting the evolution question onto the front pages of the country's newspapers. The sticking point lay less with the truth or falsity of the theory than with the question of whether it should be taught in the tax-supported, public school system.

During the early 1920s, several states devised methods to curtail the teaching of evolution. In July 1925, the nation's attention was riveted on the Scopes Trial in Dayton, Tennessee, which marked the climax of this phase. In the wake of the trial, however, many of the mainline denominations discovered that they had to contend with a widening spectrum of beliefs in their own congregations: Both liberals and conservatives sat in their pews on Sunday mornings.

This acerbic Protestant-evolution clash faded with the Great Depression of the 1930s. In 1961, however, it sprang to life with the publication of *The Genesis Flood* by John C. Whitcomb Jr. (1924–) and Henry M. Morris (1918–), which restated many of the views of Seventh-day Adventist George M. Price (1870–1963) from the 1920s. Two years later, the Creation Research Society emerged, followed in 1970 by the Creation Science Research Center in San Diego, California. The goal of the revived antievolution movement was to allot "equal time" to the theory of Creation in the public schools. Since the mainline churches now housed both liberals and conservatives, some members cheered on the creationists while others scorned their views.

From the 1970s forward, however, both liberal and conservative Protestants could agree on the dangers of recombinant DNA experiments. In 1978, conservative Baptist theologian Carl F. H. Henry (1913–   ) warned of these and other dangers, while Presbyterian theologian Paul Ramsey (1913–88) was to raise similar concerns. In 1994, an interdenominational group of liberal clerics denounced bioengineering attempts to patent human and animal life for profit. Liberal and conservative Protestant churchgoers agreed that the scientists had no license to "play God." The rise of popular environmental concerns from the 1970s forward provided yet another unifying force—an "Ecotheology"—that allowed both liberal and conservative Protestants to draw upon the biblical concept of "stewardship" of the earth's resources. Like their counterparts of a century earlier, Protestant churches concerned with the environment began to work with scientific experts on many perplexing issues.

Conclusion

Several themes emerge from the Protestant-science relationship in the nineteenth and twentieth centuries. For most of the period, the mainline churches remained either in harmony or in tandem with the sciences of the day. Consequently, the "warfare" model of science versus religion is only sporadically appropriate, involving largely the fields of biology and warfare technologies.

Moreover, as contemporary sociologists suggest, the mainline Protestant-science encounter has produced considerable engagement of both scientists and average churchgoers. Recent polls reveal that professional scientists are somewhat less involved with organized religion than the general public. Nevertheless, like the general public, they do not share a common perspective on religious matters. Those engaged in the physical sciences, such as chemistry and physics, generally remain more theologically orthodox than their counterparts in the biological, behavioral, and social sciences. Sociologists have also concluded that the average churchgoer holds "multiple realities," displaying a capacity to mix belief patterns in a manner that a logician might find inconsistent. Public-opinion polls have, at times, discovered an overlap regarding those who believe in evolution and creationism.

Finally, liberal and conservative Protestants in the mainline churches have disputed many issues, but they agree that God alone is God and that naturalistic scientific theories can never fully resolve the dilemmas of existence. Recent developments such as the big bang theory, interferon, thalidomide, the pacemaker, chemical and nuclear weapons, the Human Genome Project, and DNA have reminded Protestant theologians that science is "ambiguous." Although one might take the latest scientific information from the pages of *Nature* or *Science,* they argue, one also needs the wisdom of the Hebrew prophets and the writers of the New Testament to guide these discoveries. Hence, the Protestant-science dialogue is likely to continue unabated into the twenty-first century.

See also America's Innovative Nineteenth-Century Religions; Creationism Since 1859; Evangelicalism and Fundamentalism; Nineteenth-Century Biblical Criticism

BIBLIOGRAPHY

Barbour, Ian G., ed. *Issues in Science and Religion.* New York: Prentice-Hall, 1966.

——. *Religion in an Age of Science.* San Francisco: Harper San Francisco, 1990.

Berger, Peter L. *A Far Glory: The Quest for Faith in an Age of Credulity.* New York: Anchor Books, 1992.

Bozeman, Theodore Dwight. *Protestants in an Age of Science: The Baconian Ideal and American Religious Thought.* Chapel Hill: University of North Carolina Press, 1977.

Conser, Walter H. Jr., *God and the Material World: Religion and Science in Antebellum America.* Columbia: University of South Carolina Press, 1993.

Daniels, George. *American Science in the Age of Jackson.* New York: Columbia University Press, 1968.

Davies, Paul. *God and the New Physics.* New York: Touchstone, 1983.

Gingerich, Owen. "Is There a Role for Natural Theology Today?" In *Science and Theology: Questions at the Interface,* ed. by Murray Rae, Hillary Regan, and John Stenhouse. Edinburgh: T. and T. Clarke, 1994.

Greene, John C. *American Science in the Age of Jefferson.* Ames, Iowa State University Press, 1984.

Hovenkamp, Herbert. *Science and Religion in America, 1800–1860.* Philadelphia: University of Pennsylvania Press, 1978.

Larson, Edward J. *Trial and Error: The American Controversy over Creation and Evolution.* New York: Oxford University Press, 1989.

——. *Summer for the Gods: The Scopes Trial and America's Continuing Debate Over Science and Religion.* New York: Harvard University Press, 1998.

Mather, Kirtley F. *The Permissive Universe.* Albuquerque: University of New Mexico Press, 1986.

Moore, James B. *The Post-Darwinian Controversies: A Study of the Protestant Struggle to Come to Terms with Darwin in Great Britain and America, 1870–1900.* Cambridge: Cambridge University Press, 1979.

Numbers, Ronald L. "Science and Religion." *Osiris* 2d ser. 1 (1985): 59–80.

Numbers, Ronald L., and Todd Savitt, eds. *Science and Medicine in the Old South.* Baton Rouge: Louisiana State University Press, 1989.

Reingold, Nathan, ed. *Science in Nineteenth-Century America: A Documentary History.* New York: Hill and Wang, 1964.

Roberts, John H. *Darwinism and the Divine in America: Protestant Intellectuals and Organic Evolution, 1859–1900.* Madison: University of Wisconsin Press, 1988.

Robson, John M., ed. *Origin and Evolution of the Universe: Evidence for Design?* Kingston and Montreal: McGill-Queen's University Press, 1987.

Rosenberg, Charles E. *No Other Gods: On Science and American Social Thought.* Baltimore and London: Johns Hopkins University Press, 1976.

Szasz, Ferenc M. *The Divided Mind of Protestant America, 1880–1930.* University: University of Alabama Press, 1982.

———. *The Protestant Clergy in the Great Plains and Mountain West.* Albuquerque: University of New Mexico Press, 1988.

Warner, Deborah Jean. "Astronomy in Antebellum America." In *The Sciences in the American Context: New Perspectives,* ed. by Nathan Reingold. Washington, D.C.: Smithsonian Institution Press, 1979, 55–75.

Webb, George E. *The Evolution Controversy in America.* Lexington: University Press of Kentucky, 1994.

Wuthrow, Robert. *The Restructuring of American Religion.* Princeton, N.J.: Princeton University Press, 1988.

54. Evangelicalism and Fundamentalism

Mark A. Noll

Each of the terms defining this essay—"evangelicalism," "fundamentalism," and "science"—is ambiguous. Yet, however plastic their definitions, it is clear that, since the mid-eighteenth century, the parts of the Anglo-North American Protestant world designated evangelical or fundamentalist have been deeply engaged with the practice of science. Even more, they have been deeply involved in political and cultural contests over the role of science in public life. Because evangelicalism itself was a product of the early-modern consciousness that arose in part from an exalted respect for "science," it should not be surprising that evangelical traditions have nearly everywhere and always been preoccupied with scientific questions. This essay addresses (1) problems of definition; (2) the evangelical reliance on science; (3) the record of evangelical scientists; (4) attempts at narrowly evangelical science; and (5) evangelical concern for the larger meanings of science.

Definition

While "evangelical" has many legitimate meanings, it is used here to describe a family of Protestant traditions descended from the English Reformation, which espouses a basic set of religious convictions described by D. W. Bebbington as "conversionism, the belief that lives need to be changed; activism, the expression of the gospel in effort; biblicism, a particular regard for the Bible; and what may be called crucicentrism, a stress on the sacrifice of Christ on the cross" (Bebbington 1989, 2–3). The evangelical awakening, which began in the 1730s and affected most regions of Great Britain, Ireland, and the North American Colonies, was part of a European-wide turn toward pietism that placed new emphasis on heartfelt religion and encouraged new skepticism about inherited, traditional religious authority. The spellbinding preaching of the British itinerant George Whitefield (1714–70), the pietistic theology of the Massachusetts minister Jonathan Edwards (1703–58), and, by the 1770s, dramatic growth among churches founded by John Wesley's (1703–91) Methodist missionaries made revivalism the defining heart of evangelicalism in the United States. By comparison with its British and Canadian counterparts, American evangelicalism has usually been more activistic, oriented to the immediate, and anticlerical.

The intellectual consequences of the evangelical movement have been ambivalent. On the one hand, since evangelicalism represented only a new set of emphases within historic Christianity, much historic Christian concern for reconciling faith and reason—for working out amicable connections between revelation from the Book of Nature and revelation from the Book of Scripture—remained an important part of later evangelical movements. On the other hand, since evangelicalism promoted immediate experience over adherence to formal authorities, the individual over the collective, the Bible over tradition (even of the Protestant Reformation), and revival over less convulsive forms of Christian nurture, it has sometimes encouraged abandonment of traditional Christian thought and led to disputes with the learning of the larger world. Some evangelicals have, thus, promoted anti-intellectual attitudes. More germane to questions of science, some evangelicals have advanced conclusions about the natural world that they contend are taken from Scripture directly and so can be considered disinfected from the false science of the sinful world.

Although "fundamentalism" is now sometimes used in a generic sense for all conservative religious movements that resist the tides of modernity, the term arose to define a clearly demarcated segment of Protestant Christianity in the United States. According to one of its most perceptive students, George Marsden, fundamentalism became a distinct movement during and after World War I as a form of "militantly anti-modernist Protestant evangelicalism" (Marsden 1980, 4). Fundamentalism overlaps many other Protestant traditions, but its zealous defense of nineteenth-century revivalism and the ethics of nineteenth-century American piety separate fundamentalists (at least conceptually) from more generic Protestant evangelicalism, as well as from European immigrant pietism, the holiness movements emerging from Methodism, pentecostalism, Calvinist or Lutheran confessionalism, Baptist traditionalism, and other denominational orthodoxies.

Strife during the 1920s among Baptists and Presbyterians in the Northern United States marked the debut of a well-defined fundamentalist movement. These denominational conflicts pitted doctrinal conservatives agitated about larger changes in American society against denominational loyalists who, when it came to traditional doctrines, preferred peace to precision. When the inclusivists won these denominational battles, fundamentalists faded out of sight but not out of existence. Rather, they regrouped in powerful regional associations, publishing networks, preaching circuits, Bible schools, separate denominations, and independent churches. The tumults of the 1960s and following decades brought descendants of these cultural conservatives back to the public square.

Fundamentalist intellectual life was decisively influenced by dispensational premillennialism, a theological system first brought to America in the mid-nineteenth century by John Nelson Darby (1800–82), an early leader of the Plymouth Brethren. Dispensationalism interprets the Bible as literally as possible, and it has been preoccupied with the prophetic parts of Scripture. The heightened supernaturalism of dispensationalism also predisposes its adherents to suspect exclusively natural explanations for the physical world.

Discriminating between "evangelicalism" and "fundamentalism" is difficult, since adherents of these movements, as well as outside observers, use the terms inconsistently. Most historians, however, usually treat Protestant fundamentalism as a subsection of evangelicalism while suggesting that many kinds of evangelicals should not be considered fundamentalists.

"Science" has always been an ambiguous, negotiated term in the history of evangelicalism and fundamentalism, since, in the domains of popular culture where evangelicalism and fundamentalism flourish, the term is used with multiple (often inconsistent) meanings. In an infinite variety of actual practices, evangelicals and fundamentalists embrace, disdain, ignore, or equivocate upon these meanings—"science" as a methodological commitment to observation, induction, rigorous principles of falsification, and a scorn for speculative hypotheses ("Scientists deal with knowledge of the world derived from testable empirical hypotheses"); "science" as shorthand for generalizations about the natural world (or the human person and human society) that are thought to have been established by experts ("Scientists have shown that the Grand Canyon was formed over millions of years"); and "science" as a principle of reasoning amounting to an autonomous source of social, moral, or even political authority ("Science holds our greatest hope for the future"). Flexibility in the use of the term "science" by evangelicals and fundamentalists, as well as by the general public, accounts for considerable intellectual confusion.

Finally, the connection between evangelicals and fundamentalists, on the one side, and "science," on the other, is also beset with ambiguity. The subject can refer to practicing scientists who are evangelicals or fundamentalists (but where religious principles in the practice of science may not be distinct), to the stances of popular evangelical or fundamentalist leaders on scientific matters like evolution (but where engagement with actual research results may be next to nil), to forms of antiestablishment science promoted by ardent Bible-believers (but where other evangelicals or fundamentalists repudiate their conclusions as violating the true meaning of Scripture), or to many other possibilities. Ambiguity of definition, in sum, means that the following discussion can only sample the extraordinarily diverse facets of this protean subject.

Evangelical Reliance on Science

Evangelical commitments to the Book of Scripture and fundamentalist willingness to contest the authority of mainstream science loom large in general impressions of these groups. Yet, because evangelicalism came into existence, at least in part, as a result of its ability to exploit emphases in the increasingly scientific perspective of the eighteenth-century world, evangelicalism from the start made full use of scientific language, procedures, and warrants. Early leaders like John Wesley and George Whitefield shared much, at least formally, with the era's promoters of science—including an exploitation of sense experiences (to encourage what they called "experimental" Christianity) and an antitraditionalist reliance on empirical information. By the end of the eighteenth century, evangelicals in both Great Britain and the United States had also committed themselves fully to apologetical natural theology—the effort to demonstrate the truthfulness of Christianity by appealing in a scientific manner to facts of nature and the human personality.

In the United States, evangelical spokesmen enlisted scientific concepts to contend against the irreligion and disorder of the Revolutionary period. Led especially by the Scottish immigrant John Witherspoon (1723–94), president of the College of New Jersey (later Princeton University), American evangelicals tried to meet challenges from deism, radical democracy, and the disorderliness of the frontier with an appeal to universal standards of reason and science. In the 1790s and for several decades thereafter, evangelicals on both sides of the Atlantic recommended the natural theology of William Paley (1743–1805), even though they were often uneasy with Paley's utilitarian ethics and the ease with which he accounted for apparent waste and violence in nature.

Later, as evangelicals in America began to write their own apologetical textbooks, they drew ever more directly on methods of science. When Timothy Dwight (1752–1817) became president of Yale in 1795, he used arguments from natural theology to confront undergraduate doubts about the veracity of the Bible. Scientific arguments of one sort or another were a staple in the lengthy battles between the Unitarians and the trinitarians of New England. Widespread as the recourse to scientific demonstration was among the Congregationalists, it was the Presbyterians who excelled at what historian T. Dwight Bozeman has called a "Baconian" approach to the faith. In divinity, rigorous empiricism became the standard for justifying belief in God, revelation, and the Trinity. In the moral sciences, it marked out the royal road to ethical certainty. It also provided a key for using physical science itself as a demonstration of religious truths. In each case, the appeal was, as the successor of Witherspoon at Princeton, Samuel Stanhope Smith (1750–1819), put it, "to the evidence of facts, and to conclusions resulting from these facts which . . . every gen-

uine disciple of nature will acknowledge to be legitimately drawn from her own fountain" (Smith 1787, 3). Among both Congregationalists and Presbyterians, the most theologically articulate evangelicals in the early republic, this approach predominated in rebuttals to Tom Paine's (1737–1809) *Age of Reason* (1794–96) in the 1790s and to other infidels thereafter. Their kind of "supernatural rationalism" was also useful for counteracting the impious use of science, by making possible the harmonization of the Bible first with astronomy and then with geology.

Revivalism, perhaps the least likely feature of Antebellum evangelical life to reflect the influence of a scientific worldview, nonetheless took on a new shape because of that influence. Charles G. Finney (1792–1875), the greatest evangelist of the Antebellum period and one of the most influential Americans of his generation, did not, by any means, speak for all evangelicals. But his vocabulary in a widely read book, *Lectures on Revivals of Religion* (1835), showed how useful scientific language had become. If God had established reliable laws in the natural world, so he had done in the spiritual world. To activate the proper causes for revivals was to produce the proper effect. In Finney's words: "The connection between the right use of means for a revival and a revival is as philosophically [i.e., scientifically] sure as between the right use of means to raise grain and a crop of wheat. I believe, in fact, it is more certain, and there are fewer instances of failure" (Finney 1960, 33). Because the world spiritual was analogous to the world natural, observable cause and effect must work in religion as well as in physics.

Nowhere did the language of evangelical Protestantism and the inductive ideals of modern science merge more thoroughly than in the American evangelical appropriation of the Bible. The orthodox Congregationalist Leonard Woods Jr. (1774–1854) wrote in 1822, for example, that the best method of Bible study was "that which is pursued in the science of physics," regulated "by the maxims of Bacon and Newton." Newtonian method, Woods said, "is as applicable in theology as in physics, although in theology we have an extra-aid, the revelation of the Bible. But in each science reasoning is the same—we inquire for facts and from them arrive at general truths" (quoted in Hovenkamp 1978, 3). Many others from North, South, East, and West said the same. The best-known statement of scientific biblicism appeared after the Civil War in Charles Hodge's (1797–1878) *Sys-*

tematic Theology (1872–73), but it was a position that he, with others, had been asserting for more than fifty years:

> The Bible is to the theologian what nature is to the man of science. It is his store-house of facts; and his method of ascertaining what the Bible teaches, is the same as that which the natural philosopher adopts to ascertain what nature teaches. . . . The duty of the Christian theologian is to ascertain, collect, and combine all the facts which God has revealed concerning himself and our relation to him. These facts are all in the Bible (Hodge n.d., 1:10–11).

Such attitudes were by no means limited to the established denominations with reputations to protect. To cite just one of many possible examples, Alexander Campbell (1788–1866) led the Restorationist movement—which eventuated in the Disciples of Christ, the Churches of Christ, and the Christian Churches—in using scientific language as a principle of biblical interpretation. In self-conscious imitation of Francis Bacon (1561–1626), one of Campbell's successors, James S. Lamar, published in 1859 his *Organon of Scripture: Or, the Inductive Method of Biblical Interpretation,* in which deference to scientific thinking was unmistakable: "the Scriptures admit of being studied and expounded upon the principles of the inductive method; and . . . when thus interpreted they speak to us in a voice as certain and unmistakable as the language of nature heard in the experiments and observations of science" (quoted in Hughes and Allen 1988, 156).

Later in the nineteenth century, when new higher critical views of Scripture came to the United States from Europe, evangelicals resisted them by appealing directly to scientific principles, which they identified with inductive methods even as some of the new university science was assuming a more hypothesis-deductive approach. As they did so, an irony emerged, for America's new research universities, where higher critical views prevailed, also prided themselves on being scientific. In the 1870s and 1880s, graduate study on the European model began to be offered at older universities like Harvard and newer ones like Johns Hopkins. At such centers, objectivist science was exalted as the royal road to truth, and the new professional academics reacted scornfully to what were perceived as parochial, uninformed, and outmoded scholarship. All fields, including the study of the Bible, were to be unfettered for free inquiry. The sticking point with evangelicals was that university scholarship, in keeping with newer intellectual fashions, relied heavily upon evolutionary notions; ideas, dogmas, practices, and society all evolved over time, as did religious consciousness itself. Thus was battle joined not only on the meaning of the Bible, but also on proper uses of science.

The inaugural public discussion of the new views occurred between Presbyterian conservatives and moderates from 1881 to 1883 in the pages of the *Presbyterian Review*. Both sides, as would almost all who followed in their train, tried, as if by instinct, to secure for themselves the high ground of scientific credibility. At stake was not just religion but the cultural authority that evangelical Protestants had exercised in American society. The moderates, led by Charles A. Briggs (1841–1913), were committed to "the principles of Scientific Induction." Since Old Testament studies had "been greatly enlarged by the advances in linguistic and historical science which marks our century," it was only proper to take this new evidence into account (Briggs 1881, 558). The conservatives were just as determined to enlist science on their side. William Henry Green (1825–1900), for example, chose not to examine W. Robertson Smith's (1846–94) "presumptions" that led him to adopt critical views of the Old Testament, but chose instead the way of induction: "We shall concern ourselves simply with duly certified facts" (Green 1882, 111).

Once the terms of the debate were set in this scientific form, the evangelicals defended their position tenaciously. In 1898, one of Evangelist D. L. Moody's (1837–99) colleagues, R. A. Torrey (1856–1928)—who had studied geology at Yale—published a book entitled *What the Bible Teaches.* Its method was "rigidly inductive. . . . the methods of modern science are applied to Bible study—thorough analysis followed by careful synthesis." The result was "a careful, unbiased, systematic, thorough-going, *inductive* study and statement of Bible truth" (Torrey 1898, 1 [author's italics]).

Almost since their emergence as a distinct form of Protestantism, evangelicals adopted, promoted, and exploited the language of science as their own language. In the last three decades of the twentieth century, many evangelical and fundamentalist enterprises—including the widely used apologetic manuals of the popular evangelist Josh McDowell and the myriad presentations promoting creation science—have maintained this reliance on early-modern scientific demonstration. The fact that such full and consistent efforts to exploit the prestige of early-modern science have accompanied evangelical resistance to certain conclusions of modern scientific effort means that simple statements about evangelicals and science are almost always wrong.

Evangelical Scientists

The evangelical engagement with science includes also the professional scientific labors of self-confessed evangelicals. In both Britain and North America, evangelical scientists were especially prominent during the nineteenth century. After Darwinism and other potentially naturalistic explanations began to dominate professional science from the last third of that century, the presence of evangelicals and fundamentalists has not been as obvious, but the numbers have always been greater than the stereotype of evangelical-scientific strife would suggest.

In Britain, a lengthy roster of evangelicals enjoyed considerable scientific repute for well over a century. Among these were a trio of evangelical Anglicans—Isaac Milner (1750–1820), Francis Wollaston (1762–1823), and William Farish (1759–1837)—who occupied in succession the Jacksonian Chair of Natural and Experimental Philosophy at Cambridge. Michael Faraday (1791–1867), the renowned pioneer of electromagnetism, was the member of a small evangelical sect, the Sandemanians or Glasites (after founder John Glas [1695–1773] and major promoter Robert Sandeman [1718–71]), who zealously practiced their unusual modification of traditional Calvinism. For later evangelicals, the Victoria Institute provided an ongoing base for efforts to use respectful science in harmony with, rather than in opposition to, faith.

In Scotland, the combination of Presbyterian seriousness about learning and the empirical bent of the Scottish Enlightenment produced several notable evangelical scientists. Sir David Brewster (1781–1868), after training for the ministry, became a specialist in optics, especially the polarization of light. Eventually, he served as principal of the University of Edinburgh. The Rev. John Fleming (1785–1857) was professor of natural history at King's College, Aberdeen, and the leading Scottish zoologist of his day. Hugh Miller (1802–56), a well-known geologist, opposed evolution but not the idea that the earth could be very old. His pioneering work included investigations of fossilized fish. Until his

death in 1847, the leading Scottish minister of his age, Thomas Chalmers (1780–1847), not only supported his friends Brewster, Fleming, and Miller, but himself gave popular lectures on astronomy and offered other encouragements in scientific matters. The theological college of the Scottish Free Church, founded under Chalmers's leadership in 1843, maintained a chair of natural science whose incumbents included noteworthy theologian-scientists like John Duns (1820–1909). A final notable among British evangelicals, who was born in Ireland, was Sir George Stokes (1819–1903), professor of mathematics at Cambridge, who, for more than fifty years, was one of the most respected mathematicians and physicists of his day.

In North America, a similar roster of evangelicals gained scientific eminence. Joseph Henry (1797–1878), student of electromagnetism, diligent meteorologist, and first director of the Smithsonian Institution, was a long-time Presbyterian who, during his years as a professor at the College of New Jersey, regularly joined his friends at Princeton Theological Seminary to discuss issues at the intersection of theology and science. Asa Gray (1810–88), a botanist and taxonomist of extraordinary energy, became Charles Darwin's most active disciple in the United States but without giving up his beliefs, as an active Congregationalist, in historic Christianity or his efforts to convince Darwin that natural selection could be construed as a teleological system. James Dwight Dana (1813–95) eventually accepted a form of evolution in the last edition of his influential *Manual of Geology* (first published in 1862), but (with Gray) only in a teleological sense. The Canadian geologist and paleobotanist John William Dawson (1820–99) won his reputation through fieldwork in Nova Scotia, eventually became principal of McGill University, remained a dedicated Presbyterian, and participated actively in meetings and publications of the international Evangelical Alliance. George Frederick Wright (1838–1921) was a minister and a geologist who published important papers on the effects of glaciers on North American terrain and who encouraged Asa Gray to write essays promoting a Christianized form of Darwinism. Wright lived long enough to become disillusioned with developments in evolutionary theory, but he never lost his earlier confidence that science, properly carried out, would reinforce Christian theology, properly conceived. Just about the same could be said for several important evangelical geologist-educators of the nineteenth century, including Benjamin Silliman

(1779–1864), Edward Hitchcok (1793–1864), Arnold Guyot (1807–84), and Alexander Winchell (1824–91).

In the twentieth century, professional scientists with evangelical convictions have found a home in Britain with the Victoria Institute (founded 1865) and in the United States with the American Scientific Affiliation (founded 1941). Both groups have received the unwelcome compliment of being criticized by the scientific establishment as too religious and by their fellow evangelicals as too naturalistic.

During the nineteenth century, most self-identified evangelical scientists looked upon their research as a way of confirming design in the universe. Twentieth-century evangelical scientists usually speak with greater restraint about the apologetical value of natural theology, but they join their predecessors in viewing scientific investigation as a way of glorifying God as Creator and Sustainer of the natural world. What remains to be investigated is the extent to which specifically evangelical beliefs or practices, as distinguished from more general Christian convictions shared with Roman Catholics and Protestants who are not evangelicals, have shaped the actual practices of their science.

Narrowly Evangelical Science

In the popular stereotype, evangelicals are better known as promoters of alternative scientific visions than as participants in the scientific mainstream, and with at least reasonably good cause. The modern proponents of what is variously called Flood geology, biblical creationism, or creation science are, in fact, carrying on an evangelical tradition that is almost as old as the tradition of evangelical professional science.

Among the first generations of evangelicals, for example, were some who found congenial the anti-Newtonian science of John Hutchinson. Hutchinson (1674–1737) developed his views of the material world in direct opposition to what he held to be the materialistic implications of Newton's gravitational mechanics. If in the Newtonian world objects could attract each other at a distance with no need for an intervening medium, Hutchinson concluded, Newton was setting up the material world as self-existent and, hence, in no need of God. From a painstakingly detailed study of the linguistic roots, without vowel points, of Old Testament Hebrew, Hutchinson thought he had discovered an alternative Bible-based science. The key was the identity

of the roots for "glory" and "weight," which led Hutchinson to see God actively maintaining the attraction of physical objects to each other through an invisible ether. Moreover, by analogous reasoning from the New Testament's full development of the Trinity, it was evident that a threefold reality of fire, air, and light offered a better explanation for the constituency of the material world than did modern atomism.

Hutchinson's ideas were promoted by several dons and fellows at Oxford and by several highly placed bishops in the Church of England, but, despite their appeal to the Bible as sole authority, they never received much allegiance from evangelicals. To be sure, in Britain, several early evangelicals, including John Wesley, felt the tug of Hutchinsonianism, and William Romaine (1714–95), a leading evangelical Anglican preacher in London, held something like Hutchinsonian views. In America, there were similar indications of interest, including a respectful mention by Archibald Alexander (1772–1851) in 1812 during his inaugural sermon as first professor at the Princeton Theological Seminary. Yet, Hutchinsonianism no more caught on among American evangelicals than it did among their British colleagues. The reason probably rests in the commitments that evangelicals had made to Baconian-Newtonian ideals and to a distaste for the high-church environments in which Hutchinsonianism flourished. The fact that the most visible Hutchinsonians in both Britain and North America were Tories, high-church Anglicans, and students of the Bible in Hebrew and Greek conveyed an elitist, authoritarian ethos entirely foreign to the populist, self-taught, and voluntaristic character of the evangelical movement.

Other forms of Bible-only science gained somewhat more allegiance among evangelicals during the course of the nineteenth century. In Britain, a school of "scriptural geology," advocated by a book with that title by George Bugg (c. 1769–1851) in 1826, gained some public credibility early in the century. Bible-only approaches to science were advanced unsystematically during the 1820s and 1830s by Edward Irving (1792–1834), a leading figure of the Catholic Apostolic Church and promoter of an intensely supernaturalistic, romantic evangelicalism. Irving and his associates tended to devalue the results of natural investigation and to exalt their own interpretations of Scripture as a source of knowledge opposed to other forms of human learning. The result was a heightened supernaturalism affecting doctrines of the Bible, the Second Coming of Christ, and the special presence of the

Holy Spirit, as well as heightened supernaturalism concerning the operation of the physical world.

Irving's biblicism was far different from that promoted by Philip Gosse (1810–88), a naturalist of wide experience in Canada, the United States, and Jamaica, as well as England. Gosse was a well-respected student of marine invertebrates who came to oppose what he thought were the antibiblical implications of evolutionary theory. In his response, given fullest airing in his *Omphalos* (1857), he tried to retain both a literal interpretation of early Genesis and his own life's work as an observer of nature. To gain this end, Gosse proposed that evidence for the ancient age of the earth might be the result of God's deliberate creation of the world with the marks of apparent age.

Significantly, these varieties of Bible-only or Bible-dependent science enjoyed only modest acceptance among evangelicals. In the United States, a few evangelicals accepted Gosse's views on the apparent age of the earth, but they tended to be clerics like the Southern Presbyterian theologian Robert L. Dabney (1820–98) rather than practicing scientists like Gosse. Evangelicals were much more likely to seek accommodating adjustments between biblical authority and new scientific findings. Most prominent were efforts to finesse earlier and simpler allegiance to the early chapters of Genesis. By the start of the twentieth century, the most popular of these accommodations were the "gap theory" (in which a vast expanse of time was postulated between God's original creation of the world and the creative acts specified in Genesis 1:3 and following) and the "day-age" theory (in which the days of creation in Genesis chapter one were interpreted as standing for lengthy geological eras). At least into the twentieth century, even in debates over evolutionary theories—which began well before Charles Darwin (1809–82) published his *Origin of Species* in 1859 and which always involved much more than Darwin's own notions of development through natural selection—evangelicals were as likely to propose accommodations between biblical revelation and scientific conclusions as they were to set the Bible over against science.

So long as evangelicals took a substantial part in mainstream professional research, contrarian views of science never enjoyed more than local popularity. The success among evangelicals of Flood geology or creation science began slowly in the 1920s, precisely when tensions had emerged between evangelicals and fundamentalists, on the one hand, and proponents of university-certified specialized scientific knowledge, on the other. Unlike Hutchinsonianism and, to a certain extent, earlier forms of Bible-derived science, Flood geology or creation science has been able, especially since the 1960s, to exploit alienation from the centers of learning and to make its case in democratic, populist, and voluntarist forms that accentuate, rather than contradict, major themes in the evangelical tradition. The long history of evangelical engagements with science, however, suggests that the antagonisms promoted by creation science owe at least as much to recent developments as to historic patterns among either evangelicals or scientists.

Larger Meanings of Science

Public debates over evolution and creation science highlight the fact that evangelical engagement with science has regularly focused on grand metaphysical implications rather than on minute particulars.

In the first century after the evangelical awakenings of the 1730s and 1740s, evangelicals were ardent promoters of the age's new science, but very often for extrinsic interests. They valued the language and some of the procedures of science, not so much to increase understanding of the physical world as to refurbish natural theology for the purpose of apologetics. American evangelicals used scientific reasoning straightforwardly to defend the traditional Christian faith in an era when their countrymen were setting aside other props that once had supported the faith—respect for history, deference to inherited authorities, and a willingness to follow tradition itself. A few evangelicals in the eighteenth and nineteenth centuries occasionally complained that too much authority was being given to natural theology at the expense of simple preaching or simple trust in Scripture. But more common were attitudes like those of Thomas Chalmers, who lectured and published widely on themes from natural theology but who regularly paused to show the limited value of those arguments. In a work published in 1836, Chalmers wrote: "It is well to evince, not the success only, but the shortcomings of Natural Theology; and thus to make palpable at the same time both her helplessness and her usefulness—helpless if trusted to as a guide or an informer on the way to heaven; but most useful if, under a sense of her felt deficiency, we seek for a place of enlargement and are led onward to the higher manifestations of Christianity" (Chalmers 1844, xiv).

Evangelical apologists in the United States were somewhat more inclined to wager higher stakes on the results of natural theology, which may be one of the reasons that later clashes between fundamentalists and modernists (involving great strife over the question of who was using the proper form of scientific procedure) were sharper in the United States than in Canada or Britain, where natural theology had been promoted with Chalmers's spirit.

Modern contentions over evolution, fomented by fundamentalists and some evangelicals, have regularly begun as debates over scientific results, procedures, and verifications. But, almost invariably, they have rapidly moved on to arguments over issues only remotely related to what practicing scientists do in their laboratories or in the field. From the defenders of modern scientific procedures have come protests about professional expertise, qualifications, and decorum. From the fundamentalists and evangelicals have come protests about the decline of Western morality. In moving so rapidly to great moral questions, evangelicals have only followed a long-standing tradition, which had been expressed with great clarity by the evangelical populist William Jennings Bryan (1860–1925). For Bryan, it was necessary to oppose evolution not because it imperiled traditional interpretations of Genesis 1 or sabotaged empirical investigations but because evolution was a threat to a treasured social ideal. As Bryan put it in 1925, the year of his appearance at the Scopes Trial, human evolution is "an insult to reason and shocks the heart. That doctrine is as deadly as leprosy; . . . it would, if generally adopted, destroy all sense of responsibility and menace the morals of the world" (Bryan 1925, 51). In making this assertion, Bryan upheld a long evangelical tradition that subsumed the narrowly research-oriented aspects of science to its broad social implications.

The irony of the evangelical engagement with science is that, while evangelicalism emerged as a potent religious force in part by exploiting the prestige of science that was so important for Anglo-North American culture in the eighteenth and nineteenth centuries, descendants of this earlier evangelicalism, especially in fundamentalist forms, now view recent forms of science as a grave threat to what Christians value most. That irony, however, is also eloquent testimony to the depth and persistence of evangelical engagement with science, an en-

gagement that has always been more complicated than either the champions of, or the detractors from, evangelicalism have been willing to concede.

See also Baconianism; Creationism Since 1859; Modern American Mainline Protestantism

BIBLIOGRAPHY

Bebbington, David W. *Evangelicalism in Modern Britain: A History from the 1730s to the 1980s.* London: Unwin Hyman, 1989.

———. "Science and Evangelical Theology in Britain from Wesley to Orr." In *Evangelicals and Science in Historical Perspective,* ed. by David N. Livingstone, D. G. Hart, and Mark A. Noll. New York: Oxford University Press, 1999, 120–41.

Bozeman, Theodore Dwight. *Protestants in an Age of Science: The Baconian Ideal and Antebellum American Religious Thought.* Chapel Hill: University of North Carolina Press, 1977.

Briggs, Charles A. "Critical Theories of Sacred Scripture." *Presbyterian Review* 2 (July 1881): 550–79.

Bryan, William Jennings. *The Last Message of William Jennings Bryan.* New York: Fleming H. Revell, 1925.

Chalmers, Thomas. *On Natural Theology.* Edinburgh, 1836. Reprint. New York: Robert Carter, 1844.

Conser, Walter H., Jr. *God and the Natural World: Religion and Science in Antebellum America.* Columbia: University of South Carolina Press, 1993.

Davis, Edward B. "A Whale of a Tale: Fundamentalist Fish Stories." *Perspectives on Science and Christian Faith* 43 (December 1991): 224–37.

Finney, Charles G. *Lectures on Revivals of Religion,* ed. by W. G. McLoughlin. 1835. Reprint. Cambridge, Mass: Harvard University Press, 1960.

Green, William Henry. "Professor W. Robertson Smith on the Pentateuch." *Presbyterian Review* 2 (January 1882): 108–56.

Gundlach, Bradley John. "The Evolution Question at Princeton, 1845–1929." Ph.D. diss., University of Rochester, 1995.

Hodge, Charles. *Systematic Theology,* 3 vols. 1872–3. Reprint. Grand Rapids, Mich.: Eerdmans, n.d.

Hovenkamp, Herbert. *Science and Religion in America, 1800–1860.* Philadelphia: University of Pennsylvania Press, 1978.

Hughes, Richard L., and C. Leonard Allen. *Illusions of Innocence: Protestant Primitivism in America, 1630–1875.* Chicago: University of Chicago Press, 1988.

Livingstone, David N. *Darwin's Forgotten Defenders: The Encounter Between Evangelical Theology and Evolutionary Thought.* Grand Rapids, Mich.: Eerdmans, 1987.

———. "Darwinism and Calvinism: The Belfast-Princeton Connection." *Isis* 83 (1992): 408–28.

Marsden, George M. *Fundamentalism and American Culture.* New York: Oxford University Press, 1980.

Moore, James R. *The Post-Darwinian Controversies.* New York: Cambridge University Press, 1979.

———. "Interpreting the New Creationism." *Michigan Quarterly Review* 22 (1983): 321–34.

———. *The Darwin Legend.* Grand Rapids, Mich.: Baker, 1994.

Noll, Mark A. "Science, Theology, and Society: From Cotton Mather to William Jennings Bryan." In *Evangelicals and Science in Historical Perspective,* ed. by David N. Livingstone, D. G. Hart, and Mark A. Noll. New York: Oxford University Press, 1999, 99–119.

Numbers, Ronald L. "George Frederick Wright: From Christian Darwinist to Fundamentalist." *Isis* 79 (1988): 624–45.

———. *The Creationists.* New York: Knopf, 1992.

Perspectives on Science and Christian Faith 44 (March 1992): 1–24. Articles on the fiftieth anniversary of the American Scientific Affiliation.

Roberts, Jon H. *Darwinism and the Divine in America: Protestant Intellectuals and Organic Evolution, 1859–1900.* Madison: University of Wisconsin Press, 1988.

Smith, Samuel Stanhope. *An Essay on the Causes of the Variety of Complexion and Figure in the Human Species.* Philadelphia: Robert Aitken, 1787.

Torrey, R. A. *What the Bible Teaches.* Chicago: Fleming H. Revell, 1898.

Young, Davis A. *The Biblical Flood: A Case Study of the Church's Response to Extrabiblical Evidence.* Grand Rapids, Mich.: Eerdmans, 1995.

55. AMERICA'S INNOVATIVE NINETEENTH-CENTURY RELIGIONS

Rennie B. Schoepflin

Born into a nineteenth-century America that was committed to progress and intoxicated by a sense of divine mission, Seventh-day Adventists, Jehovah's Witnesses, Mormons, and Christian Scientists each found a unique way to blend science and religion into a popular message for their day. With a profound sense of assurance of the rightness of their various visions, each movement took to hand whatever means its culture presented to buttress and spread its views. Given the growing preeminence of science as an investigative method and an authoritative body of knowledge, it often became a tool for apologetics. These movements used it both to attack others and to defend their own claims. "True" science brought confirmation of their worldviews; science that disconfirmed their message became "false" science. They were not alone, however, in their selective use of science. Many nineteenth-century Americans, including physicians, social reformers, and political utopians, did the same—and most shared the fervent zeal that their vision was the true one.

Seventh-day Adventists

When Christ did not return to the earth on October 22, 1844, as William Miller (1782–1849) and others had predicted, "the great disappointment" left the Millerites in disarray. Although some resumed timesetting, many more abandoned the effort. However, a small faction, from which evolved the Seventh-day Adventists, believed the biblical arithmetic but spiritualized the predicted event. In their view, Jesus had never intended to return to the earth on October 22, 1844. Instead, he had moved from the first compartment of God's sanctuary in heaven, the Holy Place, into the inner chamber, the Most Holy Place, so that he might initiate a new phase of his ministry before

God on behalf of humans. Thus, Seventh-day Adventists inaugurated a universal cosmology in which heavenly and earthly events were intertwined throughout God's universe, and his secrets became unlocked in human history through prophetic interpretation.

Drawing upon the growing authority of scientific objectivity within America, Seventh-day Adventists turned the Bible into a mathematically certain road map for a predictable, confirmable, coherent, and all-encompassing journey into the future. Through their use of time charts, graphs, and tables, they transmogrified inherently ambiguous biblical passages into transparently demonstrable truths. While the Bible contained the most certain knowledge of a cosmic future, science, when "rightly understood," as Adventists often qualified it, could lead to spiritual truth. The struggle for life, so obvious in nature, presented a microcosm of the spiritual struggle between good and evil going on throughout the universe. But, just as careless or prideful study would lead to errors of prophetic interpretation, so would natural theology, when constructed by unsanctified minds, yield to "sciences of satanic origin," such as historical geology or evolutionary biology.

For nineteenth-century Seventh-day Adventists, belief in a literal six-day Creation week about six thousand years ago buttressed their observance of a seventh-day Sabbath as a memorial of God's day of rest after Creation week. But it also grounded their prophetic time schedule in the context of an established history of the earth. If the earth began ages ago in an indistinct and fuzzy past, biblical catastrophes proved difficult to reconcile with nature's geological record and gave little evidence of a divine apocalypse in the future. And if life evolved from the primeval slime, then whence came the dignity of humans worthy of inclusion in the great controversy?

On the other hand, with sure vestiges of a beginning, there remained the clear prospect of an end.

While early Seventh-day Adventists scoffed at contemporary scientists from afar, George McCready Price (1870–1963), Adventism's armchair geologist extraordinaire, launched the movement's first full-scale assault on the science of origins and advocated instead a "new catastrophism." Price and more formally trained Adventist scientists, such as Harold W. Clark (1891–1986) and Frank L. Marsh (1899–1992), maintained a continual rearguard action against evolutionists by charging them with circular reasoning, with ignoring gaps in the fossil evidence, and with accepting materialist assumptions. They insisted that Adventist biblical interpretations and the writings of founder Ellen White (1827–1915) must direct scientific investigation, and that, when the two contradicted, science must obey revelation. Although some scientists in the Church's Geoscience Research Institute rejected this approach as an intrusion of religious dogma into free inquiry, their purge in the 1970s clarified the institute's role as a "scientific" apologist for Church doctrine. Nonetheless, the work of Price and his cohorts proved effective in persuading conservative Protestants from many denominations, such as John C. Whitcomb Jr. (1924–) and Henry M. Morris (1918–), to create scientific creationism as an alternative to the dominant view of evolutionists.

Under the influence of mid-nineteenth-century health reformers and hydropaths, Ellen White experienced a vision in 1863 that irrevocably transformed healthful living into a sign of faithfulness for God's saints in the earth's final days. Not only would they possess the purity of spirit that exonerates good over evil, but, given the inseparable nature of the human soul—both mind and body, spirit and flesh—they would exercise a discipline over the body that ensured a pure spirit. Eschewing alcohol, coffee, tea, and all stimulants, which polluted the body and intoxicated the spirit, and advocating exercise, fresh air, vegetarianism, and natural remedies, Seventh-day Adventists spiritualized their habits of healthful living. To defend such practices, they selectively and expediently marshaled the science of their day for the evidence to support such beliefs and practices.

This religion of health propelled Adventists to establish clinics, sanitariums, and hospitals as "entering wedges" for worldwide evangelism. First, under the leadership of John Harvey Kellogg (1870–1963) in Battle Creek, Michigan, and subsequently at the College of Medical Evangelists, established in California in 1909 (now Loma Linda University), the Church educated the medical evangelists, physicians, nurses, and technicians required to staff its medical institutions. Soon, however, under pressures for professional accreditation and licensing, and owing to the long-standing practice of using science to defend Adventist health practices, these medical institutions fell completely under the spell of scientific medicine, which had long ago jettisoned its religious roots. Ironically, therefore, while the individual health practices of Seventh-day Adventists bore many signs of their sectarian past, Adventist medical care became secularized and virtually indistinguishable from that of any public facility.

Jehovah's Witnesses

Although raised a devout Presbyterian, Charles Taze Russell (1852–1916), the founder of what came to be called the Jehovah's Witnesses, fell under the influence of a hard-headed rationalism that led him, not unlike William Miller earlier in the nineteenth century, to reject Christianity. When Russell rediscovered his faith, through Bible study and communion with Congregational and, later, Adventist circles, he pruned away traditional Christian doctrines, such as the Trinity, the resurrection of Jesus, and an eternal hell. In their place, he developed a complex system of apocalyptic interpretation that pinpointed 1914 as the date of Christ's Second Coming. Russell and the Russellites, as his followers called themselves, began the publication of the *Zion's Watchtower* magazine in 1876 (currently *Watchtower*) to disseminate their views and to call the world to repentance. In 1884, they organized the Zion's Watch Tower Tract Society, headquartered since 1909 in Brooklyn, New York. Russell's theology, continually revised and updated until his death in 1916, appeared in a seven-volume *Studies in the Scriptures* (1886–1917) that, together with tract distribution and wide-ranging preaching, effectively transmitted his message to many Americans. Upon Russell's death in 1916, the Russellites divided, most aligning with Joseph F. Rutherford (1869–1942) and the Millennial Dawnists, who changed their name to Jehovah's Witnesses in 1931. By the 1990s, membership in the movement totaled nearly three million in North America alone, although doctrinal adjustments and continued organizational authoritarianism contributed to sizable apostasies.

Eschewing formal academic training in biblical hermeneutics and embracing a kind of commonsense inductionism, Russell believed that ordinary human reason, devoted Bible study, and the guidance of the Holy Spirit would lead the honest seeker to decipher the hidden truths of God's revelation. Jehovah's Witnesses believed that the system of biblical and prophetic interpretation used by Russell and Rutherford led to Church doctrines as certain as the "soundest laws known to science." However, just as scientists revised their understanding of the laws of nature, the biblical studies of later Church leaders led to an evolving set of Church doctrines that reflected the maturing understanding of "progressive revelation." Despite their revised apocalyptic chronologies, Witnesses believed that *"scripturally, scientifically, and historically, present-truth chronology is correct beyond a doubt"* (Penton 1985, 170).

Hand in glove with Russell's devotion to an everyman's school of biblical interpretation was an antagonism toward the formal religious training of his day and the speculative and skeptical tendencies of higher education. This was an understandable reaction to the fact that few of the distinctive truths that Russell had discovered in the Bible had received the corroboration of biblical scholars or theologians. However, more than anything else it was the supposed example of Jesus's disciples and the apocalyptic immediacy of Witness doctrine that explained the anti-intellectualism of the Jehovah's Witnesses. Jesus chose fishermen and tax collectors to herald his first coming; why would he not similarly depend on unlettered men and women in these last days before his return? The last days hastened upon the world. Sinners must be warned to repent or be lost, and the pursuit of higher education would only delay the warning. Therefore, Russell advised his followers against sending their children to college or even high school.

Jehovah's Witnesses believed that God reveals himself through nature as well as through the Bible and argued, on the basis of Romans 1:20, that an open-minded study of nature leads one to a belief in God's existence and to an understanding of many of his attributes. The power and majesty of the Great Designer is clear from an unbiased examination of the size and order of the universe, the unique nature of the earth, and the amazing design of living things. Witnesses did not, however, believe that the study of nature was sufficient for salvation; only the Bible contained those life-giving truths.

From Russell's opposition to Darwinism to the Church's later denunciation of the teaching of evolution, Jehovah's Witnesses have opposed an evolutionary understanding of the earth's origins. In 1950, the Watch Tower Society published *Evolution Versus the New World,* the first of several efforts to provide a critique of evolution and to buttress the case for special creation by using biblical chronology and the argument from design. Jehovah's Witnesses embraced a variation of the day-age theory as their basis for interpreting Genesis. According to their view, the universe may be billions of years old, but, on the first day recorded in Genesis 1, God began his creation of the earth. The days of Creation week, however, were not literal twenty-four-hour days. Instead, each day represented seven thousand years of the millennia God took to complete his work. To explain the subsequent geological transformations of the earth, early Witnesses drew on the speculations of Isaac Newton Vail (1840–1912), who had imagined watery vapors encircling the earth that periodically collapsed and caused terrestrial cataclysms.

Beyond this distinctive dating scheme and the invocation of Vail's vapor-canopy theory, the Witnesses' attack on evolution and their defense of Creation looked much like that of the so-called scientific creationists of the late twentieth century. They denied spontaneous generation, rejected the fossil record, claimed that mutations were only harmful to life, and asserted that humans appeared only about six thousand years ago. They then turned to the argument from design, arguments of probability, and the revelations of biblical prophecy to conclude that the earth and all of its living forms had been created by a benevolent and soon-returning God.

Staunchly committed to the sanctity of life, Jehovah's Witnesses opposed abortion, decried any unnecessary killing of animals, and banned the ingestion of blood. But it was not until after World War II, when blood transfusions became routine, that they took an official stand against the infusion of blood or blood particles into a member's body. Believing that the Bible proscribed transfusions when it condemned the eating of blood, Witnesses resisted the state's efforts to force transfusions on them or their children, and the resultant court tests have led to important legal precedents regarding religious freedom. However, as the techniques of scientific medicine expanded, the Watch Tower Society struggled to interpret the biblical prohibition. For example, prior to 1967, cornea, kidney, and bone transplants were allowable;

from 1967 to 1980, such transplants represented a "form of human cannibalism"; since 1980, they have again been permitted.

Mormons

Believing that he had been called by Jesus Christ and visited by an angel named Moroni, Joseph Smith (1805–44) founded a new American religion based on the historico-religious teachings revealed through his visions and published in *The Book of Mormon* (1830). Commonly known as Mormonism, this nominally Christian movement with roots in the "burned-over district" of upstate New York embodied many of the ideals that characterized nineteenth-century American culture, including individuality and community, capitalism, common sense, and progress.

The movement exploded into numerous factions after Smith's advocacy of polygamy led to riots and his subsequent murder in 1844. The largest of these groups, guided by Brigham Young (1801–77), migrated in 1847 to what came to be the state of Utah. It continued as the widely known Church of Jesus Christ of Latter-Day Saints, with headquarters in Salt Lake City. No longer practicing polygamists after the turn of the twentieth century, the majority of Mormons in Utah augmented traditional Christianity with their distinctive beliefs in the doctrine of eternal progression, preexistent souls, multiple heavens, baptism for the dead, and the revelations given to Joseph Smith. Mormonism's blend of Christianity with a mystical twist, American ideals, and a family-based community led it to become one of the fastest-growing religious denominations in the world.

Joseph Smith believed, with many of his nineteenth-century contemporaries, that the earth was only one of many inhabited worlds in the universe. Unlike many Protestant apologists, however, Smith did not use this so-called plurality of worlds concept as a natural defense of Christianity; instead, he used it as the cosmological foundation for a theological system of Mormon pluralism. According to Mormons, God created a universe with both a spiritual and a physical nature, and he filled it with numerous worlds inhabited by beings participating in a universal progression from preexistence, through mortality, to perfect immortality. Just as the plenitude of the earth's nature bore witness to the fecundity of God's plan, so must his universe of innumerable worlds be filled with sentient inhabitants. Continually to accommo-

date God's offspring and ensure their spiritual progress, these worlds come into, and pass out of, existence in an evolutionary manner; after death, their inhabitants serve as "ministering angels unto many planets" (Paul 1992, 107). By grafting Mormon beliefs in the plurality of gods, the plurality of wives, and a plurality of worlds onto a popular scientific worldview of his day, Smith and his early followers brought Mormon theology into harmony with science by way of a unique natural theology. Following the example of Mormonism's first scientist, Orson Pratt (1811–81), late-nineteenth-century Church leaders wholeheartedly embraced science as an irreplaceable way to plumb the depths of pluralism through an understanding of physics, chemistry, astronomy, and geology. But they also used science and technology as tools to make the desert blossom and to transform Utah into a successful economy.

Nineteenth- and early-twentieth-century Mormons had few difficulties in reconciling the Genesis account of Creation with the geological evidence for an old earth, and, although many rejected Darwinian evolution, they did not believe that it necessarily contradicted Mormon teaching. Acrimony arose, however, during the 1920s and 1930s, when key leaders were influenced by the fundamentalist-modernist debates and came under the influence of the creationist writings of George McCready Price. As a result, the Church affirmed divine Creation, but it allowed the days of Creation week to stand for thousand-year ages, took no formal action against Mormons who advocated theistic evolution, and refused to declare whether humans had lived before Adam or not.

Things changed in 1954, however, when Joseph Fielding Smith (1876–1972), a principal in the earlier debates and a member of the church's three-member First Presidency after 1965, published *Man: His Origin and Destiny*. Smith's claims that evolution was bad science and contrary to good Mormon doctrine gained ascendancy among many Church leaders and ushered in decades of acrimony among Mormon scientists and Church leaders that continued into the 1990s. Flood geology (which invoked the Noachian Flood as the cause of much of the geological record) acquired legitimacy among many Mormons as the best reconciliation of Genesis and geology. Evolutionary theory grew suspect, and many Mormons found it difficult to embrace the validity of contemporary scientific orthodoxy with impunity.

Like their Adventist contemporaries, early Mormons practiced a blend of primitivist faith healing, dietary reform, and sectarian medicine. They believed that much sickness could be prevented by living righteously and avoiding the stimulants found in tobacco, alcohol, coffee, and tea. However, when disease struck, early Mormons prayed for the sick, anointed them with oil, and applied herbal remedies. Many, including Joseph Smith and Brigham Young, embraced the botanical system of Samuel Thomson (1769–1843) and established a botanic board of health in Nauvoo, Illinois. Under the influence of physicians trained in the East, however, Mormons in Utah in the 1870s relinquished their botanic roots and embraced the germ theory and public-health reforms of scientific medicine. However, dietary restraints, which had been poorly enforced during the first decades in Utah, returned. Forced to give up polygamy, early-twentieth-century Mormons made abstinence from coffee, tea, tobacco, and alcohol a sign of orthodoxy among the faithful.

As with Seventh-day Adventists, well-documented longitudinal studies have demonstrated a correlation between the Mormon lifestyle and a lower incidence of cancer, heart disease, and other life-shortening diseases. Many members of both denominations believed that these results provided scientific confirmation of their health practices and proved the divine origin of their founders' visions.

Christian Scientists

Mary Baker Eddy (1821–1910) "discovered" Christian Science in 1866, when she spontaneously recovered from a severe injury after recognizing that reality is completely spiritual, while evil—especially sickness and death—is only an illusion. Eddy's understanding of the mind-body relationship and her healing techniques owed much to the principles of homeopathy and the practice of Phineas Parkhurst Quimby (1802–66), a New England mentalist and magnetic healer. However, the power of Eddy's personality, her authoritative textbook, *Science and Health* (1875), and her effective organization of the Church of Christ, Scientist, turned Christian Science into a successful worldwide movement.

All Christian Scientists practiced healing by "demonstrating" over (that is, curing) "false claims" (sickness, sin, and death), but some devoted themselves professionally to full-time service as practitioners. Although dramatic physical cures attracted the most public attention, Christian Scientists believed that healing may simply involve a process of growth and enlightenment that slowly transforms a person into the spiritual image of God's ideal.

After several schisms rocked the movement, in the 1890s Eddy centralized Church organization in Boston in a Mother Church, an official board of directors, and the Christian Science Publishing Society. Under the direction of these new organizational structures, membership grew rapidly and the movement expanded worldwide. Churches numbered about three thousand throughout the world by the 1990s, although the vast majority of their members were in the United States.

Embracing a radical idealism, Eddy affirmed that there is "no Life, Substance, or Intelligence in matter. That all is mind and there is no matter" (Glover 1876, 5). Humans and the physical universe are really perfect ideas that emanate from God and reflect his harmonious and eternal existence. Only God, his manifestations, and the synonyms that express the completeness of his nature—Mind, Spirit, Soul, Principle, Life, Truth, and Love—exist; all else, especially body, matter, error, and evil, are merely illusions, the nonexistence of which is demonstrated as humans grow to reflect God. Eddy believed that first-century Christians had understood the spiritual nature of reality and used that understanding to defeat sickness, error, and death and that the recent reappearance of these truths in the teachings of Christian Science signaled impending doom for all contemporary evil. By using the empirical evidence of these "physical" transformations, early Christians and now Christian Scientists attracted attention to the idealist ideology that had brought them about.

Christian Scientists were also empiricists of a sort. By wedding the spiritual and immaterial dimensions of Christianity with scientific empiricism and calling her teachings Christian Science, Eddy merged two widely influential nineteenth-century ideologies. She believed that Christianity could be revitalized by her discovery of the truths that had allowed Christ to heal the sick and raise the dead in New Testament times, and she appealed to the methods of science to prove the truth of her claims through reason and the empirical evidence of healed bodies. She claimed that a kind of deductive logic unified her teachings into a convincing system of doctrine. For example, if God is all that exists and he is spirit, then matter, sickness, mental illness, and death do not exist. If God is all that exists and he is good, then evil and sin do not exist; claims for their existence merely reflect the tenacity of false beliefs and the undue attention paid to the false reports of the senses. However, Eddy asserted that it became easier to grasp the authenticity of such claims when one observed the concrete results of a healed body or a transformed nature. Calling such evidence a "demonstration," she concluded that "the best sermon ever preached is Truth demonstrated on the body, whereby sickness is healed and sin destroyed" (Eddy 1875, 147). Given this peculiar blend of empiricism and idealism, aside from the evidences of these "demonstrations," Christian Scientists have had little use for natural theology or its argument from design.

At least as early as the first edition of *Science and Health*, Eddy staked out her position against both the organized Christianity and the medicine of her day. Both clergy and physicians, she believed, had lost sight of the truths revealed by Jesus Christ and, hence, struggled blindly and often ineffectively against sin and sickness. Eddy's attitudes toward nineteenth-century physicians verged on outright derision, as, for example, when she claimed that "when there were fewer doctors and less thought bestowed on sanitary subjects there were better constitutions and less disease" (Eddy 1875, 341).

Christian Science practitioners offered patients religious healing framed in the terms and concepts of medicine. They did not simply evangelize for their religious beliefs; they engaged in a healing business that offered a therapeutic alternative to many patients for whom medicine had proven unsatisfactory. The limited authority of the medical community became even clearer when physicians and Christian Scientists fought in America's courtrooms and legislative halls over the legality of Christian Science healing. Throughout these debates, Christian Scientists revealed their ambiguous status as scientific practitioners and religious healers. The 1920s witnessed the establishment of an unsteady truce between American medicine and Christian Science but an unequivocal legal standing for Christian Science healing.

See also Creationism Since 1859; Evangelicalism and Fundamentalism; Modern American Mainline Protestantism; Plurality of Worlds and Extraterrestrial Life

BIBLIOGRAPHY

Bergman, Jerry. *Jehovah's Witnesses and Kindred Groups: A Historical Compendium and Bibliography.* New York: Garland, 1984.

Cook, Melvin A., and Melvin G. Cook. *Science and Mormonism: Correlations, Conflicts, and Conciliations.* Salt Lake City, Utah: Deseret Book, 1973.

Eddy, Mary Baker. *Science and Health.* Boston: Christian Science Publishing, 1875.

Fuller, Robert C. *Alternative Medicine and American Religious Life.* 1986. Reprint. Baltimore: John Hopkins University Press, 1998.

Glover, Mrs. Mary Baker. *The Science of Man, by Which the Sick Are Healed.* Lynn, Mass.: Nichols, 1876.

Life: How Did It Get Here? By Evolution or by Creation? New York: Watchtower Bible and Tract Society of New York, 1985.

Moore, R. Laurence. *Religious Outsiders and the Making of Americans.* New York: Oxford University Press, 1986.

Numbers, Ronald L. *The Creationists: The Evolution of Scientific Creationism.* New York: Knopf, 1992.

Numbers, Ronald L., and Darrel W. Amundsen, eds. *Caring and Curing: Health and Medicine in the Western Religious Traditions.* 1986. Reprint. Baltimore: Johns Hopkins University Press, 1998.

Numbers, Ronald L., and Jonathan M. Butler, eds. *The Disappointed: Millerism and Millenarianism.* Bloomington: Indiana University Press, 1987.

Paul, Erich Robert. *Science, Religion, and Mormon Cosmology.* Urbana: University of Illinois Press, 1992.

Penton, M. James. *Apocalypse Delayed: The Story of Jehovah's Witnesses.* Toronto: University of Toronto Press, 1985.

Reid, Tim S. "Mormons and Evolution: A History of B. H. Roberts and His Attempt to Reconcile Science and Religion." Ph.D. diss., Oregon State University, 1997.

Schoepflin, Rennie B. "Christian Science Healing in America." In *Other Healers: Unorthodox Medicine in America,* ed. by Norman Gevitz. Baltimore: Johns Hopkins University Press, 1988, 192–214.

56. CREATIONISM SINCE 1859

Ronald L. Numbers

Scarcely twenty years after the publication of Charles Darwin's (1809–82) *Origin of Species* in 1859, special creationists could name only two working naturalists in North America, John William Dawson (1820–99) of Montreal and Arnold Guyot (1807–84) of Princeton, who had not succumbed to some theory of organic evolution. The situation in Great Britain looked equally bleak for creationists, and on both sides of the Atlantic liberal churchmen were beginning to follow their scientific colleagues into the evolutionist camp. By the closing years of the nineteenth century, evolution was infiltrating even the ranks of the evangelicals, and, in the opinion of many observers, belief in special creation seemed destined to go the way of the dinosaur. But, contrary to the hopes of liberals and the fears of conservatives, creationism did not become extinct. The majority of late-nineteenth-century Americans remained true to a traditional reading of Genesis, and as late as 1991 a public-opinion poll revealed that 47 percent of Americans, and 25 percent of college graduates, continued to believe that "God created man pretty much in his present form at one time within the last 10,000 years."

Such surveys failed, however, to disclose the great diversity of opinion among professing creationists. Risking oversimplification, we can divide creationists into two main camps: "strict creationists," who interpret the days of Genesis literally, and "progressive creationists," who construe the Mosaic days to be immense periods of time. But, even within these camps, substantial differences exist. Among strict creationists, for example, some believe that God created all terrestrial life—past and present—less than ten thousand years ago, while others postulate one or more creations prior to the seven days of Genesis. Similarly, some progressive creationists

believe in numerous creative acts, while others limit God's intervention to the creation of life and perhaps the human soul. Since this last species of creationism is practically indistinguishable from theistic evolutionism, this essay focuses on the strict creationists and the more conservative of the progressive creationists, particularly the small number who have claimed scientific expertise. Drawing on their writings, it traces the development of creationism from the Darwinian debates in the late nineteenth century to the battles for equal time in the late twentieth. During this period, the leading apologists for special Creation shifted from an openly biblical defense of their views to one based increasingly on science. At the same time, they grew less tolerant of notions of an old earth and symbolic days of Creation, common among creationists early in the twentieth century, and more doctrinaire in their insistence on a recent Creation in six literal days and on a universal flood.

The Darwinian Debates

The general acceptance of organic evolution by the intellectual elite of the late Victorian era has often obscured the fact that the majority of Americans remained loyal to the doctrine of special Creation. In addition to the masses who said nothing, there were many people who vocally rejected kinship with the apes and other, more reflective, persons who concurred with the Princeton theologian Charles Hodge (1797–1878) that Darwinism was atheism. Among the most intransigent foes of organic evolution were the premillennialists, whose predictions of Christ's imminent return depended on a literal reading of the Scriptures. Because of their conviction that one error in the Bible invalidated the entire book, they had little patience with scientists who, as described by the evangelist Dwight L. Moody (1837–99), "dug up old carcasses . . . to make them testify against God."

Such an attitude did not, however, prevent many biblical literalists from agreeing with geologists that the earth was far older than six thousand years. They did so by identifying two separate creations in the first chapter of Genesis: the first, "in the beginning," perhaps millions of years ago, and the second, in six actual days, approximately four thousand years before the birth of Christ. According to this so-called gap theory, most fossils were relics of the first Creation, destroyed by God prior to the Adamic restoration. In 1909, the *Scofield Reference Bible,* the most authoritative biblical guide in fundamentalist circles, sanctioned this view.

Scientists such as Guyot and Dawson, the last of the reputable nineteenth-century creationists in North America, went still further to accommodate science by interpreting the days of Genesis as ages and by correlating them with successive epochs in the natural history of the world. Although they believed in special creative acts, especially of the first humans, they tended to minimize the number of supernatural interventions and to maximize the operation of natural law. During the late nineteenth century, their theory of progressive Creation circulated widely in the colleges and seminaries of America.

The Antievolution Movement

The early Darwinian debates remained confined largely to scholarly circles and often focused on issues pertaining to natural theology; thus, those who objected to evolution primarily on biblical grounds saw little reason to participate. But when the debate spilled over into the public arena during the 1880s and 1890s, creationists grew alarmed. "When these vague speculations, scattered to the four winds by the million-tongued press, are caught up by ignorant and untrained men," declared one premillennialist in 1889, "it is time for earnest Christian men to call a halt."

The questionable scientific status of Darwinism undoubtedly encouraged such critics to speak up. Although the overwhelming majority of scientists after 1880 accepted a long earth history and some form of organic evolution, many in the late nineteenth century expressed serious reservations about the ability of Darwin's particular theory of natural selection to account for the origin of species. Their published criticisms of Dar-

winism led creationists mistakenly to conclude that scientists were in the midst of discarding evolution. The appearance of books with such titles as *The Collapse of Evolution* and *At the Death Bed of Darwinism* bolstered this belief and convinced antievolutionists that liberal Christians had capitulated to evolution too quickly. In view of this turn of events, it seemed likely that those who had "abandoned the stronghold of faith out of sheer fright will soon be found scurrying back to the old and impregnable citadel, when they learn that 'the enemy is in full retreat.'"

Early in 1922, William Jennings Bryan (1860–1925), Presbyterian layman and thrice-defeated Democratic candidate for the presidency of the United States, heard of an effort in Kentucky to ban the teaching of evolution in public schools. "The movement will sweep the country," he predicted hopefully, "and we will drive Darwinism from our schools." His prophecy proved overly optimistic, but, before the end of the decade, more than twenty state legislatures debated antievolution laws, and three—Tennessee, Mississippi, and Arkansas—banned the teaching of evolution in public schools. Oklahoma prohibited the adoption of evolutionary textbooks, while Florida condemned the teaching of Darwinism. At times, the controversy became so tumultuous that it looked to some as though "America might go mad." Many persons shared responsibility for these events, but none more than Bryan. His entry into the fray had a catalytic effect and gave antievolutionists what they needed most: "a spokesman with a national reputation, immense prestige, and a loyal following."

Who joined Bryan's crusade? As recent studies have shown, they came from all walks of life and from every region of the country. They lived in New York City, Chicago, and Los Angeles, as well as in small towns and in the country. Few possessed advanced degrees, but many were not without education. Nevertheless, Bryan undeniably found his staunchest supporters and won his greatest victories in the conservative and still largely rural South, described hyperbolically by one fundamentalist journal as "the last stronghold of orthodoxy on the North American continent," a region where the "masses of the people in all denominations 'believe the Bible from lid to lid.'"

Leadership of the antievolution movement came not from the organized churches of America but from individuals such as Bryan and interdenominational organizations such as the World's Christian Fundamentals

Association, a predominantly premillennialist body founded in 1919 by William Bell Riley (1861–1947), pastor of the First Baptist Church in Minneapolis. Riley became active as an antievolutionist after discovering, to his apparent surprise, that evolutionists were teaching their views at the University of Minnesota. The early twentieth century witnessed an unprecedented expansion of public education—enrollment in public high schools nearly doubled between 1920 and 1930—and fundamentalists such as Riley and Bryan wanted to make sure that students attending these institutions would not lose their faith. Thus, they resolved to drive every evolutionist from the public-school payroll. Those who lost their jobs as a result deserved little sympathy, for, as one rabble-rousing creationist put it, the German soldiers who killed Belgian and French children with poisoned candy were angels compared with the teachers and textbook writers who corrupted the souls of children and thereby sentenced them to eternal death.

The antievolutionists liked to wrap themselves in the authority of science, but, unfortunately for them, they could claim few legitimate scientists of their own: a couple of self-made men of science, one or two physicians, and a handful of teachers who, as one evolutionist described them, were "trying to hold down, not a chair, but a whole settee, of 'Natural Science' in some little institution." Of this group, the most influential were Harry Rimmer (1890–1952) and George McCready Price (1870–1963).

Rimmer, a Presbyterian minister and self-styled "research scientist," had obtained his limited exposure to science during a term or two at San Francisco's Hahnemann Medical College. After his brief stint in medical school, he attended Whittier College and the Bible Institute of Los Angeles for a year each before entering full-time evangelistic work. About 1919 he settled in Los Angeles, where he set up a small laboratory at the rear of his house to conduct experiments in embryology and related sciences. Within a year or two, he established the Research Science Bureau "to prove through findings in biology, paleontology, and anthropology that science and the literal Bible were not contradictory." The bureau staff—that is, Rimmer—apparently used income from the sale of memberships to finance anthropological field-trips in the Western United States. By the late 1920s, the bureau lay dormant, and Rimmer signed on with Riley's World's Christian Fundamentals Association as a field secretary. Besides engaging in research, Rimmer deliv-

ered thousands of lectures, primarily to student groups, on the scientific accuracy of the Bible. Posing as a scientist, he attacked Darwinism and poked fun at the credulity of evolutionists. He also enjoyed success as a debater.

George McCready Price, a self-trained Seventh-day Adventist geologist, was less skilled at debating than Rimmer but more influential scientifically. As a young man, Price attended an Adventist college in Michigan for two years and later completed a teacher-training course at the provincial normal school in his native New Brunswick. The turn of the twentieth century found him serving as principal of a small high school in an isolated part of eastern Canada, where one of his few companions was a local physician. During their many conversations, the doctor almost converted his fundamentalist friend to evolution, but each time Price wavered, he was saved by prayer and by reading the works of the Seventh-day Adventist prophet Ellen G. White (1827–1915), who claimed divine inspiration for her view that Noah's Flood accounted for the fossil record on which evolutionists based their theory. As a result of these experiences, Price vowed to devote his life to promoting creationism of the strictest kind.

By 1906 he was working as a handyman at an Adventist sanitarium in Southern California. That year he published a slim volume entitled *Illogical Geology: The Weakest Point in the Evolution Theory,* in which he brashly offered one thousand dollars "to any one who will, in the face of the facts here presented, show me how to prove that one kind of fossil is older than another." He never had to pay. According to Price's argument, Darwinism rested "logically and historically on the succession of life idea as taught by geology," and "if this succession of life is not an actual scientific fact, then Darwinism . . . is a most gigantic hoax."

During the next fifteen years, Price occupied scientific settees in several Seventh-day Adventist schools and authored six more books attacking evolution, particularly its geological foundation. Although not unknown outside his own church before the early 1920s, he did not attract national attention until then. Shortly after Bryan declared war on evolution, Price published *The New Geology* (1923), the most systematic and comprehensive of his many books. Uninhibited by false modesty, he presented his "great law of conformable stratigraphic sequences . . . by all odds the most important law ever formulated with reference to the order in which the

strata occur." This law stated that "any kind of fossiliferous beds whatever, 'young' or 'old,' may be found occurring conformably on any other fossiliferous beds, 'older'
or 'younger.'" To Price, so-called deceptive conformities
(where strata seem to be missing) and thrust faults
(where the strata are apparently in the wrong order)
proved that there was no natural order to the fossil-bearing rocks, all of which he attributed to the Genesis
Flood. Despite criticism and ridicule from the scientific
establishment—and the fact that his theory contradicted
both the day-age and gap interpretations of Genesis—
Price's reputation among fundamentalists rose dramatically. By the mid-1920s, the editor of *Science* could
accurately describe him as "the principal scientific
authority of the Fundamentalists."

In the spring of 1925, John Thomas Scopes (1900–
70), a high-school teacher in Dayton, Tennessee, confessed to having violated the state's recently passed law
banning the teaching of human evolution in public
schools. His subsequent trial focused international attention on the antievolution crusade and brought Bryan to
Dayton to assist the prosecution. Although the court in
Dayton found Scopes guilty as charged, creationists
found little cause for rejoicing. Some members of the
press had not treated them kindly, and the taxing ordeal
no doubt contributed to Bryan's death a few days after
the end of the trial. Nevertheless, the antievolutionists
continued their crusade, winning victories in Mississippi
in 1926 and in Arkansas two years later. By the end of the
decade, however, their legislative campaign had lost its
steam.

Contrary to appearances, the creationists did not
give up; they simply changed tactics. Instead of lobbying
state legislatures, they shifted their attack to local communities, where they engaged in what one critic
described as "the emasculation of textbooks, the 'purg-
ing' of libraries, and above all the continued hounding of
teachers." Their new approach attracted less attention
but paid off handsomely, as school boards, textbook
publishers, and teachers in both urban and rural areas,
North and South, bowed to their pressure. Darwinism
virtually disappeared from high-school texts, and for
years many American teachers feared being identified as
evolutionists. Instead of attempting to convert the world
to their way of thinking, the creationists increasingly
turned their energies inward, organizing their own societies and editing their own journals.

The Creationist Revival

In 1964, one historian predicted that "a renaissance of
the [creationist] movement is most unlikely." And so it
seemed. But even as these words were penned, a major
revival was under way, led by a Texas engineer, Henry M.
Morris (1918–). Raised a nominal Southern Baptist, and
as such a believer in Creation, Morris as a youth had
drifted unthinkingly into evolutionism and religious
indifference. A thorough study of the Bible following
graduation from college convinced him of its absolute
truth and prompted him to reevaluate his belief in evolution. After an intense period of soul-searching, he concluded that Creation had taken place in six literal days,
because the Bible clearly said so and "God doesn't lie." In
the late 1950s, he began collaborating with a young theologian, John C. Whitcomb Jr. (1924–), of the Grace
Brethren denomination, on a defense of Price's Flood geology. By the time they finished their project, Morris had
earned a Ph.D. in hydraulic engineering from the University of Minnesota and was chairing the Civil Engineering
Department at Virginia Polytechnic Institute; Whitcomb,
a Princeton alumnus, was teaching Old Testament studies
at Grace Theological Seminary in Indiana.

In 1961, they brought out *The Genesis Flood,* the
most impressive contribution to strict creationism since
the publication of Price's *New Geology* in 1923. In many
respects, their book appeared to be simply "a reissue of
G.M. Price's views, brought up to date," as one reader
described it. Beginning with a testimony to their belief in
"the verbal inerrancy of Scripture," Whitcomb and Morris went on to argue for a recent Creation of the entire
universe, a Fall that triggered the second law of thermodynamics, and a worldwide Flood that in one year laid
down most of the geological strata. Given this history,
they argued, "the last refuge of the case for evolution
immediately vanishes away, and the record of the rocks
becomes a tremendous witness . . . to the holiness and
justice and power of the living God of Creation!"

Despite the book's lack of conceptual novelty, it provoked intense debate among evangelicals. Progressive
creationists denounced it as a travesty on geology that
threatened to set back the cause of Christian science a
generation, while strict creationists praised it for making
biblical catastrophism intellectually respectable. Its
appeal, suggested one critic, lay primarily in the fact that,
unlike previous creationist works, it "looked legitimate

as a scientific contribution," accompanied as it was by footnotes and other scholarly appurtenances. In responding to their detractors, Whitcomb and Morris repeatedly refused to be drawn into a scientific debate, arguing that "the real issue is not the correctness of the interpretation of various details of the geological data, but simply what God has revealed in His Word concerning these matters."

Whatever its merits, *The Genesis Flood* unquestionably "brought about a stunning renaissance of flood geology," symbolized by the establishment in 1963 of the Creation Research Society. Shortly before the publication of his book, Morris had sent the manuscript to Walter E. Lammerts (1904–96), a Missouri Synod Lutheran with a doctorate in genetics from the University of California. As an undergraduate at Berkeley, Lammerts had discovered Price's *New Geology,* and, during the early 1940s while teaching at UCLA, he had worked with Price in a local creationist society. After the mid-1940s, however, his interest in creationism had flagged—until awakened by reading the Whitcomb and Morris manuscript. Disgusted by some evangelicals' flirtation with evolution, he organized in the early 1960s a correspondence network with Morris and eight other strict creationists, dubbed the "team of ten." In 1963, seven of the ten met with a few other like-minded scientists at the home of a team member in Midland, Michigan, to form the Creation Research Society (CRS). Of the ten founding members, five possessed doctorates in biology; a sixth had earned a Ph.D. degree in biochemistry; and a seventh held a master's degree in biology.

At the end of its first decade, the society claimed four hundred fifty regular members, plus sixteen hundred sustaining members, who failed to meet the scientific qualifications. Eschewing politics, the CRS devoted itself almost exclusively to education and research, funded "at very little expense, and . . . with no expenditure of public money." CRS-related projects included expeditions to search for Noah's ark, studies of fossil human footprints and pollen grains found out of the predicted evolutionary order, experiments on radiation-produced mutations in plants, and theoretical studies in physics demonstrating a recent origin of the earth. A number of members collaborated in preparing a biology textbook based on creationist principles. In view of the previous history of creation science, it was an auspicious beginning.

The creationist revival of the 1960s attracted little public attention until late in the decade, when fundamentalists became aroused about the federally funded Biological Sciences Curriculum Study texts, which featured evolution, and the California State Board of Education voted to require public-school textbooks to include Creation along with evolution. This decision resulted in large part from the efforts of two Southern California housewives, Nell J. Segraves (1922–) and Jean E. Sumrall (1927–). In 1961, Segraves learned of the U.S. Supreme Court's ruling in the Madalyn Murray (1919–late 1990s?) case protecting atheist students from required prayers in public schools. Murray's ability to shield her child from religious exposure suggested to Segraves that creationist parents like herself "were entitled to protect our children from the influence of beliefs that would be offensive to our religious beliefs." It was this line of argument that finally persuaded the Board of Education to grant creationists equal rights.

Flushed with victory, in 1970 Segraves and her son Kelly (1942–) joined an effort to organize a Creation Science Research Center (CSRC), affiliated with Christian Heritage College in San Diego, to prepare creationist literature suitable for adoption in public schools. Associated with them in this enterprise was Henry Morris, who resigned his position at Virginia Polytechnic Institute to help establish a center for creation research. Because of differences in personalities and objectives, in 1972 the Segraveses left the college, taking the CSRC with them; Morris thereupon set up a new research division at the college, the Institute of Creation Research (ICR), which, he announced with obvious relief, would be "controlled and operated by scientists" and would engage in research and education, not political action. During the 1970s, Morris added five scientists to his staff and, funded largely by small gifts and royalties from Institute publications, turned the ICR into the world's leading center for the propagation of strict creationism.

The 1970s witnessed another major shift in creationist tactics. Instead of trying to outlaw evolution, as they had done in the 1920s, antievolutionists now fought to give Creation equal time. And instead of appealing to the authority of the Bible, as Morris and Whitcomb had done as recently as 1961, they consciously downplayed the Genesis story in favor of what they called "scientific creationism." By 1974, Morris was recommending that creationists ask public schools to teach "only the scientific aspects of creationism," which, in practice, meant leaving out all references to the six days of Genesis and Noah's ark and focusing instead on evidence for a recent worldwide catastrophe and on arguments against evolution. Thus, the product remained virtually the same; only the packaging changed. The ICR textbook *Scientific Creationism* (1974), for example, came in two editions: one for public schools, containing no references to the Bible, and another for use in Christian schools that included a chapter on "Creation According to Scripture."

Creationists professed to see no reason why their Flood-geology model should not be allowed to compete on an equal scientific basis with the evolution model. In selling this two-model approach to school boards, creationists pressed their scientific claims. This tactic proved extremely effective, at least initially. Two state legislatures, in Arkansas and Louisiana, and various school boards adopted the two-model approach, and an informal poll of American school-board members in 1980 showed that only 25 percent favored teaching nothing but evolution. In 1982, however, a federal judge declared the Arkansas law, requiring a "balanced treatment" of Creation and evolution, to be unconstitutional, a decision endorsed by the U.S. Supreme Court five years later.

The influence of the creationist revival sparked by Whitcomb and Morris was immense. Not least, it elevated the strict creationism of Price and Morris to a position of virtual orthodoxy among fundamentalists, and it endowed creationism with a measure of scientific respectability unknown since the deaths of Guyot and Dawson. Unlike the antievolution crusade of the 1920s, which remained confined mainly to North America, the revival of the 1960s rapidly spread overseas as American creationists and their books circled the globe. Partly as a result of stimulation from America, including the publication of a British edition of *The Genesis Flood* in 1969, the lethargic Evolution Protest Movement, founded in Great Britain in the 1930s, was revitalized, and two new creationist organizations, the Newton Scientific Association and the Biblical Creation Society, sprang into existence in Britain. On the Continent, the Dutch assumed the lead in promoting creationism, encouraged by the translation of books on Flood geology and by visits from ICR scientists. Similar developments occurred elsewhere in Europe, as well as in Australia, New Zealand, Asia, and South America. By 1980, Morris's books alone had been translated into Chinese, Czech, Dutch, French,

German, Japanese, Korean, Portuguese, Russian, and Spanish. Strict creationism had become an international phenomenon.

For citations to sources quoted see under Acknowledgments.

See also America's Innovative Nineteenth-Century Religions; Evangelicalism and Fundamentalism; Evolution; Genesis and Science; Genesis Flood; Modern American Mainline Protestantism

BIBLIOGRAPHY

Eve, Raymond A., and Francis B. Harrold. *The Creationist Movement in Modern America.* Boston: Twayne, 1991.

Gatewood, Willard B., Jr. *Preachers, Pedagogues, and Politicians: The Evolution Controversy in North Carolina, 1920–1927.* Chapel Hill: University of North Carolina Press, 1966.

———, ed. *Controversy in the Twenties: Fundamentalism, Modernism, and Evolution.* Nashville: Vanderbilt University Press, 1969.

Larson, Edward J. *Trial and Error: The American Controversy over Creation and Evolution.* Updated ed. New York: Oxford University Press, 1989.

———. *Summer for the Gods: The Scopes Trial and America's Continuing Debate Over Science and Religion.* New York: Harvard University Press, 1998.

Marsden, George M. *Understanding Fundamentalism and Evangelicalism.* Grand Rapids, Mich.: Eerdmans, 1991.

McIver, Tom. *Anti-Evolution: A Reader's Guide to Writings Before and After Darwin.* Baltimore: Johns Hopkins University Press, 1992.

Moore, James R. *The Post-Darwinian Controversies: A Study of the Protestant Struggle to Come to Terms with Darwin in Great Britain and America, 1870–1900.* Cambridge: Cambridge University Press, 1979.

———. "The Creationist Cosmos of Protestant Fundamentalism." In *Fundamentalisms and Society: Reclaiming the Sciences, the Family, and Education,* ed. by Martin E. Marty and R. Scott Appleby. Chicago: University of Chicago Press, 1993, 42–72.

Morris, Henry M. *A History of Modern Creationism.* San Diego, Calif.: Master Book Publishers, 1984.

Nelkin, Dorothy. *The Creation Controversy: Science or Scripture in the Schools?* New York: Norton, 1982.

Numbers, Ronald L. *The Creationists: The Evolution of Scientific Creationism.* New York: Knopf, 1992.

———, ed. *Creationism in Twentieth-Century America: A Ten-Volume Anthology of Documents, 1903–1961.* New York: Garland, 1995.

———. *Darwinism Comes to America.* Cambridge, Mass.: Harvard University Press, 1998.

Roberts, Jon H. *Darwinism and the Divine in America: Protestant Intellectuals and Organic Evolution, 1858–1900.* Madison: University of Wisconsin Press, 1988.

Szasz, Ferenc Morton. *The Divided Mind of Protestant America, 1880–1930.* University: University of Alabama Press, 1982.

Toumey, Christopher P. *God's Own Scientists: Creationists in a Secular World.* New Brunswick, N.J.: Rutgers University Press, 1994.

Trollinger, William Vance, Jr. *God's Empire: William Bell Riley and Midwestern Fundamentalism.* Madison: University of Wisconsin Press, 1990.

Webb, George E. *The Evolution Controversy in America.* Lexington: University Press of Kentucky, 1994.

PART V

Astronomy and Cosmology

57. THE CALENDAR

LeRoy E. Doggett†

It is not mere coincidence that the principal calendars of the Western world (Jewish, Islamic, and Gregorian) were created for religious purposes. These calendars do more than order patterns of ritual for their respective religions; each provides a defining element of its faith. By following the ritual calendar, an individual proclaims adherence to the faith and joins in a characteristic practice of that faith. Although the Gregorian calendar is best known for bridging religions and cultures as the civil standard for international communications, its religious function remains.

The calendars have developed in reaction to each other. While they have in common the seven-day week, each has staked out its own weekly holy day. Each has a characteristic way of timing annual periods of penitence and celebration. Each has a characteristic way of maintaining solar and lunar cycles through calculation or observation. Efforts to follow or replicate astronomical cycles in distinctive ways have combined scientific challenge with religious quests. Only in this way can we explain the calendar controversies that have exercised some of the finest minds of their faiths.

The basic astronomical data can be briefly summarized. The tropical year (solar year, cycle of the seasons, interval from vernal equinox to vernal equinox) is currently 365.2421897 days, but it is decreasing by about half a second each century. The synodic month (lunar month, interval from new moon to new moon) averages 29.5305889 days, but it is increasing a couple hundredths of a second per century. However, the interval from a particular new moon to the next can be up to half a day longer or shorter than the average. Twelve synodic months are about 354.4 days, nearly eleven days shorter than the tropical year.

The Observational Jewish Calendar

Before the fourth century A.D., the Jewish calendar was based largely on observation. Although the week was maintained as a numerical count, months began with the first sighting of the crescent moon, resulting in months of twenty-nine and thirty days. A thirteenth month was intercalated every two or three years to ensure that Passover occurred in the spring. Without such intercalation, months would occur about eleven days earlier each solar year. The occurrence of spring was judged according to environmental conditions (for example, the ripeness of vegetation or the maturity of animal life) rather than astronomical calculations or observations of the vernal equinox. A committee of the Sanhedrin (the supreme Jewish council in Jerusalem) decided when each month began and when an intercalary month was required. Such an observational calendar, checked with knowledge of astronomical cycles, was used from the sixth century B.C. to the fourth century A.D. Because the Jewish calendar combines the lunar month and the solar year, it is called a lunisolar calendar.

The Early Christian Calendar

The early Christians faced some difficult calendrical questions in their attempts to commemorate the passion and resurrection of Christ. The Gospels assert that the resurrection occurred on Sunday. However, they date the crucifixion with respect to the time of Passover, which is the fourteenth day (full moon) in the Jewish lunar month of Nisan. Further complicating the situation, the Christians needed to know the date of Easter on the purely solar calendar of the Roman Empire, the Julian calendar of 365 days, plus an intercalary day every fourth year. As the new faith spread, there was an increasing desire to be independent of Judaism and to ensure that the faithful, from northern Africa to the British Isles, observed holy days simultaneously.

From the time of the Council of Nicaea (A.D. 325), it was generally agreed that Easter was to be the first Sunday after the full moon, occurring on or next after the vernal equinox. Calculations of full moons and equinoxes could have been based on recently constructed models of Claudius Ptolemy (second century A.D.). Instead, the Christian churches experimented with lunisolar cycles from centuries earlier. An example of such a cycle, and the one that eventually gained acceptance, is the Metonic cycle in which 235 lunar months, comprising 6,939.69 days, are nearly equal to nineteen solar years of 6,939.60 days. To implement this, seven lunar months must be intercalated over the nineteen solar years.

By adopting such cycles, early Christians ignored recent developments in astronomy but wisely minimized mathematical complexity. Although the lunisolar cycle determined a sequence of full moons, the Sunday following the full moon after the equinox still had to be determined on a solar calendar with months of thirty and thirty-one days (except for February) and a leap year every fourth year. These problems inspired the science of the computus, a system that was simple enough to be transmitted to the outposts of Christianity yet was complicated enough to inspire serious study. Not only did the computus transmit the calendar, it preserved and spread basic concepts of arithmetic and astronomy at a time when the Roman Empire was breaking down.

In the eighth century, at the height of its development, deficiencies in the computus were discovered. The problem, initially poorly understood, was twofold. The length of the Julian calendar year (365.25 days) was too long by about one day in 128 years. As a result, the actual date of the vernal equinox was shifting from its assumed date of March 21. In addition, the Metonic cycle of Moon phases was in error by one day in about three hundred years. By the thirteenth century, the ecclesiastical calendar had become a scandal among Roman Catholic scientists. The "correct" date of Easter became a hotly debated theological and scientific question.

From a scientific standpoint, the synodic month had been well determined by Babylonian and Greek astronomers. This value was not incorporated into the computus, however. The tropical year, on the other hand, was still poorly known. To the embarrassment of Christians,

the Jews and the Muslims appeared to have superior calendars.

The Calculated Jewish Calendar

Indeed, by the tenth century, the Jewish calendar had been transformed from an observational to a calculated calendar, with the rules that are in use today. The basic principles go back at least to rules made public by Patriarch Hillel II in the fourth century. With the diaspora, Jews were too widely spread to follow monthly calendrical decisions of a single, central authority. They could observe a common calendar only if it was based on calculations rather than observations. Like the Christians, the Jews based the calendar on the Metonic cycle. However, they used a better value of the tropical year and a much better value of the synodic month. Although these values were determined by Greek and Babylonian astronomers, they were implemented to produce a stable calendar.

The Islamic Calendar

The Islamic calendar that developed in the seventh century was a strictly observational lunar calendar, in which months follow the lunar-phase cycle. Each month begins (at least in principle) with the first sighting of the crescent moon after the new moon. Since months are thus twenty-nine or thirty days long, and there is no intercalation, the months gradually drift through the seasons in thirty-three years. Despite its observational basis, the calendar inspired generations of astronomers to study means of calculating when the lunar crescent becomes visible. It was part of an overall effort by astronomers working under Islamic rule (including Jews, Christians, and pagans) to recover ancient Greek astronomy and to test it philosophically as well as observationally.

Gregorian Reform

As a result of the Islamic studies, new astronomical tables were constructed with improved parameters. The most important, the Alfonsine Tables, are attributed to the court of Alfonso X of Castile (reigned 1252–84) in the late thirteenth century. The value of the tropical year given there, 365.2425 days, was adopted as the length of the calendar year in the Gregorian Reform of 1582 (named after Pope Gregory XIII [b. 1502, p. 1572–85], who promulgated it). This calendar, which serves Roman

Catholic and Protestant churches today, also features periodic adjustments to the Metonic cycle to keep the full moon-cycle synchronized with the actual phenomena.

Some astronomers of the sixteenth century advocated using accurate calculations of lunar phases to determine Easter. This was done for a time in some Protestant areas that initially rejected the Gregorian calendar. In the end, however, the Gregorian use of cycles was adopted. The Gregorian leap-year system has gradually been adopted as the international standard for communications. In it, every year that is evenly divisible by four is a leap year, except years that are divisible by one hundred. These century years are leap years only if they are divisible by four hundred.

Lunar Visibility

Today the calendrical cycles are well understood for practical calendrical purposes. The only area of lingering uncertainty is the problem of lunar visibility in the Islamic calendar. This has recently been attacked with modern tools of atmospheric physics. However, the accuracy of visibility prediction is limited by uncertainties owing to local atmospheric conditions and the ability of the observer. Even so, predictions are now more accurate than many of the observations that are accepted to begin the holy month of Ramadan. The principal problems are now political rather than scientific.

See also Copernican Revolution; Pre-Copernican Astronomy

Bibliography

Coyne, George V., Michael A. Hoskin, and Olaf Pedersen, eds. *Gregorian Reform of the Calendar.* Vatican City: Pontificia Academia Scientiarum, 1983.

Dobrzycki, Jerzy. "Astronomical Aspects of the [Gregorian] Calendar Reform." In *Gregorian Reform of the Calendar,* ed. by George V. Coyne, Michael A. Hoskin, and Olaf Pedersen. Vatican City: Pontificia Academia Scientiarum, 1983, 117–27.

Doggett, LeRoy E., and Bradley E. Schaefer. "Lunar Crescent Visibility." *Icarus* 107 (1994): 388–403.

Ilyas, Mohammad. *A Modern Guide to Astronomical Calculations of Islamic Calendar, Times, and Qibla.* Kuala Lumpur: Berita, 1984.

Kennedy, E. S. "The Crescent Visibility Theory of Thabit bin Qurra." *Proceedings of the Mathematical and Physical Society of the United Arab Republic* (1960). Reprinted in *Studies in the Islamic Exact Sciences,* ed. by D. A. King and M. H. Kennedy. Beirut: American University of Beirut, 1983, 140–3.

———. "The Lunar Visibility Theory of Ya Ôqub ibn Tariq." *Journal of Near Eastern Studies* 27 (1968): 126–32. Reprinted in *Studies in the Islamic Exact Sciences,* ed. by D. A. King and M. H. Kennedy. Beirut: American University of Beirut, 1983, 157–63.

Kennedy, E. S., and M. Janjanian. "The Crescent Visibility Table in Al-Khwarizmi's Zij." *Centaurus* 11 (1965): 73–8. Reprinted in *Studies in the Islamic Exact Sciences,* ed. by D. A. King and M. H. Kennedy. Beirut: American University of Beirut, 1983, 151–6.

King, David A. "On the Astronomical Tables of the Islamic Middle Ages." *Studia Copernicana* 13 (1975): 37–56. Reprinted in King, David A. *Islamic Mathematical Astronomy.* London: Variorum, 1986.

———. "Some Early Islamic Tables for Determining Lunar Crescent Visibility." In *From Deferent to Equant: A Volume of Studies in the History of Science in the Ancient and Medieval Near East in Honor of E. S. Kennedy,* ed. by David A. King and George Saliba. *Annals of the New York Academy of Sciences* 500 (1987): 185–225.

———. "Folk Astronomy in the Service of Religion: The Case of Islam." In *Astronomies and Cultures,* ed. by Clive L. N. Ruggles and Nicholas J. Saunders. Niwot: University Press of Colorado, 1993.

King, D. A., and M. H. Kennedy, eds. *Studies in the Islamic Exact Sciences.* Beirut: American University of Beirut, 1983.

Neugebauer, Otto. "Astronomical Commentary." In *The Code of Maimonides: Sanctification of the New Moon.* Trans. by Solomon Gandz. New Haven, Conn.: Yale University Press, 1956, 113–149.

———. *Ethiopic Astronomy and Computus.* Vienna: Oesterreichischen Akademie der Wissenschaften, 1979.

North, John D. "The Western Calendar: 'Intolerabilis, Horribilis, et Derisibilis'; Four Centuries of Discontent." In *Gregorian Reform of the Calendar,* ed. by George V. Coyne, Michael A. Hoskin, and Olaf Pedersen. Vatican City: Pontificia Academia Scientiarum, 1983, 75–113.

Obermann, Julian. "Introduction." In *The Code of Maimonides: Sanctification of the New Moon.* Trans. by Solomon Gandz. New Haven, Conn.: Yale University Press, 1956, xv–lx.

Pedersen, Olaf. "The Ecclesiastical Calendar and the Life of the Church." In *Gregorian Reform of the Calendar,* ed. by George V. Coyne, Michael A. Hoskin, and Olaf Pedersen. Vatican City: Pontificia Academia Scientiarum, 1983, 17–74.

Stevens, Wesley M. "Cycles of Time: Calendrical and Astronomical Reckonings in Early Science." In *Time and Process: Interdisciplinary Issues,* ed. by J. T. Fraser and Lewis Rowell. Madison, Conn.: International Universities Press, 1993, 27–51.

58. COMETS AND METEORS

Sara Schechner Genuth

Heavenly wonders have long been thought to announce divine displeasure or to herald calamities. In folklore, comets and meteors portended war, famine, plague, ill luck, the downfall of kings, universal suffering, the end of the world, and, occasionally, good fortune. Natural philosophers and theologians concurred until the early-modern period, when they began to reject these beliefs as vulgar superstition. Nevertheless, they continued to see comets as celestial agents of God.

Comets and Meteors as Divine Portents

In the *Meteorologica,* Aristotle (384–322 B.C.) classified comets as a type of fiery meteor that was formed when terrestrial exhalations ascended into the upper atmosphere, below the moon's sphere, and began to burn. Other fiery meteors included shooting stars, fireballs, and the aurora borealis. Comets and meteors augured windy weather, drought, tidal waves, earthquakes, and stones falling from the sky because the meteors and portended disasters were both symptomatic of hot, dry exhalations that escaped from the earth in abundant amounts. Seneca (c. 4 B.C.–A.D. 65), among others, proposed that comets were celestial objects distinct from fiery meteors, yet he believed that divination from both was possible because events were prearranged in sequence by divine agency. Aristotle's physical theory reigned supreme until early-modern times, but the natural connection he saw between meteorological phenomena and terrestrial commotion was limited. It was largely ignored by Romans, who expanded the sphere of meteoric significance. They came to view comets and showy meteoric displays as monsters, which were con-

trary to nature and augured terrible events. Roman writers like Virgil (70–19 B.C.), Marcus Manilius (fl. A.D. 9–15), and Pliny the Elder (c. A.D. 23–79) believed that the gods sent them to portend not only plague and poor harvests, but also war and the murder of great men.

Early Christians appropriated these views but saw comets and meteors as warnings from God. Medieval chronicles recorded apparitions that heralded the death of holy men and kings and augured wars of religion and civil strife. According to some early church Fathers as well as later theologians, these heavenly signs also demarcated critical periods in the history of the world and of Christianity. Thus, Origen (c. 185–251) and John of Damascus (c. 675–748) thought that the Star of Bethlehem had been a comet, whereas Jerome (c. 347–420), Thomas Aquinas (c. 1225–74), Martin Luther (1483–1546), and Thomas Burnet (c. 1635–1715) expected comets and fiery meteors to precede the Day of Judgment and the consummation of all things. Illustrations of the adoration of the Magi and the Book of Revelation (such as those to be found in the fresco by Giotto di Bondone in the Scrovegni Chapel in Padua [1304] and in the *Apocalypse* woodcuts of Albrecht Dürer [1498, 1511]) popularized these views.

During the Roman era, divination from fiery meteors had been used both to legitimate political authority and to fortify conspirators. The practice continued up to the early-modern period, when prognosticators saw fiery meteors as signs of the times (that is, as nature's reflection of power struggles between religious factions). In the sixteenth century, Martin Luther, Philip Melanchthon (1497–1560), Thomas Cranmer (1489–1556), and John Knox (c. 1514–72) saw celestial prodigies as omens of great religious and political changes as they called for church reforms. In Europe and Colonial America during the early-modern period, the popular press spread the self-serving meteoric predictions of religious and political schemers of all sorts. Meteoric propaganda was often couched in apocalyptic language because it was widely believed that current affairs fulfilled ancient prophecies. In England, for example, between the restoration of the monarchy in 1660 and the Glorious Revolution in 1688, some Nonconformists thought that comets augured the apocalypse or the millennium—either the end of the world or its renovation. Broadside ballads predicted the defeat of the Antichrist and the Second Coming. As late as the mid-nineteenth century, the Millerites in New England (a religious sect that expected the soon return of Christ) interpreted the Leonid meteor shower of 1833 and the great comet of 1843 as signs of the end of the world.

The Decline of Theological Intepretations

Medieval and Renaissance natural philosophers agreed that comets and meteors often prefigured calamity. Some, such as John of Legnano (d. 1383) and Johannes Kepler (1571–1630), looked for causal connections. Many more wrote guides to interpret the meaning of these celestial hieroglyphs. Their tracts, in both Latin and the vernacular languages, were a resource for preachers, pamphleteers, and compilers of almanacs.

In the Renaissance, new observations of the parallax, tails, and motion of comets convinced astronomers that comets were not sublunar meteorological phenomena but celestial bodies that traveled through interplanetary space. The separation of comets from meteors was complete by the end of the seventeenth century, when Isaac Newton (1642–1727) and Edmond Halley (1656–1742) established that comets traveled in elliptical orbits around the sun. In the mid-eighteenth century, scientists also began to consider extraterrestrial origins for meteors like the aurora and shooting stars.

The degree to which these scientific developments encouraged the decline of divination from comets and meteors has been much debated. The foundations of divination were also undermined, in part, by the epistemological criticism of Pierre Gassendi (1592–1655) and Pierre Bayle (1647–1706), among others, and by sociopolitical factors in Europe that encouraged elite members of society to withdraw their support of popular culture. Whatever the causes, in the late seventeenth century the learned elite of England and France (followed later by those in central and eastern Europe) came to reject as superstitious the notion that comets and meteors were miraculous signs sent by God to rebuke infidels. They no longer saw them as causes of murder, rebellion, drought, flood, or plague. Nevertheless, neither the celestial locus nor the periodic orbits of comets required believers to give up their faith in the eschatological or prophetic functions of comets. Indeed, the traditional interpretation of comets was given new life in the cosmic arena by Newton and his followers.

Although comets were represented as natural bodies following routine courses throughout the heavens, they remained apparitions of God's providence. Newton suggested that comets transported life-sustaining materials to the earth and fuel to the sun. Newton, Halley, and William Whiston (1667–1752) argued that comets played key roles in the earth's creation, Noachian Deluge, and ultimate destruction. The final conflagration would be ignited by a comet, many biblical scholars believed, and natural philosophers concurred that a blazing star could serve this function by immersing the earth in its fiery tail, by dropping into the sun and causing a solar flare, or by pushing the earth out of its orbit and transforming it into a comet. Forced to travel in a much more elongated circuit around the sun, the old earth would be scorched and frozen in turns and would become the site of hell. Therefore, widespread endorsement of the new periodic theory of comets did not mitigate the perception that comets were agents of upheaval or renewal and tools that God might use to punish the wicked or to save the elect.

In the eighteenth and early nineteenth centuries, such prominent scientists as Georges Louis Leclerc, Comte de Buffon (1707–88), William Herschel (1738–1822), and Pierre Simon Laplace (1749–1827) continued to connect comets to the creation and dissolution of planets, but they began to unlink astrotheology from celestial mechanics. Unlike their predecessors, they neither hoped nor expected to find the moral order reflected in the natural world. When catastrophism went out of style in the mid-nineteenth century, comets appeared to pose little risk or benefit to the earth. In recent years, however, the tide has turned, and the stage may be set for a new theological interpretation of comets and meteors. Most scientists now believe that comets (and their meteoric debris) may have been both the agents of death (most notably of the dinosaurs) and the conveyors of life's building blocks.

See also Earthquakes; Electricity; Macrocosm/Micro-cosm; Meteorology; Plurality of Worlds and Extraterrestrial Life

BIBLIOGRAPHY

Briggs, J. Morton, Jr. "Aurora and Enlightenment: Eighteenth-Century Explanations of the Aurora Borealis." *Isis* 58 (1967): 491–503.

Burke, John G. *Cosmic Debris: Meteorites in History.* Berkeley: University of California Press, 1986.

Curry, Patrick. *Prophecy and Power: Astrology in Early Modern England.* Princeton, N.J.: Princeton University Press, 1989.

Hellman, C. Doris. *The Comet of 1577: Its Place in the History of Astronomy.* New York: Columbia University Press, 1944.

Jervis, Jane L. *Cometary Theory in Fifteenth-Century Europe.* Studia Copernicana. No. 26. Dordrecht: Reidel, 1985.

Olson, Roberta J. M. *Fire and Ice: A History of Comets in Art.* New York: Walker and Company for the National Air and Space Museum, Smithsonian Institution, 1985.

Schaffer, Simon. "Authorized Prophets: Comets and Astronomers After 1759." *Studies in Eighteenth-Century Culture* 17 (1987): 45–74.

———. "Newton's Comets and the Transformation of Astrology." In *Astrology, Science, and Society,* edited by Patrick Curry. Woodbridge, U.K.: Boydell, 1987, 219–43.

Schechner Genuth, Sara. "Comets, Teleology, and the Relationship of Chemistry to Cosmology in Newton's Thought." *Annali dell'Istituto e Museo di Storia della Scienza di Firenze* 10 (2) (1985): 31–65.

———. "Devils' Hells and Astronomers' Heavens: Religion, Method, and Popular Culture in Speculations About Life on Comets." In *The Invention of Physical Science: Intersections of Mathematics, Theology, and Natural Philosophy Since the Seventeenth Century: Essays in Honor of Erwin N. Hiebert,* ed. by Mary Jo Nye, Joan L. Richards, and Roger H. Stuewer. Dordrecht: Kluwer, 1992, 3–26.

———. "From Heaven's Alarm to Public Appeal: Comets and the Rise of Astronomy at Harvard." In *Science at Harvard University: Historical Perspectives,* ed. by Clark A. Elliott and Margaret W. Rossiter. Bethlehem, Pa.: Lehigh University Press, 1992, 28–54.

———. *Comets, Popular Culture, and the Birth of Modern Cosmology.* Princeton, N.J.: Princeton University Press, 1997.

Stewart, Philip. "Science and Superstition: Comets and the French Public in the Eighteenth Century." *American Journal of Physics* 54 (1) (January 1986): 16–24.

Thrower, Norman J. W., ed. *Standing on the Shoulders of Giants: A Longer View of Newton and Halley.* Berkeley: University of California Press, 1990.

Yeomans, Donald K. *Comets: A Chronological History of Observation, Science, Myth, and Folklore.* New York: Wiley, 1991.

Zambelli, Paola, ed. *"Astrologi hallucinati": Stars and the End of the World in Luther's Time.* Berlin: de Gruyter, 1986.

59. Pre-Copernican Astronomy

James Lattis

Nicholas Copernicus (1473–1543) published his heliocentric theory of planetary motion in 1543. Eventually accepted in modified form in the course of the seventeenth century, Copernicanism has come to represent the end of a series of astronomical traditions that began in antiquity. The term "pre-Copernican" refers to a chronological epoch, but also to those areas of astronomy affected by the Copernican revolution. Copernicanism is a theory, which is to say a scheme for understanding or making sense of phenomena, and the areas most affected by astronomical theory are cosmology and mathematical astronomy. In addition to those areas, practical uses of the heavens, such as calendars, timekeeping, and instrumentation, demand our attention in the pre-Copernican epoch—that period before the concept of the earth as a planet was taken seriously.

Practical Astronomy

Astronomy is generally not essential to survival in an agrarian society, because the rudimentary concept of the seasons needed for successful planting and harvesting falls far short of the level of knowledge we might reasonably call astronomical. Far from being essential, astronomy probably flourishes only when agricultural prosperity permits, and this seems to have happened well before recorded history began. Some of our earliest examples of astronomical sophistication are the Neolithic sites of Europe and Britain (such as Carnac and Stonehenge), which are massive stone monuments constructed, in part, according to astronomically determined alignments that reveal considerable knowledge of solar and lunar motions. Recent research has detailed the efforts and achievements of pre-Columbian people in the Americas, who also built monumental astronomical structures. Although we have

no knowledge of why prehistoric humans created such structures, and certainly not whether the astronomical insight built into them was an end in itself, they do demonstrate that human societies were willing to devote huge efforts to astronomical matters far beyond those needed for survival.

Calendars, Navigation, Timekeeping

The ancient Egyptians marked the beginning of the Nile's flood season, and, hence, of their agricultural cycle, by the dawn (heliacal) rising of the star Sirius. However, in general, sophisticated calendars arose not out of agricultural necessity but from the desire to fix religious ceremonies with respect to celestial events, such as the solstices or phases of the moon. Ancient Mesopotamian societies employed calendars based on lunar phases, which are essentially useless for agricultural purposes, instead of the solar cycle. The "year" in a lunar calendar, which was used in the early Greek and Roman worlds, too, consists of twelve lunations amounting to only 354 days, or about eleven days short of the solar year of approximately 365 days. The inconvenient consequence of that discrepancy is that the months of the lunar year will shift rather rapidly and continuously with respect to the solar year. The problems of reconciling lunar phases and eclipses with the solar year was the focus of much ancient astronomical effort. One option was to ignore the shift and allow the lunar calendar to fall as it will during the solar year, just as the calendar used in Islam does today (though Islamic societies have often used solar calendars alongside their religious lunar calendar). Ancient calendar experts, however, contrived various solutions to reconcile the religious lunar calendar to the civil solar calendar; the result was a lunisolar calendar, such as the Jewish religious calendar. Meton of Athens (fl. c. 433 B.C.) devised a scheme, now known as the Metonic cycle, that exploited the fact that nineteen solar years very nearly equals 235 lunar months. In this scheme, the lunar calendar will resynchronize with the solar calendar every nineteen years, which means that a revolving set of nineteen different calendars will suffice to indicate where each lunar holiday falls during a given solar year. This cycle was adopted by the Council of Nicaea in A.D. 325 for fixing the (solar) dates of "moveable" feasts, most notably Easter. Known as the Nicene Paschal Cycle, it was used in the Latin Christian world until the Gregorian calendar reform of 1582.

Even a purely solar calendar poses many challenges. The Julian calendar, devised by the astronomer Sosigenes of Alexandria (first century B.C.) and instituted by Julius Caesar (100–44 B.C.) as pontifex maximus in 46 B.C., assumed a year of 365.25 days. The calendar followed a cycle of three years of exactly 365 days, and one year (the "leap," or bisextile, year) of 366 days. However, because the Julian year is slightly but significantly longer than the tropical year (the interval between recurrences of the seasons as measured by the apparent motion of the sun), the Julian calendar shifted slowly with respect to the seasons, slipping a full ten days by the mid-sixteenth century. Prominent astronomers of the fifteenth and sixteenth centuries, among them Georg Peurbach (1423–61), Regiomontanus (1436–76), and Copernicus, were consulted by the papacy on the problem. But calendar reform had important social and religious dimensions beyond the technical problem. If, for example, the official calendar is wrong, then what is the status of rites performed on the "wrong" days? The muddle of astronomical, social, religious, legal, and economic aspects of the calendar problem, not to mention the perfectly valid question of whether the "problem" really was a problem, prolonged debate and indecision for many years.

In the 1570s, Pope Gregory XIII (b. 1502, p. 1572–85) convened a commission to evaluate, select, and implement one of several proposed reforms. The presence of theologians and canon lawyers on the commission, in addition to astronomers and mathematicians, indicates Gregory's appreciation of the social and religious aspects of the project. After nearly ten years of deliberation and planning by the commission, the pope promulgated his calendar in 1582, dropping ten days to correct the seasonal discrepancy and introducing a new scheme of leap years so that the Gregorian calendar year

approximates the tropical year much more closely than did the Julian.

Religion has presented a number of challenges to practical astronomy. The daily prayer ritual of the Muslim, for example, requires that the worshiper face Mecca. To this problem emerged solutions, called *qibla*, which are methods analogous to celestial navigation for determining the sacred direction. From a fixed location, such as a given mosque, this problem need only be solved once, but a traveler must solve the problem at an arbitrary location, and that need gave rise to specialized and ingenious instruments for solving the *qibla* problem.

Marking the passage of hours, especially for establishing the time of prayer, was a constant need not only in Islam but in many Christian monastic orders as well. Sundials, which appeared in Egypt as early as 1300 B.C., served many timekeeping needs. Ancient Greek mathematicians greatly advanced gnomonics (the science of sundials) as well as the methods for making astrolabes, devices that could be used for measuring time by the positions of the stars. But the desire to schedule prayers, regardless of the availability of clear skies, led directly to the most important advances in the development of mechanical clocks, which probably occurred in English monasteries and churches in the thirteenth century.

Astral Religion and Astrology

Astronomy not only has been an aid to religion but, on occasion, has constituted the very fabric of religion. Zoroastrianism, Mithraism, and other astral religions located deities themselves, as well as the proper home of the human soul and special spiritual powers, in the heavens. Ancient Near Eastern religions commonly (though not always) associated or identified the visible planets with deities, and ancient Egyptians identified passage to the afterlife and the attainment of immortality with passage through celestial regions, such as the circumpolar zone. Whether celestial bodies were gods or merely moved according to the will of gods, it must have seemed prudent to observe and record the motions of celestial bodies for their value as omens. Detailed cuneiform omen texts from about the middle of the second millennium B.C. confirm that such practices had developed, though they may have originated as early as the Akkadian dynasty of the late third millennium B.C. By the early first millennium B.C., Babylonian astronomer-priests had devised numerical methods for predicting the motions of planets, using arithmetic sequences of numbers that expressed, as a function of time, the position and velocity of a celestial body. By this route, astral religion helped give rise to mathematical planetary astronomy in the ancient Near East. In addition, the assiduous records of Mesopotamian astronomers, spanning many centuries, provided observations that Greek astronomers would later use with great profit.

Astrology, although a Greek invention in the form in which we know it, seems to have emerged from Near Eastern astral religions. The preparation of horoscopes (the earliest of which date from the fifth century B.C.) requires knowledge of the positions of the celestial bodies so that their influences may be assessed, and this is a strong motive for the development of methods of calculating the planetary positions for some given time in the past or future. Greek astronomers approached this task employing methods that diverged widely from those of their Babylonian predecessors. While the Babylonian techniques were strictly numerical, the Greeks employed geometrical reasoning to visualize the physical path of the celestial body in space.

Causal Astronomy

Mesopotamian mathematical astronomy seems not to have arisen from consideration of the causes of celestial motions. But discovering causes on which mathematical theories could be built was a major goal of Greek astronomers. There could have been many motivations with religious overtones for that endeavor: calendrical needs, understanding the divinity of the heavens, astrological studies, satisfying intellectual curiosity, testing or justification of cosmological claims, and the like. Eudoxus of Cnidos (390–340 B.C.) created the earliest geometrical model of planetary motions on principles that would endure in Western astronomy until the early seventeenth century, namely that celestial motions are perfectly circular (or at least composed of circular motions), centered on the earth, and uniform in speed.

The planetary models of Eudoxus had serious shortcomings that stimulated development of alternative schemes. Ptolemy (second century A.D.), the great Alexandrian scholar, attributed to his predecessor Apollonius of Perga (c. 262–190 B.C.) the invention of the theoretical mechanisms of the eccentric circle and the epicycle. In these geometrical models, a small, uniformly rotating circle, the epicycle, carries the planet. The larger

eccentric circle (or "deferent"), also in uniform rotation, bears the center of the epicycle. The eccentric's center lies not at the center of the universe (which, for most of Western history, was considered to be the earth) but a point in space some distance from the earth. Though the motions of the eccentric and the epicycle are, by definition, uniform and circular, the resulting motion of the planet (or the sun or moon) perceived by the terrestrial observer is distinctly nonuniform. By adjusting the relative sizes of the circles and their speeds (and guided by Babylonian observations), Hipparchus of Rhodes (second century B.C.) succeeded in constructing quite effective models for the motions of the sun and, to a lesser extent, the moon.

Some three hundred years after Hipparchus, Ptolemy built on his predecessor's work by adding to epicycle and eccentric a third theoretical device called the equant (a point in space about which the epicycle center appears to move uniformly along the deferent). Ptolemy used the three basic mechanisms to construct theoretical models for the sun, the moon, and the planets. He then used historical observations, supplemented by his own, to establish a complete system of planetary astronomy, including the mathematical methods and tables on which the work is founded. We know this work by its Arabic title as the *Almagest*. Ptolemy's *Almagest* allowed an astronomer (or astrologer) to calculate, with tolerable accuracy, the positions of the celestial bodies at any given time. Such a feat of astronomical synthesis would not be equaled until Copernicus published his *De revolutionibus orbium coelestium* (*On the Revolutions of the Heavenly Bodies*) in 1543. And, in fact, the Ptolemaic synthesis, though translated, adapted, and improved, remained the foundation of Western astronomy until well after Copernicus's death.

The *Almagest* survived the disintegration of the classical world in the original Greek and was also translated into Arabic. It became available to medieval Europe only in the mid-twelfth century as a translation from the Arabic version into Latin. Astronomers of the Arabic world had, from roughly the tenth to the twelfth centuries, thoroughly mastered Ptolemaic astronomy and supplemented it with new observations, new instruments, new mathematical techniques, and updates such as the twelfth-century Toledan Tables. In the West, assimilation of Ptolemaic astronomy also happened gradually. King Alfonso X of Castile (1221–84) had the Alfonsine Tables drawn up in the late thirteenth century. During the thirteenth and fourteenth centuries, European scholars translated important auxiliary texts from Arabic, wrote original ones in Latin, and accumulated skills with instruments. By the fifteenth century, European astronomers, like Peurbach and Regiomontanus, had fully mastered Ptolemaic astronomy, rendering it a mature tool for scientific, ecclesiastical, and astrological applications and simultaneously laying the groundwork for Copernicus's revolution.

Cosmology and Religion

As we have seen, human beings have been observing celestial phenomena, inferring rules about them, and using those rules to predict future phenomena for a very long time. But people are also interested in what the heavens are really like: What is the nature of celestial bodies, how do they really move, what moves them, how do they affect one another, where are they, and where are we? These are questions of cosmology, and cosmological concerns go deep into history. Plato (c. 427–347 B.C.), for example, made cosmological claims when he asserted that all celestial bodies are spherical and that their motions are uniform and circular. The uniform circularity of celestial motion and the perfect centering of those motions on the earth were the mathematical principles of Eudoxus's astronomical models, but they were also accepted cosmological truths. Astronomy and cosmology have a complex relationship, sometimes informing each other, sometimes confirming, and sometimes contradicting each other. Religion and cosmology also have complex relationships. For some, cosmological insight is a way of understanding the nature and intentions of the Creator. For others, cosmology illuminates the place of humanity with respect to divine things. In yet other cases, cosmology interacts with the interpretation of sacred writings.

Cosmological thought in the ancient world spanned a broad range, and certain cosmological concepts were closely associated with particular religious cults. The Pythagoreans taught that the earth was neither stationary nor at the center of the universe; Stoics, that the universe was pervaded by a "spiritual matter" that linked the macrocosm of the universe with the microcosm of man; Epicureans, that there is an infinity of worlds like our own. All of these cosmological traditions were known, to a greater or lesser extent, in early-medieval Europe. But the cosmology of Plato's student Aristotle (384–322 B.C.)

was not at first identified with a particular religious tradition. Aristotelianism became widespread in the classical Roman world as well as in the medieval Arabic world. It entered European thought when the fundamental Aristotelian texts were translated from Arabic into Latin in the twelfth century.

Cosmology has found itself entangled with theology to the extent that the heavens were frequently associated with divinity. Plato and Aristotle, like Ptolemy half a millennium later, considered the celestial bodies to partake, in some sense, of the divine. Islamic and Christian astronomers, especially with the encouragement of Aristotle, came to think the same way. So it was natural for them to ask theological questions of cosmology. Where in the universe is God? Where are the angels (both virtuous and fallen), and where are the immortal souls of saints and sinners? Is the universe finite, as Aristotle taught, or as infinite as God is omnipotent? A serious dispute flared in the thirteenth century, when Aristotelianism was relatively new to Latin Europe, over, among other things, a number of cosmological claims about the novel Aristotelian cosmos. In 1277, the bishop of Paris condemned a number of propositions, such as that the universe is eternal and that celestial bodies are moved by their own souls. But disputes over the number or nature of celestial bodies did not contradict explicit doctrines found in any sacred texts, and, in time, theologians such as Thomas Aquinas (c. 1225–74) and others succeeded in linking Aristotelian cosmology closely to Christian doctrine. Hence, the Aristotelian cosmos ultimately survived controversies over Aristotle's metaphysical claims, and it became the dominant cosmological concept in the Western intellectual world from the fourteenth to the seventeenth centuries.

An inherent tension between Aristotelian cosmology and Ptolemaic astronomy appears clearly in the commentaries on Aristotle's works written by the Arabic philosopher Ibn Rushd (1126–98), who became known (and very influential) in Europe as Averroës. Aristotle taught that all celestial matter moves in circles around the earth, but Averroës asserted that Ptolemy's mathematical devices violated that and other Aristotelian principles and could not, therefore, be real. Defenders of Ptolemaic astronomy—Peurbach, Erasmus Reinhold (1511–52), and Christopher Clavius (1537–1612) are prominent examples—responded with a scheme of "materialized" eccentrics and epicycles (that is, theoretical celestial structures that produce motions equivalent to the Ptolemaic geometrical devices of eccentric and epicycle). The concept of the "materialized" mechanisms originated with Ptolemy himself, though in a work kept separate from the *Almagest,* and was known to both Arabic astronomers and Western writers at least as early as the thirteenth century. Ptolemy's defenders argued that the materialized constructions explained the observed astronomical phenomena and also satisfied all of the important principles of Aristotle's physics and, therefore, must be the correct description of the celestial realm.

These kinds of philosophical disputes seem not to have bothered most astronomers and astrologers, who followed Ptolemy as a practical matter, nor were they theologically important. But the contradictions between Ptolemaic astronomy and Aristotelian cosmology drove some astronomers to attempt reform, and that would have religious implications. Al-Bitruji (Alpetragius [fl. 1190]) created a novel variation on the ancient Eudoxean spheres, as did the physician Girolamo Fracastoro (1483–1553) and Giovanni Battista Amico (c. 1511–36). The latter two figures found their inspiration for astronomical reform at the University of Padua, and the same might be said of their contemporary, Copernicus, who surpassed them by abandoning not only Ptolemy but Aristotle, too. Another alternative cosmology, which may have stemmed from Stoic roots, rejected altogether the cosmological construct of celestial spheres—a concept that Copernicus retained even as he replaced so much else. Latin astronomical writers as early as the thirteenth century considered the possibility that the heavens were a fluid realm in which the celestial bodies moved freely, rather than being fixed in celestial spheres. By the late sixteenth century, some philosophers, Francesco Patrizi (1529–97) and Robert Bellarmine (1542–1621) among them, vigorously rejected the Aristotelian concept of celestial spheres in favor of fluid heavens. Bellarmine, the powerful Jesuit theologian and cardinal, based his objections to Ptolemaic cosmology squarely on the study of cosmological statements he found in Scripture.

Astronomy and cosmology must, from time to time, confront the statements of sacred writings when those statements are understood to be literal descriptions of the natural world. In general, the astronomical statements in the sacred texts of Christianity and Islam are so vague or obvious as to cause few problems. However, strict interpreters of Scripture did occasionally find conflicts with cosmological doctrines, as when Bellarmine questioned the number of celestial "heavens" counted by the Ptolemaic astronomers because that number disagreed with the three he could find mentioned in Scripture. The biggest problems emerged only when both astronomers and theologians began to take seriously Copernicus's cosmology, which not only contradicted clear statements in Scripture about the relative motions and positions of the sun and the earth, but simultaneously challenged human intuitions and preconceptions regarding the status of the earth.

See also Astrology; Calendar; Copernican Revolution; Galileo Galilei; Geocentrism; Plurality of Worlds and Extraterrestrial Life

BIBLIOGRAPHY

Aveni, Anthony F. *The Skywatchers of Ancient Mexico.* Austin: University of Texas Press, 1980.

Baldini, Ugo, and George V. Coyne.*The Louvain Lectures (Lectiones Lovanienses) of Bellarmine and the Autograph Copy of his 1616 Declaration to Galileo.* Vatican City: Vatican Observatory, 1984.

Barker, Peter. "Stoic Contributions to Early Modern Science." In *Atoms, Pneuma, and Tranquility: Epicurean and Stoic Themes in European Thought,* ed. by Margaret J. Osler. Cambridge: Cambridge University Press, 1991.

Bauer, Brian S., and David S. P. Dearborn. *Astronomy and Empire in the Ancient Andes.* Austin: University of Texas Press, 1995.

Coyne, G. V., M. A. Hoskin, and O. Pedersen, eds. *Gregorian Reform of the Calendar.* Vatican City: Vatican Observatory, 1983.

Dicks, D. R. *Early Greek Astronomy to Aristotle.* Ithaca, N.Y.: Cornell University Press, 1970.

Eastwood, Bruce. *Astronomy and Optics from Pliny to Descartes.* London: Variorum, 1989.

Grant, Edward. *Planets, Stars, and Orbs.* Cambridge: Cambridge University Press, 1994.

King, David A. *Astronomy in the Service of Islam.* London: Variorum, 1993.

Krupp, E. C., ed. *In Search of Ancient Astronomies.* New York: McGraw-Hill, 1978.

Lattis, James M. *Between Copernicus and Galileo: Christoph Clavius and the Collapse of Ptolemaic Cosmology.* Chicago: University of Chicago Press, 1994.

Lindberg, David C. *The Beginnings of Western Science: The European Scientific Tradition in Philosophical, Religious, and Institutional Context, 600 B.C. to A.D. 1450.* Chicago: University of Chicago Press, 1992.

North, John. *Norton History of Astronomy and Cosmology.* New York: Norton, 1995.

Taub, Liba. *Ptolemy's Universe.* Chicago: Open Court, 1993.

60. THE COPERNICAN REVOLUTION

Owen Gingerich

In 1543, the year of his death, Nicholas Copernicus (1473–1543) saw his life work, *De revolutionibus orbium coelestium (On the Revolutions of the Heavenly Bodies),* finally printed. A four-hundred-page technical treatise, it laid out a heliocentric framework for the planetary system, thereby providing the essential basis for the Newtonian synthesis that was to follow a century and a half later. During this same interval, the gradual overthrow of the long-accepted geocentric worldview created an upheaval in the sacred geography of the cosmos. These changes, both in technical astronomy and mechanics and in humankind's vision of its physical place in the universe, constitute the Copernican revolution.

Copernicus was born in Torun, Poland, in 1473. His father died when he was ten years old, and his maternal uncle, Lucas Watzenrode, took over responsibility for the young man's education. Watzenrode was in a successful career of ecclesiastical politics, becoming in 1489 bishop of the northernmost Roman Catholic diocese in Poland, and here he provided a position for Copernicus as canon in the Frombork (Frauenburg) Cathedral. Copernicus was never ordained as a priest, but he took minor orders and, after appropriate graduate study in Italy, served as personal physician to his uncle and as the principal legal officer of the cathedral chapter.

Precisely when and where Copernicus caught the vision of a heliocentric system we do not know. He was interested in astronomy even while an undergraduate at Cracow, and he continued to develop his understanding as he studied canon law in Bologna from 1496 to 1500. By 1514, he had written out a short precis of the heliocentric astronomy, the so-called *Commentariolus,* which was, however, not printed until its rediscovery in the 1880s. The Latin edition of Ptolemy's *Almagest* in 1515 showed Copernicus the required scope of any treatise

that would challenge Ptolemy's authority, and he began work in earnest on his *De revolutionibus.* He quickly realized that he would need a baseline of nearly twenty years' observations to establish the modern parameters for the planets, so he bided his time with a variety of duties for the cathedral as he slowly collected the fresh data. Only toward the end of his life did he finally pull together the various parts of his extensive and highly mathematical account.

The opening chapters of *De revolutionibus* lay the philosophical foundations for a moving earth and a fixed central sun, leading to the glorious chapter I,10, a powerful rhetorical defense of the heliocentric cosmology, pointing to the sun "as if on a royal throne governing the planets that wheel around it. For in no other way can we find such a wonderful commensurability and sure harmonious connection between the motions of the spheres and their sizes." The chapters that follow include a section on basic trigonometry, a catalog of fixed stars, the theory of the sun (that is, of the earth's annual orbital motion, as well as a heliocentric explanation of the precession of the equinoxes), the theory of the moon, the theory of planetary longitudes, and, finally, the theory of planetary latitudes.

Copernicus never fully explained his reasons for considering a heliocentric arrangement, and a number of hypotheses have been subsequently proposed, many unconvincing if not outright erroneous. For example, a standard account found in numerous secondary works describes the increasing disparity between actual observations and the planetary predictions based on Ptolemy's theory and the continued addition of more and more epicycles to account for these discrepancies. Eventually, this mythological account runs, the system was ready to collapse under its own weight.

In fact, there is no historical evidence for the addition of epicycles upon epicycles to increase the accuracy of the Ptolemaic system. Furthermore, the ingenious and intricately dovetailed tables provided by Ptolemy and used by all of the medieval astronomers could not be readily modified to accommodate additional epicycles. Finally, because Copernicus used the ancient Ptolemaic observations as his fundamental base, his own predictive system was not substantially more accurate than Ptolemy's, and, if accuracy of prediction were the criterion, then Copernicus's work must be deemed a massive failure. Besides, the accuracy of prediction could have been considerably improved without moving to the heliocentric arrangement. Because of the basic geometric equivalence between the two systems, not only would the predictions not be improved merely by moving to a heliocentric arrangement, but, equally important, no simple observational test could differentiate the two arrangements prior to Galileo's (1564–1642) telescopic observation of the phases of Venus in 1609.

While observational evidence could not have entered directly into Copernicus's enthusiasm for the heliocentric layout, undoubtedly aesthetic considerations played a powerful role. Copernicus describes the pleasure of a theory "pleasing to the mind." When the planets were linked together in the sun-centered arrangement, Mercury, the fastest planet, automatically fell into the innermost position, and Saturn, the slowest, fell farthest from the sun, with a gradation in between. As cited above, Copernicus commended this arrangement "that can be found in no other way." He also noticed that, in his system, the so-called retrograde motion of the superior planets was required to occur when the planet was opposite the sun in the sky, thereby giving a natural explanation to what was just an arbitrary observation in the Ptolemaic scheme.

It is quite possible that Copernicus would never have published his hypotheses except for the persuasive intervention of a young Lutheran astronomer from Wittenberg, Georg Joachim Rheticus (1514–74). Rheticus's initial account of Copernicus's ideas, Narratio prima (First Narrative [1540]), did not create the opposition Copernicus feared, so the Polish astronomer gave him permission to take a manuscript of De revolutionibus to Nuremberg for publication. The printer arranged for a local Lutheran clergyman, Andreas Osiander (1498–1552), not only to take charge of the proofreading, but also finally to add at the very beginning an anonymous warning to readers concerning the hypotheses in the work. In highly abridged form, here is the gist of Osiander's Ad lectorem (To the reader): "It is the duty of an astronomer to make careful observations, and then to make hypotheses so that the positions of the planets can be predicted. This the author has done very well. But these hypotheses need not be true nor even probable. Perhaps a philosopher will seek after truth, but an astronomer will take whatever is simplest, but neither will learn anything certain unless it has been divinely revealed to him."

When Copernicus, on his deathbed, finally received the front matter of his book (the last part to be printed), he was greatly agitated, but whether this was in disagreement with what Osiander had written, or perhaps merely the excitement of having his work completed, is unknown. Did Copernicus believe in the physical truth of his heliocentric arrangement? Certainly, some parts of the work well reflect Osiander's instrumentalist stance (for example, when Copernicus gave three different arrangements of the small circles for the solar theory, remarking with consummate illogic that "it must be one of these since they all yield the same result"). On the other hand, at the end of the cosmological chapter I,10, Copernicus declared: "So vast, without any doubt, is the handiwork of the Almighty Creator." This pious passage was later censored by the Inquisition, apparently because it made it look as if this was the way God had actually created the cosmos, but its enthusiasm suggests that Copernicus really believed that the Creator had placed the planets heliocentrically.

The Initial Reception of the Copernican Hypothesis

Whether or not Copernicus considered his work simply a mathematical hypothesis, not to be taken as a literal description of the physical world, the astronomers and theologians at the University of Wittenberg (where the book received its first detailed study) were convinced that astronomers used fictional circles in their modeling of the cosmos and that these were not to be confused with the actual physical reality sought by the professors of philosophy. Erasmus Reinhold (1511–52), Wittenberg's beloved and authoritative professor of astronomy, devoured the technical details of De revolutionibus, reveling in Copernicus's strict adherence to uniform circular motion (which corrected Ptolemy's heuristic digressions with respect to these aesthetic standards), but he essentially skipped the heliocentric cosmology. His attitude aptly illustrates what historian Robert Westman has called "the Wittenberg interpretation" of Copernicus.

Martin Luther (1483–1546), who heard of Copernicus's cosmology through his Wittenberg astronomers before its publication, made an offhand remark that was recorded in his "table talk," to the effect that "whoever wants to be a clever has to do his own thing. This is what that fool does who wants to turn astronomy upside down." His remark has gained publicity out of proportion to its significance; more important is the fact that Wittenberg became the intellectual center for teaching and publishing about Copernicus. Luther's right-hand man, Philip Melanchthon (1497–1560), referred indirectly to Copernicus in the first edition of his *Initia doctrinae physicae* (*Elements of the Knowledge of Natural Science* [1549]), saying: "The joke is not new. . . . The young should know it is not decent to defend such absurd positions publicly," but he promptly watered down his opinion in subsequent editions.

In the initial stages of the reception, any response on the Roman Catholic side was muted. Only later, in the wake of the Galileo affair in the early seventeenth century, was it discovered that a Florentine Dominican, Giovanni Maria Tolosani, had quickly written against Copernicus, but his patron died before the manuscript was printed, and his blast languished on an archival shelf. Because of the vehemence of the later Catholic response, some nineteenth-century commentators, such as Andrew Dickson White (1832–1918), hoped to give the Protestants equal time, and various anti-Copernican sentiments were attributed to John Calvin (1509–64), but careful research has been unable to substantiate any of them.

A principal point of tension in the religious community centered on various scriptural proof texts that seemed to demand a fixed earth or a moving sun. Psalm 104, "The Lord God laid the foundations of the earth that it should not be moved forever," was an often-cited verse, as was Joshua's command for the sun, and not the earth, to stand still to prolong the battle at Gibeon (Josh. 10:12–14). Rheticus supposedly wrote a "Second Narrative" defending the Copernican doctrine, but it remained lost until it was serendipitously recovered by the Dutch historian Reijer Hooykaas in 1973. Rheticus's account had been printed anonymously in the seventeenth century, in a little book now known in only two copies. Rheticus addressed the Scriptures concerning the stability of the earth by saying: "For, although on earth there occur cor-

ruptions, generations, and all kinds of alterations, yet the earth itself remains in its wholeness as it was created." He went on to argue that Scripture should be understood to mean that each object (for example, the earth or the moon) had been founded on its own stability. As for the apparent motion of the sun, he stated: "Common speech, however, mostly follows the judgment of the senses. . . . We must distinguish in our minds between appearance and reality."

The Later Protestant Reception of Copernicanism

De revolutionibus was immediately recognized as an important and magisterial book and was widely quoted in various technical contexts even in its first two decades, though rarely with respect to its cosmology. An interesting exception is Robert Recorde's (c. 1510–58) *Castle of Knowledge* (1556), in which in the dialogue the Scholar protests, "Nay syr in good faith, I desire not to heare such vaine phantasies," to which the Master rejoins, "You are to yonge to be a good judge in so great a matter." An interesting comment was given by the Louvain astronomer Reiner Gemma Frisius, who pointed out in 1555 that Copernicus had provided a reasoned explanation for the retrograde motion at opposition and that it was no longer merely a "fact in itself" as it had been for Ptolemy.

One of the first committed sixteenth-century Copernicans was the English astronomer Thomas Digges (d. 1595), who published an English translation of the cosmological chapter of *De revolutionibus* in 1576, "to the ende such noble English minds might not be altogether defrauded of so noble a part of Philosophy." He proposed that the stars extended infinitely upward and that, therefore, the sun was immovable in this frame. He also provided the first step in revising the sacred cosmology of heaven by locating "the habitacle for the elect, devoid of greefe" among the stars, "garnished with perpetual glorious shining lights innumerable."

Tycho Brahe (1546–1601), the Danish observer, remarked that "Copernicus nowhere offends the principles of mathematics, but he throws the earth, a lazy, sluggish body unfit for motion, into a speed as fast as the ethereal torches." Tycho's name is not closely associated with religion, but he had a pew in the Lutheran church on his fiefdom of Hven, and, in evaluating the Copernican system, he repeatedly said that it offended physics and Holy Scripture, always in that order. Eventually, he proposed his own geoheliocentric version of the Copernican layout, in which the sun revolved around a fixed earth, but the moving sun carried the planets in orbit around itself. The arrangement saved some of the compelling Copernican linkages but destroyed part of the beauty of the system to preserve a fixed, central earth consistent with physics and the Bible.

His contemporary, Michael Maestlin (1550–1631), a Lutheran clergyman before taking up his astronomy professorship and a virulent critic of the new "popish" Gregorian calendar reform, is probably best known for teaching Johannes Kepler (1571–1630) about Copernicus at the University of Tübingen. Maestlin concluded from his own study of the comet of 1577 that the comet's motion was best understood as being seen from a moving earth. Maestlin clearly hoped to find other circumstantial evidence for the Copernican arrangement by looking for parallel changes in the eccentricities of the planetary orbits that could be attributed simply to the change in eccentricity of the earth's orbit, but the ancient observations proved too insensitive for the test. His stance toward the reality of the Copernican system was ambiguous, and he remains an enigmatic but important transitional figure, especially because of his encouragement to Kepler.

Kepler was in the final year of the Lutheran theological program at Tübingen when he was sent as a high-school teacher to Graz in Austria. He had already become a devoted Copernican, believing that the sun-centered cosmos was an image of the Holy Trinity, with God represented by the sun, Christ by the shell of fixed stars, and the Holy Spirit by the intervening space. While in Graz he stumbled upon an imaginative explanation for the Copernican spacing of the planets, a scheme involving the five regular polyhedra. Maestlin helped him publish his book, *Mysterium cosmographicum* (*Cosmographic Mystery* [1596]), but his theological introduction was suppressed when the university senate objected. Kepler simply saved his theological defense of the Copernican system until his greatest book, *Astronomia nova* (*New Astronomy* [1609]). There he explained (as Rheticus had done earlier in his as yet unpublished *Narratio secunda* [*Second Narrative*]) that Scripture is written in common language for universal understanding and is not to be taken as a textbook of science. He wrote especially concerning Psalm 104:

I implore my reader not to forget the divine goodness conferred on mankind, and which the

Psalmist urges him especially to consider. . . . Let him not only extol the bounty of God in the preservation of living creatures of all kinds by the strength and stability of the earth, but let him acknowledge the wisdom of the Creator in its motion, so abstruse, so admirable.

Whoever is so weak that he cannot believe Copernicus without offending his piety, and who damns whatever philosophical opinions he pleases, I advise him to mind his own business and to stay at home and fertilize his own garden, and when he turns his eyes toward the visible heavens (the only way he sees them), let him pour forth praise and gratitude to God the Creator. Let him assure himself that he is serving God no less than the astronomer to whom God has granted the privilege of seeing more clearly with the eyes of the mind (Kepler 1992).

The Later Catholic Reception of Copernicanism

Among the Roman Catholics who wrote on Copernican matters was the Spanish theologian Diego de Zuñiga (1536–97), who argued that certain passages in Job could actually be read with a Copernican interpretation. The eclectic philosopher Giordano Bruno (1548–1600), who had only a very faulty technical understanding of the Copernican theory, espoused it as part of his arguments for the plurality of inhabited worlds. While the reasons for his condemnation as a heretic were many and complex, his dalliance with the Copernican doctrine gave pause to many Catholics when he was burned at the stake in 1600.

Although Galileo had written to Kepler in 1597 that he was secretly a Copernican, he kept silent on the subject until his remarkable telescopic discoveries of 1609–10. Then he became increasingly open in his suggestions about the efficacy of heliocentrism. When the question arose at the Florentine court about scriptural objections to Copernicus, his protégé Benedetto Castelli (1578–1643) announced that Galileo could no doubt answer them. Galileo was probably taken by surprise, but he promptly began a review of the relevant materials in the church Fathers and produced an essay on scriptural interpretation. The similarity of some of his arguments to those Kepler had used suggests that Galileo knew of the introduction to *Astronomia nova,* but it would have been folly for a Catholic astronomer to quote a Lutheran in such a delicate matter. Galileo's most memorable line, borrowed from the cardinal director of the Vatican Library, was that "the Bible teaches how to go to heaven, not how the heavens go."

Matters came to a head in 1616 when Galileo went to Rome in an effort to keep the Catholic authorities from banning the Copernican system. Galileo was silenced, and *De revolutionibus* was declared erroneous (but not heretical) and placed on the Index of Prohibited Books "until corrected" (along with Zuñiga's book and a few others). For the first and only time for any prohibited book, the Inquisition actually specified the corrections; in 1620 Inquisitors announced ten changes to make Copernicus's book appear more hypothetical. A recent study has shown that about 60 percent of the copies of Copernicus's book in Italy were censored, but essentially none in the other Catholic countries.

Earlier, in 1581, Christopher Clavius (1537–1612), the leading Jesuit astronomer, had written that what the Copernican system showed was that Ptolemy's arrangement was not the only possibility. Nevertheless, he held firmly to the Ptolemaic cosmology, and he was unenthusiastic when Tycho proposed his alternative geoheliocentric arrangement. After Clavius's death in 1612, and especially after Copernicus's book was placed on the Index, the Jesuits espoused the Tychonic system in their teaching. This had a curious effect on the Jesuit mission to China, which had started out teaching the Copernican system as a demonstration of the advanced state of Western science but, after 1620, rapidly backpedaled to the Tychonic arrangement, leaving Chinese students in great confusion.

At the University of Louvain, the maverick astronomer Libert Froidmond argued in 1631 that the Copernican system should be considered heretical. In France, however, Marin Mersenne (1588–1648), in a careful analysis in 1623, had concluded that the heliocentric cosmology was merely erroneous but not heretical. Earlier, in 1616, internal Vatican examiners decided that the proposition that the earth moved was erroneous, whereas the belief that the sun was fixed was actually heretical. However, their hastily prepared memorandum was not publicized. After the publication in 1632 of Galileo's *Dialogo,* a brilliant polemical defense of Copernicanism, and after his trial that followed for "a vehement suspicion of heresy," the Copernican doctrine became de facto heretical, and Copernicus's book

remained on the Index well after the matter was all but settled in scientific circles.

In 1757, action by Pope Benedict XIV (b. 1675, p. 1740–58) essentially made the heliocentric doctrine acceptable in Catholic schools; nevertheless, the original decree stood, and *De revolutionibus* still appeared in an Index published in Rome in 1819. A pivotal moment arrived when a Catholic astronomer, canon Guiseppe Settele, was refused an imprimatur for his astronomy textbook in 1820 because his book treated the Copernican system as a thesis instead of as a hypothesis. It eventually required a papal command to overrule an obstinate censor, and in 1835 a new edition of the Roman Index finally appeared without a listing for Copernicus, although it had actually been removed from the Index in 1820.

In the mid-twentieth century, Catholic physicists, still embarrassed by the Galileo affair, urged the papacy to "do something" about it. John Paul II (b. 1920, p. 1978–), a pope from Copernicus's homeland, announced to the Pontifical Academy at the time of the Einstein centennial (in 1979) that the case would be reexamined. Thirteen years later, in 1992, with little consultation with the Roman Catholic historians of science who had been commissioned to look into the matter, he made a final statement. Since Galileo had not been found guilty of heresy (as he denied believing in the truth of the Copernican doctrine) but rather of disobedience (for teaching it), Pope John Paul II's options were limited. He said that Galileo had suffered much but that times were different then. He repeated the aphorism "the Bible tells how to go to heaven, not how the heavens go" and declared that Galileo had been a better theologian than those opposing him.

See also Galileo Galilei; Pre-Copernican Astronomy; Roman Catholicism Since Trent

BIBLIOGRAPHY

Fantoli, Annibale. "The 'Galileo Affair' from the Trial's End Until Today." In *Galileo: For Copernicanism and for the Church.* Trans. by George V. Coyne. Vatican City: Vatican Observatory, 1996, 487–532.

Gingerich, Owen. *The Eye of Heaven: Ptolemy, Copernicus, Kepler.* New York: American Institute of Physics, 1993.

Hooykaas, Reijer. *G. J. Rheticus' Treatise on Holy Scripture and the Motion of the Earth.* Amsterdam and New York: North Holland, 1984.

Kaiser, Christopher B. "Calvin, Copernicus, and Castellio." *Calvin Theological Journal* 21 (1986): 5–31.

Kepler, Johannes. *New Astronomy.* Trans. by William H. Donahue. Cambridge: Cambridge University Press, 1992.

Maffei, Paolo. *Giuseppe Settele: His Diary and the Question of Galileo.* Università degli Studi di Perugia Osservatorio Astronomico, *Pubblicazioni: English Supplement to Vol. 1.* Perugia: Edizioni dell'Arquata, 1987.

Russell, John L. "Catholic Astronomers and the Copernican System After the Condemnation of Galileo." *Annals of Science* 46 (1989): 365–86.

Westman, Robert S. "The Melanchthon Circle, Rheticus, and the Wittenberg Interpretation of the Copernican Theory." *Isis* 66 (1975): 165–93.

———. "The Copernicans and the Churches." In *God and Nature: Historical Essays on the Encounter Between Christianity and Science,* ed. by David C. Lindberg and Ronald L. Numbers. Berkeley: University of California Press, 1986, 76–113.

61. THE ETERNITY OF THE WORLD

Edward Grant

Any discussion regarding whether the world is eternal depends on the meaning we assign to the terms "eternal" and "world." The usual historical sense assigned to the concept of an "eternal world" is that which Aristotle used: a world without beginning or end, so that our world may be said to have an eternal past and an infinite future. Many pagan Greeks, however, were prepared to believe that our world, and any other world that might exist, had a beginning but that the matter from which it was formed had neither beginning nor end and was, therefore, eternal.

Speculations about the eternity of the world go back at least to the early Greek philosophers of the sixth and fifth centuries B.C., who assumed the past and future eternity of matter. The worlds composed of that matter, however, were finite in duration. They would forever come into being and pass away. In the fourth century B.C., Plato (c. 427–347 B.C.) also assumed the eternity of a chaotic, ill-defined matter that was shaped into a unique world by a God who did so because of his goodness. It was Aristotle (384–322 B.C.), Plato's pupil, who left us the first reasoned defense of the eternity of a world he regarded as unique. He could find no convincing argument for supposing that our world could have come into being naturally from any prior state of material existence. For, if the world came from a previously existing material thing, say B, we would then have to inquire from whence B came, and so on through an infinite regression. Indeed, Aristotle insisted that whatever had a beginning must have an end and that what could have no end could not have had a beginning. The world was in the latter class.

With the advent of Christianity and its doctrine of a supernatural Creation, which was described in the book of Genesis in the Old Testament, Aristotle's belief in an eternal world was rejected, but the counterarguments were ineffective until A.D. 529, when John Philoponus (d. c. 570), a Neoplatonic convert to Christianity, formulated some powerful arguments against an eternal world. The world must have had a beginning or else it would already have passed through an actual infinity of years, which is absurd because an actual infinite cannot be traversed. Moreover, that actual infinite would be increased with each passing year, a consequence that Philoponus viewed as absurd, since an actual infinite cannot be made greater than it is. Philoponus's arguments had a profound influence on natural philosophers both in Islam and in the late Middle Ages in western Europe.

In the thirteenth century, Bonaventure (John Fidanza [c. 1217–74]) repeated Philoponus's arguments and elaborated on them. In the fourteenth century, some prominent scholastic natural philosophers in Europe rejected Bonaventure's solutions. First, they resorted to Aristotle's distinction between an "actual infinite" and a "potential infinite." Aristotle had rejected the concept of an actual infinite because no such thing could exist either as a number or as a magnitude. An actual infinite could never be traversed or gone through. But Aristotle had assumed that the infinite can exist potentially, in the sense that a potential infinite always has something outside it that can be added to it. Although an actual infinite time could never be traversed, years or days can always be added to a potentially infinite past time in order to reach the present.

In response to the second argument, these fourteenth-century philosophers showed that in a special sense, one infinite could, indeed, be greater than another. Gregory of Rimini (d. 1358), in 1344, adumbrated the idea of an infinite set and an infinite subset and argued that one infinite could be larger than another. For example, one might compare the infinity of the moon's revolutions with that of the sun's. Since there are twelve times as many lunar revolutions as there are solar revolutions, it follows that the sun's infinite number of revolutions in an eternal world is a subset of the moon's. And yet, as John Buridan (c. 1295–c. 1358) explained, "there are no more parts in the whole world than in a millet seed."

Although many scholastic philosophers and theologians in the Middle Ages allowed that the world might be eternal in the sense that one can always add to an infinite, most were convinced that neither the creation of the world nor its eternity was a demonstrable proposition. Thomas Aquinas (c. 1225–74) believed this and chose to reconcile the two seemingly irreconcilable assertions. He concluded that it was logically possible that God might have created a world that is eternal, with "creation" in this context meaning "dependence" (that is, God can be said to have created a world that had no beginning because it is dependent on him for its existence). He could choose to annihilate it and, therefore, deny it existence. This was a popular compromise opinion in the Middle Ages.

In the modern era, Immanuel Kant (1724–1804) regarded as equally false the opposite claims that the universe was temporally finite (that is, had a beginning and an end) and that it was eternal (that is, without a beginning or an end). Most philosophers, however, opted for one or the other. The big bang theory, formulated in 1929 by Edwin Hubble (1889–1953), shifted scientific opinion toward the notion that the world had a beginning. In the latest version of that theory, the universe is rapidly expanding and has been doing so ever since it originated from an infinitely dense point, anywhere from eight billion to fifteen billion years ago. In the modern big bang theory, the universe is assumed to have had a beginning by natural or supernatural means. Whether the world will continue to expand forever, or come to an end at some future time, is not yet determinable. But even if the big bang theory assumed a beginning and an end of our universe, we would still be confronted with the problem of what might have existed before the creation of the world and what could exist after its end. Were there universes before ours and will there be others after it is gone? In other words, might there be an eternity of successive worlds? Even if the response is negative, is there anything that can be called "existence"

before the emergence of our world? If so, would it be reasonable to call this existence a "world" and to assume that it had no beginning? If an infinite vacuum existed prior to the emergence of our world, could it be considered a world? Would the same reasoning apply to whatever follows the end of our world?

Or should we, rather, assume both a beginning and an end of the world and, thus, deny any aspect of eternity to it, as is done in the great monotheistic religions? Or that perhaps the world had a beginning but will have no end and is, therefore, eternal only with respect to the future? Whether the world should be perceived as eternal or finite in duration is as much a problem today as it was to the Greeks more than two thousand years ago.

See also Aristotle and Aristotelianism; Cosmogonies from 1700 to 1900; Stoicism

BIBLIOGRAPHY

Aquinas, Thomas, Siger of Brabant, and Saint Bonaventure. *On the Eternity of the World (De aeternitate mundi).* Trans. by Cyril Vollert, Lottie H. Kendzierski, and Paul M. Byrne. Milwaukee: Marquette University Press, 1964.

Dales, Richard C. *Medieval Discussions of the Eternity of the World.* Leiden: Brill, 1990.

Grant, Edward. "Is the World Eternal, Without Beginning or End?" In Grant, Edward. *Planets, Stars, and Orbs: The Medieval Cosmos.* Cambridge: Cambridge University Press, 1994, 63–82.

Grünbaum, Adolf. "The Pseudo-Problem of Creation in Physical Cosmology." *Philosophy of Science* 56 (1989): 373–94.

———. "Narlikar's 'Creation' of the Big Bang Universe Was a Mere Origination." *Philosophy of Science* 60 (1993): 638–46.

Murdoch, John E. "Infinity and Continuity." In *The Cambridge History of Later Medieval Philosophy from the Rediscovery of Aristotle to the Disintegration of Scholasticism, 1100–1600,* ed. by Norman Kretzmann, Anthony Kenny, Jan Pinborg, and Eleonore Stump. Cambridge: Cambridge University Press, 1982, 564–91.

Quinn, J. M. "Eternity." In *New Catholic Encyclopedia.* Vol. 5. New York: McGraw-Hill, 1967–89, 563–5.

Sorabji, Richard. *Time, Creation, and the Continuum: Theories in Antiquity and the Early Middle Ages.* Ithaca, N.Y.: Cornell University Press, 1983.

———. "Infinity and Creation." In *Philoponus and the Rejection of Aristotelian Science,* ed. by Richard Sorabji. Ithaca, N.Y.: Cornell University Press, 1987, 164–78.

Whitrow, G. J. "On the Impossibility of an Infinite Past." *British Journal for the Philosophy of Science* 29 (1978): 39–45.

62. THE PLURALITY OF WORLDS AND EXTRATERRESTRIAL LIFE

Michael J. Crowe

Few issues in the physical sciences have interacted with religious thought with more sustained intensity over the centuries than the issue of the existence of extraterrestrial intelligent life, or what was long known as the question of the plurality of worlds. More than seven centuries ago, Albertus Magnus (1193–1280) stated the matter succinctly: "Since one of the most wondrous and noble questions in Nature is whether there is one world or many . . . it seems desirable for us to inquire about it." Many religious writers have embraced the idea of extraterrestrials, whereas others have vigorously denied their existence.

Already in antiquity such atomist philosophers as Democritus (c. 460–c. 370 B.C.) and Lucretius (c. 99–55 B.C.) espoused the doctrine of other worlds, whereas Plato (c. 427–347 B.C.) and Aristotle (384–322 B.C.) opposed it. Medieval scholars also remained far from a consensus. Although Albertus Magnus and Thomas Aquinas (c. 1225–74) argued against the doctrine, the famous Condemnation of 1277, in which one of the propositions condemned was that "the First Cause [God] cannot make many worlds," opened the way to other perspectives. For example, Nicole Oresme (c. 1320–82), eventually the bishop of Paris, considered both sides of the issue, and Cardinal Nicholas of Cusa (1401–64) advocated extraterrestrials, including solarians, in his *Of Learned Interest.*

By proposing the heliocentric system, Nicholas Copernicus (1473–1543) began a process that eventually transformed the earth into a planet, stars into suns, and human beings into terrestrials wondering about their place in an immense universe. Although Copernicus never touched on this topic in his writings, others were not slow to see the possibilities that he had opened. By 1550, the Lutheran reformer Philip Melanchthon (1497–1560) noted the threat that Copernicanism's suggestion of other populated worlds posed to the belief in Christ's special and unique incarnation on the earth and the redemption solely of its inhabitants. Very different was the position taken toward the end of the century by Giordano Bruno (1548–1600), who, in a number of his books, championed the existence of extraterrestrials.

In the seventeenth century, the telescope of Galileo Galilei (1564–1642) not only intensified interest in the issue, but also enhanced hopes that scientifically secured information might resolve the debate, at least in regard to the possibility of lunarians, discussed by the astronomer Johannes Kepler (1571–1630) and by the scientist-cleric John Wilkins (1614–72). The debate became far more widespread after the publication late in the seventeenth century of two immensely popular presentations on the subject. Bernard le Bovier de Fontenelle (1657–1757) advocated extraterrestrials with such success in his *Entretiens sur la pluralité des mondes* (*Conversations on the Plurality of Worlds* [1686]) that the work went through dozens of editions and was translated into at least nine other languages. Christiaan Huygens (1629–95), writing with the credibility that came with being one of the premier scientists of the century, was scarcely less successful as an advocate when, in his *Cosmotheoros* (1698) or, in its English title, *Celestial Worlds Discover'd; or, Conjectures Concerning the Inhabitants, Plants, and Productions of the Worlds in the Planets,* he championed extraterrestrials.

More than half of the leading intellectuals of the Enlightenment discussed extraterrestrials in their writings, and nearly all supported their existence, frequently as an extension of their belief in the Principle of Plenitude, the idea that God's power and beneficence would lead him to create all possible life-forms, thereby filling out a Great Chain of Being. Poets as prominent as Alexander Pope (1688–1744) and philosophers as influential as Immanuel Kant (1724–1804) wrote from this perspective. Many astronomers, including Isaac Newton (1642–1727) and William Herschel (1738–1822), were no less enthusiastic, with Herschel advocating life even on the sun. The apparent rapprochement between religion and extraterrestrials was challenged in 1794, when Thomas Paine (1737–1809) argued vociferously in his *Age of Reason* (1794–96) that no thinking person could simultaneously accept extraterrestrials and the Christian belief in a divine incarnation and redemption. Paine used this as an argument against Christianity by claiming that the evidence provided by astronomy convincingly pointed to a plurality of inhabited worlds.

Early in the nineteenth century, a Scottish theologian, Thomas Chalmers (1780–1847), produced an extraordinarily widely read response to the position presented by Paine. Chalmers's *Astronomical Discourses on the Christian Religion in Connection with the Modern Astronomy* (1817) became one of best-sellers of the century. The attractiveness of the idea of a plurality of worlds to those who were religiously inclined is suggested by the fact that, in three major religions founded between 1780 and 1860, extraterrestrials received some prominence. The earliest of these, the Church of the New Jerusalem, or the Swedenborgian Church, was named after its prophet, Emanuel Swedenborg (1688–1772), whose writings reported conversations with inhabitants of the moon and various planets. Extraterrestrials figured prominently in the scriptures written by Joseph Smith (1805–44) for his Church of Jesus Christ of Latter-Day Saints (commonly known as Mormonism) as well as in the writings of Ellen G. White (1827–1915), founder of the Seventh-day Adventist Church.

By the mid-nineteenth century, most authors who discussed the issue of the possibility of life existing elsewhere in the universe assumed that all or nearly all planets are inhabited. Yet, the scientific evidence for such a claim was small to evanescent. William Whewell (1794–1866) shocked his contemporaries when, in his *Of the Plurality of Worlds: An Essay* (1853), he pointed out the paucity of such evidence and suggested the frailty of some of the popular theological arguments for extraterrestrials. Many authors objected to Whewell's position, but by century's end, owing partly to the writings of a self-proclaimed "Whewellite," Richard Proctor (1837–88), the solar system that Whewell had advocated had

become largely accepted. Mars provided the final battleground for life elsewhere in our solar system, especially after many authors reported detecting canals on its surface. Nevertheless, by about 1916 hopes for life on Mars had been abandoned by most astronomers.

The debate over the existence of intelligent life elsewhere in the universe and the religious implications of this possibility continued throughout the twentieth century. The single most important scientific advancement in this area was the development, after 1945, of radio astronomy, which provided a method of entering into contact with such beings, if they exist.

The three most remarkable historical facts about the debate over extraterrestrial life are its extent, the degree to which religious and astronomical considerations interacted, and the way in which this interaction occurred. The extent of the debate is suggested by the fact that, by 1916, more than 140 books (not counting works of science fiction) and thousands of articles addressing this issue had already appeared. Moreover, religious concerns powerfully affected the positions advocated not only by theological, but also by philosophical, literary, and scientific, authors. Not least surprising is the fact that authors found ways to marshal extraterrestrials in support of, or in opposition to, Christianity, deism, atheism, and dozens of other creeds and philosophies.

See also America's Innovative Nineteenth-Century Religions; Medieval Science and Religion

BIBLIOGRAPHY

Crowe, Michael J. *The Extraterrestrial Life Debate, 1750–1900: The Idea of a Plurality of Worlds from Kant to Lowell.* Cambridge: Cambridge University Press, 1986.

Dick, Steven J. *Plurality of Worlds: The Origins of the Extraterrestrial Life Debate from Democritus to Kant.* Cambridge: Cambridge University Press, 1982.

———. "Plurality of Worlds." In *Encyclopedia of Cosmology,* ed. by Norris S. Hetherington. New York: Garland, 1993, 502–12.

———. *The Biological Universe: The Twentieth-Century Extraterrestrial Life Debate and the Limits of Science.* Cambridge: Cambridge University Press, 1996.

Guthke, Karl S. *The Last Frontier: Imagining Other Worlds from the Copernican Revolution to Modern Science Fiction.* Ithaca, N.Y.: Cornell University Press, 1990.

Hoyt, William G. *Lowell and Mars.* Tucson: University of Arizona Press, 1976.

Jaki, Stanley. *Planets and Planetarians: A History of Theories of the Origin of Planetary Systems.* Edinburgh: Scottish Academic Press, 1978.

63. MACROCOSM/MICROCOSM

John Henry

The analogy between the macrocosm, the world or universe as a whole, and the microcosm, the human being (usually "man" in the historical record) as an epitome of the world, originated among the ancient Greeks and proved to be a powerful and enduring symbol of the unity of creation. As one of the most frequently invoked examples of the theory of correspondences, in which different levels in the hierarchically structured "Great Chain of Being" were held to "correspond" to one another in a variety of ways, the analogy can also be seen as a mainstay of magical belief systems.

Man was seen as a "little world," an epitome of the universe as a whole. The structure and organization of man, and even his life processes, corresponded, therefore, to the structure, organization, and natural processes of the world. As Walter Raleigh (1552–1618) put it in his *History of the World* (1614):

> His blood, which disperseth itself by the branches of veins through all the body, may be resembled to those waters which are carried by brooks and rivers over all the earth, his breath to the air, his natural heat to the inclosed warmth which the earth hath in itself . . . the hairs of man's body, which adorns or overshadows it, to the grass which covereth the upper face and skin of the earth. . . . Our determinations to the light wandering and unstable clouds, carried everywhere with uncertain winds, our eyes to the light of the sun and the moon, and the beauty of our youth to the flowers of the spring which in a very short time or with the sun's heat dry up and wither away, or the fierce puffs of wind blow them from the stalks.

Similarly, each of the parts of man's body corresponded to a different sign of the zodiac. The heart corresponded

to the sun; the head, seat of the soul and the faculty of reasoning, corresponded to the empyrean heaven; the lower abdomen, site of the anus and the genitals, corresponded to the earth, the site of generation and corruption. It was far from coincidental, therefore, that man was composed of four humors—yellow bile, blood, phlegm, and black bile—which corresponded to the four elements of fire, air, water, and earth, respectively. Man was also seen as the link between the material realm and the realm of spirit, being the only creature, apart from the universe as a whole, to be composed of both body and immaterial soul. Pursuing the analogy in the opposite direction, cosmic laws were seen as projections of those laws that governed human nature.

An important element of the broader conception was the subsidiary set of analogies between the body of man and the "body politic," on the one hand, and between the political system and the world system on the other. If society, with all of its complexity, was to run smoothly and to the best advantage of its many members, it was assumed that it, too, must reflect the same organization as the world system or as the equally complex individual human being. This gave rise to the notion, still prevalent in contemporary rhetoric, that the legitimate political system is a *natural* system ultimately established by God, and that attempts by men to impose other systems of political organization are doomed to failure because they are unnatural (though, of course, one man's natural regime is another's illegitimate system).

Man: The Measure of All Things

The origins of the analogy between the world as a whole and man as a little world remain obscure. By the time the analogy is clearly stated in ancient Greek thought, it already seems to be taken for granted. For that reason, it has not unreasonably been suggested that the notion first appeared in popular consciousness and was subsequently accepted by the first philosophers. Certainly, the analogy between the world and sociopolitical organization can be found in the very earliest thinkers, such as Thales of Miletus (fl. c. 585 B.C.), Anaximander (610–c. 546 B.C.), and Heraclitus (540–480 B.C.), who also suggest that man is made of the same things as the cosmos, and hint at parallels between man-made laws and laws of nature. Democritus (c. 460–c. 370 B.C.), founder of atomism, is usually credited with being the first to draw an explicit analogy between an animal and the universe as a whole, seen as a living creature. From then, the theme seems to have developed tentatively at first and then more systematically. Plato (c. 427–347 B.C.) developed the theme in his *Timaeus,* and it was later elaborated by the Stoics. The analogy was used both ways, seeing man as an ordered system comparable to the whole world, and the world as an organism endowed with vital powers and even reason.

One of the major influences in the transmission of the macrocosm/microcosm analogy to the Christian Middle Ages was the Roman writer Cicero (106–43 B.C.), whose treatise *De natura deorum* (*On the Nature of the Gods*) drew heavily on the analogy, including the suggestion that God bears the same relation to the material objects of the universe as the soul does to the body in the human. Macrobius's (fl.c. A.D. 400) Neoplatonic commentary upon Cicero's *Somnium Scipionis* (*Dream of Scipio*) and Chalcidius's (fourth century A.D.) commentary on the *Timaeus* were also important. The historical development of the notion of the Great Chain of Being must also have helped consolidate the analogy, since man was seen as the topmost creature in the ranks of material beings and the lowest of the spiritual beings, and, therefore, constituted a link between what was above and what was below. Parallel developments in the not unconnected theory of natural magic presumably also added extra support to the notion that man and cosmos were models of each other. Certainly by the twelfth-century revival of learning in western Europe, the macrocosm/microcosm analogy was well established.

The analogy reached the peak of its cultural and intellectual influence during the Renaissance, however, when the rediscovery of ancient texts resulted in the burgeoning of the magical tradition, and the new humanistic emphasis on the dignity of man led to considerations of man's place in nature and the flourishing of the notion of the Great Chain of Being. For medieval thinkers, man's place in the chain was absolutely fixed, as the nodal point between the material and the spiritual realms. But numerous literary works in the Renaissance took as their theme the notion that man might rise above the angels or sink lower than the beasts by the correct or false use of his reason and moral sense. The first, and most influential, exposition of this new view of man was Giovanni Pico della Mirandola's (1463–94) *Oration on the Dignity of Man* (1486). Extending earlier ideas about man as encompassing all forms of life (in medieval Aristotelianism, for example, it was believed that man had a tripartite soul: the vegetative, life-giving, soul of plants; the animal soul, which endowed motion and sensitivity; and the rational soul, which endowed immortality), Pico emphasized man's ability to become whatever form of life he chose. Partaking of all of the gifts that God had bestowed upon the rest of creation, man was said to have no fixed essence and to be outside the hierarchy of beings. Although this way of thinking seemed to remove man from the Chain of Being, allowing him to range freely rather than to represent the nodal point between purely material and purely spiritual beings, it did so by emphasizing his unique status as a recapitulation of the world as a whole.

Another characteristic aspect of Renaissance culture that relied upon and, in turn, served to reinforce the analogy between macrocosm and microcosm was introduced by artists and engineers. The rediscovery of *De architectura* (*On Architecture*) by the Roman architect and engineer Vitruvius (first century B.C.) had a major impact on Renaissance architectural theory, beginning with Leon Battista Alberti's (1404–72) *De re aedificatoria* (*On the Art of Building* [1443–52]) and continuing after the publication of a new edition of *De architectura* (1556) with commentary by the classical scholar Daniele Barbaro (1513–70) and illustrations prepared by one of the greatest Renaissance architects, Andrea Palladio (1508–80). The most influential and famous aspect of Vitruvian theory was the belief that buildings should be based upon the symmetry and proportion of the human body. Vitruvius claimed that a man's body with arms and legs fully extended can be seen perfectly to demarcate both a square and a circle. This gave rise to a new interest in the proportions of the human body, which came to be seen as the basis of all aesthetic principles and the model for all cosmic harmonies, as well as for all man-made designs (whether of buildings, towns and cities, paintings, sculptures, or other artifacts).

The most famous exemplification of this principle is the drawing of a Vitruvian figure by Leonardo da Vinci (1452–1519), in which the circle and the square are simultaneously depicted, the circle being demarcated by the man with his limbs spread-eagled, while the square is demarcated by his standing to attention with his arms outstretched to the side. There are, however, numerous other lesser depictions of the same theme, and they are not all confined to works in the fine arts. These images soon found their way into philosophical works, symbolically to illustrate the principles of the macrocosm/microcosm analogy. The most lavish of such illustrated philosophical works are those of the English physician and would-be Rosicrucian Robert Fludd (1574–1637), but his massive *Metaphysical, Physical, and Technical History of Both the Macrocosm and the Microcosm* (1617–26) is too idiosyncratic to serve as a guide to the precepts of the macrocosm/microcosm analogy. It can, however, be seen as an indication of how all-embracing the macrocosm/microcosm analogy could be taken to be. A clearer example of how ideas of proportion and harmony were absorbed into the analogy is afforded by John Dee (1527–1608) in his "Mathematical Preface" to a new edition of Euclid's Geometry (1570). In this brief account of the mathematical arts, Dee included "Anthropographie," which he defined as "the description of number, measure, waight, figure, situation and colour of every diverse thing, conteyned in the perfect body of Man." The point is, Dee wrote, that

> If the description of the heavenly part of the world, has a peculier Art, called Astronomie; if the description of the earthly Globe, hath his peculier arte, called Geographie; if the matching of both, hath his peculier arte called Cosmographie . . . why should not the description of him, who is the lesser world, and, from the beginning, called Microcosmus [have its own art, which I propose to call Anthropographie]?

The Renaissance also saw the burgeoning of the tradition of natural magic and associated occult philosophies, in which the macrocosm/microcosm analogy played a major role. Given that the Great Chain of Being and the notion of correspondences between different links of the chain formed the basis for the theory of magic, the nodal point on the chain was bound to figure

largely. But the role of man as microcosm did not simply mean that parts of his body corresponded to other features of the universe, such as his feet with the constellation of Pisces. It also meant that knowledge of ourselves allowed access to knowledge of the universe at large, and that our understanding, modeled in some way on the structure of the world, was attuned to the occult affinities of the rest of nature. For the alchemist and founder of iatrochemistry Paracelsus (1493–1541), the analogy did not simply mean that man and the greater world could be compared to each other but that they were essentially the same with regard to their power: Whatever natural forces there were in the world, man could produce them and harness them. Similar ideas are to be found in Giovanni Pico della Mirandola's *Oration on the Dignity of Man,* which was also heavily indebted to newly discovered magical texts, particularly the so-called *Hermetica,* writings attributed to the ancient Greek divinity Hermes Trismegistus but now known to have been written by various Neoplatonic thinkers in the early Christian era. One of the most influential of these early magical texts was the *Picatrix,* in which it was said that man

> has a divine power and possesses the knowledge of justice for governing cities . . . he performs miracles . . . the forms of the sciences are brought together in him . . . and God has made him the maker and inventor of all science and knowledge, able to explain all its qualities . . . to understand the treasures within everything with a prophetic spirit.

The development of the mechanical philosophy and the increasing mechanization of the world picture from the late seventeenth century onward resulted in the effective disappearance of the macrocosm/microcosm analogy from philosophical and orthodox religious thinking. When all natural objects, including human beings, came to be seen as specific conglomerates of invisible atoms or corpuscles, it no longer made any real sense to say that the world and man were structurally and organizationally similar. The only exception to this, among the ranks of the mechanical philosophers, was to be found in the philosophy of Gottfried Wilhelm Leibniz (1646–1716). Led by his highly sophisticated and complex metaphysical concerns, Leibniz asserted in his *Monadology* (1714) that the "true atoms" of nature are what he called "monads." Needing to allow for complexity within his monads (to allow them to fulfill various important roles in his metaphysical system), while simultaneously asserting their indivisibility, Leibniz insisted that they were indivisible in the sense that a person is. A man or a woman, being a true individual substance, cannot be divided. The monads also needed to be unextended, however, and immaterial, so they came to be seen like souls. But, as Leibniz wrote in Section 83 of his *Monadology,* "souls in general are living mirrors or images of the universe of created beings," and human souls "are also images of divinity itself—of the very Author of nature. They are capable of knowing the system of the universe, and of imitating it." If it is true to say that the macrocosm/microcosm analogy played a role in Leibniz's metaphysical speculations, it remains hardly possible to understand how these speculations were supposed to fit in with his mechanistic physics, in which corporeal substances were characterized in terms of force. Furthermore, Leibniz's monadology seems to have had little influence upon the subsequent development of philosophy. It remains true to say, therefore, that the rise of the mechanical philosophy saw the decline of the macrocosm/microcosm analogy.

The Human Body and the Body Politic

The subsidiary analogy between man and the "body politic" continued to flourish, however, even among orthodox thinkers. It seems fairly clear that, in spite of the dominance of the mechanical worldview, both the human body and the social and political organization of the state continued to be seen in organic terms. It made sense, therefore, to hold that the best way to organize the state was to model it on the organization of the human body. Similarly, the human body could be understood by comparing it with the complex organization of the state.

One of the most famous examples of the use of the analogy between the body and the body politic in the history of science is to be found in the works of William Harvey (1578–1657), discoverer of the circulation of the blood. The first announcement of his discovery of blood circulation, in his *On the Motion of the Heart and Blood* (1628), drew upon entirely traditional analogies straight from the standard view of the Great Chain of Being and its correspondences. The heart was "the sun of the microcosm," the sun was "the heart of the world," and King Charles I (ruled 1625–49), to whom the book was dedicated, was "the sun of his microcosm, the heart of his commonwealth." By 1649, however, when Harvey published the short defense of his ideas in *On the Circu-*

lation of the Blood, he played down the role of the heart in physiology, insisting that the blood was primary to the heart and to all other things in the body. The historian Christopher Hill has seen this dramatic change in Harvey's views about the organization of the body as an unconscious response to the political changes in Civil War England. Hill's critics have frequently misunderstood him. He did not suggest that Harvey changed his politics from Royalist to Republican and his physiology accordingly. There can be no doubt that Harvey was always a devoted Royalist. Hill's point was that the very public debates about political theory and the correct organization of the state that took place in England at that time made it possible for a thinker like Harvey to envisage a different organization of the body, which deviated from the traditional view. Just as the people took precedence over the king in the new political theory, so the blood took precedence over the heart in Harvey's later biology. Harvey's claims about the primacy of the blood have often puzzled recent commentators, and Hill's claim is the only one that makes sense of this change in his views.

Similar examples from the later history of medicine have been suggested by other scholars. Xavier Bichat (1771–1802), leading pathological anatomist and founder of histology, the study of the different types of tissue in the body, has been convincingly shown to have been influenced by the new bureaucratic organization of postrevolutionary France introduced by the government of the Directory (1795–99), in which the organization of the state comprised parallel functional systems (for example, army, education, finance) widespread throughout the whole. For Bichat, the correct way to understand the working of the body was to see it comprising parallel functional systems of different tissue types, which ramify throughout the entire body. This particular example also shows how the analogy between body and state can be made to work both ways.

In the Napoleonic period, after the demise of the Directory, the political theorist Claude Henri Saint-Simon (1760–1825) explicitly drew upon Bichat's descriptions of the organization of the human body to defend, by analogy, his theories of the correct organization of the state (which were, in fact, very similar to the reforms carried out by the Directory). Saint-Simon was deliberately trying to appropriate the authority of science in support of his political theories, but this does not mean that he did not really believe in Bichat's theories. It is more likely that he believed that his political system must be right because it so clearly reflected the organization of the body, as shown by Bichat. In Bichat's case, the influence of politics must have been more unconscious, but it seems hard to deny that it was there. Bichat discerned twenty-two different types of tissue in the human body, and these are still recognized by modern medical science. They have not been dismissed as figments of his imagination. How was it that Bichat saw in the human cadaver for the first time features that medical students today routinely accept to be there? Why had no anatomist before him noticed these supposedly obvious differences between tissue types? It is not unreasonable to suppose that before Bichat they were not regarded as significant features of the internal anatomy of the body because there was no previous model for the kind of complex organization into which the tissue types would have fitted.

Rudolf Virchow (1821–1902), founder of cellular pathology, resisted the new cell theory in biology until after his experience as a medical inspector in the mine of Upper Silesia in 1848. It can hardly be a coincidence that Virchow began to see all disease as variations of cancer, in which some cells of the body turn against others to the detriment of the organism as a whole, at just the same time that he developed his socialist political ideas in response to the exploitation of the miners by the mine owners. "The Organism is a free state of individuals with equal rights," Virchow wrote of the body, "which keeps together because the individuals are dependent on one another." It is a measure of the strength of the analogy between the human body and the body politic that Virchow, undoubtedly one of the greatest pathologists of the late nineteenth century, was very slow to recognize the validity of germ theory. Being convinced that disease, like political disorder, always resulted from internal breakdown, he could not acknowledge that disease sometimes entered the body from outside.

If the analogy between the body and the body politic still resonates in contemporary Western culture even among orthodox social and political scientists, the parent analogy between the human being and the world system as a whole resonates only among artists and poets or unorthodox thinkers, chiefly in occultist and esoteric traditions. The macrocosm/microcosm analogy played a part in the system of the French occultist Eliphas Lévi (or Alphonse Louis Constant [1810–75]), one of the major figures in the modern revival of magic. Seeing magic as a means to self-improvement, Lévi suggested that the correspondences linked the creatures and other features of the macrocosm to elements of the human psyche. The procedures of ritual magic, which used to be held to have a direct effect upon the subject to which the magic was directed, whether it be another human or some other creature or aspect of the greater world, were now held only to be means to concentrate and direct the magician's will with a view to self-mastery. The endeavor toward self-improvement was always part of the magical tradition, being particularly evident, for example, in the alchemical tradition, in which it even gave rise to the kind of mystical, nonempirical alchemy of Jacob Boehme (1575–1624). The macrocosm/microcosm analogy had already been linked to it, particularly in the theories of Paracelsus and Giovanni Pico della Mirandola, but Lévi (living in an age that could not take the analogy literally) made psychological self-improvement the whole meaning of the analogy. Lévi was himself influential among the new esoteric traditions that sprang up at the end of the nineteenth century and the beginning of the twentieth, but only the Anthroposophical Society, founded by Rudolf Steiner (1861–1925) in 1913, incorporated the macrocosm/microcosm analogy as a significant part of its speculations.

It seems fair to say, however, that such occultist uses of the analogy, unlike the uses of the body/body politic analogy, provide no generally accepted insights into the nature of man, the nature of social systems, or the world as a whole. They merely reveal the preoccupations of the occultists themselves. What was once held to be a sure guide to understanding the structure and organization of the world and of man, on the one hand, and a clear sign of our relationship to nature and to God, on the other, has now become nothing more than an arbitrary ingredient in esoteric systems of thought and an occasional image in poetry and the arts.

See also Anatomy and Physiology to 1700; Great Chain of Being; Hermeticism

BIBLIOGRAPHY

Ahern, Geoffrey. *Sun at Midnight: The Rudolf Steiner Movement and the Western Esoteric Tradition.* Wellingborough: Aquarian, 1984.

Allers, R. "Microcosmus from Anaximander to Paracelsus." *Traditio* 2 (1944): 319–407.

Conger, G. P. *Theories of Macrocosms and Microcosms in the History of Philosophy.* New York: Columbia University Press, 1922.

Debus, A. G. *Man and Nature in the Renaissance.* Cambridge: Cambridge University Press, 1978.

Godwin, Joscelyn. *Robert Fludd: Hermetic Philosopher and Surveyor of Two Worlds.* London: Thames and Hudson, 1979.

Hill, Christopher. "William Harvey and the Idea of Monarchy." In *The Intellectual Revolution of the Seventeenth Century,* ed. by Charles Webster. London: Routledge and Kegan Paul, 1974, 160–81.

Lindberg, David C. *The Beginnings of Western Science: The European Scientific Tradition in Philosophical, Religious, and Institutional Context, 600 B.C. to A.D. 1450.* Chicago: University of Chicago Press, 1992.

Lovejoy, Arthur O. *The Great Chain of Being: A Study of the History of an Idea.* 1936. Reprint. New York: Harper Torchbooks, 1960.

Pickstone, John. "Bureaucracy, Liberalism, and the Body in Post-Revolutionary France: Bichat's Physiology and the Paris School of Medicine." *History of Science* 19 (1981): 115–42.

Pouchelle, Marie-Christine. *The Body and Surgery in the Middle Ages.* New Brunswick, N.J.: Rutgers University Press, 1990.

Schmitt, Charles B., and Quentin Skinner, eds. *The Cambridge History of Renaissance Philosophy.* Cambridge: Cambridge University Press, 1988.

Singer, Charles. "The Scientific Views and Visions of Saint Hildegard." *Studies in the History and Method of Science* 1 (1917): 1–55.

Tillyard, E. M. W. *The Elizabethan World Picture.* London: Chatto and Windus, 1943.

Weindling, Paul. "Theories of the Cell State in Imperial Germany." In *Biology, Medicine, and Society, 1840–1940,* ed. by Charles Webster. Cambridge: Cambridge University Press, 1981, 99–155.

Wittkower, Rudolf. *Architectural Principles in the Age of Humanism.* London: Academy Editions, 1973.

Wright, M. R. *Cosmology in Antiquity.* London and New York: Routledge, 1995.

Yates, Frances A. *Theatre of the World.* London and New York: Routledge and Kegan Paul, 1969.

64. Cosmogonies from 1700 to 1900

Ronald L. Numbers

Late in the seventeenth century, a young English divine named William Whiston (1667–1752) criticized his contemporaries for habitually "stretching [the Six Days Work] beyond the Earth, either to the whole System of things, as the most do, or indeed to the Solar System, with which others are more modestly contented in the case." At the time, it was customary in Western science to accept the Mosaic story of Creation found in the first chapter of the Book of Genesis as a literal cosmogony, or account of how the universe began. For most, this meant that the entire cosmos, or at least the solar system, had been created by God's fiat in six successive twenty-four-hour periods, approximately four thousand years before the birth of Christ. As long as Western natural philosophers were willing to tolerate supernatural explanations within the domain of science, there was little motivation to discard this traditional cosmogony. The desire for a natural history of Creation became acute only after those pursuing science in Europe began to view their task as explaining the workings of nature without recourse to direct supernatural activity.

Descartes, Newton, and Buffon

Modern attempts to explain the origin of the solar system naturalistically date from the mid-seventeenth century. As the new science resolved one after another of nature's mysteries, the temptation to formulate a purely naturalistic cosmogony became increasingly great. One of the first modern Europeans to yield to this temptation was the French philosopher René Descartes (1596–1650). His theory of the origin of the solar system, sketched in the *Principia philosophiae* (*Principles of Philosophy* [1644]) as well as in his suppressed treatise *Le Monde* (*The World* [completed in 1633 but published

posthumously]), followed logically from his twin beliefs in the constancy of the laws of nature and the sufficiency of these laws to explain the phenomena of nature. Using vortices as a creative mechanism, he showed how the solar system could have been formed by the God-ordained laws of nature operating on a primitive chaos. Then, undoubtedly prompted by the recent experiences of Galileo Galilei (1564–1642), he cautiously added that he considered this hypothesis to be "absolutely false" and asserted his belief in the orthodox doctrine of the creation of the world in the beginning in a fully developed state.

This thinly veiled attempt to eliminate God as a necessary element in the creation of the world brought Descartes considerable notoriety. In relegating God to the remote and seemingly minor task of establishing the laws of nature, he had overstepped the bounds of seventeenth-century tolerance. His fellow countryman Blaise Pascal (1623–62) could never forgive such blatant impiety. "In all his philosophy," wrote Pascal, Descartes "would have been quite willing to dispense with God. But he had to make Him give a fillip to set the world in motion; beyond this, he has no further need of God."

Descartes fared no better with Isaac Newton (1642–1727), who consistently rejected suggestions that the solar system had been created by the "mere Laws of Nature." In the *General Scholium* at the end of the second edition of his *Principia* (1713), Newton summarized his reasons for believing in the necessity of divine action:

The six primary planets are revolved about the sun in circles concentric with the sun, and with motions directed towards the same parts, and almost in the same plane. Ten moons are revolved about the earth, Jupiter, and Saturn, in circles concentric with them, with the same direction of motion, and nearly in the planes of the orbits of those planets; but it is not to be conceived that mere mechanical causes could give birth to so many regular motions, since the comets range over all parts of the heavens in very eccentric orbits. . . . This most beautiful system of the sun, planets, and comets, could only proceed from the counsel and dominion of an intelligent and powerful Being.

Newton did not deny that natural causes had been employed in the production of the solar system, but he insisted that it could not have been made by the laws of nature alone. He stated his position clearly in a letter to Thomas Burnet (c. 1635–1715): "Where natural causes are at hand God uses them as instruments in his works, but I do not think them alone sufficient for ye creation." In particular, he could discover no cause for the earth's diurnal motion other than divine action.

Newton's own theory of the creation of the inanimate world, which he confided to Burnet, illustrates his preference for natural explanations. He regarded the Mosaic account as a description of "realities in a language artificially adapted to ye sense of ye vulgar," not as a scientifically accurate record of events. The Genesis story of Creation related primarily to developments on this globe; thus, the creation of the sun, moon, and stars had been assigned to the fourth day because they first shone on the earth at that time. Newton imagined that the entire solar system had been formed from a "common Chaos" and that the separation of the planets into individual "parcels" and their subsequent condensation into solid globes had been effected by gravitational attraction, though this possibly was the work of "ye spirit of God." Since the earth's diurnal motion probably had not begun until the end of the second day, at which time it had first become a terraqueous globe, it seemed as if the first two days of Creation week could be made "as long as you please" without doing violence to the language of Genesis.

Neither the private speculations of Newton nor the quasi-naturalistic cosmogonies offered by Burnet and Whiston succeeded in breaking the hold of a static Creation on the collective mind of the seventeenth century. Newton's widely circulated condemnation of hypothesizing about Creation by natural law and his insistence on the necessity of divine intervention left the distinct

impression, in the words of David Kubrin, that "Newtonianism and cosmogony were absolutely incompatible." Meanwhile, the general public continued to follow "those Divines" who, in the words of Burnet, "insist upon ye hypothesis of 6 days as a physical reality." Into the eighteenth century, even such well-informed cosmogonists as Immanuel Kant (1724–1804) continued to view Newton as a biblical literalist who "asserted that the immediate hand of God had instituted this arrangement [i.e., the solar system] without the intervention of the forces of nature."

Although Newton and other English cosmogonists readily utilized natural laws to assist in interpreting the events of Creation, they always did so within the context of the biblical record. They might speak of the days of Creation as long periods of time and discuss the possible role of gravitational attraction in the formation of the solar system, but they did not discard the basic features of the Mosaic story. It was in France, among the scientific disciples of Newton and the spiritual heirs of Descartes, that totally secular cosmogonies, free from all scriptural influence, first gained a foothold.

Georges Louis Leclerc, Comte de Buffon (1707–88), was one of the first French admirers of Newton; he was also one of the sternest critics of Newton's cosmogony. Whereas Newton actively encouraged the union of science and theology, Buffon demanded a complete separation. Those studying physical subjects, he argued, "ought, as much as possible, to avoid having recourse to supernatural causes." Philosophers "ought not to be affected by causes which seldom act, and whose action is always sudden and violent. These have no place in the ordinary course of nature. But operations uniformly repeated, motions which succeed one another without interruption, are the causes which alone ought to be the foundation of our reasoning." Whether or not such explanations were true was of no consequence. What really mattered was that they appear probable. Buffon acknowledged, for example, that the planets had been set in motion originally by the Creator—but he considered the fact of no value to the natural philosopher.

Buffon's repudiation of the supernatural in science led him to search for a natural history of the solar system. He was far too good a Newtonian to consider the discredited Cartesian theory of vortices, and Newton's cosmogony was out of the question; so he had no choice but to formulate his own naturalistic hypothesis. The first description of it appeared in 1749 in his *Theorie de la terre (Theory of the Earth).* Thirty years later he gave a somewhat modified version of his original ideas in *Les Epoques de la nature (The Epochs of Nature* [1778]).

The numerous uniformities in the solar system persuaded Buffon that a common cause was responsible for all planetary motions. All of the planets revolved around the sun in the same direction, and, according to his calculations, the probability is sixty-four to one that this was the product of a single cause. In addition, the planes of the planetary orbits are inclined no more than seven-and-one-half degrees from the ecliptic, and the probability is 7,692,624 to one that this could not have been produced by accident. Such a high degree of probability, "which almost amounts to a certainty," seemed to be conclusive evidence "that all the planets have probably received their centrifugal motion by one single stroke."

Though his calculations did not indicate whether the stroke had come from the hand of God, as Newton had assumed, or from some natural heavenly body, Buffon arbitrarily limited his search for an explanation to the latter type of cause. Since "nothing but comets [seemed] capable of communicating motion to such vast masses" as the planets, he confidently turned to them for the solution to his cosmogonical problem. The hypothetical production of the solar system he described in the following way:

The comet, by falling obliquely on the sun . . . must have forced off from his surface a quantity of matter equal to a 650th part of his body. The matter being in a liquid state, would at first form a torrent, of which the largest and rarest parts would fly to the greatest distances, the smaller and more dense, having received only an equal impulse, would remain nearer the sun; his power of attraction would operate upon all the parts detached from his body, and make them circulate round him; and, at the same time, the mutual attraction of the particles of matter would cause all the detached parts to take on the form of globes, at different distances from the sun, the nearer moving with greater rapidity in their orbits than the more remote.

Buffon believed the diurnal motion of the planets to have resulted from the oblique blow of the comet, which would have caused the matter detached from the sun to rotate. And he imagined that a very oblique blow would have given the planets a rotation so great that small quantities of matter would have been thrown off to form the

satellites. The fact that the satellites "all move in the same direction, and in concentric circles round their principal planets, and nearly in the place of their orbits" appeared to be a striking confirmation of this theory.

Laplace's Nebular Hypothesis

Although Buffon's cosmogony seemed "extremely probable" to him, it failed to win widespread acceptance. Nevertheless, it remained the most serious challenger to the Mosaic account of Creation through the latter half of the eighteenth century. Indeed, Pierre Simon Laplace (1749–1827), the leading Newtonian scientist in postrevolutionary France, could think of no one besides Buffon "who, since the discovery of the true system of the world, has endeavored to investigate the origin of the planets, and of their satellites."

Laplace applauded Buffon's efforts to fashion a naturalistic cosmogony but faulted him for a number of scientific errors, such as erroneously assuming that an oblique blow by a comet would necessarily impart a rotation to the planets in the same direction as their revolutions around the sun. In 1796, in a lengthy note appended to his *Exposition du systeme du monde (Explanation of a World System),* Laplace sketched out an alternative cosmogony that came to be known as the nebular hypothesis. According to his view, the planets had been created from the atmosphere of the sun, which, because of its heat, had originally extended beyond the orbit of the most distant planet. As this atmosphere condensed, it abandoned a succession of rings—similar to those of Saturn—in the plane of the sun's equator, and these rings then coalesced to form the various planets. In a similar way, the satellites developed from the planetary atmospheres. In a later edition of *Systeme du monde,* Laplace speculated that the primitive condition of the solar system closely resembled a slowly rotating hot nebula, like the cloudy bodies recently discovered by the British astronomer William Herschel (1738–1822).

Laplace's *Systeme du monde* had appeared in two English editions by 1830, but popular knowledge of the nebular hypothesis in the English-speaking world came largely from other sources, such as *Views of the Architecture of the Heavens* (1837) by the Scottish astronomer John Pringle Nichol (1804–59). Nichol congratulated Laplace for putting humans virtually "in possession of that primeval Creative Thought which originated our system and planned and circumscribed its destiny." No fewer than three of the Bridgewater Treatises on the Power, Wisdom, and Goodness of God as Manifested in the Creation, published in the 1830s, discussed Laplace's cosmogony. In *Astronomy and General Physics Considered with Reference to Natural Theology* (1833), one of the most popular volumes in the series, William Whewell (1794–1866) disarmed potential critics by pointing out that the nebular hypothesis in no way affected the much cherished argument from design:

> If we grant . . . the hypothesis, it by no means proves that the solar system was formed without the intervention of intelligence and design. It only transfers our view of the skill exercised, and the means employed, to another part of the work. . . . What but design and intelligence prepared and tempered this previously existing element, so that it should by its natural changes produce such an orderly system.

If the motions and the arrangement of the planetary bodies were the inevitable result of the operation of natural laws on nebulous matter, the design of the solar system no longer gave evidence of God and his wisdom; it revealed only what happens to nebulous matter under the influence of natural laws. But that raised the question of who established those laws. To Whewell and other like-minded Christians, the obvious answer was that they had been instituted by God and were evidence of his existence and wisdom.

Although the Scottish divine Thomas Chalmers (1780–1847) in his Bridgewater Treatise condemned the nebular hypothesis for giving aid to atheism, the theory encountered little religious opposition before 1844, when it had the misfortune of being included in the scandalous little volume *Vestiges of the Natural History of Creation,* written anonymously by the Scottish publisher Robert Chambers (1802–71). In this widely read work, Chambers brought together the nebular hypothesis, developmental geology, and Lamarckian evolution in an attempt to show how all of nature had originated as a product of natural law. Many Christian critics regarded the *Vestiges* as blatantly atheistic and roundly condemned it in both the scientific and the religious press. However, some reviewers softened their attack when dealing with the nebular hypothesis. As one writer in the *American Review* put it, he would not have rejected the nebular hypothesis "so rudely, founded as it is upon excellent proofs, if it had not come attended by a load of false conclusions, as of . . . men originating by slow degrees from monkeys."

Nevertheless, its association with the *Vestiges* left the nebular hypothesis tainted with atheism. Thus, widespread enthusiasm greeted the announcement by William Parsons (1800–67) in the mid-1840s of resolutions of nebulae. With his "leviathan" telescope, this Irish astronomer, the earl of Rosse, showed that many of the heavenly objects Herschel had formerly classed as nebulae were nothing but dense clusters of individual stars. This discovery deprived Laplace's hypothesis of what many considered to be its most convincing evidence. "The Nebular Hypothesis," wrote one American author, "vanishes as a pleasant dream, profitable though we believe it has been; and with it various systems of cosmogony, the fear of timid Christians, and the hopes of Atheistical philosophers."

The Nebular Hypothesis in America

The demise of the nebular hypothesis, however, proved to be only temporary, at least in the United States, for new evidence soon came to light suggesting that it might be true after all. In the late 1840s, an academy principal in the backwoods of Pennsylvania, Daniel Kirkwood (1814–95), discovered a simple equation, based on the nebular hypothesis, relating the rotations of the planets to their spheres of attraction. When his discovery was announced at the 1849 meetings of the American Association for the Advancement of Science, it almost singlehandedly restored the faith of American scientists in the nebular hypothesis, and they went home generally agreed "that Laplace's nebular hypothesis, from its furnishing one of the elements of Kirkwood's law, may now be regarded as an established fact in the past history of the solar system." Across the Atlantic, the analogy created a different response among men who derived no nationalistic pride from Kirkwood's accomplishment. Though some European scientists expressed admiration for what the American had done, they often remained skeptical of the analogy's scientific value and its bearing on the nebular hypothesis.

Some clever experiments by the Belgian scientist Joseph Plateau (1801–83) on globules of oil rotating in a mixture of water and alcohol also seemed to confirm the nebular theory. The spheres of oil, when rotated, abandoned rings, which ruptured and formed rotating gloves circling around the central mass. This experiment was allegedly performed in a fashionable New York City church to show how modern science supported the biblical story of Creation. At its conclusion, the congregation reportedly voted unanimously to thank the demonstrator "for this perfect demonstration of the exact and literal conformity of the statements given in Holy Scripture with the latest results of science."

This anecdote illustrates the ease with which many Christians accommodated the nebular hypothesis to their understanding of the Bible. By mid-century, many Bible believers had abandoned the notion that the Mosaic account of Creation limited the history of the world to six thousand years. One American observer estimated that, by the early 1850s, only about half of the Christian public still believed in a young earth. Orthodox Christians were not repudiating the authenticity of Genesis, but many were reinterpreting it in the light of modern science. Some chose to read the "days" of Genesis 1 as representing vast geological ages; others argued for inserting a chronological gap between the original Creation of the earth mentioned in the first verse of Genesis 1 and the allegedly much later six-day Creation described in the following verses.

The first explicit attempt to harmonize the nebular cosmogony with Genesis 1 came from the Swiss-American geographer Arnold Guyot (1807–84), who viewed the days of Genesis as six great epochs of creative activity. As he saw it, the nebular development of the solar system occurred during the first three of these epochs. The formless "waters" mentioned by Moses symbolized gaseous matter. The light of the first "day" was generated by chemical action as this gas concentrated into nebulae. The dividing of the waters on the second "day" corresponded to the breaking up of the nebulae into various planetary systems, of which ours was only one. On the third "day," the earth condensed to form a solid globe; on the fourth, the nebulous vapors surrounding our globe dispersed to allow the light of the sun to shine on the earth. This striking correlation between the cosmogonies of Moses and Laplace moved one writer to ask rhetorically: "if Moses had actually, in prophetic vision, seen the changes contemplated in this theory taking place, could he have described them more accurately, in popular language, free from the technicalities of science?" During the second half of the nineteenth century, no one did more to popularize Guyot's exegesis than the Yale geologist James Dwight Dana (1813–95).

The widespread acceptance of cosmogonical evolu-

tion before 1859 contributed significantly to the willingness of some Christians to accept organic evolution after that date. Like historical geology, the nebular hypothesis argued for an ancient world. It also promoted an interpretation of Genesis 1 congenial to theories of organic development. If the creation of the solar system resulted from an extended process rather than an instantaneous act, it seemed to increase the likelihood that the organic world also arose from a process. Advocates of biological evolution were quick to use the acceptance of the nebular hypothesis as an argument for embracing their views. As the Harvard botanist Asa Gray (1810–88) pointed out: "the scientific mind of an age which contemplates the solar system as evolved from a common revolving fluid mass . . . cannot be expected to let the old belief about species pass unquestioned." The experience of reconciling the nebular hypothesis with a theistic view of nature and with the Mosaic account of Creation gave comfort to those who might otherwise have viewed biological evolution as a threat to natural and revealed religion. After all, Laplace's theory had once been condemned by some as heretical, but time had proved them wrong.

The nebular hypothesis convinced many nineteenth-century Christians that the solar system was a product of natural law rather than divine miracle. For such persons, its acceptance permanently erased all notions of supernaturally created planetary bodies. When the scientific inadequacies of the Laplacian theory became evident around the turn of the twentieth century and cosmogonists turned increasingly to competing views (such as the planetesimal hypothesis that the solar system owed its origin to matter drawn off from our ancestral sun when a passing star approached close enough to produce a large-scale tidal effect), no one with any scientific pretensions gave consideration to miraculous explanations. Among those who expressed themselves on the subject, few seemed to care much anymore whether or not the proposed substitutes harmonized with the Mosaic story of Creation or the once cherished doctrines of natural theology. For all but the most conservative Christians, the nebular hypothesis had established natural law in the heavens.

For citations to sources quoted, see under Acknowledgments.

See also Anthropic Principle; Copernican Revolution; Pre-Copernican Astronomy; Theories of the Earth and Its Age Before Darwin; Twentieth-Century Cosmologies

BIBLIOGRAPHY

Brooke, J. H. "Nebular Contraction and the Expansion of Naturalism." *British Journal for the History of Science* 12 (1979): 200–11.

Brush, Stephen G. *A History of Modern Planetary Physics.* 3 vols. Cambridge: Cambridge University Press, 1996.

Collier, Katharine Brownell. *Cosmogonies of Our Fathers: Some Theories of the Seventeenth and Eighteenth Centuries.* New York: Columbia University Press, 1934.

Jaki, Stanley L. *Planets and Planetarians: A History of Theories of the Origin of Planetary Systems.* New York: Wiley, 1978.

Kubrin, David. "Newton and the Cyclical Cosmos: Providence and the Mechanical Philosophy." *Journal of the History of Ideas* 28 (1967): 325–46.

———. "Providence and the Mechanical Philosophy: The Creation and Dissolution of the World in Newtonian Thought: A Study of the Relations of Science and Religion in Seventeenth Century England." Ph.D. diss., Cornell University, 1969.

Lawrence, Philip. "Heaven and Earth: The Relation of the Nebular Hypothesis to Geology." In *Cosmology, History, and Theology,* ed. by Wolfgang Yourgrau and Allen D. Breck. New York: Plenum, 1977, 253–81.

Numbers, Ronald L. *Creation by Natural Law: Laplace's Nebular Hypothesis in American Thought.* Seattle: University of Washington Press, 1977.

Ogilvie, Marilyn Bailey. "Robert Chambers and the Nebular Hypothesis." *British Journal for the History of Science* 8 (1975): 214–32.

Schaffer, Simon. "The Nebular Hypothesis and the Science of Progress." In *History, Humanity, and Evolution: Essays for John C. Greene,* ed. by James R. Moore. Cambridge: Cambridge University Press, 1989, 131–64.

Schweber, Silvan S. "Auguste Comte and the Nebular Hypothesis." In *In the Presence of the Past: Essays in Honor of Frank Manuel,* ed. by Richard T. Bienvenu and Mordechai Feingold. Dordrecht: Kluwer, 1991, 131–91.

65. GEOCENTRICITY

Robert J. Schadewald

From the time the earth was discovered to be a sphere, most Western thinkers have positioned it at the center of the universe. When the heliocentric view triumphed in the centuries following Copernicus, some conservative Christians still held to geocentricity, insisting that the Bible required it. During the last third of the twentieth century, the geocentric view has even made a comeback among a few ultraconservative Christians as an adjunct to creation science.

The Pythagoreans, who were among the first to advocate the sphericity of the earth (in the fifth century B.C.), also held that the sun was the center of the universe. Although the spherical view triumphed among Greek thinkers within a century, heliocentricity quickly faded from sight. About 350 B.C., Aristotle (384–322 B.C.) argued in *On the Heavens* that the earth must necessarily be immovable and located at the center of the universe. This view became a fundamental postulate of the Hellenistic system of astronomy, which Claudius Ptolemy (second century A.D.) completed in a form that lasted for a millennium.

In the Christian church, some early Fathers maintained belief in a flat earth, but most accepted a spherical earth centered in the midst of the firmament. Influential thinkers such as Ambrose (c. 339–97), Jerome (c. 347–420), and Augustine (354–430) endorsed the latter view. By late-medieval times, Ptolemaic astronomy had been thoroughly integrated into Christian thinking.

The Copernican Revolution

Nicholas Copernicus (1473–1543) revived heliocentric astronomy in his *Revolutions of the Heavenly Bodies,* published in the year of his death. Although his system aroused great interest among astronomers, it did not gain their immediate and universal acceptance. The Danish astronomer Tycho Brahe (1546–1601), the best observer of the pretelescopic era, rejected the Copernican system and, instead, promoted a geocentric system. In the so-called Tychonic system, the sun and the moon orbit the earth, and the planets orbit the sun. In England, geographer and astronomer Nathaneal Carpenter (1588–c. 1628) advocated a modified Tychonic system, with the earth rotating on its axis daily. In France, the astronomer Jean Dominique Cassini (1625–1712) rejected the Copernican system in favor of a Tychonic system modified to use oval-shaped curves ("Cassinians") for the orbits of heavenly bodies.

Galileo Galilei (1564–1642), who first used a telescope for astronomy, adopted the Copernican system, as did Johannes Kepler (1571–1630), who discovered that planetary orbits are ellipses, with the sun at one focus. Isaac Newton (1642–1727) provided an elegant theoretical basis for a Copernican system with Keplerian orbits in his *Principia* (1687), and heliocentricity rapidly triumphed among astronomers in the following decades.

Religious opponents of Copernican astronomy cited numerous Scriptures to justify their position, while supporters of the new astronomy (like Galileo) argued that the biblical descriptions employed metaphorical or phenomonological, rather than scientific, language. Taken literally, the Bible describes an immovable earth and a mobile sun (e.g., "He has fixed the earth firm, immovable," 1 Chron. 16:30 *New English Bible;* cf. Psalms 93:1, 96:10, 104:5, and Is. 45:18). At Gibeon, Joshua commanded the sun to stand still but said nothing about the earth ceasing to rotate (Josh. 10:12). Likewise, when Isaiah moved the shadow on the dial of Ahaz, it was the sun that moved ten degrees (Is. 38:8).

Initially tolerant, the Roman Catholic Church eventually stood against Copernican astronomy. Because of Galileo's advocacy of Copernicanism, the *Revolutions of the Heavenly Bodies* was put on the Index of Prohibited Books in 1616, and Galileo was forbidden to teach heliocentricity. After he continued to do so, Galileo was charged with "a vehement suspicion of heresy" in 1633, forced to abjure, and confined under house arrest for the rest of his life. The prosecution of Galileo occurred as the heliocentric view was beginning to make rapid gains. During the following century, opposition faded, and most scientists (and Christians) accepted heliocentricity.

Sectarian Geocentric Systems

Outside the mainstream, however, geocentricity persisted among religious sectarians. Some sects developed unique astronomical systems. For example, John Reeve (1608–58) and Lodowicke Muggleton (1609–98) founded a modestly successful sect known as the Muggletonians. Their doctrines included a unique cosmology with a spherical earth, heaven no more than six miles up, a moon that shines by its own light, and lunar eclipses caused by an unseen planetary body. One sect member, Isaac Frost, published a detailed description and defense of the Muggletonian astronomical system in 1846 in *Two Systems of Astronomy*.

Lieutenant Richard Brothers (1757–1825), self-proclaimed nephew of God and prince of the Hebrews, developed another sectarian geocentric system while in a London asylum for prophesying the imminent death of King George III. In *The Universe as It Is: Describing the Sun, Moon, Stars, and Comets, with Their Daily Motions Round the Earth, Which Is at Rest!* (c. 1796), Brothers taught that the sun is an egg-shaped ball of heat and light that moves through space large-end first. The moon is a rough body of ice, and the stars also are made of ice, created (like the moon) from waters above the firmament (Gen. 1:6). Two followers, John Finlayson and Bartholomew Prescot, published works defending Brothers's astronomy. When Brothers died in 1825, for all practical purposes his astronomical system died with him.

Martin Luther (1483–1546), like most of his contemporaries, dismissed Copernicus's theory of a heliocentric universe, and perhaps that fact explains why modern geocentric beliefs seem to have been more common among Lutherans than among those of other denominations. For example, in Germany Pastor G. F. L. Knak (fl. 1868) earned the ridicule of German intellectuals for his geo-

centric views. In America, Pastor C. F. W. Walther (1811–87), the first president of the Lutheran Church Missouri Synod (LCMS), disparaged Copernican astronomy in the pages of the synod's official publication, *Der Lutheraner*. Walther's intellectual successor in the LCMS, theologian F. A. O. Pieper (1852–1931), also rejected Copernicanism. It is not surprising that most geocentric works published in America between 1870 and 1920 were written by members (mainly clergymen) of the LCMS and that geocentricity was widely taught within the synod.

In 1873, the synod's St. Louis printing office published and distributed a geocentric pamphlet entitled *Astronomische Unterredung zwischen einem Liebhaber der Astronomie und mehreren berumten Astronomer der Neuzeit* (*Astronomical Conversation between a Lover of Astronomy and Several Famous Modern-Day Astronomers*) by J. C. W. Lindemann, head of an LCMS teacher's college. Pastor J. R. L. Lange, another LCMS clergyman, published at least three geocentric pamphlets: *Die Unhaltbarkeit des kopernikanischen Systems* (*The Untenability of the Copernican System*) in 1895, *The Copernican System: The Greatest Absurdity in the History of Human Thought* in 1901, and *Antikopernikanische Aufzeichnungen* (*Anti-Copernican Notes*) in 1907. Lange advocated the Tychonian system, and his works reveal some familiarity with the history of science, especially with the history of astronomy.

Perhaps the most prolific LCMS geocentrist was Frederick E. Pasche (1872–1954), who wrote two substantial geocentric books in German: *Christliche Weltanschauung: Kosmogonie und Astronomie* (*Christian Worldview: Cosmogony and Astronomy*) in 1904 and *Bibel und Astronomie* (*Bible and Astronomy*) in 1906. In 1915, Pasche published a forty-nine-page pamphlet entitled *Fifty Reasons: Copernicus or the Bible?* As the twentieth century progressed, however, geocentricity within the LCMS largely faded from view.

Geocentricity and Modern Creationism

The modern resurgence of geocentricity began in North America in 1967, when Canadian schoolmaster Walter van der Kamp (1913–98) circulated a geocentric paper entitled "The Heart of the Matter" to about fifty Christian individuals and institutions. Van der Kamp received only four favorable responses, one from Canadian astronomer Harold L. Armstrong, who subsequently (1973) became editor of the *Creation Research Society Quarterly* (CRSQ), and another from Pastor Walter Lang, a Missouri Synod Lutheran and founder of the *Bible-Science Newsletter,* who was also sympathetic. Van der Kamp made presentations on the Tychonian system in 1975 and 1976 at conferences sponsored by the Bible-Science Association (BSA). From these seeds grew the Tychonian Society and its journal, the *Bulletin of the Tychonian Society.*

Two Cleveland astronomers, James N. Hanson and Gerardus Bouw, were among the early converts and, in the summer of 1978, they organized what was perhaps the world's first geocentric conference. Early in 1984, Walter van der Kamp retired as leader of the Tychonian Society and editor of the *Bulletin,* and Bouw succeeded him. The next year, Bouw was chief organizer of the BSA-sponsored 1985 National Creation Conference. This conference included several geocentric papers, and its grand finale was a spirited two-hour debate on the scriptural and scientific merits of geocentricity. In 1990, Bouw reorganized the Tychonian Society as the Association for Biblical Astronomy and changed the name of the *Bulletin* to *The Biblical Astronomer.* Two years later, he organized another conference on geocentricity, which was held in conjunction with a major creationism conference.

Modern geocentrists have produced several books advocating Tychonian astronomy. Bouw's two books, *With Every Wind of Doctrine* (1984) and *Geocentricity* (1992), are the most sophisticated defenses of geocentricity ever published, and the only ones written by an astronomer with a Ph.D. from a first-class university (Case Western Reserve). In 1988, Walter van der Kamp published a small geocentric book, *De Labore Solis: Airy's Failure Reconsidered.* In 1991, Marshall Hall of the creationist Fair Education Foundation published *The Earth Is Not Moving.*

All modern American geocentrists seem to be young-earth creationists who hold that the Bible compels them to reject Copernicus along with Charles Darwin (1809–82). The variant of the Tychonian system advocated by the Association for Biblical Astronomy can predict exactly the same relative motions between celestial bodies as the conventional system. This fact makes it far more coherent than Flood geology, which often is helpless to account for geologic data. Nevertheless, most creationists seem embarrassed by geocentricity. With a few exceptions, leading young-earth creationists publicly ignore (and often privately disparage) the geocentrists, who remain a small minority within the movement.

See also Copernican Revolution; Flat-Earthism; Galileo Galilei; Pre-Copernican Astronomy

BIBLIOGRAPHY

Bouw, Gerardus. *With Every Wind of Doctrine.* Cleveland: Tychonian Society, 1984.

———. *Geocentricity.* Cleveland: Association for Biblical Astronomy, 1992.

Hall, Marshall. *The Earth Is Not Moving.* Cornelia, Ga.: Fair Education Foundation, 1991.

Schadewald, Robert J. "Scientific Creationism, Geocentricity, and the Flat Earth." *Skeptical Inquirer* (Winter 1981–2): 41–7.

———. "The Evolution of Bible Science." In *Scientists Confront Creationism,* ed. by Laurie Godfrey. New York: Norton, 1983, 283–99.

Stimson, Dorothy. *The Gradual Acceptance of the Copernican Theory of the Universe.* New York: By the author, 1917.

van der Kamp, Walter. *De Labore Solis: Airy's Failure Reconsidered.* Pitt Meadows, B.C.: By the author, [1988].

66. FLAT-EARTHISM

Robert J. Schadewald

Modern flat-earthism arose in Victorian England among conservative Christians who saw conflict between conventional astronomy and a literal reading of the Bible. Though never a large or influential group, the British flat-earthers formed a raucous subculture that assaulted spherical science in lectures, books, pamphlets, and periodicals. By the end of the nineteenth century, the movement had spread throughout the English-speaking world. A faithful remnant survives.

The ancient Greeks introduced the notion of the spherical form of the earth to the Western world. The Pythagoreans (c. 500 B.C.) were among the first to hold that view. By the late fourth century B.C., Aristotle (384–322 B.C.) could cite several empirical proofs for sphericity, and most Greek philosophers considered the issue settled. The concept spread in the ancient Near East with the Hellenistic diffusion (323–30 B.C.)

The Bible never explicitly states its cosmology, but, when it is pieced together from scattered passages, it resembles the Babylonian cosmology. The Babylonians considered the earth essentially flat, with a continental mass standing above and surrounded by an ocean. The vault of the sky was a physical object resting on the ocean's waters. The biblical Creation sequence meshes well with this view. On the first day, God creates a formless, desolate earth (Gen. 1:2). On the second day, he creates the vault of heaven (the "firmament" [King James Version]) to divide the waters. The sun, moon, and stars, created on the fourth day, are inside the vault.

Elsewhere, the vault of heaven is viewed as a solid object, "hard as a mirror of cast metal" (Job 37:18 New English Bible), and an admirable feat of craftsmanship (Ps. 19:1, Job 9:8, Ps. 102:25, Is. 45:12 and 48:13). God "walks to and fro on the vault of heaven" (Job 22:14), and people below look as small as grasshoppers (Is. 40:22). An object high in the sky is visible from anywhere on the earth (Dan. 4:10–11, Rev. 1:7), and, from a high-enough mountain, one can see all of the kingdoms of the universe (Matt. 4:8). The stars are small, and all of them can fall to the earth without eradicating human life (Rev. 6:13).

The Early Church and Medieval Views

As a group, the Fathers of the Church have been, by turns, wrongly indicted for rampant flat-earthism and just as wrongly exonerated. Among the Greek Fathers, the Alexandrian school, led by Clement (c. 155–c. 220) and Origen (c. 185–c. 251), interpreted Scripture allegorically and generally accepted sphericity. The less-influential Antiochene school, however, insisted on historico-grammatical exegesis and rejected a spherical earth. For example, Antiochenes John Chrysostom (349–407), Theodore of Mopsuestia (c. 350–428), Diodorus of Tarsus (d. 394), and Severianus of Gabala (fl. 400–8) all condemned sphericity. The Latin Fathers, with notable exceptions, such as Lactantius (c. 240–c. 320), always accepted a spherical earth. With the rise of the Western church in the fourth and fifth centuries under the influence of Ambrose (c. 339–97), Jerome (c. 347–420), and Augustine (354–430), all of whom explicitly endorsed sphericity, flat-earthism rapidly became a nonissue in the Church.

In the Middle Ages, flat-earthism was rare among the educated. Theologians argued over whether the antipodes (the opposite side of the globe) could be inhabited, but no coherent intellectual tradition of flat-earthism existed in the West. Despite this fact, a persistent modern myth holds that flat-earthism was rampant at the time of Columbus (1451–1506). According to the myth, Columbus had to convince the Spanish court that the earth is a globe before Ferdinand and Isabella would finance his voyage of discovery. Then the heroic mariner had to subdue an ignorant crew whose members feared they would sail off the edge of the earth. Most of this is nonsense and is ultimately based on Washington Irving's *History of the Life and Voyages of Columbus,* first published in 1828. Irving loved a good story, and he created a dramatic scene, set at the Spanish University of Salamanca, in which Columbus argued the case for sphericity against churchmen who insisted that the earth is flat. It is all pure fiction, but it is endlessly repeated in popular writings, and even some professional historians have accepted it.

The Rebirth of Flat-Earthism

Samuel Birley Rowbotham (c. 1816–84), an itinerant lecturer and proponent of alternative medicine, founded the modern flat-earth movement in England in 1849. Under the pseudonym "Parallax," Rowbotham toured England for thirty-five years, attacking conventional astronomy in public lectures. Although he focused his lectures on scientific arguments, Rowbotham also emphasized the biblical basis of "zetetic" (flat-earth) astronomy, and he cited seventy-six scriptural passages in support of a flat earth in the last chapter of his seminal *Earth Not a Globe* (1873).

   Zetetic astronomy teaches that the known world is a vast circular plane, with the north pole at its center and an impassible wall of ice marking the "southern limit." The sun, moon, and planets circle above the earth in the region of the equator, roughly halfway between the north pole and the southern limit. Atmospheric refraction and perspective explain the rising and setting of celestial bodies and ships disappearing over the horizon. The vault of heaven encloses the known world.

   The zetetics gained enormous publicity when the famous naturalist Alfred Russel Wallace (1823–1913) foolishly accepted a challenge from zetetic John Hampden (c. 1820–91) to "prove the rotundity and revolution of the world from Scripture, from reason, or from fact." The two men wagered £500 on the outcome of an experiment performed at the Old Bedford Canal on March 5, 1870. Wallace proved the curvature of the canal's surface to the satisfaction of the stakeholder, who handed over the cash. Hampden refused to accept the result, and he

spent the next two decades vilifying Wallace in letters to the editor, pamphlets, and short-lived flat-earth periodicals such as the *Truth-Seeker's Oracle and Scriptural Science Review* (1876) and *Earth: Scripturally, Rationally, and Practically Described* (1886–8). Various legal actions kept the fiasco in the public eye, and Hampden became a zetetic hero.

   By the early 1890s, zetetic astronomy had scattered supporters among religious conservatives, especially Adventists, who interpreted the Bible literally. Adventists affiliated with the Conditional Immortality Mission in England led in the founding of the Universal Zetetic Society (UZS) in 1892. Soon afterward, the UZS journal, *Earth—Not a Globe!—Review* (1893–7), appeared under the editorship of Albert Smith (fl. 1884–1918), a former Seventh-day Adventist elder. Within a year, the UZS had members and agents all over the English-speaking world. After the *Earth Review* folded, the UZS continued under the leadership of Lady Elizabeth Anne Mould Blount (1850–after 1923), who founded *Earth,* another short-lived zetetic journal. Lady Blount lectured frequently, sometimes to audiences of a thousand or more. The London-based UZS was apparently a casualty of World War I. By then, flat-earthism was well rooted in America.

Flat-Earthism in America

A New York Zetetic Society had been organized in 1873, but it quickly faded from view. Serious flat-earth agitation in the United States began when William Carpenter (c. 1830–96), a well-known British flat-earther, immigrated to Baltimore in 1880. His pamphlet, *One Hundred Proofs That the Earth Is Not a Globe* (1885), went through more than a dozen editions, and he lectured widely in the northeast. Alexander Gleason (1827–1909), a Seventh-day Adventist from Buffalo, New York, was another well-known nineteenth-century American flat-earther. Gleason published two editions of *Is the Bible from Heaven? Is the Earth a Globe?* (1890 and 1893).

   Early in the twentieth century, Boston became the intellectual center of American flat-earthism, with its own branch of the UZS. Bostonians John G. Abizaid (fl. 1912–35), Charles W. Morse (fl. 1913), and Henry J. Goudey (fl. 1931) published works defending the zetetic view. American flat-earthism reached its pinnacle in Zion, Illinois, in the 1920s under Wilbur Glenn Voliva.

As general overseer of the Christian Catholic Apostolic Church of Zion, Voliva made flat-earthism a doctrine of the Church, and Zion's parochial schools taught that the earth is flat. Voliva lost power in Zion in the mid-1930s, and flat-earthism soon faded from view.

Postwar Revival

Samuel Shenton (d. 1971) and others revived flat-earthism in England in 1956, when they organized the International Flat Earth Society. Shenton, a sign painter by trade, was a tireless advocate, giving frequent flat-earth lectures in schools and elsewhere. Shenton gained publicity for the Flat Earth Society, but most of it was negative or frivolous. When he died, the mantle of leadership passed to Charles K. Johnson of Lancaster, California. In the *Flat Earth News,* Johnson emphasized facts from the natural world, such as that bodies of still water are flat. The Flat Earth Society has not proselytized beyond responding to inquiries.

See also Geocentricity; Pre-Copernican Astronomy

BIBLIOGRAPHY

Betten, Francis S. "The Knowledge of the Sphericity of the Earth During the Earlier Middle Ages." *Catholic Historical Review* 3 (1923): 74–90.

Carpenter, William. *One Hundred Proofs That the Earth Is Not a Globe.* Baltimore: Privately printed by the author, 1885. At least fifteen editions issued.

DeFord, Charles Sylvester. *A Reparation: Universal Gravitation a Universal Fake.* 3d ed. c. 1931. Reprint. Fairfield, Wash.: Ye Galleon, 1992.

Gardner, Martin. *Fads and Fallacies in the Name of Science.* New York: Dover, 1957.

Michell, John. *Eccentric Lives and Peculiar Notions.* San Diego, Calif.: Harcourt Brace Jovanovich, 1984.

Rowbotham, Samuel Birley (pseud. "Parallax"). *Earth Not a Globe.* 2d ed. London: John B. Day, 1873. Reissued as 3d ed. 1881. Sometimes cataloged as *Zetetic Astronomy.*

Russell, Jeffrey Burton. *Inventing the Flat Earth: Columbus and Modern Historians.* New York: Praeger, 1991.

Schadewald, Robert J. "He Knew Earth Is Round, but His Proof Fell Flat." *Smithsonian* 9 (April 1978): 101–13.

———. "The Flat-Out Truth: Earth Orbits? Moon Landings? A Fraud! Says This Prophet." *Science Digest* 88 (July 1980): 58–63.

———. "Scientific Creationism, Geocentricity, and the Flat Earth." *Skeptical Inquirer* 4 (Winter 1981–2): 41–7.

———. "The Earth Was Flat in Zion." *Fate* 42 (May 1989): 70–9.

———. "The Flat-Earth Movement." In *The Fringes of Reason: A Whole Earth Catalog,* ed. by Ted Schultz. New York: Harmony Books, 1989.

Seely, Paul H. "The Firmament and the Water Above," parts 1 and 2. *Westminster Theological Journal* 53 (1991): 227–40; 54 (1992): 31–46.

———. "The Geographical Meaning of 'Earth' and 'Seas' in Genesis 1:10." *Westminster Theological Journal* 59 (1997): 231–55.

67. TWENTIETH-CENTURY COSMOLOGIES

Craig Sean McConnell

The scientific study of the structure and the origin of the universe has changed enormously in the twentieth century. At the turn of the century, the most contentious issue was the nature of nebulae—whether they were part of our galaxy or independent "island universes" outside it. By the 1980s, big bang cosmology had become a subdiscipline of astrophysics with hundreds of practitioners and a constant place in the public eye. The interaction between cosmology and religion has also varied enormously in this period, ranging from disregard, to harmonious coexistence, to antagonistic opposition. The dynamics of this relationship have often been more dependent on the personalities of key figures in cosmology than on the intrinsic scientific content of the theories themselves.

In the nineteenth century, a careful distinction was made between the words "cosmogony" and "cosmology," the former referring only to theories of the origins of the universe or solar system, the latter to theories of the structure and the evolution of the universe after its creation. In the twentieth century, these terms have become conflated. In the first half of the century, cosmogony was used to refer to structure and evolution in addition to origins. By midcentury, the term "cosmology" was preferred, and, by the 1970s, "cosmogony" was an archaic word, unfamiliar to most. This essay traces the major developments in cosmogony, understood to be the study of both the origin and the structure of the universe, and the religious reaction to these theories. Adopting modern convention, these theories are referred to as cosmologies.

Observational and Theoretical Cosmology

For the first few decades of the twentieth century, two distinct lines of inquiry could properly be considered cosmology, but there was little religious reaction to either. The nature of nebulae was a major issue in observational astronomy that was debated in a public forum by Heber Curtis (1872–1942) and Harlow Shapley (1885–1972) in 1920. Shapley argued that nebulae were clouds of dust within our galaxy and that our galaxy was the extent of the observable universe. Curtis, echoing the work of John Herschel (1792–1871) and Jacobus Kapteyn (1851–1922), argued that nebulae were separate galaxies. The issue was settled when Edwin Hubble (1889–1953) and others observed separate stars in the Andromeda Nebula. This confirmation of the extragalactic nature of nebulae greatly expanded astronomers' estimate of the size of the universe, but it had nothing to say about the origin of the universe and attracted little, if any, religious discussion.

The other line of cosmological inquiry was opened in 1917, when Albert Einstein (1879–1955) turned his general theory of relativity to the consideration of the whole universe. Considering the interaction between gravitation and space-time at the largest imaginable scale, Einstein wrote equations that governed the whole cosmos. These equations implied a space-time that was curved, so that it was "closed," like the surface of a sphere, though it was "unbounded," in that a line without end could be drawn on the surface. The equations were also unstable, which implied that the universe was either expanding or contracting. Einstein thought that the universe was stable, so he added a term to the equations that would make the equations stable as well.

This work opened the field of modern theoretical cosmology, though few entered it right away. The mathematics that was required to consider cosmological problems in relativistic terms was notoriously difficult and esoteric, so only those concerned with these problems were able to follow the arguments they contained. Einstein's equations were soon challenged by Willem de Sitter (1872–1934), who demonstrated in 1917 that other cosmologies were possible, and by Aleksandr Friedman (1888–1925), who wrote equations in 1922 for an expanding universe, but these models were considered by most physicists to be "mathematical exercises" of no physical import. By the 1920s, a few religious writers were challenging the tenets of relativity, particularly the writings of moral relativists, but few had the mathematical skills to investigate these early theoretical cosmologies. Most of the debate about science and religion in the period before 1930 took place between creationists and evolutionists.

The Expanding Universe

Relativistic cosmology and observational astronomy were brought together in the work of Edwin Hubble and Georges Lemaître (1894–1966). Hubble's study of nebulae led him to the observation that the nebulae are all rushing away from the earth and from each other at a tremendous rate. Though there was initial confusion about how to interpret this observation, by 1930 most astronomers agreed that it meant that the universe itself was expanding. This expansion of the universe could be reconciled with Friedman's work, and Lemaître did just that. Lemaître was dedicated to linking the work of Friedman to that of Hubble, bringing observational evidence to bear on theoretical cosmology. Lemaître proposed that the expansion of the universe could be traced back to a very dense state in the distant past, in which the particles of the whole universe existed as a huge atomic nucleus. He called this nucleus the "primeval atom" and claimed that the expansion of the universe was the aftermath of a process analogous to radioactive decay that took place on a cosmic scale.

Lemaître's original publication appeared in an obscure Belgian journal, but Arthur Eddington (1882–1944) brought it to a larger audience by having it republished in the *Monthly Notices of the Royal Astronomical Society* and by featuring it in his popular book *The Expanding Universe* (1933). Eddington, a Quaker, made

overt attempts here to reconcile modern cosmology with religion, suggesting that science should include a spiritual as well as an intellectual appreciation of nature. James Jeans (1877–1946) did the same in his popular book *The Mysterious Universe* (1930). The Victoria Institute, a British association dedicated to reconciling science and religion, published a number of articles that were approving of the work of Eddington and Jeans. In particular, the distinction that was emerging between notions of an evolving universe, which might be consistent with theistic cosmology, and notions of evolving life, which seemed antagonistic to theistic descriptions of life, placated the members of the Victoria Institute.

In *God and the Universe* (1931), Chapman Cohen (1868–1954) took Eddington and Jeans to task for their conciliatory posture toward religion. This collection of essays, many of them previously published in the *Freethinker,* was sponsored by the Secular Society, a British antireligious organization. Cohen, who wanted to dismiss religion entirely, was annoyed at the presence of spiritual language in Eddington's *The Nature of the Physical World* (1928) and Jeans's *The Mysterious Universe* and was particularly irritated by the friendly reviews these books received from members of the clergy. Perhaps more influential was an attack by L. Susan Stebbing (1885–1943) in *Philosophy and the Physicists* (1937). Stebbing, who had more impressive academic credentials than Cohen, chided Eddington and Jeans for making unfounded emotional appeals to religion and for being bad philosophers as well. Subsequent popular works by both Eddington and Jeans contained fewer references to spiritual matters.

The Big Bang–Steady State Debate

Though Lemaître had hoped for an eventual synthesis of nuclear physics and theoretical cosmology, it was the work of George Gamow (1904–68) and his collaborators Ralph Alpher (1921–) and Robert Herman (1914–97) that brought the science of nuclear physics into modern cosmology. Gamow considered the heat that was required for nuclear reactions and the heat that he believed a primeval atom would contain in the first moments of its decay and proposed that the elements were formed in the first moments of this expansion. This work brought new attention to Lemaître's primeval atom and showed promise at first, but the theory suffered from several deficits. Gamow could not find a pathway of nuclear reactions to build elements of atomic number five. Worse, Hubble was refining his estimates for the age of the universe, and the figure was quite a bit shorter than the estimates for the age of the earth and the age of some stars.

A team of astronomers in England developed an entirely different cosmology in hope of setting these difficulties aside. According to their steady-state theory, the universe is eternal. The expansion of the universe has been going on forever and is not evidence of any special moment of Creation. Thomas Gold (1920–) and Hermann Bondi (1919–) developed this theory from the philosophical principle they called the Perfect Cosmological Principle. Just as Copernicus (1473–1543) had claimed that the earth does not occupy any special place in the universe, Gold and Bondi argued that the present does not occupy any special time in the universe. To explain the apparent constancy of the density of matter, they had to propose that matter is continuously created in space. A small amount of hydrogen (approximately one atom in a space the size of a school assembly hall every one hundred thousand years) would be enough to balance the observed expansion of the universe and would be so rare an occurrence that physicists would likely never see such a creation occur. While Gold and Bondi presented this theory in philosophical terms, their collaborator, Fred Hoyle (1915–) developed a relativistic field equation for the steady-state theory.

The popular and religious reaction to the debate between these competing theories—the big bang, as Hoyle derisively referred to the primeval-atom theories, and the steady-state theory—was enormous. Public lectures and debates were staged, many of them broadcast on radio and television. Pope Pius XII (b. 1876, p. 1939–58), in a speech to the Pontifical Academy of Science in 1951, endorsed Lemaître's primeval atom, an action that amused Gamow, irritated Hoyle, and horrified Lemaître. Gamow cited Pius XII in a paper he published in *Physical Review* (1952), though he tried to distance himself from the connection between cosmology and biblical Creation in his popular text *The Creation of the Universe* (1952). Lemaître, who was an ordained priest as well as a physicist, advocated a "separate spheres" approach to the issues of science and religion. He thought that they operated on different epistemological foundations and had little of merit to offer each other.

Hoyle often claimed that the religious resonance between Genesis and the big bang made people believe in the latter irrationally. His *The Nature of the Universe* (1950), ostensibly a defense of the steady-state theory, ends with a long diatribe against religion in general and Christianity in particular. Hoyle revisited these antireligious themes often, in his introductory astronomy textbook *Frontiers of Astronomy* (1955), his autobiographical musing *Ten Faces of the Universe* (1976), and his essay *The Origin of the Universe and the Origin of Religion* (1993). Ironically, some religious writers preferred Hoyle's steady-state theory on the grounds that the big bang seemed too deistic and that the hand of God was evident in a universe that was constantly balanced by the creation of new matter.

The Big Bang Paradigm

A series of observational discoveries in the late 1960s eventually settled the big bang–steady state debate in favor of the big bang, though the steady-state theory was never fully abandoned by Bondi, Gold, or Hoyle. However, the debate raged on in fundamentalist Christian circles long after the issue was considered settled among astronomers and physicists. Indeed, the steady-state theory attracted new adherents in the pages of the *Creation Research Society Quarterly*. This renewed interest in steady-state theory seems to have been largely motivated by the desire to discredit evolution by proxy—big bang cosmology and evolutionary biology were seen to be complementary theories, so a refutation of the evolutionary big bang might challenge biological evolutionary thought as well.

In an ironic bit of turnaround, Fred Hoyle's collaborator and colleague Chandra Wickramasinghe (1939–) was called as an expert witness for the creationists in the 1981 Arkansas Creation-Evolution Trial, and Hoyle's work was enlisted in the defense of creationism. Hoyle and Wickramasinghe argued for the necessity of a cosmic Creator, based on calculations estimating the probability of life originating on the earth in the available time frame. Though Hoyle remained elusive about the exact nature of this Creator, Wickramasinghe associated the Creator directly with his Buddhist beliefs. Hoyle and Wickramasinghe also made claims about extraterrestrial origins of life and were largely marginalized in the scientific community. Philosopher of science Michael Ruse, testifying on behalf of the evolutionists, occasionally conflated big bang cosmology with evolution, but, for the most part, the trial was focused on the biological sciences.

In the 1970s and 1980s, some cosmologists returned to a more harmonious representation of the relationship between cosmology and religion. British cosmologists such as Paul Davies (1946– ; emigrated to Australia in 1990) in his *God and the New Physics* (1983) have returned to speaking of cosmology and religion as addressing the same questions, while American cosmologists have largely ignored the question of the religious implications of cosmology. A noticeable exception is *The Physics of Immortality* (1994), in which Frank Tipler (1947–) claims to have reduced theology to a subdiscipline of physics. He uses cosmological arguments to demonstrate the existence of God and the certainty of an afterlife. The book sold well, though it received numerous skeptical reviews.

Consideration of cosmology by religious thinkers has typically been overshadowed by consideration of evolution. For many, cosmology is not as personally offensive as evolutionary biology. Others find cosmology so speculative that it is not worthy of protracted rebuttal. The esoteric mathematics of general relativity, the language of cosmology since 1917, makes it hard for most people to engage the arguments. Religious scientists concerned with reconciling science and religion have typically studied subjects in geology and evolution, and, in fact, many of the discussions of cosmology and theology drift back into discussions of evolution and theology.

See also Chaos Theory; Cosmogonies from 1700 to 1900; Physics; Roman Catholicism Since Trent

BIBLIOGRAPHY

Bertotti, Bruno, Roberto Balbinot, Silvio Bergia, and Antonio Messina, eds. *Modern Cosmology in Retrospect.* Cambridge: Cambridge University Press, 1990.

Hetherington, Norriss S., ed. *Encyclopedia of Cosmology: Historical, Philosophical, and Scientific Foundations of Modern Cosmology.* New York: Garland, 1993.

Jaki, Stanley. *Science and Creation: From Eternal Cycles to an Oscillating Universe.* New York: Science History Publications, 1974.

———. *God and the Cosmologists.* Washington, D.C.: Regnery Gateway, 1989.

Kragh, Helge. *Cosmology and Controversy: The Historical Development of Two Theories of the Universe.* Princeton, N.J.: Princeton University Press, 1996.

McMullin, Ernan. "Religion and Cosmology." In *Encyclopedia of Cosmology: Historical, Philosophical, and Scientific Foundations of Modern Cosmology,* ed. by Norriss S. Hetherington. New York: Garland, 1993, 579–95.

Munitz, Milton. *Theories of the Universe.* New York: Free Press, 1965.

North, John. *The Measure of the Universe: A History of Modern Cosmology.* London: Oxford University Press, 1965.

———. *Astronomy and Cosmology.* New York: Norton, 1995.

Numbers, Ronald L. *The Creationists: The Evolution of Scientific Creationism.* New York: Knopf, 1992.

Singh, Jagjit. *Great Ideas and Theories of Modern Cosmology.* New York: Dover, 1970.

Smith, Robert. *The Expanding Universe: Astronomy's 'Great Debate,' 1900–1931.* Cambridge: Cambridge University Press, 1982.

Yourgrau, Wolfgang, and Allen Breck, eds. *Cosmology, History, and Theology.* New York: Plenum, 1977.

68. THE ANTHROPIC PRINCIPLE

William Lane Craig

The Anthropic Principle is a statement of the fact that our own existence as observers acts as a selection effect determining which properties of the universe can be observed by us. The principle states that we can observe only those properties that are compatible with our own existence. When conjoined with the hypothesis that our observable universe is but one member of a wider collection of universes (a World Ensemble), the Anthropic Principle may be used to explain away the unimaginably improbable fine-tuning of our universe for intelligent life, which otherwise strengthens the evidential base of the traditional teleological argument for the existence of God. If the World Ensemble comprises universes having every physically possible combination of fundamental parameters, then by chance alone our universe will appear somewhere in the collection. Since we can observe only those combinations of properties compatible with our existence, we should not be surprised to discover that the observable universe is fine-tuned for our existence. The Anthropic Principle is, thus, significant as scientific naturalism's most recent attempt to stave off inference to a divine Designer of the cosmos.

Origin and Definition

The expression "Anthropic Principle" was originally coined in 1970 by astrophysicist Brandon Carter, who formulated the principle in an attempt to come to grips with the so-called large-number coincidences in contemporary cosmology, which had motivated exotic explanatory theories by P. A. M. Dirac and Pascual Jordan. Drawing upon cosmologist Hermann Bondi's (1919–) list of three such coincidences, Carter argued that, while the first could have been theoretically predicted by con-

ventional explanations, the second and the third could have been theoretically predicted by means of "anthropic" principles stating that what we can expect to observe must be restricted by the conditions necessary for our presence as observers. Carter's use of the word "anthropic" has occasioned confusion among subsequent writers. It was no part of his argument to single out human beings as special; rather, his concern was with "any organism describable as an observer" (quoted in Leslie 1990, 131). His claim was that, once we realize that the relevant coincidences are related to the conditions necessary for the existence of observers, then we should expect to observe such coincidences.

Unfortunately, discussion of the Anthropic Principle has been characterized by a good deal of obscurity and sloppiness. For example, Carter distinguished between a "weak" and a "strong" Anthropic Principle. The weak principle states that *our temporal location* in the history of the universe acts as a selection effect on what we can observe, while the strong principle—which Carter misleadingly formulates as stating that the universe "must be such as to admit the creation of observers within it at some stage" (Leslie 1990, 129)—asserts that *our very existence* constrains what values of the fundamental parameters of the universe we can observe. Basically, the difference between the two seems to be merely a matter of extent and does not signal a distinction in kind.

Carter's misleading language led subsequent anthropic theorizers like John Barrow and Frank Tipler to harden the distinction between the weak and the strong versions, such that the strong version affirms that "the Universe must have those properties which allow life to develop within it at some stage in its history" (Barrow and Tipler 1986, 21). This version is sometimes misrepresented as the position favored by natural theology (when, in fact, that tradition affirms God's freedom to create whatever universe he pleases). At other times, it is misconstrued to be the metaphysical affirmation of the existence of a World Ensemble, in which case the word "Universe" in the above quotation must refer to the ensemble of universes (but then it does not have a single history, as the strong version states). At the most extreme, the principle is interpreted as the outlandish "Participatory Anthropic Principle," according to which, observers retro-causally bring the universe into being.

According to Barrow and Tipler, the weak principle "is in no way speculative or controversial. It expresses only the fact that those properties of the Universe we are able to discern are self-selected by the fact that they must be consistent with our own evolution and present existence" (Barrow and Tipler 1986, 16). If the principle is to have the universal and compelling character attributed to it by Barrow and Tipler, it must be the tautologous statement that, if the universe is observed by observers that have evolved within it, then its fundamental parameters are such as to allow the evolution of observers within it. Even if we affirm the contingent statement that we are such observers, all that follows is that the fundamental parameters of the universe are such as to allow the evolution of observers within it. But why it has those parameters is left unexplained.

The World Ensemble Hypothesis

Carter claimed that a prediction based on the Anthropic Principle could be promoted to the status of an explanation by conjoining to it the hypothesis of a World Ensemble (an ensemble of universes characterized by all conceivable combinations of initial conditions and fundamental constants). Carter thus sought to explain the observed value of the gravitational coupling constant, which is finely tuned for intelligent life. In making this claim, Carter implicitly moves into territory also claimed by natural theology's teleological argument. The fine-tuning of the gravitational force is but one of a plethora of delicately balanced physical quantities, many given in the Big Bang itself as initial conditions, upon which intelligent life depends. Just as William Paley (1743–1805) compiled a vast array of evidence from eighteenth-century science for the hypothesis of intelligent design of the natural world, so Barrow and Tipler in their massive study have presented a staggering survey of the evidence from contemporary physics and astrophysics, classical cosmology, quantum mechanics, and biochemistry for the fine-tuning of our universe for intelligent life. Barrow and Tipler reject Paley's hypothesis of intelligent design in favor of Carter's anthropic explanation because (1) modern science stresses the unfinished character of nature and, thus, its dissimilarity to a completed watch (Paley's analogy); and (2) we should hesitate to draw far-reaching conclusions about ultimate reality from scientific theories that are mere approximations of the world. But Paley himself argued that, in order to recognize design, we need not be confronted with a perfectly functioning mechanism; his argument does not presuppose a completed and perfect natural world. Barrow and Tipler's second objection is Janus-faced, since they themselves embrace the speculative hypothesis of a World Ensemble to avoid the hypothesis of design.

Indeed, as the above makes clear, any explanatory power residing in anthropic explanations actually resides wholly in the World Ensemble hypothesis, not in the Anthropic Principle, which is, in itself, trivial. As Carter explicitly states: "The acceptability of predictions of this kind as explanations depends on one's attitude to the world ensemble concept" (quoted in Leslie 1990, 133). In the absence of a World Ensemble, the Anthropic Principle is explanatorily vacuous. From the obvious fact that we should not be surprised that we do not observe fundamental conditions incompatible with our existence, it simply does not follow that we should not be surprised that we do, in fact, observe fundamental conditions compatible with our existence. That such improbably fine-tuned conditions should uniquely exist is amazing, even though we should not be here to notice if they did not.

What advantage is there, then, in the World Ensemble hypothesis over against the hypothesis of divine design? John Leslie, the philosopher who has addressed most thoroughly the Anthropic Principle and the complex of issues it involves, points out that there is no evidence for any of the ensemble theories apart from the fact of intelligent life itself and that any such evidence is equally evidence for intelligent design. Moreover, each of the many-worlds theories faces formidable scientific and philosophical objections. Leslie argues that the hypothesis of divine design is neither more obscure nor less scientific than the hypothesis of a World Ensemble. Scientists should, therefore, consider the hypothesis of a divine Designer or else admit that they simply have no interest in the question.

See also Design Argument; Natural Theology

BIBLIOGRAPHY

Barrow, John D., and Frank J. Tipler. *The Anthropic Cosmological Principle.* Oxford: Clarendon, 1986.

Craig, William Lane. "The Teleological Argument and the Anthropic Principle." In *The Logic of Rational Theism,* ed. by William Lane Craig and Mark S. McLeod. Problems in Contemporary Philosophy 24. Lewiston, N.Y.: Edwin Mellen, 1990.

Leslie, John, ed. *Universes.* London: Routledge, 1989.

———. *Physical Cosmology and Philosophy.* Philosophical Topics. New York: Macmillan, 1990.

Paley, William. *Natural Theology; or, Evidences of the Existence and Attributes of the Deity, Collected from the Appearances of Nature.* 1802. Reprint. Houston: St. Thomas, 1972.

PART VI

The Physical Sciences

69. PHYSICS

Richard Olson

Physics (*physique* [French], *physicae* [Latin], or *physik* [German]) became widely used in its modern sense (that is, excluding the life sciences, geology, and chemistry) during the second half of the eighteenth century. As late as 1879, however, the major English-language textbook that covered what we call physics was Sir William Thomson (Lord Kelvin [1824–1907]) and Peter Guthrie Tait's (1831–1901) *Treatise on Natural Philosophy,* and university courses in Britain and America were still labeled courses in natural philosophy. Hence, this discussion of the religious elements in, and the implications of, physics begins about the middle of the eighteenth century and counts as physicists many figures who identified themselves as natural philosophers.

The periodization of physics is also unusual, and its labeling is inconsistent with general philosophical and literary usage. Topics treated before the middle of the last decade of the nineteenth century—mechanics, optics, heat, electricity and magnetism, hydrostatics and hydrodynamics—coupled with the theories and procedures that existed before 1897 to treat them are said to be parts of *classical* physics; whereas a group of topics that emerged after about 1895, including natural radioactivity, quantum physics (subatomic, atomic, molecular, plasma, and solid-state), as well as special and general relativity, is said to make up *modern* physics. Modern physics not only challenged the physical intuitions associated with classical physics, it also seemed to many to suggest very different religious implications. Hence, the following discussion is separated into classical and modern periods, dividing the two in the first decade of the twentieth century.

Classical Physics and Religion

During the first half of the eighteenth century, the most important and characteristic interactions between religion and natural philosophy occurred in connection with Newtonian natural theology, several features of which are important to recognize to set the stage for the religious impact of post-Newtonian developments in physics. First, Newtonian natural theology emphasized the need for some kind of active, nonmaterial agent, either God or something added by God to matter, to account for gravitational attraction. Either emphasis continued to support the matter/spirit dualism that had emerged as central to Cartesian and corpuscular philosophy during the seventeenth century. The former had special appeal for those who sought to find scientific support for belief in a God who remained continuously active within the natural universe. Second, Isaac Newton (1642–1727) insisted that the massively improbable structure of the solar system supported the argument that it had to be the product of a designer God rather than of mere chance. Finally, Newtonian natural theology acknowledged (indeed, it insisted upon) the need for God's infrequent, but unquestionably miraculous, interference with natural processes, for, without such miraculous interventions, it seemed clear from calculations based on Newton's *Principia* (1687) that instabilities in the solar system would have caused it to collapse within the duration of historical time. All of these features of the physical universe were understood to provide proofs of the existence of God.

Beginning in the middle decades of the eighteenth century, continuing developments in classical physics undermined the Newtonian position and substantially modified the way in which physics and religion were

371

understood to be connected. One of the simplest and most dramatic impacts emerged out of the development of celestial mechanics by Louis Lagrange (1736–1813) and Pierre Simon Laplace (1749–1827). In his *Exposition du systeme du monde* (*Explanation of a World System* [1796]), Laplace was able to demonstrate that the approximations Newton had used in dealing with the motions of Saturn and Jupiter had been the cause of the apparent nonperiodic element in their motions and that a more thorough solution of the problem failed to predict a collapse of the solar system. Hence, the Newtonian argument for the necessity of God's miraculous intervention in the world was vitiated. Perhaps even more important in the long run, Laplace proposed his nebular hypothesis, which offered a purely physical account of the structure of the solar system, which Newton had used to justify a belief in God. Laplace's physics came to symbolize the position of most French scientists, who argued that physics no longer offered any support for the traditional notion of God and that its implications favored pure materialism.

A quite different development of Newtonian ideas was initiated in *Theoria philosophiae naturalis* (*Theory of Natural Philosophy* [1758]) by the Serbian Jesuit Rodger Joseph Boscovich (1711–87), who also tended toward a version of materialism, but one quite unlike that of Laplace. Boscovich demonstrated that all versions of the mechanical philosophy that depended on the transfer of motion by the impact of perfectly hard particles involved a set of foundational assumptions that were logically inconsistent with each other. The problems of the mechanistic hypothesis could be avoided if one admitted that our notion of matter is drawn from our experiences of repulsive and attractive forces. Indeed, Boscovich went on to argue, particles of matter are best understood as unextended point centers of patterned forces that extend through space. Near the point center, these forces approach infinite repulsion, while, at great distances, they approach the gravitational force of attraction. Between, they oscillate between attractive and repulsive regions, accounting for such phenomena as chemical affinities, the different phases of matter, and electrical and magnetic attractions and repulsions.

By decoupling the definition of matter from its traditional grounding in extension, and by focusing on the constitutive active powers of particles of matter to attract and repel other entities, Boscovich undermined both the traditional grounds for dualistic ontologies and the

grounds for arguing that the activity of matter must be a direct manifestation of God or something added to passive matter by God. Though Boscovich's ideas seemed to many to advocate atheism or deism by challenging the need for an immanent God, they were appropriated by Joseph Priestley (1733–1804) in his *Disquisitions Relating to Matter and Spirit* (1777) in support of what he viewed as a necessary reform of Christianity. According to Priestley, an outstanding self-taught natural philosopher and the founder of British Unitarianism, the belief in a dualism between matter and spirit derived from a contamination of primitive Christianity by Greek, especially Platonist, philosophy. Moreover, it led to such perversions of true Christianity as the doctrines of the Trinity and of the immortality of the soul (which seemed to obviate the doctrine of the resurrection). It also led to hopeless philosophical difficulties like the problem of how the soul and the body could interact if one was material and the other spiritual. By breaking down this dualism, Boscovich's physics not only avoided the confusions associated with Cartesian dualism, it also pointed the way toward a recovery of what Unitarians believed was the original meaning of Christianity, including its central doctrine of the resurrection, which now became the complete reconstruction of the mortal person by God. Boscovich's revisions of Newtonian natural philosophy also suggested another central notion to Priestley: that progress in science was God's way of gradually eliminating error and prejudice, of ending usurped authority in religion and politics, and of leading to the ultimate triumph of Christianity.

In Germany, the development of Newtonian philosophy in ways similar to those of Boscovich led in a very different direction through the highly influential works of Immanuel Kant (1724–1804). In his *Metaphysische Anfangsgrunde der Naturwissenschaft* (*Metaphysical Elements of Natural Science* [1786]), Kant also argued that attractive and repulsive forces are the essence of matter and that they are, therefore, not something added by a spiritual entity. Indeed, argued Kant, no argument derived from nature could prove anything about the existence or the nature of God. For Kant, religious issues were fundamentally moral issues, and the "oughts" of morality could not be derived from the "is" of natural philosophy. This Kantian separation of science from religion had a major impact on German scientists and theologians, minimizing their interest in natural theology. Moreover, Kantian ideas entered British natural theology through the writings of William Whewell (1794–1866) and Scots such as Thomas Chalmers (1780–1847). In Britain, however, although Kantian arguments changed the character of some claims of sophisticated natural theologians, they did not undermine the traditionally close linkages between science and religion. Beginning with Whewell's *Astronomy and General Physics Considered with Reference to Natural Theology* (1833), British natural theology virtually abandoned its traditional attempts to derive the duties of Christians from the natural world, as well as its claims that natural theology actually provided proof of God's existence. Henceforth, most British works in natural theology, such as *The Unseen Universe; or, Physical Speculations on a Future State* (1875) by physicists Peter Guthrie Tait (1831–1901) and Balfour Stewart (1828–87), admitted that they could not prove God's existence. Instead, they limited themselves to demonstrating the compatibility between the structure of the physical universe and the claims of traditional Christianity.

Among the many arguments developed by Stewart and Tait, one is particularly interesting for the way in which it anticipates issues subsequently raised by theologians concerned with chaos theory in the late twentieth century. Stewart and Tait raised the theological question of how we can reconcile our experience of agency with the determinism of classical physics. In dealing with this issue, Stewart drew on his own work, analyzing the energetics of what he called "delicate," or "instable," mechanical systems—systems that we would now label "chaotic." Such systems, he argued, may be so sensitive that, if they are at all complex, the effects of any tiny change in force may be incalculable. Living beings are delicate in this way and, as a consequence, for practical purposes, they act in indeterminate ways (Stewart and Tait 1889, 185).

If nineteenth-century physics could be appropriated in the service of Christianity, it is also the case that it could be appropriated for completely different and unorthodox "religious" purposes. Some materialists, such as Ludwig Büchner (1824–99), whose *Force and Matter; or, Principles of the Natural Order of the Universe* (1855) went through seventeen German editions and twenty-two other language editions by 1920, simply claimed to be able to demonstrate that physics undermined all support for any kind of theism. A more interesting position was illustrated in the writings of the German Nobel Laureate, natural philosopher, and physical chemist Wilhelm Ostwald (1853–1932). The founder of "energetics" posited the identification of matter and energy in a single

"Monist" universe. Ostwald became convinced that scientific knowledge could replace religion as a foundation for morality and happiness, ultimately arguing that science *is* the god of the modern world. As early as 1905, he offered a formula for happiness:

$$G = (E+W)(E-W),$$

where G is the amount of happiness that an individual feels; E is the quantity of energy expended in activities that one wills to do; and W is the energy expended on activities done against one's will. Later, as chair of the German Monist League, whose conventions drew up to four thousand persons, Ostwald wrote more than two hundred scientific Sunday sermons promoting his substitute religion, offering self-hypnosis as a substitute for prayer to a higher authority, and designing naturalistic holidays to replace those of the Christian churches.

Modern Physics

After the professionalization of natural science during the nineteenth century, though it was common for physicists to seek support for their religious belief or lack of belief in a transcendent God in their science, few reported turning to scientific study primarily out of religious motivations, as had been the case during the seventeenth and early eighteenth centuries. One remarkable exception was Albert Einstein (1879–1955), for whom self-reported religious reasons played a major role in both the motivation of his own scientific work and his interpretations of the scientific work of others. Since his views, or views very much like his, have strongly influenced the attitudes of many important theoretical physicists and cosmologists well into the late twentieth century, they deserve special attention.

Einstein's religion was in no sense based on the notion of the personal God of orthodox Judaism, who demanded obedience and punished disobedience. "I cannot conceive of a God who rewards and punishes his creatures," he wrote. "Neither can I, nor would I, want to conceive of an individual that survives his physical death; let feeble souls, from fear or absurd egoism, cherish such thoughts" (Einstein 1952, 11). After a brief period of Jewish orthodoxy before he was twelve, Einstein adopted a commitment to what he later identified as Baruch Spinoza's (1632–77) entirely impersonal and entirely rational God: "A firm belief, a belief bound up with deep feelings, in a superior mind that reveals itself in the world of experience, represents my conception of God" (Paul 1982, 56). Einstein's firm conviction in the impersonal, objective aspect of God led him to the unshakable belief that the universe had a real existence, independent of all observers, and that it had to be totally causal and deterministic. Moreover, because God was completely rational, Einstein was convinced throughout his life that a complete understanding of the natural world must ultimately be accessible to the human intellect. These commitments led him to oppose both positivist assertions that science could be nothing but the systematized record of our sensations and all acausal and statistical interpretations of quantum mechanics. Indeed, because quantum mechanics failed uniquely to stipulate the state of physical systems between observations, Einstein believed throughout his life that it must be fundamentally incomplete and that it could eventually be subsumed within a more comprehensive theory that would unify his own work on general relativity and all topics dealt with by quantum mechanics.

The search for some kind of grand unified theory, or theory of everything, based on a conviction that physics must ultimately be not only consistent with our sensory experiences, but also logically inevitable and capable of accounting for everything, including the reason for the origin of the universe, continues at the end of the twentieth century among physicists. Theoreticians such as Steven Weinberg (1933–) and Stephen Hawking (1942–) allude directly to Einstein as their inspiration and persist in arguing that their work is allowing them to see into the mind of God. Experimentalists have more recently begun to take up this point of view, as evidenced by Leon Lederman's *The God Particle: If the Universe Is the Answer, What Is the Question?* (1993).

During the first half of the twentieth century, attempts to account for the character of physical phenomena on the astronomical scale depended heavily on Einstein's general theory of relativity, which posited that space was "warped" in the presence of gravitating bodies. This theory, which was to be confirmed in 1919 by the observed bending of light by the sun, offered two possible implications regarding the history of the universe. One possibility was that the universe existed in a steady state, so that, though it appeared to be expanding, its density remained constant because of the continuous formation of matter in "empty" space. Alternatively, it was possible that the universe originated in a "big bang" at some point in the past. The first of these two solutions would,

on the face of it, clearly have undermined traditional theological arguments for a creation of the universe.

In the early 1960s, empirical evidence of a residual heat radiation indicated that the big bang theory was correct, leading to a period in which a few astrophysicists and theologians (including Robert Jastrow [1925–]) optimistically suggested that the big bang theory provided new support for the creation of the universe at a point in time by a transcendent God. In 1988, however, this optimism was dealt a substantial blow by Stephen Hawking, who was able to show the possibility of a cosmology based on a fusion of general relativity and quantum mechanics, in which all observations to date could be accounted for in a finite universe that has neither spatial nor temporal bounds. As Hawking took special care to point out, in such a universe "there would be no singularities at which the laws of science broke down and no edge of space-time at which one would have to appeal to God or some new law to set the boundary conditions for space time. . . . The universe would be self-contained and not affected by anything outside itself" (Hawking 1988, 135). This argument does not disprove any Creation story, nor does it have any bearing on notions of divinity that are not transcendent, such as those associated with some variants of process theologies. But it does decouple large-scale physical phenomena from traditional supports for notions of a transcendent God.

In one of the most intriguing ironies associated with recent appropriations of physical arguments and analogies by theologians, Wolfhart Pannenberg (1928–) has argued that field theories in modern physics provide support for belief in God's continuing activity, or "effective presence" within the universe, as well as for the priority of the whole over any of its parts that plays a part in all discussions of apparent evil. The irony here is that modern field theories from Michael Faraday (1791–1867) on have been developments out of Boscovich's eighteenth-century arguments that were taken as antagonistic to the need for God's ongoing activities in nature. According to Pannenberg, on the other hand, the tendencies of field theories to undermine the importance of traditional notions of matter and to replace them with space-filling immaterial forces suggests the analogous notion that the cosmic activity of the divine Spirit is like a field of force (Pannenberg 1988, 12).

It is generally agreed that quantum mechanics, the central features of which were articulated almost simultaneously in 1926 by Werner Heisenberg (1901–76) and

Erwin Schroedinger (1887–1961) in different but logically equivalent forms, have had far more radical philosophical and theological implications than has relativity theory. As early as 1900, Max Planck (1858–1947) had shown that a correct formula for the distribution of energy in the spectrum emitted by a heated black body can be derived from the second law of thermodynamics, if energy is emitted by an oscillating charged particle only in multiples of its frequency of oscillation, the proportionality constant, h, being equal to 6.6×10^{-27} erg. seconds. In 1905, Einstein showed that the so-called photoelectric effect could be accounted for if the energy carried by a photon of light was h times the frequency. A few years later, Niels Bohr (1885–1962) was able to account for the spectrum of light emitted by hydrogen by assuming that electrons circled a positively charged nucleus without continuously radiating. When they did radiate, it was in a kind of instantaneous spasm produced when the electron dropped from one allowable energy level to another; and the allowable energy levels were governed by Planck's Constant. These and numerous phenomena that could not be understood classically all found explanations in the general theory of quantum mechanics.

Heisenberg was among the first to explore some of the counterintuitive features in his 1927 paper "On The Intuitive Contents of Quantum—Theoretic Kinematics and Mechanics." In this paper he focused on what he called the principle of indeterminacy or uncertainty. Within quantum theory, there are pairs of variables, q and p, called conjugate variables such that $qp - pq = h/2(\text{pi})\,i$, where i is the square root of minus one. Heisenberg showed that this relationship could be given a physical interpretation if one considered the experimental uncertainties in measuring p and q variables. The mathematical relationship between p and q implied that the product of the uncertainties in their simultaneous measurements was always equal to or greater than Planck's Constant divided by 2(pi). Even with theoretically perfect instruments, one could not simultaneously measure the value of conjugate variables with arbitrary precision. Moreover, since position and momentum are conjugate variables, it follows that one could never know perfectly the position and the momentum of even one particle, let alone those of all the particles of the universe, which is what Laplace had articulated as the condition that had to be met for a predictable deterministic universe. Indeed, if Heisenberg were correct, and if it is also the case that God created the universe, then it operates in such a way

that not even God can predict its precise course in advance, raising a number of theological issues regarding both the omniscience and the omnipotence of God.

If one considers Schroedinger's formulation of quantum mechanics, the uncertainty relationships are capable of a more extended and extremely interesting interpretation. In Schroedinger's system, solutions to certain equations are produced that have the form of classical wavelike functions. The product of two such functions gives the probability that, if a measurement of some variable is made, the variable will have that value. According to Heisenberg, Bohr, and Schroedinger, the Schroedinger wave functions represent the "state" of a quantum system. If we consider solutions for position, the "particle" whose position is to be measured is literally everywhere that the wave function has magnitude until a measurement is made. At that instant, the wave function collapses and the particle is found at a particular place. Many measurements of identical systems would lead to a distribution of results whose frequencies would reflect the square of the wave function at the places indicated.

This interpretation of quantum mechanics highlights several startling implications. First, it emphasizes that the uncertainty relations of Heisenberg reflect an indeterminacy or a causality that is more than a reflection of human ignorance. This is true because two measurements of identical systems are almost certain to give different results. The fact that two different consequences follow from the same laws and initial conditions violates traditional understandings of determinism (of course, at another level, the wave functions are determined; it is only the results of our observations that are not). If the universe is not deterministic, then a number of possibilities exist, including that of freedom and responsibility. Second, Schroedinger's interpretation challenges the notion, so insisted upon by Einstein, of the objectivity of the physical universe. Bohr insists that there is a strong sense in which the physical world literally does not exist in any classical way, except when it is being measured. Furthermore, since the conditions for observing are part of the formal conditions for solving Schroedinger's equation, the results of any measurement depend not only on what is being measured, but also on how the observer is interacting with it.

In 1935, Einstein, along with Boris Podolsky (1896–1966) and Nathan Rosen (1909–1995), published an article that highlighted another odd consequence of quantum mechanics and challenged the claim that quantum mechanics could ever be a complete description of physical reality. They invited consideration of the following thought experiment. They assumed that a particle composed of two protons and with a net zero spin splits into two protons with opposite spin. The two protons are allowed to travel a substantial distance in opposite directions. The two protons have equal probabilities of having right- or left-hand spins before the spin of either is measured, but the two spins must be in opposite directions. Now, suppose that the spin of one is measured to be left-handed. Instantaneously, the spin of the other will become right-handed, implying that information is passed between the two particles faster than the speed of light, which is presumed to be impossible. Clearly, according to Einstein, Podolsky, and Rosen, something is going on that is not contained within quantum mechanics itself. During the 1950s, David Bohm (1917–92) suggested a causal, nonlocal interpretation of quantum mechanics, involving hidden variables, consistent with the Einstein–Podolsky–Rosen (EPR) expectations, but it drew little attention. Since 1982, when a group of French physicists managed to carry out a near variant of the EPR experiment, the most widely held view seems to be that quantum mechanics is, indeed, complete, but that it implies that reality is nonlocal, so that how one instrument operates can, in fact, influence distant events. These results have led to a revival of interest in Bohm's work on the part of both physicists and theologians.

The upshot of quantum mechanics has been to reopen a large number of questions that had seemed closed, including the renewed possibility of God's simultaneous instantaneous knowledge and activity everywhere in the universe. One of the more intriguing readings of the implications of quantum mechanics includes a revised version of the old notion of the design of the universe by an intelligent agent, coupled with an argument for free will in humans. In 1987, British-American theoretical physicist Freeman Dyson (1923–) argued that quantum entities, such as electrons, are active, choice-making agents and that experiments force them to make particular choices from the many options open to them. At a second level, the brains of animals "appear to be devices for the amplification of . . . the quantum choices made by the molecules inside our heads. . . . Now comes the argument from design. There is evidence from particular features of the laws of nature that the universe as a whole is hospitable to the growth of mind [defined as the capacity for choice]. . . . Therefore it is reasonable to believe in the existence of a third level of mind, a mental component of the universe. If we believe in this mental component and call it God, then we can say we are small pieces of God's mental apparatus" (Dyson 1987, 60ff).

Once again, we see the key feature of the use of natural philosophy or physics in religious discourse since the beginning of the nineteenth century. Virtually no one—except those who make science into a religion—has argued for nearly two hundred years that religious propositions can be proved through physical arguments. Instead, physicists have shown a remarkable interest and aptitude in demonstrating that physical laws are consistent with, and even suggestive of, a wide variety of theological consequences.

See also Anthropic Principle; Chaos Theory; Twentieth-Century Cosmologies

BIBLIOGRAPHY

Davies, Paul C. W. *God and the New Physics.* New York: Simon and Schuster, 1983.

Dyson, Freeman J. "Science and Religion." In *Religion, Science, and the Search for Wisdom,* ed. by David M. Byers. Washington, D.C.: Bishops' Committee on Human Values, National Conference of Catholic Bishops, 1987.

Einstein, Albert. *Ideas and Opinions.* New York: Crown, 1952.

Gascoigne, John. "From Bentley to the Victorians: The Rise and Fall of British Newtonian Natural Theology." *Science in Context* 2 (1988): 219–56.

Hahn, Roger. "Laplace and the Mechanistic Universe." In *God and Nature: Historical Essays on the Encounter between Christianity and Science,* ed. by David C. Lindberg and Ronald L. Numbers. Berkeley: University of California Press, 1986, 256–76.

Hakfoort, Caspar. "Science Deified: Wilhelm Ostwald's Energeticist World-View and the History of Scientism." *Annals of Science* 49 (1992): 525–44.

Hawking, Stephen. *A Brief History of Time: From the Big Bang to Black Holes.* New York: Bantam, 1988.

Hiebert, Erwin N. "Modern Physics and Christian Faith." In *God and Nature: Historical Essays on the Encounter between Christianity and Science,* ed. by David C. Lindberg and Ronald L. Numbers. Berkeley: University of California Press, 1986, 424–47.

Lederman, Leon, with Dick Teresi. *The God Particle: If the Universe Is the Answer, What Is the Question?* New York: Houghton Mifflin, 1993.

Margenau, Henry, ed. *Integrative Principles of Modern Thought.* New York: Gordon and Breach, 1972.

McAvoy, John, and J. E. McGuire. "God and Nature: Priestley's Way of Rational Dissent." *Historical Studies in the Physical Sciences* 6 (1975): 325–404.

Müller-Marcus, Siegfried. *Wen Sterne rufe: Gespräch mit Lenin.* Wiesbaden: Credo, 1960.

———. *Der Gott der Physiker.* Basel: Birkhauser, 1986.

Odum, Herbert H. "The Estrangement of Celestial Mechanics and Religion." *Journal of the History of Ideas* 27 (1966): 533–58.

Paul, Iain. *Science, Theology, and Einstein.* New York: Oxford University Press, 1982.

Pannenberg, Wolfhart. *Systematische Theologie.* Vols. 2 and 3. Göttingen: Vandenhoeck and Ruprecht, 1991 and 1993.

———. *Toward a Theology of Nature: Essays on Science and Faith.* Louisville: Westminster, 1993.

Penrose, Roger. *The Emperor's New Mind: Concerning Computers, Minds, and The Laws of Physics.* Oxford: Oxford University Press, 1989.

Polkinghorne, John. *The Faith of a Physicist.* Princeton, N.J.: Princeton University Press, 1994.

Russell, Robert John, William Stoeger, and George Coyne, eds. *Physics, Philosophy, and Theology: A Common Quest for Understanding.* Vatican City: Vatican Observatory, 1988.

Russell, Robert John, N. Murphy, and A. Peacock. *Chaos and Complexity: Scientific Perspectives on Divine Action.* Vatican City: Vatican Observatory, 1995.

Sharpe, Kevin J. *David Bohm's World: New Physics and New Religion.* Lewisburg, Pa.: Bucknell University Press, 1993.

Stewart, Balfour, and Peter Guthrie Tait. *The Unseen Universe; or, Physical Speculations on a Future State.* 1875. Reprint. London: Macmillan, 1889.

Tipler, Frank. *The Physics of Immortality.* New York: Doubleday, 1994.

Weinberg, Steven. *Dreams of a Final Theory: The Search for the Fundamental Laws of Nature.* New York: Pantheon Books, 1992.

Wertheim, Margaret. *Pythagoras' Trousers: God, Physics, and the Gender Wars.* New York: Random House, 1995.

Whewell, William. *Astronomy and General Physics Considered with Reference to Natural Theology.* London: Pickering, 1833.

Worthing, Mark William. *God, Creation, and Contemporary Physics.* Minneapolis, Minn.: Fortress, 1996.

70. CHEMISTRY

John Hedley Brooke

For much of its history, chemistry was distinguished from natural philosophy and other protosciences by its direct association with such practical arts as metallurgy and medicine. In the eighteenth century, when claims were pressed both for its emancipation from alchemy and for its autonomy, it would be defined as the science that dealt with the decomposition and recomposition of material substances. A distinction between elements and compounds has, therefore, been fundamental to the science, which, in its post-Newtonian forms, has been concerned with the mechanism of chemical reactions as well as the units of chemical change. The appearance of a recognizably modern list of elements is usually correlated with the "revolution" achieved by Antoine Lavoisier (1743–94), whose critique of the phlogiston theory has been a cliché in symbolizing the foundations of a rigorously analytical science.

It was during the nineteenth century that controversial models of molecular structure began to appear, made possible by the atomic theory of John Dalton (1766–1844), whose study of differential gas solubilities had led to a preoccupation with the characteristically different weights of chemically indivisible "atoms" and thence to the possibility of fixing the numbers of each elementary atom in specific compounds. Developments in the new science of organic chemistry, the articulation by Edward Frankland (1825–99) and August Kekulé (1829–96) of a theory of characteristic combining powers or "valency" for each element, the reformulation of Avogadro's hypothesis by Stanislao Cannizzaro (1826–1910) in the late 1850s, and the concept of tetrahedrally directed bonds for the carbon atom, proposed independently by Joseph le Bel (1847–1930) and Jacobus van't Hoff (1852–1911) in 1874, laid the classical foundations of a science that would henceforward strive to correlate chemical properties with molecular structure.

The nineteenth century also saw the establishment of distinguished research schools in chemistry, of which the prototype was that of Justus von Liebig (1803–73) in the German university town of Giessen. Chemical institutions, such as the Institute of Chemistry in London (1877), also arose to cater to a growing band of professional chemists whose analytical skills were in demand. The most seminal innovations of the twentieth century have arguably been those in which reaction mechanisms have been explored in electronic terms, and quantum mechanics applied to atomic and molecular structures. Such developments have raised the question of whether chemistry as a science might be reduced to physics, an issue impinging on broader discussions of reductionism in which religious commentators have also claimed a stake.

The Tradition of Alchemy

The origins of chemistry lie in several ancient cultures in which the practice of metallurgy and, in some cases dyeing, encouraged the manipulation of materials. It is known that copper was smelted in the Chalcolithic and early Bronze Ages (c. 2200–c. 700 B.C.) in Britain and Europe. In the making of perfumes, pots, and paints, chemical practices also developed. Certain features were common to most forms of alchemy: the belief that metals grew naturally within the earth and the belief that all matter was ultimately one. These convictions encouraged practices of aurifacton (the making of gold), and, in seeking a transmutation, the alchemist could claim to be speeding up a process that occurred naturally. Historians have also detected differences as well as similarities among the ancient cultures of chemistry. In Chinese and Babylonian alchemy medical concerns were usually prominent, whereas in Greek alchemy the emphasis was more on metallurgy. From Chinese alchemy would come gunpowder and fireworks, allowing the speculation that the origins of the former lay, somewhat poignantly, in the quest for an elixir of life. In some contexts, alchemical practices clearly had religious meanings and connotations. An ancient Egyptian recipe conjures up the image many would have of a typical alchemical project:

> Take 28 leaves from a pithy laurel tree and some virgin earth and seed of wormwood, wheat meal and the herb calf's snout pounded together with . . . the liquid of an ibis egg and make into a uniform dough and into a figure of Hermes wearing a mantle, while the moon is ascending. . . . Let Hermes be holding a herald's staff. And write the spell on hieratic papyrus or on a goose's windpipe . . . and insert it into the figure for . . . inspiration. [Put the spell] at the feet of Hermes . . . and recite as on the altar you burn incense (Copenhaver 1992, xxxv).

In such prescriptions was a wish to control nature, with success being contingent on a form of piety. Hermes is addressed as the "prophet of events . . . who sends forth oracles by day and night." He is said to "cure all pains of mortals with . . . healing cares." Finally, he is summoned to guarantee the result: "Hither, O blessed one . . . both graciously appear and graciously render the task for me, a pious man." The image of the alchemist at prayer, striving for the correct spiritual state to effect an operation that also required divine blessing, was to be common in Renaissance Europe, reflecting, in part, the problematic status of one who sought to alter, improve, or at the very least accelerate the ordinary processes of nature. Was there not something intrinsically impious in such presumption?

From the corpus of texts ascribed to Paracelsus (1493–1541), we can see how chemistry, albeit controversially, came to be defended as a legitimate Christian activity. Among the Paracelsians, chemistry gained a higher profile, partly as a consequence of their critique of Galenic medicine. Instead of attributing illness to an imbalance of the four humors, the new emphasis fell on specific diseases of specific organs induced by specific agents external to the body. Hence the requirement for specific chemical remedies, the preparation of which,

according to Paracelsus, was a more noble and Christian task than seeking riches through the transmutation of base metals to gold. Christ, after all, by his own example, had conferred the highest sanctity on the healer. The task of the chemist was to extract from natural products the pure and efficacious ingredients that would offer relief. Against learned physicians who argued that some diseases were beyond their control, Paracelsus invoked the mercy of a God who had provided resources to cure all ailments if only they were appropriated and properly processed.

Although Paracelsus remained a Catholic, his reforming spirit has often been compared with that of Martin Luther (1483–1546). He gave chemistry an even higher profile by presenting it as the science that could best assist an understanding of the Creation narrative in Genesis. Creation was seen as a chemical process, as the elements were separated from a primordial water. There were even echoes of the Fall narrative in the chemists' toil and sweat. They labored diligently, Paracelsus affirmed, putting their fingers to the coals and the dung, not into gold rings. Through chemistry, nature was to be redeemed. When Paracelsus spoke of the last stage of the alchemical process, the tincturing of a substance to change its color, he stated that it makes all imperfect things perfect, transmutes them into their noblest essence.

In Paracelsian chemistry, there was also a reform of matter theory. The traditional doctrine of the four elements was revised to give new weight to the three principles of mercury, sulfur, and salt. Mercury was the principle of fusibility and volatility, sulfur the principle of inflammability, and salt corresponded to the noncombustible residue. Despite the vision of Paracelsian chemistry and its efforts to achieve theological credibility, its antiauthoritarian tone meant that chemical schemes for the improvement of nature were always liable to be dismissed as fantasies fueled by practices demeaning to the true scholar. When Robert Boyle (1627–91) reviewed the social standing of the chemist in post-Restoration English society, he commented on the wide gulf that separated the natural philosopher from the "sooty empirics," as the chemists were so often perceived to be. One of Boyle's aims was to bridge the gulf by conferring greater theoretical dignity on chemistry. This he hoped to achieve by making its experimental results relevant to debates on the legitimacy and scope of the "mechanical philosophy" and by offering a philosophical critique of certain analytical practices—fire analysis, for example—which were supposed to reveal the composition of substances but which, in Boyle's opinion, were too destructive. The extent to which chemistry could be exalted by making it part of a natural theology is, however, an interesting question. Physico-theologies were to enjoy a vogue during the eighteenth and early nineteenth centuries, but were not chemico-theologies conspicuous by their absence?

Chemistry and Natural Theology

Boyle's own writings on natural theology suggest one reason chemistry might prove inauspicious for the construction of design arguments. In contrast to the life sciences, it did not disclose the exquisite structures that could be correlated with final causes. Nor could it generate a sense of awe at the precision of the Divine Geometer, without whose mathematical skills, according to Isaac Newton (1642–1727), there would have been no solar system. There was little that chemistry could offer to evoke a comparable sense of divine wisdom. Jesuit philosophers had been obliged to assess the probity of alchemical practices, given contemporary associations with natural magic, but it is striking how little was their involvement compared with their support for astronomy, mathematics, and the physical sciences. Neither Paracelsus nor his successor Joan-Baptista van Helmont (1579–1644) had interpreted chemical processes in exclusively materialist terms. In introducing the word "gas," van Helmont had defined it as a hitherto unknown spirit, which can neither be retained in vessels nor reduced to a visible body. Nevertheless, as the science of material change, chemistry would exert a great appeal to later materialists, one of whom—the British radical Richard Carlile (1790–1843)—succinctly declared that all known phenomena are compounds of gases. For Carlile, chemistry, with its pretensions not merely to describe but to change the world, stood as the very antithesis of natural theology. "With the doctrine of intelligent deity," he wrote in the 1830s, "it is presumption to attempt anything toward human improvement. Without the doctrine, it is not."

Such a creed exposed what had been an incipient tension between chemistry and a conventional natural theology. In seeking to surpass nature by making new things, the chemist ran the risk of censure for usurping divine prerogatives. When attacking Paracelsian chemistry, the Lutheran humanist Andreas Libavius (1540–1616) described it as the occupation not of philosophers but of reprobates. Similarly, the notion that chemistry might facilitate the redemption of nature was qualified by Oswald Croll (c. 1560–1609) as he incorporated Paracelsian ideas within a Calvinist piety: God alone could make all things new. Whereas the natural theology of the eighteenth and early nineteenth centuries proclaimed the superiority of nature over human art, the pretensions of the chemist could be construed as an affirmation of the converse. There were, therefore, contexts in which chemistry was readily associated with political radicalism. Reflecting on the French Revolution, Edmund Burke (1729–97) slated the republicans for defying the processes of nature like an "alchymist and empiric." In short, chemistry, perhaps more than any other science, has been associated with the forces of secularization. There was nothing like chemical fertilizers, wrote Peter Burke, for changing the attitudes of European peasants (Burke 1979).

It would, however, be unbalanced to imply that chemistry had nothing to offer the religious apologist. The incorporation of chemical ideals arguably encouraged a different style of natural theology in which the emphasis fell not on an existing perfection in nature but on a collaboration between the human and the divine in the amelioration of the world. In other words, chemico-theologies tended to be process theologies in which the chemist was cocreator or, less presumptuously, comaker with God. From the time of Boyle to the middle of the nineteenth century, connections were certainly made between the aspirations of the chemist and theological discourse. They were often mediated through the relevance of chemistry to medicine and agriculture. In his *Usefulness of Experimental Natural Philosophy* (2 vols., 1663, 1671), Boyle put greater faith in medicines than in physicians: "I had much rather, that the physician of any friend of mine, should keep his patient by powerful medicines from dying, than tell me punctually when he shall die, or show me in the opened carcass why it may be supposed he lived no longer" (quoted in Cook 1990, 417).

In Newton's mind, there was to be a distinction between two forms of chemistry: the vulgar sort that imitated nature's simplest mechanical processes and a higher art that he described as a "more subtle secret and noble way of working." This was concerned with the imitation of organic processes that were dependent on the agency of a subtle vegetable spirit that owed its power and efficacy to the God who had dominion over nature. This higher form of chemistry was only for initiates precisely because it promised access to the modus operandi of the deity. During the eighteenth century, Joseph Priestley (1733–1804) would emerge as the champion of a more egalitarian chemistry in which all could participate with a minimum of apparatus and prior instruction.

Chemistry was linked to Priestley's Unitarian theology in several ways. Committed to the belief that nature was an interconnected system designed to promote human happiness, Priestley saw chemical research as one way of revealing the connections. For example, a providential system required a mechanism for replenishing the air. Experiments with aquatic plants, involving his "nitrous air" test, convinced him that the purification was the work of vegetation. Although Priestley isolated the gas that, in Lavoisier's chemistry, became known as oxygen, he described it as "dephlogisticated air" in keeping with the theory that human respiration and the combustion of metals involved the exhalation of phlogiston, the principle of inflammability. Although this theory proved vulnerable to Lavoisier's critique, it remained attractive to Priestley partly because it revealed the kind of unity and simplicity in nature that one would expect if there were a divine economy. Priestley could explain why all of the metals had properties in common (derived from the presence of phlogiston in them all) in a manner that Lavoisier could not.

There were subtle connections, too, between Priestley's radical theology and his isolation of gases. Chemistry assisted his project for the collapsing of a matter/spirit dualism because, through the manipulation of different "airs," he could rid the science of a vocabulary of "spirits," lending analogical support to a similar purge of Christian doctrine. Above all, chemistry contributed to the progress of human understanding. This was part of a historical process through which the sciences, in league with a rational and tolerant religion, would triumph over superstition. The practical application of chemical knowledge was an integral part of this process theology, and Priestley was confident that he could find medical and other uses for each of his "airs."

In preaching the virtues of chemistry to a more fashionable audience at the Royal Institution in London, Humphry Davy (1778–1829) had no difficulty developing a natural theology. The affirmation of divine purpose in the laws of nature was a unifying theme throughout his lectures. As with Priestley, Davy searched for unifying principles within his science that would impose order on an expanding list of elements to which he was himself contributing. But whereas Priestley had been vilified for his sympathies with the French Revolution, Davy found in chemistry the resources to explode the pretensions of French materialists. The fact that substances as dissimilar as diamond and charcoal were made from the same element, carbon, meant that the properties of bodies had to depend on more than the basic material of which they were made. The extraordinary contrast between the properties of laughing gas (nitrous oxide) and of what became known as nitrogen dioxide made the same point for compounds containing the same elements. As Davy's friend the Romantic poet Samuel Taylor Coleridge (1772–1834) insisted, there was more to a chemical synthesis than the juxtaposition of particles. A pioneer in electrochemistry, Davy also recognized that the reactivity of a chemical agent could be changed simply by giving it a positive or negative charge. Chemical properties, in other words, did not inhere in material particles—a conclusion that could support a natural theology. One could regard matter itself as inert and all effects produced on it as "flowing from the same original cause, which, as it is intelligent, must be divine" (Knight 1978, 68).

A natural-theology text written in the 1830s, William Prout's (1785–1850) Bridgewater Treatise, shows what a chemico-theology looked like before the genre was largely eclipsed in the following generation. Prout had earlier identified hydrochloric acid in the gastric juice and was one of the few chemists of the first half of the nineteenth century to share the conviction of Amedeo Avogadro (1776–1856) and André-Marie Ampère (1775–1836) that the molecules of elementary gases are divisible into two or more identical submolecules. Prout was conscious that he had a difficult task. In William Paley's (1743–1805) Natural Theology (1802), anatomical structures far more than chemical processes had yielded arguments for design. Prout could, nevertheless, argue that mechanical devices were subservient to chemical needs. For example, the lungs were required to oxygenate blood. To disqualify chemistry from natural theology would, therefore, be arbitrary.

Where did Prout find evidence of design? The utility of the chemical elements was an obvious source. He could rejoice in the medical uses of iodine, only recently discovered. But what of the less serviceable, even poisonous elements? Prout's answer, unsophisticated though it may be, shows how difficult it was for a chemico-theology not to be a process theology: Elements were there to be turned into compounds! But there were more sophisticated arguments for design. By the 1830s, chemistry could boast what it had largely lacked fifty years earlier: its own "laws." Prout could point to Dalton's law of definite proportions, to Gay Lussac's law of gaseous combination, and to the generalization that all gases under the same temperature and pressure contain the same number of self-repulsive molecules. As "delegated agencies," such laws pointed to the "Great First Cause."

By the time Prout wrote his book, Friedrich Wöhler (1800–82) had produced an organic compound, urea, artificially. This has often been seen as a crucial breakthrough in the elimination of vital forces, allowing a more materialistic and secular science of organic chemistry to develop. Prout's text is one of many that shows how simplistic such a view can be. He was perfectly willing to construct a vitalist physiology in which living systems were controlled by powers having a faculty "little short of intelligence." In the very act of imitating nature, the chemist clarified the superiority of nature's art. The extreme conditions required by Wöhler in the fabrication of urea only underlined the subtlety and silence of nature's operations. Drawing attention to the refractory nature of carbon, hydrogen, oxygen, and nitrogen—the four elements from which organic systems had been spun—Prout could marvel that the deity had created the human mind from charcoal. It should not be supposed, however, that vitalism and natural theology were always in alliance. There were theological critiques of vitalism based on the claim that to have quasi-intelligent principles at work in nature was to detract from the absolute sovereignty of God.

To a later generation, Prout's arguments for a deity looked decidedly weak. During the 1840s, especially in Germany, living systems were increasingly analyzed in physical terms—a reaction, in part, against the authority of the vitalist Johannes Müller (1801–58). In Britain, organic chemistry was to provide Thomas Henry Huxley (1825–95) with additional resources when, in a famous public lecture, he argued for the physical basis of life. The new principle of energy conservation made it difficult to retain a role for vital forces supposedly exempt from energy constraints, but Huxley made as much of the fact that chemical analysis had shown all cell protoplasm to be ultimately composed of the same elements. This could even support an evolutionary history of life, with Huxley championing Charles Darwin's (1809–82) *Origin of Species* (1859), which so embarrassed Paley's argument for design.

The Twentieth Century

During the twentieth century, through elaborate methods of organic synthesis, chemists have enjoyed remarkable success in imitating natural products and processes. The synthesis of vitamin B12 by Robert Woodward (1917–79) in the late 1960s is an outstanding example, in which the control of nine centers of asymmetry, once the prerogative of nature alone, was accomplished. It had once been the view of Louis Pasteur (1822–95) that, while the chemist could produce enantiomorphic pairs of optical isomers, the production of one isomer without its mirror image was a characteristic of living things. Advances in organic synthesis have rarely been undertaken with theological interests to the fore, but they have added to a body of achievement, including the elucidation of the double helix for the structure of DNA, which has given both biochemistry and molecular biology a key place in the public awareness of science. The identification of specific genes with specific sequences of bases along the DNA thread has made possible claims for a genetic reductionism that have sometimes been pressed in the service of materialism and atheism. In discussions of reductionism, a distinction is, however, commonly drawn between methodological forms in which, for the purposes of scientific inquiry, it is provisionally assumed that a reduction might be achieved, and dogmatic forms in which it is concluded that wholes are nothing but the sum of their parts. This distinction, drawn in the nineteenth century by Thomas Henry Huxley and others to rebut the charge of materialism, has been taken over by religious commentators, including scientists with religious commitments, to resist the notion that human culture can be fully analyzed in terms of genetic predispositions and genetic survival. The publicity given to the patenting of transgenic plants and animals has given a new vividness to the role of the scientist as maker, to the attendant moral issues in the discussion of which a theological voice may still be heard, and to the national economic imperatives that have come to determine scientific policies in the late twentieth century.

See also Alchemy; Natural Theology

BIBLIOGRAPHY

Anderson, Robert, and Christopher Lawrence, eds. *Science, Medicine, and Dissent: Joseph Priestley, 1733–1804.* London: Wellcome Trust/Science Museum, 1987.

Baldwin, Martha. "Alchemy and the Society of Jesus in the Seventeenth Century: Strange Bedfellows?" *Ambix* 40 (1993): 41–64.

Beretta, Marco. *The Enlightenment of Matter: The Definition of Chemistry from Agricola to Lavoisier.* Canton, Mass: Science History Publications, 1993.

Brock, William H. *The Fontana History of Chemistry.* London: Fontana, 1992.

Brooke, John Hedley. *Thinking About Matter: Studies in the History of Chemical Philosophy.* Aldershot, U.K.: Variorum, 1995.

Brooke, John Hedley, and Geoffrey Cantor. *Reconstructing Nature: The Engagement of Science and Religion.* Edinburgh: T. and T. Clark, 1998, Ch. 10.

Bud, Robert F., and Gerrylynn K. Roberts. *Science Versus Practice: Chemistry in Victorian Britain.* Manchester, U.K.: Manchester University Press, 1984.

Burke, Peter. "Religion and Secularisation." In *The New Cambridge Modern History.* Vol. 13: *Companion Volume,* ed. by Peter Burke. Cambridge: Cambridge University Press, 1979, 293–317.

Cook, Harold J. "The New Philosophy and Medicine in Seventeenth-Century England." In *Reappraisals of the Scientific Revolution,* ed. by David C. Lindberg and Robert S. Westman. Cambridge: Cambridge University Press, 1990, 397–436.

Copenhaver, Brian P. *Hermetica.* Cambridge: Cambridge University Press, 1992.

Debus, Allen G. *The Chemical Philosophy: Paracelsian Science and Medicine in the Sixteenth and Seventeenth Centuries.* 2 vols. New York: Science History Publications, 1977.

Dobbs, Betty Jo. *The Janus Faces of Genius.* Cambridge: Cambridge University Press, 1991.

Golinski, Jan. *Science as Public Culture: Chemistry and Enlightenment in Britain, 1760–1820.* Cambridge: Cambridge University Press, 1992.

Hannaway, Owen. *The Chemists and the Word.* Baltimore: Johns Hopkins University Press, 1975.

Hunter, Michael, ed. *Robert Boyle Reconsidered.* Cambridge: Cambridge University Press, 1994.

Knight, David M. *The Transcendental Part of Chemistry.* Folkestone, U.K.: Dawson, 1978.

———. *Humphry Davy: Science and Power.* Oxford: Blackwell, 1992.

Levere, Trevor H. *Poetry Realized in Nature: Samuel Taylor Coleridge and Early Nineteenth-Century Science.* Cambridge: Cambridge University Press, 1981.

Pagel, Walter. *Paracelsus: An Introduction to Philosophical Medicine in the Era of the Renaissance.* Basel: Karger, 1958.

Rocke, Alan J. *The Quiet Revolution: Hermann Kolbe and the Science of Organic Chemistry.* Berkeley: University of California Press, 1993.

Russell, Colin A., with Noel G. Coley and Gerrylynn A. Roberts. *Chemists by Profession: The Origins and Rise of the Royal Institute of Chemistry.* Milton Keynes: Open University Press, 1977.

Schwartz, A. Truman, and John G. McEvoy, eds. *Motion Toward Perfection: The Achievement of Joseph Priestley.* Boston: Skinner House, 1990.

Thiesen, Wilfred. "John Dastin: The Alchemist as Co-Creator." *Ambix* 38 (1991): 73–8.

71. ELECTRICITY

Dennis Stillings

From the beginnings of recorded history, electricity and magnetism have been associated with religious and spiritual images and ideas, such as all-pervading invisible forces, divine judgment, and the soul and its relationship to the divine. The thunderbolts of Zeus were cast down upon offenders; the lodestone, as well as amber and other electrics, were perceived as possessing a kind of soul or spirit capable of acting invisibly at a distance. For William Gilbert (1544–1603), who was the first clearly to demonstrate by scientific experiment the differences between electricity and magnetism, the earth's magnetic field was its "soul." Gilbert, as well as other early natural philosophers of the time, believed that magnetism was an analogy of God's love, the *amor Dei* that linked God with the human soul.

If magnetism seemed a far more impressive phenomenon than the static electrical effects known to Gilbert and his forebears, the situation changed dramatically with the development of the various electrical or electrostatic machines from the early eighteenth century. Developed as a result of the observation of strange lights and sparks in and around the evacuated glass chambers of air pumps, electrical machines enabled the generation of massive charges of static electricity. Francis Hauksbee (c. 1666–1713), Stephen Gray (c. 1670–1736), John Desaguliers (1683–1744), and others immediately began to use these machines to demonstrate the effects of this active power in nature. Isaac Newton (1642–1727), inspired by Hauksbee's experiments, had suggested that the electric spirit, which the new experiments seemed to suggest was present in many if not all bodies, might be the ultimate cause not only of electrical effects, but also of gravity, light, heat, and even life. These ideas and the dramatic effects of static electricity that could easily be demonstrated with the new machines came to be used to argue for and demonstrate the power of the divine in nature. As Joseph Priestley (1733–1804) commented in 1761, the electrical machine exhibits "the operations of nature, and the God of nature Himself."

It is clear from early-eighteenth-century writings on electricity that a great deal of the symbolism, and even the nomenclature, of alchemy was carried over into the new electrical theorizing. It was commonly assumed in alchemy that matter contained within it light or fire (that was often invisible) as an active principle. Electricity was the "ethereal fire," the "desideratum," the "quintessential fire," the *medicina catholica,* the "cheap thing to be found everywhere," the long-sought panacea. These terms were all used to characterize the nature and properties of the alchemical philosophers' stone. In one of his unpublished alchemical manuscripts, Isaac Newton spoke of light as an active spirit that was present in all bodies and was responsible for many of the activities of matter, because it was such "a prodigious active principle." Similar ideas appeared in print in his "Hypothesis Explaining the Properties of Light," read to the Royal Society in 1675, and in the Queries that he added at the end of his *Opticks* (1704, 1706, 1717). These ideas inspired, among others, Hermann Boerhaave (1668–1738), professor of chemistry at Leyden University, who postulated that fire was an active substance that pervaded the whole universe, penetrating even the innermost recesses of solid bodies and endowing them with many of their properties. It was an easy matter to identify Newton's light and Boerhaave's fire with electricity. When electrical machines spectacularly demonstrated how sparks of fire or light could be elicited from various kinds of matter, including even water, it seemed natural to suppose that truths foreshadowed in alchemy had been confirmed. Alchemical influence can even be seen in Otto von Guericke's (1602–86) pre-Newtonian experiments on electricity when he tried to generate electricity in a spherical terrella made of sulfur turned on a winch (1663). When rubbed, this miniature "model of the world" produced sparks of electricity. It was also a favorite pastime of the alchemists to construct terrellas, and it is perhaps more than coincidence that one of the earliest electrical generators was constructed from an alchemical alembic.

The eighteenth century was the most significant period in history for the impact of electrical theory on religion. Clerics demonstrated a special interest in electricity. John Wesley's (1703–91) *The Desideratum: or, Electricity Made Plain and Useful, by a Lover of Mankind and of Common Sense* (1760) went through several editions. The usefulness of electricity, for Wesley, lay in its potential for combating atheism. This is clear from his comments after he had attended one of the popular public demonstrations of electrical effects: "How must these [experiments] confound those poor half-thinkers who will believe nothing but what they can comprehend. But who can comprehend how fire lives in water, and passes through it more freely than through air? How there issues out of my finger, real flame, such as sets fire to spirits of wine? How these and many more as strange phenomena arise from the turning round a glass globe? It is all mystery, if haply by any means God may hide pride from man." Similar ideas flourished after Benjamin Franklin (1706–90) showed how the natural power of lightning could be used to charge a Leyden jar using a lightning conductor. As Priestley commented in his *History and Present State of Electricity* (1767): "What would the ancient philosophers, what would Newton himself have said, to see the present race of electricians imitating in miniature all the known effects of that tremendous power, nay disarming the thunder of its power of doing mischief, and, without any apprehension of danger to themselves, drawing lightning from the clouds into a private room and amusing themselves at their leisure by performing with it all the experiments that are exhibited by electrical machines?"

Priestley's history is itself historically important because of his attempt to interest the public in the performance of experiments. Public lecturers in experimental natural philosophy would display electrical phenomena in a manner that conferred authority on themselves as manipulators of the forces God had built into creation. Priestley also practiced "electroexorcism," casting out spirits by the application of static electrical sparks. "Electroexorcism" has been practiced for millennia, beginning with throwing "possessed" persons into pools filled with electric fish. This practice reemerged in modern times. The physician Carl Wickland (1861–?) claimed to use a static electrical generator to drive spirits out of his patients and into his mediumistic wife. Wickland would then converse with the spirit and convince it to quit its habitation in the patient and move on to its spiritual destiny.

In his *Theology of Electricity* (1989), Ernst Benz, a twentieth-century theologian, pursues the relationship between electricity and eighteenth-century theology, attempting to establish the claim that the "discovery of electricity and the simultaneous discovery of magnetic and galvanic phenomena were accompanied by a most significant change in the image of God." He argues that these discoveries led to a "completely new understanding of the relation of body and soul, of spirit and matter." Benz considers, in particular, the ideas of Friedrich Christoph Oetinger (1702–82), Johann Ludwig Fricker (1729–66), and Prokop Divisch (1696–1765). These "electrical theologians" saw electricity as the very light of creation, the "first light" of Genesis 1:3–4, which informs matter and is the impetus toward its evolution into higher forms. The Last Judgment and damnation for the "enemies of God" is an "Anti-Creation," involving "the deprivation of the original life force, of electricity."

The researches of Luigi Galvani (1737–98) in the 1780s (published in 1791), in which he examined electrically induced convulsions in dead frogs, gave rise to a belief that the subtle electric fluid that was assumed to be responsible for electrical effects was also present in living bodies and responsible for various life processes. Although contested, notably by Alessandro Volta (1745–1827), who insisted that the electrical effects noticed by Galvani were merely the result of connecting two different metals by a passive moist body, the notion of "animal electricity" became widely accepted. By the late eighteenth century, many prominent European physiologists were convinced that electricity was intrinsic to all life processes. During the French Revolution, experiments on the plentiful freshly decapitated corpses made it plausible that electricity was the vital fluid and that its proper application could potentially raise the dead. In 1818, the Scottish chemist Andrew Ure (1778–1857) tried to revive an executed criminal by administering electric shocks. Mary Shelley's (1797–1851) *Frankenstein; or,*

The Modern Prometheus (1818) was not, at the time, considered to be outside the realm of possibility. In fact, in the 1830s, the amateur scientist Andrew Crosse (1784–1855) earned a reputation as an "atheist, a blasphemer, a reviler of religion" for claiming to use an electrochemical process to create a living insect, *Acarus electricus*. It is small wonder, then, that electricity continued to be under theological scrutiny. As recently as the 1930s, Dr. Albert S. Hyman of New York City was accused of "tampering with providence" for his pioneering work on the artificial cardiac pacemaker, now routinely used for the electrical control of cardiac arrhythmias.

More recently, the connection of electrical phenomena with religious ideas appears in widespread cultish beliefs about the power of certain electromagnetic fields for good and evil. Electromagnetic waves, particularly those of extremely low frequency (ELF), are especially suited for attracting archetypal projections of properties normally ascribed to the divine: omnipresence (they penetrate almost anything), omnipotence (they are supposed to cause a wide variety of specific effects, from which there is virtually no protection), and invisibility.

Electricity was the last of the classical sciences to arise at a time when the rule of the materialistic, mechanistic view of nature and man was gathering momentum. The Gnostic/alchemical imagery imbedded in electrical theorizing, however, operated sub rosa as a sort of subversive quasi-spiritual factor within mechanistic scientific thought. On an unconscious level, electricity still evokes images of that paradoxical figure of alchemy, Mercurius, and of the elusive vital fluid. These unconscious associations of imagery have persisted and reemerged in our time as quantum-mechanical speculations on the role of consciousness in the material world.

See also Alchemy; Enlightenment; Hermeticism

BIBLIOGRAPHY

Benz, Ernst. *The Theology of Electricity: On the Encounter and Explanation of Theology and Science in the Seventeenth and Eighteenth Centuries.* Trans. by Wolfgang Taraba. Allison Park, Penn.: Pickwick, 1989.

Cantor, Geoffrey. *Michael Faraday: Sandemanian and Scientist.* Basingstoke, U.K.: Macmillan, 1991.

Cantor, Geoffrey, and M. J. S. Hodge. *Conceptions of Ether: Studies in the History of Ether Theories, 1740–1900.* Cambridge: Cambridge University Press, 1981.

Cohen, I. B. *Franklin and Newton.* Philadelphia: American Philosophical Society, 1956.

Hanning, Peter. *The Man Who Was Frankenstein.* London: Frederick Muller, 1979.

Heilbron, J. L. *Electricity in the Seventeenth and Eighteenth Centuries: A Study of Early Modern Physics.* Berkeley: University of California Press, 1979.

Levere, Trevor. *Poetry Realized in Nature: Samuel Taylor Coleridge and Early Nineteenth-Century Science.* Cambridge: Cambridge University Press, 1981.

Pera, Marcello. *The Ambiguous Frog: The Galvani-Volta Controversy on Animal Electricity.* Princeton, N.J.: Princeton University Press, 1992.

Priestley, Joseph. *The History and Present State of Electricity with Original Experiments.* London, 1767.

Schaffer, Simon. "Natural Philosophy and Public Spectacle in the Eighteenth Century." *History of Science* 21 (1983): 1–43.

Schofield, R. E. *Mechanism and Materialism: British Natural Philosophy in an Age of Reason.* Princeton, N.J.: Princeton University Press, 1970.

Secord, James A. "Extraordinary Experiment: Electricity and the Creation of Life in Victorian England." In *The Uses of Experiment,* ed. by D. Gooding, T. Pinch, and S. Schaffer. Cambridge: Cambridge University Press: 1989, 337–83.

Stillings, Dennis. "The Primordial Light: Electricity to Paraelectricity." *Archaeus* 2(1) (Fall 1984): 81–90.

Whittaker, Sir Edmund. *A History of the Theories of Aether and Electricity.* 2 vols. 1951 and 1953. Reprint. New York: Dover, 1989.

Wickland, Carl. *Thirty Years Among the Dead.* 1924. Reprint. London: Spiritualist Press, 1968.

72. Chaos Theory

John Polkinghorne

Although Sir Isaac Newton (1642–1727) did not think of the physical world as being merely mechanical, his theory was so precise and deterministic in its apparent character that succeeding generations, particularly in France, inclined to a clockwork understanding of the universe. Twentieth-century science has radically revalued this judgment. Not only has quantum theory revealed the existence of an imprecise and probabilistic subatomic domain, but the Newtonian equations of classical physics have been discovered to possess a large measure of unpredictability as an intrinsic property of the behavior they describe. This feature arises from an exquisite sensitivity to precise circumstances, which means that, for many systems, the slightest variation produces radically different future outcomes. In a word, the Newtonian world contains many more clouds than clocks. This insight has been given the name of chaos theory.

The first hint of this surprising discovery came to light in the researches of Jules Henri Poincaré (1854–1912) at the turn of the century. He had been studying the successive approximations used by Pierre Simon Laplace (1749–1827) some one hundred years earlier to "prove" the stability of the solar system. In fact, Poincaré found a grave flaw in the argument, which was the first indicator of the presence of sensitive dependence. It is not possible to solve the gravitational problem of even three bodies interacting with each other, in an analytic (that is, smoothly varying) form, precisely because small changes can generate increasingly large effects.

Late in the twentieth century, the burgeoning use of computers to investigate numerically the behavior of complex systems soon produced many more examples of this phenomenon. An early illustration was provided in 1961 by the work of Edward Lorenz, who was investigat- ing simple models of weather systems. A common feature of all of these examples is that their equations involve nonlinearity (that is to say, doubling the input does not double the output but causes it to change in some much more complicated way). The great sensitivity of weather systems has given rise to a classic expression of chaotic unpredictability, the so-called butterfly effect: A butterfly stirring the air with its wings in the African jungle today will have consequences for the storm systems over North America in three weeks' time.

It was soon realized, particularly through the work of Benoit Mandelbrot, that chaotic systems have their own kind of geometry naturally associated with them. Rather than the smooth curves of classical analysis, one encounters a kind of infinitely jagged entity that is called a "fractal." Fractals have approximately the same structure on whatever scale they are sampled. A crude illustration is provided by a tree made up of limbs that are made up of branches that are made up of twigs. Whether one looks at the large scale of the tree, or the small scale of the twigs, or at any intermediate scale, the same kind of forking character is to be discerned.

Chaos theory is, in many ways, an unfortunate misnomer for the phenomenon of sensitivity to circumstance. The behavior of chaotic systems is not predictable, but it is not completely random either. The future behaviors of such a system are confined within a restricted range of possibilities, which is called a "strange attractor." Chaos theory is an oxymoronic kind of subject: It has about it an ordered disorderliness.

Chaos theory has proved applicable to many different nonlinear situations. It can be used to analyze the futures markets in commodities as well as the behavior of the physical world. In its scientific applications, it origi- nated in the study of classical (Newtonian) dynamics.

However, the systems being considered soon became sufficiently sensitive for their behavior to depend upon details of circumstance at the quantum level where, in consequence, Heisenberg's uncertainty principle would intervene to forbid access to the fine detail needed for attempts at more accurate prediction. The relationship of classical chaos theory to quantum theory has been the subject of intense study and unresolved debate. The correct quantum analogue of chaotic behavior has not yet been established satisfactorily. One possible source of the difficulty lies in the fact that intrinsic quantum "fuzziness" does not permit the infinite degree of constantly replicating structure that fractal geometry requires.

Physicists thought that more than two centuries of studying Newtonian dynamics had given them a reliable understanding of its nature. The discovery of chaos theory shows that, in fact, this was not the case. All can now agree that most classical systems are intrinsically unpredictable. They are also intrinsically unisolable from their environment (that is, their behavior exhibits certain characteristics because of where they are), owing to their sensitive vulnerability to changes in their surroundings. A simple example of this latter phenomenon is provided by a billiard-ball model of air molecules colliding with each other at room temperature. After only one-ten-thousand-millionth of a second, fifty such collisions have taken place. A detailed and accurate prediction of the outcome would require taking into account the presence of an electron (the smallest particle of matter) on the other side of the observable universe (as far away as you can get) interacting through the force of gravity (the weakest natural force). Chaos theory has certainly revised, in a drastic way, our understanding of the nature of what we can know about the physical world.

It is a question for further debate whether this unavoidable epistemological defect should be taken to signal an ontological change in our account of reality. There is no logically enforceable move from epistemology to ontology, though the strategy of realism, so natural to a scientist, encourages the attempt to maximize the connection between the two. If this were to be pursued in relation to chaos theory, it would encourage the interpretation of its undoubted unpredictability as leading to an openness to the future, allowing the presence of other causal principles in bringing it about, in addition to those described by conventional physics. In that case, the deterministic Newtonian equations, from which the discussion originated, would have to be treated as approximations to some more subtle and supple reality. The debate about the possible deeper significance of chaos theory is only beginning, and it will undoubtedly continue for some time.

See also Isaac Newton; Physics; Twentieth-Century Cosmologies

BIBLIOGRAPHY

Ford, Joseph. "What Is Chaos, That We Should Be Mindful of It?" In *The New Physics,* ed. by Paul Davies. Cambridge: Cambridge University Press, 1989, 348–72.

Gleick, James. *Chaos: Making a New Science.* London: Heinemann, 1988.

Polkinghorne, John. *Reason and Reality.* London: SPCK, 1991, Ch. 3.

Ruelle, David. *Chance and Chaos.* Princeton, N.J.: Princeton University Press, 1991.

Russell, Robert J., Nancey Murphy, and Arthur Peacocke, eds. *Chaos and Complexity.* Vatican City: Vatican Observatory Publications, 1995.

Stewart, Ian. *Does God Play Dice? The Mathematics of Chaos.* Oxford: Blackwell, 1989.

PART VII

The Earth Sciences

73. THEORIES OF THE EARTH AND ITS AGE BEFORE DARWIN

David R. Oldroyd

Geology, as understood today, is a science that seeks to provide a history of the earth. It does so by examining minerals, rocks, and fossils. By investigating how they are arranged in the earth's crust, geologists endeavor to piece together a historical account of how the crust was formed and what the planet's past conditions were like. Geological inquiry involves field-work. It also deploys the results of laboratory investigations, which may attempt, for example, to simulate conditions in the earth's interior, model processes of geological change, or analyze and synthesize rocks and minerals artificially. Geologists attempt to understand the structure and behavior of the earth as a whole by formulating theories based on observations of surface features, as well as by the analysis, for example, of vibrations produced by earthquakes and the earth's magnetic properties. Geologists consider the earth to be about 4.5 billion years old, and some theorists (a minority) concern themselves with ideas about the planet's origin and its place in the cosmos. The subject, therefore, overlaps to some extent cosmology, cosmogony, and astronomy. Except in its cosmological aspects, and its use of evolutionary theory to account for the fossil record, geology today does not have much interaction with theology. Geology emerged from earlier sciences such as mineralogy toward the end of the eighteenth century.

Theories of Physico-Theology

In the seventeenth and eighteenth centuries, however, when modern science was becoming established, there was a distinctive genre of texts generally referred to as "theories of the earth." These writings sought to interweave science and theology, in what was then called "physico-theology." They sought to provide a scientific basis for theological ideas and to make religion acceptable to reason as well as to faith. But partly because, at that time, only small portions of the earth's surface had been investigated empirically, the "theories of the earth" tended to be highly speculative.

There was a long tradition within the Christian Church, going back at least to Theophilus of Antioch (fl. later second century A.D.), of attempting to determine the age of the earth by examining the texts of the Old Testament and integrating them, where gaps made it necessary, with pagan histories such as those of Greece or Egypt. Theophilus concluded that the earth was divinely created in 5529 B.C. More refined studies of this kind were made in the seventeenth century, of which the most famous in the English-speaking world was that of Archbishop James Ussher (1581–1656), Anglican primate of Ireland. Making allowance for leap years, changes in calendars, and the Jewish use of lunar months, and effecting cross-links between the biblical record and pagan histories, Ussher obtained a wonderfully precise date of October 23, 4004 B.C., for the earth's Creation. Ussher's dates, published in 1658, were often printed in the margins of the Authorized (King James) Version of the Bible and were widely accepted by Protestants until well into the nineteenth century (and, in broad terms, up to the present among some conservative Protestants). Hence, the early theories of the earth had to be accommodated in a highly constrained time frame.

Among the seventeenth-century theorists of the earth, the most important and influential was René Descartes (1596–1650). In his *Principia philosophiae* (*Principles of Philosophy* [1644]), the French philosopher sought to ground his thinking in ideas and chains of reasoning that were "clear and distinct," or self-evidently true, at least to him. Among such ideas were the notion of a nondeceiving God, whose existence was proved to Descartes's satisfaction by a version of the ontological argument and who acted as a "guarantor" of Descartes's "clear and distinct" ideas; the identity of space and matter; and the idea that the cosmos was formed of small corpuscles of various shapes and sizes, which interacted mechanically with one another, producing the various materials of the natural world. With matter and space regarded as one and the same, there could be no vacua for Descartes. So the corpuscles necessarily moved in various approximately circular orbits, or "vortices."

Descartes believed that three kinds of corpuscles were produced by the mechanical interactions of the primeval cosmic matter. There were small spherical corpuscles formed by the rubbing of the original larger pieces; very fine "rubbings" that filled the interstices between the spherical corpuscles; and larger corpuscles formed by the coalescence of the very small particles, or residues, of the originally divided matter. They corresponded approximately with the air, fire, and earth of earlier theories of matter. Descartes envisaged that the particles of the fiery element collected at the centers of celestial vortices, forming suns. But "blisters" might form at the cool surfaces of these bodies, somewhat like slag collecting on the surface of molten metal in a furnace. If these "sun spots" accumulated sufficiently, they might cover the whole surface of a sun. Its light would then be extinguished and it would become a body with a solid crust. In this condition, it might be "captured" by a neighboring vortex and become a planet to that vortex's sun. It was in this way, Descartes suggested, that the earth had been formed and had become part of the solar system.

Descartes then proposed a sequence of changes of the earth's interior, each change following naturally on the other, such that various concentric layers come into being; and mountain ranges were formed by collapses of parts of the crust into subterranean cavities. Descartes did not make it clear how much time was required for such a sequence of events, but he seems to have supposed that it might all have come about within the confines of a "biblical" time scale. Descartes's theory of the earth was an example of physico-theology not because his cosmogony was intimately linked to biblical history, but because the "mechanical" theory was philosophically (or metaphysically) grounded in rational principles that were self-evidently correct, and their truth was "guaranteed" by Descartes's nondeceiving God. Hence,

there was an intimate interweaving of Descartes's physics and his metaphysics.

Another interesting example of physico-theological ideas about the earth is provided by the English theologian Thomas Burnet (c. 1635–1715) in his *Telluris theoria sacra* (*Sacred Theory of the Earth* [1680–9]). Basing his thinking partly on Descartes's theory, Burnet supposed that the early earth was a heterogeneous fluid from which there formed a solid core surrounded by concentric layers of water and an earthy crust. This provided the conditions for an original paradise. But the crust supposedly cracked, owing to the heat of the sun, releasing the earth's internal waters and causing the Noachian Flood. The rupturing of the crust yielded mountains and ocean basins, into which the waters retreated, thus giving the earth's present irregular shape. Burnet also predicted a future desiccation of the earth, a great conflagration, ignited by volcanoes, leading to an eventual reconstitution of the earth, once again of perfect form. The interesting thing about Burnet's theory of the earth was his attempt to produce a time scheme that envisaged one great cycle, from Creation to the Day of Judgment, in accord with the Bible *and* the latest results of Cartesian physics. It was a physico-theology.

Other British examples of physico-theology were provided by naturalists William Whiston (1667–1752) in 1696, by John Ray (1627–1705) in 1693, and by John Woodward (1667–1728) in 1695. Whiston supposed that the earth originated as a comet, captured by the sun, and that the Deluge was produced by vapor from a neighboring comet's tail. Ray attributed fossils to deposition by the Deluge. Woodward thought that the earth's strata settled out, after the Deluge, according to the specific gravities of the materials and that the promiscuous mingling of rock, soil, water, and animal remains caused by the Deluge could explain the presence of fossils in hills far from the sea. But Martin Lister (1639–1712) was unconvinced of the organic origin of fossils and wrote (1671) that they were merely peculiar stones found in the earth that just happened to resemble organic remains.

Nearly all European scientific writers about the earth in the seventeenth century thought it necessary to produce a theory that accorded with the biblical account, but in such a way as to be compatible with physical principles. And because the physico-theological writers on the earth supposed that the planet was so young, they had to provide theories that (according to modern geological ideas) offered greatly accelerated geological processes. It is noteworthy, however, that the Danish physician-cum-naturalist Nicolaus Steno (1638–86), working in Tuscany, produced (1665) a hypothetical sequence of events, represented in the form of six sections, that depicted the supposed history of the region. These sections embodied the "principle of superposition," which asserted that underlying strata were deposited before those lying above them and envisaged two periods of catastrophic flooding followed by removal of sediment and collapse of strata into cavities hollowed out by running water. Interestingly, the region in Italy near Volterra, which may have inspired Steno's sections, is undergoing extremely rapid erosion, such that Etruscan tombs are exposed to view as the cliff face collapses from time to time. So perhaps Steno had empirical reasons to think that geological history could be packed into a biblical time scale. Like Descartes, by whom he was influenced, Steno was a "mechanical philosopher."

It was the presence of organic fossils, found in strata far from the sea or even near mountaintops, and the question of time, that constantly presented a challenge to physico-theology. Also, as the eighteenth century proceeded, with more information reaching Europe about the global distributions of animals and plants, the problems of direct integration of empirical information and scriptural history became more acute. It was possible to classify animals, vegetables, and minerals, but to explain their distribution satisfactorily in accordance with biblical history (especially the story of the Noachian Flood) was difficult. The Swedish naturalist Carolus Linnaeus (1707–78) suggested (1743) that the earth was originally covered by water, with a large and high island near the equator that offered a range of climatic regions. Animals could be distributed according to their appropriate climate zones, and, after a gradual fall in the level of the waters, the animals could multiply and spread around the globe to occupy their present locations. But, of course, no such island was ever found by explorers.

The French naturalist Georges Louis Leclerc, Comte de Buffon (1707–88), felt less constraint from the biblical account. He supposed (1749) that the earth and other planets were formed from pieces of the sun, knocked off by a comet. Though the motion of the universe as a whole was of divine origin, its subsequent changes were thought to occur in accordance with general physical laws. Subsequently (1778), Buffon proposed a set of seven stages, or "epochs," for a cooling earth, with a gradual "degeneration" of forms. Large animals could have entered the

Old and New Worlds from a common northern source before the continents separated by the foundering of a linking region of land.

Buffon's model fit the facts of biogeography in a more plausible way than did the hypothesis of Linnaeus. But Buffon went further, attempting an experimental determination of the age of the earth. He did this by cooling spheres of various materials, heated to as high a temperature as possible, and finding how long they took to cool to room temperature. He then estimated how long a sphere the size of the earth might take to cool through a similar temperature range and offered a very rough estimate of the age of the earth. His published figure was about seventy-five thousand years, but it is known that he speculated privately that it might be as old as three million years. Buffon's theory of the earth was condemned by the theology faculty at the Sorbonne. His account of the earth's history seemed at odds with that of Genesis, even if his number of epochs was the same as the number of biblical Days of Creation. Buffon responded that each Day might, indeed, correspond to an immense length of time; this was the loophole that many authors in the nineteenth century, and some through the twentieth, have sought to utilize. In a broader sense, however, Buffon's ideas reflected the emergence of deist thought, which looked to nature rather than the Bible for answers to the age of the earth.

Naturalistic Theories

The early theorists had their ideas about the earth linked to both divine design, as manifested in nature, and special revelation. If, however, the design argument could, by itself, be deemed sufficient to convince one of the divine construction of the cosmos, the solar system, and the earth, then revelation might seem an unnecessary intellectual requirement. This was the position adopted by deists. They held that nature itself manifested God's creative power, his "wisdom," and his design. Theirs was an exclusively natural theology, not a revealed religion.

As an intellectual movement, deism arose in the seventeenth century, but it was not until the second half of the following century that it began to play a significant role in theories of the earth. The most important figure in this movement was the Scottish gentleman-farmer James Hutton (1726–97), in his *Theory of the Earth* (1795). Totally unrestrained by the limitations of a biblical time scale, Hutton observed that agricultural soil was continually washing into the sea. It was also, he supposed, constantly being replenished by the weathering of rock. But this implied that, in time, all of the rocks of the dry land would be worn away, and then agriculture—so necessary to human existence—would no longer be possible. Hutton thought this incompatible with divine "wisdom," and so he proposed a cyclic theory of the earth.

Hutton thought it likely that the earth's interior was exceedingly hot. Sediment was consolidated under the oceans by material deposited above it and by the internal heat emanating from the earth below. Under great pressure, expansion of molten matter might occur, such that magma (as we would say) would begin to protrude into the earth's crust, elevating it and forming new mountain ranges. This process would cause tilting of strata, which might later be "planed off" by weathering and erosion. Subsequently, new sediments might be deposited horizontally on the exposed ends of dipping beds that had been formed in a previous phase of the great geological cycle. Hutton envisaged land slowly rising and then being reduced by erosive processes. His cyclic theory was such that, if true, human agriculture could continue in effect to eternity.

Hutton's theory implied that one might expect to find places where horizontal strata would lie on top of, and athwart, inclined strata, giving what geologists today call "unconformities." His prediction was successful, for in the latter part of his career he found several such structures in various parts of Scotland. If they originated as Hutton supposed, the earth was necessarily of enormous age. As his biographer, John Playfair, put it in 1805: "The mind seemed to grow giddy by looking so far into the abyss of time."

The French deist Jean Baptiste Lamarck (1744–1829), a protégé of Buffon, arrived at the notion of the immensity of geological time independently of Hutton. Lamarck's concern was with the similarities and differences between fossils and organisms found alive today. He could not envisage any processes that would lead to worldwide extinctions of species, and so he proposed that there had been slow "transmutation" of forms. Constantly, but slowly, changing environments presented organisms with new "needs," which brought about new habits. Gradual changes in form occurred slowly over many generations, as newly developed characteristics, resulting from the changed habits, were passed on. Characters could also disappear if certain bodily parts were no longer used.

Lamarck was professor of invertebrate zoology at the Muséum d'Histoire Naturelle in Paris. His colleague and rival, Georges Cuvier (1769–1832), attended to vertebrate zoology and produced a totally different theory. He showed that there were fossil mammals quite unlike those existing today and a seeming absence of intermediate forms. Cuvier's explanation (1813) was that there had been a series of great geological "catastrophes." These, he supposed, wiped out species in restricted regions, which might have been repopulated subsequently by creatures migrating from places that had escaped devastation. Cuvier's time scale far exceeded that of biblical literalism, and his ideas were not propounded for theological reasons. But Cuvier was a devout Protestant, and his theories were frequently embraced in the nineteenth century by those wishing to effect a reconciliation between science and religion. Typically, the Noachian Flood could be regarded as the last of Cuvier's catastrophes. So we have nineteenth-century "catastrophism," which offered a form of physico-theology that was attractive to many in that period (and through to the present among the proponents of creation science).

The idea of grand catastrophes, seemingly involving geological processes unlike anything known today, was an anathema to the Scottish geologist Charles Lyell (1797–1875). He wanted to place geology on a purely naturalistic theoretical and methodological basis. As a science, it should have nothing to do with providential interventions. The earth should change only according to the experimentally ascertainable laws of physics and chemistry. It should have nothing to do with the cosmogonies of the old physico-theologists. Geology should have endless reserves of time at its disposal, and its arguments should be based on field observations.

Lyell's theory was, in broad terms, similar to that of Hutton. It drew on observations of recently extinct volcanoes in the Auvergne region of central France; in particular, Lyell utilized evidence he gathered at Mount Etna in Sicily. Here a large mountain was evidently built up slowly by successive lava flows. (The details of some of these flows were known from historical records.) But the slowly accumulating mountain, which was evidently of great age in terms of human history, overlay limestones that contained fossils much the same as creatures still found in the Mediterranean. Geologically speaking, these fossils were *young*. But, in terms of human history, they were evidently *old*. Considering the whole sequence of geological strata making up the earth's crust, extending down into layers containing fossils quite different from those alive today, it was clear that the earth must be very old.

Lyell's *Principles of Geology* (3 vols., 1830–3) was subtitled *An Attempt to Explain the Former Changes of the Earth's Surface, by Reference to Causes Now in Operation.* Or, to use a well known aphorism of the nineteenth-century geologist-historian Archibald Geikie (1835–1924), Lyell held that "the present is the key to the past." Using this methodological principle, Lyell sought to sever geology and theology, and in this he was largely successful. He emphasized that the "new" science of geology should not concern itself with speculations about the earth's origin. Speculations such as these, made by the seventeenth-century physico-theologists, had given geology and geologists a bad name and should be avoided.

Lyell was quickly dubbed a "uniformitarian." He envisaged a "steady-state" earth. Species became extinct from time to time by natural causes. They also appeared from time to time, by what process Lyell knew not. The net result was a slow turnover of species, which tracked gradual changes in the environment. But so far as Lyell was concerned, there was no overall change in any particular direction—that is, no "progress."

By contrast, many of Lyell's contemporaries claimed that the stratigraphic record did show progressive change toward the present state of affairs. Moreover, certain clerical geologists (such as William Buckland [1784–1856] of Oxford and Adam Sedgwick [1785–1873] of Cambridge) were glad to link their geological findings to catastrophism, biblical history (in greatly modified form), and Christian eschatology. To an extent, they could offer an account of geological history that accorded better with empirical observations than did Lyell's uniformitarian doctrine. Sedgwick's ideas, for example, based on the results of arduous fieldwork and geological mapping in the Lake District of northern England, offered strong evidence of "catastrophic" earth movements.

Nevertheless, Lyell's geology gave the science an attractive methodological program, which sought to separate the study of the earth from both cosmogony and religion; in the twentieth century, his views have sometimes been thought essential to investigating the earth's past. Yet, some of his "biblical" opponents, who countenanced catastrophic events, including the Noachian Flood, did geological work of fundamental importance, notably in the establishment of the major boundaries of

the stratigraphic column, such as are still used today. "Diluvium," so called, could be mapped in a scientific manner, even if it was thought of as the residue of the Flood. Later it was reevaluated as glacial material.

Charles Darwin (1809–82) greatly admired Lyell's work, read it avidly during the voyage of H.M.S. *Beagle,* and sought to use Lyell's ideas of random slow changes of the relative levels of land and sea to explain geological phenomena that he saw during the voyage. As eventually formulated, Darwin's theory of evolution by natural selection accepted Lyell's ideas about the great age of the earth, the slowness of geological processes, the uniformity of the laws of nature, and the separation of geology from theology. However, contrary to Lyell's doctrine, Darwin envisaged substantive change in nature, through time, though he eschewed the idea of "higher" and "lower" forms.

It was "transformism," either Lamarckian or Darwinian, that was repugnant to many thinkers in the first half of the nineteenth century. It suggested a Creator God who operated by many small-scale changes rather than one grand act of Creation and, thus, seemed to diminish God's creative power. Moreover, some theologians viewed the transformist hypothesis as utterly incompatible with the biblical account of the earth's origin and history. As evidence in favor of transmutation gradually increased following the publication of Darwin's *Origin of Species* (1859), the Genesis account of Creation has increasingly come to be construed in a non-literal fashion.

Though Lyell is renowned for having provided one of the main supports for Darwin's theory, it is a mistake to suppose that he was a "crypto-transformist" and that all that Darwin had to do was extrapolate geological uniformitarianism to the organic world. Lyell, in fact, accepted Darwinian theory only with reluctance. Nevertheless, with a synthesis of Lyell's "gradualism," his ideas on the age of the earth, and Darwin's theory of natural selection (later supplemented by Gregor Mendel's [1822–84] theory of inheritance), a naturalistic account of the history of life on Earth could be established, which accounted in broad terms for the facts of stratigraphy (presuming that the fossil record is very incomplete). The empirical evidence furnished by the catastrophists could, thus, be seen from a gradualist perspective, given sufficient time for geological processes to occur.

The resulting synthesis of geology and biology does not logically compel disbelief in a divine Creator. But it makes a Creator a philosophical redundancy so far as geology and theories of the earth are concerned. One is left, then, with faith as to whether the earth's formation and its geological history, including the history of life, had a supernatural origin.

See also Cosmogonies from 1700 to 1900; Deism; Genesis Flood; Geology and Paleontology from 1700 to 1900; Great Chain of Being; Uniformitarianism and Actualism

BIBLIOGRAPHY

Barr, J. "Why the World Was Created in 4004 B.C.: Archbishop Ussher and Biblical Chronology." *Bulletin of the John Rylands University Library* 67 (1985): 575–608.

Brooke, John Hedley. "The Natural Theology of the Geologists: Some Theological Strata." In *Images of the Earth: Essays in the History of the Environmental Sciences,* ed. by Ludmilla J. Jordanova and Roy S. Porter. Chalfont St. Giles: British Society for the History of Science, 1978, 39–64.

———. *Science and Religion: Some Historical Perspectives.* New York: Cambridge University Press, 1991.

Brush, Stephen G. *Transmuted Past: The Age of the Earth and the Evolution of the Elements from Lyell to Patterson.* Cambridge: Cambridge University Press, 1996.

Gillispie, Charles C. *Genesis and Geology: A Study in the Relations of Scientific Thought, Natural Theology, and Social Opinion in Great Britain, 1790–1850.* Cambridge, Mass: Harvard University Press, 1951.

Gould, Stephen Jay. *Time's Arrow, Time's Cycle: Myth and Metaphor in the Discovery of Geological Time.* Cambridge, Mass., and London: Harvard University Press, 1987.

Haber, Francis C. *The Age of the World: Moses to Darwin.* Baltimore: Johns Hopkins University Press, 1959.

Hooykaas, Reijer. *Natural Law and Divine Miracle: The Principle of Uniformity in Geology, Biology, and Theology.* Leiden: Brill, 1963.

Lindberg, David C., and Ronald L. Numbers, eds. *God and Nature: Historical Essays on the Encounter between Christianity and Science.* Berkeley: University of California Press, 1986.

Numbers, Ronald L. *The Creationists: The Evolution of Scientific Creationism.* New York: Knopf, 1992.

Oldroyd, David R. *Thinking About the Earth: A History of Ideas in Geology.* London and Cambridge, Mass.: Athlone and Harvard University Press, 1996.

Porter, Roy S. "Creation and Credence: The Careers of Theories of the Earth in Britain, 1660–1820." In *Natural Order,* ed. by Barry Barnes and Stephen Shapin. Beverly Hills and London: Sage, 87–124.

Roger, Jacques. "La Théorie de la Terre au XVIIe Siècle." In *Pour une Histoire des Sciences à Part Entière,* ed. by Claude Blanckaert. Paris: Albin Michel, 124–54.

Rossi, Paulo. *The Dark Abyss of Time: The History of the Earth and the History of Nations from Hooke to Vico.* Chicago and London: University of Chicago Press, 1984.

Rudwick, Martin J. S. "Uniformity and Progression: Reflections on the Structure of Geological Theory in the Age of Lyell." In *Perspectives in the History of Science and Technology,* ed. by Duane H. Roller. Norman: University of Oklahoma Press, 1971, 209–17.

Schneer, Cecil J., ed. *Toward a History of Geology.* Cambridge, Mass., and London: MIT Press, 1969.

Toulmin, Stephen, and June Goodfield. *The Discovery of Time.* Harmondsworth: Penguin, 1967.

74. THE GENESIS FLOOD

Rodney L. Stiling

Traditions of a great flood are found in the oral and written memories of many cultures, both extant and extinct, nearly all over the world. The best-known account is that found in the biblical Book of Genesis 6–9, according to which God completely reshaped the original creation by means of a worldwide waterborne catastrophe. From the survivors of Noah's ark, both human and animal, God "replenished the earth," and human and natural history alike began anew. The precise relationship of this host of narratives to the biblical tradition is not settled. They may all stem from some singular event in the ancient past or from a number of similar, but unconnected, events. The Genesis account of the Flood also bears an obvious relationship to other ancient Near Eastern flood narratives (such as that preserved in the Epic of Gilgamesh), but the nature of that relationship (that is, the priority of literary influence) is uncertain.

Natural Questions

Early Jewish and Christian thought about the Flood was mostly restricted to discussion of the theological or the moral lessons to be drawn from the Genesis narrative or of such questions as the capacity of the ark, the height and extent of the Flood, postdiluvian animal distribution, and the geographical location of the resting place of the ark. Early Christian writers such as Tertullian (c. 160–c. 220), Ambrose (c. 339–97), Origen (c. 185–c. 251), and Augustine (354–430) occasionally defended the historicity of the Genesis Flood against contemporary skeptics by invoking the science of their day (for example, in such questions as the relative heaviness of the elements of water and earth). But speculation about the physical effects of the Flood itself remained rare

throughout late antiquity and the Middle Ages. Interest in scientific interpretations of the Flood and its natural effects did not materially emerge until the Renaissance.

The Renaissance and the New World

The discoveries that were made during the great age of exploration sparked new interest in the Noachian Flood. Although the historicity of the Flood was never disputed, the Genesis account came under close scrutiny as the reports of new lands, plants, animals, and peoples accumulated. Such influential writers as Johannes Buteo (1492–1572) in his *Opera geometrica* (*Geometrical Works* [1554]) and Athanasius Kircher (1601–80) in his *Arca Noe* (*Noah's Ark* [1675]) proposed detailed designs of the ark and defended the barge's capability to provide sufficient space for representatives of all of the animals, even those of the New World. But theories of the postdiluvial distribution of plants, animals, and peoples became all the more problematic as the scope and size of the earth were comprehended. (As early as the fifth century, Augustine had suggested that God might have performed miracles of re-creation to restock all of the far-off places with appropriate animals.) In an effort to explain the biblical text in terms of contemporary knowledge, natural historians and biblical scholars in the early-modern era speculated on the use of boats, narrow land-bridges, and modifications of migrating animals and humans owing to climatic and geographical change. Serious questions regarding the extent of human settlement on the prediluvian earth led Isaac de la Peyrère (1596–1676) to argue in his *Prae-adamitae* (1655) that the Flood had been limited to the Middle East and that some races of humans lived in land areas beyond the reach of the Flood. He also suggested that the presence of humans in the New World indicated that some humans may have been created separately from, and perhaps even before, the creation of Adam. He referred to them as Pre-Adamites. In a notable foreshadowing of an orthodoxy that was widely adopted two hundred years later, critics of his theory, such as Edward Stillingfleet (1635–99) in his *Origines sacrae* (1662) and Matthew Poole (1624–79) in his *Synopsis criticorum* (1669–76), agreed that the Flood had been geographically limited but insisted that it had been widespread enough to encompass the entire human population of Noah's day.

The natural sciences of the Renaissance and early-modern era benefited from the debates over the nature and the extent of the Flood among natural historians, who wished to integrate and harmonize natural and scriptural factors. Animal behavior and migration habits, plant and animal classification schemes, hygrometry, hydrostatics, animal and human adaptability, the volume of the oceans, and the hydrological cycle were among the subjects that received increased emphasis. However, the question of the ability of a singular event to produce the entire sequence of fossil-bearing strata of rocks, as well as such surface features as valleys, mountains, lakes, and rivers, dominated most discussions of the Flood. Physical phenomena of the earth, such as specific gravities of minerals, deposition rates of sediments, fossil sequences, and the hydrologic carrying power of moving water, took on new importance, and the Flood became the focus of the varied interests that would later combine to form the science of geology.

Fossils and Theories of the Earth

The ancients advanced two distinct, but not necessarily mutually exclusive, theories of the origins of fossils. One theory held that they were the product of inorganic natural virtues that produced lifelike designs in rocks. A second theory held that fossils were the petrified remains (or impressions) of actual organic beings. Both ideas seem to be present in Aristotle (384–322 B.C.). Marine fossils, particularly those found in elevated strata, evoked special interest. Ancient Greek writers such as Herodotus (c. 484–c. 420 B.C.) and Aristotle attributed the placement of such fossils to gradual interchanges of land and sea. A few early Christian writers, including Tertullian, argued suggestively that such fossils constituted evidence of extensive general flooding of some kind. Others, such as Procopius of Gaza (c. 465–528), argued

specifically that the fossils were relics of the Noachian Flood. How generally this view was accepted during the Middle Ages is not known. In the Renaissance era, natural historians continued to refer to all of the earlier views of the origins of fossils. By the early-modern era, however, propelled by the growth of the mechanical philosophy, the work in Italy of Nicolaus Steno (1638–86) presented in his influential *Prodromus* (1665), and the prolific writings of the "theory of the earth" school in England, general agreement emerged on two key points: first, that fossils were the petrified remains (or impressions) of actual organic beings; second, that rock strata were preserved in a kind of chronological sequence, the deeper layers and fossils having been deposited before those above them.

Thomas Burnet (c. 1635–1715) in his *Sacred Theory of the Earth* (1680–9), John Woodward (1665–1728) in *Essay Toward a Natural History of the Earth* (1695), William Whiston (1667–1752) in *A New Theory of the Earth* (1696), John Hutchinson (1674–1737) in *Moses's Principia* (1724), John Ray (1627–1705) in *Three Physico-Theological Discourses* (1693), and others in the early Newtonian era specifically sought to integrate the physical principles of mechanical philosophy with scriptural accounts of nature. In the process, a growing sense developed by the mid-eighteenth century in Britain that all or most of the fossil-bearing strata should be associated with the unique circumstances of the Noachian Flood. As this view grew in popularity, the prospect that organic forms might have become permanently extinct became all the more real, as even the vast new reservoir of plant and animals found in the New World failed to provide the living analogues of fossilized forms found in Europe. Extinction constituted a philosophical problem for some, but, to the extent that it might be thinkable, the Noachian Flood provided a reasonable explanation for it.

Diluvialism and the Deluge

In the later eighteenth century and into the nineteenth, geologists in Europe and America gradually conceded that the geological formations were simply too complex and too thick (many miles in some areas) to have been the result of a single, even if yearlong and complex, catastrophic Flood. Common observation of erosion and deposition rates suggested that the stratified rocks had been built up in discrete stages, either gradually and steadily, as the Scotsman James Hutton (1726–97) suggested in his *Theory of the Earth* (1795), or in periodic convulsions of geological violence in which continents would sink to become ocean floors or vice versa, as the French paleontologist Georges Cuvier (1769–1832) argued in his *Discours Préliminaire sur las Révolutions du globe* (*Preliminary Treatise on the Revolutions of the Globe* [1812]). Either way, those geologists who sought evidence for the Flood in the earth looked no longer to the massive thickness of stratified fossil-bearing sediments but, rather, to the layers of unconsolidated deposits at or near the earth's surface that most directly constituted the actual landscape. Cuvier even calculated that the most recent of his proposed revolutions had occurred about "five or six thousand" years ago and that its effects were everywhere visible. Valleys, canyons, lakes, grooves, scratches, boulder fields, till, rolled pebbles, and other geomorphological phenomena were routinely assigned to the Flood in such influential works as *Geological Essays* (1799) by the Irish chemist Richard Kirwan (1733–1812) and *Outlines of the Geology of England and Wales* (1822) by William Daniel Conybeare (1787–1857) and William Phillips (1775–1828). Conybeare and Phillips seem to have been among the first to employ the term "diluvium" to refer to certain surface deposits they believed had been produced by prodigious hydrological forces no longer in action, such as those that might have attended the Noachian Flood.

Thus was born "diluvialism," the idea that massive, powerful floods had from time to time swept out of the seas and over the continents with destructive and manifest results. On this view, Noah's Flood, one such diluvial catastrophe, explained the boulder fields, grooves, scratches, and other indications. Diluvialism was effectively promoted in *Reliquiae diluvianae* (*Diluvial Remains* [1823]) by the Oxford geologist William Buckland (1784–1856), who carefully left any specific correspondence between the Flood and his diluvialist theory implicit, and by the Cambridge geologist Adam Sedgwick (1785–1873), who did not. The fortunes of the Genesis Flood and diluvialism remained linked for only a short time, however. In his 1831 presidential address before the London Geological Society, Sedgwick jumped from the diluvial ark: He and other diluvialists concluded that a single Flood could not even have produced the entire complex of surface deposits. Buckland also noted (in *Geology and Mineralogy Considered with Reference to Natural Theology* [1836]) that there were no human remains in the diluvium, as one might expect in Flood-related deposits. By the late 1830s, diluvialism and the Flood had parted company. Shortly thereafter, the glacial theory promoted by the Swiss naturalist Louis Agassiz (1807–73) in his *Études sur Les Glaciers* (*Studies on Glaciers* [1840]) was able to account for the diluvial phenomena, and the Genesis Flood retired from the field as an active geological participant.

Shrinking Significance

By midcentury, even geologists committed to the inspiration of the Bible no longer held that the Flood had produced lasting geological marks. Never doubting the historical veracity of the Flood, the American geologist Edward Hitchcock (1793–1864) in his *Elementary Geology* (1840) exemplified the new understanding of the Flood by interpreting it first as a relatively tranquil worldwide event that had left no permanent marks and then simply as a significant and large-scale event that had been confined to the Middle East and Southwest Asia and that had left no visible physical indications (*Religion of Geology* [1851]). The English geological writer John Pye Smith (1774–1851) popularized this latter view in his *On the Relation Between the Holy Scriptures and Some Parts of Geological Science* (1839), which was influential in both Britain and America. Despite occasional protests by so-called scriptural geologists, many of them laymen, who insisted on a six-day Creation and a geologic column-generating Deluge, by the last third of the nineteenth century the view of the Flood as partial or limited had emerged as dominant among most English-speaking Christians, including evangelicals. Conservative Christian geologists such as the Canadian John William Dawson (1820–99) and the American fundamentalist George Frederick Wright (1838–1921) adopted this version of a nonuniversal biblical flood. Although British Museum Assyriologist George Smith (1840–76) made dramatic discoveries in 1872 and 1873 of the cuneiform record of a great flood in the Epic of Gilgamesh that stimulated interest in the literary and historical aspects of the Flood, by the end of the nineteenth century few professional geologists regarded the notion of a Noachian Flood worthy of notice, either negatively or positively. The content of Bible handbooks, encyclopedias, dictionaries, and commentaries revealed that, for most English-speaking Christians, a local, geologically insignificant flood had become the standard interpretation for reconciling the Genesis account with science and remained so well into the twentieth century.

Flood Geology and Creation Science

Since most of its retreat from geological significance took place in the decades just before the publication of Darwin's *Origin of Species* (1859), the Flood did not figure as a factor in the initial debates over Darwinism. Twentieth-century "Flood geology" (known after about 1970 as "creation science"), by contrast, constituted a deliberate strategy in the larger campaign against evolution. An echo of nineteenth-century scriptural geology, Flood geology insisted that the Genesis Flood had produced almost all of the vast sequence of fossil-bearing strata, as well as the geomorphology of the earth's surface. By positing that life appeared on earth no more than six thousand to ten thousand years ago, creation scientists argued that a long and slow process of evolution could never have occurred. This revival of an old interpretation of the Flood emerged in the first quarter of the twentieth century with the publication of a number of books by the Seventh-day Adventist teacher George McCready Price (1870–1963), notably *The New Geology* (1923). It enjoyed widespread popularity after the publication of the highly successful *The Genesis Flood* (1961) by theologian John C. Whitcomb Jr. (1924–) and hydrologist Henry M. Morris (1918–).

By the close of the twentieth century, virtually no mention of the Genesis Flood appeared in geological literature, save for an occasional suggestion by a geologist of a possible connection between the now-established evidence for large-scale postglacial meltwater flooding and flood stories in general. On the religious side, the fate of the Noachian Flood has varied. Those who embraced creation science continued to assign geological significance to the Deluge. But for most Christians, the value of the Genesis account lay in its inspiring historical and theological significance rather than in any appeal as a geological explanation.

See also Creationism Since 1859; Geology and Paleontology from 1700 to 1900; Origin and Unity of the Human Race; Uniformitarianism and Actualism

BIBLIOGRAPHY

Browne, Janet. *The Secular Ark: Studies in the History of Biogeography.* New Haven, Conn.: Yale University Press, 1983.

Cohn, Norman. *Noah's Flood: The Genesis Story in Western Thought.* New Haven, Conn.: Yale University Press, 1996.

Dundes, Alan, ed. *The Flood Myth.* Berkeley: University of California Press, 1988.

Gillispie, Charles Coulston. *Genesis and Geology: A Study in the Relations of Scientific Thought, Natural Theology, and Social Opinion in Great Britain, 1790–1850.* 1951. Reprint. Cambridge, Mass.: Harvard University Press, 1996.

Huggett, Richard. *Cataclysms and Earth History: The Development of Diluvialism.* Oxford: Clarendon, 1989.

Klaver, J. M. I. *Geology and Religious Sentiment: The Effect of Geological Discovery on English Society and Literature between 1829 and 1859.* Leiden: Brill, 1997.

Moore, James R. "Charles Lyell and the Noachian Deluge." *Journal of the American Scientific Affiliation* 27 (1970): 107–15.

————. "Geologists and the Interpreters of Genesis." In *God and Nature: Historical Essays on the Encounter between Christianity and Science,* ed. by David C. Lindberg and Ronald L. Numbers. Berkeley: University of California Press, 1986, 322–50.

Numbers, Ronald L. *The Creationists: The Evolution of Scientific Creationism.* New York: Knopf, 1992.

Rappaport, Rhoda. *When Geologists Were Historians, 1665–1750.* Ithaca, N.Y.: Cornell University Press, 1997.

Rudwick, Martin J. S. *The Meaning of Fossils: Episodes in the History of Paleontology.* New York: Science History Publications, 1976.

Rupke, Nicolaas. *The Great Chain of History: William Buckland and the English School of Geology, 1814–1849.* Oxford: Clarendon, 1983.

Stiling, Rodney L. "The Diminishing Deluge: Noah's Flood in Nineteenth-Century American Thought." Ph.D. diss., University of Wisconsin, 1991.

Young, Davis A. *The Biblical Flood: A Case Study of the Church's Response to Extrabiblical Evidence.* Grand Rapids, Mich: Eerdmans, 1995.

75. Geology and Paleontology from 1700 to 1900

Nicolaas A. Rupke

From Buffon to Darwin

During the late eighteenth and early nineteenth centuries, geology opened up a vast and unfamiliar vista of earth history. The study of rocks and fossils showed that the history of the earth had not covered the same stretch of time as the history of mankind, but extended back immeasurably before the advent of *homo sapiens*. It also appeared that prehuman earth history had not been a single period of continuity, but a great chain of successive worlds (that is, of periods of geological history), each with its own distinctive flora and fauna. Moreover, it emerged that the nature of the historical succession had been progressive: Successive worlds increasingly resembled our present world, with respect both to its inhabitants and the environmental conditions under which they had lived. This new vista of earth history equaled the Copernican revolution in its intellectual implications, reducing the relative significance of the human world in time, just as early-modern astronomy had diminished it in space.

The discoveries and theories of this new historical geology dominated the discourse of science with religion during the years 1780–1860, a period that began with the *Époques de la nature* (1778) by the Parisian naturalist Georges Louis Leclerc, Comte de Buffon (1707–88), whose book made a large and international readership familiar with the notion of periods of prehuman earth history, and ended with Charles Darwin's (1809–82) *Origin of Species* (1859). The Darwinian theory of organic evolution, which incorporated "geological time" and "progressive development," started a new chapter in the science-religion debates by denying the special creation of organic species, including humans. Until then, the question of organic origins was, to a large extent,

kept off the research agenda of the geological community.

The main sticking points of the geological theories with religion were those in which the new geology no longer fit a literal interpretation of Genesis. These points were the age of the earth, the geological effect of the Deluge, the impact of original sin on the natural world, and the question of whether or not earth history is an eschatological process. Geology and paleontology triggered controversies over these issues; yet, it should be emphasized that, in some ways, geology and religion interacted fruitfully, with reciprocal stimulation, mediated through the concepts and institutions of natural theology.

Dating the Past

Traditional sacred chronology calculated the age of the earth at some six thousand years; but there existed no consensus among chronologists, and no fewer than 140 different estimates were put forward, ranging from 3616 to 6484 years B.C. A widely used figure was 4004 B.C., worked out by the Rev. James Ussher (1581–1656), archbishop of Armagh, and published in his scholarly *Annales Veteris et Novi Testamenti* (*Annals of the Old and New Testament* [1650–4]). The principal source for these figures was the Pentateuch—in particular, the genealogies of the patriarchs recorded in Genesis. In the course of the seventeenth and eighteenth centuries, sacred chronology gained considerable scholarly weight, being made a subject of study by such giants of early-modern humanistic scholarship as the Leyden professor Joseph Justus Scaliger (1540–1609) and his Jesuit competitor Dionysius Petavius (1583–1652). One of the assumptions of sacred chronology was that the earth, having been created for man, had no fundamentally different or longer history than its human inhabitants and that, therefore, the earth's history and human history were effectively of identical duration.

Historical geology subverted biblical chronology by uncoupling earth history from world (or human) history and assigning a much greater antiquity to the earth than could be accommodated by the Old Testament genealogies. Initially, evidence for a long stretch of earth history prior to man was qualitative. The absolute age of the earth and the duration of the periods of its history could not be reliably estimated until the full sequence of rock formations and fossil communities, the very entities to be dated, had been determined. Yet, the known cumulative thickness of the sedimentary strata of the stratigraphic column, which acquired the essential outline of its modern form by the early 1840s, amounted to several kilometers, indicating the immensity of geological time. The Oxford geologist William Buckland (1784–1856) spoke of "millions of millions of years."

In one respect, sacred chronology and the new geological time scale were in agreement—namely, that the earth, irrespective of the length of its history, had a distinct beginning in time. Historical geology thus helped counter the eternalism of Enlightenment deism and, in particular, the theory of an "eternal present" expressed in the famous maxim of the Scottish naturalist James Hutton (1726–97): "we find no vestige of a beginning,— no prospect of an end."

An early quantitative method for estimating the age of the earth was based on the belief that the earth had originated as an incandescent blob and had undergone a process of secular cooling. The stretch of time from the moment that the earth had acquired a solid crust until the present day could be estimated, given a figure for the rate of heat loss. Buffon carried out ingenious refrigeration experiments and dated the earth at some seventy-six thousand years of age, the earth thus having been in existence for seventy thousand years prior to the appearance of its human inhabitants. During the 1850s and subsequent decades, this method was perfected, and the figure much increased, by the British physicist William Thomson (Lord Kelvin [1824–1907]), who calculated that the earth was maximally four hundred million years old and minimally twenty million, the minimum figure being his preferred estimate. Such numbers were regarded by the Darwinians as too conservative, however, and by this time Kelvin's figures were used less to invalidate sacred

chronology than to undercut Darwin's theory of organic evolution.

The Deluge

Some naturalists and scholars were not swayed by the stratigraphic evidence for an immense stretch of geological time. These men, the Mosaical geologists, who were not part of the leadership of the new geology that was being institutionalized in geological societies and university chairs, continued the sacred-cosmogony tradition of authors such as the Gresham College (London) professor of physic John Woodward (1667–1728), who, in his *Essay towards a Natural History of the Earth* (1695), had attributed the entire sedimentary column to the Deluge. Others who had referred many of the sedimentary and tectonic features of the earth's crust to the Deluge included the London cleric Thomas Burnet (c. 1635–1715), the Cambridge mathematician William Whiston (1667–1752), the Swiss naturalist Johann Jakob Scheuchzer (1672–1733), and such internationally less renowned figures as the Bristol vicar Alexander Catcott (1725–79), a follower of the anti-Newtonian John Hutchinson (1674–1737).

Mosaical geology survived in leading English-language geological treatises until the early nineteenth century and can be found in the first volume of the *Organic Remains of a Former World* (1804), written by the London physician and amateur paleontologist James Parkinson (1755–1824). However, by the time Parkinson published the third volume of his trilogy (1811), he had changed his mind and adopted the Cuvierian view of earth history. Mosaical geology was undermined by, among others, the French geologists Georges Cuvier (1769–1832) and Alexandre Brongniart (1770–1847), who demonstrated that successive geological formations are characterized by distinctive assemblages of fossils, concluding that these formations are the record of separate periods of geological history. Cuvier presented his synthesis of earth history in a *Discours préliminaire* (*Preliminary Discourse* [1811]) to his *Ossemens fossiles*. The English translation of the earlier work was edited by the Scottish geologist Robert Jameson (1774–1854). Not only the two periods of biblical cosmogony, ante- and postdiluvial, were recognized, but several more prior to the creation of man. These had been terminated by geological upheavals, causing the extinction of many forms of life. The last of these upheavals was generally believed to be identical with the Genesis Flood.

This perception of the history of the earth as a concatenation of prehistoric periods was sensationally confirmed by Buckland's cave researches. In his classic *Reliquiae diluvianae* ([*Diluvial Remains* [1823]), Buckland developed his so-called hyena-den theory of caves: Assemblages of bones and teeth, found fossilized in the floor of caves, are not the product of a cataclysmal event, but of a gradual accumulation over a long period of time, during which the caves were the den and larder of cave hyenas. The extinction of the cave carnivores, however, had been caused by the Deluge, which simultaneously had scooped out valleys and deposited surface detritus, the so-called Diluvium. Buckland's hyena-den theory undermined traditional diluvialism in that it limited the effect of the biblical Flood to the emplacement of loose surface sediment; the massive rock strata below it had been deposited during earlier periods of geological history.

The appearance of the *Reliquiae Diluvianae* was followed by a stream of articles and books in which Buckland's hyena-den theory and its diluted diluvialism were fiercely attacked. Most famous were *Scriptural Geology* (1826–7), written by the Oxford-educated Granville Penn (1761–1844) expressly in refutation of Cuvier and Buckland; and *New and Conclusive Physical Demonstrations, both of the Fact and the Period of the Mosaic Deluge* (1837), by George Fairholme, who, in sticking to traditional Mosaical catastrophism, put forward ingenious arguments in support of the view that the entire sedimentary column was emplaced in a single global cataclysm. The writings of these men form the intellectual roots of twentieth-century flood geology, although there is little evidence of real continuity.

Buckland's diluted diluvialism did not survive for long. By around 1830, the Geological Society of London formed the stage for a classic debate, pitching the catastrophist-diluvialists, headed by the Oxford clergymen-geologists Buckland and William Daniel Conybeare (1787–1857), against the Scottish geologist Charles Lyell (1797–1875) and his supporters. A central issue was whether valleys are diluvial or fluvial in origin. The Cambridge professor of geology Adam Sedgwick (1785–1873), initially a confirmed Bucklandian diluvialist, in his 1831 anniversary address as president of the society, dramatically recanted, admitting that Noah's Deluge had left no appreciable geological traces. The Bible, Sedgwick

more comprehensively maintained, contains information for our moral conduct, not for scientific instruction.

Sedgwick's public retraction was followed by Buckland's. In his Bridgewater Treatise, Buckland disentangled earth history from human history by arguing that the last geological catastrophe had not been Noah's Deluge, but an earlier event that had taken place just before the creation of man; the Genesis Flood, though real and historical, had been a geologically quiet event. Many of the phenomena that Buckland had attributed to the Deluge he now began seeing as the result of glacial action, and Buckland led the way in Britain when he introduced the glacial theory of the Swiss (and later Harvard) geologist Jean Louis Rodolphe Agassiz (1807–73). In other words, the Deluge was now interpreted not as a nonhistorical myth but as a nongeological event, a view that had been championed before by Scottish Presbyterians, such as the zoologist John Fleming (1785–1857) and the Edinburgh professor of physics and mathematics John Playfair (1748–1819). This vindication of the Lyellian position on the origin of "diluvial" phenomena and the removal of the Mosaical Deluge from the research agenda of London's Geological Society did not mean, however, that Lyell's anticatastrophism was generally adopted: Catastrophic occurrences continued to be postulated by the Cuvierians.

By this time, two basic schemes to reconcile Genesis with geology had become current. The first, the "day-age" exegesis, was advocated by Parkinson, the nonconformist minister Joseph Townsend (1739–1816), the Oxford chemistry professor John Kidd (1775–1851), the surgeon-paleontologist Gideon Algernon Mantell (1790–1852), and various other geologists, who suggested that the days of the Creation Week of Genesis should be understood as periods of geological time. They engaged in the complex task of demonstrating that the sequence of events of the Creation Week are exactly paralleled by the essential features of the stratigraphic column.

The second scheme, advocated by Buckland and followed by many others, such as the nonconformist divine and naturalist John Pye Smith (1774–1851) in his *On the Relation between the Holy Scriptures and Some Parts of Geological Science* (1839), made room for geology with the following exegesis. The first verse of Genesis, "In the beginning God created the heaven and the earth," is not a prospective summary of the Creation Week that follows but a retrospective reference to the primordial creation of the universe, including the earth; the first part of the second verse, "And the earth was without form and void," takes up the history of the earth following an indefinite and possibly very long interval, after the destruction of the last geological world, and just before the appearance of humans.

Buckland's scriptural interpretation had the sanction of leading Anglican theologians, including the low-church evangelical John Bird Sumner (1780–1862), bishop of Chester and later archbishop of Canterbury, and E. B. Pusey (1800–82), Regius Professor of Hebrew at Oxford and leader of the high-church Tractarian movement. The same exegesis had previously been put forward by the Scottish Presbyterian Thomas Chalmers (1780–1847), author of the Bridgewater Treatise on *The Adaptation of External Nature to the Moral and Intellectual Constitution of Man* (1833).

The advantage of this reconciliation scheme was that the earth's history was completely extricated from biblical history; the Bible covered only the history of mankind, while sacred chronology applied exclusively to the period of human existence. This perception seemed corroborated by Cuvier's observation that there were no fossil humans and by Buckland's failed attempt to find human remnants in diluvial deposits. Yet, this particular view required a further reconciliatory adjustment when, by the end of the 1850s, it became undeniable that humans had been contemporaneous with extinct mammals and, as Lyell showed in his *Geological Evidences of the Antiquity of Man* (1863), of much greater age than allowed for by biblical chronology.

There is little or no evidence to suggest that the advocates of these reconciliation schemes were influenced by higher criticism of the Bible. Higher criticism did not become a topic of major public debate in Britain before *Essays and Reviews* (1860) appeared and the bishop of Natal, John William Colenso (1814–83), published *The Pentateuch and the Book of Joshua Critically Examined* (1862), questioning the Mosaic authorship and therewith the historicity of the Pentateuch.

Extinction, Death, and Sin

The fact of extinction became established by around 1800, largely from a comparative anatomical study of fossil mammals, a study that culminated in Cuvier's monumental *Recherches sur les ossemens fossiles* (*Researches on Fossil Bones* [1812]). Initially, some naturalists

regarded extinction as incompatible with their belief in a plenitude of forms. Each species was believed to represent a necessary link in the Chain of Being, an integral part of creation as a whole, which contributed to its perfection. Destruction of a single link would lead to the dissolution of the entire chain. Divine providence would not let this happen, a belief theologically supported by the story of Noah's ark, which had preserved representatives of all species. Ironically, the notion of extinction was frowned upon also by Enlightenment "eternalists" such as Hutton because of its historicist connotation.

The eighteenth-century language of providence and the Chain of Being was gradually adjusted to the discoveries of historical geology. Some (such as Parkinson) argued that extinction was part of divine superintendence of earth history; others (such as Buckland) argued that fossils are missing links that, when added to the array of living forms, fill gaps and produce a complete Chain of Being. Hence, plenitude became a historical notion; the Chain of Being had no deficiencies when considered as a chain of history. In this way, paleontology significantly added to, and refreshed, the argument from design.

Yet, the very existence of fossils also represented a new problem: It indicated that death had occurred long before the appearance of man on Earth. Moreover, death had taken place not only by natural means, but also violently, inflicted by individuals of one animal species on those of another. This was apparent from the carnivorous anatomy of certain vertebrate fossils. Animal aggression in the geological past was depicted with savage realism in the various reconstructions of ancient landscapes and expressed by the English poet Alfred Tennyson (1809–92) in the famous lines from *In Memoriam,* "Dragons of the prime, That tare each other in their slime." The problem posed by this discovery of carnivorousness and death in the geological past derived from the traditional belief that such phenomena had not existed in the Garden of Eden and had entered the world because of, and subsequent to, the Fall of man. Old and New Testament texts formed the basis for this belief, in particular St. Paul's letter to the Romans: "Wherefore, as by one man sin entered into the world, and death by sin" (5:2). Mosaical geologists, opposed to the new geology, such as the English clergyman-naturalist George Young, were quick to point out the apparent discrepancy.

The geologists, Buckland in his Bridgewater Treatise prominently among them and also several Scottish Presbyterians, responded by using the argument of Paleyan utilitarianism: Carnivorous animals function as a "police of nature," eliminating the sick and the old who would otherwise suffer as a result of pain and a lingering death; the aggregate of animal enjoyment is, thus, increased and that of pain diminished; moreover, carnivorous animals are a check on excess numbers that would have produced a shortage of food and starvation among herbivores; therefore, carnivorousness is a "dispensation of benevolence."

The utilitarian argument did not provide a solution, however, to the problem of the prehuman existence of death. How could death be a punishment for man's sin if it already existed in prehuman geological history? In an attempt to solve this conundrum, St. Paul's letter to the Corinthians was cited: "For since by man came death, by man came also the resurrection of the dead" (15:21). The passage was interpreted to mean that, just as resurrection exclusively applies to humans, so death has been a punishment only to man and not to the creation as a whole.

Designer Fossils

An area in which the interaction of religion (in the form of a belief in providence) with the new geology proved particularly fruitful was the functionalist study of fossils. The design argument (natural theology, physico-theology), prevalent throughout early-modern times, attracted new popularity with the *Natural Theology* (1802) of the Cambridge theologian William Paley (1743–1805), cresting during the 1830s when the Bridgewater Treatises appeared. One of the most successful of these treatises was Buckland's *Geology and Mineralogy Considered with Reference to Natural Theology* (1836). The nonconfessional, general nature of the argument from design made it suitable as an instrument of interdenominational cooperation in the furtherance of science, and the use of nature as a source of design arguments made it possible that ecclesiastical sinecures were awarded to men who devoted their time to science. Both Buckland and Sedgwick, for example, lived on church incomes. In this way, natural theology became a vehicle for the introduction of geology at Oxford and Cambridge, for the promotion of this new subject at the British Association for the Advancement of Science, and for the "geologizing" by many a clergyman across the British Isles.

Paley had made the human body the main source of evidence for design, though he also used plants and animals. Geology now provided a new range of facts that exemplified adaptation and design. In particular, paleontology, with its extinct and unfamiliar forms of life, enriched the canon of design examples by adding new, in some instances bizarre, contrivances from the geological past. The megatherium, for example, one of several genera of extinct sloths, became a cause célèbre of natural theology when its seemingly monstrous frame was successfully interpreted in terms of functional anatomy. Its grotesque-looking "claws" were a perfect adaptation to the environmental conditions of the South American pampas, where the giant sloths had dug up roots or, in a modified interpretation, had wrenched tree trunks out of the ground. Natural theology did not allow for imperfections in nature and sharpened the interpretative faculties of its practitioners in perceiving functional adaptation. Many geologists, their scientific colleagues and patrons, across the diluvialist-fluvialist divide, applauded this work and added to it.

The historical dimension of paleontology provided natural theology with an altogether novel argument. Design in the world indicated a supreme designer, but this argument could be used only as a refutation of atheists. Deists, who reduced the operations of nature to those of an autonomous machine that had been designed and set in motion only at the moment of its origin, were not threatened by the argument from design. Their mechanistic worldview seemed invalidated, however, by historical geology, with its evidence of not just one single beginning but of a series of successive worlds, each with a fresh beginning and a new creation. Hence, geology served to refute not only atheists, but also deists—a function of the new science that was highlighted by its clerical practitioners.

Eschatology

In the course of the first few decades of the nineteenth century, a consensus emerged that the relationship of successive fossil worlds was one of progress or progressive development. One criterion for this was taxonomic: The lower and earlier forms of life are simpler, and the higher, or later, ones are more complex. For example, an age of fishes had preceded an age of reptiles, and this, in turn, had been followed by the rule of mammals; man, at the top of the taxonomic ladder, had come last. A second criterion was ecological: Progress was a matter of the improvement in the habitability of the earth to humans, and taxonomic progress was reduced to a subsidiary effect of environmental change.

The ecological criterion connected paleontology to the study of the earth as a planet. At this time, there was a revival of the old notion of a central heat, which stated that the earth had originated as an incandescent mass, that this mass had cooled down gradually and acquired a solid crust, and that it still retained a core of primeval heat. The central heat was believed to have influenced the climate of the earth, especially during its early stages of thermal evolution. The dominant form of life during a particular period of earth history had been the one most perfectly adapted to contemporary environmental conditions.

The progressivist synthesis strengthened the biblical Christian notion of time as a directional phenomenon, against the cyclical notion of time found in Enlightenment eternalism. It undercut the uniformitarian, steady-state model of earth history, prominently defended by Lyell in his *Principles of Geology* (3 vols., 1830–3). Subsequently, in two famous anniversary addresses to the Geological Society of London (1850; 1851), Lyell persisted in his denial that the stratigraphic record showed a progressive trend. The vertebrate paleontologist Richard Owen (1804–92) accepted the challenge and, point by point, refuted Lyell's arguments. Yet, in adopting progressivism, the natural theologians took in a Trojan horse, because the progressivist synthesis became the hard core of the argument for organic evolution in the anonymously published *Vestiges of a Natural History of Creation* (1844), written by the Edinburgh publisher Robert Chambers (1802–71). Sedgwick, one of the fiercest critics of *Vestiges,* in the famous fifth edition of his *Discourse on the Studies of the University of Cambridge* (1850), backtracked on his earlier commitment to progressivism. Ironically, some of the antiprogressionist arguments used by Lyell have become part of the armamentarium of modern-day creationists in their opposition to the Darwinian theory.

Both the taxonomic and the environmental criteria of geological progress were anthropocentric, defining progress in relation to man. Buckland ended his Bridgewater Treatise with illustrations of how the composition and structure of the earth's crust had been purposefully designed for the benefit of mankind, particularly for nineteenth-century society and most generously for Great Britain in support of industry and empire. Geological progressionism merged seamlessly with the Victorian belief in sociopolitical and economic progress.

The perception of an anthropocentric design in earth history went hand in hand with the biblical notion of history as a directional and a teleological process. Yet, to many geologists, progressive development seemed open-ended, and, as such, historical geology weakened part of the Christian view of history, namely the belief that history follows an eschatological course toward an apocalyptic conflagration and the Second Advent of Christ and his millennial reign. A fine example of an earlier historical study of the earth, couched in eschatological language, is the *Three Physico-Theological Discourses, Concerning (1) the Primitive Chaos and Creation of the World, (2) the General Deluge, Its Causes and Effects, (3) the Dissolution of the World and Future Conflagration* (1693), written by the Cambridge-educated naturalist John Ray (1627–1705).

Apocalyptic theology, especially millenarianism, had been strong as late as the seventeenth and eighteenth centuries and, in the course of the first half of the nineteenth century, experienced a new wave of popularity, especially in England, where Warburtonian lecturers (the Warbutonian Lecture at Lincoln's Inn, London, had been established to prove the truth of the Christian religion from the completion of prophecy in the Old and the New Testaments) and such popular authors as the prolific millenarian writer William Cuninghame (d. 1849) added their voices to the apocalyptic chorus, lambasting the progressivist synthesis of earth history. Among the scientists themselves, those who adhered to the "day-age" exegesis were inclined to believe that, with the reign of man, Earth's history had come to an end. The geological present, by corresponding to the seventh day of the Creation Week, marks the end of God's creative work. The Presbyterian stonemason-geologist Hugh Miller (1802–56) felt uneasy about the emphasis on progress, pointing instead to instances of degeneration in the fossil record. In his *Footprints of the Creator* (1847), he saw the final culmination of the earth's vast history in an eschatological future kingdom of Christ.

National Context

Concern with the "Genesis and geology" issue was not uniformly spread across national boundaries. For the most part, it was a British preoccupation or, more precisely, a preoccupation in the English-speaking world, as leading figures of the North American scientific community also took part in attempts to reconcile the Bible with science. Prominent among them was the Congregationalist Edward Hitchcock (1793–1864), president of Amherst College and professor of natural theology and geology. In *The Religion of Geology and Its Connected Sciences* (1851), he advocated the "day-age" reconciliation scheme, although in the second edition of his major book (1859) he let go of the need for exact correspondences, emphasizing instead that a study of nature's laws would lead us to the divine lawmaker. Many of Hitchcock's fellow American naturalists shared his interest in harmonizing the findings of geology with the biblical account of Creation, among them Hitchcock's teacher Benjamin Silliman (1779–1864), professor of chemistry and natural history at Yale University and founder-editor of the *American Journal of Science and Arts*.

On the European mainland, original literature on the "Genesis and geology" issue was relatively scarce; yet, major contributions were not altogether lacking. Already the Genevan and Calvinist naturalist Jean André Deluc (1727–1817) had presented a famous reconciliation scheme in, for example, his *Lettres sur l'histoire physique de la terre* (*Letters on the Physical History of the Earth* [1798]), arguing that the Creation days were to be understood as geological epochs and that the present epoch of earth history, conformable in length to biblical chronology, began with Noah's Deluge, which had occurred when large cavities below the antediluvial continents had collapsed, draining the oceans and exposing their floors to become our dry land. In the Netherlands, the Calvinist polymath and Romantic poet Willem Bilderdijk (1756–1831) followed Deluc's scheme in his treatise on *Geologie* (1813). A rare German contribution to the genre was *Geschichte der Urwelt, mit besonderer Berücksichtigung der Menschenrassen und des mosaischen Schöpfungsberichtes* (*History of the Antediluvian World, with Special Reference to the Races of Men and the Mosaic Creation Accounts* [1845]), written by the Lutheran professor of zoology at the University of Münich Andreas Wagner (1797–1861).

One could make a case for the thesis that the issue was of interest primarily in Protestant communities. There were exceptions to such a rule, however. The bishop of Hermopolis and minister for ecclesiastical affairs and public instruction Denis Antoine Luc de Frayssinous (1765–1841) wrote an enormously popular *Défense du Christianisme; ou, conférences sur la réligion* (*Defense of Christianity; or, Lectures on Religion* [1825]; 17 eds.), in which he argued that the days of Creation were indeterminate periods of time and that Cuvier's work had demonstrated that the Mosaical order of the

creation of living beings matched their geological occurrence. Moreover, one of the most substantial reconciliation books of the period was the *Cosmogonie de Moise comparée aux faits géologiques* (*Cosmogony of Moses Compared with Geological Events* [1838–59]), written by the Catholic naturalist and magistrate Marcel Pierre Toussaint de Serres de Mesplès (1780–1862).

Yet, it is true that, on the Continent, "Genesis and geology" never became as prominently controversial as it was in Britain and North America. In Germany, for example, none of the leading names of the geological community, such as Leopold von Buch (1774–1853), bothered to address the issue. The writings of Alexander von Humboldt (1769–1859) lacked all biblical concern. In Cuvier's *Preliminary Discourse*, too, the Pentateuch was treated not as Holy Writ but as one of several histories of nations. Such absence of reverence for the text of Genesis, however, was less the result of major differences in belief with British colleagues than of the circumstances in which Continental Europeans wrote. French and German science had nonecclesiastical, professional niches—for example, in the Parisian Muséum d'Histoire Naturelle and in the many secular universities of Germany. By contrast, English cultural and religious life was dominated by the two ancient universities of Oxford and Cambridge, in essence Anglican seminaries. This had the dual effect that science in England was supported and cultivated by the Church, but also that science had much greater difficulty in acquiring autonomy and had to be discussed in terms that were directly relevant to the education of the clergy. Both diluvialism and the geological design argument were examples of this phenomenon. In the United States, too, institutions of higher learning were, not uncommonly, denominational foundations.

Hence, the science-religion discourse developed a professional dimension: At Oxbridge, the clergymen-geologists, speaking to a largely Church-destined audience, stressed the relevance of geology to Genesis, whereas in London, at meetings of the Geological Society, the same Oxbridge dons mingled with nonecclesiastical and increasingly professional geologists, keeping Genesis as much as possible off the agenda and not infrequently taking scientific cues from their Continental colleagues.

By and large, mainstream Christian geologists and paleontologists succeeded in coming to terms with the new geology. Their reconciliation schemes provided space for scientific inquiry as well as for religious belief. Traditional Flood geology, with its tenets of a young earth and a geologically effective, cataclysmal deluge, became regarded as incorrect and antiquated. Interestingly, it has reemerged in the twentieth century, primarily among American fundamentalist scientists.

See also Creationism Since 1859; Great Chain of Being; Natural Theology; Theories of the Earth and Its Age Before Darwin; Uniformitarianism and Actualism

BIBLIOGRAPHY

Appel, Toby A. *The Cuvier-Geoffroy Debate: French Biology in the Decades before Darwin.* Oxford: Oxford University Press, 1987.

Brooke, John H. "The Natural Theology of the Geologists: Some Theological Strata." In *Images of the Earth,* ed. by Ludmilla Jordanova and Roy Porter. Chalfont St. Giles: British Society for the History of Science, 1979, 39–64.

———. *Science and Religion: Some Historical Perspectives.* Cambridge: Cambridge University Press, 1991.

Burchfield, Joe D. *Lord Kelvin and the Age of the Earth.* London: Macmillan, 1975.

Cannon, Susan Faye. *Science in Culture: The Early Victorian Period.* New York: Dawson/Science History Publications, 1978.

Conser, Walter H. *God and the Natural World: Religion and Science in Antebellum America.* Columbia: University of South Carolina Press, 1993.

Corsi, Pietro. *Science and Religion: Baden Powell and the Anglican Debate, 1800–1860.* Cambridge: Cambridge University Press, 1988.

Gillispie, Charles C. *Genesis and Geology: The Impact of Scientific Discoveries upon Religious Beliefs in the Decades before Darwin.* 1951. Reprint. New York: Harper and Row, 1959.

Haber, Francis C. *The Age of the World: Moses to Darwin.* Baltimore: Johns Hopkins University Press, 1959.

Herbert, Sandra. "Between Genesis and Geology: Darwin and Some Contemporaries in the 1820s and 1830s." In *Religion and Irreligion in Victorian Society: Essays in Honor of R. K. Webb,* ed. by R. W. Davis and R. J. Helmstadter. London and New York: Routledge, 1992, 68–84.

Hooykaas, Reijer. *Natural Law and Divine Miracle: A Historical-Critical Study of the Principle of Uniformity in Geology, Biology, and Theology.* Leiden: Brill, 1959.

Livingstone, David N. *Darwin's Forgotten Defenders: The Encounter between Evangelical Theology and Evolutionary Thought.* Grand Rapids, Mich.: Eerdmans, 1987.

Millhauser, Milton. "The Scriptural Geologists: An Episode in the History of Opinion." *Osiris* 11 (1954): 65–86.

Moore, James R. "Geologists and Interpreters of Genesis in the Nineteenth Century." In *God and Nature: Historical Essays on the Encounter between Christianity and Science,* ed. by David C. Lindberg and Ronald L. Numbers. Berkeley: University of California Press, 1986, 322–50.

North, John D. "Chronology and the Age of the World." In *Cosmology, History, and Theology,* ed. by Wolfgang Yourgrau and Allen D. Breck. New York: Plenum, 1977, 307–33.

Numbers, Ronald L. "Science and Religion." *Osiris* 2d ser. 1 (1985): 59–80.

———. *The Creationists: The Evolution of Scientific Creationism.* New York: Knopf, 1992.

Page, Leroy E. "Diluvialism and Its Critics in Great Britain in the Early Nineteenth Century." In *Toward a History of Geology,* ed. by Cecil J. Schneer. Cambridge, Mass.: MIT Press, 1969, 257–71.

Porter, Roy M. "Creation and Credence: The Career of Theories of the Earth in Britain, 1660–1820." In *Natural Order: Historical Studies of Scientific Culture,* ed. by Barry Barnes and Steven Shapin. Beverley Hills, Calif.: Sage, 97–123.

Rappaport, Rhoda. "Geology and Orthodoxy: The Case of Noah's Flood in Eighteenth-Century Thought." *British Journal for the History of Science* 11 (1978): 1–18.

Rudwick, Martin J. S. "The Shape and Meaning of Earth History." In *God and Nature: Historical Essays on the Encounter between Christianity and Science,* ed. by David C. Lindberg and Ronald L. Numbers. Berkeley: University of California Press, 1986, 296–321.

Rupke, Nicolaas A. *The Great Chain of History: William Buckland and the English School of Geology, 1814–1849.* Oxford: Clarendon, 1983.

———. "Caves, Fossils, and the History of the Earth." In *Romanticism and the Sciences,* ed. by Andrew Cunningham and Nicholas Jardine. Cambridge: Cambridge University Press, 1990, 241–62.

———. "A Second Look: C. C. Gillispie's Genesis and Geology." *Isis* 85 (1994): 261–70.

Stiling, Rodney. "The Diminishing Deluge: Noah's Flood in Nineteenth-Century American Thought." Ph.D. diss., University of Wisconsin, 1991.

Turner, Frank M. *Contesting Cultural Authority: Essays in Victorian Intellectual Life.* Cambridge: Cambridge University Press, 1993.

Van Riper, A. Bowdoin. *Men among the Mammoths: Victorian Science and the Discovery of Human Prehistory.* Chicago: University of Chicago Press, 1993.

76. UNIFORMITARIANISM AND ACTUALISM

Leonard G. Wilson

The *Oxford English Dictionary,* reflecting the time of its preparation at the beginning of the twentieth century, defines uniformitarianism as "the principles or doctrines held by the uniformitarian school of geologists, the theory of uniformity of action in the forces and processes of inorganic nature." True to its historical principles, the *OED* linked unformitarianism to the opinions of a particular school of geologists. In 1957, *A Dictionary of Geological Terms,* prepared under the direction of the American Geological Institute, defined uniformitarianism as "the concept that the present is a key to the past," a more sweeping, but less exact, definition. By contrast, the *OED* does not recognize the word "actualism" as a geological term at all, noting only its use in theological discourse. As a geological term, "actualism" is of French origin, introduced into English writings on the history of geology as late as the 1950s, with a meaning distinctly different from that of uniformitarianism.

Geology Before Lyell

In 1831, the Rev. William Whewell (1794–1866), Fellow of Trinity College, Cambridge, coined the term "uniformitarianism" to describe the geological doctrine developed by Charles Lyell (1797–1875) the year before in the first volume of his *Principles of Geology.* In the *Principles,* Lyell presented extensive geological evidence to suggest that former changes in the earth's surface could be explained by geological causes now in operation. Lyell saw the past history of the earth as continuous with the present. Throughout a long succession of geological changes that included great variations in climate, he believed, conditions on the earth's surface had remained essentially similar to those existing today. There was no separation between the modern natural world and that of the geological past; they were uniform. Whewell recognized that Lyell's viewpoint was directly opposed to that of most geologists of the time, who assumed that the elevation of sedimentary strata from the bottom of the sea to form hills and mountains, together with the extinction of successive assemblages of fossil animals, must have required "powers more energetic and extensive than those which belong to the common course of every day nature." Most geologists, said Whewell, "spoke of a break in the continuity of nature's operations; of the present state of things as permanent and tranquil, the past having been progressive and violent" (Whewell 1831, 190). In 1820, the Rev. William Buckland (1784–1856) at Oxford University had described geological causes still in action in the modern world as merely "the last expiring efforts of those mighty disturbing forces which once operated" (Buckland 1820, 5). To such belief in a progressive and violent geological past, a belief to which he himself adhered, Whewell gave the name "catastrophism."

Buckland and Whewell were both concerned to reconcile geology with the biblical account of the Creation of the world. According to Archbishop James Ussher's (1581–1656) chronology, which appeared in the margins of the Authorized, or King James, Version of the Bible, God had created the world in 4004 B.C. The violent processes suggested by catastrophism might be considered part of the process of Creation that had brought the earth to its present form. Buckland also saw in superficial sands and gravels of the English countryside effects of the biblical Flood of Noah, and he identified the bones of extinct animals in caves with those that had lived before the Flood. Nevertheless, the reconciliation of geology with a literal interpretation of the Genesis account of Creation was to become increasingly difficult as geological knowledge increased.

Between about 1790 and 1830, amid a wealth of new geological data, geologists were influenced by conflicting schools of thought. In Germany, the mineralogist Abraham Gottlob Werner (1750–1817) distinguished geological formations by their mineralogical characters and postulated that such formations were sediments deposited from a former universal ocean that had extended to the tops of the highest mountains. The oldest rock was granite, found in the cores of mountains, which had crystallized first from the primeval ocean. In Scotland, James Hutton (1726–97), while agreeing with Werner that stratified rocks had been deposited as layers of sediment beneath the sea, argued that, instead of the sea's having receded, the sedimentary strata had been elevated from the seafloor by forces derived from the internal heat of the earth. Granite, said Hutton, had been intruded from below in a molten condition. Where granite veins occurred among sedimentary strata, the heat of the molten granite had altered the sedimentary rock on either side. Granite veins were younger than the surrounding stratified rocks, as were the masses of granite connected with them in the interiors of many mountains.

By the 1820s, when British geologists generally accepted the Huttonian view that stratified rocks were former sediments that had been raised from a horizontal position beneath the sea to inclined or even vertical positions in hills and mountains, they thought that extraordinary forces must have acted formerly to bring about such elevation and dislocation. The greater former energy of geological causes appeared to fit with the eighteenth-century theory of a cooling earth, a theory supported by the increasing heat observed as one descended into deep mines. If the earth were formed originally as a molten mass that had subsequently cooled, there would have been more heat within the earth at earlier geological periods to provide the energy for violent geological change. Accounts of extinct volcanoes in central France, northern Spain, the Rhine Valley, and other localities in Europe suggested that volcanic activity was more widespread in the geological past than at present. In 1811, Georges Cuvier's (1769–1832) and Alexandre Brongniart's (1770–1847) description of the tertiary strata of the Paris Basin revealed an alternation of freshwater with marine formations that, Cuvier thought, implied repeated incursions of the sea upon the land during the tertiary period, accompanied in some cases by the wholesale extinction of animal species. Similarly, among the secondary rocks of England, geologists found that each formation possessed a particular assemblage of fossils, distinct from formations above or beneath it. The discovery in the English secondary strata of large extinct reptiles, such as Ichthyosaurus and Iguanodon, emphasized the strikingly different character of the animals that had formerly lived on the earth. In 1823, among bones found in English caves, William Buckland identified species of animals that were no longer found in England, such as the hyena and the cave bear, as animals destroyed by the biblical Flood. Taken together, such geological discoveries suggested that conditions on the earth's surface had formerly been different from those existing today and that the geological changes that had swept away former animal and plant species were large and violent.

Charles Lyell and Unformitarianism

Historically, uniformitarianism is connected inextricably with Sir Charles Lyell, especially with his *Principles of Geology*. In contrast to the view that continents had been upheaved from the ocean floor suddenly and violently, Lyell saw the elevation of land areas proceeding slowly, gradually, and steadily through geological time, in small earth movements such as may occur in earthquakes or as a result of volcanic activity. The intensity of earthquakes and volcanic action had not diminished. Such processes were occurring today just as they had done throughout the history of the earth. The location of volcanic activity shifted from one geological period to the next, but its overall amount remained unchanged. Streams and rivers wore down the land as they had always done, depositing their sediments in the sea. Lyell postulated that geological processes in the interior of the earth, on its surface, and in the surrounding atmosphere formed parts of a steady system, ceaselessly active but unhurried, that proceeded changelessly through geological time.

Earlier, James Hutton and John Playfair (1748–1819) had emphasized the gradual wearing down of the land by rain and rivers and the immense periods of time required for the accumulation of sedimentary strata, their consolidation into rock, and their subsequent elevation and dislocation to form hills and mountains. Hutton recognized that each layer of sediment represented the ruins of former land. The wearing down of land to form layers of sediment, followed by the elevation of sedimentary strata to form land, represented a cycle of processes that extended endlessly into the geological past. Hutton thought that the consolidation of soft sediments into hard rocks occurred under the influence of the internal heat of the earth and that volcanic action played an important part in the elevation of sedimentary strata. The frequently folded, inclined, or vertical positions of rock strata in hills and mountains suggested that their elevation had occurred as a result of violent disturbance of the earth's surface. Acceptance of Hutton's theory of the elevation of stratified rocks, in place of the Wernerian theory of the retreat of a formerly universal ocean, required a theory of convulsive disturbance. In 1822, the English geologist William Daniel Conybeare (1787–1857), in a tentative acceptance of the Huttonian theory to explain the elevation of mountains and continents, wrote "that when so mighty an effect is to be accounted for, the mind must be prepared to admit, without being startled, causes of a force and energy greatly exceeding those with which we are acquainted from actual observation" (Conybeare and Phillips 1822, xvii). Conybeare thought that, in the geological past, volcanic action had been much more violent and extensive than in the modern world.

When Charles Lyell began to study geology in 1819, he accepted the views then current among English geologists, but at Paris in 1823 he learned from Constant Prevost that the alternation of freshwater and marine formations in the Paris Basin was not as sharply defined as Georges Cuvier had represented it. Instead, the Paris Basin appeared formerly to have been a great bay of the sea into which rivers drained, so that, when cut off from the sea by small geographical changes, it was transformed into a freshwater lake. Cuvier and Brongniart had suggested that the ancient limestones, marls, and flint of the Paris freshwater formations were qualitatively different from the soft mud accumulated in modern lakes, but in 1824 Lyell found in Scottish lakes hard limestones and marls containing exactly the same fossils as the ancient freshwater limestones of the Paris Basin. In 1828, Lyell and Roderick Murchison (1792–1871) traveled through central France, where the white limestone resembled the secondary marine Oolite of the Cotswold Hills but was, in fact, a tertiary freshwater formation containing fossil caddis-fly larva cases and freshwater shells. Associated with the limestone were marl beds consisting of thin layers, about thirty to the inch, each layer formed from the valves of the tiny freshwater crustacean *Cypris*. Each layer represented the accumulation of *Cypris* valves of a single year, yet the marl deposit was seven hundred feet thick. It presented, therefore, an

accumulation of several hundred thousand years, but the *Cypris* valves also demonstrated that the marl had accumulated in clear, calm water, like that of modern lakes in which *Cypris* lives. Lyell and Murchison also saw red sandstones, which at first they thought corresponded to the Old Red Sandstone of Britain, the oldest of the secondary formations; however, when they found in it various freshwater fossils, they decided that it must be a much younger tertiary freshwater formation, an observation demonstrating that the appearance and the lithological characteristics of a rock had nothing to do with its geological age. The same kind of rocks had been formed repeatedly throughout earth history.

Among the extinct volcanoes of central France, Lyell noted that the freshwater strata were frequently disturbed and elevated by volcanic rocks. He decided, therefore, to visit southern Italy and Sicily to learn whether the stratified rocks in the neighborhood of the active volcanoes of Vesuvius and Etna would show signs of recent elevation. They did. At Naples, Lyell found that almost all of the tertiary fossil shells from local strata belonged to living species, whereas the tertiary Subapennine beds of northern Italy contained only about 30 percent of living species. On the island of Ischia, near Naples, Lyell found strata containing fossils of living Mediterranean species elevated more than two thousand feet. Of even greater significance to Lyell were his observations in Sicily. The great volcanic mass of Mount Etna, representing lavas poured out in eruptions occurring intermittently over hundreds of thousands of years, rested upon a platform of stratified rocks containing fossils entirely of living species. The youngest strata of Sicily were, therefore, older than Etna, as were the species living in the Mediterranean Sea. Lyell was especially startled to find near Syracuse an ancient-looking hard white limestone, containing only the casts of shells, overlying a soft marl containing shells of living Mediterranean species, still retaining their original colors. The hard white limestone was, in fact, very young. "All idea of attaching a high antiquity to a regularly stratified limestone," wrote Lyell, "vanished at once from my mind" (Lyell 1833, x–xi).

Lyell realized also that if the stratified rocks of Sicily had been elevated by the intrusion of molten rock beneath them, they must rest upon a foundation of crystalline igneous rocks, such as granite, porphyry, or syenite. Where the igneous rocks bordered sedimentary strata, they would, by their heat, convert the limestone and shale into marble and slate. If Sicily were elevated further and the overlying strata partly eroded away to reveal the metamorphosed strata and crystalline igneous rocks, the rocks of Sicily would appear much like those of the Alps today. Sicily was at an early stage of mountain building, the Alps at a later stage, and the mountains of Scotland, composed largely of granite and altered strata, were still older. Lyell thus envisioned the building up and wearing down of mountains as an unending cyclic process, marked by volcanic activity and earthquakes and proceeding through past geological ages in the same slow, gradual, and intermittent manner as today. On his return to London early in 1829, Lyell began to develop these ideas in his three-volume *Principles of Geology,* the first volume of which was published in 1830. He continued to develop them throughout his lifetime in eleven editions of the *Principles,* the last appearing in 1872, and in six editions of the *Elements* (or *Manual*) *of Geology,* published from 1838 to 1865.

Uniformitarianism as a concept was thus founded on geological observation. It was not an a priori methodological principle, but it did entail a vision of earth history as stable, cyclic, and without beginning or end. Lyell did not deny that the earth might have had a beginning, but in his time that beginning lay beyond the geologist's range of observation. The earth must have within itself a stable, continuing source of heat to provide the energy for volcanic activity and earthquakes. Lyell did not know what that source of heat might be. What he did know was that volcanic activity had occurred in past geological periods at a roughly uniform rate, with episodes of eruption separated by long intervals of quiescence, just as volcanic activity had been observed to occur in historical times.

Subsequent Developments

In 1862, the physicist William Thomson (later Lord Kelvin [1824–1907]) attempted to refute uniformitarianism by reviving the idea of a cooling earth, which must necessarily have a limited and relatively short age. Within the constraints of Kelvin's estimates of the age of the earth, which were based on cooling rates for then-known heat sources, there would be time for neither slow, uniform geological change nor organic evolution by natural selection. As a result of Kelvin's calculations, during the subsequent half-century uniformitarianism was called into question and some geologists reverted to catastrophic explanations of certain geological phenomena. The dis-

covery of radioactivity in 1896 was followed in 1903 by Ernest Rutherford's (1871–1937) demonstration that radioactive substances steadily emit heat. Rutherford suggested that, in the interior of the earth, radioactive substances might provide a constant source of heat, thereby extending enormously the possible age of the earth.

Ironically, various geologists who had estimated the length of geological periods on a geological basis to fit within Kelvin's restricted time scale resisted the vast extension of the age of the earth permitted by radioactive dating, often in the name of geological uniformity. By 1931, scientists had demonstrated from radioactive data that the earth was more than 1.4 billion years old and possibly as old as three billion years. Even the lowest of the estimates provided ample time for slow, uniform geological change. Later estimates, based on more extensive radioactive data, have increased the age of the earth to about 4.5 billion years.

The theories of continental drift, seafloor spreading, and plate tectonics, which emerged with growing force during the twentieth century, tend to support the basic principle of geological uniformity—namely, that the geological causes now at work have acted during the geological past with the same intensity as at present. Seafloor spreading and continental movements occur very slowly and steadily, at rates of one to two centimeters per year, impelled by similarly slow, steady convection currents within the semifluid interior of the earth. Geological changes brought about at the surface of the earth by such very slow, steady movements within the earth's interior must occur in a correspondingly gradual manner, marked by earthquakes and volcanic activity. The processes of mountain building, postulated by the theory of plate tectonics, proceed necessarily at very slow rates over long periods of time.

Modern Actualism

In 1959, the Dutch scholar Reijer Hooykaas (1906–94) criticized the principle of uniformity, considering it an a priori methodological principle, unjustified by the assumption that the physical laws now in operation have always been in operation. Hooykaas preferred the concept that he called "actualism," which assumed that the causes of geological change in the past were the same as those now in operation but might differ greatly in energy. Like his nineteenth-century predecessors Buckland and Conybeare, Hooykaas was attempting to maintain a view of earth history that could be reconciled with a literal interpretation of the biblical account of Creation. Hooykaas seems not to have realized that, historically, uniformitarianism represented a geological theory based upon geological evidence and must stand or fall by the test of geological evidence. If radioactivity is a physical process that has always acted as it does today, the earth is very old and the geological changes comprehended in the theories of continental drift and plate tectonics have occurred at the same slow pace as the continents themselves move—the principle that Lyell derived from his observations in France and Italy in 1828.

See also Creationism Since 1859; Genesis Flood; Geology and Paleontology from 1700 to 1900; Theories of the Earth and Its Age Before Darwin

BIBLIOGRAPHY

Albritton, Claude C., Jr., ed. *The Fabric of Geology.* Reading, Mass.: Addison-Wesley, 1963.

———. *The Abyss of Time: Changing Conceptions of the Earth's Antiquity After the Sixteenth Century.* San Francisco: Freeman, Cooper, 1980.

Buckland, William. *Vindiciae geologicae; or, The Connexion of Geology with Religion Explained.* Oxford, 1820.

Burchfield, Joe D. *Lord Kelvin and the Age of the Earth.* New York: Science History Publications, 1975.

Conybeare, W. D., and William Phillips. *Outline of the Geology of England and Wales.* London, 1822.

Davies, Gordon L. *The Earth in Decay: A History of British Geomorphology.* New York: American Elsevier, 1969.

Dean, Dennis R. *James Hutton and the History of Geology.* Ithaca, N.Y.: Cornell University Press, 1992.

Ellegard, Alvar. *Darwin and the General Reader: The Reception of Darwin's Theory of Evolution in the British Periodical Press.* Goteborg: Elanders, 1958.

Gillispie, Charles Coulston. *Genesis and Geology.* Cambridge, Mass.: Harvard University Press, 1951.

Haber, Francis C. *The Age of the World: Moses to Darwin.* Baltimore: Johns Hopkins University Press, 1959.

Hooykaas, Reijer. *Natural Law and Divine Miracle: The Principle of Uniformity in Geology, Biology, and Theology.* 1959. Reprint. Leiden: Brill, 1963.

Lyell, Charles. *Principles of Geology.* 3 vols. 1830–3. Reprint. Chicago: University of Chicago Press, 1990–1.

Rudwick, Martin. "Uniformity and Progression: Reflections on the Structure of Geological Theory in the Age of Lyell." In *Perspectives in the History of Science and Technology,* ed. by Duane H. D. Roller. Norman: University of Oklahoma Press, 1971, 209–27.

Whewell, William. "Lyell's *Principles of Geology.*" *British Critic* 9 (1831): 180–206.

Wilson, Leonard G. *Charles Lyell: The Years to 1841: The Revolution in Geology.* New Haven, Conn.: Yale University Press, 1972.

———. "Geology on the Eve of Charles Lyell's First Visit to America, 1841." *Proceedings of the American Philosophical Society* 124 (1980): 168–202.

77. GEOGRAPHY

David N. Livingstone

In the preface to the 1657 edition of his *Cosmographie,* Peter Heylyn (1600–62), a theologian and historian of high-church sympathies, remarked that an associate had brushed him aside on a London street with the scorning quip, "Geographie is better than Divinity." However Heylyn was intended to take this verbal assault, the comment serves to affirm the connections that already existed by the mid-seventeenth century between geographical matters and religious sensibilities. Such associations, in fact, were deep, lasting, and multifaceted and have exerted a considerable impact on the geographical tradition even if the subject's chroniclers have, by and large, paid scant attention to their historical significance. For analytic convenience, I address these issues on four broad fronts—religious geography, teleological geography, geography and the missionary enterprise, and the geography of religion—even while acknowledging the interplay between components of this categorization and its inadequacy to cover the subject comprehensively.

Religious Geography

By religious geography is meant the incorporation of geographical precepts and practices within systems of religious belief and ritual. Nowhere perhaps is this more conspicuously evident than in the appropriation of cartographic crafts by religious movements, such as Islam, in which spatial directions assume immense spiritual significance. Among the variety of cartographic traditions within medieval Islam, the use of *qibla* charts is worthy of special mention because the obligation to pray in a sacred direction encouraged the production of highly mathematized maps and instruments to service this devotional geography.

Spiritualized cartography, of course, has not been restricted to Islamic belief systems. In medieval Europe, a long tradition of *mappaemundi* (maps of the world) articulated in graphic form the deepest inclinations of the Christian tradition. These maps assumed a variety of configurations. And while it is mistaken to suppose that the placing of Jerusalem at the map's center was universal, there is no doubt that a Jerusalem-centered *Weltanschauung* governed their construction, notably in their orientation to the East (and, therefore, to Paradise) and, routinely, in their portrayal of the world as encircled by divine love. The medieval Ebstorf map, for example, famously depicted the sphere of the world encompassed by the head and hands of Christ. But these representations also incorporated information on key people and places in the Western religious heritage and have appropriately been considered mnemonic spatialized sermons. At the same time, their portrayal of the monstrous races served to marginalize those peoples and cultures whose differences were disconcerting to the European *mentalité.* The central theme of the *mappaemundi* was, thus, the earth as a setting or stage on which the divine drama of salvation history was played out—a salvation geography analogous to *Heilsgeschichte* (salvation history). Their primary aim, therefore, was didactic and moral rather than the communication of geographical facts as we understand them.

Closely associated with these cartographic ventures, moreover, was a tradition dealing with the geography of the Bible lands. Much of this endeavor was directed toward identifying the locations of Near Eastern place names, and thus began a tradition of printing maps in Bibles. Both Martin Luther (1483–1546) and John Calvin (1509–64), for example, deployed such cartographic material to promote their own theological views, and these maps are as enlightening for theological as for cartographic history.

The use of geographical skills in the service of religion extended beyond cartography. During the sixteenth and seventeenth centuries, for instance, geographical knowledge was mobilized to support a range of magical enterprises. Treatises on chorography, the study of the areal differentiation of the earth's surface, were frequently all-of-a-piece with works dealing with astrology, because the different regions of the globe were believed to come under the influence of the heavenly spheres. In the sixteenth-century writings of William Cunningham (fl. 1559), Thomas Blundeville (fl. 1561), and John Dee (1527–1608), these and other magical associations are readily detectable. In a similar vein, such geographical crafts as weather forecasting were domiciled in the broader framework of what has been called astrological meteorology (Leonard [d. c. 1571] and Thomas [d. 1595] Digges, for example, were Puritan advocates alike of the new science and the art of reading the signs of the zodiac).

In a variety of ways, then, geographical lore has been integrated into a range of religious and quasi-religious belief systems in such a manner as to defy efforts to extricate the "scientific" from the "religious" in at least some quarters of the geographical enterprise.

Teleological Geography

The close association between religion and geography in terms of explanation is particularly evident in the long history of what has been called physico-theology. In this tradition, such themes as the earth's surface features, its plant and animal life, its demographic characteristics, and global regional character were interpreted as evidence of divine design in the world. And while this natural-theological method of conducting geographical investigation was dominant in the seventeenth and eighteenth centuries, such teleological modes of thought persisted within geographical discourse throughout the nineteenth century and into the twentieth.

In John Ray's (1627–1705) *Wisdom of God Manifested in the Works of Creation* (1693), for example, the hydrological proportions of the globe and the character of vegetation exemplified how the natural harmonies of nature evidenced divine beneficence. In a similar vein, Ray's contemporary Thomas Burnet (c. 1635–1715), author of the *Sacred Theory of the Earth* (1680–9), deployed the design argument to advance his belief that

it was the *im*perfection of the earth's features that revealed its fittedness for sinful humanity. To him, the history of the planet displayed how it had decayed from an original perfection—dissolution in which the Deluge played a key role. But there was hope that the final conflagration would usher in a new heaven and a new earth. John Woodward (1667–1728), in his *Essay Towards a Natural History of the Earth* (1695), urged that any detectable differences between the pre- and the postdiluvial worlds only served to show how the postdiluvial earth had a constitution more suited to humanity than its predecessor, which was really only fitted for a prelapsarian race (that is, one that had existed before the Fall). To him, the "world which emerged from the diluvial metamorphosis was a world perfectly adapted to the needs of fallen man" (Davies 1969, 116). In this world, the close links between the accumulation of humus, soil erosion, and human agriculture tellingly revealed divine design.

Any rehearsal of other exemplars of this fundamentally Enlightenment tradition must include William Derham's (1657–1735) *Physico-Theology* (1713), which elucidated the teleological significance of the "Terraqueous Globe" in order to provide, as he put it in the subtitle of the work, "A Demonstration of the Being and Attributes of God from His Works of Creation." Particular attention should be drawn to Derham's application of the design argument to population theory—a move about which Süssmilch, a contemporary of Derham's who did important work on demography within a theological framework, enthused and that had also surfaced in John Graunt's (1620–74) *Natural and Political Observations Made Upon the Bills of Mortality* (1662). Works such as these displayed how population statistics could be incorporated into the fabric of natural theology.

In these renditions of teleological geography, the theme of the balance of nature played a prominent role. Later, in the writings of those like Gilbert White (1720–93), the idea of the "economy of nature" asserted itself. Thus, in White's *The Natural History of Selborne,* published in 1789, the record of the natural order of his own parish confirmed the area's complex unity in diversity precisely because providence had contrived to make "Nature . . . a great economist." Here was a political economy of nature: Everything fit together "economically." Similar sentiments are clearly discernible in the writings of Carolus Linnaeus (1707–78), K. L. Willdenow (fl. 1800), and Eberhard Zimmerman (fl. 1780), who interpreted global biogeographical patterns in providential categories.

In later generations, and in the face of the philosophical assaults of writers like David Hume (1711–76) and Immanuel Kant (1724–1804), geographical data continued to be deployed in the service of a natural-theological apologetic. Among Christian theologians, for instance, geographical phenomena were frequently called upon to sustain a belief in divine design. For popular consumption were works like Thomas Dick's (1774–1857) *The Christian Philosopher; or, The Connection of Science and Philosophy with Religion* (1825), which fastened upon such topics as the figure of the earth, the natural and artificial divisions of the globe, the features of mountains, oceans and rivers, and population size as indicative of the operations of divine providence. For more sophisticated audiences, theologians of the caliber of Robert Flint (1834–1910), the Edinburgh professor of divinity, were still by the late 1880s plundering the writings of such geographers as Carl Ritter (1779–1859) and Arnold Guyot (1807–84) for what he called their rich store of teleological data. That such sources could be called upon bears witness to the continued vitality of teleological thinking within geography. This, indeed, was recognized by H. R. Mill, who, writing in 1929 on the development of the subject in the nineteenth century, commented that "Teleology or the argument from design . . . was tacitly accepted or explicitly avowed by almost every writer on the theory of geography, and Carl Ritter distinctly recognized and adopted it as the unifying principle of his system" (quoted in Livingstone 1992). After all, Mary Somerville (1780–1872), in her *Physical Geography* (1858), argued that the patterns of human settlement demonstrated the arrangement of divine wisdom, while Arnold Guyot's ecological geography, drawing on Ritter's work, was built upon the providentially governed "grand harmonies" of nature. As for Matthew Fontaine Maury (1806–73), author of the *Physical Geography of the Sea* (1855), it was the mechanistic operations of marine and atmospheric circulation systems and of energy transfers among land, sea, and air that confirmed to him the wisdom of William Paley's (1743–1805) celebrated clock analogy.

In the twentieth century, such sentiments have not been entirely absent from the tradition. David Matless, for example, has documented the persistence of a variety of mystical modes of thinking within early-twentieth-century geography, particularly among those active in campaigns for the preservation of rural landscape and values. The Dutch geographer Gerben de Jong, as recently as 1962, rooted his conception of geography as fundamentally "chorological differentiation" in teleological soil. Here, engaging in a Ritterian reappropriation, he spoke in Kantian-sounding idiom of the region as "a form of thought" and went on to elaborate what he called a "chorological teleology." This was simply because, as he put it, "the chorological differentiation of the earth does not exist in and by itself, but is sustained by divine energies" (de Jong 1962, 62, 138).

Geography and the Missionary Enterprise

At least since the time of Britain's favorite missionary, David Livingstone (1813–73), geography's association with the missionary enterprise was firmly established in the popular consciousness. For example, Thomas Dick, to whom we have already referred, emphasized that, for Christian believers, "Geography is a science of peculiar interest [since] 'the salvation of God,' which Christianity unfolds, is destined to be proclaimed in every land. . . . But, without exploring every region of the earth . . . we can never carry into effect the purpose of God." Accordingly, directors of missionary enterprises were advised to acquaint themselves with geographical knowledge so that they would not "grope in the dark, and spend their money in vain." Christianity, therefore, had nothing but the most intimate interest in contemporary "voyages of discovery" because they were engaged in bringing to light the "moral and political movements which are presently agitating the nations" (Dick 1825, 237, 239). This moral diagnosis was particularly significant, for, alongside its topographical disclosures, geography was obviously engaged in nothing less than providing a moral inventory of the globe even while remaking it through worldwide evangelization.

Hence, it is no surprise that several missionary statesmen were closely associated with the Royal Geographical Society during the Victorian period as they reported on their exploratory endeavors. In this guise, Christianity found itself profoundly implicated in Britain's imperial ventures overseas—particularly in Africa—albeit with a humanitarian tinge. Indeed, as one observer has noted, there was a "constant interchange between missionaries, philanthropists, geographers and politicians" (Driver 1996, 119). Consider the case of Livingstone himself. Commemorated in a statue on the site of the Royal Geographical Society's modern headquarters, a missionary-explorer achieving mythic status during his own lifetime, and an ardent advocate of the twin gospels of commerce and Christianity, Livingstone cemented ties between geographical science and missionary exploit through his own mapping enterprises by having scientists accompany him on his Zambesi expedition and by contributing toward distinctively Victorian ways of representing and reading African landscapes. Indeed, Roderick Murchison (1792–1871), president of the Royal Geographical Society, described Livingstone's journey to Luanda as "the greatest triumph in geographical research which has been effected in our times" (quoted in Driver 1996, 129).

Such associations extended beyond the academic and into the popular sphere. It was through a host of missionary magazines and furlough addresses, frequently using the slide-lecture technique, that beliefs and attitudes about other people and places were formed among large numbers of the British public. Mary Slessor's accounts of the Calabar Mission Field during the last third of the nineteenth century, for example, printed in such sources as the Church of Scotland's *Missionary Record,* are illustrative. Here, she conveyed to her readers a sense of the physical landscape of Africa that combined magnificence and foreboding, her responses to local customs, and her championing of the cause of West African women. Undertakings such as these attest to the significance of missionary energies in the production of popular geographical images and imaginings during the British imperial project.

These particular cases certainly do not exhaust the geographical significance of the missionary imperative. Neil Gunson, for instance, has insisted that, in the South Pacific, missionaries authored numerous popular and learned pieces on geography and natural history for both religious and scholarly serials: "From the late 1860s, there was a steady flow of specialized articles ranging from vulcanology to linguistics. . . . Several of the missionaries played key roles in extending contemporary knowledge of the natural world" (Gunson 1994, 306). In the same regional setting, as Janet Browne has shown, the relationship between Charles Darwin (1809–82) and the mission stations at various key staging points of the H.M.S. *Beagle* voyage were of considerable significance. Not least was this in view of the connections believed to

exist between geographical conditions and the mental and moral qualities of Aboriginals. In such a context, missionaries were engaged not just in the projects of evangelization but in a "wider environmentalist scheme" in which "they were seen as front-line agents in a scientifically and biblically harmonized program of amelioration and progress" (Browne 1994, 271).

The missionary impact on the geographical tradition has been considerable, and a detailed elucidation of such historical connections remains a real desideratum.

The Geography of Religion

Thus far, we have focused on the ways in which geographical thought and practice have been incorporated into religious belief systems, the explanatory impact of teleology on the understanding of geographical distributions and environment, and the links between missionary impulses and the advancement of geographical knowledge of the globe. But religion itself also has spatial dimensions varying in manifold ways over space and time. Accordingly, various facets of religious life have been considered dependent variables and have been subjected to geographical scrutiny in ways analogous to the sociology or anthropology of religion.

Perhaps the most characteristic Enlightenment and post-Enlightenment perspective in this vein (though doubtless predecessors can be found) is what might be called ecological constructivism. In this scenario, aspects of religious belief and practice are understood as the products of distinct environmental regimes and, thus, display identifiable regional patterns. During the eighteenth century, Montesquieu (1689–1755), for example, retained a keen interest in how the religious beliefs of particular cultures were shaped by their geographical milieu. In the twentieth century, Ellen Semple perpetuated this self-same emphasis by insisting that monotheism was the product of desert environments and that conceptions of the afterlife were environmentally conditioned, while Ellsworth Huntington accounted in a similar way for different societies' conceptions of the deity. Such environmentalist theses, crystallized in Ernest Renan's (1823–92) dictum that "le désert est monothéist" ("the desert is monotheistic"), thus persisted well into the twentieth century until the disavowal of environmental determinism as a coherent or cogent set of explanatory theses.

Since then, geographers of religion have attended to a variety of other projects. In a 1962 review, for example, P. Fickeler encompassed within the sphere of the geography of religion such issues as ceremonial expression, the symbolism used by cults, sacred orientation, pilgrimage, holy places, and sacred landscapes. Understandably, perhaps, a good deal of work under this rubric has tended to focus on the visible and/or material dimensions of religion: the expression of religion on the landscape, the religious organization of space, the geography of pilgrimage, religion and demographic structure, and the geographical distribution of religious denominations. Nevertheless, there have been indications of a broader conception of the enterprise, which would encompass within its orbit the differential impact of religion on social and cultural practices. The commitment here, as Mark Billinge has put it, is to "the understanding of religion in particular places and milieux . . . by the detailed investigation of specific doctrines" (Billinge 1986, 404). Those pursuing investigations of this sort have drawn inspiration from the writings of Erich Isaac and Manfred Büttner, who have insisted on the crucial importance of "contextual knowledge of religious process and precedent" (Ley 1994, 522). For all that, the field of the geography of religion has remained in considerable disarray, and Chris Park's *Sacred Worlds* (1994) constitutes a sustained attempt to impose some coherence on a remarkably disparate field of scholarly endeavor.

The history of geography's engagements with religion in the Western tradition has been immensely varied. In some cases, geographical skills have been incorporated into religion itself; in others, religious commitment has acted as the inspiration for geographical endeavor; in yet others, religious conviction has provided the cognitive control beliefs on acceptable solutions to the problems of geographical distribution. Religion has performed a wide range of roles—as assumption underlying, sanction behind, explanation for, and subject of geographical inquiry.

See also Calendar; Ecology and the Environment; Meteorology; Natural Theology

BIBLIOGRAPHY

Billinge, Mark D. "Religion, Geography of." In *Dictionary of Human Geography,* ed. by R. J. Johnston et al. 2d ed. Oxford: Blackwell, 1986.

Browne, Janet. "Missionaries and the Human Mind." In *Darwin's Laboratory: Evolutionary Theory and Natural History in the Pacific,* ed. by Roy MacLeod and Philip F. Rehbock. Honolulu: University of Hawaii Press, 1994, 263–82.

Büttner, Manfred. "Religion and Geography: Impulses for a New Dialogue between *Religionswissenschaft* and Geography." *Numen* 21 (1974): 165–96.

Cohn, Norman. *Noah's Flood: The Genesis Story in Western Thought.* New Haven, Conn., and London: Yale University Press, 1996.

Davies, Gordon L. *The Earth in Decay: A History of British Geomorphology, 1578–1878.* London: MacDonald, 1969.

de Jong, G. *Chorological Differentiation as the Fundamental Principle of Geography: An Inquiry into the Chorological Conception of Geography.* Groningen: Wolters, 1962.

Deffontaines, Pierre. *Géographie et Religions.* Paris: Gallimard, 1948.

Delano Smith, Catherine. "Maps in Bibles in the Sixteenth Century." *Map Collector* 39 (1987): 2–14.

Dick, Thomas. *The Christian Philosopher; or, The Connection of Science and Philosophy with Religion.* 3d ed. Glasgow: Chalmers and Collins, 1825.

Driver, Felix. "David Livingstone and the Culture of Exploration in Mid-Victorian Britain." In *David Livingstone and the Victorian Encounter with Africa,* ed. by John M. MacKenzie. London: National Portrait Gallery, 1996, 109–37.

Fickeler, P. "Fundamental Questions in the Geography of Religions." In *Readings in Cultural Geography,* ed. by P. L. Wagner and M. W. Mikewell. Chicago: University of Chicago Press 1962, 94–117.

Gilbert, Edmund W. "Geographie Is Better than Divinity." *Geographical Journal* 128 (1962): 494–7.

Glacken, Clarence J. *Traces on the Rhodian Shore: Nature and Culture in Western Thought from Ancient Times to the End of the Eighteenth Century.* Berkeley: University of California Press, 1967.

Gunson, Neil. "British Missionaries and Their Contribution to Science in the Pacific Islands." In *Darwin's Laboratory: Evolutionary Theory and Natural History in the Pacific,* ed. by Roy MacLeod and Philip F. Rehbock. Honolulu: University of Hawaii Press, 1994, 283–316.

Isaac, Erich. "Religion, Landscape, and Space." *Landscape* 9 (1960): 14–18.

King, David A. "The Sacred Direction in Islam: A Study of the Interaction of Religion and Science in the Middle Ages." *Interdisciplinary Science Reviews* 10 (1985): 315–28.

Larson, James. "Not Without a Plan: Geography and Natural History in the Late Eighteenth Century." *Journal of the History of Biology* 19 (1986): 447–88.

Ley, David. "Religion, Geography of." In *Dictionary of Human Geography,* ed. by R. J. Johnston et al. 3d ed. Oxford: Blackwell, 1994.

Livingstone, David N. "Science, Magic, and Religion: A Contextual Reassessment of Geography in the Sixteenth and Seventeenth Centuries." *History of Science* 26 (1988): 269–94.

———. *The Geographical Tradition: Episodes in the History of a Contested Enterprise.* Oxford: Blackwell, 1992.

Matless, David. "Nature, the Modern and the Mystic: Tales from Early Twentieth Century Geography." *Transactions of the Institute of British Geographers* n.s. 16 (1991): 272–86.

McEwan, Cheryl. "'The Mother of All the Peoples': Geographical Knowledge and the Empowering of Mary Slessor." In *Geography and Imperialism, 1820–1940,* ed. by Morag Bell, Robin Butlin, and Michael Heffernan. Manchester, U.K.: Manchester University Press, 1995, 125–50.

Park, Chris. *Sacred Worlds: An Introduction to Geography and Religion.* London: Routledge, 1994.

Sopher, David E. *Geography of Religions.* Englewood Cliffs, N.J.: Prentice-Hall, 1967.

Woodward, David. "Medieval *Mappaemundi.*" In *The History of Cartography.* Vol. 1: *Cartography in Prehistoric, Ancient, and Medieval Europe and the Mediterranean,* ed. by J. B. Harley and David Woodward. Chicago: University of Chicago Press, 1987, 286–368.

78. EARTHQUAKES

Peter M. Hess

Terrifying in their effects and apparently random in occurrence, earthquakes have been among the most difficult of natural phenomena either to ignore or to rationalize in the Western tradition. Before the advent of rapid communications and systematic recordkeeping, it was difficult for observers to know the geographical distribution or relative magnitude of earthquakes, and knowledge about them usually came by delayed and sometimes exaggerated report. Two parallel strains of interpretation of these troubling phenomena have prevailed since antiquity. On the one hand, earthquakes have been accounted for naturalistically by contemporary scientific theories about the earth. On the other hand, a providential interpretation has been appealed to as an integral element of a theistic worldview. Until the nineteenth century, explanation often involved both, with providential and naturalistic accounts serving complementary, rather than competitive, functions. Emphasis was frequently placed on the one or the other explanation according to whether the discussion took place in a philosophical or a theological context.

In both prephilosophical Greco-Roman literature and the Judeo-Christian Scriptures, earthquakes were often reported as instances of providential divine intervention. The event accompanying the crucifixion of Jesus, for example, was miraculous in origin, testifying to the divinity of his person. In patristic and medieval literature, earthquakes were frequently, if unsystematically, interpreted as signs of divine displeasure, and even the devil was occasionally assigned responsibility for them.

Nevertheless, almost from the beginning of Western thought there was an equally persistent naturalistic tradition of interpretation. The early Greek philosophers replaced the traditional mythopoeic ascription of earthquakes to the god Poseidon with a variety of scientific explanations. Aristotle (384–322 B.C.), who treated the subject as one element of meteorology, ascribed earthquakes to the great pressures exerted by subterranean winds seeking an outlet and noted their frequent association with volcanoes. This theory was persuasive until the later Middle Ages and served as the foundation for the magisterial account of Albertus Magnus (1193–1280). Albertus pursued a thoroughly naturalistic discussion of many different theories of earthquakes in *De meteoris* (*On Astronomical Phenomena*), ultimately approving of the Aristotelian explanation in terms of subterranean winds and appealing nowhere to a theological or a moral explanation.

Although Renaissance humanism brought about increased interest in naturalistic interpretations of phenomena, this naturalism continued to share the stage with the providential explanations of earthquakes. Martin Luther (1483–1546) observed in his *Commentary on Genesis* that, while the destruction of cities by earthquakes was often assigned to natural causes, "extraordinary disasters must be regarded as a punishment inflicted by an angry God for human sin." This tension between the two different explanations continued well into the eighteenth century.

The scientific revolution of the seventeenth century provided new interpretations of geological phenomena in terms of the nascent science of chemistry. Earthquakes were increasingly judged to result from the force of subterranean explosions in deposits of "nitrous" or "sulphurous" particles. However, no general theory of the earth could as yet account in a systematic way for why tremors should occur at a given time and place. What attempts there were in the early-modern period to fit earthquakes into a comprehensive structure were often subservient to a theological program. Thomas Burnet's

(c. 1635–1715) *Theory of the Earth* (1692), for example, was as much a theological as a geological work that was in both dimensions highly speculative. Burnet regarded earth movements as divine instruments that were ordained to bring about the destruction of the antediluvian world by releasing the fountains of the deep precisely at the moment when God had decided upon the destruction of an irredeemably evil world.

The high-water mark of the theological interpretation of earthquakes coincided in the first half of the eighteenth century with a growing critical discussion of their physical causes. The following discussion reflects the fact that scholarship on this subject is imbalanced, with considerably more attention having been given to English and American Puritan responses than to Catholic and Continental discussion of these phenomena. A more balanced treatment will require extensive spadework into other early-modern interpretive traditions. Maxine Van de Wetering has examined two phases of earthquake sermons following seismic episodes in New England in 1727 and 1755 and has suggested that Puritan moralizing tended to be rationalistic and to downplay the element of mysteriousness. Puritan sermons, while assigning a moral cause to earthquakes, also paid increasing attention to the "secondary causes" of these phenomena. Although seismology would not mature into a discrete discipline until well into the nineteenth century, the discussion of earthquakes was intensifying in response to a growing awareness of the circumstances of their occurrence.

The early-eighteenth-century Puritan theological interpretation is exemplified by Thomas Paine's *Doctrine of Earthquakes* (1727). Paine (who is not to be confused with the more famous deistic author) contended that, since every part of creation has its proper function assigned by God, and since the place of the earth is to serve as a solid foundation for its inhabitants, an earthquake must be a profoundly unnatural phenomenon. "An earthquake is a prodigious, or supernatural commotion, wrought in the body of the earth . . . contrary to its nature, wrought by some extraordinary power, wherein the earth is entirely passive." There would, in fact, never be an earthquake, were not God to intervene in nature. The great Puritan synthesizer Cotton Mather (1663–1728) suggested in *The Christian Philosopher* (1721) that earthquakes are "very moving preachers to worldly-minded men." In 1727, he cataloged their natural causes in almost a dismissive fashion, asking

whether colluctations of minerals producing vapors that must have an explosion, may cause those direful convulsions in the bowels of the earth, which are felt in our earthquakes? Or, whether the huge quantities of waters, running in the bowels of the earth, may not by degrees wash away the bottom of the upper strata here and there, so as to cause their falling in? Or, whether the subterraneous fires, getting head, may not by their sulphurous bituminous exhalations in the bowels of the earth, cause a combustion that may carry all before it?

Ultimately, for Mather, this was a theological question. "Let the natural causes of earthquakes be what the wise men of inquiry please, they and their causes are still under the government of him that is the God of nature." A generation later, John Wesley (1703–91) could still argue in *The Cause and Cure of Earthquakes* (1755) that "God is himself the author, and sin the moral cause; earthquakes, whatever the natural causes may be, are a punishment for sin." Wesley did not shrink from directly connecting the deadly Jamaican earthquake of 1692 with the punishment of unrepentant blasphemers and drunken harlots among the inhabitants of Port Royal. But other preachers demonstrated a greater openness to natural causes. John Rogers (1712–89) suggested that earthquakes "are not properly miraculous or preternatural" and that the Catholic victims of the 1755 Lisbon quake were no greater sinners than the survivors or even than their American Protestant contemporaries.

In the mid-eighteenth-century—simultaneous with the flourishing of providential interpretations of earthquakes—naturalistic interpretations began to play a greater role. In his discourse *Earthquakes the Works of God, and Tokens of His Just Displeasure* (1755), American theologian Thomas Prince (1687–1758) took great pains to account for earthquakes scientifically and mentioned little about sin and divine punishment even though he situated earthquakes in the usual apocalyptic framework. His subtitle offered the reader "a brief account of the natural, instrumental, or secondary causes of these operations in the hands of God." Prince made the scientific case that God had created a dynamic earth in order to build the possibility of earthquakes into its very constitution. "Earth has a loose contexture with many caves and passages for constant circulation of air and water, with great multitudes of sulphurous, nitrous, fiery, mineral, and other substances, such as those in the clouds that cause thunder and lightning." Prince suggested that, when these substances move and strike against one another, they fly apart and expand with great violence, pushing the earth into the air. Adding to this Robert Boyle's (1627–91) calculation that the atmosphere presses with a weight of 2,592 pounds per square foot, he proposed that the earth's crust easily collapses into the subterranean spaces left by the explosion and concluded with a theological judgment: "Thus has God placed us over great and hideous vaults, ready to open when he sees it time to bury us in them."

Among the most naturalistically inclined of Puritan thinkers on this issue was the Harvard natural philosopher John Winthrop (a descendant of the famous governor [1714–79]), whose detailed "Lecture on Earthquakes" (1755) gave the providentialist interpretation a novel twist. Winthrop suggested that, while earthquakes "may justly be regarded as the tokens of an incensed deity; yet it cannot be concluded from hence that they are not of real and standing advantage to the globe in general." He contended that earthquakes play a benign and, in fact, essential role in loosening the soil and making it suitable to support vegetation, analogous to the plowing done by a farmer.

Hence, by the end of the eighteenth century, the weight was significantly shifting from providentialist to naturalistic interpretations of earthquakes. Already in 1755, Voltaire (1694–1778), in *Candide,* had ridiculed the idea that the Lisbon earthquake could in any intelligible way be interpreted as a just judgment of God. And although earthquakes still awaited constructive assimilation as natural phenomena into a theory of earth history, thinkers such as John Michell (the founder of seismology [1724–93]) and paleontologist Georges Cuvier (1769–1832) considered seismology without any reference to theology. James Hutton (1726–97) declared in his *Theory of the Earth* (1785) that

> a volcano is not made on purpose to frighten superstitious people into fits of piety and devotion, nor to overwhelm devoted cities to destruction; a volcano should be considered, as a spiracle to the subterranean furnace, in order to prevent the unnecessary elevation of land, and fatal effects of earthquakes; and we may rest assured, that they, in general, wisely answer the end of their intention, without being in themselves an end, for

which nature had exerted such amazing power and excellent contrivance.

The title of Hutton's book stood in marked contrast to Burnet's *Theory of the Earth,* published nearly a century earlier. His reference to "excellent contrivance" by a personified nature cannot obscure the fact that Hutton inhabited a very different world from providentialists of previous centuries.

Advances in seismology during the nineteenth century took the form of better catalogs of earthquakes and increased accuracy in their measurement. Important speculations were made about the connection between earthquakes and fault systems, and a number of national seismological societies were founded around the turn of the twentieth century. Although the current paradigm of plate tectonics that accounts for earthquakes by shifting faults at plate boundaries would not be developed until the 1960s, by 1900 the explanation of earthquakes among professional seismologists had become thoroughly secularized. Divine providence and judgment no longer played any meaningful role in seismological explanation.

This transformation does not mean, however, that, in the wider context of science and religion, the problem of the interpretation of earthquakes has been fully settled. Among the public and those who serve their spiritual needs, aspects of the providential interpretation of earthquakes have survived through the twentieth century, even though many who describe themselves as religious in orientation have adopted a basically naturalistic stance on this question. Meaning can still be sought regarding God's intentions, as was reported about anguished victims of the destructive Assisi earthquakes of September 1997. However, the import of that quest for meaning, while significantly broaching the subject of God's action in the world, now lies outside the scope of seismology.

See also Comets and Meteors; Electricity; Meteorology; Natural Theology

BIBLIOGRAPHY

Davison, Charles. *The Founders of Seismology.* Cambridge: Cambridge University Press, 1927.

Geschwind, Carl-Henry. "Embracing Science and Research: Early Twentieth-Century Jesuits and Seismology in the United States." *Isis* 89 (1998): 27–49.

Mather, Cotton. *The Christian Philosopher.* Ed. by Winton U. Solberg. 1721. Reprint. Urbana and Chicago: University of Illinois Press, 1994.

Oldroyd, David R. *Thinking about the Earth: A History of Ideas in Geology.* Cambridge, Mass.: Harvard University Press, 1996.

Rappaport, Rhoda. *When Geologists Were Historians, 1665–1750.* Ithaca, N.Y.: Cornell University Press, 1997.

Shute, Michael. "Earthquakes and Early American Imagination: Decline and Renewal in Eighteenth Century Puritan Culture." Ph.D. diss., University of California at Berkeley, 1977.

Van De Wetering, Maxine. "Moralizing in Puritan Natural Science: Mysteriousness in Earthquake Sermons." *Journal of the History of Ideas* 43 (1982): 417–38.

Winthrop, John. "A Lecture on Earthquakes." 1755. In *The Scientific Work of John Winthrop.* Ed. by Michael N. Shute. New York: Arno, 1980, 5–38.

79. METEOROLOGY

John Henry

Weather and its consequences have a major impact on human lives and human culture, and it seems that there has always been a tendency to seek for meaning in the vicissitudes of weather. Finding it impossible to believe that catastrophes that affected them so severely could be personally or socially insignificant, early polytheistic civilizations attributed storms, thunder, and lightning, as well as droughts and other severe manifestations of weather, to the wrath of the gods. The weather proved so important, however, that various regular meteorological observations seem to have forced themselves into popular consciousness, becoming codified in the form of weather lore. Among the ancient Babylonians, for example, it was held that a dark halo around the moon signified a month of clouds, if not of rain. In both Egypt and Babylonia from the third millennium B.C., such empirically based weather lore included observations of the heavenly bodies, which were supposed to affect many things on the earth besides the weather. This tradition of what is known as astrometeorology proved to be extremely long-lived.

The Beginnings of Naturalistic Meteorology

The earliest attempts to give a naturalistic (as opposed to religious) explanation of weather phenomena are found among the ancient Greeks. Aware of basic phenomena such as the evaporation of water on a hot sunny day and the precipitation of rain from clouds, Thales of Miletus (fl. c. 585 B.C.) seems to have groped toward an awareness of the hydrological cycle (the evaporation of surface water into the atmosphere, its condensation into clouds, and its precipitation as rain to rejoin the surface water). Anaxagoras (fifth-century B.C.) even managed to explain

summer hail, suggesting that the heat of the day might drive clouds so high that they entered a part of the atmosphere so cold that the moisture of the clouds would freeze. He believed that the heat of the atmosphere diminished with altitude because it was no longer heated by the rays of the sun reflected up from the ground.

By far the fullest and most influential account of meteorological phenomena was developed by Aristotle (384–322 B.C.) in his treatise known as the *Meteorologica*. The study of *meteora* originally meant the study of any phenomenon in the "upper part" of the world and so included astronomical phenomena, but Aristotle separated astronomy from meteorology, which was henceforth concerned only with sublunar, or what we would think of as "atmospheric," phenomena. However, since Aristotle believed that the heavens above the moon were perfect and unchanging, he supposed that transitory phenomena like shooting stars and comets must be sublunar phenomena. The word "meteor," therefore, could refer to any visible atmospheric phenomenon. It was only in the twentieth century that the word came to be restricted to shooting stars (which are, in fact, small pieces of planetary bodies, burning up owing to friction as they enter the earth's atmosphere, a notion that was inconceivable to Aristotle).

According to Aristotle, the heat of the sun drew up two kinds of evaporations: a hot and dry "exhalation" from the earth and a warm and moist "vapor" from the waters. The various different kinds of weather phenomena, or meteors, were formed as these evaporations experienced changes of heat in ascending through the air, or were subject to fluctuations in the sun's heat, or came close to the sphere of elemental fire, which was believed to be located immediately below the sphere of the moon and surrounding the sphere of air. The hot-dry exhalations could variously produce thunder and lightning, shooting stars, comets, earthquakes, and winds. The warm-moist vapors could form clouds, rain, snow, hail, dew, mist, and frost. Additionally, images like multiple suns, haloes, and rainbows were held to be caused by reflections of heavenly bodies on various vapor formations. Each of these meteors received its own specific explanation. Dew, for example, was formed when the sun's power was insufficiently strong to raise the vapor up into the air, and the vapor condensed after sunset in the cold night air. Thunder and lightning resulted when a hot exhalation was raised up by the heat of the sun, only to become trapped in the coldness of a cloud. Lightning was the flash and thunder the accompanying noise when the trapped exhalation finally burst its way out of its temporary cold prison.

Aristotle's meteorology was to prove immensely influential: It was essentially incorporated into later Greek and Roman works, including Pliny the Elder's (c. A.D. 23–79) *Historia naturalis,* and then into various encyclopedic works of the early Middle Ages. By the thirteenth century, the *Meteorologica* itself was available to the Latin West, having been translated from the Arabic by Gerard of Cremona (c. 1114–87) and from the Greek by William of Moerbeke (fl. 1260–86). From then on, Aristotelian meteorology, together with the signs for weather prognostication (many compiled by Aristotle's follower Theophrastus [c. 372–286 B.C.]), held sway until the seventeenth century. They were complemented by folk traditions (for example, Jesus clearly expected his audience to know the implications of a red sky at night and in the dawn [Matt. 16:2–3]), as well as astrometeorology, especially as it was transmitted to the West in the leading textbook of astrology, Claudius Ptolemy's (second century A.D.) *Tetrabiblos.*

Astrometeorology and Weather Magic

The assumption that the heavenly bodies affected the weather was a general belief throughout Christian Europe. Although the church was suspicious of so-called judicial astrology, which assumed that the influence of the stars operated at the level of individual human lives and seemed, therefore, to deny free will and moral autonomy, it did not deny that the heavens and the atmosphere were a dramatic setting for portents. Comets or other striking visual phenomena, like multiple suns, might signify dramatic change in human affairs, whether political or natural. The periodic pandemics of bubonic plague that swept through Europe in the premodern period were usually attributed to pestilential miasmas in the air brought about by the configuration of the heavenly bodies. Similarly, floods, droughts, storms, and other devastating aspects of the weather were linked to the stars. Ultimately, of course, God was the primary cause of such events, but the motions of the heavenly bodies were held to be instrumental in some way.

If large-scale social disruptions to the routine of human life were attributed to the wrath of God, individual or family misfortune could easily be attributed to *maleficium*—that is, to the malicious operations of a magician or a witch. The use of magic to arouse storms was included in the proscriptions against magic in Roman Law and remained as part of the common image of what magicians could do until the early-modern period. Needless to say, there was more or less continuous debate among churchmen about the possibility of the magical manipulation of the weather. Bishop Agobard of Lyon, early in the ninth century, insisted that only God could control the weather, but others clearly believed that meteorological phenomena, being natural, were subject to natural magic. Natural magic was based on the assumption that all things in creation were interconnected, so that substances could act upon other substances in occult ways (a distillation from poppies could make someone fall asleep, for example). So, as the famous Renaissance magus Pietro Pomponazzi (1462–1525) wrote, if the principles of natural magic are real, "it follows also . . . that there are herbs, stones, or other means of this sort which repel hail, rain, winds; and that one is able to find others which have natural powers of attracting them." The use of such active substances, therefore, could induce hail and rain or drive them away. Pomponazzi was assuming that such knowledge could be empirically discovered, but all too often it was assumed by Church authorities that those accused of performing weather magic to the detriment of their neighbors could not have had sufficient knowledge of the natural means of bringing about various *meteora* and must, therefore, have solicited the aid of a demon. (Demons, it should be noted, could perform weather magic only because they did know the necessary natural active substances of the kind mentioned by Pomponazzi. Demons, like magicians, had to rely on the exploitation of natural powers; only God was able to perform supernatural acts.)

Belief in weather magic declined along with other magical beliefs in the early-modern period. This decline coincided with the beginnings of a more scientific approach to meteorology, but it seems to have had as much to do with changes in religion as in scientific attitudes. The Protestant churches made a point of presenting Roman Catholicism as idolatrous, superstitious, and too much given to things that smacked of magic (for example, the host and holy water were often popularly regarded as magical objects, capable of performing extraordinary operations). Accordingly, they promoted the view of a world that was generally much less magical than the enchanted world of the Middle Ages, and they invested a great deal of effort into establishing what could be said to be genuinely natural effects (and here they borrowed heavily from the theories of the newly emerging mechanical philosophy) and what was mere superstition. The belief that weather could be magically manipulated was soon relegated to fable and story, but the astrological prediction of weather proved too useful to be rejected until some other means of prognostication began to be available.

The Development of Scientific Meteorology

More empirically based efforts at weather forecasting began to look possible with the invention of the major meteorological instruments. The thermometer, usually first attributed to Galileo (1564–1642) but improved by many others, made it possible to record air temperatures, particularly after Ferdinand II de' Medici, grand duke of Tuscany (1610–70), invented a thermometer closed to the outside air and, thus, independent of air pressure. Ferdinand's innovation, made sometime around 1640, facilitated the development of a fixed scale that allowed meaningful comparisons of temperatures in different locations. The barometer was invented by Evangelista Torricelli (1608–47) in 1643, while he was investigating the weight of the air, but its usefulness in meteorology was quickly recognized, and many natural philosophers all over Europe contributed to the development of the barometer as a practical and useful instrument. The hygrometer, for measuring the humidity of the air, was developed by Robert Hooke (1635–1703) in the second half of the seventeenth century but did not become properly useful until the innovations of the German mathematician Johann Heinrich Lambert (1728–77),

who gave the instrument its name. The rain gauge, although discussed earlier, was developed in the seventeenth century by experimental philosophers like Sir Christopher Wren (1632–1723) and Hooke. Similarly, the anemometer, for measuring the force of the wind, while mentioned by earlier writers, was developed by Santorio Santorio (1561–1636), Hooke, and others, although the modern rotating-cup type of anemometer was not invented until the nineteenth century.

The concentration of effort on the development of meteorological instruments in the seventeenth century went hand in hand with systematic attempts to draw up extensive tables of meteorological observations. Concerned to show the usefulness of their new natural philosophy, seventeenth-century thinkers turned to the weather in the hope of being able to make weather forecasting more reliable. Gathering meteorological data became one of the collective enterprises of the new scientific academies and societies that began to appear in the seventeenth century. In 1663, Robert Hooke drew up a proposed standard "Method for Making a History of the Weather," which described what observations should be included and how they should be made. Hooke's scheme was widely disseminated in Thomas Sprat's (1635–1713) *History of the Royal Society of London* (1667), which was, in spite of its title, more a manifesto for the new experimental science of the Royal Society. In 1723, James Jurin (1684–1750), Hooke's successor as secretary of the society, repeated the call for observers to send in their weather data to the society, according to strict protocols, for annual publication in the society's *Philosophical Transactions*.

This kind of data collection allowed Edmond Halley (1656–1742) to offer an explanation of the world's trade winds and draw up the first chart of the prevailing winds. Halley suggested that the trade winds were caused by the inflow of cooler air from temperate regions to replace the rising warm air at the equator. According to Halley, the westward movement of the sun over the equator accounted for the westward deflection of the air currents, but George Hadley (1685–1768) improved on this account by proposing the rotation of the earth as the reason for the deflection. Throughout the eighteenth century, numerous attempts were made to understand the behavior of storms. The Societas Meteorologica Palatina, founded in Mannheim in 1780, organized a European-wide network of reliable observers, with the result that H. W. Brandes (1777–1834) was able to draw up weather charts of Europe for every day of 1783 in which the progress of storms was clearly revealed. Johann Heinrich Lambert tried to organize a worldwide network of observation posts in 1771, and such observations were exploited by Baron von Humboldt (1769–1859) when he linked all places with the same temperature on a map of what he called "isothermals." Humboldt was thus able to see the effect of continental landmasses or oceans on climate, recognizing that continental interiors experience greater extremes of temperature than oceanic regions. The introduction of the telegraph facilitated the gathering of such worldwide observations, and in 1873 the International Meteorological Organization was established.

Developments in the scientific theories of hydrodynamics and thermodynamics allowed a much more sophisticated understanding of the movements of the atmosphere. Areas of low pressure, once assumed to be the result of cold air moving in to replace rising warm air, came to be seen as the bending of a flow of air (by the earth's rotation) into a spiral that created low pressure at the center. By the 1920s, the first major school of meteorological theory, founded at Bergen by the Norwegian mathematical physicist Vilhelm Bjerknes (1862–1951), was flourishing, thanks partly to the growing importance of aviation and its requirements. Bjerknes extended the "cyclone" theory, seeing weather patterns in terms of cyclonic disturbances running westward along the "polar front," where polar and tropical air met. This theory remains influential in spite of many advances in our understanding of atmospheric movements made in the last few decades.

Meteorology and Natural Theology

Throughout all but the latter part of the period during which scientific meteorology was being established, meteorology was regarded as another aspect of the natural theology that showed God's wisdom and omnipotence in the creation of the world. The hydrological cycle, the cycle of the seasons, the trade winds, and the beneficial aspects of climate were all seen as divinely ordained elements in the world system. By contrast, tempests, floods, famine, and other catastrophes could be used, on the one hand, to confirm the principles of theodicy and, on the other, to claim that the natural world still provided moral lessons and warnings of God's wrath. A devastating storm, therefore, could be regarded

merely as an unavoidable consequence of generally benevolent meteorological laws, an outcome that, although locally disruptive, was nevertheless part of a greater purpose in a providential order maintained by God's imminent superintendence. Perhaps one of its greater purposes was to serve as a warning to mankind.

Another aspect of the natural theology of meteorology can be seen in eighteenth- and nineteenth-century theories about the replenishing of the atmosphere. The respiration of plants was seen as God's way of ensuring that the atmosphere was continually cleansed and purified after being vitiated by the breathing of animals and the burning of fires. Sir John Pringle (1707–82) even considered tempests in this same light: "If ever these salutary gales give rise to storms and hurricanes, let us still trace and revere the ways of a beneficent Being, who not fortuitously but with design, not in wrath but in mercy, thus shakes the waters and the air together to bury in the deep those putrid and pestilential effluvia which the vegetables upon the face of the earth have been insufficient to consume." In the nineteenth century, similar ideas were assumed to make sense of the latest theories in geology about the evolution of the earth from a ball of hot gas to its present complex topography. The coal beds, for example, which testified to extensive forests of huge trees in the carboniferous system, were seen as a necessary prerequisite to the later history of the earth. The carboniferous forests were so widespread over the earth that they reduced the carbon dioxide in the atmosphere and enriched the oxygen content, thus allowing higher animals to populate the earth. The massive extinction of these trees was not, therefore, evidence of a lack of design and purpose in the world, but all part of life's rich tapestry.

The close links between meteorology and the hand of God were clearly revealed toward the end of the nineteenth century in disputes between some Anglican clergymen and British scientists. On August 24, 1860, after a very wet summer, the bishop of Oxford, Samuel Wilberforce (1805–73), instructed his clergy to include the appointed prayer for fine weather in their services. The bishops of London, Rochester, and Down and Connor in Ireland followed suit. The published title of the Rev. Charles Gutch's sermon on the matter no doubt summed up the feelings of these bishops: "The Gloomy Summer; or, God's Threatened Chastisement Deserved for National and Individual Sins" (1860). The Rev. Charles Kingsley (1819–75), however, gave an opposing sermon in which he saw praying for fair weather as an unwarranted presumption. Falling back on the tradition of theodicy, Kingsley pointed out that, for all that was known, the excessive rains may be washing away "the seeds of pestilence" and "sowing instead the seeds of health and fertility, for us and for our children after us." Although Kingsley's approach was one with its own tradition within Christianity, it was seized upon by contemporary scientists who saw it as a vindication of their own efforts to separate science from religious considerations. For John Tyndall (1820–93), writing in 1861, Kingsley and those like him were encouraging "an intelligent conflict with the real causes of disease and scarcity, instead of a delusive reliance on supernatural aid."

While we now live in an age in which science and religion are essentially separate, meteorological phenomena still seem to many to suggest a religious significance underlying physical events. Consider the extraordinary reaction to the bogus phenomena of crop circles. Now known to have been perpetrated fraudulently, these mysterious flattening of crops in complex and beautiful geometrical patterns, which originally appeared in the south of England, were for a decade (1983–92) the subject of intense efforts to explain them by natural meteorological phenomena, whether by whirlwinds or by plasma vortices surrounding ball lightning. There can be little doubt that the scientists involved failed to consider the possibility that these phenomena were fraudulently produced because they were so eager to scotch the all-too-prevalent "extraterrestrial" theories of the crop circles' existence. The serious attempt of a few meteorologists to dispose of unscientific accounts of the circles looks very like an attempt to reaffirm the supremacy of science. This pattern would seem to suggest that these meteorologists at least were concerned about antiscientific and more "supernatural" encroachments upon their intellectual territory.

By contrast, the Gaia hypothesis, put forward by two scientists, James E. Lovelock and Lynn Margulis, was quickly taken up by theologians who saw it as a reaffirmation of teleology in modern science and a powerful new statement of the argument from design. Lovelock's and Margulis's original intention was to suggest that life has a greater influence on its habitat, the earth, than has been recognized by the modern earth sciences and that, indeed, the life of the planet serves as an active control system, affecting the atmosphere, the oceans, and other aspects of the environment. Life on earth, according to the Gaia hypothesis, provides a homeostatic feedback system that stabilizes the global temperature and other aspects of the world's climate. Although the hypothesis is now taken seriously by scientists, they were initially put off, it seems, because of its appeal to theologians and other "spiritual" groups. Initially, scientists could be persuaded to discuss it only in popular forums, such as in television, newspaper, or magazine debates. In their very different ways, then, both crop circles and the Gaia hypothesis indicate that there is still a tendency among nonscientists to read cosmic significance into meteorological phenomena, while scientists, like their late-Victorian counterparts, are still keen to deny all such claims.

See also Astrology; Comets and Meteors; Earthquakes; Electricity; Magic and the Occult

BIBLIOGRAPHY

Frisinger, H. Howard. *The History of Meteorology to 1800.* New York: Science History Publications, 1977.

Heninger, S. K., Jr. *A Handbook of Renaissance Meteorology: With Particular Reference to Elizabethan and Jacobean Literature.* Durham, N.C.: Duke University Press, 1960.

Kutzbach, Gisela. *The Thermal Theory of Cyclones: A History of Meteorological Thought in the Nineteenth Century.* Boston: American Meteorological Society, 1979.

Middleton, W. E. Knowles. *A History of the Barometer.* Baltimore: Johns Hopkins University Press, 1964.

———. *A History of the Theories of Rain and Other Forms of Precipitation.* London: Oldbourne, 1965.

———. *A History of the Thermometer and Its Use in Meteorology.* Baltimore: Johns Hopkins University Press, 1966.

Schaffer, Simon. "Natural Philosophy and Public Spectacle in the Eighteenth Century." *History of Science* 21 (1983): 1–43.

Schnabel, J. *Round in Circles: Physicists, Poltergeists, Pranksters, and the Secret History of the Cropwatchers.* Harmondsworth: Penguin, 1994.

Schneider, S. H., and P. J. Boston, eds. *Scientists on Gaia.* Cambridge, Mass.: MIT Press, 1991.

Thomas, Keith. *Religion and the Decline of Magic.* London: Weidenfeld and Nicolson, 1971.

Turner, Frank M. "Rainfall, Plagues, and the Prince of Wales." *Journal of British Studies* 13 (1974): 46–65. Reprinted in Turner, Frank M. *Contesting Cultural Authority.* Cambridge: Cambridge University Press, 1993, 151–70.

Wigley, T. M. L., M. J. Ingram, and G. Farmer, eds. *Climate and History: Studies in Past Climates and Their Impact on Man.* Cambridge: Cambridge University Press, 1981.

80. ECOLOGY AND THE ENVIRONMENT

David N. Livingstone

Religion and the Metaphors of Nature

Although the term "ecology" was not coined until the nineteenth century—by Ernst Haeckel (1834–1919) in his *General Morphology* (1866)—it was fundamentally a substitute for the earlier and widespread designation "the economy of nature." Haeckel himself spoke of ecology as "the theory of the economy of nature" while, more recently, Richard Hesse defined it as "the science of the 'domestic economy' of plants and animals" (Hesse et al. 1937, 6). This metaphorical association—thinking of nature as if it were a political economy—is particularly significant for religious reasons, because early proponents of the "economy of nature" or the "polity of nature" typically cast the Creator in the role of divine economist.

Nowhere, perhaps, is this conceptual alignment more clearly revealed than in the work of the Swedish botanist Carolus Linnaeus (1707–78), whose taxonomic enthusiasm was fired by the profound conviction that he was unearthing the very order of God's Creation. Indeed, his 1749 essay "The Oeconomy of Nature" was intended to identify the hand of God in nature's order. In this system, all living things were bound together into a chain of interlocking links. To Linnaeus, God was the Supreme Economist, for the analogy was with a well-run household under the watchful eye of a beneficent housekeeper. Hence, the Linnaean system could, at once, confute atheism and justify the social order. So, too, could the political economy of nature expressed in the writings of the Anglican clergyman Gilbert White (1720–93). In *The Natural History of Selborne* (1789), he recorded the natural order of his little parish, insisting throughout that providence had contrived to make "Nature . . . a great economist" who pervasively displayed the wisdom of God (quoted in Worster 1977, 7–8).

In more or less secularized forms this economic metaphor continued to condition ecological thinking from the period of the Enlightenment right into the twentieth century. Late-eighteenth- and nineteenth-century biogeographers, for example, routinely spoke of "nations" of plants. Alexander von Humboldt (1769–1859) treated plant associations as if they were political economies, while Goethe (1749–1832) deployed the fiscal concept of "budget" in his depiction of the natural world as a perfect economy with "inviolate balances." Given such connections between political economy and the "economy of nature," it is no surprise to find figures like Thomas Ewbank (1792–1870) writing, in 1855, that the world's economy "was designed for a Factory" by the great Designer (Worster 1977, 53). In the early twentieth century, ideas about the appropriate functioning of human economies and social communities continued to condition the new science of ecology. Eugenius Warming (1841–1924) and Frederic Clements (1874–1945), for instance, believed that plant communities had what William Coleman called "a definite general economy" with a specific set of occupying life-forms (Coleman 1986).

A different, though related, metaphorical conception of nature has rather earlier roots and can be traced back at least to the Middle Ages. This was the idea of nature as an organism, a living being, and it was only with the coming of the mechanical universe of Galileo (1564–1642), Isaac Newton (1642–1727), and Francis Bacon (1561–1626) that the potency of this image began to lose its appeal. Indeed, some historians, like Carolyn Merchant, have claimed that the origin of modern environmental despoliation is to be found in the substitution of an inert, mechanistic model of nature for an earlier life-filled, organic vision. Moreover, because the organic analogy was typically construed in gendered terms—as female—a number of eco-feminists have urged that the image of the earth as a nurturing mother had a culturally constraining effect on human action. While organicist ways of thinking were progressively to diminish in the wake of the scientific revolution, they certainly did not disappear from Western consciousness. To the contrary. In the past century or so, organismic modes of thought have blossomed in the development of ecological thinking—and in its accompanying ideological preoccupations. Frank Fraser Darling, a leading conservation spokesman during the 1960s, for example, called the West to adopt "the philosophy of wholeness" or "the truth of Zoroastrianism . . . that we are all of one stuff, difference is only in degree, and God can be conceived as being in all and of all, the sublime and divine immanence" (quoted in Passmore 1974, 173). More recently, organicism has been further rejuvenated in the much publicized Gaia hypothesis (Gaia was the Greek earth goddess) advocated by James Lovelock (1919–   ), a scientist who worked for NASA (National Aeronautics and Space Administration) and Hewlett-Packard. Lovelock describes the global system as "the largest living organism" and "a complex entity involving the Earth's biosphere, atmosphere, oceans and soil; the totality constituting a feedback or cybernetic system which seeks an optimal physical and chemical environment for life on earth" (Lovelock 1979, 11).

Similarly implicated in the organic vision is the "deep ecology" movement championed by the Norwegian philosopher Arne Naess. Deep ecology is not human centered but celebrates the close partnership of all forms of life and insists on the equal right to live and blossom. Thus, the deep-ecology movement rejects the separation of humanity from the rest of the natural order and honors the intrinsic value of every form of life. While Lovelock claims scientific objectivity for his Gaia hypothesis, and the deep-ecologists call for social reform, others find in organicism inspiration for what is called the New Paganism and the restoration of worship of the Earth Goddess. In many ways, this turn of events can be seen as part of a New Age rejection of scientific rationalism and the Enlightenment, and the perpetuation of organic ways of thinking about the natural world that flourished during the medieval period.

An altogether different image of nature received impetus with the advent of the scientific revolution of the seventeenth century—that of the machine. The triumph

of this mechanical vision was due, in large measure, to the search for inexorable laws governing the physical world. Through the writings of figures like René Descartes (1596–1650), Newton, and Robert Boyle (1627–91), the triumph of the mechanical system was secured. According to some historians, the new science, particularly as championed by Francis Bacon, issued in a new ethic that sanctioned the despoliation of nature. Courtesy of the mechanical arts, nature was dominated and bound into service. This transformation from the organic to the mechanistic, moreover, was not effected in cerebral isolation from changing social conditions. Rather, it was intertwined with the lengthy and complex shift from manorial farm economics to market capitalism, with its marked ecological consequences.

If, indeed, the new science initiated profound environmental change, it was *within* the mechanical philosophy that principles of environmental management began to be enunciated. Concerned at wasteful land practices, John Evelyn (1620–1706), for example, who published in 1662 his famous *Silva: A Discourse of Forest Trees and the Propagation of Timber in His Majesty's Dominions,* responded to the alarming drop in timber supply by appealing for the institution of sound conservation practices.

As often as not, such conservation principles were built upon the assumption that the human species had been created to be God's viceroy on Earth, a perspective that received impetus from the intimate connections between the new science and the mushrooming of a natural theology designed to uncover the ways in which the orderliness of the world machine attested to the sovereignty and beneficence of its Celestial Mechanic. Within this scheme, humans were seen as having a responsibility to exercise stewardship over the natural world to ensure that the marks of its designer were not effaced. God was a wise conservationist, and people, made in his image, were to act as caretakers of his world.

This form of beneficent dominion surfaced in the writings of Sir Matthew Hale (1609–76) and William Derham (1657–1735). Hale, England's mid-seventeenth-century Lord Chief Justice, told his readers that humanity's stewardship role was for the purpose of curbing the fiercer animals, protecting the other species, and preserving plant life. As for Derham, his *Physico-Theology* (1713) outlined a range of ecologically sound principles that included population stability, ecological interdependence, and species adaptation. All of these were rooted in his conviction that the Creator's "Infinite Wisdom and Care condescends, even to the Service, and Wellbeing of the meanest, most weak, and helpless insensitive Parts of the Creation" (Derham 1727, 425).

This fundamentally *managerial* approach to environment, adapted as it was to the rationalizing tendencies of the new mechanical world order, aimed at long-term planning, the maximization of energy production, sustained yield, ecosystem control, and the application of science to policy formation. It would ultimately issue in modern cost-benefit analysis, the concept of sustainable development, and environmental-impact assessment.

The White Thesis and Its Critics

Despite the fact that it was in the period of the scientific revolution that the mainsprings of environmental managerialism are to be found, there are those who urge that it was the coming of the new science that played a crucial role in the emergence of the modern environmental dilemma. Chief among these critics was Lynn White Jr. (1907–87), whose famed diagnosis of "The Historical Roots of Our Ecologic Crisis" appeared in *Science* in 1967. His claim was that environmental devastation had its roots in the Western marriage between science and technology, a union whose intellectual origins predated the scientific revolution. During the Middle Ages, he argued, a profound dislocation in the understanding of "man and nature" had taken place. Instead of humanity's being thought of as *part of* nature, the human race was seen as having dominion *over* nature and, thus, as licensed to violate the physical environment. This attitudinal shift, when conjoined to new technology, wreaked ecological havoc. As for the origins of this exploitative turn of events, White asserted that it was the consequence of the triumph of Christianity over paganism. For Christianity, he insisted, held that nature existed for the benefit of man, who was made in the image of God. This "most anthropocentric religion," he went on, stood in stark contrast to earlier religious traditions in which every tree, spring, and stream had its own guardian spirit. Christianity, he concluded, fostered environmental indifference by eradicating pagan animism.

While it rapidly provoked a furious controversy, and a suite of refutations, White's paper should be read in the context of Bert Hall's comment that "White was a believ-

ing Christian, and in his early publications he argued for the importance of medieval Christianity in our cultural makeup" (Hall 1988). Indeed, in a 1975 commencement address to the San Francisco Theological Seminary—of which he was a trustee—White concluded that "the study and contemplation of nature are an essential part of the Christian life both because they are acts of praise, and also because they teach us how our fellow creatures praise God in their own ways" (White 1975, 11). Besides, White's diagnosis was a good deal more subtle than conventional résumés suggest. He was fully aware that Western Christianity encompassed a variety of traditions, some of which—notably that of Saint Francis of Assisi (1181/2–1226), whom he proposed as the patron saint of ecologists—were more reverential toward the created order.

White was certainly not alone in finding religious sentiments at the headwaters of the environmental crisis. Max Nicholson, for fourteen years director-general of the Nature Conservancy in Great Britain, for instance, insisted that Christianity was ecologically culpable because of the doctrine of "man's unqualified right of dominance over nature" and called for the obliteration of "the complacent image of Man the Conqueror of Nature, and of Man Licensed by God to conduct himself as the earth's worst pest" (Nicholson 1970, 264). (It is perhaps significant that he more recently insisted that the "need for theological rethinking on man's place in nature is urgent" [Nicholson 1987, 195].) Arnold Toynbee located the origins of environmental improvidence in biblical monotheism and claimed that the only solution lay in resorting to the Weltanschauung of pantheism. Similar sentiments have been expressed by many other writers, but perhaps the most articulate defender of a revisionist version of the White thesis is John Passmore, who claimed that a combination of traditional belief in human dominion over creation and Stoic philosophy encouraged a morally unconstrained use of nonhuman nature.

Despite this chorus of support, White's analysis has not escaped criticism. Lewis Moncrief expressed misgivings about attempts to account for ecological insensitivity in terms of single-factor causes, arguing instead for the significance of a range of "cultural variables," of which two were especially prominent: democratization following in the wake of the French Revolution and, in the American context, the frontier experience. The absence of a public and a private environmental morality and the inability of social institutions to adjust to the ecological crisis Moncrief attributed to these factors. The geographer Yi-Fu Tuan approached the topic rather differently by examining environmental conditions in a number of Eastern regions. It turns out that, despite their ostensibly ecologically sensitive religious traditions, their *practices* were every bit as destructive as those in the West. Hence, the "official" line on attitudes toward environment (the quiescent, adaptive line) in Chinese religions, for example, is actually vitiated by behavior as mistreatments of nature abound through deforestation and erosion, rice terracing, and urbanization.

From yet another perspective, the historian Keith Thomas argues that White and his supporters overestimate religious motivation in human behavior. For Thomas, it was the coming of private property and a money economy that fostered the exploitation of environment and the disenchantment of nature. In addition, he points to the contested character of the Judeo-Christian stance toward nature: Alongside the tradition sanctioning the human right to exploit nature's bounty was a persistent theology of human stewardship. This, too, is emphasized by Robin Attfield, who insists that the idea that everything exists to serve humanity is not the position of the Old Testament and that there is "much more evidence than is usually acknowledged for . . . beneficent Christian attitudes to the environment and to nonhuman nature" (Attfield 1983a, 369).

Historical Retrieval

Partly as a response to the charges of critics like White, a number of scholars have scrutinized the history of the Christian West to determine just what the legacy of Christianity's attitudes to nature has actually been. We have already seen that the principle of stewardship was promulgated during the scientific revolution by writers urging a restrained human use of nature. But both before and after this crucial moment in Western history, Christian voices urging environmental sensitivity were to be heard.

The case of Saint Francis of Assisi, for example, is well known. Committed to a life of poverty and a gospel of repentance, he treated all living and inanimate objects as brothers and sisters and stressed the importance of communion with nature. Some, however, have thought that these very sentiments came too close to heresy and so have turned to other sources of environmental inspiration such as Saint Benedict (c. 480–c. 543). The prin-

ciples of stewardship that he espoused amounted to an early wise-use approach to nature. Indeed, it is for this reason that René Dubos believes that Saint Benedict is much more relevant than Saint Francis to human life in the modern world. Of course, Benedict did not emerge from a theological vacuum. There were ethical resources embedded even earlier in the patristic period upon which to call. In the *Hexaemeron,* Basil the Great (c. 330–79), one of the Cappadocian Fathers, for instance, displayed a profound interest in nature, as did his contemporary Saint Ambrose (339–97) in his own writings; both sought to unveil the wisdom of the Creator in the balance and harmony of nature and to insist on the partnership between God and humanity in the task of improving the earth.

On the other side of the scientific revolution, during the eighteenth and early nineteenth centuries, theological efforts to erode an arrogant anthropocentrism began to surface. Worldwide geographical reconnaissance, expanding astronomical horizons, and an emerging sense of "deep time" all tended to diminish the significance of the human subject. But it also became more common *within* the Christian church to find those urging that all members of the Creation were entitled to be used with civility. Christian writers like John Flavel (a Presbyterian divine [c. 1630–91]), Thomas Taylor (a Seeker [1618–82]), Christopher Smart (a religious poet [1722–71]), and Augustus Montague Toplady (a Calvinist minister and hymn writer [1740–78]) variously showed that, in the Bible, animals were regarded as good in and of themselves and not just for their potential service to humanity. John Wesley (1703–91) instructed parents not to let their children cause needless harm to living things, such as snakes, worms, toads, or even flies. So powerful was this Christian impulse toward a new sensibility that Keith Thomas believes that the "intellectual origins of the campaign against unnecessary cruelty to animals . . . grew out of the (minority) Christian tradition that man should take care of God's creation" (Thomas 1984, 180).

This new sensibility manifested itself in two conceptually significant ways for the growth in ecological thinking. First, there was the enormous significance of the environmental knowledge—such as herbals and county natural histories—produced by dozens of parson-naturalists. Indeed, the natural-history pursuit in the English-speaking world was, by the middle decades of the eighteenth century, a combination of religious impulse, intellectual curiosity, and aesthetic pleasure. Second, Christian theology contributed enormously to an emerging sense of ecological interconnectedness. As Clarence Glacken amply demonstrated, the "real contribution of physico-theology . . . was that it saw living interrelationships in nature concretely. It documented them. It had already—before Darwin's 'web of life'—prepared men for the study of ecology" (Glacken 1967, 427).

The Greening of Theology

At least in part, the retrieval of some of these historical voices is a consequence of what might be called "the greening of theology" over the last quarter of the twentieth century. Joseph Sittler, for example, drew attention to the affirmation of creation in the church's liturgy and hymnody; Paul Santmire traced environmental motifs in the writings of Irenaeus (c. 130–c. 200), Augustine (354–430), Martin Luther (1483–1546), and John Calvin (1509–64); and, even more recently, James Nash recalled the ecological sensitivity of the desert Fathers and the Celtic saints, among others. Historical revisionism, however, does not exhaust the contemporary interface between ecology and religion. Prior to the publication of White's diagnosis, Sittler had been developing a theology of the earth and urging that environmental malpractice was an affront to God, while Richard Baer had spoken of environmental misuse as a theological concern. Since then, numerous pronouncements on the environment have been forthcoming from a variety of theological traditions. Drawing inspiration from the process thinking of Alfred North Whitehead (1861–1947) and Charles Hartshorne (1897–), writers like Conrad Bonafazi and John Cobb have sought to cultivate an ecological conscience. Evangelical contributions have been forthcoming from writers like Francis Schaeffer, Rowland Moss, Lawrence Osborne, Loren Wilkinson, Calvin de Witt, and the Calvin Center for Christian Scholarship. More theologically radical is the Creation spirituality championed by the American Dominican priest Matthew Fox. Roman Catholic writers like Thomas Berry and Paul Collins have developed ecological theologies, and a variety of theological eco-feminists have urged that the struggle against the domination of women is intimately connected with other forms of domination, including the environment. As these recent writings reveal, the continuing vitality of the debate over the connections between religion and ecology and the production of eco-theologies shows little sign of diminishing.

See also Views of Nature

BIBLIOGRAPHY

Attfield, Robin. "Christian Attitudes to Nature." *Journal of the History of Ideas* 44 (1983a): 369–86.

———. *The Ethics of Environmental Concern.* New York: Columbia University Press, 1983b.

Black, John S. *The Dominion of Man: The Search for Ecological Responsibility.* Edinburgh: Edinburgh University Press, 1970.

Browne, Janet. *The Secular Ark: Studies in the History of Biogeography.* New Haven, Conn.: Yale University Press, 1983.

Coleman, William. "Evolution into Ecology? The Strategy of Warming's Ecological Plant Geography." *Journal of the History of Biology* 19 (1986): 181–96.

Derham, William. *Physico-Theology; or, A Demonstration of the Being and Attributes of God, from His Works of Creation.* 8th ed. London: 1727.

Glacken, Clarence. "The Origins of the Conservation Philosophy." *Journal of Soil and Water Conservation* 11 (1956): 63–6.

———. *Traces on the Rhodian Shore: Nature and Culture in Western Thought from Ancient Times to the End of the Eighteenth Century.* Berkeley: University of California Press, 1967.

Hall, Bert S. "Lynn White, Jr., 29 April 1907–30 March 1987." *Isis* 79 (1988): 478–81.

Hesse, R., W. C. Allee, and K. P. Schmidt. *Ecological Animal Geography: An Authorized, Rewritten Edition Based on Tiergeographie auf Oekologischer Grundlage, by Richard Hesse.* New York: Wiley, 1937.

Jackson, Myles W. "Natural and Artificial Budgets: Accounting for Goethe's Economy of Nature." *Science in Context* 7 (1994): 409–31.

Larson, James. "Not Without a Plan: Geography and Natural History in the Late Eighteenth Century." *Journal of the History of Biology* 19 (1986): 447–88.

Lovelock, James. *Gaia: A New Look at Life on Earth.* Oxford: Oxford University Press, 1979.

Merchant, Carolyn. *The Death of Nature: Women, Ecology, and the Scientific Revolution.* New York: Harper and Row, 1980.

———. "Earthcare: Women and the Environmental Movement." *Environment* 23 (1981): 2–13.

Moncrief, Lewis W. "The Cultural Basis of Our Environmental Crisis." *Science* 170 (October 30, 1970): 508–12.

Naess, Arne. "The Shallow and the Deep, Long-Range Ecology Movement: A Summary." *Inquiry* 16 (1973): 95–100.

Nash, Roderick Frazier. *The Rights of Nature: A History of Environmental Ethics.* Madison: University of Wisconsin Press, 1989.

Nicholson, Max. *The Environmental Revolution: A Guide for the New Masters of the World.* London: Hodder and Stoughton, 1970.

———. *The New Environmental Age.* Cambridge: Cambridge University Press, 1987.

Passmore, John. *Man's Responsibility for Nature: Ecological Problems and Western Tradition.* London: Duckworth, 1974.

———. "Attitudes to Nature." In *Nature and Conduct,* ed. by R. S. Peters. Royal Institute of Philosophy Lectures. Vol. 8. London: Royal Institute of Philosophy, 1975, 251–64.

Thomas, Keith. *Man and the Natural World: Changing Attitudes in England, 1500–1800.* London: Penguin, 1984.

Toynbee, Arnold. "The Religious Background of the Present Environmental Crisis." *International Journal of Environmental Studies* 3 (1972): 141–6.

Tuan, Yi-Fu. "Our Treatment of the Environment in Ideal and Actuality." *American Scientist* (May/June, 1970): 246–9.

White, Lynn, Jr. "The Historical Roots of Our Ecologic Crisis." *Science* 155 (1967): 1203–7.

———. "Christians and Nature." *Pacific Theological Review* 7 (1975): 6–11.

Worster, Donald. *Nature's Economy: A History of Ecological Ideas.* Cambridge: Cambridge University Press, 1977.

PART VIII

The Biological Sciences

81. NATURAL HISTORY

Peter M. Hess

Introduction

Throughout much of Western intellectual history, the relationship between religion and the study of natural history was relatively serene, untroubled by the spectacular displays that were provoked by advances in astronomy. Indeed, during the two millennia after Aristotle (384–322 B.C.), there was little to spark significant controversy until the secular implications of biological evolution became apparent following the publication of Charles Darwin's (1809–82) *Origin of Species* (1859). Nevertheless, the many theories of natural history and the rationales underlying its practice were perennially intertwined in complex ways with the theological assumptions of the cultures in which it developed.

The term "natural history" is not susceptible to easy and consistent definition in the multiple cultural and temporal contexts through which it developed in the centuries covered by this essay. While natural history always dealt with the study of living animals and plants, during a substantial portion of its history it also included fossils, minerals, and geological formations. In the Middle Ages, it included the study of rocks and fossils, but they became detached from natural history during the eighteenth century, as recognition of the deep history of time propelled paleontology and geology toward the status of autonomous disciplines. Natural history in 1850 hardly resembled the eclectically comprehensive body of knowledge it had been in Pliny the Elder's (c. A.D. 23–79) *Natural History,* which included everything from the study of anatomy and physiology to the anthropological treatment of comparative cultures. These subjects had become separated from the topic by the mid-nineteenth century. In this article, "natural history" will be understood as refer-

ring primarily to the study of the organic world as manifested in species of plants and animals.

While making collections of curiosities was a significant dimension of natural history after 1700, the discipline never consisted merely of cataloging the elements of nature. It always involved, however unsystematically, the construction of (or at least the possibility of) philosophical interpretations of the things found. Nevertheless, natural history needs to be distinguished from "natural philosophy" not only by virtue of its subject matter but because the latter—especially from the seventeenth century onward—designated the elaboration of causal interpretations of measurable phenomena, particularly in physics and astronomy.

Underlying the relationship between religious thought and natural history in the Western tradition, one crucial paradigm shift stands out: The great sea change in thought from the classical view of nature as the immutable foundation of human affairs, which served in medieval Christendom as the backdrop for the great drama of salvation, to the modern view in which the earth, as well as biological life and the human species, have become thoroughly historicized. The natural history pursued by Aristotle and Pliny, as well as by patristic writers and medieval bestiarists, was qualitatively different from the nineteenth-century biological science practiced by Charles Darwin and integrated by such contemporary theologians as Frederick Temple (1821–1902) into a Christian, or more generally, a theistic, worldview.

The Dual Heritage

The intersection between religion and natural history in the Western tradition naturally has plural roots, three of which, at the risk of undue simplification, can be identified as being of primary significance: Greek rationality, Roman pragmatism, and the Judeo-Christian appraisal of the world as intrinsically good.

Natural history was not foremost among the interests of the pre-Socratic Greek philosophers of the sixth and fifth centuries B.C., whose speculations were primarily cosmological, nor was it particularly important for Plato (c. 427–347 B.C.). The latter's major contribution to natural history was his epistemology: His theory of Forms served to undergird the concept of species as an entity that truly existed within the divine mind, a theory that was not seriously challenged until the work of Georges Leclerc, Comte de Buffon (1707–88), in the eighteenth century. Of even greater significance was Aristotle, who made seminal contributions in at least three areas. First, his doctrine of the tripartite soul, which took vegetative, animate, and rational forms, established a crucial principle of continuity within the biological realm. However, his assertion that the source of the rational soul comes from outside the physical process of reproductive transmission set up later tensions by encouraging Christian theologians to assert that the soul was separately created by God. Second, his careful attention to firsthand observation—whether in his own work or in the reports of others—was conducive to what would become a tradition of empirical research that was pursued only intermittently until its firm establishment as a methodological approach by Francis Bacon (1561–1626). Third, Aristotle's pervasive teleology ensured that final causes would serve, at least until 1800, as a fundamental organizing principle in natural history, governing our understanding of how bodies are organized, of the purposes served by individual organs, and of the relationships between plant and animal members of the medieval "Great Chain of Being." Religion and natural history were, at best, only tangentially (and perhaps negatively) related in Aristotle's thought, however: His remote Prime Mover was unconcerned with individual plants or animals or even human beings.

Among other classical sources for natural history, one of the most influential was the work of Pliny the Elder, whose voluminous *Historia naturalis* (*Natural History*) exercised a profound influence on the West well into the Renaissance. The encounter of natural history and religion in his thought takes place against the background of his central concern to catalog and exhibit nature in all of its strange and wonderful variety. Skeptical of the existence of the gods, Pliny proceeded from

the assumption that "the world is the work of nature and the embodiment of nature itself" (2.1). Hence, his collection of facts about everything imaginable can almost literally be said to articulate his "theology." Early medieval encyclopedists drew heavily from this eclectic, unsystematic, and uncritical work and even patterned their own works after it.

The clear relationship between religion and the world in Hebrew thought is expressed in the Genesis Creation story. The sixfold divine affirmation of creation as "good" in Genesis 1 reflects the Jewish view that God's revelation does not merely designate the communication of divine truth to humankind, but involves the whole of the natural world. The sharp distinction between God and nature that was characteristic of Judaism ensured that the Creator and his creation could not be conflated, but it also opened the door to potential scientific investigation of the world. Of course, the Hebrew authors were in no sense scientists and offered no systematic account of the organic world around them. The theological structure of the first eleven chapters of Genesis clearly shows that fact. However, the positive appraisal of nature found throughout Hebrew literature would hold great significance for the development of natural history. "The heavens declare the glory of God, and the firmament shows forth his handiwork" (Psalm 19:1 Revised Standard Version). If all creatures are called upon to praise God for his creation (as in Psalm 148), the investigation of natural history becomes a worthy enterprise provoking awe and, ultimately, worship.

The Christian New Testament follows the Hebrew Scriptures in lacking any systematic interest in natural history. But the Gospels and the Pauline literature are positive in their view of nature in contrast, for example, with contemporary Gnosticism. The view of the Old Testament that the world is good is echoed in the Pauline declaration that "ever since the creation of the world his invisible nature, namely his eternal power and deity, has been clearly perceived in the things that have been made" (Romans 1:20). This passage would exert a powerful influence on the development of natural theology in Christian Europe well into the eighteenth century and, thus, serve as one rationale for the study of natural history.

From the Fathers to the Middle Ages

The portion of patristic literature that deals with natural history tends to reflect the dual heritage of Greco-

Roman science and the Hebrew-Christian affirmation of the world as God's handiwork. Especially in the writings of the Greek Fathers, nature was widely regarded as sacramental and was, therefore, considered a proper subject of investigation. As bishops and theologians, the Fathers were only amateur naturalists, but their appreciation of God's creation went far beyond merely using it as a convenient source for theological metaphors. Basil of Caesarea (c. 330–79), Gregory of Nyssa (c. 330–c. 395), and Nemesius (late fourth century) made objective observations about the plants and animals around them. These men had studied natural history as part of their general education. For example, they studied botany not merely through written sources, but by a close observation of nature that was frequently directed to practical ends, such as perfecting the cultivation of fruit trees and staple crops. On the other hand, the Fathers demonstrated an eclectic and unscientific knowledge of zoology and showed (by modern standards) considerable credulity in mixing fact with fancy. Natural history in their hands was not experimental. They diligently mined the florilegia and manuals at their disposal for scientific knowledge, which they pursued for its theological and moral use. In this respect, they demonstrated a closer affinity to Plato than to Aristotle. Hence, the revival of natural history as a constructive attempt to understand the animate world in itself would have to await the high-medieval recovery of the latter's biological works.

Natural history shared in the precipitous decline of Western intellectual culture in the period (c. 500–c. 1000) following the collapse of Roman civilization. For much of the early Middle Ages up to the twelfth century, scholarly knowledge about nature and natural phenomena was largely lost in the Christian West, and, although works from this period record considerable familiarity with local plants and their medicinal uses, no significant developments were made in the direction of a systematic understanding of natural history. Such knowledge as existed was preserved and transmitted by the medieval encyclopedias, such as Isidore of Seville's (c. 560–636) *Etymologies,* and *De proprietatibus rerum (On the Properties of Things)* by the thirteenth-century Englishman Bartholomeus Anglicus (fl. 1230–50). Ultimately, all such works descended from the anonymous Greek *Physiologus* (c. A.D. 200), and their construction reflected a continuous literary tradition more than it relied on empirical observation, which was used only infrequently to supplement excerpts made from classical texts. The knowledge

displayed in these works—especially the illuminated books of animals, known as "bestiaries"—was clearly oriented to didactic and nonscientific purposes. For example, a central theological doctrine governing the interpretation of natural history was that the Fall of Adam and Eve had effected a dramatic physical transformation in nature, including the initiation of carnivorous behavior among animals. Treatment of animals in bestiaries could not simply recount their ecological circumstances or life histories, but had also to pay attention to the natural symbolism of spiritual truths, such as the role of the serpent in the Garden of Eden or of the whale in the story of Jonah, not to mention moral qualities, such as the fox's cunning or the dog's fidelity.

With the reintroduction of the full Aristotelian corpus into the West in the thirteenth century, studies of botany and zoology began gradually to move beyond the bestiary tradition. The rediscovery of the biological works of Aristotle (and of those spuriously attributed to him) was an important catalyst to new thought, especially in the cases of Albertus Magnus (1193–1280) and Roger Bacon (1213–91). However, Pliny continued to be widely read well into the sixteenth century, and natural history remained oriented toward the dominant theological paradigm, fleshing out particular details in the "Chain of Being" between God and prime matter, in which humanity constituted the vitally important link.

From the Renaissance to Physico-Theology

The early-modern treatment of the natural-historical tradition bequeathed to it by the Middle Ages was marked by both important continuities and significant critiques. On the one hand, the ponderous weight of received tradition is illustrated by the printed floral works of the early sixteenth century, which, in some respects, merely recapitulate the themes of medieval herbals. Likewise, Conrad Gesner's (1516–65) handsomely printed *Historia animalium (History of Animals* [1551–8]) engaged the reader in the systematic study of animals but also evidenced a credulity that would be unacceptable a century later. Among the nicely drawn exempla of known species to appear in Gesner and in Edward Topsell's *History of Four-Footed Beasts* (1608) were mythical creatures such as the manticora, which was part man and part lion.

On the other hand, the invention of printing and the new humanistic scholarship together exercised a profound impact on the study of natural history, with the result that, by the fifteenth century, some biologists were beginning to examine Pliny with a decidedly critical eye. Printing offered the advantage of conveying information in the form of images, which moved well beyond a crude iconographic tradition and served to educate naturalists uniformly in far-flung parts of Europe. Albrecht Dürer's (1471–1528) detailed drawings of plants, for example, paid careful attention to their ecologies. The emblematic worldview—in which to know a creature was to know all of its literary associations—would gradually give way to the inductive methodology championed by Francis Bacon (1561–1626), in which physical observation was paramount.

Important humanist critics of the medieval tradition included Thomas Browne (1605–82), a scholar who was both deeply respectful of the authorities of the past and a scientifically minded naturalist. In his *Pseudodoxia epidemica,* or *Enquiries into . . . Vulgar and Common Errors* (1646), Browne submitted the reliability of many past writers on natural history to careful examination according to the three Anglican determinants of truth: sense, authority, and reason. His presupposition of the truth of the divinely ordained laws of nature became a touchstone of the Royal Society (founded in 1660), for whose members doing good science was a deeply religious activity. It is no accident that Nehemiah Grew's (1641–1712) important empirical researches in botany found their highest expression in his *Cosmologia sacra* (*Sacred Cosmology* [1701]). Genuine advances in scientific method and a critical understanding of phenomena fostered the empirical research of naturalists such as Robert Hooke (1635–1703) and Anton van Leeuwenhoek (1632–1723) and established biology on a firm footing by the end of the seventeenth century. Still, natural historians continued to view the evidence they accumulated in the light of received theological assumptions. As a context for interpreting his careful observations about fossils, Nicolaus Steno (1638–86), for example, posited the Noachian Flood as the source of the fossils that he meticulously described.

In the latter half of the seventeenth century, the English "physico-theology" movement developed the closest intertwining that natural history would perhaps ever enjoy with religion. The Cambridge divine and scientist John Ray (1627–1705) saw clear evidence of divine planning in the complex adaptations of plants and animals to their environments. His treatise *The Wisdom of God Manifested in the Works of the Creation* (1691) not only restated the design argument, but also offered a vast compendium of natural history that was characterized by the observation of important nuances within species and the incipient recognition of ecological relationships. The Boyle Lectures (founded in 1692) institutionalized this approach by providing a public forum for the articulation of the new science in support of traditional religious belief. The most influential course of lectures dealing with natural history that provided support for the design argument was delivered by William Derham (1657–1735) and published as *Physico-Theology; or, A Demonstration of the Being and Attributes of God from the Works of Creation* (1716). The establishment of the physico-theology tradition stands as both the embodiment of an ancient tradition wrapped in the mantle of the scientific revolution and the point from which natural history would split into two streams: one professional and increasingly secular, the other popular and persistently religious.

Eighteenth- and Nineteenth-Century Developments

If religion and natural history enjoyed a close relationship in the seventeenth century, as exemplified by the edifying structure of the physico-theology tradition, cultural and intellectual factors would erode its foundations through a variety of channels and bring about its collapse in the next century. In one degree or another, the Enlightenment exaltation of reason at the expense of revelation was implicated in most of them, but factors in the social construction of science also played an important role. In particular, four significant shifts in pre-Darwinian natural history contributed to this erosion.

First, it is important to recognize that natural history existed in two parallel traditions. The physico-theology tradition persevered with elegance until Victorian times, nourished by the religious impulses of reverence and awe at the divine wisdom revealed in the works of Creation. A classic example is the collection of observations on local flora and fauna made by the English clergyman Gilbert White (1720–93) and published in 1788 as *The Natural History of Selborne.* A far more philosophically rigorous contribution in this vein was William Paley's (1743–1805) *Natural Theology* (1802), which continued to influence a generation of students of impeccable Christian orthodoxy, including (as a young man) Charles Darwin. This popular tradition extended into the 1860s, embodying an approach to natural history that was solidly grounded in the assumptions of natural theology.

However, the tradition of natural theology had already begun to face strenuous competition in the mid-eighteenth century from professional natural historians. Although Carolus Linnaeus (1707–78), in creating his system of taxonomic nomenclature, regarded himself as a recorder of God's creation, in his work he avoided as consistently as possible any appeal to God for causal explanation of natural-historical phenomena. And from 1700 onward, the increasing sophistication of research tools and instrumentation, together with the establishment of endowed chairs in European universities, led inevitably to the professionalization of natural history. A field in which amateur collectors of specimens could still make respectable contributions was on its way to becoming the largely secular professional discipline of biology of the nineteenth century. Impelled by the research of such towering figures as Linnaeus in Sweden, Buffon in France, and Albrecht von Haller (1708–77) in Germany, natural history on the professional level discarded in theory (if not in fact) the religious assumptions of physico-theology. As scientific sophistication spread to the wider culture, discoveries that had provoked awe and reverence in the early physico-theologians were now regarded as merely commonplace.

A second shift may be seen in the eclipse of teleology and the growth of scientific naturalism. One of the most important Aristotelian legacies had been the adoption of teleology as a fundamental organizing principle in science, and it played an especially crucial role in natural history. Organisms were thought to develop according to a preconceived plan, just as organs were assumed to have been designed to serve specific purposes and animals to thrive within particular habitats, all for the service of humans. However, in the eighteenth century this basic principle began to falter, and, while it would be anachronistic to suggest that by 1859 teleological thinking already lay shipwrecked on the shoals of naturalism, the importance of its piecemeal dismantling cannot be underestimated.

Whatever personal and methodological differences there may have been among Linnaeus, Buffon, and Haller, as scientists they shared basic assumptions about the existence of final causes and immutable plans regarding the objects of their study. In contrast, their successors in the next generation of natural historians uniformly relied upon the assumptions of Enlightenment science,

discarding as useless tools the teleologies and immutable plans that had served such a vital role from Aristotle to Ray and Derham. Their intentionally nonteleological approach found philosophical legitimation in Immanuel Kant's (1724–1804) *Critique of Teleological Judgment* (1790).

Another impetus to the dissociation of natural history from a religious interpretation of nature was the extension of the seventeenth-century mechanistic cosmological model into the biological sphere. The reintroduction of Lucretius's (c. 99–55 B.C.) atomic theory of matter, purged of its atheistic elements, had reduced physical reality to matter in motion under the influence of Galileo (1564–1642) and René Descartes (1596–1650) and had already excluded the vast continuum of "vital" powers intrinsic to the Aristotelian universe. The logical sequel was to extend this reductionism to life itself and to provide a purely naturalistic explanation of life from a mechanico-chemical perspective. Even if the mechanistic interpretation of life was not ultimately successful, its presence caused some wear on the supports for a religious interpretation of nature.

A third eighteenth-century challenge to the received tradition of natural history came in the form of a secularizing "historicization" of natural history. Two growing mountains of evidence—one temporal and the other geographical—suggested that the biblical cosmogony could not be accepted literally. First, almost from the moment of the European discovery of the New World, an endless stream of information about previously unknown plants and animals began inundating the minds of natural historians. Whereas John Ray listed fifteen hundred species of animals, Linnaeus knew of fifty-six hundred species of quadrupeds alone, and further geographical exploration offered no end to this explosion of knowledge. It began to seem difficult to reconcile such an abundance of species with Creation from a central point or with the story of Noah having saved two pairs of each species in his ark, thus forcing natural historians into the increasingly uncomfortable position of having to choose between their empirical evidence and the dictates of theological tradition. The temporal factor influencing the historicization of natural history was the gradual discovery of the "deep history" of time. The evidence being gathered by the young science of geology suggested that the sedimentary strata of the earth and the fossils they contained were far older than the few thousand years that a literal reading of Genesis would allow. Consequently, by the 1830s the natural historian had every good reason to believe that the history of creation was not coterminous with human history and that species, over time, might, indeed, have come into existence and become extinct.

Nevertheless, even in these developments the importance of religious factors to natural history must not be gainsaid. It had been recognized in classical times that fauna and flora varied considerably with location, and the biblical description of a universal flood and subsequent diffusion of species from Mount Ararat served as a powerful organizing idea. Even after eighteenth-century natural historians had come to think of the Flood as a local event, the entrenched idea of the radiation of life-forms from a central point was only gradually abandoned. Likewise, the rationale for establishing botanic gardens in Europe was initially, at least in part, theological. In the sixteenth century, it had been hoped that the Garden of Eden—which, according to one tradition, had survived the destructive ravages of Noah's Flood—might be rediscovered in the course of European exploration. Disappointment in this sphere was tempered by excitement at the idea of re-creating Paradise, by reassembling from the farthest corners of the globe the many species dispersed by the Flood.

Finally, the story of pre-Darwinian natural history would not be complete without a comment on its gradual assimilation of elements of what would eventually become the new paradigm of biological evolution. From the time of Ray and Derham onward, the physico-theological tradition had paid increasing attention to the adaptations of organisms to particular environments, interpreting them through the lens of divine design. William Paley's diligent natural historical studies in *Natural Theology* masterfully rearticulated the argument for a divinely designed and providentially arranged world. Parallel to the secular work of professional natural historians, the theological interpretation of ecological adaptation persevered, both in the Bridgewater Treatises of the 1830s and in Charles Babbage's (1792–1871) argument in 1838 that the very laws governing the extinction and creation of new forms of life suitable for particular environments could be interpreted as further evidence of the benevolent, if inscrutable, purposes of God.

But, with the Darwinian synthesis, the hallowed and familiar relationship between religion and natural history became decidedly more ambiguous. Darwin's carefully substantiated case for natural selection in the *Origin of Species* found a mixed reception, with some theologians

accepting it and some scientists opposing it. While Darwin himself only gradually abandoned Christianity, after 1859 professional biologists would refer to the classic metaphor of God's "Book of Nature" with increasing rarity.

Conclusions

In the two millennia separating Aristotle from Darwin, both the assumptions underlying natural history and the express rationale for its practice were profoundly influenced by theologies in the Judeo-Christian tradition. This influence was reciprocal, as sophistication in natural-historical studies in the later medieval and early-modern periods reinforced a natural theology that had become quasi-independent of Christianity. It is perhaps significant that Aristotle and Darwin—the two thinkers who most clearly frame the period in which natural history developed into the science of biology—each operated out of a theological framework that was, in important respects, incompatible with Christianity. In the interim, the historical and metaphysical assumptions of the Judeo-Christian West provided fertile ground in which the seeds of the modern understanding of flora, fauna, and their related ecologies could take root.

The period from 1750 onward witnessed an increasingly secular approach to the practice of natural history, less and less determined by the agenda of a literal adherence to biblical dogma. The growing belief that Scripture was a historically conditioned document was paralleled by a radical historicization of the natural world and biological processes, and, since the late eighteenth century—and in a greatly accelerated fashion since Darwin—traditional theistic assumptions have been largely replaced by an underlying methodological and metaphysical naturalism. Relating theology and natural history meaningfully to each other has not become impossible, but, since the mid-nineteenth century, practitioners of each discipline have been compelled to become acutely aware of the limitations of the competencies of both as they relate to the other.

See also Aristotle and Aristotelianism; Charles Darwin; Early Christian Attitudes Toward Nature; Ecology and the Environment; Evolution; Genesis Flood; Geography; Great Chain of Being; Natural Theology; Taxonomy

BIBLIOGRAPHY

Ashworth, William B. "Natural History and the Emblematic World View." In *Reappraisals of the Scientific Revolution,* ed. by David C. Lindberg and Robert S. Westman. Cambridge: Cambridge University Press, 1990, 302–32.

Barber, Lynn. *The Heyday of Natural History, 1820–1870.* New York: Doubleday, 1980.

Bates, Marston. *The Nature of Natural History.* Princeton, N.J.: Princeton University Press, 1950.

Brooke, John. *Science and Religion: Some Historical Perspectives.* Cambridge: Cambridge University Press, 1991.

Browne, Janet. *The Secular Ark: Studies in the History of Biogeography.* New Haven, Conn.: Yale University Press, 1983.

Clark, Willene B., and Meradith T. McMunn. *Beasts and Birds of the Middle Ages: The Bestiary and its Legacy.* Philadelphia: University of Pennsylvania Press, 1989.

Crombie, A. C. *Augustine to Galileo.* Cambridge, Mass: Harvard University Press, 1961.

Gillespie, Neal C. "Natural History, Natural Theology, and Social Order: John Ray and the 'Newtonian Ideology.'" *Journal of the History of Biology* 20 (1987): 1–49.

Glacken, Clarence. *Traces on the Rhodian Shore: Nature and Culture in Western Thought from Ancient Times to the End of the Eighteenth Century.* Berkeley: University of California Press, 1967.

Goerke, Heinze. *Linnaeus.* Trans. by Denver Lindley. New York: Scribner's, 1973.

Hoeniger, F. D., and J. F. M. Hoeniger. *The Growth of Natural History in Stuart England from Gerard to the Royal Society.* Charlottesville, Va.: University Press of Virgina for the Folger Shakespeare Library, 1969.

Jardine, N., J. A. Secord, and E. C. Spary, eds. *Cultures of Natural History.* Cambridge: Cambridge University Press, 1996.

Knight, David M. *Natural Science Books in English, 1600–1900.* London: Batsford, 1989.

Larson, James L. *Interpreting Nature: The Science of Living from Linnaeus to Kant.* Baltimore and London: Johns Hopkins University Press, 1994.

Lenoir, Timothy. *The Strategy of Life: Teleology and Mechanics in Nineteenth-Century German Biology.* Dordrecht: Reidel, 1982.

Lindberg, David C. *The Beginnings of Western Science: The European Scientific Tradition in Philosophical, Religious, and Institutional Context, 600 B.C. to A.D. 1450.* Chicago: University of Chicago Press, 1992.

Pelikan, Jaroslav. *Christianity and Classic Culture: The Metamorphosis of Natural Theology in the Christian Encounter with Hellenism.* New Haven, Conn.: Yale University Press, 1993.

Prest, John. *The Garden of Eden: The Botanic Garden and the Recreation of Paradise.* New Haven, Conn.: Yale University Press, 1981.

Rehbock, Philip F. *The Philosophical Naturalists.* Madison: University of Wisconsin Press, 1983.

Roger, Jacques. "The Mechanistic Conception of Life." In *God and Nature: Historical Essays on the Encounter between Christianity and Science,* ed. by David C. Lindberg and Ronald L. Numbers. Berkeley: University of California Press, 1984, 277–95.

Rudwick, Martin J. S. *Scenes from Deep Time: Early Pictorial Representations of the Prehistoric World.* Chicago: University of Chicago Press, 1992.

Sloan, Phillip R. "John Locke, John Ray, and the Problem of the Natural System." *Journal of the History of Biology* 5 (1972): 1–53.

———. "Natural History, 1670–1802." In *Companion to the History of Modern Science,* ed. by R. C. Colby et al. London: Routledge, 1990, 295–313.

Stannard, Jerry. "Natural History." In *Science in the Middle Ages,* ed. by David C. Lindberg. Chicago and London: University of Chicago Press, 1978, 429–60.

Wallace-Hadrill, D. S. *The Greek Patristic View of Nature.* Manchester, U.K.: Manchester University Press, 1968.

82. THE GREAT CHAIN OF BEING

William F. Bynum

Alfred North Whitehead (1861–1947) once famously remarked that the European philosophical tradition consists "of a series of footnotes to Plato." Along with his pupil Aristotle (384–322 B.C.), Plato (c. 427–347 B.C.) provided the foundation for one of the most pervasive themes within Western science, the notion that all creation may be conceived as a vast, graduated chain of beings, stretching, in the words of a later poet, "from nothing to the Deity." Called by various other names, such as the scale of nature *(scala naturae),* or the ladder of beings, the Great Chain of Being was the subject of a classic monograph of that title by the American historian of ideas Arthur O. Lovejoy (1873–1963).

Lovejoy argued that the Chain of Being rested on three related principles, or "unit ideas": plenitude, continuity, and gradation. Plenitude came from Plato's exposition of the idea of the Good in the *Republic,* and his account in the *Timaeus* of Creation by a force he called the Demiurge (divine craftsman). Plenitude identified goodness with fullness and implied that a good, powerful Creator would have created every possible kind of being ("it takes all kinds to make a world"). It also justified the existence of seemingly noxious creatures such as poisonous snakes and spiders. Continuity presupposed that there could be no gaps between adjacent beings; otherwise, creation would be less than full and, hence, less than perfect. Gradation, more closely associated with both Aristotle's biological and metaphysical work, guaranteed that the Chain of Being was vertical and that some kinds of beings were "higher" than others. At one practical level, this meant that Aristotle graded organisms in relation to their "likeness" to the highest, which were human beings. Thus, monkeys were higher in the scale than worms. In addition, the "higher" also incorporated the attributes of the "lower": Rational man also partook of the sensation

and motion of animals, the growth, nutrition, and reproduction of plants, and the substantiality of inanimate things like stones.

Lovejoy overstated the precision with which these three principles were actually expounded by Plato and Aristotle, but they certainly did provide the framework for a series of ongoing theological, metaphysical, and scientific debates in the Christian era. The church Fathers, from Augustine (354–430) and Pseudo-Dionysius (fl. c. 500) to Thomas Aquinas (c. 1225–74), attempted to reconcile the implicit necessitarianism of plenitude (Did God *have* to create every possible kind of being? Could he have chosen to create a less than perfect world?) with the notion of divine free will. Aquinas distinguished between God's "absolute" and "ordained" powers, so that the world he chose to make is the actual world we live in. Its ordained fullness is an expression of his goodness and providence, but in his omnipotence he could have created a different world. As William Paley (1743–1805) was to conclude in his *Natural Theology* (1802), "It is a happy world after all." Others, from Raymond Lull (c. 1232–1315) to the founders of the Royal Society of London in the mid-seventeenth century, sought to organize human knowledge in ways that were consonant with the hierarchical principle of gradation ("from Nature up to Nature's God").

From the late Middle Ages to the early nineteenth century, however, four specific sets of issues characterized the ongoing interaction between scientific discoveries and speculations, on the one hand, and the theological and metaphysical precepts inherent in the idea of the Chain of Being. They are: (1) the plurality of worlds, (2) the possibility of biological extinction, (3) the nature of a biological species, and (4) the historicity of nature.

Plenitude and the Plurality of Worlds

Both the influence of Neoplatonism during the Renaissance and the astronomical discoveries during the scientific revolution raised the conceptual and physical possibility that an infinite variety of beings required infinite space in which to exist, that the earth was only one of a large number of inhabited planets, and that "out there" existed beings as far superior to mankind as man was to the apes. At one level, this heady idea was merely a small part of the scientific realization, beginning in the sixteenth century, that the earth was not the center of the universe but was, rather, an average-size planet rotating around an average-size star, the sun. Other larger stars, which the telescope could reveal, might have their own planets with their own rational beings. Such a notion obsessed the scientific mystic and martyr Giordano Bruno (1548–1600), who died at the stake (though probably for his interest in magic rather than his devotion to plenitude). Nevertheless, Bruno's fate highlights the fact that ideas of the plurality of worlds were hard to square with the biblical account of man's place in the cosmos and with the Fall and unique Incarnation of Jesus. The plurality debate did not die with Bruno, however, but was revived periodically during the next two centuries and more: by the French savant Bernard Fontenelle (1657–1757) in the seventeenth century, the English astronomer William Herschel (1738–1822) in the eighteenth, and the Scottish clergyman Thomas Dick (1774–1857) in the nineteenth. More recent discussions of the possibility of extraterrestrial life are usually based on notions of chance and probability and owe more to the theory of evolution than to theology.

Fossils and Biological Extinction

Medieval and early-modern notions of the Chain of Being were static: God had created the universe only a few thousand years ago, and the fullness of his handiwork had existed from the final day of Creation. Voyages of exploration began to reveal many kinds of plants and animals unknown in Europe. On the one hand, these new and often exotic organisms seemed to be empirical confirmation of plenitude, since they could be related to the familiar flora and fauna of the Old World and thus fill in gaps in the Chain of Being; on the other, they reminded scholars that only a tiny portion of the earth's lands and seas had been systematically scrutinized, thus

making it reasonable that newly discovered fossilized bones and shells, which did not seem to belong to any known living species, might eventually be found alive and well in far-off parts. One school of thought argued that these "fossils" (meaning, literally, "something dug up") represented nature's abortive attempts at life, having the forms but not the functions of living creatures. From the late seventeenth century, however, naturalists increasingly accepted them as the hardened remains of once-living plants and animals, and their present-day descendants had either to be discovered or the world accepted as less full than it once was, because some organisms had died out completely. This belief had implications for both the age of the earth and the conventional elaboration of plenitude, since, if whole species had disappeared, the world was not so complete as it once was or might be. By the early nineteenth century, biological extinction became generally accepted, largely through Georges Cuvier's (1769–1832) reconstructions of the giant vertebrate fossils discovered in geological strata around Paris.

What Is a Species?

Common sense and ordinary language show that organisms differ and that words like "dog" or "geranium" have a definite meaning. Plato had been concerned with the relationship between the individual and the type (this particular dog and universal characteristics of "dogness"). Likewise, it was not always clear whether plenitude and continuity pointed toward a universe with all possible types or one in which there was a multiplicity of individuals, and any abstraction beyond the individual object was merely a handy convention invented by human beings. A real continuum requires that adjacent points can always be subdivided, and eighteenth-century Europeans liked to point out that human beings varied from angelic-like Newtons to apelike Hottentots. Maybe, as the French naturalist Georges Leclerc, Comte de Buffon (1707–88), put it, nature knows only the individual, and all higher taxonomic groupings are artificial, conventionally useful but not "natural." Buffon announced this radical conclusion in the 1740s, but two further decades of observing, describing, and experimenting with a wide variety of animals convinced him that there are natural boundaries between different species. These limits are reflected in intraspecific reproductive capacities and the sterility of most hybrids produced by closely related species, such as mules from crossing a horse and a donkey. At the same time, Buffon and many others were intrigued by the extent of variability within a species, such as the vast range of size, shape, and other characteristics in different breeds of dogs. This raised the question of the relationship between variability that is observed at present and the nature of the original species as created by God. With the introduction of time, natural history as a static, descriptive enterprise gradually became transformed into something concerned with the history of nature.

The Temporalization of the Chain

During the second half of the eighteenth century, naturalists such as Charles Bonnet (1720–93) and Jean Baptiste Robinet (1735–1820) struggled with the temporal relationships between kinds of organisms and with the possibility that the fullness of Creation was not achieved once and for all ("In the beginning"), but was a dynamic process. Only through time could all potential forms become actual. Various alternative models were proposed to replace the notion of a static, hierarchical chain or ladder, ranging from a kind of escalator, whereby all living forms somehow developed in tandem, to a three-dimensional grid, which seemed better to relate the complex attributes of awkward species, such as highly intelligent mammalian sea creatures like dolphins, or the hydra, which seemed to possess both animal and vegetable characteristics in almost equal measure. The widespread acceptance of the vast antiquity of the earth and its inhabitants, combined with advances in geology, comparative anatomy, and paleontology, led to a complete revolution in scientific thinking in the early decades of the nineteenth century. Jean Baptiste Lamarck's (1744–1829) *Philosophie Zoologique* (*Zoological Philosophy* [1809]) offered a synthesis that would later be described as evolutionary. Significantly, Lamarck had a deep revulsion to the possibility of species extinction, arguing instead for organic change as organisms were confronted with the challenges of new environments.

After about 1800, the three "unit ideas" that constituted the Great Chain of Being continued severally to influence scientific as well as philosophical thinking. Plenitude surfaced in German Romanticism. Continuity

was preserved in the evolutionary notion of a "tree of life" and in the fascination with "missing links." The modern sense of progress embodied aspects of the hierarchical associations of gradation. As an integrated conceptualization of the structure of nature, however, the chain was dismantled in the early nineteenth century. Its cosmic optimism had never been an entirely convincing solution to the problem of noxious creatures, and its theological foundations were never completely reconciled with traditional Christian doctrine. The secular sciences of the nineteenth century rested on alternative foundation beliefs about the nature of things.

See also Macrocosm/Microcosm; Natural History; Plurality of Worlds and Extraterrestrial Life; Taxonomy

BIBLIOGRAPHY

Bowler, Peter J. *The Fontana History of the Environmental Sciences.* London: Fontana, 1992.

Brooke, John Hedley. *Science and Religion: Some Historical Perspectives.* Cambridge: Cambridge University Press, 1991.

Bynum, W. F. "The Great Chain of Being After Forty years: An Appraisal." *History of Science* 13 (1975): 1–18.

Crowe, Michael J. *The Extraterrestrial Life Debate, 1750–1900: The Idea of a Plurality of Worlds from Kant to Lowell.* Cambridge: Cambridge University Press, 1986.

Dick, Steven J. *Plurality of Worlds: The Origins of the Extraterrestrial Life Debate from Democritus to Kant.* Cambridge: Cambridge University Press, 1982.

Formigari, Lia. "Chain of Being." In *Dictionary of the History of Ideas,* ed. by Philip P. Wiener. Vol. 1. New York: Scribner's, 1973, 325–35.

Funkenstein, Amos. *Theology and the Scientific Imagination from the Middle Ages to the Seventeenth Century.* Princeton, N.J.: Princeton University Press, 1986.

Journal of the History of Ideas 48(2) (1987). Special Issue on Lovejoy and His Work.

Knuuttila, Simo, ed. *Reforging the Great Chain of Being: Studies of the History of Modal Theories.* Dordrecht: Reidel, 1981.

Kuntz, Marion Leathers, and Paul Grimley Kuntz, eds. *Jacob's Ladder and the Tree of Life: Concepts of Hierarchy and the Great Chain of Being.* New York: Peter Lang, 1987.

Lovejoy, Arthur O. *The Great Chain of Being: A Study of the History of an Idea.* 1936. Reprint. New York: Harper Torchbooks, 1960.

Oakley, Francis. *Omnipotence, Covenant, and Order: An Excursion in the History of Ideas from Abelard to Leibniz.* Ithaca, N.Y., and London: Cornell University Press, 1984.

83. TAXONOMY

David M. Knight

Taxonomy is the art or science of identifying and classifying natural objects by type. It addresses the questions why is the world so diverse and how are we to make sense of it all? Putting things into groups is like explaining. It can be a dry activity, painstakingly carried out in a museum, but it has also seemed to appeal to some scientists as a way of understanding God's plan in creation. To them, the order and the variety of nature seemed designed, evidences of a world in which the needs of every creature were provided for.

"That's a chaffinch, not a bullfinch," we say. We classify people and things all the time; language and thought depend upon it. The natural world has long been seen as composed of three kingdoms: animal, vegetable, and mineral. Indeed, this classification can form the basis of a quiz game. All languages lump various creatures together, such as fishes, birds, or flowers, though they may differ about difficult cases such as the whale, the ostrich, and the mushroom. Within these big groups, we recognize that the bullfinch, the chaffinch, the hawfinch, and the greenfinch are different, but very similar, birds and rather unlike mallard ducks and eider ducks; and our ordinary speech reflects this intuition of our ancestors. In the Old Testament, naming had overtones of power; but we, more matter-of-factly, take it for granted that there are real groupings in nature and that we can find them out.

We know that the way we classify human beings, by gender, ethnicity, and status, reflects the particular structure and interests of a society. Émile Durkheim (1858–1917) used evidence from Australian Aborigines to argue that all of our fundamental categories express forms of social organization. If this were so, then our feeling that our divisions reflect nature would be an illusion; they would simply be a social construction. The naturalist Frank Buckland, catching a train in Victorian England, found that he had to pay for his monkey, since it was a dog; but his tortoise, as an insect, went free. We accept that such categories are unscientific. Belief that taxonomy is involved with nature rather than society is reinforced partly by the great edifice of modern science, but also partly because studies, such as that of the Kalam of New Guinea, for example, show that peoples who differ widely in their social arrangements do classify animals in a reasonably similar fashion.

Taxonomy in Antiquity

The word "taxonomy" comes from ancient Greek, and it is with the Greeks that our scientific classification seems to have begun. Plato's (c. 427–347 B.C.) system of division into twos characterized mankind as "the featherless biped." In his thinking, we also find the idea of nature as a Great Chain, or ladder, stretching up from the lowliest creatures to mankind and then on through the orders of angels. The task of the naturalist was to find the missing links in God's chain and, thus, display the wisdom and the benevolence that lay behind it all. This image of a chain or ladder was a very attractive and powerful one right down to the early nineteenth century. In its classic form, it was static. There was no movement up or down. There was a place (higher or lower) for everything, and everything would be found to be in its place. If Durkheim is right, this would fit well with a world of little social movement.

Plato was not primarily a naturalist, but his great pupil Aristotle (384–322 B.C.) was a doctor's son and a keen zoologist, who dissected many different kinds of animals, notably fish. He perceived animals as falling untidily into family groupings of various sizes rather than neatly into twos or onto a chain. Aristotle, for whom humans were "the rational animal," gave particular weight to reproduction. Dividing animals into bipeds and the rest is wrong because it puts us with the birds, which lay eggs, and separates us from dogs and sheep, which bring forth their young alive and suckle them and, thus, have much in common with us. In more complex cases, we must not be misled by appearances. Vipers bear their young alive (the story was that the new generation gnawed their way out), but they do not suckle them, and they have no placenta to nourish them in a womb; hence, they are properly put with other reptiles. The dolphin bears young as we do, so, although it looks like a fish, it is not one. Taxonomy is a complicated business. In detail, any plan is hard to discern.

Aristotle moved toward the distinction between homologous and analogous organs. Homologous ones have the same structure but may have a different function, like the dog's leg and the dolphin's flipper. Analogous ones perform the same function but have a different structure, like the wings of birds and bees. It is homologies that guide us in taxonomy. Aristotle divided the animals into those that have red blood and those that do not. They are almost equivalent to our vertebrates and invertebrates. The lowest animals he believed to be spontaneously generated from mud. For example, he saw that some creepy-crawlies like spiders and grasshoppers lay "perfect" eggs from which little versions of their parents emerge, while the eggs of butterflies are "imperfect" because a grub comes from them, which, in due course, turns into another egg, the chrysalis. These observations were reflected in his family groupings. Aristotle's pupil Theophrastus (c. 372–286 B.C.) was a botanist, who classified plants according to whether they were herbs, shrubs, or trees. But most people were interested in botany primarily for medicinal purposes. Herbals, in which plants were classified as much by the diseases they cured as by their resemblances, were the major publications in botany down to the middle of the seventeenth century. These herbals contained many tall stories, such as that of the mandrake that shrieked when pulled up (a job best done by a dog), as did the medieval bestiaries, in which animals with human faces sadly confront us and the zoology owes as much to Aesop (the sixth-century B.C. author of fables) as to Aristotle. According to medieval herbalists, God made us stewards of animals and plants, which were, therefore, to be studied more for human purposes than for their own sake. Plants and animals had both symbolic and practical value. Lions made us feel brave

and foxes cunning. God might have provided in Europe the remedies for diseases endemic there, or he might have intended us energetically to explore and find our medicines in the Indies. The shapes of leaves, roots, or flowers were seen as God-given clues to their intended uses.

The Renaissance and the Scientific Revolution

Arabic scholars who translated and added to Greek works knew of different regions with their fauna and flora. At the end of the fifteenth century, the Portuguese reached and passed the southern tip of Africa on their way to India and beyond, while the Spaniards discovered and began colonizing America. They found in temperate areas very different plants and animals from those of Europe, and in the tropics many more. The English Puritan William Turner (1510–68) recognized that attempts to match up ancient Greek descriptions of plants with those he knew were hopeless, because different plants grow in different places. The whole business of describing and classifying so many different kinds was daunting.

In 1660, John Ray (1627–1705) published a flora of Cambridge, a pioneering work. He delighted in the variety of nature, which demonstrated for him the wisdom and goodness of God. He became one of the great taxonomists, seeking, like Aristotle, to place organisms by considering their whole range of characters, though giving more weight to some. His method involved intuition rather like the connoisseurship of the art historian and could best be learned by working with him for some time. This was too slow for the surgeon or the seaman off to foreign parts; during the first half of the eighteenth century, Carolus Linnaeus (1707–78) proposed a convenient "artificial" system for plants, based on the number of sexual parts in the flower. This usually, but not always, went with the intuition of the experts. Linnaeus's greatest innovation was the use of two Latin words, the generic and the trivial name, to characterize species: Thus, the Canada goose is *Branta canadensis,* and the Barnacle goose *Branta leucopsis.* This international language proved very efficient. In his classic *Systema naturae* (*System of Nature* [10th ed., 1758]), the pious Linnaeus put the orangutan, *Homo sylvestris,* beside the human, *Homo sapiens.* Rather than describe mankind, he simply wrote: "Nosce te ipsum" ("Know thyself"). In modern systems, we are further from apes, but Linneans saw no problem, since species were fixed, separate creations, with no question of a common ancestry or a blurring of the line between us and them.

After 1789

Especially in France, taxonomists were unsatisfied with the Linnean system, and Michel Adanson (1727–1806) and the dynasty of the Jussieus persisted in the search for the natural method that would really reflect nature. In 1789, the year of the French Revolution that upset all European society and faith, Antoine de Jussieu (1748–1836) published his *Genera plantarum (Genera of Plants)*. Although this work formed the basis of subsequent botanical systems, ever since its publication there has been controversy between "splitters," who divide up groups into numerous species, and "lumpers," who regard many of them as varieties or subspecies. Jussieu's older contemporary Georges Leclerc, Comte de Buffon (1707–88), had proposed that two creatures belong to the same species only if they are interfertile, an idea that led to messy and inconclusive experiments with dogs and wolves. By 1800, it had become clear that some sorts of creatures were no longer with us—and Buffon's test could not be applied to fossils. The fact of extinction worried those who believed that God had made the best of all possible worlds, in which any change must be for the worse. If it was good to have mammoths, then how could God allow them to die out? And if not, then why had God made the mistake of creating them in the first place? In 1809, Jean Baptiste Lamarck (1744–1829) put the Chain of Being into motion, insisting that all animals and plants were moving upward. The gloomy message that mammoths had become extinct was replaced by the cheerful tidings that they had evolved into elephants.

Lamarck specialized in the classification of invertebrates, as Charles Darwin (1809–82) was to do. Like Darwin, he was aware of the enormous number of species, very hard to tell apart, which seemed to cry out for evolutionary explanation. His contemporary and rival, the staunchly Christian Georges Cuvier (1769–1832), reconstructed chiefly mammalian fossils and saw how the bones were correlated. While he accepted that there had been different faunas at different times, he could not believe in a chancy or an occult process of evolutionary change. Dissections of mummified cats from Egypt established that they were just like present-day cats. Instead of a chain, Cuvier proposed classifying all animals in four great branches: the vertebrates, the mol-

luscs, the articulata (including insects), and the radiata (like starfish and sea urchins). To most of us, this looks like an evolutionary tree, but to contemporaries it did not, and Cuvier was famous for his hostility to the idea. Every part of every creature was so adapted that slow transition was impossible; for him, the changes in faunas and floras to be seen in the rocks were the result of great catastrophes.

Two of Cuvier's most eminent followers were Richard Owen (1804–92) in Britain, who reconstructed from a single bone the moa, an extinct giant bird from New Zealand; and Louis Agassiz (1807–73), who classified extinct and living fishes and inferred that there had been ice ages. Agassiz went from his native Switzerland to America, where at Harvard he became the most celebrated naturalist of his day. Both Owen and Agassiz saw species as an expression of ideal types. For them and for most contemporaries, terms like "genus" and "family," which imply relationships, were only metaphors. Both became important figures in the scientific establishment, and, although Owen seems privately to have accepted that species might change over time, in public he took a conservative stance.

Agassiz was perplexed about the way animals are distributed around the world. He came to believe that species (expressions of a celestial idea) might have been created in more than one place. Thus, the European and the American populations of mallards might not have had a common ancestor. For ducks, this notion may seem far-fetched but harmless; for mankind in the late 1850s, the period before the American Civil War, it was an explosive notion. If Black and White people were not all descendants of Adam and Eve, brothers and sisters under the skin, then perhaps one group could justifiably enslave the other just as we domesticate horses or sheep. Owen's friend Bishop Samuel Wilberforce (1805–73) was among those who were keen to evangelize in Africa and who believed that we all belong to one species and, hence, to one moral community. Slavery, and any attempt to justify it scientifically, was, thus, abhorrent to him.

Linnaeus's system for plants had definite numbers and a shape to it: Flowers can have only so many stamens and pistils. But the natural method seemed to give no shape to the order of things. Cuvier's tree looked like a messy kind of shrub, in need of pruning and tidying. In Britain, W. S. MacLeay, William Swainson ([1789–1855] a high-churchman trying to read God's mind), and a few others devised the "Quinary System," based upon repeating patterns of circles at different levels, which for a time in the 1820s and 1830s seemed to promise to make sense of the arrangement of animals. This system aroused some interest among natural historians, but most felt that nature was being forced into a preconceived mold, where often fanciful resemblances were used to put creatures into circles. Charles Darwin, home from his voyage on the H.M.S. *Beagle* and getting down to establishing a reputation, wrote his taxonomic volumes on barnacles (1851–8) partly as an assault upon the Quinarians.

Barnacles were an interesting group, because it was only in the 1820s that their closeness to the crabs and lobsters was established. Previously, they had generally been put with the molluscs, but baby barnacles look like little shrimps, which then settle down on rocks, groins, or ships and become immobile. They are, therefore, a group that has gone down in the world. Moreover, in some species the male seemed to have degenerated into a stomach and sex organs living within the shell of the female; this was far from the Victorian ideal. Again, the small but definite differences between the different species seemed to Darwin to indicate development from a common ancestor rather than a Creator working from scratch each time. Instead of patterns of circles, he looked for family trees to make sense of the system. Seeing individuals and species making their way in the world, he rejected notions of "up" and "down": There is no hierarchy or chain in a world in which suitable niches must be sought and found.

When the *Origin of Species* was published in 1859, Darwin discussed the imperfection of the fossil record. That any particular animal or plant should be fossilized was highly unlikely; that the fossil should be found and brought to the attention of a scientist was also most improbable. After 1859, knowledge of fossils rapidly improved, especially as the American West was opened up with the building of the railroads. Thomas Henry Huxley (1825–95), content to be known as "Darwin's bulldog," realized that dinosaurs were not especially like lizards or crocodiles and that the structure of their pelvises indicated that some of them ran on their hind legs and were more like ostriches. The extraordinary bird fossil archaeopteryx indicated to him the closeness of birds and reptiles. Counterintuitive though it may be, descendants of the dinosaurs come to our gardens in search of the crumbs that fall from our tables. Evolutionary preoccupations, allied with careful comparative anatomy, had led to a new understanding of the place of two great groups of creatures.

Cuvier and natural theologians like William Paley (1743–1805) noted that an organism is a harmonious whole whose various parts perform a specific function: Hence, they invoked a Designer. In contrast, Darwin's "natural selection" ensured that every creature is well fitted for its environment. But he focused upon the blemishes or contraptions of nature, such as the vestigial organs (our appendix, for example), which do not benefit the creature but may reveal lineages. Everybody knew that horses and donkeys were close species. They are even interfertile, but the offspring (mules and hinnies) are not themselves fertile. Zebras also indubitably belong to the same group; and Darwin had found from breeders that stripes are not uncommon on donkey foals. While there were no horses in America when the Spaniards landed there, in the American West there were the fossils of horselike creatures taking back a line of descent to a small animal with five toes. This common ancestor of our different species of horses represented the first convincing evolutionary family tree. But, in fact, the fossils represent distinct species, and we do not find a steady gradation of intermediate forms in the record. There is dispute about just how smoothly, and how fast, evolution works and whether, as Lamarck and some of Darwin's circle believed, it can be seen as progressive (that is, as evidence for God working out his purpose).

Following his debates with Owen and Wilberforce in 1860, Huxley published his *Man's Place in Nature* (1863). He urged his readers to imagine themselves as unprejudiced scientists from Saturn, who could have no doubts, given the evidence, that humans belonged in the same group as the apes. For Aristotle, we had been with the other mammals; in the Great Chain, next to the orangutan. But these placings had all been part of God's grand design: As rational beings, we were quite distinct from our neighbors and bore God's image and superscription. For Huxley, we and the apes had a common ancestor. Rather than contemplate creatures as types in God's mind, we should search for our fossil forebears. And in the twentieth century, they have duly been found. The basis of taxonomy is history, with all its messiness, rather than theology or geometry.

In our time, evidence from comparative anatomy has been supplemented by biochemistry. The scales of reptiles and the feathers of birds have the same chemical composition. Analysis of egg-white proteins led to the birds of paradise being put in the same group as the starlings. Now studies of DNA enable us to infer common ancestry with much more certainty than Huxley and his contemporaries could. Taxonomy based upon descent, called cladistics, is widely used, but some empirically minded scientists, seeing the dangers of imposing a pattern like the Chain of Being or the Quinary System, prefer numerical taxonomy. This feeling goes back to Adanson, who believed that one should record all characteristics, without any weighting or preconceptions, and see where the majority of them placed the creature. With computers, this can be a valuable method of placing organisms in groups. But with the progress of science, characteristics Adanson never dreamed of are now noted, and no doubt our successors will find more and classify creatures differently.

In science as in life, there is no escape from a measure of theory and judgment. Ernest Rutherford (1871–1937) is supposed to have said that all science is either physics or stamp collecting. Taxonomy must have been his target, but even physicists have to classify their fundamental particles, and chemists their elements. Taxonomy is not just a more or less convenient filing system but an attempt to understand why the world is the way it is and how we can speak about it. It used to be seen by many taxonomists as a means of uncovering God's plan, and a static arrangement of perfectly designed animals and plants—little watches with their place in the great clockwork of the universe—was generally accepted. So was a short time scale, in which no change in cats over a period of two thousand years proved that species did not change over time. Darwin's revolution gave them a different picture, open-ended and fluid, of a world in which species must adapt or die over eons as their environment changes. At a particular time, most species are distinct, though splitters and lumpers will differ over particular cases like the two kinds of English oak. But taxonomy has become perforce a matter of dealing with entities that are essentially unstable in the long run. Meteorologists classifying clouds have long had to wrestle with such problems. Those seeking God's plan in nature have to expect something less definite, but perhaps with more grandeur.

See also Evolution; Great Chain of Being; Natural History

BIBLIOGRAPHY

Agassiz, Louis. *Essay on Classification.* Ed. by E. Lurie. 1857. Reprint. Cambridge, Mass.: Harvard University Press, 1962.

Blunt, Wilfred, and Sandra Raphael. *The Illustrated Herbal.* London: Frances Lincoln [1979].

Browne, Janet. *Charles Darwin: Voyaging.* London: Jonathan Cape, 1995.

Bynum, W. F., E. J. Browne, and R. Porter, eds. *Dictionary of the History of Science.* London: Macmillan, 1981.

Desmond, A. *Archetypes and Ancestors: Palaeontology in Victorian London, 1850–1875.* London: Blond and Briggs, 1982.

———. *Huxley: The Devil's Disciple.* London: Michael Joseph, 1994.

Gage, A. T., and W. T. Stearn. *A Bicentenary History of the Linnean Society of London.* London: Academic, 1988.

Jardine, N., J. A. Secord, and E. C. Spary, eds. *Cultures of Natural History.* Cambridge: Cambridge University Press, 1996.

King, Ronald. *The World of Kew.* London: Macmillan, 1976.

Knight, David. *Ordering the World.* London: Burnett, 1981.

Linnaeus, C. *Species plantarum,* Ed. by W. T. Stearn. 1753. Reprint. London: Ray Society, 1957–9.

———. *Systema naturae, regnum animale.* 10th ed. 1758. Reprint. London: British Museum (Natural History), 1956.

Linnean Society. *Lectures on the Development of Taxonomy* and *Lectures on the Practice of Botanical and Zoological Classification.* London: Linnean Society, 1950 and 1951.

Lovejoy, Arthur O. *The Great Chain of Being.* Cambridge, Mass.: Harvard University Press, 1942.

Lukes, Stephen. *Émile Durkheim: His Life and Work.* London: Alan Lane, 1973.

Majnep, Ian Saem, and Ralph Bulmer. *Birds of My Kalam Country.* Auckland: Auckland University Press, 1977.

Ray, John. *Flora of Cambridgeshire.* Trans. and ed. by A. H. Ewen and C. T. Prime. 1660. Reprint. Hitchin, Herts, U.K.: Wheldon and Wesley, 1975.

Rudwick, Martin. *The Meaning of Fossils.* London: Macdonald, 1972.

Rupke, N. *Richard Owen: Victorian Naturalist.* New Haven, Conn.: Yale University Press, 1994.

Stearn, W. T. *Botanical Latin.* Newton Abbot, U.K.: David and Charles, 1966.

Turner, William. *Libellus de Re Herbaria.* 1538. *The Names of Herbes.* 1548. Facsimile. London: Ray Society, 1965.

Walker, Margot. *Sir James Edward Smith, 1759–1828: First President of the Linnean Society.* London: Linnean Society, 1988.

Winsor, Mary P. *Starfish, Jellyfish, and the Order of Life: Issues in Nineteenth-Century Science.* New Haven, Conn.: Yale University Press, 1976.

84. THE ORIGIN AND UNITY OF THE HUMAN RACE

David N. Livingstone

Throughout the Middle Ages, European scientific conceptions of human origins, expressed in the tradition of tripartite *mappaemundi* (maps of the world)—conventionally known as T in O maps—assumed the literal truth of the biblical narrative that the varieties of the human race were descended proximately from three sons of Noah and, ultimately, from Adam and Eve. To be sure, classical writers like Anaximander (c. 610–546 B.C.) had promulgated what look like proto-evolutionary accounts of the human race. And Gregory of Nyssa (c. 330–c. 395) had argued the case for Adam's physical body being derived from animal forebears. Because he believed that everything existed in spermatic potential from the initial divine impulse of Creation, Gregory could and did advance a developmentalist account of the origin of life-forms and urged that the human body had been created through the inherent activity of the elements of the earth. But, in large measure, such speculations received little support in the Christian West, though later Christian evolutionists would look back to figures like Gregory to legitimate their own doctrinal orthodoxy. For all that, cartographic representations routinely associated the three known continents—Asia, Africa, and Europe—with the three sons of Noah—Sem (Shem), Cham (Ham), and Jafeth—thereby integrating a three-fold continental schema with a tripartite racial taxonomy.

Challenges to Convention

Challenges to the standard biblical account were to emerge from several different sources. From *within* the confines of the Old World, the increasing availability of what were called pagan chronicles posed a considerable threat to received wisdom, as did overland expeditions to "the East." Indeed, for chronologists of world history, one of the greatest moral problems was that the annals of pagan history seemed to confirm the speculations of those infidels who claimed the existence of genealogies predating the biblical Adam. Concurrently, in some versions of the *mappaemundi,* depictions of what were called "the monstrous races" began to feature as cartographic marginalia, as they also did in a range of medieval encyclopedic chronicles. The existence of such more or less exoticized species raised some troubling questions about the nature and status of Adam's descendants. But they performed the perhaps even more significant role of providing what might be called a suite of anthropological templates into which peoples hitherto unknown to Europeans might be fitted. Accordingly, these images were intimately connected with challenges to conventional Christian anthropology that came from *outside* the Old World and, in particular, from the Americas. Thus, in the pictorial representations of cosmographers like Sebastian Münster (1489–1552) and Andrô Thevet (fl. late sixteenth century), legendary races simply occupied the same spaces as newly encountered peoples.

It was the European discovery that the "hidden islands" were inhabited, then, that prompted figures like Paracelsus (1493–1541), Giordano Bruno (1548–1600), Thomas Hariot (1560–1621), and Walter Raleigh (1552–1618) to flirt with the suspicion that all races might not be descended from the one biblical Adam. Indeed, such encounters shook the intellectual foundations of the Old World and largely displaced the authority hitherto resident in those ancient texts that had long guided Europe's moral economy, even if the concepts—though not the terminology—of the "ignoble savage" were deeply rooted in European consciousness.

La Peyrère and the Preadamite Heresy

One means of coping with challenges such as those out-lined above was the beguilingly simple theory that the biblical Adam was simply not the first human being. The idea of preadamic humans had been long hinted at, for example, in the writings of Moses Maimonides (1135–1204) and Yehuda Halevi (c. 1075–1141). But it was in "the monumentally heretical doctrine" of Isaac de la Peyrère (1596–1676), promulgated in his *Prae-Adamitae* (1655), that the preadamite theory found its first sus-tained champion. The basic thrust of the treatise was that only the Jews were descended from the biblical Adam and that the other world peoples were derived from non-Adamic progenitors. At once, this fundamentally polyge-netic account of human origins relieved the biblical text of the burden of pagan history and provided a compelling account of the genesis of New World peoples. Such attrac-tions, however, were not widely felt as the doctrine received widespread condemnation and its author was branded a skeptic. For all that, Anthony Grafton, in an exploration of "Isaac La Peyrère and the Old Testament," has made the observation that, in accounting for the intellectual transformation that was effected between the burning of Noël Journet in 1582 for his querying of Scripture and Pierre Bayle's (1647–1706) *Historical and Critical Dictionary* (1692), "no one did more to make this revolution happen than the little-remembered French Calvinist Isaac La Peyrère" (Grafton 1991, 205). Not surprisingly, this earned for Peyrère an established place in the annals of anthropological history.

In the Peyrèrian formula, internal matters of biblical interpretation and chronology provided one source of speculation; indeed, La Peyrère's critical stance toward the Old Testament documents has earned him a reputa-tion as a precursor of biblical criticism. A second factor was the pressure deriving from the voyages of reconnais-sance. Peyrère had long followed their progress and was fascinated, in particular, by questions having to do with the settlement of Greenland and Iceland, finding the standard account of migration from the Old World unconvincing.

Despite the aroma of heresy that long clung to Preadamism, the theory attracted an increasing number of sympathetic critics and outright advocates in succeed-ing generations. In some cases, those who rejected the theory were altogether hesitant in their dismissal; others

set about modifying the basic Peyrèrean formula to suit their own purposes. Some opted for a kind of secular preadamism—basically polygenism—while others sought to retain its theological significance. Accordingly, we will attend now to the debates between the monogenists and polygenists as a prelude to reviewing the continued apolo-getic significance of preadamism in the efforts to keep ethnology and theology in conceptual tandem.

Monogenism and Polygenism

The eighteenth and nineteenth centuries witnessed a prolonged and acrimonious feud between monogenists and polygenists. Perhaps the most conspicuous chal-lenge to the traditional monogenism that underlay stan-dard interpretations of the Genesis narrative came from Henry Home (Lord Kames [1696–1782]), who, in 1774, published his *Sketches of the History of Man*. Uncon-vinced by Montesquieu's (1689–1755) environmentalism and by Georges Leclerc, Comte de Buffon's (1707–88), resort to climate to account for human diversity, Kames was helplessly attracted to polygenism. To him, climate did not produce human variety; rather, human varieties were created for particular climates. Whatever his hesi-tancy, Kames did much to advance the polygenetic cause, and others—less unnerved by its seeming profanity—promulgated the thesis with considerable vigor. Polygenic theories provided an appealing naturalistic solution, too, to the new anthropological challenges that came from places like Tahiti, Easter Island, and the Solomon Islands during the Enlightenment era.

Kames's proposals were deeply troubling to many, however, and not least to Samuel Stanhope Smith (1750–1819), president of Princeton and a transatlantic advo-cate of the self-same Scottish Common Sense philosophy in which Kames himself was intellectually domiciled. To Smith, human variability was entirely explicable in terms of human adaptation to climate, and he vigorously protested both the doctrinal propriety and the scientific plausibility of polygenism. His motivation for so doing, however, was intensely political. Plural origins of the human race, Smith believed, necessarily disrupted the uni-versal human nature of the species and, thus, subverted the very possibility of a public moral order. His own envi-ronmentalist schema, by contrast, preserved a common and a cosmopolitan, if flexible, human constitution. To Smith, then, Kames's polygenetic speculations were not only scientifically erroneous, they were morally repugnant and politically subversive.

The Kames-Smith exchange did not secure closure on this controverted issue. In nineteenth-century America, for example, figures like Samuel G. Morton (1799–1851), Josiah Nott (1804–73), George R. Gliddon (1809–57), and Louis Agassiz (1807–73) deployed "scientific" polygenism in the cause of racial apologetic. The ostensible motivation of these individuals was anthropological and archaeological, but their collective project was an ideologically driven one. Thus, while polygenism came to pervade pre-Darwinian American anthropology, the enterprise was profoundly implicated in the manipulation of anthropometric data so as to ensure lower scores on what were perceived to be key variables for certain racial groupings.

In Britain, broadly similar conceptual alignments are also detectable. *The Natural History of the Human Species* (1848) by Lieutenant-Colonel Charles Hamilton Smith, for example, was decidedly polygenist in tone as Smith elaborated on the regional homelands of what he took to be the three major racial types. Indeed, when an American edition of the work was brought out in 1851, it was under the editorial care of Samuel Kneeland, a Boston medical naturalist and polygenist who was known to confirm Morton's measurements of Hindu crania. In an introduction that amounted to nearly a quarter of the length of the whole book, Kneeland provided a detailed review of scientific works on race, ever biasing his judgments toward polygenism and confirming the orthodoxy of Agassiz-type creationism. As we shall presently see, polygenetic sentiments—whether of secular, theological, or quasi-religious stripe—were also to the fore at the Ethnological Society of London and its more racialist alternative, the Anthropological Society of London. Indeed, as George Stocking Jr. remarks: "wherever the physical anthropological viewpoint was manifest, it contained a strong polygenist impulse" (Stocking 1987, 67). In the present context, however, it is fitting to turn to the deployment of such theories in attempts to retain good relations between ethnology and theology.

Reconciling Ethnology and Theology

Where efforts were made, throughout a good deal of the nineteenth century, to maintain cordial relations between ethnology and theology, versions of the preadamite theory persistently reasserted themselves. To be sure, many rejected its polygenetic ethos and retained a monogenist environmentalism. But, with the prevailing polygenetic savor of contemporary anthropology, the preadamites were frequently conscripted into the service of Christian apologetic. In 1800, for example, Edward King, a Fellow of the Royal Society, urged that the Genesis narrative depicted two quite distinct Creation stories, the first dealing with humankind in general, the second with an individual Adam, and concluded that "*the commonly received opinion, that all mankind are the sons of Adam . . .* is directly contrary to what is contained" in Scripture (author's emphasis). The same emphasis is plain in an 1856 volume entitled *The Genesis of the Earth and Man,* which was edited, introduced, and endorsed by the distinguished British archaeologist and orientalist Reginald Stuart Poole (1832–95). The anonymous author, Edward William Lane (1801–76), was an Arabic scholar, lexicographer, and traveler. His intention was to integrate biblical religion with the findings of the pioneer American anthropologists, and, in doing so, he turned to the preadamite theory. To him, the scheme had considerable advantages, not least for philological concerns, and he launched an attack on K. J. Bunsen (1791–1860) and F. Max Müller's (1823–1900) monogenetic account of linguistic development. His own formulation, based on the discrimination of monosyllabic, agglutinate, and amalgamate forms, proposed a polygenetic taxonomy of language systems that necessarily presupposed that "there have existed Pre-Adamites of our species" (Poole 1856, 201). Crucially, the schema also required a recent Adam as a linguistic forebear, and it thus assumed an extended preadamic chronology.

As already indicated, during the early decades of the nineteenth century, the preadamite theory continued as part of the conventional discourse of the new sciences of anthropology and ethnology. At the Ethnological Society of London, for example, John Crawfurd (1783–1868), an Indian army doctor turned Orientalist, steadfastly promoted preadamism from a variety of perspectives, ranging from physical anthropology to philology. In his mind, it had "pleased the Creator—for reasons inscrutable to us—to plant certain fair races in the temperate regions of Europe, and there only, and certain black ones in the tropical and sub-tropical regions of Africa and Asia, to the exclusion of white ones, but it is certain that climate has nothing to do with the matter." So committed was Crawfurd to this scheme that he dismissed James Cowles Prichard's (1786–1848) monogenism as a "monstrous supposition" hardly worthy of "serious refutation" (quoted in Livingstone 1992).

Such a strategy was far from unique. Reginald Stuart Poole, for example, explicitly endorsed the double-Adamism of his uncle Edward Lane in an 1863 presentation to the Ethnological Society, though he hastened to dissociate himself on Christian grounds from the nasty racialist implications that some had drawn from polygenism. The Rev. Frederic W. Farrar (1831–1903) presented the same society in 1865 with superabundant scientific testimony to the fixity of type and the impotence of climate.

Perhaps the most sustained mid-Victorian effort to use preadamism to maintain—as the subtitle of his treatise put it—"the Harmony of Scripture and Ethnology" was Dominick McCausland's *Adam and the Adamite* (1864). His passion was to uphold the *detailed* accuracy of Scripture in the face both of scientific challenges and of the higher criticism of Bishop John William Colenso (1814–83) and *Essays and Reviews* (1860). If the standard monogenetic account continued to receive support, he argued, the challenges of the geologists, historians, archaeologists, philologists, and ethnologists would reduce the Book of Genesis "to the fanciful speculations of some visionary mythologist" (McCausland 1864, 3). Happily, such a judgment would be too precipitate, for the biblical Adam was only the last of a series of human types that God had created. Adam was superior to his forebears, and his creation ex nihilo (from nothing) in the image of God was recorded for all posterity, although in a short time the pure Adamic line would be sullied through intermarriage with preadamite stock. In McCausland's case, as earlier with Lane, the preadamite theory was deployed to safeguard the integrity of Scripture from the assaults of higher critics—a quite remarkable reversal of its earlier engagement as a source of skepticism.

That the polygenist thesis was finding favor with Christian apologists and scientific racists alike certainly does not mean that monogenist adherents to the traditional Adamic narrative had disappeared. Throughout the middle decades of the nineteenth century, the conventional monogenist history continued to be defended by successors of Stanhope Smith and James Cowles Prichard. In America's Southern states, for example, some ministers stood out against what they saw as the malign implications of Mortonite polygenism. John Bachman (1790–1874), a Lutheran clergyman and naturalist, and Thomas Smyth defended the unity of the

human race on scientific *and* scriptural grounds by arguing that polygenism was born in infidelity and nurtured in skepticism. Yet, this certainly did not imply that they were committed to egalitarianism. The idea of Black inferiority was just too ingrained for that. Bachman, for example, staunchly defended Southern slavery and argued, on the basis of the biblical curse on Ham, that the Black race was designed, and destined, for servitude. For Bachman, polygenism threatened not only the authenticity of Scripture, but also the ideological fabric of what he considered Christian civilization.

Among American Roman Catholics, a sustained opposition to polygenism was forthcoming. Drawing on Cardinal Nicholas Wiseman's (1802–65) insistence that polygenism threatened *the* foundation of Catholicism, American Catholics saw it as the greatest challenge of nineteenth-century science, more significant even than uniformitarian geology or Darwinian biology. To them, the consanguinity of the human race had to be preserved at all costs, and this theological-control belief prompted some, like Clarence Walworth (1820–1900), actively to pursue alternative theories of heritable variation and organic saltation.

Darwinian Transformations

While on the surface it might seem that the advent of Darwinism must have sounded the death knell to preadamic and polygenetic speculations, in fact polygenism lingered long in the thinking of post-Darwinian anthropologists. What is also readily detectable is that, among some scholars with Christian commitments, preadamite theories were rejuvenated to meet the newest challenge of evolutionary theory. Typically, such champions severed preadamism from polygenism by arguing that Adam had human, or protohuman, predecessors from whom he was descended.

Perhaps chief among those whose thinking prepared the way for such moves was Alexander Winchell (1824–91), a leading American geologist and Methodist whose *Adamites and Preadamites* (1878) earned him considerable notoriety at the time, including dismissal from Vanderbilt University. Winchell's version of the theory departed from much historical precedent in that he argued for a monogenetic rendition of the doctrine that indirectly enabled him to retain a Lamarckian account of evolution. By this move, Winchell opened up a prebiblical chronology that could be exploited for scientific purposes. And while he did not explicitly connect preadamism with evolutionary theory, his rupturing of the ties between preadamism and polygenism helped prepare the way for an apologetic use of monogenetic preadamism as a strategy for harmonizing biblical anthropology and human evolution.

Not all deployments of preadamism in the post-Darwinian period, of course, were pro-evolutionary in sentiment. In Britain, Sir John Ambrose Fleming, F.R.S. (1849–1945), president of the Victoria Institute, first president of the Evolution Protest movement, and for forty-one years professor of electrical technology at University College, London, resorted to preadamism to square biblical religion with the evidence for Neanderthal man excavated in 1856 at Düsseldorf, in 1887 near Spy in Belgium, and in the years up to 1914 at Krapina, Croatia, and in southern France. Fleming speculated that the Neanderthals were a preadamic stock, whereas the specially created Cro-Magnons were the Adamic antediluvians of the biblical narrative.

Yet for all that, late-nineteenth- and early-twentieth-century incarnations of the preadamite were routinely marshaled into the service of accommodating Christianity to evolutionary theory. In varying ways, both Protestant and Roman Catholic harmonizers resorted to the scheme. Two instances will suffice by way of illustration. A. Rendle Short (1880–1953), Royal College of Surgeons Hunterian Professor, was a distinguished surgeon and vigorous apologist for evangelical Christianity. Accordingly, in the latter capacity, he took up the subject of the "Problem of Man's Origin" in a volume on science and the Bible that appeared during the 1930s. Here he hinted at the possibility that there "might conceivably have been pre-Adamite creatures with the body and mind of a man, but not the spirit and capacity for God and eternity." By 1942, such speculations had become convictions: Now he was confident that the Neanderthals could well be preadamite and that it was likely that the biblical Adam was formed by the infusion of spiritual qualities into some preadamic creature.

Among Roman Catholic partisans, Ernest Messenger's *Evolution and Theology* (1931) is illustrative. In his detailed examination of the "the origin of man," he argued that the emergence of the human race by way of phylogenetic descent was entirely compatible with Catholic tradition and that opposition from modern theologians stemmed from an over-literalistic reading of the Old Testament. Once the possibility of preadamite human forms was entertained, the need for postulating a creationist account of Adam's physical form withered away, and the theological propriety of a divine employment of secondary causes in the creation of the human race was confirmed.

Preadamism Redivivus

In the second half of the twentieth century, the preadamite theory and variants thereof continued to find advocates among those of conservative theological conviction for whom the story of a literal Adam occupied an important place in the salvation of human beings. Figures like Derek Kidner, John Stott, R. J. Berry, and Bernard Ramm have given the *imago Dei* a theological, rather than psychical or physiological, meaning, thereby leaving room for the evolution of *homo sapiens* prior to its transformation into *homo divinus,* the biblical Adam. Indeed, whole tracts have been composed endeavoring to show that preadamism is a fertile means of retaining good relations between science and Christianity. R. K. Victor Pearce's *Who Was Adam?,* first published in 1969, for example, was specifically written to substantiate preadamic claims from a detailed reading of the biblical text as much as from the field evidence of prehistoric anthropology and archaeology. More recently, Dick Fisher (1996) explicitly sought to retrieve the preadamite theories of La Peyrère and McCausland in his proposed solution to the origins question.

See also Creationism Since 1859; Genesis and Science; Theories of the Earth and Its Age Before Darwin

BIBLIOGRAPHY

Alberstadt, Leonard. "Alexander Winchell's Preadamites: A Case for Dismissal from Vanderbilt University." *Earth Sciences History* 13 (1994): 97–112.

Astore, William J. "Gentle Skeptics? American Catholic Encounters with Polygenism, Geology, and Evolutionary Theories from 1845 to 1875." *Catholic Historical Review* 82 (1996): 40–76.

Fisher, Dick. *The Origins Solution: An Answer in the Creation-Evolution Debate.* Lima, Ohio: Fairway, 1996.

Friedman, John Block. *The Monstrous Races in Medieval Art and Thought.* Cambridge: Cambridge University Press, 1981.

Gossett, Thomas F. *Race: The History of an Idea in America.* Dallas: Southern Methodist University Press, 1963.

Grafton, Anthony. *Defenders of the Text: The Traditions of Scholarship in an Age of Science, 1450–1800.* Cambridge, Mass.: Harvard University Press, 1991.

———. *New Worlds, Ancient Texts: The Power of Tradition and the Shock of Discovery.* Cambridge, Mass.: Harvard University Press, 1992.

Grayson, Donald K. *The Establishment of Human Antiquity.* New York: Academic, 1983.

Hannaford, Ivan. *Race: The History of an Idea in the West.* Baltimore: Johns Hopkins University Press, 1996.

Harris, Marvin. *The Rise of Anthropological Theory: A History of Theories of Culture.* New York: Crowell, 1968.

Hodgen, Margaret T. *Early Anthropology in the Sixteenth and Seventeenth Centuries.* Philadelphia: University of Pennsylvania Press, 1964.

Lestringant, Frank. *Mapping the Renaissance World: The Geographical Imagination in the Age of Discovery.* Trans. by David Fausett. Oxford: Polity, 1994.

Livingstone, David N. *The Preadamite Theory and the Marriage of Science and Religion.* Philadelphia: American Philosophical Society, 1992.

McCausland, Dominick. *Adam and the Adamite; or, The Harmony of Scripture and Ethnology.* London: Richard Bentley, 1864.

Noll, Mark A. *Princeton and the Republic, 1768–1822: The Search for a Christian Enlightenment in the Era of Samuel Stanhope Smith.* Princeton, N.J.: Princeton University Press, 1989.

Pagden, Anthony. *The Fall of Natural Man: The American Indian and the Origins of Comparative Ethnology.* Cambridge: Cambridge University Press, 1982.

Pearce, R. K. Victor. *Who Was Adam?* Exeter: Paternoster, 1969.

Poole, Reginald Stuart, ed. *The Genesis of the Earth and of Man; or, The History of Creation, and the Antiquity and Races of Mankind, Considered on Biblical and Other Grounds.* London, 1856.

Popkin, Richard H. "The Pre-Adamite Theory in the Renaissance." In *Philosophy and Humanism: Renaissance Essays in Honor of Paul Oskar Kristeller,* ed. by Edward P. Mahoney. Leiden: Brill, 1976, 50–69.

———. *Isaac la Peyrère (1596–1676): His Life, Work, and Influence.* Leiden: Brill, 1987.

Smith, Roger. "The Language of Human Nature." In *Inventing Human Science: Eighteenth-Century Domains,* ed. by Christopher Fox, Roy Porter, and Robert Wokler. Berkeley: University of California Press, 1995, 88–111.

Stanton, William. *The Leopard's Spots: Scientific Attitudes toward Race in America, 1815–59.* Chicago: University of Chicago Press, 1960.

Stocking, George W., Jr. "The Persistence of Polygenist Thought in Post-Darwinian Anthropology." In Stocking, George W., Jr. *Race, Culture, and Evolution: Essays in the History of Anthropology.* Chicago: University of Chicago Press 1982, 43–68.

———. *Victorian Anthropology.* New York: Free Press, 1987.

Trigger, Bruce G. *A History of Archaeological Thought.* Cambridge: Cambridge University Press, 1989.

Voget, Fred W. *A History of Ethnology.* New York: Holt, Rinehart, and Winston, 1975.

Wokler, Robert. "Anthropology and Conjectural History in the Enlightenment." In *Inventing Human Science: Eighteenth-Century Domains,* ed. by Christopher Fox, Roy Porter, and Robert Wokler. Berkeley: University of California Press, 1995, 31–52.

Wood, Paul B. "The Science of Man." In *Cultures of Natural History,* ed. by N. Jardine, J. A. Secord, and E. C. Spary. Cambridge: Cambridge University Press, 1996, 197-210.

$85.$ EVOLUTION

Peter J. Bowler

Of all of the topics that have fueled the antagonism between science and religion, evolutionism remains perhaps the only one with power to stimulate debate even today. Following on from the impact of geology and paleontology in the early nineteenth century, evolutionary theories challenged the story of human origins recounted in sacred texts. By rendering humankind a product of nature, evolutionism broke down the barrier between human spirituality and the mentality of the "brutes that perish." Equally seriously, some of the more materialistic theories of evolution undermined the traditional belief that nature itself is a divine construct. In the Darwinian theory of natural selection, struggle and suffering are the driving forces of natural development and, hence, the root cause of our own origin. Not surprisingly, there are many who still think that the human species must be the product of a more purposeful mode of development, and some who wish to retain the traditional view that we are divinely created.

Despite the ongoing sources of conflict, historians have shown that the conventional image of nineteenth-century Darwinism sweeping aside religious belief is an oversimplification. There were, indeed, great controversies, and Darwinism was supported by liberal intellectuals, who had good reason to be suspicious of the ways in which the image of a divinely created universe had been used to sustain a conservative model of the social order. Conservative thinkers quite correctly pointed out the materialistic implications of Charles Darwin's (1809–82) theory. It was Darwin's supporter Thomas Henry Huxley (1825–95) who coined the term "agnosticism" to denote the critical state of unbelief generated by a scientific approach to nature. Yet, historians have shown that the materialistic aspects of Darwin's theory were suppressed by many of the first-generation evolutionists; even Hux-

ley did not accept the theory of natural selection. In the so-called Darwinian revolution, evolutionism was popularized only by linking it to the claim that nature is progressing steadily (if a little irregularly) toward higher mental and spiritual states and by making the human species both the goal and the cutting edge of that progressive drive. A sense of purpose—and, for many, it was still a divine purpose—was built into the operations of nature itself. The more materialistic implications of Darwin's thinking became widely accepted only in the twentieth century, when biologists at last became convinced that natural selection was the driving force of evolution. As scientists began to insist that we must learn to live with the idea that we are the products of a purposeless and, hence, morally neutral natural world, so the modern creationist backlash began.

Early Evolutionism

In the seventeenth century, naturalists believed that the world was created by God only a few thousand years ago. Books such as *The Wisdom of God Manifested in the Works of Creation* by John Ray (1627–1705) argued that each species was perfectly adapted to its environment because it had been created by a wise and benevolent God. This view was repeated in the *Natural Theology* (1802) of William Paley (1743–1805) and was still popular in conservative circles in the early nineteenth century. In the eighteenth century, however, the worldview of what would now be called simple creationism was challenged. In part, this was a product of the discoveries made by geologists and paleontologists. The world was clearly much older than a literal interpretation of the Genesis story would suggest. There was increasing evidence from the fossil record that some species had become extinct in the course of geological time and had been replaced by others. Following the work of Georges Cuvier (1769–1832), these conclusions became inescapable.

Even before this, however, materialist thinkers such as Georges Leclerc, Comte de Buffon (1707–88), and Denis Diderot (1713–84) had begun to suggest that life could be created on the earth by natural processes (spontaneous generation) and that the species thus produced might change in response to natural forces. By the end of the eighteenth century, Erasmus Darwin (1731–1802) and Jean Baptiste Lamarck (1744–1829) were beginning to suggest comprehensive theories of transmutation in which life had advanced slowly from primitive origins to its present level of development. The adaptation of species to their environments was explained by supposing that individual animals modified their behavior in response to environmental change, and any resulting changes in their bodily structure were inherited (the inheritance of acquired characteristics, now often called Lamarckism). Paley's defense of the claim that adaptation indicated design by a benevolent God was a reaction to these new ideas.

Historians used to assume that Lamarck's views were dismissed by most of his contemporaries. Cuvier may have demonstrated that new species must appear from time to time, but he and his followers did not believe that natural evolution was the source of new species. In Britain especially, conservative geologists invoked the image of a series of divine creations spread through geological time, thereby accounting for the evident discontinuity of the fossil record. Recent work by Adrian Desmond (1989) has shown that radical anatomists, especially in the field of medicine, were using materialistic theories such as Lamarckian transformism to attack the image of a static, designed universe that sustained the traditional social structure. Evolutionism became firmly linked to materialism, atheism, and radical politics. In Britain, the anatomist Richard Owen (1804–92) gained his reputation by holding back the demands of the radicals. Owen modernized the view that all species are divinely created by stressing the underlying unity of structure among all of the members of each animal group: The Creator had instituted a rational plan for his universe that could be deciphered by the comparative anatomist. Unity of design, rather than a list of particular adaptations, offered the best illustration of the Creator's handiwork.

In 1844, an effort to make evolutionism acceptable to a middle-class audience was made in an anonymously published book, *Vestiges of the Natural History of Creation,* actually written by Robert Chambers (1802–71). The book proclaimed a message of progress through nature and human history but attempted to circumvent the charge that transmutationism was atheistic by arguing that progress represented the unfolding of a divine plan programmed into nature from the beginning. *Vestiges* clearly explored the implications of the view that the human mind was a product of nature by linking transmutationism to phrenology (the belief that the brain is the organ of the mind). For Chambers, the human mental and moral faculties were generated by the enlarged brain produced by progressive evolution in the animal kingdom. On this count, his book was roundly condemned as materialistic by conservative scientists such as Hugh Miller (1802–56).

By the 1850s, however, the possibility that the divine plan might unfold through the operations of natural law, rather than by a sequence of miracles, was being taken increasingly seriously even by conservative naturalists such as Owen. As science grew more powerful, it became necessary to bring the operation of creation under the control of law, provided the law was seen as having been instituted for a purpose by the Creator of the universe. The mathematician and philosopher Baden Powell (1796–1860) argued that design was seen more obviously in the operation of law, rather than in capricious miracles, and noted that one implication of this view was that the introduction of new species would have to be seen as a lawlike process. The threat to the status of the human mind remained, however, a potent check to full exploration of this idea.

Darwinism

In 1859, the situation was changed dramatically by the publication of *Origin of Species* by Charles Darwin. Darwin proposed new lines of evidence to show how evolutionism could explain natural relationships, but he also suggested a new and potentially more materialistic mechanism of evolution. He had developed his theory of natural selection in the late 1830s, following his voyage of discovery around the world aboard the survey vessel H.M.S. *Beagle.* In the Galapagos Islands, Darwin found evidence that new species were produced when populations became separated in isolated locations and subject to new conditions: In these circumstances, several different "daughter" species could be produced from the

parent form. Darwin then went on to develop the theory
of natural selection to explain how the separated populations might change to adapt to their new environment. In
this theory, it was assumed that the individuals making up
a population differ among themselves in various ways; the
differences have no apparent purpose and are, in that
sense, "random." Following the principle of population
expansion suggested by Thomas Malthus (1766–1834),
Darwin deduced that there must be a "struggle for existence," in which any slight advantage would be crucial.
Those individuals with variant characters that conferred
such an advantage would survive and reproduce, passing
the character on to their offspring. Those with harmful
characters would be eliminated. This process of natural
selection would, thus, gradually adapt the species to any
changes in its environment. The philosopher Herbert
Spencer (1820–1903) called it the "survival of the fittest."
Darwin almost certainly began as a progressionist but
gradually lost his faith in the idea that evolution moved
toward a morally significant goal. As understood by
modern biologists, his theory implied a branching model
of relationships, in which there could be no single goal
toward which life has tended to evolve and no inevitable
trend toward higher levels of organization.

Darwin had delayed publication of his theory, partly
to wait for a change in the climate of opinion. An intense
controversy followed the publication of *Origin of Species*
(Ellegard 1958). Radical scientists such as Huxley proclaimed that Darwin's new insights at last opened up the
subject to rational investigation. Conservative opponents
labeled the theory as the most extreme manifestation of
the atheistical tendency inherent in the basic idea of evolution. Not only were humans reduced to the status of
animals, but the natural world that produced us was
reduced to a purposeless sequence of accidental changes.
It is clear that the evolutionists carried the day: By the
1870s, the vast majority of scientists and educated people
had accepted the basic idea of evolution. The question
that historians now ask is: In what form did they accept
the theory? Was it the radical materialism of the theory
of natural selection, or was it a less threatening version of
evolutionism, a compromise in which some form of purpose was retained by assuming that natural developments tended to progress toward higher states?

The most comprehensive accounts of the religious
debate (Livingstone 1987; Moore 1979) suggest that, in
the long run, there was as much compromise as confrontation. This does not mean that passions were not
aroused: The issues were important, and the conflict
between conservatives and radicals was intense. Huxley
and Spencer hated the way in which the idea of design
was used to block aspirations for social change and
wanted to see humankind firmly embedded in a universe
subject to change under natural law. But, in the end,
both sides came to accept evolution, and neither wanted
a worldview based on nothing but chance and suffering.
Faced with the even greater threat of natural selection,
conservatives took up the (once radical) argument that
evolution represented the unfolding of a divine plan.
They concentrated their efforts not on blocking the case
for evolution but on showing that the process could not
be driven by a purely haphazard mechanism such as natural selection. Radicals wanted a changing universe
based on natural law but assumed that the changes
would, in the end, be beneficial and moral. They were
more willing to let individual effort determine success in
this world but were comforted by the fact that success
depended not on brute force, but on the old Protestant
virtues of thrift and industry. As James Moore (1985b)
has noted, this allowed liberal Protestants to accept
Spencer's philosophy of cosmic evolutionism, in which
the old human values were now built into nature itself as
the driving force of progress. Since the agnostics also
argued for a purposeful universe, those religious thinkers
who wanted to keep up with the times could accept that
the new cosmology was not antithetical to their beliefs.
The old image of Spencer and Darwin destroying all
moral values and sweeping Western culture immediately
into an age in which the only measure of worth was brute
force is, thus, a myth. It took many decades for the full
implications of Darwin's thinking to become apparent,
and much "social Darwinism" has its sources in other
models of nature.

Human Origins

The most controversial issue at first was the evolutionary
origin of the human race. Huxley was engaged in an
intense debate with Owen over the degree of relationship
between humans and apes. He is popularly supposed to
have demolished Samuel Wilberforce (1805–73), bishop
of Oxford, at the 1860 meeting of the British Association
for the Advancement of Science by declaring that he
would rather be descended from an ape than from a man
who misused his position to attack a theory he did not
understand. It has now been suggested that the popular

story of this confrontation is also a myth: Huxley certainly did not convert his audience to Darwinism overnight. But the animal ancestry of man was increasingly taken for granted over the next decade, and everyone had to grapple with the implications of it.

Darwin had been aware from the start of his theorizing that evolutionism would affect our ideas about human nature in a way that would undermine the traditional concept of the soul. His mature views on this issue were eventually presented in his *Descent of Man* (1871). He believed that many aspects of human behavior are controlled by instincts that have been shaped by natural selection. Our moral values are merely rationalizations of social instincts built into us because our ape ancestors lived in groups. Spencer had already proposed an evolutionary psychology, and evolutionists such as George John Romanes (1848–94) built upon Darwin's work to propose evolutionary sequences by which the various mental faculties had been added in the progress toward mankind.

A few evolutionists, including the codiscoverer of natural selection, Alfred Russel Wallace (1823–1913), were so concerned that they refused to endorse such views, holding that some supernatural intervention was still required to explain the appearance of the human mind. The Roman Catholic anatomist St. George Jackson Mivart (1827–1900) argued that, while the evolution of the human body might be explained naturally, the soul must be a divine creation. Mivart defined what would eventually become the Roman Catholic position on this issue, although it would take some time for this compromise to become widely accepted by the Church hierarchy.

Most Darwinists believed that an ad hoc discontinuity marking the advent of the human spirit violated the logic of the evolutionary program, and the image of a distinct human spiritual character was abandoned. The situation was made bearable by assuming that traditional moral values were not at variance with nature but were built into nature in a way that ensured their emergence in the human mind. For religious thinkers such as Henry Drummond (1851–97), the highest moral value, altruism, was the foundation of the evolutionary process. Drummond's *Ascent of Man* (1894) presented cooperation, not competition, as the driving force of progressive evolution and implied that the human race, with its expanded sense of altruism, was the inevitable culmination of the development of life. Another way of minimizing the emotional shock of the idea of human evolution was adopted by paleontologists such as Henry Fairfield

Osborn (1857–1935). He attempted to block early creationist attacks (discussed below) by suggesting that we had evolved not from the disgusting apes but from some more remote (and, hence, less immediately threatening) animal ancestor.

The potentially disruptive implications of the integration of humankind into nature became apparent only as early-twentieth-century thinkers began to explore the possibility that the world might not, after all, be evolving toward ever-higher states. Sigmund Freud (1856–1939) built on the idea of evolution to argue that our subconscious thoughts are shaped by instincts from our animal past. The loss of faith in progress precipitated by World War I also helped create a framework in which the more pessimistic implications of Darwinism might be explored.

Design in Nature

If the traditional gulf between humankind and the animals was bridged, it was made possible for most thinkers by rejecting the Darwinian theory of natural selection in favor of a more purposeful or morally acceptable process. From the start, there were many objections to the selection theory by conservatives who wanted to believe that nature must still exhibit evidence of design by God, even if individual species were produced by natural law. But radicals also found natural selection hard to accept: Huxley was never happy with the theory, and Spencer was an avowed Lamarckian. Non-Darwinian evolutionary mechanisms allowed everyone to believe that there was something more to natural development than mere trial and error. The Lamarckian theory seemed to imply a more purposeful evolutionary process because it allowed individual self-improvement to be inherited (the main point in Spencer's social philosophy) and implied that purposeful changes in animals' behavior was the directing agent of evolution.

It was the opponents of natural selection who correctly identified its materialistic implications. They saw that, in a universe governed solely by random variation and the survival of the fittest, the existing state of nature must be the outcome of trial and error, not of purposeful intention. In a letter to Charles Lyell (1797–1875), Darwin reported that Sir John Hershel (1792–1871) had called natural selection "the law of higgledy-piggledy" (quoted in Burkhardt and Smyth 1991, 423). Hershel certainly expressed his preference for the view that the history of life must be under the control of divinely planned laws of development. The biologist William Benjamin Carpenter (1813–85), while accepting evolutionism, argued that the exquisite structures of the single-celled Foraminifera could only be the product of design. The duke of Argyll (George Douglas Campbell [1823–1900]) claimed that the beauty of many birds was intended by their Creator for us to appreciate, and he saw rudimentary organs as structures being prepared for future use.

The most effective collection of antiselectionist arguments was assembled by St. George Jackson Mivart in his *Genesis of Species* (1870). His strategy was to demonstrate that evolution was under divine control. He argued that a wide range of characters cannot be explained by mere utility to the individual; they are the products of trends built into evolution by the God who established the laws of development. As evidence for the existence of such trends, he pointed to many cases of parallel evolution, in which several branches of the animal kingdom seem to have moved independently in the same direction. Mivart's arguments were linked to his claim that the origin of the human spirit could not be explained by natural evolution: both formed part of his strategy for reconciling the Roman Catholic Church to aspects of the new biology. He argued that the writings of the Church Fathers did not rule out the natural evolution of the body. Although his efforts were at first welcomed by the Church, by the end of the century he encountered increasing hostility and was excommunicated.

Darwin rejected the claim that there were aspects of the evolutionary process that were not susceptible to a natural explanation. For him, bright colors were developed by sexual selection because they conferred an advantage in the struggle to obtain a mate, and rudimentary organs were merely relics of what had once been useful in the past. The disparity between his theory and what has become known as theistic evolutionism (evolutionism under the control of a divine plan) became evident in a controversy with the American botanist Asa Gray (1810–88). Gray defended Darwin vigorously against those who rejected evolution, but, in a series of papers collected in his *Darwiniana* (1876), his views on design forced him to express doubts about natural selection. Having tried to defend the position that any form of lawlike production of species was compatible with belief in a Creator who established the laws, Gray was forced to admit that selection based on random variation seemed to eliminate any real sense of design in nature. He suggested

that the variation within each population was somehow led along beneficial lines, thus removing the need for the elimination of unfit variants. Darwin protested that all of the evidence from plant and animal breeders proved that variation was purposeless. If someone builds a wall by picking out useful pieces of stone fallen from a cliff, the design is in the selection of the stones: No one would suggest that nature was set up in such a way that stones split from the rock with useful shapes (Darwin 1882, II, 427–8).

For many evolutionists wishing to retain the belief that nature is somehow the expression of the divine will, Lamarckism seemed to solve the problem highlighted by Gray. Animals acquire useful characters by learning new habits that encourage them to use their bodies in different ways. The fact that the animals can make a deliberate choice of a new behavior pattern in a new environment seems to imply a kind of creative input by the organisms themselves. American neo-Lamarckians such as Edward Drinker Cope (1840–97) used this aspect of the inheritance of acquired characters to argue that the Creator had delegated his creative power to life itself. This position also accepts a continuity between animal and human mental faculties: Even the most primitive animals have rudimentary mental powers, which enable them to make conscious choices when faced with an environmental challenge.

In Britain, similar points were made by the novelist Samuel Butler (1835–1902) in a series of antiselectionist books beginning with his *Evolution Old and New* (1879). Butler recognized the force of Mivart's arguments but thought that the answer was to invoke not design built into the laws of nature but a nature that was itself creative. Natural selection was a "nightmare of waste and death," but Lamarckism made life self-creative in a way that fit a more general belief in the purposeful character of nature. Butler's arguments were taken up by many literary figures who had moral objections to natural selection, including the playwright George Bernard Shaw (1856–1950) and the author Arthur Koestler (1905–83). Butler himself alienated the scientific community by his personal attacks on Darwin, but, by the end of the nineteenth century, his views were becoming more acceptable. Many early-twentieth-century scientists participated in a widespread moral reaction against Darwinism based on the belief that evolution must be a purposeful process designed to enhance mental and moral progress.

The Roman Catholic Church began to adopt a different position, accepting that evolution might be an indirect mechanism of creation for the body but refusing to extend the argument to include the creation of the soul. By the 1920s, a significant body of opinion began to build up among Roman Catholic scholars in favor of the position that Mivart had defined in response to Darwinism. Works such as Ernest Messenger's *Evolution and Theology* (1931) argued that there was nothing in the writings of the Church Fathers that prevented acceptance of evolution, provided the process was seen as a manifestation of divine creativity. This movement paved the way for the modern Roman Catholic view of evolution, in which natural processes (assumed to be of divine origin) have formed the human body, while the soul has been introduced by direct divine intervention.

Modern Darwinism

Although many nonscientists felt strongly that natural selection was unacceptable for moral and philosophical reasons, the biologists themselves gradually began to believe that Darwinism might, after all, be the most promising theory. To a large extent, this was a product of the emergence of modern genetics, which undermined the credibility of Lamarckism by showing that acquired characters cannot be reflected in the organism's genes. Genetic mutation also supplied a plausible source of the random variation that Darwin had noticed in populations. By the 1930s, the "modern synthesis" of genetics and Darwinism was being constructed, a theory that has remained the dominant force in scientific evolutionism. Some modern Darwinians, including Julian Huxley (1887–1975), have tried to defend the view that evolution is progressive in a way that reflects human values. Julian Huxley even endorsed the theistic evolutionism of Pierre Teilhard de Chardin (1881–1955), according to which the development of life is tending toward an "omega point" of spiritual unification (Teilhard de Chardin 1959). But other founders of the modern synthesis, especially George Gaylord Simpson (1902–84), argued that Darwinism is essentially materialistic: There is no purpose in nature and no goal toward which evolution is striving (Simpson 1949). The human race simply has to grow up and realize that the values it cherishes are not respected by nature. Such a position had, in fact, been anticipated by Thomas Henry Huxley at the end of his career. His 1893 lecture on "Evolution and Ethics" had denied progress in nature and insisted that moral values are not products of the evolutionary process.

Indeed, he had proclaimed, nature may be actively hostile to our moral feelings. In such a view, we are, indeed, the products of a cosmic accident.

Not surprisingly, these developments in science have been resisted both by religious thinkers and by those who want to see human moral values as having some natural foundation. Two very different stands of protest can be identified. The best known is that leading to what is now known as creationism, in effect the return to a preevolutionary worldview in which species (especially the human species) have been directly created by God. In its most extreme manifestation, creationism has led to a complete repudiation of the geological time scale and a renewed acceptance of a literal interpretation of the Genesis account of Creation. Less well known is a current of anti-Darwinian thought emanating from both religious and philosophical critics of Darwinism who unite around the claim that the development of life cannot have been brought about by a process as purposeless as natural selection. This movement generates continued support for non-Darwinian evolutionary mechanisms in defiance of the geneticists.

The creationist reaction has received more publicity in recent years. It began in America during the 1920s, when many ordinary people, especially in the rural South, began to see Darwinism as a symbol of the moral corruption that was undermining traditional values. To treat humans as animals, they claimed, was to invite the evils of hedonism and social Darwinism. In 1925, the state of Tennessee passed legislation forbidding the teaching of evolution in the public schools. This was challenged in the famous "monkey trial" of John Thomas Scopes (1900–70), who was convicted after a much-publicized court case in which he was prosecuted by William Jennings Bryan (1860–1925) and defended by Clarence Darrow (1857–1938). Although much of the resulting publicity ridiculed the creationists, evolutionists prudently kept their subject out of biology textbooks for several decades.

In the 1960s, the now-confident Darwinians again tried to reintroduce evolutionism into the American school curriculum, precipitating the most recent outburst of creationism. Fundamentalist Protestantism now had a much wider power base in American society, and efforts had been made to establish a "creation science," in which the earth's geological structure was explained as the result of Noah's Flood. In several states, creationists urged legislation requiring equal time in high school classes for what they presented as a scientific alternative to evolutionism. In a series of much-publicized trials, this legislation was banned by the courts as unconstitutional on the ground that creation science was little more than an attempt to claim the literal truth of the Genesis story.

A far less visible campaign continued throughout the twentieth century by religious thinkers and moralists who accept evolution but argue that a more purposeful process than Darwinism must be involved. In Britain, this campaign was sparked by the inclusion of a Darwinian view of evolution in *The Outline of History* (1920) by H. G. Wells (1866–1946). The Catholic writer Hilaire Belloc (1870–1953) challenged Wells, proclaiming that Darwinism was by now dead even in science. Spirit could play a role in human history because spiritual factors were involved in evolution itself (although Belloc did not accept the evolutionary account of human origins). Unfortunately for Belloc, and for moralists such as George Bernard Shaw, who shared his distaste for selectionism, the biologists were by this time beginning to argue that theories of purposeful evolution were untenable and that selectionism would have to be accepted as the principal mechanism of evolution. Biologists such as J. B. S. Haldane (1892–1964) responded to Belloc and the anti-Darwinians and may even have been prompted to think more carefully about Darwinism by the challenge.

The rise of scientific Darwinism in the last half of the twentieth century has, however, been matched by a continued reluctance on the part of outsiders to admit that the theory can offer a complete explanation of the development of life. The popularity of Teilhard de Chardin's evolutionary mysticism is but one example of an ongoing rejection of the selection theory by those who think that nature must be based on principles that guarantee progress toward a spiritually significant goal and that the human race itself must be the highest product of such a process. For some, however, it is the origin of the human spirit that remains the chief stumbling block. As a Jesuit, Teilhard had been refused permission to publish during his lifetime because his vision included human origins, illustrating a tension within the Roman Catholic Church's position. Modern religious opposition to Darwinism thus runs the whole gamut from a creationism that rejects the orthodox scientific explanation of the geological record, through more sophisticated versions in which occasional creations are required to establish the main groups of animals and, of course, the human species. Even more liberal are those who accept a completely evolutionary worldview, so long as the Darwinian mechanism is marginalized in favor of something that allows for progress and purpose in nature. This latter position is maintained by many who would claim that their concerns are motivated by philosophical or moral, rather than purely religious, principles.

See also Charles Darwin; Creationism Since 1859; Evolutionary Ethics; Geology and Paleontology from 1700 to 1900; Great Chain of Being; Taxonomy

BIBLIOGRAPHY

Bowler, Peter J. *The Eclipse of Darwinism: Anti-Darwinian Evolution Theories in the Decades around 1900.* Baltimore: Johns Hopkins University Press, 1983.

———. *Theories of Human Evolution: A Century of Debate, 1844–1944.* Baltimore: Johns Hopkins University Press, 1986.

———. *The Non-Darwinian Revolution: Reinterpreting a Historical Myth.* Baltimore: Johns Hopkins University Press, 1988.

———. *Evolution: The History of an Idea.* 2d ed. Berkeley: University of California Press, 1989.

Burkhardt, Frederick, and Sydney Smyth, eds. *The Correspondence of Charles Darwin.* Vol. 7. Cambridge: Cambridge University Press, 1991.

Chambers, Robert. *Vestiges of the Natural History of Creation.* 1844. Reprint. Chicago: University of Chicago Press, 1994.

Corsi, Pietro. *Science and Religion: Baden Powell and the Anglican Debates, 1800–1860.* Cambridge: Cambridge University Press, 1988.

Darwin, Charles. *The Variation of Animals and Plants Under Domestication.* 2 vols. 2d ed. London: Murray, 1882.

Desmond, Adrian. *The Politics of Evolution: Morphology, Medicine, and Reform in Radical London.* Chicago: University of Chicago Press, 1989.

Ellegard, Alvar. *Darwin and the General Reader: The Reception of Darwin's Theory of Evolution in the British Periodical Press, 1859–1872.* 1958. Reprint. Chicago: University of Chicago Press, 1990.

Gillispie, Charles Coulston. *Genesis and Geology.* New York: Harper, 1959.

Greene, John C. *The Death of Adam: Evolution and Its Impact on Western Thought.* Ames: Iowa State University Press, 1959.

———. "The Interaction of Science and World View in Sir Julian Huxley's Evolutionary Biology." *Journal of the History of Biology* 23 (1990): 39–55.

Jensen, J. Vernon. "Return to the Wilberforce-Huxley Debate." *British Journal for the History of Science* 21 (1988): 161–79.

Koestler, Arthur. *The Ghost in the Machine.* New York: Macmillan, 1967.

Larson, Edward J. *Summer for the Gods: The Scopes Trial and America's Continuing Debate Over Science and Religion.* New York: Basic Books, 1997.

Livingstone, David. *Darwin's Forgotten Defenders: The Encounter between Evangelical Theology and Evolutionary Thought.* Edinburgh: Scottish Universities Press/and Grand Rapids, Mich.: Eerdmans, 1987.

McQuat, Gordon, and Mary P. Winsor. "J. B. S. Haldane's Darwinism in Its Religious Context." *British Journal for the History of Science* 28 (1995): 227–31.

Messenger, Ernest. *Evolution and Theology: The Problem of Man's Origin.* London: Burnes, Oates, and Washbourne, 1931.

Moore, James R. *The Post-Darwinian Controversies: A Study of the Protestant Struggle to Come to Terms with Darwin in Great Britain and America, 1870–1900.* New York: Cambridge University Press, 1979.

———. "Evangelicals and Evolution: Henry Drummond, Herbert Spencer, and the Naturalization of the Spiritual World." *Scottish Journal of Theology* 38 (1985a): 383–417.

———. "Herbert Spencer's Henchmen: The Evolution of Protestant Liberals in Late Nineteenth-Century America." In *Darwinism and Divinity,* ed. by John Durant. Oxford: Blackwell, 1985b, 76–100.

———. "Of Love and Death: Why Darwin 'Gave Up Christianity.'" In *History, Humanity, and Evolution,* ed. by J. R. Moore. Cambridge: Cambridge University Press, 1989, 195–230.

Numbers, Ronald L. *The Creationists: The Evolution of Scientific Creationism.* New York: Knopf, 1992.

Ospovat, Dov. *The Development of Darwin's Theory: Natural History, Natural Theology, and Natural Selection, 1838–1859.* Cambridge: Cambridge University Press, 1981.

Richards, Robert J. *Darwin and the Emergence of Evolutionary Theories of Mind and Behavior.* Chicago: University of Chicago Press, 1987.

Simpson, George Gaylord. *The Meaning of Evolution.* New Haven, Conn.: Yale University Press, 1949.

Sulloway, Frank. *Freud: Biologist of the Mind.* London: Burnett, 1979.

Teilhard de Chardin, Pierre. *The Phenomenon of Man.* London: Collins, 1959.

Turner, Frank Miller. *Between Science and Religion: The Reaction to Scientific Naturalism in Late Victorian England.* New Haven, Conn.: Yale University Press, 1974.

86. ANATOMY AND PHYSIOLOGY TO 1700

Emerson Thomas McMullen

Anatomy and Teleology

A key guiding assumption in anatomy and physiology, from ancient times through the scientific revolution, was the idea that nature exhibited purpose. Plato (c. 427–347 B.C.) and Aristotle (384–322 B.C.) addressed the question of the origin of the universe in different ways, but both included purpose in their explanations. Plato rejected a chance beginning of the universe and intuited that the Demiurge (Divine Craftsman) had made the cosmos according to design. The idea of a designed universe leads directly to the concept of purpose in nature. Purpose is different from function or description. The diagram of a clock gives the plan of its workings, and, while an explanation of how each part functions may exist, the designed purpose, the reason for which the clock exists, is to tell time. Plato's approach to science, besides explaining how nature operated, also asked why it functioned in the way it did.

Aristotle rejected the belief that the universe had been created by a creator/designer, arguing that it was eternal. Nevertheless, he agreed with Plato that the cosmos was purposeful and not governed by chance. If the heavens had an origin, Aristotle wrote in *On the Parts of Animals* (I.1, 641b), it did not come about by chance but by purpose. He reasoned that everything had an ultimate goal or end *(telos);* hence, his view was teleological. This key premise is found at the beginning of his *Generation of Animals:* "There are four causes underlying everything: first the final cause, that for the sake of which a thing exists" (715a). Aristotle applied this cause throughout his science. For example, he begins Chapter Two of his *Gait of Animals* with the statement that, in this particular study, he will employ the principles that he customarily used for his scientific investigations. The first principle is "that Nature creates nothing without a purpose" (704b). Aristotle thought of purpose as a universal principle that appears in all of nature's work. Aristotle's biological treatises, as well as those on the history and motion of animals, laid the groundwork for subsequent studies of anatomy and physiology.

During the Western Middle Ages, of course, belief in design in nature shifted from Plato's limited Demiurge and Aristotle's Nature to the unlimited God of Christian revelation. God had, of his own free will, created the heavens and the earth and everything in them. Subsequent natural philosophers might continue to write that nature does nothing in vain, but by this phrase they meant that God had created nature with purpose in mind.

The Medical Tradition

The most influential physician, anatomist, and physiologist from Roman times until the mid-sixteenth century was Galen of Pergamum (A.D. 129–c. 210). His investigations into anatomy and physiology contributed significantly to the effort to base medicine on scientific principles that had begun in Greece more than five hundred years earlier. One of Galen's research techniques was to apply Aristotle's teleological approach, which he summed up in the dictum that "nature does nothing in vain." In his scientific program, Galen tried to elaborate the teleological connection between anatomy and physiology. His appeal to purpose is nowhere more evident than in one of his greatest works, *De usu partium (On the Usefulness of the Parts).* More than a medical treatise on anatomy and physiology, it is a natural theology in which every dissection reveals a miniature universe. This study of the microcosm simultaneously demonstrated the purpose and craftsmanship of both Plato's Demiurge and Aristotle's Nature.

One example of Galen's use of purpose in science was the way in which he rejected the urine-formation theory of Lycus the Macedonian (second century A.D.). Both agreed on the structure and the basic function of the kidneys. However, Lycus thought that urine is only the residue of the kidney's nutrition. Galen disagreed. He judged that, if this physiological interpretation were so, the kidneys' blood vessels should be relatively small. Instead, they appeared to him to be larger than required by Lycus's theory. Galen concluded that there had to be another theory that explained why "the Creator, who does nothing without a purpose, inserted such large arteries into the small bodies of the kidneys." He reasoned that any theory that does not explain why these vessels are relatively large must be wrong (*De usu partium* V.5).

Galen was familiar with Judaism and Christianity, and he mentions them in *De usu partium*. He understood that his concept of deity, the Demiurge, was limited when compared to the unlimited God of the Jews. Galen wrote that, according to Moses, everything was possible for God. God could even make a horse out of ashes. However, Galen believed that the Demiurge would never attempt such a thing, choosing instead what is best to be done from what is possible. Although Galen was critical of the Judeo-Christian tradition, his acknowledgment of the validity of the argument from design made possible his rehabilitation by Christian thinkers. Moreover, his medical system, which proved so encyclopedic and influential, was used to support Christian orthodoxy during the Middle Ages in much the same way that Aristotle's system of natural philosophy was allied to Christian teachings.

According to the Galenic system of physiology, ingested food was concocted in the stomach into the milky fluid (*chyle*) and transported to the liver, where it underwent further concoction into venous blood. The blood, held to contain "natural spirit," was distributed around the body through the veins to bring nourishment to all of the parts. During this general distribution, some of the venous blood was delivered to the right ventricle of the heart and seeped through invisibly small pores in the interventricular septum (the thick muscular wall between the ventricles), where this small proportion of the venous blood was mixed with air, brought in from the lungs via the pulmonary vein, and concocted into arterial

blood containing "vital spirit." The vital spirit was then distributed to all parts of the body via the arteries to bring heat and life to the parts. In turn, some of the arterial blood was distributed to the brain, where a final concoction produced the even more subtle "animal spirits," which were then distributed to all parts of the body through the nervous system, endowing motion and sensitivity on the parts. Galen's system seemed to provide a neat account of what the major parts of the body were intended for. The liver, heart, lungs, and brain all had important parts to play. The vital and animal spirits could be identified with the Aristotelian vegetative and animal souls. And the four humors of the pre-Galenic Hippocratic tradition—blood, phlegm, yellow bile, and black bile—could be associated with one of the major organs: yellow bile with the liver, blood with the heart, phlegm with the brain, and black bile with the spleen. Assumptions about the nature of pathology and the corresponding system of therapeutics were also derived from this physiological system. All disease was held to be the result of an imbalance in the normal constitution of the four humors. The doctor's role was to restore the balance of the patient's humors. Adjustment was brought about by bleeding, or by administering emetics, expectorants, diuretics, or laxatives, as well as by keeping the patient warm or cold, as appropriate, and administering "cold" or "hot" (or "moist" or "dry") medicaments.

From the Middle Ages to the Renaissance

Ingenious and intellectually satisfying though Galen's physiology was, it was at least to some extent (particularly in details that are beyond the scope of this restricted account) based upon erroneous anatomical beliefs. Galen was forbidden by societal mores to dissect human bodies and, hence, had to rely on the dissection of animals, chiefly pigs and apes. His errors were propagated throughout the Middle Ages, when his authority was nearly unquestioned. There were, however, a few who challenged Galen's opinions. One was Ibn al-Nafis al-Qurashi (d. 1288), a Syrian physician who questioned Galen's assertion that blood passed through the cardiac septum. If the blood did not take this path, al-Nafis concluded, it had to go through the lungs in order to get from the right to the left side of the heart, a concept that is sometimes called the lesser circulation of the blood.

Western anatomists, like Henri de Mondeville (1260–1320), a graduate of Montpellier and a body physician to Philip the Fair, and Mondino de' Luzzi (c. 1265–1326), professor of anatomy at Bologna, were more concerned to use their work to extend its teleological and natural theological lessons rather than to engage with technical anatomical details. In the introduction to his *Anatomy,* for example, Mondino listed four reasons why man is upright in stature. The fourth reason given is "the end to which he was made," that he may understand. In other sections, he wrote that the purpose of the womb is chiefly conception and that the pericardium is made to guard the heart from injuries and to prevent it from coming into contact with other organs during expansion. Similarly, nature ordains eyebrows to guard the eyes from things coming from above and eyelids to guard the eyes from things coming from the front. While some of Mondino's statements may seem to be merely affirming the self-evident, they illustrate the practice of his first asking the purpose of a part of the body, to which he provides an answer. This often involved stating the obvious simply because the purpose of some body parts, such as eyes and teeth, is apparent. However, the purpose of other parts was not as manifest to early investigators.

The guiding assumption of purpose in nature continued into the Renaissance but, with the increasing skepticism toward ancient authority, brought about by the discovery of alternative philosophical systems, and the concomitant emphasis on personal experience and observation, it was only a matter of time before Galen's authority was challenged. The usual practice of anatomical instruction in university medical schools had been to read from one of Galen's anatomical works while a barber-surgeon, usually called in from the town and unable to understand the Latin being read out, did the actual dissection. This practice was completely changed by Andreas Vesalius (1514–64), professor of surgery at the University of Padua, who undertook to dissect bodies himself in front of the students. Teaching anatomy in this way, Vesalius claimed that he had discovered more than two hundred errors in Galen's anatomical works. The most important was his discovery that there are no pores in the heart's interventricular septum. This, in itself, was enough to undermine Galen's physiology, but Vesalius was content merely to announce his skepticism on this particular detail of Galen's system without taking it further.

The problem confronting Vesalius and other anatomists was that Galen's system was so wide ranging that it

was impossible to point to uncertainty in one aspect of his system without throwing the rest into doubt. In the absence of an equally all-encompassing replacement system, it seemed inconceivable that the new discoveries demanded anything more than ad hoc adjustments to Galen's theories. Continued faith in Galen was particularly supported by practicing physicians, who were making a good living out of applying Galenic therapeutic procedures. How could these therapies work if Galen was wrong?

The discovery of the valves in the veins provides a clear example of a discovery that seemed to demand not a thorough revision of physiology but merely a refinement of Galenic ideas. Usually said to have been discovered by Hieronymus Fabricius of Aquapendente (1533–1619), William Harvey's professor at the University of Padua, but known earlier to Vesalius, Salomon Alberti (1540–1600), and possibly others, the purpose of the valves eluded anatomists until Harvey. Fabricius theorized that the purpose for which "nature has formed them" is to slow the blood's flow to the extremities. If the blood flowed too fast to the hands and feet, the upper limbs would be undernourished and the hands and feet would be permanently swollen. Therefore, the function of the venous membranes was to retard the flow of blood, and their purpose was to provide proper nourishment to the body and an even distribution of the blood.

The other major development in Western physiological theory before Harvey, the discovery of the lesser, or pulmonary, circulation, was also seen merely as a refinement of Galenic theory until Harvey's more sweeping changes. First suggested by Michael Servetus (1511–53) in a radically reformist theological work, *Christianismi restitutio* (*The Restitution of Christianity* [1553]), the theory did not receive due prominence until it was rediscovered by Realdo Colombo (1510–59) and published in 1559. Colombo's reasoning was much more familiarly in the tradition of teleological anatomy. According to Galen, the pulmonary artery, leading from the right side of the heart to the lungs, was intended just to take nourishment to the lungs, but in Colombo's judgment it was far too large for this. Moreover, whenever in dissections he opened the pulmonary vein (leading from the lungs to the left side of the heart), he found that it was full of blood, and the valves guarding the entrance to this vessel seemed to be fully competent and to allow flow only from the lungs into the heart. According to Galen, this vessel was intended, on the one hand, to bring air into the left side of the heart from the lungs and, on the other, to evacuate the noxious fumes left over from the concoction of venous blood and air to form vital spirits/arterial blood. Colombo became convinced that all of the blood arriving at the right side of the heart was transported through the pulmonary artery to the lungs and, from there, to the left side of the heart through the pulmonary vein. No air made its way into the heart, and no waste gases could have escaped from the heart through the valves at the opening of the pulmonary vein.

William Harvey

The fact that William Harvey (1578–1657) used purpose as an integral part of his science is shown in both of his two main books. The most famous is his *Exercitatio anatomica de motu cordis et sanguinis animalibus (An Anatomical Disputation on the Motion of the Heart and Blood in Living Creatures* [1628]), usually abbreviated to *De motu cordis.* In it, Harvey spoke of the valves in the veins being made to ensure a one-way flow of blood through the veins and of nature ordaining that the blood should go through the lungs. He wrote that the parts of the circulatory system were arranged as they are "by the consummate providence of nature." Similarly, Harvey's *Exercitationes de generatione animalium (Exercises on the Generation of Living Creatures* [1651]) overflows with phrases involving design in nature. One example concerns the parts of the hen, which are "destined by nature for purposes of generation . . . for nothing in nature's works is fashioned either carelessly or in vain." Because "Nature does nothing in vain, nor works in any round-about way when a shorter path lies open to her," Harvey was certain "that an egg can be produced in no other manner than that in which we now see it engendered, viz., by the concurring act of the cock and hen." He drew many similar conclusions using purpose as a working principle.

After Harvey had joined the Royal Society of Physicians in London, he gave a lecture series on anatomy. His unpublished notes, "Prelectiones anatomiae universalis" (Lectures on the Whole of Anatomy [1616]), provide clues to how he discovered the circulation of the blood. Harvey had read both Alberti and Fabricius and knew of their differences over the interpretation of the membranes in the veins. He chose Alberti's interpretation. He referred to the valves in the veins as one-way and consistently used the Latin terms for "valve" (*valvulae, valvulis,*

valvulas) for the membranes. Conversely, Harvey rejected both Fabricius's terminology (*ostiola*) and his interpretation (that it slows blood flow). Writing later in *De motu cordis,* he explained that Fabricius and others "did not rightly understand" the purpose of the venous valves (*valvulas*).

Harvey carefully and clearly differentiated between function and purpose. In *De motu cordis,* he wrote that "the function of the valves in the veins is the same as the three sigmoid valves which we find at the commencement of the aorta." On the other hand, the purpose of the venous valves was to keep the blood from flowing "from the greater into the lesser veins, and either rupture them or cause them to become varicose." His description of how the membranes operate as one-way valves relates to function. His answer to why they are one-way valves involves purpose. A close reading of Harvey's lecture notes and *De motu cordis* reveals that the membranes in the veins were the key to his discovery of the blood's circulation. Concerning their structure, Harvey noted that, no matter where they are located in the body, the edges of the membranes all point to the heart. This means that, if they function as one-way valves, as the cardiac valves do, blood motion is only toward the heart, and it would be impossible for the blood to nourish the body. Harvey was also impressed by the membranes' relative abundance in the veins, especially when compared to the arteries, where there are no membranes, except for the aortic valve. Concerning function, he accepted Alberti's description of how the venous membranes act as one-way valves, like the valves of the heart. Accepting this explanation meant that both Galen and Fabricius were wrong about how the blood moves in the veins. It followed from this that they were also wrong about why there are valves in the veins in the first place. Yet, there had to be a reason since nature does nothing in vain.

Harvey struggled to determine the purpose of these one-way, relatively abundant, venous valves. This struggle led him to posit other factors, which included the consideration that the veins and the arteries, especially those near the heart, were, in his judgment, too large for their function in Galenic physiology. Just as Galen had done in his analysis of Lycus's urine-formation theory, and as Colombo had done in his consideration of the pulmonary artery, Harvey surmised that there had to be another reason that these vessels and conduits are so large. Additionally, because of their size, an abundance of blood must move through them in a short time. Harvey roughly estimated (indeed, to make his point more forcefully, he well and truly underestimated) how much blood might be expelled into the aorta (the main artery leading from the heart) at each heartbeat. He concluded that, even in half an hour, the amount of blood passing through the left ventricle could not possibly be supplied by the liver concocting chyle. The only alternative, Harvey believed, was to assume that the same blood was reappearing over and over again in the heart.

Finally, then, Harvey came to the realization that the blood moves in a circle, flowing out from the heart into the arteries and then returning in the veins. The valves in the veins allow the blood to move toward the heart, but, if the blood flow reverses, the blood pushes open the membranes, blocking any further movement of the blood away from the heart. Even if a valve were defective, Harvey reasoned, the relatively large number of the venous valves would combine to prevent reverse flow of the blood. Hence, the assumption of purpose was vital in Harvey's logic of discovery.

Harvey's assumption of purpose was not just motivated by Galen and Aristotle. Harvey was a Christian who mentioned Jesus Christ in his scientific works ("Lectures on the Whole of Anatomy" and *On Parturition*). He believed that, in doing research, God's book of nature could also be considered along with his book of revelation. For instance, he differed with Aristotle over where life first appears. His own studies indicated that life appears first in the blood. He supported this claim in *On Generation* by stating that "the life, therefore, resides in the blood (as we are informed in our sacred writings)," referring to an Old Testament passage (Leviticus 17:11 and 14).

Harvey demonstrated his new theory of blood circulation with what, from our perspective, seem to be unambiguous and incontrovertible experiments. Nevertheless, for many of Harvey's contemporaries his arguments and evidence were by no means convincing. A major part of his difficulty stemmed from the fact that, although his theory of the heart and blood, if accepted, would have completely undermined Galenic physiology, Harvey had nothing to put in its place. Harvey's theory meant that the Galenic function of the liver was completely misconceived, but he offered no alternative suggestion as to what the function of the liver might be. His theory, in turn, seemed to imply that the brain might not function as Galen said it did. Even the role of the lungs was problematic in Harvey's scheme. While Galen believed that the lungs were essential in bringing air to the blood, Harvey had been misled by comparative studies of lungless animals into supposing that the lungs were not an essential part of the heart/blood system (he failed to recognize the role of gills when he dissected fish, for example). Harvey concluded that the heart/blood system was a closed circuit that did not need to be supplied with anything from the lungs. This conclusion raised the problem of the purpose of the lungs, which Harvey failed to solve. Furthermore, Harvey's new scheme made absolutely no difference to medical practice: It offered nothing to replace the traditional humoral pathology and suggested no workable therapeutic techniques (although some dangerous experiments with blood transfusion were carried out for a brief period by the Royal Society and the Paris Académie des Sciences).

Mechanical Physiology

Another aspect of Harvey's work that proved disagreeable to many of his contemporaries was its vitalism. For Harvey, the blood was a living principle that animated the rest of the body but needed nothing else (not even air) to maintain its own vitality. Harvey likened the blood to a spirit, even seeming to declare that there was no need to postulate a separate soul distinct from the blood. This kind of talk was unacceptable to the new mechanical philosophers. René Descartes (1596–1650) accordingly developed a more mechanistic version of circulatory theory. Descartes postulated that, as blood entered the left ventricle from the coolness of the lungs, it was immediately and forcefully rarefied by the heat in the ventricle. As a result, the heart expanded and ejected the rarefied arterial blood out into the aorta. The emptied heart would then collapse, ready to repeat the cycle as more blood entered from the lungs. On this view, the active stroke of the heartbeat was the expansion of the heart (*diastole*). In this, Descartes agreed with Galen; Harvey had argued that the active stroke was the heart's spontaneous contraction (*systole*).

Descartes's more mechanical version of the circulation won a number of adherents, but the experimental support that Harvey provided for his theory proved hard to deny, and it was taken up not only by Harvey's English followers but by a number of Continental medical writers as well. Moreover, subsequent research began to establish such matters as the function of the liver and the lungs and the nature of the nervous system. More mechanistic accounts of the circulation were developed that did not deviate from Harvey's theory about the active stroke of the heart, and before too long Harvey began to be represented (falsely) as a mechanical philosopher who had held the heart to be nothing more than a pump. Meanwhile, the mechanical philosophy extended into other areas of physiology, providing what were seen at the time as plausible accounts of digestion, responses to stimuli, muscular movement, and other aspects of the workings of the body.

The antivitalistic aspects of the mechanical philosophy, together with its perceived similarity to ancient atomism, meant that it was all too frequently identified with atheism. Devout proponents of the new physiology took extra care, therefore, to insist that their theories could be used to combat atheism. Accordingly, new theories of anatomy and physiology featured prominently in the burgeoning tradition of natural theology. This new alliance became all the more prominent when the microscope made it possible to show undreamed of intricacies in plant and animal forms. As is clear from Robert Hooke's (1635–1703) *Micrographia* (1665), the microscope magnified the gap between the "perfection" of nature's artistry and the imperfection of human artifacts. This contrast was used by John Ray (1627–1705) to emphasize the wisdom of God discernible in nature. In this respect, the microscope was a boon to natural theology.

See also Natural Theology; Premodern Theories of Generation

Bibliography

Adelman, H. B. *Marcello Malpighi and the Evolution of Biology.* 5 vols. Ithaca, N.Y.: Cornell University Press, 1966.

Bates, Don G. "Harvey's Account of His Discovery." *Medical History* 36 (1992): 361–78.

Baumer, Anne. "Christian Aristotelianism and Atomism in Embryology." In *Science and Religion—Wissenschaft und Religion,* ed. by M. Buttner and A. Baumer. Bochum: Brockmeyer, 1989.

Bylebyl, J. J. "Boyle and Harvey on the Valves in the Veins." *Bulletin of the History of Medicine* 56 (1982): 351–67.

Cunningham, Andrew. "Fabricius and the 'Aristotle Project' in Anatomical Teaching and Research at Padua." In *The Medical Renaissance of the Sixteenth Century,* ed. by A. Wear et. al. Cambridge: Cambridge University Press, 1985, 195–222.

Frank, Robert G., Jr. *Harvey and the Oxford Physiologists: Scientific Ideas and Social Interaction.* Berkeley: University of California Press, 1980.

French, Roger. *William Harvey's Natural Philosophy.* Cambridge: Cambridge University Press, 1994.

French, Roger, and Andrew Wear, eds. *The Medical Revolution of the Sixteenth Century.* Cambridge: Cambridge University Press, 1989.

Galen. *On the Usefulness of Parts.* Trans. by M. T. May. Ithaca, N.Y.: Cornell University Press, 1968.

Gorham, Geoffrey. "Mind-Body Dualism and the Harvey-Descartes Controversy." *Journal of the History of Ideas* 55 (1994): 211–34.

Grene, Marjorie. "The Heart and Blood: Descartes, Plemp, and Harvey." In *Essays on the Philosophy and Science of René Descartes,* ed. by Stephen Voss. New York: Oxford University Press, 1993.

Hunter, R. A., and I. Macalpine. "William Harvey and Robert Boyle." *Notes and Records of the Royal Society of London* 13 (1958): 115–27.

Keynes, Geoffrey. *A Bibliography of Dr. William Harvey, 1578–1657.* 3d ed. Winchester: St. Paul's Bibliographies, 1989.

Lang, Helen S. "Aristotelian Physics: Teleological Procedure in Aristotle, Thomas, and Buridan." *Review of Metaphysics* 42 (1989): 569–91.

McMullen, Emerson Thomas. "Anatomy of a Physiological Discovery: William Harvey and the Circulation of the Blood." *Journal of the Royal Society of Medicine* 88 (1995): 491–8.

Nutton, Vivian. *Galen on Prognosis: Edition, Translation, and Commentary.* Corpus Medicorum Graecorum. Vol. 5. Berlin: Akademie-Verlag, 1979.

O'Malley, C. D. *Andreas Vesalius of Brussels, 1514–1564.* Berkeley: University of California Press, 1965.

Pagel, Walter. *New Light on William Harvey.* London: Karger, 1976.

Reines, Brandon P. "On the Role of Clinical Anomaly in Harvey's Discovery of the Mechanism of the Pulse." *Perspectives in Biology and Medicine* 34 (1990): 128–33.

Roberts, K. B., and J. D. W. Tomlinson. *The Fabric of the Body.* Oxford: Clarendon, 1992.

Ruestow, Edward G. *The Microscope in the Dutch Republic: The Shaping of Discovery.* Cambridge: Cambridge University Press, 1996.

Sanders, J. B., and C. D. O'Malley. *Andreas Vesalius Bruxellensis: The Bloodletting Letter of 1539.* New York: Schuman, 1947.

Shea, William R. *The Magic of Numbers and Motion: The Scientific Career of René Descartes.* Canton, Mass: Science History Publications, 1991.

Siraisi, Nancy G. *Medieval and Early Renaissance Medicine.* Chicago: University of Chicago Press, 1990.

Temkin, Owsei. "A Galenic Model for Quantitative Physiological Reasoning?" *Bulletin of the History of Medicine* 35 (1961): 470–5.

Wear, Andrew. "William Harvey and the 'Way of the Anatomists.'" *History of Science* 21 (1983): 223–49.

Whitteridge, Gweneth. *William Harvey and the Circulation of the Blood.* London: Macdonald, 1971.

Wilson, Catherine. *The Invisible World: Early Modern Philosophy and the Invention of the Microscope.* Princeton, N.J.: Princeton University Press, 1995.

87. PREMODERN THEORIES OF GENERATION

Charles E. Dinsmore

Living things reproduce themselves, a simple observation that, to the creative human imagination, presents a formidable intellectual challenge. Although numerous explanatory hypotheses about the central processes of generation have been proposed over the past twenty-five hundred years, they actually form a limited number of categories based on commonly shared experience, observation, and analogy. These categories include (1) the familiar sexual reproduction, in which two more or less discrete sexes of the same species participate in the act of procreation; (2) asexual reproduction, or parthenogenesis, in which a single individual in the absence of copulation produces another individual of the same species; and (3) spontaneous generation, typically understood as the production of an organism from inert matter.

Within the above categories, a theory of generation may embrace either intrinsic or extrinsic regulation of the process. The question of natural as distinct from supra- or supernatural governance, respectively, then becomes a significant component of the theory. That context interjects into the postulates fundamental beliefs about the presence or absence of divine guidance in the natural world. Such theories tend also to reflect the social, technical, and philosophical terrain of any given period, and, while framed by mutually accessible facts, competing theories may derive mutually exclusive conclusions.

This particular dichotomy among theories of reproduction emerged with the early Greeks and continued into the twentieth century. Some theories contained an element of supernatural intervention or a vital principle (for example, entelechy, *vis essentialis,* élan vital) as central to the process. Theories of this nature remove an essential component of the process of generation from scientific investigation by conferring on it a metaphysical foundation, unavailable to scientific scrutiny. For example, seventeenth- and eighteenth-century theories of preformation by preexistence denied that generation occurs at all. Rather, they asserted that all organisms—past, present, and future—have existed since the time of Creation, though as infinitesimally small, preformed replicas that simply unfold.

Alternative theories of generation expressly omitting or simply not necessitating supernatural explanations appeared as early as the time of Hippocrates (c. 460–377/359 B.C.). Later theories of "epigenesis" (the generation of organisms from unformed matter) represent another such example. While unable to explain ultimate mechanisms, the ancient Greeks began a tradition of analyzing natural phenomena and rationally debating natural explanations. Animal dissection and comparative anatomy provide explicit examples of their seeking intrinsic explanations for body-related functions, such as reproduction, at a macroscopic level. With the advent of microscopic exploration of living nature in the late seventeenth and early eighteenth centuries, new theories appeared that augmented the development of material-based concepts of generation.

Distinctions between natural and supernatural components of theories, however, are not always unambiguous; technical limitations of a given period often determine the point at which an unknown "essential force" or an unknowable divine intervention might be invoked. However, fundamental philosophical differences set apart theories that assume commitment to a material view of a nature with intrinsic laws from those that invoke extrinsic or supernatural powers.

Sexual Reproduction

In the Western tradition, the ancient Greek philosophers, some of whom were also physicians, developed a method of skeptical inquiry and reasoning from analogy in seeking natural causes to account for natural processes. Reproductive issues find significant representation in their surviving works. For instance, the embryological treatises among the Hippocratic writings include a theory of the nature of generation. One short work entitled *The Seed* includes unequivocal statements about human generation: During coitus, seminal fluids or semen from both the male and the female mix and solidify, resulting in the generation of an embryo within the uterus. Furthermore, the treatise postulates a pangenesis mechanism: Semen formation draws "fluids" containing miniature representative structures from each part of the adult body. This material hypothesis of sexual reproduction granted generation a purely natural basis. While obviating supernatural intervention, it had the additional advantage of accounting for common observations such as the variable resemblance of children to both parents. More than two thousand years later, the French mathematician and naturalist Pierre-Louis Moreau de Maupertuis (1698–1759) published similar views in his *Vénus physique* (*Physical Venus* [1745]). At the same time, he suggested experimentally testing a theory that anticipated the inheritance of acquired characteristics. In the next century, Charles Darwin (1809–82) also endorsed pangenesis and called the semen's hereditary units, derived from both sexes, "gemmules."

Aristotle's (384–322 B.C.) biological treatises also contain an elaborate theory of generation. In *Generation of Animals* (1.1), he distinguished viviparous and oviparous animals, which "come into being from the union of male and female," from those that "come into being . . . from decaying earth and excrements" or through spontaneous generation. His theory of sexual generation derives from male and female "principles," designated as the efficient cause and the material cause, respectively. He nevertheless rejected pangenesis, replacing it with a theory of subtly defined "residues." The menstrual blood constituted the material residue for creating the embryo, while an ethereal constituent of male semen provided a "motion" or animating force. That introduced an immaterial soul (*anima*) into the process of generation, thereby reestablishing supranatural or extrinsic influences in reproduc-tion. His assignment of a passive, subordinate role to femaleness and an active, dominant role to maleness influenced central social-theological dogma in Western European intellectual circles for more than fifteen hundred years.

A theory of generation also appears in Galen's (A.D. 129–c. 210) *On the Natural Faculties.* It borrows heavily from Aristotle, invoking an animating male principle as well as assuming that female menstrual blood contributes the material of the embryo, but its liberal use of "faculties" and "qualities" betrays its greater reliance on teleology and vitalism. For example, Galen believed that the uterus retains the conceptus through a "retentive faculty" and proposed an imaginary "principle of proportionate attraction" to explain differentiation. Such undefined forces of attraction were to reappear in eighteenth-century theories of generation as potential biological laws. In the interim, Galen's authority and strong endorsement of teleological principles as driving forces in generation did little to encourage experimental inquiries into the process.

Preformation and Preexistence

In the late seventeenth century, polarized opinions about the nature of generation demonstrated explicitly a divergence in philosophical convictions. From one point of view, a divine power beyond the comprehension of mortals actively regulated nature; from another, naturalist-philosophers accorded nature a comprehensible sovereignty, rejecting theological opinion by removing God from natural phenomena. Consequently, explanations of generation were forged either to conserve a role for God or to supplant God with an autonomously regulated nature. Preformation tended largely to depict the former worldview.

Preformation theories generally assert that new individuals, or at least their component parts, occur prefabricated in the parental body prior to birth. Generation might take place through the admixture of male and female semen or simply by a preformed embryo preexisting as a "germ" either in the female semen (ovism) or in the male semen (animalculism). René Descartes (1596–1650) considered that preformation might actually account for plant development, though not for animal generation. He pointed out that, since plant seeds are constructed of solid, hard materials, the embryonic parts might necessarily be prearranged. Animal semen, on the contrary, is very fluid, clearly warranting an epigenetic mechanism of generation. Another issue central to the ensuing debate, as framed during the late seventeenth and early eighteenth centuries, was an accommodation of observations to theological dogma. Maintaining that unorganized matter might autonomously generate an organized and living body, even in a preformation theory, had serious theological consequences. A felicitous alternative depicted an uninterrupted chain of preexistent beings and maintained that all complex organic forms had existed since Creation. Such preformation by preexistence had the additional advantage of concordance with concepts of predestination.

Partisans of preformation were often religious individuals for whom the soul's place in the process of generation became a key concern; hence, their writings in natural history fit within a larger matrix of Christian apologetics. One of the great Protestant intellectuals, the German mathematician and philosopher Gottfried Wilhelm Leibniz (1646–1716), established and defended a theologically based, mechanistic hypothesis of generation in his *Theodicy* (1710); his preformation theory relied on a preexistence mechanism. Particular metaphysical assumptions about the soul led him to couple soul to matter in an ambiguous concept of "monads," comparable to Aristotle's "entelechies." These vital units, or "true atoms of life," thus created a metaphysical link between his theology and contemporary natural history and mathematics.

Leibniz's contemporary, the French priest-philosopher Nicolas de Malebranche (1638–1715), also championed the primacy of religious goals in observing nature. His *Search After Truth* (1674) contains the fully articulated *emboîtement* (encasement) model of preformation. This landmark among theological theories of generation favored ovist preformation, maintaining that females of all originally created animals, including Eve, contained eggs bearing the actual individuals of all future generations. It assumed that each successively encased generation had been completely formed at Creation. That sentiment, mirroring predestination, transcended the boundaries of major Christian communions, thus also gaining adherents in non-Roman Catholic countries.

Charles Bonnet (1720–93), a Genevan naturalist-philosopher, became one of the most zealous and influential proponents of preformation theory. He was formally educated at the School of Calvin in Geneva, where he

assimilated the theory of preexistent "germs" in a theological context. He read Abbé Noël Pluche's (1688–1761) *The Spectacle of Nature* (1732), Malebranche's *The Search after Truth,* and Jan Swammerdam's (1637–80) *The Book of Nature.* As a result of his study of insects and their reproductive strategies in the year 1740 (when he was only twenty years old), Bonnet was able to demonstrate conclusively (in his *Traité d'insectologie* [*Treatise on Insectology,* 1745]) asexual reproduction (parthenogenesis) in aphids. In that same year, 1740, his cousin Abraham Trembley (1710–84) discovered that a bisected hydra regenerates two new individuals (published 1744; English translation by Lenhoff and Lenhoff 1986), an observation disturbing for the concept of animal souls. Bonnet subsequently constructed a comprehensive theory of generation based on preexistent germs to accommodate both of these enigmatic observations in natural history into his philosophy. His later reading of Leibniz's *Theodicy* provided him with a "decisive confirmation of the system."

Beginning with Malebranche's encasement theory of ovist preformation, Bonnet eventually theorized that "germs" of body parts might be disseminated throughout an organism to account for both regenerative and reproductive abilities. In his highly influential and widely read *Considérations sur les corps organisés* (*Reflections on Organized Bodies* [1762]), he not only provided a synthesis of contemporary theories of generation, promoting his own, but also repudiated the various systems of epigenesis, which he considered heretical. With the first volume of the *Corps organisés,* Bonnet mounted an unrelenting attack on epigenetic theories of generation in general and on the noted French naturalist Georges Louis Leclerc, Comte de Buffon's (1707–88), model in particular, which he described in correspondence as "atheistic" (Sonntag 1983). Preexistence theories explained the origins of complex form and function associated with life by including explicit reference to Creation. Insinuating a discrete role for God in generation effectively eliminated the problematic origin of form. Alternatives, such as the epigenetic theories described below, failed in this regard.

Another partisan in the epigenesis-preformation debate was Albrecht von Haller (1708–77), who, at different times in his life, eloquently supported both preformation and epigenesis. As a medical student, Haller had espoused the animalculist-preformation account of generation, but Trembley's hydra-regeneration discovery made him convert to epigenesis. He developed an explanatory mechanism that postulated "attractive forces" guided by "divine laws." His retreat from epigenesis toward ovist preformation in the early 1750s coincides with his growing concern as an orthodox Calvinist about the theological issues at stake (for example, in his references to "a Creative Mind," "the all-governing Divinity," "connection to contemporary Christianity" [Sloan 1981]), a concern markedly missing from his epigenetic phase. Reviewing Buffon's theory of generation, which clearly neglected mention of God's role in the process, Haller found it "prejudicial to revelation" and, in correspondence with Bonnet, described Buffon as "reasoning like an Atheist" (Sonntag 1983). His return to preformation, therefore, exhibits strong religious motives.

Epigenesis

The preformation-epigenesis dichotomy appears in Aristotle's biological treatises, in which Aristotle seems to have favored epigenesis over preformation, at least for higher-animal development. Nevertheless, William Harvey's (1578–1657) De generatione animalium (On the Generation of Living Creatures [1651]) offers a more complete rendering of an epigenetic model of generation. Acknowledging a debt to Aristotle, Harvey in addition coined the term "epigenesis" (per epigenesin) and framed its underlying concept: Embryos arise by the sequential construction of parts from unformed matter. This he contrasted with metamorphosis, defined as the transformation of one preexistent form into another, such that all constituent parts appeared simultaneously. Just as a stamp impressed into clay inscribes all of the image at once, so, too, does metamorphosis convert all of the parts contained within a caterpillar directly into all of the parts of a butterfly. Thus, he explained such insect transformations not as examples of true generation but merely as metamorphosis.

Harvey's French contemporary René Descartes also included a theory of generation in his philosophical system, based on concepts of matter and motion. He applied this notion to the two-semen hypothesis as a potential mechanism for explaining differentiation from otherwise homogeneous fluids. As an epigenesis theory, it invoked a gradual, sequential differentiation of the embryonic parts, beginning with the heart. He proposed that fermentation-like heat, as from wet hay or bakers' yeast, animated the seminal fluids. Thus, while he considered preformation of relatively solid matter to account for

plant development, he embraced an epigenetic model of animal development in view of the relative fluidity of animal tissues in general, but of animal semen in particular.

Descartes's theory of generation was a part of, and consonant with, his philosophical works, which he tested among friends. Extant letters, however, document his anxiety about the theological implications of his system. He expressed concern that Church dogma had become so imbued with Aristotelian philosophy that to propose alternative theories would be perceived as contrary to faith. Consequently, the details of his theory of generation appeared in 1664, well after his death.

The next significant epigenetic theories of generation appeared nearly one hundred years later, as new observations further illuminated flaws in preformation hypotheses. In his Vénus physique (1745), the mathematician Pierre-Louis Moreau de Maupertuis meticulously dissected preformation theories, ridiculing the logical consequences of their central assumptions. For example, the emboîtement theory required belief in inconceivably small organisms contained within each other. Moreover, ovist preformation neglected paternal resemblance in children, just as animalculist preformation overlooked maternal resemblance. Maupertuis countered with an epigenetic model of generation, which he acknowledged as fundamentally similar to the Hippocratic views on sexual reproduction. To the pangenesis version of the two-semen hypothesis, he appended "attractive forces" to account for the segregation of those particles during embryonic differentiation. Maupertuis sought to explain the sequential development of embryonic form by analogy with the recently established principles of chemical attraction, gravitation, and magnetism. He succeeded to a certain degree in creating an epigenetic theory independent of a vital principle, but it failed to convince preformation advocates. Christian naturalists associated his theory with spontaneous generation and quickly denounced it.

Another epigenetic theory of generation appeared in 1749, published in the second volume of Buffon's Histoire naturelle (Natural History), which bore many similarities to that of Maupertuis, with whom Buffon shared his ideas in the early 1740s. Buffon pointed out that preformation theories placed the issue of generation beyond scientific inquiry, but his intentional omission of divine guidance from his natural history drew the ire of the Sorbonne's Faculty of Theology. Buffon noted that cubes of sea salt grow through the accretion of other, smaller cubes of the same composition and hypothesized that comparable "organic molecules" account for the generation and growth of both plants and animals. To account for the origin of complex form, he postulated species-specific "internal molds," which selected and organized the organic particles into an appropriately formed individual. Though promoted under the banner of epigenesis, Buffon's theory was sufficiently ambiguous and untestable to allow alternative interpretations. In fact, his organic molecules, as irreducible units of life, necessarily place the model in the vitalist category.

It is clear, then, that preformation theories of generation developed in the eighteenth century in opposition to epigenetic theories. They sprang almost invariably from deep religious commitments to biblical literalism or to theological doctrines that specifically denied fundamental autonomy to the process of generation. Both the published accounts from the different schools of thought and the extensive correspondence between several prominent naturalists (see Castellani 1971 [Bonnet-Spallanzani]; Sonntag 1983 [Haller-Bonnet]) clearly indicate a religious point of view among the preformationists. Similarly, epigenesists like Maupertuis and Caspar Friedrich Wolff (1733–94) framed their arguments in terms independent of an appeal to supernatural intervention, adopting the naturalistic point of view of the contemporary Enlightenment philosophes. They included acknowledged deists, who rejected belief in supernatural powers acting in the present world, as well as agnostics and atheists.

Asexual Reproduction, or Parthenogenesis

Aristotle allowed, in the second book of his *Generation of Animals,* that, if there were animals in which only one sex (presumably female) were found, they would be able to generate young ones from themselves. He also related, in his *History of Animals,* the apocryphal anecdote that dissections of pregnant Persian mice revealed pregnant female embryos. And he repeated a story of asexual reproduction whereby, in the absence of a male, the female mice became pregnant by licking salt. Though asexual reproduction in higher animals did not appeal to commonsense experience, Aristotle allowed that it was at least suspected in some quarters.

On the other hand, production of plants from cuttings constitutes perhaps the most widely observed and practiced example of asexual reproduction. The actual

occurrence of asexual reproduction in animals, though inferred prior to the eighteenth century, was not unequivocally demonstrated until Bonnet performed his studies on isolated aphids (1742). Raising several successive generations of individual aphids in isolation, he confirmed the possibility of insect parthenogenesis, yet observed that the same organisms were also capable of sexual reproduction. His discovery provided further fuel for the epigenesis-preformation controversy and, for preformation partisans, lent strong support to the ovist theory of generation. It apparently confirmed the predictions of both Leibniz and Malebranche concerning "zoophytes" (microorganisms), thereby acquiring even greater philosophical weight.

Trembley had almost simultaneously undertaken an elaborate set of observations and experiments on freshwater hydra, or polyps (published in 1744). He discovered their previously unsuspected regenerative abilities, particularly their multiplication by the simple expedient of sectioning, which caused substantial discussion among both epigenesists and preformationists. Contemporary models of epigenesis readily accommodated this extreme of animal regeneration, but Bonnet soon revised his concept of preformed germs, locating them throughout the body of animals like hydra or in particular organs of animals, like crayfish and salamanders, found to have limited regenerative abilities. Generation and regeneration had, thus, become irrevocably linked in these organisms, and theories formulated to address generation from then on would also need to account for regeneration.

Spontaneous Generation

Aristotle had also pioneered a theory of spontaneous, or equivocal, generation. In both *Generation of Animals* and *History of Animals,* he reported that some insects arise from decaying plant and animal matter. John Farley (1977) adds a further, clearly modern, interpretation by distinguishing abiogenesis (in which living things arise from inorganic matter) from heterogenesis (in which spontaneous generation is limited to organic substrata such as decaying plant or animal matter). Heterogenesis also includes the belief that parasites may arise spontaneously within living hosts. In any event, chance or random events define spontaneous generation, making it a theologically objectionable issue. Belief in spontaneous generation also required an associated epigenetic mechanism to account for the generation of complex form from homogeneous, unformed matter. It was, nevertheless, a widely believed mechanism of generation in the first half of the seventeenth century and not only among the uneducated. Its fundamental premise was an extrapolation of the Cartesian principle that all nature was reducible to matter and motion, the clock analogy appearing in several discussions. But counterarguments, including the observation that two clocks placed side by side never produced a little clock, brought the preformation theory back into prominence. "As a result defense of preexistence and attacks upon spontaneous generation became a central tenet of the Christian faith" (Farley 1977, 29).

Francesco Redi's (1626–97) famous experiments of 1668 represent the beginnings of the scientific dismantling of spontaneous-generation theory. But, though Redi provided experimental evidence against the equivocal origin of maggots in decaying meat, he believed that spontaneous generation was possible among microscopic organisms. The ensuing century brought increased scrutiny to the newly discovered microscopic world. John Turberville Needham (1713–81), a French-trained English priest, performed a series of experiments on boiled broths and infusions, which appeared in a report to the Royal Society in London in 1748. Needham claimed to have demonstrated that new organisms arose spontaneously in his boiled and stoppered flasks of broth. But fifteen years later, Lazzaro Spallanzani (1729–99) repeated those experiments, proving that Needham's method was flawed and that his sealed flasks had become contaminated. It now appears that the microscopic animalcules observed by both Needham and Spallanzani were protozoans (single-celled organisms). Bacterial and viral organisms, yet to be discovered, and the process of fermentation provided further examples of potential spontaneous generation for the next century and for Louis Pasteur's (1822–95) final assault on, and dismantling of, that theory.

See also Anatomy and Physiology to 1700; Enlightenment

BIBLIOGRAPHY

Aristotle. *The Complete Works of Aristotle.* Ed. by Jonathan Barnes. 2 vols. Rev. Oxford ed. Princeton, N.J.: Princeton University Press, 1984.

Bonnet, Charles. *Traité d'insectologie ou Observations sur les Pucerons.* Paris: Chez Durand Librairie, 1745.

Buffon, George Louis le Clerc, Comte de. *Histoire naturelle, générale, et particulière, avec la description du Cabinet du roy.* 15 vols. in quarto. Paris: De l'Imprimerie royale, 1749–67.

Castellani, Carlo, ed. *Lettres à M. l'Abbé Spallanzani de Charles Bonnet.* Milan: Episteme Editrice, 1971.

Darwin, Charles. *The Descent of Man and Selection in Relation to Sex.* London: Murray, 1871, Chapter 8.

Dunstan, G. R., ed. *The Human Embryo: Aristotle and the Arabic and European Traditions.* Exeter: University of Exeter Press, 1990.

Farley, John. *The Spontaneous Generation Controversy from Descartes to Oparin.* Baltimore: Johns Hopkins University Press, 1977.

Galen. *On the Natural Faculties.* Trans. by Arthur John Brock. Loeb Classical Library. Cambridge, Mass.: Harvard University Press, 1979.

Gasking, Elizabeth. *Investigations into Generation, 1651–1828.* Baltimore: Johns Hopkins University Press, 1967.

Gilbert, Scott F., ed. *A Conceptual History of Modern Embryology.* Vol. 7 in *Developmental Biology: A Comprehensive Synthesis,* ed. by Leon W. Browder. New York: Plenum, 1991.

Horder, T. J., J. A. Witkowski, and C. C. Wylie, eds. *A History of Embryology.* New York: Cambridge University Press, 1986.

Leibniz, G. W. *Theodicy.* Ed. by A. Farrer. 1710. Reprint. La Salle, Ill.: Open Court, 1985.

Lenhoff, S., and H. Lenhoff, trans. *Hydra and the Birth of Experimental Biology, 1744: Abraham Trembley's Memoirs Concerning the Natural History of the Freshwater Polyp with Arms Shaped Like Horns.* Pacific Grove, Calif.: Boxwood, 1986.

Lloyd, G. E. R. *Greek Science After Aristotle.* New York: Norton, 1973.

Malebranche, Nicolas. *The Search After Truth.* Trans. by Thomas M. Lennon and Paul Olscamp. 1674. *Elucidations of the Search After Truth.* Trans. by Thomas M. Lennon. *Philosophical Commentary,* by Thomas M. Lennon. Columbus: Ohio State University Press, 1980.

Maupertuis, Pierre-Louis Moreau de. *Vénus physique, contenant deux dissertations, l'une sur l'origin des hommes et des animaux: et l'autre, sur l'origine des noirs.* The Hague: Husson, 1745.

Needham, Joseph. *A History of Embryology.* 1959. Reprint. New York: Arno, 1975.

Pluche, l'Abbé Noël-Antoine. *Le Spectacle de la Nature; ou, Entretiens sur les Particularités de l'Histoire Naturelle, Qui ont paru les plus propre à rendre les Jeunes-Gens curieux, & à leur former l'esprit.* Paris: Chez La Veuve Estienne, and Jean Desaint, 1732–5.

Roe, Shirley A. *Matter, Life, and Generation: Eighteenth Century Embryology and the Haller-Wolff Debate.* New York: Cambridge University Press, 1981.

Roger, Jacques. *Les Sciences de la vie dans la pensée française du XVIIIe siècle: la génération des animaux de Descartes à l'Encyclopédie.* Paris: Armand Colin, 1963.

Savioz, Raymond. *Mémoires autobiographiques de Charles Bonnet de Genève.* Paris: Librairie Philosophique J. Vrin, 1948.

Sloan, Phillip R. *Haller on Buffon's Theory of Generation* (selections). In John Lyon and Phillip R. Sloan, eds., *From Natural History to the History of Nature: Readings from Buffon and His Critics.* 1751. Reprint. Notre Dame, Ind.: University of Notre Dame Press, 1981, 311–27.

Sonntag, Otto. *The Correspondence between Albrecht von Haller and Charles Bonnet.* Bern: Hans Huber, 1983.

Trembley, Abraham. *Mémoires, pour servir à l'histoire d'un genre de polypes d'eau douce, à bras en forme de cornes.* Leiden: Verbeek, 1744.

88. GENETICS

Richard Weikart

Religious scientists have contributed much to advances in genetics, from the discoveries of the Austrian monk Gregor Mendel (1822–84) to the work of Francis S. Collins (1950–), the director of the Human Genome Project, who was converted to Christianity by reading C. S. Lewis (1898–1963). However, cooperation has not always characterized the relationship between genetics and religion. Some pioneering geneticists have been materialists searching for a material basis of life. More recently, religious groups have expressed concern over the ethics of genetic experimentation and the uses of genetic technology.

Notions of heredity before the dawn of Mendelian genetics were heavily influenced by philosophical and religious ideas, for no one knew how heredity worked. Biologists in the late nineteenth century debated the merits of Jean Baptiste Lamarck's (1744–1829) theory of the inheritance of acquired characteristics, which had many adherents. Lamarckism waned after 1900, however, when the significance of Mendel's experiments with peas in his monastery garden in the 1860s was recognized. Mendel's work founded genetics by suggesting that peas have pairs of genetic factors that segregate during gamete formation and distribute randomly to offspring. Hugo de Vries (1848–1935), one of the rediscoverers of Mendel, and William Bateson (1861–1926), who coined the term "genetics" in 1905, both believed that Mendelian genetics supported a theory of evolution through saltation. Thomas Hunt Morgan (1866–1945) and Hermann J. Muller (1890–1967), two early pioneers in genetics, adopted the chromosome theory of hereditary transmission, which bolstered their materialist convictions.

Religious opponents of evolution have, since the 1920s, hailed Mendelian genetics as confirmation of their creationist views, since it showed that hereditary changes were primarily the reshuffling of genetic material already present rather than the introduction of new traits. They rejected the prevailing view among biologists that genetic mutations could account for the introduction of beneficial traits. Many Christians and Jews, however, embraced evolutionary theory. One of the major contributors to the Darwinian synthesis, which combined Mendelian genetics with Darwinian natural selection, was Theodosius Dobzhansky (1900–75), a Russian Orthodox Christian.

A great breakthrough in genetics occurred in 1953, when Francis Crick (1916–) and James D. Watson (1928–) proposed the double-helix model for the DNA (deoxyribonucleic acid) molecule, paving the way for molecular genetics. Both men were motivated by their materialist philosophy, hoping that their research would demonstrate that biology can be reduced to physics and chemistry. Indeed, many materialists have interpreted molecular genetics as evidence for their philosophy; more recently, some sociobiologists have argued that religion is merely a genetic trait.

The religious implications of DNA have been interpreted differently by others. The painter Salvador Dali (1904–89) said: "And now the announcement of Watson and Crick about DNA. This is for me the real proof of the existence of God." The complexity of the genetic code is awe inspiring, and apologists for the theistic origins of life have used probability theory to show the impossibility of DNA's arising spontaneously through time and chance.

Greater knowledge of molecular genetics made genetic engineering possible, sparking controversy in the 1970s. Debate over the ethics of genetic experimentation and the use of genetic knowledge intensified in the late 1980s with the advent of the Human Genome Project (HGP), an attempt sponsored by the U.S. government to map all human genes. The HGP set aside 5 percent of its budget to explore the ethical, legal, and social implications of genetics, which include religion. It funded two conferences on "Genetics, Religion, and Ethics" in Houston, Texas, in 1990 and 1992, and also supported studies undertaken by the Center for Theology and the Natural Sciences in Berkeley, California.

The World Council of Churches (WCC) established a commission on genetics and religion in 1971 and issued several statements on genetics thereafter. A statement issued in 1989 supported most forms of genetics research and somatic gene therapy but opposed genetic engineering of the human germline and embryo research. The National Council of Churches' statement of 1986, "Genetic Science for Human Benefit," is very positive about genetics. The United Methodist Church, the United Church of Christ, and the Church of the Brethren have all issued official statements on genetics; generally, they approve of genetic research but want to limit genetic engineering and screening. The American Scientific Affiliation, an association of evangelical Protestant scientists, stated its support for genetics research in 1987 but cautioned against eugenics. Pope John Paul II (b. 1920, p. 1978–) also endorsed genetics research to help cure genetic diseases but opposed the use of genetic knowledge for eugenics or to promote abortion. In May 1995, leaders of every major religious denomination in the United States signed a statement opposing the patenting of genes.

Genetic screening has been a contentious issue in some religious circles because of its implications for abortion. Catholics and conservative Jews and Christians generally oppose prenatal genetic screening except for therapeutic purposes. Almost all Christian and Jewish religious bodies oppose prenatal genetic screening for sex selection. Orthodox Jews in New York and Israel, who suffer from a high incidence of genetically transmitted Tay-Sachs disease, have implemented premarital genetic screening to identify carriers of the disease. The government and the Orthodox Church in Cyprus mandated a similar program of premarital genetic screening for thalassemia, which had almost eliminated the disease by 1986.

Although controversy still surrounds the issue, some geneticists and psychologists have conducted studies allegedly demonstrating a genetic basis for certain forms of behavior, such as alcoholism, homosexuality, and violence. Some argue that genetic determination of behavior invalidates the traditional Christian doctrine of sin. For example, though most Anglican leaders oppose his stance, the bishop of Edinburgh, Richard Holloway, stated in May 1995 that God "has given us promiscuous genes" and that adultery is a God-given genetic trait. However, a small number of religious leaders, including the chief rabbi of England and a few ultraconservative Protestants, have argued that sinful genetic tendencies should be treated as genetic defects and eliminated through genetic engineering.

Most religious leaders and organizations who have addressed the topic have tried to encourage genetic research for the benefits it can confer on humanity but have urged restraint on genetic engineering. They staunchly oppose any attempt at human eugenics, and some oppose altering any species, because they fear that humans will be usurping God's role.

See also Eugenics

BIBLIOGRAPHY

Bowler, Peter J. *The Mendelian Revolution: The Emergence of Hereditarian Concepts in Modern Science and Society.* Baltimore: Johns Hopkins University Press, 1989.

Cole-Turner, Ronald. *The New Genesis: Theology and the Genetic Revolution.* Louisville, Ky.: Westminster/John Knox, 1993.

Crick, Francis. *Of Molecules and Men.* Seattle: University of Washington Press, 1966.

Herron, Frank, ed. *Genetic Engineering.* New York: Pilgrim, 1984.

Kevles, Daniel J., and Leroy Hood. *The Code of Codes.* Cambridge, Mass.: Harvard University Press, 1992.

Nelson, J. Robert. *On the New Frontiers of Genetics and Religion.* Grand Rapids, Mich.: Eerdmans, 1994.

Olby, Robert. *The Path to the Double Helix.* Seattle: University of Washington Press, 1974.

Oosthuizen, G. C., et al., eds. *Genetics and Society.* Oxford: Oxford University Press, 1980.

Wallace, Bruce. *The Search for the Gene.* Ithaca, N.Y.: Cornell University Press, 1992.

Watson, James D. *The Double Helix: A Personal Account of the Discovery of the Structure of DNA.* London: Weidenfeld and Nicolson, 1968.

89. EUGENICS

Edward J. Larson

The theory of eugenics, which dominated American and northern European scientific thinking about human heredity during the early twentieth century, split the religious community along its modernist/traditionalist fault line. Many liberal Protestants, especially those willing to accommodate their religious beliefs to scientific authority, readily accepted a hereditarian view of human physical, mental, and spiritual progress and endorsed the eugenic remedies that followed from that point of view. Roman Catholics and conservative Protestants, in contrast, typically rejected the concept that human progress could be reduced to biology and denounced proposals to limit reproduction by the eugenically "unfit."

English scientist Francis Galton (1822–1911) coined the term "eugenics" in 1883 to identify the science of improving human stock through selective breeding. During the ensuing half-century, Galton's new word and the underlying theory that he had begun to develop from the evolutionary concepts advanced by his cousin Charles Darwin (1809–82) spread throughout North America and northern Europe. Early-twentieth-century developments in genetics bolstered Galton's theory, prompting many prominent scientists to agree that various forms of mental illness and retardation, criminality, and epilepsy were strictly hereditary. Led by the work of biologist Charles Davenport (1866–1944), psychologist H. H. Goddard (1866–1957), and biometrician Karl Pearson (1857–1936), biological and social scientists compiled the staggering toll in crime, degeneracy, and welfare costs allegedly resulting from reproduction by the mentally unfit. They proposed compulsory sterilization, sexual segregation, and marriage restrictions as means to address these social problems. Dozens of American states, Canadian provinces, and northern European countries adopted and enforced such restrictions during the first half of the twentieth century. Perhaps because of the church's traditional authority over issues involving the family and marriage, religious leaders played a major role in the public-policy debate over eugenics.

Eugenicists actively courted the favor of reform-minded clerics. In the United States during the 1920s, for example, the American Eugenics Society (AES) formed a committee for cooperation with the clergy that, among other activities, sponsored eugenics sermon contests. These competitions apparently tapped a reservoir of support because they attracted hundreds of sermons from across the country, mostly by Protestant ministers. The sermons typically proclaimed Christian authority for selective breeding and linked the spiritual advancement of humans to their hereditary endowment. Some traced the eugenic attributes of Christ's pedigree, while others foresaw the millennium arriving through the genetic improvement of humanity. Harry Emerson Fosdick (1878–1969) of New York's prestigious Riverside Church, University of Chicago theologian Charles W. Gilkey, Federal Council of Churches President F. J. McConnell, and other prominent American religious leaders served on AES committees and endorsed eugenic solutions to social problems. At the state level, progressive ministers assumed a visible position lobbying for eugenic-sterilization legislation and marriage restrictions.

The same pattern followed in northern Europe. In England, for example, the convocation of the Church of England and several key Methodist Church leaders endorsed the 1912 Mental Deficiency Bill, a highly controversial eugenics proposal. Leading British eugenicists regularly appealed for support from liberal religious audiences, and Anglican cleric William Inge, Dean of St. Paul's (1860–1954), assumed a prominent role in the national eugenics movement. Theologically liberal ministers provided similar support for eugenic lawmaking in Scandinavia and other Protestant regions of Europe. This apparent alliance of scientific and religious authority in support of eugenic doctrines may simply have reflected the recognition that ministers were effective public spokespersons for the cause, but, clearly, many of these clerics willingly allowed scientific theories to inform their spiritual beliefs.

Despite this visible Protestant support for eugenic doctrine, Galton, Davenport, and other leading eugenicists bitterly denounced the Christian church for opposing scientific progress. In part, these attacks reflected the timing of the eugenics movement, which occurred at the height of the antievolution crusade in America and at a time when secular scholars generally perceived Christianity as historically hostile to science. Eugenicists felt this hostility primarily in the form of vigorous Roman Catholic opposition to sterilization laws, marriage restrictions, and other eugenic measures designed to improve the human race.

Based on its religious commitment to the sanctity of all human life regardless of biological fitness, the Roman Catholic Church emerged as the first major organization to challenge eugenic doctrines. Catholic resistance stiffened as the eugenics movement began advocating sterilization, which the church denounced as violating the "natural law" that linked sexual activity to procreation. Pope Pius XI (b. 1857, p. 1922–39) formally condemned eugenics in a sweeping 1930 encyclical on marriage. Biting essays from the pen of popular British author G. K. Chesterton (1874–1936), a convert to Catholicism, did much to undermine support for eugenics among the educated classes throughout the English-speaking world. Church publications and pronouncements picked up on many of Chesterton's themes and carried them to a wider audience. Wherever eugenic legislation surfaced, local Catholic clergy, lay leaders, and physicians took the lead in opposing it. This opposition proved decisive in defeating eugenic-sterilization laws in such heavily Catholic states as Pennsylvania, New York, and Louisiana; it helped stop eugenics legislation in Britain and prevented the spread of eugenic restrictions to the Catholic regions of Europe and the Americas.

Many conservative Protestants also voiced religious objections to eugenic legislation, especially in the American South, where fundamentalism was strong. Protestant opponents of eugenics generally did not articulate their position as clearly as either Protestant supporters of the cause or its Catholic opponents. Nevertheless, the legislative record is littered with comments by individual Protestants denouncing eugenics as unchristian. Taken as a whole, these comments reflect the view that God controls human reproduction and that neither science nor the state should interfere.

At most, religious objections slowed the spread of eugenic thinking. It took a coalition of critics to defeat it. By the 1930s, an increasing number of social scientists began to favor environmental explanations for human development. Biologists and geneticists also began to question eugenics, especially in response to the excess of Nazi eugenics. Following World War II, scientific support for eugenics disappeared, and religious commentators increasingly cited Nazi practices as an object lesson in the dangers resulting from a society guided by scientific materialism.

See also Genetics

BIBLIOGRAPHY

Allen, G. "The Eugenics Record Office at Cold Spring Harbor, 1910–1940." *Osiris* 2 (1986): 225–64.

Haller, M. *Eugenics: Hereditarian Attitudes in American Thought.* New Brunswick, N.J.: Rutgers University Press, 1963.

Kevles, D. *In the Name of Eugenics: Genetics and the Uses of Human Heredity.* New York: Knopf, 1985.

Larson, E. "The Rhetoric of Eugenics: Expert Authority and the Mental Deficiency Bill." *British Journal for the History of Science* 24 (1991): 45–60.

———. *Sex, Race, and Science: Eugenics in the Deep South.* Baltimore: Johns Hopkins University Press, 1995.

Reilly, P. *The Surgical Solution: A History of Involuntary Sterilization in the United States.* Baltimore: Johns Hopkins University Press, 1991.

Weindling, P. *Health, Race, and German Politics between National Unification and Nazism.* Cambridge: Cambridge University Press, 1989.

PART IX

Medicine and Psychology

90. MEDICINE

Darrel W. Amundsen and Gary B. Ferngren

Medicine may be defined as the art of preserving or restoring health and treating disease, illness, or physical dysfunction by means of drugs, surgical operations, or manipulations. The history of medicine is the history of both the changing concepts of health and disease and the greatly varied social roles and ethical responsibilities of those who seek to preserve or restore health. The former is properly an aspect of the history of science in general and of the biological sciences in particular. The impact of religion on the history of science, in its broadest sense as well as in some of its specific disciplines, is reflected in the history of changing concepts of health and disease. The roles and responsibilities of medical practitioners, while affected by changing scientific concepts, are less features of the history of science than of social, religious, moral, legal, and economic history.

A variety of definitions of health have been given at different times and in different cultures. Health is an imprecise concept. The words for "health" in many languages are semantically related to ideas of wholeness and are virtually synonymous with wellness and even well-being. They may refer to the body, the mind, and the soul. Metaphorical uses of health are virtually limitless. The basic definition of the concept is the absence of disease. The spectrum of disease includes sickness, infirmity, illness, mild physical discomfort, dysfunction, disability, and deformity. Like "health," "disease" and related terms can be used metaphorically and applied to body, mind, and soul.

The World Health Organization has defined health as a "state of complete physical, mental, and social well-being, and not merely the absence of disease or infirmity." This well-known definition makes health virtually indistinguishable from happiness and is so broad as to be essentially meaningless. When health is so construed, it occupies too profound a place in the economy of goods and probes too deeply into questions of ultimate reality and meaning to be limited to the realm of medicine alone. When applied to the history of medicine, especially in its relationship to religion, one must ask whether so comprehensive a definition of health clarifies or obfuscates the pertinent issues.

Sacral Medicine

It is probable that prehistoric peoples melded the natural and the supernatural into a cohesive whole. Well-being depended on living in a state of harmony with all aspects of the environment, which was animated by vague numinous or spiritual presences and able to be manipulated through a complex variety of magico-religious mechanisms that were employed either to maintain or to restore a harmonious equilibrium. Every disturbance could be understood only by discerning the identity and motives of the responsible supernatural agent or human practitioner of malevolent magic. Common physical ills that aroused no awe were viewed symptomatically and treated by the sufferer or family members with herbs or other healing substances. The efficacy of this empirical folk medicine depended on the performance of appropriate magico-religious procedures. We know of no specifically medical practitioners in prehistoric societies; we assume that some individuals may have been sufficiently skilled in treating common ailments that people outside their immediate family solicited their assistance. More serious illness was believed to be a disruptive intrusion of numinous powers. Prehistoric people appear to have believed that every disease was an intrusive entity that required the intervention of the community's shaman, witch doctor, or medicine man. His role, as the culture's most powerful religious authority, was to preserve or restore the health of his community in its broadest sense. Only a part of his responsibilities, however, involved the treatment of illness.

The earliest historical (that is, literate) civilizations of the Near East arose in Egypt and Mesopotamia at the beginning of the third millennium B.C. Although Egyptian and Mesopotamian cultures differed from each other in a variety of ways, they were similar to prehistoric cultures in their conception of the cosmos as divine. Well-being was maintained by being in a state of harmony with deified nature. Any disruption of that state necessitated employing the appropriate religious or magico-religious mechanisms for restoring harmony. If Egyptians or Mesopotamians were afflicted with a condition for which an immediate natural cause was suspected or identifiable, they (or a member of their immediate family) might employ empirical techniques and substances or they might consult a medical craftsman (the *asu* in Mesopotamia, the *swnw* in Egypt), who, in treating acute symptoms, used a wide range of empirical methods supplemented and rendered more effective by a limited use of prayers and incantations.

Egyptians and Mesopotamians viewed any but the most common diseases etiologically rather than symptomatically. The cause was the disease. Determining the identity of the agent was essential for diagnosis and treatment. The agent could be a god, a demon, a dead person, or someone who had the ability to manipulate supernatural powers through malevolent magic. Those afflicted had recourse to a variety of healers, including a priest, a sorcerer, or an exorcist (in Egypt the *sau* and the *wabw*, in Mesopotamia the *ashipu*), who relied on prayer, libations, and incantations. These healers would occasionally employ healing substances such as herbs and drugs.

In primitive and ancient Near Eastern cultures, the all-inclusive concern of religion for the community's health provided the context for a much more limited concern of medicine for the health of the body. The folk medicine employed by family members or by such empirical practitioners as the *asu* and the *swnw* was not based on any theory of disease. The magico-religious medicine practiced by the medicine man (*sau, wabw,* and *ashipu*), however, was the product of a magico-religious classification of disease. Hence, a compatibility prevailed between medicine and religion because the aims of medicine were entirely subordinated to those of religion, and both the system of classification and the therapeutic

model were religious or magico-religious. Since everything that was not readily explicable was believed to have happened for a purpose, sickness had meaning that the magico-religious construct of reality provided through its interpreters. The breaking of a taboo could precipitate divine anger. Sometimes divine anger struck capriciously. Both pernicious supernatural powers and humans who were gifted in the use of malicious magic could inflict disease. The tendency to moralize sickness by rendering its victims sinners in need of repentance was, however, a late development in Egyptian and Mesopotamian religions. Furthermore, in these monolithic, sacral cultures, all aspects of what we call medical ethics (that is, all moral considerations that arise in the actual diagnosis and treatment of sickness) were inseparable from religion.

The ambience changes significantly when we shift our attention to the ancient Hebrews. Insofar as they are known through the Hebrew Scriptures (the Old Testament), they differed considerably from other peoples of the ancient Near East. Their ethical monotheism was predicated upon the belief that God (Yahweh), the Creator of all things, existed apart from nature and that nature depended upon him for its very existence. With the Fall of Adam and Eve in the Garden of Eden, sin and its consequences had entered the world. Suffering, in all of its forms, was effected by God's curse upon both humanity and nature, a curse that included, however, a promise of the reconciliation of God with fallen humanity. The Jews believed that God entered into a special relationship with the descendants of Abraham, who became his chosen people. He established a covenant with them that promised blessings for their faithfulness to him and suffering, including sickness in general and pestilence in particular, if they spurned his love and worshiped other gods.

Biblical Hebrew contains no word for bodily health. *Shalom,* typically translated as "peace," but sometimes as "prosperity, health, wholeness, and safety," occurs more than 250 times in the Old Testament. It was used as the standard Hebrew valediction. While it denoted an inclusive concept of health, *shalom* remained an inherently spiritual well-being that depended on a functional holiness. Illness in the Old Testament was consistently described in spiritual rather than medical terms. Hence, it is surprising that, although Hebrew priests enforced a code of personal and social hygiene and diagnosed various dermatological conditions (including leprosy), there was in Israel no sacerdotal medical practice as there was in Egypt and Mesopotamia. Ample evidence exists that the Jews employed empirical medicine for common ailments, but without the ancillary role of magic, which Hebrew law strictly forbade. While it is possible that some Jews practiced a folk medicine within their communities, there is no evidence of a distinct medical profession.

Desacralized Medicine: The First Phase

In ancient Greece before the late sixth or early fifth century B.C., illnesses appear to have been categorized as either mysterious (and, hence, of divine origin) or common (and, therefore, natural). Empirical medical knowledge and folk medical practice were undoubtedly a part of Greek culture from very early times. As early as the period of the Homeric epics (c. eighth century B.C.), we see medical craftsmen *(iatroi),* who practiced empirical medicine but with little or no reliance on the magico-religious procedures of their ancient Near Eastern counterparts. Their reliance on therapeutic processes rather than on supernatural power suggests a climate conducive to the development of rational medicine.

Mere knowledge of symptoms and use of moderately effective medical techniques do not constitute what may properly be termed a body of knowledge. To be such, medical techniques must be placed within, and made subordinate to, a theoretical framework. Attempts by Ionian philosophers beginning in the sixth century B.C. to explain the world in terms of natural processes rather than by using mythopoeic categories provided the catalyst for the development of rational-speculative medicine by the late fifth century B.C. The development of rational medicine is evidenced in the disparate treatises that came to form the Hippocratic corpus. Shamanistic healers *(iatromanteis)* disappeared from the scene and were replaced, in part, by a variety of healing cults, the most important being that of the god Asklepios, and by the *iatroi,* who were evolving into what may properly be called physicians and whose purview included the entire range of physical ills understood in natural terms.

Naturalistic causality of disease was viewed as primarily physiological rather than ontological. Health was viewed as balance, symmetry, and harmony, while sickness arose from their disturbance. The view that came to prevail, especially as systematized by Galen (A.D. 129–c. 210), was the "humoral theory," which saw health as

the proper binary combination of the four basic elements in nature (earth, air, fire, and water) and the four principal humors of the body (phlegm, blood, yellow bile, and black bile), and sickness as dissonance in their relationship. This model of health and sickness remained dominant until the seventeenth century. Health was, thus, a state in accordance with nature, while disease was contrary to nature. This teleologically based biological model lent itself to a limited moralization of health and disease, insofar as the latter was understood to be precipitated by the individual's lack of self-discipline, especially in diet and sexual activity.

The development of rational medicine did not entail a rejection of traditional Greek religion. Medicine was a divinely bestowed art, and Apollo was its major patron deity. Philosophical naturalism did not make physicians atheists. Greek and (later) Roman religion accommodated without conflict a medical rationalism that understood illness as a natural process without excluding religious explanations of ultimate causality. The kaleidoscopic character of Greek and Roman polytheistic religions and philosophical systems, from the Hellenistic period (323–30 B.C.) on, permitted a rich diversity of explanations of the meaning of sickness, although sickness itself was most commonly seen through a grid of naturalistic causality. This is not to suggest, however, that, after the advent of rational-speculative medicine, no Greek or Roman attributed sickness to demons, magic, or other supernatural sources.

Contact with Greek civilization during the Hellenistic era provided Jews with a rational-speculative medicine that, in its theoretical framework, was religiously neutral when disengaged from the pagan philosophical cosmology that had made its theoretical development possible. Desacralized medicine's religious neutrality allowed for divine explanations of ultimate causality but provided for natural processes of proximate causality within God's created order. As expressed by Jesus ben Sirah (early second century B.C.), since God created both medicine and physicians, a sensible person will not despise them. One should not rely on them apart from God, however, because healing comes from God. Hence, when sick, one should both pray to God for healing and heed the physician who also relies on God (Ecclesiasticus 28:1–14).

The attitudes toward medicine expressed in Christian literature of the first several centuries were, for the most part, as congenial as those that arose in contemporary Judaism. Although some scholars insist that the writers of the New Testament accepted an exclusively demonic causality of disease, apart from reported cases of demon possession (in which there typically is no mention of any abnormal condition other than the possession itself), the authors of the New Testament assumed a naturalistic causality of disease, as did early Christians generally. If they sometimes spoke in a manner that blurred the distinction between ultimate and proximate causation, it was because they believed that the immanent presence of God was operative in natural forces. They viewed Jesus's exorcisms and miraculous healings as signs that the kingdom of God had come, not as normative models for either the understanding of ordinary disease or its healing. All of the church Fathers believed that God's creation was essentially good (that is, that created matter was not inherently and intrinsically evil). They also affirmed that God provided for humanity to sustain itself through the proper use of nature. Hence, it was appropriate for Christians to avail themselves of the services of physicians and the art of medicine but always with the caution that one must not rely exclusively on them, for God may choose to heal through them, to heal without them, or to withhold healing. While prayer for healing without recourse to medicine was always appropriate, recourse to medicine without prayer was thought to be inappropriate.

Furthermore, the Fathers were convinced that healing could be effected by spiritually pernicious forces, whether demonic or magical. Although they were well aware that the art of medicine could be used for egregious and sinful ends, they also recognized its potential for good. The charitable use of medicine was an obvious means of extending Christ's love by applying his command to love one's neighbor as oneself. The visitation, care, and comfort of the sick were duties incumbent upon all believers. Christian physicians were especially commended when they viewed the care of their patients' bodies as an extension of their concern for their souls. By late antiquity, many physicians were also priests. The clerical practice of medicine found its primary outlet in cenobitic (community) monasticism. It was out of the early Christian charitable concern for the sick that the first hospitals arose.

Aggressive missionary activity spread Christianity and Christian attitudes toward medicine and healing throughout Europe. During the early Middle Ages, the church was engaged in a concerted effort to suppress folk paganism. The alternatives that the church offered to the magico-religious healing practiced by the semi-christianized pagans were supernatural healing (medi-ated through sacraments and the cult of saints or relics) and secular medicine (practiced by physicians, many of whom were monks). By the twelfth century, magical-healing practices were regarded less as residual elements of paganism than as heresy.

By the end of the Middle Ages, clerical medical practitioners had, for the most part, been replaced by a secular and licensed medical profession as part of a general laicization of European society. The combination of an effort on the part of the church to suppress the practice of magical healing, especially by women, and the medical profession's sustained struggle to eliminate all unlicensed competitors (regardless of the type of healing that the latter practiced) resulted in a somewhat uneasy but enduring alliance of religious orthodoxy with medical orthodoxy.

Desacralized Medicine: The Second Phase

The Protestant Reformation brought about the breakdown of the religiously monolithic society of the Middle Ages. It had little immediate effect, however, on the understanding of disease and the practice of medicine. The physiological model of disease, which had been dominant since antiquity, was attacked by various disease ontologists like Paracelsus (1493–1541). In spite of the work done in the seventeenth century by Johannes-Baptista van Helmont (1579–1644), William Harvey (1578–1657), and Thomas Sydenham (1624–89), a verifiable doctrine of specific etiology had to await the germ theory of disease, made possible by the invention of the microscope and dramatically confirmed by Robert Koch's (1843–1910) discovery of the tubercle bacillus in 1882. During these centuries, a radical Cartesian dichotomy of body and soul helped foster a mechanistic physiology and pathology. The humoral theory of disease as a state contrary to nature gave way in some quarters to the model of "man against nature" in his war against disease. Although the medical materialism of the Enlightenment encouraged this view, the Romantic movement reemphasized health as a natural state by glorifying primitive man (the "noble savage") in robust health, undefiled and undebilitated by civilization and its attendant ills.

The concept of "diseases of civilization" occasionally manifested itself in the nineteenth-century view that civilization was itself a disease. Although some proponents developed this concept into an ideological model that had implications far beyond medicine, it was difficult to deny that civilization fostered disease, especially given the unwholesome features of urban overcrowding that accompanied the industrial revolution. This awareness stimulated public health and sanitary measures in the nineteenth century, in which scientists, physicians, politicians, and clergy sometimes worked hand-in-hand (though not always without conflict).

It was in the nineteenth century, too, that Darwinism and its stepchild, social Darwinism, made their distinct mark on biological and social concepts of health and disease, along with such secular constructs as psychology and some schools of neurophysiology. The new disciplines, theories, and movements met a variety of reactions from Christians, ranging from welcome acceptance to cautious adoption to strong opposition. The same, however, cannot be said of religious reaction to the major developments that typified medical advances of the nineteenth and early twentieth centuries. Spectacular advances in the fields of anatomy and physiology lent support to philosophically crafted theological arguments for the existence of a natural order in which a Creator appeared to be self-evident. At the same time, the increasing desacralization of medicine was welcomed by many religious bodies. The process was essentially completed in the mid-to-late nineteenth century, when the sometimes uneasy alliance between theological orthodoxy and medical orthodoxy was greatly strengthened. This alliance was precipitated by two developments. First, there was a reaction by mainstream Christianity, on both sides of the Atlantic, against the appeal that medical heterodoxies such as botanical medicine, homeopathy, hydrotherapy, and mind-cure had for a variety of religious sects. Second, the scientific revolutions that established anatomy, physiology, biochemistry, pathology, and bacteriology as the foundational disciplines of medicine made its practitioners appear to be quintessential "objective neutrals" in the theological arena.

The thorough desacralization of classificatory and therapeutic models, which removed medicine and its practitioners from the realm of religion, was to remain a fundamental feature of what became the dominant scientific model of medicine in the West. Nevertheless, until quite recently, the compartmentalization of medicine and religion was not complete. An overlap remained between religion and medicine because Western society was, although not monolithic, united by a moral consensus, in which Judeo-Christian morality governed medical ethics. In the last third of the twentieth century, a new prevailing model of social policy and law began to emerge. As Western societies rapidly became pluralistic and secular, the Judeo-Christian consensus broke up; Christianity was aggressively pushed out of the public sphere and, with it, the Judeo-Christian basis of medical ethics. A utilitarian approach (now called consequentialism) took its place. Medical ethics came to be defined by the lowest common moral denominator and increasingly regulated by econometrics and cost-benefit analysis. Owing to this growing compartmentalization of medicine and religion, tension arose between those who promoted a secular model and those who (mostly from a religious point of view) regarded its results and implications in the clinical arena, in the courts, and, indeed, in the community at large as gravely detrimental to society's health.

Tensions continued to exist between the practitioners of secular medicine and the small minority of Christians who regarded supernatural intervention as the only appropriate form of healing. Compatibility, however, has been and generally remains the defining characteristic of the relationship of Christianity and secular medicine, although it is still not uncommon to encounter the popular misconception that Christianity has traditionally sought to obstruct the advancement of science in general and medicine in particular. So compatible has this relationship become that it has contributed to the nearly total demise of the age-old Christian conviction that not all healing comes from God and is necessarily consistent with his purposes. Moreover, throughout the history of Christianity, sickness has regularly been emphasized in spiritual literature as a salutary catalyst to personal self-examination and repentance from sin. This theme is so contrary to the spirit of the late twentieth century that it too has largely disappeared.

Resacralized Medicine

Religion has never been well served when it has ignored current scientific models. But it has been seriously weakened when it has sought to adapt its understanding and articulation of ultimate verities to contemporary paradigms (including models of health and disease), which over time have tended to give way to new ones. The medical materialism of Enlightenment secularism led some optimistic observers, especially during the nineteenth century, to believe that science would prove man to be a wholly material being. A few even looked forward to a time when the clergy would be supplanted by physicians and to a utopia in which all disease and even death itself would be conquered.

In the twentieth century, many infectious "killer" diseases have been conquered only to be replaced by new ones, especially by those that afflict the increasingly large proportion of the population who are elderly. Old enemies such as cancer have remained, while new contagious threats like HIV/AIDS and ebola have come to mock modern medical security. Although statistical life expectancy has continued to rise, the biological life span has remained unchanged. For realists, the hope of a utopia of unlimited health has faded. At the same time, however, the clergy have been increasingly displaced by physicians and therapists. Religion has come to be gradually, and not always subtly, subsumed under medicine, as the realm of medicine has expanded to include physical or emotional therapy for virtually every perceived personal or social ill, inadequacy, or dysfunction. In a modern therapeutic society, religion has begun, in some circles, to be redefined and absorbed by medicine. This new pattern perhaps reflects the hope of achieving the ultimate realization of the World Health Organization's definition of health, but in a manner so broad that it either demedicalizes the concept of health altogether or medicalizes every deviation from its nearly absolute ideal of well-being. It has resacralized society within the cocoon of a new spirituality constructed along therapeutic lines that, as an inversion of sacral medicine, with which we began, is in many respects not dissimilar to it.

See also Anatomy and Physiology to 1700; Epidemic Diseases

BIBLIOGRAPHY

Amundsen, Darrel W. *Medicine, Society, and Faith in the Ancient and Medieval Worlds.* Baltimore: Johns Hopkins University Press, 1996.

Amundsen, Darrel W., and Gary B. Ferngren. "Medicine and Religion: Pre-Christian Antiquity." In *Health/Medicine and the Faith Traditions: An Inquiry into Religion and Medicine,* ed. by Martin E. Marty and Kenneth L. Vaux. Philadelphia: Fortress, 1982, 53–92.

———. "Medicine and Religion: Early Christianity Through the Middle Ages." In *Health/Medicine and the Faith Tradi-*

tions: An Inquiry into Religion and Medicine, ed. by Martin E. Marty and Kenneth L. Vaux. Philadelphia: Fortress, 1982, 93–131.

Brown, Michael L. *Israel's Divine Healer.* Grand Rapids, Mich.: Zondervan, 1995.

Ferngren, Gary B. "The Imago Dei and the Sanctity of Life: The Origins of an Idea." In *Euthanasia and in the Newborn: Conflicts Regarding Saving Lives,* ed. by R. M. McMillan, H. T. Engelhardt Jr., and S. F. Spicker. Dordrecht and Boston: Reidel, 1987, 23–45.

———. "Early Christian Views of the Demonic Etiology of Disease." In *From Athens to Jerusalem: Medicine in Hellenized Jewish Lore and in Early Christian Literature,* ed. by S. Kottek, G. Baader, G. Ferngren, and M. Horstmanshoff. Rotterdam: Erasmus, 2000.

Kinnier-Wilson, J. V. "Medicine in the Land and Times of the Old Testament." In *Studies in the Period of David and Solomon,* ed. by I. Ishida. Winona Lake, Ind.: Eisenbrauns, 1982, 337–65.

Kocher, Paul H. "The Idea of God in Elizabethan Medicine." *Journal of the History of Ideas* 11 (1950): 3–29.

Léonard, Jacques. "Women, Religion, and Medicine." In *Medicine and Society in France,* ed. by Robert Forster and Orest Ranum. Baltimore: Johns Hopkins University Press, 1980, 24–47.

Numbers, Ronald L., and Darrel W. Amundsen, eds. *Caring and Curing: Health and Medicine in the Western Religious Traditions.* 1986. Reprint. Baltimore: Johns Hopkins University Press, 1997.

Numbers, Ronald L., and Ronald C. Sawyer. "Medicine and Christianity in the Modern World." In *Health/Medicine and the Faith Traditions: An Inquiry into Religion and Medicine,* ed. by Martin E. Marty and Kenneth L. Vaux. Philadelphia: Fortress, 1982, 133–60.

Pagel, Walter. "Religious Motives in the Medical Biology of the Seventeenth Century." *Bulletin of the Institute of the History of Medicine* 3 (1935): 97–120.

Sheils, W. J., ed. *The Church and Healing.* Studies in Church History 19. Oxford: Blackwell, 1982.

Tackett, Timothy. *Priest and Parish in Eighteenth-Century France: A Social and Political Study of the Curés in a Diocese of Dauphiné, 1750–1791.* Princeton, N.J.: Princeton University Press, 1977.

Temkin, Owsei. *Hippocrates in a World of Pagans and Christians.* Baltimore: Johns Hopkins University Press, 1991.

Walsh, James J. *The Popes and Science: The History of the Papal Relations to Science During the Middle Ages and Down to Our Own Time.* New York: Fordham University Press, 1908.

Watson, Patricia Ann. *The Angelical Conjunction: The Preacher-Physicians of Colonial New England.* Knoxville: University of Tennessee Press, 1991.

91. EPIDEMIC DISEASES

Darrel W. Amundsen and Gary B. Ferngren

The word "epidemic" is often employed metaphorically, but it is sometimes difficult to tell whether a literal or a metaphorical meaning is intended, in such phrases as "an epidemic of sports injuries" and "an epidemic of smoking-related deaths." Epidemics, as we shall use the word, are diseases that suddenly strike a community and in time either entirely abate, or nearly so, or else become endemic (long-term but not especially alarming) features of a society's pathological environment, once their virulence has significantly diminished. Such terms as "plague" and "pestilence" are typically used as conceptually imprecise synonyms of the word "epidemic."

As far back as human history extends, we find accounts of communities' having been afflicted by widespread diseases that eventually subsided. The reaction of any given society to these phenomena is, in some ways, similar to its reaction to disease generally. Hence, in societies in which reality is seen primarily through a magico-religious lens, all sicknesses for which an obvious "natural" cause is not discernible necessitate the intervention of experts who can determine the causal agent and his (or her or its) motives. Propitiating that agent's wrath or counteracting his power are essential to restoring wellness. Homer's (second half of the eighth century B.C.) *Iliad* provides a well-known example. The poem begins by describing a plague that has afflicted the Greek forces besieging Troy. The Greeks had no doubt about who inflicted this calamity on them. Apollo, "who strikes from afar," had for nine days been aiming his pestilent arrows at his victims, with the result that piles of corpses were being burnt. On the tenth day of the affliction, a seer was consulted to determine why Apollo was angry. The cause was easily discerned, the deity propitiated, and the plague removed.

Rational-speculative explanations of the causes of illness in general and of specific illnesses in particular developed with the rise of Hippocratic medicine in Greece in the fifth century B.C. As a result, the mysterious features of *immediate* causality disappeared or at any rate diminished significantly in popular perceptions. The development of a rational-speculative framework for practicing medicine produced an expectation that physicians were, first and foremost, products of a "scientific" training and orientation. In other words, a popular expectation arose, which has henceforth prevailed in the Western world, that physicians deal with disease and other physical ailments both rationally and empirically, not magically, mystically, or superstitiously. The frequent failure of the therapeutic procedures that were the products of nosological systems, which, we can say today, had little if any "scientific" basis, typically did not reduce popular respect for these systems and their interpreters. Popular stirrings of skepticism for medical practitioners, however, were sometimes stimulated by epidemics because they could do virtually nothing other than explain, consistently with prevailing nosological paradigms, the causes of epidemics and their own incapacity to treat their victims efficaciously.

In 430 B.C., during the second year of the Peloponnesian War (431–404 B.C.), Athens was stricken with a devastating plague. The historian Thucydides (c. 460–c. 400 B.C.), who himself was afflicted with the plague, gives a nearly clinical (but still inconclusive) description of the symptoms and course of the disease. He notes that physicians were unable to help the afflicted because they did not know the disease's nature, origin, or causes (*Peloponnesian War* 2.47.4 and 48.3). He describes the devastating effects of the plague on public morals. No fear of gods or law of men restrained the basest, for they believed that the worst penalty they could suffer was the plague itself, which was indiscriminately laying waste both the pious and the impious (2.52.3 and 53.1–4). Thucydides laconically remarks that supplications at sanctuaries and appeals to oracles were all futile, and, as the plague continued to flourish, people desisted from such religious exercises (2.53.4).

The naturalistic understanding of disease causality contributed, in some quarters, to philosophical attacks upon religion. Epicureanism, the doctrines of which are summarized in the *De rerum natura (On the Nature of Things)* of Lucretius (c. 99– 55 B.C.), is the best-known example. Lucretius's didactic poem breaks off with an explanation of the nature of disease that culminates in a gripping description of the great plague of Athens. Although he does not include a denunciation of religion in this probably unintended conclusion to his work, the pervasive theme of the entire poem is that naturalistic understanding of the natural order itself frees humanity from the fear that both created and sustained religious beliefs and practices. It is ironic that the tranquility of mind that Epicureanism sought to foster should be undercut by the dramatically crafted description of the agony and hopelessness of humanity in the face of an exceptionally virulent plague.

The nonreligious perspective of Thucydides and the antireligious emphasis of Lucretius did not typify popular attitudes in classical antiquity. Especially devastating natural disasters (whether floods, famines, or plagues) have stimulated not only popular religious fervor, but also the tendency to look for scapegoats. During the early centuries of the Christian era, natural disasters evoked persecution of Christians on the ground that toleration of these "atheists" had provoked the wrath of the gods. Christians had themselves inherited a tradition that attributed natural disasters, including epidemics, to God's wrath. Not only had God inflicted "plagues" on the Egyptians and later on various enemies of the children of Israel, but, when the Hebrews left Egypt, God promised them blessings if they were faithful to him and sufferings if they spurned his love. Repeatedly in the Hebrew Scriptures (the Old Testament), God (Yahweh) juxtaposed threats of punishment for unfaithfulness with the promise of restoration for repentance and blessings for covenant faithfulness. Prominent among the threats was the triad of sword, famine, and pestilence (mentioned fourteen times in Jeremiah alone). Apocalyptic passages also warned of eschatological horrors that included plagues

and pestilences (for example, Is. 19:22; Zech. 14:12 ff.). This theme became an important feature of New Testament apocalyptic in the Book of Revelation.

Christian theology has typically accepted the natural causality of disease, while at the same time it has asserted the belief in God's ultimate sovereignty and inscrutable providence in all spheres of nature and history. Because epidemic diseases cause widespread and extensive human suffering, they have often been seen either as evidence of God's wrath or as portending the last times. Even when their natural etiologies have been explained to the satisfaction of both the medical community and popular opinion, epidemics have excited religious explanations of their ultimate purpose and meaning. Sixteen waves of plague afflicted Europe from A.D. 541 to 767. As a result, many Christians initially relapsed into pagan practices. But the long-term effect was to stimulate repentance and renewed attention to religious observances. After a lull of several centuries, Europe was smitten by the devastating Black Death of 1348–9. Attempts to explain its etiology consistently with prevailing nosological models were varied, imaginative, widely accepted, and therapeutically ineffective. Efforts by the church to diagnose and treat the moral or spiritual ills that were believed to have precipitated the plague sometimes conflicted with medical advice to guard against it and civic efforts to contain it. Seeking scapegoats in various groups, especially among Jews, in some communities was spawned by the combination of terror, helplessness, and popular prejudice.

After the Black Death, periodic episodes of plague swept Europe until the 1660s. Popular reactions to the Black Death and subsequent scourges of plague ranged from calls to repentance to a sometimes cavalier and sometimes despairing licentiousness, as its real causes— hence, its prevention and cure—continued to elude medical understanding. Clergy stressed repentance as the best prophylactic; physicians, a healthy regimen; and governmental officials, restrictive containment. What all three of these groups typically shared was a conviction that natural disasters, especially epidemics, were visitations of the wrath of God upon humanity for sin in general or for prevailing sins in particular. Usually, they identified the most rampant sins of the community as having precipitated God's righteous judgment, which he intended to lead to conviction, repentance, reformation, and spiritual restoration. When the "epidemic" of what was later called syphilis arose in 1494, even though the venereal nature of its transmission soon became patent, the primary sources indicate that the theological response of clerics, physicians, and magistrates was to view this new scourge as God's wrath visited upon society because of a variety of egregious sins, among which sexual immorality was not prominently named.

The seventeenth century witnessed the beginning of widespread epidemics of smallpox, which reached their peak in the eighteenth century. In the nineteenth century, a number of pandemics of cholera occurred. These two diseases (smallpox and cholera) are benchmarks in the history of the relationship of epidemiology to religion. Although smallpox was initially subject to theological explanation or interpretation, it soon faded with the development of effective means of prevention. The fight against smallpox was led in North America by the Puritan minister Cotton Mather (1663–1728), who, in 1721, promoted inoculation through variolation. He was opposed primarily by some members of the medical profession (as well as by James Franklin and his newspaper) who argued that the procedure was not only unsafe, but also interfered with God's will. As variolation was replaced by the safer and more effective technique of vaccination, clerical support for inoculation continued, and medical opposition nearly ceased. Even William Douglass (c. 1691–1752), Mather's chief critic, endorsed inoculation before the mid-eighteenth century.

When pandemic outbreaks of cholera occurred in the first half of the nineteenth century, they provoked the same theological responses that earlier epidemics had drawn. Repentance and moral reformation were seen as the only prophylaxis. But, by the 1860s, the cause of cholera had been convincingly traced to contaminated water supplies. Improved sanitation was manifestly its only truly effective preventive. During the next decade, the germ theory of disease stimulated bacteriologists to search for microbial causes of most diseases, including those that we call epidemic.

Belief in God's direct and immediate involvement in human sickness had long before begun to diminish, however, even in the minds of the devoutly religious, with the rise of rational-speculative medical theories. But it persisted, even for the nominally religious, as a means of accounting for epidemics for which there were no explanations that could be translated into prevention or cure. When smallpox was shown to be preventable through inoculation, and cholera through sanitation, and when the etiologies of other diseases were rendered comfort-

ably specific by germ theory, God receded into irrelevance, or at least into the background, for the vast majority of people. But as the *pax antibiotica* that has created the apparent medical security of the modern age recedes in the face of HIV/AIDS, with its moral implications, and new viral scourges such as ebola, concerns about the meaning of epidemics will direct some people to their religious traditions for explanations. Within the theistic traditions, the explanation of disease in terms of natural causation does not preclude belief in an ultimate cause in terms of God's action in the world, even if his specific purposes remain hidden from human understanding by the mystery of divine providence.

See also Medicine; Theodicy

BIBLIOGRAPHY

Amundsen, Darrel W. "The Moral Stance of the Earliest Syphilographers, 1495–1505." In Amundsen, Darrel W. *Medicine, Society, and Faith in the Ancient and Medieval Worlds.* Baltimore: Johns Hopkins University Press, 1996, 310–72.

Biraben, J.-N., and Jacques LeGoff. "The Plague in the Early Middle Ages." In *Biology of Man in History: Selections from the Annales: Economics, Sociétés, Civilisations,* ed. by R. Forster and O. Ranum. Trans. by E. Forster and P. M. Ranum. Baltimore: Johns Hopkins University Press, 1975, 48–80.

Cipolla, Carlo M. *Faith, Reason, and the Plague in Seventeenth-Century Tuscany.* Ithaca, N.Y.: Cornell University Press, 1979.

Coleman, William. *Death Is a Social Disease: Public Health and Political Economy in Early Industrial France.* Madison: University of Wisconsin Press, 1982.

———. *Yellow Fever in the North: The Methods of Early Epidemiology.* Madison: University of Wisconsin Press, 1987.

Cook, Noble David, and W. George Lovell, eds. *"Secret Judgments of God": Old World Disease in Colonial Spanish America.* Norman: University of Oklahoma Press, 1992.

Duffy, John. *Epidemics in Colonial America.* Baton Rouge: Louisiana State University Press, 1953.

Gribben, William. "Divine Providence or Miasma? The Yellow Fever Epidemic of 1822." *New York History* 53 (1972): 283–98.

Jones, Colin. "Plague and Its Metaphors in Early Modern France." *Representations* 53 (1996): 97–127.

Klairmont, Alison. "The Problem of the Plague: New Challenges to Healing in Sixteenth-Century France." *Proceedings of the Fifth Annual Meeting of the Western Society for French History* 5 (1977): 119–27.

Lobo, Francis M. "John Haygarth, Smallpox, and Religious Dissent in Eighteenth-Century England." In *The Medical Enlightenment of the Eighteenth Century,* ed. by Andrew

Cunningham and Roger French. Cambridge: Cambridge University Press, 1990, 217–53.

Martin, A. Lynn. *Jesuit Accounts of Epidemic Disease in the Sixteenth Century.* Kirksville, Mo.: Sixteenth Century Journal Publishers, 1996.

Nutton, Vivian. "The Seeds of Disease: An Explanation of Contagion and Infection from the Greeks to the Renaissance."

Medical History 27 (1983): 1–34. Reprinted in Nutton, Vivian. *From Democedes to Harvey: Studies in the History of Medicine.* London: Variorum Reprints, 1988, XI 1–34.

Rosenberg, Charles E. *The Cholera Years: The United States in 1832, 1849, and 1866.* Chicago: University of Chicago Press, 1962.

92. EUROPEAN PSYCHOLOGY

Wade E. Pickren

While the history of psychology as a distinct academic discipline in Europe is relatively short, its origins can be traced to a matrix that was formed by religion and philosophy. Accounts of the beginnings of modern psychological inquiry usually begin with developments that occurred in the seventeenth century, when a change occurred in the dominant discursive practice, from a focus on the moral and the religious to the epistemological (that is, how we know). This shift made the psychological, rather than the theological, central.

British Empiricism and Its Critics

It was John Locke (1632–1704) who provided the intellectual foundation on which a protopsychology could be erected. Locke developed his views on the nature of mind in a complex political and religious context. He came of age during the turmoil of the English Revolution, which had pronounced religious overtones, and he began his philosophical writing as the monarchy was being restored. Disturbed by the civil and religious conflict, which he saw as emanating from an overemphasis on personal ambition and extreme self-centeredness, yet unwilling to deny the importance of individual rational choice and action in both religion and politics, Locke sought an explanation for human thought that would retain individual instrumentality in these matters as well as provide an orderly basis for civil society. By the time of the publication of his *Essay Concerning Human Understanding* (1690), Locke had succeeded in developing a conception of human nature that was individualistic, atomistic, and mechanical. By focusing on epistemology, Locke was able both to avoid an overt clash with theology and to give an account of human knowing that was

based principally on the senses. His empiricism insisted that sense evidence was foundational for accurate knowledge and that only this evidence was necessary for making truthful propositions about what can be known.

Locke's work was part of a larger debate about the nature of ideas, whether they were immaterial or corporeal, and was related to the question of the role of God in inspiring thought or making it possible. Locke asserted that there are only two sources of ideas: sensation and reflection. Sensation is the result of sensory stimulation, in which the things and objects of the material world impinge upon our sense organs. Reflection is the innate faculty of the mind that enables humans to perceive, organize, and examine the sensations provided by our sense organs. Reflection, then, is for Locke the psychologizing of human experience and understanding. It is not due to the direct action of God, though God or divine reason may be the ultimate source of the faculty of reflection. Ideas, what humans know and can know, and the limits and possibilities of human understanding are the result of experience. By establishing the sources of human understanding in sense experience, Locke suggested the limits of what can be known. We know ourselves by intuition and we know God by reason; all other knowledge is due to sense experience. Locke's approach, while acknowledging God, was secular, and it incited a great deal of controversy.

The chief points on which the debate centered were the nature of soul and the basis of human understanding. By the end of the controversy, the immortal soul was no longer the topic of serious philosophical discussion, and the senses were established as the principal source of human knowledge. While many tomes addressed the issues, most of them by individuals who are no longer of major interest, the work of Bishop George Berkeley

(1685–1753) remains significant. Berkeley provided the first enduring philosophical response to Locke.

Like Locke, Berkeley worked from an empirical standpoint: The senses were the ultimate fount of knowledge. Unlike Locke, however, he wished to ground knowledge once again in theology in order to avoid the skepticism that was possible if Locke's epistemology was followed to its conclusion. Berkeley interpreted Locke's epistemology as placing the final ground of knowledge in sensation apart from God. If ideas form the base of knowledge, and if we perceive ideas of real objects, how can there be assurance of correspondence between our ideas and the real objects? Berkeley answered that matter is never directly perceived. Belief in matter comes through inference, and it is perception that gives substance to our inferences. In Berkeley's famous phrase, *Esse est percipi* (To be is to be perceived). How ideas correspond to objects in the "real" world is not the question, since there is no direct apprehension of matter, only perception. Perception, in turn, is grounded in God. God's perception of the physical world is what makes it possible, and he allows our ideas to correspond to the physical world, thus giving us a sense of knowing the real world. Berkeley's assertion of the primacy of God in sustaining the world and our perception of it is at the heart of his argument, while his theory of visual perception is the introduction to his main argument. In this view, which has been termed "idealism" or "immaterialist monism," there is no division between matter and spirit. The universe is spiritual, sustained by God, and animated by his will.

While Berkeley's works were well known, their arguments were unable to counter the movement toward secular explanations of psychological phenomena. The Newtonian metaphor of mechanics, at first applied to the natural world and then to humans, which was apparently supported by sensationist and associationist accounts of human knowing and perceiving, was nearly irresistible to the intelligentsia of England and much of Continental Europe. One of the last grand attempts to marry older theological notions to the new empiricist, mechanical accounts was made by the English physician David Hartley (1705–57). Hartley employed the Lockean principle of the association of ideas and the Newtonian understanding of sensations as vibrations to forge a programmatic account of the human mind and behavior. His doctrine of vibrations supposed that environmental stim-

uli caused vibrations in nerves, which, in turn, caused vibrations in the brain. The latter are experienced as ideas, the mental representation of the environmental event that caused the vibrations in the nerves to begin with. When we experience events close in time, they become associated in memory, Hartley added, and the more frequently they are experienced together, the stronger the association. Such associations, if repeated often enough, will become permanently represented in the brain. The principles apply even to groups of experiences. Entire clusters of associated experiences can become linked to one another in such a way that the reexperiencing of any one association may lead to the recall of the entire cluster. The context of these proposals by Hartley was solidly religious. Hartley developed his theory to show that Christianity is true and compatible with natural theology.

If Hartley's approach can be viewed as an attempt, like Berkeley's, to keep God in accounts of human knowing, then David Hume (1711–76) can be viewed as agreeing with Berkeley that we can know only our subjective experience. In his accounts of human knowing, Hume, a skeptic and practical atheist, rejected the necessity of God. He did not believe that God guaranteed the veracity of our perceived relation between our ideas and the physical world. Further, he was not certain that our ideas did, in fact, correspond to the physical world. His *Treatise of Human Nature* (1739–40) addresses the possibilities and limitations of human understanding.

Hume's *Treatise* is an attempt to offer a complex and complete psychological theory on which to build a true science of man. The British associationist and empiricist tradition finds its most articulate expression in this work. Hume begins by offering a categorization of the contents of human minds. Perceptions, which are based on experience, are of two types: impressions and ideas. Impressions include sensations and strong emotions. Ideas are copies or the residue of impressions. Impressions and ideas may be simple or complex. A simple impression is an unanalyzable sensation, while complex impressions are due to input from multiple sensory sources. Simple ideas are copies of simple impressions, and complex ideas are due to the association of simple ideas. Impressions, for Hume, are more reliable than ideas because they have a closer connection with perceptual reality. Truth may be arrived at by analyzing ideas into their constituent impressions, so that, when ideas are found to have no empirical content, they are to be rejected. Hume argued that ideas of theology are in this category, and he rejected them.

Hume was not the first to use the principles of association of ideas, but he developed them in a novel way. For Hume, these principles were the chief tools of philosophical and psychological inquiry. He asserted three basic principles of association: resemblance, contiguity, and cause and effect. Resemblance is the principle that similar ideas will cluster together; contiguity is the principle that, when things are experienced together in time, they become associated with each other; cause and effect is the principle that, when we experience things together, the one that occurs first leads us to perceive it as the cause and the second event as the effect. Hence, cause and effect originate in contiguity; one notices A first, then B, and draws the conclusion that A caused B. Hume asserted that we can never directly perceive causes. Since our perception is subjective, we can never know with certainty that our conclusions about cause and effect are true. How, then, do humans come to believe in cause and effect? Through experience. Throughout our lives, we regularly experience many conjunctions of events in which the preceding event appears to cause or lead to the second event, and so we come to believe in cause and effect. We cannot, however, rationally prove cause and effect.

Hume reduced cause and effect to a psychological experience and opened the door to a radical skepticism. Even the experience of self is cast into doubt, since all we can experience is a perception of self. These experiences are linked together in an associative manner to give us a sense of self-coherence, but, upon close inspection, this coherence may dissolve. In this sense, Hume may be seen as the first to make the psychological a central issue in philosophy. Humans operate within the natural world, not above it. In formulating human nature and understanding in this manner, Hume stepped outside religion and theologically based explanations of human nature. He established the foundation of human knowledge, belief, and identity on the psychological.

A counter to the skepticism of Hume was the approach of the Scottish school, principally Thomas Reid (1710–96) and his student Dugald Stewart (1753–1828). Both insisted on a commonsense account of knowledge. We can, Reid asserted, believe our senses and so know the world in a direct, unmediated way. Reid argued against associationism and espoused a nativist position: Humans are born with certain innate faculties that facilitate knowledge of the world and are imbued with moral qualities. Reid and Stewart were intent on establishing a natural philosophical base for moral behavior. Accounts of human understanding were necessary to establish such a base.

The Continental Enlightenment

While British thinkers debated the role of God in psychology during the eighteenth century, the situation was different in France. Those who were concerned with giving an account of human understanding were, for the most part, clearly anticlerical in their views. Psychological inquiry held a prominent place among the French philosophes of the Enlightenment. The tone of much of this inquiry was frankly irreligious. Influenced by Locke's empirical psychology and René Descartes's (1596–1650) speculative physiology, French philosophes sought to place all knowledge on a strictly human basis. From La Mettrie's concept of man as a machine to Condillac's reductionist sensationalism to Claude Helvetius's (1715–71) extreme environmentalism, French naturalism postulated a psychology that did not need a metaphysics to undergird it.

The mechanistic approach of Julien Offray de La Mettrie (1709–51) may serve as one example. In a revisionist reading of Descartes, La Mettrie claimed that Descartes's true message was a materialistic account of all human thought and action. His *L'Homme Machine* (*Man a Machine* [1748]) claims a continuity of thought from the lowest animal to the highest. All are part of nature and differ only in degree. All activity, including the highest form of human activity, is due to physiological laws and so can be explained mechanically. In La Mettrie's view, man is best studied by science, not theology; in fact, theologians are not even qualified to explain human activity. Another example of French materialist approaches to psychological ideas is found in the work of Étienne Bonnot de Condillac (1715–80). Working in the Lockean tradition, Condillac proposed an even more materialist account of human understanding by suggesting that all mental experience is derived from simple sensations. Imagine a statue, Condillac suggested, that has the sense of smell and is sensitive to pleasure and pain. No other faculties are initially present in this statue. Through these simple experiences (sensations), the statue could accumulate more and more complex experiences and eventually come to know as humans know. Condillac, in this proposal, denies even the necessity of powers of reflection and attention, with which Locke had begun his epistemology. These French philosophes were typical in that they sought to understand what it means to be human without reliance on theological or moral categories.

While empiricist and sensationist philosophers proposed passive accounts of the human mind and understanding—that, prior to experience, the mind is blank and experience actively fills the blank—the influential German philosopher Immanuel Kant (1724–1804) sought to show that the human mind is active and participates in providing a basis for human knowledge. The mind, Kant argued, is regulated by principles inherent in it. Hence, it cannot be explained by principles of association based in experience alone; it must organize and structure our experience of the world. For example, Hume had proposed that we believe in cause-and-effect relationships because we learn by association to do so; it is a mental habit. Kant proposed instead that we believe in cause and effect because there are mental structures that humans have that organize our experience in this way. The world is constructed so that every event is determined, and our experience can never violate that truth. The possibility of thinking in terms of causation does not come from experience, in other words, but is a priori and independent of experience. The mind has innate categories that structure our experiences; sense data are transformed and given meaning on the basis of preexistent categories. These innate categories include concepts of unity, totality, cause and effect, reality, negation, possibility/impossibility, and existence/nonexistence.

Behind this world of things seen, the phenomenal world, Kant suggested that there exists a world of *noumena,* or things-as-they-are. In this noumenal world, there may be things that do not follow the laws of the world as it is seen. Moral responsibility and freedom belong to this noumenal world, as does God. Since human reason does not apply to this world of things-as-they-are, it is useless to try to prove the existence of God. God is never known directly and, hence, cannot be proved to exist or not to exist. Although Kant asserted that there cannot be an empirical psychology because its data cannot be objective and thus quantifiable, his work has had an enduring effect on psychology. From Kant's time onward, the debate about the relative importance of innate factors versus the necessity of experience has con-

tinued and still influences work in child development, perception, and language.

Nineteenth-Century British Psychology

By the nineteenth century, psychology had become secularized, and religious issues had ceased to be central to discussions of human understanding. By the end of the century, religion was an afterthought in the scientific work, if not the personal lives, of most of those who saw themselves as psychologists. While Locke, Hume, Condillac, and, to a lesser degree, Kant had developed their psychologies in the context of religious and theological controversy, those who were most directly their legatees in the development of psychology as an academic scientific discipline seldom addressed religious topics. Man's place in nature, assumed for so long to be distinct from and above the rest of nature, was called into question by the publication of Charles Darwin's (1809–82) *Origin of Species* (1859). If Darwin was correct, then man was not a special creation but on a continuum with all other animals, while mind was part of nature.

The consequences of Darwin's thought for psychology were many. His work led to an emphasis on the function of the mind and the role that mind plays in man's adaptation to the demands of survival. Through the work of his cousin Francis Galton (1822–1911), Darwin influenced the development of a psychology of individual differences and the study of the psychology of religion. Galton investigated a wide array of topics during his lifetime. He was a developer and promoter of the use of statistics to measure psychological abilities. Galton employed the use of correlational techniques to investigate the efficacy of prayer. He concluded that there was no correlation between being prayerful and being healthy, living long, or having influential children. Galton also studied the use of religious imagery and reverence.

The influence of Darwin may also be found in James Ward (1843–1925), the father of modern British psychology, who adopted a functionalist approach to psychology. He first trained as a minister, then as a physiologist, before turning to psychology and, finally, to philosophy. An early crisis of faith turned him away from the ministry and led him to reject associationist notions of knowledge. In his research and writing, which became increasingly philosophical, Ward rejected atomistic accounts and proposed that the role of perception and intellect is to facilitate human adaptation to the environment. Although Ward rejected traditional Christianity, he developed a theistic position that argued for purpose in the universe, a position that, he held, depended on faith rather than on empirical evidence.

Continental Psychology

Meanwhile, in Germany during the nineteenth century, the influence of Kant on psychology was manifold: It inspired both an idealist and an empirical approach to philosophical and psychological inquiry. Indeed, Kantian idealism gave to psychology its principal subject matter and problem: consciousness. The great post-Kantian idealist Gustav Fechner (1801–87) developed psychophysics as the first true measurement of psychological functions. His work was informed by a panpsychism in which all material substances, including humans, animals, plants, and the earth, have consciousness, their "souls" all being part of the one great "soul" of the universe. Fechner sought to discover the exact relation between mind and body by quantitatively measuring the relation between physical stimulation and the experience of sensations.

Another Kantian, Wilhelm Wundt (1832–1920), developed a cultural or folk psychology that was concerned with a broad social perspective on psychological processes. In this regard, Wundt was following Friedrich Hegel (1770–1831), who had argued for the primacy of the social and the group over the private and the individual. Wundt argued that the higher mental processes, including language, myth, and religion, could be understood only by taking this broad perspective. Wundt attempted to place religion within an evolutionary framework that begins with humans projecting their emotions onto material objects. These projections lead to myth, which eventually leads to religion. Religion is the higher expression, which seeks to connect our experience to meaning.

Following in this tradition, Karl Girgensohn (1875–1925) used laboratory-based empirical methods of experimental introspection to investigate the psychological aspects of religious experience. Girgensohn eventually formed his own school, known as the Dorpat School of Religious Psychology, whose members investigated many psychological aspects of the religious life, with their results usually published in their own scholarly journal. A rival group, the Vienna Research Institute for the Psychology of Religion, was formed in 1922 by Karl Beth (1872–1959) and his followers. The Vienna group sought to go beyond the strictures of the laboratory to investigate individual differences in religious experience. In particular, the question of developmental processes in religion concerned Beth and his colleagues.

Investigations of the relation between psychology and religion in Germany in the years between the World Wars included the work of Otto Grundler on the structure of religious acts and of Wilhelm Koepp on the typology of religious experience. Eduard Spranger (1882–1963), a student of the great polymath Wilhelm Dilthey (1833–1911), was a philosopher, psychologist, and educator. Spranger formulated a complex typology of personality within an existential-interpretive framework. In particular, he was interested in what he called the religious type, who is wholly oriented to the intense experience of the highest values.

The psychodynamic tradition that emerged from the work of Sigmund Freud (1856–1939) also addressed religion. Freud was openly antireligious, claiming that religious beliefs are rooted in Oedipal processes of fear of the all-powerful parent. Religion is the product of the human psyche and is irrational. Psychoanalysts in the Freudian tradition typically continued this critique of religion, though there were a few, such as Oskar Pfister (1873–1956), who saw religious belief as an aid to growth. Carl Jung (1875–1961), the Swiss psychiatrist who had a brief and intense friendship with Freud, took a very different approach to religion in his depth psychology. Jung argued that religion is an essential function of the human experience. Self-actualization, according to Jung, is promoted by an integration of archetypes that are symbolic expressions of the deepest and most enduring aspects of human reality. Religion has been one avenue for the expression of these archetypes, Jung believed, and may serve the individual in the process of growth and integration of the personality.

In France, the principal relation between psychology and religion developed within the broader context of philosophy and was furthered in the context of psychopathology. Maine de Biran (1766–1824) is often cited as the father of modern French psychology. He suggested that psychological knowledge could be gained through introspection, physiological studies, and comparative work, as well as psychopathology. Biran also suggested that religious feeling and mystical experience were part of a total psychology. Auguste Sabatier (1839–1901) argued that psychological factors were the foundation of religious life. Sabatier was widely influential, for example, on the young Jean Piaget (1896–1980).

Biran's influence is seen most profoundly in the work of French psychopathologists, who were the first to investigate the clinical relationship between religion and psychological dysfunction. Jean Charcot (1825–1893), Pierre Janet (1859–1947), Theodule Ribot (1839–1916), and Ernest Murisier (1867–1903) all were interested in the similarities between mystical-ecstatic religious states and various types of psychological disturbance. This emphasis on psychopathology of religious states drew an enduring response from the Roman Catholic Church. Henri Delacroix (1873–1937), a Catholic psychologist, argued that the unusual experiences of Christian mystics reflected psychological health rather than disorder. Additional works by Catholic psychologists extended Delacroix's argument and eventually led to the establishment of a journal of psychology and religion, which ended publication only in 1960.

During the early twentieth century, a distinguished line of French and Swiss psychologists helped shape the modern psychological view of religion. Theodore Flournoy (1854–1920) investigated religious phenomena associated with both normal and pathological states. He addressed the question of individual differences in religious experience and wrote about his work with mentally disordered individuals who had profound religious experiences. Flournoy's influence was present in the development of a tradition of the scholarly study of psychology and religion that was centered in Geneva. The most prominent figure in this tradition was Georges Berguer (1873–1945). Berguer advocated a scientific theology that was deeply psychological. He drew on the work of Jung and other depth psychologists to illuminate the importance of symbolic representations of divinity to psychological growth and health. Psychology, in Berguer's approach, was a means to fostering a deeper spirituality. Meanwhile, Pierre Bovet (1878–1965) focused on religious development. A longtime director of the Jean Jacques Rousseau Institute in Geneva, Bovet advocated a developmental sequence of religious feeling that moves from a focus on the parents to a focus on nature to a focus on God.

Jean Piaget is best known for his work on cognitive development in children. Less well known is the role that religion played in Piaget's life. As a youth, Piaget combined his burgeoning interest in science with an intense involvement in the Swiss Christian youth movement.

When Piaget took a position at the Rousseau Institute in 1921 at the age of twenty-five, he organized a group to investigate the psychology of religion. His principal question was how to balance faith with scientific objectivity. Along with presenting papers on the topic, Piaget began his lifelong research into cognitive development in children. A primary focus in these early years was the development of moral reasoning in children. Piaget came to reject any need for a transcendent element in moral reasoning. His psychology of religion was parallel to his psychology of cognitive development: As the latter proceeded from egocentrism and concreteness to objectivity and abstractness, so religious development proceeded from dogmatic belief to liberal Protestantism based on immanence.

See also Baconianism; Phrenology; Psychology in America; Theories of Religious Insanity in America; Theories of the Soul

BIBLIOGRAPHY

Arens, Katherine. *Structures of Knowing: Psychologies of the Nineteenth Century.* Dordrecht: Kluwer, 1989.

Ash, Mitchell G., and William R. Woodward, eds. *Psychology in Twentieth Century Thought and Society.* Cambridge: Cambridge University Press, 1987.

Boring, Edwin G. *A History of Experimental Psychology.* New York: Appleton Century Crofts, 1957.

Burnham, John C. "The Encounter of Christian Theology with Deterministic Psychology and Psychoanalysis." *Bulletin of the Menninger Clinic* 49 (1985): 321–52.

Funkenstein, Amos. *Theology and the Scientific Imagination from the Middle Ages to the Seventeenth Century.* Princeton, N.J.: Princeton University Press, 1986.

Gay, Peter. *The Enlightenment: An Interpretation.* Vol. 1: *The Science of Freedom.* New York: Knopf, 1969.

Hearnshaw, L. S. *A Short History of British Psychology, 1840–1940.* London: Methuen, 1964.

Hergenhahn, B. R. *An Introduction to the History of Psychology.* Belmont, Calif.: Wadsworth, 1986.

Leahey, Thomas H. *A History of Psychology: Main Currents in Psychological Thought.* Englewood Cliffs, N.J.: Prentice-Hall, 1987.

MacLeod, Robert B. *The Persistent Problems of Psychology.* Pittsburgh: Duquesne University Press, 1975.

Richards, Graham. *Mental Machinery: The Origins and Consequences of Psychological Ideas.* Part I: *1600–1850.* Baltimore: Johns Hopkins University Press, 1992.

Richards, Robert J. *Darwin and the Emergence of Evolutionary Theories of Mind and Behavior.* Chicago: University of Chicago Press, 1987.

Spiegelberg, Herbert. *The Phenomenological Movement.* The Hague: Nijhoff, 1965.

Symondson, Anthony, ed. *The Victorian Crisis of Faith.* London: SPCK, 1970.

Teich, M., and R. Young, eds. *Changing Perspectives in the History of Science.* Dordrecht: Reidel, 1973.

Turner, Frank M. *Between Science and Religion: The Reaction to Scientific Naturalism in Late Victorian England.* New Haven, Conn.: Yale University Press, 1974.

Wagar, W. Warren, ed. *European Intellectual History Since Darwin and Marx.* New York: Harper Torchbooks, 1966.

Woodward, W. R., and M. G. Ash. *The Problematic Science: Psychology in Nineteenth-Century Thought.* New York: Praeger, 1982.

Wulff, David M. *Psychology of Religion: Classic and Contemporary Views.* New York: Wiley, 1991.

Young, R. M. *Mind, Brain, and Adaptation in the Nineteenth Century.* New York: Oxford University Press, 1990.

93. PSYCHOLOGY IN AMERICA

Jon H. Roberts

P rior to the late nineteenth century, when psychologists began to detach themselves from the field of philosophy and align themselves with the natural and social sciences, Americans characteristically regarded the investigation of the nature and operation of the human mind and behavior as a "science of the soul" (Fay 1939, 6). No group more avidly participated in developing that science than clergymen and religious thinkers. Although Roman Catholics were preoccupied with setting down roots in American soil and dealing with "bricks-and-mortar" issues, American Protestants, vitally interested in expressing their faith within theological categories, made concerted efforts to address psychological issues in analyzing the nature of the divine-human encounter. As a result, theology and psychology existed in a complex and often intellectually rich symbiosis.

The Colonial Period

During the seventeenth century, medieval patterns of thought had not yet entirely given way to more modern categories of analysis. Psychological discussion in the British Colonies of North America was almost exclusively the preserve of American clergymen-theologians in the Protestant Reformed tradition. These individuals conceived of the human being as a microcosm of the entire universe. In common with the way in which they viewed other aspects of nature and society, they tended to analyze the powers, or "faculties," that humans possessed in hierarchical terms. At the apex of this hierarchy was the endowment that distinguished human beings from other living things: a "rational soul." There was essential unanimity among Americans who discussed human nature that this soul comprised the understanding and the will and that those two faculties had been weakened

and distorted by original sin. As a result, the self was a "troubled monarchy" (Holifield 1983, 48) that was constantly threatened with rebellion from the lower appetites and passions. Insofar as psychological issues evoked controversy at all in the seventeenth century, it tended to center on the precise nature of the hierarchical relationship between the will and the understanding. A few clergymen were "intellectualists," who held that the will was subordinate and obedient to the understanding. Most, however, took the "voluntarist" position that the will could act independently of the understanding, often exploiting human emotions—the "affections"—in sinful ways.

For the clergy who participated in psychological discussions, knowledge of the nature of the human mind was not simply a matter of abstract interest. It was, rather, an issue crucial to their vocation as pastors charged with the responsibility of caring for their parishioners' souls and helping them interpret their religious experience. Reformed theology bred introspection, and, although the clergy were convinced that only God could extend the grace necessary for salvation to sinful humanity, they believed that, through skillful interaction with their parishioners—a kind of seventeenth-century variant of psychotherapy—they could help allay doubts, temper sinful proclivities, cultivate piety, and encourage members of their flock to confess before God their faithlessness, their idolatry, their pride, and their disobedience as a prelude to the repentance necessary for salvation.

During the eighteenth century, views of human nature continued to shape and, in turn, be shaped by analyses of the divine-human encounter and the scheme of redemption. Undoubtedly, the event that was most decisive in shaping these analyses was the Great Awakening of the 1730s and 1740s. Both the supporters and the opponents of the often dramatic events associated with the Awakening could agree in embracing a dualistic view of the relationship between mind and body and a hierarchical view of human faculties. They also agreed that the Fall had disrupted the proper balance of those faculties. Nevertheless, the Awakening served as the occasion for intense debates over the relative importance of the understanding and the affections in shaping the lives of human beings, the degree to which the will obeyed the understanding in shaping lives, and the nature of conversion. Supporters of the Awakening tended to emphasize the preeminence of the affections as God's instrument in conferring his grace on human beings. They also characteristically viewed conversion as a dramatic supernatural infusion of divine grace. Opponents of the Awakening, by contrast, tended to emphasize the salience of the understanding in humanity's encounter with God and a more gradual, less crisis-oriented view of spiritual rebirth.

A few religious intellectuals, most notably Jonathan Edwards (1703–58), used the Awakening as the occasion for promulgating an essentially new vision of human nature, characterized by the inseparable unity of the will, the affections, and the understanding within the soul. Such a unity, Edwards maintained, more clearly captured the complexity of the soul and God's interaction with it than either an emotional or an intellectualist view of spirituality. Edwards also borrowed John Locke's (1632–1704) concept of "simple ideas" to convey his belief that the converted enjoyed an immediate, inward apprehension of spiritual truth. No less important, in his intellectually masterful *Freedom of Will* (1754), which sought to reconcile Calvinist views of predestination with Christian affirmations of human responsibility, Edwards set the terms for discussions about the nature and freedom of the will that continued for more than one hundred years.

Psychology and Religion to 1870

The debates concerning human nature sparked by the Awakening continued throughout the eighteenth century and did much to ensure that psychological issues would continue to occupy center stage in much of the discourse of American intellectuals. By 1800, however, the penchant of clergymen and theologians for thinking in hierarchical terms and the sense of the ubiquity of supernatural activity that underlay those debates had somewhat waned. In their place were a more egalitarian view of the faculties and a more staid, predictable view of

the divine-human encounter. In large measure, these new emphases were a function of a heightened appreciation for balance and intelligibility, fostered by the Enlightenment. In colleges and pulpits alike, Americans expressed their allegiance to the more moderate precepts of the Enlightenment by embracing Locke's emphasis on experience and the importance of the understanding, Baconian empiricism, and Scottish Common Sense realism. As a result of these commitments, psychological concerns continued to play an important role in shaping the philosophical and theological perspectives of educated Americans.

By the 1820s, professors of mental and moral philosophy and natural theology in American colleges were routinely commending the "scientific" study of the mind in accordance with the inductive methodology of Francis Bacon (1561–1626). This methodology, which involved the careful use of introspection to observe the data of consciousness, disclosed the existence of a set of principles, or "laws," that shaped human thought and behavior. The "science of the soul" that emerged from this procedure constituted the foundation of philosophy and theology alike. The nature of the human mind, pedagogues urged, provided the basis for assertions about the nature of God and the operations of divine government. Just as often, however, American moral and mental philosophers held that the existence of God constituted the basis for believing in the veracity of the perceptions and inferences made by the human beings created in his image. However, academic philosophers chose to relate human psychology and Christian apologetics, though they united in proclaiming their commitment to the desirability of creating a Christian civilization. This commitment led them to shift the emphasis away from truths conveyed in the Scriptures and from the converted—the beneficiaries of a special infusion of divine grace—and to focus on truths about nature and society that were accessible to all people. This more open, democratic orientation extended to their view of the individual mind as well. Increasingly, they abandoned a hierarchical view of the faculties in favor of an emphasis on the desirability of a balanced harmony of the intellect, the emotions, and the will.

Although clergy at the parish level acknowledged the importance of understanding the human mind, they valued this understanding primarily because they believed that it would assist them in altering sinners' wills and changing their hearts. In the more Arminian theological climate of the nineteenth century, sin came to be viewed less as a state of being than a determinate act of volition. Thus, to these clergy it was of paramount importance to exploit the affections and the intellect in persuading human beings to use the power of their wills to turn away from sin.

Underlying the views of Christians concerning human nature in the period prior to 1870 was their conviction that a sharp distinction existed between mind and body. Not surprisingly, therefore, most Christians in the United States looked with great suspicion on any doctrine or theory that questioned that conviction. One such view was phrenology, a doctrine developed during the early nineteenth century by the German physician Franz Joseph Gall (1758–1828) that sought to move the study of the mind from the realm of philosophy to that of biology. Gall and his disciples maintained that the faculties of the mind, the sites of distinct personality traits, were localized in specific areas of the brain and that the relative strength of these faculties determined the shape of the brain and, in turn, the shape of the skull. From this perspective, they reasoned that it would be possible to account for human character traits and behavior by examining the protrusions, or "bumps," of the skull. When phrenology came to the United States during the 1820s, it attracted a great deal of attention and support in some scientific circles. However, Christian thinkers commonly assailed it as a materialistic and deterministic theory masquerading as science. One writer in the Unitarians' *Christian Examiner,* for example, denounced phrenology for turning the "beautiful region of mental philosophy . . . into a barren *Golgotha,* or place of sculls. . . . [T]his carnal philosophy, with its limited conceptions, its gray truisms, its purblind theories, its withering conclusions, and its weary dogmatism is to supplant the lofty faith of antiquity, and the sublime philosophy of the Bible, and to sit in judgement on the Infinite and Eternal!" (Davies 1955, 68). Although a number of practicing Christians within the scientific community, such as Benjamin Silliman (1779–1864) and Edward Hitchcock (1793–1864), insisted that concerns about phrenology's irreligious implications were unfounded, phrenology remained the object of a good deal of suspicion within the American religious community.

The Growth of Psychology, 1870–1945

Although the popularity of phrenology in the United States waned after 1850, it proved to be merely the advance guard for a series of concerted and successful efforts to convert psychology into a discipline that was oriented toward natural science. In the late nineteenth century, many American thinkers committed themselves to bringing to the study of the human mind an approach comparable in rigor to that already employed in studying natural phenomena in the physical and biological worlds. The largest group of these thinkers were the "new psychologists" in the nation's burgeoning colleges and universities. These individuals became convinced that it was time to separate psychology from speculative philosophy by applying the methods associated with the natural sciences to the study of the human psyche. The theory of organic evolution, which denied that human beings were utterly unlike other animals and held that the human mind, like the human body, was a product of transmutation, was instrumental in convincing these thinkers that the mind was a legitimate object of scientific investigation. No less important, the work of European physiologists and psychologists, which suggested the interdependence of mental and neurophysiological processes, furnished American psychologists with a number of experimental techniques that proved useful in examining and measuring human consciousness.

Notwithstanding the fact that proponents of the new psychology were often strident in their support of experimentalism, this mode of investigation only supplemented philosophical speculations; it did not replace them. Many of the pioneers in modern scientific psychology, such as William James (1842–1910), George Trumbull Ladd (1842–1921), G. Stanley Hall (1844–1924), and James Mark Baldwin (1861–1934), hoped to use psychology to refute materialism and preserve at least some role for spiritual values. Often, psychologists sought to ingratiate themselves with college officials and gain the support of the American public by implying that psychological experimentation would undermine the efforts of those intent on reducing the data of consciousness to neurophysiological processes. In the end, however, scientific psychology proved instrumental in extending the realm of naturalistic discourse into the human mind.

The work of the new psychologists, coupled with the ideas of Sigmund Freud (1856–1939) and other partisans of psychotherapy, found an interested—and often concerned—audience among American religious thinkers. As in the earlier period, Protestants dominated the discussion within the public arena. During the late nineteenth century, American Protestant thinkers, motivated by the desire to make Christianity seem credible and relevant, emphasized the centrality of human experience in their discussions of God and the Christian scheme of redemption. As a result, their interests inevitably converged with those of psychology. This convergence was more diffuse and generally less fraught with heated exchanges among the partisans than the well-known disputes over Darwinism and other issues surrounding the biological and physical sciences. Nevertheless, students of American history who are interested in showing the persistence of tension between science and religion during the twentieth century can hardly do better than to look at issues relating to the nature of the human mind, for mind and personality have continued to be contested turf throughout the twentieth century.

During the period after 1870, psychology impinged on religious thought in three major ways. First, it provided a means of analyzing religious phenomena. Psychologists of religion such as Edwin Diller Starbuck (1866–1947), George A. Coe (1862–1951), and James Leuba (1867–1946), used autobiographical records, introspection, and questionnaires to analyze religious experience, the nature of conversion, the components of worship, and a variety of other religious ideas and practices. The most notable of these works was undoubtedly William James's *The Varieties of Religious Experience* (1902), which quickly became a classic in the literature of Christian spirituality as well as the psychology of religion. James presented detailed accounts of the religious experience of individuals of widely disparate beliefs, historical eras, and geographical areas to show that religion made significant differences in the way people thought and lived. James, though not personally pious, remained sympathetic to religious impulses throughout his life. For him, the human subconscious was the path through which God "actually exerts an influence, raises our centre of personal energy, and produces regenerative effects unattainable in other ways" (James 1902, 523).

The work of psychologists of religion promoted existing tendencies toward an anthropocentric rather than a theocentric orientation of religion and tended to discount the significance of theology. Not surprisingly, the response of American Protestant thinkers to the psychological approach to religion was strongly dependent on prior theological commitments. Liberal Protestants, wedded to science, tended to look on the psychology of religion and its implications with approval. By contrast, evangelicals, fundamentalists, and those half-siblings of

liberals during the 1930s—the neo-orthodox—repudiated psychologism and its approach to religion. In fact, the work of psychologists of religion was one of a number of factors that proved decisive in prompting conservative Protestants to assume a more aggressive stance in defending theism in general and Christian theology in particular. It was equally important in convincing the neo-orthodox that the psychological approach to religion was a dead end and that renewed emphasis should be given to theology.

Psychology also provided Americans in the period after 1870 with a series of therapeutic strategies intended to help people realize their potential and modify their behavior. As in the case of their response to the psychology of religion, Christians' response to psychotherapy was strongly informed by prior theological commitments. Whereas conservatives tended to see problems associated with humanity's emotional, and even intellectual, life primarily in terms of sin, liberals tended to be more willing to use the secular language of maladjustment. While conservatives described their goals in terms of eternal salvation, liberals were more inclined to assume that personality integration on a high moral plane—"self-realization"—was an appropriate end in itself. Even most liberals, however, acknowledged that mere mental "health" was a woefully modest object of human aspiration. In this spirit, Granville Mercer Williams (1889–1980), the pastor of St. Paul's Episcopal Church in Brooklyn, New York, reminded his readers that Christians "are called not only to make men happy, which is the goal of psychology; but to go further, and make men saints, which is the goal of religion" (Williams 1927–8, 209).

Finally, in the name of science, psychologists advanced a series of propositions about the nature of mind and its relationship to the external world. In the case of both behaviorism and Freudianism, the two most comprehensive approaches to psychology in the twentieth century, these propositions embraced both scientific naturalism and determinism. More generally, these interpretations of mind seemed to many psychologists to be incompatible with religious concepts such as the soul and spiritual interpretations of mind and personality. It is, therefore, little wonder that, in both 1916 and 1934, questionnaires indicated that psychologists were less likely to believe in God and immortality than any other group of scientists. For their part, Protestant liberals, evangelicals, fundamentalists, and the neo-orthodox joined forces with Roman Catholics in denouncing those versions of psychology as unscientific and dangerous. It seems clear that those religionists were successful in convincing Americans that individuals can play a significant role in shaping their destinies. Prior to 1945, the source on which most Americans drew, in their reflections about the mind and self and their place in nature and society, was not experimental psychology, psychoanalysis, or even the multifarious secular "self-help" traditions; it was religion.

The Postwar Period

After about 1945, many Christians in the United States, in common with other Americans, turned a more favorable eye toward secular psychology. Although they continued to reject psychological propositions that conflicted with major tenets of their faith, their opposition became, as one historian has put it, "increasingly selective" (Burnham 1985, 341). They also became more enamored of the therapeutic dimensions of psychology. In large measure, this was because the ideas and the language of many of the most popular psychologists of the day—Erich Fromm (1900–80), Erik Erikson (1902–94), Carl Jung (1875–1961), Carl Rogers (1902–87), and, more recently, M. Scott Peck (1936–)—were somewhat more solicitous toward religion than had been those of their predecessors. In some respects, the seeming rapprochement was misleading. Psychologists continued to be among the least religious members of the academic community. Moreover, psychotherapists have remained less favorably disposed toward traditional religious beliefs and values than the American population as a whole. Nevertheless, the period since World War II has seen a greater emphasis on pastoral psychology and an increase in psychotherapeutically oriented works among liberal Christians. Proponents of "New Age" religions have also given hearty endorsement to the works of Carl Jung, Carl Rogers, and other psychotherapists sympathetic to religion. Even evangelicals have become more positive in their attitudes toward psychology. To be sure, they have continued to warn against substituting faith in psychology for faith in the Christian gospel, and they have remained convinced that the emotional problems attending human life can be truly resolved only by attending to the Christian message of sin and salvation. But they have become more amenable to psychotherapy's interpretation of the human condition. Some, most notably Clyde

M. Narramore (1916–) and James Dobson (1936–), have even devoted sustained attention to the task of presenting psychotherapeutically oriented works from an evangelical perspective. Meanwhile, at least a minority of academic psychologists sympathetic to the Christian worldview have argued that, in light of the important similarities between religious and scientific approaches to understanding the cosmos, it is now time to develop a more "constructive" relationship between psychology and religion. All in all, the support of Americans sympathetic to the spiritual dimension of life is one of the major reasons for the rise of the postwar "therapeutic culture" and for psychology becoming, as one recent commentator has put it, "the creed of our time" (Herman 1995, 1).

See also Baconianism; European Psychology; Phrenology; Theories of Religious Insanity in America; Theories of the Soul

BIBLIOGRAPHY

Albanese, Catherine L. *America, Religions, and Religion.* 2d ed. Belmont Calif.: Wadsworth, 1992.

Beit-Hallahmi, Benjamin. "Psychology of Religion, 1880–1930: The Rise and Fall of a Psychological Movement." *Journal of the History of the Behavioral Sciences* 10 (1974): 84–90.

Blau, Joseph L. *Men and Movements in American Philosophy.* Englewood Cliffs, N.J.: Prentice-Hall, 1952.

Browning, Don S. *Religious Thought and the Modern Psychologies: A Critical Conversation in the Theology of Culture.* Philadelphia: Fortress, 1987.

Burnham, John C. "The Encounter of Christian Theology with Deterministic Psychology and Psychoanalysis." *Bulletin of the Menninger Clinic* 49 (1985): 321–52.

Davies, John D. *Phrenology, Fad and, Science: A Nineteenth-Century American Crusade.* New Haven, Conn.: Yale University Press, 1955.

Fay, Jay Wharton. *American Psychology Before William James.* New Brunswick, N.J.: Rutgers University Press, 1939.

Fiering, Norman. *Jonathan Edwards's Moral Thought and Its British Context.* Chapel Hill: University of North Carolina Press, 1981a.

———. *Moral Philosophy at Seventeenth-Century Harvard: A Discipline in Transition.* Chapel Hill: University of North Carolina Press, 1981b.

Fuller, Robert C. *Mesmerism and the American Cure of Souls.* Philadelphia: University of Pennsylvania Press, 1982.

Herman, Ellen. *The Romance of American Psychology: Political Culture in the Age of Experts.* Berkeley: University of California Press, 1995.

Holifield, E. Brooks. *A History of Pastoral Care in America: From Salvation to Self-Realization.* Nashville: Abingdon, 1983.

James, William. *The Varieties of Religious Experience: A Study in Human Nature.* 1902. Reprint. New York: Longmans, Green, 1914.

Jones, Stanton L. "A Constructive Relationship for Religion with the Science and Profession of Psychology: Perhaps the Boldest Model Yet." *American Psychologist* 49 (1994): 184–99.

Leuba, James H. *The Belief in God and Immortality: A Psychological, Anthropological, and Statistical Study.* Boston: Sherman, French, 1916.

———. "Religious Beliefs of American Scientists." *Harper's Monthly* 169 (1934): 291–300.

Meyer, D. H. *The Instructed Conscience: The Shaping of the American National Ethic.* Philadelphia: University of Pennsylvania Press, 1972.

Misiak, H., and V. M. Staudt. *Catholics in Psychology.* New York: McGraw-Hill, 1954.

Narramore, Clyde M. *Counseling with Youth at Church, School, and Camp.* Grand Rapids, Mich.: Zondervan, 1966.

O'Donnell, John M. *The Origins of Behaviorism: American Psychology, 1870–1920.* New York: New York University Press, 1985.

Roberts, Jon H. "The Human Mind and Personality." *Encyclopedia of the United States in the Twentieth Century,* ed. by Stanley I. Kutler. 4 vols. New York: Scribner, 1996, 2:877–98.

Vitz, Paul C. *Psychology as Religion: The Cult of Self-Worship.* Grand Rapids, Mich.: Eerdmans, 1977.

Watt, David Harrington. *A Transforming Faith: Explorations of Twentieth-Century American Evangelicalism.* New Brunswick, N.J.: Rutgers University Press, 1991.

Williams, Granville Mercer. "Psychology and the Confessional." *American Church Monthly* 22 (1927–8): 197–209.

Wulff, David M. *Psychology of Religion: Classic and Contemporary Views.* New York: Wiley, 1991.

Young, Robert M. "The Role of Psychology in the Nineteenth-Century Evolutionary Debate." In *Historical Conceptions of Psychology,* ed. by Mary Henle, Julian Jaynes, and John J. Sullivan. New York: Springer, 1973, 180–204.

94. THEORIES OF RELIGIOUS INSANITY IN AMERICA

Ronald L. Numbers, Janet S. Swain, and Samuel B. Thielman

The association of excessive religious enthusiasm with madness dates back to antiquity, but it was not until the seventeenth century that the former acquired definition as a distinct disease. In *The Anatomy of Melancholy* (1621), the Anglican vicar Robert Burton (1577–1640) coined the term "religious melancholy" to describe the often intense religious experiences of Puritans and other sectarians. As the medical historian George Rosen observed in a pioneering essay on religious enthusiasm, "it is quite likely that the sectarian ranks included individuals whose mental and emotional balance was at the least precarious," but it seems equally probable, as the historian Michael MacDonald has argued, that the "ruling elite" at times used the concept of religious insanity to discredit socially disruptive religious dissidents such as the Puritans.

With the rise of Methodism in the eighteenth century, talk of religious insanity in the English-speaking world shifted from the Puritans to the even more enthusiastic followers of John Wesley (1703–91). Under the influence of Wesley's preaching, anxious listeners would sometimes drop "as dead," experience temporary blindness, tremble violently, tear their clothes, or groan and shout loudly. Wesley reported numerous cases of madness associated with his ministry, and, between 1772 and 1795, the Hospital of St. Mary of Bethlehem in London (better known as Bedlam) admitted ninety patients allegedly suffering from "religion and Methodism." By the middle of the eighteenth century, writes MacDonald, "the idea that religious zeal was a mental disease had become a ruling-class shibboleth," widely acknowledged by both medical and lay opinion. By the nineteenth century, medical authorities commonly used the term "religious insanity" to connote an etiologically distinct mental disease.

In the first major American work devoted to the subject of insanity, *Medical Inquiries and Observations Upon the Diseases of the Mind* (1812), Benjamin Rush (1746–1813), arguably the most influential physician in the United States in the early nineteenth century, noted that 10 percent of the fifty "maniacs" then residing in the Pennsylvania Hospital owed their misfortune to "erroneous opinions in religion," especially ones that burdened the pious with unbearable guilt. Rush expressed particular concern about the baleful effects that often accompanied "researches into the meaning of certain prophesies in the Old and New Testaments," noting that madness associated with such activity arose "most frequently from an attempt to fix the precise time in which those prophesies were to be fulfilled, or from a disappointment in that time, after it had passed."

American Revivalism

The wave of revivals that passed over the United States in the early 1800s, characterized by protracted meetings that involved days of nearly constant preaching and praying, seemed only to confirm the connection between religious enthusiasm and insanity. For example, the American evangelist Charles G. Finney (1792–1875), who rose to prominence in the mid-1820s, sometimes reduced whole congregations to wailing and writhing, ostensible manifestations of the Holy Spirit. When on occasion the excitement and fear generated by his sermons pushed a poor soul over the brink of sanity, Finney tended to blame the victim, saying that he had "made himself deranged by resisting" the Spirit.

Such goings-on naturally attracted the attention of physicians who cared for the insane—and prompted one of them, Amariah Brigham (1798–1849), to write a controversial book on religion and mental health, in which he attributed the "outward signs" associated with revivals to overstimulation of the nervous system rather than to the "*special outpouring of the Spirit of God.*" In New England and New York alone, for the period from 1815 to 1825, Brigham knew of more than ninety instances in which "religious melancholy" had led to suicide—and an additional thirty cases that had resulted in attempted murder. The implication that clergymen could not distinguish between "the ravings of the insane or semi-insane and the operations of the Holy Spirit," to use Frederick A. Packard's (1794–1867) description, did not go unchallenged. As Packard explained in the *Princeton Review:* "An enthusiast preaching wildly would at once pass among us for an insane man, and his influence would extend but little if at all beyond those who are predisposed to the same class of mental aberrations or already under their power."

The American religious revivals of the early nineteenth century coincided with—and indirectly encouraged—a boom in asylum building that saw the opening of approximately two dozen new asylums in America between 1810 and 1850. The annual reports of these institutions, which customarily included statistical tables listing the supposed causes of insanity, provided apparent scientific confirmation of the connection between religious excitement and mental illness. When the New Hampshire Asylum for the Insane opened in 1842, the first patient to enter its doors was a Millerite believer in the imminent end of the world, and twenty-one of the first seventy-six admissions to that institution were thought to have suffered from religious excitement, more than twice as many cases as were attributed to ill health, the second leading cause. When the New York State Lunatic Asylum at Utica opened the next year, it, too, listed "religious anxiety" as the number one cause of insanity. A recent analysis of patients admitted to the Hartford Retreat for the Insane during its first twenty years, 1824–43, reveals that "twenty-two percent involved cases of religious insanity directly linked to evangelism" and that admissions for religious insanity corresponded strikingly to outbursts of revival activity in Connecticut.

The 1840s seems to have been particularly conducive to the production of religion-based insanity, if the experiences of the McLean Asylum for the Insane at Boston (opened 1818) and the State Lunatic Hospital at Worcester, Massachusetts (opened 1833), were typical. As Table 1 indicates, the number of "religiously insane"

patients in the decades before the Civil War reached a peak in the 1840s.

TABLE 1: RELIGIOUSLY INSANE ADMISSIONS

	1820–29	1830–39	1840–49	1850–59
McLean	9	19	48	30
Worcester	—	75	161	81

In both theory and practice, mid-nineteenth-century physicians commonly attributed each case of insanity to two causes: predisposing and exciting. The former cause, such as inherited tendencies and poor physical health, made persons vulnerable to mental illness but did not directly cause it. The latter cause, which allegedly precipitated abnormal behavior, could involve anything from excessive study, disappointed love, and physical abuse to mesmerism, Mormonism, Swedenborgianism, Fourierism, and Grahamism (vegetarianism)—all of which appeared as exciting causes of insanity in the reports of American asylums during the 1830s and 1840s.

Millerism

During these decades, no religious development generated more psychological excitement than Millerism, a movement that arose in response to the prediction of William Miller (1782–1849), a Baptist farmer and lay minister from upstate New York, that Christ would soon return to the earth. On the basis of the biblical prophecy found in Daniel 8:14—"Unto two thousand and three hundred days; then shall the sanctuary be cleansed"—Miller calculated that the end would come "about the year 1843" (later revised to October 22, 1844), twenty-three hundred years after Artaxerxes of Persia issued a decree to rebuild Jerusalem.

In his annual report for 1843, the superintendent of the State Lunatic Hospital at Worcester noted that nearly 7 percent of all admissions during the previous year—and more than half of all cases resulting from religious causes—could be charged to Millerism. He believed that, in the other asylums of New England, Millerites constituted an even larger percentage of the patient population. Although he regarded it as unusual for a "popular religious error" to have "produced so much excitement in the community and rendered so many insane," he professed to understand why so many minds were unsettled by Millerism: "the subject is momentous, the time fixed for the final consummation of all things so near at hand, and the truth of all sustained by unerring mathematics." At Worcester, the Millerite cases fell into two categories: the true believers so "full of ecstacy [sic]" that some refused even to eat or drink, and the unconverted who feared that Miller's prophecy might be correct, "who have distracted their minds by puzzling over it, thinking about it, and dreading its approach, who have sunk into deep and hapless melancholy."

Brigham also addressed the Millerite problem in his annual report for 1843—and devoted an entire article to the subject in the first volume of the *American Journal of Insanity,* which he founded and edited. In Brigham's opinion, the insidious effects of Millerism stemmed less from its peculiar teachings than from its tendency to deprive "excitable and nervous persons" of needed sleep while they attended protracted meetings. He acknowledged that, "for the most part," Millerites were "sincere and pious people." However, he believed that their teachings threatened the mental health not only of the present population, but also of generations yet to come, who, because of their ancestors' errors, would enter the world predisposed to insanity. Such prospects prompted him to rank Millerism above even yellow fever and cholera as a threat to the public's health. By the late 1840s, Millerism had come to occupy a prominent place in the literature of American psychiatry as the stereotype of epidemic "religious insanity."

In the 1850s, as admissions of Millerites to American asylums dwindled, superintendents began noting with alarm that spiritualism was playing the same role then that Millerism had played in the previous decade. "'Millerism'" in its day, sent many victims to most of our hospitals," noted the head of the Pennsylvania Hospital for the Insane in a typical statement, "and what is now called 'spiritual investigations,' is a not less prolific cause of the disease." In the 1870s, psychiatrists shifted their concern again, this time to the evangelistic campaigns of Dwight L. Moody (1837–99). According to one medical observer, his emphasis on "conviction of sin" and "a sense of divine wrath" seemed to be upsetting "the mental equilibrium of many a youth, at least temporarily."

The Decline of Religious Insanity

Meanwhile, in the psychiatric community, skepticism regarding the usefulness of identifying the supposed causes of insanity, such as religious excitement, grew rapidly. In 1863, a leading American psychiatrist observed that "the proportion of cases attributed, in our hospital reports, to 'Causes unknown,' has been steadily rising from zero to half or more of the whole number," thus destroying, "at a blow, a great deal of fancied knowledge." That same year, Brigham's successor as editor of the *American Journal of Insanity* noted an apparent "decrease of religious anxiety, as an attributed cause of insanity," owing, he thought, to "the steady progress of medical knowledge," which was beginning to emphasize the organic, rather than moral, causes of mental illness. His own opinion, undoubtedly still a minority view, was that "religious anxiety is rarely, if ever, a cause of insanity."

Despite such sentiments, many American psychiatrists continued to subscribe to the notion that religious excitement produced insanity. A survey of about sixty American asylums in 1876 revealed that religious excitement was thought to be the probable exciting cause of insanity for 5.79 percent of all patients; it ranked among the top four or five causes in a list of more than thirty. Statistics from the Pennsylvania Hospital for the Insane giving the average number of admissions per year attributed to religious excitement suggest that significant change may not have come until the 1880s. For the years 1841–9, the average number of yearly admissions was 6.8; for 1850–9, it was 6.6; for 1860–9, 4.5; for 1870–9, 6.4; and for 1879–85, 2.1. After the death of a longtime superintendent in 1883, religious excitement disappeared entirely from lists of supposed causes at the Pennsylvania Hospital, and his successors attributed only one new case during the 1880s to religion. This pattern lends credence to Barbara Sicherman's observation that "the older view that religious revivals themselves caused insanity had generally declined by 1880."

Contemporary explanations for the decline of religious insanity varied widely. We have already noted that one observer attributed it to a growing agnosticism about the etiology of insanity. Others thought it resulted from increased knowledge about the somatic origins of mental disorders. Some writers credited the decline to the secularization of the modern mind, which dwelt less and less on religious subjects, while one Boston psychiatrist attributed it to changing theological fashions. "The number of persons actually made insane by religious excitement," he wrote in 1877, "has probably diminished with the gradual softening of the rigors of orthodox belief." With the appearance of new nosological systems toward the end of the century, psychiatric authorities tended increasingly to view religious agitation as a *symptom* of dementia praecox (schizophrenia) or some other disease, and the term "religious insanity" slowly disappeared from the vocabulary of medicine.

The Twentieth Century

During the early years of the twentieth century, psychiatry in the United States and Europe underwent a number of changes, most notably an increasing emphasis on social progress and the general welfare of society. Several forces—especially psychoanalysis, but also an evolving body of literature on the psychology of religion and the intellectual marginalization of religious fundamentalism—shaped the psychiatric stance toward things religious. Diagnostically, psychiatrists increasingly turned from classifications based on the course and prognosis of disease to underlying causes. The American Adolf Meyer (1866–1950), for example, came to view designations such as religious insanity and religious mania, based on the content of a delusion, as irrelevant to classifying and treating mental disorders. He focused instead on the deeper causes of delusions, causes that he believed were best understood through a thorough psychological knowledge of the patient. "It is natural that in the interpretation of cases of this kind the desire for a clean-cut issue has led to the emphasis of the delusion formation as the supposed backbone of the whole mental affection," he wrote. "It is, however, to say the least[,] fairly possible that we deal only with an end-production, a kind of adjustment on the surface."

Though the notion of religious insanity had faded by the twentieth century, it lived on in some form in the ideas of Sigmund Freud (1856–1939), who typically avoided seeing religion in terms of individual psychopathology. Rather, in several of his writings, such as *Totem and Taboo* (1913), *The Future of an Illusion* (1927), *Civilization and Its Discontents* (1930), and *Moses and Monotheism* (1939), he outlined his views of religion and the problems it created for humans. In *The Future of an Illusion,* in particular, he portrayed religion as something of an atavistic social phenomenon, a pathology of culture that had failed over thousands of years to cure the insecurities and unhappiness of the human race. Freud saw even the religious impulses of otherwise normal people as a primitive defense mechanism that few persons should need.

Several positive developments relating to psychology and religion in the early and mid-twentieth century

pushed psychiatric thinking away from notions of religious insanity. Some liberal Protestants integrated the insights of psychoanalysis into pastoral care through such organizations as the Emmanuel Movement, and many seminaries began offering "clinical pastoral education" that used psychoanalytic insights in the training of pastors. Forces friendly to religion existed even within the American psychiatric establishment. Karl Menninger (1893–1990), in particular, explored the relationship of religion and mental disorders. Despite the general abandonment of psychoanalytic notions and the ascendancy of the neurosciences in the last decades of the twentieth century, psychiatric interest in religion continued. For example, a 1968 report on "The Psychic Function of Religion in Mental Illness and Health" by the Group for the Advancement of Psychiatry noted that religious themes often surfaced during psychotherapy. The authors of the report treated religious faith and practice respectfully, distinguishing between religion as a ubiquitous human phenomenon and the psychopathology of patients who exhibited symptoms associated with religion.

During the last quarter of the twentieth century, an explosion of knowledge in the neurosciences and psychopharmacology once again transformed psychiatry, making the assumptions of classical psychoanalysis increasingly tangential to the concerns of practicing psychiatrists, who came to rely more and more on physiologically based diagnoses and on pharmacological treatments. The attempts of some psychiatrists and psychologists to use psychiatric terms to stigmatize cults and new religious movements generally failed, though some mental-health professionals justified efforts to "deprogram" cult members on the grounds that cult leaders used mind control to influence their followers. In 1989, the American Psychiatric Association judged it unethical for a psychiatrist to diagnose mental illness solely on the basis of membership in a new religion or cult.

However, one residue of earlier interest in religious insanity remained in the glossary of the third edition of the American Psychiatric Association's *Diagnostic and Statistical Manual of Mental Disorders (DSM-III).* Despite the absence of any terms that implied a religious origin of mental illness, the glossary tacitly linked religion and mental illness by frequently using examples of psychopathology associated with religious content. Criticism of the manual for its implicit bias against religion resulted in a greater sensitivity to religious belief in the fourth edition, known as *DSM-IV* (1994). *DSM-IV* also included a diagnostic code, "Religious or Spiritual Problem," which could be used with patients who were experiencing distress as a result of conversion, a loss of faith, or a questioning of spiritual values. In this way, the manual sought to avoid a materialistic or reductionistic bias in psychiatric diagnosis and recognized the importance of religion in the lives of many people.

In 1990, the American Psychiatric Association issued a statement on possible conflict between a psychiatrist's religious commitments and therapeutic practices, condemning any use of psychiatry to promote religious (or political) values. In doing so, the association affirmed the psychological importance of religion, which therapists needed to handle with care. The Association also backed one more step away from the concept of religious insanity and from the positivistic approach to psychiatry that had come to characterize so much of nineteenth- and twentieth-century thought on the subject.

For citations to sources quoted, see under Acknowledgments.

See also European Psychology; Psychology in America

BIBLIOGRAPHY

American Psychiatric Association. *Diagnostic and Statistical Manual of Mental Disorders (DSM-IV)*. Washington, D.C.: American Psychiatric Association, 1994.

Burnham, John C. *Psychoanalysis and American Medicine, 1894–1918: Medicine, Science, and Culture*. New York: International Universities Press, 1967.

———. "The Encounter of Christian Theology with Deterministic Psychology and Psychoanalysis." *Bulletin of the Menninger Clinic* 49 (1985): 321–52.

Committee on Psychiatry and Religion, Group for the Advancement of Psychiatry. "The Psychic Function of Religion in Mental Health and Illness." *Reports and Symposiums*. Vol. 6. Report No. 67 (January 1968): 642–725.

Dimond, Sydney G. *The Psychology of the Methodist Revival: An Empirical and Descriptive Study*. Oxford: Oxford University Press, 1926.

Donat, James G. "Medicine and Religion: On the Physical and Mental Disorders That Accompanied the Ulster Revival of 1859." In *The Anatomy of Madness: Essays in the History of Psychiatry*, ed. by W. F. Bynum et al. Vol. 3. London: Routledge, 1988, 124–50.

Grob, Gerald N. *Mental Illness and American Society, 1875–1940*. Princeton, N.J.: Princeton University Press, 1983.

"Guidelines Regarding Possible Conflict Between Psychiatrists' Religious Commitments and Psychiatric Practice (Official Actions)." *American Journal of Psychiatry* 147 (1990): 542.

Hill, Teresa Lynne. "Religion, Madness, and the Asylum: A Study of Medicine and Culture in New England, 1820–1840." Ph.D. diss., Brown University, 1991.

Larson, David B., et al. "Religious Content in the DSM-III-R Glossary of Technical Terms." *American Journal of Psychiatry* 150 (1993): 1884–5.

MacDonald, Michael. "Religion, Social Change, and Psychological Healing in England, 1600–1800." In *The Church and Healing*, ed. by W. J. Sheils. Studies in Church History. Vol. 19. Oxford: Blackwell for the Ecclesiastical History Society, 1982, 101–25.

Meissner, W. W. *Psychoanalysis and Religious Experience*. New Haven, Conn.: Yale University Press, 1984.

Meyer, Adolph. "The Treatment of Paranoiac and Paranoid States." In *The Modern Treatment of Nervous and Mental Diseases*, ed. by William A. White and Smith Ely Jelliffe. 2 vols. New York: Lee and Febiger, 1913, 2:616.

Numbers, Ronald L., and Janet S. Numbers. "Millerism and Madness: A Study of 'Religious Insanity' in Nineteenth-Century America." *Bulletin of the Menninger Clinic* 49 (1985): 289–320.

Porter, Roy. *Mind-Forg'd Manacles: A History of Madness in England from the Restoration to the Regency*. Cambridge, Mass.: Harvard University Press, 1987.

Post, S. G. "DSM-III-R and Religion." *Social Science and Medicine* 35 (1992): 81–90.

Rosen, George. "Enthusiasm." *Bulletin of the History of Medicine* 42 (1968): 393–421.

Rubin, Julius H. *Religious Melancholy and Protestant Experience in America*. New York: Oxford University Press, 1994.

Sena, John F. "Melancholic Madness and the Puritans." *Harvard Theological Review* 66 (1973): 292–309.

Screech, M. A. "Good Madness in Christendom." In *The Anatomy of Madness: Essays in the History of Psychiatry*, ed. by William Bynum et al. Vol. 1. London: Tavistock, 1985, 25–39.

Ungerleider, J. Thomas, and David K. Wellisch. "Deprogramming (Involuntary Departure), Coercion, and Cults." In *New Religious Movements: A Report of the American Psychiatric Association*, ed. by Marc Galanter. Washington, D.C.: American Psychiatric Association, 1989, 244.

95. Phrenology

Lisle W. Dalton

Phrenology is the belief that the brain is a collection of "organs" that localize mental function and can be discerned from the shape of the skull, thus giving an estimate of innate mental capacity, character, and intelligence.

Basic Concepts and History

Though speculation about the precise relationship of the brain to mental ability and character can be traced to antiquity, Austrian doctor Franz Joseph Gall (1758–1828) formulated phrenology in the modern sense in the late eighteenth century. Gall claimed that the human brain was actually a composite of twenty-seven distinct measurable organs, which accounted for all mental activity and behavior. Later phrenologists would add to this total, but most followed Gall in organizing the mental organs into two general classes: animalistic traits like the sexual instinct and self-preservation, and qualities exclusive to human beings like religious sentiment and comparative wisdom. General considerations looked to the size of the organs in this second "moral and intellectual" group, particularly in proportion to the more "animal" organs of the first group, as an index of intelligence, moral vigor, and religious devotion.

Gall's ideas were subsequently disseminated throughout Europe, North America, and Australia. Key advocates like German Johann Gaspar Spurzheim (1776–1832), Scotsman George Combe (1788–1858), American Orson Fowler (1809–87), and Spaniard Mariano Cubi y Soler (1801–75) saw phrenology as a positive new "science of the mind" and promoted it as the basis for a variety of reforms, including temperance, public education, the treatment of the mentally ill, and penology. At the popu-

lar level, phrenology was best known for its "head readings," which purported to reveal personality and character through the careful examination of the shape of the cranium. Although nominal interest in phrenology developed among virtually all social strata, its core constituents were the rising middle classes and artisans who were keenly interested in both social reform and finding new ways of fashioning personal identity in the face of rapid industrialization. Despite ongoing criticism from both scientific and religious sources, enthusiasm for phrenology grew robustly throughout the first half of the century. Thereafter, support fell off sharply, although pockets of adherents survived into the twentieth century.

Phrenology and Religion

Controversy regarding the religious and moral implications of phrenology dogged the movement throughout its history. Critics charged that the phrenological understanding of the mind was a new version of materialism, a reduction of mental function to the anatomy and physiology of the brain, which denied any significant role for a soul or a transcendent God. Furthermore, since the organs were viewed as innate, phrenology was accused of fostering fatalistic expectations regarding moral behavior and intellectual ability. Often, these critics were Protestant and Catholic authorities who became increasingly wary of phrenology as it grew as a popular movement. Anti-phrenological sermons and pamphlets were commonplace in Great Britain and the United States, and Catholics frequently censured important phrenological works.

Phrenologists met this challenge in a variety of ways, the most prominent of which touted the advantages of a naturalistic understanding of religiosity and morality while explicitly disavowing materialism. In Baconian fashion, phrenologists often boasted of replacing the metaphysical speculation that usually surrounded discussions of religion and morality with an empirical science based upon quantifiable categories and universal laws. Characteristics such as hope, veneration, conscientiousness, and benevolence were viewed as natural qualities of the brain and, therefore, as integral to the human constitution as digestion or respiration. Gall even claimed to have found a new proof for the existence of God by isolating a cranial organ dedicated to divine worship.

In the context of promoting social reform, phrenologists softened their ostensibly deterministic scheme of innate faculties to include the possibility that the quality of the brain might be improved. Though phrenological analysis could set parameters and give evidence for general inclinations and abilities, the proper cultivation was thought to bring about an increase in the size of the desirable organs. This served to deflect accusations of materialism and fatalism and also contributed to the generally optimistic, albeit often proscriptive, tenor of phrenological literature. To help individuals reach their full mental and moral potential, phrenologists advocated both institutional reconfiguration, such as penal and educational reform, and rigorous self-discipline, which included temperance, antitobacconism, vegetarianism, and the reduced consumption of vanity goods.

Appeals to theism, social optimism, and personal improvement helped phrenologists find a receptive audience among some religious groups, particularly liberal Protestants in Great Britain and the United States. Converts included prominent clergymen like Anglican Archbishop Richard Whately (1787–1863) and the popular American preacher Henry Ward Beecher (1813–87). This success, however, did not fully allay fears that the general tenor of the phrenological message eroded the authority of revealed theology and Scripture. With some prominent freethinkers, radicals, and nonbelievers among its devotees, many religious critics continued to suspect that phrenology promoted infidelity. The equivocal religious orientation of major figures in the phrenological movement, such as Spurzheim, Combe, and Fowler in particular, doubtlessly added to the confusion and suspicion surrounding phrenology. Although all at times made overtures to Christian belief and practice, at the core of their thought were many essentially deistic attitudes. They included an emphasis on a creator God who works through natural law, the elaboration of the concept of natural religion (a manifestation of the brain), distrust of clerical authority, antipathy toward sectarianism, and frequent calls for religious tolerance.

Much of the deistic perspective of the major phrenologists flowed from their strongly teleological understanding of nature that, while rooted in the design arguments of traditional natural theology, also actively embraced emerging theories of organic evolution. Akin to Anglo-American intellectuals in the tradition of Archdeacon William Paley (1743–1805), phrenologists evidenced a fascination with the intricacies of natural structures, particularly brains and skulls, and hoped to extrapolate from them objective knowledge of divine intelligence and cosmic purpose. Few were content with static design, however, and, decades before Darwinism came into prominence, many phrenologists championed a variant of Lamarckian evolutionism that correlated human social progress with organic development.

Ongoing efforts to discredit phrenology eventually took their toll. Anatomists and physiologists regularly assailed phrenological assumptions about the physical structure and functioning of the brain, while many religious intellectuals disdained the movement's pretensions toward establishing a completely naturalistic understanding of the mind. Others noted the irony of an allegedly empirical science that was brimming with metaphysical mental categories. By the last quarter of the nineteenth century, phrenology was well on its way to its present pseudoscientific reputation. Nevertheless, the brief and widespread interest in phrenology around mid-century contributed to the birth of the more reputable human sciences of psychology, anthropology, and sociology. Often, these disciplines dealt with similar issues, including the localization of mental function, the relationship of the brain to behavior, the application of scientific perspectives to social reform, and the meaning of organic evolution. Insofar as wrangling persisted over the theological and moral implications of such endeavors, phrenology can be reckoned as a significant influence upon the interaction of religion and science in the late nineteenth century.

See also Psychology in America

BIBLIOGRAPHY

Combe, George. *The Constitution of Man Considered in Relation to External Objects*. With an additional chapter, "On the

Harmony Between Phrenology and Revelation," by Joseph A. Warne. 9th Amer. ed. Boston: Ticknor, 1839.

Cooter, Roger. *The Cultural Meaning of Popular Science: Phrenology and the Organization of Consent in Nineteenth-Century Britain.* Cambridge: Cambridge University Press, 1984.

Davies, John D. *Phrenology, Fad, and Science: A Nineteenth-Century American Crusade.* New York: Archon Books, 1971.

Fowler, Orson. *Religion, Natural and Revealed.* New York: Fowler and Wells, 1843.

Gall, Franz Joseph. *On the Functions of the Brain and of Each of Its Parts.* Trans. by Winslow Lewis Jr. 6 vols. Boston: Marsh, Capen, and Lyon, 1835.

Spurzheim, Johann Gaspar. *Phrenology; or, The Doctrine of Mental Phenomena.* 2 vols. Boston: Marsh, Capen, and Lyon, 1833.

Stern, Madeleine. *Heads and Headlines: The Phrenological Fowlers.* Norman: University of Oklahoma Press, 1971.

Temkin, Owsei. "Gall and the Phrenological Movement." *Bulletin of the History of Medicine* 21 (May/June 1947): 275–321.

Young, Robert M. *Mind, Brain, and Adaptation in the Nineteenth Century: Cerebral Localization and Its Biological Context from Gall the Ferrier.* Oxford: Clarendon, 1970.

96. THEORIES OF THE SOUL

Peter G. Sobol

The concept of the soul probably dates back to humanity's earliest attempts to understand the nature and fate of living things and may even be older than *homo sapiens sapiens*. The Neanderthals' ritual burial of their dead may reflect a belief in the continued existence, within or beyond the grave, of some component of the deceased person. From the earliest dynasties of ancient Egyptian civilization to the twentieth century, theologians, philosophers, and scientists have assumed the presence of an animating principle in living things and sought to discover whether it was material or immaterial, mortal or immortal, limited to individuals or shared with the world at large. The widely held belief that each human being possesses a soul that survives the death of the body profoundly affected both religious and moral teaching, as well as efforts to understand the physiological, emotional, and intellectual aspects of human life. The concerns of religious inquirers regarding this issue were largely distinct from the concerns of natural philosophers and scientists. Because few individuals pursued both lines of inquiry, reconciliation of the religious soul and the scientific soul has been rarely attempted.

Classical Antiquity

The philosophers of classical antiquity envisioned two distinct roles for the human soul. From Greek Orphism and Pythagoreanism emerged the idea of the soul as a divine entity imprisoned in the terrestrial realm by an endless cycle of reincarnation (the moral soul). With proper guidance for leading its incarnate life and the knowledge necessary to navigate hazards after death, the soul could avoid punishment between incarnations and ultimately escape to the divine realm of its origin. From the speculations of Pre-Socratic materialists such as Her-

aclitus (540–480 B.C.), Alcmaeon (fl. 500 B.C.), and Democritus (c. 460–c. 370 B.C.) emerged the idea of the soul as a subtle, vivifying matter that enabled an organism to perform the acts that defined living plants, animals, and humans (the vital soul).

The Moral Soul

Those who saw the soul as a moral agent faced different problems from those who saw the soul as a vital power. The dialogues of Plato (c. 427–347 B.C.), which concentrate on the soul as a moral agent, address such questions as the reason for the soul's incarnation in a human body, the effect of that incarnation on the soul, the consequences of incarnate behavior for the soul's existence after death and in its subsequent incarnations, and the ultimate fate of the soul. Plato's early Socratic dialogues understand the soul (*psychē*) as the true self, an entity that continues to exist after death in a state dependent on the choices it makes while incarnate in the human body. Socrates (469–399 B.C.) urges his interlocutors to care for their souls by acquiring wisdom and by overcoming the soul's own ability to do evil (*Charmides* 156D). In the *Phaedo,* which is set at Socrates's execution and dates from Plato's middle period, Socrates argues that human souls exist before incarnation in a world in which they have direct knowledge of absolutes such as equality and goodness. The pursuit of philosophy purifies the soul of its corporeal pollution (67C) and may ensure that it escapes the cycle of reincarnation (114C).

When Plato's focus shifted to the composition of the state, his views of the composition of the soul changed as well. The tripartite soul in the *Republic* has reason (*nous*), spirit, and appetite, which parallel the three divisions of the citizens of the state: the philosophers, the guardians, and the workers (441C). So long as reason rules in either realm, the actions of the lower powers contribute to the good of the whole. The *Republic* concludes with the Myth of Er, which illustrates both the reward for virtue and the punishment for vice that await the soul after death. The *Phaedrus* (246B) presents a similar picture of the soul, with *nous* as a chariot driver who must control two horses, one noble *(kalos),* the other ignoble *(enantios).* Where the *Republic* echoes the assertion of the *Phaedo* that the body hinders the soul from its pursuit of truth (611C), the *Phaedrus* allows that, even during its existence in the heavens, reason as charioteer may fail to control its horses, leading to the soul's descent into a body (248C). Once incarnate, only by attending to the beauty in material things can the soul hope to recall true beauty and ascend again to the realm beyond the heavens, where truth dwells (249E). The body-soul dualism of Plato was to influence philosophy throughout the classical period.

In the "probable account" (29D and elsewhere) of Creation that is presented in the *Timaeus* (a late dialogue), Plato broadens his inquiry to include the vital soul. The *Timaeus* describes human souls as impure portions of the material used by the Demiurge (divine craftsman) to fashion the World Soul. Each is initially placed in its own star (41E), where souls learn what to expect in their incarnate lives (42A). Some are then placed in human bodies constructed by lesser daimons (42E). Extending the tripartite division of powers in the *Republic,* the *Timaeus* locates the divine *nous* in the head, safely separated by the isthmus of the neck from the mortal irrational powers, themselves divided into a better part, located in the chest above the diaphragm, and a worse part, located below the diaphragm. Despite its divine origin, the *nous* is afflicted by humoral imbalance in the brain, just as the irrational powers are afflicted by imbalance in their organs (87A). After death, the soul faces judgment and either escapes the cycle of reincarnation or returns to a suitable terrestrial body (90C). Cowards and miscreants return as women. Men who were guided solely by their souls' mortal irrational powers return as wild animals (90A-E).

The dialogues suggest that Plato elaborated upon Socrates's devotion to the care of the soul by proposing the soul's divinity, preexistence, and transmigration. They also reveal Plato's ambivalence about whether poor decisions arise from within the soul or follow from the soul's preoccupation with the body. Plato's foray into the vital soul raised, but did not resolve, the problem of how an immortal, immaterial soul can occupy and interact with a physical organ.

The Vital Soul

The soul as vital power received its authoritative statement in Aristotle's *De anima (On the Soul).* Aristotle (384–322 B.C.) criticized materialist theories of the soul as well as Pythagorean and Platonic concepts that portrayed the soul as a temporary inhabitant or user of different types of human bodies. In his own theory, the soul was, in effect, the ability of a natural body to perform its vital functions. The souls of plants allowed them to absorb nourishment, grow, and reproduce. The souls of animals empowered them to perform the vegetative functions of nutrition, growth, and reproduction, as well as the functions of sensation and movement. The vegetative, sensitive, and motive functions all require organs. Animals digest food by virtue of their natural heat. Eyes see because, lacking any color of their own, they readily receive color. Ears hear because their internal air, completely still, lacks any sound of its own. The human soul confers not only the vegetative and the sensitive powers possessed by animals, but also the power of mind *(nous).* By virtue of the mind, humans contemplate universal concepts, draw conclusions from premises, overcome immediate desires in order to achieve long-term benefits, and perform guided searches (recollection) through their stores of memory. Where materialists derived these abilities from the blood (so Empedocles [c. 492–432 B.C.]) or from various types of atoms (so Democritus), Aristotle was led by analogies with the function of sense organs to argue that the mind can have no organ. Because the eye must be potentially any visible color, it can have no actual color and, hence, is transparent. Because the mind must be potentially all things that can be thought, it can have "no actual existence until it thinks" (429a23). Were the mind to have any actuality before thinking, it would suffer a limitation in what things it could become when it thinks, in the same way that a jaundiced eye is limited in what color it can become when it sees. Furthermore, because every change in nature, including a new thought, must occur by virtue of something that acts and something that is acted upon, the mind must have an active part and a recipient part. In a difficult passage, Aristotle concluded that the active part of mind is immortal *(athanatos,* 430a23).

The extent of Aristotle's commitment to an immaterial *nous* or to an immortal part of the human soul remains unclear. Aristotle remarked in the first book of *De anima* that intellectual acts may be the soul's only function independent of the body, but that the functions of the mind may depend upon the organic power of imagination (403a5–12), just as the function of vision depends upon the eyes. Both *De anima* (431a17) and *De memoria* (*On Memory* I, 449b31) assert that thinking cannot occur without images (*phantasmata*). Aristotle's very definition of soul as form and "first actuality" of a living body implies the soul's mortality. By emphasizing the passages that supported their differing views, medieval and Renaissance scholars were able to derive either the immortality (so Thomas Aquinas [c. 1225–74]) or the mortality (so Pietro Pomponazzi [1462–1525]) of the soul from *De anima*.

Later Antiquity

The vital soul remained of interest to both Epicureans and Stoics. Both viewed the soul as a special kind of matter that, although it continued to exist after death, did not preserve anything of the deceased. The Stoic doctrine of the psychic *pneuma*, which animated living bodies and returned to the *pneuma* of the World Soul at death, had a wide influence. For centuries, physicians and philosophers drew upon the concept of *pneuma* to describe a subtle spirit that animated the living body and acted as mediator between body and soul.

Study of the moral soul continued in late antiquity in the works of the Neoplatonists and the Christian Fathers. The Neoplatonists, led by Plotinus (205–70), saw the cosmos as an emanation from a series of divine entities beginning with the One. Plotinus affirmed the divinity of human souls as emanations from the World Soul and, ultimately, from the One. He argued that the descent of these divine entities into bodies was natural, as shown by the astrological correlation between celestial alignments and events and temperaments in incarnate life. Yet, he also admitted that the incarnate soul, overly attracted to the body it had created, could unnaturally cut itself off from the divine realm. When the soul returned to its source at death, it lost any individuality that it possessed while incarnate. Both the Neoplatonic concept of descent and the Gnostic concept of capture (described below) held forth the possibility of the soul's reascent or escape to the divine realm of its origin. The hope of such a reunion

drove the development of mysticism and, later, ceremonial magic and the Cabala.

Continuing a trend that had begun in Judaism, concern for salvation and a future life assumed a central place in early Christianity. In the earliest texts of the Old Testament, the souls of the dead of all nations go to the underworld, Sheol, whence only the soul of Samuel returns when summoned by Saul (I Sam. 28). Under the duress of the Exile (586 B.C.) and the promise of unfulfilled prophecies of restoration in Isaiah 60 and Ezekiel 37, the Jews began to see Yahweh not merely as the resurrector of the nation, but also as the resurrector of individuals. Jewish writers began to propose the resurrection of the body (for example, Dan. 12:2). The *Wisdom of Solomon* (second century B.C.) speaks of eternal life for the virtuous and death for the impious.

Christians both inherited the problems faced by Greek writers on the moral soul and faced new ones as well. Where do souls come from? If the soul of an unborn child is directly infused by God, at what point during fetal development does the infusion occur? Why would a good God subject souls to the misery of life in the flesh? Will the souls of the dead be judged at death or on the day of judgment? Who will perform the judgment and upon what basis? Does God not already know the outcome of the judgment? Gnostic Christians answered that the soul was a captive stranger in the cosmos. One Gnostic prophet, Mani (c. 216–c. 276), taught that humans had been created in a universe in which the two coeval powers of light and darkness were already at war. The cosmos was an elaborate prison constructed by the world of darkness to hold, in the form of human souls, tiny sparks of the world of light. Humans who recognize their status as prisoners have taken the first step toward the knowledge needed for escape. The Gnostic solution, with its salvation based on *gnosis* (knowledge) rather than faith or good works, was vigorously opposed by representatives of Christian orthodoxy. Within that orthodoxy, however, in the second and third centuries A.D., the latitude of acceptable beliefs regarding the soul remained wide. Tertullian (c. 160–c. 220) believed that the soul of each newborn, like its body, was produced by its parents (traducianism). Origen (c. 185–c. 251) believed in the preexistence of souls.

Mani's message attracted the nineteen-year-old Augustine (354–430), who could not attribute to God the misery of the soul's incarnation in the flesh. After ten years as a Manichaean hearer, however, Augustine turned to Christianity, desiring "to know God and the soul" (*Soliloquies* 1.2.7). Augustine retained an essentially Platonic view of the soul as an entity capable of existing on its own and achieving its perfection only when it left the body behind, although he departed from Platonism in his belief that God created the soul of each human being and infused it at some point (he never decided when) during fetal development. In Augustine's view, the body cannot affect the soul. Only if the soul allows its gaze to be drawn to the body and away from higher things can it become distracted from its proper search for God and truth. The pursuit of that search, despite the body's interference, shows that the human soul shares in the immortality of what it seeks. Without God, however, humans are powerless to acquire knowledge or salvation. Drawing upon the Allegory of the Cave in Plato's *Republic,* Augustine constructed an analogy that related the roles of the sun and the eye in vision to the roles of God and the mind in the acquisition of knowledge. The mind must act to acquire knowledge, yet is insufficient to do so in the absence of divine illumination. Augustine believed that each human inherits the sin of Adam and requires, in addition to baptism, prevenient grace in order to seek salvation, and cooperative grace in order to attain it. His belief in God's omniscience and in the complete dependence of humans on God for salvation led him to argue that God has already determined who will be saved and, at the same time, to insist that humans retain free will in their ability both to sin and to reject divine grace. Other fifth-century Christian theologians argued that such predestination denied human free will, the efficacy of prayer, and the universal offer of individual salvation.

Middle Ages

From the fifth to the twelfth centuries, while the intellectual life of Europe survived in monasteries, writers on the soul explored Augustine's theories of grace, predestination, and free will. In the tenth and eleventh centuries, Europeans began to grapple with such problems as the nature of universals. The debate focused on the ontological status of taxonomic categories such as "horse" and "animal." With the recovery of Aristotelian and Islamic philosophy in the twelfth century, academic interest expanded to natural philosophy, including the vegetative, sensitive, motive, and intellectual powers of the vital

soul. Despite objections raised at the University of Paris—the premier faculty of theology in Europe—against assertions in the Aristotelian corpus contradictory to Christian faith (including the mortality of the soul in *De anima*), Aristotle's works became the core of the arts curriculum. Theologians did not begrudge the arts masters' claim to the vital soul and even permitted philosophical speculation about how the disembodied soul suffers punishment after death. As the century progressed, however, the relationship between arts and theology at Paris began to deteriorate. Certain masters of arts, faced with explaining how a single human can know a universal concept, followed the Cordovan Muslim philosopher and physician Averroës (1126–98) in asserting that, according to Aristotle, all humans share one universal intellect. Other masters of arts, following the Greek commentator Alexander of Aphrodisias (fl. second or third century), held that Aristotle had taught the mortality of the soul because, as the form of the living body, the soul cannot exist in a separated state. Christian theologians could accept neither thesis, however, because both denied the survival of the individual after death that was necessary for punishment or reward. Thomas Aquinas strove to derive human individuality and immortality from Aristotle's works, in part, by arguing that, although the soul is the form of the body, it must persist after death because, even when incarnate, its intellectual functions use no organ. Despite Aquinas's efforts, the bishop of Paris in 1277 condemned 219 propositions ostensibly drawn from the teaching of arts masters, including several that bear upon the Averroist and Alexandrist denial of individual immortality.

By the end of the thirteenth century, most scholars had come to believe that the human soul was a separable form with a natural predilection for incarnation, and they had formulated a set of inquiries that continued to engage them well into the Renaissance. Virtually every commentator on Aristotle's *De anima* asked, for example, whether the soul has a location in the body. Many authors concluded that the soul is wholly in every part of the body, paralleling the theological statement that God is wholly in every part of the cosmos. Scholars also examined the nature of the "sensible species," which permitted sensation of distant qualities, the number and function of the internal senses, the nature of "intelligible species," and the roles of the possible and agent intellects in human thinking and their relation to the body. One dissenting voice came from Duns Scotus (c. 1265–c. 1308), who argued that the will was superior to the intellect and that intellectual functions alone did not prove the immortality of the soul because these functions may exist only in living humans.

The Renaissance and the Reformation

Behind the debates over human cognition of objects and concepts that were fueled by the claims of Duns Scotus and William of Ockham (c. 1280–c. 1349), the views of Alexander of Aphrodisias and Averroës remained appealing philosophical alternatives to the view of the human soul as a separable form well into the sixteenth century. Pope Leo X (b. 1475, p. 1513–21), at the eighth session of the Fifth Lateran Council in 1513, expressly forbade the teaching of the mortality of the intellect or a single intellect for all humans. The decree had little effect. In 1516, Pietro Pomponazzi, no stranger to controversy, published his *De immortalitate animae (On the Immortality of the Soul)*. Philosophy, he argued, teaches that the intellect is mortal because it is either organic or entirely reliant on organic powers.

The Protestant Reformers of the sixteenth century were more concerned with the fate of the immortal soul after death than with philosophical arguments proving or challenging the soul's immortality. Their insistence upon God's sovereignty and the insufficiency of human will to achieve salvation brought them back to Augustinian predestination. Both Martin Luther (1483–1546) and John Calvin (1509–64) saw human beings as wholly depraved, unable to save themselves, and, hence, in need of God's grace. Protestants based their doctrines on explicit scriptural teaching rather than on ecclesiastical tradition. Thus, the Reformers denied the existence of Purgatory, an intermediate abode for the souls of those Christians who required purification through suffering before entering heaven. Instead, the souls of the dead went immediately to their final resting place.

Some historians trace the beginnings of the modern science of psychology to the sixteenth century, during which the term *psychologia* was first used. Earlier inquiries had emphasized the distinction between the soul's intellectual powers and its sensitive and vegetative powers. Sixteenth-century scholars began to consider the relationship of the intellectual powers to the senses and the imagination. The skeptic Gianfrancesco Pico della Mirandola (1470–1537), in his *De imaginatione*

(*On the Imagination* [1501]), argued that the content of the intellect and, hence, a person's desires and actions could be directed by controlling the content of his or her sense images. The Spanish humanist Juan Luis Vives (1492–1540), in his *De anima et vita (On the Soul and Life* [1538]), examined the intellect's susceptibility to emotions.

Some Italians, drawing upon their training in philosophy and medicine (which had been combined in their university curricula since the late thirteenth century), explained thinking itself in physiological terms. Physicians from the time of Hippocrates (c. 460–377/359 B.C.), unencumbered by philosophical arguments for an immaterial intellect and eager to bring all human maladies within their purview, had always included thinking among the organic powers. The same tendency continued in Renaissance Italy and led Girolamo Fracastoro (1483–1553) and Bernardino Telesio (1509–88) to offer organic explanations of intelligence. Having done so, they struggled, with debatable success, to salvage a role for the immortal human soul in incarnate human life.

A further complication, considered infrequently in the Middle Ages, also emerged in the sixteenth century. If intellect is, indeed, the exclusive possession of humans, then animals lead their complex and successful lives on the strength of sensitive powers alone. How much, then, of human accomplishment might be explained without recourse to intellect? And if human intellect is an organic power, how, precisely, are humans and animals different? A persuasive and congenial answer came from René Descartes (1596–1650). His division of the universe into what is extended (*res extensa*) and what thinks (*res cogitans),* and his limitation of *res cogitans* to humans, had happy consequences for religion. At a time when many people perceived a threat to religion in the growing popularity of the mechanical philosophy, Cartesians pointed out that, by ceding nature and the human body to mechanists, Descartes's philosophy allowed one to understand living bodies without the empty concepts of animism and to prove to oneself one's own immortality. If one thinks, then one possesses *res cogitans,* which, because it is unextended, can never decay. Nevertheless, Cartesian dualism faced a host of critics. The ascendancy of Newtonian over Cartesian physical science inspired John Locke (1632–1704) and, later, David Hume (1711–76) to attempt the construction of an analogous science of the mind, in which innate ideas were rejected and the soul's spirituality and immortality were seen as only probable.

Descartes's denial of *res cogitans* to animals, based on their limited behavioral repertoire and their lack of language, became a popular debating point between Cartesians and a broad spectrum of critics. The latter combed through the works of Roman and medieval encyclopedists looking for examples of intelligent animal behavior and resurrecting arguments for the rationality of animals and even for their use of language. Discomfort with Descartes's dualism led Baron d'Holbach (1723–89) and other atheist philosophes to deny the existence of a soul distinct and separable from the body. Baruch Spinoza (1632–77) and Gottfried Wilhelm Leibniz (1646–1716) developed theories in which mind and matter derived from a single substance, as did Julien Offray de La Mettrie in his (1709–51) notorious *L'Homme machine* (*Man a Machine* [1748]).

The Eighteenth Century

During the eighteenth century, the dichotomy between animism and mechanism began to break down in the face of the ever more bewildering capabilities discovered in animals. Ironically, the reassertion that life is more than matter and motion came not from the contemplation of the classically nonorganic powers of the intellect but from the failure of mechanical philosophy adequately to deal with such "vegetative" functions as homeostasis, fetal development, and regeneration. Just as Isaac Newton (1642–1727) had gone beyond strict mechanical philosophy by admitting centripetal force into his dynamics, so Albrecht von Haller (1708–77) proposed that living matter possessed sensibility and irritability. He neither explained these traits in mechanical terms nor explicitly stated their irreducibility. Many of Haller's contemporaries, however, believed that living matter operated under the direction of a power or pattern irreducible to mechanics. Charles Bonnet (1720–93), sometimes called the founder of physiological psychology, not only retained the term "soul" to name the guiding power, but also proposed a naturalistic explanation of survival after death and regeneration of individual humans and animals. Bonnet was one among many who continued to search for the "seat of the soul" in animals, although few any longer associated the irreducible vital power with the immortal human soul.

Belief in the material basis of mental powers led Franz Joseph Gall (1758–1828) and Johann Gaspar Spurzheim (1776–1832) to quantify human personality traits by noting how the skull had grown to accommodate development in the region of the brain responsible for the trait. The phenomena of rapport and somnambulism discovered by pupils of Franz Mesmer (1734–1815) suggested that the will itself was subject to some form of material influence. To some eighteenth-century Catholics, certain aspects of the somnambulic state bore a worrisome resemblance to demonic possession. In the nineteenth century, Popes Gregory XVI (b. 1765, p. 1831–46) and Pius IX (b. 1792, p. 1846–78) deplored, but did not formally condemn, mesmerism.

By the end of the eighteenth century, the vital soul had given way to vital powers. Vitalism retained scientific respectability into the twentieth century, although theoretical reliance on vital powers became less often an assertion of the autonomy of living matter and more often a stopgap until a mechanical explanation was found. François Magendie (1783–1855) argued that the only nonmechanical entities licit in physiology were those governed by quantitative laws.

Except among atheist materialists, belief in the moral soul—the immortal self—remained unshaken, although the grounds for that belief were much reduced. Immanuel Kant (1724–1804) made of the soul a *noumenon*, something we can never know in itself but can know only through the medium of experience, just as we know objects in the external world. Reason, he claimed, can neither prove nor disprove the immortality of the soul, the free will of the soul, or the existence of God. Yet, the immortality of the soul follows from the disparity between human characteristics, especially the moral sense, and mere "earthly utility." Free will, undemonstrable in the phenomenal world, may arise from within the unknowable world of *noumena*, wherein soul and matter may interact.

The Nineteenth Century

Nineteenth-century science seemed further to weaken the scientific basis for belief in the uniqueness and the autonomy of the human soul. Toward the end of his *Origin of Species* (1859), Charles Darwin (1809–82) predicted that, as a consequence of his theory of natural selection, "psychology will be based on a new foundation, that of the necessary acquirement of each mental power and capacity by gradation. Light will be thrown on the origin of man and his history." This new challenge to the special status of humans and to scriptural veracity drew no formal condemnations, even following the publication of

The Descent of Man (1871) and *The Expression of Emotion in Man and Animals* (1872), in which Darwin argued that the human mind, like the human body, was a product of descent with modification.

The nineteenth century also produced great strides in physiological psychology and witnessed the beginnings of clinical psychology, psychiatry, and psychoanalysis. Although he moved away from neurology in his later work and did not offer a neurological distinction between the id, ego, and superego, Sigmund Freud (1856–1939) continued to believe that the mind arose from the brain. Carl Jung (1875–1961), however, found in his theory of the Collective Unconscious evidence of an immaterial and divine human soul. Some educated people in the late nineteenth and early twentieth centuries, scientists included, for whom religious faith alone offered insufficient assurance of a "life after death," turned to spiritism for communication with the "other side" through spirit mediums. The picture of the afterlife gleaned from such communication, and the communication itself, were unacceptable to mainstream Christians. The desire to prove the existence of a nonphysical component in humans also lay behind the growing interest in psychical research, reincarnation, and out-of-body and near-death experiences.

The Twentieth Century

While studies of such paranormal phenomena have yielded inconclusive results, efforts to discover the mind's dependence on the brain have had impressive success. New technology for monitoring brain activity has augmented the knowledge of brain function gained from the study of patients with specific areas of brain damage and allowed researchers to correlate certain brain states with certain subjective states. The emerging field of cognitive science grapples with the nature of consciousness and its relationship to the nervous system. Some practitioners have argued that mental states are identical with brain states, in effect denying the existence of consciousness, while others believe that mental states arise out of brain states.

Some late-twentieth-century theologians referred to the human person as a self instead of a soul, thereby acknowledging the interdependence of mind and body and avoiding the duality of body and soul that remains a modern legacy of the Greeks. Their efforts to understand the survival after death and the resurrection of the body assume the same interdependence. The orthodox Christian (including Roman Catholic, evangelical Protestant, and Orthodox) commitment to an immortal, immaterial soul remains evident in the abortion debate. The majority of Catholic theologians condemn all abortions, believing that the soul is infused at fertilization. Others adopt a more Aristotelian attitude and state that the soul cannot be infused until the brain, which is required for intellectual activity, is sufficiently developed. Should research in artificial intelligence ever produce a nonhuman person, or should ethology ever persuasively show language in animals, the religious concept of the soul as an exclusively human possession will face its greatest challenge.

See also Aristotle and Aristotelianism; The Cabala; Cartesianism; Epicureanism; European Psychology; Mechanical Philosophy; Plato and Platonism; Psychology in America; Stoicism

BIBLIOGRAPHY

Barrett, William. *Death of the Soul: From Descartes to the Computer.* Garden City, N.Y.: Anchor, 1987.

Blumenthal, H. J. *Plotinus' Psychology: His Doctrine of the Embodied Soul.* The Hague: Nijhof, 1971.

Brandon, S. G. F. *The Judgement of the Dead: An Historical and Comparative Study of the Idea of a Post-Mortem Judgement in the Major Religions.* London: Weidenfeld and Nicolson, 1967.

Bremmer, Jan. *The Early Greek Concept of the Soul.* Princeton, N.J.: Princeton University Press, 1983.

Carter, Richard B. *Descartes' Medical Philosophy: The Organic Solution to the Mind-Body Problem.* Baltimore: Johns Hopkins University Press, 1983.

Denzinger, Heinrich. *The Sources of Catholic Dogma.* Trans. by Roy J. Deferrar. St. Louis: Herder, 1955.

Driesch, Hans. *The History and Theory of Vitalism.* Trans. by C. K. Ogden. London: Macmillan, 1914.

Everson, Stephen, ed. *Psychology.* Companions to Ancient Thought. Vol. 2. Cambridge: Cambridge University Press, 1991.

Gregory, Richard L., ed. *The Oxford Companion to the Mind.* Oxford: Oxford University Press, 1987.

Hothersall, David. *History of Psychology.* Philadelphia: Temple University Press, 1984.

Kenny, Anthony. *The Anatomy of the Soul: Historical Essays in the Philosophy of Mind.* New York: Barnes and Noble, 1973.

Kretzmann, Norman, Anthony Kenny, and Jan Pinborg, eds. *Cambridge History of Later Medieval Philosophy.* Cambridge: Cambridge University Press, 1982, 595–628.

McDougal, William. *Body and Mind: A History and Defense of Animism.* 1911. Reprint. Boston: Beacon, 1961.

Onians, Richard Broxton. *The Origins of European Thought About the Body, the Mind, the Soul, the World, Time, and Fate.* Cambridge: Cambridge University of Press, 1951, 13–122, 480–505.

Pegis, Anton Charles. *St. Thomas and the Problem of the Soul in the Thirteenth Century.* 1934. Reprint. Wetteren, Belgium: Universa, 1983.

Reeves, Joan Wynne. *Body and Mind in Western Thought.* Harmondsworth: Penguin, 1958.

Robinson, Thomas More. *Plato's Psychology.* 2d ed. Toronto: University of Toronto Press, 1995.

Rosenfield, Leonora Cohen. *From Beast-Machine to Man-Machine: Animal Soul in French Letters from Descartes to La Mettrie.* 1940. Reprint. New York: Octagon, 1968.

Schmitt, Charles B., ed. *Cambridge History of Renaissance Philosophy.* Cambridge: Cambridge University Press, 1988, 455–534.

Smith, Roger. "Does the History of Psychology Have a Subject?" *History of the Human Sciences* 1 (1988): 147–77.

Von Eckardt, Barbara. *What Is Cognitive Science?* Cambridge, Mass.: MIT Press, 1995.

PART X

The Occult Sciences

97. ASTROLOGY

Laura A. Smoller

Astrology is the study of the effects of the heavenly bodies on earthly events, encompassing in its broadest sense both popular star lore and the intricate mathematical computations of professional astrologers that are termed "technical astrology." Technical astrology arose in the last few centuries B.C. and was an important part of the Western worldview (and inseparable from astronomy) through the seventeenth century, after which it became increasingly popularized and vulgarized, resulting in the newspaper and magazine columns that are familiar today. Technical astrology has undergone a minor revival in the twentieth century, largely at the hands of self-styled pagans, magicians, and occultists, who claim to have revived ancient esoteric knowledge and religious practices. Throughout its long history, astrology has had links to science, religion, and magic. It has also come under attack on numerous occasions on both rational and theological grounds.

Whereas popular astrology takes notice of only the most obvious changes in the heavens (for example, the phases of the moon, the position of the sun along the zodiac), technical astrologers calculate planetary positions with respect both to the background of the so-called fixed stars and to the observer's position on Earth. Technical astrology came to possess four distinct branches of predictions: general predictions, nativities (also known as genethlialogy or horoscopic astrology), elections (or catarchic astrology, the choice of astrologically auspicious moments to begin any undertaking), and interrogations (answering questions based upon the configuration of the heavens at the moment of questioning). In all branches, the astrologer's fundamental tool has been the chart plotting the positions of the heavenly bodies with respect both to the twelve zodiacal signs and to a division of the heavens into twelve mundane houses (also called

places) that are determined by the observer's location on Earth. The first mundane house begins with the point marking the intersection of the ecliptic (the sun's apparent path) and the horizon, termed the ascendant, or *horoscopus*. The importance of this signifier for astrological prediction has led to a misleading dubbing of the entire chart a "horoscope." Each of the twelve mundane houses is said to have significance over some aspect of the subject's life. Interpretation of a chart takes into consideration what planets and signs fall within each house, as well as the planets' angular relationships to one another (aspects), their relative strengths, information based on individual degrees within zodiacal signs, and additional signifiers, such as the Lot of Fortune and other lots.

Babylonian Roots of Astrology

Ancient astrologers asserted that some 490,000 years worth of Babylonian observations underlay their science. While modern scholars are agreed in dismissing such claims, they have disagreed to some extent about astrology's origins. Historians concur that technical astrology proper arose in Hellenistic Egypt in the second century B.C. They debate, however, the relative importance of Babylonian and earlier Greek contributions to the science. One group of nineteenth-century scholars asserted that astrology was entirely of Babylonian origin, while most later scholars have followed the conclusions of Otto Neugebauer, who argued that technical astrology originated in a blend of Greek mathematical astronomy with a cruder Babylonian star lore. Recently, however, scholars have labored to highlight the extent to which a systematic astrology was present in ancient Mesopotamia and to downplay the role of Greek "rationalism" in the development of an astrological science.

The Babylonians were responsible for many key components of technical astrology. Babylonian star lists and celestial-omen lists date from the second millennium B.C. The most famous is the *Enūma Anu Enlil,* which was written down in the seventh century B.C. but incorporates much older material. Under the Persian Empire, Mesopotamian omen literature spread to Egypt, Greece, the Near East, and India. A Babylonian list of constellations along the ecliptic, some of which are retained in the modern zodiac, dates from c. 1000 B.C. By the seventh century B.C., there were organized teams of observers throughout the kingdom who kept records of eclipses and planetary movements, which, by the sixth century B.C., were plotted with reference to twelve thirty-degree divisions of the ecliptic. The most recent evidence points to the invention of the horoscope (or chart) in ancient Babylonia as well. The earliest-known Babylonian horoscopes, which describe nativities, date from 410 B.C. The oldest Greek horoscope describes an event in 62 B.C.

The Birth of Technical Astrology

Technical astrology proper originated in Hellenistic Egypt in the second century B.C. The earliest Hellenistic astrological texts come from the same Alexandrian milieu that produced the *Corpus Hermeticum,* a group of philosophical, magical, astrological, and alchemical writings. These texts attribute the founding of astrology to two mythical figures, Nechepso and Petosiris, under whose names are given descriptions of astral omens, horoscopic astrology (including instructions for computing the length of life), astrological medicine (with clear links to the other Hermetic material), and the connection between various plants and stones with the stars. Already in these texts, one sees a fully systematized astrology, the doctrines of which were passed on in later manuals, such as those of Marcus Manilius (fl. A.D. 9–15), Dorotheus of Sidon (late first–early second century A.D.), Vettius Valens (second century A.D.), Ptolemy of Alexandria (second century A.D.), and Julius Firmicus Maternus (composed in A.D. 334–7).

The reasons most frequently given for the rise of astrology in Hellenistic Egypt have to do, first, with migrations from Persia in the wake of Alexander the Great's (reigned 336–323 B.C.) conquests and, second, with the receptive philosophical climate of the Hellenistic world. According to legend, astrology was brought to Greece by the third-century B.C. Babylonian priest

Berossus, who settled on the island of Cos, or by the Babylonian diviner Sudines (third century B.C.). These stories highlight the many cultural lines of communication opened up after Alexander's conquests. Further, Hellenistic philosophy in general supported notions that would facilitate the growth of astrology. Philosophers saw in a human being an image of the cosmos at large, a microcosm that reflected the macrocosm. Both Platonic and Aristotelian cosmologies taught the superiority of the celestial spheres over the terrestrial. Stoicism, with its stress on Fate, and, much later, Neoplatonism (which arose in the third century A.D.), with its emphasis on an animated cosmos, could justify astrological notions also. Certain political developments may have furthered astrology's rise as well. One recent historian has linked it to the political upheavals of the late Roman Republic and the quest of various Roman generals for one-man rule.

Astrology Under the Roman Empire

Greek philosophers brought astrology to Rome in the second century B.C., and the science became an important means for politicians and battling generals to proclaim legitimacy in the strife-torn Roman Republic of the first century B.C. In the civil war that took place after Julius Caesar's (100–44 B.C.) assassination, the future emperor Augustus (63 B.C.–A.D. 14) used Capricorn (his birth sign) as a symbol against his enemies. As emperor (31 B.C.–A.D. 14), he published his horoscope and had coins issued with Capricorn on them, asserting that the stars gave testimony to his destiny to rule. Evidence indicates that astrology quickly became fashionable among the Roman elite. Under Augustus's rule, the planets' names were assigned to the days of the week, and poets portrayed traditional seers as knowledgeable about the stars. That the Romans took astrology seriously is also attested by the appearance of edicts directed against astrologers, who were repeatedly expelled from Rome beginning in 139 B.C. In A.D. 11, Augustus forbade the consultation of astrologers concerning the date of a person's death. Roman historians frequently linked astrologers with both emperors and would-be usurpers of the imperial title. According to Suetonius (c. 69–c. 140), the Emperor Domitian (b. 51, r. 81–96) exiled and then executed a man whose horoscope indicated an ascent to the imperial throne.

Astrology was not without its critics, particularly among Skeptical and Epicurean philosophers. Cicero

(106–43 B.C.) attacked its doctrines in his *On Divination*; his and most later arguments against the science derive from objections first laid out in the second century B.C. One objection decried the lack of free will in a world in which the stars determine all; another, raised by the Skeptics, questioned the ability of astrologers to make accurate predictions. Even those Stoics who linked astrology to the chain of causes they dubbed "Fate" frequently had only scorn for actual practitioners of the art.

Astrology was not without its links to Roman religion and, later, to the mystery cult of Mithraism and to the solar cults of the later Roman Empire. Romans began calling the planets by the names of gods during the late Republic, the same period in which astrology came to prominence. Astrology seems to have been particularly important to the Mithraic cult, a popular religion of the late Empire. Mithraic temples contained considerable astrological symbolism, and the seven grades of initiation bear the names of the seven planets. The solar cult instituted by the Emperors Elagabulus (b. c. 203, r. 218–22) and Aurelian (b. c. 212, r. 270–5) in the third century A.D. may also reflect a transformation of astrological lore. Finally, authors of ancient astrological manuals may have deliberately organized their material in a confusing manner in order to imitate the layers of arcane knowledge gained by the initiate into a mystery religion.

The early Christians inherited a healthy hostility to diviners and astrologers from the Judaism of the Old Testament, but they were not wholly immune from the cultural favor shown to astrology in late antiquity. (Jewish attitudes toward astrology had softened as well in the last two centuries B.C.) The Gospel of Matthew (2:1–12) relates the well-known incident of the Magi, who learned of Christ's birth from observing the heavens. While the appearance of the star of Bethlehem lent legitimacy to Christianity, later theologians explained that the episode neither sanctioned the use of astrology nor implied that God was subject to the stars. Tertullian (c. 160–c. 220) argued that the Magi had learned of Christ's birth through astrological science but that the art was no longer valid. Another solution was to argue that baptism freed one from the stars' control. Still other writers insisted that the star of Bethlehem was no ordinary star and that the coming of the Magi, therefore, gave no support to the Christian use of astrology.

By the time Christianity became a majority religion in the fourth century A.D., astrology was viewed as a serious rival. Christian writers were hostile to astrology for several reasons. In the first place, astrology offered a competing system of prophecy. Second, it had clear links to both pagan religion and heresies, such as Manichaeism, Gnosticism, and later (in the fifth and sixth centuries) Priscillianism. Third, astrology in its most fatalistic form denied the fundamental Christian principle of the freedom of the human will. Early Christian theologians consequently denounced astrology as a wrongful form of divination that could expose one to the intervention of harmful demons. This attitude found its most vigorous expression in the writings of Augustine of Hippo (354–430), who used many of the older pagan arguments against astrology to attack it on both rational and theological grounds. If astrologers ever spoke correctly, he concluded, it could only be by the occult prompting of evil spirits. The nascent church moved to implement this condemnation by prohibiting the practice of astrology at the Councils of Toledo (400) and Graga (560–5).

Astrology in the Middle Ages

Scholars disagree about the extent of astrological practice in the Latin West in the early Middle Ages. Many have assumed that the vigorous opposition of Catholic authorities led to a decline of interest in astrology at that time. Against this view, M. L. W. Laistner proposed that a lack of proper instructional manuals, and not the censure of the church Fathers, caused astrological practice to drop off in these centuries. More recently, Valerie I. J. Flint has maintained that there was, on the contrary, a considerable practice of astrology in the early Middle Ages. She suggests that astrologers could carry on their business by word of mouth or via single-sheet charts (although one can argue that only a very rudimentary form of astrology could survive in this manner). Further, Flint hypothesizes that shrewd church authorities actually bolstered astrology and some other forms of magic in order to counter what they perceived to be more dangerous forms of divination.

Whether actively aided by church authorities or not, astrology found its way back to intellectual respectability during the High Middle Ages. Some found imaginative ways to christianize the zodiac by equating the twelve signs with, for example, the twelve apostles, the twelve tribes of Israel, or individual biblical figures, such as Mary as Virgo and Adam and Eve as Gemini, the twins. In a simpler fashion, the zodiacal signs came to stand for the twelve months of the year, as one sees in the calendar on the cathedral of Amiens. In the twelfth century, a revived interest in the natural world, combined with the beginnings of a wave of translations from the Arabic, brought the Latin West into contact with the sophisticated astrological science of the Muslim world. Scholars now had access to the tables and textbooks they had previously lacked, along with a new theoretical basis upon which to justify astrology, namely Aristotelian cosmology.

The astrology that Europeans learned from their Muslim neighbors was an elaborated version of the science that had been laid out by ancient writers like Ptolemy of Alexandria and Firmicus Maternus. In Iran under the Sassanian Empire (founded in A.D. 226), scholars had translated both Greek and Indian astrological works into Pahlavi. (Indian astrology itself was a blending of Greek genethlialogy and some native traditions.) Sassanian scholars also began applying horoscope techniques to make general predictions about the fate of the Empire or the world as a whole, by assigning one thousand years to each of the twelve zodiacal signs, by discerning epochal changes with certain conjunctions of Saturn and Jupiter that occurred every 960 years, or by assigning to each planet a lengthy period to rule in turn. In the eighth and ninth centuries, vast numbers of these texts, along with Greek and Sanskrit works, found their way into Arabic translation. The astrological system that emerged contained more complex versions of many features of Hellenistic astrology (for example, a vast multiplication of the number of Lots) but also placed more emphasis on the general predictions developed by the Sassanians.

With the influx of astrological knowledge from Islam, one begins to see in European records competent practitioners of astrology. The Holy Roman Emperor Frederick II (b. 1194, r. 1215–50) had two skilled astrologers at his service. At the same time, Christian thinkers of the twelfth and thirteenth centuries had to struggle with the problem of reconciling the renewed interest in astrology with the condemnations of the early church Fathers. In general, most outlined a compromise like that articulated by Thomas Aquinas (c. 1225–74). Aquinas maintained that the stars had no direct power over the human soul but that they did influence material things, including the body, directly. The heavens, consequently, might incline people to certain actions by affecting the senses, but Aquinas insisted that a person was always free to override such impulses. He added, however, that few people resist their

passions. Such a position saved the important practice of astrological medicine (whereby medicines and treatments were timed according to the stars), yet refuted claims that astrology implied a determinism that was repugnant to Christianity. When astrology in its most fatalistic form came under attack in the late thirteenth and fourteenth centuries, defenders of the science continued to assert that they advocated only the natural, licit astrology outlined by Aquinas and not the superstitious, fatalistic type that the church rightly condemned.

The importance of astrology in the later Middle Ages is attested by its prominent place both in royal courts and as a handmaiden to prophecy. The French king Charles V (b. 1337, r. 1364–80), for example, commissioned translations of astrological texts and amassed a library in which works of astrology and divination held a prominent place. Astrological predictions of the king's death played a decisive role in a major scandal during the reigns of Henry VI (b. 1421, r. 1422–61 and 1470–1) in England that ended with the execution of one astrologer for treason in 1441. Astrology's importance to church as well as state derived from general predictions that were elaborated by the Arabic astrologers. In particular, conjunction theory pointed to times for changes in empires and religions. From the thirteenth century, many scholars embraced the possibility of using astrology to predict the end of the world. Widely circulated prophecies drew upon astrological language, and no less a figure than Cardinal Pierre d'Ailly (1350–1420) brought astrological calculations to bear upon the major ecclesiastical crisis of his day, the Great Schism (1378–1417). Medieval thinkers managed to reconcile astrology with Christian theology in a compromise that survived through the seventeenth century.

Astrology in Early-Modern Europe

From the fifteenth through the seventeenth centuries, technical astrology reached its zenith in Europe. Many humanists of Renaissance Italy, together with their aristocratic patrons, eagerly embraced astrology, while a few attacked it. Some humanists tied the theme of renovation or a new epoch in their own times to conjunction theory; others, like Marsilio Ficino (1433–99), pursued an astrologically based magic. Late in his life, Giovanni Pico della Mirandola (1463–94) issued a scathing denunciation of astrology, initiating a wide-ranging debate about the science but with no visible effects on its practice, save a tendency to discredit any accretions to the science since Ptolemy. Key astrological texts enjoyed a broad circulation and readership in the fourteenth and fifteenth centuries and were among the earliest printed books. With the invention of printing, astrological principles reached new and larger audiences through the media of prognostications and almanacs, in which form astrology gained popularity in seventeenth-century America as well. Astrologers, both Catholic and Protestant, seized upon the appearance of a major conjunction of the three superior planets in Pisces in 1524 to issue scores of pamphlets that interpreted its significance, usually in confirmation of their own religious faith or political sympathies. Of the major reformers, Philipp Melanchthon (1497–1560) wholeheartedly supported astrology, while Martin Luther (1483–1546) and John Calvin (1509–64) attacked it (although Calvin defended astrological medicine). Astrology was fashionable at courts throughout Europe in the sixteenth and seventeenth centuries, but its clients were not merely courtiers. The English astrologer William Lilly (1602–81) received as many as two thousand consultations a year. Astrologers enjoyed unprecedented popularity and influence during the English Civil War and Interregnum of 1642–60.

By the early eighteenth century, however, European elites were abandoning technical astrology, leaving its principles to survive in the watered-down form of the almanac and as "popular superstition." Historians have differed in their explanations of the science's demise. Many have attributed its decline to the new cosmology of the scientific revolution that removed the earth from the center of the heavens. Johannes Kepler (1571–1630), however, was committed to astrological principles, as were many of the scientific elite of seventeenth-century England, who argued for a reformed astrology but not for its wholesale rejection. Furthermore, astrological almanacs did much to popularize the new theories about the heavens, when Ptolemy was still being taught in the universities. Nor were scientists the most vigorous critics of astrology but, rather, clergymen and, by the early eighteenth century, satirists.

Other scholars have pointed to religious reasons for the decline of astrology. For some, the hostility of the Protestant Reformers and the Catholic Church after the Council of Trent (1545–63) explains astrology's demise. Keith Thomas, however, argued that the Reformation fostered a rise in astrology. After the Reformation, Thomas believes, the English Church was bereft of the magical arsenal of cures and blessings it possessed in the Catholic Middle Ages. Hence, an opening appeared in which all sorts of magical practitioners (among whom he numbers astrologers) could flourish, and clergymen saw these practitioners as direct competitors. Magic and astrology declined, he argues, only with the rise of a spirit of rational self-help in the course of the seventeenth century, so that something like fire insurance would deal with the uncertainty that formerly drove clients into astrologers' consulting rooms.

For still other historians, the abandonment of scientific astrology forms part of the larger trend of the retreat of European elites from popular culture. At least in the English case, this shift was a result of the political upheavals of the seventeenth century and the prominent role played by astrology in the Civil War. After 1660, English elites associated astrology with the radical sects that flourished during the years of the Civil War, and they feared the power of astrological predictions to incite the people to rebellion and unrest. Further political turmoil in the 1670s and 1680s cemented this fear of astrology's link to popular instability and led to the exclusion of astrology from the dominant culture, despite a number of attempts at a reformed astrology.

Astrology After 1700

Astrology survived in its popular form after European elites abandoned technical astrology, and it has undergone a number of revivals since 1700, largely linked to spiritualist impulses. People continued to read and buy almanacs, and a number of middle-class astrologers practiced their art in rural areas during the eighteenth century. Astrological doctrines were joined to some of the antirationalist movements of the late eighteenth century, which included mesmerism, Freemasonry, and animal magnetism. Astrologers writing under the pen names Raphael (Robert C. Smith [1795–1832] or John Palmer [1807–37]) and Zadakiel (Richard James Morrison [1794–1874]) created and sustained a middle-class audience for astrology by publishing a series of almanacs that began in 1825. A revival of astrology in the late nineteenth century was linked to the rise of theosophy after 1875, which spawned interest in horoscopes in England and Germany in particular. Adolf Hitler (1889–1945) was reported to have consulted astrologers. In 1930, the London *Sunday Observer* published the first horoscope in a newspaper, thus engendering a popularized form of astrology that has survived to the present. The rebirth of a more sophisticated form of astrology, with roots in the occultist movement, began in Britain in the late nineteenth century and still thrives. Although abandoned by the scientific establishment, astrology has persisted in the modern West by renewing its ties with religion in the form of occult and New Age movements.

See also Alchemy; The Cabala; Hermeticism; Magic and the Occult; Numbers

BIBLIOGRAPHY

Barton, Tamsyn. *Ancient Astrology.* Sciences of Antiquity. London and New York: Routledge, 1994.

Bouché-Leclercq, Auguste. *L'Astrologie grecque.* 1899. Reprint. Aalen: Scientia Verlag, 1979.

Butler, Jon. "Magic, Astrology, and the Early American Religious Heritage, 1600–1760." *American Historical Review* 84 (1979): 317–46.

Capp, Bernard. *English Almanacs, 1500–1800: Astrology and the Popular Press.* Ithaca, N.Y.: Cornell University Press, 1979.

Carey, Hilary M. *Courting Disaster: Astrology at the English Court and University in the Later Middle Ages.* New York: St. Martin's, 1992.

Curry, Patrick. *Prophecy and Power: Astrology in Early Modern England.* Cambridge, U.K.: Polity, 1989.

Eade, J. C. *The Forgotten Sky: A Guide to Astrology in English Literature.* Oxford: Clarendon, 1984.

Flint, Valerie I. J. *The Rise of Magic in Early Medieval Europe.* Princeton, N.J.: Princeton University Press, 1991.

Garin, Eugenio. *Astrology in the Renaissance: The Zodiac of Life.* Trans. by Carolyn Jackson and June Allen. London and Boston: Routledge and Kegan Paul, 1983.

Godbeer, Richard. *The Devil's Dominion: Magic and Religion in Early New England.* Cambridge: Cambridge University Press, 1992.

Hübner, Wolfgang. *Zodiacus Christianus: Jüdisch-christliche Adaptationen des Tierkreises von der Antike bis zur Gegenwart.* Beiträge zur klassischen Philologie 144. Königstein: Anton Hain, 1983.

Kay, Richard. *Dante's Christian Astrology.* Philadelphia: University of Pennsylvania Press, 1994.

Kennedy, Edward S. "Ramifications of the World-Year Concept in Islamic Astrology." *Proceedings of the Tenth International Congress of the History of Science* (1962): 23–43.

Laistner, M. L. W. "The Western Church and Astrology During the Early Middle Ages." *Harvard Theological Review* 34 (1941): 251–75. Reprinted in Laistner, M. L. W. *The Intellectual Heritage of the Early Middle Ages: Selected Essays.* Ed. by Chester G. Starr. Ithaca, N.Y.: Cornell University Press, 1957, 57–82.

Lemay, Richard. *Abu Ma'shar and Latin Aristotelianism in the Twelfth Century: The Recovery of Aristotle's Natural Philosophy through Arabic Astrology.* Beirut: American University Press, 1962.

Luhrmann, T. M. *Persuasions of the Witch's Craft: Ritual Magic in Contemporary England.* Cambridge, Mass.: Harvard University Press, 1989.

Neugebauer, Otto, and H. B. Van Hoesen. *Greek Horoscopes.* Memoirs of the American Philosophical Society 48. Philadelphia: American Philosophical Society, 1959.

North, John D. *Horoscopes and History.* London: Warburg Institute, 1986.

———. *Chaucer's Universe.* Oxford: Clarendon, 1988.

Pingree, David. "Astrology." In *Dictionary of the History of Ideas.* Vol. 1. Reprint. 1968. New York: Scribner's, 1973; 118–26.

Schumaker, Wayne. *The Occult Sciences in the Renaissance: A Study in Intellectual Patterns.* Berkeley: University of California Press, 1972.

Smoller, Laura Ackerman. *History, Prophecy, and the Stars: The Christian Astrology of Pierre d'Ailly, 1350–1420.* Princeton, N.J.: Princeton University Press, 1994.

Tester, S. J. *A History of Western Astrology.* Woodbridge, Suffolk: Boydell, 1987.

Thomas, Keith. *Religion and the Decline of Magic.* New York: Scribner's, 1971.

Wedel, Theodore Otto. *The Medieval Attitude towards Astrology, Particularly in England.* New Haven, Conn.: Yale University Press, 1920.

Zambelli, Paola, ed. *"Astrologi hallucinati": Stars and the End of the World in Luther's Time.* Berlin and New York: de Gruyter, 1986.

98. Magic and the Occult

William Eamon

Magic may be defined as the use of preternatural forces to control and manipulate nature. Although such powers may or may not be supernatural, being outside the normal course of nature, they are held to be responsible for the magic's extraordinary productions. Magical events are, thus, distinct from miracles in the sense that magic manipulates natural, though hidden, forces, while miracles are caused solely by supernatural powers. Whether assisted by angels or demons or done by purely natural means, magic seeks to place control of nature in human hands.

There are commonalities as well as sharp differences among magic, religion, and science. Magic has been so intertwined with religion as to be virtually indistinguishable from it; yet, from the standpoint of official religion, it is a forbidden art. Like religion, magic invokes extraordinary realities and beings, but it adopts a manipulative attitude toward them, while religion venerates and supplicates the gods. Historically, magic has occupied an equally ambiguous status with respect to science. Like science, magic uses empirical techniques, but its secretiveness and its supposed "superstitious" character are anathema to science. While magical and quasi-magical ideas have profoundly influenced natural philosophy, modern science categorically rejects magic.

Early Christianity and Magic

The emergence of Christianity coincided with a revival of magic and occult science in the Roman Empire. By the time the Romans made their first major contacts with the Greek world, the philosophical tradition of the Periclean age had given way to a preoccupation with the occult "mysteries of nature." Equally significant was the revival of Pythagoreanism, not merely as a formal philosophy but as a religious cult and way of life. Neo-Pythagoreanism became the principal stimulus to the codification of Greek magic, which developed in the eastern provinces of the Roman Empire and spread westward.

The most important works associated with the revival of magic were the so-called Hermetic treatises, supposedly consisting of the revelations of the Egyptian god Thoth, called Hermes Trismegistus ("Thrice-Great Hermes") by the Greeks. Composed between the first and third centuries A.D., the Hermetic texts promised access to "secrets of nature" that would enable one to master nature's occult forces. To an age terrorized by angry divinities and the omnipotence of fate, the Hermetic teachings were popular and influential. The *Corpus Hermeticum* became the most famous magical text in the West. According to the teachings of Hermes, the secrets of nature were absolutely opaque; they could be known only by revelation. Science was practically indistinct from religion. It was no longer rational understanding, but *gnosis* (revealed knowledge), an outcome of piety. Because of its quasi-religious character, the early Christians were ambivalent about Hermeticism. Lactantius (c. 240–c. 320) dressed Hermes in the garb of a Christian prophet, while Augustine of Hippo (354–430) attacked him as an idolater. Part divine and part diabolical, Hermetic doctrines were both food for heretical thought and grist for polemical mills.

Kyranides, a second-century treatise, illustrates the character of Hermetic magic. Supposedly a compilation of the writings of a certain Harpocration of Alexandria (first or second century A.D.) and King Kyranos of Persia, the work consists of four books divided into chapters arranged according to the letters of the Greek alphabet. Each chapter describes the magical properties of the animals, plants, or stones beginning with that letter. Under the letter alpha, for example, are entered *ampelos* (grape vine), *aquila* (eagle), *aetitis* (eagle-stone), and *aquila* (eagle-ray). All have marvelous virtues that are cunningly related to one another. From the grape, wine is made; the root of the grapevine cures epilepsy and drunkenness. The stone found in the head of the eagle-ray prevents someone from getting drunk. If you sketch the form of an eagle on an eagle-stone and place it by your door with an eagle's feather, it will act as a charm to ward off evil. According to *Kyranides,* every natural object possesses magical virtues. Hence, the realm of natural philosophy was scarcely distinguishable from the realm of mysticism and the occult.

The matrix of early Christianity was a Palestinian Judaism that had been permeated by Hellenistic influences. During the early centuries of Christianity, magic (despite its deviant religious status) constituted a strong undercurrent in Judaism. Jewish magic became part of the Christian heritage. The Gospels record numerous instances of miracles performed by Jesus that resemble magical practices, including exorcisms, healing, wonder-working, and nature miracles. The pagan writer Celsus (second century A.D.) claimed that Jesus, like other magi, learned the magical arts in Egypt.

The early Christians were also accused of practicing magic. Such charges seemed plausible in light of the numerous quasi-magical acts attributed to the apostles. Peter's shadow was said to have the power to cure (Acts 5:12–16), as had aprons and handkerchiefs Paul touched (Acts 19:11). On several occasions, the apostles overcame the power of competing magicians. Celsus charged that Christians got their powers by demonology and incantations. Although the Christians responded that their power came from God acting within them, from the pagan viewpoint they seemed merely to be claiming a superior form of magic.

Pagan and Christian Magic

Both pagans and Christians condemned magic, but for different reasons. For pagans, magic was reprehensible because it was secretive, antisocial, and a threat to the social order. Christians, on the other hand, condemned magic because it was the work of demons. Augustine, in his influential *City of God,* insisted that all magic is demonic. Augustine maintained that demons taught people how to perform magical rituals and how to make

use of the occult power of stones, plants, and animals. He acknowledged certain marvelous natural powers, such as magnetic power or the power of goat's blood to shatter a diamond. But magic, he concluded, attacking Hermes, was diabolical.

From the early fourth century, when Christianity became the official Roman religion, magic became a capital offense. In earlier centuries, Roman law had punished magic only when it was used to inflict harm (*maleficium*). In general, the Romans tolerated sorcery and divination except when such practices were seen to be politically dangerous. Thus, in A.D. 11, the Emperor Augustus (b. 63 B.C., r. 31 B.C.–A.D. 14) issued an edict that forbade publishing the emperor's own horoscope or prophesying anyone's death date. Nor were the legal measures introduced by Christianity effective against magic. Indeed, some authorities of the early Christian church acknowledged magic's strength by accommodating Christian practices to pagan magic. Such accommodation to pagan culture was a common and effective missionary strategy in the early Middle Ages. Pagan temples were reconsecrated as Christian shrines. Missionary monks tolerated magical charms and amulets, requiring only that the names of Christian saints, instead of pagan deities, be invoked. Competition among healers, diviners, and priests offering access to spiritual powers caused some early Christian missionaries to assimilate rival pagan practices, thus encouraging the growth of magic.

Despite magic's illicit status, the practice of magic was quite common in the early Middle Ages. The parish priests who practiced medicine as part of their duties did not think of themselves as magicians; yet, without scruples, they used charms and magical plants to combat illnesses. Secular healers also used magic. The eleventh-century Anglo-Saxon medical manual *Lacnunga* explained how to cure "elf-shot," or diseases caused by mischievous elves or spirits. The names of apostles and saints were also invoked for their healing powers. Amulets made of plants and animal parts were used to ward off illness and to protect the bearer from witchcraft. An eleventh-century lapidary by Marbode of Rennes described the magical properties of stones. The agate is an antidote to poison and can be used to strengthen eyesight. Chrysolite, worn as an amulet, drives away demons, while selenite reconciles quarreling lovers. Divination and fortune-telling, including astrology, the interpretation of dreams, casting dice, and reading thunder claps, were also common. Although the magical books provide but a glimpse into the magical world of the early Middle Ages, they suggest that the practice of magic was widespread throughout Europe.

The distinction between "white" (helpful) magic and "black" (harmful) magic was not always easy to make, since techniques for sorcery were essentially the same as those for medical or protective magic. However, sorcery (magic used with evil intent) was strictly forbidden. Women, who often performed roles as midwives, healers, matchmakers, and finders of lost objects, were particularly vulnerable to charges of sorcery. Early Christian writers believed that women were especially prone to magical practices because of their supposed credulity and moral debility. Tertullian (c. 160–c. 220) wrote that demons took advantage of women's inherent character flaws and taught them knowledge of magical herbs.

Learned Magic

During the twelfth century, European intellectual life underwent a transformation as a result of the introduction of Arabic learning into the West, which acquainted Europeans with the rich philosophical and scientific tradition of Greco-Roman antiquity. However, because ancient philosophy came into the West through Arabic sources, it came as a potpourri of genuine philosophical treatises and pseudepigraphical tracts on the occult sciences, which the medieval scholastics had difficulty distinguishing from the original ancient works. The Hermetic writings had exerted a powerful appeal among radical Muslim sects. The Ismaili, a Shiite sect, added their own works on alchemy, astrology, and magic to the already sizable *Corpus Hermeticum*. One of the most influential magical textbooks in the medieval West, the notorious *Picatrix,* was a translation of a work produced by the Brethren of Purity, a radical Ismaili sect.

The appeal of the Arabic magical books to medieval intellectuals is revealed by Roger Bacon's (1213–91) enthusiastic assessment of the *Secretum secretorum* (*Secret of Secrets*), a ninth-century Arabic work attributed to Aristotle (384–322 B.C.). Couched in the form of a letter from Aristotle to his pupil Alexander the Great (356–323 B.C.), the work described the rules of statecraft, including the use of astrology and magic to defeat one's enemies. Bacon thought that the *Secretum* contained "the greatest natural secrets which man or human invention can attain in this life."

The *Secretum secretorum* was a key text in the formation of the image of the magus, which found an especially favorable reception in the medieval courts. Whether in the form of casting horoscopes for princes or using sorcery to gain a prince's favor, magic and fear of magic were pervasive in courtly society. In 1159, John of Salisbury (1115–80) warned that magicians were particularly active in the courts, where ambitious servants used whatever devious means were available to them to curry favor with princes. The engineer Konrad Kyeser of Eichstatt (fl. fourteenth century), in dedicating his treatise on military technology to the emperor Rupert, portrayed himself as a magus in possession of powerful secrets.

The tendency to overlap magic and technology caused Bacon to distinguish carefully between them in his letter *On the Secret Works of Art and Nature* (c. 1260). Bacon contrasted magic, which he considered to be demonic, with legitimate experimental science, or "art using nature as an instrument." Similarly, Albertus Magnus (1193–1280) explained that the Three Magi "were not sorcerers.... For a magus is different from the astrologer, enchanter, or necromancer; properly a magus is only a great man who, with the requisite knowledge, produces marvels" (*Commentary on the Book of Matthew*). Bacon's concept of "art using nature as an instrument" was the core idea underlying what would later be called "natural magic."

Despite the nearly ubiquitous presence of magical books after the twelfth century, magic had a marginal status in relation to conventional scholastic philosophy. According to Aristotle, the dominant medieval authority on scientific methodology, science (*scientia*) meant knowledge of universal, necessary causes of quotidian phenomena. Magic, however, had to do with the manipulation of the occult properties of matter, which could not be apprehended by the senses, although their effects could be known empirically. (The attractive virtue of the magnet, for example, is an occult quality, although its effect upon iron is manifest.) Some medieval thinkers, such as Thomas Aquinas (c. 1225–74), traced the origin of occult properties to the heavens, while others attributed them to the "substantial form" of matter itself.

Perhaps no work better illustrates the assimilation of the occult sciences into scholastic philosophy than the *Liber aggregationis (Book of Collections),* attributed to Albertus Magnus but, in fact, composed by an unknown thirteenth-century scholastic. By far the most famous medieval book of "experimental" magic, the work was a compilation of "secrets" and "experiments" drawn from a variety of classical and medieval sources. The *Liber aggregationis* was essentially a treatise on employing the "secret" or marvelous virtues of plants, stones, and animals. The work is obviously indebted to the occult tradition leading back to the Hellenistic era. However, what makes it so different from the Hermetic books is pseudo-Albertus's unwillingness to accept that marvels are *merely* marvelous. Instead, he attempted to explain them according to the principles of scholastic science. In his tract, *De mirabilibus mundi (The Marvels of the World),* appended to the *Liber aggregationis,* pseudo-Albertus argued that marvels are, in fact, natural events caused by the "rational virtues" in things, even though these causes may be hidden from the intellect.

In making this argument, pseudo-Albertus adopted a conventional scholastic strategy to explain occult qualities. Although certain qualities in nature may be insensible or idiosyncratic, he argued, it is, nevertheless, possible to find rational, physical explanations for them—unless, of course, they are caused by demons. In the fourteenth century, Nicole Oresme (c. 1320–82) devoted an entire scholastic treatise, *De causis mirabilium (The Causes of Marvelous Things)* to arguing that "marvelous" phenomena do not require supernatural causes to explain them. Oresme contended that all of the events that people generally regard as marvelous proceed instead from natural causes that are overlooked, or they result from perceptual errors. Once their causes are known, they are no longer marvelous.

To the growing number of scholars whose curiosity was aroused by magic, the religious and academic establishment issued a stern warning. Hugh of St. Victor (c. 1096–1141), writing in the 1120s, categorically denounced magic, charging that "it seduces [people] from divine religion, prompts them to the cult of demons, fosters corruption of morals, and impels the minds of its devotees to every wicked and criminal indulgence" (*Didascalicon* 7.15). Hugh's denunciation of magic, like virtually all "official" medieval pronouncements on the subject, was essentially a restatement of the Augustinian position. However, underlying the medieval hostility toward magic was a deep and pervasive suspicion of intellectual curiosity in general. In contrast to legitimate intellectual inquiry, magic was considered to be a form of aimless erudition *(curiositas),* the "passion for knowing unnecessary things."

Although *curiositas* referred to any form of intellectual inquiry carried to excess, magic was the medieval world's paradigmatic example of forbidden knowledge. For the boundary between "natural" and demonic magic was ambiguous. Hence, magic of any kind might tempt practitioners into making pacts with demons in order to learn the secrets of creation. So, in the Renaissance, Faust would sell his soul to Satan in order to know the secrets of nature. Not only did the magus pry into nature's hidden recesses and steal its secrets, he used his illicitly won knowledge to glorify himself and to impress the world with his "marvels." According to medieval accounts, pride and curiosity about secret things caused Gerbert of Aurillac (c. 945–1003), who later became Pope Sylvester II (999–1003), to leave his monastery and journey to Spain in order to study astrology and magic under Saracen teachers—at the price of his soul. Gerbert, whose insatiable thirst for knowledge was legendary, was but the most famous medieval example of the overly curious cleric who crossed the boundary of legitimate intellectual inquiry to dabble in the forbidden art. Similar stories implicated Roger Bacon, Albertus Magnus, Robert Grosseteste (c. 1168–1253), and Michael Scott (c. 1175–c. 1230). Indeed, any medieval scholar who had a reputation for his knowledge of natural science was a potential antihero in this rich legendary tradition.

Renaissance Magic

Magic's reputation and intellectual standing underwent a dramatic reversal beginning in the fifteenth century. In 1463, the humanist Marsilio Ficino (1433–99) translated the *Corpus Hermeticum* into Latin at the request of his patron, Cosimo d'Medici (1389–1464). In developing a theory of magic, Ficino maintained that the key to magical power was the *spiritus mundi,* a subtle material substance that is diffused throughout the universe and acts as a medium for influences between celestial bodies and the sublunar world. Using magic, Ficino argued, one can attract the "spiritual" influence of any planet by employing talismans, music, scents, and foods appropriate to that planet. Such influences, channeled through the cosmic spirits into humans, act as powerful medicines.

Within a few decades of Ficino's translation of the *Corpus Hermeticum,* magic became a respectable, even pioneering, humanistic subject. Dozens of treatises reflecting this new "learned magic" appeared in the Renaissance, while Hermetic influences turn up in art, literature, philosophy, theology, and politics. Ficino's famous *Oration on the Dignity of Man* (1489) is replete with magical influences and references. Another proponent of magic, Heinrich Cornelius Agrippa von Nettesheim (1486–1535), brought magic to a broad academic audience in his influential *De occulta philosophia* (*On the Occult Philosophy* [1533]), which proclaimed magic to be the most perfect knowledge of all.

To some extent, Renaissance magic was an attempt to unify nature and religion. Thus, Paracelsus (1493–1541) condemned Aristotle on both scientific and religious grounds. The Paracelsians maintained that Aristotle was a heathen author whose natural philosophy was inconsistent with Christianity. Therefore, it had to be replaced by a Christian Hermeticism that attempted to account for all natural phenomena in a manner that was consistent with Scripture.

Magic found particular favor in the Renaissance courts. The Holy Roman Emperor Rudolf II (b. 1552, r. 1576–1612) was passionately devoted to magic, and his court at Prague became a center of magical studies. Not coincidentally, Rudolf's court was also a thriving center of scientific research. Both Tycho Brahe (1546–1601) and Johannes Kepler (1571–1630) lived at Rudolf's court. In many instances, magic served as an impetus to science, promoting experimentalism and mathematics and creating a positive image of the scientist as a magus.

Another center of Renaissance magical activity was Naples, where the philosophical naturalism of Bernardino Telesio (1509–88) took root. Telesio's vitalistic naturalism provided the philosophical foundation for what Renaissance philosophers called "natural magic," an experimental approach to nature that attempted to use occult forces for practical ends. Telesio's followers established experimental academies with the goal of discovering natural "secrets." They wrote learned treatises on astrology, physiognomy, and the occult secrets of nature.

The most famous Neapolitan magus was Giambattista Della Porta (1535–1615). His *Natural Magic* (1558) was not only the Renaissance's most famous book of magic, it was also, for a time, a highly respected scientific work. Della Porta argued that natural magic was not demonic; it manipulated solely natural forces. Della Porta's ideas made a deep impression on the Dominican friar Tommaso Campanella (1568–1639), who used natural magic as part of his scheme to establish a utopian community in southern Italy. The abortive revolt of Cala-

bria, which Campanella led in 1599 to eject the Spanish from the Kingdom of Naples, was framed by an ideology pervaded with magical ideas.

Hermeticism was immensely popular among Renaissance humanists and intellectuals. Its adherents numbered some of the leading intellectuals of the day, including Giovanni Pico della Mirandola (1463–94), Giordano Bruno (1548–1600), and John Dee (1527–1608). Renaissance magic invoked both natural and supernatural powers and, to that extent, became linked to both science and religion, arousing debate and controversy from both sides.

Despite attempts to create an occult theory based solely on nondemonic principles, magic continued to be the focus of religious controversy. Although natural magic looked innocent to some, it claimed to produce the same effects as religion without any supernatural agencies. Hence, critics charged, it bordered dangerously on atheism. Thus, on two separate occasions, Della Porta was brought before the Inquisition and questioned about his magical activities. In the 1580s, he was implicated in a famous dispute over witchcraft between the French jurist Jean Bodin (1529–96) and the German physician Johann Wier (1515–88). Arguing, in his *De prestigiis daemonum* (*On the Sorceries of Demons* [1564]), against the persecution of witches, Wier cited Della Porta's experiment demonstrating that the "witch's salve," supposedly used to transport witches into flight, could be understood according to naturalistic principles. Della Porta maintained that the witch's salve was, in reality, a hallucinogenic drug that caused the supposed witches to fantasize their nocturnal flights. Attacking Wier in his *Démonomanie des sorciers* (*Demon Mania of the Sorcerers* [1580]), Bodin brought Della Porta into the dispute, damning him as "the great Neapolitan sorcerer."

The sixteenth-century debate over magic is best understood within the context of Counter-Reformation politics. The Roman Catholic Church, determined to consolidate its monopoly over supernatural forces, saw any attempt to utilize occult powers as a threat to its jurisdiction over the miraculous. The history of Inquisitorial processes in the sixteenth century confirms the Church's growing concern about magic. After about 1580, illicit magic replaced doctrinal heresy as the most common charge brought before the local tribunals of the Holy Office. In most of these cases, the accused were charged with using charms, incantations, and magical devices to heal physical complaints, to detect thieves, to find stolen objects and buried treasure, or to incite sexual passion. Formerly, such popular practices were considered harmless. But, in its attempt to protect the faithful from the demonic magic, the Church condemned all magic as heretical. In the heat of the Reformation conflict, natural magic was caught in the net along with popular superstitions, witchcraft, and sorcery.

The sixteenth century also witnessed the publication of countless "books of secrets" that professed to reveal the occult secrets of nature to general readers. The most famous of these tracts was Alessio Piemontese's famous best-seller, the *Secreti* (1555). This work was, in fact, a book of experiments and recipes compiled by the humanist Girolamo Ruscelli (c. 1500–66) in his Academy of Secrets at Naples. Alessio's *Secrets* was widely reprinted in the sixteenth and seventeenth centuries and became the prototype of a huge popular genre. Meanwhile, the fictional Alessio became the ideal of a new kind of scientific magus: the wandering empiric who travels throughout the world in search of the secrets of nature, which he publishes "for the benefit of the world." Other writers on secrets included the Flemish physician Levinus Lemnius (1505–68), whose *Occulta naturae miracula* (*Secret Miracles of Nature* [1559]) assembled occult phenomena, natural prodigies, herbal lore, and folk beliefs, all deployed to prove that "in the smallest works of nature the Deity shines forth"; and Girolamo Cardano (1501–76), who compiled a massive encyclopedia of secrets entitled *De subtilitate* (*Of Subtlety* [1550]).

The New Philosophy

Many historians believe that magic had a profound impact on the scientific revolution of the sixteenth and seventeenth centuries. They argue that Renaissance magic contributed to the emergence of a new conception of the scientific enterprise: the idea of science as a hunt for nature's secrets. Not satisfied with understanding nature on the basis of external appearances, the "new philosophers" insisted upon penetrating nature's hidden recesses and uncovering the occult causes of phenomena. According to the epistemology of the hunt, nature's secrets were hidden from ordinary sense perception; hence, they had to be sought by extraordinary means. Instruments had to be made to enable researchers to penetrate nature's interior. Experiments were devised that would enable researchers to force out nature's secrets. New methods of reasoning had to be found to

take the place of scholastic logic, which, according to the new philosophers, was incapable of reaching nature's inner recesses and laying bare its secrets.

The advent of the hunt metaphor in the scientific discourse of the early-modern period testifies to the emergence of a new philosophy of science. Instead of viewing nature through the texts of the ancient authorities, the new philosophers tended to think of science as a search for new and unknown facts and of causes concealed beneath nature's outer appearances. This conception of science rested, in turn, upon a new definition of scientific knowledge. Whereas in medieval natural philosophy unexplained facts had no place in science, in the new philosophies facts (in the sense of novel, unexplained data) began to take on powerful significance. In the tradition of natural magic, such novel, previously unnoticed facts were signs ("signatures") that guided investigators to nature's arcana. Della Porta wrote: "True things be they ever so small will give occasions to discover greater things by them."

The hunt metaphor also underscores a reevaluation of the status of occult qualities in natural philosophy. For the epistemology of science as a hunt rested upon a distinction between knowledge of nature gained by common sense, which revealed only nature's outer appearances, and knowledge of the inner causes of phenomena. Early-modern natural philosophers understood this difference in terms of the distinction between manifest and occult qualities, a problem that was at the focus of heated controversy in the sixteenth and seventeenth centuries. Instead of banishing occult qualities, the new philosophers embraced them and sought explanations for what the scholastics conceded was, in principle, unknowable. All qualities (in the sense of physical causes) are occult, they argued, but are nevertheless knowable. In the new philosophies, the concept of occult qualities was not an ending point but a beginning of inquiry.

But if occult qualities were, in principle, knowable, by what means could they be known? The new philosophers were in general agreement that access to nature's secrets could be gained only by adopting a two-fold strategy that consisted of right method combined with instruments to aid the senses. In the 1680s, Robert Hooke (1635–1703) formulated such a strategy for the Royal Society of London in his *General Scheme; or, Idea of the Present State of Natural Philosophy,* which embodied many of the ideals of the new experimental philosophy. According to Hooke's formula, the natural defects of the senses would be overcome by scientific instruments, while proper experimental methodology would overcome defects in human reasoning.

The repeated references to the occult "secrets of nature" in the scientific literature of the seventeenth century should not be dismissed as mere rhetoric. Far from being a mere hackneyed metaphor, the appearance of that well-worn phrase indicates a fundamental shift in the direction of natural philosophy. The concept of nature's "secrets"—the idea that the mechanisms of nature were hidden beneath the exterior appearances of things—was the foundation of the new philosophy's skeptical outlook and of its insistence upon getting to the bottom of things through active experimentation and disciplined observation. The scholastics had been too trusting of their senses, the new philosophers asserted. Their naive empiricism was responsible for the erroneous belief that nature exhibits its true character on the outside. In reality, nature's causes are hidden. The unaided senses do not reveal reliable information about what makes nature tick any more than observing the hands of a clock reveals how the clock works. All of the dogmatic pronouncements of scholastic philosophy were but chimeras based upon unreliable foundations.

The Decline of Magic

The rise of the mechanical philosophy in the seventeenth century dealt a nearly fatal blow to magic, as far as its relevance to science was concerned. As formulated by its leading proponent, the French philosopher René Descartes (1596–1650), the mechanical philosophy rested upon two assumptions: First, all phenomena could be explained in terms of particles of passive matter in motion, and, second, the only way the motion of any particle could be changed was by direct contact with some other particle. In theory, the mechanical philosophy banished occult qualities from natural philosophy by reducing explanations of phenomena to mechanical causes.

Nevertheless, because of the inadequacy of the mechanical philosophy to offer a plausible and comprehensive view of the physical world, the status of occult qualities continued to be debated. The focus of the controversy was Sir Isaac Newton's (1642–1727) theory of universal gravitation. In the *Principia mathematica* (1687), Newton postulated the existence of a force that existed among all bodies in the universe. To many natural philosophers, Newton's gravitation resembled the discredited occult forces of Renaissance magic. Somewhat unconvincingly, Newton responded that he "feigned no hypotheses" about the causes of gravity. But the physical interpretation of gravity continued to vex scientists throughout the eighteenth century.

The occult sciences came under sustained attack during the Enlightenment. In the seventeenth century, Sir Francis Bacon (1561–1626) had condemned magic for its secretiveness and its exclusivity. The Enlightenment philosophes, who believed that nature was completely rational, agreed. Such a position left little room for belief in the occult. In the popular tradition, however, belief in magic and the occult continued, giving rise to such movements as mesmerism and spiritualism. Mesmerism, the brainchild of Franz Anton Mesmer (1734–1815), was a form of healing supposedly based upon the channeling of "animal magnetism" through the human body. His system descended directly from the vitalistic natural magical theories of the Renaissance. Although mesmerism was extremely popular in France during the 1780s, the system was roundly condemned by the academicians.

A number of prominent nineteenth-century scientists were adherents of spiritualism, the belief that spiritual forces operate in the natural world. Alfred Russel Wallace (1823–1913), the codiscoverer of the theory of evolution by natural selection, was convinced that natural selection was unable to account for intellectual and moral evolution and, hence, invoked an occult spiritual force to account for human development. An avowed spiritualist, Wallace attended seances and investigated seance phenomena. Other prominent spiritualists included the physiologist and Nobel Prize–winner Charles Richet (1850–1935), who carried out extensive research on psychic phenomena, and the physicist Oliver Lodge (1851–1940).

Psychic phenomena continued to be the subjects of scientific inquiry in the early twentieth century, notably by Joseph Banks Rhine (1895–1980), who founded the Society for Psychical Research. However, because its results proved too difficult to replicate, parapsychology was not accepted by the scientific community. Nowadays, scientists adamantly resist attempts to include paranormal phenomena in research programs. Efforts to obtain funding for such research are generally met with silence or scorn. From the standpoint of modern science, the separation of physical from spiritual and occult phenomena is, in principle, virtually complete.

See also Alchemy; Hermeticism; Spiritualism

BIBLIOGRAPHY

Albertus Magnus (Ps.). *The Book of Secrets of Albertus Magnus of the Virtues of Herbs, Stones, and Certain Beasts. Also a Book of the Marvels of the World.* Ed. by Michael R. Best and Frank H. Brightman. London: Oxford University Press, 1973.

Aune, David E. "Magic in Early Christianity." In *Aufstieg und Niedergang der römischen Welt: Geschichte und Kultur Roms im Spiegel der neueren Forschung,* ed. by Hildegard Temporini and Wolfgang Haase. Part II: Principat. Vol. 23/2. Berlin: De Gruyter, 1980, 1507–57.

Clark, Stuart. *Thinking with Demons: The Idea of Witchcraft in Early Modern Europe.* Oxford: Clarendon, 1997.

Copenhaver, Brian. "Astrology and Magic." In *Cambridge History of Renaissance Philosophy,* ed. by C. B. Schmitt and Q. Skinner. Cambridge: Cambridge University Press, 1988, 264–300.

———. "Natural Magic, Hermetism, and Occultism in Early Modern Science." In *Reappraisals of the Scientific Revolution,* ed. by David C. Lindberg and Robert S. Westman. Cambridge: Cambridge University Press, 1990, 261–302.

———, ed. and trans. *Hermetica: The Greek "Corpus Hermeticum" and the Latin "Asclepius" in a New English Translation, with Notes and Introduction.* Cambridge: Cambridge University Press, 1992.

Eamon, William. "Technology as Magic in the Late Middle Ages and the Renaissance." *Janus* 70 (1983): 171–212.

———. *Science and the Secrets of Nature: Books of Secrets in Medieval and Early Modern Culture.* Princeton, N.J.: Princeton University Press, 1994.

———. "Natural Magic and Utopia in the Cinquecento: Campanella, the Della Porta Circle, and the Revolt of Calabria." *Memorie Domenicane* 26 (1995): 369–402.

Festugière, A.-J. *La Révélation d'Hermès Trismégiste.* 4 vols. Paris: Librairie Lecoffre, 1950–4.

Flint, Valerie I. J. *The Rise of Magic in Early Medieval Europe.* Princeton, N.J.: Princeton University Press, 1991.

Hansen, Bert. "Science and Magic." In *Science in the Middle Ages,* ed. by David C. Lindberg. Chicago: University of Chicago Press, 1978, 483–506.

Hutchison, Keith. "What Happened to Occult Qualities in the Scientific Revolution?" *Isis* 73 (1982): 233–53.

Kiekhefer, Richard. *Magic in the Middle Ages.* Cambridge: Cambridge University Press, 1989.

Luck, Georg, ed. and trans. *Arcana Mundi: Magic and the Occult in the Greek and Roman Worlds.* Baltimore: Johns Hopkins University Press, 1985.

Nauert, Charles G., Jr. *Agrippa and the Crisis of Renaissance Thought.* Illinois Studies in the Social Sciences. No. 55. Urbana: University of Illinois Press, 1965.

Neusner, Jacob, Ernest S. Frerichs, and Paul V. M. Flesher. *Religion, Science, and Magic: In Concert and in Conflict.* Oxford: Oxford University Press, 1992.

Rossi, Paolo. *Francis Bacon: From Magic to Science.* Trans. by S. Rabinovitch. Chicago: University of Chicago Press, 1968.

Thomas, Keith. *Religion and the Decline of Magic.* New York: Scribner's, 1971.

Thorndike, Lynn. *History of Magic and Experimental Science.* 8 vols. New York: Columbia University Press, 1923–58.

Vickers, Brian, ed. *Occult and Scientific Mentalities in the Renaissance.* Cambridge: Cambridge University Press, 1984.

Walker, D. P. *Spiritual and Demonic Magic from Ficino to Campanella.* Notre Dame, Ind.: University of Notre Dame Press, 1975.

Westman, Robert S., and J. E. McGuire. *Hermeticism and the Scientific Revolution.* Los Angeles: William Andrews Clark Memorial Library, 1977.

Yates, Francis. *Giordano Bruno and the Hermetic Tradition.* Chicago: University of Chicago Press, 1964.

99. ALCHEMY

Lawrence M. Principe

Alchemy is a discipline roughly comparable to chemistry, which, in its millennium-and-a-half of existence, encompassed such broadly diverse topics as the transmutation of metals, the making of chemical pharmaceuticals, the refining and assaying of metals and ores, and the production of chemical products, including dyes, pigments, inks, artificial gems, and alloys. While alchemy is often artificially separated from chemistry, the two words were used interchangeably until the eighteenth century and referred to the same topics.

Historical Overview

The history of alchemy is roughly divisible into three chief epochs: the Hellenistic, the Islamic, and the Latin periods. Hellenistic alchemy (third to sixth centuries A.D.) was closely allied to metalworking and the craft traditions, from which it probably draws its origins. Few pure texts survive from the period, but the extant fragments reveal the beginnings of many important theoretical constructs and attitudes that characterized later alchemy. The earliest texts are the Papyri of Leiden and of Stockholm, dating from the third century A.D., which recount metallurgical processes and contain coded recipes. The writings of "Cleopatra" show knowledge of distillation and sublimation techniques. The writings of Zosimus of Panopolis (third or fourth century), the most respected and prolific author of the period, display a developed system of alchemical theory, and particularly a complex set of literary imagery, drawn predominantly from pagan religious mysteries, to describe alchemical operations.

During the Islamic period (seventh to fourteenth centuries) the theoretical, empirical, and experimental content of alchemy was enormously expanded. The eighth-to-tenth-century texts attributed to Jabir Ibn Hayyan (fl. late eighth or ninth century) were probably actually compositions of the obscure Isma'li sect, the Ikhwan as-Safa, or Brethren of Purity. They laid down what became the chief alchemical theory for the composition of the metals and minerals. "Jabir" taught that the metals were composed of two principles he called Mercury and Sulfur. Neither of these substances was equivalent to the common elements known today by the same names. They were, instead, conceived as material principles analogous to them in properties. Mercury in a body gave fusibility, weight, and metallicity, while Sulfur gave color, smell, and inflammability. Consequently, easily fusible metals like tin and lead were believed to contain a preponderance of the liquid principle Mercury; hard, refractory metals that are burned in fire (like iron and copper) contained much Sulfur. Only gold, the perfect metal, contained perfectly pure Mercury and Sulfur strongly united in perfect proportion. The Mercury-Sulfur theory draws its origins from Aristotle's (384–322 B.C.) *Meteorologica,* in which the philosopher postulated the existence of two exhalations—one moist and vaporous, the other dry and smoky—that arose from the center of the earth and then condensed and combined under the earth into stones and minerals. The Muslim alchemists made significant contributions to the knowledge of the properties, preparations, and uses of mineral and animal substances and salts and devised several pieces of apparatus to improve the important processes of distillation, sublimation, and digestion.

The knowledge of the Muslim alchemists first appeared in Latin Europe in 1144, when Robert of Ketton translated an alchemical treatise from Arabic into Latin as *De compositione alkimiae (On the Composition of Alchemy).* Translations of Jabir al-Razi (c. 865–c. 925), and others followed. By the mid-thirteenth century, original European alchemical writings began to appear. Chief among these early works was the *Summa perfectionis (Compendium of Perfection),* which appeared in the late thirteenth century under the name of "Geber," a pseudonymous attribution to the authoritative Arabic author Jabir. The *Summa,* now shown to be the composition of the Franciscan Paul of Taranto, borrowed considerably from Arabic style and theory but was cast into a predominantly scholastic framework. Alchemy developed and diversified greatly in Europe over the following five centuries, reaching its greatest development in the seventeenth century.

Branches of European Alchemy

European alchemy contained several subsets, each with its own diverse schools of thought. Perhaps the chief subset (and the most popularly recognized as alchemy) was chrysopoeia—the making of gold from base metals—an endeavor whose origins reach back without interruption to the Hellenistic period. Transmutation of the metals had theoretical backing from the alchemical theory of the composition of metals from substances common to them all. If all metals were composed of Mercury and Sulfur and were distinguished only by the relative proportion and purity of these common ingredients, then it should be possible to transmute one metal into another by simple manipulation. Furthermore, it was believed that all metals tended toward the perfection of gold, the king of the metals. Deep inside the earth, base metals, gently cooked by subterranean warmth and washed with subterranean water, gradually matured over the centuries into gold. Some alchemists wrote accordingly that base metals were all unripe gold. The task for the chrysopoeian alchemist was to complete in his workshop-laboratory in a short time what occurred naturally under the earth over thousands of years. While some writers believed that this process was to be carried out by manual manipulation involving lengthy processes of purgation and purification, most alchemists chose, instead, to seek an agent of metallic transmutation that could effect these changes more rapidly and easily. This agent was termed the Philosophers' Stone, an alchemical preparation that, when cast upon hot mercury, molten lead, or another base metal, was supposedly able to transmute it in a few moments into pure gold. The first

expressions of belief in the existence of such a transmutatory agent occur in Hellenistic alchemical texts, in which it is called either *lithos tōn philosophōn* (Stone of the Philosophers) or *xōrion,* a word meaning medicine in the form of a powder. The medieval Islamic alchemists, who greatly elaborated upon the notion of the Stone they had inherited from Greek sources, added the Arabic definite article to the Greek stem, producing *al-iksir.* This word, transliterated into the Latin West, became "elixir," a term synonymous with the Philosophers' Stone and much later transferred to various medicinal preparations of exaggerated virtue.

The preparation of the Philosophers' Stone was a closely guarded secret, never to be mentioned openly. The chief problem for aspiring alchemists was the identification of the correct substance with which to begin. Some alchemists looked in gold, seeking to propagate the "seed of gold," believing that minerals, like plants and animals, should, in some sense, contain within themselves a principle of propagation (although the use of the expression "seed" does not necessarily imply a vitalistic view of metals). Others looked in salts or minerals, and some (although they were ridiculed by most) in dung and urine. The alchemical texts that deal with the Stone are often a maze of riddles, allegories, allusions, and metaphor carefully crafted both to conceal and to reveal the author's knowledge. No alchemist ever published a supposed route to the Stone openly but, rather, covered the names of substances to be used under a set of secret names and codes. Often, these allegorical descriptions are quite extravagant, speaking of the marriage of a "red man" with a "white wife," of the making of hermaphrodites, of the activities of green lions, black dragons, or bursting toads. The knowledge of making limitless supplies of gold or even good imitations of gold was potentially dangerous, as it would lead to debasement of the value of currency and subsequent political and social turmoil. Hence, Pope John XXII (b. 1249, p. 1316–34) issued a bull against transmutatory alchemy in 1317, which was followed by similar edicts in France and England around 1400. There were equally compelling religious reasons for secrecy.

In the late Middle Ages, the goals of alchemy began to include the preparation of medicines. One of the early medical exponents was the fourteenth-century radical Franciscan John of Rupescissa. Later, the Swiss physician and iconoclast Theophrastus von Hohenheim, called Paracelsus (1493–1541), emphasized medicinal preparations over the transmutation of metals and other alchemical goals. Paracelsus's trademark was his general assault on all authorities, scientific, medical, and religious. His unorthodox views and violent, arrogant temperament caused his expulsion from several of his places of residence. Paracelsus introduced new, often bizarre, conceptions of matter and nature. His books are difficult to understand for he freely created barbarous words of uncertain meaning and often wrote quite contradictory statements. Nonetheless, he gained an extremely wide following. At about the same time, the Philosophers' Stone itself took on the added property of being a potent, perhaps universal, medicine. Just as it "cured" the base metals of their defects and turned them into gold, so (it came to be believed) the Stone could "transmute" sickness into health. This deployment of alchemy for pharmacological uses is called "iatrochemistry," and it constituted a large and important branch of the discipline in the sixteenth and seventeenth centuries. The introduction of chemical medicines by the iatrochemists, who were generally followers of Paracelsus, was generally opposed for two centuries by the predominantly Galenist medical establishment, whose pharmacopeia was based on plant and animal preparations and who believed (with some accuracy) that Paracelsian or iatrochemical medicines prepared from minerals and metals were harmful.

One of the more widely accepted innovations of Paracelsus and his followers was their codification of the variable quantity of earth, which was present in metals and minerals (according to some Islamic writers), into a third principle termed Salt. Salt was supposed to confer the properties of hardness and brittleness. These three—Mercury, Sulfur, and Salt, or the *tria prima*—were then extended to be the ingredients of all substances, not just of minerals and metals. Later writers, about 1600, began to include two further principles—Phlegm and Earth—that were passive compared to the active ingredients of Mercury, Sulfur, and Salt. Attempts to separate the *tria prima* from mixed bodies, to purify them, and then to recombine them into purer, more powerful, regenerated forms made up yet another subset of alchemy termed "spagyria," from the Greek words *span* (to separate) and *ageirein* (to combine).

In the seventeenth century, all of the different subsets and schools of alchemy coexisted. Some alchemists pursued only chrysopoeia and had no interest in medicine; others gave up the quest for the Stone and concentrated on medicinal preparations; still others combined activities in both spheres. Alongside all of these developments were numerous charlatans, who gave the subject a bad popular reputation. Some such cheats hawked supposedly miraculous cures, while others promised to complete the Stone for patrons at a price but were more adroit at extracting money from the wealthy than essences from metals. Numerous royal and princely courts in Europe employed court alchemists, who were supported on the supposition that they were close to solving the problem of transmutation. The court of the Holy Roman Emperor Rudolf II (b. 1552, r. 1576–1612) at Prague was a renowned locus of such activity. But in the early eighteenth century, belief in the possibility of profitable chrysopoeia waned considerably, and, as new theories of the constitution of matter were advanced, spagyria declined as well. While these branches survived in a few locales in Germany until the late eighteenth century, by the end of that century they were essentially extinct. Iatrochemistry and some other aspects of alchemy continued to evolve, flowing into modern chemistry and pharmacy.

Modern Interpretations of Alchemy

Since its demise, several schools have advanced interpretations of alchemy. The rationalist temper of the Enlightenment rejected alchemy as fraudulent and irrational. In the nineteenth century, there arose the esoteric or occultist interpretation, which claims that alchemy was predominantly or exclusively a spiritual endeavor dealing with the soul of man rather than the manipulation of matter. This view draws its origins from popular Victorian occultism and continues to attract numerous adherents, even though it is refuted by historical evidence. The psychoanalytic school, founded by Carl Jung (1875–1961) and drawing upon the wealth of alchemical imagery, proposes that alchemical texts describe the projection of the unconscious onto matter and that what the alchemists describe is not the actual transformation of material substances but, rather, manifestations of psychological processes within the alchemists themselves. In its rejection of the real laboratory aspects of alchemy and its lack of support from historical evidence, the Jungian interpretation is largely a recasting of the occultist view (to which it owes a great debt) in more sophisticated terminology. In the light of recent questions regarding Jung's motives and credibility, the psychological interpretation is shaky at best, in spite of which it still attracts numerous devotees. At the other end of the interpretational spectrum, positivists and presentists (echoing Enlightenment sentiments) have dismissed alchemy as unproductive and misguided and claim it to have been, at best, a pseudo-science. This interpretation is likewise flawed, for, while alchemy differs in significant ways from modern chemistry, it nonetheless contained a well-developed theoretical framework with competing schools of thought. Many alchemists pursued logically constructed experimental programs directed toward their goals, however unattainable. The chrysopoetic, spagyric, and iatrochemical branches of alchemy (not to mention its more technical aspects) had positive and profound influences on the development of modern science in both theory and practice. Recent work on the Paracelsian iatrochemists leaves little doubt as to their contributions to science and medicine. Many important figures of early-modern science, such as Robert Boyle (1627–91) and Isaac Newton (1642–1727), were strongly influenced by alchemy and pursued it avidly. Boyle was a firm believer in the reality of chrysopoeia and spent much time seeking for preparation of the Stone.

Alchemy and Religion

From the earliest times, there have been cross-influences between alchemy and religion. In the Hellenistic period, many Gnostic elements appeared in alchemical writings. Zosimus's system relies upon a conception of matter as composed of "body" and "soul," with the active principles referred to the soul. As already mentioned, one of the most important corpora of Islamic alchemical texts arose out of the Ikhwan as-Safa, an esoteric Muslim brotherhood. In Europe, the processes of alchemy were widely viewed as emblems or parallels to religious truths. Paracelsus and some of his followers linked the material *tria prima* of Mercury, Sulfur, and Salt into a web of correspondences, which included the Triune Godhead and the threefold nature of man—spirit, soul, and body. While there can be no doubt of the important interconnections between alchemy and religion—for alchemical texts are full of religious or metaphysical expressions and references—such linkages have gained an exaggerated importance in the common view that alchemy is *essentially* linked to spiritual or religious topics. The link between alchemy and religion is primarily analogical and pious rather than intrinsic; the great majority of

alchemists did not claim their art to be supernatural or miraculous but, rather, purely physical and natural. The importance of the role of religious and spiritual elements in alchemy has been artificially magnified since the mid-nineteenth century by the distortions of the occultist and Jungian schools.

Only a few alchemical authors write of supernatural or spiritual agencies and powers. Paracelsus's world system, for example, is populated with a vast number of supernatural beings and elemental spirits, and natural and sympathetic magic played a central role in his organic cosmos. Certain other developments blurred the lines between magical, spiritual, and religious practices and alchemy. One chief contributor was the Renaissance influx of the Hermetic corpus, Neoplatonism, and the Cabala, plus heightened interest in natural magic and the juxtaposition of these topics to alchemical notions by writers like Giovanni Pico della Mirandola (1463–94) in Italy and the Abbot Trithemius (1462–1516) and Agrippa von Nettesheim (1486–1535) in Germany. Likewise, the later writings of self-styled Rosicrucians like Robert Fludd (1574–1637) and Thomas Vaughn (1622–66) combined alchemical notions with natural magic and mystical cosmologies. Yet, concurrent with these developments—these extensions of alchemy into more peripheral domains—most chrysopoeian and iatrochemical authors did not directly ally the fundamentals of their art with spiritual matters even if they did recognize important metaphorical correspondences between their art and religion. Alchemists, in general, were at pains to emphasize that their art proceeded by purely natural and physical means. Indeed, the theological arguments over the licitness of alchemy from the thirteenth century to the seventeenth hinged upon the natural processes involved in the art and the identical physical natures of natural and alchemically prepared gold.

Readers of alchemical texts will be immediately struck by their religious tone. Authors invoke the necessity of divine revelation for the successful uncovering of grand alchemical secrets; the Philosophers' Stone, in particular, was considered a true *donum Dei* (gift of God). The alchemical masters, or *adepti,* were considered an Elect, favored by God with the knowledge of the secrets of nature. The students, or Sons of Art, needed, in addition to assiduous study, sanctity and humility before God in order for success to flow to them as a grace from the Almighty. This doctrine of initiation and sanctity, ubiquitous in alchemical books, is already present (though far less pervasively) in Geber's thirteenth-century *Summa perfectionis*. The author invokes God's blessing on the aspiring adept, claiming that such a blessing is necessary for success. The origin of these religious imprecations has been traced to Islamic sources, particularly to "Jabir's" *Liber de septuaginta (Book of Seventy)*, whose style "Geber" emulated. This exalted status of alchemy intensified the need to cover alchemical writings in secrecy, to avoid, in alchemical parlance, "casting pearls before swine" by making the fruits of divine inspiration indiscriminately available to the vulgar. Some later European alchemists argued for a divine origin of alchemy, claiming it as a crucial part of the *prisca sapientia* (ancient wisdom), which had been revealed by God directly to Adam, to one of his sons, or to the patriarchs. This view maintained that Solomon's wisdom included great alchemical knowledge, and it was through his art that the gold for the temple of Jerusalem was produced. Supporters also argued that the mythical founder of alchemy, the Egyptian Hermes Trismegestus, himself learned the art from inscriptions on pillars engraved by ancient patriarchs before the Flood.

The most immediately apparent interface between alchemy and religion occurs in the almost ubiquitous use of religious imagery as a source of metaphor for alchemical texts. By the fifteenth century, a fairly well-developed set of correspondences or parallels had been set up between alchemical theory and religious truths. The fifteenth-century *Rosarium philosophorum* (*Rose Garden of Philosophers*), for example, attests to such development with its use of Christ as an emblem for the Philosophers' Stone—the matter of the Stone undergoes "death" and "resurrection" like Christ. The parallel between Christ the Savior and Redeemer and the Philosophers' Stone, "the medicine of men and metals," recurs repeatedly in scores of texts. As Christ frees mankind from its sins, so the Stone both frees base metals from their imperfections by exalting them into gold and frees sick men from their illnesses. The colors through which the forming Philosophers' Stone was supposed to pass were also related to theological truths. The matter must first turn black, the prime indication of correct practice. This *nigredo* (blackening) was seen as a sign of death and putrefaction: "Unless the grain of wheat fall into the ground and die, increase you may not get." The duration of this black color was sometimes described as a purgatory, during which the impurities and superfluities were removed by the action of the continuous fire under the

flask. The subsequent whitening symbolized resurrection, and the final red stage the glorified body that could no longer be hurt by either fire or corruption.

Many authors considered the work of making the Philosophers' Stone as emblematic of the greater process of the history of salvation or, in other cases, of Creation. Biblical passages were, thus, often applied to alchemical operations. One writer, Melchior Cibiensis, purports to expound the whole secret of making the Stone under the imagery and text of the Mass. Some writers believed or expected that alchemical processes should show similitudes to the greater processes of Creation or salvation (the famous Hermetic dictum, "as above, so below," was often interpreted in just this way) and, therefore, employed theological truths or Scriptural passages to guide their experimental practice.

These close links, which many alchemists made between alchemical and religious belief, were an expression of minds more pious, and more accustomed and attuned to the drawing of parallels and the reading of signs and emblems than ours, and also of a time in which modern divisions between domains of knowledge (such as science and religion) were not sharply drawn. The use of metaphorical language does not countenance the conclusion that alchemical authors necessarily meant to imply some mystical union between events alchemical and religious or that they intended such metaphors to act as explanations of alchemical processes. The alchemists' observations of the appearances of chemical processes and changes and their subsequent attempts to explain or describe them would naturally have led to the construction of such similitudes. The need for alchemical secrecy greatly intensified this tendency as alchemical writers (particularly chrysopoeians) strove to create an intricate set of *Decknamen* (cover names) under which to hide their secrets, within allusive or metaphorical frameworks of correspondences that drew freely on ancient mythology, everyday experience, or religious doctrine and imagery. While the common affirmations that personal sanctity and God's blessing are required for success may strike the modern reader as evidencing an especially close link between alchemy and religion, it can be argued that such expressions do not reveal anything uniquely about alchemy but, rather, evidence the greater piety and religious sentiments of the premodern period in general.

The almost universal use of religious imagery in alchemy was mirrored by a much less prevalent employment of alchemy in religion. The chief such writer was

Jacob Boehme (1575–1624), the cobbler, autodidact, and Lutheran mystic of Görlitz. After his first ecstatic religious experience in 1600, Boehme began to compose an elaborate (and sometimes contradictory) vision of the world and God's creative power within it. In his mystical descriptions, he employed the terminology of alchemy: Mercury, Sulfur, and Salt presented cosmic powers and functions. Central to his early writings was the concept of *Salitter,* a divine substance containing within itself the sum of all creative forces and the means of things coming to be and passing away. The properties he attributes to it make up an analogy to the physical properties of the alchemists' *sal nitrum* (saltpeter, potassium nitrate). Boehme was aware of the alchemical, especially Paracelsian, tradition and principles and adapted them to his mystical purposes. The subsequent school of Behmenists propagated Boehme's alchemical metaphor, and his notions strongly colored the theology of eighteenth-century Pietists.

See also The Cabala; Hermeticism; Magic and the Occult

BIBLIOGRAPHY

Baldwin, Martha. "Alchemy and the Society of Jesus in the Seventeenth Century: Strange Bedfellows?" *Ambix* 40 (1993): 41–64.

Browne, C. A. "The Rhetorical and Religious Aspects of Greek Alchemy." *Ambix* 2 (1938): 129–37; 3 (1939): 15–25.

Debus, Allen G. *The English Paracelsians.* London: Oldbourne, 1965.

———. *The French Paracelsians.* Cambridge: Cambridge University Press, 1991.

Dobbs, Betty Jo Teeter. *The Hunting of the Green Lion: Foundations of Newton's Alchemy.* Cambridge: Cambridge University Press, 1975.

———. *The Janus Face of Genius: The Role of Alchemy in Newton's Thought.* Cambridge: Cambridge University Press, 1990.

Figala, Karin. "Die exacte Alchemie von Isaac Newtons." *Verhandlungen der Naturforschenden Gesellschaft in Basel* 94 (1984): 157–228.

Ganzenmüller, W. *Die Alchemie im Mittelalter.* Ch. 3, "Alchemie und Religion." 1938. Reprint. Hildesheim: Olms, 1967.

Halleux, Robert. *Les alchimistes grecs.* Paris: Les Belles Lettres, 1981.

Hooykaas, Roger. "Die Elementenlehre des Paracelsus." *Janus* 39 (1935): 175–87.

———. "Die Elementenlehre der Iatrochemiker." *Janus* 41 (1937): 1–28.

Jabir Ibn Hayyan. *Book of Definitions (Kitab al-idah).* Trans. by E. J. Holmyard. *Proceedings of the Royal Society of Medicine, Section of the History of Medicine* 16 (1923): 6–57.

Kopp, Hermann. *Die Alchemie in Alterer und Neuerer Zeit.* 1971. Reprint. Hildesheim: Olms, 1986.

Lippmann, E. O. von. *Entstehung und Verbreitung der Alchemie.* Berlin: Springer, 1919.

Newman, William. *The Summa perfectionis of the Pseudo-Geber.* Leiden: Brill, 1991.

———. *Gehennical Fire: The Lives of George Starkey, an American Alchemist in the Scientific Revolution.* Cambridge, Mass: Harvard University Press, 1994.

Newman, William R., and Lawrence M. Principe. "Alchemy vs. Chemistry: The Etymological Origin of a Historiographic Mistake." *Early Science and Medicine* 3 (1998): 32–65.

Principe, Lawrence M. *The Aspiring Adept: Robert Boyle and His Alchemical Quest.* Princeton, N.J.: Princeton University Press, 1998.

Principe, Lawrence M., and William R. Newman. "Some Problems in the Historiography of Alchemy." *Archimedes* 4 (2000).

Schuler, Robert M. "Some Spiritual Alchemies of Seventeenth-Century England." *Journal of the History of Ideas* 41 (1980): 293–318.

van Martels, Z. R. W. M., ed. *Alchemy Revisited.* Leiden: Brill, 1990.

100. HERMETICISM

Jole Shackelford

Hermeticism (or Hermetism) refers to a diverse body of religious, magical, astrological, and alchemical teachings associated with the ancient Egyptian god Thoth, whom the Greeks called Hermes Trismegistus. These teachings originated c. A.D. 100–500 in the chaotic social and political climate of Greco-Roman Egypt, which nourished a melange of religious cults. A number of treatises attributed to Hermes or involving him and his descendants survived these cults and disseminated an arcane, fragmentary knowledge of alchemy, astrology, magic, and religion to Byzantium, echoes of which reverberated in the West, often in the specialized and secretive world of chemists, metallurgists, astrologers, and healers. By the late European Middle Ages, the name "Hermes" was connected to such esoteric knowledge, much of which had come to the Latin West by way of Islam. One well-known example of this literature is the Emerald Table of Hermes, which was embedded in the Arabic alchemical works attributed to Jabir Ibn Hayyan (Geber), who flourished in the eighth or ninth century. It presents thirteen aphoristic statements that were fundamental to medieval and Renaissance occult philosophy, including the well-known statement of the harmony between the macrocosm and the microcosm, "that which is above corresponds to that which is below." However, a Hermetic religious text, the *Asclepius,* was also known to Christian scholars in Latin translation since the time of Augustine (354–430).

Hence, when a Greek manuscript comprising fourteen of seventeen texts, known today as the *Corpus Hermeticum,* was brought from Byzantium to Florence and translated by Marsilio Ficino (1433–99) in 1463, contemporaries were already familiar with the name Hermes and eager for the ancient sources of the true Christian theology it seemingly contained. Ficino's Latin edition was published in 1471 and accompanied by an introduction in which he dated Hermes to the time of Moses on the basis of patristic chronologies and on the internal evidence of the Hermetic texts themselves, which "foretold" the coming of Christianity. Ficino's misdating of the *Corpus* by fifteen hundred years added to its appeal as an early source of divine wisdom. The *Corpus* itself was immensely popular and was republished many times in the sixteenth century, when three new texts were added and a Greek edition was published, including Hermetic fragments that were collected by Stobaeus about A.D. 500. Hence, early-modern scholars were faced with two kinds of Hermetic tracts, the "theoretical Hermetica" of the *Corpus,* which are not very magical but teach a contemplative, ascetic, sometimes Gnostic religion, and the diverse "technical Hermetica," which pertain to magic and the occult sciences.

In modern times, the Hermetica concerned mainly orientalists, occultists, and historians of Renaissance religion until the mid-1960s, when Frances Yates identified the "Hermetic tradition" as an important source for the cosmology of Giordano Bruno (1548–1600). She credited Ficino with reviving Hermetic magic and establishing a philosophical tradition leading from the *Corpus* to Bruno. Bruno's visionary, sometimes modern-sounding cosmology intrigued historians of science, some of whom saw in Bruno's execution by the Roman Catholic authorities an emblem of a more general suppression of scientific freedom by an entrenched religious orthodoxy. But Yates's work painted a picture of Bruno as a Hermetic magician, not as a misunderstood modern, and suggested that this Hermetic tradition may have played an important role in reorienting natural philosophers' attitudes toward human will and the ability to control nature, both factors considered important to the ideology of the new science of the seventeenth century. This spurred historians of science to reexamine the roots of modern science, taking cognizance of a wide intellectual context that includes the occult sciences and religious views of early scientists such as Nicholas Copernicus (1473–1543), Johannes Kepler (1571–1630), and Isaac Newton (1642–1727).

Recent studies have challenged Yates's conclusions, pointing out that the emphasis on magic and control of nature found in the work of Ficino and his followers cannot have come from the *Corpus* but, instead, represents a broad synthesis of ancient philosophy, astrological medicine, and Renaissance Platonism. They argue that the term "Hermetic" ought to be used in the restricted sense, referring only to doctrines with a specific textual basis in the *Corpus,* the Stobaean fragments, and the *Asclepius.* However, this narrow philological definition privileges the theoretical Hermetica of the *Corpus,* which may actually have been selected from a larger body of Hermetic literature precisely because they lacked explicit alchemical and magical content and, therefore, represent only the religious side of Hermeticism. Furthermore, although such a precise definition is useful to the student of texts, it does not fit the actual usage of the term in the early-modern period and, therefore, offers little help to the historian of ideas, for whom "Hermeticism" conjures up a diffuse philosophical matrix of ideas about the origin and structure of the world.

When early-modern occult philosophers and their critics wrote of "Hermetic medicine" and "Hermetic doctors," as, for example, in the title of Hermann Conring's (1606–81) criticism of occult philosophy, *De hermetica medicina* (1648), they did not have in mind the *Corpus* or any other particular body of texts but, rather, a cosmology that was based on a vitalistic, Neoplatonic metaphysics that embraced astrology and alchemy: a worldview that was allegedly rooted in ancient philosophy and theology and associated with the Hermes who wrote the Emerald Table. Vestiges of this broader use of "Hermetic" survive to this day in the phrase "hermetically sealed," which comes not from the *Corpus Hermeticum* but from the technique used by "Hermetic" chemists to provide a vessel with an air-tight seal. Hermeticism will likely be used for a long time with both of these meanings: as a reference to a body of religious texts and as a general term for a Renaissance worldview. However, we are well advised not to judge by this dual meaning that there are any close doctrinal connections between Hermeticism as

an occult philosophy and the theoretical works of the *Corpus Hermeticum.* This explains why Hermetic philosophy continued to demand serious consideration well after the *Corpus* was convincingly redated in 1614 by the humanist philologist Isaac Casaubon (1559–1614). The *Corpus* subsequently lost its credentials as a divine source of Mosaic wisdom, but the Hermetic worldview itself remained a viable alternative to Aristotelian philosophy until it was transformed and replaced by corpuscular hypotheses in the late seventeenth and eighteenth centuries.

See also Alchemy; Astrology; The Cabala; Magic and the Occult

BIBLIOGRAPHY

Primary

Copenhaver, Brian P. *Hermetica: The Greek Corpus Hermeticum and the Latin Asclepius in a New English Translation.* Cambridge: Cambridge University Press, 1992.

Nock, A.D., and A. J. Festugière. *Corpus Hermeticum.* 4 vols. 1946–54. 3d ed. Paris: Belles Lettres, 1972–3.

Scott, Walter. *Hermetica: The Ancient Greek and Latin Writings Which Contain Religious or Philosophic Teachings Ascribed to Hermes Trismegistus.* 4 vols. 1924–36. Reprint. London: Dawsons, 1968.

Secondary

Copenhaver, Brian P. "Natural Magic, Hermetism, and Occultism in Early Modern Science." In *Reappraisals of the Scientific Revolution,* ed. by David C. Lindberg and Robert S. Westman. Cambridge: Cambridge University Press, 1990, 261–301.

Festugière, A. J. *La Révélation d'Hermès Trismégiste.* 4 vols. Paris: J. Gabalda, 1950–4.

Merkel, Ingrid, and Allen G. Debus, eds. *Hermeticism and the Renaissance: Intellectual History and the Occult in Early Modern Europe.* Washington, D.C.: Folger Shakespeare Library, 1988.

Nebelsick, Harold P. *Circles of God: Theology and Science from the Greeks to Copernicus.* Edinburgh: Scottish Academic Press, 1985.

Plessner, M. "Hermes Trismegistus and Arab Science." *Studia Islamica* 2 (1954): 45–59.

Shumaker, Wayne. *The Occult Sciences in the Renaissance: A Study in Intellectual Patterns.* Berkeley: University of California Press, 1972.

Silverstein, Theodore. "Liber Hermetis Mercurii triplicis De VI rerum principiis." *Archives d'histoire doctrinale et littéraire du moyen age* 30 (1955): 217–302.

Tester, S. J. *A History of Western Astrology.* Bury St. Edmunds: Boydell, 1987.

Walker, Daniel. P. *Spiritual and Demonic Magic from Ficino to Campanella.* Studies of the Warburg Institute. No. 22. London: Warburg Institute, 1958.

———. *The Ancient Theology: Studies in Christian Platonism from the Fifteenth to the Eighteenth Century.* London: Duckworth, 1972.

Westman, Robert S., and J. E. McGuire. *Hermeticism and the Scientific Revolution.* Los Angeles: Clark Memorial Library, 1977.

Yates, Frances A. *Giordano Bruno and the Hermetic Tradition.* London: Routledge and Kegan Paul, 1964.

———. "The Hermetic Tradition in Renaissance Science." In *Art, Science, and History in the Renaissance,* ed. by Charles Singleton. Baltimore: Johns Hopkins University Press, 1968.

101. NUMBERS

Peter G. Sobol

In virtually every culture, numbers have enjoyed sacred or symbolic value. Many cultures have also had a tradition of numerology, in which they have assigned mystical or magical properties to numbers. The traditional spiritual significance that is often associated with numbers comes from a belief in their supposed revelatory power. This belief springs from two largely distinct traditions, both dating to antiquity. In the philosophical tradition initiated by the Greek philosopher Pythagoras (sixth century B.C.), numbers are the elements of the natural world, and the world is best known by discovering the properties of numbers. In the mantic tradition, which is probably at least as old as the invention of writing, words and names reveal hidden meanings and associations when interpreted as numbers.

Pythagoras

The assignment of meanings to certain numbers may date back to the origin of counting. Pythagoras and his followers adopted traditional meanings for the numbers in the decad (the numbers from 1 to 10), but they also expanded upon traditional meanings in numbers by attending to arithmetical properties. Despite their belief that even numbers were feminine and weak, while odd numbers were masculine and strong, the number 10 evoked their special reverence, in part because it represented at once the decad and the sum of the first four numbers of the decad (1+2+3+4 = 10).

Pythagoras himself may have discovered that the two parts of a string that is stretched over a moveable bridge yield consonant harmonic intervals when the lengths on either side of the bridge make up small whole-number ratios (2:1 for the diapason, or octave; 3:2 for the diapente, or fifth; and 4:3 for the diatesseron, or fourth).

This discovery may have persuaded the Pythagoreans not only that numbers can be used to describe reality, but also that numbers *are* reality. Therefore, they believed, the discovery of nature is best pursued not by observation of natural phenomena but by contemplation of the properties of numbers. Their devotion to 10 led them to propose a cosmology with 10 celestial bodies, including the sun and the earth, which orbit a central fire *(hestia)*. The seven known planets (moon, Mercury, Venus, sun, Mars, Jupiter, and Saturn), the earth, and the sphere of the fixed stars yielded only nine bodies, so (much to Aristotle's [384–322 B.C.] indignation at *On the Heavens* 2.13.293a 23–27) they proposed a tenth celestial body, a counterearth *(antichthon),* which was never visible from the habitable regions of the earth. The Pythagoreans believed that each celestial body, by virtue of its speed of revolution around the *hestia,* produced a musical note (higher notes for faster planets, lower notes for slower). These notes combined in a celestial harmony that, because it always sounded, remained inaudible.

Plato

The idea that proportion and harmony are at the basis of nature appealed to other Greek thinkers. Plato (c. 427–347 B.C.) mentions the inaudible music of the spheres in the Myth of Er at the end of *Republic* 10 (617b). Whether Pythagorean number mysticism lies behind Plato's use of specific numbers is unclear. Plato probably chose 5,040 as the number of households in the ideal city described in *Laws* 5 (737e) because it has sixty factors, including the first ten digits, and, hence, allows for flexible division of responsibility, rather than because of any mystical significance. Scholars continue to puzzle over the meaning and even the value of Plato's "nuptial number," which was to guide human reproduction (*Republic* 8. 546).

Christianity

The Old and New Testaments refer to various numbers, such as the six days of Creation, the dimensions of the ark, and the 153 fish caught by the disciples (John 21:11), all of which had special meaning for biblical commentators. For Augustine of Hippo (A.D. 354–430), the reason that God created the world in six days arose from the properties of the number 6. Following the Pythagoreans, Augustine held that numbers equal to the sum of their factors are perfect. Since 6 is the first perfect number (6 = 1+2+3), the six days of Genesis reveal the perfection of creation.

Rules for extracting meanings from numbers became enshrined in the seven liberal arts in the works of Macrobius (fl. c. A.D. 400), Martianus Capella (fl. 480), and Boethius (c. 475–525). Although these rules yielded contradictory meanings for any given number, they offered an appealing form of explanation applicable to Scripture and natural philosophy alike. The stability and balance of the number 4 explained why there were four elements, four humors, four seasons, and four winds. Four was the number that represented things at rest, as the earth was at rest in the center of the cosmos. To match the fourness of the world, God sent four evangelists to write four Gospels. The five senses of animals explained their creation on the fifth day, while the perfection of humans explained their creation on the sixth.

Johannes Kepler

Implicit in such reasoning was the belief that God had created the world in agreement with the properties of numbers. Johannes Kepler (1571–1630) accepted this view, but Kepler's God was a geometer not a numerologist. Kepler recognized that seven bodies (moon, Mercury, Venus, sun, Mars, Jupiter, Saturn) orbited the central earth according to the Aristotelian and Ptolemaic planetary systems, while only six bodies (Mercury, Venus, Earth, Mars, Jupiter, and Saturn) orbited Copernicus's (1473–1543) central sun. Yet, he nevertheless chose not to support the Copernican theory by reference to the perfection of 6, as his follower Georg Rheticus (1514–74) did in his *Narratio prima* (*First Narrative* [1540]). Instead, Kepler showed in his *Mysterium cosmographicum* (*Cosmographic Mystery* [1596])

that the five regular Platonic polyhedrons could be used to define orbits for six bodies, implying that the heliocentric cosmos followed from God's geometrical plan.

In *Harmonice mundi* (*Harmonies of the World* [1619]), Kepler retained the Pythagorean belief that the cosmos revealed divinely established harmonies. He obtained for each planet a musical interval that was derived from the ratio of its maximum and minimum orbital speed. He also discovered the constant proportion between the square of each planet's orbital period and the cube of its mean orbital radius, which became his third law of planetary motion. An appendix that was critical of the number mystic Robert Fludd (1574–1637) initiated a debate between Kepler and Fludd over the extent and numerological significance of harmonies in the cosmos.

The Mantic Tradition

In the ancient Greek and Hebrew alphabets, letter characters doubled as numerals. Consequently, every word and every name was also a number. The ancient practice of *gematria* (a cabalistic method of interpreting the Hebrew Scriptures) assumed that a word or a name with a certain numerical value was equivalent to other words or names of equal value. *Gematria* was one of several methods incorporated into the Jewish mystical theology, called Cabala, which developed in the early centuries of the Christian era. Integral to both Jewish Cabala and its Christian expressions was the belief that the Hebrew Scriptures contained hidden meanings that *gematria* and other techniques could disclose. Cabalists revealed the identity of the three men who appear to Abram in Genesis 18:2 by noting that the phrase "and, behold, three men" has the same numerical value as the phrase, "these are Michael, Gabriel and Raphael." Twentieth-century numerology employs the reduction of name-numbers by addition to a single or two-digit number (supplemented by a separate sum for vowels and consonants), in which personal information is revealed.

See also The Cabala; The Copernican Revolution; Hermeticism; Macrocosm/Microcosm; Magic and the Occult; Plato and Platonism

BIBLIOGRAPHY

Bell, Eric Temple. *Numerology.* Baltimore: Williams and Wilkins, 1933.

———. *Magic of Numbers.* New York: McGraw-Hill, 1946.

Burkert, Walter. *Lore and Science in Ancient Pythagoreanism,* 372–77. Cambridge, Mass.: Harvard University Press, 1972, 465–80.

Butler, Christopher. *Number Symbolism.* London: Routledge and Kegan Paul, 1970.

Field, Judith V. "Kepler's Rejection of Numerology." In *Occult and Scientific Mentalities in the Renaissance,* ed. by Brian Vickers. Cambridge: Cambridge University Press, 1984, 273–96.

Hopper, V. F. *Medieval Number Symbolism: Its Sources, Meaning, and Influence on Thought and Expression.* New York: Columbia University Press, 1938.

Peck, Russell A. "Numbers as Cosmic Language." In *By Things Seen,* ed. by David L. Jeffrey. Ottawa: University of Ottawa Press, 1979, 47–80.

Seidenberg, A. "Ritual Origin of Counting." *Archives for the History of the Exact Sciences* 2(1) (1962): 1–40.

Westman, Robert S. "Nature, Art, and Psyche: Jung, Pauli, and the Kepler-Fludd Polemic." In *Occult and Scientific Mentalities in the Renaissance,* ed. by Brian Vickers. Cambridge: Cambridge University Press, 1984, 177–207.

102. The Cabala

Peter G. Sobol

The expulsion of the Jews from Spain in 1492 brought to public awareness among Jews and Christians alike the existence of a Hebrew esoteric mystical theology, the Cabala, that included cosmogonical and psychological doctrines, as well as methods for discovering supposed hidden meanings in the text of the Torah. Christian humanists, with their interest in ancient languages and their respect for ancient wisdom, were drawn to the Cabala seeking evidence to support their faith. Aspects of the Cabala appealed also to the Renaissance penchant for magic, and it continued to appeal to occultists into the twentieth century.

The Cabala, as it was revealed in the early sixteenth century, had only recently coalesced from several much older ideas about Creation and salvation. As early as the second century A.D., Jewish thinkers were using in their cosmogonies concepts of emanation and of entities intermediate between God and creation. Jewish interest in eschatology and in the postmortem existence of the soul dates back to the Babylonian exile (sixth century B.C.). Scholars continue to debate whether these periods of upheaval sparked innovations from within the Jewish religious community or opened that community to Gnostic and other ideas from without.

The Texts

The central texts of the Cabala in the early sixteenth century were the *Sefer Yezira (Book of Formation),* the *Sefer Bahir (Luminous Book),* and the *Sefer Zohar (Book of Splendor).* The *Sefer Yezira,* a brief and abstruse work written between the third and sixth centuries, explains creation in terms of the first ten numbers and the twenty-two letters of the Hebrew alphabet, together making thirty-two "paths of wisdom." These mysterious teachings formed the roots of two of the Cabala's basic tenets: the existence of ten divine powers or manifestations, often called *sefirot* (singular *sefira*), which represent God or mediate between God and creation; and the creative and magical power of words and names.

The *Sefer Bahir (Luminous Book),* a compilation of brief texts and fragments made in southern France late in the twelfth century, places the *sefirot* in a particular formation, a "secret tree," and likens the arrangement to the image of a primordial man. The *Bahir* also assumes the occurrence of *gilgul* (reincarnation via transmigration of souls), a belief with scant prior development in Jewish thought.

Several teachers in Germany, France, and Spain in the twelfth and thirteenth centuries pursued both the speculative aspects of the Cabala (the nature of the *sefirot* and *gilgul*) and the more practical aspects, including various techniques for extracting hidden meanings from the text of Scripture. One such technique, *gematria* (a cabalistic method of interpreting the Hebrew Scriptures), can be applied to any written language in which letters also serve as numerals (which is true of Hebrew, Greek, and Latin) with the consequence that any word or name can also be understood as a number. Cabalists believed that words and numbers in Scripture could be replaced with words or numbers of equal value to reveal hidden meanings. Using *notarikon,* Cabalists treated each letter of a difficult word as if it were the initial letter of a word in a phrase. Conversely, the initial letters of a phrase could be combined to form a word that contained all of the power of the phrase. *Temurrah* entailed the anagrammatic reconstruction of scriptural passages.

In the late thirteenth and early fourteenth centuries, Moses de Leon (c. 1240–1305) disseminated copies of a *midrash* (commentary on the Hebrew Scriptures) and other works in Hebrew and Aramaic attributed to Simeon ben Yohai (fl. mid-second century A.D.) under the title *Sefer Zohar (Book of Splendor)*. Modern scholars agree that Moses himself was their author. In the *Zohar*, the *sefirot* acquire several levels of meaning. God is their source, yet they are not distinct from God. They are at once a manifestation of God's powers and the image both of the created world and of its microcosmic representation, man. God himself is *en sof*, limitless and beyond human comprehension.

The appearance of the *Zohar* marked a turning point in the history of the Cabala. It amplified the Gnostic ideas implicit in earlier texts and widened the debate among rabbis and scholars over the value of the Cabala. Advocates argued that, by insisting on the divine inspiration of even obsolete legal sections of the Torah (believing that deeper levels of meaning lay encoded therein), Cabalists retaliated against interpretations of the Torah offered by Moses Maimonides (1135–1204) and other rationalist philosophers. Opponents argued that Cabalistic doctrines, so at odds with tradition and possibly infected with Christian ideas, posed a greater threat than rationalism.

Isaac Luria

Cabalists driven from Spain in 1492 joined others, who had emigrated earlier, in the Palestinian city of Safed. The most influential of the Safed Cabalists, Isaac Luria (1534–70), elaborated on Zoharic psychological doctrines, enhancing their Gnostic tenor. Lurianic Cabala analogized the exile of the human soul from its celestial home with the exile of Israel and with a coeval flaw in the cosmos itself. While successive reincarnations sufficed for an individual soul to achieve *tikkun* (restoration), the *tikkun* of Israel and of the cosmos required a messiah. The penetration of these ideas into the mainstream of Jewish life led to a popular belief in the immanent advent of a messiah and contributed to the Shabbatean movement in the seventeenth and eighteenth centuries. The Lurianic tenet that prayer and meditation could hasten the messiah's arrival influenced the development of Hasidism in the eighteenth century.

Historians of science have shown that natural philosophers in the sixteenth and seventeenth centuries esteemed several concepts, such as the importance of harmony and proportion, traceable to Neoplatonic and occult traditions. The influence of specifically Cabalistic ideas on scientific thought remains largely unexplored. Recent studies have suggested a role for the Cabala in the thought of Johannes Kepler (1571–1630) and Gottfried Wilhelm Leibniz (1646–1716).

The Christian Cabala

Christian interest in the Cabala began with the Italian humanist Giovanni Pico della Mirandola (1463–94). Pico's recourse to the Cabala for more than one hundred of his nine hundred daring *Conclusiones philosophicae, cabalisticae, et theologiae (Philosophical, Cabalistic, and Theological Theses* [1486]) drew attention to the existence of a vast esoteric literature with broad appeal for early-modern Christian intellectuals. Some Christians came to believe that the Cabala contained the record of a primordial revelation. Others believed that it contained ancient indications of Jesus's coming and hoped to draw upon those texts in their efforts to convert Jews to Christianity. Ties between the Cabala and hermetic doctrines attracted Rosicrucians, alchemists, and magi, including Henry Cornelius Agrippa von Nettesheim (c. 1486–1535), Robert Fludd (1574–1637), and Athanasius Kircher (1601–80). The practical Cabala promised the diligent magus a means of discovering profound secrets and constructing words of power. The speculative Cabala reinforced his belief that he was a microcosm, able to harness celestial influences, and that, with knowledge and preparation, his soul could ascend through the *sefirot* and unite with God.

Christian students of the Cabala in the eighteenth and nineteenth centuries who could not read Hebrew relied upon the two volumes of *Kabbalah denudata (Cabala Revealed* [1677–84]) by Christian Knorr von Rosenroth (1636–89), a German Protestant. He supplied Latin translations of texts from the *Zohar* along with essays by himself and others. The Cabala continued to play a role in modern occultism in the nineteenth and twentieth centuries in the work of Alphonse-Louis Constant (Eliphas Lévi [1810–75]), Helena P. Blavatsky (1831–91), and Aleister Crowley (1875–1947).

See also Judaism to 1700; Judaism Since 1700;
    Macrocosm/Microcosm; Numbers

BIBLIOGRAPHY

Blau, Joseph Leon. *The Christian Interpretation of the Cabala in the Renaissance.* 1944. Reprint. Port Washington, N.Y.: Kennikat, 1965.

Clulee, Nicholas H. *John Dee's Natural Philosophy: Between Science and Religion.* London and New York: Routledge, 1988.

Coudert, Allison P. *Leibniz and the Kabbalah.* Dordrecht: Kluwer, 1995.

Idel, Moshe. *Kabbalah: New Perspectives.* New Haven, Conn.: Yale University Press, 1988.

McGinn, Bernard. *Cabalists and Christians: Reflections on Cabala in Medieval and Renaissance Thought.* Dordrecht: Kluwer, 1994.

Müller, Ernst. *A History of Jewish Mysticism.* 1946. Reprint. New York: Barnes and Noble, 1995.

Ruderman, David B. *Kabbalah, Magic, and Science: The Cultural Universe of a Sixteenth-Century Jewish Physician.* Cambridge, Mass.: Harvard University Press, 1988.

———. *Jewish Thought and Scientific Discovery in Early Modern Europe.* New Haven, Conn.: Yale University Press, 1995.

Scholem, Gershom. *Kabbalah.* New York: Meridian, 1978.

Waite, A. E. *The Holy Kabbalah.* New York: University Books, 1929.

Walton, Michael T., and Phyllis J. Walton. *The Geometrical Kabbalahs of John Dee and Johannes Kepler: The Hebrew Tradition and the Mathematical Study of Nature.* Dordrecht: Kluwer, 1997.

103. SPIRITUALISM

Deborah J. Coon

Spiritualism has two broad definitions. In the older, more technically philosophical usage, it means simply a spiritual rather than a material view of things. Since the late nineteenth century, with the advent of the modern spiritualist movement, the term has come more narrowly to stand for the belief in a system of communication with the spirits of the dead.

Spiritualism is often conflated with psychic research, but the two can be viewed as distinct. While spiritualism entails a belief in the afterlife and in human immortality, research concerning extrasensory perception (ESP) does not require such beliefs. Psychic research presupposes only the possibility that some living creatures are able to communicate with other living (not dead) creatures through extraordinary means. Some proponents of psychic research have believed in the afterlife and the possibility of spiritistic communication; others have not and have stressed the distinction between spiritualism and psychic research in an attempt to demarcate their own research as scientific.

The History of Spiritualism

Communication with spirits has had a long history in various societies, including Indian, African, Near Eastern, and Native American cultures. Nineteenth-century antecedents to the spiritualist movement of the 1850s can be found in American Shaker communities beginning in the 1830s and in the writings of the Swedish scientist-turned-mystic Emanuel Swedenborg (1688–1772) and his American followers beginning in the 1840s. R. Laurence Moore (1980) points out that, whereas Swedenborg claimed that he was divinely and uniquely endowed with the ability to communicate with the spirit world, the subsequent spiritualist movement in America had a democratizing influence.

Anyone, even those of the most humble origins, could potentially communicate directly with spirits.

The modern spiritualist movement traces its beginnings to 1848 in a small town near Rochester, New York, where two adolescents, Kate and Margaret Fox, were reported to have heard repeated rapping sounds in their home. The Fox sisters revealed these sounds to be the messages of a dead peddler, murdered and buried in the basement of their farmhouse. Prominent Rochester Quaker abolitionists, relatives of the youngsters, investigated the mystery and decided it was not a fraud (although the girls were discredited years later). With their help, the Fox sisters quickly rose to fame in radical reform circles and, from there, moved into public lecture halls and elite parlors, where they demonstrated their abilities to interested gatherings. As word of the Fox sisters spread, increasing numbers of people began reporting their own abilities to communicate with spirits. Popular interest in, and enthusiasm for, spiritualism grew rapidly in the 1850s and 1860s, fueled by the staggering death toll of the Civil War, as large numbers of people hoped to communicate with lost relatives. At the same time, the development of wireless telegraphy sparked the popular imagination with possible scientific explanations of spiritualistic communication. Perhaps there was a sort of "celestial wireless" that made possible communication between the souls of the living and the dead. The discovery of Roentgen rays in the 1890s showed the potential of science to discover previously unknown forms of energy, which added to hopes that scientists might eventually uncover the even more subtle types of mental and spiritual energy that purportedly underlay communication with spirits.

Within spiritualism, the term "medium" was applied to those persons who provided the means of communication with the spirit world. While mediums could be either male or female, the majority in the late nineteenth century were female. The term "spirit-control" was used to denote the particular spirit that was said to communicate by controlling the voice and movements of the medium. Many mediums had a specific spirit-control, who was believed to be regularly in attendance at their séances and who was alleged to help them contact other spirits. A séance was a session during which a given medium would act as the communicator between the spirit-control and a small circle of attendees, many of whom were devotees of a particular medium. Some mediums performed in front of larger audiences, filling lecture halls at the height of spiritualism's popularity in the 1870s and 1880s. During a séance, attendees attempted to contact deceased loved ones through the medium, often asking questions concerning life in the afterworld. To test the authenticity of the medium, attendees would also ask questions about themselves or their living friends and families that no one other than the questioner and the dead loved one could be expected to know. Correct answers from the medium provided empirical "proof" that he or she was in direct contact with spirits. Extant transcriptions of séances from the late nineteenth century also include less personal queries about the spirit world's opinions on current social, political, and religious movements.

Science and Spiritualism

For some followers, spiritualism was an alternative system of belief and a form of unorthodox religion. It did not require belief in God but provided its own proofs of spiritual immortality, as well as its own forms and rituals of spiritual union with beings beyond the veil. Spiritualism was a product of the modern scientific era as well, in that spiritualists believed in using empirical evidence to prove the existence of spiritual phenomena, and many believed that verification and validation by scientists were crucial to the spiritualist cause. Thus, authenticity of mediums was challenged and demonstrated empirically at each séance.

Those who developed an interest in spiritualism included a broad range of thinkers in a number of countries. Among the most prominent was the American philosopher and psychologist William James (1842–1910). James urged psychologists to study spiritualistic and psychic phenomena because, if real, they fell within the purview of psychological science. He argued that psy-

chology was too new a science to dismiss such reported phenomena a priori and urged that psychologists undertake disinterested scientific research to determine whether or not any of the reported phenomena were real. James also viewed spiritualism as a plausible form of new popular religion. In personal correspondence, he revealed his belief that perhaps the best hope of the social and moral regeneration of society lay in new phenomenological proof of an afterlife, such as that produced by the spiritualist movement. He urged that scientists become involved in the movement because they would be popularly considered more trustworthy judges than would laypeople, and their support would lend credibility to the movement. Throughout his career, he was sympathetic to the efforts of spiritualists and psychic researchers, and he was a founding member of the American Society for Psychical Research. The majority of scientists who declared their views of spiritualism in the late nineteenth century, however, were scientific naturalists who rejected the claims of the spiritualists and their scientific adherents.

The "New Psychology" that arose in the 1880s and the 1890s was intended by its founders to be an experimental natural science of the mind and soul. Early psychologists attempted to "secularize the soul," divorcing it from its theological or metaphysical foundations and explaining its phenomena through natural means. However, many members of the lay public expected these new psychologists to address their interests in spiritualism, mental telepathy, and clairvoyance, and wealthy donors to several early psychology laboratories stipulated that their funds be used for spiritualistic and psychic research. Some of the most prominent early psychologists, such as Theodore Flournoy (1854–1920) in Switzerland and Charles Richet (1850–1935) and Pierre Janet (1859–1947) in France, were also interested in these phenomena. Hence, spiritualism and psychic research became contentious issues within the new science. While some early psychologists conducted research that investigated spiritualistic phenomena, others, such as Joseph Jastrow (1863–1944), G. Stanley Hall (1844–1924), and Hugo Münsterberg (1863–1916), created new research fields in the psychology of belief and deception that attempted to discredit the research supporting such phenomena. Perhaps the most famous program in psychic research was carried out by Joseph Banks Rhine (1895–1980) and Louisa Rhine at Duke University beginning in the 1930s. Psychic research has remained a controversial issue within scientific psychology in the twentieth century. While interest in spiritualism as a potential topic of scientific pursuit has largely died away, spiritualism as a popular phenomenon experienced a resurgence of interest in the 1960s and later in the New Age movement.

See also Pragmatism; Psychology in America; Theories of the Soul

BIBLIOGRAPHY

Barrow, Logie. *Independent Spirits: Spiritualism and English Plebeianism.* London: Routledge and Kegan Paul, 1986.

Brandon, Ruth. *The Spiritualists: The Passion for the Occult in the Nineteenth and Twentieth Centuries.* New York: Knopf, 1983.

Braude, Ann. *Radical Spirits: Spiritualism and Women's Rights in Nineteenth-Century America.* Boston: Beacon, 1989.

Cerullo, John. *The Secularization of the Soul: Psychical Research in Modern Britain.* Philadelphia: Institute for the Study of Human Issues, 1982.

Collins, Harry, and Trevor Pinch. *Frames of Meaning: The Social Construction of Extra-Ordinary Science.* London: Routledge, 1982.

Coon, Deborah J. "Testing the Limits of Sense and Science: American Experimental Psychologists Combat Spiritualism, 1880–1920." *American Psychologist* 47(2) (1992): 143–51.

Davis, Andrew Jackson. *The Harmonial Philosophy: A Compendium and Digest of the Works of Andrew Jackson Davis.* London: Rider, 1917.

Doyle, Arthur Conan. *The History of Spiritualism.* 2 vols. New York: Doran, 1926.

Gauld, Alan. *The Founders of Psychical Research.* New York: Schocken, 1968.

Hess, David J. *Science in the New Age: The Paranormal, Its Defenders and Debunkers, and American Culture.* Madison: University of Wisconsin Press, 1993.

Kerr, Howard. *Mediums, and Spirit-Rappers, and Roaring Radicals: Spiritualism in American Literature, 1850–1900.* Chicago: University of Illinois Press, 1972.

Kerr, Howard, and Charles L. Crow, eds. *The Occult in America: New Historical Perspectives.* Urbana and Chicago: University of Illinois Press, 1983.

Leahey, Thomas H., and Grace Evans Leahey. *Psychology's Occult Doubles: Psychology and the Problem of Pseudoscience.* Chicago: Nelson-Hall, 1983.

Mauskopf, Seymour, and Michael McVaugh. *The Elusive Science: Origins of Experimental Psychical Research.* Baltimore: Johns Hopkins University Press, 1980.

McClenon, James. *Deviant Science: The Case of Parapsychology.* Philadelphia: University of Pennsylvania Press, 1984.

Moore, R. Laurence. *In Search of White Crows: Spiritualism, Parapsychology, and American Culture.* New York: Oxford University Press, 1977.

———. "The Spiritualist Medium: A Study of Female Professionalization in Victorian America." In *Women's Experience in America: An Historical Anthology,* ed. by Esther Katz and Anita Rapone. New Brunswick, N.J.: Transaction Books, 1980.

Murphy, Gardner, and Robert O. Ballou, eds. *William James on Psychical Research.* New York: Viking, 1960.

Oppenheim, Janet. *The Other World: Spiritualism and Psychical Research in England, 1850–1914.* Cambridge: Cambridge University Press, 1985.

Owen, Alex. *The Darkened Room: Women, Power and Spiritualism in Late Victorian England.* Philadelphia: University of Pennsylvania Press, 1990.

Turner, Frank Miller. *Between Science and Religion: The Reaction to Scientific Naturalism in Late Victorian England.* New Haven, Conn.: Yale University Press, 1974.

Index

D

Darrow, Clarence, 463
Darwin, Charles, 100–105, 302
  atheism alleged of, 102, 187
  and *Beagle* voyage, 101, 395, 417, 459
  on causation, 18, 19, 36
  and conflict thesis, 6, 8, 12, 13, 15, 77
  The Descent of Man, 49, 62, 103, 203, 226, 292, 461, 522
  on design argument, 66
  on ethics, 199
  on fossil record, 450
  on Genesis, 77
  on heredity, 473, 479
  on instinct, 461, 498
  life of, 100–104
  and materialism, 49, 180
  on moral values, 461
  on natural theology, 61, 62
  religious views of, 102, 104, 187, 196, 442
  See also Darwinian evolutionary theory; *Origin of Species*
Darwin, Emma Wedgwood, 102–103, 104
Darwin, Erasmus, 187, 459
Darwin, Francis, 103
Darwin, William, 103–104
Darwin and the Modern World View (Greene), 7
Darwinian evolutionary theory, 3, 18, 19, 197, 459–460
  and antievolution movement, 314–316
  on common descent, 22
  creation–evolution debate, 9, 21–23, 101, 295, 304, 305, 313–314, 460
  versus design argument, 461–463
  and epistemology, 24
  formulation of, 101–103, 395
  fundamentalist attack on, 212
  on gender, 226
  and Genesis account of creation, 77, 101
  on God's causation, 36
  humanist defense of, 212
  instinct in, 461
  Jehovah's Witnesses's attack on, 309
  and materialism, 49, 458, 460, 461
  and Mendel's genetics, 277
  modern synthesis of, 463–464
  and natural history, 442
  of natural selection, 8, 61, 62, 66, 101–102, 180, 187, 314, 395, 442, 450, 458, 459–460
  versus natural theology, 62
  and nature philosophy, 175
  Protestant response to, 292–293
  and psychology, 498, 521–522
  and scientific naturalism, 2–3
  in Scopes trial, 5, 22, 463
  taxonomy in, 450
  and theodicy, 74–75
  unscientific labeling of, 19, 21, 22
  See also Darwin, Charles; evolutionary theory
Darwinian Heritage, The, 9
Darwiniana (Gray), 462
Darwin's Metaphor, 7
Davenport, Charles, 481
Davidson, Donald, 197
Davies, Paul, 294, 365

Davis, Edward B., 201, 281
Davy, Humphry, 40, 126, 172, 174, 381
Dawkins, Richard, 18, 62, 66
Dawson, John William, 77, 302, 313, 314
De anima et vita (On the Soul and Life) (Vives), 520
De anima (On the Soul) (Aristotle), 115, 517, 518, 519
De architectura (On Architecture) (Vitruvius), 345
De causis mirabilium (The Causes of Marvelous Things) (Oresme), 536
De compositione alkimiae (On the Composition of Alchemy) (Robert of Ketton, trans.), 541–542
De divina omnipotentia (Peter Damian), 34
De generatione animalium (On the Generation of Living Creatures) (Harvey), 475
De Genesi ad Litteram (Augustine), 69
De hermetica medicina (Conring), 548
De imaginatione (On the Imagination) (Mirandola), 520
De immortalitate animae (On the Immortality of the Soul) (Pomponazzi), 520
De incarnatione (Athanasius), 70
De Labore Solis: Airy's Failure Reconsidered (van der Kamp), 358
De memoria (Aristotle), 518
De meteoris (On Astronomical Phenomena) (Magnus), 420
De mirabilibus mundi (The Marvels of the World), 536
De motu cordis (Harvey), 469
De natura deorum (On the Nature of the Gods) (Cicero), 65, 141, 345
De occult philosophia (On the Occult Philosophy) (Nettesheim), 537
De partibus corporis humani sensibilibus et irritabilibus (Haller), 165
De prestigiis daemonum (On the Sorceries of Demons) (Wier), 537
De proprietatibus rerum (On the Properties of Things) (Anglicus), 439
De re aedificatoria (On the Art of Building) (Alberti), 345
De rerum natura (On the Nature of Things) (Lucretius), 123, 129, 184, 492
De revolutionibus orbium coelestium (On the Revolutions of the Heavenly Bodies) (Copernicus), 331, 334, 336, 338
De subtilitate (Of Subtlety) (Cardano), 538
De trinitate (Augustine), 69
De usu partium (On the Usefulness of the Parts) (Galen), 466–467
De vero bono (On the True Good) (Valla), 129
deanimation, 40
death, science *versus* religion, 405
Death of Adam, The (Greene), 6
Death of Nature, The (Merchant), 228
decision, theory of, 92
Decisive Treatise on the Harmony Between Religion and Philosophy (Averroës), 254
Decknamen, 545
deconstruction, 231–233
Dee, John, 346, 415, 537
deep ecology, 430

Défense du Christianisme; ou, conférences sur la réligion (Defense of Christianity; or, Lectures on Religion) (Frayssinous), 407
deism, 45, 48, 99, 152, 153, 158–160
  adherents of, 158
  and atheism, 185
  basic beliefs of, 158, 285, 393
  diversity of, 159
  Enlightenment, 208–209
  and Newtonians, 158–159, 209
  on salvation, 159
  and science, 49, 158, 159
  and secular humanism, 208–209
  theories of earth, 393–396, 405
déistes, 158
Delacroix, Henri, 500
Della Porta, Giambattista, 537
Delmedigo, Joseph, 240
Deluc, Jean André, 407
Deluge. *See* Flood, Noah's
demarcation of science and religion, 17–23
  creation–evolution debate, 21–22
  future view, 22–23
  historical view, 19–21
  issues related to, 17–19
Dembski, William A., 65, 66–67
"Demise of the Demarcation Problem, The" (Laudan), 19–20
Demiurge (Divine Craftsman), 53, 58–59, 65, 111, 201, 262, 444, 466, 467
Democritus
  atomism of, 122, 123, 155, 176, 201
  on design argument, 66
  and Epicureanism, 129
  on macrocosm/microcosm, 345
  materialism of, 176
  on plurality of worlds, 342
  on soul, 516, 517
Démonomanie des sorciers (Demon Mania of the Sorcerers) (Bodin), 537
demons
  and illness, 488
  and weather, 425
Dennett, Daniel, 181
Derham, William, 42, 415, 430, 440
Desaguliers, John, 384
Desargues, Gérard, 90
Descartes, René, 5, 51, 56, 90, 91, 185, 205, 231
  and atomism, 125–126
  and Augustine, 136
  and causation, 33–34
  on "*Cogito ergo sum*", 143, 146
  cosmogony of, 350–351
  death of, 146
  dualism, 146, 372
  generation theory, 473–474, 475
  on materialism, 178
  mechanical philosophy of, 41, 54–55, 59, 124, 146, 150, 151, 155, 172, 282, 392, 393, 430, 470, 539
  on miracles, 69
  and providentialism, 55
  on skepticism, 143, 144, 146, 147
  on soul, 146–147, 520–521
  theological conservatism of, 147

H